DATE DUE

			PRINTED IN U.S.A.

Poetry
Criticism

Guide to Gale Literary Criticism Series

For criticism on	Consult these Gale series
Authors now living or who died after December 31, 1959	*CONTEMPORARY LITERARY CRITICISM (CLC)*
Authors who died between 1900 and 1959	*TWENTIETH-CENTURY LITERARY CRITICISM (TCLC)*
Authors who died between 1800 and 1899	*NINETEENTH-CENTURY LITERATURE CRITICISM (NCLC)*
Authors who died between 1400 and 1799	*LITERATURE CRITICISM FROM 1400 TO 1800 (LC)* *SHAKESPEAREAN CRITICISM (SC)*
Authors who died before 1400	*CLASSICAL AND MEDIEVAL LITERATURE CRITICISM (CMLC)*
Authors of books for children and young adults	*CHILDREN'S LITERATURE REVIEW (CLR)*
Dramatists	*DRAMA CRITICISM (DC)*
Poets	*POETRY CRITICISM (PC)*
Short story writers	*SHORT STORY CRITICISM (SSC)*
Black writers of the past two hundred years	*BLACK LITERATURE CRITICISM (BLC)*
Hispanic writers of the late nineteenth and twentieth centuries	*HISPANIC LITERATURE CRITICISM (HLC)*
Native North American writers and orators of the eighteenth, nineteenth, and twentieth centuries	*NATIVE NORTH AMERICAN LITERATURE (NNAL)*
Major authors from the Renaissance to the present	*WORLD LITERATURE CRITICISM, 1500 TO THE PRESENT (WLC)*

ISSN 1052-4851

Poetry Criticism

Excerpts from Criticism of the Works of the Most Significant and Widely Studied Poets of World Literature

VOLUME 22

Carol T. Gaffke
Anna J. Sheets
Laura A. Wisner-Broyles
Editors

GALE

DETROIT · LONDON

STAFF

Laura Wisner-Broyles, *Editor*

Anna Sheets, Larry Trudeau, *Associate Editors*

Susan Salas, Debra A. Wells, *Assistant Editors*

Susan Trosky, *Permissions Manager*
Kimberly F. Smilay, *Permissions Specialist*
Sarah Chesney, *Permissions Associate*
Stephen Cusack, Sandra K. Gore, Kelly Quin, *Permissions Assistants*

Victoria B. Cariappa, *Research Manager*
Michele P. LaMeau, *Research Specialist*
Julie C. Daniel, Tamara C. Nott, Tracie A. Richardson,
Norma Sawaya, Cheryl L. Warnock, *Research Associates*

Mary Beth Trimper, *Production Director*
Carolyn A. Fischer, *Production Assistant*

Randy Bassett, *Image Database Supervisor*
Michael Ansari, Robert Duncan, *Scanner Operator*
Pamela Reed, *Photography Coordinator*

Library of Congress Catalog Card Number 91-118494
ISBN 0-7876-2013-0
ISSN 1052-4851

Printed in the United States of America

10   9   8   7   6   5   4   3   2   1

Contents

Preface vii

Acknowledgments xi

Preface

A Comprehensive Information Source on World Poetry

Poetry Criticism (PC) provides substantial critical excerpts and biographical information on poets throughout the world who are most frequently studied in high school and undergraduate college courses. Each *PC* entry is supplemented by biographical and bibliographical material to help guide the user to a fuller understanding of the genre and its creators. Although major poets and literary movements are covered in such Gale Literary Criticism Series as *Contemporary Literary Criticism (CLC)*, *Twentieth-Century Literary Criticism (TCLC)*, *Nineteenth-Century Literature Criticism (NCLC)*, *Literature Criticism from 1400 to 1800 (LC)*, and *Classical and Medieval Literature Criticism (CMLC)*, **PC** offers more focused attention on poetry than is possible in the broader, survey-oriented entries on writers in these Gale series. Students, teachers, librarians, and researchers will find that the generous excerpts and supplementary material provided by *PC* supply them with the vital information needed to write a term paper on poetic technique, to examine a poet's most prominent themes, or to lead a poetry discussion group.

Coverage

In order to reflect the influence of tradition as well as innovation, poets of various nationalities, eras, and movements are represented in every volume of *PC*. Each author entry presents a historical survey of the critical response to that author's work; the length of an entry reflects the amount of critical attention that the author has received from critics writing in English and from foreign critics in translation. Since many poets have inspired a prodigious amount of critical explication, *PC* is necessarily selective, and the editors have chosen the most significant published criticism to aid readers and students in their research. In order to provide these important critical pieces, the editors will sometimes reprint essays that have appeared in previous volumes of Gale's Literary Criticism Series. Such duplication, however, never exceeds fifteen percent of a *PC* volume.

Organization

Each *PC* author entry consists of the following components:

- **Author Heading:** the name under which the author wrote appears at the beginning of the entry, followed by birth and death dates. If the author wrote consistently under a pseudonym, the pseudonym will be listed in the author heading and his or her legal name given in parentheses in the lines immediately preceding the Introduction. Uncertainty as to birth or death dates is indicated by question marks.

- **Introduction:** a biographical and critical essay introduces readers to the author and the critical discussions surrounding his or her work.

- **Author Portrait:** a photograph or illustration of the author is included when available.

- **Principal Works:** the author's most important works are identified in a list ordered chronologically by first publication dates. The first section comprises poetry collections and book-length poems. The second section gives information on other major works by the author. For foreign authors, original foreign-language publication information is provided, as well as the best and most complete English-language editions of their works.

- **Criticism:** critical excerpts chronologically arranged in each author entry provide perspective on changes in critical evaluation over the years. All individual titles of poems and poetry collections by the author featured in the entry are printed in boldface type to enable a reader to ascertain without difficulty the works under discussion. For purposes of easy identification, the critic's name and the publication date of the essay are given at the beginning of each piece of criticism. Unsigned criticism is preceded by the title of the journal in which it originally appeared. Publication information (such as publisher names and book prices) and parenthetical numerical references (such as footnotes or page and line references to specific editions of a work) have been deleted at the editor's discretion to enable smoother reading of the text.

- **Explanatory Notes:** introductory comments preface each critical excerpt, providing several types of useful information, including: the reputation of a critic, the importance of a work of criticism, and the specific type of criticism (biographical, psychoanalytic, historical, etc.).

- **Author Commentary:** insightful comments from the authors themselves and excerpts from author interviews are included when available.

- **Bibliographical Citations:** information preceding each piece of criticism guides the interested reader to the original essay or book.

- **Further Reading:** bibliographic references accompanied by descriptive notes at the end of each entry suggest additional materials for study of the author. Boxed material following the Further Reading provides references to other biographical and critical series published by Gale.

Other Features

- **Cumulative Author Index:** comprises all authors who have appeared in Gale's Literary Criticism Series, along with cross-references to such Gale biographical series as *Contemporary Authors* and *Dictionary of Literary Biography*. This cumulated index enables the user to locate an author within the various series.

- **Cumulative Nationality Index:** includes all authors featured in *PC,* arranged alphabetically under their respective nationalities.

- **Cumulative Title Index:** lists in alphabetical order all individual poems, book-length poems, and collection titles contained in the *PC* series. Titles of poetry collections and separately published poems are printed in italics, while titles of individual poems are printed in roman type with quotation marks. Each title is followed by the author's name and the volume and page number corresponding to the location of commentary on specific works. English-language translations of original foreign-language titles are cross-referenced to the foreign titles so that all references to discussion of a work are combined in one listing.

Citing *Poetry Criticism*

When writing papers, students who quote directly from any volume in the Literary Criticism Series may use the following general formats to footnote reprinted criticism. The first example pertains to material drawn from periodicals, the second to material reprinted from books:

[1]David Daiches, "W. H. Auden: The Search for a Public," *Poetry* LIV (June 1939), 148-56; excerpted and reprinted in *Poetry Criticism*, Vol. 1, ed. Robyn V. Young (Detroit: Gale Research, 1990), pp. 7-9.

[2]Pamela J. Annas, *A Disturbance in Mirrors: The Poetry of Sylvia Plath* (Greenwood Press, 1988); excerpted and reprinted in *Poetry Criticism*, Vol. 1, ed. Robyn V. Young (Detroit: Gale Research, 1990), pp. 410-14.

Comments Are Welcome

Readers who wish to suggest authors to appear in future volumes, or who have other suggestions, are cordially invited to contact the editors.

Acknowledgments

The editors wish to thank the copyright holders of the excerpted criticism included in this volume and the permissions managers of many book and magazine publishing companies for assisting us in securing reproduction rights. We are also grateful to the staffs of the Detroit Public Library, the Library of Congress, the University of Detroit Mercy Library, Wayne State University Purdy/Kresge Library Complex, and the University of Michigan Libraries for making their resources available to us. Following is a list of the copyright holders who have granted us permission to reproduce material in this volume of *PC*. Every effort has been made to trace copyright, but if omissions have been made, please let us know.

COPYRIGHTED EXCERPTS IN *PC*, VOLUME 22, WERE REPRODUCED FROM THE FOLLOWING PERIODICALS:

Allegorica, v. V, Winter, 1980. Reproduced by permission.—*The American Book Review,* v. 6, January-February, 1984. 8 1984 by *The American Book Review.*— *Arizona Quarterly,* v. 15, Winter, 1959 for "Joyce's 'Chamber Music': The Exile of the Heart," by James R. Baker. Copyright © 1959, renewed 1987 by the Regents of the University of Arizona. Reproduced by permission of the publisher and the author—*Chasqui,* v. IV, November, 1974; v. XXIII, November, 1994. Both reproduced by permission.—*Comitatus,* v. 1974. Reproduced by permission.—*Critical Inquiry*, v. 13, Spring, 1987 for "Political Poetry and the Example of Ernesto Cardenal" by Reginald Gibbons. Copyright © 1987 by The University of Chicago. Reproduced by permission of the publisher and the author.—*English Studies,* v. 68, 1987; v. 73, 1992. Copyright © 1987, 1992. Swets & Zeitlinger. Both reproduced by permission.— *The Explicator,* v. 55, Spring, 1997. Copyright © 1997 Helen Dwight Reid Educational Foundation. Reproduced with permission of the Helen Dwight Reid Educational Foundation, published by Heldref Publications, 1319 18th Street, NW, Washington, D.C. 20036-1802.—*French Forum*, v. 13, January, 1988. Copyright © 1988 by *French Forum*, Publishers, Inc. Reproduced by permission.—*French Studies*, v. XXXVII, April, 1983. Reproduced by permission.— *The Georgia Review,* v. 34, Spring, 1980; v. XLV, Spring, 1991. Copyright © 1980, 1991, by the University of Georgia. Both reproduced by permission.—*The Hollins Critic,* v. XXIX, February, 1992. Copyright (c)1992 by Hollins College. Reproduced by permission.—*The Hudson Review,* v. XXI, Summer, 1968; v. XXXIV, Spring, 1981; v. XLII, Spring, 1989. Copyright © 1968, 1981, 1989 by The Hudson Review, Inc. All reproduced by permission.— *The Iowa Review,* v.15, Winter, 1985 for a review of "The Dead and the Living" by Carolyne Wright. Copyright. © 1985 by The University of Iowa. Reproduced by permission of the author.— *James Joyce Quarterly,* v. II, Summer, 1965; v. 18, Winter, 1981; v. 1, Spring, 1994. All reproduced by permission.—*The Journal of Asian Studies,* v. 53, May, 1994. Reproduced with the permission of the Association for Asian Studies, Inc.— *Journal of English and Germanic Philology,* v. 90, October, 1991 for "Success and Glory in 'Beowulf'" by Richard J. Schrader; v. 92, January, 1993 for "Prey Tell: How Heroes Perceive Monsters in 'Beowulf'" by Ward Parks. Both reproduced by permission of the publisher and respective authors.—*The Journal of Ethnic Studies,* v. 12, Winter, 1985. Copyright © 1985 by *The Journal of Ethnic Studies.* Reproduced by permission.— *Journal of the American Oriental Society,* v. 96, January-March, 1976; v. 104, April-June, 1984. Both reproduced by permission.—*Kentucky Romance Quarterly*, v. 27, 1980. Copyright © 1980 Helen Dwight Reid Educational Foundation. Reproduced with permission of the Helen Dwight Reid Educational Foundation, published by Heldref Publications, 1319 18th Street, NW, Washington, DC 20036-1802.—*The Journal of Medieval and Renaissance Studies*, v. 24, Winter, 1994. Copyright © 1994 by Duke University Press, Durham, NC. Reproduced by permission.— *Library Journal,* v.121, January, 1996 for a review of "The Wellspring" by Christine Stenstrom Copyright © 1996 by Reed Publishing, USA, Division of Reed Holdings, Inc. Reproduced from *Library Journal,* a Division of Reed Publishing, USA, by permission of the author.—*Literature East and West*, v. XXI. Reproduced by permission.—*The Literary Review,* v. 37, Fall, 1993 for "'Never Having Had You, I Cannot Let You Go': Sharon Old's Poems of a Father-Daughter Relationship" by Brian Dillon. Copyright © 1993 by Fairleigh Dickinson University. Reproduced by permission of the author.— *Medieval Studies,* v. 54, 1992. Reproduced by permission.—*Medium Aevum,* v. XXIX, 1960. Published by The Society for the Study of Medieval Languages and Literature by Basil Blackwell. Reproduced by permission.—*MELUS,* v. 21, Spring, 1996. Copyright, MELUS, The Society for the Study of Multi-Ethnic Literature of the United States, 1996. Reproduced by permission.—*Modern Language Quarterly*, v. XXVIII, March, 1967. Copyright © 1967 by the University of Washington. Reproduced by permission of Duke University Press.—*Mosaic,* v. 29, March, 1996. © *Mosaic* 1996. Reproduced by permission.—*The Nation,* New York, v. 239, October 13, 1984; October 7, 1991. © 1984, 1991 *The Nation* magazine/ The Nation Company, Inc. Reproduced by permission— *Neophilologus,* v. XLVII, 1963. Reproduced by permission.— *New England Review,* v. 14, Fall, 1992. Copyright © 1992 by Kenyon Hill Publications, Inc.

COPYRIGHTED EXCERPTS IN *PC* VOLUME 22, WERE REPRODUCED FROM THE FOLLOWING BOOKS:

Bucknell University Press, 1996. Copyright © 1996 by Thorpe Running. All rights reserved. Reproduced by permission.—Willis Barnstone with Jorge Luis Borges. From **Borges at Eighty: Conversations**. Edited by Willis Barnstone. Indiana University Press, 1982. Copyright © 1982 by Indiana University Press. All rights reserved. Reproduced by permission.

PHOTOGRAPHS AND ILLUSTRATIONS APPEARING IN *PC* VOLUME 22, WERE RECEIVED FROM THE FOLLOWING SOURCES:

Borges, Jorge Luis, photograph. The Library of Congress.—Cardenal, Ernesto, sitting, serious expression, wearing a black beret, photograph, 1983. AP/Wide World Photos. Reproduced by permission.—Joyce, James (Ulysses), photograph. The Library of Congress.—Levine, Philip, standing, outside, mountains in background, photograph. Reproduced by permission.—Olds, Sharon, standing in dark blazer, long hair flowing over her shoulders, photograph. Reproduced by permission.—Princess Shakuntala, heroine of Kalidasa's greatest drama, Indo-Persian, 18th century, miniature painting. The Granger Collection. Reproduced by permission.—Villa, José Garcia, photograph. AP/Wide World Photos. Reproduced by permission.

Beowulf
Circa Eighth Century

Old English epic poem.

INTRODUCTION

Beowulf is the earliest surviving long poem in Old English and has been described as the greatest of its kind. Although the origins of this account of Dark Age warrior cultures and of heroes and monsters battling one another remain for the most part a mystery, many scholars agree that *Beowulf* was probably composed in the eighth century and that its unknown author, as well as the poem's early audience, possessed at least a basic familiarity with Christianity. The only extant manuscript of *Beowulf* was damaged by fire in 1731, before it could be transcribed; thus, portions of the poem are missing. This fact, along with the difficulty of rendering the poet's elusive style and many allusions to events and legends long past, has made the process of interpreting *Beowulf* both a challenge and a source of debate for modern literary critics.

Plot and Major Characters

The plot of *Beowulf* can be divided into two parts. In part one, the Geatish hero, Beowulf, who is remarkable for his extraordinary strength and courage, sails to Denmark to defeat Grendel, a terrifying monster that has been preying on the warriors—or "thanes"—of the aging Danish king, Hrothgar, at Heorot Hall. After slaying Grendel, Beowulf enjoys the gifts and banquet provided for him by the grateful Danes. Later that night, however, Grendel's avenging mother interrupts the celebration by attacking the Hall, thus obliging Beowulf to fight and kill her. Having freed Heorot of these evil menaces, Beowulf returns home. Part two is set many years later in the land of the Geats, where Beowulf has long since become king. Now, as an aging ruler himself, Beowulf must defeat a dragon that threatens his people. With the help of his faithful young retainer, Wiglaf (the rest of his men have fled in fear), Beowulf destroys the dragon but receives a mortal wound during the battle. After his cremation and burial along with the dragon's treasure hoard, ill fortune is predicted for the Geatish nation. In addition to this main plot, the narrative is also interspersed with several digressions, which allude to other heroes or stories and serve as commentary on the main action of the poem.

Major Themes

Among the numerous themes identified in *Beowulf,* a principal one is that of friendship, known in the context of the poem as *comitatus,* or the closeness which exists between

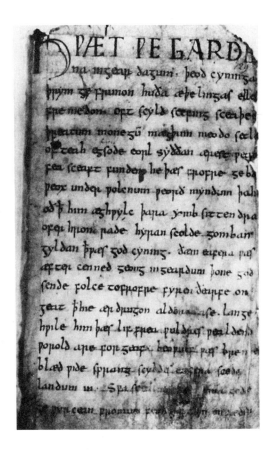

a ruler and his men. According to the precepts of *comitatus,* a leader rewards his thane—such as Beowulf in the first part of the poem or Wiglaf in the second—for his acts of courage and loyalty by granting him material gifts and high social status. Closely related to *comitatus* is the tradition of the feud, a custom of avenging oneself and one's people for harm done by an enemy. Critics observe that the theme of feuding applies not only to the warrior cultures represented in the poem, but also to Grendel's mother, who attacks Heorot to avenge her son's death. Finally, commentators have perceived in the somber, elegiac tone at the close of *Beowulf* the culmination of such themes as aging, the destructive and endless nature of feuding, the shortness and brutality of life, and the death of the pagan heroic code—a system of belief which offered immortality only through fame. Additionally, many critics have argued that the poem represents the waning of pagan traditions as they were superseded by the values of Christianity.

Critical Reception

Largely because its exact origins are unknown, *Beowulf* has elicited much critical disputation. Many early critics faulted the poem's organization, arguing that *Beowulf's* numerous digressions detract from its aesthetic unity. Several scholars have suggested that these divagations imply that the poem was in part edited by individuals other than the original author-monks, for example, who endeavored to give the poem a Christian rather than a pagan emphasis. Alternatively, some scholars have asserted that the poem achieves unity only if it is read as a Christian allegory with the hero, Beowulf, as a Christ-like figure. More recently, critics have argued that its themes of revenge and the brevity of life, unifying mood, and complementary structural elements—such as Beowulf's series of heroic battles—provide for coherence in the poem. The nature of the *Beowulf* poet has also been a source of considerable critical interest. Some have speculated as to his religious background, inquiring if the poet was Christian or pagan. Others have explored the details of the poem's composition, whether as oral or written literature. Lastly, while some critics describe the somber ending of *Beowulf* as a condemnation of its hero's pagan beliefs, others see the conclusion as a solemn farewell to a moral code replaced in the subsequent Christian era.

CRITICISM

Margaret E. Goldsmith (essay date 1960)

SOURCE: "The Christian Theme of *Beowulf*," in *Medium Aevum,* Vol. XXIX, No. 2, 1960, pp. 81-101.

[*In the following excerpt, Goldsmith contends that the story and symbolism of* Beowulf *are coherent only when the poem is given a Christian interpretation rather than a secular, pagan one; however, Goldsmith warns that the character Beowulf is not meant to be regarded as Christ-like.*]

I

The poem **Beowulf** as we have it contains indisputably Christian sentiments and vocabulary, and handles familiarly and allusively certain Biblical stories. Yet there lingers a belief that these are extraneous trappings, that the feeling of the poem is essentially pagan, or at the best only half-heartedly Christian. I shall seek to show that it gains considerably in coherence and significance if we allow ourselves to be guided by the poet's own emphases in the choice and presentation of the stories and his moral reflections upon them. A literate Anglo-Saxon poet would in the normal course of things have learnt to read in a monastery, where his daily reading would be much on the Psalms and certain other parts of the Bible, and where his attitude to the meaning of meaning would be formed by the traditional exegetic methods of the homilists. To such a man, Cain, the giants, the dragons, would be historical realities and at the same time symbols of spiritual strife continually existing. On the secular plane, the poem falls apart, not merely into two scarcely related adventures with monsters, but into a number of fragmentary scraps

which can only be accounted for as concessions to the fantastic weakness of the putative audience for 'digressions' or to the inability of the poet to restrain himself from going off at a tangent. Considered as a poem of ideas rather than of physical action, it has a pattern, a progression, and a purpose which explains the structure of the narrative.

There are certain false critical assumptions about the poem which do the poet some disservice.

First: that the hero Beowulf is the poet's ideal. Many notable scholars have convinced themselves that Beowulf is presented as the saviour of his people, like a Christian knight, or even like Christ himself, in spite of the fact that even in the final eulogy there is no hint of this. Beowulf is presented as a noble hero, but not as the complete paragon of kingly virtue. One can imagine a comparable Christian poem about King David: there would be much to praise in the hero, but no-one would suggest that his every act was held up for imitation by the poet's patron.

Second: that the poet's beliefs can be identified with those which motivate his characters, in spite of the fact that he himself stands apart as commentator.

Third: that the poem only makes sense if one has learnt, from other sources, the unmentioned details or later consequences of the events described. From this assumption comes a good deal of unnecessary puzzlement. The tidy version of the stories, as sifted from the analogues by the editor, often looks much more remote from the argument of the poem than those features of the stories which the poet has chosen to recall. This is nowhere better illustrated than in the episode of Sigemund and Fitela (ll. 874-986), where the poet tells of a hero and his nephew who were comrades in many a battle with giants and in much human strife, though the uncle stood alone when he killed the great dragon and carried off its treasure in his ship. Loyalty and treachery among kin, giant-slaying, dragon-fights, treasure hoards, are all integral parts of what the poet is writing about, and these are the aspects of Sigemund's life-story which bear upon the tale of Beowulf as he has conceived it. The incestuous begetting of Fitela, the curse upon the Nibelung's treasure, are discarded, if known, as irrelevant here. By the same critical method one can reconstruct the Finn story so that it appears to be a lay in honour of the Danes, disregarding the ironic comparison between the pent-up passions (like the winter waves locked in the bond of ice) of the Danes forced to swear allegiance to Finn, and the concealed hatred which will destroy Hrothgar's family.

If we look at the story as the poet presents it, we shall remember the foreign queen Hildeburh when we learn of the betrothal of Freawaru, and recall the burning of Finnsburg when Beowulf reminds us of the unquenchable hatred between Ingeld's men and the followers of his bride. There are other and different purposes in the telling of this lay: the swift transition from the splendid description of the Scylding king's gifts to Beowulf to the glittering splendour of the gold on Hnæf's funeral pyre has the same effect as the sudden picture of devouring fire superimposed on the first account of the splendours of Heorot. The delayed revenge of Hengest may be recalled when Beowulf must take the throne from his lord's slayer, Onela. These and other links with the 'main plot' may easily be obscured if we concern ourselves with the quasi-historical puzzles of the Finn affair, on the assumption that the allusive method of writing demands much knowledge in the audience. The only demand on the listener, as I see it, is that he shall remember what has gone before in the poem. To our generation this is not easy, but this demand on the memory appears to be inherent in this kind of narrative technique, which constantly foreshadows coming events. Each thunderstorm is presaged by a cloud no bigger than a man's hand. A poet who adopts a method of this sort is likely to be a man who sees his work whole and chooses his effects with deliberation.

I believe that we have here a skilled Christian poet who has chosen to retell the story of a pre-Christian hero in such a way as to impart certain moral lessons. The danger of celebrating a pagan hero he has ingeniously avoided by giving his characters a pre-Christian setting, as if they had lived B.C. Like the Israelites of the Old Testament, they can be presented as servants of the Lord, under the moral obligations of the 'Old Law'. There were giants in the world of Genesis (c. 6, 4), enemies of God. There was divinely sanctioned blood-vengeance (c. 9, 5-6). There was strife between the kin of Cain and the men of God. Thus the whole Beowulf story of feuds between men and supernatural creatures, and amongst men, can without inconsistency be conceived as belonging to that primitive world, with its hero, like another Samson, as the (not immaculate) champion of God.

The poet quite evidently means to show that the strife with the Grendel kin is part of the uncompoundable feud between God's people and the race of Cain. Beowulf's victory in this strife is symbolized by the hilt of the giant-made sword which he used, with God's help, to behead the monsters. When the trophy of victory is examined in Heorot, it is seen to bear an engraving which depicts the antediluvian war between the giant-race and the Creator. This engraving is so unnecessary to the adventure story of Beowulf the Geat, and so essential a part of the religious theme, that it makes a very significant pointer to the poet's conception of his work.

It must not be forgotten that the devil and his crew have their place in the Genesis-world. When Hrothgar is made to speak (in ll. 1740 ff.) of arrows of the devil which wound a man's soul while its guardian sleeps, his phrasing is Christian, but there is nothing anachronistic in the doctrine. The sin of pride, against which Hrothgar is warning the victorious hero, is older than Adam's fall.

If all the poet had done were to draw the poison from a heathen heroic lay, we should have to treat him as a reviser rather than a creative artist. But his work is not by any means of a negative kind. He has not only seen the adventures of Geatish Beowulf in a new perspective: he has joined them with other material, so as to compose a poem of a new kind, for which the name heroic elegy is the best so far found. He has woven in two themes: the theme of *dom* and the theme *sic transit gloria mundi*. Neither of these themes is in itself Christian: *Hávamál* is sufficient evidence to the contrary. If the poem were simply about the inevitability of death and decay, and the endurance of fame after death, God would have no necessary place in it, and Beowulf's piety would be incidental. Many scholars have looked at the poem like this. But they have been puzzled by one thing: why, with so many heroic stories at his command, did the poet choose Beowulf's fights with the Grendel kin and the dragon as the high points of his poem? I do not find any satisfactory answer to this, except the answer offered by Professor Tolkien, that the monsters, though indisputably living and breathing creatures, are symbolic of the powers of evil.

But I do not find the whole answer here. There are still awkward questions to be asked. What have Hrothgar's moral discourse and the dragon's cursed treasure to do with one another? Why, if Beowulf is the champion of good against evil in his last fight, does he not openly put his trust in God, as he does before the other fights?

We can offer solutions to these puzzles in two different ways. We can say that the poet, in reworking an older story, was content to leave some of the heathen motivation in the latter part, ignoring the discrepancies thus caused. Or we can argue that the poet knew his craft, and deliberately prepared for the nature and outcome of the last contest, using his common device of foreshadowing the future, in the scene of Hrothgar's warning to young Beowulf (ll. 1698-1784). The second way seems to be more in accord with our general assessment of the poet's qualities as narrator.

Most interpreters of the poem take no account of the change in Beowulf's character as it is revealed in the last section of the poem. We do not see the processes of change: we are confronted with old Beowulf, on whom time and success and worldly prosperity have left their mark, and we see middle-aged Beowulf only through his own reminiscent eyes. In the dragon affair we do not find the Beowulf of the Grendel fight. The old man is no less courageous, no less physically strong, but he is overcome, because he is arrogantly confident of his power to assay the contest unaided, and his expressed motives are worldly. Such a moral deterioration Hrothgar had foreseen. The ageing Beowulf is boastful of his previous successes, whereas the young champion was comparatively reticent (see his reply to Hygelac's invitation to recount what happened to Grendel, ll. 2093-6) and was careful to give the credit to God, and to include his companions in his first account of his exploit (l. 958). Old Beowulf parted from his thanes for the last time, spurning their help.

> Nis þæt eower sið,
> ne gemet mannes, nefne min anes . . .
>
> (ll. 2532-3)

The tragedy of Beowulf is more than a contrast between Youth and Age: Beowulf does not fall because he is old, but because *Sigora Waldend* is not with him.

The poem is not only about the hero Beowulf, and in what follows I have looked afresh at the narrative in the light of my two assumptions, that the poet was a man whose thinking was moulded by traditional Christian teaching, and that the presentation of the stories is our best guide to his governing purpose. In the space available to me, I am forced to select only the most noteworthy instances of the poet's Christian teaching, but I am convinced that the treatment of the rest can be shown to support my general contentions.

II

Consider the opening: up to l. 193 the hero does not appear at all. Why, we may ask, begin with Scyld? The usual explanation, to show the glory of the Danish dynasty, seems to miss the point. Almost half the lines concerning Scyld are descriptive of the treasure loaded upon his funeral ship. Not Scyld's mysterious childhood, not the great battles of his kingship, but the splendid futility of his funeral is what the poet dwells upon. The magnificent hoard sailed no man knows where, but Scyld went *on Frean wære* (l. 27). Pagan as Scyld was, no-one is to begin to think that he made a triumphant voyage to Valhalla. There is no anachronism here: the poet believes that God sent Scyld to the lordless Danes; into God's keeping he went. This passage is typical of the poet's handling of his pre-Christian heroes; God ruled them as he rules all men:

> Metod eallum weold
> gumena cynnes,   swa he nu git deð.
>
> (ll. 1057-8)

Whenever he has to tell of mysterious or supernatural happenings the poet repeats this affirmation, sometimes bluntly, as here, sometimes with great delicacy, as when the sword melting in the monster's poisonous blood is likened to the melting ice which the Father sets free from winter's bond (l. 1608), or when the unearthly light in the underwater cavern is likened to *rodores candel,* so that the hearer is reminded of the Creator who

> gesette sigehrepig   sunnan ond monan,
> leoman to leohte   land-buendum.
>
> (ll. 94-5)

The poet moves swiftly from Scyld's treasure-ship to Hrothgar's towering palace of Heorot, greatest monument to his worldly success. And at once he turns it to a blackened ruin before our eyes. It will be destroyed in the blaze kindled by a passion of hatred between the king and his son-in-law. We need no footnote on the Heathobard feud to explain the impact of this. It is enough that vengeful hatred will destroy this great work of men's hands, and that the hatred will spring up where there should be most loyalty. The story of Freawaru's marriage has its place in the narrative, but the poet is not so inept as to

tell it here, when the stark facts of the splendour and the ruin make his point.

The hint of treachery and hatred is enough to lead into the Cain-theme which dominates the first part of the poem. Cain could not endure that his brother's worship was acceptable to God while his own was not: the Hymn of Creation sung by a Dane in Heorot rouses the same malicious envy in Grendel, one of Cain's brood. In the terror of Grendel's attacks, some Danes turn to the worship of idols: hell is in their hearts. The poet speaks with horror of their prospect of damnation, infinitely worse than the earthly ills which have driven them to this desperation (ll. 175-88).

Beowulf comes as a God-sent deliverer 'to cleanse Heorot'. Both he and Hrothgar acknowledge God's governance, and I find no difficulty in the fact that the hero uses proverbial expressions, such as 'Gæð a wyrd swa hio scel' (l. 455). Only in the last part of the poem does Beowulf speak of Fate without speaking also of God's control of Fate, and this is in keeping with my contention that the old king has lost his trust in God. I see no reason to suppose that the *poet's* view of *wyrd* would differ from that of Boethius. The Alfredian version of the *De Consolatione Philosophiæ* shows the English Christian's way of using the old word *wyrd:*

> Ðæt ðætte we hataþ Godes foreþonc and his
>   foresceawung . . . siððan
> hit fullfremed bið, ðonne hataþ we hit *wyrd.*

The next event in the narrative is Unferth's challenge and Beowulf's reply. This interchange reveals more than the story of the swimming-match. Unferth's envy makes an attempt to stir up strife, but Beowulf is not roused to offer him violence, in spite of the provocation. This un-aggressive quality of the mighty hero is a part of his character stressed by the poet, nowhere more than in his funeral dirge:

> Cwædon þæt he wære
> Manna mildust ond monþwærust.
>
> (ll. 3180-1)

Though we see him in the grip of righteous wrath when he pitilessly destroys Grendel and his dam, we are also in sundry ways made aware that he is not a man governed by passion or a fighter for the love of fighting. The brief mention of his despised boyhood (ll. 2184-8) I believe to be retained from the old tale to reinforce this impression that Beowulf was not by nature savage and wild. His reluctance to fight without good cause earned him the reputation of cowardice, until he had proved himself in his early monster-fights. The contrast which is made between him and Heremod is in part a contrast between the hero whose mind controls his mighty strength and the strong man who misuses his great gift because he cannot govern his passions (ll. 1711-19).

The interchange with Unferth also reveals the nature of this trusted counsellor of King Hrothgar. Beowulf's retort makes the accusation that Unferth has killed his own brother. It can hardly be accidental that the sins of Cain—envy and the murder of kin—are thus disclosed as an evil within Heorot. A little later we infer that the same evil is a canker in the heart of Hrothulf (ll. 1018-19) and that this will cause the death of the sons of Hrothgar.

Concerning the Grendel-fight, I would only observe that Beowulf trusted in God (ll. 685-7) and God gave him victory (ll. 696-7) over his superhuman foe, who would gladly have fled from him to hide himself amidst a concourse of demons (l. 756).

After the victory comes a time of gaiety, when songs and lays are sung by the Danes. It is in the choice of these entertainments, which are not dictated by the action of the Beowulf story, that we ought to discern very clearly what was in the poet's mind. I have already spoken above of the Sigemund lay. The poet draws the threads together very skilfully here: Sigemund's dragon-treasure loaded in the bosom of his ship is not only to be recalled when Beowulf learns of *his* dragon and its hoard; it also has a function here to recall, in the scene of Beowulf's triumph, that other treasure-laden ship which carried dead Scyld away. The lay of Sigemund brings in a lay of Heremod, whose early fame was like Sigemund's, whose promise as a prince was like Beowulf's, but who later brought sorrow to his people and met a miserable death through treachery. Just as earlier the poet threw a shadow over Heorot, he now ends the fêting of Beowulf with the harsh, terse comment on Heremod: *hine fyren onwod* (l. 915). Beowulf is his people's hope, as young Heremod was, and even more beloved (l. 915). What will Beowulf's end be?

It is usually said that Heremod's rôle in the poem is 'to serve as a foil to the exemplary Beowulf'. The poem is treated as a jigsaw puzzle, with a few missing pieces, and the commentator rearranges it so as to produce a pattern of his own devising. Here a neat chiasmus is proposed: Heremod's early promise, Heremod's wretched death, contrasted with Beowulf's glorious end, following his despised youth. But this is not the contrast the poet makes. When Beowulf's 'slothful' boyhood is mentioned (l. 2187) there is nothing to bring Heremod to our minds. When King Hrothgar uses the example of Heremod in his moral discourse, it is as a warning to young Beowulf, who has yet to prove himself as king (ll. 1722-4).

After the Heremod lay has been sung by the Danish *scop*, there comes a thanksgiving to God for their deliverance, and then preparations for a feast. The poet, thinking of Grendel trying to run away from death as he made tracks for the hellish pool, offers one of those serious comments which are so often taken as melancholic asides, or even as interpolations, touched off by the action but bearing no direct relevance to it:

> No þæt yðe byð
> to befleonne—fremme se þe wille—
> ac gesecan sceal sawlberenda
> nyde genydde, niþða bearna,

> grundbuendra gearwe stowe
> þær his lichoma legerbedde fæst
> swefeþ æfter symle.

                                (ll. 1002-8)

The sentiment of the sleep of death after the feast of life is commonplace; the poet's skill lies in the use he has made of it. From Grendel vainly running from death over the wastes we have been brought back to the comfort of Heorot, where the Danes are celebrating, with a feast, *their* escape from death. But after that feast, Æschere is killed, and even when the avenging monster is overcome, death still waits for the Scyldings in the smiling face of Hrothulf: hence the lines

> Nalles facenstafas
> þeod-Scyldingas þenden fremedon.

                                (ll. 1018-19)

At the feast, Beowulf and the Geats are royally rewarded for their valour, but the poet reminds us that it was God who used Beowulf's courage to end the reign of terror (ll. 1056-7). Hrothgar pays *wergild* for the Geat whom Grendel slew (ll. 1053-5). The death of the man devoured before Beowulf's eyes has been a stumbling-block to many students of the poem, since it seems a blemish on the hero. This episode was, I suppose, a feature of the older story which the poet did not want to reject, because it makes Grendel's savagery actual and immediate in the fight scene. He is not troubled that Beowulf may be thought a little less of on this account, but I think he may have been concerned lest his audience should question why God stayed his hand. Hence he follows this passage of reflection on Grendel's final attack with a passage more openly didactic than he usually permits himself:

> Forþan bið andgit æghwær selest,
> ferhðes foreþanc.

                                (ll. 1059-60)

As this appears in the translations, it seems to be an irrelevant platitude, if indeed it makes any sense at all. *Andgit* and *foreþanc* have meaning here only if we know how they were used by Anglo-Saxon churchmen. *Andgit* is the best of man's faculties: it translates the Psalmist's *intellectus,* the God-given intelligence by which man can know God. Ælfric makes St. Agnes say, 'Se geleafa ne bið on gearum, ac bið on glæwum andgitum'. *Foreþanc* is the word used of God's Providence (see above), though here it means the human counterpart: 'provision (for the soul)'. Men must understand that God permits evil-doing, and allows both good and ill to come to men, but he is *witig* (l. 1056): he sees and governs all. Sudden death may be in store for any man; it is not for him to question God's will, but to look to the future of his soul.

The Danes enjoy their respite from fear, untroubled for the first time for many years. The feast is followed by song, and we hear the lay of Finn, a tale of treachery and sudden slaughter, its relevance to the court of Hrothgar brought home by the irony of Queen Wealhtheow's speech, in which she speaks of her son's future and her trust in Hrothulf's loyalty. Once more the end of the story of Heorot is foreshadowed, more subtly this time, by the use of an analogous tale.

We turn from the puzzles of the Finn episode to the puzzle of the four lines devoted to Hama. As I read the lines, Hama is shown as a robber who repented: having possessed himself of the most precious necklace in the world, he gave it up for the lasting good of 'treasure in heaven'—*geceas ecne ræd* (l. 1201). Not so King Hygelac, to whom his loyal nephew Beowulf gave the wonderful necklace which he had received from Hrothgar. The necklace was about Hygelac's throat when he was slain in Frisia, trying to defend the plunder he had set off in his pride to win.

> Hyne wyrd fornam
> syþðan he for wlenco   wean ahsode
> fæhðe to Frysum.
>
> (ll. 1206-7)

By means of this passage, the poet turns the listeners' thoughts from envious contemplation of Beowulf's rich rewards to the contemplation of that same gold ripped by the despoilers from dead Hygelac's breast. Hama chose the lasting good; Hygelac courted death for the sake of more wealth, only to leave to his enemies his costly adornment, and to his people a legacy of bitter enmity. We have the evidence of Hrothgar's sermon, the reiteration of the fall of Hygelac, and the manner of Beowulf's own death, to substantiate this interpretation. If the poet's purpose were only to remind us of the transience of human splendour, there would be no need to show, as he does, the human motives which underlie the ruin of Heorot and the overthrow of the Geats.

After the feasting, the men of Heorot sleep. Their pitiful preparedness does not save Æschere when the second monster revives the feud that night. So Beowulf is asked to carry vengeance to a place that sounds like an Anglo-Saxon Christian's idea of the very mouth of hell. He accepts the duty unhesitatingly:

> Ure æghwylc sceal   ende gebidan
> worolde lifes;   wyrce se þe mote
> domes ær deaþe;   þæt bið drihtguman
> unlifgendum   æfter selest.
>
> (ll. 1386-9)

This sentiment would not be out of place in a wholly heathen context, but we cannot fail to be reminded of the very similar words in *The Seafarer,* where the ideal of earthly glory is merged with the hope of heavenly reward for the hero. Both poets agree that the best life for a man is a life spent fighting in the unending feud against the devil and all the enemies of God,

> deorum dædum   deofle togeanes.
>
> (*Seafarer,* l. 76)

In this spirit Beowulf fights, with *dom* as his reward—not only the earthly fame symbolized by the barrow on Hronesness, but *soðfæstra dom;* the heavenly judgement of his deserts among all the just souls. In this unending fight, the hero's strongest weapon is faith.

Beowulf realizes this truth in the moment of crisis in the underwater chamber, when the sword Hrunting, lent him by Unferth, fails him in his need. He casts it from him, and trusts once more in his God-given strength. When he ceases to care for his own life and puts all his strength into the struggle, God comes to his aid, and he is victorious. He leaves the pool cleansed of its evil and returns to Heorot with his trophies, Grendel's head and the giant sword-hilt.

This palace-scene asks for special attention because, like the lays we have discussed, it is not required by the movement of the plot, and its length suggests its importance to its creator. Note first Beowulf's humility; he gives the credit for his victory to God:

> oftost wisode
> winigea leasum.
>
> (ll. 1663-4)

Hrothgar is given the sword-hilt to examine, and we learn the significance of the engraved design, the design of the giant-feud, which I have already discussed. Because of the previous emphasis on Grendel's origin, we perceive that Beowulf's fights have been a small part of this Holy War. But the devil, whose servants he has overcome, will not withdraw from the contest, as old King Hrothgar clearly sees. So far Beowulf has borne his might and his fame wisely, acknowledging the source of his strength. But, while he praises him for this, King Hrothgar warns the young man to take heed of the example of King Heremod, to whom God gave like strength, and then power over men. As king, Heremod failed to govern himself: 'Learn by this', says the wise old king to Beowulf. And then, as if to still any murmurs of dissent, he speaks at length of the special dangers that await the man whom God has given wisdom, royal rank, a land to govern. To that man, prosperity may prove a worse enemy than fierce assailants. When he thinks himself safe from his enemies, he forgets that earthly life and power are short-lived, and a great arrogance and a desire for worldly splendour grow within him. Thus the arrows of the devil pierce his unguarded heart. When he dies, his power is at an end, and his hoarded wealth passes into other hands.

> Bebeorh þe ðone bealoníð,   Beowulf leofa,
> secg betsta,   ond þe þæt selre geceos,
> ece rædas;   oferhyda ne gym,
> mære cempa!
>
> (ll. 1758-61)

This wisdom Hrothgar has learnt from his own chastening experience with Grendel. He knows that two paths lie before young Beowulf: one leads to *ece rædas,* the eternal reward (which Hama chose); the other, to pride in possession of this world's solaces, and spiritual decline. Above all, the triumphant hero must guard himself against the sin of pride: *ofer-hyda ne gym.*

The significance of this sermon is slowly unfolded in what follows. We have been told already that King Hygelac of the Geats will die in his pride as he seeks for more wealth. The Geat people, like the Scyldings, will suffer misery, but their disaster springs from different causes. The Scyldings' ruin will come about through envy and murderous hatred among those who should be most loyal to Hrothgar: the spirit of Grendel still darkens Heorot. Gradually we learn what is in store for the Geats; bit by bit the causes of the smouldering enmity of the Swedes and Frisians and Franks are made known, so that we become aware that only the might of the Geatish king stands between his people and subjugation by their foes. We remember the plight of the lordless Danes before God took pity on them (ll. 14-16), and we remember Hrothgar's words to Beowulf in the last part of his homily (ll. 1769-81), in which he speaks of his own chastening reversal of fortune. The first part of the poem comes to an end with Beowulf enthroned beside his uncle Hygelac, modest, loyal, sagacious (he foresees the failure of the Heathobard marriage pact), covered with honours and praised by all. Hrothgar's words have prepared us for Beowulf's later coronation, and also for the hero's trial to come, where the enemy is the devil, and one of his weapons worldly success. Beowulf's spirit is too noble to fall into the grosser sins of a Heremod, as the poet obviously means to emphasize in his lines on Beowulf's character (ll. 2177-88). But Hrothgar too was a good and noble king until the long years of having his own way made him careless of spiritual well-being. It needed the coming of Grendel to make him aware of his actual weakness.

It is with no surprise, therefore, that we find ourselves lifted across fifty years in a few lines (l. 2200 ff.), to see Beowulf placed in the position of Hrothgar when Grendel made his first attack. After many years of prosperous rule, his peace is broken by an invading monster.

Whether the dragon is symbolic of anything or nothing has been much debated. One argument asks a kind of sympathy for the outraged dragon, who 'is nowhere called God's enemy, or a fiend, or joyless; in fact no words of moral disapprobation are applied to him'. This R.S.P.C.A. attitude, which in the past has also embraced Grendel's dam, would, I am sure, be incomprehensible to the Anglo-Saxon Christian. The malice of the dragon is something very different from the righteous wrath of a man who has been robbed. Before he has made the mound his home, he is called *eald uht-sceaða* and *nacod nið-draca;* he holds the countryside in terror (ll. 2274-5). He is not called 'joyless', because he is not, like Grendel, corroded with hopeless desire for the comfortable life of men from which he is cast out. He finds his satisfaction in possessing his hoard and in the terror and suffering that he can cause. The dragon, like Grendel, is essentially malicious, essentially a destroyer.

It is impossible to be precise about the degree of symbolism involved in the poet's conception of the dragon and Grendel. It is certain that they are not abstractions or fictional creatures: water-trolls and fire-breathing dragons were part of popular belief. Trolls eat people and dragons lie upon gold. The Christian poet accepted these creatures as part of God's world, because he had in Genesis an explanation of their origin, and he has been very careful to recount that origin in the case of Grendel. Why is there no comparable explanation of the dragon? Surely because *wyrm* and *draca* are recognizably creatures of hell in Christian lore? The OE poem of *Genesis* also has a *wyrm:* this is the disguise of the Tempter in the Garden of Eden. In the Latin Bible the dragon and serpent are interchangeable symbols for the devil. See what Bede thought of dragons, in his commentary upon the Book of the Apocalypse: in c. 20, 2, the Bible has *Et apprehendit draconem serpentum antiquum.* Bede's note is: *Draco ergo, propter nocendi malitiam: Serpens, propter fallendi astutiam.* The dragon is an appropriate image of the devil because of his malice. Note also that Bede's comment on c. 12, 9, *Et projectus est draco ille magnus in terram . . . ,* begins: *Antiquus hostis de spiritualibus expulsus, arctius in terrenos includitur.* The **Beowulf** poet uses the English equivalent of *antiquus hostis,* i.e. *eald-gewinna,* of Grendel (l. 1776): Bede regards it as an alternative for *draco ille magnus.* This in itself would suggest that there is no fundamental difference of attitude towards the two monsters. I have no doubt that the poet and his audience would share Bede's opinion of the essential nature of a *draca* or *wyrm,* and would be familiar with this monster as a shape of the devil and his henchmen.

Only if we refuse to admit that the **Beowulf** dragon is a Christian's dragon can we be confused into thinking that he is not God's enemy, as much as, and more than, Grendel is. The poet has added his Christian lore about these creatures to the commonly received pre-Christian beliefs about them. It would be absurd to suppose that he sub-divided the *genus draco* in his mind into Biblical species and Germanic species. In Germanic folk-lore, dragons lust after gold, they are covetous and *frætwum wlanc,* though gold is useless to them. In Christian legend, the devil is seen as a serpent or dragon: his sin is arrogance. We have seen how the sins of the Danish court were reflected in Grendel: is it no more than coincidence that Hygelac the Geat died through pride and lust for gold? We have been warned in Hrothgar's sermon that as a successful king Beowulf would face the temptation of thinking himself self-sufficient:

> him eal worold
> wendeð on willan;   he þæt wyrse ne con—
> oð þæt him on innan   oferhygda dæl
> weaxeð ond wridað . . .
>
> (ll. 1738-41)

So it was with Satan before his fall. Young Beowulf was humble and not covetous—he did not desire Grendel's gold, nor did he keep back for himself anything of the royal rewards he gained in Heorot. But observe how, in Hrothgar's sermon, the prosperous ruler's growing pride and disregard of conscience gave the devil his opportunity to prompt him to further sin:

þinceð him to lytel,   þæt he lange heold,
gytsað grom-hydig.

(ll. 1748-9)

So spoke Hrothgar of his hypothetical ruler, who becomes fiercely covetous of yet more wealth. Yet, lift
that last phrase from its context, and it might equally
well form part of the description of Beowulf's dragon, savagely lusting after new treasure. This desire for
wealth is one aspect of the evil Beowulf has to fight.
The arrogance of Satan is the greater evil which menaces him: *'oferhyda ne gym, mære cempa!'* The dragon does not conquer him, but it is a mortal struggle,
and he does not win alone. As Hrothgar needed his
help, he will need Wiglaf's.

It is unfortunate that some details of the dragon story are
uncertain because of damage to the manuscript. We can,
however, be sure that some Geat—*secg syn-bysig*—
entered the dragon's mound unwittingly, when in need of
a refuge from *hete-swengeas*. Finding himself in a trea-
sure-chamber, he seizes a jewelled goblet, and makes off
with it, apparently because with it he can buy his life.
(So, Beowulf's father Ecgtheow fled from his home after
killing a man, and later bought peace with treasure sent
on his behalf by Hrothgar.) The thief's petition is granted, and his lord receives the goblet:

frea sceawode
fira fyrngeweorc   forman siðe.

(ll. 2285-6)

It is not stated whether this *frea* is Beowulf or another.
A hundred and twenty lines later, another terse statement,
which certainly refers to Beowulf, tells us—

him to bearme cwom
maðþumfæt mære   þurh ðæs meldan hond.

(ll. 2404-5)

The *melda* is his informant; whether he is one and the
same as the thief is unclear. The implication of Beowulf
in the consequences of the theft is more reasonable if we
suppose that he was in fact the receiver of the stolen cup.
Whatever the details of the affair, Beowulf eventually
keeps the goblet.

The dragon's rage on discovering the theft is terrible; he
can scarcely wait for vengeance. The poet makes the
curious observation, *apropos* the danger the thief was in
when he crept by the dragon's head:

Swa mæg unfæge   eaðe gedigan
wean ond wræcsið   se ðe Waldendes
hyldo gehealdeþ.

(ll. 2291-3)

The force of this is only seen if we look forward once
more to the time when Beowulf nears the dragon. The
thief was saved in his moment of peril because God was
with him, sinner though he was. Beowulf faced the dragon's fire without *Waldendes hyldo:*

wende se wisa,   þæt he Wealdende
ofer ealde riht   eccan Dryhtne
bitre gebulge;   breost innan weoll
þeostrum geþoncum,   swa him geþywe ne wæs.

(ll. 2329-32)

Beowulf took the dragon's visitation as God's chastise-
ment. It should be noted that the thief's motives mitigate
his sin. He made no attempt to enrich himself from the
hoard, though he was destitute and a fugitive. The dragon
did not molest him. Beowulf, on the other hand, challenged the dragon with these parting words to his thanes:

'Nis þæt eower sið,
ne gemet mannes,   nefne min anes,
þæt he wið aglæcean   eofoðe dæle,
eorlscype efne.   Ic mid elne sceall
gold gegangan,   oððe guð nimeð
feorhbealu frecne   frean eowerne!'

(ll. 2532-7)

Beowulf, like Hygelac before him, was tainted with
the sins of the dragon, arrogance and love of treasure.
Before the earlier monsterfights, he committed himself to God. This time, he boasts to his men that he
alone will win the gold. When he faced Grendel, the
poet told us

Huru Geata leod   georne truwode
modgan mægnes   Metodes hyldo.

(ll. 669-70)

Like the thief, he trusted then in *Metodes hyldo.* When
he came to face the dragon—

strengo getruwode
anes mannes;   ne bið swylc earges sið.

(ll. 2340-1)

The variation is significant. Old Beowulf was still brave,
but bravery is no substitute for *Metodes hyldo* in such a
fight.

What was this 'heathen gold' which Beowulf gave his life
to win? It was the piled-up wealth of a dead people. I do
not think any reader of the Bible could hear the 'Lay of
the Last Survivor', or the description of the treasure hoard
as Wiglaf saw it, tarnished and rusty, without being reminded of the lines from St. Matthew's Gospel, 6, 19:
*Nolite thesaurizare vobis thesauros in terra, ubi aerugo
et tinea demolitur, et ubi fures effodiunt et furantur;
thesaurizate autem vobis thesauros in cælo . . .* It does
not appear to me likely that our poet would have effected
this resemblance coincidentally, in view of the pattern of
thought which now emerges. Christ's admonition here is
the ultimate source of the earnest advice given by King
Hrothgar:

'Bebeorh þe ðone bealonið,   Beowulf leofa,
secg betsta,   ond þe þæt selre geceos,
ece rædas.'

(ll. 1758-60)

Thesaurizate thesauros in cælo is but another way of saying *geceos ece rædas,* and the evil Beowulf must shun is that of lusting after earthly wealth. With his usual astonishing sense of what is historically fitting, the poet has not given Hrothgar the actual words of Christ, but his use of this admonition, together with the rust on the treasure and the thief breaking in, leaves me with no doubt that this gospel passage was in his mind throughout the poem. It provides a key to our understanding of the matter of the buried treasure, and it is a key which the poet's postulated audience would not need to seek. Constantly, from the Scyld prelude to the pyre of Beowulf, the poet uses gold as a setting for death and destruction; constantly, in the last part of the poem, he warns us that no good comes from buried treasure. Because of this buried hoard, death will come upon Beowulf's people. The poet sums up this belief just after his prophecy of the downfall of the Geats (ll. 3028-30). First he gives another description of the treasures, *omige, Þurhetone,* and a mention of the curse on them which God alone could circumvent. Then he says:

Þa wæs gesyne,   þæt se sið ne ðah
þam þe unrihte   inne gehydde
wræte under wealle.

(ll. 3058-60)

To the Christian poet, the burial of gold is not only futile, it is actually *unrihte,* for it goes directly against Christ's command, *Nolite thesaurizare [v.l. condere] vobis thesauros in terra.*

Thus the poet has taken the legend of cursed heathen gold and turned it to his purpose. His intention in the lines I have discussed is plain; his handling of the curse itself reads awkwardly, as if he were not sure himself what power of evil incantatory spells might hold. One thing is certain, that God holds this evil power in check if He so wills. The corollary is that He allowed it to compass Beowulf's death, though the hellish torments the curse places on the despoiler did not fall upon him or upon the other Geats who touched the hoard. This is not to say that Beowulf's death was caused by a blind fate, in spite of the fact that Wiglaf and the king himself sometimes speak as though it were. Wiglaf says of Beowulf, for example:

heold on heah-gesceap.

(l. 3084)

But that this is a manner of speaking rather than a philosophical statement is clear from the context. This is the closing line of his speech beginning:

Oft sceall eorl monig   anes willan
wræc adreogan,   swa us geworden is.

(ll. 3077-8)

He implies that Beowulf acted wrongly. The difference between the Christian and heathen outlook on Fate is this: the Christian believes that a man is responsible for his acts, whatever the circumstances. The Geats' distress was caused *anes willan,* by Beowulf's choice of strife with the dragon for the sake of the gold. Had he not desired to win this gold, the curse would not have touched him. I think this may be what the poet is trying to say in the couplet which ends the account of the horrors of the curse (ll. 3074-5) though it would be hazardous to build any argument on a passage so obscure. All I would remark is that the sentence as it stands does not preclude such an interpretation, and there is no need to assume any special contextual meanings (as is often done) *unless* we are trying to exculpate Beowulf. Shorn of its complications, the sentence appears to read:

Næs he . . . gearwor hæfde . . . est ær gesceawod
(ll. 3074-5)

The verb *sceawian* has been used previously of the lord's gazing upon the stolen cup (l. 2285), and the same combination of *gearo* and *sceawian* is used of Beowulf's dying eagerness to look upon the buried treasure. He says to Wiglaf:

Bio nu on ofoste,   þæt is ærwelan
goldæht ongite,   gearo sceawige
swegle searogimmas,   þæt ic ðy seft mæge
æfter maððumwelan min alætan
lif ond leodscipe,   þone ic longe heold.

(ll. 2747-51)

Since *est,* used concretely, normally means 'a mark of favour', 'a gift', it seems to me reasonable to interpret this *agendes est* (l. 3075) as 'the gift of the possessor', i.e. the stolen cup which first roused Beowulf's desire to win the dragon's hoard. The doubtful adjective *goldhwæte,* 'rich in gold', appropriately describes this *maÞÞumfæt mære* which came into Beowulf's possession; *ær* would then refer to the first occasion on which he saw the cup. We are left with the logical puzzle of *næs . . . gearwor,* 'not at all more readily'; I should like to interpret this as marking the contrast between Beowulf's reluctant acceptance of the stolen cup and his later eagerness to examine the buried board. The context of the curse apart then, I would regard the following as a likely rendering: 'Very much less readily before had he looked upon the gold-encrusted gift of the possessor'. But if it be argued that the postulated connexion between *agendes est* and the stolen cup is too tenuous, we are driven to taking *est* in some vaguer sense, as some previous 'mark of favour' given to Beowulf. I should still consider the two lines a virtual statement that Beowulf had sought this cursed hoard more eagerly than he had sought other treasure in the past. Putting these two lines into their context, we have a sequence: that no man knows where he will meet death; Beowulf did not know the cause of his death; did not know there was a curse on the treasure when he sought the dragon fight, desiring that treasure more than other treasures he had looked upon. This is coherent, whereas the usual view, that the last two lines stress Beowulf's *lack* of covetousness, provides us with a malign curse, falling, *with God's approval,* on Beowulf's *innocent* head.

The curse, as I see it, is retained to symbolize the evil power of hoarded gold. This interpretation gives point to the otherwise gratuitous

> Sinc eaþe mæg
> gold on grunde   gumcynnes gehwone
> oferhigian.
>
> (ll. 2764-6)

It also brings the curse into line with Hrothgar's homily. It must not be suggested that Beowulf died in mortal sin. I take it that the dragon fight, in which he was slain in slaying the monster, represents the struggle with temptation, so often described in saints' lives in terms of a physical contest. After the fight, his soul leaves his body:

> secean soðfæstra dom.
>
> (l. 2820)

The word *soðfæst* translates the Vulgate Latin *justus,* the righteous man, and the phrase used here appears to be the equivalent of the Patristic Latin *justorum judicium.* Beowulf has lived most of his life according to the *eald riht,* and though he falls short of Christian ideals, he goes after death as a good man to judgement, not, like an Unferth, to damnation. The gold the hero gave his life for lies useless in the ground, but his noble life has won him the hope of eternal reward.

There is a great deal more in the latter half of the poem, but it is all subordinated to the theme of the treasure which is Beowulf's bane and the cause of the overthrow of the Geats. Two passages stand out from the 'historical' matter. One is the description of the death of Hrethel's heir and the old man's heart-break. The other is Wiglaf's condemnation of the cowardly retainers.

The first of these passages has been admirably discussed by Professor Whitelock, who shows the point of departure of the simile in which Hrethel's grief is compared with that of an old man whose son is hanged. The extension of the simile seems to ask for other explanation. It rouses an emotion which will be transferred to old Beowulf, who grieves as he faces death that he has no son to whom he could pass on his rich possessions. There may be some bitterness in Beowulf's last words on Hrethel:

> eaferum læfde,   swa deð eadig mon,
> lond ond leodbyrig,   þa he of life gewat.
>
> (ll. 2470-1)

Beowulf himself has no *eafera* to cherish what he has won. The poet has seized upon the historical event of King Hrethel's decline after the death of his eldest son to elaborate upon the human desolation of the man who has no use for his riches. Hrethel ceased to take delight in the comforts of this world:

> gumdream ofgeaf,   Godes leoht geceas.
>
> (ll. 2469)

There is a hint in the choice of these words describing his death, that Hrethel may have found a higher consolation when human joy was denied him. The ultimate effect of the whole passage is to increase our sense of the futility of amassing earthly wealth, even for the sake of passing it on to a son.

The other passage I mentioned, the condemnation of the retainers who fled, at first sight seems to bear little relation to the themes I have been discussing. Yet even this conventional and obviously unavoidable part of the story has been made to bear upon the poet's chief preoccupations. The men whose loyalty Beowulf has bought with rings and weapons turn and flee when they see him being worsted. Only Wiglaf will risk his life for his lord, for there is for him the greater bond of kinship:

> Sibb æfre ne mæg
> wiht onwendan   þam þe wel þenceð.
>
> (ll. 2600-1)

This is the obverse of the story of Heorot, where men plot the murder of their kin. Wiglaf does not think of his own possible advancement if Beowulf dies. His love and loyalty sustain Beowulf, and together they overcome the dragon.

The poem ends with the king's funeral rites and the committal of the hard-won treasure to the earth:

> eldum swa unnyt,   swa hit æror wæs.
>
> (ll. 3167-8)

As his memorial is raised, his followers sing a lament in which Beowulf's deeds are praised. They celebrate his mildness and gentleness and his desire for fame. This is a very odd epitaph for a Germanic warrior, yet it is in keeping with the poet's view of the hero (in ll. 2177-83). It befits the old man who could boast in his last hour:

> ne sohte searoniðas,
>
> (ll. 2738)

and who rejoiced that God could not reproach him with the slaying of kinsmen (ll. 2741-2). That he has *not* murdered any of his family seems a curiously negative virtue for the old king to take pride in: the only reason for the insistence appears to be the poet's obsession with Cain, the fratricide.

It is important to realize that to Bede, and hence, most certainly, to the ***Beowulf*** poet, Cain was more than the first murderer and the progenitor of giants. Bede explains:

> Sicut ab initio seculi incipientis in occisione Abel passiones sanctorum; in livore autem et persecutione Cain perfidiæ sunt insinuatæ reproborum, quæ ad finem usque sæculi erunt ambæ in mundo permansuræ; sic et in civitate quam ædificavit Cain typice intimabatur, quod spes tota pravorum in hujus sæculi regno esset ac felicitate figenda, ut pote qui futurorum bonorum aut fidem aut desiderium nullum haberent.

Cain typifies the wicked, who cause the innocent to suffer. The wicked, the race of Cain, build their cities in this world because all their hope lies here: they have no faith in *ece rædas*.

Thus the two halves of the poem come together in one. 'Treasure upon earth' is the desire of the followers of Cain, and envy, treachery, and killing attend its satisfaction. Hrothgar, forgetting his mortality in the pride of his palace, is no less a part of the Cain-motive than Unferth killing his brother or Hrothulf scheming to gain the throne. Hrothgar, chastened by Grendel's visitation, warns Beowulf against coveting the glory and wealth of this world. Beowulf's temptation takes symbolic shape in the dragon's cursed treasure, for which the king, in his pride, would have given his life in vain, had it not been for Wiglaf, who rated the love of kin higher than his own life.

The poem was obviously not composed as an allegory, in the way that *Piers Plowman* was composed. The stories existed, and the poet, I believe, saw symbolic significance in them, which he has pointed and elaborated by his manipulation of the tales. He has treated the story of heathen Beowulf as an exegete might have treated, say, the story of Samson, by drawing a moral lesson from the hero's deeds. Above all, in his treatment of the 'digressions' he has concentrated his listeners' thoughts on certain aspects of the cleansing of Heorot and the burial of the treasure, so as to emphasize, not just a morbid sense of decay and doom, but his faith in the greater good of lasting wealth, the wealth of the spirit. In this respect *Beowulf* seems to me no different in intention from the other Old English elegies we have. The chief inspiration of such poems is ultimately the Psalms.

Besides the Psalms, the poet obviously had in mind some of the teachings of Gregory and Augustine. A Gregorian source has been argued for Hrothgar's homily, and others have seen the influence of Augustine in the portrayal of the virtues of the ruler. The theme of the whole poem as I have outlined it is Augustinian in spirit; the ultimate source may be found in St. Paul's First Epistle to Timothy. Some phrases from this epistle have become proverbial, though their context is less well known. Together, in c. 6, we find three thoughts which seem to me the essence of the doctrine the poet wished to bring home:

> Radix enim omnium malorum est cupiditas, quam quidem appetentes erraverunt a fide et inseruerunt se doloribus multis.
>
> (v. 10)

> Certa bonum certamen fidei, apprehende vitam æternam.
>
> (v. 12)

> Divitibus huius mundi non sublime sapere neque sperare in incerto divitiarum, sed in Deo vero . . . bene agere, divites fieri in bonis operibus . . . thesaurizare sibi fundamentum bonum in futurum, ut apprehendant veram vitam.
>
> (v. 17)

Paul sees the good man as a fighter in the war against evil, who by freeing himself from *cupiditas* lays up for himself heavenly treasure. I suggest that the *Beowulf* poet saw, in the legendary life of a heathen hero, an opportunity to write of this fight against the devil and the seed of Cain. In the strife which forms the background of the story, he saw the sins of Cain still causing suffering to the innocent; in the gold of Heorot and the buried treasure, he saw the hope and achievement of those who, like Cain, have no faith in a future good; in the monsters, he saw the embodiment of the evils which the devil has let loose upon the world. So, in the heroic tragedy of *Beowulf,* he showed his audience that many of the old Germanic virtues might be used in the service of God, in that unending feud which began before Adam was created.

Jack Durant   (essay date 1962)

SOURCE: "The Function of Joy in *Beowulf,*" in *Tennessee Studies in Literature,* Vol. VII, 1962, pp. 61-69.

[*In the excerpt that follows, Durant defines three types or "levels" of joy in* Beowulf *and demonstrates how these levels work to unify the poem's structure, present its major plots, and support some of its themes.*]

Critics rarely fail to remark the heavy aura of gloom surrounding **Beowulf.** To Klaeber, for example, the Beowulf-poet evidences an "especial fondness" for "feelings of grief and sadness." [All citations to **Beowulf** are taken from Fr. Klaeber's third edition (Boston, 1950) of the poem.] Tolkien goes even so far as to style the poem an heroic-elegy. "In a sense," he writes, "all its first 3136 lines are the prelude to a dirge." Even the joy in **Beowulf** is largely looked upon as a foil for sorrow. Thus Adrien Bonjour observes that joyful settings often provide frameworks for anticipations of woe. Herbert Wright points up the dramatic contrasts of joy and sorrow. And Arthur Brodeur finds the joy in **Beowulf** to be a significant relief mechanism—a mechanism used to keep the reader fresh for the poem's periodic horrors. By no means, however, is the well-guarded gloom of **Beowulf** outraged by the suggestion that joy in this poem exists for its own sake. Out of a synthesis of the poem's many references to joy and rejoicing arises the suggestion that three fairly distinct levels of joy are apparent in **Beowulf;** and it is further demonstrable that the interactions of these levels serve variously (1) to define certain of the conflicts, (2) to strengthen the structural unity, (3) to delineate the major plots, (4) to support several of the themes, and (5) to clarify the heroic nature of the central figure.

At the outset it should be said that the levels of joy in **Beowulf** are but slightly discernible in verbal connotations. "Wyn(n)," the most frequent of the joy words, is used variously to express earthly joy ("worolde wynne," 1080; "eorþan wynne," 1730, 2727), convival joy ("hearpan wynne," 2107), and joy of might ("mægenes wynnum," 1716, 1887). Similarly diverse are the uses of "dream" and "gefea." Since the selection of joy words seems largely to have been governed by the demands of alliteration or by the principles of variety (rather than by specialized connotations), the levels of joy are most easily discernible through contexts. And while expressions of joy are frequently formulaic, no one of them seems to be superfluous, to be psychologically unjustifiable, or to be significantly ill-suited to its context.

I

The most prominent level of joy in **Beowulf** might suitably be labeled "social joy." Basically, this is the joy of participation in the *comitatus,* and it exalts virtually every aspect of the *comitatus* relationship. The joy of the *principes,* for instance, finds expression in Wealhtheow's exhortation to Hrothgar, "'bruc þenden þu mote / manigra medo'" (1177b-78a), and it is further reflected in Hrothgar's reference to the joys of rule, "'on eþle eorþan wynne'" (1730). Evidences of the joy of the *comites* are apparent in passages describing the revelry in Heorot and (more poignantly) in the joy experienced by the Geats upon seeing their prince return to them out of the mere (1626-28). Also contributing to social joy is the joy of the heroic *dom.* This, of course, is the joy of personal achievement, the pleasure to be derived from the prospect of fame and from the admirations of tokens of glory. Sigemund experiences this joy as he takes personal pleasure in the hoard he has won (893-895); and with similar satisfaction Beowulf, whose awareness of his own fame is indisputable, delights in the treasures which go with him from Denmark (1880-82a).

It is worth noting, I think, that social joy in **Beowulf** has little dependence upon devotion to God. Just as godly men (such as Beowulf and Hrothgar) suffer woe, so ungodly men (such as Unferth) participate in social joy. God, of course, is exalted in the singing of the scop (89-98); His power is the acknowledged source of greatness (1724-34), but He remains upon the periphery of social joy. And while His laws are certainly outraged by the behavior of a Heremod, Heremod's evils are predominantly social evils. His violation of the *comitatus* sends him alone from the joys of men (1714-15).

It is to be agreed, of course, that in being "dreamum bedæled" (721), Grendel, like Cain, is bereft of joys both social and spiritual. On more than one occasion, however, we are given to know that Grendel is capable of his own sort of grim exultation. And his joy, "diabolic joy," suggests the second of the broad levels of joy in **Beowulf.** When Grendel sees the Geats sleeping in Heorot, for example, his heart exults: "Þa his mod ahlog" (730). He experiences the very sensation Beowulf had imagined his having—the upshot of a happy diabolism: "he lust wigeð." Beowulf had said, "swefeð ond snedeþ" (599b-600a). The firedrake, too, experiences this grim joy. For while he is not a man-eater, a man-hater he certainly is; and he takes pleasure in this hatred, rejoicing in the imminence of his encounter with Beowulf: "hwæðre *wiges* gefeh, / bea(du) [we] weorces" (2298b-99a). It is against this attitude of happy belligerence that the third level of joy, "spiritual joy," stands diametrically opposed.

Interestingly enough, the discernment of spiritual joy is not involved in vague references to the joys of heaven. So uniformly secular is the poet's vocabulary of joy that his one use of the phrase "heofones wynne" (1801) is simply a kenning for "sun." All his references to joy, then, partake of a common secular vocabulary; all are identifiable with practical human experience. Thus, surely, the joy in his poem was to his audience (as it is to us) peculiarly meaningful and quite readily realizable. As I mean to illustrate, spiritual joy in **Beowulf** is perceived in terms of social joy.

Inasmuch as spiritual joy figures prominently in considerations of the poem's themes and in the character of its hero (matters discussed below), it is enough here to say that Beowulf alone participates in this joy. The attitudes in which it is discerned suggest themselves in his motivations to heroism: chiefly his readiness to serve and his respect for human brotherhood. And these attitudes resolve themselves into joy when, lying mortally wounded, he reflects upon the conduct of his life and when he rejoices in the treasure-hoard he has won.

In **Beowulf,** then, there are three levels of joy: social joy, diabolic joy, and spiritual joy. At the outset it was suggested that the interaction of these levels serves variously (1) to define certain of the conflicts, (2) to strengthen the unity, (3) to delineate the major plots, (4) to support themes, and (5) to clarify the heroic nature of the central figure. Demonstration of the first two of these functions requires further analysis of diabolic joy.

II

Adrien Bonjour seems quite conclusively to have answered T. M. Gang's contention that "the dragon is altogether a different sort of creature from the Grendel-tribe." Indeed, Bonjour has corralled quite an impressive list of parallels between the firedrake and the two monsters from the mere. Like them, for example, the dragon is invulnerable to ordinary swords; he bears a latent grudge against mankind; he is a night-raider; he is a solitary fighter; he is a scourge of the people. And it should further be said that he is a participant in diabolic joy. Since, however, this participation allies him with Grendel only (and not with Grendel's dam) it is necessary that distinctions be drawn among the conflicts motivating Beowulf's three great encounters.

In the light of diabolic joy it becomes apparent that the malice which delights Grendel and the firedrake is not shared by Grendel's dam. At no times does the she-wolf rejoice in her opportunities for vengeance, nor does she demonstrate an unreasonable jealousy of social joy. She is uniformly sorrowful even as she acts upon a principle enunciated by Beowulf himself: "Selre bið ægwhæm, / þæt he his freond wrece, þonne he fela murne'" (1384-85). Thus Beowulf's excursion to the mere is predicated on the same retributive policy that brings Grendel's dam to Heorot. Because of Beowulf's grand moral stature, there is justice in his victory; but since the combatants fight under equal causes, there is also justice in the severity of their strife.

A distinction, then, is to be made between Beowulf's conflict with Grendel's dam and his conflicts with Grendel and the firedrake. It has been argued that the firedrake suffers outrage and that the Beowulf-poet is somewhat sympathetic to him. But these attitudes are not really tenable. The poet obviously resents the dragon's seizure of a treasure-hoard for which he has no earthly use ("ne byð him wihte ðy sel," 2277b). Such hoards, says the poet, are joy-giving ("Hordwynne," 2270). They contribute to the functions of the *comitatus,* to social order, to social joy. In principle, then, the dragon's *raison d'etre* is as objectionable as Grendel's. And when he renews his strife with mankind, he brings with him the same delight in the purposes of destruction that Grendel had brought. Beowulf seems himself to be aware of this parallel; for when he arms himself for combat against the dragon, he recalls his fight not with Grendel's dam but with Grendel, insisting that were he certain to make his vow good, he would now renounce his weapons, "swa ic gio wið Grendle dyde" (2521b).

In helping to define conflicts, diabolic joy also strengthens the unity of *Beowulf.* It does this by pointing up an A B A structure in the sequence of the three great encounters—a structure which, to the modern mind at least, effects a unity far stronger than does the A A B structure implied in Gang's argument or the A A A structure implied in Bonjour's.

III

The two major plots in *Beowulf* involve (1) the heroic actions of the central figure, and (2) the destinies of the peoples to whom his energies are dedicated. By examining the joy relative to these two large plot strains, it becomes apparent that delineation of plots is significantly supported by the interplay of social joy and spiritual joy.

It is frequently remarked that the first half of the poem is predominantly cheerful. Its tone befits, as Professor Malone suggests, a period of youth. In the midst of this cheer, however, there is always the menacing anticipation of sorrow—a sorrow which (according to many critics) permeates the second half. "In Part II," writes Brodeur, "there is no present weal to afford contrast with impending woe; instead, the unrelieved darkness of the theme contrasts bleakly with the recollected splendor and glory of Part I." Indeed, there is discernible in the poem a gradual shading-out of joy. The burst of exultation which accompanies Beowulf's first "beot" (his announced determination to destroy Grendel) is sustained in the glorious celebration of his victory. But the second return from the mere is as sober and stately as is the first one jubilant; and the feast celebrating the destruction of Grendel's dam is significantly less joyous (at least in duration) than is the celebration accompanying Grendel's own demise. After Beowulf's return to Geatland, joy almost "has to be divined" (to use H. G. Wright's phrase). And while happy times are recalled in the hero's account of his experience, these joys, alas, are purely reflective. I think, however, that Brodeur is only partially right in saying that in Part II "the unrelieved darkness of the theme contrasts bleakly with the recollected splendor and glory of Part I." For it should be noted that the contrast he points applies only to social joy and that it involves the secondary plot: that treating the destinies of the peoples to whom Beowulf's energies are dedicated. Spiritual joy at last arises in rapid counterpoint. This joy is applicable solely to the primary plot; and it continues to flourish, even while social joy fades.

The fading of social joy in *Beowulf* is, of course, rich in thematic values. Most significantly, it provides a grim parable for social man, pointing up the necessity of human interdependence. The blood-greedy Heremod (1719), the drunken spearsman at the court of the Heathobards (2042), the man driven by need to molest the dragon (2223)—all these men violate their responsibility to social order; thus social joy dies. Also exemplified in the fading of social joy is the validity of Wiglaf's observation:

> Oft sceall eorl monig anes willan
> wraec adreogan, swa us geworden is.
>
> (377-78)

This observation illustrates, of course, the guiltless man's liability to sorrow. It enlarges upon the total theme of social joy by suggesting that while one is never free from the menaces of human frailty, one can minimize the frequencies of sorrow by scrupulous observation of social decorum and by uncompromising respect for social order. It should further be noted that the death of social joy provides a striking contrast for the spiritual joy which at the close of the poem is very much alive. Through spiritual joy, themes are further articulated; further insight into the character of the central figure is gained.

IV

Before encountering the firedrake, Beowulf, who is not characteristically sorrowful ("swa him geþywe ne wæs," 2332b), experiences a long moment of deep depression. He reproaches himself for having somehow offended God (2329-31a). He sadly anticipates his own death (2419-24). He identifies himself with the sorrowful history of the Geats, recalling the tragedies of Herebeald and Hæthcyn, lamenting the miseries of Hrethel (2426-2509). Thus sadly, but with heroic determination and with full awareness of his social duties (his "eorlscype," 2535), he faces the dragon. At last, however, the sickness of heart which accompanies him to battle stands in dramatic contrast to the joy he experiences as he lies mortally wounded. In a long speech (2724-43a), he there reviews the successes of his rule, affirming that he has guarded his own people well, that he has sought no treacherous quarrels, nor sworn many an oath unjustly. And although he is sick unto death, he now has joy: "Ic þæs ealles mæg / feorhbennum seoc gefean habban'" (2739b-40).

It was earlier suggested that this expression of joy resolves itself out of attitudes which throughout the poem are reflected in Beowulf's behavior: his readiness to serve ("heold min tela," 2737b) and his respect for human broth-erhood ("me witan ne ðearf Walden fira / morðorbealo maga." 2741-42a). It is appropriate, of course, that broth-erhood be quite strongly emphasized in this speech, for the brotherhood motif (an important thematic strain) here has its culmination.

Beowulf's contribution to this motif is reflected in many of the poem's episodes: it is apparent, certainly, in the altercation with Unferth (where disrespect for brother-hood is summarily condemned, 587); it is apparent in the Cain-spirit embodied in Beowulf's great adversaries. And it is especially apparent in the spirit with which Beowulf presents his newly won treasure to Hygelac. He tenders his gifts with pleasure, taking joy in the strong bond of kinship which binds him to his king. "'Gen in eall æt ðe / lissa gelong,'" he says to Hygelac (2149b-50a). And so characteristic of Beowulf is the warm spirit of brother-hood reflected in these words that the poet pauses to comment on its significance to his life (2177-83a), caus-ing it, at last, to be a source of joy to the dying hero.

Beowulf's life of service (the second of the virtues cul-minating in his final joy) finds keen expression not only in his long reflection upon the conduct of his life (2732-43, summarized above) but also in his eagerness to see the gold he has won in overcoming the firedrake (2747-51). Wiglaf views this gold rejoicing in victory ("sigehre-ðig," 2756), and for a moment one recalls the joys of the victorious Sigemund. Beowulf, of course, evidences none of the energetic exultations Wiglaf enjoys, but he finds comfort in the hoard; and the comfort thus taken has given rise to perplexities.

Miss Bertha Phillpots, for example, finds this episode contradictory to the Christ-image Klaeber has seen in Beowulf: "Would it not be too strange an irony," she writes [in *Essays and Studies,* 1913], "if the author had such a prototype in his mind, to make the dying hero exult in the dragon's gold, and insist on seeing it as he lies dying—gold which is buried with him, 'as unprofit-able to men as it had been before'?" There is irony, of course, in the fact that Beowulf must lay down his life for a worthless heap of treasures. After his death, the hoard comes . . . to symbolize "the joys now to pass for ever from the Geats." But Beowulf does not participate in this grand irony. His joy in the gold is a joy which derives from the principles of service, not from a lust for riches:

> Ic ðara frætwa Frean ealles ðanc,
> Wuldurcyninge wordum secge,
> ecum Dryhtne, þe ic her on starie,
> þæs þe ic moste minum leodum
> ær swyltdæge swylc gestrynan.
>
> (2794-98)

The Sigemund episode, an obvious parallel to Beowulf's fight with the firedrake, helps to define the peculiar com-fort taken by Beowulf in the treasure-hoard. The poet is careful to tell us that the treasures won by Sigemund were his to enjoy at his own discretion: "he beahhordes

brucan moste / selfes dome" (894-895a). Sigemund's joy, then, is social joy. His gold will provide him with phys-ical comfort and prestige. It is pertinent to the practical interdependences of men. Beowulf, however, is at the end of his life. He can look for no physical comfort, but he can find spiritual comfort in the universal principles of brotherhood and service.

Professor Malone has observed [in "Beowulf," *English Studies,* XXIX (1948)] that Beowulf is really a virtuous pagan. "He is made as Christ-like as the setting permits, but all his virtues can be explained quite naturally as grow-ing out of the heroic ideals of conduct traditional among the English as among the other Germanic peoples." Thus it is that considered as isolated sources of pleasure, the joys Beowulf evidences at the close of his life are social joys: brotherhood, service, delight in winning and giving gold. But the imminence of his death removes these joys from the realm of social function. It abstracts them into universal principles—the principles upon which Beowulf's heroic nature is in large part based and through which he gains his "soðfæstra dom" (2820). Spiritual joy, then, is perceived in terms of social joy. And it enlarges upon the themes of social joy by suggesting that while a custom-ary observation of the principles of service and brother-hood may contribute to an impermanent temporal joy, devotion to the ideals of these principles gives rise to a joy not subject to the irresponsibilities of men or to the menaces of Fate.

Taylor Culbert   (essay date 1963)

SOURCE: "Narrative Technique in *Beowulf,*" in *Neophilo-logus,* Vol. XLVII, No. 1, 1963, pp. 50-61.

[*In the excerpt that follows, Culbert examines the points of view used and the excitement generated in each of Beowulf's three battles, and concludes that Beowulf's last two battles—with Grendel's mother and with the dragon, respectively—are relatively anticlimactic.*]

In recent years, attention has been called to the artistry exhibited by the *Beowulf*-poet in his depiction of Beowulf's three fights. Through skillful use of various narrative techniques, he created interest in the accounts of the hero's combats with Grendel, Grendel's dam, and the dragon. Lumiansky, for instance, has described the use of a dramatic audience as a means of enhancing the interest of the combats. And Moorman has stated that the poet used various points of view to maintain interest in the fights. The present paper will explore further certain narrative techniques employed by the *Beowulf*-poet for the depiction of the three combats. It will show that the combat with Grendel is reported three times, and that each version is differentiated from the other two. Both Beowulf's other combats are likewise reported three times, but in neither case do the accounts reveal narrative artistry of as high an order as that evinced in the presen-tation of the fight with Grendel.

For the narration of the entire poem, the **Beowulf**-poet adopted the point of view of an omniscient author, of an epic teller, who observes and records the physical action, describes what Beowulf or any other character said, comments on the action, and allows himself to look into the minds and hearts of Beowulf, Hroðgar, and even of Beowulf's non-human adversaries so that he can report what they hoped, feared, and thought. That the poet is telling the story in his own person is indicated by his use of *w* in line 1 and by the many references to himself, the narrator, as *ic* in lines 38, 62, 74, 1011, 1027, 1196, 1197, 2163, 2172, 2694, 2752, and 2773. [All line references and quotations are from **Beowulf,** ed. Fr. Klaeber (3rd ed., Boston, 1941).] The poet also refers to himself by the words *m ne gefræge* that appear in lines 776, 837, 1955, 2685, and 2837. Although this may be a stock phrase, it reveals the vantage point from which the tale is told.

The epic teller observes the physical action even when he is theoretically not present. When Beowulf fights Grendel's dam in her cave, there is no witness; yet the poet reports the actions of both combatants: for example, Beowulf seizes Grendel's dam by the shoulder (lines 1537-38), and she attacks the hero and draws her dagger (lines 1545-46a). The story-teller also relates what is said, directly by quoting speeches verbatim and indirectly by asserting that such-and-such a character said so-and-so. Thus the poet quotes Beowulf's first person report to Hroðgar concerning his fight with Grendel's dam (lines 1651-76). The fact that during this speech Beowulf refers to himself as *ic* (lines 1655, 1659, 1662, 1668, etc.) does not signify that the point of view has changed. The epic teller—omniscient author—is still reporting what he heard and saw. He prefaces his report with the words "Beowulf maþelode, bearn Ecgþ owes" (1651); and he heard Beowulf give a speech in these very words. The teller occasionally presents indirectly what his characters said. The watchers on the shore are pictured as talking about Beowulf and saying that they no longer had hopes of seeing him again, though their actual words are not given (lines 1591-99). Finally, the narrator describes what went on in the minds of characters, both human and non-human. He says, for example, that Beowulf rejoiced in his work (line 1569b), that Grendel's dam hoped to avenge her son (lines 1546b-47a), that Grendel was struck with fear and wished to flee (lines 753b-756a), and that Beowulf remembered some words that had been spoken earlier (lines 758-759a).

Now, from this point of view, the author looks particularly at some one element of the scene before him: at Beowulf, at Grendel, at the watchers, or whatnot. This object that is looked at is the narrative focus. To present Beowulf's thoughts, for instance, the narrator adopts the point of view of an omniscient author and gives us a glimpse into Beowulf's mind; or he causes Beowulf to reveal his private thoughts by having him declare them through a public utterance. In either case, a reader's attention is directed toward Beowulf. The subject that is presented to the reader's gaze, Beowulf in this case, is the focus of the narrative at this particular juncture. In

practice, the point of view in **Beowulf,** that of the epic teller, remains constant, but the narrative focus varies frequently.

Moorman has asserted [in "Suspense and Foreknowledge in *Beowulf*," *College English,* 15 (April 1954), 379-383] that the poet relied almost entirely upon two "points of view" for the first description of Beowulf's encounter with Grendel; he presented the fight principally from the "points of view" of Grendel and of the watchers in the hall, but made very sparing use of Beowulf's "point of view". In fact, he finds only four brief passages narrated through the hero's eyes. Although his term "point of view" seems to be misleading, Moorman's conclusion that "the **Beowulf** poet is able to create a good deal of audience interest in the actual battle sequence by maneuvering the possible points of view by which he may describe his scene" at least calls attention to an important element in the presentation of this episode. It is clear that the poet is aware of point of view (or narrative focus), that he has made little use of Beowulf as a possible focal point for relating the Grendel combat, and that he has adopted several points of focus to achieve, among other results, a pleasing variety in the depiction of this fight. There is a real possibility, however, that the apparent neglect of Beowulf was deliberate and that the poet postponed use of this perspective so that he might exploit it more fully in the two later reports of the fight where the hero's views could be presented under more appropriate circumstances.

The general scheme of the poem required a description of the battle with Grendel when it occurred; a second account of the fight was demanded for the benefit of Hroðgar following the battle; and a third version, Beowulf's report of his adventures upon his return to Hygelac, was also necessary. The obvious danger of inartistic repetition inherent in presenting three versions of the same encounter was avoided in two ways: (1) by adroit handling of narrative focus so that Beowulf's two personal reports of the action, the second and third versions, stress aspects of the combat other than those stressed in the first and more nearly complete account, and (2) by the revelation of previously undisclosed details in each version of the fight, with the result that notice must be taken of all three versions in order to arrive at a complete picture of the combat.

In the initial presentation of Beowulf's fight with Grendel, six passages are focused upon the hero: lines 736b-738, Beowulf's observation of Grendel's actions; lines 748b-749, Beowulf's reactions to Grendel's advance; lines 758-760, the hero's recollection of his boasts and his attack upon the foe; line 761b, his movement toward the escaping adversary; lines 788b-794a, Beowulf's refusal to allow Grendel to escape; and lines 818b-819a, the statement that Beowulf won glory for this deed. In view of the extent of this account of the struggle, lines 710 to 824, and in view of the fact that it would seem likely that the bulk of the fight should be focused upon Beowulf—he is, after all, the hero—the few brief uses of this narrative focus are quite surprising. There must be some very good reason, in addition to a desire to vary the narrative focus, for the poet's adoption of this unusual procedure.

The explanation becomes apparent when Beowulf's report to Hroðgar is examined. After Hroðgar has thanked Beowulf for delivering him and his hall from Grendel's depredations (lines 925-956), Beowulf presents his account of the combat. At this time, what the hero tried to accomplish, what he did achieve, and particularly what he thought during the battle can be reported with greater naturalness and appropriateness than at any other time. His speech contains several direct references to himself: *wē* in line 958 and *ic* in lines 960, 963, 967, and 968. As a result of the quotation of Beowulf's exact words and of the personal references within the speech, the hero himself is thrust prominently before the reader. In addition, the narrative focus of Beowulf's report is divided between himself and his foe, with more than half the lines (59%, 957-970a) dwelling upon his own part in the combat. But even in lines 970b-979 (41%), in which the narrative focus rests upon Grendel, Beowulf himself, because he is the speaker, is not removed completely from the picture. Throughout the entire speech, the story-teller maintains his omniscient point of view and focuses upon Beowulf by reporting verbatim Beowulf's words to Hroðgar. In the first part of Beowulf's speech, there is in effect a double focus upon the speaker; and in the second part, the focus of the story-teller remains upon Beowulf whereas the focus of Beowulf's own words rests upon Grendel. Thus in one way or another Beowulf is on display throughout the entire passage.

Upon his return to his own land, after the encounters with Grendel and Grendel's dam, Beowulf is obliged to relate to Hygelac his adventures in Hroðgar's realm. For the duration of Beowulf's entire report, the narrative focus of the omniscient author rests upon Beowulf as he speaks to Hygelac. But within the context of the speech, the narrative focus of the speaker rests at various times upon the speaker himself, upon his adversary, and upon the bystanders. Throughout the speech, Beowulf devotes 37% of the lines to himself (lines 1999-2009a and 2091b-96a), and regards the other men in the hall 12% of the time, just long enough to mention the slaying of Hondscio (lines 2076-80); the remainder of his speech that is concerned with the combat (lines 2069b-75, 2081-91a, and 2096b-100, 51% of the total) is focused upon Grendel, describing his actions and intentions. Like his previous account of the fight, this version gives prominence to Beowulf in that his words are reported directly; and at the same time it achieves an air of vigor and movement through a shifting focus within the speech itself.

Not only has the ***Beowulf*-**poet rendered each telling of the battle distinctive by his handling of narrative focus, but he has further differentiated each version of the fight by the presentation of new information, with the result that a complete account of the battle can be obtained only by considering all three passages dealing with it. The second report of the fight, that delivered by Beowulf

to Hroðgar, adds to our knowledge of the combat by revealing the hero's thoughts and feelings during the actual contention. We learn, for example, that "Ic hine hrædl ce heardan clammum / on wælbedde wrī þan þōhte" (lines 963-964), that "ic hine ne mihte, þa Metod nolde, / ganges getwæman" (lines 967-968a), and that "nō ic him þæs georne ætfealh, / feorhgenī ðlan" (lines 968b-969a). The third account, that presented to Hygelac, adds several specific details to the picture of the battle. We are told in the first account of the fight that Grendel seized and ate a sleeping warrior (lines 739-745a), but we learn here for the first time the name of the warrior who was eaten by Grendel: Hondscio (line 2076). We hear too in this third report of the glove or pouch that Grendel carried and of his intention to stuff Beowulf and other men into it:

> Nō ðy ær ūt ða gēn   īdelhende
> bona blōdigtōð, bealewa gemyndig,
> of ðam goldsele gongan wolde;
> ac hē mægnes rōf mīn costode,
> grapode gearofolm. Glōf hangode
> sīd ond syllīc,   searobendum fæst;
> sīo wæs orðoncum eall gegyrwed
> dēofles cræftum ond dracan fellum.
> Hē mec þær on innan unsynnigne,
> dīor dædfruma gedōn wolde
> manigra sumne.
>
> (lines 2081-91a)

In addition, we are told that it was Grendel's right arm that was torn off and preserved as a trophy of the combat: "hwæþre him s o sw ðre swaðe weardade / hand on Hiorte" (2098-99a).

The depiction of Beowulf's combat with Grendel's dam exhibits traces of the same narrative methods, although they are not developed and handled with equal skill and firmness of hand. Like the Grendel combat, this fight is described three times, once as it occurs, once in the form of a report to Hroðgar, and once as the hero's account of his achievements to Hygelac. The point of view adopted for the narration of all three versions is that of the omniscient author; and from this vantage point the poet focuses upon the three participants in the action: Beowulf, the adversary, and a dramatic audience composed of watchers on the shore.

The preliminaries of this combat include the initial attack by Grendel's dam (lines 1251-309), Hroðgar's appeal to Beowulf to undertake this exploit (lines 1310-82), and Beowulf's agreement to fight, his arming, and his statements to his companions (lines 1383-491). Throughout this introduction, the narrative focus remains rather constantly upon the hero. The account of the combat itself starts with Beowulf's trip to the bottom of the lake and concludes with the slaying of the foe (lines 1492-572a). To these lines must be added the closely related post-combat events (lines 1572b-650), which include the activities of Beowulf in his adversary's lair and the reactions of the watchers on the shore during and immediately after the combat.

Because the fight takes places beneath the water, in the lair of Grendel's dam, where obviously none can be present except the two combatants, the poet had no choice but to adopt the point of view of an omniscient author and to focus the narrative upon one and then the other participant. He starts with a description of Beowulf's approach through the water (lines 1492-96), and then switches to the adversary for her discovery of the invader, her initial seizure of him, and her subsequent conveyance of him into her abode (lines 1497-512a). The next stage of the combat is portrayed by focusing upon Beowulf; he perceives that he is in an under-water cave, his sword does not bite, and he is compelled to rely upon his hand-grip (lines 1512b-44). The focus moves back to Grendel's dam for the continuation of the struggle and for a brief mention of her motive for fighting, vengeance for her son (lines 1545-47a). Finally, the focus of narration returns to the hero for the account of his discovery of another sword and the slaying of his foe (lines 1547b-72a). Up to this point in the fight, Beowulf has held the center of the stage; 78% of the lines have been focused upon him and 22% upon Grendel's dam. The accounts of Beowulf's activities immediately after the combat (lines 1572b-90 and 1605b-25) are interrupted by a glance at the warriors waiting on the shore who note the blood-stained waters and infer that Beowulf has been slain (lines 1591-605a). The final passages pertaining to this combat are concerned with Beowulf's rejoining his faithful companions and their return to Heorot and Hroðgar (lines 1626-50). In this case, the dramatic audience cannot be used as it was in the Grendel combat as a means of commenting upon the fight while it is actually in progress; here, it can be employed only after the fighting is completed and the effects of the combat, the blood in the water, are observed. Even if the post-combat actions of Beowulf in the cave and the reactions of the dramatic audience are added to the fight itself, the narrative focus rests on Beowulf for 64% of the lines (1011/2), on Grendel's dam for 11% of the lines (18), and on the dramatic audience for 25% of the lines (391/2). Although the poet has concentrated upon the three elements of the scene that he worked with previously and has shifted the focus frequently from one element to another, it is apparent that he has not kept Beowulf in the background as he did in the corresponding account of the Grendel combat.

As was done in the case of the Grendel combat, a report is given by Beowulf to Hroðgar shortly after the termination of the fight (lines 1651-98a). The report is necessary because Hroðgar was not a witness to the combat; and, after all, it was at his request that Beowulf undertook to fight Grendel's dam. As soon as he reaches Heorot, Beowulf gives his version of the fight in his own words. Once more, there is a double focus: the introductory words, "Bēowulf maþelode, bearn Ecgþēowes" (line 1651), followed by the hero's actual words indicate that the focus of the narrator rests throughout the speech upon Beowulf. Within the speech, however, *ic* is the subject of virtually every sentence, an indication that the narrative focus is upon Beowulf himself. Beowulf says that "Ic þæt unsōfte ealdre gedīgde" (line 1655), that "Ne meahte ic

æt hilde mid Hruntinge/with gewyrcan" (lines 1659-60a), and that "Ic þæt hilt þanan / fēondum ætferede" (lines 1668b-69a). This is a logical focus to adopt for the presentation of this particular version of the combat. Of the two combatants, only Beowulf survived; and there were no witnesses to the combat itself. This view of the action serves to stress the hero; but it is robbed of some of its effectiveness because the same focus was exploited extensively in the first account of the fight. As part of his report, Beowulf displays the hilt of the sword that he used to slay Grendel's dam; and it is examined by all the persons in the hall (lines 1677-98a). In this manner, some use is made of the bystanders as a point of focus.

The third report of the fight with Grendel's dam is given by Beowulf to Hygelac upon his return to Hygelac's court (lines 2115-43). The poet focuses upon Beowulf as the speaker while Beowulf focuses first on his foe (lines 2115-30) and then upon himself (lines 2131-43). The first phase deals with the attack by Grendel's dam and the slaying of Aeschere; the second treats in very general terms Beowulf's behavior in the combat. The focus of the speech is divided more or less equally between the two participants; 55% of the lines (16) are concerned with the monster and 45% (13) with the hero. This passage—the third account of the Grendel's dam fight—follows a few lines after Beowulf's version of his fight with Grendel, which ends at line 2100. The technique employed for narrating both affairs is similar. In each case, the bulk of the lines are focused upon the hero and his foe. Because it exhibits no new or striking narrative method, the second report, that dealing with Grendel's dam, seems to be a continuation of the first and thereby loses novelty. It is true that the first fight led directly to the second, but, for artistic purposes, they might better have been treated separately as they were in the initial versions.

Although the three versions of the battle with Grendel's dam do not differ greatly from each other, the poet has introduced bits of new information and altered the emphasis slightly so that no one version is an exact duplicate of another. In the second telling of this fight, no new details are presented during the recital of the actual combat (lines 1651-70); however, the gold hilt of the sword used for the slaying of the foe, though mentioned both at the time of the fight and during Beowulf's report of the encounter to Hroðgar, is displayed and described in detail (lines 1677-98a). In a sense, this exhibit does add to our knowledge of one aspect of the fight.

The third report of this combat (lines 2115-43) is little more than a summary of the information given in the other two versions. Only the fact that Beowulf cut off the head of his foe is added here to our total knowledge of this fight (lines 2138b-40a). It is somewhat surprising, in view of the careful treatment of the three reports of the fight with Grendel, that this reference to the fight with Grendel's dam should be so perfunctory. It seems almost as if the poet were including it merely for the sake of symmetry, in order to complete his scheme of reporting each fight three times.

Some skill appears to mark the handling of narrative focus in the presentation of Beowulf's fight with the dragon. Because the hero will not be alive at the end of the combat to give his own account of the fray and also because the poet seeks to reveal all facets of the hero in the role of king—his character as well as his prowess—it is necessary to concentrate upon him during the actual fighting. As a result, considerable attention (581/2 lines or 34%) is devoted to Beowulf in the initial account of the fight. Even greater stress (861/2 lines or 49%), however, falls upon the actions and thoughts of Wiglaf and the *comitatus*. By developing this focus, the poet is able to suggest some consequences of the combat, to comment obliquely on the fierceness of the fight, and to gain suspense by interrupting the action with an explanation of Wiglaf's relationship to Beowulf. Once again, there are two other references to this combat, though admittedly they are rather inchoate. A very short version is given by Wiglaf to the members of Beowulf's *comitatus* after the fight is over (lines 2877-83), and another sketchy report is made by the messenger sent by Wiglaf to announce Beowulf's death to his subjects (lines 2900-10a).

In the initial account of the fight with the dragon (lines 2538-711a), four points of focus are employed: the description concentrates upon Beowulf, the dragon, both combatants together, and the bystanders—Wiglaf and the other members of the *comitatus*. With the exception of a long passage devoted to the *comitatus* (lines 2596-668), no one element is held before the reader's gaze for any considerable time; rather, the author's strategy is to shift rapidly from one focal point to another, affording the reader constantly changing points of focus. Ten times during the narration of the fight the focus rests upon Beowulf, seven times upon his adversary, three times upon both combatants together, and three times, including the long passage concerning Wiglaf and his sword, upon the *comitatus*. A representative passage reveals the poet's method: lines 2583b-91a deal with the failure of Beowulf's sword; lines 2591b-92 describe the resumption of the combat; lines 2593-94a treat the renewal of courage in the dragon's heart; and then the focus turns to Beowulf and his plight (lines 2594b-95). Thereafter the narrative is concerned with the flight of the *comitatus,* Wiglaf's loyalty, an account of his sword, his rebuke to his comrades, and his words of comfort to Beowulf (lines 2596-668). The result is a description of a fight in which the motion of the narrative focus creates an impression of violent activity corresponding to the vigor and movement of the struggle itself.

The second report of the battle (lines 2877-83), that given by Wiglaf to the other members of the *comitatus,* is dramatically necessary as a means of reproaching them for their cowardly behavior. Apparently they were not in a position to observe the fight closely, and some comment upon the battle is required to show them the results of their defection and to justify Wiglaf's charge (lines 2882b-83) that too few of them assisted him in the fight. Within his speech, Wiglaf deals particularly with his own actions and thoughts. He refers, for example, to the fact that "Ic him līfwraðe \tley meahte / ætgifan æt gūðe"

(lines 2877-78a), that "þonne ic sweorde drep / ferhðgenīðlan, f\yr unswīðor / wēoll of gewitte" (lines 2880b-82a). His words are not really a summary of the fight but rather comments upon one aspect of it, his aid to his lord and the consequences of the failure of the *comitatus* to do its duty. By focusing upon himself, Wiglaf can show his companions what they should have done; they, after all, were in a situation similar to his and could have acted as he did.

The messenger dispatched by Wiglaf to report the leader's death to the king's anxious subjects presents in a few lines a third account of the dragon combat (lines 2900-10a). He mentions Beowulf's inability to wound his foe and his death and then refers to Wiglaf and his loyalty in guarding his lord. The messenger is primarily concerned with the consequences of the fight, not with the fight itself, as his subsequent words (lines 2910b-3030a) indicate.

Neither the second nor the third report contributes new information about the combat. Nor is this illogical, for the original version of the encounter was detailed and lengthy (1731/2 lines). After the death of Beowulf, both Wiglaf and the messenger stress the outcome of the struggle, rather than the actual fighting, as the basis for predicting trouble for Beowulf's realm (lines 2884-91 and 2910b-3030a). To dwell upon the action at greater length would emphasize the manner in which the hero was killed and not the tragic consequences of his death. Nevertheless, because the poet in the second and third reports did not draw attention to the fighting, as was done in the accounts of the other two combats, the depiction of this combat is less emphatic, is likely to be less distinct in the reader's mind.

When we evaluate the results of the employment of these modes of narrating Beowulf's three fights, we conclude that the poet is most effective at precisely the wrong points in the poem. Greater narrative skill was employed in the depiction of the fight with Grendel than was displayed in the narration of either of the other combats. Because the poet controlled the narrative focus so well in this case, because he rendered the second and third accounts of that combat absolutely necessary for a full picture of the encounter, that fight strikes the reader as the most dramatic and vivid of the three. The fight with Grendel's dam follows immediately after the struggle with Grendel and loses some effectiveness simply because it is fundamentally the same kind of contention: heroic warrior versus monster. Although the poet did much to differentiate the two fights by varying the locales and the details of the fighting and made good use in each case of a dramatic audience, the impression still remains that the second is to some extent an inartistic repetition of the first. The reader even feels that the fight with Grendel's dam reveals no significant aspect of the hero that was not better exhibited in the first combat. Whereas the first two battles reveal Beowulf in the role of youthful warrior, the dragon fight displays his exemplary behavior as a mature king. Yet, in spite of the national significance attributed to the dragon affair as a consequence of

Beowulf's kingship, that fight never impresses the reader as forcibly as does the battle with Grendel. Certainly, the less adroit handling of narrative focus, the fact that this is the third occasion on which Beowulf has performed in a difficult situation, and the greater attention devoted to Wiglaf, the *comitatus,* and the ramifications of the combat—all these contribute to the comparatively ineffective picture of this fight.

Theoretically, perhaps, the dire consequences attributed to Beowulf's death and the climactic position of the dragon fight within the story should elevate that struggle above the other two. But when we weigh these abstract considerations against the very striking effects achieved through narrative skill in the depiction of the Grendel episode, the fact is that we are more impressed by the Grendel fray. We seem to encounter the dramatic climax early in the story with two more combats still to be presented. To make the reader feel, as well as understand, that the dragon fight is the real climax, the poet should have subordinated the fights with Grendel and Grendel's dam and concentrated all his artistry, all the skill that he has displayed in the depiction of the first combat, upon the last.

Charles Moorman (essay date 1967)

SOURCE: "The Essential Paganism of *Beowulf,*" in *Modern Language Quarterly,* Vol. XXVIII, No. 1, March, 1967, pp. 3-18.

[*In the following excerpt, Moorman identifies a pessimistic tone running through* Beowulf *and argues that it is the product of a pagan rather than a Christian view of life.*]

One has only to glance at the criticism devoted to *Beowulf* in the last sixty years to see how firmly entrenched the so-called Christian interpretation of our chief Anglo-Saxon poem has become. Specialized studies, such as M. B. McNamee's interpretation of the poem as an "allegory of salvation," Marie Hamilton's view of the poem as reflecting the Augustinian doctrines of grace and providence, and the patristical studies of D. W. Robertson, Jr., R. E. Kaske, and Morton W. Bloomfield, as well as the more general treatments of A. G. Brodeur and Dorothy Whitelock, have apparently solidified Frederick Klaeber's original assertion that "Predominantly Christian are the general tone of the poem and its ethical viewpoint" and have thoroughly discredited the early arguments of H. M. Chadwick and F. A. Blackburn that the Christian sentiments expressed by characters and author are mere "colorings" in a poem which "once existed as a whole without the Christian allusions" (Blackburn). And certainly no student would wish to argue against such opponents that both the *Beowulf* poet and his audience were not possessed of the rudiments of Christianity or that, save perhaps in a few passages (168-69, 180-88, 1740-60), the Christianity expressed in the poem as it has come down to us is not a part of its original design. [The line numbering in my text is that of Klaeber's edition.

However, in order to facilitate reading, I have throughout the article quoted from R. K. Gordon's translation of **Beowulf,** in *Anglo-Saxon Poetry,* Everyman ed. (New York, 1926).]

Yet one feels that the scholars may have protested too much. The subject matter, the narrative line, and, more important, the tone of **Beowulf** are far removed from the more patently Christian poems of the Old English period, not only from the saints' lives and biblical paraphrases, but from those poems—*Andreas* and *Judith,* for example—that, like **Beowulf,** boast a strongly heroic character. The difference between **Beowulf** and these poems is ultimately more qualitative than quantitative: it is not so much a matter of more or less Christian coloration, or even of more or less specifically Christian subject matter, but one of point of view, of language and diction, and, especially, of tone. Compare for a moment the ending of **Beowulf** with the closing passages of *Judith* and *Andreas,* which, although they derive from the Old Testament and from Christian folk tradition rather than from specifically Christian scriptural sources, nevertheless share with **Beowulf** the heroic attitude:

> *Judith:* Judith ascribed the glory of all that to the Lord of hosts who endued her with honour, fame in the realm of the world and likewise reward in heaven, the meed of victory in the splendour of the sky, because she ever held true faith in the Almighty. At the end she doubted not at all of the reward which long while she had yearned for. Therefore glory for ever be to the dear Lord who in his own mercy created the wind and the airs, the skies and spacious realms, and likewise the fierce streams and the joys of heaven. (Gordon, p. 358)

> *Andreas:* and then they worshipped the Lord of glory, called aloud all together, and spoke thus: "There is one eternal God of all creatures! His might and his power are famously honoured throughout the world, and his glory gleams over all on the saints in heavenly majesty, with beauty in heaven for ever and ever, eternally among the angels. That is a noble King!" (Gordon, p. 233)

> **Beowulf:** The warriors began to rouse on the barrow the greatest of funeral-fires; the wood-reek mounted up dark above the smoking glow, the crackling flame, mingled with the cry of weeping—the tumult of the winds ceased—until it had consumed the body, hot to the heart. Sad in heart, they lamented the sorrow of their souls, the slaying of their lord; likewise the woman with bound tresses sang a dirge . . . the sky swallowed up the smoke. . . .

> Thus did the men of the Geats, his hearth-companions, bewail the fall of their lord; they said that among the kings of the world he was the mildest of men and most kindly, most gentle to his people and most eager for praise. (Gordon, pp. 69-70)

It should be obvious, even from these brief quotations, that while *Judith* and *Andreas,* like *The Fates of the Apostles* and *The Dream of the Rood*—all of which end with death and unhappy events—conclude with paeans of triumph and rejoicing in the victories of the servants of God, *Beowulf,* save for a single reference to Beowulf's soul having sought out the judgment of the righteous (2820), ends in tragedy and disillusionment. Beowulf's death, however heroic it may have been, has unleashed the forces that will destroy his people, and the last three hundred lines of the poem, despite all the appeals of Whitelock to "things that last for ever" are pessimistic and foreboding in the extreme.

The difference between *Beowulf* and these other poems, moreover, does not lie merely with the fact that *Beowulf* ends tragically and the others with assertions of the joyful victories of the saints, though the conclusions of the three poems define an important part of that difference. For the whole of *Beowulf,* despite its Christian elements, is strongly and most un-Christianly pessimistic in its view of life and history. The narrative framework of the poem, the story of Beowulf's encounters with his monstrous opponents, demonstrates that although even the most heroic of men may for a time overcome the powers of darkness, he in time will be defeated by them. The background of Scandinavian history before which the action of *Beowulf* takes place and to which the poet constantly alludes makes precisely the same point of the fates of nations: societies rise only to perish, and it is only a few generations from Scyld Scefing to Hrothulf and from Hrethel to Wiglaf. In the end, no matter how great the personal valor, how strong the *comites,* how determined the heroic struggle, the dragons prevail and Heorot burns. It is thus no surprise that *Andreas,* which reflects an essentially optimistic Christian philosophy of history, ends with the followers of the saint praising the everlasting glory of God and his saints, and *Beowulf* concludes with a lonely funeral pyre and the lamentations of the Geats.

I bring forward this pronounced difference in tone between *Beowulf* and these patently Christian poems not in order to deny the presence of the many obviously Christian sentiments in *Beowulf,* but simply to reassert in the face of almost all recent criticism the essential paganism of the poem. However important to our view of *Beowulf* the principal Christian elements—the allusions to free will, Hrothgar's sermon on humility, Beowulf's moderation and thanksgivings to God, the identification of Grendel with the race of Cain—may be, they are essential neither to its narrative nor even to its major theme—the unyielding, though profitless, struggle of man against the forces of a malevolent nature. In the final analysis, the Christian elements are peripheral; they need appear in no paraphrase of the poem, they contribute nothing to its over-all effect, and they in no way affect either its structure or its thematic unity.

More important for this discussion, however, is the fact that in concentrating upon the Christian elements of the poem, we have failed to plumb the depths of its paganism. For just as the Christianity of the poem is at best conceived of as a surface coloration, so its paganism is the very hue of the material from which it is made. It is

a comparatively easy process, for instance, to amass evidence to show that at the time the poem was written, the stern Germanic Wyrd (like Dame Fortuna) had become softened and shaped into an agency of the Christian God; indeed, it may have been so considered by the poet. But the action of the poem, if not always the comments of characters and author, asserts man's fate to be fixed and tragic; as Charles Kennedy has remarked, there is no evidence either in plot or in tone "to imply control of Fate by the superior power of Christian divinity." Hrothgar's speech on humility may well be an interpolation, but even if it is not, its sentiments are hardly in agreement with what we know of Hrothgar's actions in the poem; Brodeur, for example, frankly regards him as a pagan king. And while Beowulf may well be "brave and gentle, blameless in thought and deed, the king that dies for his people" (Klaeber, p. li), he is, nevertheless, of all men the "most eager for praise," and his actions in the poem are always those of the pagan Germanic chieftain rather than of the "Christian Saviour" that Klaeber thought him to be. He recognizes as binding all the customs and laws of the *comites,* including the obligations of the warrior to revenge himself on his enemies; he undertakes his exploits primarily out of a desire for both glory and gold; his last thoughts are "sad, restless, brooding on death" (2419-20); he feels just before his death that he has somehow angered a vengeful God (2327-31); and his final wish is to see the treasure hoard he has won (2743-51). Compared with these fundamental actions and attitudes, Beowulf's brief thanksgivings to God seem superficial, so much so that J. R. R. Tolkien remarks, "We have in Beowulf's language little differentiation of God and Fate." The much discussed identification of Grendel with the race of Cain can hardly be called Christian at all, though its source is scriptural; it is best taken simply as a means of expanding and intensifying the poet's vision of the evil forces of pagan nature that Beowulf faces. Moreover, as Klaeber said, we have in the poem no mention at all of the items of specifically Christian experience such as are found in the religious poems of the period: "we hear nothing of angels, saints, relics, of Christ and the cross, of divine worship, church observances or any particular dogmatic points" (p. xlix).

Its paganism, on the other hand, is essential to the thought and action of *Beowulf.* The externals of paganism—the omens, heathen sacrifices, pagan burials—are as peripheral as the externals of Christian sentiment. But the great concepts that determine the structure and theme of the poem—the unmitigated pessimism, the doctrine of an unyielding fate, the poet's insistence upon the code of the *comites* and upon the obligations of kinship and the vendetta, the praise of worldly heroism, and the glorification of prowess and courage for their own sakes—these are indispensable to any interpretation of *Beowulf.* All of these concepts point toward a deep-seated pagan tradition of thought and action which the Christianity of the poem has managed to color, but not to erase or disguise.

I suspect that we have fallen into the habit of seeing *Beowulf* as a Christian poem simply because we know more about late medieval Christianity than we do about the Germanic paganism of the Dark Ages. It is far easier to look back at *Beowulf,* Church Fathers in hand, from the Christian vantage point of the late Middle Ages than from the pagan point of view of earlier centuries from which so little information has come down. The remnants of paganism that did survive in Britain—the scattered altars, the maimed rites and dances, the denunciations from Rome and local clergy—tell us almost nothing. The precise relationships among the English, German, and Scandinavian mythologies are blurred. The very fact that a number of historians fall back upon *Beowulf* itself in order to "see therein much of the workings of the primitive English mind" should demonstrate the scantiness of our information concerning pagan Britain. Whitelock, for example, can be most explicit about the degree of Christian knowledge held by the poet's audience; she is, of necessity, silent concerning that same audience's knowledge of pagan doctrines. Yet whether or not one wishes to accept Margaret Murray's theory of a continuing English pagan tradition, one must accept the fact that the audience of *Beowulf* must have been very close indeed to its pagan heritage and could still understand and appreciate in its own terms a pagan tale, even though that tale might be shaped and rendered respectable by a poet with an eye cocked toward the local clergy.

There would also seem to be in the poem layers of pagan thought directly below those that appear on its surface. For example, there is far more emphasis on kinship and on its relationship to kingship and to the *comites* than appears at first sight. Historians disagree somewhat as to the importance of the family in Anglo-Saxon aristocratic society. Earlier historians argued that the Saxon invaders brought to England a tribal system of government in which the ties of kinship and the obligations of family duty determined both the social and the economic systems. But later historians, basing their conclusions on the evidence of what was known of Germanic institutions (information derived chiefly from Tacitus' *Germania*), seem agreed that Anglo-Saxon society was founded not so much on the old Germanic allegiance of kinsman to kinsman as on that of the devotion of thane to lord. "The most powerful bond in this new society," says Peter Hunter Blair [in *Roman Britain and Early England,* 1963], "was that which united lord and man in a close relationship which was neither national nor tribal but personal." Both groups, interestingly enough, use *Beowulf* as source.

It seems clear, however, that both the family and the *comites,* both kinsman and lord, claimed a large measure of the devotion of the Anglo-Saxon warrior. The story of Cynewulf and Cyneheard in the *Anglo-Saxon Chronicle* for 755 demonstrates that the duties to lord and kinsman might come into conflict and that, in this one instance at least, the obligation to lord proved stronger. Of the two claims, however, that of the family is admittedly older, and certainly in Anglo-Saxon times the demands of family loyalty must still have been heartfelt indeed: witness the grief of Hrethel upon the death of his oldest son, Herebeald, and his frustration at being unable to revenge his son's death. *Beowulf* is filled not only with constant allusions to kinship—the most obvious being the use of

patronymic epithets—but also with statements that emphasize the importance of family relationships, particularly as they affect royal succession, to the plot, action, and theme of the poem.

The poem itself begins with a genealogy, that of the descendants of Scyld Scefing, from whom the throne of Denmark descends generation by generation, son to son, until it passes to Heorogar. The natural succession is broken with Heorogar, for the throne does not come down to his son Heoroweard, who is mysteriously passed over, but falls, disastrously, to Hrothgar, a brother of Heorogar. Presumably because of the weakness of his own sons, Hrothgar becomes involved toward the end of his life in a bitter contest for the throne with his son-in-law Ingeld. When Hrothgar dies, his nephew Hrothulf usurps the throne, at least temporarily, and in the resulting civil wars Heorot is burned and the noble Scylding dynasty comes to an end.

Much the same emphasis on the importance of family succession can be seen in the Geatish royal house. Herebeald, who is Hrethel's proper heir, is accidentally killed by his brother Haethcyn, who is in turn killed by the Swedes and is succeeded by Hygelac, the youngest of Hrethel's sons. After Hygelac's death the throne passes to his son Heardred, although Hygd, Hygelac's widow, first offers it to Beowulf. Heardred is soon killed by the Swedes, and the throne passes to Beowulf. But Beowulf has no sons, and upon his death the rule passes to Wiglaf, the last of the Waegmundings and the last of the Geatish kings.

The history of the two tribes, as given in the poem, points toward a general concept which seems to be germane to its theme: that rightful succession and, more generally, right family relationships assure peace and good fortune in the state, while interruptions in due succession and the disregard of blood ties result not only in bitter family feuds but in the overthrow of kingdoms.

This general theme of kinship and its relation to the fortunes of state is reinforced incidentally throughout the poem. Unferth is damned by Beowulf as the murderer of his brother, a fact which not only presages his future alliance with Hrothulf, but also perhaps links him with Cain and hence with Grendel. Certainly, he is to be contrasted with Beowulf; logically, Unferth should have been the man to whom Hrothgar and Wealtheow turned in trouble. Yet since Unferth was unfaithful to his own kinsman, Hrothgar makes at least a tentative offer of foster sonship to Beowulf, who later may have ruled over Hrothgar's kingdom (3004-07). Unferth is thus in a sense the false son whose treachery destroys the state, Beowulf the true son who might have saved it.

The emphasis on family relationships may also explain the large place given to Wealtheow in the poem. In her concern for her sons, she is to be compared to the lamenting Hildeburh, the Danish wife of Finn, who sees her son and her brother killed in battle, just as Hygd, Hygelac's widow, loses her son in battle, and is later compared with Queen Thryth. By some curious transference—though this I would not insist upon—Wealtheow may be contrasted in the poem with Grendel's dam, who has also lost a son, but whose desire for revenge may well be contrasted with Wealtheow's great sorrow.

Time and again, the **Beowulf**-poet repeats the theme of kinship, along with its resulting entanglements and feuds: in the rebellion of Eanmund and Eadgils against their uncle, in Finn's war against his brother-in-law, in Heremod's seizure of the Danish throne from his brother and his resulting degeneracy, in Hygd's fears for Heardred. And Beowulf himself begins his final lament with the regret that he has no son to whom he may pass on his armor and that Fate has swept away all of his kinsmen save Wiglaf.

Although family loyalty as such is of course quite compatible with Christianity, the vendetta is not, and it is clear that in the Anglo-Saxon period, even down to the time of King Alfred, as Dorothy Whitelock says [in *Beginnings of English Society,* 1952], "it was unavoidable that there should be a clash between Christian and pre-Christian ethics in this matter of vengeance." As we have seen, the stern ethical code which stems from family loyalty and its effects upon society are far more central to the action of **Beowulf** than is the Christian code of conduct, which not only forbids family feuds and acts of revenge no matter how well justified, but in fact demands that all family relationships be put aside if necessary so that the Christian ideal of forgiveness and mercy may be followed.

But the insistence on family and rightful succession and on the identification of private and public weal may point toward a deeper (though perhaps by the time of **Beowulf** an almost forgotten) layer of pagan thought and practice. Beginning with Frazer, anthropologists and literary critics have seen as a ruling motif both in primitive society and in literature the ritual sacrifice of the sacral king as a means of assuring the continuing fertility of the land and the prosperity of the tribe. In *The God of the Witches,* Murray says:

> The underlying meaning of the sacrifice of the divine victim is that the spirit of God takes up its abode in a human being, usually the king, who thereby becomes the giver of fertility to all his kingdom. When the divine man begins to show signs of age he is put to death lest the spirit of God should also grow old and weaken like its human container. . . . When the changes inevitable to all human customs gradually took place, a substitute could suffer in the king's stead, dying at the time the king should have died and thus giving the king a further lease of life.
>
> (pp. 165-66)

One need not accept Murray's highly conjectural theories regarding Joan of Arc and Thomas à Becket as substitute victims in order to grant the basic truth of her assertion that the sacrifice either of the king or of his substitute was a fundamental part of the Germanic paganism which infused England in the Anglo-Saxon period and continued well into the Christian Era. The *Ynglinga*

saga records that the Swedish King Domaldi was sacrificed by his people in order to improve a series of bad harvests, and Snorri records that Olaf the Wood-Cutter, one of the ancestors of the kings of Norway, was sacrificially burned in his house after a number of crop failures. And almost certainly the old sacrificial rituals, as E. K. Chambers says, lingered "in the country, the pagan, districts" and so "passed silently into the dim realm of folklore," most notably in England, according to Chambers, in the village festival play.

I would hardly claim that **Beowulf** is filled with references to human sacrifices disguised for court consumption by a pagan posing as a Christian. But I think it entirely possible that the matter of the poem does reflect something of the pagan notion of kingship and ritual sacrifice. No one would deny that after fifty years as king, Hrothgar has outlived his period of effective rule. Old age has robbed him of his youthful strength (1886-87). His dreams of glory in building Heorot have been shattered by the raids of Grendel, who in twelve years has completely demoralized the whole Danish court: the thanes no longer attempt to sleep in the hall at night, nor will Grendel consent to be bought off. Hrothgar himself is powerless even to approach his own throne, and in desperation the court abandons whatever shallow Christianity it professes and turns to pagan gods. In Murray's terms, the "spirit of God" has grown old within Hrothgar and has weakened "like its human container." Nor, apparently, can Hrothgar's son deal with the situation. The task of cleansing Heorot thus falls upon the young Beowulf, who replaces the old king in destroying Grendel and his mother and who is almost, but not quite, accepted by Hrothgar as foster son and heir.

His ineffectualness in dealing with Grendel is not the only sign of Hrothgar's decrepitude. The revolt of Ingeld during the old king's lifetime and the seizure of the throne by Hrothulf after his death are attributable to Hrothgar's senility and lack of judgment, a failing which Wealtheow plainly shares and which she clearly evidences in her trust of Hrothulf and in her plea to Hrothgar to be generous first of all with his own kinsmen and to leave to them, not to Beowulf, his subjects and kingdom. It is noteworthy that after Wealtheow's speech Hrothgar never again alludes to the "new kinship" he has offered Beowulf; instead, he proposes rewards of gold and riches for the killing of Grendel's mother and, after Beowulf has successfully destroyed this second menace, sends him home to Hygelac with a sermon on humility and the prayerful hope that in time Beowulf will become king of the Geats and will remain friendly to the Danes.

The point is, I think, that Hrothgar is allowed to live too long, that his prolonged rule brings about the destruction of his nation, and that Beowulf, who might have assumed Hrothgar's throne by virtue of his having saved the Danes, does not do so (or, if he does, does so only after the forces of revolt have destroyed the nation).

The second part of the poem helps to clarify the first. As Brodeur points out, the tragic conflict between the two parts is strikingly clear: Hygelac is dead, the Danes have been destroyed, and Beowulf, now an old man who, like Hrothgar, has ruled his fifty years, is now himself faced with Hrothgar's problem—a deadly monster and a group of cowardly thanes. Even before the dragon appears, the poet forecasts the death of Beowulf and begins to anticipate with increasing frequency the approaching destruction of the Geatish nation. And although Brodeur insists that the contrast between the closing lines of Part I, which show "the hero at home in his uncle's court . . . , Hygelac . . . alive and powerful, his realm . . . rich and strong," and the beginning of Part II, with its "terrible antithesis" to Part I, is "sufficient in itself, without irony," the comparison between Hrothgar and the Beowulf of Part II is surely both intended and ironic. Suddenly the young hero who saved an old king is himself an old king, the slayer of dragons is now about to be slain by a dragon, the savior of Heorot finds his own hall destroyed, and he who had ridiculed Hrothgar's untrustworthy thanes is now surrounded by cowards.

If we are to make sense of Beowulf's last foreboding, bitter speeches, and hence of the last half of the poem, we must read them in this context. For they are not the speeches of a Christian hero who is satisfied with the fruits of his life's work and, having made his peace with God, is assured of his place among the saints. Even his last apologia (2724-51) is filled with regret that he has no son, that Fate has deprived him of kinsmen, that his only monument will be a hoard of treasure. He takes pride, of course, in the facts that he has kept the peace and that he has not sworn many unjust oaths or stooped to cunning attacks or killed his own kinsmen. But these are in the main negative accomplishments and are hardly the boasts of a triumphant soldier of Christ. These final speeches make it clear that Beowulf realizes that his struggles have been for the most part in vain, that Wiglaf is the last of the Waegmundings, and that the Geats are doomed. In the end his only thanksgiving to God is for the treasure he has been able to win for his people, a treasure which, ironically, is buried with him.

The picture of Beowulf presented in these scenes, especially those of Section XXXIII, which immediately precede the fight with the dragon, is disturbing in a number of ways. The poet says of him that he thought that by "breaking established law [*ealde riht*], he had bitterly angered God, the Lord everlasting. His breast was troubled within by dark thoughts, as was not his wont" (Gordon, p. 52). The usual interpretation of these lines is that suggested by Klaeber, that Beowulf "did not yet know the real cause of the dragon's ravages" (p. 211). Both Klaeber and Wrenn take the *ealde riht* to which the poet refers to be God's commandments, but the poet has made no mention of Beowulf's breaking any such laws, and it may well be that the passages of Section XXXIII following the statement of Beowulf's despair are actually attempts to explain the nature of the *ealde riht* that Beowulf has violated.

Having described the ravages of the firedrake and prophesied again the deaths of both Beowulf and the dragon, the poet tells us that Beowulf

scorned to seek the far-flier with a troop of men, with a great host. He feared not the fight, nor did he account as aught the valour of the dragon, his power and prowess; because ere this, defying danger, he had come through many onslaughts, wild attacks, when he, the man of victory, purged Hrothgar's hall. . . .

(Gordon, p. 53)

This passage, coming immediately after one of the many prophecies of Beowulf's death, lays emphasis on the hero's great pride in his own strength and on his self-confidence, qualities which seemed perfectly fitting in the young hero, but strangely out of place in an old man brooding darkly on his transgressions. The poet would seem to be establishing here yet another comparison with Hrothgar and, incidentally, with Hygelac, this time in terms of their pride. Hygelac's raid against the Frisians so weakened the Geats that they were unable to aid Hrothgar's sons in their struggle with Hrothulf. Hrothgar in his pride had built Heorot, only to find that he could not inhabit it. Beowulf here scorns the safety of numbers in his self-assurance that he is still the same man who, fifty years before, defeated Grendel and his mother. Taken in this context, the sermon on humility delivered by Hrothgar to the young Beowulf suddenly makes sense, not as a Christian exposition of the follies of pride spoken by a pagan king, but as an explicit warning to Beowulf of the trap into which any aged king may fall, that of regarding himself as immune to the ravages of old age and faltering judgment and of thus disregarding the *ealde riht* of Germanic kingship. Beowulf, like Hrothgar, has failed to relinquish his throne while still in his prime; perhaps it is his realization of this failure that prompts his sudden despair.

The next few verses, moreover, provide an alternative, or more likely a supplementary, explanation of Beowulf's depression. Recounting the death of Hygelac at the hands of the Frisians, the poet says that Beowulf alone escaped the battle by swimming, this time carrying thirty suits of armor, "over the stretch of the gulfs" (Gordon, p. 53) back to his homeland. Although this incident is another example of Beowulf's remarkable strength and skill in swimming, it is out of keeping with our idea of the Germanic hero and of the *comitatus* spirit, which demanded, above all, loyalty even unto death in battle. We should have expected Beowulf to have died at Hygelac's side, and it may well be that his flight is the violation of an *ealde riht* of the *comites* which he recalls and laments at the end of his life.

The next few lines (2369-79) introduce a possible third explanation of Beowulf's dejection, one that also reflects Beowulf's failure in the past to understand the laws of both kingship and *comites*. The poet recalls that when Beowulf returned to the Geats, Queen Hygd, distrusting her own son's ability to protect the kingdom, had offered Beowulf the crown and that he had refused it, as Adrien Bonjour says, [in *The Digressions in 'Beowulf,'* 1950], "out of sheer loyalty towards the rightful heir." Subsequent events prove that it would have been better for his countrymen if Beowulf had accepted the queen's offer.

Heardred is killed by the Swedes, and the war between Swedes and Geats culminates in an uneasy truce, which lasts only during Beowulf's lifetime. Although I agree with Bonjour that one purpose of the reference is to establish still another image of Beowulf's power, I think that the poet, by placing the passage so close to the descriptions of the dragon's ravages, of Beowulf's enduring pride, and of his retreat from Hygelac's battle with the Frisians, makes a subtle but quite definite allusion to another failure in substitution, that of Beowulf for Heardred.

An account of Beowulf's revenge upon Onela for the death of Heardred follows immediately and quite naturally; here again, the poet's aim may be to explain Beowulf's melancholy in terms of his having broken *ealde riht.* Beowulf, of course, supports Onela's nephew in his revolt against his uncle, an engagement that results in Onela's death. Yet one must wonder at Beowulf's action, since the text clearly states that after Heardred's death, Onela departed for Sweden and permitted (*let*) Beowulf to hold the Geatish throne. I strongly suspect also that the *god cyning* of line 2390 is Onela, whose attitude toward Beowulf is here praised. If this reading is correct, then Beowulf's later action against Onela is inexcusable, the action of a proud Heremod who becomes improperly involved in what we should call "the internal affairs of another nation" in order, for the sake of revenge, to strike down a benefactor.

It is certainly possible that I am here guilty of overreading, or perhaps even misreading, the text, that—as the commentators have maintained—the poet introduces these incidents not to bury Beowulf, but to praise him. Yet, the allusions to Beowulf's pride, his escape from the battle with the Frisians, his refusal of the Geatish crown, and his role in the death of Onela, coming as they do immediately after the description of his melancholy and his feeling that the dragon's onslaught is a result of his somehow broken *ealde riht,* may perhaps serve to explain his dejection in terms of his violations of the pagan laws of kingship and the code of the *comites.* He in his pride has ruled too long, he has deserted the side of his dead lord, he has refused to take the place of an unworthy king in order to preserve his nation, and he has slain his benefactor. There is little wonder that "his breast was troubled within by dark thoughts."

To return to the main argument, I think it clear that the Beowulf of the second half of the poem is not that of the first. Fate, youth, his thanes, and at the end even his boundless self-assurance have deserted him. It is Wiglaf who now comes to the fore and, like the young Beowulf, is seen by his lord as a foster son. Yet again the substitution comes too late, and the words of Wiglaf, whom the Swedes hate, and the messenger leave us in no doubt of the heavy days to come. Having ruled too long, the old king dies, and with him the nation whose welfare had depended upon his strength and virility.

I am perfectly aware that in tracing, however cursorily, these vestiges of the sacral kingship in **Beowulf,** I may seem to have chosen my evidence overscrupulously, considered passages out of their contexts, and largely ignored the comments made by the Christian author on these passages, and that I may consequently be guilty of misinterpreting the characters and actions of the poem. Yet such is not wholly the case. Even though the actions of Section XXXIII that I have seen as reflecting the guilty thoughts of Beowulf just before his encounter with the dragon have been interpreted by others as praise of the hero, the poet himself in no way indicates that such is the case. The whole of the section is reported with an objectivity rare in the poem. In the same way, the sermon of Hrothgar, Wealtheow's plea that Beowulf protect her son, and the final speeches of the hero are presented without authorial comment. Moreover, the references to the Christian God are notably fewer in these harsh final passages than in the Grendel episodes. Save for Beowulf's own reference to the approval of the Ruler of Men (2741), the poet's statement that Beowulf's soul has joined those of the righteous (2820), and the hero's reflection that he has perhaps angered God (2330), these Christian references take the form either of rather colorless incidental allusions or of the poet's usual references to the will of God, which in these final scenes are matched by an almost equal and quite indistinguishable number of references to the power of pagan Wyrd.

The point is that, in its second half, the essential paganism of the poem is more evident than in the first. As the tragedy of Beowulf approaches, the Christian poet finds little to say concerning the hero's Christianity and little consolation in its assurances of the comforting thoughts of its saints. Beowulf dies a lonely death; he finds no real solace either in the thoughts of his accomplishments, which will be of no lasting value to his people, or in any expectation of future glory. And, unlike the authors of the religious poems of the period, neither does the **Beowulf**-poet, though we are assured by the religious references in the poem that he was himself at least nominally a Christian.

I would suggest that, in the end, the archetype of the poem, or at least the folk elements from which it sprang, comes to dominate its mood and theme. The pessimism of Nordic mythology finally overshadows whatever brighter Christian colors the poem had in its conception displayed; its hero is revealed not as a Christian martyr whose life of trials and sacrificial death had advanced the cause of God in the world, but as an old man who, though permitted by Fate to win with the help of the young his last battle, nevertheless dies knowing that he has accomplished nothing of permanent value. And in this regard Beowulf is far closer to the heroes of the medieval epics that are obviously more pagan than Christian—the *Nibelungenlied* and the *Njáls saga,* for example—than to those of such patently Christian poems as the *Chanson de Roland.* For although the *Nibelungenlied* and the *Njáls saga* were presumably written by Christian poets, their heroes are in every way pagan in attitude and spirit. Gunnar and Njál, Siegfried and Rudeger perish as the result of feuds that are in the end as meaningless as they are futile. They do not die on behalf of noble causes, nor do they really serve their parties' best interests by dying, however well they die. Scandinavian mythology presented a negative, pessimistic view of history in which man and earth and giants were to be destroyed as the final act of a conflict between gods and giants in which all men, living and dead, were to take part. Although a new heaven and earth might eventually arise from the ashes of the old, the present life of man was marked not only by struggle, but by a sense of the futility of struggle.

It is into this literary and religious context that **Beowulf** best fits, not into that of the *Andreas* and the *Chanson de Roland,* whose heroes die assured of personal glory after death and of the eventual triumph of their causes. Beowulf is of the same age as the dragons he fights, an age in which the families of men were still more real than the Communion of Saints, in which the well-being of the land still depended upon the vigor of the king, and in which the forces of nature could still assume the shapes of trolls and dragons against which no man or *comites* could either endure or prevail.

Jane C. Nitzsche   (essay date 1980)

SOURCE: "The Structural Unity of *Beowulf:* The Problem of Grendel's Mother," in *Texas Studies in Literature and Language,* Vol. 22, No. 3, Fall, 1980, pp. 287-303.

[*In the excerpt that follows, Nitzsche discusses the contrast between Grendel's mother and the feminine ideal and also analyzes her fight with Beowulf as a transitional link between Beowulf's battle with Grendel and with the dragon.*]

The episode in **Beowulf** involving Grendel's mother has been viewed as largely extraneous, a blot upon the thematic and structural unity of the poem. If the poem is regarded as two-part in structure, balancing contrasts between the hero's youth and old age, his rise as a retainer and his fall as a king, his battles with the Grendel family and his battle with the dragon, then her episode (which includes Hrothgar's sermon and Hygelac's welcoming court celebration with its recapitulation of earlier events) lengthens the first "half" focusing on his youth to two-thirds of the poem (lines 1-2199). [The edition of **Beowulf** used throughout is Frederick Klaeber, *Beowulf and the Fight at Finnesburg,* 3rd, ed. (Boston, 1936, with 1941 and 1950 supplements).] If the poem is regarded as three-part in structure, with each part centering on one of the three monsters or the three fights, then the brevity of her episode again mars the structural balance: her section, roughly 500 lines (1251-1784), is not as long as Grendel's, roughly 1100-1200 lines (86-1250), or the dragon's, 1000 lines (2200-3182). Even if her episode is lengthened to a thousand lines (from line 1251 to 2199) so as to include Hrothgar's sermon and Hygelac's court celebration, still Grendel's mother hardly dominates these events literally or symbolically as do Grendel and the dragon the events in their sections.

But her battle with Beowulf (and this middle section of the poem) is more than merely a "transition between two great crises," even though it is "linked with both the Grendel fight and the Dragon fight." The key to her significance may indeed derive from her links with the other two monsters in a way Bonjour did not envision when he made these statements [in "Grendel's Dam and the Composition of *Beowulf,*" *English Studies* 30 (1949)].

Grendel and the dragon have been interpreted recently as monstrous projections of flaws in Germanic civilization portrayed by the poet as "Negative Men." Grendel is introduced as a mock "hall-retainer" (*renweard,* 770; *healoegn,* 142) who envies the men of Heorot their joy of community; he subsequently attacks the hall in a raid that is described through the parodic hall ceremonies of feasting, ale-drinking, gift-receiving, and singing. The dragon is introduced as a mock "gold-king" or *hordweard* (2293, 2303, 2554, 2593) who avariciously guards his barrow or "ring-hall" (*hringsele,* 3053), and attacks Beowulf's kingdom after he discovers the loss of a single cup. The envy of the evil hall-retainer and the avarice of the evil gold-king antithesize the Germanic *comitatus* ideal first enunciated in Tacitus' *Germania* and pervading heroic and elegiac Anglo-Saxon literature: the *comitatus'* well-being depended upon the retainer's valor in battle and loyalty to his lord and the lord's protection and treasure-giving in return.

Like these monsters, Grendel's mother is also described in human and social terms. She is specifically called a *wīf unhyre* (2120), a "monstrous woman'," and an *idesaglæcwīf* (1259), a "lady monster-woman." "Ides" elsewhere in **Beowulf** denotes "lady" and connotes either a queen or a woman of high social rank; outside **Beowulf,** primarily in Latin and Old English glosses, *ides* pairs with *virgo* to suggest maidenhood, as when on *idesan* equals *in virgunculam.* In addition, as if the poet wished to stress her maternal role she is characterized usually as Grendel's *mōdor* or kinswoman (*mage,* 1391), the former a word almost exclusively reserved for her, although other mothers appear in the poem. It seems clear from these epithets that Grendel's mother inverts the Germanic roles of the mother and queen, or lady. She has the form of a woman (*idese onlīcnes,* 1351) and is weaker than a man (1282ff) and more cowardly, for she flees in fear for her life when, discovered in Heorot (1292-93). But unlike most mothers and queens, she fights her own battles. *Maxims* I testifies that, "Battle, war, must develop in the man, and the woman must flourish beloved among her people, must be light-hearted."

Because the poet wishes to stress this specific inversion of the Anglo-Saxon ideal of woman as both monstrous and masculine he labels her domain a "battle-hall" (*nīosele,* 1513; *gīosele,* 2139). (The dragon's barrow he describes equally appropriately, given the monster's avaricious symbolic nature, as a "ring-hall," as we saw previously.) In addition, he occasionally uses a masculine pronoun in referring to her (*sē þe* instead of *sēo þe* in 1260, 1497; *hē* instead of *hēo* in 1392, 1394). Such a change in pronoun occurs elsewhere in the poem only in reference to abstract feminine nouns used as personifications and to concrete feminine nouns used as synecdoches. Other epithets applied to her are usually applied to male figures: warrior, *sinnige secg,* in 1379; destroyer, *mihtig manscaoa,* in 1339; and [male] guardian, *"gryrelīcne grundhyrde,* in 2136. Indeed, in the phrase *ides aglæcwīf* applied to Grendel's mother as a "lady monster-woman" the *aglæca* not only means "monster," as it does when directed at Grendel (159, 425, 433, 556, 592, 646, 732, 739, 816, 989, 1000, 1269) or the water monsters (1512), but also "fierce combatant" or "strong adversary," as when directed at Sigemund in line 893 and Beowulf and the dragon in line 2592. Such a woman might be wretched or monstrous because she insists on arrogating the masculine role of the warrior or lord.

Her episode is thus appropriately divided like her monstrous but human nature and her female but male behavior into two parts to illustrate the various feminine roles—of the mother or kinswoman (*mōdor*) and queen or lady (*ides   glæcwīf*)—she inverts. The poet constantly contrasts the unnatural behavior of Grendel's dam with that of the feminine ideal by presenting human examples as foils in each of the two parts. We turn first to an examination of the female ideal in **Beowulf,** then to a detailed analysis of the episode involving Grendel's mother and its two parts, and finally to some conclusions regarding the structural unity of the entire poem.

I

The role of woman in **Beowulf** primarily depends upon "peace-making," either biologically through her marital ties with foreign kings as a peace-pledge or mother of sons, or socially and psychologically as a cup-passing and peace-weaving queen within a hall. Wealhtheow becomes a peace-pledge or *friousibb folca* (2017) to unite the Danes and Helmings; Hildeburh similarly unites the Danes and Frisians through her marriage; and Freawaru at least intends to pledge peace between the Danes and Heathobards. Such a role is predicated upon the woman's ability to bear children, to create blood ties, bonds to weave a "peace kinship."

In addition, woman functions domestically within the nation as a cup-passer during hall festivities of peace (*freoþo*) and joy (*drēam*) after battle or contest. The mead-sharing ritual and the cup-passer herself come to symbolize peace-weaving and peace because they strengthen the societal and familial bonds between lord and retainers. First, the literal action of the *freoouwebbe* (peace-weaver, 1942) as she passes the cup from warrior to warrior weaves an invisible web of peace: the order in which each man is served, according to his social position, reveals each man's dependence upon and responsibility toward another. For example, after Wealhtheow gives the cup to Hrothgar she bids him to be joyful at drinking as well as loving to his people (615ff). Then she offers it to the *duguo* (old retainers), then to the *geoguu* (young retainers), and finally to the guest Beowulf. Second, her peace-weaving also takes a verbal form: her speeches accompanying the mead-sharing stress the peace and joy contingent upon the fulfillment of each man's

duty to his nation. At the joyous celebration after Grendel's defeat Wealhtheow concludes her speeches with a tribute to the harmony of the present moment by reminding her tribe of its cause, that is, adherence to the *comitatus* ethic. Each man remains true to the other, each is loyal to the king, the nation is ready and alert, the drinking warriors attend to the ale-dispenser herself (1228-31). Yet minutes before she attempted to forestall future danger to her family and nation by preventive peace-weaving: she advised Hrothgar to leave his kingdom to his sons, and then, as if sensing the future, she reminded Hrothulf, his nephew, of his obligations to those sons (obligations he will later deny). Third, the peace-weaver herself emblematizes peace, for she appears in the poem with her mead-vessel only after a contest has been concluded. Thus Wealhtheow enters the hall only after the contest between Unferth and Beowulf (612); she does not appear again until after Beowulf has overcome Grendel, when the more elaborate feasting invites the peace-making speeches mentioned above. After Grendel's mother is defeated the poet preserves the integrity of the pattern of feminine cup-passing after masculine contest by describing the homecoming banquet at Hygelac's court, where Hygd conveys the mead-vessel. This structural pattern to which we shall return simultaneously weaves together the Danish part of the poem with its Geatish part.

Most of the other female characters figure as well in this middle section so that the female monster's adventures are framed by descriptions of other women for ironic contrast. The role of mother highlights the first half of the middle section with the scop's mention of Hildeburh (1071ff) and the entrance of Wealhtheow, both of whom preface the first appearance of Grendel's dam (1258) in her role as avenging mother. Then the introduction of Hygd, Thryth, and Freawaru after the female monster's death (1590) stresses the role of queen as peace-weaver and cup-passer to preface Beowulf's final narration of the female monster's downfall (2143). The actual adventures of Grendel's mother cluster then at the middle of the middle section of the poem.

II

In the first part of the female monster's section, the idea is stressed that a kinswoman or mother must passively accept and not actively avenge the loss of her son. The story of the mother Hildeburh is recited by the scop early on the evening Grendel's mother will visit Heorot. The lay ends at line 1159; Grendel's mother enters the poem a mere hundred lines later when she attacks the Danish hall, as the Frisian contingent attacked the hall lodging Hildeburh's Danish brother in the *Finnsburh Fragment.* The **Beowulf** poet alters the focus of the fragment: he stresses the consequences of the surprise attack rather than the attack itself in order to reveal Hildeburh's maternal reactions to them.

Hildeburh is unjustly (*unsynnum,* 1072) deprived of her Danish brother and Finnish son, but all she does, this sad woman (*geōmuru ides,* 1075), is to mourn her loss with dirges and stoically place her son on the pyre. In fact, she can do nothing, caught in the very web she has woven as peace-pledge: her husband's men have killed her brother, her brother's men have killed her son. Later the Danish Hengest will avenge the feud with her husband Finn, whether she approves or not, by overwhelming the Frisians and returning Hildeburh to her original tribe. The point remains: the peace-pledge must accept a passive role precisely because the ties she knots bind *her*—she *is* the knot, the pledge of peace. Her fate interlaces with that of her husband and brothers through her role as a mother bearing a son: thus Hildeburh appropriately mourns the loss of her symbolic tie at the pyre, the failure of her self as peace-pledge, the loss of her identity. Like Hildeburh Grendel's dam will also lose her identity as mother, never having had an identity as peace-pledge to lose.

As if reminded of her own role as mother by hearing of Hildeburh's plight, Wealhtheow demonstrates her maternal concern in an address to Hrothgar immediately after the scop sings this lay. In it she first alludes to Hrothgar's adoption of Beowulf as a son: apparently troubled by this, she insists that Hrothgar leave his kingdom only to his actual kinsmen or descendants when he dies (1178-79). Then she urges her foster "son" Hrothulf (actually a nephew) to remember his obligations to them so that he will "repay our sons with liberality" (1184-85). Finally, she moves to the mead-bench where the adopted Beowulf sits, rather symbolically, next to her sons Hrethric and Hrothmund (1188-91). The *past* helplessness of the first mother, Hildeburh, to requite the death of her son counterpoints the anxiously maternal Wealhtheow's attempts to weave the ties of kinship and obligation, thereby forestalling *future* danger to her sons. Later that night, Grendel's mother intent on avenging the loss of her son in the *present* attacks Heorot, her masculine aggression contrasting with the feminine passivity of both Hildeburh and Wealhtheow. Indeed, she resembles a grieving human mother: like Hildeburh she is guiltless and *galgmōd* ("gloomy-minded," 1277); her journey to Heorot must be sorrowful (1278) for she "remembered her misery" (1259). But a woman's primary loyalty as peace-pledge was reserved for her husband, not for her son, according to the Danish history of Saxo Grammaticus. Perhaps for this reason Grendel's mother is presented as husbandless and son-obsessed—to suggest to an Anglo-Saxon audience the dangers inherent in woman's function as *friousibb*.

However, her attempts to avenge her son's death could be justified if she were human and male, for no *wergild* has been offered to her by the homicide Beowulf. The role of the masculine avenger is emphasized throughout the passage (1255-78) in defining her motivation to attack: she performs the role of avenger (*wrecend,* 1256) "to avenge the death of her son" (1278). Whatever her maternal feelings, she actually fulfills the duty of the kinsman. Unlike Hildeburh, she cannot wait for a Hengest to resolve the feud in some way; unlike Freawaru, she cannot act as a peace-pledge to settle the feud. Tribeless, now kinless, forced to rely on her own might, she seizes and kills Aeschere, Hrothgar's most beloved retainer, in an appropriate retribution for the loss of her own most beloved "retainer" and "lord"—her son.

The monstrosity of her action is at first not evident. Hrothgar suspects she has carried the "feud" too far (1339-40). And from the Danish and human point of view she possesses no legal right to exact compensation for her kinsman's loss because Grendel is himself a homicide. However, Beowulf later implies that the two feuds must remain separate, as she desires her own "revenge for injury" (*gyrnwracu,* 2118). Because she is legally justified in pursuing her own feud given the tribal duty of the retainer to avenge the death of his lord, regardless of the acts he has committed, she behaves monstrously then in only one way. For a mother to "avenge" her son (2121) as if she were a retainer, he were her lord, and avenging more important than peace-making, is monstrous. An analogy conveying her effect on the men in Heorot when she first appears suggests how unusual are her actions in human terms. Her horror "is as much less as is the skill (strength) of maidens, the war-horror of a woman, in comparison to a (weaponed) man, when the bound sword shears the one standing opposite" ("Wæs se gryre læssa / efne swa / micle, swa bio mægþa cræft, / w ggryre w fes be wæpnedmen, / þonne heoru bunden . . . andweard scireo," 1282-87). In their eyes recognizably female, she threatens them physically less than her son. But because female "peacemakers" do not wage war, the analogy implies, by litotes, that her unnatural behavior seems *more* horrible.

In the second part of her adventure she no longer behaves solely as an avenging monster, antitype of Hildeburh and Wealhtheow, who are both through marriage "visitors" to a hall like Grendel and his dam. Such hall-visitors contrast with the hall-rulers of this second part: the *merew f* as queen or guardian (*grundhyrde,* 2136) protects her "battle-hall," the cave-like lair, from the visiting hero like the regal dragon guarding his ring-hall, and like King Beowulf his kingdom, in the last section of the poem. Accordingly, the stress on the relationship between mother and son delineated in the first part of her adventure changes to a stress on the relationship between host and guest.

As a tribeless queen or lady (*ides aglæcwīf*) she rudely receives her "hall-guest" Beowulf (*selegyst,* 1545, *gist,* 1522) by "embracing" him and then "repaying him" for his valor not with treasure but with "grim grips" ("Hēo him eft hraþe andlean forgeald / grimman grapum," 1541-42) just as the dragon will "entertain" him in the future. Indeed, the parody of the hall-ceremony of treasure-giving is complete when a "scop" (Beowulf's sword, acting as bard) sings a fierce "war song" off the side of her head ("hire on hafelan hringmæl g l/ grædig gūolēoo," 1521-22). It is interesting to note that this "hall-celebration" of the mock peace-weaver to welcome her valorous guest Beowulf following her attack on Heorot and her curiously listless "contest" with Aeschere duplicates the pattern of mead-sharing ceremonies involving peacemakers which follow masculine contests throughout the poem.

It is also interesting to note that the contest between this apparently lordless "queen" and her "guest" contrasts in its mock-sensual embracing and grasping with the other two major battles of the hero—the briefly described arm-wrestling between Grendel and Beowulf, and the conventional sword-wielding of Beowulf against the fire-breathing dragon. Indeed, before Beowulf arrives at the "battle-hall" Hrothgar introduces the possibility of a Grendel's father in addition to the mother, even though they do not know of such a father (1355), and of possible additional progeny of such a father or even of Grendel himself (through an incestuous union with his mother?): "hwæþer him ænig wæs ær acenned / dyrnra gasta" (1356-57). His ostensible point is to warn Beowulf of additional monsters lurking nearby, but it serves as well to remind the reader that Grendel's mother has an animal nature very different from that of a human lady. For during the passage describing their battle the poet exploits the basic resemblance between sexual intercourse and battle to emphasize the inversion of the feminine role of the queen or hall-ruler by Grendel's mother. This is achieved in three steps: first, the emphasis upon clutching, grasping, and embracing while they fight; second, the contest for a dominant position astride the other; and third, the use of fingers, knife, or sword to penetrate clothing or the body, the latter always accompanied by the implied figurative kinship between the sword and the phallus and between decapitation and castration.

First, she welcomes him to the *mere* with an almost fatal embrace similar to the "embrace" (*fœom*, 2128) to which Aeschere has succumbed. She "grasped then towards him" (1501), seizing him with "horrible grips" (1502) envisioned earlier by the hero as a "battle-grip" (1446) and a "malicious grasp" (1447). Second, inside the "castle" (*hof*, 1507) where she has transported him both grapple for a superior position over the other. After his sword fails him, for example, he "grasped her by the shoulder," hurling her to the ground. The poet, conscious of the monster's sex and Beowulf's definitely unchivalrous behavior, drily protests that in this case "the lord of the Battle-Geats did not at all lament the hostile act" (1537-38). Then, as "reward for his valor, this lady "repaid" him with the treasure of her "grimman grapum," forcing him to stumble and fall (1541-1544), after which she climbs, rather ludicrously, on top of her "hall-guest" (*selegyst*, 1545), intent on stabbing him and thereby (again) avenging her only off-spring (1546-47). Third, the battle culminates in very suggestive swordplay, and wordplay too. Earlier her "hostile fingers" (1505) tried to "penetrate" ("ourhfōn," 1504) his locked coat-of-mail; now she tries unsuccessfully to pierce the woven breast-net with her knife. Previously Beowulf discovered his own weapon was impotent against the charm or spell of the "sword-greedy" woman (*heorogīfre*, 1498), who collects the swords of giants. Now the "sword-grim" hero substitutes one of these swords, an appropriate tool to quell such a woman. The "sword entirely penetrated [ourhwōd] the doomed-to-die body" (1567-68). After this final "embrace" of the "grasping" of her neck, the sweord wæs swatig secg weorce gefeh" ("the sword was bloody, the warrior rejoiced in the work," 1569). The alliteration links *sweord* and *secg*, to identify the bloody sword with the rejoicing, laboring "man-sword" (*secg*); the "battle" appropriately evokes erotic undertones. The equation of the sword and warrior, with the subsequent sexual connotations, resembles the synecdoche controlling Riddle Twenty, "The Sword," in which the sword becomes a retainer who serves his lord through celibacy, foregoing the "joy-game" of marriage and the "treasure" of children, and whose only unpleasant battle occurs with a woman, because he must overcome her desire while she voices her terror, claps her hands, rebukes him with words, and cries out "ungod." Similarly in *Beowulf* once the sword finally penetrates the body its blade miraculously melts—like ice into water—either from the poison of Grendel's blood or of his mother's, the poem does not specify which (1601). And even the *mere* itself, approached through winding passageways, slopes, and paths, and in whose stirred-up and bloody waters sea monsters lurk and the strange battle-hall remains hidden, almost projects the mystery and danger of female sexuality run rampant.

Such erotic overtones in descriptions of battles between a male and female adversary are not especially common in Anglo-Saxon literature but can be found in various saints' lives in the Old English *Martyrology* (ca. 850) and in Aelfric's *Lives of the Saints* (ca. 994-early eleventh century), and in another epic poem also contained in the same manuscript as *Beowulf, Judith.* In the saints' lives a large group of thirty-four portrays a physical conflict between a Christian woman and a pagan man wishing to seduce her physically or spiritually. The description of the torture the saint undergoes to preserve her chastity often veils with obvious sexual symbolism the act of intercourse, or else it lovingly lingers over the description of the virgin's rape (see, for example, the life of St. Lucia). The reason for such descriptions should be clear to those acquainted with the Canticum Canticorum and its celebration of the love of the Sponsa for the Sponsus (of man's soul for God, of the Church for Christ), providing an analogous basis for the holy sacrament of marriage. The woman saint as a type of the soul longs to be joined, as in intercourse, with her spouse Christ; the threat of seduction by a human male must be read as an assault on the soul by the Devil.

In *Judith,* a work like *Beowulf* contained . . . the fragmentary epic portrays similar sexual overtones in Judith's "battle" with Holofernes. As in *Beowulf* a warrior battles a monster: the blessed maiden grapples with the "drunken, vicious monster" (*se inwidda,* 28) Holofernes. However, the sexual role behavior of *Beowulf* occurs in reverse in *Judith:* Holofernes parallels Grendel's dam, but whereas the *wīf* is aggressive and sword-greedy, Holofernes seems slightly effete (his bed enclosed by gold curtains, for example) and impotent from mead-drinking: "The lord fell, the powerful one so drunken, in the middle of his bed, as if he knew no reason in his mind" (67-69). These hypermetrical lines heighten the irony of his situation, for the warrior swoons on the very bed upon which he intended to rape the maiden. Having lost his head to drink in a double sense he himself is penetrated by the virgin's sharp sword, "hard in the storm of battle" (79), thereafter literally losing his head. But first Judith draws the sword from its sheath in her right hand, seizes him by the hair in a mock loving gesture (98-99), then pulls him toward her "shamefully" ("teah hyne folmum wio hyre weard / *bysmerlice,*" 99b-100a). The "b" alliteration in line 100 ("bysmerlice, ond þone bealofullan") draws attention to *bysmerlice,* which as a verb (*bysmrian*) elsewhere suggests the act of "defiling" (intercourse). In this line what seems shameful is apparently her embrace of the warrior's body while she moves it to a supine position. As in ***Beowulf,*** the female assumes the superior position; she lays him down so that she may control (*gewealdan,* 103) him more easily in cutting off his head. The ironic embrace and mock intercourse of this couple parallels that of Beowulf and the *ides aglæcwīf:* the aggressive and sword-bearing "virgin" contrasts with the passive and swordless man (Holofernes, Aeschere, and even Beowulf are all momentarily or permanently swordless). The poet's point in each case is that a perversion of the sexual roles signals an equally perverse spiritual state. Holofernes' impotence is as unnatural in the male as the *wīf*'s aggression is unnatural in the female; so the battle with the heroine or hero in each case is described with erotic overtones to suggest the triumph of a right and natural sexual (and social and spiritual) order over the perverse and unnatural one. In the latter case Grendel's dam and her son pose a heathen threat to Germanic society (the macrocosm) and to the individual (Beowulf the microcosm) as Holofernes and the Assyrians pose a heathen threat to Israelite society (the macrocosm) and to the individual (Judith the microcosm).

In this second part of her adventure, Hygd and Freawaru contrast with the *wīf* as queen or cup-passer as Hildeburh and Wealhtheow contrasted with Grendel's dam as mother in the first. Hygd, the first woman encountered after the defeat of Grendel's mother, as truly fulfills the feminine ideal of *Maxims* I as does Wealhtheow. Her name, which means "Thought" or "Deliberation," contrasts her nature with that of the bellicose *wīf* and possibly that of the war-like Thryth, whose actions, if not her name, suggest "Strength" (only in a physical sense; the alternate form of her name, "Modthrytho" or "Mind-Force," implies in a more spiritual sense stubbornness or pride). Although Hygd like the *wīf* and Thryth will be lordless after Hygelac's death, she does not desire to usurp the role of king for herself: doubting her son's ability to prevent tribal wars she offers the throne to Beowulf (2369ff). In addition, this gracious queen bestows treasure generously (1929-31), unlike the *wīf* and Thryth, the latter of whom dispense only "grim grips" and sword blows upon their "retainers."

The Thryth digression is inserted after Hygd enters to pass the cup upon Beowulf's return to Hygelac. Its structural position invites a comparison of this stubborn princess and the other two "queens," Hygd and the *wīf.* She appears to combine features of both: she begins as a type of the female monster, but upon marriage to Offa changes her nature and becomes a much loved queen. According to the poet, Thryth commits a "terrible crime"; she condemns to death any retainer at court caught staring at her regal beauty. That she abrogates her responsibilities as a queen and as a woman the poet makes clear: "Such a custom—that the peace-weaver after a pretended injury deprive the dear man of life—is not queenly for a woman

to do, although she be beautiful" (Ne bio swylc cwēnlic þēaw / idese tō efnanne, þ ah oe hīo ænlicu sy, / þætte freoouwebbe fēores onsæce / æfter ligetorne lēofne mannan," 1940-43). The label "peace-weaver" (*freoouwebbe*) seems ironic in this context, especially as she does not weave but instead severs the ties of kinship binding her to her people and the bonds of life tying the accused man to this world. That is, for any man caught looking at her "the deadly bonds, hand-woven, were in store; after his arrest it was quickly determined that the sword, the damascened sword, must shear, make known death-bale" ("ac him wælbende weotode tealde / handgewriþene; hraþe seoþ an wæs / æfter mundgripe mēce geþinged, / þæt hit sceadenm lscyran mōste / cwealmbealu cyan," 1936-40). If she weaves at all then she weaves only "deadly hand-woven bonds" binding him to a grisly end. The "peace-weaver" cuts these bonds—imprisoning ropes—with a sword, simultaneously shearing the bonds of life to "make known death-bale." She resembles that other ironic peace-weaver, the *wīf,* who tried to penetrate the braided breast-net of Beowulf with her knife.

Both antitypes of the peace-weaving queen behave like kings, using the sword to rid their halls of intruders or unwanted "hall-guests." Unlike Thryth, the monstrous *wīf* remains husbandless, having lost her son, "wife" only to the *mere* she inhabits both in life and in death. At this moment in the poem, both Thryth and Grendel's mother belong to the past. If they represent *previous* inversions of the peace-weaver and cup-passer, and Hygd who is now passing the mead-cup to Beowulf's weary men in celebration signifies a *present* cup-passer, so the poet introduces a final queen, this time a cup-passer of the *future* who will fail in her role as the first woman, Hildeburh, failed in hers.

Freawaru, like Hildeburh, seems innocent of any crime. She is envisioned by Beowulf as a queen married to Ingeld of the Heathobards in a digression (2032-69) immediately preceding his summary of the battles with Grendel and with his mother. She will fail in her role as peace-weaver because of an underlying hostility—an old Heathobard warrior's bitterness over ancient Heathobard treasure acquired through previous wars and worn by a young Danish man accompanying the new queen. The fragility of this role is heightened even further when, in the third section involving the dragon, Beowulf inhabits a queenless kingdom and when Wiglaf must become the cup-passer, pouring water from the "cup" of Beowulf's helmet in a futile attempt to revive his wounded lord.

Indeed, three women characters appear outside this middle section to convey dialectically the idea that woman cannot ensure peace in this world. First, Wealhtheow, unlike other female figures, appears in the first (or Grendel) section of the poem to pour mead after Grendel's challenge has been answered by the hero. This first entrance symbolizes the ideal role of Germanic woman as a personification of peace, as we have seen. In antithesis, Beowulf's account of the fall of the *wīf unhyre* appropriately ends the poem's second (Grendel's mother) section which has centered on this role: the personification of discord, the antitype of the feminine ideal, has been destroyed. But in the poem's third section a synthesis emerges. The nameless and unidentified Geat woman who appears, like the other female characters, after a battle—this one between Beowulf and the dragon—mourns at the pyre. That is, the efforts of the peacemaker, while valuable in worldly and social terms, ultimately must fail because of the nature of this world. True peace exists not in woman's but in God's "embrace" (*faeþm*, 188).

III

This idea is implied in Hrothgar's sermon (1700-84), like the court celebration of Hygelac a part of the middle section belonging to Grendel's mother but apparently unrelated to it. In it Hrothgar describes three Christian vices in distinctly Germanic terms. Impelled by envy like Grendel, Heremod kills his "table-companions" (1713-14). Next the wealthy hall-ruler in his pride is attacked by the Adversary while his guardian conscience sleeps within the hall of his soul (1740-44). So the monster that specifically epitomizes pride in *Beowulf,* as in Genesis, is female—Grendel's mother—thematically related to Thryth or Modthrytho, whose name (if it can be said to exist in manuscript in that form) means "pride." Grendel's mother substitutes war-making for the peace-weaving of the queen out of a kind of selfish pride—if she were capable of recognizing it as such. Finally, this same hall-ruler "covets angry-minded" ("gytsa gromhydig," 1749) the ornamented treasures God has previously given him by refusing to dispense any to his warriors. So the mock gold-king dragon avariciously guards his treasure. Although the poet portrays the monsters as antitypes of Germanic ideals, his integument conceals a Christian idea. The city of man, whether located in a Germanic or Christian society, is always threatened by sin and failure.

Such sin alienates Christian man from self, neighbor, and God; it alienates Germanic man primarily from other men. Note that although in *Beowulf* each of the three monsters is described as guarding or possessing a hall, whether Heorot, a watery cavern, or a barrow, each remains isolated from humanity (and from each other—Grendel and his mother live together, but they never appear together in the poem until he is dead). Ideally when the retainer, the queen, and the gold-lord cooperate they constitute a viable nucleus of Germanic society: a retainer must have a gold-lord from whom to receive gold for his loyalty in battle; the peace-weaver must have a "loom"—the band of retainers and their lord, or two nations—upon which to weave peace.

Despite the poet's realization that these roles cannot be fulfilled in this world, this Germanic ideal provides structural and thematic unity for *Beowulf.* Grendel's mother does occupy a transitional position in the poem: as a "retainer" attacking Heorot she resembles Grendel, but as an "attacked ruler" of her own "hall" she resembles the dragon. As a monstrous mother and queen she perverts a role more important socially and symbolically than that of Grendel, just as the queen as peace-pledge or peace-weaver ultimately becomes more valuable than the retainer but less valuable than the gold-giver himself.

If it seems ironic that a Germanic ideal that cannot exist in this world *can* exist in art, unifying the theme and structure of the poem, then Grendel's mother, warring antitype of harmony and peace, must seem doubly ironic. The structural position of her episode in the poem, like woman's position as cup-passer among members of the nation, or as a peace-pledge between two nations, is similarly medial and transitional, but successfully so.

Jacqueline Vaught   (essay date 1980)

SOURCE: "*Beowulf:* The Fight at the Center," in *Allegorica,* Vol. V, No. 2, Winter, 1980, pp. 125-37.

[*In the following excerpt, Vaught argues that Beowulf's battle with Grendel's mother is more exciting than is his earlier battle with Grendel and that it is also more important to the poem's focus on heroism.*]

Among the most helpful of recent approaches to *Beowulf* are those that have increased our understanding of the rise of the hero in the first part of the poem—in Tolkien's terms, the first of "two great moments in a great life . . . first achievement and final death." In showing how the poem attains that first "moment," the best of recent studies have drawn out implications that illuminate not only the social import of Beowulf's heroism, but the psychological and cosmological import as well. Until recently, that first moment of heroic achievement has been located in the fight with Grendel; correspondingly, the "entire episode . . . involving Grendel's mother has been viewed as largely extraneous, a blot upon the thematic and structural unity of the poem" [according to Jane C. Nitzsche, *Tennessee Studies in Literature and Language,* Vol. 22 (1980)]. The effect of this critical consensus has been to raise many unanswered questions about the poem, including several that specifically involve Grendel's mother.

In the past year, however, both Michael N. Nagler and Jane C. Nitzsche, from different perspectives, have attempted to shift the weight of critical emphasis to the second fight. Nagler, working on "*Beowulf* in the Context of Myth," has located that particularly "climactic moment" at the bottom of the mere rather than in Heorot; and Nitzsche has addressed herself to proving that the dam, far from being an extraneous extension of Grendel, is "more important socially and symbolically" than her son.

I wish to affirm the essential rightness of these views and to explore further the importance of Grendel's mother, the mere, and Beowulf's heroic victory there. The subsequent discussion will summarize Beowulf's heroic achievement, consider several ways in which the poem itself signals the importance of the fight in the mere, and suggest what is most important there—socially, cosmologically, and psychologically—to the hero. In doing so,

I hope to show some of the advantages of the specific shift in critical emphasis from the first part of the narrative to the second.

In the most elementary sense, Beowulf does not conquer the forces threatening Heorot until he kills the dam and decapitates Grendel in the mere. As Klaeber says, "The fight with Grendel is rather monotonous and seems altogether too short and easy to give much opportunity for excitement." [Fr. Klaeber, ed., *Beowulf and The Fight at Finnsburg,* 3rd ed. (Lexington, Mass.: Heath, 1950), p lii. All references to the Old English text of **Beowulf** are from this edition.]

Nevertheless, the critics of **Beowulf** have usually joined the Geats and Danes in proclaiming Beowulf the hero after his fight in Heorot. We should remember, however, that the festivities prove ironically premature—the celebration being destroyed when Grendel's mother seeks vengeance for her son. Far from completing his quest, Beowulf's so-called victory in Heorot serves as a prelude that will amplify his fight against Grendel's mother, much as his verbal exchange with the coastguard prefigures his successful introduction to the king. It is not until the fight in the mere that Beowulf fulfills his development as the hero.

Stanley Kahrl's discussion of the word "feud" (*fæhð*) offers useful insights into Beowulf's role as hero. Comparing two lines that describe Beowulf in the second fight (l. 1534b and l. 1537b) with two lines describing Grendel earlier in the poem (ll. 135-7), Kahrl concludes that the passages suggest a similarity between Beowulf and Grendel since neither cares about the consequences of a feud. But, as Kahrl argues, the "normative maxim" (*swa sceal man dôn*) [So should a man act] applied to Beowulf in the mere shows that

> Beowulf's attitude is praiseworthy, whereas Grendel's is not. . . . The distinction is that which we regularly make between the reckless courage of the criminal who has abandoned all hope and whose actions are purely selfish and the selfless courage of the hero who places the good he is defending before his instinct for self-preservation.

It is true that the selfish criminal is subtly contrasted with the selfless hero. Yet throughout the poem, similar contrasts are made between the kings and monsters who are destructive through greed and selfishness and the kings and heroes who exhibit generosity and selflessness. The importance of the lines describing Beowulf lies less in the concept of *fæhð* than in the context of the immediately ensuing defeat of Grendel's mother. As much as they stress Beowulf's selflessness, they signal the moment in the poem when he attains his selfhood and gains victory over Grendel and his mother.

Still, we can take a cue from the "normative maxim" that distinguishes the heroic Beowulf from the monstrous Grendel. That expression, *swa sceal man dôn,* calls attention to the fact that Beowulf fights in the mere, not

with animalistic instincts of rage or fear, but with something potentially heroic and particularly human. That something is precisely the "unyielding will" (that, if realized, defines the hero) which Tolkien and others since him have claimed for Beowulf in the first fight.

That Beowulf is capable of an heroic exertion of will has been anticipated in the poem by his eagerness to fight for the Danes and by his initial power to overwhelm Grendel with fierce determination:

> Forð nēar ætstōp
> nam þa mid handa   higeþihtigr.e
> rinc on ræste,   ræhte ongēan
> fēond mid folme;   hē onfēng hraþe
> inwitþancum   ond wið earm gesæt.
> Sona þæt onfunde   fyrena hyrde,
> þæt hē ne mētte   middangeardes,
> eorþan scēata   on elran men
> mundgripe m ran: hē on m de wear
> forht on ferhðe;   nō þæy ær fram meahte.
> Hyge wæs him hinfūs,   wolde on heolster flēon . . .
>   (ll. 745b-55b).

> [Grendel stepped nearer and with his hands seized the strong-hearted warrior in bed, reached toward him, the fiend with his hands. Beowulf quickly took on the hostile purposes and with his arm sat up. Instantly, the keeper of crimes found that he had never met on middle-earth, from the corners of the earth, in any other man a greater grip. In his heart he became frightened in spirit; nor might he leave there for all that. His heart was eager to get away, wished to flee into his hiding-place.]

Yet in Heorot Beowulf's will is not taxed to the point of having to stand with unflinching resolve in the face of inevitable death. The ordeals he endures in the mere, however, test the full strength of his will. With no retainers to aid him and no weapon to protect him after Hrunting fails, Beowulf's will remains firm in his resolve to fight—despite the fact that the dam has overpowered him and that he despairs of his life. Instead of recoiling in fear as Grendel did in Heorot, Beowulf faces his opponent and proves himself the hero, defeating Grendel's mother in an act of pure will. As only a man can do, Beowulf stands firm against the powers of destruction at the moment he physically stands against the dam:

> Him on eaxle læg
> brēostnet brōden;   þæt gebearh fēore,
> wið ord ond wið ecge ingang forst d.
> Hæfde ða forsīðod   sunu Ecgþēowes
> under gynne grund,   Gēata cempa,
> nemne him heaðobyrne   helpe gefremede,
> herenet hearde,—   ond halig God
> gewēold wīgsigor;   wītig Drihten,
> rodera Rædend   hit on ryht gescēd
> æyðelīce,   syþðan hē eft astōd
>
>   (ll. 1547b-56b).

[On his shoulders lay the woven breast-net; that protected his life, withstood the entry of point and edge. The son of Edgetheow, champion of the Geats, would have perished then under the wide ground had not his battle-shirt, his hard war-net, brought him aid.—And the holy God granted victory; the wise Lord, the Ruler of the heavens, decided it rightly, easily, as soon as Beowulf stood up again.]

Nagler, while agreeing that the mere is the central scene in *Beowulf,* argues that the "climactic moment" of the poem occurs a few lines later, in the ten lines (ll. 1563-72a) that describe Beowulf's seizing the Giants' Sword, his decapitating Grendel, and the light's shining through the mere. Although I think it right to regard these ten lines as the climax of a basic Indo-European myth that Nagler reconstitutes, I think it wrong to accept them as the climax of the poem as we have it. In *Beowulf* that decisive moment occurs when Beowulf stands against the dam, and it is marked at that moment by God's assurance of victory.

It is because Beowulf has already completed his development as the hero that God so easily (l. 1556a) grants him the victory. And it is because Beowulf has already defeated the monsters with the strength of his will that he then has the power to raise the Giants' Sword (a sword no other man could lift) with which he will physically conquer them.

The achievements and miracles that follow Beowulf's heroic stance—the seizure of the sword, the killing of the dam, the light's shining, the decapitation of Grendel, the melting of the blade, and the cleansing of the mere—all constitute the denouement, poetically reiterating and amplifying Beowulf's original heroic achievement. Thus, it is not his success in Heorot, but his stance in the mere that is the decisive victory socially, cosmologically, and psychologically toward which the first half of the poem has led. In the most literal reading of the poem, Beowulf accomplishes in the mere what he had originally intended when he came to Heorot. The hall is safe, and all is cleansed.

Long before Beowulf kills Grendel's mother in the mere, the poem indicates, chiefly through surprise and dramatic suspense, that the victory there is the climactic achievement that completes the rising movement of the first part of the poem.

Whereas there is never any doubt about whether Beowulf will overwhelm Grendel in Heorot, the audience remains as ignorant as Beowulf about the outcome of the second fight—that is, until the moment he regains his feet. R. M. Lumiansky finds no essential difference between the predictions of victory which occur *before* the fight with Grendel and the assurance granted *in* the fight with the dam. But as Richard Ringler notes [in *Speculum* 41 (1966)], the fight in the mere is "fraught with uncertainty, suspense and alarm in a way that the Grendel fight is not."

The intense uncertainty about the second fight is the culmination of dramatic suspense which arises from the moment Grendel's mother abruptly appears in the poem:

> Þæt gesæyne wearþ,
> wīdcūþ werum, þætte wrecend þa gæyt
> lifde æfter laþum, lange þrage,
> æfter gūðceare; Grendles mōdor . . .
>
> (ll. 1255b-58b).

[Then it became evident, widely known to men that an avenger yet lived after the hostile one, for a long time after the grievous strife—Grendel's mother.]

As Irving notes [in *Introduction to Beowulf,* 1969], "She breaks into the poem as she breaks into the hall, out of nowhere." Though long-abiding (l. 1257b), this menacing "wrecend" is as surprising to the Geats and Danes, and to Beowulf, as she is to the audience.

After the dam's appearance, the marked increase in emotional tension continues to build through Hrothgar's description of the mere, which contains the suggestion that the mere is fatally hostile to society, and through the long march there. The dramatic technique of *Beowulf* is "cumulative, as when the poet first reveals Hrothgar's genuine fear of Grendel's lake . . . followed by the difficult march, the finding of Aeschere's severed head on the brink, and the slaying of the 'nicor.'" As they march to this *dæygel lond,* the men move increasingly away from the known into the unknown, leaving behind both the familiar lands around the hall and society itself. The path becomes increasingly narrow until the men are forced to walk in single file; finally they reach the mere that Beowulf will enter alone. The tension is "felt rather than seen" and "grows with each line."

The cause of this tension is certainly felt, if not seen, by Beowulf when Grendel's mother seizes him in the mere and proves to be stronger than she had appeared on land. Then, in "almost total ignorance of what to expect," Beowulf is left in a state of extreme uncertainty that does more than simply sustain dramatic suspense. It is a state of uncertainty thematically equivalent to the Unknown—that which Beowulf must enter willingly and alone if he is to become the victor.

In a poem so obviously concerned with social loyalty (and the difficulty and transience of that), the fact that Beowulf is alone when he enters the mere is one of the largest signals that his experiences there are central to the meaning of the poem. As Nitzsche points out, isolation in *Beowulf* is a characteristic of the monsters, those alienated from and opposed to society: and the dam's isolation is one of the many manifestations of her perversity that comment ironically on the maintenance and ethics of the *comitatus.* Yet in the fight in the mere and during the Breca swimming match—the two episodes in the poem in which Beowulf is successful in slaying monsters—Beowulf shares this "monstrous" characteristic of solitude.

The Breca episode has several parallels with the fight against the dam. As in the mere, Beowulf, alone, conquers the monsters with a sword; light shines and the waterways are cleared:

> . . . on mergenne   mēcum wunde
> be yðlafe   uppe lægon,
> sweo [r] dum aswefede,   þæt syðþan na
> ymb brontne ford   briml ðende
> lade ne letton.   Lēoht ēastan cōm,
> beorht bēacen Godes,   brimu swaþredon . . .
> (ll. 565a-70b).

> [. . . the morning found them (the sea-monsters) lying in the leavings of the waves, dead from the sword-wounds, killed with the sword, so that thereafter nothing around the deep waterways hindered the passage of the seafarers. Light came from the east, the bright beacon of God; the sea became still.]

Much as he does in the mere when careless of his life (l. 1536b), Beowulf gains the reward that can be attained only by an "immersion of the individual in the sea of experience . . . ready to risk all in the meeting."

Yet Beowulf has not become the hero in the Breca episode. His "heroic" actions there are more accidental than willed. Meeting a boyhood challenge, Beowulf and Breca face the sea together to test their powers, not to use them for the benefit of society. Only accidentally does Beowulf become separated from his friend; and while fighting to stay alive, he inadvertently serves society by clearing the waterways of the sea monsters.

In the fight with Grendel, the more experienced Beowulf is prepared to endure the ordeal in order to help society. And although he attempts to fight Grendel alone and without arms (an attempt that marks him as the potential hero), Beowulf does not fulfill his quest as the hero—precisely because he is still within society, literally inside the walls of Heorot and the circle of his men. As the poem makes clear, no hand, however powerful, that is still connected to the hands of society is free to wield the blow that would conquer the forces threatening that society. It is thus particularly ironic that Grendel's arm is raised to the roof of Heorot as a sign of victory:

> Þæt wæs tacen sweotol,
> syþðan hildedēor   hond alegde,
> earm ond eaxle —þær wæs eal geador
> Grendles grape—   under gēapne hr (ōf)
> (ll. 833b-36b).

> [It was a clear sign when the brave in battle set the hand, arm, and shoulder—there was all together, Grendel's grasp—under the vaulted roof.]

Although closely aligned to an entire set of hand imagery representing the interdependence of society, the arm and hand of Grendel are actually signs of mockery rather than of victory. As the Geats and Danes discover after Beowulf's first fight, chaos still reigns over Heorot.

In order to save society, the potential hero must leave the necessarily restrictive bounds of society and confront, as Beowulf did only accidentally in his youth, the destructive force directly. He must, paradoxically, become like the monsters, alienated from society—become the *wrǣcca* (meaning "wretch, miserable outcast, outlaw") in order to be the *wrǣcca* (also meaning "hero, avenger, champion"). Beowulf must symbolically leave his own country, then the familiar walls of Heorot—the "civilized world" that is "distinctly inside"—and follow the *wrǣclastas* [exile tracks] of Grendel's mother into the alien waters of the mere.

This motif is continued in the battle with Grendel's mother when Beowulf discovers that Hrunting, the chief protecting weapon of society that "næfre hit æt helde ne swa c / manna ængum" (ll. 1460b-61a) [never had it in battle failed any man], is ineffective in subduing the dam. As Nagler points out, some scholars have thought that "the failure of Hrunting when Beowulf seems to need it most is part of Unferth's plot against Beowulf." Others, such as Thomas A. Shippey, have argued that Hrunting fails only because its conquering function in a core tale has been transferred in **Beowulf** to the Giants' Sword. Yet as Nagler convincingly argues, the two swords serve significantly different functions: the hero must learn that "whatever (relatively) ordinary, earthly weapons he brings with him are of no avail" in battling his opponent: he "must have recourse to the demon's own weapon" or to "a weapon that is in the demon's possession."

Although Nagler concentrates on the mythic and psychological levels of **Beowulf,** his point about the swords has social import. In order to defeat the force threatening society, it is necessary for Beowulf to learn that he cannot defeat it with Hrunting which, representing the "order and degree in human society" that weapons in **Beowulf** usually mean, is as incapable of defeating that force as Beowulf is within the civilized world of Heorot. When he stands alone in the face of impending death and, consequently, proves stronger than the threatening power of the mere, Beowulf makes manifest the heroic inner strength that then enables him to execute that strength in physical action. Only then is he able to lift the Giants' Sword, associated with "primordial conflict," and complete his quest as the savior of society.

That Beowulf's heroic quest has cosmological as well as social significance has been recognized by several readers. It is not surprising that most of them have, until recently, concluded that it is in the fight at Heorot, the symbolic "center of the universe," that Beowulf acts in a god-like manner by repeating the original act of creation. Nor is it surprising to find that Grendel's mother, who seeks to avenge her son (l. 1278b), is generally considered to be a humanized extension of Grendel's chaotic energy. Similarly, the mere is considered to have only human, rather than cosmological, proportions.

Certainly, Grendel assumes cosmological significance in the poem, hating (as both Bernard F. Huppé and Raymond J. S. Grant note) not only the men in the hall and the joy there, but the Song of Creation in particular. When Grendel hears the song (ll. 86a-92b), his fury and pain establish him as a force of destruction, utterly opposed to the force of creation. But just as the fight in Heorot only anticipates Beowulf's victory for society in the mere, the cosmological import of the first fight only anticipates that of the second.

Heorot has been recognized as being, symbolically, the "center of the universe, i.e., the place from which creation . . . was begun": and if the mere-hall is accepted as an inversion of Heorot, then it may also be recognized as the symbolic "center" of chaos, the place from which destruction springs. The mere, itself, with waters indistinguishable from the clouds (ll. 1373a-76a), suggests uncreated, unformed chaos. Almost exclusively identified with the mere and the mere-hall, Grendel's mother is more of an extension of primal, chaotic energy than a humanized extension of Grendel. She is, notably, Grendel's *mother*—the source from which he and his destructive powers spring. This is one of the reasons that the dam, at home in the symbolic center of chaos, proves stronger there than she had appeared to be on land and why her fury is characteristically irrational and instinctive, whereas Grendel, if not exactly rational, approaches Heorot with premeditated cruelty (ll. 710a-34b). It is the dam who is most nearly identified with the cosmological force of chaos and Grendel who, to some degree, represents the humanized extension of that destructive power.

The cosmological significance of Beowulf's victory in the mere is most clearly signaled by the two similes in that scene:

> Lixte se lēoma,   lēoht inne stōd.
> efne swa of hefene   hadre scīneð
> rodores candel
>
>   (ll. 1570a-72a).

[The beam brightened, light shone within, just as the sky's candle from heaven clearly shines.]

>   Þa þæt sweord ongan
> æfter heaþoswate   hildegicelum,
> wīgbil wanian: þæt wæs wundra sum,
> þæt hit eal gemealt   īse gelīcost,
> ðonne forstes bend   Fæder onlæteð,
> onwindeð wælr pas,   s geweald hafað
> sæla ond mæla: þæt is sōð Metod
>
>   (ll. 1605b-11a).

[Then, because of the battle-sweat, that sword began to diminish, war-sword into battle-icicles. That was a wondrous thing—that it all melted, most like ice when the Father who watches over the times and seasons, loosens the frost's bond, unwinds the water-fetters. That is the true God.]

Both similes make connections between events in the mere and ones that carry connotations of the divine. Furthermore, the light's shining like heaven's candle suggests the first act of creation—a reading that follows not only from Nagler, but also from Grant's suggestion [in *Leeds Studies in English*, Vol. 8, (1975)] that light in *Beowulf* is "an image of creation or fire under control." Being rare in Old English poetry, the similes call attention to this special moment of Beowulf's god-like victory over chaos.

Yet the creative act on either the social or cosmological level is finally only a metaphor for the creative act potentially within every man. As the similes make clear, Beowulf's actions are only *like* a god's; however heroic, they are fundamentally human.

The confrontation between Beowulf and Grendel's mother is, psychologically, a concrete form of the abstract "battle of the inner self" [according to Jeffrey Helterman, *ELH*, Vol. 35, (1968)]. That battle may mean courage overcoming fear, will overcoming instinct, the conscious overcoming the unconscious, or any process in which the uncontrolled, potentially destructive energy of the psyche is conquered and converted into a constructive force. That process is the creation, or re-creation, of the self. In the poem, that process is presented in the form of Beowulf's facing the female monster, the antithesis of all his constructive, heroic qualities. That destructive force must be faced directly: avoiding it or repressing it may cause it to become manifest in a new and more powerfully destructive form—much as driving Grendel from Heorot leads to the mother's rising from the mere.

In order to earn the decisive victory, the hero must enter the unconscious, a symbolic landscape of the irrational and the unknown that can be entered only willingly and alone. In a passage that well applies to the episode in the mere, Joseph Campbell writes [in *The Hero with a Thousand Faces,* 1949] that the journey of the hero is

> fundamentally . . . inward—into depths where obscure resistances are overcome, and long lost, forgotten powers are revivified, to be made available for the transfiguration of the world. This deed accomplished . . . life becomes penetrated by a knowledge of its own unconquered power. Something of the light that blazes invisible within . . . breaks forth, with an increasing uproar.

As he enters the mere, Beowulf makes his journey inward. Rapidly he discovers that neither society nor even his own physical strength can help him in this internal battle. But when he stands, he also finds the center of himself, the strength of his unyielding will: the Giants' Sword is revivified; light breaks through the opaque mere as Beowulf discovers his own power and emerges from the mere as the hero.

John D. Niles   (essay date 1983)

SOURCE: "Ring Composition," in *"Beowulf": The Poem and Its Tradition,* Harvard University Press, 1983, pp. 152-62.

[*In the following excerpt, Niles explains how the author of* Beowulf *used a repeating structural design known as "ring composition" to organize his poem and to draw connections between characters such as Beowulf and Grendel.*]

The overall structure of **Beowulf** was once believed to be a product of a series of mistakes or fortuituous accidents. The author (or authors, for he was multiplied) was given credit for his fine sentiments and noble style, but not for his sense of form. Like most readers today, I believe that this view is based on a misapprehension of the poet's concept of what constitutes narrative form, and I want to help lay the view to rest by examining certain ways in which the poem shows patterning in its larger structure as well as on the level of the formulaic word or phrase.

One feature of the poem's patterning that deserves attention is *ring composition,* a chiastic design in which the last element in a series in some way echoes the first, the next to the last the second, and so on. Often the series centers on a single kernel, which may serve as the key element, so that the design as a whole may be thought of as an *ABC . . . X . . . CBA* pattern capable of indefinite expansion.

In her illuminating study of the rhetorical paterns used by Old English poets in extended verse paragraphs, Adeline Courtney Bartlett cites a number of passages that are organized according to what she calls an "envelope" pattern, in which the same word, phrase, or idea both begins and ends the passage. A good example of ring composition based on a verbal "envelope" not cited by Bartlett occurs early in **Beowulf,** in lines 12-19, which tell of the coming of Scyld's son, Beow (or Beowulf, as the scribe mistakenly calls him):

> Đæm eafera wæs   æfter cenned
> geong in geardum   þone God sende
> folce to frofre;   fyrenðearfe ongeat
> þe hie ær drugon   aldorlease
> lange hwile;   him þæs Liffrea,
> wuldres Wealdend   woroldare forgeaf:
> Beowulf was breme   —blæd wide sprang—
> Scyldes eafera   Scedelandum in.

> To him in time   a son was born,
> young in the land,   whom the Lord sent
> to comfort the folk;   He knew the dire need
> they had suffered earlier,   lacking a king
> for a long time.   The Lord of life,
> Ruler of glory,   granted them grace for this.
> Beow[ulf] was famous,   his name rang widely,
> Scyld's son,   in the lands of the North.

This self-contained verse paragraph clearly is framed by the word *eafera,* "son." Less obviously, it is built up not only as an envelope but as a ring. The second element in the ring is a phrase descriptive of Scyld's son, Beow: first he is said to be "young in the land" (13a), then he is described as "famous" (18a). Third is the equivalent of the phrase "God sent him as a blessing to the people" (13b-14a, 16b-17). The kernel of the passage is the reference to the Danes' long years of misery before the coming of Scyld (14b-16a). The poet uses ring composition as a means of traveling from the immediate reality (the Danes under Scyld's son, Beow) to an "other," legendary reality that is used as a point of comparison (the Danes in their previous years of misery), then back again to the present reality. Ring composition enables the poet to ease into and out of a picture of past terrors, as the Danes' previous sufferings are safely enclosed within the envelope of God's mercy.

Ring composition in archaic and oral narrative poetry is not confined to the short verse paragraph. It may be used as a way of organizing long passages as well, or even entire poems. In **Beowulf** it is a technique of major importance from beginning to end. The poet relies so greatly on this sort of patterning that, for him, balance and symmetry of thought must have been almost second nature. Of course, certain instances of ring composition in the poem might be dismissed as obvious and practically inevitable. The two sea voyages, for example (lines 205-228 and 1880b-1924), show a kind of symmetrical structure that could hardly have been avoided: *journey down to the shore, embarcation, voyage across the high seas, disembarcation, journey up from the shore.* Other instances of fairly simple ring composition are identified by Bartlett and by Constance B. Hieatt in their discussions of "double envelope" and "triple envelope" patterning in **Beowulf.** I call attention here to certain additional ways in which the poet built up his narrative using chiastic patterning of a sort that is neither obvious nor inevitable. The parts of the poem I single out are the episodes that tell of the midnight struggle between Beowulf and Grendel (702b-836), the subsequent feud between Beowulf and Grendel's mother (1279-1802a), and the battle many years later between Beowulf and the firedrake (2200-3136). A close study of these episodes shows that the **Beowulf** poet used ring composition not only as a minor rhetorical device or an occasional linking tool, but as a means of giving form to the most important events of his story.

All the preliminary action of the poem leads up to a single event, the hero's hand-to-hand struggle in Heorot. Before the fight begins, Grendel stands for a moment at the door of Heorot and laughs to see his sleeping prey (730b). When the fight is over, it is Beowulf who stands at the door rejoicing (827b). The act that initiates the fight—Grendel's devouring the young warrior Handscioh, even his feet and hands—is balanced later by Beowulf's similar act of brutish violence in wrenching Grendel's arm from his body. When the monster first grapples with Beowulf, the poet notes the deadly effect of Beowulf's grip on Grendel's hand ("his fingers burst," 760b) and indicates that the ogre "wished to flee" (*wolde fleon,* 755b). Toward the end of the fight the poet reverts to a similar bone-crushing image ("his joints burst," 818a) and indicates that Grendel "had to flee" (*scolde . . . fleon,* 819-820a). At the climax the poet twice calls attention to the uproar in the hall and to the fear that grips the listening Danes (767-770, 782b-788a). All the details of the fight radiate about a single kernel, the moment of extreme violence when Heorot itself seems about to fall (771-782a). Formless though the episode might seem at first, owing in part to the repetitive, stop-and-go narrative movement that has been described rather generously as "lack of steady advance" [see Frederick Klaeber, ed., *Beowulf and the Fight at Finnsburg*, 3rd ed. with 1st and 2nd supp. (Boston, 1950), p. lvii.], the narrative coheres. Important events align themselves into contrastive pairs that center about the moment of awesome fury when the mead hall begins to splinter around the two antagonists, whose struggle is still unresolved.

Longer and more complex is the account of the events that occur from sunset of the second day until sunset of the third day of the hero's stay in Denmark. The episode centers on the critical fight between Beowulf and Grendel's mother on the floor of the mysterious pool that serves as the monsters' home.

At the start of the day, Hrothgar, Beowulf, and their companions emerge from their chambers and learn of the attack made by Grendel's mother during the night. In a long speech Hrothgar recounts the death of his chief thane, Æschere, and describes the monsters' pool (1321-82). In a short reply Beowulf expresses his determination to average Æschere's death (1383-96). Toward the end of the day these two speeches are answered by another pair, a brief address in which Beowulf reports on his success (1651-76), and Hrothgar's long, homiletic speech on the subject of pride (1700-84). In like manner, the journey of the Danes and Geats to the pool (1399-1421) is later balanced by the briefly described triumphant return of Beowulf and his men to Heorot (1632-50). On the journey out, the narrow trail taken by the men is called an "unknown path" (1410b); on the return trip, the same route has become "known ways" (1634a). Each journey culminates in the image of a severed head—first Æschere's, then Grendel's. When the Danes and Geats first come to the banks of the pool, they gaze with horror on the blood welling there, the blood of Æschere. After Beowulf has emerged from the mere, the poet again calls attention to the blood staining the water, now the blood of the monsters. Other details echo back and forth in similar fashion: the ceremonious arming of Beowulf in his helm and byrnie (1441b-54) and the swift removal of his helm and byrnie after his return (1629-30a); the hero's solemn farewell before the fight and his comrades' joyous greeting of him afterward; his descent through serpent-infested waters and his later ascent through the same waters, now miraculously "all cleansed" (1620). From first to last, events on the third day in Denmark succeed one another not haphazardly, but in the order imposed by a sustained narrative intelligence.

Some of these correspondences are admittedly of little consequence. If the hero survives his descent through the waters of the pool, for example, he can be expected to swim back up; if he journeys overland from Heorot to the pool, he can be expected to return. All the same, the consistency with which events after the fight echo earlier events is a special characteristic of the *Beowulf* poet's style. One observes little patterning of this sort in, for instance, the corresponding episode of *Grettir's Saga* (chaps. 65-66), in which the story is nearly linear in its development. In *Beowulf,* few narrative events stand alone; most are linked to others in complex interrelationships.

Equally characteristic of the poet's style is the way in which thesis is answered by antithesis. The horror of the second night in Heorot is answered by the calm of the third; solemn farewells are answered by joyful greetings; the once infested waters become miraculously cleansed. Rarely in *Beowulf* is an event repeated in the same terms and with the same emotional coloring. More often, one event is balanced by another that resembles it in certain respects but contrasts with it in others. Between the monster's midnight attack and Beowulf's triumphant return from the pool, events seem clouded. Fear of the unknown hangs over all, making even familiar paths look weird and unknown. After the fight, events seem to take place in the clear light of the sun.

Less elegant in its patterning, though in some ways still more interesting, is the third great episode, the story of the aged hero's fight against the firedrake. Apart from certain transitional lines that summarize some of the chief events of the preceding years (2200-10a, 2354b-96), this episode occupies the whole of the second great part of the poem up to the final fitt. Although any scheme that claims to account neatly for all the events in this part would be an oversimplification, the episode does not lack form. In this section—the loftiest and most magnificent of the poem—speeches, journeys, allusions to Swedish-Geatish hostilities, and references to the splendor of the dragon's hoard are ranged in complementary pairs about the scene of the hero's final combat and death.

Although the fight itself and its immediate aftermath are recounted linearly, this kernel episode too reveals the poet's tendency toward stylization and patterning. Three times the dragon attacks before Beowulf and his young kinsman Wiglaf cut him down (see 2569, 2669-70, 2668); three times the wounded king speaks before he dies (2724-51, 2792b-2808, 2813-16). Framing this central episode like a pair of trumpet cells are two speeches that express in brief the code of conduct on which both Beowulf and Wiglaf have based their actions. In the first of these Beowulf addresses his comrades and kinsmen for the last time and affirms in emphatic words his intention to live and die by the heroic ideal (2535b-37). The second speech is Wiglaf's. It concludes with an equally emphatic approach to the same comrades and kinsmen, who in the meantime have been found conspicuously lacking in the stuff of heroism: "Death is better / for any man than a life of shame!" (2890b-91). Framing these two speeches are two longer ones alluding to ancient Swedish-Geatish hostility, which threatens to erupt again into war. Beowulf addresses the first of these to the Geats (2425-2509); the second, the "Messenger's Prophecy," is spoken by an unnamed Geat who is given the gloomy task of bearing the news of the fight to his countrymen (2900-3027). The dangers of war, which had seemed hypothetical, are now both real and immediate, and the messenger depicts them with grim precision.

In this episode as in other parts of the poem, ends and beginnings are intertwined. The initial account of the dragon's hoard (2231b-70a) finds a counterpart in the later description that introduces the theme of a charm or curse laid on the treasure (3047-57). In each passage the poet dwells with evident delight on the splendor of the hoard: the rings and cups plated with gold, the swords, the helms, the byrnies. After the later description, the rifling of the barrow's treasures by eight chosen Geats answers to the event that set this episode in motion, the rifling of the barrow by an unknown fugitive. Even the "Lament of the Last Survivor" (2247-66), the celebrated digression in which the last survivor of an ancient tribe is depicted in the act of bequeathing his tribe's treasures to the earth, finds an echo in Wiglaf's solemn address to his fellow Geats as they stand over their dead king (2864-91).

Wiglaf's speech is the last in the poem, and it is heavy with the melancholy tone that has been sounded throughout this episode. Its speaker has more than a little in common with the speaker of the earlier "lay." Wiglaf too is a last survivor, as Beowulf makes clear in his final speech, when he addresses him as "the last of our tribe, the Wægmundings'" (2813-14a). Wiglaf too has lived to see the death of his former lord. He stands gazing on the same treasure that the last survivor had held so lovingly, and he buries it "as useless to men as it had been before" (3168). The last survivor witnessed the breakup of a kingdom. Wiglaf fears the same fate for the Geats. Between the speech of the last survivor and Wiglaf's concluding speech, between the first rifling of the treasure and the last, there is little advance in tone. The same sense of impending doom hangs over all.

In the main, one may conclude, the poem consists of three major episodes of different length and complexity, each one of which shows ring patterning. The question remains: How are these episodes articulated into a single coherent story of epic length?

If the reader does not become lost in the many byways of the narrative, the large-scale symmetry of its design will be evident: (*A*) introduction, (*B*) fight with Grendel, (*C*) celebrations, (*D*) fight with Grendel's mother, (*C*) celebrations, (*B*) fight with dragon, (*A*) close. The three great fights that constitute the main body of the poem are separated by two substantial interludes in which the hero's triumphs are celebrated with gifts, feasting, and songs and speeches alluding to legendary heroes. Surrounding the whole—enveloping it in the wraps of eternity, as it were—are passages of opening and closing that look deep into the past, in the story of Scyld, and far into the future, in the dark forebodings of the "Messenger's Prophecy" and in the building of a barrow for the dead king that is to stand ever after "as a remembrance to my people" (2804).

In the grand design as well as in its parts, events answer to one another. The poem ends where it begins, with a eulogy for a dead king. And before and after these eulogies? Stories of the kings' funerals. In a way too consistent

to be the result of chance, events in the poem's gradual unfolding find a reply in events from the poem's gradual close. Although these events are like one another in some ways, they are antithetical in others. Scyld is an ideal king, for example, but is preeminently a king of war and conquest. Beowulf, an equally ideal king, is renowned for his keeping of the peace: of all worldly kings he is "mildest and most gracious to his people" (3181-82). The fight with Grendel is the young Beowulf's first great test, and he meets it with extraordinary vigor. The moment he puts his hands on Grendel, the joyful outcome of the fight is no longer in doubt. The fight with the dragon is the aged Beowulf's last test of all, and he meets it with almost superhuman fortitude. In this fight, the narrator's frequent and all too clear asides (2341b-44, 2419b-24, 2511a, 2589-91a, and 2725b-28) impress on the audience the dark end that is drawing near.

Most of the chief correspondences that knit the poem together are obvious. Others, less obvious, appear with equal force when one reflects on them. Hrothgar's command to build Heorot, for example (67b-76a), has a parallel in Beowulf's request to have his barrow built (2802-08). Each edifice, adorned with gold in magnificent quantities, is to stand high (*hlifade*, 81b; *hlifian*, 2805a) over the surrounding countryside, a monument to future generations of the glory of the past. Each is given a special name—*Heorot, Biowulfes beorh*—and each shines bright (311, 2803a). Heorot echoes with the song of the Creation (90b-98), and over the barrow is heard the lamentation of the Geats (3148b-55a).

To a remarkable extent, the structure of **Beowulf** can be described in terms of a series of major and minor pairs. The two great parts of the poem—the parts that together make up Tolkien's "balance" and "opposition of ends and beginnings"—are the largest pair. Another contrasting pair consists of the Grendel fight and the dragon fight. Somewhat smaller are the sea voyages to and from Denmark. Smallest of all are minute echoes of diction that ring too clear to be fortuitous, such as "unknown path" (1410b) and "known ways" (1634a).

Many of these correspondences, great and small, converge on a single narrative event of great intensity: the hero's struggle against Grendel's mother in the depths of the monsters' pool. The choice of this event as the structural center of the epic is not casual. At this point in the narrative the young hero has his closest brush with death; he is in fact given up for dead by the Danes, who think that the blood welling to the surface of the pool is his. Insofar as Beowulf is marked out as "a mythic figure of death and resurrection," as Albert Lord has maintained, it is here that he can be said to suffer symbolic death. Thereafter, the hero returns to his native land to take his rightful place in society as a mature and respected adult.

Readers of the *Odyssey* will note a curious and appropriate parallel between the ring structures of these two poems. As others have observed, the adventure that forms the kernel of the story of Odysseus' wanderings (books 9-12) is the Nekyia, the tale of his journey to the land of the dead. The corresponding event of the *Aeneid* will leap to mind: book 6, Aeneas' descent to the underworld to consult the shades of the dead. Like Homer and Virgil, the *Beowulf* poet had the narrative genius to develop his story around its point of greatest mystery. In doing so, he called to mind the greatest story of Christendom as well. By repeatedly associating Grendel and his mother with the creatures of hell, he presents Beowulf's descent in terms that call to mind Christ's legendary harrowing of hell, as recounted in the apocryphal Gospel of Nicodemus. Such echoes may have been unintentional, of course. There is no way of knowing if the narrator was consciously alluding to Christ's descent, although he evidently drew on established conceptions of the mouth of hell. Virgilian influence in the poem is uncertain, and direct Homeric influence can be ruled out. In developing a narrative that has points in common with certain critical parts of the *Odyssey,* the *Aeneid,* and the story of Christ, the author may unconsciously have been drawing on the same age-old popular traditions (or the same psychic depths) that inspired Homer, Virgil, and the early disseminators of the Christian myth. All one can say with confidence is that to an audience familiar with these mythically cognate materials, such associations between Beowulf and other legendary heroes are an appropriate means of enriching the poem. Thanks largely to the way in which it centers on a complex of events that resonates deeply with famous stories of the past, *Beowulf* is transformed from what it might have been—a fairly straightforward tale of the deeds of a good man—into a work of superb psychological and mythic suggestiveness.

Far from having been an unskilled compiler of separate tales, the poet was endowed with a keen (although always flexible) sense of narrative form. His epic develops in a leisurely manner, as events in the poem's gradual beginning eventually find their equivalents in the poem's gradual close, so that the work as a whole has the solidity and grace of a well-planned piece of architecture. *Beowulf* is no mere collection of "fabulous exploits redolent of folktale fancy" (Klaeber, p. xii). It is no sightless narration, nor is it a clumsy joining of two tales. It is a well-wrought epic poem. Its chief materials may be highly disparate, but in ordering them the poet shows his competence in relating a long, cohesive verse narrative.

While it is tempting to believe that the structural patterning of *Beowulf* has some relation to the poem's special conditions of oral performance or to the conditions of oral composition among hypothetical prototypes of the text, this relation is too problematical to be assessed here. Patterning of any sort is mnemonically useful to an oral poet or to a performer of oral poems, just as it is useful to any stage performer (whether singer, storyteller, actor, musician, toastmaster, or nightclub entertainer) who does not rely on a fixed text as the basis of his or her performance. Ring composition could serve as one elementary type of mnemonic patterning: as Cedric Whitman observes, "The oral poet, having mentioned A, B, and C, picks them up later on in the order C, B, and A, since it is natural to reconstruct a chain of thought backwards." All the same, oral texts taken from the field have

not been shown to exhibit complex ring structures comparable to those evident in the *Iliad* and *Beowulf.* Perhaps these structures exist, but the necessary field work and analysis have not been done. Moreover, even some polished literary works (such as *Tom Jones* and *Paradise Lost*) show complex ring patterning. The various sorts of ring composition in *Beowulf* may plausibly be taken as traits that would be useful to an oral poet or performer, but further conclusions are premature.

More important, perhaps, is the question of audience response. What aesthetic effect would the patterning in the structure of *Beowulf* have had on an audience of Anglo-Saxons listening to the poem? And what is the aesthetic effect of such patterning on a person reading the poem today?

Assuming that the poem was composed for oral presentation, one might think that an audience of Anglo-Saxon monks or thanes could hardly have been cognizant of the poem's close-knit design. If the poem was recited during a single evening, how could listeners have held the Scyld episode in mind until the poem reached Beowulf's funeral? How or why would they be thinking of Grendel at the time of the dragon's attack? If the performance was drawn out over several sittings, the audience's perception of patterning would be yet more faint. All the same, one suspects that the patterned structure of *Beowulf* would not have been wholly without aesthetic effect. No concern is purely structural; one cannot conceive of structural phenomena in literature that are devoid of aesthetic implications. To the question of whether or not Homer's audience could possibly have caught the signs of such "fearful symmetry" in the *Iliad,* Whitman replies, "The human mind is a strange organ, and one which perceives many things without conscious or articulate knowledge of them, and responds to them with emotions necessarily and appropriately vague. An audience hence might feel more symmetry than it could possibly analyze or describe." An audience of Anglo-Saxons listening to a performance of *Beowulf* might well have had certain definite, though unarticulated, expectations about the proper way of conducting such an epic song. Among these may have been the expectation that in a well-wrought tale, no one narrative event would stand alone; no event would be thought of as random or isolated, without antecedents or consequences. The story of the coming of Scyld, for example, might have set up certain expectations that would not have been satisfied until the singer came to tell of the passing away of Beowulf. The story of the young hero's rout of Grendel, a monstrous creature whose eyes blaze like fire, who has been ravaging a king's hall in midnight attacks, and who reminds one of the walking dead, might likewise have set up expectations that would not have been satisfied until the poet came to sing of the hero's last fight against the dragon, a more terrible creature, whose mouth breathes fire, who has razed a royal hall in a midnight attack, and who comes as inexorably as death itself. The probability that such expectations would have been unconscious makes them no less real. Moreover, one need not assume that they were unconscious. An audience that had heard a story told often, with variations, might have become sufficiently discerning to appreciate even subtle instances of thematic echo.

To a modern reader able to review the text in detail, comparing event with event, speech with speech, and word with word, the poem has a readily apparent symmetry of design that exerts a clear aesthetic effect. In *Beowulf,* it would appear, human success and failure are conceived of as an inseparable pair. As in other poems of the Anglo-Saxon corpus, joy does not occur apart from sorrow, creation apart from dissolution, human success apart from failure. The founding of the Scylding dynasty is answered in time by the tribal dissolution facing the Geats. Æschere's head demands Grendel's. Heorot gives way to war or flames, and in its place stands a barrow. In *Beowulf,* as Joan Blomfield has pointed out, there is no simplistic development of either character or plot. In a tale such as this, "the concluding affairs must be implicit in the beginning," as one is made to see "the ever-present identity of seed in fruit and fruit in seed." John Leyerle has put the matter more pessimistically: "The sudden reversals inherent in the structure . . . give to the whole poem a sense of transience about the world and all that is in it . . . With each reversal the elegiac texture is tightened, reminding us of impermanence and change, extending even to the greatest of heroes, Beowulf . . . A bright and golden age of a magnanimous man vanishes, even as it seems hardly to have begun."

The dominant mood created by this recurrent play of joy against sorrow, creation against dissolution, may strike some readers as fatalistic, and it may well be; but if so, the poem's fatalism stems from a realistic understanding of the limits that bound earthly success. The poet seems to have lived enough of life to appreciate the awful ease with which time and an indifferent fate blot out even the most glorious of human achievements. Possibly the realistic fatalism of *Beowulf* may be the melancholy of a person looking back upon a former heroic age whose virtues he admired intensely. Possibly—more plausibly, it seems to me—such fatalism is an innate part of the heroic view of life. Whatever the explanation, the poem has power to move, and that is its reason for being.

Richard Butts   (essay date 1987)

SOURCE: "The Analogical Mere: Landscape and Terror in *Beowulf,*" in *English Studies,* Vol. 68, No. 2, 1987, pp. 113-21.

[*In the following excerpt, Butts maintains that the* Beowulf *poet's description of Grendel's mere, or pool, is meant to be nightmarish rather than realistic.*]

The description of Grendel's mere in Hrothgar's speech to Beowulf (1345a-1379b) is an extended metaphor for terror. [The text of *Beowulf* used throughout this paper is that of Friedrich Klaeber's edition, *Beowulf and The Fight at Finnsburg,* 3rd. ed. (Lexington, Mass., 1950).] The difficulty of reconciling all the features of the landscape surrounding the mere into a realistic picture has been noted by previous commentators. But to take an unsympathetic view of the poet's accomplishment here and read the description as an unsuccessful attempt to accurately and realistically render a natural landscape is to misread it. The poet gives us Hrothgar's description not so as to present a natural landscape but in order to point to the realm of the supernatural. The supernatural, thus evoked, allows for a mode of language and thought which is ideally suited for expressing the poet's prime concern: the collective terror of men in the face of the unknown. The purpose of the poet is less to describe a particular topography than it is to communicate some sense of men's imaginative and psychological response to Grendel.

Even the most cursory examination of the principal imagery associated with Grendel's mere reveals the highly unnatural character of the landscape. The morning after the attack of Grendel's mother on Heorot, Hrothgar tells Beowulf of the two "ellorgæstas' (1349a) and the place from which they come in a speech which, although detailed, is also highly elusive. That Grendel represents something beyond the experience of the Danes—something beyond the limits of the natural and social order with which they are familiar—is reinforced by an imagery which suggests that the monster is part of a world which is both temporally and physically distinct from the world of contemporary men. From Hrothgar, we learn that 'þone on geardagum Grendel nemdon / foldbuende' (1354a-1355a). The phrase 'on geardagum' recalls a legendary time, existing at the extreme edge of human memory. Hrothgar's knowledge of it is fragmentary and tentative; it is a time so far removed from the understanding of contemporary men that knowledge of it is preserved only in the songs of the scop, of 'se þe cuþe / frumsceaft fira feorran reccan' (90b-91b). From this dark and mysterious time, Grendel has come to terrorize the Danes. Figuratively, this earlier time is a time of darkness; it signals a dark prehistory before the dawning of the Danish civilization which culminates in Hrothgar's reign and the building of Heorot, the 'beahsele beorhta' (1177a). Grendel is consistently characterized as a creature of the darkness. The first reference to him in *Beowulf* describes him as 'se þe in þystrum bad' (87b). Grendel is the 'deorc deaþscua' (160a) who lives in a darkness quite literally beyond the understanding of men:

> [Grendel] sinnihte heold
> mistige moras; men ne cunnon,
> hwyder helrunan hwyrftum scriþaþ.
>
> (161b-163b)

Consonant with the temporal alienation of Grendel from the world of the Danes is the physical separation of his territory from the haunts of men. Hrothgar tells Beowulf that Grendel and his mother are 'micle mearcstapan' who 'moras healdan' (1348). The severity of the terrain over which Hrothgar leads Beowulf and his retainers in order to reach Grendel's lair further underlines this separation of the world of monsters from the world of men; the men travel by:

steap stanhliþo, stige nearwe,
enge anpaþas, uncuþ gelad,
neowle næssas, nicorhusa fela.

(1409a-1411b)

The technical challenge which the **Beowulf** poet must overcome in relation to the mere is the inadequacy of language to convey a complex and subtle state of mind, in this case, the psychological mood of men toward Grendel and all the greater unknown which he represents. The principal difficulty encountered in describing a psychological mood is that it resists most forms of univocal description. The linguistic problem points to a deeper epistemological one. Hrothgar tells Beowulf: 'No þæs frod leofaþ / gumena bearna, þæt þone grund wite' (1366b-1367b). The Dane's reference to the bottom of Grendel's mere is as much a figurative emblem of the limits of what can be known and said by men as it is an allusion to the depth of a body of water. Rendering a psychological mood poses a similar problem of description for the poet insofar as a state of mind or psychological mood is not as readily an object of sense as is, say, a 'sincfæt' or a 'guþsweord geatolic'. When the mind is turned inward to focus on a psychological mood as an object of knowledge, the mind must perceive it more intimately and less through the medium of sense; the process is more intuitive than it is empirical. Yet in spite of this rather formidable obstacle to communication, the poet does succeed in offering to his readers an understanding of a dominant psychological mood which is simply too exquisite to be contained within the conventional conceptual dimension of language. He communicates this mood through an analogical mode of thinking and description in which details of the physical landscape are consciously manipulated to evoke a psychological landscape.

Hrothgar calls the land in which Grendel and his mother live the 'dygel lond' (1357b). The dominant chord struck by the landscape description is one of otherworldliness, an intimation of the supernatural conveyed by the threatening images of the

[. . .] wulfhleoþu, windige næssas,
frecne fengelad, þær fyrgenstream
under næssa genipu niþer gewiteþ,
flod under foldan.

(1358a-1361a)

The image of the 'wulfhleoþu' mediates between the natural and supernatural resonances of the landscape. Wolves do move in the natural landscape with which Hrothgar and Beowulf would be familiar, but these animals are also traditionally associated with death and the horrors of the battlefield where warriors pass from the world they know to the unknown beyond. The disappearance of the 'flod under foldan', with the 'fyrgenstream' flowing under the darkness of the headlands—foreshadowing Beowulf's descent into the water to do battle with Grendel's mother—is also emblematic on a more general level of this passage from light and the natural world to the mysterious darkness of whatever lies beyond it. The supernatural character of Grendel's mere is enhanced by the 'hrinde bear-

was, / wudu wyrtum fæst' (1363a-1364b) which overshadow the water and the eerie spectacle which may be seen there each night, the 'niþwundor' (1365b) of the 'fyr on flode' (1366a). Perhaps the most powerful evocation of the supernatural, almost magical mood associated with Grendel's mere comes at the climax of Hrothgar's speech where the old king, in his attempt to impress upon Beowulf the very fearful and unnatural aspect of the place, tells the young Geat the story of the 'heorot hornum trum' (1369a), the extraordinary hart which gives up its life to the hounds rather than brave Grendel's mere.

I have suggested that the poet's manipulation of details to evoke a supernatural landscape is supported by an analogical mode of thinking and description. The poet's interest in the supernatural signals, I believe, a concurrent interest in the psychological: the landscape which the poet has offered us with his description of Grendel's mere is, in effect, the landscape of dreams. For example, the odd combination of frost and fire—the frost of the 'hrinde bearwas' (1363b) and the fire of the 'fyr on flode' (1366a)—juxtaposed in the same scene seems inappropriate to what we would expect of a natural landscape. But such phenomena might easily be combined by the associative logic of dreams or visionary experiences. In fact, such a juxtaposition of elemental symbolism, and particularly the oxymoronic figure of the 'fyr on flode', is highly characteristic of the surrealistic heightening of consciousness that we associate with dreaming.

A similar combining of disparate images distinguishes the poet's description of the mere itself. Overshadowed by the 'wudu wyrtum fæst' (1364a) and fed by the falling 'fyrgenstream' (1359b), the mere has been described by some commentators as an inland lake. Influenced by the corresponding scene in the *Grettissaga,* Klaeber remarks that the 'outlines' of Grendel's mere are 'fairly well understood' as a 'pool surrounded by cliffs and overhung with trees, a stream descending into it, and a large cave behind the fall'. But the 'windige næssas' (1358b) and 'næssa' (1360a) are more suggestive of formations along the seacoast than they are of inland hills. And the closing imagery of Hrothgar's speech, the turbulent images of the 'yþgeblond' (1373a) of Grendel's mere which 'up astigeþ / won to wolcnum, þonne wind styreþ / laþ gewidru' (1373b-1375a) seems less appropriate to the site of an inland pool than it does to the open ocean. Later, when Hrothgar, Beowulf, and their retainers visit Grendel's mere, they find the water populated with fierce *sea* creatures:

Gesawon þa æfter wætere wyrmcynnes fela,
sellice sædracan sund cunnian,
swylce on næshleoþum nicras licgean,
þa on undernmæl oft bewitigaþ
sorhfulne siþ on seglrade,
wyrmas ond wildeor.

(1425a-1430a)

The poet's conflation of lake and sea imagery thwarts any clear picture of Grendel's mere; each cluster of imagery undermines the signifying power of the other. Details of the description of Grendel's mere are manipulated by the poet to produce a subversive rhetoric, subversive to the extent that it militates against its own cognitive content. The poet is quite capable of describing a scene closely and realistically when he chooses to do so, but here, in spite of the accumulation of realistic details built into Hrothgar's speech, we are left with what is, I think, an intentionally contradictory picture. And this is not an undesirable feature of the description. Because the cumulative and overwhelming force of this tension between conflicting clusters of images inhibits any single cognitive perception of the scene, it necessitates a non-intellectual, almost emotional response in the reader; the reader is left with the impression of having submitted to a subtle sensual experience rather than to a carefully marshalled description of a body of water. Such a poetic strategy is quite consistent with the kind of appeal the poet wishes his description to make: it recreates the appeal of the elusive yet symbolic landscapes of the dreams which embody our most profound and primal fears. It is morning when Hrothgar delivers this speech to Beowulf; traditionally the time in Old English poetry of misery without consolation, it is of course also the time when the night's dreams are remembered.

The scenic confusion of the lake and sea imagery also functions to render Grendel's mere more terrifying. The sea represents a source of the hostile unknown; it is a place from which come 'niceras' (422a), the 'wedera cealdost' (546b) and invading 'searohæbbendra / byrnum werede' (237a-238b). To the extent that it is bound up with the imagery of an inland lake, the sea is brought closer to home, and consequently, made more threatening. Symbolically, the sea and what it represents is internalized: as this source of terror is associated with an inland lake, it is seen to have invaded the terrestial home of the 'foldbuende' (1355a). The figurative entry of the sea into the land parallels the narrative action of Grendel's nightly raids on Heorot. Hrothgar's beguilingly simple statement to Beowulf 'Nis þæt feor heonon / milgemearces, þæt se mere standeþ' (1361b-1362b), underlines just how much the very source of terror lies within the literal and the psychological domains of men.

Hrothgar's story of the 'hæþstapa' (1368a), the hart which surrenders to the hounds rather than escape by entering Grendel's mere, is an elegiac testimony to the fear all creatures have of Grendel:

> þeah þe hæþstapa hundum geswenced,
> heorot hornum trum holtwudu sece,
> feorran geflymed, ær he feorh seleþ,
> aldor on ofre, ær he in wille,
> hafelan [beorgan].
>
> (1368a-1372a)

In a characteristic understatement, Hrothgar adds 'nis þæt heoru stow' (1372b). It is significant that the poet has chosen to designate his fugitive animal a 'heorot' (1369a); 'heorot' is, of course, the eponym for Hrothgar's great hall, the symbol of the prosperity and security of the Danish kingdom. The poet was no doubt sensible of the

figurative and poetic overtones of such a word here at the climax of Hrothgar's speech, especially as this is the only occurrence of 'heorot' as a common noun in *Beowulf.* The noun allows the poet to sum up the collective fear of the Danes into the vivid metonymy of the fleeing hart. This metonymic shrinking of men's fear into the image of the fugitive hart has the typical function of condensation in dreams: there is conveyed an intensity of impression that could not have been achieved by the mere statement that all creatures, including men, fear Grendel. Hence, Hrothgar's elegy for the hart is as much an elegy for Heorot, the 'healærna mæst' (78a), and the people whom it represents. In the death of the hounded hart, we may even find a metonymic prophecy of the fall of Heorot itself in the Heatho-Bard conflict.

A recurrent theme in Hrothgar's speech is the ability, or the inability, of men to know. Hrothgar's 'selerædende' (1346a) describe the appearance of Grendel and his mother 'þæs þe hie gewislicost gewitan meahton' (1350). The poet underlines just how little knowledge the 'fold-buende' (1355a) possess about the monsters: 'no hie fæder cunnon, / hwæþer him ænig wæs ær acenned / dyrnra gasta' (1355b-1357a). With respect to Grendel's mere itself, 'No þæs frod leofaþ / gumena bearna, þæt þone grund wite' (1366b-1367b). And Hrothgar warns Beowulf 'Eard git ne const, / frecne stowe, þær þu findan miht / sinnigne secg' (1377b-1379a). Clearly linguistic features of the description of Grendel's mere are bound up with epistemological features. And underlying the organization of the description is the simple proposition that phenomena begin to elude verbal expression the more they approach the limits of human knowledge. But the striking corollary to such a proposition is that phenomena beyond the limits of human knowledge are beyond *most* forms of verbal expression. (Practically speaking, from the historical perspective of the Danes, Grendel and his mother come from some preternatural realm outside the bounds of human knowledge.) Such phenomena are accessible, however, through an analogical mode of expression. The poet's mode of description in Hrothgar's speech corresponds to a form of analogical language which Northrop Frye, in *The Great Code,* calls the metonymic mode. Although the term 'metonymic' carries several meanings, Frye primarily uses it to denote a form of language in which 'the verbal expression is "put for" something that by definition transcends adequate verbal expression'. In Hrothgar's speech, aspects of the landscape are 'put for' the collective and psychological response of the Danes to Grendel. It is not surprising that Hrothgar's ironic understatement 'nis þæt heoru stow' (1372b) is cast as a negative construction. Because of the preternatural character of the place he is describing, it is much easier for him to say what it is not than what it is.

The poet offers several very specific clues in the text to indicate that he is working within the sphere of analogy and that he is describing no ordinary landscape but rather the landscape of the soul. Of some interest is his use of the verb *reotan* in the clause 'roderas reotaþ' (1376a). The verb *reotan*, 'to weep', would seem more appropriate to a human agent, but here, as it is used to describe the action of the skies over Grendel's mere, it suggests an analogical mode of thought: it intimates that features of the landscape bear an analogical relationship to things human. The diffuse light at the mere contributes to the analogue of the melancholy mood by creating a dark and shadowy atmosphere. While the skies pour rain down on the mere, the air becomes gloomy ('lyft drysmaþ'—1375b). Like the 'weeping' of the personified skies, the narrative event of the air becoming gloomy has emotional overtones, introducing a melancholy, despairing quality, even as it suggests, from a visual perspective, the darkening of the landscape. Earlier, Hrothgar has told Beowulf that trees overshadow the mere ('wæter oferhelmaþ'—1364b). This imagery of shadows and darkness associated with the mere has a subtle affinity with a corresponding human darkness, perhaps even a terrifying and unexplored darkness within the soul. We can read the progress of the 'fyrgenstream' (1359b) under the 'næssa genipu' (1360a) in this context of analogy as a symbolic entry into the dark interior of the souls of men.

The most substantial indication the poet offers of this analogical mode—an indication so obvious as to be perhaps overlooked—is that Grendel and his mother, the two 'ellorgæstas' (1349a), are cast in almost-human forms. According to what Hrothgar has been told, Grendal's mother 'wæs . . . idese onlicnes' (1349b-1351a). And Grendel himself 'on weres wæstmum wræclastas træd, / næfne he wæs mara þonne ænig man oþer' (1352a-1353b). While there are very few explicit similes in *Beowulf,* the poet is quite sensitive to the nuances of analogical thought. He likens Grendel to a man 'næfne he wæs mara' (1353a) not simply as a device to aid his reader to visualize the monster (although the comparison does serve that function) but as part of his sophisticated program to intimate that while the monster may move through the exterior landscape, it also inhabits the human—the psychological—landscape. Grendel and his mother represent a horrific and primitive force, something far below the level of the conscious mind; yet the effect of the poet's description is to identify the monsters intimately with men.

Earlier the poet offered a somewhat sympathetic description of Grendel's mother after the death of her son. Highly understandable in human terms, her motive for attack on Heorot is maternal vengeance: 'Ond his modor þa gyt/ gifre ond galgmod gegan wolde / sorhfulne siþ, sunu deoþ wrecan' (1276b-1278b). But what is particularly striking about this portrait of Grendel's mother is that it seems like a demonic parody of maternal love, coming as it does less than one hundred lines after Wealhtheow publicly presents Beowulf with the Brosings' necklace and asks him to act as a protector to her sons, Hrethric and Hrothmund: 'ond þyssum cnyhtum wes / lara liþe! Ic þe þæs lean geman' (1219b-1220b). And some one hundred lines previous to Wealhtheow's appeal, Hrothgar's scop tells of the conflict with the Frisians and of how, among other things, the Danish Hildeburh, a symbol of victimized and grieving maternity, loses her son (as well as her brother Hnæf and her husband Finn) in the ensuing battles:

unsynnum wearþ
beloren leofum æt þam lindplegan
bearnum ond broþrum; hie on gebyrd hruron
gare wunde; þæt wæs geomuru ides!
(1072b-1075b)

This close succession of maternal figures either solicitous for or grieving for their sons, first Hildeburh (1071a-1080a; 1114a-1118b), then Wealhtheow (1180b-1191b; 1219b-1220b; 1226b-1227b) and finally Grendel's mother (1276b-1278b), serves to draw attention to the suggestive affinities between the mothers of warriors and the mothers of monsters.

This association of the human and the demonic is nowhere more succinctly captured than in Hrothgar's final challenge to Beowulf: 'sec gif þu dyrre!' (1379b) says Hrothgar of the dangerous place where Beowulf may find the 'sinnigne secg' (1379a). Although Old English poetry is renowned for its litotes, the *Beowulf* poet does have a more than adequate vocabulary at his disposal with which to describe Grendel's mother as a monster, demon, or some such other fitting adversary for Beowulf, for example, 'aglæca' (wretch, monster, demon, or fiend), 'laþ' (hostile or hateful one), 'manscaþa' (wicked ravager or evildoer), 'bana' (slayer or murderer), and 'feond' (enemy or fiend) to name only a few. It might then appear as something of a disappointment that he has designated her with the neutral and rather common 'secg'. Certainly we have come to expect a more colourful language at such dramatically crucial moments. Yet if we are sensitive to the nuances which the poet is manipulating in Hrothgar's speech, we will find that he has made a particularly apposite choice of words. The noun 'secg' in most contexts means 'man'. But as it refers in this instance to the monster, it economically captures the weird and intimate affinity of the human and the demonic in the single image of the 'sinnigne secg' (1379a). Such an otherwise slight noun is freighted with sinister connotations by virtue of its local context; it adds an even more disturbing and ominous subtext to Hrothgar's challenge to 'sec gif þu dyrre' (1379b), hinting at the possibility—a possibility of which Hrothgar himself may be unaware—that the fiend which Beowulf must face is as much within as it is without.

Linda Georgianna   (essay date 1987)

SOURCE: "King Hrethel's Sorrow and the Limits of Heroic Action in *Beowulf,*" in *Speculum,* Vol. 62, No. 4, October, 1987, pp. 829-50.

[*In the excerpt that follows, Georgianna studies the lengthy, meditative speech that Beowulf gives just before his fateful battle with the dragon in the second half of the poem.*]

Just prior to his last fight, Beowulf delivers a long speech on the headlands above the dragon's cave (ll. 2425-37). [*All references are to line numbers as given in the edition* of Frederick Klaeber, *Beowulf and the Fight at Finns-burg,* 3rd ed. with 1st and 2nd suppls. (Boston, 1950).] It is, with the exception of his report to Hygelac on returning from Heorot, Beowulf's longest and perhaps his most puzzling speech. Little has been written about the speech as a whole; in fact, rather little attention has been paid to any of Beowulf's speeches, which is perhaps not surprising given Beowulf's stated preference for deeds over words. "It is better for a man to avenge his friend than to mourn much," Beowulf tells Hrothgar, and indeed in a heroic narrative we might ordinarily expect actions to take precedence over words. So it dismays those who would judge the poem primarily as a heroic narrative to find, as Klaeber did, that despite the hero's initial appearance as "an aggressive war hero of the Achilles or Sigfrit type," Beowulf is in fact "somewhat tame, sentimental, and fond of talking," and nowhere more so than in this speech.

When viewed primarily in terms of whether or not it "advances the action," Beowulf's speech before the dragon fight must seem inept. Not only does the rambling monologue itself delay the fight, but the central story told in the speech concerns the sorrow and death of a hero and king for whom heroic action is delayed endlessly. Deferral or delay, evident throughout the poem in its style and structure, emerges here to become a subject of the narrative, suggesting that the poet's interests may not lie solely in fostering what Klaeber calls "true epic movement." On the contrary, in the speech under discussion as well as in the second part of the poem generally, the poet seems intent on disengaging his audience from the forward movement of the heroic story in order to suggest the limits of heroic action and perhaps of heroic narratives as well.

In the Danish episodes, at least, action predominates. Beowulf's words in Heorot seem for the most part mere extensions of his deeds. His boasts, while polite, are also fairly direct and squarely focused on the deeds of courage he is about to perform. References to history or to circumstances are subordinated to the promise of action. The poem's opening lines, "We have heard about the glory of the Spear-Danes in the old days . . . , how those princes did brave deeds," herald in a major key the theme of old heroic deeds and the fame such actions have brought.

But in what is usually regarded as the poem's second half or movement (ll. 2200-3182), the focus shifts. Edward Irving remarks [in *A Reading of Beowulf,* 1968] that in **Beowulf** "history is made in Part I, while it is studied in Part II." In the Heorot episodes deeds are done. Memories seem fresh, manageable, and close at hand, and although we sometimes see further than the characters—the poet's remarks on the devil worship of the Danes are a notorious example—for the most part such moments seem exceptional intrusions upon an otherwise unmediated view of Beowulf's glorious deeds. But in the poem's second half, deeds are talked about and meditated upon, described over and over from different angles of vision and at different paces. The revisionary impulse seems at

work here, creating a complicated context for the text of Beowulf's deeds by emphasizing causes, connections, and circumstances. In fact, so involved does the poem become in what could be called deep background that the central *act* of part two—Beowulf's fight with the dragon—is at times all but lost sight of.

In the first part of the poem one can hardly miss the fight with Grendel, which is prepared for with what has been described as fine cinematic skill. In most cases everything but the poetic present is clearly labeled a digression, often in the form of a scop's song concerning some self-contained and chronologically remote episode. But in part two, it is the present itself that seems the digression. Beowulf's fight with the dragon at times seems a thin, brief, somewhat dreamlike moment all but overwhelmed by the involved, repetitive accounts of past action and forecasts of the future: how the treasure came to be here, how the dragon came to be here, how Beowulf came to be here, and what will become of them all and the Geatish people with them. The heroic moment, the present, so significant at the poem's beginning, is in the second part almost bled of significance and reality as meaning shifts to the past and future.

Nowhere are these distinctions between the two parts of the poem more apparent than in the poet's preparation for Beowulf's last fight. Nearly two hundred lines separate Beowulf's ordering his shield from his using it, lines dense with historical material spanning the history of the Geatish people. More than half of these lines make up Beowulf's speech, delivered as he sits on the headlands above the dragon's cave. The hero's "gilp-cwide" of part one (ll. 407-56), delivered to Hrothgar as a tactful but confident piece of self-advertisement, is replaced here by a retrospective, highly digressive, meditative speech, less a preamble to action than an amble through various related and unrelated memories of childhood, both joyful and sorrowful, memories of the brave deeds of kinsmen and finally of his own glories as a hero. Out of this odd blend of elegiac stasis and heroic affirmation Beowulf shapes his resolve to fight the dragon. But the speech has a different effect on the audience, I would argue, distancing us from Beowulf's coming battle and from his heroic world, undermining the value and effectiveness of heroic action at precisely the moment when the hero is most relying on it.

The speech consists of a series of dissociated memories juxtaposed without comment: early childhood memories of Beowulf's happy youth in the hall of his grandfather, King Hrethel; the story of Herebeald's accidental death at the hands of his brother Haethcyn; the even more digressive simile comparing Hrethel's sorrow to that of the father of an executed felon; and finally a brief recalling of the Swedish-Geatish feud that follows upon Hrethel's death. Beowulf ends his reverie by reaffirming his loyalty to Hygelac, proved by his hand-to-hand combat with Daeghrefn, presumably Hygelac's slayer. The poet breaks the speech briefly here, then resumes with Beowulf's boast, which closely follows the phrasing of his earlier boasts, a promise to attempt to perform a "great deed" (*mærþu fremman,* l. 2514) and win fame and treasure.

The speech, which situates Beowulf for the first time in a personal as well as dynastic and national history, is treated by most critics as evidence of Beowulf's age and new depth of character. It certainly represents a side of the hero we have not seen before. For a character so often associated with the action of the moment, this speech represents a real turn in showing Beowulf reflecting in an almost leisurely way on Hrethel's sorrow and unheroic death. Beowulf's meditative mood is especially surprising in that he is virtually at the dragon's door. The hero has pondered his possible guilt, ordered his shield, assembled his men, and hastened to the cave; the time for reflection seems long since passed. John Pope explains the speech as the poet's way of representing the hero's old age realistically in terms of Beowulf's experience and frame of mind without having to portray him as subject to the "ordinary infirmities of age." In Pope's careful reading the speech serves the double purpose of preparing at the same time for Beowulf's death and for his battle: the stories of Hrethel and the mourning father serve the first purpose, while the stories of more recent Geatish feuds and Beowulf's own triumph serve the second. Edward Irving further develops the relationship between these two purposes in terms of character, arguing that for Beowulf the case of King Hrethel serves as a negative example of his own current situation. Thus "the will to act is defined by its opposite, the world without action," a reading which might help to explain Klaeber's enigmatic note, "The king's morbid surrender to his grief is significant." Although King Hrethel could find no remedy for his sorrow, Irving argues, Beowulf is still free to act and gain revenge from the dragon just as his kin did in the Swedish-Geatish feud. His meditation on King Hrethel and the nameless father causes him to hesitate but ultimately feeds his resolve to act, thus increasing his stature in our eyes. The poet, according to Irving, presents a new standard of heroism, involving sympathy and understanding in addition to "the capacity to act in total dedication." Eamon Carrigan, somewhat less sympathetic to the hero than Irving, at least sees Beowulf's turn from elegy to heroic affirmation as logical: Beowulf "now sees the acceptance of feuding as an escape from the elegiac hopelessness" of Hrethel's death. Rejecting despair, he quickly recalls those kin who could and did gain vengeance and fame, Haethcyn for the attack by the Swedes, Hygelac for the death of Haethcyn, and Beowulf himself for the death of Hygelac. Such memories propel him toward his final boast announcing his intention of performing a deed of fame.

Such interpretations, which emphasize the psychological coherence of the speech and its function as a preamble to the poem's final action, are useful and are preferable to the critical tendency to treat apparent inconsistencies or shifts in point of view in this poem as evidence, in and of themselves, of interpolation, loss of lines in the manuscript, or a happy disregard for coherence. Yet there is also a danger in underplaying inconsistencies and gaps in this poem, especially when it is done in the name of

"realistic" character development. In reading the speech as an indication of Beowulf's maturity, readers have to work hard to smooth out inconsistencies, supply needed transitions and logic, and in general remold the speech into a more modern "dramatic monologue" than perhaps it is. For Beowulf is not Prince Hamlet, nor was he meant to be. His transitions connecting joyful childhood memories to the tragedy of Herebeald's death, the mourning of the nameless father, King Hrethel's death, and the Swedish-Geatish feud are by no means smooth, but rather abrupt, confusing, and disorienting. They tell us more about the poet's methods and habits of mind than Beowulf's growing sensitivity to sorrow. The emphasis on delay, introspection, and indirection describes the Beowulf poet more aptly than Beowulf the character; indeed certain parts of the speech, such as the reference to Hrethel's having "chosen God's light," are distinctly out of character, and thus all the more disconcerting to an audience. A better explanation for the structure and subject of the speech lies not in Beowulf's character but rather in the poet's method, particularly in the poem's second half, of disorienting his audience by suddenly shifting the terms of his story. The effect, rather than encouraging a closer sympathy with Beowulf in his old age, is to force the audience to distance itself from the hero and the action of the narrative present. In short, the poet engages in what might nowadays be called a revolt against the narrativity of the poem's first half. He frustrates our desire for narrative progress and logic even as he frustrates his hero's need for clarity of vision and purpose in this speech, which is itself an interruption of the narrative and, in addition, has as its subject a hero's inability to act as a heroic narrative would require. This is not a new idea. What now might be called antinarrativity was described years ago in a famous section of Klaeber's commentary titled "Lack of Steady Advance." What is new is the modern or postmodern taste for subversive elements in narratives. For Klaeber, they were simply "trying."

The story of Herebeald's death and Hrethel's sorrow forms the imaginative center of the speech. As the earliest episode in Geatish history related in the poem, it is roughly equivalent to the Scyld Scefing story in Danish history, the story with which the poem begins. Yet, unlike the story of Scyld, with its ceremonial, epic grandeur, the story of Herebeald's death seems in its very ordinariness out of place in a heroic tale. In addition the story is introduced not as an archetypal moment from the distant past that somehow captures the essence of a nation's history, but rather as an almost random piece of personal history, unexpectedly recalled. Finally the story is disorienting because it is so abruptly introduced (at l. 2435) after Beowulf's "joys of the hall" reverie, which appears to introduce the speech but contradicts its tone. The speech begins:

> In my youth I survived many battle storms,
> times of war. I remember all that.
> I was seven winters old when the lord of treasure,
> friend of the people, took me from my father.
> King Hrethel received and kept me,
> remembered our kinship, gave me treasure and feast.

As a man in his stronghold, I was to him in life
no more hated than his own sons,
Herebeald, Haethcyn, and my dear Hygelac.
For the eldest, undeserved
a murder bed was spread by a kinsman's deed,
when Haethcyn, with an arrow from his horn-bow,
struck down his friend and lord,
missed the mark, and shot his kinsman;
one brother shot the other with a bloody arrow.
That was a fight without a price, a wrong wickedly
     done,
wearying to the heart and mind. Nevertheless, the
     noble prince
had to lose his life and die unavenged.

                              (ll. 2426-43, emphasis mine)

The center of treasure, feast, and kinship becomes the setting for a "murder bed" spread by a kinsman, a movement both sudden and unexplained. The outlines of the story of Herebeald's death are clear enough, but the details further intensify the confusion surrounding the event. The eldest son of Hrethel and heir apparent is tragically killed by a stray arrow shot by his younger brother Haethcyn. We are given no further circumstances directly, but because arrows were only rarely used in battle, the suggestion is that the accident probably occurred not during a battle, but during a moment of leisure, perhaps at a sporting contest, making the tragedy all the more unexpected. Herebeald, the king's eldest son and presumably a hero, meets his fate not on the battlefield but in an almost careless, arbitrary way. Instead of hitting his target, his brother simply "missed the mark," hitting Herebeald instead. The event itself therefore seems as much a deviation from the stuff of epic as the telling of it is from Beowulf's usual discourse. If, as Klaeber notes, boys were frequently sent to court at a young age for their education, then we might well wonder, given his earliest memories, just what Beowulf learned there.

To confuse matters further, the poet's diction stresses contradictory sides of the event. On the one hand, he emphasizes the inherent pathos of a man who unwittingly kills a kinsman who was both "friend" and at least potentially his "lord." The image of the arrow stained with a brother's blood combines the accidental nature of the death with the tragedy of kin-killing. But on the other hand, the poet treats the death not as an accidental tragedy, but as a wicked crime. Haethcyn makes for his brother what the poet calls a "murder bed," a unique compound found only in this poem and one which stresses the domestic circumstances of the kinsman's deed. The act is called a "crime wickedly done" (*fyrenum gesyngdad*), an unavenged death described in the cold terms of economics and law as "a fight without a price" or recompense (*feohleas gefeoht*). Suddenly and without warning or transition the kinsman's tragic "dæd" becomes a fight, a feud (*fæþo*), and the doer becomes a life-slayer (*feorh-bonan, l. 2465*).

This dual representation has confused many readers. As though to argue with the text, Benjamin Thorpe adds a note to his transcription insisting that accidental homicide was punishable. Some imaginative readers, eager to see this deed avenged, interpret the simile of the mourning father which immediately follows as a reference to Hrethel himself, mourning the hanging of his second son for the murder of his first. David Williams, in keeping with his interest in the Cain motif, treats the event almost exclusively as intentional fratricide, hinting that Haethcyn may have had his brother in mind as his target all along. But in spite of our critical desire for certainty (if not for revenge), the poet simply refuses to let us have it one way or the other, either as tragic mishap or as wicked crime. In part the confusion can be traced to contemporary secular and ecclesiastical law, which treat the deed of homicide itself as crime or sin, regardless of the intent or motive. Old English penitentials, for example, distinguish accidental from intentional homicide but nevertheless treat both as punishable offenses. However, although accidental homicide was theoretically punishable, this particular case represents a further complication, as Dorothy Whitelock established many years ago. Insofar as this event is considered a fight, it does have its price or *wergild,* but because the deed was done by a kinsman, there is no appropriate person of whom to demand the price. King Hrethel, whose duty as the victim's kin is to exact vengeance or compensation from the killer's family, is also the killer's father. Thus there can be no avenging Herebeald's death and no resolving Hrethel's dilemma.

While evidence from Anglo-Saxon culture may help to clarify the backgrounds of Hrethel's dilemma, the poet's diction seems calculated to emphasize not clarity but the confusion of the events. That is, it is precisely the unresolved nature of Herebeald's death in the mind of Hrethel that holds the poet's attention in this passage. In addition to grieving for the loss of his son, he seems to grieve for the loss of a whole system of values that had seemed coherent, a system centered on kin loyalty and the satisfaction gained by vengeance. In a sense, Hrethel dies of ambivalence:

              So the Weder-King
carried in his heart surging sorrow
for Herebeald; in no way could he
settle the feud with the life-slayer,
nor the sooner could he hate the warrior [Haethcyn],
or do hateful deeds against him, though he was not
     dear to him.

                              (ll. 2462-67)

To be unable to act, as Achilles tells Odysseus in the underworld, is a hero's idea of hell, which we recall also in Bryhtnoth's frustration before the battle of Maldon. But worse is not to know how to act. Bryhtnoth knows what he must do; the tide merely keeps him temporarily from meeting his enemy on the battlefield. But all the time in the world will not help Hrethel, whose resolve to act is itself caught between love and hate, between the opposing duties of hero, king, and father. Able only to brood over a predicament whose solution eludes categories he formerly recognized as separate and stable, Hrethel chooses despair and death.

The simile of the nameless mourning father expands both the causes and effects of a grief like Hrethel's, again focusing on the death of a son, this time not an accidental or unexpected death but the sanctioned execution of a felon. Like Hrethel, this father is helpless "when his son hangs, a joy to the raven, and he, although very old and wise, cannot perform any help for him." The stress on performing or accomplishing (*gefremman*) again reinforces the loss of purpose. Further intensifying the mourning father's bitterness is that he, unlike Hrethel, has no more sons. To outlive one's children is to outlive one's own future, to *un*redeem time. Perhaps that is why the father's "song" quickly becomes a highly generalized *ubi sunt* lament:

> Full of sorrow, he looks on his son's dwelling,
> deserted wine-hall, wind-swept resting place,
> bereft of joy. The rider sleeps,
> warrior in the grave. There is no sound of the harp,
> no pleasures in the courtyard, as there were before.
> (ll. 2455-59)

Surely this passage describes not only the loss of an individual but of a whole way of life, summed up in the lost joys of the hall; it is reminiscent of the so-called lay of the last survivor in *Beowulf* (ll. 2247-66) and of the great brief elegies as well. If this mourner is not the last of his race, he might as well be. Cut off from his future as well as his past, set adrift from society itself (because society condemned his son to an unavengeable death), the father, like the last survivor, sings a lament, this one both for and by a solitary: "an æfter anum" (l. 2461), literally, "one for another," or perhaps, "one here for one gone." For this father, as for King Hrethel, all connections between one and another have broken down, depriving the world of its definition and shape. The last we hear of the nameless father is that "þuht him eall to rum, / wongas ond wicstede" (ll. 2461-62), "all seemed to him too roomy (or open), the land and the house." The poet makes the highly suggestive phrase "eall to rum" the point of contact between the nameless father and King Hrethel, to whose case he now returns. In part, the image of roominess is an amplification of "windy resting place" of a few lines above and refers to the emptiness and perhaps the imagined disrepair of the empty hall. The hall's inside now seems indistinguishable from the outside, and the father retreats to his bed (l. 2460), a smaller enclosure, perhaps to find the protection and comfort formerly afforded by the hall as a whole. But in this highly generalized version of the idea—*all* seemed too roomy—we are reminded that for a father who is no longer a father, contemplating a hall which is no longer a hall, the world as a whole has lost its definition and its limits. Early in the poem, the construction of a hall was given almost mythic status; the building and naming of Heorot seemed to represent Hrothgar's success in asserting order and control over the dangerous chaos of the dark world outside. Now we witness the opposite process, as we are invited to imagine the disintegration of the hall and the protection it once afforded.

The suddenness of the transition from the final thoughts of the nameless father back to Hrethel's condition supports such a generalized reading of these lines. For Hrethel's hall is not, in fact, empty. On the contrary, it still awaits its moment of glory and great prosperity in the reigns of Hygelac and Beowulf, a glory already evoked for the audience in the poet's description of the splendor of Hygelac's reception of Beowulf on his victorious return from Heorot (ll. 1888-2000, 2152-99). But for Hrethel, as for the mourning father of the simile, confusion, paralysis, and chaos have replaced duty and definition. Both men are insiders who suddenly see themselves as outsiders, sufferers of a form of internalized exile. The world seems to them too roomy in part because they feel they have no place to go. Time as well as space has been permanently altered for these two fathers. As Edward Irving remarks, "In the world of no action, present time can blur with future or past; time no longer matters because it is wholly unredeemable."

In suspending narrative time while he has Beowulf tell these stories of the past, the poet reproduces in the audience feelings similar to those experienced by Hrethel and the nameless mourning father. Not only have we been diverted from Beowulf's upcoming battle with the dragon, which seems continually pushed further and further into the future as we regress further into the past, but in addition we have been invited as we follow Hrethel's perspective to dismiss the future of the Geats altogether, a future which includes the entire narrative present of the poem. Hygelac, the figure who looms so large throughout the rest of the poem, is not even named in this passage, but is merely one of the "sons" to whom Hrethel leaves his lands (ll. 2470-71). Furthermore the poet as it were sandwiches the analogy of the mourning father between the two parts of Hrethel's story, producing in the audience some of the same confusion and collapse of distinct categories experienced by Hrethel. The poet's abrupt juxtaposition of Herebeald's unavenged death with the execution of a criminal is inherently confusing and disorienting, as is shown by the bizarre theories put forth by critics to explain the connection. Even Whitelock's sensible explanation of the passage in terms of the similar helplessness of the two fathers to gain revenge or compensation, while important for its cultural insight, does not fully account for the obvious disparity in the two situations. In so suddenly moving from the accidental death of a guiltless royal heir to the shameful execution of a nameless felon, the poet encourages his audience to seek similarities and thus blur distinctions ordinarily regarded in Anglo-Saxon poetry as representing opposing categories. The innocent and the guilty merge, victim and villain are treated as one, and the criminal or outcast operating at the very edges of his society is as much mourned as a noble prince living at the very center of his world. The king's own confusion, described as "wearying to heart and mind" (l. 2442), stems from his identification with both the victim and the villain, and the poet's diction and patterning encourage the audience to share in Hrethel's crisis of identity.

Significant narrative effects result from the poet's choice to include Hrethel's story at this point in the narrative, and to tell it in such a way as to duplicate Hrethel's confusion in the audience. The primary effect of the poet's treatment of Hrethel's sorrow, it seems to me, is to underscore the limits of heroic action, and to distance the audience from the forward movement of the heroic narrative. In destabilizing or confusing the categories of innocence and guilt, victim and villain, insider and outsider, the poet begins to undo the basis of heroic action as it is represented in the poem's first half.

In the Heorot episodes Beowulf's heroic actions depend upon a context of freely chosen battles against enemies clearly identified as outsiders. Faced with evidence of the bloody death of Æschere, Beowulf says exactly what a hero is expected to say when he announces that "it is better to avenge a friend than to mourn much." The heroic "emergency," considered essential to epic protagonists, already exists, awaiting only an appropriate hero to confront the obviously monstrous adversary. It is true that early on in the epic the poet toys with the idea of presenting Grendel as a complex and even sympathetic figure, but Beowulf's arrival in Heorot serves in itself as an act of clarification, shedding light on the shadowy figure of Grendel. All doubt and ambiguity about the mysterious "hall thane" are resolved as Beowulf lies in the dark hall and observes the awful otherness of this monster: he *eats* thanes, "feet and hands" (l. 745).

In the dragon episode of part two, however, the closer Beowulf moves toward performing a heroic feat, the more confusion and ambiguity the poet infuses into the narrative, diverting our attention from the dragon fight and toward a more distant and critical view of the heroic world within which Beowulf so confidently and so splendidly operates. The death of Herebeald, conceived of as a fight without recompense (*feohleas gefeoht*), calls into question the coherence and meaning of the heroic world, which depends substantially on vengeance and fame to lend meaning to death. Herebeald's death is seen as incomprehensible not only in its causes—whether viewed as an accident or as a crime, the randomness of the event is what is stressed—but also in its effects: the king's immobilizing sorrow, the breakdown of his relationship with his next surviving son (an essential tie in this society), and ultimately the king's death followed by the release of violence on Sorrow Hill. The poet further expands the consequences of a single arrow that missed its mark when he juxtaposes Hrethel's sorrow with that of the father who sees in the death of his executed son the disintegration of the joys of the hall and even of the hall itself. In fact, Herebeald's death and Hrethel's hopeless sorrow threaten the coherence of the heroic world in something of the same way that Grendel did earlier when his nightly raids rendered Heorot "useless" (*unnyt*, l. 413), actions as incomprehensible to the Danes as the feeless fight is to Hrethel, and similarly conceived of by the Danes as a "feud" which Grendel refuses to settle with compensation (*fea,* l. 156). But in the case of Hrethel's sorrow, the feud has no traceable (and therefore eradicable) origins, and the enemy, if he is an enemy, is not an alien monster but a member of the family.

I do not mean to suggest that Beowulf himself sees the story in this way. On the contrary, the poet's emphasis on Hrethel's confusion and his narrative technique, which encourages a similar disorientation in the audience, mark a distinct divergence at this point between Beowulf's concerns and our own. Until now, although we sometimes know more than Beowulf knows, our knowledge rarely interferes with his heroic purpose, but rather supports it. The approach of Grendel's mother is a good example: we have already seen the hero respond splendidly to the immediate threat of one monster, and our knowledge of the approach of another, which precedes Beowulf's knowledge, calls up our expectation that the hero will once again rise to the heroic occasion. If anything, our foreknowledge actually anticipates, and in some sense even produces, another victory for Beowulf. But in his treatment of the attack of the dragon, which initially seems to provide a similar heroic emergency, the poet complicates our response to the hero's efforts by continually intruding to provide the audience with knowledge of which the hero is necessarily ignorant.

A prime example occurs just prior to the story of King Hrethel, in the poet's insertion, by way of another confusing digression, of the history of the dragon's treasure, a story told to us but not to Beowulf (ll. 2231-77). The last survivor of a race, we are told, buried his people's treasure, their final legacy, because there was no one left to protect and use it. It would seem that such treasures were not meant to be resurrected or made useful again (the poet's inclusion later of the curse on the treasure [ll. 3051-57] only reiterates the point), and thus Beowulf's attempt to win the treasure seems misdirected or out of joint with its narrative context. Although the poet does not criticize Beowulf himself, who cannot be faulted for his ignorance of the treasure's history, nevertheless our knowledge does interfere with Beowulf's heroic pursuit and with the narrative process itself. Not only does the story of the treasure delay our hearing of Beowulf's fight with the dragon, but also the subject of the last survivor's story, which is the *end* of all heroic stories as the race of heroes dies out, urges reflection and elegy rather than action and narrative progress. As we listen to one hero consign his people's now useless legacy to the earth, it is hard for us to anticipate with any shared pleasure another hero's delight in winning the same treasure.

In the case of Beowulf's speech on the headlands an even more vexed relationship between hero and audience is established. Here it is Beowulf himself who delays the action to tell a nonheroic story of suffering and paralysis which occurs not because of some monstrous invasion calling for heroic action, but as the result of a mishap. Furthermore the story describes Beowulf's legacy more fully than it has ever been described before. At important points in the narrative Beowulf has been identified with artifacts described as "Hredles lafe," Hrethel's heirlooms, literally the remains of Hrethel. It is only now that we learn that in addition to heroic treasures, Hrethel also left a legacy of impotence and sorrow. But the story of Hrethel's sorrow, which revises our vision of heroic history, seems to have only a momentary effect upon the hero who tells it. Those who would argue that the speech is designed to show Beowulf's new depth of character seldom discuss the movement of the speech as a whole. After telling us that Hrethel gave up the joys of men and "chose God's light" (an odd image for a pagan to use, especially one about to choose immortal fame through heroic action instead), Beowulf abruptly turns, with what might be described as relief and certainly a sense of pride, to the kind of story he knows best, the fast-paced, heroic history of the Swedish-Geatish feud which erupts upon King Hrethel's death: "My kinsmen avenged that [a Swedish attack], the feud and the crime, as was well known!" He treats the story in terms of the triumph of heroic action reasserting order after the slaughter of many Geats on Hreosnabeorh, or Sorrow Hill (l. 2477). The place of battle is aptly named, for the story, as Beowulf tells it, suggests that for heroes the most appropriate response to the sorrow and hopelessness of death is heroic action. This half of Beowulf's speech is dominated by the heroic language of strict reciprocity, described in simple economic terms: Haethcyn "bought" revenge but paid with his life, a "hard bargain"; Hygelac had no need to "buy" warriors elsewhere, because Beowulf "repaid" him in battle for the gold he was given. In the place of an incomprehensible "feeless fight," Beowulf posits the language of heroic economy, which emphasizes action and reaction, with payment in kind delivered immediately.

To be sure, this is the sort of story the hero needs to support his resolve to act bravely against great odds. Like many of his critics, Beowulf seeks from his stories a certain clarity and single-minded purpose, which provide the grounds for a conventional epic boast. But for the reader alert to the poet's reflective methods, the context of Beowulf's last battle becomes increasingly complex. As though to emphasize the limitations of the heroic perspective, the poet late in the poem provides a retelling of the story of the Swedish-Geatish feud told earlier by Beowulf in the speech we have been examining. The messenger's long speech following Beowulf's death (ll. 2922-98) supplements and counterpoints in several ways Beowulf's speech on the headlands before the dragon fight. Both are substantial speeches centrally occupied with Geatish history, and with the history of the Swedish-Gaetish feud in particular. The messenger refers repeatedly to "Hrethel's people," a somewhat unusual name for the Geats in this poem, and one which recalls the recently told story of Hrethel's sorrow. But in spite of the ways in which the speech recalls Beowulf's version of heroic history, the differences are more striking. The messenger's version of the feud, seven times as long as Beowulf's, emphasizes not the triumph of one side or the other but the frenzied action, the abrupt reversals of battle, and the brutal violence unleashed by both sides. In particular, the messenger follows the hunting down and killing of the Swedish king Ongentheow. While in Beowulf's version Ongentheow's death is briefly described as suitable payment for the death of Haethcyn, in the later, expanded retelling, Ongentheow is portrayed not as an enemy, but as something like Beowulf's double, an "old," "wise" king who dies protecting his "hoard," here defined with pathos as consisting of his wife and children.

At the moment when he is "brought to bay"—the animal image is typical of the poet's treatment of this battle—he is referred to with great sympathy as the "shepherd of his people," hunted down by two Geats whose names mean wolf and boar. If for Hygelac the feat of killing the old king calls for a ceremonious exchange of treasure (including even, as Eofor's prize, Hygelac's daughter in marriage [ll. 2989-98]), to the messenger himself the only reciprocity involved is summed up in his grim description of how the treasure was gathered: "one [live] warrior plundered another [dead] one."

Although many feuds are alluded to in the poem, the Battle at Ravenswood is the only one described in any detail, and the poet waits until almost the end of his poem to focus on this grim representation of feuding. When only briefly alluded to, the vengeance and fame obtained in battle may seem, as they do to Beowulf, the heroic alternative to immobilizing, hopeless sorrow. Indeed that was precisely the case earlier when the brooding Hrothgar "leaped up" (*ahleop*, l. 1398) upon hearing Beowulf choose vengeance over mourning. But as the audience's perspective widens in the poem's second half, and particularly with this close-up view of the very feud Beowulf described not long before in such positive heroic terms, we see as the hero cannot that the differences between fighting and despairing are more apparent than real. For all of the action involved in the Battle of Ravenswood, the hopelessness of the heroic cycle of battle and vengeance seems just as clear. Heroic battle is not finally represented in the poem as an antidote to Hrethel's sorrow; rather it is in many ways another version of the same thing.

Finally it is the poet's blurring of the distinction between action and paralysis that most seriously unsettles the basis of heroic action. In the stories of Hrethel's sorrow and Ongentheow's death the poet shows us how severely limited heroic action is in overcoming or explaining that which remains for the characters the "wonder" of death. Early on in the poem we were invited to view the devil worship of the Danes as the desperate act of a benighted, unredeemed people:

> Such was their custom,
> the hope of the heathen; they thought of hell
> in their hearts, knew not the Ruler,
> Judge of deeds, nor acknowledged the Lord God,
> nor indeed knew how to praise heaven's Protector,
> King of glory. Woe be to him who,
> when in terrible trouble, must shove his soul
> into the fire's embrace, expect no comfort,
> nor change in any way. Well be it for him who may,
> after his death-day, seek the Lord,
> and in the Father's embraces, wish for peace.
>   (ll. 178-88)

But so early in the epic, this view of heathen hopelessness could easily be dismissed as an intrusion in the narrative process; after all, Beowulf was on his way precisely to offer Hrothgar comfort (*bot*, l. 281; *frof[or]*, l. 628); and change (*edwenden*, l. 280). Beowulf's actions not only restore the Danes to Heorot but also restore the swift pace of the heroic narrative, which depends on an unhesitating, active response to the challenge of life's sudden reversals—its *edwenden*-ness. Only at the poem's end do we sadly come to recognize that for all its grandeur and epic possibility heroic action provides at best only the illusion of hope and change.

This is not to say that the poet asks us to dismiss Beowulf's heroism. On the contrary, even in the passage just cited, which treats the poem's pagan characters with uncharacteristic moral sternness, regret outweighs condemnation as the poet repeatedly stresses what the heathen "did not know" and could not know about an afterlife in "the Father's embraces," rather than the "fire's embraces." Furthermore, if the poet here seems to satisfy even the strictest demands of Alcuin, who dismissed his heroic ancestors as "pagan . . . and damned kings," he also immediately follows this statement with a skillful, vivid narrative of an unequivocal heroic emergency—a good king's hall rendered useless by the monstrous attacks of the worst example of an enemy, one who not only feuds with his neighbors but eats them—and an exemplary hero, whose generosity, courage, and strength provide exactly what seems needed to counter the foe. Even Alcuin would have to admit that in the war against the forces of chaos, Beowulf fights on God's side, if not on God's behalf.

But this is not the only story the poet has to tell, nor his only way of telling a story. And in the accumulation of his stories, as well as in his method of juxtaposing, delaying, and retelling stories—in short, his lack of steady advance—the poet is able to lead his audience first to embrace the efforts of the poem's pre-Christian heroes, then slowly and regretfully to recognize that the hope of the heathens—*hæthenra hyht*—is no hope at all. The brave hero kills the monster, but the monsters keep on coming, and more and more the outsiders come to resemble the kin and folk whom the hero would protect. King Hrethel's confusion and paralysis, instigated by what he views as a mysterious, random act, and resulting in what is imagined as the irrevocable loss of the joys of the hall, serve for us, if not for Beowulf, as an example of a more general confusion and paralysis at the heart of heroic society, the cause of which is ultimately a lack of belief in and hope for meaningful or permanent change. Beowulf knows as well as any Christian that "lif is læne," but Beowulf's choices in the face of life's transitoriness come to seem extremely limited, especially in the light of such stories as that of King Hrethel's sorrow. A man either fights as a hero or flees as a coward, and each fight requires this heroic choice, without regard for what may lie beyond the next fight or even the last fight. The rewards the hero seeks in return for fighting—fame, vengeance, and treasure—come to seem equally limited and shortsighted. Beowulf deserves and gains all of these rewards before he dies, but the Christian poet cannot help asking his audience to consider, even if only from time to time, what such gains are ultimately worth. Ultimate values, causes, and effects are not invoked often in the poem, which commemorates more often than it moraliz-

es the past, but when they are invoked, the result is to unsettle the narrative profoundly, to disorient the audience enough to disengage it from the lure of heroic narrative. In short, lack of steady advance, rather than being a defect of the poem, is the point. By the end the poem is not so much a heroic narrative as it is *about* heroic narratives, in which, the poet suggests, advances and retreats are equally illusory.

The story of King Hrethel's sorrow, like that of the last survivor and the Battle of Ravenswood, is part of this process of gradually revealing the limits of all heroic action, even that of a hero as courageous and strong as Beowulf. This story, unlike the poet's earlier representations of the Danes' devil worship, presents the hopelessness of the heathens primarily in secular terms. A nonheroic story whose telling itself delays the hero's pursuit of revenge and fame, the story is also about the disillusionment visited upon a hero who can no longer make effective choices or gain fitting rewards. Caught between conflicting duties and loyalties, apparently expecting neither "comfort" nor "change," Hrethel can only choose death.

Within the context of the issue of heroic choice the metaphor used by the poet to describe Hrethel's death is particularly unsettling:

> He then, amid that sorrow, too grievous that befell him,
> gave up the joy of men, chose God's light,
> left to his sons, as a happy [or blessed] man does,
> his land and towns, when he went forth from life.
> (ll. 2468-71)

The Christian reference seems quite out of character for a heathen hero and has attracted a good deal of attention. Most editors treat the phrase "godes leoht geceas" as a "Christian euphemism" or "periphrasis" for "he died." In Beowulf's discourse the phrase seems to serve as little more than an inert metaphor, attributable to the poet's habit of characterizing his heroes as generally pious, if not committed to specific church doctrines. But the poet's phrase—his phrasis—cannot be gotten around quite so easily. Similar references elsewhere in Anglo-Saxon poetry are unambiguously Christian, referring to the choice between the transitory joys of this world and the eternal rewards of a life of Christian renunciation. Hrethel has certainly experienced the transitoriness of his earthly joy, his "gum-dreamas," and in his choice of phrase the poet may express his own hope that the fact that Hrethel "gave up" worldly joy comes close enough to a rejection of earthly rewards and pleasure to win him God's favor. But at the same time, in the context of this resolutely secular speech, the phrase has other, contrary effects. Here Beowulf, who still thinks of himself as free to choose heroic action in the pursuit of fame and treasure, but who is at the same time unaware that he has a "sawle hord" which is about to depart (ll. 2420-22), dwells upon what seem to him the devastating effects of Hrethel's lack of choice. In this context the reference to Hrethel's choosing God's light seems painfully ironic, for it points to the one choice which the poet believes could help Hrethel, were it available to him. But Hrethel cannot choose "God's light." In fact he chooses death precisely because as a pagan hero he cannot hope to transcend the need for earthly joy. If the poet's choice of phrase suggests that he holds out some slight hope for Hrethel (as he does later for Beowulf), the same phrase also reminds us that Hrethel imagines none for himself. Thus the Christian reference serves to express both respect and deep regret for Hrethel's dilemma, by reminding a Christian audience of the gulf separating even noble pagans from Christians. Looked at across this gulf, Hrethel's immobilizing sorrow and Beowulf's heroic choice do not seem altogether different.

Richard J. Schrader   (essay date 1991)

SOURCE: "Succession and Glory in *Beowulf*," in *Journal of English and Germanic Philology,* Vol. 90, No. 4, October, 1991, pp. 491-504.

[*In the following excerpt, Schrader traces Beowulf's involvement in the lines of succession for both Danish and Geatish kingship, and illustrates how earthly glory and valor serve as important but fragile marks of distinction for these pagan rulers.*]

At the opening of **Beowulf** the poet celebrates the glory (*þrym*) and valor (*ellen*) of the ancient Danish kings (*þeodcyninga, æþelingas*). [All **Beowulf** quotations are from *Beowulf and the Fight at Finnsburg*, ed. Fr. Klaeber, 3d ed. (Lexington, Mass.: Heath, 1950).] For more than sixty lines he traces these qualities from their apparent beginning with Scyld Scefing to their culmination in Hrothgar, a great-grandson. This is the full Scylding line to that point, but the poem makes clear that there were earlier rulers of the Danes, presumably living before Sceaf, men such as Heremod and Hnæf. They are not mentioned until other themes require them; here the poet has established a *translatio gloriae* in which they have no part. The nature of the glory and the means of its transmission will have important consequences in Danish history (as presented in the poem), and similar ideas attached to succession appear in the Geatish section as well.

The celebration of glory has such emphasis because human praise is the highest goal of the pagan characters, providing justification for individuals and a collective heaven for nations in a world where nearly all the apparent motion leads to dead ends. The poet may well have absorbed these lessons from the *City of God*, where Augustine contrasts earthly and heavenly (true) glory and speaks of pagans even more high-minded about the other things of this world than the Scandinavians of **Beowulf:**

> Wherefore, when the kingdoms of the East had been illustrious for a long time, it pleased God that there should also arise a Western empire, which, though later in time, should be more illustrious in extent and greatness. And, in order that it might overcome the grievous evils which existed among other nations, He purposely granted it to such men as, for the sake of honour, and praise, and glory, consulted well for their country, in whose glory they sought their own, and whose safety they did not hesitate to prefer to their own, suppressing the desire of wealth and many other vices for this one vice, namely, the love of praise. . . . But since those Romans were in an earthly city, and had before them, as the end of all the offices undertaken in its behalf, its safety, and a kingdom, not in heaven, but in earth—not in the sphere of eternal life, but in the sphere of demise and succession, where the dead are succeeded by the dying [sed in decessione morientium et successione moriturorum]— what else but glory should they love, by which they wished even after death to live in the mouths of their admirers? . . . For as to those who seem to do some good that they may receive glory from men, the Lord also says, "Verily I say unto you, they have received their reward"

[Matt. 6:2].

I

After a destitute youth Scyld was a terrorizer of his neighbors. His glory (*weorðmyndum*, l. 8) was such that they were compelled to obey him (*hyran scolde*, l. 10) and pay tribute; that, emphatically, was a good king (l. 11). At death, he goes to the same Lord (*frea*, l. 27) that gave worldly glory to his son and successor, Beowulf Scylding (l. 16). It is a self-ordered funeral, like that which closes the poem, and he carries with him considerable treasure. As if in ironic compensation for the way he arrived (taking ll. 43-46 as litotes), all the pieces that are specified are war gear. Under a viking banner (*segen*, l. 47) he goes they know not where.

The interjected description of his son Beowulf adds that the people had suffered long from lordlessness before Scyld arrived, establishing a clear break with whatever had come before. God sent the young man to prevent a recurrence and gave him glory, which spread widely (*woruldare*, l. 17; *blæd*, l. 18). After summarizing the qualities of the good, if warlike, king, the poet has portrayed the worthy successor, a young man who uses his time as heir apparent to prepare for kingship (ll. 20-25). With his father out of the way—and the poet takes pains to underscore Scyld's passing (ll. 55-56)—the portrait resumes, but with few additional details except that this Beowulf was beloved (l. 54).

Even fewer lines are devoted to Healfdene, the next to rule the glorious (*glæde*, l. 58) Scyldings, and *his* children are merely listed. It is tempting to follow Klaeber's reconstruction (p. xxxvi) based on Scandinavian sources and assume that we are to understand that Healfdene was killed by Ingeld's father, Froda, chief of the Heathobards, but the poem is silent on the matter. We learn later that his son Heorogar succeeded him, then Hrothgar. Neither they nor Halga are seen as his avengers.

The field of view has progressively narrowed until the focus is exclusively on Hrothgar. Now it will open to describe his contributions prior to the coming of Grendel. To this point we have been given an outline of Danish history down to the poem's present. Outside this *Stammbaum*, which is an introduction that sets the standards by which to judge Hrothgar, there is also in the poem a fragmentary prehistory which is not so glorious. The poet looks in two directions by having Hrothgar's scop celebrate Beowulf's triumph over Grendel with a mention of Sigemund's carrying off a dragon's treasure in a boat (ll. 895-97); though presumably not considered a Dane, he was known for his *ellen*-deeds (l. 900). Beowulf leaves Denmark with a boatload of treasure, and all of the dragon's hoard is buried with him when he leaves Geatland. The glory and valor shown in his climactic fight have ambiguous results, and the reburial of the treasure signifies the end of his tribe's glory, unlike Scyld's passing from the Danes.

The poet contrasts Sigemund with the notorious Heremod, whose *ellen* subsided (ll. 901-2) and who did not live up to his ancestral rank (*fæderæþelum*, l. 911). The poet's language makes it clear that he was a Danish king and predecessor if not father of Scyld. He was ignored at the opening because the *translatio* begins when the Danish Beowulf succeeds the eponym, Scyld. Later on, Hrothgar himself elaborates on Heremod's offenses. He says that his Geatish rescuer will be a comfort (*to frofre*, l. 1707) to his people as Heremod was not to the Danes—and we recall the same phrase used of the former Beowulf (l. 14). Heremod was part of a disordered past outside the continuum of glory. Here the Danes are called Ecgwela's retainers for the only time, and in the next half-line Honor-Scyldings (l. 1710). I think that the balancing of the two is deliberate: Ecgwela is an unknown king, a "mythical" figure even to Hrothgar and part of a tradition before Scyld, as Scyld (only once) is son of the absent Sceaf (l. 4). Heremod was forced into exile and killed (l. 1714), creating a lordless situation of the kind it was the function of Scyld to alleviate. ([Adrien] Bonjour goes so far as to claim that Heremod's death was followed by the very interregnum that Scyld ended.) And when in power he would not reward the Danes for glory (*dome*, l. 1720).

To this same "mythical" time we should presumably assign Hnæf, slain at Finnsburg, and his father Hoc. Hnæf was a Danish chief sung about by Hrothgar's scop not long after the Sigemund-Heremod vignettes. Hnæf's people are called Half-Danes, Danes, and Scyldings, but their relation to the Danish royal house as it is presented in the poem is obscure. For the scop it is a story that shows the vengeful Danes in a good light, but it is not told in his voice. It has been paraphrased and structured in such a way as to make prominent the sorrows of Hildeburh, Hnæf's sister, rather than to celebrate the revenge ethic. In fact it is another tragedy of lordlessness (cf. l. 1103). It says of those on the pyre that their glory (*blæd*, l. 1124) was gone.

So the true line begins with Scyld. Fittingly, the first words about his great-grandson Hrothgar are that he was given success in war, glory (*weorðmynd*, l. 65) in battle,

but this good king's retainers *eagerly* obeyed (*georne hyrdon*, l. 66). The warlike Scylding kings have sufficiently pacified the realm that a great meadhall can be built. None was mentioned for the Danes before this, and Scyld was instead known for destroying those of others (l. 5). That the glory of Hrothgar, at least, soon will end is made clear at once. Heorot will burn, probably during a feud with his son-in-law in a failed attempt to use marriage to keep peace. And before that he must deal immediately with Grendel (l. 86). He says at one point that prior to this invasion he was always able to protect his people (ll. 1769-76), maintaining the tradition started by Scyld.

For now his court is ideally ordered, reflecting the stability of the dynasty. To enter that court and be accepted by it, Beowulf must undergo a succession of challenges by persons of increasing importance. He is passed from one to another in an initiation that culminates in formal adoption, and so he enters Scylding history as if a Dane in the great tradition. First he encounters the coastguard, where the issue is whether these alien seafarers (ll. 254-55) are wanderers arriving in the style of Moses-like Scyld or march-haunting Grendel (l. 103). The coastguard wants to know their lineage, and Beowulf reveals the names of his uncle and father (ll. 252, 260-63). When satisfied, this servant (*ombeht*, l. 287) guides them (l. 292) to Heorot.

There they must deal with another *ombiht* (l. 336), the herald Wulfgar. He too wants to know about their noble lineage (*æþelum*, l. 332), but feels that they come not as exiles but out of heart's greatness / glory (*higeþrymmum*, l. 339). With that, Beowulf finally discloses his name (l. 343). Hrothgar adds to the Geat's family tree when he supplies Beowulf's grandfather, telling Wulfgar that he indeed knows the recent history of that family (ll. 372-75) and bidding him to inform Beowulf that he knows his *æþelu* (l. 392). Wulfgar guides them in (l. 402).

Later on, after the formal introduction to Hrothgar, Unferth makes his problematical challenge. Among other things, he is disturbed that Beowulf's glory (*mærða*, l. 504) is greater than his, and among Beowulf's rejoinders is the charge that Unferth slew his own brothers (ll. 587-88), which the poet later confirms (ll. 1167-68). Even if this test is a formal flyting, it forces one to consider whether the Scylding heritage is sufficient to handle a military problem that involves not the destruction of a meadhall but the spiritual pollution of it. Beowulf's particular glory, soon to be engrafted onto that of the Danes, is that he alone can cleanse Heorot.

Finally, he meets Wealhtheow, who should be associated with these challengers. She makes no demands at this point, but her mead-dispensing precipitates Beowulf's vow (ll. 611-41). Her relevance to the process under discussion becomes clearer after the slaying of Grendel and the adoption of Beowulf, when Beowulf moves back through the same series of persons (or their equivalents) and out of Danish history. On this occasion she finds Hrothgar sitting with and trusting the suspicious Hrothulf and

Unferth. Her function here is to make Beowulf aware that his adoption is not to be at the expense of the Danish royal line, which will in time have enough troubles from within. She properly addresses her husband first, enjoining him to leave the kingdom to their sons (ll. 1178-80), even though that kind of succession is not inevitable in the world of the poem. Somewhat fitfully she trusts that Hrothulf would be a good regent (ll. 1180-83) and asks Beowulf to be kind in instruction, gentle in deeds to her boys (ll. 1219-20, 1226-27), that is, to take no more upon himself than what she expects of Hrothulf, citing the loyalty of the court about him as an (ironic?) example of what she means (ll. 1228-31). Later, Beowulf promises Hrothgar that he will protect his son (ll. 1836-39), and events prove that he had no designs on the throne.

Unferth (mentioned twice in passing after his challenge) reenters the action as a supporter of Beowulf in the encounter with Grendel's mother. He lends him a sword that had done *ellenweorc* (l. 1464), though he himself lost glory (*dome*, l. 1470) by not daring the venture himself. In that, he represents all the Scyldings, and the same might be said of the sword. It fails to help Beowulf, though he expected to work glory with it; for the first time its glory ceased (*dom*, ll. 1491, 1527-28). Beowulf returns it, with thanks (ll. 1807-12). He had already exchanged for it what may be the sword Hrothgar gave him for killing Grendel (ll. 1023, 1488-90).

Beowulf does not reencounter Wulfgar, the *ombiht*, herald, and guide who came before Unferth in the prior (reverse) sequence. The only other *ombiht* is a Geatish attendant to whom Beowulf entrusted his sword before the fight with Grendel (l. 673). But another Danish hall-thane does appear on the night before Beowulf's departure (l. 1794). He guides him (l. 1795) not to another encounter but to bed.

So too the final meeting with the coastguard is entirely amiable. Beowulf gives him (or another attendant) a gold-wound sword (ll. 1900-1901). Perhaps, in challenging the fifteen Geats alone, the coastguard had shown more of the old glory than any other Dane Beowulf met. Like Scyld, the hero departs in a boat laden with treasure (ll. 1896-98), but he does not leave much hope behind.

The Danes are first made hall-less and then are lordless in their reversion to disorder. The Heathobard feud involving Hrothgar's son-in-law Ingeld will destroy Heorot, in the customary understanding of those early allusions to its burning. Beowulf imagines a scene (ll. 2032-69) like that which he heard Hrothgar's scop portray in the Finnsburg lay, where a man is goaded to take vengeance on the slayers of his lord. Beowulf cannot know the full outcome, but the poet evidently does. And then Hrothulf, by all indications, will take the throne after his uncle Hrothgar dies. They were friends *then* (ll. 1019, 1164), when Beowulf visited. Wealhtheow expects that Hrothulf will be good to her boys *if* he remembers how well she and Hrothgar treated him when a child (ll. 1180-87). Beyond this "admirable subtlety," in Klaeber's words (p. xxxii), the poet does not go. No matter what happened

in "real" history, he implies trouble ahead. If this does not fit facts exterior to the poem, then we should remember that he also makes Sigemund a dragon-slayer and contrives a demise for the Geats: poetic facts are made to serve themes. Further, it is significant that Hrothulf is not assigned the kind of glory he receives as Hrólfr Kraki in Scandinavian lore. The poet does not bother to detail the Danish succession, leaving us to infer that the *translatio* ends with Hrothgar—or Beowulf.

His first words to Hrothgar affirm that he is Hygelac's kinsman (l. 407), but he says less about his ancestry than what he told either the coastguard or Wulfgar. We could be meant to assume that he knows what Wulfgar would report, but it is also a gesture of courtesy, identifying himself with a formulaic phrase as a kind of verbal handshake with a man who knows him already—Hrothgar (in his first words) tells him without qualification why he had come (ll. 457-72). He is not reading the visitor's mind: all signs imply that Ecgtheow, Beowulf, and Hrothgar were well acquainted with each other. Beowulf came to return the favor performed for his father, when Hrothgar paid wergeld to end a feud at the very time he was consolidating his own power after the death of his brother Heorogar (ll. 465-69); the fates of the two families were linked thereafter.

For the first time, Hrothgar voluntarily gives control of the hall to another (l. 655), bidding him to remember glory (*mærþo*) and display mighty valor (*mægenellen*) (l. 659). These are the qualities that will make him worthy of association with the Scylding line laid out for us at the beginning. But Hrothgar already knows that only Beowulf, not any of the Danes, has them in sufficient measure to qualify for the task. Beowulf later says to his men that God will assign the glory (*mærðo*, l. 687) in the battle, and it is given to Beowulf (*guðhreð*, l. 819). The happy Danes speak of his *mærðo* (l. 857). They say that no one is more worthy of a kingdom (l. 861), though they do not find fault with Hrothgar, for "þæt wæs god cyning" (l. 863), and after the second fight Hrothgar will say the same thing about the young man's royal qualifications (ll. 1845-53). Both in their way are worthy Scyldings.

Hrothgar ratifies his honorary lineage by adopting him into a new kinship (*niwe sibbe*) while praising nonetheless, in Biblical terms, the woman who bore him (ll. 942-49). Hill has explored the complexities of the scene, noting that "Hrothgar first spiritually adopts Beowulf and then seems to offer the right of succession," signs of which are the four treasures; "Hrothgar offers something that falls between legal adoption and mere fraternal spirit." That ambiguity—along with Beowulf's never indicating that he wants to take over and his stressing his loyalty to Hygelac upon returning home—is the poet's way of maintaining the *spiritual* nature of the succession. Beowulf acknowledges the *ellenweorc* (l. 958) that brought this about, nicely pointing out that Grendel is *feasceaft* (l. 973). The reader can associate this with the original condition of Scyld (l. 7), the only times the word is used in this part of the poem: "feasceaft funden; he þæs frofre gebad" ([he was] found destitute; for that he received help). Not so for Grendel: "feasceaft guma frofre gebohte" (the destitute man [has not] bought help). Grendel has sunk back into the primordial disorder from which the Scyldings have always escaped thus far. Among the gifts Hrothgar gives Beowulf is a *segen gyldenne,* like the one bestowed on Scyld for his last voyage (ll. 47, 1021).

As he prepares to fight Grendel's mother, Beowulf reminds Hrothgar of the adoption, that is, that he is now fighting as his son (ll. 1474-79). The poet calls him a Scylding warrior—"freca Scyldinga" (l. 1563)—and the sense of that genitive plural is the same as in the appellation of his namesake, "Beowulf Scyldinga" (l. 53). Beowulf pointedly remarks that Hrothgar need no longer fear harm "from *that* side" (l. 1675), that is, *external* threats, once he has defeated Grendel's mother. Hrothgar responds by affirming that Beowulf's glory (*blæd,* l. 1703) has been established, that he will be a help (*to frofre,* l. 1707) to his people, the language used of Beowulf Scylding (ll. 14, 18). His advice includes a warning that Beowulf's present *blæd* of his might (l. 1761) will wane, which is why he should learn from the story of Heremod and from Hrothgar's own failure to protect his people. For now, though, Beowulf is confident enough to promise help to the king if he should be terrorized by his neighbors ("ymbsittend egesan þywað," l. 1827), presumably the neighbors terrorized into submission by Scyld:

> egsode eorl[as] . . .
> oð þæt him æghwylc ymbsittendra
> ofer hronrade hyran scolde.
>
> (ll. 6, 9-10)

That Beowulf takes his filial role seriously is reflected by the first thing he reports to Hygelac about Hrothgar: "he seated me with his own sons" (l. 2013; cf. ll. 1189-91). The first treasure he commands to be brought in is the banner (l. 2152), as it was the first treasure Hrothgar gave him (l. 1021). Another connection with dynastic matters is the armor he likewise turns over (ll. 2155-62). He says that Hrothgar told him to tell Hygelac that Heorogar, his older brother and predecessor, deliberately passed over his own loyal son in giving the armor to him. It has not gone to Hrothgar's natural sons, either. Now it passes to Hygelac as a permanent reminder of the favor done for a Geatish exile at the time Hrothgar took the throne. Unfortunately, Beowulf will never again have a chance to act as a male peace-weaver for the Danes, as the succession evidently bypasses all of Hrothgar's sons.

Beowulf's great opponents in Denmark may be thought of as an opposing dynasty, remnants of another time and place of disorder. They too have a pedigree, connecting them by a vague and metaphorical "thence" (l. 111) to the race of Cain: giants, elves, evil spirits. These physical progeny were destroyed by the Flood; Grendel and his mother are their spiritual heirs. He is also the antithesis of Scyld. For instance, he comes at the end of a line and not the beginning. A destroyer of his neighbors, he nonetheless spares their meadhall, where he had total rule and fought against the right (l. 144). While "men knew not" where Scyld traveled in the afterlife, they know not where Grendel goes here and now (ll. 50, 162). It is both a usurpation and a parody of all the conquering that has gone on before. Fittingly, he is *feasceaft* at his end (l. 973), not his beginning, and is succeeded by a parent, not an offspring.

With the arrival of his mother we are given the same genealogy and the same "thence" (l. 1265). The two are all the more mysterious and terrible to the Danes for having no pedigree *they* know of (ll. 1355-57). Having admitted ignorance of their ancestry, Hrothgar goes on unwittingly to reveal their spiritual heritage by describing the hellish mere. The monsters' hall is on the other side of the mirror. When they enter the Danish world it is to fight against "the right." Since they are absurd inversions, it is not surprising that (in a much-remarked role and gender reversal) mother is the successor and avenger of son.

Their world has relics of the antediluvian giants with whom they are associated. Whereas "old sword made by giants" is a reflexive formula in the later part of the poem (ll. 2616, 2979), it takes on real substance in the underwater lair, where Beowulf enters prehistory, outside any surviving lines of human descent. Beowulf uses such a sword (ll. 1558, 1562, 1679) when the gift from the Danish court fails. Its hilt then undergoes a *translatio.* Having already outlasted the giants and the Grendel clan, it now passes from Beowulf to Hrothgar (ll. 1677-86). The "origin of the ancient strife" is written on it (ll. 1687-93), along with the death of the giants, but that is another story Hrothgar does not know. In entering the modern world, the weapon has lost its edge; only its wisdom remains. So too the wisdom of Hrothgar is the chief relic of Scylding glory.

II

The Geatish succession, by contrast, is not as richly imagined, and an element of disorder obtains in all of it before Beowulf. The only figure named who might precede Hrethel is Swerting, the uncle or grandfather of Hygelac (l. 1203). The Geats of the story are most properly Hrethlings (l. 2960). Like Healfdene he has three sons and a daughter, and like Hrothgar he takes Beowulf into his family (ll. 2428-34). The long process seen in the first part, where Beowulf crowned and ended Danish glory, is here foreshortened in a series of disasters that brings Beowulf to the throne, when the history of disorder ends until the dragon arrives. Hrethel's son Hæthcyn accidentally kills his brother Herebeald, after which their father dies of grief and hostility with the Swedes ensues (l. 2472). Hæthcyn is killed by Ongentheow at Ravenswood when the Geats attacked out of arrogance (l. 2926), leaving them lordless (l. 2935). Like a Scyld, Hygelac rescues them from that condition, arriving under viking banners (l. 2958). We already know that he will not live up to what is promised here, dying under a banner during another needless raid, his body and treasures passing (*gehwearf,* l. 1210) into the hands of inferior warriors.

Beowulf does not seize the kingdom; it "passed" to his

control when Hygelac and his son Heardred died, as the sword "passed" to Hrothgar (*gehwearf,* ll. 1684, 2208). Hygelac's widow Hygd had wanted him to play the part of Hrothulf and displace his cousin when the king died, not trusting her young son's abilities (ll. 2369-72). But these *feasceafte* ones (l. 2373) could not prevail upon him to supersede Heardred, who rules until his death in the Swedish wars. Then it is Beowulf's natural turn.

The transition had begun long before, when Beowulf merged his part in Danish history with the future of the Geats on the occasion of his return. His recapitulation and his yielding of treasures to Hygelac are acts of obeisance. Also, Beowulf has "few [that is, no] near relatives" except for the king (ll. 2150-51)—a situation that anticipates his lonely end. The first thing brought in from Hrothgar's bounty is a banner (l. 2152), perhaps to be thought of as the one carried on Hygelac's fatal raid. A bit later he gives Hygd Wealhtheow's present of a necklace (l. 2172), which had already been associated with that venture (l. 1195). If the Hrethling dynasty is a story of decline, Beowulf's life has been one of increasing glory, from a youth who was thought worthless (ll. 2183-88) to one now given Hrethel's sword and enough land to make him an underking (ll. 2190-99). All of this is toward the end of the first part.

In the second, Beowulf is proud that none of his neighbors (*ymbesittendra,* l. 2734) had been able to oppress the Geats with terror (*egesan,* l. 2736). He founded new glory for the Geats, as had Scyld for the Danes, and prevented those surrounding him from repeating Scyld's viking depredations. The treasure buried with him included a golden banner (l. 2767), chronologically the last of these viking symbols in the poem, and what glory there is in the viking way for the Geats passed with him. His demise and, later, that of the Geats are owed to entanglement in two problematical successions. First, Beowulf becomes involved in the Swedish matter as king by helping the *feasceaft* Eadgils (l. 2393), grandson of Ongentheow, whom Hygelac's men had slain at Revens**wood. Eadgils and his brother Eanmund had fled the wrath of their uncle Onela (who, along with their father Ohthere engaged in slaughter of Geats at a time before Ravenswood [l. 2475]) and were protected by Heardred, Hygelac's son. Onela invaded, killing Heardred and Eanmund. With the aid of Beowulf's people, Eadgils returned to kill the king and take the throne. It develops that Wiglaf is carrying the sword of Eanmund, whom his father had slain; it was a reward from Onela (ll. 2602-19). The matter is complicated, difficult for anyone to take in at one reading (or hearing), and even so the poet is careful to establish that there is a line, one that enters the poem's history with Ongentheow, though with the usual hint of a prehistory in the epithet Scylfing for the Swedes. And again the Scylding pattern is reversed, with a destitute youth coming at the end of a line whose purpose in the poem is to rob the Geats of what little glory there is before and after Beowulf.

The second "succession" involves the dragon and a reenactment of the Danish adventure with new twists. Like Hrothgar Beowulf had lived through many *ellenweorca* (l. 2399) beforehand, and his own hall is burnt (ll. 2324-27). His final *ellenweorc* (l. 2643) costs him his life, as Hrothgar's warning proves accurate. In one sense the dragon is the successor of Grendel, introduced in the same way ("oð ðæt an ongan," ll. 100, 2210) and ruling with the same power (*rixode / 2rics[i]an,* ll. 144, 2211), the only times those expressions are used. In another sense his career is the opposite of Beowulf's, *beginning* with a treasure barrow on a bluff by the sea (ll. 2241-43). He enters the poem as the successor of the "last survivor," guarding the hoard for three hundred years before a cup is stolen by a *feasceaft* man (l. 2285)—as with Eadgils, the sign of an ending about to occur. Only the lair has an eternal (*ece*) aspect to it, being the work of giants (ll. 2717-19) and surviving from Geatish prehistory like Grendel's antediluvian sword. The treasure, vainly cursed by men of old (ll. 3051-57), was meant to stay there until Doomsday (l. 3069), as was the dragon (l. 3083). In fact the gold is still in the ground, thanks to its burial with Beowulf, as useless to men as ever (ll. 3163-68).

The *translatio* of the gold had been wrongly continued by the thief, leaving Beowulf no choice but to fight its rightful guardian. Antiheroically, this wretch finds no ceremonial progression in his approach to Beowulf's throne (ll. 2281-83?, 2403-5) and remains nameless; like the earlier servants and not the hero, *he* does the guiding (l. 2409) when it is time to meet the dragon. This intruder from the deep past—not, like Grendel, a spiritual heir of anything—is the Geats' nemesis, and the end of the tragedy will be the primal terror worked by men like Scyld (*egesan,* l. 3154), as the female mourner rightly predicts, for all their praise of Beowulf's valor-work and glory (*ellenweorc,* l. 3173; *lof,* l. 3182).

That will be the outcome of long-standing feuds, however, not their present lordlessness, for there is one last inheritor of Danish and Geatish glory. As Beowulf had "few [no] near relatives" when making his act of obeisance to Hygelac, so when, while dying, he passes regalia to Wiglaf (in lieu of a son [ll. 2729-32]), he remarks that Wiglaf is the last of their race, the Wægmundings (ll. 2813-14)—probably Swedes, but their relation to the Geatish royal family is unstated. Wiglaf is also called a Scylfing (Swede) and a kinsman of the unknown Ælfhere, to cloud the issue further (ll. 2602-4), and his father had fought for the Swedes. In any event, having been informally adopted by Beowulf he stands in the same relation to the Hrethlings as Beowulf does to the Scyldings, the fifth, adoptive, and last true successor to the eponymous founder. Beowulf's failure in his dying speech to predict disaster like the messenger or the female mourner is a judicious signal of confidence in Wiglaf and further evidence that he regards him as the next king.

However, Wiglaf's refusal to take a share of the treasure, magnanimously attributing the victory to Beowulf, is a way of burying all the glory of the Geats. The tribe is now *feasceaft* in every sense. Its history from the beginning had been one of unwisdom until Beowulf, who alone represented the same *prymm* achieved by the Danes before Grendel intruded. The Danes had experienced ever-broadening glories, safe from external threats, while the Geats seem never uninvolved in feuds before Beowulf. His intervention in the Danish succession had happy results and represented a new pinnacle for those people. Similar interventions in Geatland only ensure the downfall of his own people, whose chaotic history compares poorly with that of the Danes.

Fidel Fajardo-Acosta   (essay date 1992)

SOURCE: "Intemperance, Fratricide, and the Elusiveness of Grendel," in *English Studies,* Vol. 73, No. 3, June 1992, pp. 205-10.

[*In the following excerpt, Fajardo-Acosta argues that Grendel acts as an instrument of divine punishment against the immoral Danes and that he can only be defeated by someone like Beowulf, who is virtuous and self-restrained.*]

One of the most difficult and baffling puzzles posed by the story of Grendel and his enmity with the Danes in *Beowulf* is perhaps that which refers to the extreme difficulties experienced by the Danes in disposing of the monster. The strength and size of Grendel together with his supposed invulnerability to swords and his habit of striking at night under the cover of darkness account partially for the helplessness of the Danes in dealing with their enemy. These explanations, however, cannot in any way be considered as fully satisfactory or even approach the challenge of wholly accounting for the nature of the problem. The idea that a relatively sophisticated society of warriors, such as the tribe of Hrothgar, could find no solution to the nightly ravages of Grendel and endured his outrages for nearly twelve years suggests that an investigation is required in order to clarify the precise nature of the Danes' failure to get rid of the monster. Beowulf's success in his man-to-man wrestling match with Grendel clearly points out the fact that Grendel was in no way invincible and that both his strength and courage had well defined limits. Why was it then that the Danes could not put together a large enough army to confront and defeat the monster? Surely the lack of courage and fighting power could not have been a factor in a society of individuals who made their living as pirates and pillagers accustomed to face and defeat fierce enemies both at home and abroad. The very regularity of Grendel's behavior in his nightly ambushes of Heorot Hall hints at the fact that even if the monster was indeed exceedingly strong, a cunning counter-ambush could have been prepared by Hrothgar's troops to imprison and destroy the enemy. Neither the powers of strength and martial prowess nor the treacherous stratagems of war could possibly have been lacking or unknown to Hrothgar and his men. That in spite of their knowledge of war and the tricks of fighting the Danes failed for twelve years to stop the monster and had to be in the end shamefully rescued by a foreigner is indeed strong evidence of the fact that the figure of Grendel and the problem that is posed for the seemingly defenseless Danes embody a

mysterious and symbolic significance which it is the purpose of this study to help elucidate.

Studies of the nature and character of Grendel often point out the idea that in spite of his undeniably human characteristics Grendel can be seen as a symbol of evil in general, possessing all the attributes of the devil as they were perceived by Christians in the early Middle Ages. The references in the text to Grendel as a descendant of Cain (Il. 107, 1261) have also attracted the attention of scholars and helped in the characterization of the monster as a destructive force connected to the concept of radical evil in the Judeo-Christian tradition. [All textual references in this study refer to the text of *Beowulf* in *Beowulf and the Fight at Finnsburg,* ed. Fr. Klaeber (Lexington, Mass., 1950).] In his character as a supernatural, demonic force, it is perhaps simple to understand the enormous power of Grendel over the society of the Danes. The reason why the Danes are deserving of and vulnerable to the attacks of the devil is, on the other hand, a different question. The *Beowulf* poet seems to suggest that indeed the Danes had themselves made their society open to the attacks of the devil through their own heathen way of life and their worship of demonic forces:

> Hwilum hie geheton æt hærgtrafum
> wigweorþunga, wordum bædon,
> þæt him gastbona geoce gefremede
> wið þeodþreaum. Swylc wæs þeaw hyra,
> hæþenra hyht; helle gemundon
> in modsefan, Metod hie ne cuþon,
> dæda Demend, ne wiston hie Drihten God,
> ne hie huru heofena Helm herian ne cuþon,
> wuldres Waldend.
>
> (***Beowulf:*** 175-183)

> Sometimes they offered at heathen temples
> sacrifices to idols, they vowed words
> that the soul-slayer would help them
> against distress. Such was their custom,
> the hope of heathens. Full of hell
> in their spirits, they did not recognize the Ruler,
> the Judge of deeds; they did not know the Lord God,
> nor indeed did they praise the Protector of Heaven,
> the Lord of glory.

Therefore, according to the *Beowulf* poet, the presence and ravages of Grendel among the Danes appear to be a phenomenon directly related to the behavior and character of the Danes themselves. Elsewhere I have argued that indeed Grendel appears to be himself a Dane sent into exile for mysterious reasons by either Hrothgar or his predecessors. Whatever the literal identity of Grendel, however, in his role as an evil spirit with a mission to torture and punish Hrothgar and his people, Grendel seems indeed a sort of manifestation of a divine decree against the way of life of the Danes. Both the character and behavior of Grendel appear in some sense to mirror and reflect the immoral essence of the character of the Danes whom he so viciously victimizes.

The idea that the Danes, as individuals and as a tribe,

suffer from severe moral shortcomings which make them deserving of the curse of Grendel is well supported by the internal, textual evidence in the poem. The criticism of the Danes seems in fact a very understandable impulse on the part of a Christian, Anglo-Saxon poet interested in condemning the way of life of the barbarian Danish tribes who not only adhered to a semi-pagan ideology and lifestyle but who were also the proverbial enemies of the newly-Christianized and relatively more civilized groups inhabiting the English islands at the time when the ***Beowulf*** poet was composing his epic. The creation of Grendel and his characterization as the very embodiment and epitome of evil appears to have as much to do with the condemnation of un-Christian principles and ways of life in general as with the criticism of the Danish people in particular on the grounds of their failure to adopt a more civilized and Christian way of life.

The vices of intemperance in the consumption of alcoholic beverages and the drunken, brutish, destructive, and often criminal behavior associated with alcoholism appear to stand foremost in the mind of the poet in the articulation of his criticism of the Danish people. Unferth, Hrothgar's ineffectual champion, is the particular figure in the story which the poet seems to have chosen to represent the essence of the moral problems plaguing the Danes and the consequences of those problems in rendering even the greatest of the Danish warriors into boastful but useless defenders of the kingdom against the threat of Grendel. In his response to Unferth's challenges during the party preceding Beowulf's confrontation with Grendel, Beowulf accuses Unferth of being 'beore druncen' (l. 531; 'drunk with beer') and also notices the fact that the reputation of the Danish champion is tarnished by the crime of fratricide:

. . . ðu þinum broðrum te banan wurde,
heafodmægum; þæs þu in helle scealt
werhðo dreogan . . .

(***Beowulf***: 587-589)

you became your brother's slayer,
your close relative; therefore you shall in hell
suffer damnation.

The faults that Beowulf sees in Unferth appear to be part of a larger problem associated with the character and behavior of the Danes in general. As Geoffrey Hughes suggests [in *English Studies*, Vol. 58 (1977)], it appears that 'something is rotten in this state of Denmark.' The situation that the poet seems to consider as representative of the essence and consequences of that problem is the very one embodied in the scenes depicting celebrations in the beer-hall. In general, after the warriors have become blind-drunk during such celebrations, they seem to forget the distinction between friends and enemies and are very apt to commit the worst atrocities, including, as in the case of Unferth, the slaying of one's own relatives. Such a situation appears to stand behind the infamous Finnsburg episode, the story told by the minstrel in ***Beowulf*** recounting the tragic fight that broke out between Danes and Frisians during a feast and which ended with the slay-

ing of the Danish king Hnaef and his nephew, along with many other men. Excessive drinking turned the initially friendly gathering of Danes and Frisians into what the poet characterizes as 'morþorbealo maga' (line 1079; 'the slaughter of kinsmen'). It is perhaps interesting to note that in another work—Shakespeare's *Hamlet*—similar to ***Beowulf*** in the fact of its being the product of a Christian, English author writing about the Danes of the early Middle Ages, the attitudes presented concerning the character and behavior of the Danish people are also similar to those in the Old English epic. In *Hamlet* we not only find a character, Claudius, who, like Unferth, is guilty of both intemperance in drinking and fratricide but we also hear from Hamlet's own mouth a clear statement of the reputation of drunkards enjoyed by the Danes among other peoples. After noting that Claudius plans to spend the night drinking and carousing, Hamlet tells Horatio:

But to my mind, though I am native here
and to the manner born, it is a custom
more honored in the breach than the observance.
This heavy-headed revel east and west
makes us traduced and taxed of other nations.
They clepe us drunkards and with swinish phrase
soil our addition, and indeed it takes
from our achievements, though performed at height,
the pith and marrow of our attribute.

(*Hamlet* 1. iv: 14-22)

The image of the monstrous Grendel feasting to his heart's content on the bodies of the Danes in the midst of Heorot Hall acquires a larger significance when juxtaposed with the notion of the Danes' intemperance and the crimes generally committed in the beer-hall under the influence of a few too many cups of mead. The idea that for twelve years starting right after the construction of Heorot Hall, night after night an invisible monster visits the beer-hall and mutilates and devours thirty of Hrothgar's warriors begins to appear under this perspective more than as a literal explanation of the disaster, as a figurative account of the devastations caused by the warriors' own drunkenness and brutish violence, Grendel—a monster who because of his voracious appetite and his links to the figure of Cain stands in the story as an unequivocal symbol of intemperance and fratricide—needs therefore to be interpreted as a mirror image and symbolic representation of the vices and flaws in the character of the Danes themselves, vices which indeed are very costly to the Danish society and whose effects could be compared to those of a monster revaging the country. [John] Leyerle correctly notes [in *University of Toronto Quarterly*, Vol. 37 (1967)] that "in ***Beowulf*** monsters are closely associated with the slaying of friends and kinsmen. They function in part as an outward objectification and sign of a society beset by internecine slaughter between friend and kin."

The elusiveness of Grendel, his enormous strength, his seeming invulnerability to weapons, the idea that he attacks at night and completely unseen by either victims or survivors, and the fact of his virtually complete dominance of the Danes are facets of the monster's characterization which make perfect sense when considered from the perspective that Grendel is a symbolic rather than a literal monster in the epic. Indeed it is quite impossible for the baffled Danes to capture and destroy a monster who only manifests itself after the warriors have fallen victim to the effects of alcohol and who proceeds to quickly conceal itself within each and every one of the revelers once the effects of the drink have dissipated. Grendel is a highly elusive 'evil spirit' who is an integral part of the character and personality of the Danes themselves. As [James W.] Earl points out [in *Thought*, Vol. 57 (1982)], *Beowulf* is characterized by a "pervasive language of spiritual warfare, in which the enemy has been internalized and the battlefield is the soul." The problem which the Danish people confront in the menace of Grendel is none other than that posed by their own brutish behavior—the monster is therefore primarily an internal enemy which can never be defeated with weapons and whose presence can only be exorcised through a process of self-examination and personal transformation which the Danes seem incapable of bringing about. [Stephen C.] Bandy notes [in *Neophilologus*, Vol. 56 (1972)] that 'these benighted warriors of Hrothgar cannot learn. They are the slaves of their appetites. In Bandy's view, the Danes are victims of 'self-indulgence (and specifically drunkenness).'

Not surprisingly, it is only a foreigner, a non-Dane who holds the key to the solution of the Grendel problem. In the figure of Beowulf, the Danes find a man whose ability to defeat Grendel is grounded not so much on pure brute, physical force but on a miraculous sort of strength generated by certain gifts of moral character and which are characterized by the poet as God-given. In particular, the poet chooses to emphasize the idea that Beowulf is different from Unferth and from the rest of the Danes in the fact that he seems able to control both his violence and his consumption of alcohol. That degree of temperance and self-control are then characterized as being intimately related to his awesome physical strength:

> Swa bealdode bearn Ecgðeowes,
> guma guðum cuð, godum dædum,
> dreah æfter dome; nealles druncne slog
> heorðgeneatas; næs him hreoh sefa,
> ac he mancynnes mæste cræfte
> ginfæstan gife, þa him God sealde,
> heold hildedeor.
>
> (*Beowulf* 2177-2183)

> Thus he showed himself brave, the son of Ecgtheow,
> a man known in battles, of good deeds,
> he acted according to discretion; when drinking he slew
> no hearth-companions; his spirit was not violent,
> but he of mankind the greatest strength,
> a generous gift that God gave him,
> held as a warrior.

Beowulf's ability to defeat Grendel is a function of his temperance and self-restraint. He is the only one in the entire company of Geats that accompanied him to the adventure in Denmark who manages to stay sober enough to perceive the entrance of Grendel into Heorot Hall. Bandy notes the 'remarkable wakefulness of Beowulf and further suggests that 'only the warrior who is first defeated by his own weakness can become the prey of Grendel and his evil.' Thus, as a man capable of temperance and self-restraint, Beowulf easily catches the fierce Grendel and holds him by the hand in a wonderful allergorical representation of precisely the manner in which the virtuous man holds in check his own violent passions and appetites. Although fated to succumb to the temptations posed later in the story by the fiery dragon, in the Grendel adventure Beowulf exhibits a degree of self-control and moral virtue which make it possible to see the Geatish hero as a sort of spiritual warrior engaged in a dangerous psychomachia or internal battle from which he emerges victorious as the vanquisher of the monstrous passions and violent tendencies which lurk inside his own heart and the hearts of all human beings. In this manner, Beowulf achieves a moral victory for himself and for the Danes which has to do with the importance in a human society of finding certain individuals of outstanding moral character who can serve as an example to others of the possibility of defeating the monster within. The joy of the Danes at the success of Beowulf in his encounter with Grendel can then be understood as a celebration of the opening of avenues of human character and behavior up till then unknown in Danish society. From this perspective it is then possible—though not entirely accurate—to compare the figure of Beowulf to that of Jesus Christ as a spiritual hero and redeemer of humanity. Such a comparison however should never be allowed to obscure the fact that for all its seeming virtue and goodness, the behavior of Beowulf, as a warrior and mercenary engaged in the pursuit of wealth and fame, remains highly problematic from a Christian point of view and determines the fact that the hero is doomed to tragedy and failure in the ultimate confrontation with the dragon, the symbol of all evil and the strongest of the satanic forces in the universe of *Beowulf.*

Ward Parks (essay date 1993)

SOURCE: "Prey Tell: How Heroes Perceive Monsters in *Beowulf*," in *Journal of English and Germanic Philology*, Vol. 92, No. 1, January, 1993, pp. 1-16.

[*In the essay that follows, Parks focuses on the ambivalent nature of all three monsters in* Beowulf *but particularly on that of Grendel, whose shifting status as both animalistic predator and human-like opponent adds to the terror associated with him.*]

Since ancient times, the bestiality of man has been a topic of such resonance in the discourse of high culture as to suggest that it strikes upon deep tensions in the human psyche. While certain features of this problematic relationship between the human and infrahuman are fairly stable, in different eras it has been conceived through radically differing paradigms. The Christian ascetic, for example, while acknowledging the bestial within the human soul, castigated it as the source of fleshly temptations that distract the pilgrim in his ascent to God. Seeking a mechanism of relationship on the material rather than the spiritual plane, Charles Darwin shocked the religious sensibilities of his day by postulating that the kinship is genetic and evolutionary, that man is literally descended from the ape. In the last few decades, the rapidly maturing sciences of ethology and sociobiology have vastly enlarged the body of evidence concerning the social behavior of higher life forms and the role of such patterns in an evolutionary process. In this study I would like to bring some of these modern behavioral perspectives to bear on an ancient poet's delvings into the same basic issue. For the ambiguous standing of the *Beowulf* monsters, and more specifically the liminality of the brood of Grendel, who is neither fully human nor fully bestial, is an essential defining characteristic of the particular challenge to human community that the poet wishes to pose. And Beowulf's response, heavily laden with symbolic gesture, is designed to reconstitute this catastrophe in terms acceptable to the heroic world view.

The fundamental ambivalence that Grendel embodies and that Beowulf must resolve relates to the distinction between predatorial and agonistic aggression. In brief, Grendel wants to ravage like a predator, whereas Beowulf insists on contesting with him like a conspecific adversary (that is, as a member of the same biological species). The association between the poem's horrific imagery and mood—especially in its early movements—and the theme of predation is very clear. Consider the famous passage that immediately precedes the Beowulf-Grendel encounter. The *glæca* (monster) has just made his way from the dark and misty moors into the great Danish hall of Heorot, finding there a delectable *comitatus* of savory, sleeping Geats. Seeing no need for delay, Grendel proceeds directly to the feast:

> ac hē gefēng hraðe forman siðe
> slæpendne rinc, slat unwearnum,
> bāt banlocan, blōd ēdrum dranc,
> synsnædum swealh; sōna hæfde
> unlyfigendes eal gefeormod,
> fēt ond folma.

(but he seized quickly on the first pass a sleeping warrior, he tore him up with ease, bit his body, drank blood in streams, swallowed huge chunks; at once he had devoured the entirety of that lifeless man, feet and hands.) [See *Beowulf and the Fight at Finnsburg*, ed. Fr. Klaeber, 3d ed. (Lexington, Mass.: D.C. Heath, 1950), ll. 740-45. All subsequent textual citations will refer to this edition. Translations are my own.]

Now much of the ghastliness of this passage derives from the fact that Hondscioh—Grendel's victim (l. 2076)—is not just killed but physically *eaten;* the *Beowulf*-poet underscores this point through the graphic detail with which he describes the monster's gory meal. This is not a heroic contest between champions but a lion pouncing on a helpless deer. Were it not that we, the human audience, are perennially susceptible to this very concrete,

very creaturely terror, the scene would not grip us as it does. The symbolic accomplishment of Beowulf the hero is to reject the role of prey and to establish himself as Grendel's worthy opponent. In the process, he begins to modulate aggressive violence in the poem out of the predatorial pattern of stealthy-attack-and-flight into that of formal, agonistically styled contesting.

Before focusing on the poem in detail, I need to state more fully the differences between the predatorial and agonistic aggressive patterns. The distinction between these aggressive modes in *Beowulf* can most clearly be seen in terms of three variables: objective, style, and interrelationship of the adversaries in terms of biological species. The objective of predation is obvious enough: hunters stalk their prey in order to make them their food. By contrast, formal agonistic contesting is usually undertaken for the control of some external resource (such as territory or mating prerogatives), or simply for the exhilaration of "winning." And so contest rivals need only to be beaten, not eaten. This difference in aim engenders contrasting combat styles. For predators, ceremonial display addressed toward prospective victims would in most cases be counterproductive; their purposes are better served by a secretive than by a well-advertised approach. Agonistic combatants, on the other hand, attach a great premium to such intangibles as high dominance ranking or "honor and glory" since, within their communities, these abstract gains are often betokened by and translate into concrete benefits. For these reasons they exhibit a penchant for elaborate battle ceremony accompanied by flamboyant threat displays and predictable styles of combat, preferably conducted in public arenas. Finally, the aggressive mode correlates significantly (though not absolutely) with comembership or lack of comembership in a species; that is, predators usually prefer victims from other species whereas agonistically styled duels generally match conspecifics. The converse does not hold true: interspecific aggression is not always predatorial, and violence among fellow-members of a species is frequently unceremonialized, as in the case of a stealthy murder. One might, moreover, cite exceptions, such as cannibalism, or elaborate game strategies in interspecific encounters. In general, nonetheless, predators prefer to hunt creatures over whom they enjoy overwhelming fighting advantages; and this state of affairs is best brought about interspecifically. By contrast, the ceremonialization of combat flourishes best amid symmetrical, thus intraspecific, opposition.

There are, of course, other types of aggression besides the predatory and agonistic. Indeed, the integrity of "aggression" as a scientific category has from time to time been questioned; and the accent of much recent research has fallen on its physiological determinants. Yet behavioral differentia cannot be disregarded, particularly in literary study where the subjects of investigation are, in a biological sense, nonexistent; and in the behavioral terrain that "aggression" seems conventionally to designate, the distinction between high-display *agonia* and low-display predation has a real heuristic value. In a recent study Robert O'Connell (1989) has made this point, showing that the alternation between predatory and "intraspecific" (i.e., agonistic) patterns has been a persisting theme in the history of weaponry and its deployment. Even in animal combat, he points out, that weaponry (such as a stag's antlers) biologically engendered for intraspecific combat is both more spectacular and less destructive than the weaponry of predation. Human warfare, he maintains, has witnessed a tension between the impulse toward an intraspecific ceremonialization that limits (though it by no means eliminates) bloodshed and an increasingly impersonal and destructive weapons technology that confers the advantage to those who wage war predatorially, without restraint. O'Connell's book is replete with superb examples, such as the Anglo-American naval establishment's stubborn distrust of the invisible and subversive submarine. Completed before I became aware of O'Connell's work, my own study of verbal dueling in heroic epic (1990) recognized a similar distinction. For the bragging and abuse exchanged between heroes joined in an agonistic encounter is fundamentally akin to threat displays between conspecific mammals, such as the roaring matches with which red deer preface their clashing of antlers. Predatorial encounters do not feature such bilateral symmetrical displays to anything approaching the same degree.

While the **Beowulf**-poet's artistry draws upon this contrast, of course we must recognize that neither he nor his fictional creations understood it through these same analytic categories. Yet a mouse trapped by a cat, while it may never have read Konrad Lorenz or E. O. Wilson, knows perfectly well that it has a problem; and so do the Danes. Moreover, the sheer gruesomeness of the Danish catastrophe makes it plain where the poet's sympathies lie. Modern readers critical of martial idealism are sometimes disposed to valorize the viewpoints of Grendel and his mother, arguing that their "monstrosity" is no worse than that of their human foes. John Gardner's *Grendel* plays on something of this sensibility. Yet such most emphatically is not the standpoint of the **Beowulf**-poet. His outlook is thoroughly homocentric—or, if I may unleash the neologism "anthroscopic," whose syllable -*scop*-, derived from the Greek verb *skopein* 'to see' puns with the Anglo-Saxon word for "poet." Such parochialism may be easily derided by persons who have seldom been exposed to physical violence; but when one's survival is in question, decentered and dehumanized viewpoints quickly lose their appeal. Critics who assume an impartial response to the massacre of the Danes have not sufficiently grappled with the imagistic horror of those scenes. In warlike times, or in their recent memory, mythic narratives of atrocities against human community are no joke. Neither the Scandinavians within the action of the poem nor the poet-audience group witnessing it has any sympathy to waste on demonic ravagers whose "lifedays" they, like Beowulf, "reckon beneficial to none of the [human] nations" (ll. 793-94). The only good predator is a dead predator: so say the prey.

The poet's predatorial coloring of the original crisis implicitly imputes nonhumanity to Grendel; and other strokes in his portraiture accentuate this effect. He in-

habits an inaccessible, underwater den and stalks the misty moors beyond the margins of human community outreach. Possessed of overpowering strength, he nonetheless prefers not to attack frontally but to 'ensnare' (*besyrwan*, l. 713) through stealthy nighttime assaults, carrying off in his *glōf* (l. 2085) what he does not devour at the time. When he enters Heorot he sees not prospective worthy adversaries by whom he might enhance his glory but only the 'expectation of a plentiful meal' ("wistfylle wēn," l. 734). Although it seems he could not "approach the throne" (ll. 168-69), whether God's or Hrothgar's, in all other respects Grendel exhibits disregard if not outright disdain for the symbols and ceremonies of human order, including even the civilities of warfare. Thus he eschews formal challenge and prebattle flyting—not, we must assume, out of fear but mere contempt. Similarly, he will not undertake the postbattle restoration of peace through "wergild" (ll. 154-58), such as one might hope for in intertribal feuding. These implied attitudes on Grendel's part are thoroughly predatorial: why should a cat come to terms with mice? Further—and this is a particularly telling detail—human weaponry is unavailing against him. And in this connection we should recall, as O'Connell points out, that the weaponry as well as the defensive strategy that evolution has designed for intraspecific combat is often useless or unused against predators. Thus the experience of the Danes and Geats echoes that of other prospective prey when they discover that, against Grendel, their swords do not bite (ll. 801-5).

That Grendel and his mother are indeed predators par excellence is underscored in one of the poem's most striking anecdotes. After Grendel's defeat has provoked the counterattack by his mother, Hrothgar sets about describing their lair to Beowulf. To highlight the baneful aura surrounding Grendel's Mere which the Geat will soon have to brave, Hrothgar introduces an explicitly predatorial figure (ll. 1368-72):

Đēah þe hæðstapa hundum geswenced,
heorot hornum trum holtwudu sēce,
feorran geflymed, ær hē feorh seleð,
aldor on ōfre, ær hē in wille,
hafelan [beorgan]; nis þæt hēoru stōw!

(Although the heath-stalker hard-pressed by hounds, the strong-horned hart should seek the forest, put to flight from afar, sooner will he give up his life on the bank than go in to save his neck [lit.: head]; that is not a nice place!)

This passage works through an implied comparison of degree whose constant term is predatorially inspired terror. The hart is more frightened by the mere possibility of the death lurking beneath the waves than by its certitude at the teeth of the pursuing hounds. By so much, then, does the horror of Grendel's clan exceed that of other killers. Further, since Hrothgar's obvious intention is to give Beowulf a frank warning about the risks he is asking him to run, his anecdote implies comparison between the fate of the stag and that of any man who assails Grendel's abode. This association is strengthened by the fact that one of the terms in this passage for the hart, *heorot* (l. 1369), serves also as the name for the Danish hall. That men can be food for monsters Hrothgar knows all too well—no one better. Thus when the moment arises for him to summon his greatest descriptive powers to the imaginative construction of terror, it is a predatorial figure that he calls upon.

Yet while Grendel's man-eating habits dehumanize him, in other respects he is much akin to his human victims. This kinship has indeed a literal aspect. For on two parallel occasions, immediately prior to the first attacks of Grendel and his mother, the poet inserts ring-framed meditations (ll. 99-114 and 1255-78) on the lineage of these monsters that traces back to Cain, the original fratricide and child of the original human parents. Of course, the fact that *eotenas, ylfe, orcnêas,* and *gīgantas* are also descended from Cain (ll. 112-13) mitigates the force of this genealogical association between monsters and men as evidence of cohumanity. Nonetheless, the hostilities between these races are described in the language of feuding (*fæhðe,* l. 109) and resonate against an all-too-human background of intertribal warfare. Moreover, Hrothgar specifically reports that the two *mearcstapan* ('border-walkers,' l. 1348) bear human likeness: the mother has 'the likeness of a woman' ("idese onlīcnes," l. 1351) while her son is in 'the form of a man' ("weres wæstmum," l. 1352). It is true, however, that he is 'larger than any other man' ("mara þonne ænig man ōðer," l. 1353), so much so that four of Beowulf's retainers are required to carry just his head (ll. 1634-39). This size difference seems to imply the extreme unlikelihood of interbreeding between Grendel's kin and Hrothgar's; and in this connection we should recall that the ability of male and female to procreate is one of the marks of comembership in a species. Then again, Grendel and his mother exhibit human life habits and may have mastered certain human arts. Like humans, they occupy a hall (albeit an underwater hall) whose approach is guarded by a *comitatus* of sorts, if one wishes to view the *nicors* in this way; on the other hand, the exile imagery marking the comings and goings of the Danes' marginalized foes colors them with a contrary yet equally humanizing stroke. Moreover, even though Grendel does not seem to know the mastery of such 'good things' ("gōda," l. 681) as swords, his mother can put a dagger ("seax," l. 1545) to use, and they own a sword heirloom whose hilt records runically a piece of family history (ll. 1677-98), if we can assume that giants whom the flood killed are Grendel's distant relations. Taylor has gone so far as to argue that Grendel knows speech and writing, although he never displays these skills in the poem. Further lexical corroboration for Grendel's intermittent humanity can be found in Tripp's comprehensive table of terms for him and his kin, which indexes a mixture of associations human, monstrous, and diabolical. My point, in sum, is that Grendel is irreducibly ambiguous with respect to the human-nonhuman dichotomy; and this very liminality is essential to the poet's designs. Because Grendel devours Danes like so many rabbits, he casts the survivors into an insufferable role. Yet because he exhibits so many human traits, he is susceptible to the radicalizing agonistic challenge

of the hero. Thus the poetic narrator and the hero collaborate in his transformation. To try to fix him and his mother into one category of the other would be to deny one of the poem's most essential acts.

I would like to emphasize that the distinction this essay is exploring, while of real bearing at certain points in the poem, is nonetheless of limited importance; in no way does it constitute the controlling theme around which all other elements in the poem are organized. Grendel's nature has dimensions that the distinction cannot elucidate. For example, Norse analogues (such as *Grettir's Saga*) suggest his literary affiliation with the *draugr* and other supernatural miscreants of legend and saga. While these literary traditions may themselves feed occasionally on the interplay between predator and agonistic rival, they have a full life of their own these terms cannot explain away. Moreover, as Tripp's table details in full, Grendel is at times characterized as an infernal creature—a 'fiend in hell' ("fēond on helle," l. 101), 'hell's captive' ("helle hæfton," l. 788), an 'alien spirit' ("ellorgast / ellorgæst," ll. 807, 1617, 1621), a companion of 'devils' (l. 756), indeed, a devil himself, if we accept that the reference of "d ofla" in line 1680 includes him. Russom has gone so far as to argue that Grendel lives in hell quite literally. His diabolical pedigree is reinforced by the repeated allusions to the feud between God and Cain's progeny. This world of Christian mythological reference and resonance implicates far more than just the interrelations between the human and infrahuman; indeed, Grendel's ambiguous predatoriality is less essential to his representation than these other associations are. Yet there is no need to unravel and rank these threads in his nature. Other illustrious monsters—such as Homer's Polyphemos or the cultured yet man-eating rakshasas of the Indian epics *Mahabharata* and *Ramayana*—show similar blends of traits predatorial, human, and superhuman or supernatural. Each of these imparts to the resulting monstrous personality its own distinctive coloring, and none is reducible to another.

The ambiguity in Grendel's representation is exploited by Beowulf, who refuses to accept the premise of inequality that the predator-prey relationship presupposes but insists instead on conducting his anti-monstrous campaign in the high style, as between conspecific adversaries. It is true that most of his ceremonial display is directed toward his human cohorts, not the monsters; yet Grendel himself must bear much of the blame for this, since his reliance on surprise attack does not allow for dialogue. Nonetheless, the Grendel affair lies at the heart of Beowulf's intertribal dealings, which are notable for their altruistic motives and honorable course. Nowhere is this more evident than in his initial generous offer to risk his life for the benefit of a foreign people. To be sure, he has a family debt to repay, incurred when his father Ecgtheow was bailed out by Hrothgar during a difficult feud with the Wylfings (ll. 457-72); yet in the subsequent Danish crisis Beowulf presents himself without being asked and renders services that far exceed his obligations. Further, he binds himself to the Grendel venture with formal, unilateral pledges, first in his dialogue with the Danish coast guard (ll. 237-300), and later with Hrothgar himself (ll. 407-90). The culminating stage in this process arrives in his flyting with Unferth, where the Geat's heroic credentials are called up for inspection and wagered as the stake for victory or loss. This heroic flyting is an instance of a widely diffused contest genre whose defining characteristic is an oral contract binding one or both of the flyters to a martial test by which the quarrel will be adjudicated. In this case Beowulf and Unferth are the contestants, the right to claim heroic superiority is the prize, and Beowulf's fortunes against Grendel will measure their rival claims. The interesting point is that, since Grendel is unavailable for challenges and cannot be flyted with, his projected fight with Beowulf has now been woven into the structure of a larger intraspecific (man-against-man) contest that adumbrates a heroic ethos and conforms to a code of honor. Thus Beowulf's campaign against Grendel has been invested through his association with agonistic rather than antipredatorial overtones.

Since Grendel has been so thoroughly alienated from the homocentric (or anthroscopic) sensibilities of the poem, Beowulf's expedient of redirecting ceremonial display from monsters to men provides an acceptable substitute in bringing about the symbolic transformation that he desires. After all, the human community is trying to convince itself that it can combat with Grendel agonistically; Grendel's opinion on the likelihood of their success in such a project is thoroughly unwanted. Nonetheless, in his final boast at bedtime (ll. 677-87), Beowulf makes him the immediate beneficiary of a sincere and courageous heroic gesture. Ignorant of the charm by which, evidently, Grendel has rendered himself invulnerable to sword-blows (ll. 804-5), Beowulf renounces the use of weaponry on the grounds that Grendel, despite his great strength, is unversed in these arts. For the Geat does not consider himself inferior to his rival in war-strength (ll. 677-78) and wants to establish this in a fight where both enjoy the same advantages and limitations. God will assign glory as seems right to Him (ll. 685-87); and by this allusion to external witnessing (the third-stander) and supernal judgment Beowulf is calling upon one of the basic principles of the formal contest. In all of this Beowulf is distancing himself from the ruthless pragmatism typifying the self-protective stratagems of prey confronted with the overwhelming superior force of predators. To the contrary, he wants a fair fight between matched warriors; and as O'Connell points out repeatedly, the intraspecific fighting mode features symmetrical weaponry. Of course, all of this heroic idealism is quite lost on Grendel, one might say, since the brief moment of their encounter leaves Cain's man-eating descendant with no time to reflect on his opponent's gallantries. Yet again, this is quite beside the point. For the heroic service which Beowulf means to perform is for the benefit of the human community to whom he broadcasts these noble sentiments, not for his monstrous *feond*.

Many readers have noted the lack of dramatic tension in the actual Beowulf-Grendel fight. For the moment that Grendel recognizes the quality of his foe, he becomes

"hinfūs" (l. 755), 'eager to escape' to his 'hiding place' ("heolster," l. 755) in the fens. Yet the poet tells us explicitly that his strength is greater than his mother's (ll. 1282-87). Why, then does the *aglæca* perform so poorly in this his death-struggle? Of course, he does not enjoy the home-court advantage that his mother does when Beowulf encounters her in her lair. Yet the more basic reason is that he has not come prepared to contest with a heroic equal; his reaction typifies that of a predator suddenly meeting up against more than he has reckoned on. Despite the bench-bashing and wall-shaking, his fight with Beowulf never emerges into the full status of an agonistic contest.

Such is not the case with Grendel's mother, who has been alerted by her son's misfortune to the presence of an adversary who cannot be dispatched with the ease that his predecessors were. Nonetheless, in keeping with the habits of her clan, she too introduces herself to the Danes predatorially. Waiting until the revellers have gone to sleep, she sneaks into Heorot, snatches Æschere, and escapes into the darkness; and that she has made a good meal of the worthy thane is to be inferred from one of the most ghastly images of predatory violence in the poem in the Danes' discovery of his head on the cliff beside her mere (ll. 1417-21). All the same, while her behavior is predatory, her motives are not. The poet tells us specifically that she made her woeful journey "sunu dēoð wrecan" 'to avenge the death of her son' (l. 1278); and in his speech to Beowulf the next morning Hrothgar characterizes her assault as an act of vengeance within a feud (ll. 1330-45), not a food-foraging expedition. Moreover, Beowulf's encounter with her proceeds much as a battle of champions. His approach is proclaimed as a kind of challenge by the blowing of a horn (ll. 1423-24) and the shooting of a *nicor* (ll. 1432-36); and before plunging into the waters he arms himself in the formal heroic manner (ll. 1442-54) and engages in a decorous exchange with Hrothgar and his former rival and new friend, Unferth (ll. 1455-91). Thus a predatorially styled initiative has been countered by a ceremonious, agonistic response; and in the fight that follows, it is Beowulf's policy that prevails. For this epic struggle is conducted not as a predatorial massacre but as a single combat on fairly equal terms. Both tear at each other by hand; each deals the other an unsuccessful stroke with a blade. And here a further symmetry emerges: for the inability of Hrunting (Unferth's sword-gift) to injure her (ll. 1519-28), which recalls Grendel's invulnerability against sword-blows (ll. 801-5), is paralleled by the success of Beowulf's corselet in turning aside her dagger-thrust (ll. 1545-54). In the end Beowulf slaughters her with her own sword. With this act, and with the retrieval of Grendel's head as a display and token of his victory, Beowulf has finally and decisively cast off the image of predatory victim with which the human community has been straddled from the outset of the poem. And in the process he has vindicated agonistic heroism as a means of dealing with such problems.

Readers have often noted that the dragon in **Beowulf** is quite dissimilar from his monstrous foregoers, and this observation certainly holds regarding the issue under study here. In fact, the dragon is neither so predatorial nor so human as Grendel is. True, he destroys Geatland with ruthless violence and evident contempt for the opposition. Yet he never actually *eats* anyone, at least that we hear of; and even if one wishes to argue that the poet simply omitted to mention this detail, the omission is itself significant. Gone from this portion of the poem are gory images of a monster tearing limbs from a helpless man, slurping blood, and gulping hunks of flesh. The terror, though no less real, is less corporeal. Yet while he is not a predator, the dragon does not project the image of a champion or conspecific adversary either. He does fit into certain human stereotypes—that of the guardian (*weard* and *hyrde*), the hall-dweller, the miserly and vengeful king. Yet he lacks a *comitatus,* does not appear to enjoy active membership in a tribe or clan, and boasts no genealogy. Further, he is serpentine, and thus conspicuously nonanthropomorphic, in physical appearance. This is a monster truly alien to human kind. The contrast between predator and conspecific adversary simply does not comprehend him. And since he does not inhabit the margins between these categories, he cannot be transformed through the same process.

Beowulf's response to his challenge nonetheless incorporates many agonistic movements; the Geat's heroism is indeed founded on agonistic paradigms to such a degree that he cannot eschew them entirely. Thus he prefaces his assault with formal boasts before his retainers and apologizers for the necessity of armor (ll. 2510-37); soon after, he broadcasts his arrival at the dragon's barrow with a shout of challenge (ll. 2550-53), not unlike flyting, that succeeds indeed in arousing the ire of the *wyrm.* Yet his realistic recognition of the need for sword and shield and byrnie, in view of the anticipated battle-fire and poison (ll. 2522-24), shows that certain agonistic proprieties have had to cede place to expediency. The dragon's menace is simply too overwhelming to permit overscrupulousness regarding the niceties of formal dueling. The battle that follows, while certainly a supreme contest in a sense, is characterized more by an asymmetrical parity than by a genuine matching up according to a single system of rules. Fire clashes against shield, fang against corselet, sword against bone, advance by foot against an uncoiling and slithering: Beowulf and the dragon do not share a single common term in weaponry or styles of attack and defense. Finally and perhaps most tellingly, Beowulf cannot, despite his boast, defeat his opponent single-handed; the dragon dies only when Beowulf and Wiglaf team up. In short Beowulf, despite his heroic preferences, has had to yield to necessity. The dragon simply must be killed, whatever the means; and while the spirit of agonistic adventurism has not been quenched altogether, cooperation between fellow warriors has emerged into greater prominence.

Thus agonistic heroism no longer stands in antithesis to predation. This dichotomy, so crucial to the Grendel sequence, has faded entirely out of view. At the same time I would like to suggest that the vacuum created by the disappearance of this concern is filled by another newly emerging problem that exhibits a certain metaphoric likeness on the level of human community to the threat that predation posed on the level of individual corporeal existence. From its outset the story has been played out against a background of intertribal friendships and feuds. In the last thousand lines, however, the frequency and duration of these digressions increases markedly. To my reading, some of the most horrific imagery unfolds in these passages, as when the terrible Swedish king Ongentheow drives the wound-weary Geats into Ravenswood and serenades them the night long with threats to hack them open with swords and leave them swinging from gallows-trees for the sport of birds (ll. 2936-42). What the Geatish messenger who recollects this episode from tribal history wishes to convey is that, with the dissemination of the bad news of Beowulf's death and the cowardice of his retainers, bloody assaults like this are only what the Geats have to expect. In a figurative sense, then, the Swedes and other enemies are threatening to dismember the Geatish nation and "consume its substance," as it were. We would be wise not to press this analogy too far. No one ever implies that the Swedes or Franks practice cannibalism or genocide; nor can we gloss over the distinction between the graphically concrete violence of Dane-gobbling and the more abstract violence in the "rending of a community." The former inspires terror of a stark, bodily variety, the latter, a somewhat intangible mood of oppression and sense of impending doom. Nonetheless, the relationship between the devouring of persons and of tribes is sufficient to ensure that the disappearance of corporeal predation from the poem's surface texture does not cause a loss of momentum and let-down in dramatic power.

The burden of this argument is not to promote the positivistic reduction of **Beowulf** into some kind of Darwinian allegory. The poem stands as a mighty expression of the human spirit; and its sweep and majesty are in no sense curtailed by its willingness to engage terrors of the most creaturely sort. Indeed, these fears occasion much of the supreme heroism in the poem and thus make possible the vindication of human courage in the face of a hostile world.

FURTHER READING

Baker, Peter S. "Beowulf the Orator." *Journal of English Linguistics* 21, No. 1 (April 1988): 3-23.

> Focuses on Beowulf's speeches to prove that Anglo-Saxon poets and their audiences admired flowery and highly ornamented language.

Bandy, Stephen C. "*Beowulf:* The Defense of Heorot." *Neophilologus* LVI, No. 1 (January 1972): 86-92.

> Argues that because the Danes are caught sleeping when Grendel attacks they are a symbol of their own moral blindness.

Barnes, Daniel R. "Folktale Morphology and the Structure of *Beowulf*." *Speculum* XLV, No. 3 (July 1970): 416-34.

Applies classic folktale structure to the poem *Beowulf* to prove that it owes its origin to early folktales.

Baum, Paull F. "The *Beowulf* Poet." *Philological Quarterly* XXXIX, No. 4 (October 1960): 389-99.

Examines critical reactions to the difficult language and two-part structure of *Beowulf* while speculating on the nature and intentions of its unknown author.

Benson, Larry D. "The Originality of *Beowulf*." In *The Interpretation of Narrative: Theory and Practice,* edited by Morton W. Bloomfield, pp. 1-43. Cambridge: Harvard University Press, 1970.

Contends that the unknown *Beowulf* poet did not rely heavily or mechanically on earlier sources and is instead a more original author than most critics suggest.

Bjork, Robert E. "Speech as Gift in *Beowulf*." *Speculum* 69, No. 4 (October 1994): 993-1022.

Compares speech-making to gift-giving in *Beowulf,* arguing that each custom is crucial to the health of Danish as well as Geatish society but that both customs ultimately fail.

Brennan, Malcolm M. "Hrothgar's Government." *Journal of English and Germanic Philology* LXXXIV, No. 1 (January 1985): 3-15.

Analyzes the levels of government at work in the poem and how the Geatish Beowulf is processed through the Danish bureaucracy.

Brodeur, Arthur Gilchrist. *The Art of 'Beowulf.'* Berkeley: University of California Press, 1959, 283 p.

A book-length discussion of the poem's diction, setting, action, structure, and style, including an examination of its Christian and pagan elements.

de Looze, Laurence N. "Frame Narratives and Fictionalization: Beowulf as Narrator." *Texas Studies in Literature and Language* 26, No. 2 (Summer 1984): 145-56.

Focuses on the "Father's Lament" (told by Beowulf shortly before he battles the dragon) as the only so-called fictional tale in the poem.

Earl, James W. "Apocalypticism and Mourning in *Beowulf*." *Thought* LVII, No. 226 (September 1982): 362-70.

Approaches *Beowulf* as an "act of cultural mourning" that uses the religious myth of the apocalypse to bid farewell to the pagan heroic world and to replace it with Christian culture.

Florey, Kenneth. "Grendel, Evil, 'Allegory,' and Dramatic Development in *Beowulf*." *Essays in Arts and Sciences* XVII (May 1988): 83-95.

Examines those aspects of the poem's first half which encourage us to interpret the characters at more than face value, so that Grendel stands for "Evil" and Beowulf stands for "Good."

Frank, Roberta. "The *Beowulf* Poet's Sense of History." In *The Wisdom of Poetry: Essays in Early English Literature in*

Honor of Morton W. Bloomfield, edited by Larry D. Benson and Siegfried Wenzel, pp. 53-65. Kalamazoo: Medieval Institute Publications, 1982.

Maintains that the *Beowulf* poet shows an understanding of history by giving a consistent, complex depiction of Scandinavian society circa A. D. 500.

Fry, Donald K., ed. *The 'Beowulf' Poet: A Collection of Critical Essays.* Englewood Cliffs: Prentice-Hall, Inc., 1968, 177 p.

Presents eleven essays by well-known critics on a variety of topics concerning *Beowulf* including diction, point of view, and audience.

Greenfield, Stanley B. "*Beowulf* and Epic Tragedy." *Comparative Literature* XIV, No. 1 (Winter 1962): 91-105.

Discusses the differences between epic tragedy and dramatic tragedy, and explains how *Beowulf* qualifies as an epic tragedy.

————. "A Touch of the Monstrous in the Hero, or Beowulf Re-Marvellized." *English Studies* 63, No. 4 (August 1982): 294-300.

Argues that there is proof in the poem that Beowulf should be regarded as superhuman.

Halverson, John. "*Beowulf* and the Pitfalls of Piety." *University of Toronto Quarterly* XXXV, No. 3 (April 1966): 260-78.

Pursues the debate as to whether or not *Beowulf* is a Christian or pagan poem, pointing out that the god presented in the poem is "not uniquely Christian."

Hansen, Elaine Tuttle. "Hrothgar's 'Sermon' in *Beowulf* as Parental Wisdom." *Anglo-Saxon England* 10 (1982): 53-67.

Argues that Hrothgar's speech, given after Beowulf defeats Grendel's mother, represents fatherly advice that would be considered appropriate by the *Beowulf* poet's audience.

Harris, Anne Leslie. "Hands, Helms, and Heroes: The Role of Proper Names in *Beowulf*." *Neuphilologische Mitteilungen* LXXXIII, No. 4 (1982): 414-21.

Suggests that the *Beowulf* poet used word play to develop some of the poem's themes.

————. "The Vatic Mode in *Beowulf*." *Neophilologus* LXXIV, No. 4 (October 1990): 591-600.

Identifies and discusses the different types of prophecy at work in the poem.

Harris, Joseph. "Beowulf's Last Words." *Speculum* 67, No. 1 (January 1992): 1-32.

Analyzes the structure and impact of Beowulf's dying speech after his battle with the dragon in the final part of the poem and compares it to last words in other epics.

Helder, William. "The Song of Creation in *Beowulf* and the Interpretation of Heorot." *English Studies in Canada* XIII, No. 3 (September 1987): 243-55.

Argues that we are meant to see the building of the Hall of Heorot as symbolic of human goodness rather than of human pride.

Hill, John M. "*Beowulf,* Value, and the Frame of Time." *Modern Language Quarterly* 40, No. 1 (March 1979): 3-16.

Refutes the argument that as a Christian, the *Beowulf* poet distances himself from the pagan world of his hero.

Huffines, Marion Lois. "OE *aglaeca:* Magic and Moral Decline of Monsters and Men." *Semasia* 1 (1974): 71-81.

Speculates on why the Old English word *aglaeca,* the meaning of which involves both terror and magical powers, is applied to men as well as monsters in *Beowulf.*

Irving, Edward B., Jr. "The Nature of Christianity in *Beowulf.*" *Anglo-Saxon England* 13 (1984): 7-21.

Disagrees with the view that the close of the poem amounts to a Christian condemnation of Beowulf's life as a pagan.

————. "What to Do with Old Kings." In *Comparative Research on Oral Traditions: A Memorial for Milman Parry,* edited by John Miles Foley, pp. 259-68. Columbus, Ohio: Slavica Publishers, Inc., 1987.

Looks at the manner in which old age is treated in *Beowulf.*

————. *Rereading 'Beowulf.'* Philadelphia: University of Pennsylvania Press, 1989, 183 p.

Examines the characterization, style, plot, and symbolism of *Beowulf* while emphasizing the oral nature of the poem.

Kahrl, Stanley J. "Feuds in *Beowulf:* A Tragic Necessity?" *Modern Philology* 69, No. 3 (February 1972): 189-98.

Traces the Old English word "feud" as it occurs repeatedly in the poem and discusses its thematic importance.

Kinney, Clare. "The Needs of the Moment: Poetic Foregrounding as a Narrative Device in *Beowulf.*" *Studies in Philology* LXXXII, No. 3 (Summer 1985): 295-314.

Analyzes the effects resulting from the poem's shifts among past, present, and future, as well as between different points of view.

Lawrence, William Witherle. *'Beowulf' and the Epic Tradition.* New York: Hafner Publishing Company, 1963, 349 p.

With a view toward a general audience, Lawrence discusses the subject matter and story-telling traditions which the *Beowulf* poet relied on to compose this heroic tale.

Leyerle, John. "Beowulf the Hero and the King." *Medium Aevum* XXXIV, No. 2 (1965): 89-102.

Explains the "interlace" pattern organizing *Beowulf* into a coherent whole, and follows that pattern to the poem's contradictory major theme.

McNamee, M. B. "*Beowulf*—An Allegory of Salvation?" *Journal of English and Germanic Philology* LIX (1960): 190-207.

Presents the poem as a Christian allegory, with the hero Beowulf functioning as a Christ-like figure.

Moorman, Charles. "Suspense and Foreknowledge in *Beowulf.*" *College English* 15, No. 7 (April 1954): 379-83.

Argues that while the outcome of each of Beowulf's battles is foreshadowed, the *Beowulf* poet's inventive presentation of these fights ensures that no excitement is lost.

Nagler, Michael N. "*Beowulf* in the Context of Myth." In *Old English Literature in Context,* edited by John D. Niles, pp. 143-56. Totowa: Rowman and Littlefield, 1980.

Asserts that *Beowulf* is mythic because it deals with universal mythological themes.

Niles, John D. *'Beowulf': The Poem and Its Tradition.* Cambridge, Mass.: Harvard University Press, 1983, 310 p.

Looks at *Beowulf* as a product of an oral tradition which catered to an aristocratic, Anglo-Saxon audience.

Nist, John. "*Beowulf* and the Classical Epics." *College English* 24, No. 4 (January 1963): 257-62.

Compares *Beowulf* with the *Iliad,* the *Odyssey,* and the *Aeneid* and concludes that the *Beowulf* poet was unfamiliar with the classical epics.

Oetgen, Jerome. "Order and Chaos in the World of *Beowulf.*" *The American Benedictine Review* 29, No. 2 (June 1978): 134-52.

Asserts that the poem's structure, plot, and images reflect a concern with order and chaos as well as the belief that chaos will prevail on earth but not in heaven.

Overing, Gillian R. *Language, Sign, and Gender in 'Beowulf.'* Carbondale: Southern Illinois University Press, 1990, 137 p.

Takes a theoretical and feminist approach to *Beowulf,* with a look at women's roles as "peace-weavers" or resolvers of feuds via marriage.

Pearce, T. M. "Beowulf's Moment of Decision in Heorot." *Tennessee Studies in Literature* XI (1966): 169-76.

Contends that Beowulf makes an accepted, tactical decision to sacrifice his man, Hondscioh, in order to take Grendel by surprise.

Pearsall, Derek. "*Beowulf* and the Anglo-Saxon Poetic Tradition." In his *Old English and Middle English Poetry,* pp. 1-24. London: Routledge & Kegan Paul, Ltd., 1977.

Discusses the poem's history—its background, style, and possible date, and discounts the theory that it was composed orally.

Puhvel, Martin. *"Beowulf" and Celtic Tradition.* Waterloo, Ont.: Wilfrid Laurier University Press, 1979, 142 p.

Compares the poem to Celtic folktales and proposes the theory that the *Beowulf* poet might have been influenced by Celtic literary traditions.

Renoir, Alain. "Point of View and Design for Terror in *Beowulf.*" *Neuphilologische Mitteilungen* LXIII (1962): 154-67.

Asserts that the *Beowulf* poet skillfully used different points of view to make the poem visually exciting for listeners.

————. "Oral-Formulaic Context in *Beowulf:* The Hero on the Beach and the Grendel Episode." In his *A Key to Old Poems: The Oral-Formulaic Approach to the Interpretation of West-Germanic Verse,* pp. 107-32. University Park: The Pennsylvania State University Press, 1988.

Studies examples from the poem to support the suggestion that *Beowulf* was created by someone well-versed in oral composition.

Robinson, Fred C. *'Beowulf' and the Appositive Style.* Knoxville: University of Tennessee Press, 1985, 106 p.

　　Examines the stylistic and thematic ways in which the *Beowulf* poet conceives of "pagan heroic life" through a Christian point of view.

Short, Douglas D. "*Beowulf* and Modern Critical Tradition." In *A Fair Day in the Affections: Literary Essays in Honor of Robert B. White, Jr.,* edited by Jack D. Durant and M. Thomas Hester, pp. 1-23. Raleigh, N. C.: The Winston Press, 1980.

　　Presents an overview of modern editions of *Beowulf* and critical writings on the poem beginning with the late 1920s.

Smithers, G. V. "Destiny and the Heroic Warrior in *Beowulf.*" In *Philological Essays: Studies in Old and Middle English Language and Literature in Honour of Herbert Dean Meritt,* edited by James L. Rosier, pp. 65-81. The Hague: Mouton, 1970.

　　Acknowledging the existence of Christian elements in *Beowulf,* the essay looks at the poem's secular and pagan aspects which function as "submerged layers of meaning."

Tarzia, Wade. "The Hoarding Ritual in Germanic Epic Tradition." *Journal of Folklore Research* 26, No. 2 (May-August 1989): 99-121.

　　Compares archaeological finds with the treasure hoards mentioned in *Beowulf* to draw conclusions about Anglo-Saxon poetry.

Tolkien, J. R. R. "*Beowulf:* The Monsters and the Critics." *Proceedings of the British Academy* XXII (1936): 245-95.

　　Argues that critics have been treating *Beowulf* as a historical document instead of focusing on its merits as a poem.

Wentersdorf, Karl P. "*Beowulf:* The Paganism of Hrothgar's Danes." *Studies in Philology* LXXVIII, No. 5 (Early Winter 1981): 91-119.

　　Attempts to reconcile the pagan and Christian references in *Beowulf.*

Whallon, William. "The Christianity of *Beowulf.*" *Modern Philology* LX, No. 2 (November 1962): 81-94.

　　Argues that the *Beowulf* poet's rudimentary Christian beliefs serve mainly to unify what is principally a set of pagan tales of heroes and monsters.

Williams, David. *Cain and Beowulf: A Study in Secular Allegory.* Toronto: University of Toronto Press, 1982, 119 p.

　　Focuses on the biblical story of Cain as legendary rather than theological in its use by the *Beowulf* poet.

Woolf, Henry Bosley. "On the Characterization of Beowulf." *ELH* 15, No. 2 (June 1948): 85-92.

　　Examines the ways in which the poet successfully delineates Beowulf as heroic.

Additional coverage of Beowulf is contained in the following sources published by Gale Research: *Classical and Medieval Literature Criticism,* **Vol. 1.**

Jorge Luis Borges
1899-1986

(Also wrote with Adolfo Bioy Casares under joint pseudonyms of B. Lynch Davis, H[onorio] Bustos Domecq, and B. Suarez Lynch) Argentine short story writer, essayist, poet, translator, critic, biographer, travel writer, novelist, and scriptwriter.

INTRODUCTION

Borges is best known for his erudite short stories, which blend fantasy and realism to address complex philosophical problems. Involving such thematic motifs as time, infinity, identity, and memory, Borges's stories combine elements of fiction and personal essay in hybrid forms that resist classification. Earlier in his career Borges wrote poetry and criticism almost exclusively. At this time he associated with the Ultraístas, an avant-garde literary group whose works fuse elements of Dadaism, Imagism, and German Expressionism. However, he later broke with the Ultraístas in favor of a more traditional mode of versification. Summarizing contemporary critical thought concerning Borges's poetry, Keith Botsford deemed the Argentine's later poems "among the most skillful and immaculate in Spanish. Strict in their rules and sober in their imagery, gentle in tone, recollected in tranquillity, they are elegiac, formal, symmetrical."

Biographical Information

Borges was born in Buenos Aires, where he lived for most of his childhood. His father, Jorge Guillermo Borges, was a respected lawyer, author, and educator. From an early age, Borges absorbed a wide range of world literature and learned to read English before Spanish due to the influence of his English grandmother. When the Borges family became stranded in Switzerland in 1914 by the advent of World War I, Borges enrolled at the Collège de Genève and received his degree in 1918. In the following year, he traveled to Spain, where he published critical reviews, essays, and poetry, and associated with the avant-garde Ultraístas, whose literary works appeared in the journal *Ultra*. Rejecting the traditional rhymed verse and baroque ornamentalism common to nineteenth-century Spanish poetry, the Ultraístas championed metaphor as a predominant mode of expression and strove in their poetry to transcend boundaries of time and space. Their influence permeates much of Borges's early work, particularly *Fervor de Buenos Aires* (1923), his first poetry collection. Borges returned to Buenos Aires in 1921, and helped launch several noted Argentine publications, including the literary magazine *Prisma* and the journal *Proa*. In the 1920s

Borges continued to focus his attention on poetry, publishing two more volumes of verse, *Luna de enfrente* (1925) and *Cuaderno San Martín* (1929). During this time, Borges, an acclaimed editor and essayist, produced his highly-regarded volumes of early essays, *Inquisiciones* (1925) and *El idioma de los argentinos* (1928).

The following decades witnessed Borges's increasing interest in prose fiction, though he continued to write poetry throughout his life. An itinerant lecturer and teacher in the 1940s, Borges published his short story collection *Ficciones* in 1944; it is generally regarded as his most significant work. In 1955, he was named director of the prestigious National Library of Argentina and later awarded the Premio Nacional de Literatura, the country's highest literary honor. Yet Borges remained largely unknown outside Latin America. In 1961, he and Irish dramatist Samuel Beckett shared the Prix Formentor, an international prize recognizing authors whose work will "have a lasting influence on the development of modern literature"; this achievement helped establish his reputation throughout the world. Beginning in the late 1950s, Borges's eyesight had started to fail.

Although his increasing blindness slowed his literary output, he continued to publish volumes of stories, poetry, and essays. In 1985, Borges was diagnosed with liver cancer. He left Buenos Aires for Geneva, Switzerland, where he married his companion and former student, María Kodama. Three weeks later, at age eighty-seven, he died.

Major Works

Although Borges is best known for his short stories, he wrote a significant amount of poetry, which has gained increasing critical attention. In his first collection, *Fervor de Buenos Aires,* he utilized Ultraíst concepts to portray colorful individuals and events in Buenos Aires. His next volume of poetry, *Luna de enfrente,* contains confessional and love poetry. Both collections are thought to anticipate Borges's later concerns with such topics as time, memory, and the architectural features of Buenos Aires. *Cuaderno San Martín* consists chiefly of tributes to deceased poets, among them Francisco López Merino, Borges's friend and associate, who committed suicide.

In his later poetry, Borges adopted a neoclassic approach, availing himself of the poetic elements of rhyme and meter discarded by the avant-garde poets. Moreover, he applied some of the principles used in his prose, such as intertexual reference and the articulation of the whole. *El hacedor* (1960; *Dreamtigers*), a collection of brief poems, quotations, and parables, uses the tiger as an ambivalent symbol of unnatural evil and natural change. In the title poem of *Elogio de la sombra* (1969; *In Praise of Darkness*) Borges proposed the paradoxical notion that old age and blindness may signify deep happiness because of the imminence of death. Dualities involving physical blindness and spiritual sight also pervade *El oro de los tigres* (1972; *The Gold of Tigers*).

Critical Reception

A prolific writer in many and mixed genres, Borges is recognized as one of the most influential and innovative Latin American authors of the twentieth century. His experiments with the intermingling of fantasy and realistic detail presaged the realist style of writing practiced by such major Latin American authors as Gabriel García Marquez and Julio Cortázar; the latter writer referred to Borges as "the leading figure of our fantastic literature." His insights into the nature of learning, literature, and the fictive process have established him as one of modern literature's most philosophically accomplished authors. Although Borges has largely been recognized for the stylistic originality of his essays and the metaphysical experimentation of his short fiction, critics have also frequently praised his poetic works for their formal precision and mellifluous tone.

PRINCIPAL WORKS

Poetry

Fervor de Buenos Aires　1923
Luna de enfrente　1925
Cuaderno San Martín　1929
Poemas, 1923-1943　1943
Poemas, 1923-1953　1954
Poemas, 1923-1958　1958
El hacedor [*Dreamtigers*] (poetry and prose)　1960
Obra poética, 1923-1964　1964
Para las seis cuerdas　1965
Obra poética, 1923-1966　1966
Obra poética, 1923-1967 [*Selected Poems, 1923-1967*]　1967
Elogio de la sombra [*In Praise of Darkness*]　1969
El otro, el mismo　1969
El oro de los tigres [*The Gold of Tigers*]　1972
Siete poemas sajones / Seven Saxon Poems　1974
La rosa profunda　1975
La moneda de hierro　1976
The Gold of Tigers: Selected Later Poems　1977
Historia de la noche　1977
La cifra　1981
Los conjurados　1985

Other Major Works

Inquisiciones (essays)　1925
El tamaño de mi esperanza (essays)　1926
El idioma de los argentinos [with Jose Edmundo Clemente] (essays)　1928
Evaristo Carriego [*Evaristo Carriego: A Book About Old Time Buenos Aires*] (biography)　1930
Discusión (essays and reviews)　1932
Historia universal de la infamia [*A Universal History of Infamy*] (short stories)　1935
Historia de la eternidad (essay)　1936
El jardin de senderos que se bifurcan (short stories)　1941
Seis problemas para Isidro Parodi [*Six Problems for Don Isidro Parodi*; with Adolfo Bioy Casares, under pseudonym H. Bustos Domecq] (short stories)　1942
Ficciones [*Fictions*] (short stories)　1944
Dos fantasías memorables [with Adolfo Bioy Casares, under pseudonym H. Bustos Domecq] (short stories)　1946
Un modelo para la muerte [with Adolfo Bioy Casares, under pseudonym B. Suarez Lynch] (novel)　1946
Nueva refutacion del tiempo (essay)　1947
El Aleph [*The Aleph and Other Stories, 1933-1969*] (short stories)　1949
Aspectos de la literatura gauchesca (essay)　1950
Antiguas literaturas germánicas [with Delia Ingenieros] (essay)　1951
La muerte y la brújula (short stories)　1951
Otras inquisiciones [*Other Inquisitions, 1937-1952*] (essays)　1952

El Martín Fierro [with Margarita Guerrero] (essay)
1953

Obras completas. 10 vols. (prose and poetry) 1953-67

La hermana de Eloísa [with Luisa Mercedes Levinson]
(short stories) 1955

Leopoldo Lugones [with Bettina Edelberg] (essay) 1955

Los orilleros. El paraíso de los creyentes [with Adolfo
Bioy Casares] (screenplays) 1955

Manual de zoología fantástica [*The Imaginary Zoo*;
with Margarita Guerrero; also published as *The Book
of Imaginary Beings*] (essays) 1957

Cuentos (short stories) 1958

La poesía gauchesca [with Adolfo Bioy Casares] (essays) 1960

Antología personal [*A Personal Anthology*] (prose and
poetry) 1961

Labyrinths: Selected Stories and Other Writings (short
stories and essays) 1962

Introducción a la literatura inglesa [*An Introduction
to English Literature*; with María Esther Vázquez]
(essay) 1965

Crónicas de Bustos Domecq [*Chronicles of Bustos
Domecq*; with Adolfo Bioy Casares] (short stories)
1967

Nueva antología personal (prose and poetry) 1968

Dialogo con Borges (interviews) 1969

El informe de Brodie [*Dr. Brodie's Report*] (short
stories) 1970

El Congreso [*The Congress*] (short story) 1971

Introducción a la literatura norteamericana [*An Introduction to American Literature*; with Esther Zemborain de Torres] (essay) 1971

Borges on Writing (lectures) 1973

Les Autres: Escenario original [with Adolfo Bioy
Casares and Hugo Santiago] (screenplay) 1974

El libro de arena [*The Book of Sand*] (short stories)
1975

Prólogos (essays) 1975

Qué es el budismo? [*What is Buddhism?*; with Alicia
Jurado] (essay) 1976

Nuevos cuentos de Bustos Domecq [with Adolfo Bioy
Casares] (short stories) 1977

Rosa y azul (short stories) 1977

Borges oral (lectures) 1979

Obras completas en colaboración [with others] (short
stories, essays, screenplays, and novel) 1979

Narraciones (short stories) 1980

Siete noches [*Seven Nights*] (lectures) 1980

Borges: A Reader (prose and poetry) 1981

Nuevos ensayos dantescos (essays) 1982

*Veinticinco agosto 1983 y otros cuentos de Jorges Luis
Borges* (short stories and interview) 1983

Atlas [*Atlas*; with María Kodama] (prose and poetry)
1984

Ficcionario: Una antología de sus textos (short stories) 1985

En voz de Borges (interviews) 1986

Libro de dialogos (interviews) 1986

*Textos cautivos: Ensayos y reseñas en 'El Hogar' 1936-
1939* (essays and reviews) 1986

El aleph borgiano (reviews) 1987

Biblioteca personal: Prologos (essays) 1988

CRITICISM

David William Foster   (essay date 1962)

SOURCE: "Borges and Dis-Reality: An Introduction to
His Poetry," in *Hispania,* Vol. XLV, No. 4, December,
1962, pp. 625-29.

[*In the following essay, Foster argues that Borges creates an atmosphere of "dis-reality" in* Fervor de Buenos Aires, *which transcends the ordinary boundaries
of time and space.*]

> No habrá sino recuerdos
>
> . . . . .
>
> como parte de una Realidad innegable.

Reality and ir-reality are common words in our daily
vocabulary. However, in the realm of art, there are not
two "realities," but three. The other is a "dis-reality," a
type of atmosphere created in which both reality, what is
verisimile, and ir-reality, what is fantasy, are partaken of.

This paper will attempt to discuss *Fervor de Buenos Aires,*
an early work of Borges, as an example of extremely
localized poetry (Buenos Aires), but possessing a style
which makes use of elements of dis-reality. We want
to consider as a basis for our discussion Anderson Imbert's comment: "'Reducción de la lírica a su elemento
primordial: la metáfora' había sido su primera fórmula"
[E. Anderson Imbert, *Historia de la Literatura hispan-
oamericana,* 1957]. The first poem of this collection,
"Las Calles," [*Fervor de Buenos Aires*] fittingly employs a metaphorical image to preface the poems which
follow:

> Hacia los cuatro puntos cardinales
> se van desplegando como banderas las calles;
> Ojalá en mis versos enhiestos
> vuelen esas banderas.

Anderson Imbert goes on to celebrate the fact that the
poet does not quite realize his intent in this and subsequent books of poetry. So be it; we may still be permitted
the examination of the devices which he does use and the
extent to which he employs them. But going beyond this
one book of poetry, it is necessary for the critic to discuss as separate entities the metaphysical ideas which
Borges expresses. In order to do this, we shall refer to a
volume of short stories, *El Aleph,* which appeared in 1949
and which represents more or less a synthesis and a depu-
ration of Borges' concepts, now fully matured, which
appear in the poetry and which in the short stories are
made into fictional narrations.

The metaphysical elements which constitute Borges' poetry are Time, Space and Consciousness. In *Fervor de
Buenos Aires* we are localized within a fixed time-space

boundary, but the poet soars off on tangents, which, like complex geometrical creations, raise the subject matter to third, fourth and fifth dimensional planes.

> Son aledaños suyos tiempo y espacio
> son arrabales de alma
> con las herramientas y son las manos del alma
> y en desbaratándose está,
> juntamente caducan el espacio, el tiempo, elmorir,
> como al cesar la luz
> se acalla el simulacro de los espejos.

"La luz" is, of course, mental and physical consciousness, as the cessation of light ending the continuing reflection and re-reflection of mirrors, so does death and the continuum of human consciousness. These verses point out a very common poetic and metaphysical device: the labyrinth. These labyrinths are a manifestation of the poet's belief in a "fifth" dimension—a continuing circle of existence which by nature of its essential indestructibility transcends the bounds of Time and Space. The synthesis of this belief is to be found in his short story "El immortal." With particular reference to the poetry, the belief and employment of a transcending essence raises the "local" themes of Buenos Aires to a much higher level of importance. Such a "trick" may be accused of shallowness and may be criticized as the bringing of sophomoric philosophies into poetry. This may be a valid criticism, for a philosopher. However, as poetry, what is important is the degree to which the poet succeeds in using his elements to create a vivid impression and an enlightening vision. Through recourse to the poetry, we may examine these labyrinthal metaphors.

> En supremo aislamiento
> cada árbol está conmovedoramente perdido
> y son sus vidas tan incomunicadas y hurañas
>
> . . . . .
>
> cual espejos que profundizen habitaciones distantes
> o como el soñar de muchos durmientes
> que reúne idéntico techo.

The labyrinth is established in these lines by the mirrors which give profundity. One mirror alone lacks the ability to create depth, but several mirrors face to face echo and re-echo a vision to unrecognizable and hence profounder extents. The metaphor, with relation to the trees, is particularly effective, for we have all been fascinated by the reflecting qualities of two mirrors: "Sirena / La eternidad espera en la encrucijada de estrellas." Here, the "crossroads of the stars" seems to hold a secret for eternity which eternity, in turn, waits on. The canvas of stars appears on a clear night as a complex of dots—a labyrinth. In this way the concept of a secret of eternity locked in a maze of dots is familiar and reappears in Borges' work "La escritura del Dios," in which the configurations on a tiger's back hold the key to the universe. There is an element of surrealism inherent in this concept—the hypnotization induced by the configuration, either of stars or lines producing *from the subconscious* a new vision or reality. But Borges never carries his images or metaphys-

ical suggestions this far and continues to function in a realm of dis-reality, the realm of the transcendent metaphor.

> La llamarada salta y disporrotea.
> . . . Yo paso junto a la llama; yo escucho
> lo que quiere proclamar su lengua de
> fuego, . . . doy palabras y voz a lo que
> susurra esa llama.

The poet feels in this passage that he is able to decipher the flame's message, the flame whose burning and movements also have a compelling and hypnotic effect and whose existence seems to carry a meaning behind and beyond its physical presence. It is the penetration into the flame's meaning and profundities which gives rise to the labyrinthal metaphor in this case.

In a sense, the whole pattern of Buenos Aires forms a complex for the poet. His sense of aloneness, discussed further on, and the effect which the mere walking of the city's streets, tracing the complexes, has upon him tend to make one believe that all of this is a labyrinth and his poetry is his attempt to capture the essence and mood of the city by deciphering each object's meaning and significance—the part each component plays in the complete form:

> Quizá esa hora única
> aventajaba con prestigio la calle
> dándole privilegios de ternura
> haciéndola real como una leyenda o un verso:
> lo cierto es que la sentí lejanamente cercana
> como recuerdo que si parece llegar cansado de lejos
> es porque viene de la propia hondura del alma.

I have discussed the labyrinths and given a few examples to show how these metaphors give a deeper meaning to the images than would a superficial reality.

The dis-reality of Space furnishes the poetry of ***Fervor de Buenos Aires*** with one of its principal elements. In poetry we often find the element of Space restricted to a real fixed point, which with the union of all points forms the totality of the universe. Or one finds, on the other hand, a complete disregard for spatial localization, in which case we have the "eternal" or "heavenly" or "universal" or such emotion—emotions and images which possess no localization. In this poetry we have the dis-real element of spatial intensification introduced. By this it is meant that a point or locale becomes intensified to the degree that it moves beyond its union with the other points of the universe and assumes either a primordial position or a bimundial position. The primordial position is called an "Aleph" and is evidenced in the story called "El Aleph": "Aclaró que un Aleph es uno de los puntos del espacio que contienen todos los puntos." The bimundial position is a point which exists simultaneously in two realms of consciousness (cf. "The Crystal Egg" by H. G. Wells).

Clearly, Buenos Aires itself represents a primordial point in Space: "La ciudad está en mí como un poema . . ."

What is within knows no spatial boundaries, and becomes important as an ego-centric object. Or note, the "Aleph" quality which the poet evokes with his patio scenes:

> Patio, cielo encauzado.
> El patio es la ventana
> por donde Dios mira las almas.
> El patio es el declive
> por el cual se derrama el cielo en la casa.

or

> Los patios agarenos
> llenos de ancestralidad y eficacia,
> Pues están cimentados
> en las dos casas más primordiales que existen:
> en la tierra y el cielo.

Many of the poems' images have a final quality, such as "en el Juicio Final de cada tarde!" This finality arises from a suprareal situation, as the fixed point (Buenos Aires and the poet's vision) which represents all points (the conscious universe and the totality of the poet's experience). Thus a single event is a total event.

Much more complex and extensive is the dis-reality of Time, which either stands still and is primordial, or which refuses to stop and is universal (and must therefore again be primordial). "Quizá es hora única" expresses the idea of a moment in time being unique—time for the poet seems to either stand still or be removed from reality in order to allow him to contemplate his vision, and he goes on to say: "la sentí lejanamente cercana." This oxymoron completely establishes this dis-reality.

Time also is conceived of with a labyrinthal metaphor, as in this verse fragment: ". . . por las malezas del tiempo." Time is indeed a "thicket" to the poet, a complex which has no real value: "va poblando el tiempo usurpado." Time as an infinite repertoire of possibilities is expressed in these lines: "La causa verdadera / es la sospecha universal y borrosa / de las metafísicas posiblidades del Tiempo." One of the "metaphysical possibilities" is observed in this statement:

> (Al salir vi en un alboroto de niñas
> una chiquilla tan linda
> que mis miradas en seguida buscaron
> la conjetural hermana mayor
> que abreviando las prolijidades del tiempo
> lograse en hermosura quieta y morena
> la belleza colmada
> que balbuceaba la primera).

Here we observe both Time and Space dis-reality functions. In the first place, the child plays a role in two worlds, having her location through two points in Time-Space—she is a vision of "la primera." In order to accomplish this, the poet must succeed in "abreviando las prolijidades del tiempo." And finally, by being picked out of "un alboroto de niñas," the poet catches her as a pri-

mordial vision—the focal point of his perspective even though seemingly confused in a group.

Time can be used in a metaphor in which it is devoid of meaning and importance just because it *is* "real" time: "cuyo reloj austero derrama / un tiempo ya sin aventuras ni asombro / sobre la lastimosa blancura." The comment that this is time "ya sin aventuras" implies that there is a time "con aventuras": the Time which we have examined above.

We arrive now at the final and most extensive element of dis-reality—Consciousness. Consciousness is manifested in four ways: 1) Nihil novum sub sole—man and events are reflections of men and events which have preceded them—life is seen as a dynamic continuum interrupted only by the various failures to recognize this, i.e., individual existences; 2) Consciousness of man and Consciousness of God, two opposing forces; 3) Being and un-being, the former failing to have a recognizable existence, since man in general is unaware of the eternity of existence, and 4) All of which in turn depend upon the elements of Time/Space dis-reality. Borges' interesting view of Consciousness is summarized in "El inmortal": "Encarados así, todos nuestros actos son justos, pero también son indiferentes. No hay méritos morales o intelectuales. Homero compuso la Odisea; postulado un plazo infinito, con infinitas circunstancias y cambios, lo imposible es no componer, siquiera una vez, la Odisea. Nadie es todos los hombres. Como Cornelio Agrippa, soy dios, soy héroe, soy filósofo, soy demonio y soy mundo, lo cual es una fatigosa manera de decir que no soy." Experience is eternal and man lacks singular existence from too much essence. Turning again, as we always must, to the poetry, we see these impressions emerging vividly:

> Nos place la quietud
> equivocamos tal paz de vida con el morir
> y mientras creemos anhelar el no-ser
> lanzamos jaculatorias a la vida apacible.

How can we "anhelar el no-ser"—destroy a lack of existence. Clearly we can't, as well as we are not able to become individuals entirely—we belong to a past that is eternal, as the "nina del alboroto" above.

"Sólo el vivir existe." Life is eternal. This is not to be taken in a Christian sense, in which the soul lives on either in punishment or in reward, but as an expression of a life-continuity which is not unakin to the Hindu concept of transmigration:

> Ahí estaban las causas y los efectos y me
> bastaba ver esa Rueda (ef. the Hindu "wheel
> of life") para entenderlo todo, sin fin.
>   (La escritura de Dios)
> alma mía que se desparrama por corazones y calles,
> fuera milagro que alguna vez dejaran de ser,
> milagro incomprensible, ináudito
> aunque su presunta repetición abarque con grave
>   horror la existencia.

Dead they may be; yet they exist still! "Quejambre mora / bordeando oscuramente ambas eternidades / del cielo gigantesco y delas leonadas arenas." We have seen the eternity of both the earth and the sky established in the labyrinthal metaphors introduced above. "Pueda persistir algo en nosotros inmóvil," expresses well enough the concept of an essence before and after the individual consciousness; it is "la maciza realidad primordial." One can see these ideas matured and brought to an excellent narrative-life in "Historia del Guerrero y de la cautiva," whence: "Comprendió que un destino no es mejor que otro, pero que todo hombre debe acatar el que lleva adentro." Or, in this poetry: ". . . cuando tú mismo eres la continuación realizada / de quienes no alcanzaron su tiempo / y serán otros a su vez tu inmortalidad en la tierra." Observe in this quote the confusion of living and dead; and the perpetuation of all until "El último dios . . . el último día."

> Hoy el olvido borra su censo de muertes,
> pues que son parciales los crímenes
> si los cotejamos con la fechoría de Tiempo,
> esa inmortalidad infatigable
> que anonada con silenciosa culpa las tazas
> y en cuya herida siempre abierta
> que el último dios habrá de restañar [;] el último día
> cabe toda la sangre derramada.

And, a dead man is not just a dead man, but a personification of death. "Inconmensurable, abstracto, casi divino / desbaratadas las tarduras del ser, / el muerto ya no es un muerto: es la muerte." Therefore, the poet arrives at his reality through the dis-reality of these visions: "Ya casi no soy nadie, / soy tan sólo un anhelo / que se pierde en la tarde." And he feels the tenuous experience of life:

> No hay más que una sola tarde
> la única tarde de siempre
>
>   . . . . .
>
> hora amanecer en que le sería fácil a Dios
> matar del todo la amortiguada existencia.

Our wandering through the labyrinths of Time and Space, through mazes of Reality and Dis-reality have brought us to our ultimate task—that of making a final value judgement of this style and setting. If one believes that the purpose of poetry is the continual search and development of devices to evoke the eternal qualities of life, Borges will assume an undeniably great place in poetry. He has chosen tenuous perhaps even absurd metaphysical devices and images to raise the reader above the banality of Reality towards a Supra-reality of the essence of Being. Although he has centered *Fervor de Buenos Aires* around strictly local themes, his elements of dis-reality penetrate their commonplaceness to bring out hidden values and to cause them, literally, to transcend the bounds of Time and Space. Borges' poetic style is, as we have amply seen, built on a series of often complex and bewildering metaphors; but, like the Baroque writers, whom he so closely resembles, his obfuscation of reality is not an end in itself which could become a rhetorical toy, but

rather a means of achieving a higher reality, the essense of human experience. As he says:

> perseveraremos con ensalzadas minucias,
> levantados a divinidad, trasmutados,
> pero inmutablemente individuales,
>
>   . . . . .
>
> como parte de una innegable Realidad.

John C. Murchison   (essay date 1972)

SOURCE: "The Greater Voice: On the Poetry of Jorge Luis Borges," in *Prose for Borges,* edited by Charles Newman and Mary Kinzie, Northwestern University Press, 1972, pp. 256-66.

[*In the following essay, Murchison argues that Borges's poetic voice is at once humble and intended to be the voice of the eternal creator.*]

Not much has been written about Borges' poetry in Spanish, and still less in English. [This article was written for publication in 1970. Since then, of course, Seymour Lawrence has brought out a splendid edition, *Jorge Luis Borges: Selected Poems 1923-1969* (New York, 1971), to which I refer the reader.] Borges himself has done a fair job of belittling his own production, dismissing most of it with a sad, slightly contemptuous gesture; but it is this very depreciation that illuminates certain aspects of his poetry. We cannot, after all, lightly gloss over Borges' poetic production; that privilege may be his but not ours, since the poetry itself looms large in his work, and steadily. His first book of poems, *Fervor de Buenos Aires* (*Fervor of Buenos Aires*), was published in 1923, shortly after his return from Europe; his latest, a mixture of prose and verse—like the earlier *El hacedor* (*The Maker*) [Published in English as *Dreamtigers.*]—*Elogio de la sombra* (*In Praise of Darkness*), appeared in 1969. Over the intervening forty-six years, several others appeared—*Luna de enfrente* (*Moon across the Way*), *Cuaderno San Martín* (*San Martín Copybook*), *El otro, el mismo* (*The Self and the Other*), *Para las seis cuerdas* (*For the Guitar*)—well over two hundred poems, and Borges is still going strong. For a writer who professes to be no more than a versifier, such zeal in versifying seems suspect. One can legitimately claim that Borges is, in fact, being too modest in his own appraisal, and even a cursory glance at the poems is enough to convince one that here is a rich terrain indeed, and virtually unexplored.

But Borges' modesty is a major clue to understanding his poetry. It is a peculiar modesty, grounded not only in character but also in metaphysics. Time and again, Borges has stated that he would like to be remembered as the creator of a few good lines; even in his own terms, this, as we shall see, is asking a great deal.

Borges' fictions very often are, in effect, parables of the creative process, its possibilities and limitations. Stories—

meditations—on the writing of stories, they deal at heart with the power of the word to capture and re-create a reality which might be termed "objective" when it lies within. This, which may seem no more than a quibbling way to speak about "reality" and "fantasy," nevertheless reflects a vital point; for Borges, *both* are equally real. If "the fantastic" seems a quality inseparable from Borges, it is owing precisely to the fact that fantasy is as real to him, as immediate and pervasive, as a blade of grass is to Whitman.

The problem, then, lies in using words in order to re-create an ambient state, whether objective or subjective. For that re-creation to be effected, the *anima* becomes the decisive factor, the telling element without which the re-creation is stillborn. And the search for that *anima,* that spirit, is what moves Borges, and brings him at last to the realization that the spirit, not the poet, is the creator of the living lines. The potential of enormous power lies within the word, and thus poetry, dealing more closely even than prose with the power of words, has always been a predominant mode of expression for Borges. [Between 1929 and 1943, it is true, Borges wrote exactly five poems; but considering the fourteen-year gap, the extent of his poetic output is all the more remarkable.] Indeed, so vital is poetry to Borges that even in the earliest poems we come across the idea of poetry as an all-encompassing phenomenon which antedates the poem and culls from it some of that poetry, while at the same time making the poet aware of the encompassing existence of Poetry. Tacitly, these poems reflect a Platonic idea of Poetry as an archetype from which all poems derive, and are thereafter more or less perfect reflections of the whole; though never quite perfect, since by their nature they are limited in time and space, in opposition to the archetype which necessarily transcends these limitations. The heart of the matter—what Borges is *about*—lies in the adjustment of the poem to Poetry, in the transcendence of the work of man, and thus of man himself. In the splendid, early **"Vanilocuencia"** (**"Vain Words"**), from *Fervor de Buenos Aires,* Borges says:

> The city is within me like a poem
> I've not been able to catch in words.
> > [Unless otherwise credited, all translations
> > are by the author and are from Borges'
> > ***Obra poética 1923-1967.***]

Seen within this context, his love for that city, for Buenos Aires, grows beyond the proportions of the parochial; the city is a surrounding symbol of Poetry, an endless spatial dimension which indeed spontaneously brings the endless temporal dimension—and the concomitant awareness of a limited self on the part of the poet—into play:

> On one hand, the exception of a few lines;
> on the other, cornering them,
> life hastens over time
> like a terror
> overtaking the soul.

The City, as a felt presence, is seen as an intimation of Poetry, and it is the latter, more than Buenos Aires itself,

which is the subject of the poem. This helps to explain why, in a book ostensibly dedicated to Buenos Aires, we surprisingly come across a poem to **"Benares,"** in which Borges writes about a city as distant and unreal as Samarkand. The poem sings that city into being for us, and, as in **"Vain Words,"** the City—the Poetry—is richer than the poem:

> And to think that,
> while I play with uncertain metaphors,
> the city I sing, lives. . . .

The difference between the two poems lies in the attempt—in **"Benares"**—to re-create imaginatively a place unseen. It is striving, in fact, to conquer the limitations of the senses, of the realization—brought about in **"Vain Words"** by the perception of an encompassing reality—of the self bound in time and space. But in the appeal to fantasy, more clearly limitless than objective reality, the attempt to translate the mind's intimation of extensional continuity into a poem brings about equally the consciousness of the limited self as the manipulator of limited means—of words which, because tied to Borges, coming from him, are caught, as is he, in the net of time and space.

Just as **"Benares,"** the deprecated conjuring of an unknown city, claims a logical place in *Fervor de Buenos Aires,* so does **"Forjadura"** (**"The Forging"**), a poem on the imminence of fervor, of mastery. Here, the attempt itself is the key to the poem and its subject. In comparison with **"Vain Words"** and **"Benares," "The Forging"** seems exultant, with the poet as a giver of life:

> . . . to the sower of words
> night is land lying fallow.

There is good reason for the underlying optimism. While the poem meditates on the ability to give life—Poetry—to words, it is also a love poem, written by a young man. For that young man, no higher praise can be found for the woman he loves than to admit that his love for her allows him to achieve what he has so often sought in vain.

In **"Forjadura,"** in the forging of language, we also notice the seed of another idea—that of the poem as a thing somehow apart from the poet himself, a maverick, unwilling if not unable to express the poet's sense of Poetry. The creator has to contend now with his creation, which differs from himself. In **"Jactancia de quietud"** (**"Gladly Still"**) from *Luna de enfrente,* the idea is clearly expressed.

> I ask my verse not to contradict me, and that is a
> great deal.

At bottom, this is again a preoccupation with the word as a tool by essence unfit to do the job it must. Timebound, spatially circumscribed, words cannot succeed in reproducing that which, by definition, is limitless. At his best, then, the poet manages to do no more than allude. Still, the attempt to do more than simply allude is an urgent necessity and, as such, becomes a central issue in Borges' poetry. In another poem, in a later book, *El otro, el mismo (The Self and the Other)*, Borges will try to capture that elusive reality, free from all bounds, by stalking a single object. The success of **"The Other Tiger,"** perhaps Borges' best known poem, may be partially explained as that same single-minded search for just one splendid iota of reality. Because everything else is sacrificed to the quest, the quest itself—the quest for "the other tiger, the one beyond the poem"—becomes crucially problematic. Morris' "And the craft that createth a semblance . . . ," which Borges uses as the epigraph for the poem, thus acquires poignant meaning. In **"The Other Tiger,"** there is an almost desperate attempt to re-create reality, not merely to set down its verbal semblance. The three stanzas invoke three tigers: each is different from the preceding in degree, and each is the cause of the next. The first is the poet's tiger, his imagination at work. The second is born of the knowledge that the first is a false re-creation, and constitutes a search for the "real" tiger; the third tiger, barely mentioned, finally, is the "other" tiger, the real animal which is brought to our collective inner eye as readers, while, paradoxically, its occurrence in the poem again traps it in the world of craft and semblance, in the world of words—a flawless poem about the failure of the poet, himself flawed in his ability to re-create a flawless reality.

Sensing the imperfection of words, and knowing that they are his only tools, the only link between his intimation of a total reality (whether objective or fantastic) and its expression, leads Borges to despair of his own work, and from despairing to disparagement. The awareness of the conflict between an essentially infinite vision and its essentially finite expression involves the awareness of the risks he must take in order to overcome the limitations of his means. Since the conflict stems from the need to reduce the timeless and spatially infinite vision of Poetry to words, Borges is impelled to attempt, in every poem, something he knows beforehand to be impossible—the task of freeing the word from the warp and woof of time and space, the net in which he himself, through pondering his creations, feels caught. What makes the risk enormous is that in every instance Borges, clearly sensing the infinite in the shape of Poetry, is forced to face his own felt mortality, his own lonely finitude.

Not surprisingly, at times he seems almost unwilling to assume creative responsibility. As if wishing to maintain some sort of distance between himself and his creations, with their reminders of mortality, he quotes FitzGerald as a measure of self-effacement in the epigraph of his third book, *Cuaderno San Martín (San Martín Copybook)*:

> As to an occasional copy of verses, there are few men who have leisure to read, and are possessed of any music in their souls, who are not capable of versifying on some ten or twelve occasions during their natural lives: at a proper conjunction of the stars. There is no harm in taking advantage of such occasions.

The book was published in 1929; by that time, Borges had found his poetic voice in a grave, resonant, baroque song. It dovetailed exactly with his strongly metaphysical themes, which began to undergo a series of complex variations. These variations deal with the ways—ingenious, pathetic, comic, tragic—in which men have tried to use their highest intelligence to avoid the trap of time and space. Beyond the aesthetic pleasure derived from examining these intellectual constructs, Borges feels the nobility of their vision, along with their admixture of vain hope and useless courage. A fine example of this struggle to be rid of limits is found in **"The Cyclical Night,"** from *The Self and the Other.* Here the organ-like words ring every change, in a harmonious fugue which seems stolen from a greater harmony, and indeed refers to it. Here is the City as an elusive symbol of words frozen into stone:

> This, here, is Buenos Aires. Time, which brings
> Either love or money to men, hands on to me
> Only this withered rose, this empty tracery
> Of streets with names recurring from the past
> In my blood. . . .
>
> $\qquad\qquad\qquad\qquad\qquad\qquad$ (*SP, 79*)

And at the end of the poem, the endless hope: the poem, like the city, and rising from its contemplation, seems to be saved from the ravages of time by time itself, repeating, cyclical—like the poem:

> It returns, the hollow dark of Anaxagoras;
> In my human flesh, eternity keeps recurring
> And the memory, or plan, of an endless poem
> $\quad$ beginning:
> "They knew it, the fervent pupils of Pythagoras . . ."
>
> $\qquad\qquad\qquad\qquad\qquad\qquad$ (*SP,* 81)

The last verse repeats the first, in an attempt to merge the eternal with the temporal, in an effort to equate Poetry with the poem, and thus to save it.

But these are, after all, only technical representations of the games so dear to Borges, which toy with mankind's "elegant hopes." On a deeper level, the poem itself, as a mass of words, must become a bulwark against ravaging time. For that to happen, the old distinction between the thing and its verbal symbol, between *res* and *signum,* must cease. The distinction is temporal in essence: words are tied to time, to the temporal consciousness of their speaker. Things, on the other hand, being free from the consciousness that inhibits, partake of the Infinite, and so are beyond the words that so imperfectly represent them. Borges is well aware of this lack of adjustment between the two.

In **"Matthew XXV: 30,"** another of the poems—again from *The Self and the Other*—that have come to constitute his "canon," Borges says:

> From the unseen horizon
> And from the very center of my being,
> An infinite voice pronounced these things—

Things, not words. This is my feeble translation,
Time-bound, of what was a single limitless Word:

"Stars, bread, libraries of East and West,
Playing cards, chessboards, galleries, skylights, cellars,
A human body to walk with on the earth,
Fingernails, growing at nighttime and in death,
Shadows for forgetting, mirrors busily multiplying,
Cascades in music, gentlest of all time's shapes,
Borders of Brazil, Uruguay, horses and mornings,
A bronze weight, a copy of the Grettir Saga,
Algebra and fire, the charge at Junín in your blood,
Days more crowded than Balzac, scent of the
  honeysuckle,
Love and the imminence of love and intolerable
  remembering,
Dreams like buried treasure, generous luck,
And memory itself, where a glance can make men
  dizzy—
All this was given to you and with it
The ancient nourishment of heroes—
Treachery, defeat, humiliation.
In vain have oceans been squandered on you, in vain
The sun, wonderfully seen through Whitman's eyes.
You have used up the years and they have used up
  you,
And still, and still, you have not written the poem."

                                                          (*SP*, 93)

Several things are to be noticed here. The first is the very title of the poem, referring to the biblical verse "And cast ye the unprofitable servant into outer darkness: there shall be weeping and gnashing of teeth." We will examine this more closely in due course. Another is the conjunction of the two visions of infinity mentioned earlier—that of an objective reality, and fantasy, or subjective reality. Another oddity is the sounding of a voice—the voice implied in the epigraph. And finally, we begin to see why "chaotic catalogues" are so dear to Borges: they are catalogues of *things,* shorn, insofar as possible, from any context which might tie them down to *words.* As such, in fact, they are the least imperfect reflections of a limitless reality. Their very mention provides an intimation of infinity, and a refuge from temporality. In **"Poema del cuarto elemento" ("Poem of the Fourth Element")**—also from *The Self and the Other,* Borges addresses water the way others would a god—namely, as a savior:

Water, I beseech you. By this vague
Web of numerical words I speak,
Remember Borges, your swimmer, your friend.
Fail not my lips at the end.

These intimations of the Infinite given through the contemplation of things, of objects devoid of their verbal representations as far as possible, posit the question, as we see in "Matthew," of a greater voice than the poet's, "an infinite voice" which is able to transcend the human voice—and its concomitant limitations—against which Borges' poetry struggles. In a sense, the new presence of a greater voice is a form of belief hard won at the end of

despair. Time after time in Borges' cosmogony, a voice emerges from long and painful meditation—verbal meditation on his mortality. In **"Matthew,"** this severing of tonalities produces almost shy references to the poet who sees himself as the "unprofitable servant," the translator of another and greater voice. But in his very next poem, **"Compass,"** the pathos of such modesty, such insufficiency, has become secondary to the strong voice of adherence—Borges is now more the advocate, the priest:

All things are words of some strange tongue, in thrall
To Someone, Something, who both day and night
Proceeds in endless gibberish to write
The history of the world. . . .

                                                          (*SP*, 97)

Here, the sight of an object leads the poet to meditate on the word for it, on its *signum,* and from there to the idea of a Writer, from whom "all things are words." In this context, the word triumphs over temporal and spatial limitations, since it is uttered by a speaker who is beyond them.

Thus the belief that things, when they are the words of a greater voice, provide salvation from the threat of time leads to the larger question, and the unanswerable one: Who is able to utter that word? In **"Compass,"** it is "Someone, something"; not quite the recognition of a theological deity, the statement paves the way for such a recognition's coming about. In no sense, however, is this an approach to religious, or orthodox, faith. Rather it reflects Borges' passionate involvement with words—the beginning of the poet's faith, not that of the priest. It is true that the "infinite voice" of "Matthew" implies the voice of God in the traditional Judeo-Christian sense; but it is the concept of God as a semantic term—as the Word, simply—devoid of its theological attributes.

The poet, then, creates the poem, but not its endurance, since both creator and creation are bound in time; what persists of the poem is Poetry, imposed on the poem by a Greater Voice, in whom are intertwined the attributes of deity (the essence of creative will and power) and the absence of human limitations. Borges, wishing with apparent modesty to be remembered "for a few good lines," is, in fact, wishing to equate himself with the creative godhead, not so much out of pride as out of love for Poetry. For himself, and for his fellow poets, he claims no more than the meager role of amanuensis. In **"El otro" ("The Other One")** he bluntly states that

The pityless, nameless god gives
His chosen tool to his chosen few. . . .
His is what remains in the memory
Of man. Ours the rubble.

When we explore Borges' road to his Greater Voice, we skirt dangerous ground. Borges' reputation as an ironclad agnostic precedes him and seems incompatible with any idea remotely similar to the orthodox Judeo-Christian belief in God. Still, as has been suggested earlier, Borges' faith in the Word springs from his faith in the power of

Poetry as a web of words, and to that must be added his passion for our common Hebraic tradition and its Christian revitalization. In some ways, Borges' approach to his Greater Voice bears close parallels to mysticism, in the sense of union between the soul ("the very center of my being") and the infinite ("the unseen horizon"), so that coming face to face with God is, in the deepest sense, an awareness of self. It is fitting, then, that in his latest published work of poetry, *Elogio de la sombra* (*In Praise of Darkness*), all these factors should unite in an extraordinary poem, **"John I: 14."** The biblical title, as in the case of **"Matthew,"** and its reference ("And the Word was made flesh . . ." are telling. All the themes which have appeared dispersed in other poems are presented here in a single, humble, and humbling statement. The strains between creator and creation; the awareness of the eternal—and, with it, of our own sorry temporality—leading to the realization that at best we are not truly creators, but creatures translating as best we can, into our own dimension, a larger harmony of ineffable Spirit; the concrete presence of that Spirit itself, in true poetic Eucharist—all blend to integrate this complex work. Slowly the reader is made aware of the identity of the speaker, who is God Himself:

> This page will be no less a riddle
> than those of My holy books
>
> . . . . .
>
> I who am the Was, the Is, and the Is To Come
> again condescend to the written word,
> which is time in succession and no more than an
>   emblem.

[This and the following excerpts are from the
translation by Norman Thomas di Giovanni published
in *The New Yorker*, February 12, 1972]

And Borges goes on to describe—again the "chaotic list"—the wonderment of the Word made flesh:

> I knew memory,
> that coin that's never twice the same
>
> . . . . .
>
> I knew wakefulness, sleep, dreams,
> ignorance, the flesh,
> reason's roundabout labyrinths,
> the friendship of men,
> the blind devotion of dogs.

He also describes the Word's human bewilderment at the variety of his own creation:

> My eyes saw what they had never seen—
> night and its many stars.
> I knew things smooth and gritty, uneven and rough,
> the taste of honey and apple,
> water in the throat of thirst,
> the weight of metal in the hand,
> the human voice, the sound of footsteps on the grass,
> the smell of rain in Galilee,
> the cry of birds on high.

These verses indicate how far Borges has come along his own road leading toward the admission of a Greater Voice in the creation of Poetry. There is a tacit and very noble theory of poetry imbedded in these lines—that the poet does no more than set down, as best he can, the voice of the Spirit. But Borges does it with supreme success, managing to communicate to the reader not simply *what* he believes but *how* he believes. As we have earlier felt and shared his anguish when confronted by the disparity between his vision of infinity and the limited means at his disposal with which to render it faithfully, now we are able to share, also, his calm humility; and this enables us as it does him:

> I have entrusted the writing of these words
>   to a common man;
> they will never be what I want to say
> but only their shadow.
> These signs are dropped from My eternity.
> Let someone else write the poem, not he who
>   is now its scribe.

The New York Review of Books (review date 1974)

SOURCE: A Review of *In Praise of Darkness*, in *The New York Review of Books*, Vol. XXI, No. 5, April 4, 1974, p. 44.

[*In the following review, the unsigned critic responds to the idiosyncratic imagination of Borges's poetry in* In Praise of Darkness.]

Borges is the modern poet who best expresses not the power of the imagination but the seductiveness of the imaginative intellect, not one who evokes emotion raw or lyrical on the page but one who offers a highly idiosyncratic consciousness just prior to the awakening of an emotion or just after the emotion has passed. Immediacy has always been lacking in his works. And yet the world of Borges has its own majesty, its own penetrating cadences and charm, full of spheres within spheres, thought about thought, a parabolic shadow play continually unfolding, doubling back, and then returning (to use one of Borges's persistent motifs) like a river to its unimaginable source.

In Borges, of course, there can be no release from these cyclic modes of consciousness: "I think (what I have thought before) / that this winter holds in it all winters past, / back to those of the elders who wrote / that our way is marked out, / that we already belong to Love or to Fire." So when he tells us that "perhaps universal history is the history of a few metaphors," he is really describing his own sparse particular art, his meditative way of eliciting the illusion of freedom or chance from among the iron-bound laws of time, his lonely eloquent way of celebrating the labyrinth that is man's fate.

If these new poems have a certain twilit convalescent air, recording Borges's familiar fascination with mirrors and mazes, to which have been added two new themes, "old age and ethics," they nevertheless have the beauty of faded cameos, of museums of shifting forms, as well as Borges's poignant, stoical apprehension of his approaching death: "I reach my center, / my algebra and my key. . . . Soon I shall know who I am."

Willis Barnstone   (review date 1974)

SOURCE: A review of *In Praise of Darkness*, in *The New York Times Book Review*, Section 7, August 11, 1974, pp. 6-7.

[*In the following review, Barnstone offers a positive assessment of* In Praise of Darkness.]

Like Miguel de Cervantes, about whom he often writes, the Argentine Jorge Luis Borges sees himself primarily as a poet. But Cervantes's quixotic notion of being a great poet was wrong, for the Spaniard's verses are largely mannered imitations in the Italian style and meter of the other Golden Age poets. Conversely, Borges, known largely for his *ficciones,* has now published his fifth volume of poems [titled **In Praise of Darkness**], a unified sequence of profound observations about people and things, dreams and darkness, showing that Borges, in giving primacy to poetry, is right. Yet with typical shiftiness, Borges also claims there is really no difference between his *ficciones* and his poems, that anyway he would "like to be remembered less as a poet than as a friend," that he too "dislikes them [the poems]," and finally, reversing himself, he speaks about "the book which in the end may justify [him]."

"Poetry is no less a mystery than anything else on earth," he writes ambiguously in his introduction, and so he includes among the poems some forms of prose, asking us to read the volume as a volume of poems. In itself the book is nothing, a thing among things; and the esthetic act, he says, occurs only when it is written or read. The reader controls the latter. Borges likes to shift from one perplexity to another, to what he calls "his mysterious habit," to what "we call metaphysics." In **In Praise of Darkness** (*Elogio de la sombra*) the blind Argentine master of historical spoof, exotic violence, of mirrors, labyrinths and the circular ruins that lead us to the border of knowledge, has again taken us to the instant of recognition—where he stops, stationing us in mystery, in order to save us from false knowledge. As in all Borges, the events outside are a whimsical journey to the paradox of self-discovery. In speaking of the Gauchos, he writes:

> They lived out their lives as in a dream, without
>   knowing who they were or what they were.
> Maybe the case is the same for us all.

This latest book by Borges is unified and dominated by darkness and sight, with often an ecclesiastic note as he recreates Heraclitus or the Apostle John or fragments from an apocryphal gospel. Borges is blind and therefore sees everywhere. Yet his is not an Isaiahan vision of heaven and destruction, and when he speaks through biblical figures it is as if he were talking to an old Argentine friend over a cup of *maté.* Indeed, he slips through historical and imaginary time periods in such a way as to prove that man is always man, always alone, caught in the beast of his body, the labyrinth, while living out the dream or illusion of a vision beyond the labyrinth. In the poem **"May 20, 1928,"** he takes us into the eyes of the young poet Francisco López Merino, about to commit suicide, as he looks at his double in the mirror and tries to reach and to understand the other side of darkness:

> He will go down to the lavatory. There, on the
>   chessboard-patterned floor tiles, water will
>   wash the blood away quite soon. The mirror
>   awaits him.
>
> He will smooth back his hair, adjust his tie (as
>   fits a young poet, he was always a bit of a
>   dandy) and try to imagine that the other man—
>   the one in the mirror—performs the actions and
>   that he, the double, repeats them. His hand will
>   not falter at the end. Obediently, magically, he
>   will have pressed the weapon to his head.
>
> It was in this way, I suppose, that things
>   happened.

Borges's sight extends even into what he calls *las cosas,* plain things. All the things we remember or forget, "a file, an atlas, doorways, nails, the glass / from which we drink—serve us like silent slaves." Because these things are sightless "they will live on / familiar, blind, not knowing we have gone." Clearly the elegiac theme pervades the volume. So in the manner of Simonides, he writes poems of historical praise for Israel, tracing the Jew from Eden through the Book of the cabalists, the death chambers and the battlefield. He praises his native city of Buenos Aires with the morbidity of a Palatine epigrammist:

> It's a certain corner of Jeru Street,
> where Julio César Dabove told us
> that the worst sin a man can commit
> is to father a son and sentence him
> to this unbearable life.

And above all, as in the earlier famous **"The Maker,"** where he roams through the vision of the blind poet Homer, he sees old age as a time of happiness, a coin shining under rain, and possibility. This is not resignation or silly euphoria but rather the last steps toward his search. Like Constantine Cavafy in "Ithaka," he tells us in his apocryphal gospel to seek the pleasure of seeking, not of finding. The title poem **"In Praise of Darkness"** brings us to the edge:

> Old age (this is the name that others give it)
> may prove a time of happiness.
> The animal is dead or nearly dead; man and soul
>   go on . . .
> To think, Democritus tore out his eyes; time has
>   been my Democritus.

This growing dark is slow and brings no pain;
it flows along an easy slope and is akin to
eternity.

Old age has led men to write impossibly conflicting documents. In "De Senectute" Cicero argued tediously and proved the value of old age because a Roman senator himself carries the distinction of *senex* (old man) in his title. Yeats raged as a deprived sensualist while Cavafy simply erased age's sterility by re-creating in poems a real or imaginary past. Vicente Aleixandre speaks with the bitter authority of a poet whose word and vision acquire sharper pathos as he confronts oblivion. Borges speaks with several voices. His blindness, as he states in many earlier works, has prepared him for the vision of darkness, for the uncertainty of waking to dream or of dreaming of nothing. Death may be violent in the act, but it holds no terror for him. He affirms that he (or we) know nothing certain while we are alive. Possibility of knowledge lies only where there is no where and when there is no when. He has lived with

Emerson, and snow, and so many things.
Now I can forget them. I reach my center,
my algebra and my key,
my mirror.
Soon I shall know who I am.

This last verse in the volume is Borges's one line of prophecy. For the reader who wants to overhear secrets, the poet is again elusive, like the ultimate knowledge he seeks; he does not have it yet, and, moreover, when he does it will belong to him alone, for he will be dead. Although Borges has again escaped, giving us "a symbol or something we are about to understand, but never quite do," we are convinced, at last, that his *elogio* (praise) is real, and that one day we will be the speaker in the poem.

The translation of the book is by Norman Thomas di Giovanni in collaboration with the author (except for one poem translated by John Updike). As in other skillful translations by this team, one cannot really speak of loss but of transformation. Borges's fiction and poems work equally well in Spanish and English, and the reader need not fear disparities. In some cases, Borges tells us, he has modified the Spanish original as a result of the kind of reading demanded by the act of translation. The last two poems, including the title poem, were translated back into Spanish from the English draft.

Borges is a clever metaphysician who has given us an enormous and varied literature, ranging from re-creations of an ancient Chinese "Book Guardian" to the characteristics of imaginary beasts. His influence on younger generations, in many countries, is pervasive. Although the Royal Swedish Academy failed to give its award to the blind Homer, and failed again in the case of Cervantes (though here Borges has carefully preserved the maimed author of the "Quijote"), there is no reason for further delay in regard to the sightless Argentine. Let the Academy awake and redeem itself.

H. Ernest Lewald with Jorge Luis Borges (interview date 1974)

SOURCE: "Borges: His Recent Poetry," in *Chasqui,* Vol. IV, No. 1, November, 1974, pp. 19-33.

[*In the following interview, Lewald and Borges discuss several common themes in Borges's poetry.*]

[H. Ernest Lewald]: *In this interview I would like to ask a few questions about certain themes that I feel recur in your poetry . . .*

[J. L. Borges]: Go ahead.

I shall name just a few and then I'll just ask about seven specific questions.

Seven is the magic number, no?

Maybe.

Yes, there are seven planets, seven days of the week . . .

Right.

Seven wonders of the world . . .

And I think according to Aristotle man becomes mature at 49, but it's just a game.

It's a game; the same with us. People say that Adam was born at the age of 33 in order to identify him with the second Adam, no? Christ. They also draw a parallel between the Cross and the Tree of the Knowledge of good and evil.

Well, the themes I have would be these: the cult of courage, Nordic spell, the remembrance of forefathers, and a zeitgeist of Buenos Aires; and there are three new themes that I have seen in your last collections.

Let's go over them one by one. Now the first one . . .

The first one would be what I consider the cult of courage; that there exists a fascination for the opposite.

Well, I think it came from the fact that many of my forefathers were soldiers. For example, my great-grandfather won the Battle of Junín. Then he fought the gauchos of Rosas whose cousin he was. Afterwards he fought in the war of Brazil. My grandfather died in action way back in 1874 and four years previously he married an English lady and they lived on the border of western civilization in the town of Junín . . . So there was a military tradition in the family . . . of course, I knew my eyesight was defective since my father, my maternal grandmother, and my great-grandfather, Dr. Edward N. Haslan, died blind. So that I knew that blindness was awaiting me at the end of the road. But still at home and around I was seeing all those pictures of my military forefathers and swords and things of that kind. For example, when I was young—

when I was a boy—in Buenos Aires the worship of courage was very common. But nowadays . . . nobody dreams of asking whether he's a brave man or not. But in those days among the first things to be said about somebody was whether this person was brave or not. And not only by the hoodlums but also by the gentlemen. For example, I remember it was held against Rosas that he was a coward; it was held against General Roca; well, he wasn't as much as he might have been, but nowadays people hardly think of those things.

Yes, but now what about the gaucho as a hoodlum? You once talked to me several years ago about Martín Fierro being nothing but a hoodlum. Now the gaucho as such; wouldn't he also be included in the cult of courage—because you do have poems dedicated to gauchos?

Well, yes, but in the case of Martín Fierro, I don't think that Martín Fierro should be a typical gaucho at all. Of course, after all, he was a soldier. He went over to the Indians because he was not paid what he should be paid. Then he became a killer, a hoodlum, but I don't think most of the gauchos were like him. Nor were the Indians part of our history at all. I can understand, let's say, the kind of cult of the Indians in other parts of Latin America. Let's understand that they had a culture of their own. But here the Pampa Indian and the Araucans were really barbarians who could only count up to four. They counted this way; well, as I told you, my grandmother told me: "I'll teach you the whole of Pampa Indian mathematics." I stared at her; I was but a child, and I said, "I don't think that I will understand it." "Oh, yes," she said, "you will." And she held up her hand and then she began counting, "One, two, three, four, many."

Now, how about the orillero; *you have written stories like "El hombre de la esquina rosada" set in the Buenos Aires of 1900. Are these people now, outside of courage, are they admirable in any way? Do you just feel attracted to them because of their courage?*

Well, since then they have died out, I think.

Oh, yes; but I mean . . . you can still feel attracted to them?

Yes, but in a wistful way; a wistful way because . . . well, I knew many of them personally. I can tell you one thing about them. You see, they were not thieves; they despised pimps. They were poor men, who, of course, had no religion whatever. And so they had in a sense to build their own kind of religion and that religion was, let's say, the cult of being brave, for a man, being able to fight anybody else, and it was being able to do it with a knife and not with firearms. Firearms, they stand for marksmanship and not for courage. When you are fighting a duel with another man and you have only a knife then it's not enough to be skillful . . . you must be brave to do it. For example, the idea of a man killing someone by surprise or killing somebody with a revolver, that would be beyond the code. The fighting had to be done in equal circumstances and

there was even a word for a man who took advantage of somebody and suddenly killed him. That word was—wait a bit, there were two words, *pegadores* and *ventajeros.* A brave man was supposed to do the whole thing in a slow way to give his adversary the opportunity of having it out with him. For if somebody jumped on somebody else and killed him, then people would label him as being a coward.

Now, let me cite you one of your recent poems, "Tankas," in which you lament "No haber caído como otros de mi sangre en la batalla."

I wrote that as a kind of exercise, no?, versifying after the Japanese fashion, no? But, of course, nothing of myself. I think of the many people of my blood who fell in action.

Would you have liked to have had a destiny, I mean, emotionally, of a similar kind?

Yes, and you will find that in many of my stories also.

"El sur," I would say; wouldn't that be an example?

Yes, because in "El sur" I am implying all the time that the whole thing is a dream. The man died under the knife during liberation and then afterwards he had a dream of a kind of death he would like to have. The man stands for myself. For my people have *estancias* in the north of Buenos Aires. I have seen them. They are breeding Aberdeen Angus cattle now. Well, when this man had his *estancia* in the south some of my people were English, and this man came of German stock; so, in a sense, all the circumstances are worked in on purpose.

Now you seem to have a genuine love for what I would call Nordic essence. Could that be a parallel for a sort of a yearning that comes from placing action above thought when you mention "la espada del sajón" or "del danés," Morris' Völsunga Saga, "el oro de Sigurd"?

Yes, and I can give you proof of that. My Saturdays are dedicated to the study of Old English.

I knew that the last time we met you were studying Old English.

And now I am also going in on Sundays, I'm going in for the study of Old Norse, of Icelandic, those are kindred tongues—Old English and Icelandic. In English there are many Scandinavian words. I don't know if you know that the word "sky" is a Scandinavian word; the word "law"; the word "ill"; the word "tick" for example. The Saxons had *neman* akin to the German *namen.*

Then you do feel an affinity for the epic spirit?

For the epic spirit, yes. I think the epic spirit is found both in Old English and in Old Norse literature. For example, if you think in terms of Old English literature—

what?—think of Beowulf, in fact it is all over and you can find it anywhere in the sagas.

Do you think there is somehow a yearning in you that might be parallel to the cult of courage because the dramatic mythology did allow for the warrior to be picked up by the Valkyrie?

Yes, and in Old Norse *Valkyrie* means "the chosen of the slave."

Now in some of your old poems like **"Dulcia Linquimus Arva"** *and . . .*

That was a long time ago so I don't have to feel guilty about this.

Your collections from the 1920's like **Fervor de Buenos Aires** *shows a sort of zeitgeist that's rooted in, on, let's say, the time of Evaristo Carriego and the porteño milieu of 1910.*

Well, I knew Evaristo Carriego personally because he used to come to dinner with us every Sunday; and he knew many of those hoodlums personally also because they all lived in the neighborhood.

Yes, but you show a great love for Buenos Aires—the simple streets that you used to walk, a theme that even repeats in the poem "Buenos Aires" that has not been written too long ago. Is there a continuity or is there a change in your view of the Buenos Aires that is, of course, gone, that no longer exists except in your mind?

Well, I think I must surely feel that this country is going to the dogs, no? In 1910 or thereabouts when Buenos Aires was quite a small city we felt the city to be a growing city, no? While today we feel that things are going from bad to worse, no? Because believe it or not, this country was a fine country way back in 1910. But today, of course, with weak governments or even bad governments, and even governments for the sake of dictatorship and so on, that people are in a hopeless mood but most of all they're downcast. Of course, many people think that's the kind of thing we shouldn't say, but after all, I think I owe you my personal sincerity, no?

Right, and it's for export only, anyhow. Well, let me talk now briefly about the new themes that I have seen in your poetry and . . .

I wonder if you have seen my last book called ***El oro de los tigres***?

Yes, I have it right here . . .

That's the last piece I wrote. Then I've written some half a dozen stories, but I won't be publishing them until the book comes out next year. Then there'll be, let's say, some ten stories and some quite long.

Who will publish this book?

The publishers will be as usual Emecé.

Now the next theme I have is that of the Doppelgänger *which appeared in "Borges y yo" and now in "El centinela" and . . .*

And then I have written another story in this book called "El otro" where I have taken the same subject. Of course, that concept—it is common to most nations. I think in Scotland and Ireland they call the *Doppelgänger* the "fetch" because you see yourself and then you've come to fetch yourself, no? And you find your way into death. I think that is used by Cicero in the sense of the friend being an *alter ego*. Another self, it may have spun from the same magic idea, don't you think so?

It might. Now what I would . . .

Alter ego, no? Another self that's, of course, to be used in the sense of a friend being an *alter ego*. But suppose that the phrase *alter ego* were the common form and really stood for something like the Celtic "fetch" or the German *Doppelgänger,* no?

The critics today have devised a new term; that is to say, there are two types of doubles—the Jekyll and Hyde split personality and the autoscopic double which means the one who criticizes the other part of himself as you seem to do in **"El centinela."** *You take a very harsh position toward yourself.*

Yes, I do. Of course, that subject was chosen in a sense by Oscar Wilde—I think of *The Picture of Dorian Gray*—and of course there was Jekyll and Hyde and I think there was a story by Henry James called *The Private Life*—about a man leading a public and a private life and being two men really, no?

Could you say anything personal about what dictated your writing of **"El centinela"** *since you do talk, for instance, about "esclavitud" and about "el otro me impone su memoria" and . . .*

Yes, I think it comes really from a feeling I have every morning on waking up. Because when you're asleep . . . then, well, you're everything, nothing, everybody, nobody, and so on. Then when you wake up you find that you're tied down to being . . . well, to being somebody in particular who will be sorting memories linked to him and sorting duties to fulfill that day and assorted things. I have that feeling every morning. Now I was talking to a lady friend of mine and she told me that every morning when she woke up she felt that way. She said she felt "What a pity . . . now I am So-and-so once more."

But in this poem you do seem to play roles, I mean we all play roles, and you seem to feel it so much this time.

Yes, and I think that you will also find the idea of a double . . . well, many times over . . . in the poetry of William Butler Yeats.

How about the very last line that will get us to the next question. That is what I would call a confrontation with age or even with death . . . When you talk about "la puerta del suicide está abierta" but that you will be there on the other side. That's pretty grim.

Yes, it is grim, but if I remember the poem rightly, and I may be wrong for all that I know; I don't think I said that. I said that the theologians say I find myself . . .

Oh, yes. "Afirman que en la sombra ulterior del otro reino estaré yo, esperándome"; but to me that means that suicide would not be feasible because you would be there on the other side.

Yes, of course.

Now would you want to find yourself or would you not want to find yourself in a future life?

No, because I really wanted to die utterly, let's say now I hope to die wholly.

Would you like to be somebody else? We all do . . . I know I would like to be somebody else.

Yes, I would. If I were somebody else I would just be somebody else . . . and I want to be . . . myself, for example, no?

*To continue this topic, you wrote something in **"El triste"** about "El resignado ejercicio del verso no te salva." Is there any special reason?*

I wrote that poem, well . . . I was generally an amateur with a woman, no? And I was thinking that whenever you love and the love is unanswered then in that case all things are felt to be useless. Of course, they aren't really useless, but you feel they are useless, at least for the moment.

*Yes. Now, as to the title **"H. O.";** does it stand for anything and, if so, would you mind telling what it stands for?*

From *El oro de los tigres?*

*Yes, where it says: "Esa piedra quiero, de dos fechas abstractas y de olvido." The poem is called **"H. O."***

Well, these are not really the initials but they stand for the initials of a lady but I didn't want to be asked an indiscreet question or even to trouble her, no?

I understand.

So I used initials—well, of course, she knows, I suppose, that she's present in the poem that I'm speaking of, but the initials are not the real ones, of course. Because then I would be giving the whole thing away, no?

But as I interpret this line it does have to do with the death wish, is that right?

Of course, of course. There is the tombstone, the dates.

Well, I just want to make sure because critics read too many things into writers.

Well, why shouldn't they, no?

Yes, but I feel . . .

The writers are truly grateful to them, no? Reading things into one's work, no? It's a thing the Germans call *Hineinlesung,* to read into something.

Or Nachempfindung, *verbally, "to feel after the writer."*

Yes, that's it.

Well, this gets us actually to the next to the last theme which is that of the eternal female that appears more and more in your later poetry.

As one gets older, one thinks more and more about women, no? Especially, when one has been unhappily married and separated. And so on.

There is always the aging Faust and Goethe saying: "Das ewig Weibliche zieht uns hinan," the lure of the eternal female.

Yes, as George Bernard Shaw said, the idea was driving us all the time and getting us nowhere.

*Yes, well, in **"Lo perdido"** you have, for instance, the line: "Pienso también en esa compañera que me esperaba y que tal vez me espera"—would this be symbolic of or be directed to a certain person?*

No. Those things are aimed at somebody who, I am sorry to say, is hardly interested in the subject.

Well, this happens to most of us.

When a nephew of mine was engaged and then the girl told him that she was in love with somebody else, well, I said this belongs to every man's life, no? For example, all of us have fallen off a horse, no? That's part of the Argentine biography, no? Who has not fallen off a horse or a bicycle or has been crossed in love? Of course, when it happens it is pretty grim.

*Yes, you have a poem called **"El amenazado"** that I confess is one poem that is very difficult; it's very intriguing . . .*

It's not intriguing at all; it's a very outspoken poem.

Yes, but it starts, for instance, "Tendré que ocultarme o huir."

Yes, I was a newlywed; I was in love with her; I was hopelessly in love, no? So that I said to myself: well, what can I do now? I merely have to take myself and run away, hide myself, and forget all about it.

You also say "la hermosa máscara ha cambiado pero siempre es la única." Would this refer to the woman or to something else?

No. It is a personal fact that the mask changes; the woman's face changes. But what you feel about it is essentially the same. It is really the mask that changes.

You mean the woman's appearance?

No, no. I'm just saying that you fall in love with a lady whose name happens to be A, and another B, another C, and another D, another E, and so on, but you feel the same way about them. What changes is the mask, you know?

Well, you would have then sort of a symbol of womanhood that's the eternal female more than any one given person that would represent the grand amour as the French would certainly call it.

Yes, I see it, of course. That's what I'm saying in so many words. The lovely mask changes, but only the mask. But the way you feel about it is the same.

That would also tie in with the very end of the poem "El amenazado": "Me duele una mujer en todo el cuerpo."

Yes, exactly.

That would be woman, the eternal female?

No. No, in the end I'm referring to a particular "H. O." of the poem.

A particular person?

Yes, a person.

What we have left is to talk about two symbols. You elaborate on the symbol of gold and of tigers. Is there any special attraction that you feel toward these recurring symbols? They are powerful symbols and, of course, they have been used before in literature.

Of course, "Tiger, Tiger, burning bright," and so on.

Exactly. And Darío has used the gold in many ways.

I suppose he has, and all poets have.

Yes, yes. You use it often in the sense of "el oro triste" or "el or cansado."

In the sense of the sun that sets, no? The sun sets and you find gold all over. A lot of it. You also find it in Old English poetry—you also find gold. How does it run? "Mod Godes glaed modnesse." I mean "glaed-mod," I

mean in a glad mood referring to warriors and "briht gold" and gold bright and shining with gold; "gold-beorht," gold bright, all the same worlds. As to the use of "Tiger" in the title of the poem, when I was a boy I used to go and watch the tigers in the zoo. And now my sight is failing me because I'm almost blind, and I can make out light—I can make out windows—I can make out darkness; I can make out, let's see, white colors; I can't make out your face. But the one color left to me is yellow.

The gold of the sun in a sense like sun—gold as an archetypal symbol.

Yes, I call the book *El oro de los tigres* and explain that in the very last poem. For the first color I spoke of was yellow. Now the one color left to me is yellow. Because, for example, if I see something red, I'm not quite sure if it's really red or blue or brown or green. But yellow stands out being the most vivid of all colors or at least a certain kind of yellow.

It's a life-giving color, of course. And as such it is important to you because you have the interplay of life in shades and gold.

Yes.

Well, I think the tape has just about run out. I thank you very much.

Nancy B. Mandlove (essay date 1980)

SOURCE: "Chess and Mirrors: Form as Metaphor in Three Sonnets of Jorge Luis Borges," in *Kentucky Romance Quarterly,* Vol. 27, No. 3, 1980, pp. 289-98.

[*In the following essay, Mandlove explores Borges's use of archetypal patterns in his sonnets "Ajedrez I," "Ajedrez II," and "A un poeta del siglo XIII."*]

> "To the Looking-glass world it was Alice that said,
> 'I've a sceptre in hand, I've a crown on my head;
> Let the Looking-glass creatures, whatever they be,
> Come and dine with the Red Queen, the White
>   Queen and me!'"
>
> Lewis Carroll

The mirror appears frequently in Borges' work as a symbolic representation of the infinite multiplication and repetition of human experience. In his short stories, Borges often uses mirrors and mirror images to show that human nature endlessly repeats itself, that a single character exists in both the past and in the future, or that he exists simultaneously in places widely remote from each other. The mirror image in the short stories generally serves to reflect and support the theme of the work. A very different use of the mirror image appears in much of Borges' more recent poetry, where the form of the poem itself becomes a mirror which captures and reflects the infinite variety of human experience. Through the image of the mirror, form becomes metaphor; the structure of the poem points beyond itself to the structure of human existence.

Critics Guillermo Sucre and Zunilda Gertel have both emphasized the fact that Borges turns away from the visionary images and free verse of the early *ultraísta* period (1918-1929) in favor of traditional, timeless metaphors and conventional poetic forms in the later work (1958 to the present). According to Sucre: "el poeta, para él [Borges], es aquél que busca secretamente los arquetipos, las formas esenciales; aquél que busca un orden superior de la que la obra sea un símbolo y donde el azar se vea cada vez más reducido" [*Borges, el poeta*]. The more recent poetry of Borges is then, a search for forms, for forms which reveal a superior order, the order of the universe itself. The work becomes symbolic of a higher order because Borges uses archetypal images and metaphors within conventional poetic forms in such a way that both the formal structure and the content of the poems reflect the same basic structural pattern of human existence. The archetypal content of the poems is a metaphorical representation of a higher order. The form of the poems, too, becomes metaphorical through the image of the mirror. Ana María Barrenechea has observed that the mirror image in Borges' work alludes to "the Gnostic idea that the universe is an inverted copy of the celestial order" [*Borges: The Labyrinth Make,* trans, Robert Lima, 1965]. Functioning like a mirror, the formal structure of the poem directly reflects a greater structure, that of the universal order. Thus one finds in Borges' work not just a harmony of form and content, but poems in which both form and content are parallel vehicles of a metaphor in which the tenor is the greater, universal structure. The poems produce an ever expanding pattern of reflections, mirror images into which the reader too, is drawn, recognizing himself as part of the pattern, as one of the multiple reflections in the mirror of the poem. As Borges notes in "Arte poética:" "A veces en las tardes una cara Nos mira desde el fondo de un espejo; / El arte debe ser como ese espejo / Que nos revela nuestra propia cara."

It is Borges' use of the sonnet which, as the most ordered and conventional of poetic forms, best illustrates the way in which form becomes metaphor. In a sonnet entitled **"A un poeta del siglo XIII,"** Borges suggests that the sonnet form—the structure of the sonnet—is archetypal, that it is not the result of trial and error, of an arbitrary arrangement of quatrains and tercets on the part of the great poet Petrarch, but rather the reflection of a divinely revealed archetypal structure. The sonnet form itself is a mirror, a metaphor reflecting another, greater structure.

Vuelve a mirar los arduos borradores
De aquel primer soneto innominado,
La página arbitraria en que ha mezclado
Tercetos y cuartetos pecadores.

Lima con lenta pluma sus rigores

Y se detiene. Acaso le ha llegado
Del porvenir y de su horror sagrado
Un rumor de remotos ruiseñores.

¿Habrá sentido que no estaba solo
Y que el arcano, el increíble Apolo
Le había revelado un arquetipo,

Un ávido cristal que apresaría
Cuanto la noche cierra o abre el día:
Dédalo, laberinto, enigma, Edipo?

In the first stanza, before the original sonneteer has finished his poem, it appears that the composition of the sonnet is a matter to be determined by the creative power of the poet as he labors meticulously over his work. The random arrangement of tercets and quatrains indicated by the words *arbitraria* and *mezclado* suggests that the poet is seeking the proper form for his expression through an act of his own creative will. However, in the second stanza, when he suddenly discovers the precise combination of stanzas for the sonnet, what were once "tercetos y cuartetos pecadores" now seem to be distant and timeless echoes of a dimly intuited sacred form.

In the first tercet Borges speculates on the possibility that the random pattern selected by Petrarch for the sonnet is not a matter of chance or freely determined creative activity, but the recognition of a greater, archetypal, pattern older than poetry. He associates the revelation of the form with Apollo, god of beauty, law, civilization and supreme authority in matters of ritual [Apollo "is often associated with the higher developments of civilization, approving codes of law. . . . In matters of ritual especially purification, his oracles are commonly regarded as the supreme authority" (*The Oxford Classical Dictionary,* ed. N. G. L. Hammond and H. H. Scullard, 2nd ed., 1970], suggesting that the form itself is, in some way, a reflection of an Ideal structure, a structure basic to human civilization which acquires ritualistic dimension through its repetition in diverse areas of man's endeavor.

In the last stanza, Borges compares the form to a mirror which both contains and reflects "cuanto la noche cierra o abre el día." The form captures and contains all the possibilities of human existence, the dark, evil, malevolent as well as the enlightened; at the same time, it serves as a direct formal reflection of those polar opposites because it too is part of the same pattern. The last line of the poem mirrors the four part structure of the sonnet and incorporates the opposites introduced in the preceding line by "noche" and "día." It begins with Dedalus, the archetypal representative of man's highest aspirations, and ends with Oedipus, symbolic of man's deepest anguish. In the middle is the form—a labyrinth, a mysterious mixture of chaos and order, a puzzle. The sonnet is a formal structure which mirrors another, greater formal structure, whose pattern is known, but whose meaning remains an enigma. The form is a mirror image of its content and, as the content may comprise the full spectrum of human existence, the structure of the sonnet, according to Borges, is a microcosmic reflection of the structure of the macrocosm. The form becomes a metaphor linking the lesser world with the greater world.

In two sonnets dedicated to the subject of chess, Borges expands and elaborates the concept of the sonnet as an archetypal pattern which mirrors the structure of man's existence. In these two sonnets, the mirror image is not presented directly, but is created through formal patterns which are mirror images of each other. The black and white pattern of the chessboard becomes the background for a cosmic game in which man is both player and pawn. In **"Ajedrez I"** the sonnet structure reflects the structure of the chess game, creating a pattern within a pattern. Metaphorical structure mirrors metaphorical content.

En su grave rincón, los jugadores
Rigen las lentas piezas. El tablero
Los demora hasta el alba en su severo
Ambito en que se odian dos colores.

Adentro irradian mágicos rigores
Las formas: torre homérica, ligero
Caballo, armada reina, rey postrero,
Oblicuo alfil y peones agresores.

Cuando los jugadores se hayan ido,
Cuando el tiempo los haya consumido,
Ciertamente no habrá cesado el rito.

En el oriente se encendió esta guerra
Cuyo anfiteatro es hoy toda la tierra.
Como el otro, este juego es infinito.

The first stanza of this sonnet sets the stage for the interplay of opposing forces which gives form to both sonnets. The setting in which the chess game takes place is stripped of all but the essential details. It is completely impersonal, formal and almost abstract. The game takes place in a "grave rincón," a "severo ámbito." The adjectives "grave" and "severo" lend formal dignity to the game, while the noun "rincón," the place where the nameless players sit, reflects the square shape of the chessboard. Neither the players nor the pieces are named in this stanza. The game proceeds almost mechanically according to strict, logical rules, without haste or emotion. When night falls and the game is suspended, the pieces are frozen, motionless and trapped in their fixed pattern until the game continues. The last line of the stanza ("ámbito en que se odian dos colores") is both abstract and impersonal, yet charged with tension and emotion. The two sides of the game are reduced to pure antithesis, black against white, which implies the opposition of all opposing forces. At the same time, the verb "odiarse" makes the antagonism between them something personal and emotional which is then not confined to the two opposing factions, but spreads out to dominate the entire atmosphere in which the struggle takes place.

While the first stanza presents the exterior, logical, rational nature of chess, the second stanza elaborates the interior, irrational logic which operates within the game. The chessmen on the board are subject to a rigorous set of rules which govern their moves and appear to be of a formal, logical nature and yet behind that logic there are irrational, mysterious forces at work. The figures on the board are not pieces now but forms, a change which raises them from mere markers in a game to the level of archetype. Each form is named and modified to correspond to its function in the game, according each one a character of its own.

In the tercets, Borges moves away from the temporal and specific into the realm of the eternal. The chess game is a ritual, a rite symbolizing the perpetual struggle between opposing forces. The last stanza links chess, a game of war to the greater game, the microcosm to the macrocosm, for "el oriente" refers both to the Eastern origins of chess and to the dawn of man and civilization. The world is now a chessboard and the game is infinite.

In **"Ajedrez I"** Borges presents the game of chess as an archetypal conflict between opposing forces by reducing the game to an essential pattern of forms in opposition, black versus white. He locates that pattern within another archetypal pattern, the sonnet, which is a direct reflection, a mirror image of the same archetypal structure. The sonnet, like the game of chess, is subject to a rigid and predetermined pattern. Both forms are based on the number four, a number symbolic of rational order, of human civilization and logic. The game of chess is played on a four-sided (square) board divided into eight rows, each one composed of alternating colors—four black and four white. The pieces, too, are based on the number four: bishop, knight, rook and pawn governed by the king and queen. [The original game which in Sanskrit was called Chaturanga, "army," literally meant "four arms." . . . A link between the ancient and the modern versions of the game is still apparent. . . . See Henry A. Davidson, *A Short History of Chess,* 1949.] The structure of the game reflects the structure of human society. The terminology used to designate the pieces changes according to the culture and period in which it is played, from terms implying strategic warfare to those reflecting the European court structure, but the game is universal and the patterned movement of the pieces never varies. Whether viewed as a game of war or of court intrigue, chess is an archetypal representation of man's attempt to reconcile chaos and order, to provide a rational, logical structure for the irrational conflict of opposing forces. The sonnet structure into which this game of chess is woven represents the same symbolic ordering of threatening, chaotic oppositions. It too is based on the number four: four stanzas, including two quatrains, symbolic of rational order. Just as the chessboard is composed of symbolic opposites, the sonnet structure also reflects a balance of oppositions. The two tercets complement the quatrains and represent (through the symbolic number three) the irrational dimension of existence, the world beyond man and his society. The tightly knit rhyme scheme of the sonnet further supports the integration of symbolic opposites and contributes to the tensive nature of oppositions held in perfect balance. In the quatrains, the ABBA rhyme scheme, dependent on two rhymes, reflects the tension found in the content between the pairs of opposites: black and white, the opposing players. The CCD/EED rhymes of the tercets also support the tension between opposing forces in the two rhyme sequence found in each tercet, but the pattern here goes beyond that of the quatrains to include a third rhyme when the tercets are considered together, thus contributing to the irrational dimension symbolically represented in the tercets by the number three.

In **"Ajedrez I"** Borges uses the pattern of the two quatrains to reflect the pattern of the chess game. The form of the game, like the quatrains, represents the external, rational, human ordering of forces in conflict. In the tercets, however, the game extends beyond the limits of the chessboard and encompasses the greater world. The three line stanzas reflect the internal, irrational dimension of the game which is now cosmic. While the order which governs the opposing sides in the game extends, in Borges' poem, to include the universal order, logic is lost when the game becomes infinite. Both the sonnet and the game of chess are man's civilized attempts to bring order out of chaos, to provide a logical structure for irrational forces, to encompass the infinite within the finite, to control the uncontrollable. In chess the moves of each piece are limited and well defined, while the possible variations within those limitations are infinite. In the sonnet, too, the form is limited and pre-determined, but the material contained is limitless. Thus, this sonnet is a mirror image of its content, an archetypal pattern reflecting an archetypal pattern. The form of the poem is a metaphorical vehicle of the same nature as the content and points beyond itself to a higher order.

In **"Ajedrez II"** the archetypal pattern is extended still further to add two more dimensions to the same structure. In **"Ajedrez I"** the symbolic chess game expanded in space, converting the world into a chessboard where man waged war against chaos. In **"Ajedrez II"** the pattern expands in time as well as space and incorporates the literary tradition into the archetypal pattern.

> Tenue rey, sesgo alfil, encarnizada
> Reina, torre directa y peón ladino
> Sobre lo negro y blanco del camino
> Buscan y libran su batalla armada.
>
> No saben que la mano señalada
> Del jugador gobierna su destino
> No saben que un rigor adamantino
> Sujeta su albredrío y su jornada.
>
> También el jugador es prisionero
> (La sentencia es de Omar) de otro tablero
> De negras noches y de blancos días.
>
> Dios mueve al jugador, y éste, la pieza,
> ¿Qué dios detrás de Dios la trama empieza
> De polvo y tiempo y sueño y agonías?

In the first stanza Borges again names the chess pieces and modifies each with an adjective which both designates its function in the game and contributes to the personification of the individual forms. The black and white pieces, personified by such adjectives as "tenue," "sesgo" and "encarnizada" appear to function as free agents ("buscan y libran su batalla armada"). The pattern of the board, which was represented as a static, spatial pattern in **"Ajedrez I,"** now becomes an active pattern extending into the dimension of time. The opposing pieces are no longer in fixed positions, but are actively pursuing their own destinies in time and space "sobre lo negro y blanco del camino." The quatrains present the relationship between player and pawn. In the first stanza the chessmen appear to forge their own destinies, while in the second the illusion is broken by the hand of man which controls their every move. But it is still the rational world of human civilization, in which man assumes control by methodically ordering his circumstances.

In the tercets of **"Ajedrez II,"** Borges extends the game to include the universal order—the order beyond man and his world. The alternating black and white pattern of the static chessboard in sonnet I became, in the tercets, a spatial pattern encompassing the world. In sonnet II the alternating black and white path followed by the chessmen becomes the eternal cycle of day and night in which man is a prisoner. The pattern expands in time now, as well as in space. In the final stanza, the levels of the game extend to encompass the universal order where the relationship of player and pawn is an infinite series of master and subject. Once again the order is precise, logical and predetermined, but the rational gives way to the irrational when the game becomes infinite, for although the order is clear, the meaning is a mystery. The function of the three line stanzas again contrasts with that of the four line stanzas by providing the irrational dimension.

The form of sonnet II, like that of sonnet I, is a mirror image of its content, a pattern within a pattern. However, in the second sonnet Borges includes still another representation of the pattern which was only hinted at in the first sonnet. The image of the eternal cycle of day and night as a chessboard on which man works out his destiny is not only a continuation of the theme the poet presents in the first stanza, but is a direct reference to *The Rubaiyat* of Omar Khayyam ("la sentencia es de Omar"). "'Tis all a Chequer-board of Nights and Days / Where Destiny with Men for Pieces plays: / Hither and thither moves, and mates, and slays, / And one by one back in the Closet lays" [Trans. Edward Fitzgerald, 1952]. Thus Borges incorporates within a twentieth century Argentine sonnet, an image taken from a twelfth century Persian poet based on the same archetypal pattern. The Persian poet weaves together the pattern of man's fate and the pattern of the chessboard. Borges fuses that pattern, now a part of the literary tradition, with his own re-creation of the same archetypal concept of order and uses the sonnet form, a literary convention to mirror that structure. Furthermore, the version of the original poem which Borges relies on for his poem, is that translated for the modern world in the nineteenth century by Edward Fitzgerald who has added his own stamp to the archetypal pattern. [The Persian poet does not refer to the pattern of the chessboard as the board was not so marked at that time in history. The colored pattern is an elaboration by Fitzgerald; see Davidson, *A Short History of Chess*.] The result is a complex structure of interwoven patterns: the chess pattern within the sonnet pattern, two literary traditions within a literary convention.

While in **"Ajedrez I"** the incorporation of the literary tradition was not as central to the poem as it is in **"Ajedrez II"** it was, nevertheless present, and added resonance to the sonnet. In the second stanza of that poem where he named the chess pieces, Borges referred first of all to the rook calling it, "torre homérica," giving an epic quality to the struggle between opposing factions. The reference to Homer in this context also calls to mind the Trojan War and the strategic Trojan horse designed like a giant chess piece in which the real players are contained. That brief allusion to the literary tradition recalls a whole series of archetypal references which support the pattern of the poem: the parallel between war and chess, man as a pawn in a greater game, the infinite repetition and variation of the epic struggle between opposing forces.

The last line of **"Ajedrez II,"** ("de polvo y tiempo y sueño y agonías") despite the fact that it is an ordered, parallel construction conforming to the symmetrical structure of the sonnet, reveals a certain sense of chaos and mystery. Even though man imposes order on his creations, God orders man's world and an infinite series of gods behind God impose the same order on their creations, the meaning is still an enigma. The sonnet form, like the game of chess, is an attempt to capture and reflect the universal order, but there is a point at which, when it becomes infinite, the order breaks down and reveals the chaos and disintegration which are the other side of order. The last line of Borges' **"Ajedrez II"** recalls that of Góngora's famous sonnet in which the perfectly ordered world of physical beauty disintegrates with the passing of time, "en tierra, en humo, en polvo, en sombra, en nada" [Luis de Góngora y Argote, *Poemas y Sonetos,* 1940]. The world of order once again returns to chaos, to nothingness. Whether by design or by coincidence arising from the archetypal nature of both sonnets, Borges' sonnet is linked to Góngora's which expands the literary resonance of that last line to include another tradition.

Finally, returning full circle, the last line of **"Ajedrez II"** forms a direct parallel to the last line of Borges' own sonnet, **"A un poeta del siglo XIII,"** in which he speculates on the archetypal nature of the sonnet. "Dédalo, laberinto, enigma, Edipo." "De polvo, y tiempo y sueño y agonías." The sonnet form captures and reflects the human experience. It gives order to experience but it does not explain it. The form reflects the full spectrum of existence, the chaos and mystery as well as the order. In **"Ajedrez II"** Borges moves from the specific archetypal content of **"A un poeta"** to a more general archetypal

content when he questions the meaning of the whole pattern. The archetypes, whether embodied in a symbolic hero, form or concept—Dedalus and Oedipus, the sonnet and chess, the labyrinth—provide man with a symbolic framework in which to order his experience, but again, the order is lost when the concept becomes infinite. When these two last lines are contrasted, Dedalus (and by extension, all man's aspirations) returns to dust, the labyrinth is an eternal labyrinth of time, the enigma is the infinite world of dream and Oedipus is only one representation of man's eternal anguish in the face of the unknown.

The artistry of Borges' sonnets does not depend on the themes, which are common, on the form, which is conventional, nor on the uniqueness of the language, but on the skillful manipulation and inter-weaving of archetypal patterns. The sonnets work through the pattern itself which expands in ever widening circles and produces the effect of a mirror with infinite reflections. The theme of free will versus predetermination apparent in **"A un poeta del siglo XIII"** is reflected in the sonnet structure. The same theme predominates in the two sonnets on chess but it acquires greater dimension by becoming fused with the pattern of the game and with the parallel structure of the sonnet, creating a multiple fusion of the pattern. The chess pattern then expands in time and space through the literary tradition and through the extension of the game to universal proportions. Borges suggests that the pattern is universal but the variations are infinite. The reader identifies with the archetypal content of the sonnets, recognizes the same archetypes in the literary tradition incorporated within the poems and becomes a participant in the expanding pattern. Thus the world of Alice, the Red Queen and the White Queen with which this essay begins is, in a sense outside the sonnets, and yet a part of them, for it is another variation, another extension of the same pattern into which Borges has drawn the reader and the reader's own experience. The multiple pattern in the sonnets triggers a reaction in the reader which tempts him to continue expanding that pattern, to see Lewis Carroll's White Queen as part of Omar Khayyam's pattern of days and nights, to watch the chessmen work out their destiny against the background of Stendhal's *The Red and the Black,* to see himself on the chessboard through the looking-glass of the sonnet.

Willis Barnstone with Jorge Luis Borges (interview date 1982)

SOURCE: "The Nightmare, That Tiger of the Dream," in *Borges at Eighty: Conversations,* edited by Willis Barnstone, Indiana University Press, 1982, pp. 135-52.

[*In the following interview, Borges discusses the poetic influences of Walt Whitman, Edgar A. Poe, and others.*]

[Willis Barnstone]: *In the years that we have known each other we have spoken almost exclusively about poetry.*

[Jorge Luis Borges]: Yes. It's the only subject, really.

A few days ago when we took a plane in New York, you asked what the name of the airline was, and I said TWA. You asked what that stood for, and I said Trans World Airlines. Do you remember what you said?

Yes. I said that that stood for Walt Whitman Trans World. He would have enjoyed that.

What about that pioneer transworld pilot?

I think that what I have to say now is what I said quite some time ago in an essay ["Nota sobre Walt Whitman," *Discusion,* 1932]: the fact, forgotten by many people, that Whitman thought of *Leaves of Grass* as an epic, not as a series of short poems. Now, the epic has been attempted many times, but there always was a central figure. *Arma Virumque canō.* I mean you always had a character larger than life. For example, you had Ulysses, you had Beowulf, you had Roland. But when Walt Whitman thought of writing an epic, Sewuld he thought, well, this should be an epic of democracy, and so I can't have a central figure. In one of his poems he says: "There are painters who give us pictures of crowds, and one of them has a halo. But I want all of my characters, all the people in my pictures, to have halos." And then he came to a very strange scheme, and nobody seems to have remarked it, since the people who imitated, or tried to imitate, Walt Whitman did not imitate his method but the results of his method. I am thinking of very important poets, for example, Carl Sandburg, Pablo Neruda, Edgar Lee Masters. Since Whitman had to write an epic of democracy, he created a character and that character is a very strange trinity, and yet many people mistake him for the writer. But the writer is not the character. When Walt Whitman began, he thought of his own life. He thought of having been born on Long Island, but he thought that this isn't enough: I should have been born all over America. Then he created that very strange character, Walt Whitman, not to be taken for the writer of the book, the Brooklyn journalist, who had written a novel about alcohol—he had written, I think, a tract in favor of slavery. But here he attempted a very daring experiment, the most daring and the most successful experiment in all literature as far as I know. The experiment was this. The central character would be called after the author, Walt Whitman, but he was, firstly, Walt Whitman the human being, the very unhappy man, who wrote *Leaves of Grass.* Then a magnification, or transmogrification of that Walt Whitman, called Walt Whitman, who was not the real Whitman at all, or at least not the Whitman his contemporaries knew, but a divine vagabond. And that man was a real character in "Walt Whitman, a kosmos, of Manhattan the son, / Turbulent, fleshy, sensual, eating, drinking and breeding." ["Song of Myself," 24, lines 497-98.] It appears from the biographies that those facts are not quite true. We find many distressing things about Whitman, but not about Walt Whitman. And then, since that character had to be a trinity—for he thought of it as a trinity—he introduced a third person. That third person is the reader.

So Walt Whitman is compounded of Walt Whitman the man, of Walt Whitman the myth, and also of the reader, because he thought of the reader as being also the hero of the book, being also the central man of the picture. So the reader speaks to Walt Whitman, and asks him: "What do you see, Walt Whitman? What do you hear, Walt Whitman?" And then Whitman answers back, "I hear America" or, for example—I'm an Argentine and I have chosen this particular example:

> I see the gaucho crossing the plains, I see the incomparable
>   rider of horses with his lasso on his arm,
> I see over the pampas the pursuit of wild cattle for
>   their hides.
>
>> ["Salut Au Monde," lines 122-23. In Whitman's
>> version "gaucho" is "Wacho," a member of a
>> Caddoan Indian Tribe, Texas.]

"The incomparable rider of horses." That is taken of course from the last line of the *Iliad*: "Hector, tamer of horses." But had Whitman written "the incomparable rider," he would have written nothing, but "rider of horses" gives it that peculiar strength.

And so we have this very strange character: the Whitman whose dates are given in the dictionaries and is forgotten, the Whitman who died in Camden, the magnification of Whitman, and then the reader. And the reader is made to stand for all future readers, and he thought of them as being all Americans. He did not know that he would be known the world over. He never thought in terms of that. He thought in terms of America, and of America the democracy.

Sometimes Whitman tells things of himself. But since he wanted to be everybody, he said something that no poet had ever said. I think the verses go thus:

> These are really the thoughts of all men in all ages
>   and lands,
>   they are not original with me,
> If they are not yours as much as mine they are
>   nothing,
>   or next to nothing,
> If they are not the riddle and the untying of the
>   riddle
>   they are nothing,
> If they are not just as close as they are distant
>   they are nothing.
> This is the grass that grows wherever the land is
>   and the water is,
> This common air that bathes the globe.
>   ["Song of Myself," 17, lines 355-60]

Other poets, for example, Edgar Allan Poe or one of his disciples, Baudelaire, were trying to say uncommon things. They were trying to surprise the reader. Poets still keep on working at that game. But Whitman went further. Whitman thought of his thought as being the "thoughts of all men in all ages and lands." "They are not original with me." He wanted to be everybody else. He wanted to be all men. He even saw himself as a pantheist, but the world is rather priggish. I think it comes from a deep feeling in Whitman. Now I wonder if that has been detected, because people read, and they don't think that they are one of the persons in that trinity which is Walt Whitman. And yet that was Whitman's idea. He wanted to stand for all America. In one of his poems, he writes:

> Now I tell what I knew in Texas in my early youth,
> (I will tell not the fall of Alamo,
> Not one escaped to tell the fall of Alamo,
> The hundred and fifty are dumb yet at Alamo,)
> ["Song of Myself," 34, lines 871-74]

Well, he never was in Texas in his life. And he also wrote: "As I have walk'd in Alabama my morning walk." ["Starting from Paumanok," II, line 148.] He never went to Alabama, as far as I know. But in another poem he says that he remembers having been born in the South. Of course I don't think he was born in several places at once, a kind of miracle. But still that made him into a great poet. Nobody seems to have attempted anything like it. They have just copied his intonation, his use of Biblical free verse, but nobody seems to have seen how strange was his personal experiment.

And even Walt Whitman did not live up to that one epic, because afterwards, there came the Civil War, and Walt Whitman was not all Americans. He was a partisan, as may be expected, on the side of the North. He did not think of himself as being also Southern, as he had felt himself in the beginning. And then in a sense he became less of Walt Whitman. He became someone in particular. He was no longer all men in all ages and lands. He was a contemporary of the War between the States. But should we say those things, since perhaps he wrote the most beautiful lines at the end of the book, when he says "Camerado"—he thought he was using Spanish but he was inventing the word [The Spanish word for "comrade" (masculine and feminine) is *camarada*.]:

> Camerado, this is no book,
> Who touches this touches a man,
> (Is it night? are we here together alone?)
> It is I you hold and who holds you,
> I spring from the pages into your arms—decease
>   calls me forth.
> ["So Long!" lines 53-57]

And then:

> I am as one disembodied, triumphant, dead.
> ["So long!" line 71]

The book ends with that single word of one syllable, *dead*. But the book is living. The book is still living, and every time that we open the book, every time that we go back

to it (and I'm doing that all the time), we become part of that trinity. We are Walt Whitman. So I am grateful to Whitman, not for his ideas—after all, I have no personal use for democracy myself—but democracy was a tool needed by Whitman in order to form that extraordinary epic called *Leaves of Grass,* and changed from edition to edition. Emerson said that that book when it appeared was the "finest piece of wit and wisdom that America had yet contributed."

I think of Walt Whitman not only as a myth but as a friend of mine. I think of him as having been rather unhappy, and having worked himself into singing joy and happiness, and that has been done perhaps by another poet, perhaps in Spanish, by Jorge Guillén, who really gives us a sensation of happiness. And now and then Shakespeare. As for Whitman, you can always see that he was doing his best to be happy, although he really wasn't happy, and that is part of the interest he has for us. Well, now you should say something, I have been talking far too much, Barnstone.

One thing I wanted to ask you was—

Why one thing, many things!

—what you think of Whitman's notion of writing one book all his life. And you mentioned Jorge Guillén as one who also wrote one book for at least thirty-one years, Cántico. [Guillén (b. 1893) later added two more books, *Clamor* and *Homenaje,* which he incorporated into one book, *Aire Nuestro,* 1968.]

A very fine book.

The way Baudelaire also wrote one book, Les Fleurs du Mal.

Yes, alas, he did.

What do you think of the notion of a writer, in the prophetic manner of Whitman, who dedicates his life to the elaboration of one long book?

Personally, I suppose all writers are writing the same book over and over again. But I suspect that every generation rewrites, with very slight variations, what the other generations wrote. I don't think a man can do much by himself since, after all, he has to use a language, and that language is a tradition. Of course he may change that tradition, but at the same time that tradition takes for granted all that came before it. I think Eliot said that we should try to renew with a minimum of novelty. And I remember that Bernard Shaw said, in a very unjust, derogatory way, of Eugene O'Neill: "There is nothing new about him except his novelties," meaning that novelties are trivial. As for one book—well, I wonder. All my writings have been bound together in a single volume. Maybe a few pages may survive.

It is very curious that Poe for Europe is what Whitman is for the Americas.

Yes, and we owe that to France; we owe that to Baudelaire and to Mallarmé. When I was a boy, Poe was known to us through the French.

But why was Walt Whitman for the New World what Poe was for the Old World? Virtually every Latin American poet, including yourself, has a poem to Walt Whitman.

I think that Whitman appealed to Europe also. I remember reading Whitman through a fine German translation by Johannes Schlaf. He also appeals to Europe. The fact is that America has given the world at least three names that cannot be thought away without changing everything. And those names are Whitman, the second one is Poe, and as to the last, I would choose Robert Frost. Other people might choose Emerson perhaps. You can do your own choosing. But America gave the world three men that cannot be thought away. They are essential. All contemporary literature would not be what it is had it not been for those two very different and those two very unhappy men, Edgar Allan Poe and Walt Whitman.

What specifically in the prosody of Whitman do you think the other writers imitated? Or if not prosody, what aspect of Whitman appealed to other writers?

Of course Whitman was one of the many inventors of free verse, perhaps the most conspicuous. You read the psalms and you read Walt Whitman. You can see that of course he had read the psalms, but the music is different. Every poet evolves a music of his own, and almost a language of his own. After a great poet has passed through a language, then the language is no longer the same. Something has changed. And in the case of Walt Whitman, it did change. Now, Whitman went in for the vernacular. And at the same time, one feels that he did not know how to use it very well. And you find very ugly lines now and then. For example: "Americanos! conquerers! marches humanitarian!" ["Starting from Paumanok," 3, line 37]. That is highly offensive, and he could write things like that. But those who mastered the vernacular used it after him. I mean two such diverse men as Mark Twain and Sandburg. They used the vernacular easily, while in the case of Walt Whitman, he rather floundered. He used French words, Spanish words, not too happily. At the same time I know that when I discovered Walt Whitman I was overwhelmed. I felt of him as the only poet. I had the same feeling afterwards with Kipling, I felt it with De Quincey, who wrote poetry in prose, and they were very different poets. But I thought of him at the time as being *the* poet, the man who had found the right way, the way in which poetry should be written. Of course there are many ways of writing poetry, all of them different from each other.

Would you be willing to comment on the poem you wrote about Whitman?

Well, I don't recall the poem. Go ahead, I am very curious. Why don't you read it in the English translation where it will be greatly bettered? I know you will be very disappointed. That poem is no good.

"CAMDEN 1892"

The smell of coffee and of newspapers.
Sunday and its boredom. It is morning.
Some allegorical verses are adorning
The skimmed over page: the vain pentameters
Of a happy colleague. The old man lies
Stretched out and white in his respectable
Poor man's room. Lazily he fills
The weary mirror with his gaze. His eyes
See a face. He thinks, now unsurprised: that face
Is me. With fumbling hand he reaches out
To touch the tangled beard and ravaged mouth.
The end is not far off. His voice declares:
I am almost gone, and yet my verses scan
Life and its splendor. I was Walt Whitman.
                    [Trans. Willis Barnstone.]

It's quite good, eh? Not too good but quite good, as far as it goes. That's the human Whitman only, not the myth.

Whitman thought of himself as a prophetic figure, writing a kind of Bible.

Well, he did!

Frequently in your stories and poems, you don't write a Bible, but you aspire to secrets, to enigmas, to a single word.

I am constantly being baffled by things.

You go different routes. Your work gets simpler and simpler, fewer and fewer words.

Yes, I agree.

If Whitman could throw in an adjective, he did so.

He did only too often, I should say.

His work might have been called Broad Leaves of Grass, *because he usually added words to intensify, often not with the best results. What do you think of the fact that this poet, who is marvelous and uneven, manages—*

But he *is* marvelous and uneven. Silvina Ocampo said to me that a poet stood in need of bad verses. If not, the others would not stand out. We were commenting on Shakespeare. I said he has many bad verses. And she said: "That's all to the good. A poet should have bad verses." Only secondary poets write only good verses. Out of politeness you should have bad verses.

Eliot said there should be weaker words among the stronger ones so that the lines do not become crabbed. But among the hack works which you claim you have done was to translate a book of Walt Whitman's poetry. You say that Walt Whitman was your poet and meant so very much to you. What did he teach you?

He taught me to be straightforward. That was the one lesson I learned from him. But teaching, after all, is not important. The fact is that I was overwhelmed by emotion, that I knew pages and pages of his work by heart, that I kept on saying them to myself in the day and in the night. I think that what's important is the way a man is moved when he reads poetry. If a man doesn't feel poetry physically, then he doesn't feel poetry at all. He had better become a professor or a critic. I think of poetry as being a very personal and a very important experience. Either you feel it or you don't. If you feel it, you don't have to explain it.

I am listening so intently that it wipes out further thoughts and questions. I stand in need of Edgar Allan Poe. Would you speak now about Poe?

Every writer is undertaking two quite different works at the same time. One is the particular line he is writing, the particular story he is telling, the particular fable that came to him in a dream, and the other is the image he creates of himself. Perhaps the second task that goes on all throughout life is the most important. In the case of Poe, I think that our image of Poe is more important than any of the lines on the pages that he wrote. We think of Poe as we may think of a character in fiction. He is as vivid to us as Macbeth or Hamlet. And creating a very vivid image and leaving that to the memory of the world is a very important task. As to the verses of Edgar Allan Poe, I know some of them by heart, and I think them lovely, and others are not so good. For example, I will begin by verses I learned:

> Was it not Fate that, on this July midnight—
> Was it not Fate (whose name is also Sorrow)
> That bade me pause before the garden-gate,
> To breathe the incense of those slumbering roses? . . .
>
> (Ah, bear in mind this garden was enchanted!)

["To Helen," lines 21-24, 30. This poem was written for Mrs. Sarah Helen Whitman.]

And also this very strange line from his first book, *Al Aaraaf.* I am not sure. My erudition is but dim:

> The eternal voice of God is passing by
> And the red winds are withering in the sky!
>   [Lines 131-32]

And at the same time, when I think of the raven, I think of it as a stuffed raven. I cannot take it seriously! When the raven speaks, "Quoth the Raven 'Nevermore,'" that seems to me to be ineffective. Rossetti, who had read "The Raven" of course, did it better. He was inspired by Poe, but he wrote thus:

> Look in my face; my name is Might-have-been;
>   I am also called No-More, Too-late, Farewell. . . .

[Sonnet 97, "A Superscription," from *The House of Life.*]

There is also that wonderful word invented by Bishop Wilkins in the seventeenth century, a word so fine that no poet has ever dared to use it. He invented two words. One, *everness,* and I was bold enough to use that as the title for a sonnet of mine, **"Everness."** Because *everness* is better than *eternity.* It goes with the German *Ewigkeit.* Then another word like *doom,* a word far better than that line I like so much in Dante: *Lasciate ogni speranza voi ch'entrate* "Abandon all hope you who enter here." That single word invented, given to the English language by Bishop Wilkins and never used because all those poets have stood in fear of it, that terrible, that beautiful, word is *neverness.* That could be done into German perhaps as *Nimmerkeit.* It can't be done into Spanish, I know. You see, *everness* is a fine word and *neverness* is a desperate word. Edgar Allan Poe wrote many verses and I don't think much of them, but there is one story of his that stands out, and that story is "The Narrative of Arthur Gordon Pym." You have Arthur and Edgar, both Saxon names, then Gordon and Allan, both Scottish. Then Pym goes for Poe. Now the first chapters of that long tale are not too memorable, I should say. But the last chapters are a nightmare. And they are, strangely enough, a nightmare of whiteness, of white being thought of as being terrible. Of course Herman Melville had read "The Narrative of Arthur Gordon Pym," and he wrote *Moby Dick, or the White Whale.* There he used the same idea, the idea of white, not scarlet or black, as being the most terrible of colors. You find that both books, *Moby Dick* and "The Narrative of Arthur Gordon Pym," are a nightmare of whiteness.

And of course Edgar Allan Poe created a genre. He created a detective genre. It seems to me that everything that has been done afterwards, all those things had already been thought out by Poe. You remember "The Mystery of Marie Rogêt," "The Murders in the Rue Morgue," "The Purloined Letter," and "The Gold Bug." Then you have all those many fine books that came afterwards. After all, Sherlock Holmes and Watson are but Poe and his friend, the Chevalier Auguste Dupin. Poe thought of many things. He thought that detective novels were artificial, so he did not seek a close reality. He placed them in France. His detective is a French detective, because he knew that it would be easier to deal with Paris—I don't think he knew Paris—the French—though he hardly knew them—than to write stories about contemporary happenings in New York. He was quite aware that detective fiction is a form of fantastic fiction. He invented all the conventions. He also invented something else. He invented the *reader* of the detective story. That is to say, when we read any detective story, when we read, for example, Eden Phillpotts, or Ellery Queen, or Nicholas Blake, we are really being created by Edgar Allan Poe. He created a new type of reader. That of course has made for thousands of books all over the world. I have attempted the genre myself, writing detective stories, but I knew all the time that real writer was Edgar Allan Poe. So he has given us many things. He also gave us an idea, which I think is mistaken, but is very interesting: the idea that poetry can be made through reasoning. I suppose you remember what he wrote about "The Raven." He said that when he began he needed a word with an *o* and an *r*. That gave him *nevermore*. Then he had the problem of why in the world it should be repeated at the end of every stanza, because he thought in terms of ending every stanza with the same word. He said: Why should a reasonable being keep on saying *nevermore?* Then he thought of an unreasonable being—and at first he thought of a parrot. But of course a parrot is green and would do him no good. Then he thought of a raven. A raven's black. That's the right color. Then the black had to stand out, so he thought of marble, and that gave him the bust of Pallas, and so on. So through a link of reasoning he came to the poem "The Raven." He said the poem should not be too long since, if it is read at two sittings, then attention dissolves, and it cannot be followed. It cannot be too short either, because a short poem would not be intense. So he said to himself, I will write a poem of a hundred lines. In fact, he wrote a hundred and seven or ninety-seven, or whatever it may be. He also thought: What is the most tragic subject on earth? And he immediately answered: The most tragic subject on earth is the death of a beautiful woman. And who can lament her death best? Of course he thought her lover. That gave him the lover and the death of a perfect woman. But he thought that poetry could not happen in too wide a scope, so he needed a closed room. Then he thought of a library, and that of course would be the right place for the bust of Pallas. Then there should be a contrast. Since the raven had to enter into the poem, he would have to be driven in by the stormy night. Thus, by a link of reason, he went on to write down his poem. I suppose this is merely a hoax. Poe was very fond of hoaxes. I don't think anybody could write a poem in that way. But let us suppose that we accept the first of his arguments. Well, he might have argued: I need an unreasonable being, let's say, a madman. But no, he chose a bird, a raven. From my own poor experience, I know that poems do not get written in that way, and Poe wrote much that were poems according to that system. But I think of writing poetry and of reasoning as being essentially different. I should there are two ways of thinking. One is the argument and the other is the myth. The Greeks could do both things at the same time. In, for example, that last conversation of Socrates before he drinks the hemlock, you find reason and myth wound together. But today it seems we have lost that capacity. We are either using arguments or we are using metaphors or images or fables. I suppose the real way of writing poetry is to let yourself be passive to dream. You do not try to reason it out. Of course you will reason out the details, the meter, the patterns of rhymes you will follow, the cadences, but as to the rest, it is given to you in the form of myths. Now all this comes out of our image of Edgar Allan Poe. And it is important that I should think of him as being unhappy. Unhappiness is part of that image, as much as unhappiness is part of the image of an old character, Hamlet. And were I to choose from the works of Poe, I suppose I would choose "The Narrative of Arthur Gordon Pym." But why choose? Why not have all the stories? Why not have, for example, "The Facts in the Case of M. Valdemar," "The Pit and the Pendulum," "The Gold Bug." All those stories are quite different from each other, and yet in all of them we hear the voice of Poe, and we are still hearing it at this moment.

One of Whitman's myths was that he was dealing with the common man and woman, that he was dealing with vernacular speech, with historical events such as the Civil War, with the death of Lincoln, which he celebrated in "When Lilacs Last in the Dooryard Bloomed," another historical event. In your own writing, you have this aspect of dealing with the vernacular, with hooligans, with rough people, with death, ordinary life.

Well, those are literary tricks.

Are not the literary tricks of the ordinary man, meaning what you have in common with Whitman, complemented by some other aspects of Poe, that is, the nightmare, the dream, the invention, the imagination, the erudition, sometimes sham, but there, sometimes the spoofing at erudition, the hoax, are you in part Poe and Whitman?

I am indebted to both of them, as all contemporary poets are, and as all contemporary poets should be. As to nightmare and Poe, it's very strange. I have read many books of psychology, and little is said of the nightmare, and yet the nightmare stands apart. In Spanish the word for it is quite ugly, *pesadilla,* it can hardly be used. In Greek they have a fine word, *ephialtēs,* standing for the demon of the night. Now, I have a nightmare every other night. I am often haunted by nightmare. And I feel that were I a theologian—happily I am not—I might find an argument in favor of hell. It is very common to be unhappy, but when we are unhappy, we do not get the nightmare touch, the uncanny touch, the eerie touch. That is given us by the nightmare itself. The nightmare has a peculiar horror to it. The nightmare, that tiger of the dream. It has a peculiar horror that has nothing to do with things that happen to us in waking life. And that horror might be a foretaste of hell. I don't believe in hell, of course, but there is something very strange about the nightmare, and nobody seems to have noticed that. I have read many books on dreams— Havelock Ellis, for example. But I have never found any reference to that uncanny and very strange taste of the nightmare. Yet there it is, and it may be a gift, for all we know. I have been given plots for stories in nightmares, and I know them only too well, I have them very often and they always follow the same pattern. I have the nightmare of the labyrinth. I always begin by being at some particular place in Buenos Aires. Now that place may be a street corner I know well. It may be, for example, Venezuela or Perú or Arenaldes, Esmeralda. I know that is the place, but it is quite different. In nightmare what I see is actually marshes, mountains, hills, sometimes cattle and horses. But I know that I am on that particular street in Buenos Aires, which is quite unlike what I see, and I know that I have to find my way home and that I won't. And then I know that this is the nightmare of the labyrinth. Because I keep on moving and coming back to the same place over and over again, to the same room over and over again. One of the nightmares. The other is the nightmare of the mirror. I see myself looking up, and then I see somebody I don't know, someone unknown to me, and I know that I am that being, and when that happens I awake and I am trembling all over. So my nightmares always follow the same pattern. But we seem to be straying farther from Poe.

I think we have strayed from Poe because you have strayed into that strange notion of reality, meaning dream and nightmare, which is so characteristic of your work and Poe's work.

Poe's work of course and also of idealism. As to thinking of the world as unreal I am always thinking of it and am always surprised by the world, by the things that are happening to me. For example, last year I was eighty, and I thought nothing can happen to me. Then after that I underwent a successful but very painful operation. After that I went on a wonderful trip to Japan, a country I now greatly love and had not known before, and now strangely enough, here I am in Indiana, talking to you. All those things the future had in store for me, all those gifts, and I was quite unaware of it. And now it has come. And I keep on expecting more gifts from the future. Since the one thing we know about the future is that it will be quite unlike the present. People only think of the future in terms of the twentieth century magnified and distorted. But I know firstly that there will be many futures, and secondly that things that we think of as being important will be frivolous and irrelevant in the future. For example, men will not be politically minded, men will no longer be equal—it is an illusion—men will not think in terms of circumstances, of success, of failure. I expect a quite different world, and many different worlds. Not the brave new world of Huxley, which is merely a transformation of Hollywood. I know that many futures are about to come. Why speak of *the* future? That has no meaning.

I wonder whether we could finish our talk by your saying something about Robert Frost. Perhaps you remember by heart his poem "Acquainted with the Night"?

> I have been one acquainted with the night.
> I have walked out in rain—and back in rain.
> I have outwalked the furthest city light.

And at the end, we get the same line "I have been one acquainted with the night." In the beginning, at the first reading, you think that acquainted with the night means: I have walked through a city at night. But then you foresee, as you come to the last lines, that the night stands for evil, especially for sensual evil as felt by a Puritan, because

> One luminary clock against the sky
> Proclaimed the time was neither wrong nor right.
> I have been one acquainted with the night.

And that, I think, is the chief achievement of Frost. He could write poems that seem simple, but every time you read them you are delving deeper and finding many winding paths and many different senses. So Frost has given us a new idea of metaphor. He gives us metaphor in such a way that we take it as a simple, straightforward statement. And then you find that it is a metaphor. "And miles

to go before I sleep / And miles to go before I sleep." There we see that the same words have two different meanings. In the first of the last two verses, the words stand for miles and going and sleeping. And in the 1st line, sleep stands for death. But in a very unobtrusive way. He was a shy man, I suppose. But I think of him as being, perhaps, the greatest poet of the century, if "greatest poet" means anything. I think of Frost as being perhaps a finer poet than the other candidate, and that would be William Butler Yeats. I prefer Frost, but that would be a personal bias. Of course I revere Yeats. When I think back to such lines as "That dolphin-torn, that gong-tormented sea." That of course is gorgeous writing, the kind of writing that Frost tried to avoid, that I try to avoid also. But Yeats could also write straightforward verses. For example:

> How can I, that girl standing there,
> My attention fix
> On Roman or on Russian
> Or on Spanish politics?

Then:

> And maybe what they say is true
> Of war and war's alarms,
> but O that I were young again
> And held her in my arms!

[Audience]: *I would like to know what you think of the Nobel Prize, and what Borges, the other Borges, thinks of it.*

I think that both of them feel very greedy about it. But they'll never get it.

The Nobel Prize committee keeps failing each year.

[Audience]: *I'd like to hear you speak more about Old English, perhaps only because I love it also, Anglo-Saxon.*

I remember a disciple of mine, a fellow student, who said: "What a pity, what a pity, the battle of Hastings! Now Anglo-Saxon has come down to English, and we have to put up with Shakespeare. What a pity!" Really, I fell in love with Old English. I think that perhaps the Old English sounds, the open vowels, the hard Scottish *r*s, are better than the hushed English we speak today. It has a more resonant ring to it. That's the reason. My memory is full of Old English verses. In Old English poetry we are getting the impression that the poems have been composed, have been chanted by or, rather, given to the brave and simple man. They did not abound in vanity. Vanity might have been found in the kennings. But the Anglo-Saxons very soon found out that the kennings did them no good and so they became merely synonyms. They were the first to speak out. I remember the elegies, the beginning of *The Seafarer*: "I can now tell a true song about myself. / I can tell my travels," *Maeg ic be me sylfum soðgied wrecan, / siþas secgan.* [Lines 1-2]. There the first lines are really Walt Whitman. In Old English poetry you get something essential, not only to England, but to all the world. You get the sea. The sea is always around the corner in Old English poetry. Even in that very dreary poem *Beowulf,* you find the sea in the beginning:

> Men ne cunnon
> secgan to soðe, seleræedende,
> hæleð under heofenum, hwa þæm hlæste onfeng.
> [*Beowulf,* lines 42, 50-52]

There is the sea. And of course in *The Seafarer,* where he speaks of the bitterness and of the attraction of the sea. People have thought of *The Seafarer* as being a dialogue. That, I think, is wrong. We should think of it as being written by one man who had been defeated by the sea, who had suffered but went on loving it. Perhaps that piece is the best of all we have left of Anglo-Saxon literature. But there is also a poem written after the Battle of Hastings, and done into English by Longfellow. The poem "The Grave." Longfellow translates: "Doorless is that house, / And dark it is within." [Lines 24-25.] But if you go back to the original you find still better: *Durelass is ðæt hus / And deerc hit is wiðinnen.*

[Audience]: *Could you elaborate more on your relationship with Ariosto, or your feelings about Italian literature and Dante?*

I think that the *Divine Comedy* is perhaps the peak of all literature. And I think I am in the right, because there is no other cause that would make me love that thing. For example, I have no Italian blood as far as I know. I am not a Catholic. I cannot accept the mythology of the poem. I cannot think of hell, of purgatory, and of heaven. And yet I know that Dante is right every time. In the case of Shakespeare, we are being let down at any moment. In the case of Dante, he is very dependable. He won't let you down. He knows what he's doing. There is another strange point I would like to tell you. It is Dante's idea that in a lifetime there is only a single moment. That moment stands for years and years of life, or stands for a man. For example, we are told nothing whatever of Paolo and Francesca. We know nothing about their political opinions, if any, of their ideas, if any, but we know that they were reading a book that came out of Brittany and that suddenly they knew that the characters in the book were themselves, and they knew that they were in love. That is sufficient. So Dante chooses a moment in every life. That is sufficient for him, since from that particular moment he gives us the whole character of the man and his whole life. That character may last three verses, and yet, there he is, forever. That is one of the feats of Dante. One of the many feats of Dante. As I have never studied Italian, I began by reading Longfellow's translation. And reading the notes. Then I had a bilingual edition, and I read, firstly, the English text, a canto, then the Italian text. I went on, and when I refound myself in purgatory, I could do without the English text and go on reading in Italian. To try to translate Dante into Spanish is a mistake, since the two languages are so much alike that anybody can understand them both. Besides, the Italians have made a very fine job of it. I have read the *Divine Comedy* through

already some ten or twelve times. Every time in a different edition, and have been given new interpretations. Ariosto has also meant much to me. In fact, I wrote a poem called **"Ariosto and the Arabs."** Therein I lamented that nobody seemed to read Ariosto since the *Arabian Nights* had taken over, and we don't even read the *Arabian Nights* as we should. But we have forgotten Ariosto and we should not forget him. Those two works, the *Furioso* and the *Arabian Nights,* resemble each other in the fact that they are really endless. And the fact that we are reading very long *is* a virtue. They have to be long. A labyrinth has to be long.

Linda S. Maier   (essay date 1994)

SOURCE: "Borges' Early Love Poetry," in *Chasqui,* Vol. XXIII, No. 2, November, 1994, pp. 48-53.

[*In the following essay, Maier endeavors to establish Borges's early poetry as romantic love poetry.*]

The name Jorge Luis Borges rarely comes to mind in a survey of Hispanic love poets. The omission may be attributed to a general lack of familiarity with Borges' poetry, in particular his early work written as a young man during the late 1910s and 1920s. [Borges began his literary career in Spain with the publication of the poem **"Himno del mar"** in *Grecia* on 31 Dec. 1919. This and other early works, such as **"Paréntesis pasional"** (*Grecia* 20 Jan. 1920), contain sensual and erotic imagery related to the love theme. Between 1919 and 1926, Borges published at least nine poems and two prose vignettes with similar motifs in Spanish journals. In addition to the two pieces already mentioned, the others include the following: **"Alejamiento,"** *Alfar* Jan. 1924: 25; **"Casa Elena** (Hacia una estética del lupanar en España),"** *Ultra* 30 Oct. 1921; **"Catedral,"** *Baleares* 15 Feb. 1921; **"Distancia,"** *Ultra* 30 April 1921; **"Escaparate,"** *Tableros* 15 Jan. 1922; **"Gesta maximalista,"** *Ultra* 20 Feb. 1921; **"Insomnio,"** *Grecia* 15 Sept. 1920: 9; **"Mallorca,"** *El Día* 21 Nov. 1926; **"Trinchera,"** *Grecia* 1 June 1920: 6. These works have been reprinted in Meneses, **"'Mallorca,' un poema en el olvido"** 1010, and *La poesía juvenil* 57-76, and Videla 187-95.] In any case, the myth of Borges as a cold, cerebral author untouched by human concerns persists even among those personally acquainted with him. For example, the Argentine writer Estela Canto, with whom Borges was romantically involved for years between 1944 and the early 1950s, has portrayed him as "un escritor que nunca escribe sobre mujeres, como no sea como complemento o pretexto para una situación dramática que prescinde de ellas."

On the other hand, any account of Borges' life calls attention to the many women who nurtured, sustained, and influenced him. These include his mother, Doña Leonor Acevedo de Borges; his sister, the artist Norah Borges; the many women with whom he was linked romantically—Concepción Guerrero, Haydée Lange, Cecilia Ingenieros,

Estela Canto, Elvira de Alvear, the mysterious H. O. and I. D.; his numerous female collaborators (Betina Edelberg, Margarita Guerrero, Delia Ingenieros, Alicia Jurado, Luisa Mercedes Levinson, María Esther Vázquez, Esther Zemborain de Torres), and, of course, his two wives, Elsa Astete Millán (1967-70) and María Kodama (1986). In countless interviews, Borges has stated his preoccupation with the loves of his life:

> La mujer está siempre presente en mi vida y quizá escribo para olvidarme un poco de mi obsesión por ella.

> Con cierta tristeza descubro que toda la vida me la pasé pensando en una mujer u otra. Creí ver países, ciudades, pero siempre hubo una mujer para hacer de pantalla entre los objetos y yo.

> Yo siempre estuve enamorado. . . .

> Enamorarse es producir una mitología privada y hacer del universo una alusión a la única persona indudable.

Though a number of scholars have perceived the love theme in Borges' poetry, it remains a problematical issue open to further study. Martin Stabb acknowledges the introspective nature of Borges' early poetry [in *Jorge Luis Borges,* 1970] which includes love poems and "poems of deep personal involvement." Alicia Jurado has also recognized that "[e]n los poemas juveniles . . . están . . . sus emociones más intensas: el amor a alguna mujer . . . ." Emir Rodríguez Monegal has noted the pervasive love theme of the early poetry and [in *Genio y figura de Jorge Luis Borges,* 1964] has even described *Fervor de Buenos Aires* as "a sort of diary of a young poet in love" [in *Jorge Luis Borges: A Literary Biography,* 1978]. Other critics have suggested that specific early poems illustrate this recurrent theme. Carlos Meneses notes the restrained eroticism of the pre-*Fervor* poems published in Spain and the poet's pessimistic outlook on romance (*Poesía juvenil.* . . . In his study on *Borges' Ultraist Movement and its Poets* Thorpe Running examines several love poems that depart from the avant-garde norm of anticonfessionalism and display Symbolist influence. In his essay on the "Poesía amorosa de Borges," E. Caracciolo Trejo relates this theme to the Borgesian idea of the essential unreality of individual identity; even he yields, however, to the widespread notion that "[e]l tema del amor no ocupa una posición central en la obra de Borges." On the other hand, Carlos Cortínez has concluded [in *Revista Canadiense de Estudios Hispánicos,* Vol. 3, 1978-79] that the theme of unrequited love is a constant in Borges' poetry; in his article, "Lo que no se dice en un poema de Borges," he speculates about the identity of the woman who inspired a poem of *El oro de los tigres* (1972) and provides close textual analysis. Borges' own early declaration that "[t]oda literatura es autobiográfica, finalmente. . . . [T]oda poesía es plena confesión de un yo, de un carácter, de una aventura humana" can be substantiated by his own writings which clearly reflect his romantic relationships and the omnipresent female image (*El tamaño de mi esperanza*). Indeed, a reevaluation of Borges' early love poetry not only dispels "la absurda consideración de situar al poeta ajeno a la vida amorosa" [Carlos Meneses, *Cartas de juventud de J. L. Borges (1921-1922),* 1987] but also reveals the nature and representation of the woman, reduced to her "elemento primordial" (Borges, **"Ultraísmo"**) of image which becomes only further accentuated in the later poetry.

A number of the poems of *Fervor de Buenos Aires* (1923), *Luna de enfrente* (1925), and *Cuaderno San Martín* (1929) form a poetic chronicle of a love affair, similar to Neruda's *Veinte poemas de amor y una canción desesperada* (1924). However, rather than being the central focus, the woman in Borges' poetry is the backdrop to other, more philosophical concerns. Nonetheless, these early poems sketch a portrait of Borges' first love.

After a seven-year stay in Europe (1914-21), the Borges family returned to Buenos Aires aboard the *Reina Victoria Eugenia* in March 1921, and later that year or early the following year the 22-year old Borges met and fell in love with Concepción Guerrero, a local girl six years his junior (Meneses, *Cartas*). The young couple often met at the home of their mutual friends Norah and Haydée Lange, Concepción's neighbors (Milleret). In a letter of April 1922 to his Mallorcan friend and fellow Ultraist poet Jacobo Sureda Borges outlines his plans to marry Concepción and describes their meetings:

> [E]s bastante probable,—sin bromas—que en dos o tres meses me encuentre situado en la calle del Rhône e incluso en el Colegio Viejo [de Ginebra], pues quiero hacer prosáicamente mi bachillerato, para regresar aquí, entrar en la Facultad de Filosofía y Letras, hacer en dos años la hazaña de 3, obtener un título y—casarme con Concepción—. . . . El azar hace que nosotros nos veamos siempre cerca del crepúsculo, en casa de Norah Lange, que nos deja solos en el jardín o en el salón bastante deteriorado. Hablamos poco, graves, distraídos, en la garganta una especie de angustia oscura de felicidad, hasta el momento en que se interpone la oscuridad de la noche y el rostro de Concepción cerca de mí se hace casi lejano. Cuando yo la abrazo, se estremece toda. . .

> (Meneses, *Cartas*)

Borges' poems provide a composite portrait of his *novia*. She is a dark-eyed brunette who wears her hair in braids. She has a very fair complexion and possesses a taciturn, somewhat haughty personality. The poet describes her in **"Mi vida entera"**: "He querido a una niña altiva y blanca y de una hispánica quietud" (*Luna*). In his letter to Sureda of 29 May 1922, the young poet remains "enamoradísimo" and characterizes the girl as "una muy admirable niña de diez y seis años, sangre andaluza, ojazos negros y una grata y apacible serenidad, con mar de fondo de ternura" (Meneses, *Cartas*).

At first indifferent to her suitor, the girl seems inaccessible to the poet. He admires her from afar like an "espectador de [su] hermosura," as he writes in **"Trofeo,"** but she remains aloof and does not return his affection (*Fervor*). Nevertheless, he dedicates the poem **"Sábados,"** celebrating their weekly late afternoon trysts, to her: "Para mi novia, Concepción Guerrero." Here, she treats him with cold disdain: "A despecho de tu desamor / tu hermosura / prodiga su milagro por el tiempo. / . . . / Ya casi no soy nadie, soy tan solo un anhelo / que se pierde en la tarde" (*Fervor*).

However, even as the relationship advances on one level, the poet remains a distant observer of the female form. In the poem meaningfully titled "antelación de amor" Borges employs a familiar artistic convention: contemplation of a woman in repose. Notwithstanding the inherent sensuality of such a scene, the poet reveals that their relationship has not been physically consummated ("tu cuerpo, aún misterioso y tácito"), and he beholds her as a separate and remote being: "Como Dios ha de verte, / . . . / Sin el amor, sin mí' (*Luna*). Merely the sound of the woman's voice is enough to stir the poet's imagination in "A la doctrina de pasión de tu voz." Just as in Neruda's Poem 15 of the *Veinte poemas* ("Me gustas cuando callas porque estás como ausente"), the poet feels privileged even to hear the woman speak:

> Tu voz a la que deberíamos creerle todo,
> es el sonido de la pasión del amor
> ¡ay de nosotros que la hemos escuchado sin
>   merecerla
> y de tu voz que sabe más que tu vida! . . .
> pero tu voz es la del poderío de la pasión
> y anega las palabras que dice.
> ¿Cómo olvidar lo que no debimos oír,
> cómo olvidar tu voz de pasión, . . .
>
> (*Cuaderno*)

Indeed, such poems reflect Borges' growing romantic involvement with Concepción. By mid-winter 1922, they met more often, two or three times a week, and in a letter of 25 July of that year, Borges confides to Sureda: "Me afianzo en mi enamoramiento. . . . Nos seguimos escudriñando el alma, bañándome yo el corazón en apacible romanticismo y dulzura" (Meneses, *Cartas*). The young poet had become so enamored that the idea of even a brief separation from Concepción in August or September 1922 caused him to despair to his friend: "Estoy alejado de mi novia, dos eternas semanas pasarán sobre mí antes que logre verla otra vez, me siento dejado de la mano de Dios, a mi soledad" (Meneses, *Cartas*). In spite of the physical distance between them, the poet retains the vivid memory of his girlfriend: "y es tu recuerdo como un ascua viva / que nunca suelto / aunque me quema las manos" ("**Ciudad**," *Fervor*). Her spirit pervades the city of Buenos Aires and imbues Borges' first collection of poetry with "lo que en [sus calles] supe de amor, de pena y de dudas" ("**A quien leyere,**" *Fervor*).

In fact, a sense of loneliness, pain at parting, and absence characterize Borges' early love poetry. A second family trip to Europe in 1923 precipitated the hasty publication of *Fervor de Buenos Aires* and forced the young lovers apart, but their correspondence kept the relationship alive. Poems such as "**Despedida**" (*Fervor*) and "dualidá en una despedida" (*Luna*) record the sorrow and desponden-cy occasioned by departure: "Entre mi amor y yo han de levantarse / trescientas noches como trescientas paredes / y el mar será un milenio entre nosotros. / . . . / No habrá sino recuerdos" (*Fervor*). For the poet, whose memory conjures up an idealized vision of the girl, his "horror de ausencia" ("**Alquimia**," *Fervor*) only intensifies his feelings; he does not merely preserve her image in his mind but rather embellishes and reinvents it. The poem "**Ausencia**" best captures the abstract nature of the poet's vision: "Habré de levantar la vida inmensa / que aún ahora es tu espejo: / piedra por piedra habré de reconstruirla" (*Fervor*). As Running suggests, Borges "refers not to the real woman but to her image reflected in his mind."

The end of the affair initially provokes regret which, over time, evolves into total repudiation of the romantic episode. In the prologue to *Luna de enfrente,* the poet warns the reader to expect to find a sense of lost love: "Verás [en este libro] . . . la soledá de un amor que fué." His homecoming occasions not a reunion with the girl he left behind but rather a permanent dissolution of their relationship. In "**La vuelta a Buenos Aires,**" the poet mourns the loss of love and pledges himself to the city:

> Son forasteros en mi carne los besos y único el
>   viento es abrazador de mi tronco. [t/o]
> Ya no sabe amor de mi sombra.
> Yo te rezé mis palabras todas, mi patria, y me ves
>   tan aislado co
> mo el viento. [t/o]
> Acaso todos me dejaron para que te quisiese sólo a
>   vos:
> Visión de calles doloridas: mi Buenos Aires, mi
>   contemplación, mi
> vagancia. [t/o]
>
> (*Luna*)

The poet blames himself for the breakup and appeals to the reader for compassion: "A una muchacha traté mal; no se si ella era buena, peró sí se que era linda. / Pobre de amor yo fuí' (*Luna*). In the end, however, he manages to rationalize his actions in his own mind and in fact, ultimately represses the entire incident: "no he sabido ningún amor" (*Cuaderno*).

Borges' early love poetry provides an undisguised account of his failed romance with Concepción. Their correspondence during Borges' second stay in Europe maintained the relationship until mid-1924, when the young poet returned home to find a changed, more mature Concepción, a young woman very different from the image he had preserved of her. Their relationship ended with Borges' intention to marry her unfulfilled ("Quiero la novia que sea luego la esposa") (*Luna*), thus establishing a pattern for Borges' future romances: "[A] Borges los amores no lo conducen al clásico final feliz."

However, Borges' early poetry is suffused by the at times ethereal and mostly absent woman whose poetic representation is based on the poet's first love, Concepción Guerrero. It has been suggested that the subtle influence of various women define Borges' life and literary career:

Una de las características de la obra de Borges es que cada uno de sus libros está unido a un grupo de personas que giran alrededor de una determinada mujer. . . . Es como si él no sólo se hubiera enamorado de una mujer, sino del ambiente que rodeaba a esa mujer. . . . El nunca cortaba definitavamente una relación y, cuando se desvanecía el amor por una mujer, continuaba enamorado de los momentos líricos que había tenido con ella.

Estas constelaciones de personas marcan etapas en el desarrollo intelectual y moral de Borges.

[Estela Canto, *Borges a contraluz,* 1989]

But for Borges, the aftereffects of love provide an even more fruitful source of inspiration. The ineffable female image continued to obsess the poet; as Borges has stated: "What you really value is what you miss, not what you have."

Throughout the years Borges incessantly revised his poetry, practically erasing the woman from his early collections. The female figure becomes progressively more and more abstract, ever more remote from her concrete origins. For example, in the dedication to the poem "Sábados," Borges reduces the woman simply to her initials, "A. C. G." This device recurs in the poem "**H. O.**" from *El oro de los tigres,* in which the woman is signified only by her initials and voice (Cortínez). Through a process of abstraction and reduction, the poet shapes the desired image of the woman. As Caracciolo Trejo has suggested [in *Revista Iberoamericana,* Vol. 43, 1977]: the woman becomes "más ficción que alusión concreta a una experiencia. . . . [L]a amada es . . . un producto de su mente."

In his later years Borges acknowledged his propensity to write intellectual poetry, a paradoxical synthesis of abstractions and concrete imagery (**"Prólogo,"** *La cifra*). Indeed, Borges has confessed his repudiation of material and temporal reality in favor of a few eternal images; rather than being in love with a particular woman, he has admitted to being "enamorado de una imagen que había creado." The poem **"La dicha,"** included in Borges' penultimate collection of poetry dedicated to his second wife, universalizes the individuals in the love relationship: "El que abraza a una mujer es Adán. La mujer es Eva." The Borgesian idea that one man is all men applies also to woman. The female figure is ultimately replaced by an indelible, yet depersonalized image. Of Borges' relationship with Elvira de Alvear, as he writes in the poem dedicated to her in *El hacedor* (1960), he retains only the memory of her smile (*Obra poética*). In **"Two English Poems"** from *El otro, el mismo* (1964) the poet recalls a lost love and strives to preserve her image, literally her reflection in a mirror: "I want your hidden look, your real smile—that lonely, mocking smile your cool mirror knows. / What can I hold you with?" (*Obra poética*). It is this image of woman that endures in **"El enamorado"** from *Historia de la noche* (1977): "Sólo tú eres" (*Obra poética*).

The image of woman emerges transcendent in Borges' poetry. As he writes in **"Posesión del ayer"** included in his last verse collection, *Los conjurados* (1985), also inscribed to María Kodama, Borges' failures, romantic and otherwise, survive: "Sé que he perdido tantas cosas que no podría contarlas y que esas perdiciones, ahora, son lo que es mío. . . . Nuestras son las mujeres que nos dejaron." In **"La larga busca,"** another poem from the same book, he acknowledges that the Absolute is often sought in "la mirada de una mujer." Years earlier, in the poem **"Elegía"** from *El otro, el mismo* Borges summarizes his life in which the face of a girl from Buenos Aires remains etched in his imagination: "y no haber visto nada o casi nada / sino el rostro de una muchacha de Buenos Aires" (*Obra poética*). In life she was physically distant from the poet who lamented her absence, transforming it into a presence that remains in Borges' poetry.

Thorpe Running (essay date 1996)

SOURCE: "The 'Secret Complexity' of Jorge Luis Borges's Poetry," in *The Critical Poem: Borges, Paz, and Other Language-Centered Poets in Latin America,* Bucknell University Press, 1996, pp. 125-38.

[*In the following essay, Running studies the "secret complexity" of Borges's poetry, which arises from the poet's awareness of the ambiguity of language and of human experience.*]

Ever since the final years of the Ultraist decade of the twenties in Argentina, Jorge Luis Borges (Argentina, 1899-1986) tried to undo or to discredit almost everything that he believed or wrote during those years. This purposeful rejection of what was, after all, a synthetic approach to art, a catchall of avant-garde theory and practice, led him into new areas of literary investigation that placed him once again paradoxically in the forefront of current theoretical development. In fact, Borges is now commonly mentioned in the same breath with some of the leading poststructuralist theoreticians. It is well known by now that many of those thinkers about literature, particularly the French-language ones—such as Maurice Blanchot, Michel Foucault, Gérard Genette, and Jacques Derrida—have used Borges as a starting point for certain of their concepts. [Emir Rodríguez Monegal, "Borges y la 'nouvelle critique'," in *Jorge Luis Borges,* ed. Jaime Alazvaki, 1976. See also Emir Rodríguez Monegal, "Borges and Derrida Apothecaries," in *Borges and His Successors,* ed. Edna Aizenberg, 1990.] Their interest in Borges has generally stemmed from themes found in his prose fiction. Borges's poetry, in its own ambitious trajectory, actually expands on some of those same themes.

Although Borges rejected the militant tone of his early Ultraist pronouncements, as well as a belief in the supreme powers of the metaphor they expressed, he kept trying, in a more unassuming way, to discover—to rescue—the basis for a true poetic image. In contrast to the Ultraists' contrived metaphors—which ranged from difficult to brilliant to silly as they tried to bring together ever more "distant realities"—Borges later "modestly" advised us that his more mature poetry had a "secret complexity" underlying its apparently ordinary language.

Such "secret complexity" is the key to the critical poetry that Borges cultivated over the last twenty-five years of his life. Unfortunately, the "secret" part has its own very complex elements. Underlying that secret is Borges's skepticism toward language, which fits in with his general skepticism toward the world, as Arturo Echeverría has pointed out [Arturo Echeverría, *Lengua y literatura de Borges*, 1983]. . . . Even Borges's prose writing owes its original and easily identifiable technique to his belief that language does not have the ability to "name" things, as Sylvia Molloy has shown in her article on "simulacrum and textual causality" in his fiction [Sylvia Molloy, "Dios acecha en ios intervalos': Simulcra y causalidad textual en la ficción de Borges," *Revista Iberoamericana*, Vol. 100-101, July-December 1977]. This concern becomes an even greater dilemma for the poet, as Borges explains in his postscript to ***Historia de la noche*** (1977):

> La materia de que dispone el lenguaje, es, como afirma Stevenson, absurdamente inadecuada. ¿Qué hacer con las gastadas palabras—con los Idola Fori de Francis Bacon—y con algunos artificios retóricos que están en los manuales?
>
> [Jacques Derrida, *Positions*, 1972]

> [The material that language is made up of is, as Stevenson affirms, absurdly inadequate. What can be done with the worn out words—with Francis Bacon's Idola Fori—and with some rhetorical artifices that are in the manuals?]

And he then elaborates on the "inadequacy" of what he elsewhere calls "ambiguous language":

> Whitehead ha denunciado la falacia del diccionario perfecto: suponer que para cada cosa hay una palabra. Trabajamos a tientas. El universo es fluido y cambiante; el lenguaje, rígido.

> [Whitehead has denounced the fallacy of the perfect dictionary: supposing that there is a word for each thing. We grope our way along. The universe is fluid and changing; language, rigid.]

That "fluid" universe makes the idea of a "rigid" language a fallacy, as Borges often shows. Sylvia Molloy puts it this way: "Borges delights in pointing out the transformations of a word repeated and yet different, the many ways in which a term, or a series of terms, considered fixed and final, may drift" [Sylvia Molloy, *Signs of Borges*, trans. Oscar Montero and Sylvia Molloy, 1994]. This is looking very much like the troubled view of language that [can be seen] . . . in Paz and Juarroz and some of the French thinkers. In fact, considered as fluid and drifting, the word now almost fits Jacques Derrida's concept of the "floating signifier" (*signifiant flottant*), which re-

sults from "the absence of a transcendental signified" (*l'absence de signifié transcendentale*) [Jacques Derrida, *L'écriture et la différence*, 1967]. Derrida's term for that ungraspable sign is the "trace," which Borges again almost echoes with the words "vástago" (descendent) and "reflejo" (reflection) in these two selections from the poems **"A Johannes Brahms"** and **"Juan 1, 14"**:

> Mi servidumbre es la palabra impura,
> Vástago de un concepto y de un sonido;
> Ni símbolo, ni espejo, ni gemido,
> Tuyo es el río que huye y que perdura.

> [My obligation is the impure word,
> descendent of a concept and a sound;
> neither symbol, nor mirror, nor moan,
> yours is the river that flees and that remains.]

> He encomendado esta escritura a un hombre
>   cualquiera;
> no será nunca lo que quiero decir,
> no dejará de ser su reflejo.

> [I have entrusted this writing to any man at all;
> it will never be what I want to say,
> it will be nothing but its reflection.]

> [Jorge Luis Borges, ***Obra poética (1923-1967)***, 1977. All references in the text to Borges's poetry are from this volume, unless otherwise indicated.]

In Borges's later poetry this inability to "name" and the frustration with a "worn-out" and "ambiguous" language are ever-present concerns; his famous poem **"El otro tigre"** (**"The other tiger"**) from ***El otro, el mismo*** (1969), clearly illustrates this preoccupation, which carries into all of the subsequent volumes. In the last line of the first quotation above ("yours is the river"), we see part of the reason why the inadequacies of language hold such fascination for a writer whose favorite topic is time. For Borges, the failings of language are linked with human weaknesses, since both share a temporal nature; language is both worn out and undermined by time (a "fluid and changing universe"), as are the people who use that language. But he is not content to stay at this skeptical level; he does not simply turn the "game of signification," as Derrida would call it, into a "spiral of echoes" (in Octavio Paz's phrase). We could start our look at the other side of this coin, as it were, with the prologue to ***La moneda de hierro*** (The iron coin). In this essay, as he discusses the limitations of art, Borges points out that in spite of its shifting meanings, language—the word—literally has a future:

> Cada sujeto, por ocasional to tenue que sea, nos impone una estética peculiar. Cada palabra, aunque esté cargada de siglos, inicia una página en blanco y compromete el porvenir.

> [Each subject, however occasional or tenuous it may be, imposes a peculiar aesthetic on us. Each word, even

though it may be loaded down by centuries, initiates a blank page and compromises the future.]

In the face of an impure language and his own mortality, he insists on establishing a poetry with a durable meaning, and this insistence is personal and solidly affirmative, in spite of the "secret" (and ever so "critical") aspects that this process will entail.

The first way in which Borges's texts face up to an ambiguous language is by demonstrating how a word "loaded down by centuries" can have an almost unlimited richness and a multiplicity of meanings. The well-known poem **"El otro tigre"** does just that, showing that, as Roman Jakobson says, "the context is variable and each new context gives the word a new signification. In that fact resides the creative force of the literary sign" [Roman Jakobson, *Lingüistica,* 1981]. **"Blake,"** a poem in *La cifra* (The cipher), contains the same kind of assertion about its subject, the rose, saying it "can be" a long list of possible things [Jorge Luis Borges, *La cifra,* 1981]. It is important to note that Borges is not casual about selecting these subjects: both the rose and the tiger are words that already have poetic (or as Borges would say, "archetypal") associations, and as such they are what Greimas would term "classemes." Another poem on the same topic, with the English title **"The Unending Rose,"** carries this idea of a multiplicity of meanings within a single word—much like Lacan's "chain of signification"—to an almost unlimited degree, a concept reinforced by the title of the book that contains it: *La rosa profunda.* That adjective, "profundo" (deep), is one that Roberto Juarroz also uses in his *Poesía vertical* in order to indicate the unlimited verticality—the open-ended depth of signification—of the poetic word. At the end of **"The Unending Rose"** it is evident that "the rose" has taken on a wealth of associations. Addressing the rose, the poet says:

> Cada cosa
> Es infinitas cosas. Eres música,
> Firmamentos, palacios, ríos, ángeles,
> Rosa profunda, ilimitada, íntima,
> Que el Señor mostrará a mis ojos muertos.

> [Each thing
> Is infinite things. You are music,
> Firmaments, palaces, rivers, angels,
> Profound rose, unlimited, intimate,
> That the Lord will show to my dead eyes.]

An awareness that the word in poetry has the potential to evoke a vast range of meanings within the reader underlies, then, all of Borges's mature poetry, and is an important part of his poetry's "secret complexity." Although in **"The Unending Rose"** Borges shows how a word's endless implications can provide poetic depths, he does not focus exclusively on this idea, which some poets also see as the way to unlimited expression; for Roberto Juarroz, as we saw, the open-ended signifier is the key to a *poesía explosiva.* Rather, Borges seems

to turn his back on this penetrating vision of what an ambiguous and unlimited language can do, incongruously insisting on *consciously* disregarding that knowledge. He explains the contradiction in his poem **"El ingenuo"** (**"The naïve person"**) from *La moneda de hierro*:

> Cada aurora (nos dicen) maquina maravillas
> Capaces de torcer la más terca fortuna;
> Hay pisadas humanas que han medido la luna
> Y el insomnio devasta los años y las millas.
> En el azul acechan públicas pesadillas
> Que entenebran el día. No hay en el orbe una
> Cosa que no sea otra, o contraria, o ninguna.
> A mí sólo me inquietan las sorpresas sencillas.
> Me asombra que una llave pueda abrir una puerta,
> Me asombra que mi mano sea una cosa cierta,
> Me asombra que del griego la eleática saeta
> Instantánea no alcance la inalcanzable meta,
> Me asombra que la espada cruel pueda ser hermosa,
> Y que la rosa tenga el olor de la rosa.

> [Each dawn (they tell us) fabricates marvels
> Capable of twisting the most stubborn fortune;
> There are human steps that have measured the moon
> And insomnia devastates years and miles.
> Public nightmares lie in wait in the blue
> And make the day gloomy. In the sphere there is
> Nothing that is not another or contrary thing, or
>   nothing.
> Only the simple surprises disturb me.
> It amazes me that my hand may be a certain thing.
> It amazes me that the Greek's
> Instantaneous Eleatic arrow does not reach the
>   unreachable goal,
> It amazes me that the cruel sword can be beautiful,
> And that the rose can have the smell of a rose.]

The poem is, in spite of its title, anything but a reflection of naïveté. To be sure, it is *about* the voice in the poem thinking himself naive. And following the lead of the title, we will most likely read the poem as such: as an expression of bewilderment in the face of modern "progress" and a preference for a contemplation of the (not so simple) "simple surprises." But I think we can also read these lines as a description, or perhaps an allegory, of the new poetics that we are watching Borges develop. For this reading, "El otro, el mismo" would have been a more fitting title. Here, the poem's first half is a demonstration of "modern" or avant-garde poetics, and the second half a listing of the now preferred "simple surprises" (or secret complexities— it's pretty much the same thing, as we will see). The opening seven lines are constructed in a way that makes them representative—technically—of the kind of exotic images that have characterized all modernist poetry, and their subject matter also reflects developments of modern society. This imagery becomes almost a parody of avant-garde verse. As in the Ultraists' poetry there is dehumanization: human elements are referred to through metonymy (human steps, insomnia, public nightmares), but the images in these lines are formed by the Ultraists' favorite means, personification ("each dawn fabricates marvels," for example). The verbs used are in the Creationist mold—dynamic and assertive (fabricate, twist, measure, devastate, lie in wait). At the end of these seven verses ("there is nothing that is not another or contrary thing"), the text restates Borges's frequently expressed belief that there is an excess of analogies and nihilistic pessimism in both the world and in language.

In contrast to that conscious "modernity" of both expression and content, the second half of the poem deals with unremarkable things that nevertheless "astonish" the author, and the style changes to an apparently flat and prose-like one, as the poem maintains its strict form, with its fourteen-syllable lines and consonantal rhyme. How can these simple things (the hand and the rose's smell, at least, have no obvious complexity at all) "astonish" the Borges whom we see in this poem? They cannot surprise him if he is truly naive. But there is a complexity to these things if one is aware of it, or has pondered what lies behind those simple phenomena. Why do humans have two hands and two feet, why do we have five fingers on each hand and not two or eight, for example? Why does a rose smell like a rose and not a lilac or a skunk? How can a sword that has the function of killing also be beautiful? Contrary to the title, the poet here has decided *not* to be naive, *not* to accept the apparent simplicity of these "obvious" things. This is a conscious decision made out of a deep philosophical awareness. In the light of this poem we can now more easily see what lies behind the term "secret complexity" in this statement from the prologue to *El otro, el mismo*:

> Es curiosa la suerte del escritor. Al principio es barroco, vanidosamente barroco, y al cabo de los años puede lograr, si son favorables los astros, no la sencillez, que no es nada, sino la modesta y secreta complejidad.
>
> [Jorge Luis Borges, *El otro, el mismo*, 1969]

> [The writer's fortune is curious. At first it is baroque, vainly baroque, and over years he can reach, if the stars are favorable, not simplicity, which is nothing, but, instead, a modest and secret complexity.]

Like the "simple surprises" of the previous poem, the "secret complexity" here is Borges's understated rebellion against the more obvious "baroque" difficulties of modernist or imagist poetry. But the answer does not lie in simplifying the text. That, Borges says, would be "nothing." Borges, typically, doesn't tell us exactly what he has in mind here. Rather, we are left to ponder a bit, and if we do that we soon realize the only things left to be simplified are the author and the reader. As contradictory as this new turn seems, after all of Borges's demonstrations of the problems inherent in language, we can now see the secret complexity as being the need to consciously disregard all those problems. This would be difficult, of course, and Borges has several poems that explore a more direct way around the problem of a fluid language. In

"Browning resuelve ser poeta" (Browning resolves to be a poet) Borges explains one possible, if merely wishful, plan of attack against exactly that other kind of critical poetry, including his own, which seems always to look for difficulties:

> Como los alquimistas
> que buscaron la piedra filosofal
> en el azogue fugitivo,
> haré que las comunes palabras
> —naipes marcados del tahúr, moneda de la plebe—
> rindan la magia que fue suya
> cuando Thor era el numen y el estrépito,
> el trueno y la plegaria.

> [Like the alchemists
> who looked for the philosophers' stone
> in fleeting mercury,
> I will make the common words
> —cards marked by the gambler, common coins—
> produce the magic that was theirs
> when Thor was divine and noisy,
> thunder and prayer.]

This idealized approach to language that the poet plans to create will have two important aspects. It will involve magic and alchemy and will want to create a *hard* word ("stone," "coins") out of what is now a fluid medium ("fleeting," "mercury"). The magic is associated with the far removed past—the time of the Vikings. Another poem recalling this same epoch and with a similar insistence on solid words is **"Un sajón"** (**"A Saxon"**).

> Era tenaz. Obraron su fortuna
> Remos, redes, arado, espada, escudo;
> La dura mano que guerreaba pudo
> Grabar con hierro una porfiada runa.

> [He was tenacious. These things worked out his fate:
> Oars, nets, plow, sword, shield;
> The hard hand that fought was able
> To carve with iron a stubborn rune.]

The second line here consists of only five words—five simple, hard, essential, and almost symbolic things. Their importance is even dynamic, since they are the personified subject of the verb "obrar" (work). *They* were the *real, active* protagonists. The person, who is even reduced metonymically to a hard hand, nevertheless was able to carve out a solid and lasting image, a rune, into stone. This poem's final four stanzas further describe the original process of language formation, which had the magical quality Borges is working toward in his own verse.

> Para cantar memorias o alabanzas
> Amonedaba laboriosos nombres;
> La guerra era el encuentro de los hombres
> Y también el encuentro de las lanzas.

Su mundo era de magias en los mares.
De reyes y de lobos y del hado
Que no perdona y del horror sagrado
Que hay en el corazón de los pinares.

Traía las palabras esenciales
De una lengua que el tiempo exaltaría
A música de Shakespeare: noche y día,
Agua, fuego, colores y metales.

Hambre, sed, amargura, sueño, guerra,
Muerte y los otros hábitos humanos;
En arduos montes y en abiertos llanos,
Sus hijos engendraron a Inglaterra.

[To sing of memories or praises
He coined laborious names;
War was the collision of people
And also the clash of spears.

His world was one of magic on the seas,
Of kings and wolves and fate
That does not pardon and of the sacred horror
That lies in the heart of the pine groves.

He brought the essential words
Of a language that time would raise
Into Shakespeare's music: night and day,
Water, fire, colors, and metals.

Hunger, thirst, bitterness, sleep, war,
Death and other human habits;
In arduous forests and in open plains,
His children will produce England.]

Even for the purpose of singing, the archaic linguistic development is described here as a hard, solid "coining" operation (the new, solid word could well be seen, then, as a "moneda de hierro," the title of Borges's 1976 book). But this was a magical, longed-for world, where such an immediate and unmediated relationship between the word and the world could still exist. Significantly, those iron coins are "essential words" describing "human habits," the words and the functions to which Borges wants magically to return through the "alchemy" he mentioned in the "Browning" poem. This recapturing of a magical experience with the most ordinary words recalls the astonishment seen in the four-times-repeated "me asombra" (it astonishes me) that Borges expressed in connection with "simple" things in the poem **"El ingenuo"**; those lines in turn are summarized in this one from **"El mar"** (**"The Sea"**): "the astonishment that elemental things leave."

Borges makes even more explicit his attraction to ancient linguistic origins, to a "language of the dawn," as he calls it, in **"Al iniciar el estudio de la gramática anglosajona"** (**"On beginning the study of Anglo-Saxon grammar"**), from the same book.

Símbolos de otros símbolos, variaciones
Del futuro inglés o alemán me parecen estas palabras

Que alguna vez fueron imágenes
Y que un hombre usó para celebrar el mar o una
    espada;
Mañana volverán a vivir,
Mañana *fyr* no será *fire* sino esa suerte
De dios domesticado y cambiante
Que a nadie le está dado mirar sin un antiguo
    asombro.

[Symbols of other symbols, variations
Of the future English or German are these words
That at one time were images
And that a man used to celebrate the sea or a
    sword;
Tomorrow they will live again,
Tomorrow *fyr* will not be *fire* but rather that kind
Of domesticated and changing God
Which nobody is allowed to see without an ancient
    astonishment.]

Again it is the original word as metaphor ("symbols of other symbols"), along with the experience of the emotional relationship between word and element, that Borges describes here. And he wants the ability to use that new/old word in order to "compromise the future" ("tomorrow they will live again"). The desired effect will be to once again experience a sense of astonishment that goes back to the original magical relationship—an "ancient astonishment."

Of course, it is not that easy. And Borges knows that. On the one hand there is the ideal of the "iron" word, coined out of an indelible experience. On the other is the continuing awareness of a failed language. In the "Inscription" at the beginning of **Los conjurados** (The conspirators), his last book of poetry, Borges writes of the tension that develops between the magic of the pure experience and the uncertainties of a fluid language:

Escribir un poema es ensayar una magia menor. El instrumento de esa magia, el lenguaje, es asaz misterioso. Nada sabemos de su origen. Sólo sabemos que se ramifica en idiomas y que cada uno de ellos consta de un indefinido y cambiante vocabulario y de una cifra indefinida de posibilidades sintácticas. Con esos inasibles elementos he formado este libro.

[Jorge Luis Borges, **Los conjurados,** 1985]

[To write a poem is to practice a minor magic. The instrument of that magic, language, is quite mysterious. We know nothing of its origin. We only know that it branches into different languages and that each one of them has an indefinite and changing vocabulary and an indefinite cipher of syntactic possibilities. With those ungraspable elements I have formed this book.]

The beginning of a poem from **La cifra,** called **"Happiness"** (**"La dicha"**), brings up this very same quandary. The last line of the poem indicates at least part of its resolution, and thus the happy title. Here are its first lines:

El que abraza a una mujer es Adán. La mujer es
  Eva.
  Todo sucede por primera vez.
  He visto una cosa blanca en el cielo. Me dicen que
  es la luna,
pero
  qué puedo hacer con una palabra y con una
  mitología.

[The one who's embracing the woman is Adam. The
  woman is Eve.
  It's happening for the first time.
  I've seen a white thing in the sky. They tell me
  it's the moon,
but
  what can I do with a word and with a mythology.]

Here he asks not what he can do with just any word, but
the moon, a subject scorned during the Ultraist period as
being nothing but an outworn poetic cliché (just recall
the Ultraists' scorn for Lugones's *Lunario sentimental*).
The poem's last line, as mentioned, provides an additional, if not the essential, clue to the equation that will allow
us to see further into Borges's "secret complexity":

  El que lee mis palabras está inventándolas.

  [The one who reads my words is inventing them.]

The reader's response, an active and creative one—an
invention—is an important part of the solution. A further,
final, clarification of this whole equation comes together
in the poem **"La luna" ("The moon")**, which explains
the "secret" of how that most outworn of words—"luna"—
can be used even one more time.

  El secreto, a mi ver, está en usarla
  Con humildad. Es la palabra *luna*.

  [The secret, in my view, is in using it
  With humility. It is the word *moon*.]

That word "humility," as will shortly be clear, looks like
a rather typical Borges-type understatement, except in
this case it is a particularly enormous understatement. At
the very least, it implies here an extreme degree of self-
awareness. In the next stanza he states that he does not
dare spoil the moon "with a vain image"—an indictment
of both Modernismo and Ultraism—explaining in the following verses that the word "luna" already provides sufficient "complexity":

  Sé que la luna o la palabra *luna*
  Es una letra que fue creada para
  La compleja escritura de esa rara
  Cosa que somos, numerosa y una.
                    [Borges, *El otro, el mismo*]

  [I know that the moon or the word *moon*
  Is an inscription that was created for
  The complex script of that rare
  Thing that we are, numerous and one.]

Now we have the key, and it brings us, and Borges, back
to the concept of "secret complexity." Here we see that
it already exists in the "complex script" of human experience. On one level the complexity lies in the multiple
associations a word has gathered over the centuries
(and we cannot simply wish those associations away).
But, at the other, the level of human complexity (which
we share yet experience individually), a self-conscious
ingenuousness is required. For this, the writer and,
ideally, the reader, must ignore—or consciously strip
away—the word's timeworn complications in order to
experience a new astonishment that will match what
the original fabricators of language felt when they made
their first metaphorical connections between words and
objects. Now a word as overused as "luna" can be experienced as an "inscription," a hard runic engraving that
has all the solidity we can give it. This process is all
too ironic, of course. A return to a new naïveté (an ironic concept in itself) can be attained only by virtue of a
finely honed critical awareness. The "humility" with which
the voice of these poems uses words is thus necessarily the result of a complex and highly self-conscious
process, and those inner workings must be hidden, or
secret. But they need to remain secret only for an instant—and this is yet another key. Françoise Collin provides some insightful comments on this factor of the
equation. She sees in Borges's work "an intensification
of the presently lived moment," [Françoise Collin, "From
Blanchot to Borges," in *Borges and His Successors,*
ed. Alzenberg.] In his texts, she says, "the concentration of the unlimited in one instant transforms distress
into jubilation."

That instantaneous "concentration of the unlimited" well
expresses Borges's desire to see the problem of an unlimited, fluid word resolved through a momentary vision
or "invention" of that word as a newly minted one. This
is by no means a permanent or "real" solution to a fleeting language (just as Borges's famous "new refutation"
of time, for all its cleverness, could not really do away
with time). As Collin says, we cannot "hide the unlimited." But we can "apprehend it in a [different] mode." This
different mode of perception, she continues—and this
balancing of total knowledge and complete ignorance also
makes Borges possibly the most "critical" of all the poets,
[to study] . . . —is "a form of refutation of knowledge."
Exactly. The complexity must remain secret. For Borges
the key is to understand all the pitfalls that underlie language, in order to consciously adopt a new, momentary
naïveté, or a willing suspension of disbelief.

FURTHER READING

Criticism

Aizenberg, Edna, ed. *Borges and His Successors: The
Borgesian Impact on Literature and the Arts.* Columbia:
University of Missouri Press, 1990, 296 p.

Collection of essays that link postmodern texts to their roots in Borges's writing.

Borges, Jorge Luis. "Foreword." In *Homage to Walt Whitman: A Collection of Poems from the Spanish,* translated and annotated by Didier Tisdel Jaén, pp. xiii-xvii. University of Alabama Press, 1969.

Borges discusses Whitman's influential weaving together of biography and myth.

Collmer, Robert G. "Donne and Borges." *Revue de Littérature Comparée* 43, No. 2 (April-June 1969): 219-32.

Traces Borges's interest in the poetry of John Donne.

Molloy, Sylvia. "'The Coveter of Souls': A First Step toward Fiction." In *Signs of Borges,* pp. 10-11. Durham, N. C.: Duke University Press, 1994.

Briefly studies the "textual voyeurism" of Borges's early poetry.

Monegal, E. R. Review of *Selected Poems 1923-1967* and *Doctor Brodie's Report. The New York Times Book Review,* Part 1 (May 7, 1972): 4, 18.

Observes the sources and development of Borges's poetry.

Ortega, Julio. "Borges and the Latin-American Text," in *Poetics of Change: The New Spanish-American Narrative.* Austin: University of Texas Press, 1984, pp. 20-32.

Examines Borges's works in the context of Spanish-American culture.

Review of *Selected Poems 1923-1967. The New York Times Book Review,* Section 7 (June 4, 1972): 29.

A positive assessment of Borges's collected poetry.

Interviews

Botsford, Keith. "About Borges and Not About Borges." *The Kenyon Review* XXVI, No. 4 (Autumn 1964): 723-37.

Combines interview notes and personal ideas to present a characterization of Borges.

Burgin, Richard. "Tales and Meanings; Favorite Poems; The Gifts of Unhappiness; A Girl from Buenos Aires; Homer; Parables . . ." In *Conversations with Jorge Luis Borges,* pp. 66-80. New York: Holt, Rinehart and Winston, 1968.

Burgin and Borges discuss the latter's favorite poems and parables.

Additional coverage of Borges's life and career is contained in the following sources published by Gale Research: *Authors & Artists for Young Adults,* Vol. 19; *Contemporary Authors,* Vol. 21-24R; *Contemporary Authors New Revision Series,* Vols. 19, 33; *Contemporary Literary Criticism,* Vols. 1, 2, 3, 4, 6, 8, 9, 10, 13, 44, 48, 83; *Dictionary of Literary Biography,* Vol. 113; *Dictionary of Literary Biography Yearbook,* Vol. 86; *DISCovering Authors; DISCovering Authors: British; DISCovering Authors: Canadian; DISCovering Authors: Most-Studied Authors Module; DISCovering Authors: Multicultural Authors Module; Hispanic Literature Criticism; Hispanic Writers; Major 20th-Century Writers; Short Story Criticism,* Vol. 4; *World Literature Criticism.*

Ernesto Cardenal
1925-

Nicaraguan poet and nonfiction writer.

INTRODUCTION

A poet and Roman Catholic clergyman, Cardenal is a leading figure in the revolutionary literature of Latin America. Frequently compared to such distinguished authors as Ezra Pound and Pablo Neruda, Cardenal composes most of his poetry in a montage style that unites political ideology with theological reflection. His work critiques the values and ideology of modern capitalism in an effort to initiate societal change.

Biographical Information

Born in Granada, Nicaragua, Cardenal studied philosophy and letters at Mexico's National University and later attended Columbia University in New York City. During his college years, Cardenal composed love poems wherein he frequently incorporated news clippings or historical documents. He returned to his native country in the early 1950s and became involved in subversive activities directed against the regime of President Anastazio Somoza. After Somoza's murder in 1956, Cardenal experienced a spiritual conversion and entered the Trappist Monastery of Gethsemani, in Kentucky. Illness forced Cardenal to leave the monastery in 1957; two years later, he entered the Benedictine community at Cuernavaca, Mexico, and composed *Gethsemani, Ky.* A year after his ordination to the priesthood in 1965, Cardenal founded Solentiname, a Christian commune devoted to a life of manual labor, prayer, and scholarship. In 1977 the Nicaraguan government destroyed Solentiname, forcing Cardenal into exile in Costa Rica. When the Marxist Sandinistas seized control of Nicaragua in 1979, Cardenal was appointed Minister of Culture; however, Sandinistan human rights atrocities and ecclesiastical disapproval eventually forced him to resign.

Major Works

Cardenal's verse explores themes such as spiritual love and the quest for the transcendental life. *Gethsemani, Ky.*, for example, espouses a lyrical interpretation of the universe as having been formed by the outpouring of God's mercy. Likewise, *El estrecho dudoso* combines biblical rhetoric with prosody to show readers that history has an anagogical dimension. Echoing the form and content of the Old Testament psalms, the poems in *Salmos* frequently relate humanity's joy in beholding creation. In addition to religious motifs, Cardenal's poetry also manifests strong social and political concerns. Many of his works, including *With Walker in Nicaragua and Other Early Poems, 1949-1954,* examine Nicaragua's history, elucidating the

roots of conflict in Central America. Critics have found that Cardenal's later verse is markedly more explicit regarding the author's political sympathies. The poems in *Zero Hour,* for instance, mix archaic biblical prophetic teaching with contemporary Marxist ideology. The dialectic between the past and the present is similarly explored in *Homage to the American Indians;* recapturing the quality of pre-Columbian life, Cardenal's descriptions of the psychic wholeness of extinct Mayan, Incan, and Nahuatl civilizations are contrasted with the superficiality of modern imperialism.

Critical Reception

Critical reaction to Cardenal's work has been mixed. Some reviewers have denounced his poetry as didactic and propagandistic; many have found his Marxist treatises incompatible with his Catholic beliefs, yet others have praised the prophetic insight of his writing. Commentators have pointed out that Cardenal's poetry bears many similarities to Ezra Pound's verse. Like Pound, he borrowed the short, epigrammatic form from Catullus and Martial, masters of Latin poetry, whose works Cardenal has translated. Critics have also maintained that in his use of factual information, crosscutting, and contrast, his poetic technique resembles that of documentary filmmakers. His complex narrative *El estrecho dudoso,* for example, relates the history of destruction in Central America; through comparison and juxtaposed images, however, critics note that the poem becomes a commentary on contemporary political and cultural exploitation.

PRINCIPAL WORKS

Poetry

Ansias lengua de la poesía nueva nicaragüense 1948
Gethsemani, Ky. 1960
Horo 0 1960
Epigramas: Poemas 1961
Oración por Marilyn Monroe y otros poemas [*Prayer for Marilyn Monroe and Other Poems*] 1965
El estrecho dudoso 1966
Antología de Ernesto Cardenal 1967
Salmos [*The Psalms of Struggle and Liberation*] 1967
Homenaje a los indios americanos [*Homage to the American Indians*] 1974
Poesía escogida 1975
Apocalypse, and Other Poems 1977
Zero Hour and Other Documentary Poems 1980
Tocar el cielo: poesias 1981
Antología: Ernesto Cardenal 1983
With Walker in Nicaragua and Other Early Poems, 1949-1954 1985
From Nicaragua with Love: Poems 1979-1986 1986
Golden UFOs: The Indian Poems 1992

Other Major Works

Vida en el amor [*To Live is to Love*] (meditations) 1970
En cuba [*To Cuba*] (nonfiction) 1972
El Evangelio en Solentiname [*The Gospel in Solentiname*] (dialogues) 1975
La paz mundial y la Revolución de Nicaragua (nonfiction) 1981

CRITICISM

Jorge H. Valdés (essay date 1986)

SOURCE: "Cardenal's Poetic Style: Cinematic Parallels," in *Revista Canadiense de Estudios Hispánicos,* Vol. XI, No. 1, 1986, pp. 119-29.

[*In the following essay, Valdés discusses the cinematic images and techniques Cardenal utilizes in his poem "Oráculo sobre Managua."*]

In commenting on the ethical purpose and art of the poet, Cardenal writes in his poem **"Epístola a monseñor Casaldáliga":**

> No es tiempo ahora de crítica literaria.
> Ni de atacar a los gorilas con poemas surrealistas.
> ¿Y para qué metáforas si la esclavitud no es metáfora
> ni es metáfora la muerte en el Río das Mortes
> ni lo es el Escuadrón de la Muerte?

These lines declare even as they demonstrate a belief in the avoidance of highly figurative language, and they suggest the reasons for this belief. Indeed, the reader of **Hora 0, Salmos,** and the poetry that follows will be struck by the abundant use of literal, commonplace details and the paucity of figurative language. The details include historical and current events, ordinary household objects, commercials, well-known biblical references, the names of some of Cardenal's friends, and familiar, twentieth-century political figures, all having an existence apart from the subjective world of the poet, all verifiable, as it were, in external reality. This is not to say that the poetry of Cardenal is devoid of similes, metaphors, or symbols. One need only turn to the evocative, intimate poems of **Gethsemani, Ky.** to find several examples of figures of speech. In Cardenal's poetic work as a whole, however, one discovers not only the predominance of literal images but an ever-increasing use of prosaic detail, particularly in the poetry written after 1960—such as **Homenaje a los indios americanos,** "Canto nacional," "Oráculo sobre Managua," and the epistles to Casaldáliga and José Coronel Urtecho. In order to explain the poetic advantages of this technique, we need, first, to consider it by itself and, then, within a poetic structure or form. In doing the former, it will prove useful to invoke a parallel with the artistry of film, and, in doing the latter, to apply the language of film to an analysis of the structure of the first sequence of Cardenal's most ambitious poem, **"Oráculo sobre Managua."** But before doing either, it is necessary to discuss what led Cardenal to use literal detail so extensively.

Cardenal's penchant for a concrete language, often journalistic in style, can be explained partly by his faithful adherence to the principles of *exteriorismo,* a tendency predominant in Nicaraguan poetry since the 1950's. For Cardenal, the foremost exponent of this poetic tendency

> El exteriorismo no es un ismo ni una escuela literaria. Es tan antiguo como Homero y la poesía bíblica (en realidad es lo que ha constituido la gran poesía de todos los tiempos).

> El exteriorismo es la poesía creada con las imágenes del mundo exterior, el mundo que vemos y palpamos, y que es, por lo general, el mundo específico de la poesía. El exteriorismo es la poesía objetiva: narrativa y anecdótica, hecha con los elementos de la vida real y con cosas concretas, con nombres propios y detalles precisos y datos exactos y cifras y hechos y dichos. En fin, es la poesía *impura.*

> Poesía interiorista, en cambio, es una poesía subjetivista, hecha sólo con palabras abstractas o simbólicas como:

rosa, piel, ceniza, labios, ausencia, amargo, sueño, tacto,
espuma, deseo, sombra, tiempo, sangre, piedra, llanto,
noche . . .

Cardenal's affinity for *exteriorismo* cannot be explained solely in aesthetic terms, as this passage seems to suggest. It is, rather, the result of combined aesthetic and ethical interests. Indeed, in most instances, his aesthetic interests are subservient to his strongly ethical concerns. From the early *Epigramas* to the present, his poetry is patently didactic. As he emphatically states in the prologue to his anthology *Poesía nueva de Nicaragua*: "La literatura debe prestar un servicio. Debe estar—como todo lo demás en el universo—al servicio del hombre. Por lo mismo la poesía también debe de ser política. Aunque no *propaganda* política, sino *poesía* política." Thus, Cardenal's poetry seeks to inform, convince, and, ultimately, through immersion in apparently objective detail, move the reader beyond reflection into action. It seeks, in Robert Pring-Mill's words, "to provoke him [the reader] into full political commitment, thus fostering the translation of the poet's more prophetic visions into sociopolitical fact" [*Ernesto Cardenal: "Zero Hour" and Other Documentary Poems,* edited by Donald D. Walsh, 1980]. Exteriorist poetry, Cardenal feels, with its emphasis on the details of external reality is the mode most capable of rendering the troubled sociopolitical reality of Latin America, and, because of its sensory immediacy and readily verifiable frame of reference, the one most effective in engaging the reader.

Although in his definition of *exteriorismo* Cardenal focuses on the type of language employed by the poet, what mostly distinguishes his *exteriorismo* from "interiorist poetry" is the *way* in which he employs "los elementos de la vida real y . . . cosas concretas." The word "sangre," for instance, included by Cardenal in his catalogue of interiorist terms, is not uncommon in his exteriorist poetry, as we see in the following passage from **"Oráculo sobre Managua"**:

> Puertas destrozadas hierros retorcidos techo de zinc
> perforado por la avioneta las paredes con grandes
>   huecos
> sangre en el patio un colchón ensangrentado en el
>   baño
> pedazos de camisas calzonetas pañuelos llenos de
>   sangre
> sangre en la cocina los frijoles regados tapas de
>   parras
> con goterones de sangre en el patio la casa llena de
>   humo . . .

In all cases in which "sangre" appears in this passage, it is employed as one of many visual, concrete details depicting sensorially and directly the aftermath of Leonel Rugama's shootout with Somoza's forces. The term thus functions strictly as a literal image.

Cardenal therefore remains true to his exteriorist poetic credo, not by restricting his poetic language to certain words as he suggests, but by using visual details in a literal way. The literal use of concrete language allows him

to create a reality external to the speaker. At times, the speaker appears to be totally independent of this reality, as when Cardenal writes in **Hora 0**:

> En abril, en Nicaragua, los campos están secos.
> Es el mes de las quemas de los campos,
> del calor, y los potreros cubiertos de brasas,
> y los cerros que son de color de carbón;
> del viento caliente, y el aire que huele a quemado,
> y de los campos que se ven azulados por el humo
> y las polvaredas de los tractores destroncando;
> de los cauces de los ríos secos como caminos
> y las ramas de los palos peladas como raíces;
> de los soles borrosos y rojos como sangre
> y las lunas enormes y rojas como soles,
> y las quemas lejanas, de noche, como estrellas.
>
> En mayo llegan las primeras lluvias.
> La hierba tierna renace de las cenizas.
> Los lodosos tractores roturan la tierra.
> Los caminos se llenan de mariposas y de charcos,
> y las noches son frescas, y cargadas de insectos,
> y llueve toda la noche. En mayo
> florecen los malinches en las calles de Managua.

The end of winter in the first stanza and the coming of spring in the second are described with such realism and objectivity that the passage seems almost a random documentation of external reality. The faithfulness to concrete detail on the part of the poet and his restraint in withholding his emotional attitude allow the reality its autonomy. In depicting places and events which immerse the reader in the physical world about him, Cardenal's poetry operates much like a camera recording elements and events that can be responded to with sensory immediacy. Such poetry Robert Pring-Mill calls "documentary poetry."

Whereas Cardenal's documentary poetry makes extensive use of physical reality, it cannot be called objective. Regardless of how faithful Cardenal may remain in his depiction of external reality, intervening between the reader and that which is depicted, is the poet's selection of details and ordering of events. In fact, Cardenal's documentary poems rely heavily on the techniques of selection and ordering to bring the reader into communication with a physical world seen *exclusively* from the poet's point of view.

In the passage quoted above from **Hora O,** for instance, Cardenal has carefully selected a number of visual details to emphasize the arid and barren fields (e.g., "los campos están secos"; "las polvaredas de los tractores"; "los ríos secos como caminos") and to depict the termination of life (e.g., "las quemas de los campos"; "los potreros cubiertos de brasas"; "los cerros . . . color de carbón"; "el aire que huele a quemado"; "los campos . . . azulados por el humo"; "las quemas lejanas"). These visual details function with great immediacy as an objective correlative which prepares us to accept Cardenal's subsequent, explicitly stated view, that "abril en Nicaragua es el mes de la muerte." Moreover, the juxtaposition of the third strophe which portrays the tragic consequences of the aborted April

Rebellion reveals that the death previously evoked is not only that of nature but, more importantly, that of Adolfo Báez Bone and other revolutionaries:

> En abril los mataron.
> Yo estuve con ellos en la rebelión de abril
> y aprendí a manejar una ametralladora Rising.

Thus, what at first appeared as a documentation of a reality from which the poet was independent is now perceived as a description strongly tinted by the poet's point of view.

In its reliance on the selection and use of details and on the juxtaposition of events and descriptions, Cardenal's documentary style closely parallels the artistry of the documentary film. In documentary film the director's point of view is conveyed through the eye of the camera which selects what the viewer is to see, including effects of montage. This does not mean that Cardenal has consciously adopted the techniques of film, but there are parallels between the techniques of his poetry and those of film which ultimately enhance our appreciation of his artistry and our understanding of his thought. Given Cardenal's use of unconventional poetic techniques—many of which find filmic equivalents—the parallels provide us also with a critical terminology for analyzing his poetic strategy.

In order to demonstrate the usefulness of talking about Cardenal's documentary poetry in filmic terms, I will concentrate on the condensed opening lines of **"Oráculo sobre Managua"** (ll. 1-35). Before narrowing our focus to this section, however, it is necessary to give some sense of the section in the context of the poem as a whole.

Written in the aftermath of the earthquake which destroyed the center of the capital on December 23, 1972, **"Oráculo"** presents a comprehensive view of the inextricable relation of man, history, and nature. Its twenty-four sections, comprising almost a thousand lines, may be grouped into five distinct, though conceptually interrelated, sequences. The first one, consisting of just the first section (ll. 1-35), serves a function comparable to that of the establishing shot in film by giving an overview of a prehistoric site. The overview, in establishing the notion of an evolutionary-revolutionary process, provides a context for what follows, a context that gives fuller meaning to the particulars in subsequent sequences.

The second sequence, comprised of sections two and three (ll. 36-140), links the starving inhabitants of present-day Acahualinca, a shantytown near the prehistoric site, with the political prisoners tortured by Somoza, and with the prehistoric inhabitants fleeing in terror from a volcanic eruption. These ancient people are the same inhabitants whose footprints Cardenal points to in the opening establishing sequence. Thus, through what might be called a poetic visual montage, Cardenal successfully equates the terrorizing force of the prehistoric volcano with that of the victimizing Somoza.

The longest of the sequences, the third one, includes sections four through seventeen (ll. 141-588). In this sequence, through a variety of cutting techniques and camera-like movements, Cardenal develops the notion depicted visually by the examination of the archeological layers in the first section: an evolutionary-revolutionary dialectical process which encompasses both nature and man, prehistory and history. Although not made explicit in the opening section, this process is now conceived as an overall, though not constant, progression toward integration and union. According to Cardenal, the progression takes place both in the physical world and in the realm of human consciousness. It will yield "Un hombre nuevo un tiempo nuevo una nueva tierra" (I. 474).

Introducing yet another aspect of this process—revolutionary change in society—the fourth sequence, sections eighteen through twenty-one (ll. 589-767), portrays Leonel Rugama's battle against the Somoza regime as a struggle toward union. The revolutionary activity of society is parallel to the revolutionary activity of nature, seen as the volcanic eruption in the first sequence. These dramatic changes in society and nature, Cardenal maintains, result ultimately in the union of people (e.g., the union of people fighting in solidarity for economic and social justice, and the union of the ancient inhabitants in common flight from the erupting volcano).

Finally, in sections twenty-two through twenty-four (ll. 768-993), the fifth sequence employs, in effect, a pan shot of the drastic physical changes brought about by the earthquake. Analogous to the volcanic action of the first sequence, the earthquake is viewed by Cardenal as "un preludio telúrico de la revolución" (I. 892). The poem concludes with an integrating notion: sudden changes in the natural world (e.g., ancient volcanic eruption and modern earthquake) and revolutionary changes in society and the political state are understood as quickened steps in the pilgrimage toward a new social order. This order, characterized by union, is for Cardenal tantamount to love: "En medio de la tendencia general a la desintegración / hay una tendencia inversa / a la unión. Al amor" (ll. 165-67).

Although parallels to filmic techniques abound in all five sequences, they show themselves in greatest concentration in the opening sequence which lays the groundwork for the rest of the poem. An account of these parallels, using the terminology of film, yields the following interpretation: Introducing the sequence is a medium shot of a yarn and textile factory, as the narrator recalls it from before the earthquake. There follows immediately a flash shot of the tremor. The flash shot, signaled by a parenthetical statement—"(si ha quedado / la fábrica tras el terremoto)" (ll. 1-2)—establishes the idea of evolutionary change central to the meaning of the poem. A pan or horizontal camera-like movement to show a drainage channel near a lake leads to a series of close-ups of "basuras, bacinillas rotas, / . . . huellas, impresas en estrato volcánico" (ll. 3-4). The adverse conditions of the present are thus linked visually to the prehistoric footprints which resulted, as we soon learn, from equally adverse conditions. A visual montage of chamber pots and footprints further develops the notion of time and change suggested in the early flash shot. A sudden flashback achieved through the equivalent of two wipe cuts reinforces the idea of an evolutionary process: "Tal vez sin tejido textil, y ni siquiera cerámica, / ocuparon esta área de Managua junto con el bisonte. / Vivían de la caza y la pesca y la recolección de alimentos" (ll. 5-7). Concomitantly, the flashback serves as a basis for a contrast between the fertile conditions of the past and the decaying resources of the present. A sharp cut back to the present, followed immediately by a second flashback, shows that the present site of three lakes was in ancient times a single, active volcano. Three close-ups of footprints, separated by pan shots in the direction of the lake suggest the flight of the ancient people away from the volcano, and prepare us for understanding evolution as a long pilgrimage which will continue even in the present aftermath of the earthquake. Two flash shots, again signaled by parenthetical statements, provide specific details of the people in flight: "huellas huyendo del volcán / unas hundidas más (indica que algunos llevaban cargas) / no corriendo (los pasos son cortos y regulares)" (ll. 14-16). A close-up of other tracks of fleeing animals changes to a dissolve, denoted by three periods in succession. This dissolve serves, in turn, as a smooth transitional pointer to a shot of the eruption in progress. A quick cut returns us to the present site of Acahualinca where the poet begins to examine in a vertical movement or tilt shot the various layers of the subsoil beginning with the most ancient ones (at the bottom) and concluding with the most recent ones (at the surface). Whereas movement by itself suggests a process at work, the verticality of this movement suggests Cardenal's belief in a progression within the process. This progression is conveyed in specific terms by Cardenal's focus on artifacts. There is progress in the very creation of artifacts, and there is also progress in the evolution of the artifacts from utensils to objects of art:

> . . . y finalmente la capa superior de tierra
> con la primera cerámica. Maya. Monocroma. De
>   Nicoya
> (polícroma). De la época de Cristo. Cerámica Luna
> (lacas blancas y motivos de líneas finas). Monos
> jaguares rojos con fondo blanco, incensarios.
>
> **(ll. 30-34)**

At the surface level of the archeological site lies the rubbish of contemporary times: "Y encima / trozos de Coca Colas y llantas Goodyear y bacinillas" (ll. 34-35). Cardenal's choice of details such as Coca-Cola bottles, Goodyear tires, and chamber pots and the juxtaposition of these to the artistic pottery of Mayan times indicate the decadence of a consumer, capitalist society. This montage is particularly effective in communicating Cardenal's attitude toward present society as a retarder of progress, a theme he develops at length in the third sequence of the poem. For Cardenal, the division into classes and the rise of capitalism represent an unfortunate by-product of a dialectical evolution toward an absolute communal society. The slowing down of the evolutionary-revolutionary process, however, is seen, ultimately as a transitory irregularity in the course of evolution. Likewise, the contrasting

revolutionary changes in nature and society are presented as quick leaps in the evolutionary continuum.

The establishment of parallels between Cardenal's poetic strategy and various filmic techniques provides us with an approach well-suited to a study of the Nicaraguan's documentary style. This approach enables us to concentrate on the visual aspects of the poetry and to analyze the relation of its parts (its structure). The poet's documentary-like depiction of the world of external, objective reality, in combination with his restraint in the direct manifestation of subjective attitudes, enables the reader to *experience* Cardenal's perspective with sensory immediacy and, in several instances, with journalistic objectivity. Yet, as in film, the documentary approach is not as objective as it appears. As we have seen, beneath the surface lies a strongly personal interpretation of reality conveyed by means similar to those of film. These consist of the selection and use of details; quick, bold cuts from present to past events and continuous movement in the depiction of the setting, both to suggest an evolutionary-revolutionary process and to give the reader a felt sense of continual change; visual montages of events and elements in nature and society to establish parallels and contrasts which, in turn, convey the poet's attitudes; various distance shots to emphasize details or to set them in a meaningful context; and an establishing sequence to provide an overview to which the successive parts of the poem can be related.

In using "filmic" devices, Cardenal attempts to make the readers of "Oráculo" undergo, in two ways, the same dialectical process of integrating and unifying nature, man, history, and prehistory which he sees taking place in the universe: (1) through the readers' visual responses as they experience movement and change and (2) through the readers' conceptual responses as they relate and integrate what they experience in the poem. As a result of these responses, readers are made receptive to the poet's views, namely, that the earthquake that shook Managua is not an isolated event, but one in a long chain of evolutionary-revolutionary changes moving us toward the creation of an all-integrating consciousness and universal love. To the extent that readers accept this view, it is because Cardenal makes **"Oráculo"** a means of actively engaging his audience in the pursuit of his own goal, and he achieves this largely by using means that can be readily identified through cinematic parallels.

Reginald Gibbons (essay date 1987)

SOURCE: "Political Poetry and the Example of Ernesto Cardenal," in *Critical Inquiry*, Vol. 13, No. 3, Spring, 1987, pp. 648-71.

[*In the following essay, Gibbons places Cardenal within the context of Latin American politics and examines the major themes of his political poetry.*]

Perhaps the subject of political poetry is so inextricable from specific poems and poets at particular historical moments that one can discuss only examples. Ernesto Cardenal is an interesting one, not least because the cause for which he long spoke, the release of the Nicaraguan peasantry from the oppressive burdens of economic exploitation and arbitrary rule by force, was victorious; the Sandinista victory gave him an opportunity, or an obligation, to become a poet of praise and victory after he had been a poet of compassion and wrath:

De pronto suena en la noche una sirena
de alarma, larga, larga,
el aullido lugúbre de la sirena
de incendio o de la ambulancia blanca de la muerte,
como el grito de la cegua en la noche,
que se acerca y se acerca sobre las calles
y las casas y sube, sube, y baja
y crece, crece, baja y se aleja
creciendo y bajando. No es incendio ni muerte:
   Es Somoza que pasa.

Suddenly in the night there's a siren
of alarm, long, long
the gloomy howling of the siren
of a fire engine or the white ambulance of death,
like the cry of a mourner in the night,
that comes nearer and nearer over the streets

and houses and rises, rises, and falls
and grows louder, louder, falls and goes away
rising and falling. It's neither fire nor death:
   It's Somoza going by.

In Latin America Cardenal is generally regarded as an enduring poet. He brought a recognizably Latin American material into his poetry, and he introduced to Spanish-language poetry in general such poetic techniques as textual collage, free verse lines shaped in Poundian fashion, and, especially, a diction that is concrete and detailed, textured with proper names and the names of things in preference to the accepted poetic language, which was more abstract, general, and vaguely symbolic. But what is notable in Spanish-language poetry is not only Cardenal's "craft," in the sense given this word by Seamus Heaney to mean manipulation of poetic resources; there is also this poet's "technique," which in Heaney's sense means a "definition of his stance toward life." Cardenal's characteristic poetic stance has been admired because he addresses the political and social pressures that shape—and often distort, damage, or destroy—life and feeling. This is apparent even in the earliest poems Cardenal has chosen to preserve. **"Raleigh,"** for example, is a dramatic meditation from 1949 in which the treasure-hunting explorer marvels at the expanse and wealth of the American continents and out of sheer pleasure recounts some of the triumphs and hardships of his travels. Although his alertness and wonder make him sympathetic, this Raleigh's vision of the New World as a limitless source of wealth is forerunner to the economic exploitation of the land and people.

One might ask, What are the political and social circumstances which, rather than distorting and damaging life

and feeling, nurture and preserve them? Perhaps one might answer that, paradoxically, destructive conditions of life have many times proven insufficiently powerful to prevent the creation of poetry. And some poetry has even arisen in reaction to the destructive: such conditions produce resistance, which, if it cannot heal the spirit, can lend it strength. One might answer further that it is not Cardenal's or any artist's responsibility to establish what circumstance will form a fruitful matrix for art, but only to work as honestly and as hard as political, social, and artistic circumstances will permit.

Poetry, perhaps of all arts, is least demanding of physical materials: mere scraps of paper and a pencil, or nothing at all but a good memory, may suffice for its creation. Its medium is the currency of our thinking and feeling, language; and its creation is individual, solitary, and takes place in response to, or despite, every known social and political situation. States may seek to suppress it by making publication difficult or impossible and by attacking its creators, the poets. But no state has found a way to expedite the writing of great poetry or to improve the quality of poetry generally.

However, one sees Cardenal seeking at times, especially in his most recent works, to praise conditions and possibilities which he regards as favorable to life and to art, and which he locates in the promises and principles, if not always the achievements, of the Sandinista government. Most such poems are less convincing than those which speak not for any form of social organization but for other persons in their suffering or happiness, or which represent a critical intelligence and speak against the destructive.

Indeed, in Cardenal's work as a whole there are two recurring contradictions which are never resolved convincingly, as far as I can tell. The first is between on the one hand poetic experiment and on the other hand a desire to write as accessibly as possible; that is, a contradiction between the poet answering his own expressive needs or the political needs of the audience (as he conceives them). The second is between on the one hand poems of anger and hope which speak *against* (against injustice, suffering, materialism, oppression both historical and contemporary, and so on) and which enjoy the advantages of a stance of independence, critical thinking, and resistance, and on the other hand poems which speak *for* (for compassion, for justice, for delight, and—or but?—for revolution, then for the Sandinista victory) and which may adopt a voice of consensus or even obligatory ideals. Both of these patterns of contradiction are also congruent with the modern dilemma of the artist-intellectual: "the unresolved conflict at the heart of the Romantic-democratic concept of art" is a "dual commitment both to 'high' literature (as the expression of transcendent personal genius) and to a literature that represents 'the people' at large," in the succinct wording of Sacvan Bercovitch, writing of the classic (North) American writers [*Critical Inquiry,* Summer, 1986].

A common though blandly favorable reaction to Cardenal's poetry outside Latin America goes like this: "His poems deserve attention both for the ideas expressed (whether one agrees with them or not) and for their intrinsic poetic merit." We are often so asked to divide poetry into two constituent parts, its technical virtues and its expression of belief, and to suspend or quality our judgment of the latter. But is the division desirable, necessary, useful, or reliable as a representation of how we read, experience, and evaluate poems? How do the two elements function? What part of poetic *meaning* is constituted by belief? How is that meaning created and conveyed, how far is it subject to evaluation apart from the poem, and how generally may the poem be evaluated if it expresses belief?

These questions go beyond the broad notion of the inherently "subversive" nature of art, as in Marcuse's formulations. All art may indeed stand in a subversive or at least critical relationship to established institutions, to ideology, to "common sense," conventional wisdom, and habits of feeling. (I will return to this idea below, in discussing the rhetoric of poetry.) But that antagonistic relationship is flexible enough to permit artworks to decorate corporate buildings or to please tyrants. Equally problematic is the intention of authors whose essentially subversive works (such as surrealist poems) prove too difficult to be understood by those whom they would either attack or liberate. And when art, including poetry, professes belief or takes a perceptibly political stance toward life or allies itself explicitly with certain historical figures, movements, or causes, there can also be surprising contradictions. If Pound and Cardenal are, for instance, completely opposed politically, they nonetheless share not only a poetic technique but also the (related?) assumptions that the structure of society and of institutions, if changed, could improve the spiritual and material conditions of man, and that poetry may participate in the attempt to change what exists. How may the devices and powers of narrowly read literary works so participate? One answer derives from Kenneth Burke: literature may function as a kind of "symbolic action" which confronts that which cannot be effectively confronted by "real" action, either categorically (such as death) or effectively (such as a war). (Symbolic action joins in spirit other forms of action that confront mutable realities such as the social and political organization of the human community.) This symbolic action has the power to satisfy our impulse to act, to *move* (as in political "movements"), our desire to be moved (as in "[e]motion"), and our need for solace and joy, which we seek even in "emblems of adversity." By no means does this amount to a mere "acting out," which would be a kind of blindness to reality; it is instead a clearer seeing of the world, an elucidation of reality by artistic means.

An example is the poem quoted at the head of this essay. This early work of Cardenal's uses the devices of poetry, including the enacted rhythms of perception, the chimes of similar sounding phonemes (especially assonance on the vowels *e-a* and *a-a*), and the dramatic possibilities of syntax to create first a perceptible sense-impression and then to reveal the source and thus the meaning of that sense-impression. Especially significant is the assonance on *e-a*, which links the words *suena* ("it sounds"), *sirena*

(the siren), *cegua* (the "mourner"—a deliciously complicated word, of which more in a moment), *acerca* ("it comes near"), *calle* ("street"), and *aleja* ("it goes away").

Cegua is a Central American regionalism, a word indigenous to the world Cardenal is describing. It derives from the Aztec *cihautl,* "woman," and means a woman weeping, or even a hired mourner; but it's also a kind of apparition, a village bogey with the body of a woman and the head of a horse, which screams in the night and is popularly believed to be a ghost. The *cegua*'s presence in folklore is pre-Columbian, so with this word Cardenal establishes the cry in the night as an ancient protest, heard by the humblest persons (to whose imagination and lives the *cegua* mostly speaks). The *e-a* assonance *is* the *cegua*; the assonantal words enact its approach and withdrawal through the streets. Cardenal plays on contradiction at the end of the poem, when he writes that the sound is not in fact that of a fire truck or an ambulance rushing to some emergency with which a mourner might be associated. The siren comes from Somoza's convoy of police, yet the ghost-soul in torment cries out at the passing of the tyrant, as if at fire and death. The tyrant is not the fact of fire and death but the ever-present threat. The *cegua* is not only his announcement of his passing but also the curse laid on him by the common people through the image of this supernatural mourner.

The terrible sound moves, as Somoza does, and the unmoving listener who hears it escapes simply because Somoza goes by without stopping. Is the deftness of the manipulation of expectation and surprise simply an ornament to the poetic contention that Somoza is an active, destructive force, against whom the passive citizen can do nothing except bear bitter witness? Or is this oscillation between opposites or containment of them something essential to the poem, and even to poetry generally?

The poem is "political" in that by means of its allusion and devices it attacks the dictator of Nicaragua. In terms proposed by Thomas McGrath [reprinted in *North Dakota Quarterly,* Fall, 1987], this would appear to be more of a "tactical" revolutionary poem, aimed at local and specific circumstances, than a "strategic" poem, whose effect is to "expand" the consciousness of the reader:

> One [. . .] kind of poetry [. . .] might be called tactical, about some immediate thing: a strike, let's say; some immediate event. The poet should give it as much clarity and strength as he can give it without falling into political slogans, clichés, and so on. I also thought we needed another kind of poetry that is *not* keyed necessarily to immediate events, a poetry in which the writer trusts himself enough to write about whatever comes along, with the assumption that what he is doing will be, in the long run, useful, consciousness raising or enriching. A strategic poetry, let's say. There have been a lot of tactical poems directed to particular things, and those poems now are good in a certain sort of way, but the events they were about *have moved out from under them.* Somebody asked Engels, "What happened to all the revolutionary poetry of 1848?" He

replied: "It died with the political prejudices of the time." That is bound to be the fate of a lot of tactical poetry. [. . .] On the other hand, we take a poem like Neruda's *Canto General,* a marvelous big poem, but it's not there to help in some immediate kind of situation; it's a *strategic* poem. But anyone who reads it will have his consciousness expanded by the reading of it. . . . The ideal thing of course is to bring the tactical and the strategic together so that they would appear in this massive poem of pure lucidity, full of flying tigers and dedicated to the removal of man-eating spinning wheels from the heads of our native capitalists—absolute lucidity and purest, most marvelous bullshit. That's the poem I would like to have, because there's a place where those two are the same. That's in the archetypal heavens of course.

The value of Cardenal's best work, even when it is most specific to Nicaraguan life, is that it is—in McGrath's terms—strategic as well. For does one have to know who Somoza is for the poem to make sense? Doesn't an inference of his nature suffice? One cannot substitute the name of a humane benefactor—Mother Teresa, Hippocrates—without introducing an absurd contradiction into the poem; but it *is* possible to substitute the name of any historical or literary figure identified with state terror, or any political figure identified by some audience, somewhere, as tyrannical and violent, without changing the poem's meaning, only its focus.

Nonetheless, the poem's strongest gesture is in its naming of Somoza, and if a substitution of names reveals a deeper value, still the act of naming—ancient and consecrated to poetry—is crucial. Here the naming is not, as in some poems, a blessing, but a curse. And the poem is political not only in delivering the curse that is Somoza's name but also in its demonstration, within the terms of the descriptive diction, of a political relationship between the one who listens passively, powerless and vulnerable, and the one who raises sounds of fright and threats of harm. Both Somoza and the listener are "political" agents in their participation in Nicaraguan society. But the powerless agent—namer, witness, and giver of detail—has only the language and his poem, which by virtue of its artistic effectiveness is emotionally empowering, with which to "act" (symbolically), while the agent of power acts but has no voice of his own (in the poem), only the accompanying mournful cry of the *cegua,* which is at once the sound of his own destructiveness and the wail of those whom he harms. In life, Somoza's voice rules persons; in poems, Cardenal's can hope to rule only time (as poets have always hoped their poems would outlive themselves and their subjects).

When, with his fellow poet José Coronel Urtecho, Cardenal formulated his new poetics, which was intended in part to make a kind of political comment aesthetically possible in poetry, he gave it the name *exteriorismo* and offered a rationale for density of detail, use of documents, and free form. Aesthetically, "exteriorism" was influenced not only by Pound's introduction of materials formerly foreign to poetry but also by his advice to the Imagists to avoid subjectivity in their work and to prefer a precise description of the thing outside the self. One of several explanations:

> *Exteriorismo* is a poetry created with images of the exterior world, the world we see and sense, and that is, in general, the specific world of poetry. *Exteriorismo* is objective poetry: narrative and anecdote, made with elements of real life and with concrete things, with proper names and precise details and exact data, statistics, facts, and quotations. . . . In contrast, interiorist poetry is a subjectivist poetry made only with abstract or symbolic words: rose, skin, ash, lips, absence, bitterness, dream, touch, foam, desire, shade, time, blood, stone, tears, night.

But beyond this aesthetic influence and preference, exteriorism seems also shaped by unmistakable political considerations. In the context of long-suppressed civil liberties and gross economic exploitation of the peasantry, exteriorism looks like an attempt to find a poetic principle that would disallow the kind of language that was characteristic of, or acquiescent to, political and commercial powers. The acquiescence of poetic interiority and ethereality to arbitrary state power or capitalist exploitation would be forestalled if a poem contained the true names of things and the textures of perceived reality. No one who is unfamiliar with the clichés of bad poetry in Spanish can appreciate how bitter is the gesture of Cardenal's list of despised "subjectivist" words.

I see Cardenal's poetry as a sphere in which we are called as individuals to react not only to a poet's perceptions but also to feeling, conviction, and belief as they be related to us in our own lives.

—*Reginald Gibbons*

While it is unfair to expect manifestos to be reasonable, there are two objections to this one. First, if subjectivist words are indeed a poetic liability (as, in our poetry, the repetitive later work of W. S. Merwin seems to demonstrate with a similarly reduced symbolic vocabulary), it was nonetheless with such a brief poetic word list that Paul Celan created powerful—but not at all "exteriorist"—responses to the historical reality of the German concentration camps and the murder of so many Jews. A prescription for poetic diction cannot guarantee the truth of poetry, even if the example of Cardenal shows how one poet freed himself from an oppressive poetic context with just such a prescription (which excluded a few things and, more important, included many things). Second, as Czeslaw Milosz has written, "Not every poet who speaks of real things necessarily gives them the tangibility indispensable to their existence in a work of art. He may as well make them unreal." I take him to mean that the mere naming of things is insufficient to suggest their reality to the reader, and such a failing has little to recommend it over its opposite poetic failing, mystification. But however valid these two objections may be generally, Cardenal's exteriorist poetics nonetheless empowered him to write a kind of poetry, and a poetry of distinct successes, not seen before in Spanish. The exuberance and plenitude of descriptive detail even in the early **"Raleigh,"** and the American materials and occasions of this and other poems, attest to this. If these same two objections have more weight against Cardenal's later poems, that is another issue in a poetic career inextricably rooted in his changing political circumstances in Nicaragua, to which I will return.

The influence of both the ventriloquistic and autobiographical passages in Pound's *Cantos* is also apparent in Cardenal's early **"La vuelta a América"** or **"León,"** although Pound's poems are denser and more far-ranging in their allusions. The irony of Cardenal's use of Pound's poetics—the leftist poet profiting from the reactionary's poetic achievements and discoveries—shows that those devices have no inherent relation to any particular political position but in larger terms simply accommodate the presence of political and historical materials in poetry. [In *Poetry East,* 1986] McGrath has warned against unthinkingly equating traditional poetic forms with reactionary political belief and has pointed out that "most of the inventors [of free verse] were political reactionaries, even Fascists. Why should they smash up the traditional forms?" (Indeed—why should they? The topic is complex. The communist Hugh MacDiarmid, for example, used both traditional forms and meter, and free verse.) McGrath suggests unexceptionably that free verse "has often been used to bring new materials, attitudes and feelings into poetry. In this century, it always flourishes when poets interest themselves in social-political matters, when they take sides, even tentatively or unknowingly, in the class struggle." McGrath doesn't specify on what side, and one thinks not only of Pound but also of Williams Carlos Williams, Allen Ginsberg, Aimé Césaire, and others in this context.

In keeping with this more general connection between free verse and political *materials,* and even before his political position is as clear as it will later be, Cardenal employs poetic detail in his early work simply to suggest the complex and unhappy effect of the first Europeans on the native cultures of America. His judgment of them as individuals is not at all sweeping; in **"Los filibusteros" ("The Freebooters")** he writes:

> Hubo rufianes, ladrones, jugadores, pistoleros.
> También hubo honrados y caballeros y valientes.
>
> There were rogues, thieves, gamblers, gunmen.
> There were also decent men, gentlemen, and brave
>   men.

So these early poems are "political" in the sense of being concerned generally with a moral judgment of social and political relations and therefore with the historical record of conquest and governance in America. For, as Kenneth Burke puts it in an early essay, "The Nature of Art Under Capitalism," both "pure" art and "propaganda" arise partly out of the relationship between "work-patterns and ethical patterns" [*The Philosophy of Literary Form: Studies in Symbolic Action,* 1973]. That is, all poetic response is in some way tied to the ways in which the people around the poet live, work, and die. But, despite our being able to invoke Burke's symbolic action and McGrath's terms "tactical" and "strategic," the artistic accomplishment of a poem may well seem insufficient to a poet whose daily life brings him the sight of peasants debilitated, impoverished, and even murdered by their own government. Some poets and readers will always feel that in terms of its concrete effect on life, the poem is arguably of less value than bread would be, even though Milosz says that the experience of Poland shows that when bread is scarce, poetry becomes most valuable. Cardenal's exteriorism, as a linguistic gesture, seems to be an attempt to bring the power of naming—as when he cursed Somoza in the poem quoted above—to bear on everything that could be named in the life around him, and his poetic faith in the power of naming is striking, one might even say touching, in the face of hopelessness. But exteriorism was an artistic solution to an artistic problem, not a political solution to anything.

After the successful revolution, Cardenal can be seen to move from the anecdotal and narrative textures of some of the exteriorist poems, juxtaposed against each other and against other kinds of quotation and poetic material, toward something simpler with, if anything, a renewed presence of names and naming, but more like homily that includes exemplary incidents or facts. The short postrevolutionary poems, while they sometimes have a lyric intensity missing from Cardenal's exteriorist poems, can also seem pieces of a larger work that he has not accomplished, perhaps hasn't wanted to accomplish. He prefers the tactical to the strategic *after* the revolution, one might say. Under the surface of many of the later poems is a felt, implicit obligation to make use of poetry as an inspiriting, uplifting kind of exhortation and for praise of revolutionary accomplishment.

Cardenal's case is less unusual in Latin American terms than in North American ones. The Latin American tradition of education and art differs from our own, first in grouping the artist with the relatively small caste of intellectuals, and second in expecting the intellectual (and artist) to be sensible of a social obligation to the rest of society. Latin American intellectuals and artists tend to be more involved in political activity than their North American counterparts: when governments are sufficiently acceptable to them, writers have often served them, and when governments are unacceptable to persons with humane values, writers have tended to oppose them not only with words but also with acts. When Cardenal writes in a spirit of solidarity with the revolutionaries against Somoza or the impoverished peasants or later the Sandinista government, he is keeping faith with the intellectuals' social responsibility as he has inherited it. Is he likely to be charged with breaking faith with a responsibility more familiar and more highly touted among North American writers—to independence from all constraints, from all responsibilities but those felt as personal? He might answer that the responsibilities he feels are indeed, to him, the stuff of conscience. Is the objection then to conscience itself, when conscience brings not only consciousness of "wrong," but also responsibilities of "right"? After all, in his major early work, ***Hora 0*** (1960), we see, as the poem itself says of Sandino, "poeta convertido en soldado por necesidad (a poet converted by necessity into a soldier)."

In the social context in which Cardenal has lived and written, preserving a strictly "personal" independence might be regarded not as a responsibility but as an intellectually irresponsible withdrawal from social and political life.

Cardenal's position as the first minister of culture of Nicaragua, dating from his appointment by the Sandinista government in 1979, is a circumstance that one cannot help pondering when reading his most recent work. After all, his poems closely identify him with the contemporary history of Nicaragua. The trajectory of his work moves from outrage and lament over suffering and injustice to a sense of triumph and an active encouragement of those who rebelled against Somoza, overthrew him and his army, and took control of the nation's government. With these views many North American literary intellectuals have no complaints. Ernesto Cardenal has done the right thing, has been politically correct—this is the viewpoint of the North American left (and, of course, of others whose stand is political because it arises out of moral repugnance at the inhumane dictatorship which the Sandinistas overthrew).

It is far more common in Latin America than in North America for a writer to join a political party or cause; this is the accepted, indeed expected, course of political conscience. If a party wins power, it may be just as common for those who have joined or supported it to find themselves in the position of having to choose to work for the new government or to be considered an enemy for having declined to serve. I do not know either the nature of the Sandinista government's invitation to Cardenal or his feelings about accepting it. But if his present position is no surprise, it is probably a reflection not only of conviction but also of political necessity. For this reason I am not sure Cardenal can be considered an architect of the political regime which eventually was established, insofar as it is not ideal. The practical necessities and compromises of political power will crush the scrupulosity of intellectual and artistic inquiry and experiment, even where these have had the apparent advantage in their formation of a consciousness of social responsibility. And even if ministers of culture had much power, the historical record shows few such officials who could bring their artistic scruples to the exercise of their personal power. But we so seldom see a serious artist in a position of state power that we may forget the inevitable conflicts of conscience that must face any intellectual whose public being is not outside power and devoted to critique but subservient to a power group and at least partly conscripted for the presentation and protection of that power.

Speaking in Chicago in 1985, Cardenal ridiculed as a perversion of the humanistic tradition the bizarre appendix on "Literary Resources" in the contra pamphlet circulated by the CIA. His justifiable scorn for this absurd little essay and its author follows from the assumption that poetry by definition can have no hand in violence against the innocent or in violation of humane ideals such as the sanctity of life or the desirability of education or medical care. Yet because of Cardenal's own conversion from poet to soldier—and understandably—there come moments even in his poems when some of these values are abandoned. If a revolution is to win a military victory it must usually succeed in killing and capturing a sufficient number of the ruling forces. Revolutionaries weigh the violence they must commit against the violence suffered by those on whose behalf they fight. Others weigh the justice of that cause. Poets may side with revolutionaries, or against them, or neither; but their weighing of the same moral dilemma remains a "symbolic" act, in that poems, even when they move readers, do not carry arms. If it is true, as has been said, that Che Guevara carried poems of Pablo Neruda in his pack, it is also uncertain whether poems are sought in such circumstances because they encourage, or console.

It is no surprise when a great and political poem like Neruda's "Alturas de Macchu Picchu" prizes life over death, but a political (and especially a revolutionary) poem must also begin to say *whose* life. When Pound bitterly laments in poems the waste of life in World War I, the "enemy" is not Germany—no more than it is England—but a deadly failure that the political leadership of both nations share. In Cardenal's earlier work the lives of the powerless, the vulnerable, and the persecuted are movingly memorialized; perhaps, in such fierce work, it is impossible not to prize their lives above the lives of their tormentors or oppressors. In his postrevolutionary work the compassion narrows further. If it was true that there were no "innocent" victims on the side of Somoza, and that one cannot invite the murderous oppressor into one's own house, there is nonetheless something disappointing in the poet who makes such frequent reference to a Christian commune based on love, but who, in **"Preguntas frente al lago" ("Questions Beside the Lake")**, sounds not wise but strained when he writes that "God is something that is in everyone, / in you, in me, everywhere." The exteriorist poetic cannot justify or redeem some of Cardenal's later poems, nor convince the reader to admire them solely for their value as sentiment or statement.

Another recent poem recounts the young Sandino's fury at seeing a trainload of American soldiers come to occupy Nicaragua for the benefit of American investment:

> y el chavalo se puso furioso
> > y dijo que deseaba colgarlos a todos de los palos.
> Lo interesante de este cuento es que este chavalo
> > después pudo realizar lo que deseaba.

> and the boy became enraged
> > and said he wanted to hang them all from the trees.
> The interesting thing about this story is that this boy
> > later was able to do what he wanted.

Again, one doesn't by any means expect to see a forgiving hand offered to the contras and ex-Somocistas who are still committing crimes of violence; one wonders only if the prophet of democratic, humane ideals can sustain his vision when he must speak for a regime—any regime—rather than against one. The lives of "men and women who find themselves in history's path" tend to be so much expendable currency to those who rule, and even to those who would rule. Cardenal's deep—and convincing—allegiance was to those who *are* ruled. In his much earlier poem **"Apocalipsis"** (**"Apocalypse,"** published 1973) he rewrites the Revelation of Saint John and includes these lines:

> y el ángel me dijo: esas cabezas que le ves a la
>   Bestia son dictadores
> y sus cuernos son líderes revolucionarios que aún
>   no son dictadores
> pero lo serán después
> y lucharán contra el Cordero
>
> and the angel said to me: those heads you see on
>   the Beast are dictators
> and its horns are revolutionary leaders who are not
>   yet dictators
> but will be afterward
> and will fight against the Lamb

This frightening prophecy only confirms, to my mind, the humane sensibility and values in Cardenal's work. It does not alter my own understanding that the revolution against Somoza for which he hoped and which he supported did indeed rescue many people from violent or impoverished death, and has led to a life at least marginally better—especially regarding education and medical care—for many, perhaps most of the citizens of Nicaragua. But these early lines seem dangerously ironic in the present political context.

Cardenal's comments in Chicago sought to establish an intimate, essential link between poetry and the Sandinista revolution. Yet the U.S-sponsored counterrevolution of the contras against the Sandinista government, which has put the former revolutionaries in the position of defending an established order, had inevitably driven him to a position we often call in English "artistic compromise." Now, in Spanish the word "compromised" does not have a pejorative connotation but means the same as the French *engagé*—committed to a belief and to a participation in the possibilities for action that follow from that belief. *Comprometido* connotes not "I will yield my interests and in part accept yours" or "I have cheapened my character" but "I am committed to what I have promised, in solidarity with you." Does this merely rationalize, or does it justify, not only Cardenal's lament for the deaths and deprivations suffered under Somoza but also his desire to find glory as much as tragic loss in revolutionary death?

Among poems that present us with the issue of the "political," then, there are those which express identifiable party, ideological, or historical positions (the tactical poetry of a revolutionary). There are others that happen rather to represent human life in such a way that inevitably some of the social and political contexts of feeling and action are depicted, pondered, or enacted by the poet (the strategic poetry of a socially conscious writer). There may also be implied politics in a poem caught willy-nilly in a powerful sociopolitical context. Even the poem intended to be "pure" (a species deriving from Mallarmé and Valéry, and one whose value was much debated in Spain in the first half of this century) may come to seem political or reveal its political meaning (and its strategic value) in the context of repressive state power. The state, in permitting, perhaps undermines some art and, in attacking, foregrounds in art the humane values it would destroy (as with Mandelstam or Lorca). Less apparently political art may be attacked as forcefully as overtly oppositional works because its expressive power can be just as memorable, and because it too threatens to bear witness far into the future against the state.

I think what distinguishes the strategic sort of poetry is that it *resists* ideology in favor of an insistence on the intrinsic value of life and the political value of life lived freely. Such poetry often shows an encompassing compassion. These very values can of course be claimed by an ideology—and as Burke notes, "the ideal act of propaganda consists in imaginatively identifying your cause with values that are unquestioned." But the political practice of ideology will inevitably belie the rhetoric. (For example, Cardenal has said that there is no poetry of the contras, not could there be; but even if there were, it would be bound up with the likes of Ronald Reagan's absurd claim of virtue for the contras when he calls them "freedom fighters" while at the same time condemning black revolutionaries who have far greater cause to rebel against the South African government.) The values that can truly claim the widest adherence, and which repressive states will strive actively to eradicate, or with bureaucratic structures will wear down, or with the manipulation of language and image will subvert and discredit, are those which in essence make a plea for peace, freedom from danger, mutual respect and compassion between persons, and an orderly social organization that forbids arbitrary power and fosters justice. Thus artistic works expressive of these values must unavoidably offer witness to the relationship between individual and state; to memory, as against forgetting (the cardinal point of Milosz's conception of poetry); and, quite simply, to life as against death.

I believe there is an identifiable rhetoric of poetry—a poetics, general across several historical periods, languages, and cultures (at least in the West), which is subtly and complexly entangled with these values. It is a rhetoric of observable techniques common to many poets—perhaps all of which belong to a general intention to write in such a way as simply to please the memory that recalls the poem. Perhaps the pleasure to memory of the wrought thing, the poem, partly accounts for the admiration and preservation even of poetry whose ostensible subject is pitiable or unpleasant. This does not mean subject is secondary or irrelevant; on the contrary, this shows that the poet's manipulation of poetic devices and resources (Heaney's "craft") tends to please the senses and to evoke one's admiration for the poet's gift, while the poet's "stance toward life" (Heaney's "technique") gratifies the spirit and emphasizes one's overcoming, with the poet, the distances between men. Thus Heaney says one can find poets of wobbly craft who nonetheless have a strong technique. like Patrick Kavanagh, but the most common failing is the poet of some craft who is lacking a technique, a stance toward life. Technique implicates the poet's materials, subjects, and occasions: Homer's craft becomes a source of pleasure and the vehicle of ancient lore, while Homer's technique makes one reread the poems to feel again our astonishment at them.

Obviously, poems of the sort that present what Terrence Des Pres calls [in *Tri Quarterly,* Winter 1986] "the *concrete* relations of men and women who find themselves in history's path" tend no less than any others to utilize this rhetoric, and we often call these poems "political" only in the most general sense of the word. But to see this is nonetheless to catch a glimpse of the politics indeed inherent in all use of language. In English, the poetic rhetoric seems generally to privilege acute discriminations and vividness of detail, memorable freshness of diction, and strength of syntax. No better description of it exists than Coleridge's in chapter 14 of his *Biographia Literaria,* which implies the power of poetry to contravene the *habits* of perception, feeling, and thought and thus to confront us with a more profound sort of truth than we are used to, as well as giving us pleasure in the art. This quality of newness ("defamiliarizing," in the critical vocabulary) is what William Carlos Williams meant when he wrote in "Asphodel, That Greeny Flower":

My heart rouses
            thinking to bring you news
                        of something
that concerns you
            and concerns many men. Look at
                        what passes for the new.
You will not find it there but in
            despised poems.
                        It is difficult
to get the news from poems
            yet men die miserably every day
                        for lack
of what is found there.

The values inherent in such a poetic rhetoric would inevitably contend on some level with all bureaucratic and state powers. Is it for this reason that tyrants prefer music to poetry for their aesthetic pleasure? Music draws one, sometimes dizzily, into the self, as one responds to what Suzanne Langer called music's formal "morphology of feeling"; but poetry is unavoidably an utterance that presumes a connection between the one who writes and the one who, when reading, experiences not only a kind of dynamics of feeling but also the recognition of the referents outside the poem and of the concrete being of others. Totalizing powers, such as those of governments and bureaucracies, must be blind to the feelings and suffering of others in order to function: they fail to respond to individuals except as antagonists whom they would dis-

tract, coopt, suppress, or destroy. The rhetoric of poetry, in this context, is inherently critical; and its essence is a kind of quicksilver gleaming that cannot be eradicated.

Perhaps the poetic rhetoric I have described is natural to all literary works of enduring value; it collects, constellates, presents, transforms, and otherwise alters the names and descriptions of things, acts, and mental states in such a way as to produce in us a responsiveness to the descriptive detail and to the minutest functions and powers of language. To take an outwardly unlikely example, even such a programmatically generalized work as Samuel Johnson's *Rasselas*—where in chapter 10 Imlac offers a famous definition of a poetic rhetoric quite opposite to the one I have just sketched—presents us nonetheless with a literary text to which we respond as to none other: we apprehend not only the descriptive specificities of the text and the unique substance and embodiment of Johnson's thinking but also the admired and inimitable rhythms and textures of Johnson's sentences. Thus the poetic rhetoric of details and oppositions, in congruence with the moral values with which I have associated it, suggests that the nature of literary works is to resist tendencies in the reader to totalize, summarize, paraphrase, or abstract, just as the nature of those values is to stand against the effort of states and bureaucracies to oppress individual citizens, to generalize and quantify them, and thus to convert them from unique individuals to manipulable groups. Poetry's nature is to prize its own contravention of the political or social norm, even in a period when the poet considers himself an exponent of the norm, for the great poem defies above all the mediocrity of the other poems that form its literary context.

Even though individual poetic temperament may often be more important than any other factor in the poet's craft, some interesting generalities about individuality itself can be seen. In much eastern European poetry, the idea of privacy seems a defiance of state powers of surveillance, an insistence that individual powerlessness imposed by the state will not succeed in eradicating identity. The laconicism and antitraditionalism of such poetry are a kind of refusal of any tone of voice that might be interpreted as august, formal, "stately." What is wanted by the poet is the right to a thoroughly private life. This value, expressed in a poem, is political. In poetry written under parliamentary governments the idea of individuality seems often to be a defiance of market manipulation and an insistence on the irreducible identity constituted by genuine feelings. Yet what this poet wants is the ability to speak *for* others (beyond those found in the publishing "marketplace" as the relatively few buyers and readers of books of poems), to associate with others on terms of feeling rather than on grounds of economic or other statistical status (what the staffs of American commercial magazines call "the demographics"). The categorizing of the individual by either state power or advertising analysts is no more accurate, and no less false, than a précis of a novel or a paraphrase of a poem, for these always fall into more general categories of types. (My having to summarize in this discussion some of Cardenal's works and certain positions, opinions, and attitudes in those works is unfortunately also false, although imposed necessarily by the limited space of an essay.) To pursue this parallel: in some sense, paraphrase and literary taxonomy are census—and we might recall that after a census, the ancients felt a need to bathe, to cleanse themselves in order to restore their identities.

Now, compared to English, the Spanish language has less of the sort of concrete texture that I have been saying was a defining aspect of poetic rhetoric; by this I mean simply that Spanish has a smaller number of words for the naming of things, and that these tend to fall into less various levels of diction. Is it merely a coincidence that when less precision is wanted in English, diction can become latinate and periphrastic, as in bureaucratic prose that aims at an authoritative and procedural, even ceremonial tone? Borges thought English a superior medium for poetry to Spanish, for reasons related to the poetic rhetoric I have characterized above. In formulating "exteriorism," Cardenal was reacting artistically against an apparently narrow tonal range in Spanish, *so that* poetry could speak against social and political circumstances which the old poetic diction had been inadequate either to resist or criticize. In order to attack more forcefully the "subjectivity" of accepted poetic diction, he exaggerated it somewhat; in truth it can indeed be physically evocative in Antonio Machado, even if etherealized in Juan Ramón Jiménez. But Cardenal found his preferred poetic models in Pound and other North American poets. I think the artistic defense of this poetic posture is that, in requiring poetry to refer to the tangible and historical world in a literal as well as a symbolic way, it draws attention to the *occasions* of poems as well as their *subjects*; Cardenal requires that there be an apprehensible occasion outside the poet, not solely an interior "poetic" subject like love or longing or death. Bad poems, in this view, are simply too vague and misty, and ask of the reader a familiar rather than a fresh response of feeling and thought. This would imply that poems bearing traces of ideology (of any sort) would also tend to echo propagandistic points of view (wrong not because they are already established but because they falsify with slogans and simplifications). The rhetoric of politics may prize either action or passivity, depending on the nature of the structure of government, and in either case a familiarity of statement, a mere reference; the rhetoric of poetry prizes the vital re-experiencing of feelings and thoughts, and vision—in both senses, and vividly. The rhetoric of politics prizes persuasion; that of poetry prizes perception (the sight of what is visible) and insight (the understanding of what is hidden). Of course this does not rule out political content in poems, but it does discount those poems bearing a heavy load of the ideological.

Poetry, with its peculiar rhetoric, calls us thus to respond to an intense and vivid presentation of the human condition, and Cardenal's poetry is a particularly compelling instance of this.

—*Reginald Gibbons*

How one means to use the word "ideology" is crucial. The conflict is very wide—between the rhetoric of poetry and, on the other side, the highly developed modern rhetoric and media of persuasion, cultural and political amnesia, and the falsification of information by those who control its preservation and dissemination. Before the successful revolution of the Sandinistas against Somoza in 1979, Cardenal frequently used the word "propaganda" in the customary pejorative sense to mean precisely the language of state power and advertisements, as for instance in his first psalm:

> Bienaventurado el hombre que no sigue las
>   consignas del Partido
> ni asiste a sus mítines
> ni se sienta en la mesa con los gangsters
> ni con los Generales en el Consejo de Guerra
> Bienaventurado el hombre que no espía a su
>   hermano
> ni delata a su compañero de colegio
> Bienaventurado el hombre que no lee los anuncios
>   comerciales
> ni escucha sus radios
> ni cree en sus slogans

> Será como un árbol plantado junto a una fuente

> Blessed is the man who does not follow the orders
>   of the Party
> nor attend its meetings
> nor sit at the table with gangsters
> nor with Generals in councils of war
> Blessed is the man who does not spy on his
>   brother
> nor inform on his school-mate
> Blessed is the man who does not read
>   advertisements
> nor listen to their radios
> nor believe in their slogans

> He will be like a tree planted beside a fountain

Paradoxically, this moral high ground remains to some extent a luxury of the powerless, who in challenging ruling powers exercise a critical function that is more congruent with the rhetoric of poetry, with the artist's "criticism" of life itself. A successful revolution brings with it meetings and slogans, although these are certainly the most innocent of the sins denounced in this first psalm. As I have already noted, Cardenal's poetry falls perhaps unsurprisingly into two groups; there is a troubling difference between poems condemning injustice, mostly written before Somoza's fall, and poems praising the new political and social order, written afterward. Take Yeats as a counterexample: one can go so far as to ignore the contours of his (reactionary) politics and note simply that as an individual who actively sought to intervene in the political history of his nation, he remained relatively powerless because he was in the opposition. Therefore his two critical functions, as poet and as opposition political figure, were in a crucial way not at odds with each other, and he did not experience the torsions of the poetic impulse felt by Cardenal, who went from being a hunted conspirator against the Somoza regime to being the minister of culture of Nicaragua.

Earlier, I suggested a congruence between art's critical nature and a "speaking against." [In his *Art and other Serious Matters,* 1985] Harold Rosenberg's analysis of the relationship between the artist's engagement with politics and the use by political power of artistic method led him to hold that the artist is the most valuable critic of propaganda, for "as an expert in the fabrication of appearances and realities, he has the training needed to penetrate the fabrications of politics." Some of Cardenal's prerevolutionary poetry, aimed against the manipulation of politics and political information by Somoza, demonstrates this critical impulse. Such artistic expertise is needed, according to Rosenberg, because

> politicians have become fiction makers, competitors and collaborators of fiction writers. One recalls, for instance, that mystery-story writers were invited to participate in think tanks on national military strategy [just as, I would add, more recently some science fiction writers have had a hand in advocating the so-called Star Wars Strategic Defense Initiative, in opposition to the expertise of some genuine scientists]. . . . A former assistant secretary of state declared on a radio program in which I participated that propaganda can no longer be successfully carried on by waiting for events to happen, and then interpreting them to support one's policies. It is necessary, said he, to create the events that verify the soundness of the policies one advocates.

Rosenberg held in the same essay that art could have almost no impact on politics, but that "the impulse to intervene in political life hovers like a ghost over the art of our century, perhaps because of the crisscrossing of fact and illusion which art and politics share."

But as one can infer from Milosz's *The Witness of Poetry,* the impulse to bear witness *is* a kind of indirect intervention—a small act, at the very least, in the larger discourse of which politics forms a sometimes dominant part. It is in the realm of politics, too, that the only decisive answer to this indirect intervention may be given, either as persecution or state approval, neither of which should be wanted. The task of criticism, then, in addition to pondering artistic intervention in political life, should be to weigh political intervention in imaginative life, to which political poetry is in part a response. With regard to poems, criticism should consider not only expressed belief or conviction or political position but also the expressive significance of the poem's formal qualities *and* the formal value, in the overall structure of the poem, of the expressed belief or conviction.

And no one should suppose that an opposition between poetry and a state that uses literary devices to manipulate information and opinion leaves poetry altogether unharmed. The "competition" of opinions and of versions of information, like that of products, extends—as a circumstance of commercial life and also as an ideology dear to the industrialized, parliamentary states—into the very production and distribution of books of poems. The effect of this incursion is destructive because in the frenzies and failures of publicity it promotes not a genuine sorting out of artistic value but a race between public images and literary fashions. Inevitably, competition in this sense affects in a dubious manner the dissemination of artistic works in society, by whatever means (including all the phenomena related to the writing and reading of poetry: readings, workshops, writers' conferences, and so forth).

Therefore, even if poetry can usefully preserve humane values which stand against the inhumane, which show men and women suffering in the path of history, this political engagement of the art is not free from a reverse damage which the marketplace and the pervasive manipulated language of politics work on all language. The fundamental contradiction of poetry's engagement with politics is that if, especially when it's "political," poetry tries to intervene in history, then in all its forms poetry is subject to the intervention of politics and economic relations—both in terms of language and in terms of the very conditions of life (and sometimes death) of the poet. So in some sense writers generally work *against* "history"; for if, as Des Pres writes, "history has often shown us the long-term victory of truth," we might also concur with him in noting, less cheerfully, that history (that is, the surviving record) has also—and often—concealed the long-term victories of falsehood.

The critic is not immune to this sometimes unwitting falsification. It is the victor and his beneficiaries, however removed, who enforce the context of historical interpretation, which includes even poetry. Many examples testify to the susceptibility of evaluation and canon formation to political distortion. The phrase "evaluation of political poetry" can only suggest the phrase "political evaluation of poetry." We can play a game with adjectives revealing how difficult it is to untie the knots already tightly pulled at the heart of the evaluation of poetry. If one can speak of the "evaluation of a political poem," one might also substitute for "political" such words as "historical," "psychological," "philosophical," or "religious" without suggesting anything out of the ordinary in the history of literary criticism. But if one takes the altered phrase, "the political evaluation of poetry," and makes the same substitutions for "political," a whole range of different *sorts* of criticism presents itself, not many of them practiced with distinction. To place any adjective in front of "evaluation" is to play the victor, to abdicate a larger and more significant responsibility in favor of a smaller and less significant one (albeit more immediately *useful* to the concerns of various intellectual fields of inquiry), and to enforce an unresponsive, partial context of evaluation on the work evaluated. Our task should be, instead, to read the poetry for the sake of investigating every aspect of its participation in the life of the people in whose society it was created (even if that is our own); then to ask what it brings to those (even ourselves, in our most conscious moments) not overly distanced from that society and that poem by history or by greater or smaller cultural heritage, or by our individual formation as readers; then to ask what it brings to those who are indeed at such a distance. In such contexts of expectation, what was once tactical may turn strategic—the poem written in response to a given historical and political circumstance may finally reveal its resonance to wider human situations and command our admiration, evoke our pleasure, and compel us to preserve it.

Cardenal has written political poetry of both a general and a partisan kind, and some of the poems (mostly, but not entirely, written before the revolution) are enduring work, while others seem flawed by simplification and service to a political position enforcing idealization. (This is a practical judgment, an evaluation—the result of my reading his work through—which I must assert for lack of sufficient space to demonstrate.) Is it possible to go further and to open a generally valid theoretical avenue to the problem of evaluation of "political poetry"? I do not believe so.

The individual reader's judgment and evaluation are much shaped by experience and temperament. This acknowledgment may come less readily from critics, who tend to prefer theoretical consistency, than from writers, who are often and unavoidably engaged in informal evaluation and make little pretense to being "objective" about it. Their own artistic needs compel them to evaluate the work of others so as to determine whether and how to make use of it. Cardenal did this with the works of Pound and other English-language poets and took from them what he needed—but not Pound's politics, or his entire aesthetic, and certainly not his technique (his stance toward life).

[In *Canons,* edited by Robert von Hallberg, 1984], Barbara Herrnstein Smith has noted how thoroughly the question of evaluation has been neglected by academic criticism for decades, and she has expounded an impressive theoretical examination of evaluation. Her essay leads me to two points. First, neglect of evaluation is itself an ideological and evaluative act which, in removing the question of evaluation from ostensible concerns while continuing unavoidably to participate in a myriad of implicitly evaluative acts, is partly responsible not for "the decline of the humanities" but for the general decline of *regard* for the humanities (even among some engaged in humanistic study). When literary criticism shows no overt concern for the evaluation of individual works but only for abstract goals like "critical thinking" or "humanities," it contributes to the opinion held all too widely that there is little *value* in the humanities, only a teachable method. Thus the scientistic longings of criticism, when they do achieve some result, end merely in a self-destructive explosion.

Second, it is not possible to construct any theoretical model of evaluation because the terms "theoretical" and "evaluation" are at odds. Can there be a "theoretical," that is, often "hypothetical," evaluation, except as a kind of mental role playing? Evaluation is an act of mind that may issue in conviction as well as proceed from it—a specific act of a specific individual, who if he or she evaluates a literary work solely in terms of a theoretical position may violate his or her own identity as a person, for we pursue evaluation—as Smith notes—with a larger portion of our being than that which contemplates theoretical possibilities, and rightly so. In Christopher Lasch's terms, we might say that we cannot evaluate solely as voices of

reason, but do so also as voices of conscience and imagination [*Salmagundi,* Spring/Summer, 1986]. To do otherwise is to narrow the critical act of evaluation to a partial act of analysis, as I attempted to demonstrate with my lists of adjectives for the phrase "the ___ evaluation of poetry."

Thus evaluation is always, in larger terms, the incorporation into criticism of the assessment and judgment of beliefs. But whereas a technical analysis or theoretical disquisition requires, for interest's sake, almost no prior or anticipated consensus except around the notion that criticism should be interesting to read, evaluation and judgment do require prior or anticipated consensus on the standards or values by which poetry, or any human endeavor, is to be judged as good, fruitful, acceptable, mediocre, bad, destructive, or whatever.

To substantiate a claim with regard to value, one can argue from verities perceived as eternal, as from religion, or from those perceived to survive over time, as from tradition, or from those perceived to lie in scientifically validated evidence, as from the natural world. The first method tends to seek its justification in the divine, the second in the people, the third in principles deduced to be inherent in the human creature because inherent in the physical universe. There is no great clarity here because from any one of these one can also argue to another—if there are apparently universal principles governing the nature of life on this planet, I can infer a divine order. If there is, as in Kenneth Burke's view, a "constellation" of human values such as courage, love, freedom, which are demonstrably present in cultures widely separated in time and space, I can infer from this tradition some universal and eternal aspects of human nature. And so on.

Sociological and Marxist thinking have insisted on the "socially constructed" nature of every value. Although based on the incontrovertible evidence that most human experience and all values held in common by human beings are affected by historical circumstance, finally this seems to lie just beyond the point of truth. (It would be hard to prove that the experiences of the rush of adrenaline when one is in danger, of the wearying heaviness of grief, of the ecstasy of orgasm, are socially constructed in any appreciable way.) Essentialist and politically reactionary thinking has insisted on the firm, inalterable, and flawed core of human nature, and, although based on incontrovertible evidence that across huge barriers of history, culture, and race, certain central human experiences find their unmistakable echoes in others, this too of course lies beyond the point of truth. (It would be hard to prove that the particular choices of one's active response to physical aggression, one's outward behavior at the death of one's child, or one's notions of romantic love, are not socially constructed almost in their entirety.)

So if a poem is called "political" and presents itself to our eyes as a tangle of poetic craft (which we judge by one conventional set of standards) and poetic technique, or "stance toward life," or "belief" (which we judge by another, subtly related set of standards), our response is diagnostic not only of the nature of the poem but also of the nature of our assumptions about art and politics. Most valuable among these, perhaps, is the assumption that works of art and human actions may be—should be—judged against one another, some to be preferred and some abhorred. Because evaluation is the act of an individual mind at a given moment, to evaluate Cardenal's political poetry is to evaluate individual poems against other individual poems, and to do so in the realm of both conviction and pleasure, both solace and connoisseurship, as well as that of literary history. Persons will disagree on the priority assigned to human values and will disagree on poems: I believe that some of Cardenal's poems are enduring works, and perhaps more important than that, I see his poetry as a sphere in which we are called as individuals to react not only to a poet's perceptions but also to feeling, conviction, and belief as they may be related to us in our own lives. Work like Cardenal's forces us to make ourselves as conscious as we can of the implicit assumptions affecting our evaluative decisions. Poetry, with its peculiar rhetoric, calls us thus to respond to an intense and vivid presentation of the human condition, and Cardenal's poetry is a particularly compelling instance of this. When criticism denies or ignores this call, it turns against its own subject.

Geoffrey R. Barrow (essay date 1987)

SOURCE: "Tradition and Originality in the Denunciatory *Salmos* of Ernesto Cardenal," in *La Chispa '87: Selected Proceedings,* edited by Gilbert Paolini, Tulane University, 1987, pp. 15-22.

[*In the essay below, Barrow provides a stylistic and thematic analysis of Cardenal's psalms.*]

What Anita Brookner has said of Germaine Greer might be applied to the contemporary Latin American poet, Ernesto Cardenal. He is like Delacroix's portrait of liberty, marching forward with his banner, rallying the troops in his commune of Nuestra Señora de Solentiname, doomed to the eminence of a figurehead as the current Nicaraguan Minister of Culture and chained to the concept of permanent struggle. He has now given up writing, however, in order to dedicate himself to ministerial duties since, at least for this Catholic priest and Marxist poet who was radicalised by his visit to Cuba in 1970, the Revolution is the same thing as the Kingdom of God. Cardenal embraces the plight of the poor in Central America as well as the sufferings of the Nicaraguan people under the Somoza dynasty. He attacks issues of judicial corruption in politics, torture by the secret police, deployment of the military in furtherance of domestic political matters, American influence in Latin American affairs, and the threat of nuclear holocaust. His poetry embodies some of the most contentious issues of our times, and Robert Pring-Mill claims stentoriously that Cardenal's ideas are "clearly around to stay and must be reckoned with" [in his introduction to *Zero Hour and Other Documentary Poems*, by Ernesto Cardenal, 1990].

The foundations of Cardenal's radicalism are biblical and meditative. In a revealing interview at his commune of Solentiname, just before being outlawed by Somoza, he explained:

> En realidad, yo me he politizado con la vida contemplativa. La meditación, la profundización, la mística es la que me ha dado a mí la radicalización política. Yo he llegado a la revolución por el Evangelio. No fue por la lectura de Marx sino por Cristo. Se puede decir que el Evangelio me hizo marxista.

("Conversación")

The gospel, of course, finds the good news in the bad news. Broken of self and self-sufficiency by the rigors of Trappist training and seminary preparation, Cardenal saw the face of Christ in the primitive community of peasants and fisherman at Solentiname. Among the poor and humble of Central America he finds the hope of resurrection, and it is instructive to examine his *Salmos* in order to comprehend the literary effects of revolutionary Christianity. Composed during his training for the priesthood in Colombia and illuminated by contemplation, the collection is patently Christian. Moreover, if his own statement about the foundation of his Marxism in Christian meditation counts, as it should, then the collection is central to an understanding of his work.

The immediate issues are whether the poems are indeed psalms and, if so, what sort and what literary qualities do they display. Critical analysis will show, I think, that Cardenal's *Salmos* are felicitous imitations that stretch mind, imagination, and sensibility. They also contain a basic element of revolutionary dogma, namely, that society is riven by unappeasable strife that will be overcome by the liberation of the poor and oppressed. In these poems, divine intervention is the sole agent of renewal; within a decade, God's agent becomes a Marxian proletariat. Religion legitimates, as it were, the new social order.

Unlike translators, imitators do not aspire to faithfulness. Cardenal had already encountered Pound's translations from the classics while at Columbia University in New York, and this experience led him to produce versions of Catullus and Martial (*Epigramas*). One does not have to read far to see that there is nearly always a gap, and sometimes a chasm, between Cardenal and his model. The result is a commentary on Cardenal as much as on the original, and the omissions are as telling as the imaginative departures. This dialogue between old and new also pervades the *Salmos,* although the origins are not strictly literary but liturgical. The chief characteristics of Trappist life are liturgical prayer, contemplation and absolute silence. As a Trappist monk and then as a Catholic seminarian, Cardenal recited the psalms daily in the Divine Office. Their intrinsic spiritual depth and beauty form the backbone of public and private prayer. Cardenal, however, strives to produce a version of the Vulgate Bible psalms that the ancient author would have given us had he been born in Central America. The result is a contemporary work capable of standing on its own feet, and some *Salmos* have been used in rather unorthodox liturgies in Latin America. In treating the Bible as a source of supply, Cardenal looks both backward and forward. On the one hand he seeks to enhance his dignity by close links with the past; on the other he likes to experiment with old material and create new effects with it. The title of the English translation of *Salmos, Psalms of Struggle and Liberation*, bluntly underlines Cardenal's emphasis, but, in fact, his stance is closer to Mertonian non-violence.

Cardenal selects twenty-five of the one hundred and fifty psalms that are his source of supply, while he preserves the ordering of his source. He chooses what suits him: certain topics receive unusual emphasis while others, equally important, are peremptorily neglected. The principle of selection is to take what corresponds with his own outlook. There are several kinds of biblical psalms: penitential and imprecatory, praise and thanksgiving, supplication, royal and messianic, wisdom and songs of ascents. However, Cardenal changes the proportion of these ingredients in his *Salmos*, so that there is a fundamental shift of emphasis towards supplication and imprecation. Certainly, the psalms of praise offer Cardenal opportunities for imaginative poetic treatment, in modern scientific terms, of God's wonders in creation. Yet he reduces the whole range of relations between God and man which is the subject matter of the Psalms, giving attention to those psalms which provide expression for his own ideas. His fresh adaptations show clear traces of their ancestry, but the overall focus is different. In short, Cardenal's central themes are the power of wicked dictators, the sufferings of oppressed innocents, and the desire to see God's vengeance upon the wicked. Ferocious hatred, indignant self-pity, and passionate desire for God's retributive justice give a fiery Old Testament tone, although the image of God is painted with shades of a peasant *caudillo*.

The forms that Cardenal's versions assume offer some insight into his purpose. He takes as many precious stones as he can from the mosaic of biblical heritage and uses them to construct his own pattern. Some are intermittent paraphrases, others contain brief allusions and are so free that they are scarcely recognizable as adaptations of the Psalms. The degree of proximity, therefore, varies. Cardenal's psalms bear the original stamp of independent creations but they have transfusions of foreign blood in their veins. For example, the surprise ending to psalm five adds a new dimension to its source. The closure of the original, in a familiar English rendering from the Book of Common Prayer, is as follows:

> For there is no faithfulness in their mouth; their inward parts are very wickedness.
>
> Their throat is an open sepulchre; they flatter with their tongue.
>
> Destroy them, O God; let them perish through their own imaginations; cast them out in the multitude of their ungodliness; for they haverebelled against thee.
>
> And let all them that put their trust in thee

rejoice; they shall ever be giving of thanks, because thou defendest them; they that love thy Name shall be joyful in thee;

> For thou, Lord, wilt give thy blessing unto the righteous, and with thy favourable kindness wilt thou defend him as with a shield.

This is a prayer for deliverance from personal enemies, but Cardenal combines biblical features with certain contemporary realities in such a way as to make them imaginative with a dual significance in biblical lament on the one hand and Nicaraguan reality on the other:

> Hablan con la boca de las ametralladoras
> Sus lenguas relucientes
>   son las bayonetas . . .
> Castígalos oh Dios
>   malogra su política
> confunde sus memorandums
>   impide sus programs
> A la hora de la Sirena de Alarma
> tú estarás conmigo
> tú serás mi refugio el día de la Bomba
>
> Al que no cree en la mentira de sus anuncios
>   comerciales
> ni en sus campañas publicitarias ni en sus
>   campañas políticas
>   tú lo bendices
> Lo rodeas con tu amor
>   como con tanques blindados
>   **(*Salmos* 13-14)**

Time does not allow a thorough and detailed study of all the verses which Cardenal retains or abandons in his selections, but this sample exhibit shows the nature of his renderings, at least when he follows the original relatively closely. He pushes and pulls against his source. The spirit of unshakable faith remains together with the psalm's function of providing comfort, inspiration and strength. He frequently alters, however, the disposition of the individual elements. Elsewhere, in the first psalm for example, the contrasting fate of the righteous and the wicked is still the basis of Cardenal's version; but the depiction of the wicked occupies twice as much space as in the source. The extended simile for the righteous, "He is like a tree planted by streams of water, that yields its fruit in its season and its leaf does not wither. In all that he does, he prospers" (vs. 3), is reduced simply to the closing line, "Será como un árbol plantado junto a una fuente." Yet the remainder of the poem is taken up with the depiction of the wicked in contemporary sociopolitical terms. Curiously, the disastrous end of the wicked described in the second half of the original is omitted completely. This changed selection and arrangement transforms the model into an exercise in denunciation. Cardenal bases himself on two of the original six verses (vs. 1, 3), so that the balance shifts.

Cardenal has intensely absorbed his biblical material, but the original stamp of his free imitations shows his independence. His frame of reference is restricted. The goal is an effective means of expression, fluent and moving, not an exact reproduction. The Psalms are turned into a collection of endorsements to back his own moral judgements, which spring from his own Nicaraguan experience. The imitation of a biblical model with less than absolute precision, therefore, is a means to an end. At the stylistic level, there is a clear recollection and recitation of biblical fragments:

> "Escucha mis palabras oh Señor
>   Oye mis gemidos
> Escucha mi protesta"
>
> > **(Salmos 5)**

> "Líbrame Señor"
>
> > **(Salmos 7)**

> "Cantaré Señor tus maravillas"
>
> > **(Salmos 9)**

> "Y séante gratas las palabras de mis poemas Señor,
>   mi libertador."
>
> > *(Salmos 18)*

However, the echoes are intricately blended in a new amalgam. The key lines that seize Cardenal's attention are clearly appropriated, but the bottles are new. Apart from the psalms of praise (18, 93, 103, 113, 148, 150), the predominant tone is one of denunciation and lamentation.

The Psalms, of course, contain a good portion of maledictions. They freely express hatred and invoke divine judgement, since wrong is offensive to both God and the victims of wickedness. The simple life of the righteous is contrasted with the luxury, extravagance, and cruelty of the sinful. Moreover, since the Psalms display characteristic stylistic features of ancient Hebrew lyric, notably, parallelism, patterning, and hyperbole, it is worth looking at the rhetoric and diction of Cardenal's reworkings. He typically expresses indignation by highlighting the antithesis between oppressor and oppressed in order to denounce the wicked:

> Sus ametralladoras están emplazadas
> > contra nosotros
> y los slogans de odio nos rodean
> los espías rondan mi casa
> los policías secretos me vigilan
> > de noche
> estoy en medio de los gangsters
>
> > **(Salmos 26)**

Luxury is exaggerated and presented by means of polysyndeton and auxesis:

> (Señor, líbrame de)
> los que tienen repletas las refrigeradoras
> y sus mesas llenas de sobras
> y dan de caviar a los perros.
>
> > **(Salmos 26)**

Parallelism and anaphora are distinctive features of the Psalms and Cardenal exploits these rhetorical schemes to produce a rhetoric of blame.

The appearance of the villains in the **Salmos** becomes aggressively monotonous. "Gangsters, generales, Consejos de Guerra, dictadores, Ministros de Justicia, Cortes Supremas de Justicia, Fuerzas Armadas, Policía Secreta, Primer Ministro, asesinos llenos de condecoraciones," all populate the scene. Reflecting the temper of the times, their weapons are "anuncios comerciales, slogans, la prensa, radio, memorandums, campañas publicitarias, periódicos, propaganda, testigos falsos." These are in essence the lying lips of the Hebrew Psalms. The oppressed suffer from "campos de concentración, bombas, armas atómicas, el detector de mentiras, alambradas electrizadas, tortura." How banal the forces of repression are. However, if it were not for these agents of destruction, so necessary to the revolutionary code, the world could be freed for the poor and oppressed, superior in their splendid covenant with God to all the creatures by whom they have been exploited.

Cardenal's **Salmos** are radical not because the speaker holds contemporary views but because he expects history to submit to him, not *vice versa.* Sanctity, love, and humility, appear to give way to spiritual pride, self-righteousness, and a persecuting zeal. There may not yet be freedom at the end of Cardenal's struggle in Nicaragua, but it is unfortunate that his new political eminence prevents him from writing poetry. **Salmos** are important as much because of his biblical expression of modern indignation as because of the creative expression of wonder and gratitude in his psalms of praise. But the psalms of praise will be a subject for another time.

Tamara R. Williams (essay date 1990)

SOURCE: "Ernesto Cardenal's *El estrecho dudoso:* Reading/Re-writing History," in *Revista Canadiense de Estudios Hispánicos,* Vol. XV, No. 1, 1990, pp. 111-21.

[*In the following essay, Williams analyzes the epic structure and subject matter of* El estrecho dudoso, *maintaining that the poem is both secular and religious.*]

Ernesto Cardenal's **El estrecho dudoso** (1966) is a book-length poem of over 3,000 lines. Divided into twenty-five cantos, the text's primary focus is on the historical events linked to the area now generally referred to as Mesoamérica, with a specific (but not exclusive) interest in Nicaragua. The poem concentrates on the first one hundred years of activity following the arrival of the Spanish on the American continent. It opens with Columbus' fourth voyage and his discovery of Terra Firma near the present Cape of Honduras in 1502, and concludes with a cataclysmic finale which narrates the destruction of the City of León, Nicaragua, by the volcano Momotombo in 1603.

The most remarkable feature of **El estrecho dudoso** is that it is constructed almost entirely from fragments of texts gleaned from an array of historical documents dating from the period in which the story takes place (1500-1650). The poet's use of history is not gratuitous; it serves the purpose of constructing a discourse which appeals to the reader as "authoritative" and evokes the illusion of truthfulness, objectivity, and adherence to fact rather than fancy and invention.

The concern for a narrative that is an accurate and truthful representation of the selected sequence of events is stated metapoetically. In Canto XXI, this concern is mediated through the quotation of metahistorical statements made by Bernal Díaz del Castillo in his *Historia verdadera de la conquista de la Nueva España.* Citing the *Verdadera Historia,* **El estrecho** outlines Bernal Díaz's reasons for writing his "verdadera historia." He wishes to tell the story of all those explorers and discoverers, conquerors and colonizers whose names were ignored and omitted in the chronicles of the period. Berating the inaccuracies of Francisco López de Gómara's *Historia de las Indias y conquista de México,* and advancing the need for a rewriting of history, Castillo initially expresses his insecurity about his abilities to write, actually abandoning the project for a time. Finally, motivated by the falsities and omissions of the chronicles and histories that precede his, he takes up the task of re-writing the "true" history of the conquest. These metahistorical statements establish "truth" as the basic criterion for the writing of history. They advance the need to rewrite history, if necessary, to attain the most accurate account and explanation of the historical sequence selected for narration:

> El viejo ha vuelto a leer otra vez esas crónicas
> y ve que no cuentan nada de lo que pasó en Nueva
>   España.
> Están llenas de mentiras. Ensalzan a unos capitanes
> y rebajan a otros. Dicen que estuvieron en las
>   conquistas
> los que no estuvieron en ellas. Entonces coge la
>   pluma
> y empieza otra vez a escribir, sin elegancia,
> sin policía, sin razones hermoseadas ni retórica,
> según el común hablar de Castilla la Vieja.
> Porque el agraciado componer es decir la verdad.
> Aunque tal vez no haga sino gastar papel y tinta . . .
> Porque él nunca había escrito. El es sólo un
>   soldado.
> Pero escribe también para sus hijos y sus nietos,
> para que sepan que él vino a conquistar estas
>   tierras.
> Su historia si se imprime verán que es más
>   verdadera
> ¡Y ahora que lo escribe se le representa todo
> delante de los ojos como si fuera ayer que pasó!
> Irá escribiendo con su pluma, despacio, despacio,
> corrigiendo los errores con cuidado, como el piloto
> que va descubriendo las costas, echando la sonda . . .

El estrecho dudoso, in constructing a historical account through a careful re-reading, selection and re-combination of events recorded in "esas crónicas," embodies this same critical, corrective approach to the making of history. Like the old "regidor" from Medina del Campo, the poet in **El estrecho** scans the "viejas crónicas"

like a pilot readjusting his compass and his direction, mapping out alternative coasts, new horizons, new contours of truth, and, ultimately, new meaning.

More specifically, the historical account presented to us in **El estrecho dudoso** is one that the author has deciphered and interpreted according to a particular set of religious beliefs. It is an account ordered into a relatively finite context in the sense that all historical activity is mediated within a specific ethical/theological imperative, which in turn, is informed by the author's vital commitment to Liberation Theology. In this account, Cardenal emplots historical events into an eschatological framework, rendering a story that is apocalyptic in structure and in tone, embracing the past and, in that past, looking forward to the future. Moreover, this eschatological framework, by invoking a specific theological imperative, creates a moral space in which all action is judged, or sanctioned, characters are saved or damned according to the will of a Supreme God who militantly intervenes on behalf of "those who are persecuted in the cause of right."

Cardenal himself is a self-declared, renowned liberation theologian; however, his writings on the subject have been mainly applied in nature. His three-volume collection titled *Evangelio en Solentiname,* for example, is a series of transcribed meditations on the Bible by numerous individuals from the viewpoint of liberation. For this reason, we turn to Gustavo Gutiérrez, the pre-eminent theologian from Peru, who offers a succinct explanation of this Biblical interpretation in his book, *The Power of the Poor in History.* Several points that are central to the liberationist perspective deserve mention because they shed light on the operating belief system that informs the explanation of historical events that **El estrecho** offers.

Crucial to this interpretation is the assumption that the Bible tells the story of a people; it is seen as a historical account of the Jews. Furthermore, this history is perceived as a struggle for liberation from Egypt throughout which God reveals Himself and in which humankind proclaims Him. Besides revealing Himself in history, the God of the Bible is a God who not only governs history, but who orients it in the direction of the establishment of justice and right. He is more than a provident God, He is a God who actively sides with the poor and the afflicted in their struggle for liberation from misery, poverty, slavery and oppression.

This history from which Faith springs, argues Gutiérrez, is an open-ended history; it is open to the future. Its core—the Jews' struggle for liberation from Egypt—is an event that should be read and re-read for it prefigures other historical interventions of Yahweh. To find such interventions of Yahweh, finally, Gutiérrez insists that readings of history must be undertaken from the viewpoint of the poor, the oppressed and the enslaved. Claiming that "the history of humanity has been written with a white hand" he calls for the recovery of the memory of the struggles of "the scourged Christs of America" (which is how Bartolomé de las Casas referred to the Indians of the American continent), adding that "this memory has never died and has a latent existence in the cultural expression and resistance against the institutionalized church." Re-reading history from the viewpoint of those in the struggle, finally, makes the subversion and the re-making of history possible:

> . . . *rereading history* means *remaking* history. It means repairing it from the bottom up. And so it will be subversive history. History must be turned upside down from the bottom, not from the top. What is criminal is not to be subversive, struggling against the capitalist system, but to continue being *"super*versive"— bolstering and supporting the prevailing domination. It is in this subversive history that we can have a new faith experience, a new spirituality—a new proclamation of the Gospel.

Cardenal's *El estrecho dudoso* is a brilliant and creative articulation of these concepts. It is a rereading/remaking of history of the Spanish Conquest of America, told from the vantage point of those struggling for freedom rather than from the viewpoint of the victors and perpetrators of violence and injustice. Using authoritative historical documentation, the poem explores God's presence and alliance with the victims in their struggle for life and renewal. The author remakes a history where God exhibits a clear "preferential option" for the underdogs in the struggle for justice and right. In this history, His name is proclaimed and Faith in Him and the future is renewed. He intercedes on behalf of the gravely afflicted, promising them a better world to come. Canto XVII of *El estrecho,* citing fragments of the book of prophesies of *Chilam Balam,* prophesies to the afflicted Maya that the dawning of a new age is at hand:

> Es ella la insignia de Hunab-ku erguida;
> el tronco del árbol enhiesto vendrá a anunciar a las
>   gentes
> que surge la nueva aurora para el mundo.
>
>   (123)

As is appropriate to the serious nature and subject of his story, Cardenal emplots the series of events into a discernible epic structure that most resembles a Christian contrast epic. In it, one series of actions involves characters in ironic human situations, and another outlines the origin or continuation of a divine society. Fragments are selected and recombined to reveal a cycle with close metaphorical identification with the Biblical structure, where the movement is from a situation of apparent exile from God toward the arrival of messengers of faith, and finally to a sign of God's redemption and revelation.

The ironic pole in *El estrecho* results primarily from an elaborate and innovative development of the quest theme. As the title of the poem suggests, *El estrecho dudoso* devotes particular attention to what may be deemed in retrospect as the Spanish obsession, particularly during the XVIth century, with locating an interoceanic waterway—un "estrecho"—that would enable them to navigate west directly to Calicutt and the Moluccas, avoiding the hostility of the Portuguese (who had virtual control over the African route to *La Especiería*). "El estrecho du-

doso" is in fact "un estrecho ansiado." In Cardenal's poem, the elusive strait constitutes a pivotal object of desire; it is the object of repeated quests, the motivation for complicated and violent action, and the cause of war. The quest for the delusive strait, moreover, becomes metaphorically identified with the con-quest, that is, with the subduction of the "other" and the corruption of power which ensues. These are ultimately revealed, however, as the unattainable, as false objectives, misguided quests that invariably result in catastrophic action.

These episodes typically involve a materialistically inclined explorer on a perilous journey that promotes a temporary *agon* and a subsequent death struggle, or *pathos,* that he is rarely able to survive. The struggle pits these individuals' grossly idealized preconceptions and fabricated illusions regarding the still unexplored and unknown totality of the New World against the overwhelming, diverse, and threateningly harsh and cruel reality of the American continent. In an ironic reversal, the greedy expectation of a materialistic utopia is met instead by a hellish world of chaos and anarchy marked by labyrinthine marshes, impenetrable tropical forests, catastrophic earthquakes, volcanic eruptions and fierce maritime storms. Where the Spanish explorers hope to find gold and emeralds in infinite abundance, they instead encounter death. Extremes of heat or cold kill them off in the most grotesque manner or simply drive them to a lonely, pathetic insanity. Thirst and hunger lead the few survivors to drink sea water and eat poisonous plants and raw shellfish. Some resort to cannibalism.

A related field of action associated with the ironic pole of the contrast epic in *El estrecho dudoso* is one involving the events of war. Here again the action entails a quest, but the quest moves beyond the desire to control geographical territory to include that of conquering peoples. Hence the confrontation between man and nature is substituted for the violent confrontation between two opposing peoples.

Cardenal draws from segments of Bernal Díaz's *Verdadera historia,* and from Francisco Fuentes y Guzmán's *Recordación Florida* to develop this quest series. Hernán Cortés, the conqueror of México, and Pedro de Alvarado, the conqueror of Guatemala, are the central figures in these episodes. They are initially portrayed as individuals of heroic dimensions, marked by their overall strength, character and daring. They invariably appear flanked by a loyal entourage of soldiers, pages, messengers, cooks, and priests. Their stature is further enhanced by colorfully waving flags, pennants and banners.

The primary obstacle the conquerors face is the resistance of the Native American peoples. Unlike the aforementioned life-threatening struggle with an antagonistic nature, this one concludes with a relatively easy Spanish victory. The domination of the Native population in these episodes is facilitated by a combination of Spanish military superiority and aggressiveness, Amerindian collusion with the conquerors (La Malinche being the classic case—Canto VIII), and the generally well-meaning and peaceful Amerindian predisposition.

The success of the conqueror, however, turns against itself when the Amerindian becomes the irreversible underdog and victim. Unable to measure their power, the conquerors become perpetrators of prolonged and unnecessary brutality. This is exemplified by the unwarranted execution of Cuauhtemoc in Aclan ordered by an over-suspicious Cortés and narrated in Canto VIII, or the ruthless burning of villages and people alike by Alvarado in his conquest of Guatemala, narrated in Canto XIII. These "executive-type" episodes are supported by the more "deliberative-type" episodes involving the speeches and letters of figures such as Bartolomé de las Casas and Antonio de Valdivieso, which graphically describe the injustices being committed and are a reminder of their moral consequences.

The successful conqueror's remarkable achievements and heroic dimensions appear, therefore, marred by the fundamental imperfection inherent in his misguided and unbridled power. This short-coming is signalled by the introduction of an omen such as "el más extraño quetzal," which haunts Alvarado in Canto XIII. The devices utilized portend an eventual fall. The conqueror's transgression, which elicits Divine disfavor of fatal consequence, is his abuse of power in the service of oppression.

Finally, the ironic pole in *El estrecho* reaches its highest level of expression in the actions described that involve the foundation and government of cities by the Spanish in the New World. To this series belongs the ominous centrality of the governor-tyrant figure, represented by Pedrarías Dávila, Rodrigo de Contreras, and his two sons, Pedro and Hernando de Contreras.

Under the supposed aegis of the governor, life takes on nightmarish proportions. Cities are founded on greed in commercial ventures requiring extensive exploitation of the native population and resources. Mining and pig farming, metaphorically degrading tasks, are promoted as the major sources of revenue, along with the trading of slaves. Simply put, the governor-tyrant violates all the ethical codes of Christian governorships. He is the antithesis of the ideal ruler.

The turning point in *El estrecho* comes in Canto XXIV, when Hernando de Contreras, one of Rodrigo de Contreras' sons, seeks revenge against Antonio de Valdivieso for his role in ousting Rodrigo de Contreras from the Nicaraguan governorship. Hernando Contreras savagely murders the bishop in the town of León in the wake of a more generalized rebellion against Spain in 1550. Valdivieso, represented as a messianic figure selflessly devoted to delivering Nicaragua from evil, emerges at this point as a hero, introducing the anagnorisis.

The triumph of the hero is dramatically supported by the closing Canto of the poem. In an episode inspired by a segment of Fray Antonio de Remesal's, *Historia de las Indias Occidentales,* the Canto narrates the "excommunication" of the accursed city of León, Nicaragua, site of the murder of the bishop who is, like Christ himself, a "servant of God." God hands down his wrathful judge-ment in the shape of darkness, storms, plagues, periods of infertility, violent earthquakes, and consequent torrential landslides that virtually submerge the city in a murky sea of sulphuric-smelling mud.

From amidst the sinking city, however, emerges a sign of redemption. The text closes and the story ends with the image of a wall stained by the bloody handprint of the murdered Antonio de Valdivieso: "Su mano ensangrentada quedó pintada en la pared. / Siempre quedó la sangre viva y roja, dicen, como si acabara de salir de sus venas . . . El agua seguía subiendo y la ciudad *maldita,* con la mano de sangre en el muro todavía pintada se iba hundiendo y hundiendo en el agua" (169-70). The image of the blood-stained hand is a reminder of the violence suffered by Valdivieso, but it also signals vengeance, repossession of the city, its deliverance from sin and the dawn of a new era, thus fulfilling the earlier mentioned prophecy from the *Chilam Balam* which appeared in Canto XVII. The closing, both terrible and wondrous, coincides with an episode of the Book of Revelations, which reads as follows:

> And the Angel whom I saw standing on sea and land lifted up his right hand to heaven and swore by him who lives for ever and ever, who created heaven and what is in it, and the sea and what was in it, that there should be no more delay, but that in the days of the trumpet call to be sounded by the seventh angel, the mystery of God, as he announced to his servants the prophets, should be fulfilled. (Rev. 10: 5-7)

Concurrent with the narration of the deluded Colonial quest, its progressive corruption and ultimate self-destruction is the contrasting field of action narrating the origin and continuation of a divine society.

In Cardenal's poem, the original society is the society of the New World, in other words the society that the Spanish found in place when they reached what they believed to be the Indies. It is portrayed well within the realm of the divine community struggling against a sudden onslaught of Spanish injustice, disease and oppression, threatening their very survival and existence. However, the *Estrecho* goes beyond the superficial treatment of the topic of the noble savage in its adherence to Bartolomé de las Casas' argument that the Amerindian is a creature (and a creation) of God, and, as such, should be embraced freely and indiscriminately into His flock. In *El estrecho dudoso,* the emphasis is overwhelmingly on those qualities (both individual and societal) of the Native peoples of America that point to their rightful membership to the human race and the Christian community at large.

The *Estrecho* thus undermines and ultimately inverts the stereotypical savage/civilized opposition. The Amerindian is portrayed as the virtuous, civilized and Christian victim of the lawless, fierce, godless Spanish tyrant. A selection from the XVIIIth Canto of the *Estrecho,* which draws almost entirely on Las Casas' *Brevísima relación de la destrucción de las Indias,* refers to this inversion very directly, using animal imagery reminiscent of the Biblical Psalms in opposing the wolf and the tiger (the oppressors) to the lamb (the oppressed): "Y los españoles llegaron como lobos y tigres, / como lobos y tigres donde estas ovejas mansas . . ."

It would be inaccurate to limit the portrayal of the American Indian in *El estrecho* to the extreme consequences of this inversion, which would render what would really amount to a romanticized or allegorical characterization of limited complexity. The inversion, an overcompensation and reverse stereotipification, functions on one level as a reminder of the indigenous peoples' deserved membership in the community of man and of Christ. In assuming this membership, the text assumes its implications. Once the Amerindians are inscribed in the community, their words are uttered, their voices are heard, and their actions carry a weight beyond the "othering-type" of discourse of manners and customs. Their utterances, ranging from moral judgements to prophetic messages, the most notable being the speeches of Panquiaco (Canto IV), Nicaragua (Canto VI), Cuauhtemoc (Canto VIII), and Lempira (Canto XVII), and their actions (including the abortive attempts of armed resistance by Lempira in Canto XVII and the defeat of Cortés by the Aztecs in Canto XXI) become a vital component, a resisting force, in the complexity and violence of colonial reality as the *Estrecho* reads it.

Like the afflicted children of Israel, the Amerindian peoples, finally, are portrayed as a chosen people of God. Through a fragment selected from the Mayan book of prophecies by Chilam Balam, a selection which in itself reveals the poem's commitment to the idea that the native Americans were in fact "the scourged Christs of the Indies," it is revealed that, following a sustained period of discord and anarchy, one just and merciful God will come to guide and protect the people of Itzá, marking the dawn of light and the age of renewal. The inclusion of this millenial prophecy and others like it suggests a metaphorical identification with the Babylonian captivity, in that they both deal with a community experiencing a seemingly endless period of servitude and captivity, infernal darkness, victimization and destruction preceding the coming of a new heaven and a new earth.

> Adoradla, oh Itzalanos. Debéis adorar esa insignia
> enhiesta
> y creer en la palabra del verdadero Dios
> que viene del cielo a hablaros.
> Multiplicad vuestra buena voluntad oh Itzalanos,
> ahora que está el nuevo amanecer por iluminar
> universo
> y la vida está por entrar en una Edad Nueva.
> Tened fe en mi mensaje, yo soy Chilam Balam
> y he interpretado la palabra del verdadero Dios.
> (123-24)

"La palabra del verdadero Dios" is brought to the chosen Native American society by two exemplary messengers of Christ, Antonio de Valdivieso and Bartolomé de las Casas. Profoundly committed to the community which the Spaniards had thus far considered insignificant,

irrelevant, nameless and disposable, Las Casas and Valdivieso dedicate their Christian ministry to the renewal of the life and wellbeing of a culture and a people who, since the advent of the Conquest, have been systematically denied the right to life, freedom and cultural integrity.

The Defender of Indians emerges well within the dimensions of a Messianic hero, whose divinely inspired messages and actions struggle to rescue a beleaguered society from the demonic control of tyranny restore peace, order, and fertility in a world of hellish confusion on the brink of death.

Valdivieso, as was mentioned earlier, dies in the struggle as a murder victim of a threatened enemy, Hernando Contreras. His death shares close parallels with Christ's crucifixion in that Valdivieso dies symbolically for the repossession of life, justice, and peace in the midst of a decaying and violently corrupt society. Las Casas lives on in the struggle, leaving the reader with some degree of confidence and hope in the continued fight for a better world to come.

The poem displays the characteristic expansiveness of the epic, achieved primarily through the theme of the quest. On the one hand, the materialistically motivated discoveries and explorations, the quests for (to use the Augustinian model) "the city of man," its conquest and colonization lead the reader through an ample and heterogeneous physical territory ranging from coastal areas, jungles, forests, swamp lands and estuaries, to more populated spaces: villages, towns and cities. These quests could be said to constitute the horizontal spatial axis in the text. On the other hand, and projected onto this horizontal spatial axis, is a quest of a moral kind—the divinely inspired quest for the just and the right—"the city of God"—which is engendered through the figures of Las Casas and Valdivieso. It constitutes a vertical spatial axis in its metaphorical identification with heaven and hell. The vertical spatial axis and its thematic associations—God/Satan, good/bad, order/disorder, darkness/light, barrenness/fertility—modify the quality and desirability of the horizontal spatial axis and combine with it to create a poem that embraces an eschatological world. This world embraces both history and myth; it is both physical and spiritual, human and providential.

Robert Pring-Mill (essay date 1992)

SOURCE: "Cardenal's Treatment of Amerindian Cultures in *Homenaje a los indios americanos*," in *Renaissance and Modern Studies*, Vol. 35, 1992, pp. 52-74.

[*In the following essay, Pring-Mill traces the development of Cardenal's life and poetry, and relates this growth and change to his portrayal of Native American peoples in* Homenaje a los indios americanos.]

In any examination of the ways in which the Americas have been perceived, and of the struggle to make sense of the continent and come to terms with the effects of cultural change and conflict, the range of images of its indigenous peoples found in literature is an obvious area for scrutiny. How have these been treated, and how has their 'treatment' helped to shape our present-day awareness of the identities of different Amerindian cultures? 'Treatment'—as used in the title of this article—is not merely a matter of 'attitudes' or 'views expressed', but also a matter of the 'modes of representation' which a writer employs (starting with his choice of genre, but including such stylistic features as rhetorical devices, register, symbolism, and tone). Hitherto, more critical attention has been devoted to the treatment of indigenous peoples and cultures in prose fiction than in poetry, yet poetry can offer different kinds of insight. It should be read in the light of its original context, however, and the reader must guard against the rash but common assumption that 'historical' poetry can safely be read as 'history' (thus, absurd though such an assumption would seem to the historian, many Latin American readers have taken Neruda's *Canto general* to be a reliable account of what did actually occur). It should also be stressed that some of the most revealing 'insights' which poetry can offer will be insights into things quite different from the alleged 'realities' which it ostensibly presents.

The Amerindian poems of the Nicaraguan poet-priest Ernesto Cardenal (1925-) are a case in point: whereas the title of his *Homenaje a los indios americanos* (first published in 1969, but later expanded) appears to promise a eulogy of things Amerindian for their own sake, one must never forget that he is above all a Spanish-American 'committed poet'—indeed the foremost one since Pablo Neruda. His determination to change the world around him, and to change his readers so that they should contribute to its improvement, is always uppermost: consequently, although much of the source-material of *Homenaje* is historical, archaeological, or anthropological, the subtext of all its poems is focussed on the present and the future, whatever their overt topic. Cardenal's basic approach to the cultures he depicts can, therefore, only be properly understood when studied in the light of the social and political context in which the poems were written, just as their changes of attitude and focus require to be examined in the light of a series of shifts of interest linked to major changes in the poet's life.

Cardenal came from a wealthy upper-class Nicaraguan family, firmly opposed to the Somozan dictatorship. During the early 1950s, after a period studying in Mexico (1943-47) and another in New York (1947-49), Cardenal—like many of his fellow-students—became involved in Nicaraguan revolutionary politics (notably in an abortive plot to bring down the first Somoza which ended with the detention, and slaughter, of some of the poet's closest friends in 1954). This period also saw the production of his *Epigramas,* whose clandestine circulation brought him immediate fame, as well as the writing of *Hora 0 (Zero Hour).* Both the gift for curt aphoristic turns of phrase perfected in the epigrams and the more expansive 'documentary' techniques of *Hora 0* were to be further exploited in *Homenaje,* only a few years later. But this collection might never have been written had Cardenal not experienced a religious conversion in 1956—the first of three

major turning-points which were to determine both the course of his life and the direction taken by his revolutionary poetry.

His conversion led him to enter the Cistercian Abbey of Gethsemani, in Kentucky, in May 1957. Cardenal's period at Gethsemani proved decisive for the genesis of *Homenaje* for two reasons. On the one hand, the novice-master was Thomas Merton, who convinced him of the rightness of Gandhi's doctrine of non-violence—without any diminution of his revolutionary zeal. Cardenal's commitment to non-violence was to last until the events of the late 1960s convinced him that 'civil disobedience' could never succeed against a tyrannical regime, and it coloured his approach to Latin American history throughout the formative years of *Homenaje.* On the other hand, his poetic imagination was fired by Merton's fascination with pre-Columbian cultures—an interest which deepened after he left Gethsemani, because of ill-health, in August 1959.

Cardenal's decision to leave the Trappists was the second turning-point, exposing him to new influences and directing his vocation away from monasticism towards religious action in the world. After a year and a half in Mexico with the Benedictines in Cuernavaca—where the earliest poem of *Homenaje* was composed—he went on to complete his training for the priesthood in Colombia at the seminary of La Ceja, near Medellín, from 1961 to 1965. Significantly, his years as a seminarist coincided with the time of ferment when the Second Vatican Council (1962-65) was at last committing the catholic church to the promotion of social justice, freedom, and the defence of human rights. In Latin America, these issues acquired increasing prominence with the rapid rise of 'liberation theology', and they loom larger in Cardenal's thought and writing as *Homenaje* progresses. The third turning-point came six months after his ordination, when he founded the small community of Nuestra Señora de Solentiname on a remote island in Lake Nicaragua early in 1966, and this was where the greater part of *Homenaje* was written. The establishment of such a religious commune, untrammelled by any monastic rule yet able to bring its spirituality to bear on society through its influence on individuals in the outside world, had been in his mind ever since he was a novice under Thomas Merton, and Merton remained Cardenal's spiritual guide until his death in December 1969, only a few months after the publication of the first edition of *Homenaje.*

It is within this framework that Cardenal's poetic development must be viewed. His poetic techniques are quite as revolutionary as his politics, and rather more surprising because they have an English-language source: although his concerns and thought-patterns are firmly Spanish American, he discarded the stylistic influences of Rubén Darío and Neruda—which had dominated his adolescent verse—when he discovered the poetry of Ezra Pound while studying in New York. Pound's influence was already apparent in the taut satire of the *Epigramas,* but all his later poetry has also exhibited four further Poundian features: total rejection of metaphor, the highly selective use of documentary sources, collage, and an air of extreme (yet only apparent) objectivity. This elimination of overtly subjective elements became enshrined in the poetic doctrine of *exteriorismo,* which Cardenal has defined as

> a poetry made out of elements taken from the external world. Interiority expressed through images taken from the external world surrounding us. A poetry made out of events, persons, and things. This poetry can include everyday realities, anecdotes, and the proper names of people and places . . . and also dates and numbers when required.

He praises Pound's poetry for its directness, describing it as being made up of 'the contraposition of images, of pairs of things which are either dissimilar or similar, but which produce another image when they are placed beside each other—a device which Ezra Pound had compared to the structure of Chinese ideograms but which Cardenal equated with the way film-shots are handled in the cutting-room. Pound's impact brought about a technical renovation of Cardenal's vernacular inheritance in much the same way as the impact of Italian Renaissance poetry on Garcilaso—four centuries earlier—had revitalized Spanish peninsular lyric poetry at the beginning of the Golden Age.

Cardenal's poetic revolution differs from Garcilaso's, however, in that the latter's merely involved renewing the poetry of one Romance language by cross-fertilization from another, whereas what Cardenal learnt from Pound proved to be the first positive contribution made by any aspect of North American English-language culture to the growth of Spanish-American poetry. This unexpected benefit is the more paradoxical given Cardenal's Latin American distaste for the generality of North American social and political attitudes, including that 'cultural imperialism' which most Latin American intellectuals believe to be a conscious feature of United States foreign policy. Beneath that Poundian surface, however, Cardenal's lines of thought remain much closer to Spanish-American tradition than the 'exterior' of his poetry suggests, as will be apparent throughout the poems of *Homenaje*.

Besides their common *exteriorista* approach, these Amerindian poems have numerous specific—and significant—technical links not only with *Epigramas* and *Hora 0* (both written before his spiritual conversion) but also with important aspects of four of Cardenal's other poetic collections whose composition actually overlapped with that of *Homenaje*: a series of taut vignettes called *Gethsemani, Ky.,* based on his spiritual notebook from Kentucky but only polished into poetry in Cuernavaca; a versified history of the conquest of Central America and its colonial aftermath called *El estrecho dudoso (The Doubtful Passage),* written during the second half of his period in Mexico; a slim pamphlet called *Oración por Marilyn Monroe y otros poemas (Prayer for Marilyn Monroe and other poems,* 1965), started in Cuernavaca but only completed in La Ceja; and the *Salmos* (first published in 1964), a sequence of twenty-five updated psalms all written in La Ceja, which overlapped both with *Oración* and with the first expansion of his Amerindian poetry.

What Cardenal's manner of proceeding in *Homenaje* takes over from his *Epigramas* is not just its penchant for aphoristic statement but also a marked tendency to make its major points by implication rather than by 'explicitation'. From *Hora 0,* besides the subtleties of documentary collage, *Homenaje* takes over the symbolic use of natural phenomena—plants, animals, the seasons, the cycles of reproduction and the agricultural year—whose implications in each specific context are normally left to the imagination of the intelligent reader: this update of the 'pathetic fallacy' became one of Cardenal's favourite techniques for the 'implicitation' of subtextual meaning, once it had been perfected (chiefly as a means of hinting at unstated spiritual feelings) in the tranquil meditative poems of *Gethsemani, Ky.* during his first few months at Cuernavaca. Similarly, *El estrecho dudoso* provided the model for his treatment of pre-Columbian cultures by handling an explicit 'chronicle' of past injustice in such a way that it would read as an implicit commentary on the modern world, while the satirical approach to modern culture used whenever *Homenaje* makes any explicit mention of western life and values was developed in some of the more ironic poems of *Oración*. Lastly, it was also at La Ceja that Cardenal began to experiment with prophetic utterance—a very significant mode at a certain stage in the development of *Homenaje*—by applying Old Testament texts to modern situations, not only in the *Salmos* but also in the longest poem in *Oración*: '**Apocalipsis**', which is a forceful rewriting of the Book of Revelation as a vision of the aftermath of nuclear holocaust. Each of these various techniques and strategies is unobtrusively employed at one stage or another in the poetry of *Homenaje,* whose composition spanned many years, with changes of course or emphasis as time went by.

I spent much of the summer of 1972 in Solentiname, working with Cardenal with a view to establishing the documentary sources of all his poems to date (including those of *Homenaje*), as well trying to disentangle the order of their composition. The chronological issue was complicated by three things: firstly, his collections had not been published in the order of their completion; secondly, they had frequently overlapped in composition (not merely in the cases mentioned above); and, thirdly, he had often been engaged concurrently on drafts of various poems (his longer ones may be months in the writing, with much pruning and revising and frequent regrouping of their constituent 'units'). Thus the fact that the first *Homenaje* had not appeared till 1969 did not mean that all its fifteen poems were later than those in 'earlier' collections, nor was their sequence in the volume any help since they had not been arranged in order of composition—or even in the historical order of the situations they described.

As well as the original fifteen, we discussed both of the two additional poems included in the Chilean edition (Santiago, 1970). He was then already working on the early typescripts of "**Sierra Nevada**"—the first of two further poems added in the Barcelona edition of 1980, which includes all the nineteen Amerindian poems completed prior to the Sandinista revolution. Their arrangement within that collection: is relatively unimportant in the present context. What matters, rather is their order of composition (see below). In any event, Cardenal himself clearly regards the series as open-ended: since he ceased to be minister of culture, twelve new Amerindian poems have appeared—together with nine of the earlier ones—in a separate volume called *Los ovnis de oro* (Mexico City, 1988), and it is his expressed intention to bring all his Amerindian poems together under 'un nuevo titulo'.

For reasons of space, however, the present study must concentrate on *Homenaje,* placing particular emphasis on the poems composed between 1959 and 1968: nine of its nineteen texts were written during these ten years, and they show a steady development which brings up in turn all of the main critical issues raised by Cardenal's treatment of past and present Amerindian cultures. But it is impossible to understand either their stylistic evolution, or the progressive maturation of his attitudes towards those cultures, without relating these key poems both to the shifts in his career and to the nature of his other writings during the same period. The ten remaining poems of *Homenaje* will be discussed in far less detail, since they—and the new texts which joined the series in *Ovnis*—merely continue lines of thought and modes of treatment which had all made their appearance by the end of 1967, although there were to be various significant shifts of emphasis and coverage which cannot pass unmentioned in this study.

The earliest one of all was **"Las ciudades perdidas" ("The Lost Cities")**, a Mayan poem written within nine or ten months of Cardenal's arrival in Cuernavaca in August 1959, and something of a romantic digression from the two spiritual projects then engaging most of his attention (**"Gethsemani, Ky."** and the mystical prose meditations of *Vida en el amor*). **"Ciudades"** deserves the longest discussion, since it establishes the basic paradigm for *Homenaje.* It was completed before he tackled any serious historical research, such as would be required towards *Estrecho* (an 'epic' project suggested by José Coronel Urtecho only a few months later), and this may partly explain why a certain romantic nostalgia took priority over scholarly content. Back in Gethsemani, Merton had awakened his interest in the ancient Maya, and **"Ciudades"** was inspired by an article about the ruins of Tikal which Merton had pinned up on the noviciate noticeboard. Fascinated, Cardenal had looked further: **"Ciudades"** is chiefly based on notes taken in Gethsemani from Merton's copies of Thompson's *The Rise and Fall of the Mayan Civilization* (1954) and the much enlarged 3rd edition of Morley's *The Ancient Maya* as revised by Brainerd (Stanford, 1956). In the late 1950s, these were still the last word on the subject among non-specialists. Although their interpretation of Mayan history was soon to undergo a drastic revision, these volumes remained Cardenal's favourite source of archaeological information on the Mayan area—fleshed out in later poems by recourse to the thought and terminology of the *Chilam Balam* and the *Popol Vuh.*

Overtly, **"Ciudades"** seems merely the nostalgic evocation of a happier world, yet almost all its explicit statements contain some implied criticism of modern civilization—for instance its reference to there being 'no names of generals on the stelae'. It contrasts the ruins of Tikal (the earliest Mayan city), where the jungle animals once 'stylized in the frescoes' now roam, with an apparently idyllic past admired as much for the things which it—significantly—lacked (such as having 'no word for *master* nor for *city wall*') as for its 'progress in religion, mathematics, art, astronomy' or for the benevolent paternalism of its theocratic social structure:

> Their cities were cities of temples . . .
> Religion was the only bond between them,
> but it was a religion freely accepted,
> imposing no burden. No oppression.
> Their priests had no temporal power
> and the pyramids were built without forced labour.

There may perhaps be some small element of truth in this highly idealistic picture, though it is clear even from Morley that the development of a highly organized priesthood 'composed of astronomers, mathematicians, prophets, and ritualists, and, as it grew more complex, [also] skilled administrators and statesmen' must have replaced the poet's non-exploitative two-tiered Eden—if that ever existed—long before the building of Tikal, in the fourth century A.D. What Cardenal would seem to have done is to project onto such Classic Mayan cities the monastic values of shared work and prayer which he had encountered in Gethsemani, and which naturally also ruled the Benedictine priory at Cuernavaca where the poem was written (in the modern catholic church the 'communism' of the early Christians, which Cardenal so greatly admires, survives only in the monastic orders).

Accepting Morley's vision of the Classic Maya, such a projection was not beyond the bounds of credibility, and Cardenal's belief that even a high culture could once have been both peaceful and bloodless deepens his evident nostalgia. Since then, advances in the decipherment of Mayan inscriptions (together with the reinterpretation of Mayan iconography) have shown that even the Classic city-states were bloodthirsty: 'regionally oriented, dynastic and warlike' and full of monuments which were 'glorifications of individual kings' (rather than 'abstract representations of calendar priests'). How does this affect Cardenal's **"Ciudades"**? Had he wished to teach the 'historical truth' about the past by putting it into verse (Neruda's stated aim in much of *Canto general*) then anything which disproved the 'facts' would have 'falsified' the poem as history. But Cardenal was using the evocation of a certain social complex (which he then happened to believe had once existed) as the springboard for an implicit attack on present evils—and the relevance of the criticism is undiminished by the ahistoricity of the chosen springboard. Long afterwards, Cardenal did actualize much of the idyllic vision of **"Ciudades"** in his own island commune, but here his glowing evocation of the early Maya performs the same function as the classical myth of the 'golden age' in Greco-Roman and Renaissance poetry.

Lines stressing the (presumed) absence of personality cults among the ancient Maya are directed at the Somozas, but their message also had a wider relevance in the aftermath of 'destalinization' (the worldwide repercussions of Kruschev's speech at the Twentieth Party Congress, in 1956, were far from over). Equally, the anti-militarist thrust had not only an immediate local relevance (coming so soon after the events of 1954 in Guatemala) but also a wider significance in the context of United States support for military regimes all over Latin America. Its vibrantly uncompromising tone was, however, also partly attributable to the recency of the poet's own conversion to nonviolence: the pacific 'model' which he conjures up reads like an answer to the petition 'Lord guide our feet into the way of peace' (one of the antiphons used to introduce the 'Benedictus' at morning prayer).

Cardenal's nostalgia was intensified by his fascination with the Mayans' cyclical notion of time—'They used the same katuns for past and future / in the belief that time was re-enacted'. While extremely conscious that 'the Pan American jet flies high above the pyramid' today (his one explicit reference to our modern world) he ends by asking 'will the past katuns one day return?'. This was no rhetorical question, and it has nagged him ever since. "Ciudades" also includes the first example of his delight in discovering Amerindian analogies for Christian beliefs or practices: 'They knew Jesus as the God of the Maize / and gave him simple offerings of maize, of birds, of feathers'. As well as being a 'gloss' on the past, this is an allusion to current rural Mayan syncretism, with peasant offerings to Jesus and the saints perpetuating those to the various gods who mattered most to farmers.

Cardenal wrote no more Amerindian poems for several years, until late in his time at La Ceja and after his background knowledge had been much broadened by the research for *Estrecho* in the libraries of Cuernavaca and Mexico City. He had also become much better acquainted with the heritage of Nahuatl poetry. The first two volumes of Garibay's bilingual *Poesía náhuatl* (1964, 1965) appeared while he was at La Ceja, where his interest in the past and present of the Amerindian peoples was also extended by direct contact with several 'primitive' communities (he paid two visits to the Cuna, also travelling in the Upper Amazon basin) and by research in the anthropological collections of Medellín and Bogotá. He was planning a book on primitive peoples which would explore the resemblances between primitive and Christian ritual, but soon dropped the project, feeling that such stress on ritual practices was out of step with the post-conciliar church—as well as with the kind of Christian community he now planned to establish (under Merton's tutelage) once he had been ordained. But none of this anthropological work was wasted, since his prose drafts were later reworked into poetry.

The La Ceja poems were **"Cantares mexicanos (I)"** and **"Nele de Kantule"**, and he also began work on **"Economía de Tahuantinsuyo"**. The phrase 'Cantares mexicanos' is an allusion to a famous manuscript in the National Library of Mexico, and **"Cantares (I)"** develops its implicit parallels between pagan and Christian beliefs through a reworking of lyric texts by the most famous of all pre-Columbian poets, Nezahualcóyotl (ruler of Texcoco), who seemed to voice

in Mexican terms the same sense of *desengaño* (a disillusionment provoked by the transience of earthly things) which overshadows Spanish Golden Age poetry and spirituality: 'Necklaces of shells or jade are scattered . . . / Even a temple pyramid / will crumble / We [poets] are here / to leave a few illuminated manuscripts / But will those who come after comprehend the Codex?'. The stock *ubi sunt* motif is applied to the reigns of Mexican rulers, and it is only in the final sequence that Quetzalcóatl's rebirth as the Morning Star is taken as a sign that he will 'bring me back from Mictlan' (land of the dead)—just as Christ's resurrection is the Christian's guarantee of immortality. But the main thrust of Nezahualcóyotl's faith in immortality was picked up only two years later, in **"Cantares (II)"**.

The other Amerindian poem completed in La Ceja, **"Nele de Kantule"**, is more positive. It grew out of his first visit to any non-Christian society, that of the Cuna Indians of the San Blas Islands (off the Caribbean coast of Panama), where he was welcomed into a peace-loving community whose pagan values seemed profoundly Christian and whose spirit of mutual cooperation was wholly at variance with our competitive society. He was told about the *neles* (wise men) the most famous of whom was Kantule, who had not only learnt the wisdom of his people but studied abroad, had led an Indian rebellion against the Panamanian government in 1925 (which won a guarantee of Cuna autonomy), and had wisely decided just how much 'progress' could be accepted without weakening the Cuna culture (he bought a motor vessel to service the islands, built schools and libraries, negotiated an agreement with the Americans governing conditions of employment for Indians in the Canal Zone, and obtained scholarships for his young men to learn such skills on the Panamanian mainland as could be of benefit to the community). The fact that he used his office to serve his people and not as a source of power, together with the continued strength of Cuna mythology and tribal wisdom, entranced Cardenal, and much of the poem is taken up with retelling the local Creation myth. Kantule's death-bed baptism is mentioned (almost incidentally), but what is stressed is that when the missionary told him that he would now see God, he replied 'I am already seeing God'. This visit to the Cuna showed Cardenal that perfect communities did still exist in the 'real world' and might even provide him with a viable model: his own foundation, on an island in the Solentiname Archipelago, may have owed almost as much to the example of the Cuna islanders as it did to Christian monastic tradition.

With **"Tahuantinsuyo"** we are back in another world, in more senses than one. Cardenal turns to the Incas, but since he had not yet been to Peru his knowledge of its past and present were both still excessively bookish (a disadvantage he had overcome by the time he wrote his second Inca poem). The Incas are praised above all for their moneyless economy ('since there was no money / there was no prostitution or theft', whereas modern Peru was corrupt, poverty-stricken, and inflation-ridden), but also because 'The heir to the throne / succeeded to his father's throne / BUT NOT TO HIS POSSESSIONS'. Furthermore 'Religious truth / and political truth / were a single truth for the people'. Yet Cardenal was not blind to the totalitarian aspects of the regime: after mentioning Neruda's name, to imply dissent from what he—erroneously—took to be uncritical praise of the 'socialist empire of the Incas' in the *Alturas de Macchu Picchu,* he says 'Not everything was perfect in the "Inca Paradise" / They censored history . . . / There were free motels . . . / but no freedom to travel'. Nonetheless, while 'there was no freedom / there *was* social security'.

Unlike **"Ciudades",** there is much explicit criticism of modern conditions (including a side-swipe at the stock markets, where futures drop on the forecast of good crops) but **"Tahuantinsuyo"** ends on the same note, enquiring whether the virtues of the pre-Columbian past will ever return. Stylistically it is much more experimental, with extensive temporal crosscutting, and making its impact chiefly by using cinematographic sequences of discontinuous 'shots' whose juxtapositions invite the reader to infer the meaning behind the 'collisional montage' (a technique exploited further in later poems). This distinguishes it as the product of a different poetic generation from that of Neruda's *Alturas*: conceptually, however, it lacks the depth of the earlier classic, and the name-dropping which invited the comparison was just belated juvenile bravado (in 1965 Cardenal was already forty, while Neruda was sixty-one and still at the height of his powers).

Cardenal returned to Managua in the summer of 1965 and was ordained on the Feast of the Assumption. He then went back briefly to Gethsemani (for the first time in six years) to discuss his plans for Solentiname with Merton, and on his return journey he visited the Pueblo Indians of New Mexico (his first visit to any indigenous North American people). **"Tahuantinsuyo"** was completed immediately afterwards, and in February 1966 Cardenal and two friends began clearing a space for their huts on the tropical island of Mancarrón. The abundant birdlife of the archipelago (with its striking seasonal changes) provides much of his best supporting and contrastive imagery thereafter, starting with one of the earliest poems he wrote in Solentiname: **"Kayanerenhkowa"**. Its title means 'The Great Peace' and it extends the scope of *Homenaje* to North America, describing the sixteenth-century 'League of the Five Nations'—the famous Iroquois Confederacy. But it was not completed until 1967, because establishing the settlement left scant time for poetry during their first eighteen months.

"Kayanerenhkowa" begins with the autumnal arrival of migrating birds from the States. Cardenal uses their journey to link back to New York's Central Park, and so to the United Nations, thus providing a backdrop for a meditation on an Amerindian 'League of Nations' which he views as authentic antecedent of the UNO: conceived—by a happy coincidence—on almost the same site, one afternoon when the Huron chieftain Deganawida 'camped on the banks of the Mohawk (New York) / sat down beneath a tree and smoked his pipe'. Historically, Deganawida's *Pax Iroquoia*—in which all were to 'eat the one beaver out of the one plate' and bury the hatchet forever—did

not spell peace except between the five confederated Nations. To their neighbours, it meant a war 'characterized by frightfulness, the object of which was power and glory' (in Wissler's phrase). Cardenal, however, was inspired by those who admired the vision behind its organization (according to some authorities it even served as the model for England's ex-colonies to form their own confederacy), so what he evokes is only its 'Good News of Peace' and the absence of treachery among the Nations themselves. After an extended exposition of religious symbolism, he retells the foundation of the League in modern terminology, blames the recrudescence of war on the greed of the fur-traders, and contrasts the peaceful formations of migrating birds with those of military aircraft.

This time the concluding question is strictly modern: 'And where are the jet-planes going? / Do they fly / towards Vietnam?'. However profoundly Cardenal is moved by the symbolic aspects of Indian life and beliefs (those passages have great poetic beauty), his crosscutting between the past and the present is nonetheless directed at the contemporary world. Although there is no allusion to the war until that final question, he is as deeply troubled by Vietnam as Merton, who expressed his despair in a long letter to Cardenal as early as October 1966 and began publishing his own—far more explicit—denunciations of the war while **'Kayanerenhkowa'** was being completed. It is characteristic of Cardenal that the poem's most immediate relevance should be an unstated moral, while even the positive nature of his response to Indian symbolism is something which the reader must infer from his objectively *exteriorista* exposition.

Over the next eighteen months, he wrote two further Mayan poems (**"Mayapán"** & **"Katún 11 Ahau"**) and two more grounded in Nahuatl poetry (**"Cantares mexicanos (II)"** & **"Netzahualcóyotl"**). **"Mayapán"** and **"Katún"** overlapped, although **"Katún"** was probably the first to be completed, but **"Mayapán"** stands—both conceptually and stylistically—between **"Ciudades"** and **"Katún"** and should therefore be considered first. It is a longer and weightier poem, and caused a considerable impression when Cardenal read it aloud in Mexico in September 1967, when he went to attend the ordination of his brother Fernando (who later became well-known as the Jesuit architect of Nicaragua's literacy crusade, and subsequently Sandinista minister of education).

Set in the Postclassic age, **"Mayapán"** is concerned with the evils brought by militarism once the—unhistorical—'peaceful coexistence' depicted in **"Ciudades"** had given way to the values of warring city-states (values which, as we now know, prevailed far earlier than Cardenal supposed). Thus whereas in **"Ciudades"** there was 'no word for *city wall*', the very name of Mayapan means 'She who has walls'. Both poems use their Mayan precedents to comment on our times (either through the implicit contrast between a tranquil past and a fraught present, or by more overt parallels between two periods of decadence), but whereas **"Ciudades"** was also permeated by nostalgia for the supposed past, here the whole thrust is contemporary—Mayan decadence is chiefly a convenient basis for the present-day polemic.

The poem documents the decay of Classic Mayan culture, as art proliferates but the carving grows more crude— crosscutting between English and Spanish to compare the spread of skyscrapers to the multiplication of stelae ('el skyline de Tikal . . . / "Building Boom" en Guatemala y / "Estela Boom". . .'). But at least Mayan urban spread did not consist of 'Commercial Centers / sino centros ceremoniales, Ceremonial Centers' whose only advertisements were the poems on the stones. Weapons multiplied (like modern armaments), palaces outdid the temples, there were even dynasties of tyrants. But the tyrants were ultimately overthrown and Mayapan was destroyed: 'MAYAPAN "SHE WHO HAS WALLS" FELL. . . . / In Katun 8 Ahau *Mayapan fell"* / (says the CHILAM BALAM OF CHUMAYEL)'. Mayapan stands for the same things as Babylon in **"Apocalipsis"** but, since Mayan time is cyclical, there is an added twist. On this occasion, Cardenal accepts—at least for poetic purposes—that each 260-year katun will be repeated and that every **"Katun 8 Ahau"** sees parallel events. Thus, although the Katún 8 Ahau when Mayapan collapsed was specifically 'The Mayan Ides of March', the event must happen again—the prophecies of the Chilam Balam have still not lost their power.

After a collage of truncated texts from the *Chilam Balam,* Cardenal begins to speak without mediation, prophesying in the first person: 'I say that Mayapan will fall / In this katun walled Mayapan always falls' (the biblical echo of Jericho is clearly one of the intended resonances). The archaeological record suggests that Mayapan flourished for no more than about a katun—'Thompson says / 1200-1450 A.D.'—and Cardenal, rather tellingly, leaves it to the reader to work out that one has only to add 260 years twice over to reach 1970. Immediately after quoting Thompson's dates, the poem ends with a trick:

> Esta es la
> Este-
> la

['This is the Stela']

Cardenal's own text is, thus, itself the graven stone. This lengthy poem's three outstanding features are the linking of his earlier use of historical precedents to the Mayan notion of cyclical time, the poet's self-identification with the Mayan chilan (which lets him speak in the first person when applying the resonances of the *Chilam Balam* to our age), and the fact that—just as in **"Kayanerenhkowa"**—his Amerindian source-material is clearly being deployed primarily so that it may serve a topical Central American purpose.

"Katún 11 Ahau" discards the archaeology but continues the prophetic line, dealing with the present entirely in terms of the *Chilam Balam.* Cardenal's approach is slightly too enigmatic: not even many Nicaraguans know that 11 Ahau is the katun in which the *conquistadores* reached Mayan territory, so missing the title's 'message' that we live in a matching period (thus weeping 'for the books that were burnt' applies as much to Somozan censorship

as to the destruction of the Mayan sacred writings by the Spanish church). The savage opening jeremiad switches at line 48 ('But the Katun of Cruel Men will pass') into a prophecy of better times, when the Katun of the Tree of Life is established and we no longer 'have to keep our voices low'. The abruptness of the central switch underscores the implied message that present evils portend changes for the better.

Despite the Mayan idiom, this Cardenal who speaks as a chilan is like an Old Testament prophet in his combination of 'denunciation' and 'annunciation' (*denunciar* and *anunciar* were the paired terms he used when we discussed the nature of his ***Salmos*** again, in San José de Costa Rica, just ten days before the Sandinistas entered Managua). When a seminarian, he had naturally studied the dual functions of prophetic writing, and he had already used them himself when updating the Psalms and the Apocalypse. At the end of **"Katún 11 Ahau"**, however, the Mayan chilan is credited with more than purely prophetic powers:

> The Chilan:
>   he who reads the sacred scriptures
> and studies the skies by night [. . .]
> in order that the time to till the land be known,
> the time to harvest maize [. . .]
> to search the woods for deer.
> The Chilan: he sets the days for rain.
> The days when men shall sing.
> The ending of the rainy season.
> Wards off both plagues and hunger.
> Distributes food should hunger come.
> Invigilates the carving of the stelae,
>   designs new temples,
> delivers tablets which predict eclipses.

The poem is itself just such a tablet, predicting a (political) eclipse which presages the downfall of Somoza.

It is no accident that the chilan is shown playing such a prominent part in society. This is the role which Cardenal has set aside for the modern poet-priest as the initiator of social change. Although not every item is applicable—not even Cardenal can 'set the days for rain'!—much of that catalogue applies to the social role he was already starting to assume as the Solentiname commune evolved, particularly in his prophetic-cum-paternalistic stance vis-à-vis the *campesions* who flocked to his Sunday mass and joined in the distinctly 'revolutionary' discussions of the scripture-readings. In this context, two further lines deserve particular comment: 'It is the time to build a new pyramid / upon the basis of the old'. At the end of each period of time, Mayan temples were rebuilt not by demolishing the earlier ones but by removing the superstructure and enclosing the earlier pyramid inside a larger and better one, on which the new altars were erected. The implicit moral is clear: our existing social structures should not be utterly swept away, because the core deserves to be preserved within the improved structure of a New Society. Nor was this New Society wholly intangible: its values had already taken shape at the micro level, in Solentiname.

The last two poems of this cluster were both Mexican: **"Cantares mexicanos (II)"** and **"Netzahualcóyotl"**. **"Cantares (II)"** merely continues the earlier **"Cantares (I)"**—written in La Ceja—in a like-minded meditation on poetry and immortality, again reworking Nezahualcóyotl and providing another pagan parallel to Christian doctrine (one can see why Cardenal was happy to link them more closely when he later used them as the first two sections of an extended **"Cantares mexicanos"**); it needs no further comment here. Internal evidence suggests that it preceded **"Netzahualcóyotl"**, but their composition may have overlapped. Whereas both of the original 'Cantares' are spoken in the first person by Nezahualcóyotl, the poem named after him is a praise-poem, and this panegyric—which is likewise inspired by Texcocan court poetry—is the last poem requiring detailed consideration on this occasion: while the ten remaining texts do indeed continue to evolve, they do so within the existing parameters.

"Netzahualcóyotl" is a complex celebration of a poet-prince who is also 'a Mystic, an Astrologer, a Legislator and an Engineer / [who] made verses, and also dikes / talking about bridges and new poetry'. It raises a wealth of points in its 541 lines, most of them propounded in eminently quotable form—but there are far too many such 'statements' for it to be possible to discuss all of them here. One important innovation is the shift from drawing simple direct parallels or contrasts (whether implicit or explicit) between the past and the present to exploring a major pre-Columbian confrontation between Good and Evil in ways which either imply or underline its presumed present-day significance (often achieving this with great economy simply by using terminological crosscutting between the two periods). Thus the 'Philosopher-King' was previously 'a guerrillero-King', who overthrew 'tyrants and military juntas', and who also disagreed 'with human sacrifices [because] that was not his [kind of] religion'.

Nezahualcóyotl built his pyramid to the Unknown God ('el Dios Desconocido') without images or sacrificial altars, opposite the pyramid of 'Huitzilopochtli-Nazi': Huitzilopochtli was the most bloodthirsty of all Aztec gods (at the dedication of whose temple in 1487 literally thousands of sacrificial victims had their hearts torn out) but, since that fact is common knowledge in Mesoamerica, Cardenal need only add the adjective to juxtapose the holocausts, and so—by implication—the regimes. Where the military destroyed books and rewrote history, Nezahualcóyotl imposed the death penalty on historians who knowingly travestied the truth, as well as on anyone accepting bribes. He also established compulsory universal education and fostered the arts: 'The Ministry of Poetry / open all day. That of War almost always closed'.

As both Lyons [in *Ernesto Cardenal: The Poetics of Love and Revolution*, unpublished doctoral dissertation, 1981] and Borgeson [in *Hacia el hombre nuevo: poesía y pensamiento de Ernesto cardenal,* 1979] point out, the act of describing Nezahualcóyotl as wearing blue-jeans—Cardenal's normal dress—contributes to the identification of the Philosopher-King with the modern poet. Those jeans are, however, part of a whole code of modern nouns: Nezahualcóyotl's fellow-poets are his *cuates*—pals—and his guerrilleros sang *corridos* like Sandino's followers. Nonetheless the identification is correct: Cardenal even makes Nezahualcóyotl say 'My ideology is Non-Violence'. Of course all this is anachronistic: Brotherston, speaking as an Amerindianist, describes Cardenal's response to Nahuatl lyrics as 'vitiated . . . by a reluctance to admit . . . the original context [of] the martial and homosexual rites that informed them as song'. But, while the observation is correct, that comment seems to miss the point of what Cardenal was actually doing.

His evocation of the Texcocan circle of artists and poets is partly an idealization of what Solentiname might become, and partly a vision of what the cultural elite ought to be like in the New Society. Cardenal has a somewhat 'two-tiered' view of an ideal world in which, while everyone should have the opportunity to realize his full potential (and the humblest campesino has unrecognized gifts), the upper tier consists of those who have already done so and now use their talents in the service of the *pueblo* in a mildly paternalistic way. Except for that principle of Non-Violence (an ideal which Cardenal dropped about 1970), this Texcocan court-circle bears a quite remarkable resemblance to the Sandinista directorate of *comandante*-poets: men with a middle-class background and a good education, determined to give all citizens the right to come up to their level, within the framework of an egalitarian constitution. But when he wrote **"Netzahualcóyotl"** Cardenal could not yet see how the Solentiname 'model' could be applied on a larger scale: setting up a viable commune was relatively easy (communes were multiplying throughout the western world) but to create a Latin American republic grounded in social justice and 'the option for the poor' was something different.

At first sight, it may well look as though Cardenal were merely projecting his picture of the modern world onto the pre-Columbian past in order to be able to transform it into a source of handy precedents. But perhaps there is also a kind of 'reverse process' at work: a process of 'rethinking' which can best be understood by referring back to the *Salmos*. The major part of the canonical 'hours' (the backbone of communal monastic prayer) consists of the antiphonal chanting of the psalms, and when Cardenal had first been brought into continuous contact with these in Gethsemani, he could only make them meaningful—as he was reciting them in choir—by mentally transposing them to our modern world, all of whose joys and terrors had their parallels in the Old Testament. The series of *Salmos* he later composed in La Ceja was merely a written application of this same devotional technique, and he described them as 'translations' (when we discussed them once more in San José in 1979). This whole process of what might be termed 'decontextualization' and 'recontextualization' comes quite naturally to anyone using the psalms in prayer. But it has a further consequence: intertextuality works both ways (for authors as for readers) and Cardenal rapidly discovered that the interplay of meaning between the 'old' and the 'new' was beginning to deepen his experience of both 'readings'.

The relevance of this reciprocal process to what he is doing in his historical poems would appear to be as follows: while he may well have begun by using his pre-Columbian sources chiefly as springboards for contemporary messages, by the time he writes **"Netzahualcóyotl"** he would seem to be reading them in the same way as the psalms: namely, not just seeking out their modern 'relevance' through the discovery of parallels but also finding the originals themselves enriched by virtue of the fact that such parallels enabled him—and other modern readers—to empathize with their creators. This way of apprehending pre-Columbian Nahuatl poetry is certainly anachronistic, and it will doubtless offend the purist (primarily concerned to uncover their original 'meaning', like an archaeologist who excavates a buried city). But it does make that poetry 'meaningful' to modern readers in the modern world, and—with the advent of 'reception theory'—this means that it is a 'reading' which has to be taken seriously by critics.

Furthermore, the reciprocal relationship between the old text and the new has an important linguistic dimension. Just as happens in the case of the psalms, the interplay between different levels of historical experience which underlines their situational parallels is linguistically reinforced by the ebb-and-flow of resonant associations between two very different linguistic codes of reference. In the case of the *Salmos,* the interaction lies between the often deliberately clichéd terms of Cardenal's modern Spanish, and the Latin of the psalms as he had experienced them in the pre-conciliar church. In the case of **"Netzahualcóyotl"** or **"Mayapán"**, it involves the interaction between the modern vernacular idiom (which may include crosscutting between Spanish and the clichés of political or commercial American English) and the indigenous terminologies and registers of Nahuatl poetry and the *Chilam Balam,* as these have been absorbed by Cardenal through the intermediary of scholarly translations. The 'remote' documentary sources are, admittedly, not being read in their original language—in either case—, but one should recognize that using Amerindian prose or poetry in translation is, after all, really no different from using the Old Testament in Jerome's Latin!

No major new issues arise in the subsequent poems, although they all have points of interest. The next one he began was **"La danza del espíritu"**, exploring the symbolism of North American ritual dances in the context of Tecumseh's vision of a peaceful Indian confederacy (in the first decade of the nineteenth century) and the brief-lived, late-nineteenth-century Ghost Dance cult predicting the coming of an Indian Messiah. It ends with a reminiscence of Cardenal's visit to Taos Pueblo in 1965. During the course of its composition he wrote two more brief Mayan pieces making prophetic use of the *Chilam Balam*: **"8 Ahau"** and **"Ardilla de los tunes de un katú"**. In 1968, he composed his third North American poem—**"Tahirassawichi en Washington"**—about the symbols and rituals of the Pawnees. To my way of thinking, this is the best of Cardenal's North American poems.

The most recently composed of the fifteen poems in the 1969 *Homenaje* are the two shortest: **"La carretera"** (only 16 lines) and the 35-line **"Milpa"**, the former a Mayan vignette, and the latter about a *milpa* (maize-field) near the ruins of Cobá. This quiet meditation has an echo of the scriptural grain of wheat that dies to bring forth fruit (John 12.24), which becomes a veritable topos in elegies for martyred guerrilleros (Cardenal had already used it himself both in *Epigramas* and in *Hora 0*), but there is a neat extension of this idea in **"Milpa"** which brings together many lines of thought from earlier poems: 'Beneath the earth the grains, step by step / one step each day, / are raising up the pyramid of the maize'.

Of those first fifteen poems, [one] concerned the Incas, seven were on Mayan topics, three were grounded in pre-Columbian Nahuatl poetry, three had North American themes, and only [one] concerns a contemporary Amerindian community—but it is noteworthy that Cardenal gave this one pride of place at the beginning of the collection. It has a double immediacy which does set it apart: firstly the vividness of direct and joyful observation, and secondly its 'contemporaneity'—dealing with a present which has a message for the future but scarcely any history. It is as *exteriorista* as the rest, communicating strictly through the coordination of external data, but the intensity of concealed subjective feeling (which is almost always present in these poems, though perhaps at its most urgent in the Mayan prophecies) is nearest the surface here—and only in this instance does one feel that the overt Amerindian subject is at least as important to the poet as its wider social relevance. The same distinction, both in meaning and in tone, between the 'historical' poems and those about 'contemporary' Amerindian peoples holds good throughout the body of his later Amerindian poems.

Both of those which were added in the 1970 edition were written shortly before his first visit to Cuba: **"Marchas pawnees"** links back to **"Tahirassawichi"** in its sources, and to **"Kayanerenhkowa"** in its crosscutting between the exploitative modern world and a wise traditional society (in which goods were bartered 'in an exchange which was not commercial but religious'). The second one, **"Oráculos"**, was written some two months later, soon after the completion of his elegy for Thomas Merton. It is in the same Mayan prophetic line as **"Katún"**, but with the addition of such explicitly revolutionary statements as 'The people will take over the Government [and] the Bank'. After Merton's death, Cardenal's stress on non-violence diminished, though he still proposed the Gandhian model in his earliest discussions with Carlos Fonseca at about this time. What proved decisive were, firstly, his visits to Cuba—which persuaded him that many things he had thought unattainable at the macro level could indeed be achieved (if only by an armed revolution which could bring about radical changes in the social order)—and, secondly, the growth of a Theology of Liberation willing to contemplate the waging of 'just wars' against tyranny. But none of this surfaces in the last two poems added to *Homenaje*: **"Sierra Nevada"**, the one on which he was engaged when I was in Solentiname, and **"Grabaciones"** (completed in either 1972 or early 1973).

The former explores the spiritual world of the Koguis (in Colombia's Sierra Nevada). Cardenal was fascinated by the continued existence of a way of life which regards the world as a physical-cum-spiritual continuum ruled by an all-pervasive force of love (an idea he developed considerably further in his own non-Amerindian poems of this period). Although he never succeeded in reaching the Koguis, this poem has almost the immediacy of **"Nele de Kantule"**—perhaps because it was inspired by what he heard in person from an anthropologist who had lived among them (Reichel-Dolmatoff whom he got to know in Bogotá). This pursuit of present-day primitive societies was to be taken further in various of the new poems added in *Ovnis,* whereas 'Grabaciones de la pipa sagrada'—the fifth and last of his North American Indian poems—represents the end of quite a different line of thought.

Despite its title, it was inspired not so much by Black Elk's accounts of the rites of the Oglala Sioux in *The Sacred Pipe* (first published in 1953) as by the more historically oriented 'oral testimony' recorded by John G. Neihardt in *Black Elk Speaks*: although this had originally appeared as early as 1932, it unexpectedly turned into a 'current youth classic' during the 1960s, and Cardenal certainly first met it in Gethsemani. Just before the composition of **"Grabaciones"**, it suddenly 'exploded into surprising popularity' once more when Neihardt was interviewed on television in 1971. **"Grabaciones"** is in many respects the most nostalgic of the five North American poems, and its placing at the very end of *Homenaje* highlights its seemingly positive response to the question posed in the final line of **"Ciudades"**: there, Cardenal had ended by asking whether the past katuns would ever return; here, Black Elk closes the poem by saying 'The ball'—a ritual object standing for the universe (and for whose possession the players strove in a symbolic game which represented the course of man's life)—'will again return to the centre: / and they will be at the centre with the ball'. As these lines stand in the poem, they are the more resonant for having been left somewhat enigmatic. But their fuller implications would seem to require a knowledge of their original context in the closing paragraph of *The Sacred Pipe*:

> At this sad time today among my people, we are scrambling for the ball, and some are not even trying to catch it, which makes me cry when I think of it. But soon I know it will be caught, for the end is rapidly approaching, *and then it will be returned to the center, and our people will be with it.* It is my prayer that this be so, and it is in order to aid in this "recovery of the ball," that I have wished to make this book. [My italics.]

Cardenal could have said as much of *Homenaje,* but it is characteristic of his preference for 'implicitation' over 'explicitation' that he does not spell this out, while his treatment of Black Elk's testimony is equally typical of his idiosyncratic (or even cavalier) handling of the written sources on which he depends for so much of the raw material of his poems.

The appearance of *Ovnis* in 1988 has altered both the historical and the geographical balance of Cardenal's coverage of Amerindian cultures but not the range of basic attitudes, nor has it pioneered any fresh stylistic approaches. It contains no further North American poems but extends the Mexican coverage by five items (four ancient and one modern): the expanded **"Cantares mexicanos"**, two further poems about pre-Columbian Nahuatl poetry, an extended enquiry into all the meanings ever attached to either the person or the myth of 'Quetzalcóatl', and a 'snapshot' of an Indian girl today. There is one more Mayan item—his only poem to date about the life of present-day Mayan Indians (set in the highlands of the Quiché and with an ominously understated hint of a military presence)—and one further look at the Incas (**"El secreto de Machu-Picchu"**). This poem contains more—and far sterner—criticism of modern Peru than **"Tahuantinsuyo"** and, since the new poem (unlike its predecessor) is firmly grounded in personal knowledge of the Peruvian scene, it also has a greater feeling of testimonial immediacy.

Of the six other new poems, only one is historical: **"La Arcadia perdida"**. This provides a very positive account of the Jesuit *reducciones* in Paraguay (a topic which I had myself brought to Cardenal's attention in Solentiname, in 1972, as an example of benevolent priestly paternalism not dissimilar to his own experiment). Its nostalgia is, however, countered by the depiction of the misery of a jungle tribe in Paraguay today. . . . The remaining four are all concerned with other present-day 'primitive' peoples: **"Los yaruros"** deals with a Venezuelan tribe which Cardenal had visited in 1977, now shrunk to a tragic remnant, while [another poem] is based on a similar visit to a Colombian coastal settlement (today dispossessed of its lands and reduced to 'just 250' individuals). The others, by contrast, take him back to his old friends the Cunas of San Blas, revisited with delight during his years as Sandinista minister of culture, where developers had wished to build a great hotel 'but Torrijos assured me "There will be no Hilton"'.

It is clear that the balance of Cardenal's interests had shifted quite considerably during the eight years between the Barcelona printing of *Homenaje* and the appearance of *Ovnis* (years which broadly coincided with his period in office as the Sandinista minister of culture—although much of the groundwork of some of the new poems dates back to before he left Solentiname in 1977 to go into exile). *Ovnis* does not only extend Cardenal's Amerindian coverage: more importantly, the main emphasis of the new poetry has moved away from his former preoccupation with the discovery of 'messages' in the past to giving at least equal attention to the anthropological description of today's endangered peoples, conducted in a substantially more 'documentary' mode. No less than six out of the twelve new texts relate to present-day Amerindian societies, where only one of the nineteen poems in *Homenaje* had done so.

Nevertheless, the two main conclusions to be drawn from the closer examination of the nine poems of *Homenaje* composed between 1959 and 1968 remain valid for the entire corpus of his Amerindian poetry: (1) while the Past is diligently—and often lovingly—explored in search of useful precedents and resonant prophecies, the poet's real concern has always focussed on the Present and the Future; consequently (2) it is only the present-day communities he represents which ever get treated primarily 'in their own right'—and it is therefore only in these cases that one could describe his treatment as helping to shape an accurate awareness of Amerindian cultures.

While it follows that one should never consult his pre-Columbian poems in search of 'accurate' history or archaeology, they deserve just as serious a scrutiny as the others with a view to understanding, firstly, the nature of their intended 'relevance' to the development of the society for which they were actually written and, secondly, the ways in which Cardenal makes use of literary means to his didactic ends—as well as simply to enjoy the poems as poetry!

They all come under the heading of 'The Poetry of Useful Prophecy' (coined by Ronald Christ in 1974). All of them are intended to be 'useful', and they are also all 'prophetic', in so far as Cardenal is invariably looking forward even when he seems to be merely looking back (as in **"Ciudades"**). He is always interpreting his sources like a priest in the pulpit, who seeks to apply his biblical texts to 'the cure of souls' and the curing of society itself. For, just as Scripture is traditionally read by Christians for the furtherance of Salvation, History (as it is interpreted in the light of Latin American liberation theology) is used by Cardenal to further the establishment of the Kingdom of God on this earth.

FURTHER READING

Criticism

Cohen, Jonathan. Introduction to *With Walker in Nicaragua and Other Early Poems, 1949-1954,* by Ernesto Cardenal, translated by Jonathan Cohen, pp. 3-17. Middletown, Conn.: Wesleyan University Press, 1984.
Provides an overview of Cardenal's life and work.

Elias, Edward. "Prophecy of Liberation: The Poetry of Ernesto Cardenal." In *Poetic Prophecy in Western Literature,* edited by Jan Wojcik and Raymond-Jean Frontain, pp. 174-85. London: Associated University Presses, 1984.
Examines how Cardenal communicates a prophetic message by mixing historical documents, the language of pre-Columbian civilizations, biblical quotations, and colloquial Spanish in his poetry.

Pring-Mill, Robert. Introduction to *Marilyn Monroe and Other Poems,* by Ernesto Cardenal, translated by Robert Pring-Mill, pp. 7-32. London: Search Press, 1975.
Outlines Cardenal's life and career, focusing on his poetry's changing style and content.

Randall, Margaret. "Talking with Ernesto Cardenal." *Fiction International* 16, No. 2 (Summer-Fall 1986): 47-60.
Interview in which Cardenal discusses his literary influences, the Nicaraguan revolutionary struggle, and the relation of poetry to spiritual life.

Salmon, Russell O. Introduction to *Golden UFOs: The Indian Poems,* by Ernesto Cardenal, translated by Carlos Altschul and Monique Altschul, pp. ix-xxxv. Bloomington: Indiana University Press, 1992.
Provides an analysis of Cardenal's poetic technique in *Golden UFOs.*

Schaeffer, Claudia. "A Search for Utopia on Earth: Toward an Understanding of the Literary Production of Ernesto Cardenal." *Crítica Hispánica* IV, No. 2 (1982): 171-79.
Examines the major themes of Cardenal's work.

Valdes, Jorge H. "The Evolution of Cardenal's Prophetic Poetry." *Latin American Literary Review* XI, No. 23 (Fall-Winter 1983): 25-40.
Determines the objectives of Cardenal's poetry.

Williams, Tamara. "Reading Ernesto Cardenal Reading Ezra Pound: Radical Inclusiveness, Epic Reconstruction and Textual Praxis." *Chasqui* XXI, No. 2 (November 1992): 43-52.
Discusses the influence of Ezra Pound on Cardenal's poetry.

James Joyce
1882-1941

(Full name James Augustine Aloysius Joyce) Irish novelist, short story writer, poet, dramatist, memoirist, and critic.

INTRODUCTION

Joyce is considered one of the most prominent literary figures of the first half of the twentieth century. His experiments in prose contributed to a redefinition of the form of the modern novel. As a poet, Joyce's contribution has been regarded as much less noteworthy than that of his fiction, and some critics describe him as a "minor" poet.

Biographical Information

Joyce was born in a suburb of Dublin to middle-class parents. He was educated by Jesuits and underwent the same emotional hardship and intellectual discipline as Stephen Dedalus, the hero of his first novel, *A Portrait of the Artist as a Young Man.* In 1902 Joyce graduated from University College after earning a degree in Romance languages. He then left Ireland and studied at the Bibliothèque Nationale in Paris. His mother's serious illness caused his return to Dublin in 1903. Following his mother's death in 1904, Joyce moved permanently to the continent with his future wife, Nora Barnacle. Settling in Trieste, a city located in the Austro-Hungarian empire, he struggled to support himself and his family by working as an English-language instructor at a Berlitz school.

Two months before the birth of his daughter Lucia in 1907, a collection of Joyce's poems, *Chamber Music,* was published. He would continue throughout his life to write poetry, but would make little effort to develop his technique beyond the form of these early poems that he had begun before he left Dublin. His first major success, the short fiction collection *Dubliners,* depicts middle- and lower middle-class Dublin life. While composing these short stories, Joyce was also writing a novel, *Stephen Hero,* which he abandoned to turn his attention to *A Portrait of the Artist as a Young Man.*

With the onset of World War I, Joyce moved to Zurich, Switzerland, in 1915. He used the next four years to complete most of his novel *Ulysses,* which was published in 1922. In 1920 Joyce moved to Paris. Following the international renown accorded *Ulysses,* Joyce gained the financial patronship of Harriet Shaw and was able to devote himself exclusively to writing. He spent nearly all of his remaining years composing his final work, *Finnegans Wake.* Joyce's final years were darkened by the worsening insanity of his

daughter Lucia and by several surgical attempts to save his failing eyesight. After the publication of *Finnegans Wake* in 1939, Joyce fled Paris and the approaching turmoil of the Second World War. He died in Zurich of a perforated ulcer.

Major Works

Joyce's first book of verse, *Chamber Music,* was started during his youth as a college student in Dublin in the late 1890s and published after he had moved to the continent in 1907. A wide range of influences—from Victorian love ballads, Irish songs, and the poetry of William Butler Yeats, Paul Verlaine, and Horace—can be detected in the poems comprising the volume. Most of the poems are brief, simple, and unambiguous. In 1927 Joyce published his second book of poetry, *Pomes Penyeach,* a collection of thirteen lyric poems. He composed most of them over a period of eleven years, between 1913 to 1924, though one poem, "Tilly," dates back to 1903. With little stylistic variation, they are noteworthy for their distinct rhythm and diction as well as their autobiographical content.

Critical Reception

Upon its publication, *Chamber Music* received mixed critical attention. Critics recognized the lyrical qualities of the poems, but faulted them for a lack of innovation and emotion. However, as Joyce's reputation grew, some commentators have reassessed the verses comprising *Chamber Music*. Later critics have examined Joyce's use of biblical and classical allusions in the poems. Other commentators have analyzed the thematic and stylistic connections between the poems and Joyce's later fiction. His second collection, *Pomes Penyeach,* received more praise upon publication than his first volume, and many critics view these later poems as more direct, distinctive, and expressive than those of *Chamber Music.*

PRINCIPAL WORKS

Poetry

Chamber Music 1907
Pomes Penyeach 1927
Collected Poems 1936

Other Major Works

Dubliners (short stories) 1914
A Portrait of the Artist as a Young Man (novel) 1916
Exiles (drama) 1918
Ulysses (novel) 1922
Finnegans Wake (novel) 1939
Stephen Hero: A Part of the First Draft of "A Portrait of the Artist as a Young Man" (novel) 1944
The Critical Writings of James Joyce (essays) 1959
Letters of James Joyce (correspondence) 1966
Giacomo Joyce (memoir) 1968

CRITICISM

M. D. Z. (essay date 1930)

SOURCE: "The Lyrics of James Joyce," in *Poetry: A Magazine of Verse,* Vol. XXXVI, No. 4, July, 1930, pp. 206-13.

[*In the following review, the critic offers a mixed assessment of poems comprising* Chamber Music *and* Pomes Penyeach.]

The interest aroused by the ever-expanding design of the *Work in Progress* [*Finnegans Wake*], as it appears in quarterly installments in *transition,* as well as by the inclusion of three segments of this prose epic among the poems which the Messrs. Ford and Aldington have gathered in their recent *Imagist Anthology, 1930,* is probably sufficient reason for recalling that among Joyce's achievements is a small group of lyrics which certain readers still claim as his most beautiful work. Throughout his career Joyce has been regarded in many quarters as fundamentally a poet. When *Ulysses* appeared in 1922, its first readers and critics, encountering problems for which their earlier experiences with revolutionary forms of art had not prepared them, at once sought refuge behind the large assumptions that go disguised under the name of poetry. Most of the early notices called it "essentially a poem," "a poet's concept," etc., and thus gave support to a view of Joyce's genius which the autobiographical evidence in his stories, as well as the anecdotes of friends like Æ [George William Russell] and Colum who picture him as a typical visionary of the Irish revival in the nineties, had already encouraged. His first published book was the collection of lyrics, *Chamber Music* (1907), and in earlier poems like **"Tilly"** (1904) he had sketched in himself the familiar traits of poetic adolescence, enraged at the stupidity of life:

> Boor, bond of the herd,
> Tonight stretch full by the fire!
> I bleed by the black stream
> For my torn bough.

The reportorial naturalism in *Dubliners* was illuminated by a lyric clairvoyance and sympathy, the story "Araby" first describing the restless creative temper which victimized Joyce's undecided youth. Ultimately, when Stephen Dedalus took shape as Joyce's fictional counterpart, he was a poet charmed by liturgical cadences, by the creative vitality of words, and by the treasury of coined phrases stored in his mind, any one of which—

> A day of dappled seaborne clouds—

could set the train of creative enthusiasm running.

In spite of this testimony, we have little evidence that Joyce is not fundamentally a genius in prose. *Ulysses* may rely on Homeric symbolism, and, if we are to follow Foster Damon, on "the spiritual planes of the *Divine Comedy,* and the psychological problem of *Hamlet,*" together with a somewhat less convincing use of Blake's mechanism of the epic. The *Work in Progress* may require its exegetes to make use of far-scattered verse analogies. But, conventional definitions apart, his novels lack specific poetic elements, as well as poetry's absolute sublimation of experience. It is equally apparent that his lyrics are the marginal fragments of his art, minor in theme and too often, for all their precise and orderly felicities, undecided in quality. To the thirty-six poems in **Chamber Music** he added the thirteen which in 1927 came from the press of Shakespeare & Co., Paris, under the title **Pomes Penyeach,** eight having originally appeared in 1917 in *Poetry.* Though an extremely small part of his entire production, this body of lyrics is large enough to disclose changes and adjustments through which Joyce's mind has passed, as well as the creative impulses by which it has been guided.

The verse in **Chamber Music** has not the finality of single intention. Its deficiencies have been ascribed to the fact that, where it does not reflect the vaporous mysticism of the early Yeats, Æ, and the other Irish revivalists, it is a patent imitation of the Elizabethan song-books. Examination reveals in these poems little more than a superficial verbal similarity to the poetry of the Celtic twilight whose obvious accents appear only in **"XXXVI"** "Oh, it was out by Donnycarney." Whatever Joyce retained from the bardic songs (or their modern translations) in the way of simplified expression and elegiac motives, was overlaid with the formal decorum, yet enlivened by the lucid sensibility, of Jonson and Herrick, or of those poems by Byrd, Dowland, and Campion which he knew from boyhood. To read **Chamber Music** with its familiar refrains is to revive sensations first gained from the *Book of Airs* or *A Paradise of Dainty Devices.* Yet the overlay of artificial elegance never conceals wholly a nerve of sharp lyric refinement. Little more than elegance is present in **"VI"**:

> I would in that sweet bosom be
>   (O sweet it is and fair it is!)
> Where no rude wind might visit me.
>   Because of sad austerities
> I would in that sweet bosom be.

Adjusted to the courtly tone of Suckling and the Cavaliers, it reappears in **"XII"**:

> What counsel has the hooded moon
>   Put in thy heart, my shyly sweet,
> Of love in ancient plenilune,
>   Glory and stars beneath his feet—
> A sage that is but kith and kin
> With the comedian capuchin?

It is clear that in such poems one has, instead of direct and unequivocal poetic compulsion, a deliberate archaism and a kind of fawning studiousness which attempt to disguise the absence of profounder elements. Yet the archaism which exists at its extreme level in **"X"** and **"XI,"** or, phrased as *vers de société,* in **"VII,"** was converted into Joyce's own material in two or three lyrics which, for spiritual suavity and logic, approach the minor work of Crashaw, or at least of Crashaw's descendants in the nineteenth century, Thompson and Lionel Johnson. One of them is **"XXVI"**:

> Thou leanest to the shell of night,
>   Dear lady, a divining ear.
> In that soft choiring of delight
>   What sound hath made thy heart to fear?
> Seemed it of rivers rushing forth
> From the grey deserts of the north?
> That mood of thine, O timorous,
>   Is his, if thou but scan it well,

> Who a mad tale bequeaths to us
>   At ghosting hour conjurable—
> And all for some strange name he read
> In Purchas or in Holinshed.

It has been remarked before, by Edmund Wilson, that Joyce was closer to continental literature during his apprenticeship than to current English and Irish. In a writer so intentionally derivative, affiliations are natural. They can probably be traced here to the kind of lyric impressionism that grew, by a curious process of inversion, out of Dehmel and Liliencron toward the broken accent of expressionism as one finds it in Werfel, Joyce's closest ally among the figures of later German poetry. Through his lively contemporaneity and his curious sympathy with modern French art, Joyce was undoubtedly attracted by the inferential subtlety of the Symbolists. But his lyricism, like Dowson's or Rilke's, betrays too much diffusion to enable him to approach Mallarmé's faultless penetration or Rimbaud's intense discipline. It was more readily susceptible to the colors and moods of Verlaine's songs.

> All day I hear the noise of waters
>   Making moan,
> Sad as the seabird is when going
>   Forth alone
> He hears the winds cry to the waters'
>   Monotone.

This is very nearly a tonal and metrical equivalent of the *Chanson d'automne,* whose lyric values, and those on other pages of the *Poèmes Saturniens* or *Jadis et Naguère,* are present in **Chamber Music.** But Joyce was testing his lyric gift by a stricter training, by a reading of Rimbaud and Samain perhaps, or of Meredith. The latter's homelier phrases in *Love in a Valley* are echoed in **"XXIV,"** and his unexpected power to order the material of allegory lies behind the last poem in **Chamber Music,** the magnificent lyric whose Yeatsian tendency has yielded to the vigor of Meredithian symbolism as one finds it in *Lucifer in Starlight* or *The Promise in Disturbance*:

> I hear an army charging upon the land
>   And the thunder of the horses plunging, foam
>   about their knees.
> Arrogant, in black armor, behind them stand,
>   Disdaining the reins, with fluttering whips, the
>   charioteers.

The later lyrics in **Pomes Penyeach** go so far in integrating these disparate elements that Joyce achieved in the little booklet his own poetic character for the first time. The sedulous understudy which kept him from attaining intimacy or a unifying personality in his earlier work is largely avoided. The style may be defined by devices. It consists in the marked alliteration of **"On the Beach at Fontana"** and **"Tutto e sciolto"**; in the persistent periphrasis of words like *rockvine, greygolden, slimesilvered, moongrey, loveward,* and *loveblown* (all suggestive of *Ulysses*); and in the transparent choral tonality of **"She Weeps over Rahoon"** and **"Watching the Needle-boats at San Sabra."** Archaisms are still present, and the humid emotionalism of impressionist verse still prevails in **"Alone"** and **"Bahnhofstrasse."** But the pattern is constricted by severer form, the lyric accent gains edge, and the emotional content is more secure in its power. Ultimately the tragic surge and wrath of *Ulysses* finds voice in **"A Prayer"** and in **"A Memory of the Players in a Mirror at Midnight"**:

> This grey that stares
> Lies not, stark skin and bone.
> Leave greasy lips their kissing. None
> Will choose her what you see to mouth upon.
> Dire hunger holds his hour.
> Pluck forth your heart, saltblood, a fruit of tears,
> Pluck and devour.

Even within this narrow range, Joyce's eclecticism, the long reach of his artistic interests, is revealed. Yet one sees likewise the limitations which have kept his lyric output small. The real functions of free-verse have escaped him, and his lyric ideas must otherwise submit to conventional stanzaic formalities. Diffusion mars the outline of many poems, and unnatural sobriety and caution hinder the spontaneity of others. But in four or five pages he has achieved a complete fusion of rapture and lucidity, and written with mastery. **"Simples"** must rank as one of the purest lyrics of our time: . . .

> Of cool sweet dew and radiance mild
> The moon a web of silence weaves
> In the still garden where a child
> Gathers the simple salad leaves.
>
> A moondew stars her hanging hair
> And moonlight kisses her young brow,
> And gathering, she sings an air:
> *Fair as the wave is, fair art thou!*
>
> Be mine, I pray, a waxen ear
> To shield me from her childish croon,
> And mine a shielded heart for her
> Who gathers simples of the moon.

The lyric motive and discipline have not been forgotten by Joyce among the problems and ingenuities of his prose epics. Wherever *Ulysses* avoids parody or satire, it is likely to soar in a lyric utterance; the river symphony at the beginning of the *Work in Progress* is one of the brilliant phonetic evocations in modern literature. His power to synthesize and formulate the swarming resources of his mind has demanded prose for its proper extension. Yet the poetic temper which has played an indubitable part in his career has given us, by the way, a small offering of exquisite poems, valuable both as diversions of one of the first literary geniuses of our day, and as lyrics which at their best have the mark of classic beauty upon them.

James R. Baker (essay date 1959)

SOURCE: "Joyce's *Chamber Music:* The Exile of the Heart," in *Arizona Quarterly,* Vol. 15, No. 4, Winter, 1959, pp. 349-56.

[*In the following essay, Baker considers love as the unifying theme in* Chamber Music.]

A common practice in much Joyce criticism is to dismiss **Chamber Music** as youthful trivia. Such an estimate is tempting because the thinness of the poems is indeed blatant when they are compared even with the fiction not far removed in conception, *Dubliners* and *Stephen Hero.* Confirmation of this now traditional disparagement is found in Joyce's own flippant rejection of the poems as "a capfull of light odes." While his critics are hardly to be blamed for neglect of obviously slight verse, the result has been a blind spot in our understanding of Joyce the man and his total accomplishment: if we ignore **Chamber Music** we lose additional evidence of the amazing unity of his work, and we lose a dimension in our view of at least one of his characteristic themes.

Critical analysis of the technical aspects of the **Chamber Music** sequence has been adequate. Since the early review by Arthur Symons, assessments of the competence of the verse and of the various influences which went into its making have been offered by Morton Dauwen Zabel, Hugh Kenner, and William York Tindall. But among these commentators only Kenner and Tindall have undertaken discussion of theme.

Tindall's preface to the Columbia University Press edition of these first poems offers valuable commentary on the textual problems and supplies much biographical data. In the discussion of theme, however, he insists upon the self-limiting terms of "Freudian" analysis or, alternatively, upon the Joyce-had-a-clever-but-nasty-mind reading which detects cloacal overtones throughout the sequence. Though there is no doubt that Tindall's methods allow him to discover a surprising subtlety and suggestiveness in these youthful verses, his interpretations are often over-erudite and labored. The effect is to eclipse a theme which had its first expression in the poems and was to be repeated in all subsequent work. **Chamber Music** is Joyce's initial exploration of the conflict of love and creativity, a dilemma which never lost its power to absorb Joyce, both as artist and as man.

Hugh Kenner's analysis, a brief chapter in his *Dublin's Joyce,* recognizes that the anonymous maiden of **Chamber Music** reappears with modulated though basically similar symbolic status as "E. C." in *Portrait of the Artist,* as Beatrice in *Exiles,* and as Iseult in *Finnegans Wake*; but he does not trace her presence in **"A Prayer"** of **Pomes Penyeach,** in several of the stories in *Dubliners,* and in *Ulysses.* While Kenner is to be credited with a sketch of this pervasive feminine force, the complete job remains to be done. That undertaking, however, will be hampered until we see more clearly that **Chamber Music** must be the point of orientation.

The sequence of lyrics depends upon a quite conventional metaphor for its unity, which reminds us once again that young Joyce was familiar with the lyric and sonnet-sequence traditions of the English Renaissance. The three-fold cycle in the evolution of the love-relationship is paralleled with the spring-summer-autumn seasonal cycle and (though with less consistency) the dawn-noon-evening progression of the day. Each of the seasons of love finds its appropriate symbolism in the corresponding season of nature and, when useful in a particular lyric, the period in the day of love is rendered in terms of the mood and atmosphere of the hour. The winter season, which is only implied, follows the closing of the thirty-six poem sequence and serves a double purpose: it marks the end of the love cycle, in which the lovers, recognizing the degeneration of their passion, accept the bleakness of their separate ways; and thus, in terms of the mature insights achieved near the end of the autumnal stage, the entire experience (at least for the boy) appears to have been a time of "deep slumber" and "death."

This final inversion of the seasonal symbolism points to the vital theme of the entire sequence—the initiation of the lovers into the limitations of the passional experience. Poems I-XIII develop the romantic-sentimental phase wherein each of the lovers is absorbed in a fearful duelling for possession of the other. Attracted by the siren-like song of the maiden, the youth abandons his book, the symbol of intellectual motives, and leaves the insular security of his room to join his temptress:

> I have left my book,
> I have left my room,
> For I heard you singing
> Through the gloom.
>
> ("V")

In the following lyric ("VI") the consciousness of the youth retreats from the "austerities" implicit in his initial solitude and the logic of bookish motives, and he begs the girl to admit him into her love. In subsequent poems this shirking of his lonely destiny is overcome. Thus in terms of the metaphor before us at the moment, their love should be regarded as the womb from which the creative spirit is to be born.

> I would in that sweet bosom be
>   (O sweet it is and fair it is!)
> Where no rude wind might visit me.
>   Because of sad austerities
> I would in that sweet bosom be.
>
> I would be ever in that heart
>   (O soft I knock and soft entreat her!)
> Where only peace might be my part.
>   Austerities were all the sweeter
> So I were ever in that heart.
>
> ("VI")

In poem "XII" "the bridal wind is blowing / For love is at his noon." In "XIV" (Stanislaus Joyce suggests echoes of "The Song of Solomon") the lover addresses his be-

loved as "my dove." And so, though he has earlier called for a surrender of her virginal sentiments ("X," "XI," "XII"), phase one closes in an aura of idealism and holiness, soon to be dispelled by the awakening and consequent dialectics of the emerging season. As Joyce explains in a letter to G. Molyneux Palmer, "The central song is "XIV" after which the movement is all downwards until "XXXVI" which is vitally the end of the book. "XXXV" and "XXXVI" are tail-pieces just as "I" and "II" are preludes."

In the second stage (poems XIV-XXII) the conflict between love and creativity emerges in explicit form. The lover, and to some extent the maiden, develops an awareness of the limitations of the love-relationship. Here begins the divorce of spirit which is to culminate in the ascendancy of the male. His evolution to a superior position is foreshadowed in the nature of the disillusionments experienced. While the maiden sentimentalizes the loss of her virgin charms and laments the loss of her moral status, the voice of the lover enters the duo to complain that the exclusiveness of their relationship has destroyed the male companionships in which he found resources necessary for his growth (XIX-XVIII). Poem "XV," therefore, "From dewy dreams, my soul, arise / From love's deep slumber and from death," marks the turning point in his values: henceforth he is to argue for the Daedalian destiny of his soul and while admitting the fascination of his former "sweet imprisonment" he insists that "Love is aweary now." For the first time, the male clearly recognizes his confinement and forsees the spiritual masochism which a continuance of the relationships would demand:

> Of that so sweet imprisonment
>   My soul, dearest, is fain—
> Soft arms that woo me to relent
>   And woo me to detain.
> Ah, could they ever hold me there
> Gladly were I a prisoner!
>
> Dearest, through interwoven arms
>   By love made tremulous,
> That night allures me where alarms
>   Nowise may trouble us;
> But sleep to dreamier sleep be wed
> Where soul with soul lies prisoned.
>
> ("XXII")

Thus the impulse to retreat from "austerities," first expressed in lyric "VI," is here re-experienced, this time with a defeating self-consciousness lacking in the earlier episode.

In the concluding poems of the sequence (XXIII-XXXVI) the lover comes to rate the values of the passional experience as naive, impermanent—subordinate to the potential creativity of the immanent separate ways:

> Love is past
> That had his sweet hours many a one;
> Welcome to us now at the last
> The ways that we shall go upon.
>
> ("XXX")

Since he is now capable of transcending his passion, the coy charms of his beloved are seen as "witchery," evil powers which threaten to enchant him and so destroy his impulse for freedom:

> I pray you cease to comb out,
>   Comb out your long hair,
> For I have heard of witchery
>   Under a pretty air.
>
> That makes as one thing to the lover
>   Staying and going hence.
>
> ("XXIV")

He urges that they enjoy the last moments of a failing love ("XXV") before the "rivers rushing forth/From the grey deserts of the north" overwhelm them with the full sense of their separate destinies ("XXVI"). Yet, though the sound of the rivers strikes fear into the heart of his beloved, the youth identifies it with the sound of Alph, the sacred river; and this he inevitably associates with a triumph of the poetic imagination. His lonely way is now definitely linked with the exile of the artist.

As the lovers wander in the "brown land" of the autumnal phase, their former passion now reduced to a mere friendship, he attempts to console his brooding partner: "The leaves—they do not sigh at all / When the year takes them in the fall." The closing of the love cycle, like the closing of the year, is not an occasion for grief but a time of harvest, presaging a future rich in promise: "Grieve not, sweetheart, for anything— / The year, the year is gathering."

Having achieved this somber triumph, the lover is to discover his naivete. He is now confronted with the loss of the innocent rest he had known ("XXXIV") and is haunted by the loneliness of the journey which lies before him:

> All day I hear the noise of waters
>   Making moan,
> Sad as the sea-bird is, when going
>   Forth alone,
> He hears the winds cry to the water's
>   Monotone.
>
> The grey winds, the cold winds are blowing
>   Where I go.
> I hear the noise of many waters
>   Far below.
> All day, all night, I hear them flowing
>   To and fro.
>
> ("XXXV")

In the last poem of the sequence the lover suffers all of the terrors of the fledgling exile. The host of triumphant forces which have been released into his being, now that he has escaped his "sweet imprisonment," rushes upon him as he enters the world. Determined, but terribly alone, the army of fears (actually benevolent enemies of love) assaults his dreams, and he cries out the tortuous ambiv-

alence of his state:

> My heart, have you no wisdom thus to despair?
> My love, my love, my love, why have you left me
>   alone?
>
> ("XXXIV")

The "love" of the last line seems to be not so much the girl he has abandoned but the state of loving, the "sweet imprisonment" in which he can no longer rest.

This reading of the poems does not reduce the sequence to a juvenile apologue of the artist's escape from society, homeland, and church (a miniature *Portrait of the Artist*), as Kenner suggests. Actually, the milieu in which the tensions are awakened and resolved is quite abstract. Nor does it render the cloacal tones which Tindall ingeniously derives. The result of endowing *Chamber Music* with the irony and subtlety of the mature Joyce is simply to obscure the obvious thematic tie between verses and the later works.

"A Prayer" in *Pomes Penyeach*, for example, shows this characteristic duality. On the one hand there is a strong and almost sentimental commitment to the confining demands of passion; on the other, the will to freedom and exile. In a masochistic ecstasy the aroused and enthralled lover submits to the vampire-like powers of his lady:

> Draw from me still
> My slow life! Bend deeper on me, threatening head,
> Proud by my downfall, remembering, pitying
> Him who is, him who was!

Yet we have also a repetition of that ambivalent outcry in the last lines of *Chamber Music*, for in the midst of his appeal the suppliant maintains the tension and division of motives typical of Joyce's artist-lovers:

> O have mercy, beloved enemy of my will!

And finally, this blatant outcry:

> Subduer, do not leave me! Only joy, only anguish,
> Take me, save me, soothe me, O spare me!

The "beloved enemy" is a figure who reappears in various guises throughout Joyce's work. She is the young initiate of *Chamber Music* and the prototype for the Joyceian female. In *Dubliners* she is Little Chandler's wife, Annie, representing (as she usually does) the paralyzing force of convention which has penetrated the soul of her husband, a minor poet in potential. In *A Boarding House* she is the girl and the mother who conspire to cage in marriage the young life of the seducer. In *Portrait of the Artist* she is the Emma who comes to symbolize for Stephen the several means of convention which are the enemies of his destiny. But in the *Portrait*, Dedalus, like his precursor in *Chamber Music*, is so caught up in the naive romanticism of rebellion that he manages to escape. The price he is to pay for his aloofness is seen in *Ulysses* where, still fearful of involvement, he is dependent upon the amusements afforded by prostitutes—a dependence which functions as a symbol of his fears and the sterility of his creative instinct.

At the opposite pole is Bloom. His utter failure to even attempt the extrication of his potentials from the web of convention is epitomized in the Circe episode. There his submerged will is humiliated by the "enemy" as she appears in several symbolic costumes. Culminating in *Finnegans Wake,* this pervasive feminine force is the Iseult of Earwicker's dream, a link with **Chamber Music** which Kenner has noted.

If we appraise these many love-relationships for their symbolic import, it becomes clear that Joyce conceived of creativity as a power whose maintenance depends upon an ideal balance between the slavish submission of Bloom and Earwicker, on the one side, and the sterile objectivity of Dedalus on the other. Looking, then, to the psychologic overtones of these tortured alliances, it is obvious that they go deeper than the chamber-pot reading of **Chamber Music** or the other works will allow. The theme of the "beloved enemy of my will" is operative in everything that Joyce wrote. Yet it remains to be explored thoroughly, and perhaps an even more challenging and delicate mission awaits future biographers.

Marvin Fisher   (essay date 1959)

SOURCE: "James Joyce's 'Ecce Puer': The Return of the Prodding Gaul," in *University of Kansas City Review,* Vol. 25, No. 4, June, 1959, pp. 265-71.

[*In the following essay, Fisher explores thematic links between Joyce's poem "Ecce Puer" and his works of fiction.*]

"Ecce Puer" is a slender poem, simply yet gracefully eloquent. To both critics and cultists it is recognizable as one of James Joyce's greatest single lyrical achievements, a poem that is worthy of praise without compensatory references to his more distinguished prose efforts. **"Ecce Puer"** need borrow none of the accumulated luster of the better known prose works beginning with *Dubliners* and culminating in *Finnegans Wake,* since the poem contains rather the most satisfying splendor that can be effected by an economy of means in the hands of the most methodical writer in modern literature. Here is the poem:

> Of the dark past
> A child is born;
> With joy and grief
> My heart is torn.
>
> Calm in his cradle
> The living lies.

> May love and mercy
> Unclose his eyes!
>
> Young life is breathed
> On the glass;
> The world that was not
> Comes to pass.
>
> A child is sleeping:
> An old man gone.
> O, father forsaken,
> Forgive your son!

The common reader's conception of James Joyce has been influenced by the mildly hostile nature of much of the popular Joyce criticism, by the mere bulk of *Ulysses,* and most of all by the unique, multi-levelled, and admittedly difficult verbal medium of *Finnegans Wake.* This reader, confronted with the plain facts of **"Ecce Puer,"** may well ask whether the poem is at all typical of or integral to Joyce's work. Is not the author's real nature more truly represented by the highly complex but skillfully interwoven themes and motifs that are incorporated in the polysyllabic vagaries of *Ulysses* and *Finnegans Wake?* What can the tersely restrained simplicity of this poem, which contains only one word of more than two syllables, have in common with the complexity that characterizes so much of *Ulysses* and is climaxed not in the unconscious but in the subconscious nature of *Finnegans Wake?* How can the economy and restraint of **"Ecce Puer"** be even remotely connected with over seven hundred and fifty pages which profess to represent eighteen hours in the lives of three major characters in a most limited physical environment on a typical, even trivial day in June, 1904?

Nevertheless, this poem, seemingly unlike the bulk of Joyce's work, summarizes the most significant of his recurrent themes. For, strangely enough, the half a hundred words of this poem contain a coalescence of the elements and materials used by Joyce in his four best known and individually distinctive prose works. The poem is in part a return to the flawless technique of *Dubliners* and the compacted experiences of *A Portrait of the Artist as a Young Man.* Each of the four stanzas is a miniature epiphany; and taken together they represent a revelation that is continually expanding in concentric many-meaninged circles to reproduce the unending rhythm of birth and death. Just as evident here as the form and method of *Dubliners* are some of the themes and occurrences of *Ulysses,* and the philosophical framework of *Finnegans Wake.*

In a sense, the two words which constitute the title are the most important of the entire poem, for they indicate the direction or the thrust of the poem. The title, **"Ecce Puer"** [behold the boy], is both a play on words and a redefining of the original Christian myth, or at least, a restatement of its central meaning in immediate, personal terms. Joyce is only too well aware of the phrase "ecce homo" [behold the man] and its significant context. He intentionally uses a derivative title in order to bring to the poem a set of nonliterary associations which are at the heart of the religious beliefs of the West. The crucifixion of Jesus, the event so obliquely alluded to, is described in John xix.5:

> Pilate therefore went forth again, and saith unto them, "Behold, I bring him forth to you, that ye may know that I find no fault in him." Then came Jesus forth, wearing the crown of thorns, and the purple robe. And Pilate saith unto them, "Behold the man!" When the chief priests therefore and officers saw him, they cried out, saying, "Crucify him, crucify him." Pilate saith unto them, "Take ye him, and crucify him: for I find no fault in him." The Jews answered him, "We have a law, and by our law he ought to die, because he made himself the Son of God."

The salient points of the episode, in addition to the redemptive death of Jesus, are His total innocence and the suggestion of suffering prior to death—the meaning of the thorns.

Further evidence of the implicative nature of the title is the lack of apparent connection between it and the secondary materials of the poem—those thoughts or events in experience which lie behind the imagized concepts which constitute the structure of the poem. **"Ecce Puer"** is ultimately derived from two events in Joyce's life, both of great importance to him. Written in 1932, this poem combines the celebration of the birth of Joyce's grandson with the almost coincidental mourning for the death of his father.

The poem, however, undergoes a process of depersonalization. Both the old man and the child are first viewed as people, not as members of Joyce's immediate family. The exact designations are "a child" and "an old man." Nothing could be less definite, less specific, or more intentionally anonymous.

The first two lines of the poem ("Of the dark past / A child is born") are a succinct summation of one of the most difficult and most criticized phases of *Ulysses,* the hospital scene where Mrs. Purefoy delivers her child out of the dark past of linguistic development. The very fact the child is born "of the dark past" binds him to those same elements which constitute the past. The act of birth marks the act of creation, of giving form and meaning to a pre-existent void. Through the evolution of language, beginning with the involved constructions of Latin style and continuing through the Medieval period, parodying the notably English men of letters and reaching its consummation in a verbal pandemonium, Joyce correlates the embryonic development of the foetus with ages of language both living and dead. Joyce's method here seems to follow Jung's theory of a "collective unconscious," a racial mythology which has its origins not in the personal unconscious, but which stems from a backlog of racial memory, an echo of Stephen Dedalus' "uncreated conscience of my race."

Jung's thesis complements another theory which Joyce drew upon, that of the Italian philosopher Vico, who held that human history progressed in cycles, each of which contained the same four phases. Joyce's debt to Vico has been adequately documented; and it should be sufficient to say that Vico's cyclical theory was the irreducible historical process which Joyce, the creative artist, used as a structural basis in *Finnegans Wake* to equate, transpose, and merge his own myth with innumerable correspondences and associations, secure in the knowledge that his creation would coincide with the general pattern of human history. Both Jung's racial unconscious and Vico's historical cycle seek the common ground of a general pattern, and were thus attractive to Joyce. It is in the last two stanzas of the poem that a cyclical view becomes explicit.

The remaining lines of the first stanza ("With joy and grief / My heart is torn") contain the tensions, the divergent and explosive forces that affect the poet. This is the condition of the martyr (a pose not unknown in Joyce—St. Stephen) or of one who is sympathetically aware of the martyr. More specifically, joy is the hope for the future—a hint of the Messianic ideal, which has been already prophesied by Joyce's echoing the words of the Christmas hymns: "Rejoice, a child is born." And grief is indicative of the dismal view of the past voiced by the autobiographical Stephen Dedalus.

Soft, fluid "l" sounds quiet the reader in the next two lines, but beneath the lull of "Calm in his cradle / The living lies" is the implication, perhaps only an unvoiced questioning, of a parallel condition in the dead. Central to this suggestion is the explicit mention of the "cradle" as a container for the living (the unspoken association being the coffin and the dead). Then too, the immediately following supplication ("May love and mercy / Unclose his eyes!") is so fervently and compassionately voiced that one is made aware that the living has something in common with the unliving, the lack of any profound sight. The two lines are reminiscent of the blessing said of the dead—"May the Lord have mercy on his soul." Also suggested here is Stephen Dedalus' unfailingly dark view of the past—"History is a nightmare from which I am trying to awake," literally to open his eyes and disengage himself from the bad dream that man's past evokes. Hence, the later and more imperative admonition, "Finnegans, Wake!" But this still does not explain the use of "unclose," a word that certainly does not seem to belong. That the word should be a negative imperative is important. The eyes of a dead person are closed, as are the eyes of the foetus: therefore to undo death or to begin life, one must unclose those eyes. Joyce has used a single strange word to focus his meaning. The whole quality of the stanza recalls that magnificently phrased coda in the last paragraph of "The Dead," the concluding story in *Dubliners*: "His soul swooned slowly as he heard the snow falling faintly through the universe and faintly falling, like the descent of their last end, upon all the living and the dead."

"Young life is breathed / On the glass; / The World that was not / Comes to pass." Here Joyce is, on one level at least, relating the flickering beginning of life, the evident organic miracle, that is to be found in the phenomenon of generation. A deeper level is established by the symbolic departure of "glass." Could this be the looking glass, that instrument that functions solely to reflect objectively and transpose the continuous activity that is life? Remotely perhaps connected with Stephen's vivid symbol of Irish art, this mirror more obviously represents an early medical test for the existence of life, a test used only when life is indistinguishable from death. But with this new implication, the mirror completes a pattern, constructs a symmetrical view of any object or event, and integrates the reality with the illusion or the physical object with its reversed image. Everything and its contrary reflection may be viewed simultaneously in this mirror which has already reflected the coffin inherent in the cradle—the death coexistent with life. The "glass" becomes a symbol which unites and reconciles two hitherto unrelated areas—what Jung has called a mediator between the conscious and the unconscious and between all other pairs of opposites.

Conjectural as this may seem, it serves as a support for the previously mentioned world view of Vico. This view, which is explicit in the remainder of the poem, which constitutes one of the philosophical rhythms of *Ulysses,* and which supplies the structural concept of *Finnegans Wake,* is further borne out by the subtle ambiguity in "The World that was not / Comes to pass." Here in quasi-biblical phraseology is a reminder of that dark past of primal chaos indicated in the first line of the poem as well as restatement of the theme of becoming and being, of void and form. But it is the word "pass" that produces the ambiguity. The more obvious sense of the word is "to be accomplished" or "to come into existence." Still, "to pass" retains the sense of "to pass by" or "to overtake." Another reading indicates "to pass an inspection or test successfully; to attain the required standard." And a reading still different could hold out for "to pass away" or "to be concluded." (The words "to pass" are so flexible that they might also indicate that "the world that was not" comes to be regarded as valid—unheeded or unchallenged.) All these readings of the two words contribute to the idea of a cycle of nothing, becoming, being, and returning to nothing. They differ, however, as to what stage of that cycle each one refers.

Stephen, walking along Sandy-mount Beach, ponders the "ineluctable modality," the generations of man linked by a mystical umbilical cord, and the consubstantiality of Father and Son. The common element in these thoughts of young Dedalus is indeed striking. Individual existence, that is, existence apart from the predetermined pattern, is metaphysically denied. Even the dog on the beach is "looking for something lost in a past life" (metempsychosis). Bloom, also, is aware of the cycle—"Molly. Milly. Same thing watered down . . . Life. Life." "Every Friday buries a Thursday if you come to look at it." The thought of a unifying cycle appears to Bloom in a less meditative though probably as emotionally colored an association as Stephen's, but there is, ironically enough, too much of the worldly about Bloom for him to dwell on the subject. Nevertheless, the "wheels within wheels." The "same old

dingdong always. Gas, then solid, then world, then cold, then dead shell drifting around . . ." are Bloom's own passing attentions to the pattern. Significantly enough, both the funeral and the occasion at the maternity hospital hold such associations for Bloom. Quite evidently, Joyce was constantly attracted by the possibilities of a mythic cycle which allowed him to merge creation, history, and personal experience.

Supplementing Vico and Jung with the writings of an earlier Italian philosopher, Giordano Bruno, Joyce reinforced his cyclical conception of reality. If, as Bruno said, each thing serves as the origin of its contrary, then Joyce could encompass birth and death, joy and grief, the cradle and the coffin, in one coincidental paradox that resolves itself into a continuous circle—"The world that was not / Comes to pass," and immediately following: "A child is sleeping: / An old man gone." The idea of Bruno's coinciding contraries is consistent with the simultaneous inversion of the looking glass, but no longer necessary is the objective symbol which effects the reconciliation of opposites. This paradoxical reconciliation assumes a metaphysical validity and shapes the material out of which Joyce continues the poem.

Strongly explicit in the concluding stanza are the particular, personal experiences of the seemingly remote author.

> A child is sleeping:
> An old man gone.
> O father forsaken
> Forgive your son!

The first two lines juxtapose the child and the old man, life and death, the coinciding contraries mentioned earlier. Next to this two-line summary of the poem's action is a plea from the heart of the poet to the spirit of his dead father, a plea too late to be effectual even though it constitutes the culmination of Joyce's looking glass revelations. The last two lines, recalling the Biblical overtones of the title and initial stanza, supply a reversed image of the last words of Jesus before his death: "Father, forgive them; for they know not what they do," and the final cry, "My God, my God, why hast thou forsaken me?" Joyce has from the title onward expanded the meaning of the poem in a manner that has become as ritual to him. The meanings of the poem may be said to expand in the same fashion as ripples in a pool form concentric circles always moving outward, till the last circle has become so large that its edges are blurred and its area is indefinite. One circle encloses the experience of the Joyce family. Another circle takes in greater area and more meaning—perhaps Joyce has suggested that this is the experience of any man. This aim at a more universal scope results from the anonymity of the people involved. A third circle confirms the universality of the experience and defines the history of the generations of man, the experience of Everyman. The final circle is achieved through the mythic—in this case the pattern of Christ's origin, death, and resurrection. Obliquely, perhaps, Joyce is also utilizing the myth of the Phoenix, the bird that is reborn out of its own ashes, just as the child is born out of the death of its grandfather, or the future is born at the death of the present.

In *Ulysses* Bloom is not only the archetypal Everyman; he is, in various situations which Joyce views as correspondences, Moses, Elijah, Jesus, and even God. In this poem, too, Joyce has reflected the Nativity—and coincidentally the Crucifixion—in a culturally corresponding situation, and moreover, he has employed the epiphany in its original sense, the revelation of Christ to the Magi. Equally evident in this final stanza are the specific parallels with *Ulysses*. A child has been born of the same dark past, an old man has died, and a son has deserted his father. It is not for sentimental reasons that Joyce has recast his material.

No, the sentimental is no part of Joyce as he, like Milton's Satan, revisits now with bolder wing the same argument that occupied so much of both the *Portrait* and *Ulysses* and even pervades the mind of the sleeping Earwicker. The cry: "O, father forsaken / Forgive your son!" could have no greater power even on the tongue of a repentant Satan. It consolidates Stephen's haunting remorse for his stubborn and proud refusal to ease his mother's death, the "agenbite of inwit," with Joyce's most recurrent theme, the question of paternity. Overtones of a religious denial—of the young man who has denied the faith of his forebears—are likewise present and ought not be suppressed. But even in *Ulysses,* Stephen is not the only one who has deserted his father, who has denounced his church, and who inwardly has no armor against the prodding guilt, the gall of remorse and of additional suffering. Bloom, who as the fatherless son stands before the mirror and sees himself the sonless father, Bloom, who recalls his dead father quoting Abraham from Mosenthal's drama—"Nathan's voice! His son's voice! I hear the voice of Nathan who left his father to die of grief and misery in my arms, who left the house of his father and left the God of his father"—also possesses this dual guilt toward his dead father and toward his abandoned faith. From the time that Stephen defines paternity as a mystical estate, until he refuses to acknowledge the paternal advances of the vicariously divine Bloom, we follow with anticipation and ultimate disappointment his quest for a father and a faith. And finally it is Joyce himself who in the course of his own personal life cycle has assumed the role of the father, and who can, with remorseful maturity, view in retrospect the bitter arrogance of his youthful *Non serviam*. He is the Icarus who had to *swim* to safety in order to become Dedalus, in order to "unclose his eyes."

The complex and paradoxical synthesis of the many resources of language so evident in this poem—one set of qualities providing instructions for the interpretation of the meaning which emerges from another set—characterizes Joyce's novels and the fifteen cantos of *Dubliners*. Just as any synthesis, the poem can be successfully examined as an isolated whole, or it can be subjected to an approach which attempts to realize the elemental components of the poem in a larger context—not to demolish its unity of structure but to clarify and even reinforce it. Either approach produces evidence that Joyce, the artificer, could vary his external style, but was possessed of an inner compulsion that would not permit him to abandon his most familiar materials. As a creative artist, he could find no mode of expression not contained in the materials of the very nets that once pinioned his newly tried wings. Like the resurrected Finnegan who begins to build anew in the very same pattern, James Joyce returns also to the cycle that nursed him, the cycle that has indelibly etched on his consciousness the *already* created conscience of his race.

Virginia Moseley   (essay date 1964)

SOURCE: "The 'Perilous Theme' of *Chamber Music,*" in *James Joyce Quarterly,* Vol. I, No. 3, Spring, 1964, pp. 19-24.

[*In the following essay, Moseley discusses allusions to the book of Ezekiel in Joyce's* Chamber Music.]

One "portrait of the artist" in *Finnegans Wake* characterizes him as "a sensible ham," who having "with infinite tact in the delicate situation seen the touchy nature of its perilous theme . . . spat in careful convertedness a musaic dispensation about his *hearthstone.*" Placed alongside a reference to "chamermissies" and the promise, "if one has the stomach to add the breakages, upheavals distortions, inversions of all this chambermade music one stands . . . a fair chance of actually seeing . . . the mystery of himsel in furniture," these allusions by the mature Joyce to his earliest work, **Chamber Music,** seem admissions that his first attempt at turning image into symbol necessarily concealed more than it revealed.

Joyce repeatedly connects his first and last works with a paraphrase of the biblical theme, "the last shall be first, and the first last" (e.g. "So warred he from first to last," FW; and "the lubricitous conjugation of the last with the first," FW). In *Stephen Hero* the "ham" artist desired to imitate in his "first fruits" (a lyrical sequence) the "fascinating enigmas of the disdainful Jesus," avoiding the "hell of hells wherein everything is found to be obvious"; and this semi-autobiographical fragment, like *A Portrait,* developed toward a momentous decision: the hero's choice among three careers—singing, the priesthood, and writing. This choice is followed in *A Portrait* by a flight into exile. When Davin asked Stephen Dedalus if it were true he was going away and why, Stephen responded, "the shortest way to Tara was *via* Holyhead" (*Portable James Joyce*), implying that the glory of ancient Ireland envisioned in Moore's "The Harp That Once in Tara's Halls" could be restored best from across the sea with "Holyhead" as vantage point.

All this evidence suggests that Stephen-Joyce's decision to become a writer in exile and his method of arriving at it were ultimately theological. The pun on Holyhead (pronounced "hollyhead" in Britain) and the reference to **Chamber Music** as a "musaic dispensation" seem particularly meaningful. "Self exiled in upon his ego," the young artist saw in the "priest of the imagination" a potential means of combining three careers in one. He could "sing" while creating a "mosaic" of poetic indirection; to keep the "Mosaic Law" imposed by his superego (home, church, and country), he would, because of the "delicate situation," displace through "careful convertedness" the "perilous theme" of "touchy nature" in "delicate" songs.

Is it not probable then that hidden in the biblical overtones of "chamermissies" lies a statement of the young Joyce's own dilemma ("mystery of himsel"), resolved by a choice he was known to regard as perhaps a mistake for eternity, and of his reasons for flight? Such a possibility has remained largely unexplored by exegetes, other analogies being more obvious, although in his edition of the poems, W. Y. Tindall does point to connections with both the Song of Solomon and the Garden of Eden and identify the poet as the "Word."

The title alone of **Chamber Music** recalls, in addition, the following biblical phraseology: "a bridegroom coming out of his bride-chamber"; the dark "chambers of imagery" in which each ancient of Israel deceived himself (Ezekiel 8:12); and the elaboration of the New Testament commandment, "Thou shalt love thy neighbor as thyself . . . walk honestly, as in the day . . . not in chambering and impurities" (Romans 13:9). And words with religious association occur throughout: antiphon, heaven, soul, entreat, cherubim, divine, enaisled, irreverent, confess, raimented.

Ambiguity and a concern with love and deception are typical of Joyce's other works. But as might be expected of a budding symbolist consciously trying to throw his basic conflict completely off center, it is the least likely of the passages above which appears on careful analysis to supply a key to the fundamental struggle of the lyrics and, in fact, provide them with a structural unity—the one from Ezekiel. Numerous cross-references in *Finnegans Wake* support this interpretation.

Added significantly as tailpieces, the last two poems show Ezekiel was in Joyce's mind. **"XXXVI"** is almost a paraphrase of Ezekiel 38, describing the army of God with its horse and horsemen which will bring about "a great commotion in the land of Israel" to purge it before restoration. There is a direct use of language from Ezekiel 43:2 in **"XXXV,"** "the noise of many waters"; God's voice is so imaged when He descended to the temple of the re-established Israel in the "vision of the city." Following the clue of these visionary lyrics, one notices also a remarkable similarity between the images of the sequence and those in this book of prophecy: river, air, fire, book, watchman, captivity, trees (especially the willow and cedar), harps, winds, hair, love, glory, doves, exile, valleys, windows, gates, garden, bending and descent—even the pot (parable of the boiling pot).

Joyceans find that what may be far-fetched at first glance becomes entirely logical and suitable once the right key is turned—and **Chamber Music** is no exception. Ezekiel marked the beginning of that apocalyptic type of litera-

ture whereby the later prophets sought to make their messages impressive and arouse the intellectual activity of their hearers. Alternating between discursiveness and vision, God instructed Ezekiel to use images and symbols in order to illuminate and make effective His teachings. Where else could a young artist so thoroughly steeped in Christian theology have discovered a surer model for his first attempt at the symbolic method? Perhaps it was in acknowledgement of this source and its method that Joyce wrote in *Finnegans Wake*, "graced be Gad, . . . in whose words were the beginnings" and "It's haunted. The chamber. Of errings."

For the book of Ezekiel, like **Chamber Music,** is actually a love story—an ironic one—tracing the courtship, marriage, and separation of God and His chosen people. A warning in *Finnegans Wake* recognizes this correlation, it seems, and relates infancy (early work), mystery (elusive pattern), and continued practice (final Amen): "Hold him here, Ezekiel Irons, and may God strengthen you! . . . Where misties swaddlum, where misches lodge none, where mystries pour kind on, O sleepy! So be yet!"

The twilight atmosphere of both the lyrics and Ezekiel is appropriate to the Celtic twilight of Ireland during Joyce's youth "beside the rivering waters of, hitherandthithering waters of. Night!" And Ezekiel, like the lover of the poems, as well as Joyce himself, was by a river (Chebar) when appointed to act as God's spokesman to His chosen people languishing in Babylonian exile with their harp, the national instrument of the Hebrews, hung figuratively upon the willows (Psalm 137:2). In **"I"** and **"III,"** designated by Joyce as the prelude, the strings of the harp (national instrument of the Irish also) unite the earth and air with music "by the river where / The willows meet." Responsible for this harmony is the wind blowing in the trees, a controlling image throughout **Chamber Music**; and God's voice directs his prophet from a whirl-wind. Joyce's lover, "lonely watcher of the skies" (**"III"**), is asked if only he awakes to hear "harps playing unto Love to unclose / The pale gates of sunrise." To Ezekiel alone, divinely commissioned "watchman of the house of israel" (3:17), does God reveal that He has not abandoned Israel in the darkness of captivity.

Death hangs like a pall over love from the beginning of both **Chamber Music** and Ezekiel; reminiscently, poem **"XXX"** explains, "We were grave lovers." In each instance responsibility for the gravity of the affair and its apparent lack of consummation rests in the character of the beloved. The image of the loved one (**"V"**) is "golden-hair"; poem **"VIII"** pictures "my own true love . . . with springtime all adorning her." So was Israel at first, God remembers: "I passed by thee, and saw thee; and behold thy time was the time of lovers" (16:8). Through His prophet He reminds her that His love had been extraordinary, yet after lavishing all sorts of rich raiment and jewels upon her He had found her prostituting herself to everyone passing by (16:15). As early as poem **"VII,"** the "mien so virginal" in **Chamber Music** is forebodingly shown to be coquettish, self centered, wooed by "gay winds," and in "light attire / Among the apple trees."

Stephen Hero expressed a fondness for the Holy Saturday service, when the seventh prophecy is read from Ezekiel's "vision of the plain of dry bones," where the "living dead" are organized, clothed, vitalized, and raised to become a living army, the new Israel ("but deeds bounds going arise again. Life . . . is a wake"). Personified by the Three Marys in this Holy Saturday service are the three natures of God's chosen people as well as those of the sweetheart in Joyce's lyrics—the virgin (**"IV"** and **"VIII"**); the mother (**"VI"**); and the temptress (**"X"** and **"XVII"**). It is these three natures which are questioned perhaps in the last line of the final poem (**"XXXVI"**), "My love, my love, my love, why have you left me alone?", an echo of Jesus's words on the Cross and of a leave-taking in keeping with the young Joyce's departure into what he considered a necessary exile from his three loves which had sheltered yet betrayed him.

Because of the loved one's duplicity in both Ezekiel and *Chamber Music,* there is, as *Finnegans Wake* puts it, "a split in the infinitive from to have to have been to will be. . . . This is the glider that gladdened the girl that list to the wind that lifted the leaves." Poem **"XI"** employs the imagery presaging the nearness of God in Ezekiel 9 and 10 ("When thou hast heard his name upon / The bugles of the cherubim"); the "glory" of Love fills poem **"XII"** as "the brightness of the glory of the Lord" shines over the cherubim in the prophet's vision; yet "a wind of spices" implying burial blows in the Epithalamium of **"XIII."** Immediately after poem **"XV,"** where the bridegroom comes forth from his bridechamber, **"XVI"** reveals that the valley in which "many a choir is singing now" has not been reached, and **"XXVII"** admits, "Nor have I known a love whose praise / Our piping poets solemnize." Since at the death of a wife the Hebrews caused pipes to be played, the analogy indicates love remains unconsummated.

The justice of God requires that Israel be punished for having placed uncleannesses in her heart (14:3), but at the same time His mercy establishes a covenant with her to be pacified in the end (16:60). Warned that if he allows the righteous to remain unwarned, "I will require his blood at thy hand" (3:20), the prophet is given to eat a roll of a book filled with lamentation. In poem **"XXVII"** the lover vows, "I but render and confess / The malice of thy tenderness," and a pledge is made in **"XVI"** that once the valley of harmony is reached "there, love, will we stay."

To signify the fate of Israel: a third part to be destroyed by fire, a third part by the knife, and a third part, although scattered by the winds, to survive ("ever a wynd had saving closes"), Ezekiel divides his hair and beard into three parts. Joyce may have seen in this three-sided act a parallel to his own three-faceted dilemma. In the climactic **"XIV"** "the odorous winds are weaving a music of sighs"; later, in **"XXIX,"** "shall love dissolved be / When . . . the wild winds blow."

The remnant of Israel escaping God's judgments are "like doves of the valley, all of them mourning everyone for his iniquity (7:16). Dove imagery is prominent in *Chamber Music;* in poem **"XIX"** "they" are "sadder than all tears; their lives ascend as a continual sigh." Through the possible dove imagery of **"XVIII"** the "man of sorrows" who "shall have rest" only by reconciliation with his "bride in exile" is suggested. The reversal of roles in **"XIV"** to show the bride resting on the breast of the bridegroom supports this inference; and the "lying clamour" over which the sweetheart grieves (**"XIX"**) recalls the victimizing of both Israel and Joyce by lying prophets. "I would we lay in deep . . . pine-forest enaisled" is a sad wish bearing in its choice of words hints of the church (**"XX"**); it displays perhaps Joyce's own sadness at being unable to follow the letter of the law as well as its spirit. Lines in poem **"XXIX"** are reminiscent of the transfiguration scene and Gethsemane: "How is your beauty raimented" and "Desolate winds assail with cries / The shadowy garden when love is." Correlations with the Song of Solomon already noted by Tindall affirm the link between the Old Testament Israel and the New Testament church as the bride in exile.

Although God acknowledged them as His "hope" and "all His riches" ("This heart that flutters near my heart / My hope and all my riches is . . . as in some mossy nest. . . . I laid those treasures I possessed," **"XXIII"**), the surviving Israelites were long to be abroad among the Gentiles gathering wealth (4:13). As in poem **"XXII,"** "soul with soul lies prisoned"; nevertheless, since exile is necessary before the land of promise can be regained, "the ways that we shall go upon" (**"XXX"**) are welcome. The rain which grays the world is a sign of eventual renewal (**"XXXII"**); yet during the period of exile there can be no real peace: "They will seek for peace and there shall be none" (7:25). Hence the paradox of poem **"XXXIV,"** "vitally" the end of the book, Joyce said in a letter to Geoffrey Palmer (quoted in Tindall's edition of *Chamber Music*). "Vitally the end" of Joyce's works, ALP's farewell in *Finnegans Wake* could well be the resolution of the affair in *Chamber Music*:

> And it's old and old it's sad and old it's sad and weary
> I go back to you, my cold father, my cold mad father,
> my cold mad feary father . . . I rush, my only, into your
> arms . . . I sink I'd die down over his feet, humbly
> dumbly, only to washup . . . There's where. First . . .
> The keys to. Given!
>
> (628)

In Ezekiel the whole ironic affair between God and Israel is epitomized by the "parable of the two eagles and a vine." One of the eagles sets the highest branch of the cedar, a tree prized in biblical times for its durability and odor, in a city of merchants, and plants the seed of the land along great waters as a willow tree. The growing seed becomes a vine of low stature. At first it leans toward the eagle which planted it, like Joyce's beloved, but soon it bends toward the second eagle (Joyce's jester with "cap and streamers . . . in the hollow," **"X"**). God declared that the cedar would be exalted in the end, while the willow would wither in the leaves of spring. In *Chamber Music* the land of the willows becomes autumnal as the sequence wanes, but the lover in the poem of climax, **"XIV,"** waits significantly by the cedar.

According to the arrangement of his lyrics Joyce preferred, judging from his letters, **"XXI"** would come first. Read in light of the analogy with Ezekiel it pointedly associates "that high unconsortable one" with the lover, Joyce, Jesus, and God Himself. Each had "glory lost," had found no "soul to fellow his / Among his foes in scorn and wrath / Holding to ancient nobleness." Joyce's own decision to become an exiled "priest of the imagination," if it is the "perilous theme" of "touchy nature," was expressed in *Chamber Music* as a pledge which can be recognized as fulfilled now in the canon of his succeeding works.

Robert Scholes   (essay date 1965)

SOURCE: "James Joyce, Irish Poet," in *James Joyce Quarterly,* Vol. II, No. 4, Summer, 1965, pp. 255-70.

[*In the following essay, Scholes provides a thematic and stylistic analysis of "Tilly" and "Ecce Puer," and places Joyce's verse within the context of Irish poetry.*]

> —They drove his wits astray, he said, by visions of hell. He will never capture the Attice note. The note of Swinburne, of all poets, the white death and the ruddy birth. That is his tragedy. He can never be a poet. The joy of creation . . .
>
> [Mulligan to Haines of Stephen, at "The Ship": *Ulysses*]
>
> . . . I am a poor impulsive sinful generous selfish jealous dissatisfied kind-natured poet . . .
>
> . . . *one day* you will see that I will be something in my country . . .
>
> . . . the Abbey Theatre will be open and they will give plays of Yeats and Synge. You have a right to be there because you are my bride: and I am one of the writers of this generation who are perhaps creating at last a conscience in the soul of this wretched race. . . .
>
> [Joyce to his wife in letters of 23, 24 Dec. 1909 and 22 Aug. 1912—MSS at Cornell]

The first of the two quotations prefixed to this essay is not merely an excerpt from a work of fiction. It represents Joyce's view of the attitude present in certain Dublin quarters toward his own artistic ambitions, and specifically toward his pretensions to being a poet. The second, made up of excerpts from three letters to his wife from Dublin, presents Joyce's view of himself and his rightful position in the literary firmament of the Irish capitol. Whatever his success in the various literary centers outside Ireland, Joyce's thoughts always turned, on publication of one of his works, to its reception at home. Was it being reviewed in the Dublin papers? And what were they saying of it there and thinking of him there? In these questions he never lost interest. His letters to his London publishers are full of requests for information about the Irish reviews of his books. In a particularly hubristic

moment he even wrote his wife that he hoped to "be able to give you the fame of sitting beside me when I have entered into my kingdom" (c. 21 Aug. 1912—MS at Cornell). And he meant this kingdom to be a literary one, located specifically in Dublin.

Joyce's desire for a very specific kind of success—in Dublin, as a poet—accounts for some peculiar and interesting facets of his work. I have begun here by asking the reader to consider this rather limited and specialized side of Joyce's literary intention as a prelude to offering for consideration a much more complex aspect of his approach to the creation of literature. I think we can safely say that Joyce began and ended his literary career with a desire to be an Irish poet. From *Chamber Music* to *Finnegans Wake* his concept of the meaning of "Irish poet" no doubt evolved considerably, beginning with a notion of someone who was born in Ireland and wrote elegant verses, but culminating with the idea of squeezing the universe inside the four walls of a Dublin pub. In just this manner we must expand out own concept of what an Irish poet might be, in order that we may encompass and accommodate Joyce's peculiar genius.

We do not usually think of Joyce as a poet. He wrote some verse, but it seems unmistakably minor—both in relation to the work of those poets whom we think of as "major" and in relation to his own work as a whole. Yet we cannot easily think of him as anything else. He is not a dramatist, though he wrote two plays, nor is he really a novelist either. As a novel, *Finnegans Wake* is an absurdity, and even *Ulysses,* though there is a novel in it, is obviously something more than a novel also. Many of us would be ready to abandon the distinction between prose and verse as a criterion for distinguishing the poet from the non-poet. The Dean of the Education School at the University of Wisconsin has published a volume of verse—but this does not make him a poet. And, conversely, many would agree that passages of Joyce's prose (the close of "The Dead," or of Chapter 4 of *A Portrait,* or of *Finnegans Wake,* for examples) might properly be called poetic. But there are other assumptions about the nature of poetry, more subtle and more significant than the mere distinction between prose and verse, which color our usual application of the word poet and raise special problems when we think of applying that word to Joyce. Since the Romantics, poetry has generally been considered to be at the emotional border of the domain of literature, far removed, by its very nature, from things learned and things intellectual. We are certain that Dylan Thomas is a poet. But, like Matthew Arnold, we have our doubts about Alexander Pope. We are not likely to think of praising a poet nowadays in such terms as occurred to the fifteenth-century English poet John Metham when he set out to commend one of his contemporaries for both his learning and his "craffty imagynacionys off things fantastyk." The highest praise that Metham could think of was, "that hys contynwauns made hym both a poyet and a clerk." In our time, we like to believe, the true poet is to be found only far from Academe, in a tavern, or, better still, a coffee-house. We are suspicious of poetry which is either too ratiocinative or too learned.

As an intellectual gesture typical of the current attitude, we can find a bright and aggressive graduate student of English in one of our respected literary quarterlies, attacking *Finnegans Wake* as "over-intellectual" and "cute." Though some would disagree with these criticisms, a large body of serious modern readers would probably agree that it is not good for a literary work to be too intellectual, and especially not for a work which aspires to the condition of poetry, as *Finnegans Wake* and all Joyce's works seem to do. The charge against *Finnegans Wake* in the attack we are considering here is that it is too clever and complicated; that it does not make the direct and moving appeal to the heart, imagination, and intellect that a work like Mann's *Joseph and His Brethren* obviously does; that it is, in a word, a book written for professors to use as a show-case for their ingenuity. If we accept the notion that learning and intellect are separate from and opposed to emotion and imagination through some sort of segregation in the psyche; if we accept the "dissociation of sensibility" as an actuality and not a concept; then perhaps we may be right to dismiss Joyce's greatest effort as a triumph of pedantry and an artistic failure—a colossal non-poem. But need we accept this view of the psyche and the esthetic which follows from it? To the individual with no interest in theology, Dante's "Paradiso" is not much fun. Does that mean we must declare it, also, a non-poem?

Though Joyce thought of himself at times as a "classicist" rather than a "romantic," he was really neither. By inclination and training his mind approached most closely—more closely than any other modern writer's—the spirit of the later Middle Ages and the emerging Renaissance. His intellectual affinities are with the humanists, allegorizers, and systematizers: with Pico and Bruno, with Dante and Spenser, with Joachim of Flora and Giambattista Vico. And the best defense of the poetry of *Finnegans Wake* is to be found in part twelve of the fourteenth Book of Boccaccio's *Genealogia Deorum Gentilium:*

> But I repeat my advice to those who would appreciate poetry, and unwind its difficult involutions. You must read, you must persevere, you must sit up nights, you must inquire, and exert the utmost power of your mind. If one way does not lead to the desired meaning, take another; if obstacles arise, then still another; until, if your strength holds out, you will find that clear which first looked dark. For we are forbidden by divine command to give that which is holy to dogs, or to cast pearls before swine.

[trans. by Charles C. Osgood]

To consider Joyce as a poet, we must conceive of poetry not as the Romantics did but as the humanists did. And we must avoid the common absolutistic feeling that we of the mid-twentieth century have in our ultimate wisdom finally arrived at the only true definition of poetry. Boccaccio says (*Genealogia*, XIV, vii) that "whatever is composed as under a veil, and thus exquisitely wrought, is poetry and poetry alone." And in dealing with Joyce, Boccaccio will be more helpful to us than Coleridge, or

Richards, or even Whitehead. What Boccaccio means by "composed as under a veil" is that poetry always approaches the condition of allegory. Where most moderns have accepted the notion that literature holds a mirror up to nature, Boccaccio believed that poetry "veils truth in a fair and fitting garment of fiction." And so, for that matter, did Sidney, though he phrased it differently. We have heard of *The Mirror and the Lamp*; now we must think for a moment of the implications of the mirror and the veil. To the Renaissance mind, delighting in the play of intellect over the accumulations of history, literature, and philosophy, a poem which encouraged this kind of mental activity was the ideal kind of poem. When Spenser called the *Faerie Queene* a "dark conceit," he meant that in it truth was veiled, and he certainly intended some of the reader's pleasure to come from the intellectual exercise which the continued allegory would afford. Of course, he required a learned and intelligent reader. To such a reader he was willing to give helpful hints, as in his letter to Raleigh, which is really aimed at a larger audience and was in fact incorporated into the book by an early printer. Joyce's habit, in giving such men as Stuart Gilbert, Frank Budgen, and Samuel Beckett clues to the meaning of *his* dark conceits, is not some modern aberration of eccentric genius but behavior characteristic of all allegorical poets. In this Joyce resembles not only Spenser but Dante as well, whose famous letter to Can Grande della Scala is analogous to Spenser's to Raleigh.

One place where we can see Joyce's allegorical habit of mind in action on a small scale is in his verse. The only critical attempt thus far to see this verse as allegorical has been Professor Tindall's [the editor] reading of **Chamber Music** as an elaborate dirty joke. If Joyce's allegory is to lead us only into the blind alleys of scatology, perhaps we might do well to abandon any plan of considering him as an allegorist, or poet in Boccaccio's sense. But there are other avenues of exploration open to us. A more usual approach to Joyce's verse than the scatological is the biographical. For this approach there is not only precedent, but obvious justification as well; and it has clearly had its successes in illuminating Joyce's works. His prose as well as his verse can often be traced back to its sources in the actualities of his own life. But this is not necessarily the best and most fruitful way to approach either his minor or his major works. Joyce is an allusive writer as well as an elusive one. But the great question we must face in dealing with his allusiveness is the nature and the context of his allusions. By emphasizing one context of allusion or another in reading his work, we can place it in a variety of perspectives. The usual practice has been to emphasize the biographical allusions. The argument about to be developed here is that we often (and perhaps always) would do more justice to Joyce as a poet if we would subordinate the biographical approach to a more purely literary one. Let us consider two poems: one clearly a success, and one, just as clearly, an enigma. The first is **"Ecce Puer,"** a dramatic lyric written long after **Chamber Music** and **Pomes Penyeach,** on the occasion of Joyce's becoming a grandfather.

"Ecce Puer"

Of the dark past
A child is born
With joy and grief
My heart is torn

Calm in his cradle
The living lies.
May love and mercy
Unclose his eyes!

Young life is breathed
On the glass;
The world that was not
Comes to pass.

A child is sleeping:
An old man gone.
O, father forsaken,
Forgive your son!

This does not appear, at first glance, to be an auspicious poem on which to base the argument that the biographical method for penetrating the veil of Joyce's poetry is not the best one. For that reason it is of especial importance for us. If it can be established that the effects of this poem depend more on another context of allusion than the biographical, then we shall have come a long way toward accepting the view that the biographical context should not be the dominant one in any reading of Joyce. For this poem is both personal and occasional. In it Joyce celebrates the birth of his grandson and mourns the recent death of his father. Our knowledge of Joyce's life and of the problems and difficulties he faced both as a son and as a father, cannot fail to invest the poem for the biographically knowledgeable reader with greater significance and emotion than it might otherwise have. But the question is not whether biographical knowledge can add to our appreciation of poetry. Almost always it can. The question here is whether or not it the most important context of allusion in this poem.

To answer this question we should first consider what the poem might mean to a reader deprived of this context. Such a reader could be expected to note that the speaker is torn between joy over the birth of a boy-child and grief over the passing of an old man. The inference which jumps most readily to the reader's mind is that the dead man is the speaker's father, the child his son. As the last lines indicate, this poem, like *Ulysses* is deeply concerned with the relationship between fathers and sons. The poem, then, would be seen as presenting the universal emotions appropriate to a speaker mourning his father's death and celebrating his son's birth. The apparently close juxtaposition of the two events in time enables the poet to heighten both emotions by their proximity and the dramatic conflict this proximity engenders in the heart of the speaker. The old man and the child represent also the past and the future between which the speaker himself is poised. In the last two lines the exclamation of the speaker leads us to believe that he has left his father at some time in

the past and now, too late, asks forgiveness. It also must raise the unspoken question of what will be the relationship between the speaker and his son in he future. If the sensitive but un-biographically oriented reader we have postulated here should finally turn to biography for further help—would that help be forthcoming? From the biographical data he would learn much about Joyce's father that might add poignancy to the poem for him. But he would also learn that the child involved was not Joyce's son but his grandson. The neat trinity of the three generations—analogous to that of Laertes, Odysseus, and Telemachus which Joyce remarked in the *Odyssesy*—would be spoiled by the biographical facts, if those facts were allowed to dominate the poem. But it may well be that while time and fate chose to juxtapose the death and birth over a span of four generations, the poet in Joyce saw, in this situation which moved him as a man, the possibility for the even more moving and dramatic juxtaposition of the two events spanning only three generations. Thus he did not in the poem specify names, relationship, or generations and he left that reader whom Fielding called sagacious to make the inference which was right for the poem though wrong for the facts.

> Though Joyce thought of himself at times as a "classicist" rather than a "romantic," he was really neither. By inclination and training his mind approached most closely—more closely than any other modern writer's—the spirit of the later Middle Ages and the emerging Renaissance.
>
> —*Robert Scholes*

But the poem does not depend for its effect on the inferable dramatic situation alone. There is a context of allusion here which adds, for the knowledgeable reader, overtones and reverberations which enhance the poem and raise its intensity to a higher pitch. The last two lines allude to the primal Christian archetype of the confrontation between father and son: the "My God, My God, why hast thou forsaken me" of Matthew and Mark, and the "Father, forgive them; for they know not what they do" of Luke. Joyce's lines

O, father forsaken,
Forgive your son!

are a witty conflation and inversion of the Biblical expressions, but the wit is poet's wit, designed to control, even while it displays, a deep emotion. Within the reader who pierces the veil of allusion (surely not too difficult a task in this case) an emotion corresponding to that of the speaker is also engendered. Perhaps we can paraphrase Eliot and say that here Joyce has employed an allusive correlative. The cries of Jesus and of the speaker in this poem are cries for atonement—in all the senses of that word—and the human cry may be the more poignant of the two because it is made too late, to ears that cannot hear it.

The alert reader, having seen this much, will also see how the title of the poem alludes to the same context. Pilate's exclamation, "Ecce Homo," which has been used as the title for countless paintings of Christ's passion (including one by Munkacsy on which Joyce wrote a youthful essay) is modified here to apply to the birth of a boy-child rather than to the passion of the Son of Man. In this title there is perhaps more of Christmas than of Easter. But the speaker is a son, also, and it is *his* passion which the poem dramatizes and expresses through an intense combination of situation and allusion.

The other poem to be presented here as an example of Joyce's allusive art is a more difficult one. It was first published in **Pomes Penyeach** under the title **"Tilly,"** which refers primarily to the fact that it is the extra item in this baker's dozen of poems. But it had previously existed for a long time in manuscript under the titles of **"Cabra"** and **"Ruminants."** The **"Cabra"** version was the first, and had been written as early as 1903, when Stanislaus Joyce referred to it in his diary (*The Dublin Diary of Stanislaus Joyce,* ed. G. H. Healey, Cornell: 1962).

"Cabra"

He travels after the wintery sun,
Driving the cattle along the straight red road;
Calling to them in a voice they know,
He drives the cattle above Cabra.

He tells them home is not far.
They low and make soft music with their hoofs.
He drives the cattle without labour before him,
Steam pluming their foreheads.

Herdsman, careful of the herd,
Tonight sleep well by the fire
When the herd too is asleep
And the door made fast.

At some later date this version acquired the title **"Ruminants,"** a significant change in the light of the final version of the poem. As **"Cabra"** the poem is a brief pastoral idyll. The change to **"Ruminants"** suggests Joyce's shifting attitude toward his subject, and is probably meant—as the final version would indicate—to include the herdsman as well as the herd, emphasizing their common bond of placid animality. When it appeared as **"Tilly"** in **Pomes Penyeach** the poem read this way:

"Tilly"

He travels after a winter sun,
Urging the cattle along cold red road,
Calling to them, a voice they know,
He drives his beasts above Cabra.

The voice tells them home is warm.
They moo and make brute music with their hoofs.

He drives them with a flowering branch before him,
Smoke pluming their foreheads.

Boor, bond of the herd,
Tonight stretch full by the fire!
I bleed by the black stream
For my torn bough!

The differences between the two versions have been dealt with in considerable detail by Chester Anderson (*PMLA,* LXXIII, 3) and will not be rehearsed here. The change in attitude is reflected in many changes in diction throughout the poem, but primarily through the introduction of a new image and the dramatic specification of the speaker's situation. The herdsman now drives his herd with a flowering branch, apparently torn from the living bush or tree which is the speaker of the poem.

The only two previous attempts to treat this poem seriously which have come to my attention are those of Chester Anderson and Richard Ellmann. Both relate the poem to the biographical context of allusion. Mr. Anderson (in the essay cited above) suggests that the poem is about Joyce's relationship with J. F. Byrne (the "boor" of the poem in this reading); Mr. Ellmann suggests that the poem is about the death of Joyce's mother (the "bough" in this reading—see *James Joyce,* New York: 1959). For a number of reasons another context than the biographical seems preferable in the case of **"Tilly,"** First of all, Joyce was still making new copies of the **"Cabra"** version of the poem as late as 1916, which he would certainly not have done if he had supplanted it by the opposed **"Tilly"** version (see MSS No. 54 in the Cornell University Joyce Collection), and as late as 1919 the old version, with the title changed to **"Ruminants,"** was the current version (see MSS No. IV.A.—in the University of Buffalo Joyce Collection). The drastically revised version of the poem probably dates from shortly before its first publication in 1927. (The only known holograph manuscript [in private hands] is of that date.) This removes the poem in time from the psychological moments of composition appropriate to either J. F. Byrne or Joyce's mother as subject matter, making either subject dubious on biographical grounds alone. Furthermore, a purely literary context exists which will provide us with a reading more satisfactory than the biographical. The bleeding bush or tree is a poetical image used by many of the greatest poets, including some Joyce most admired and knew best. The context to which Joyce is alluding here is a literary one, the knowledge of which will open the poem easily to us and enable us to perceive both its meaning and its excellence.

Vergil used this image in Book III of the *Aeneid* (24-68). Here Aeneas, himself now a wandering exile, seeks to prepare an altar for a sacrifice to his mother, Venus. On plucking some myrtle boughs he is horrified to see black blood welling from the injured tree. The tree speaks. It is Priam's son Polydorus who had been sent abroad, exiled for safety's sake by his father, only to be betrayed and slaughtered treacherously on the shore of Thrace.

In Book VIII of the *Metamorphoses* (which provided Joyce with the epigraph for *A Portrait.*) Ovid introduced an oak tree which bled when struck with an axe, and spoke to warn that its death would be avenged. But the image of the bleeding tree was employed most powerfully of all by Dante, in Canto XIII of "The Inferno." There, beside the boiling river of blood, Dante and Vergil enter the wood of the Christian suicides. At Vergil's bidding Dante plucks a small branch from a thorn tree and is startled to see the tree bleed and to hear words bubbling forth with the dark blood. Vergil reminds Dante that he has recounted such a wonder in the *Aeneid*, and he asks the tree to tell Dante of its history. The tree in life had been Pierre delle Vigne, poet, scholar, and advisor to Frederick II of Sicily. Through envy Frederick was led to accuse his counselor of treason and ultimately to have him blinded, banished, and imprisoned, driving him to suicide.

In Book I, Canto ii of the *Faerie Queene*, Spenser employed the bleeding tree in a similar context. Taking shelter under two "goodly trees" the Redcross Knight plucks a bough to make a garland for the false Duessa, whom he knows as Fidessa. The tree begins to bleed and speak, telling of how as a man he had been seduced by Duessa and betrayed, existing now "enclosed in wooden walls full faste / Banished from living wights." Spenser here was following Ariosto (Orlando Furioso, VI, stanzas 26-56), whose French knight Astolfo was seduced by Alcina and then transformed to a myrtle tree on the shore of a magic island far from his home. The exile and betrayal of Polydorus, the betrayal and banishment of the blinded Pierre delle Vigne, the seduction, betrayal, and banishment of Astolfo and Fradubio—these provide us with the context against which **"Tilly"** must be considered. Joyce's poem is a variation on a traditional theme.

Through the image of the bleeding tree, with its rich heritage in literary history, Joyce has established as a context for **"Tilly"** an atmosphere of betrayal and banishment. The specific details of the speaker's situation are not developed as in the narrative poems of Vergil, Dante, Ariosto, and Spenser. They must be worked out by the reader inferentially, employing his awareness of the poem's allusiveness. For the reader who does this, what seems originally to be an enigma will be found to yield its meanings once it is seen in its proper and necessary contexts of allusion. In addition to the context suggested by the image of the bleeding tree itself, we may also turn to the context suggested by the themes of betrayal and exile which cluster about the image as an accumulation from its literary past. In *A Portrait of the Artist as a Young Man*, the play *Exiles*, and *Ulysses* these themes are of considerable importance. The reverberations set up between **"Tilly"** and these larger works add to the poem's richness of meaning and to the satisfaction of that kind of reader whom Boccaccio desired for poetry. The reader alert to the literary history of the image of the bleeding tree, and to the importance of the themes of exile and betrayal in Joyce's work as a whole, will readily perceive in the boor with the flowering branch driving the herd another of Joyce's characterizations of the stay-at-homes of Irish literature, who cater to the rabblement (as

Joyce accused Yeats's Irish Literary Theatre of doing in "The Day of the Rabblement"), flourishing the garlands they have usurped from the true poet, who has been banished for trying to create the conscience of his race. With the boor we must associate a gallery of characters, ranging from the sympathetically treated Gabriel Conroy of "The Dead," to Malachi Mulligan, the "usurper" of *Ulysses*, and including Cranly in *A Portrait*, and Robert Hand in *Exiles*. Richard Rowan, the autobiographical character in *Exiles*, derives his name from the rowan tree, the ash with its bell-like berries, believed to have magical properties and often cut for switches, wands, and walking sticks. In Richard and Robert we can readily see the torn bough and the tearing hand. Joyce's interest in the themes of betrayal and banishment was a continuing preoccupation, which he never kept long out of his writing, from his first literary production, the lost "Et tu, Healey," to *Finnegans Wake*.

His interest in the theme of exile, in particular, may have brought to his attention a poem of Yeats's on this theme, in which we find exile and a torn bough closely juxtaposed. It first appeared as the dedication to a collection of Irish tales edited by Yeats and published in 1891. (Stanislaus Joyce said that his brother had read "all of Yeats," and there is no reason to think there is much exaggeration in the statement, especially as far as the early Yeats is concerned.) In its first appearance the poem was simply called "Dedication":

> There was a green branch hung with many a bell
> When her own people ruled in wave-worn Eri,
> And from its murmuring greenness, calm of faery
> —A Druid kindness—on all hearers fell.
>
> It charmed away the merchant from his guile,
> And turned the farmer's memory from his cattle,
> And hushed in sleep the roaring ranks of battle,
> For all who heard it dreamed a little while.
>
> Ah, Exiles, wandering over many seas,
> Spinning at all times Eri's good tomorrow,
> Ah, world-wide Nation, always growing Sorrow,
> I also bear a bell branch full of ease.
>
> I tore it from green boughs winds tossed and hurled,
> Green boughs of tossing always, weary, weary,
> I tore it from the green boughs of old Eri,
> The willow of the many-sorrowed world.
>
> Ah, Exiles wandering over many lands,
> My bell branch murmurs: the gay bells bring laughter,
> Leaping to shake a cobweb from the rafter;
> The sad bells bow the forehead on the hands.
>
> A honied ringing! under the new skies
> They bring you memories of old village faces,
> Cabins gone now, old well-sides, old dear places,
> And men who loved the cause that never dies.

In 1892 Yeats included the poem in his volume *The Countess Kathleen and Various Legends and Lyrics*.

Joyce may well have come to know the poem in this edition, for one of his favorite Yeats poems, "Who will go drive with Fergus now," was originally a song in the play "The Countess Kathleen" in this volume. If not in this edition he would probably have found it in the *Poems of 1895* or in one of the many later reprints of this volume. We should not have to be concerned with the various reprintings of the "Dedication" poem, were it not that its history parallels the history of **"Tilly"** in a very interesting way. In the *Irish Statesman* of 8 November 1924 Yeats published a new version of the poem under the title "An Old Poem Re-written":

> There was a green branch hung with many a bell
> When her own people ruled this tragic Eire;
> And from its murmuring greenness, calm of Faery,
> A Druid kindness, on all hearers fell.
>
> It charmed away the merchant from his guile
> And turned the farmer's memory from his cattle,
> And hushed in sleep the roaring ranks of battle:
> And all grew friendly for a little while.
>
> Ah, Exiles wandering over lands and seas,
> And planning, plotting always that some morrow
> May set a stone upon ancestral Sorrow!
> I also bear a bell-branch full of ease.
>
> I tore it from green boughs winds tore and tossed
> Until the sap of summer had grown weary!
> I tore it from the barren boughs of Eire,
> That country where a man can be so crossed;
>
> Can be so battered, badgered and destroyed
> That he's a loveless man: gay bells bring laughter
> That shakes a mouldring cobweb from the rafter;
> And yet the saddest chimes are best enjoyed.
>
> Gay bells or sad, they bring you memories
> Of half-forgotten innocent old places:
> We and our bitterness have left no traces
> On Munster grass and Connemara skies.

This new, more somber version then replaced the old in the section called "The Rose" of the collected *Early Poems and Stories* of 1925. It may be found today in this section of the standard editions of Yeats's verse, not far from "Who Goes with Fergus," which was dropped from the play "The Countess Kathleen" and added to "The Rose" in the *Poems* of 1912. These dates are important, for **"Tilly"** did not appear in print until Joyce's **Pomes Penyeach** volume of 1927. We know that as late as 1919, Joyce had not re-written **"Tilly,"** but we do not know exactly when he did re-write it. The suggestion offered here is that he may well have re-done his old poem after encountering Yeats's "An Old Poem Re-written" in the *Irish Statesman* of 1924 or the *Early Poems and Stories* of 1925 (where the new version appeared under the original title). The theme of exile in the two poems, combined with the striking image of the torn branch, links them in fact, whether or not Joyce's poem was intended to be an answer to Yeats. It is tempting, however, to see in **"Tilly"** a direct answer of sorts—an address to the tearer of boughs and leader of the rabblement by the torn and rejected arch-exile himself. But we ought not to think of merely substituting Yeats for J. F. Byrne or any other individual in our reading of the poem. The function of the contexts of allusion Joyce has invoked in the poem is to establish a frame of reference which is at once general and specific. Once aware of these contexts we are in no doubt that this is a poem about betrayal and exile, about the contrast between the contented ruminants who are located specifically in Cabra, Ireland, and the speaker, bleeding from his torn bough by some nameless dark stream. Unlike **"Ecce Puer"** this poem does not have any situational level which can be apprehended in realistic terms. Cabra and the black stream are as far apart as "that . . . country" and Byzantium in Yeats's "Sailing to Byzantium." If we seek merely to particularize the poem, to equate Byrne or Yeats or Gogarty or any other individual with the leader of the herd, we succeed only in diminishing the poem's meaning and its importance. It is a song of exile, a bitter echo brought to life, perhaps, by Yeats's "gay bells," but itself awaking reverberations, answering notes from our cultural and literary tradition. In his introduction to the anthology of Irish tales for which he wrote this "Dedication" poem, Yeats observed that "No modern Irish writer has ever had anything of the high culture that makes it possible for an author to do as he will with life, to place the head of a beast upon a man, or the head of a man upon a beast, to give to the most grotesque creation the reality of a spiritual existence." Joyce aspired to the kind of culture Yeats had in mind here and sought in his most ambitious works to invest his own grotesque creations with "the reality of a spiritual existence." And in **"Tilly"** it is precisely this culture which justifies the grotesque image of the bleeding tree. Joyce did not, of course, merely aspire to high culture. He went a long way toward achieving it. In 1902 George Russell (AE) had written to Yeats, "I want you to meet a young fellow named Joyce whom I wrote to Lady Gregory about half-jestingly. He is an extremely clever boy who belongs to your clan more than to mine and more still to himself. But he has all the intellectual equipment, culture and education which our other clever friends here lack.". . .

Joyce, in a way, was just the kind of young man Yeats and his friends who cared for Irish literature were hoping would arise—a man with enough culture and education as well as the genius to be a great poet. Though Joyce's independence—apparent to Russell and Yeats from the start—only grew as he matured; though he went into voluntary exile from Ireland, blasting Yeats and Russell and both their "clans" with his broadside verses *The Holy Office*; Yeats in particular must have derived some well deserved satisfaction in having seen what Irish literature needed in 1891, and having later recognized it in Joyce, who had not been ten years old when Yeats wrote his introduction to the Irish tales. He did more than merely recognize talent in Joyce. He was of considerable practical assistance in getting this difficult young man reviewing work which kept him alive in Paris in 1902 and 1903 and in introducing him to people who could help him, including finally Ezra Pound, who was an enormous help to Joyce when he needed it most. All this assistance, of course, did not prevent Joyce from developing a sense of injured merit, and it did not stop him, in particular, from measuring himself as a poet against Yeats and Russell and their proteges. If Joyce wished, in some way, to see **"Tilly"** set off by Yeats's "Dedication," he may also have wished to see **"Ecce Puer"** set off against another of Yeats's poems. No artistic work is produced without connection with past works of similar kinds. The metrical scheme of **"Ecce Puer"** did not come to Joyce out of nowhere as the appropriate vehicle for the celebration of the birth of his grandson. He undoubtedly used the scheme he did because Yeats had employed almost the identical meter and rhyme scheme for a similar poem. (Again, this poem is to be found in the "Rose" section of the standard collections of Yeats's poems.)

"A Cradle Song"

The angels are stooping
Above your bed;
They weary of trooping
With the whimpering dead.

God's laughing in Heaven
To see you so good;
The Sailing Seven
Are gay with His mood.

I sigh that kiss you,
For I must own
That I shall miss you
When you have grown.

Joyce rhymed only the second and last lines of each stanza, while Yeats rhymed the first and third as well, but aside from the minor difference the similarity in prosody and situation is striking. Even the juxtaposition of the new-born and the dead in Yeats's first stanza anticipates the contrast between the generations which is the dramatic fulcrum of Joyce's poem.

Joyce consistently measured himself against other Irish artists, and he was always more interested in the reviews of his work in Irish periodicals than in any others. In *Dubliners* he had deliberately set out, with George Moore's collection of Irish stories *The Untilled Field* in hand, to write better stories than Moore or any other Irishman could write. Even in *Finnegans Wake* he was partly motivated, no doubt, by a desire to show that when he wanted to he could do more with Irish mythology than Lady Gregory and Yeats and the rest of the Irish Literary Revival put together. It is also likely that in the two dramatic lyrics we have been considering, **"Tilly"** and **"Ecce Puer,"** he was driven by the same desire to measure himself against the best in poetry that Ireland could produce—and he had no doubt that Yeats was the best.

In his introduction to that collection of tales dedicated to the Irish exiles, Yeats had remarked, "Most things are changed now—politics are different, life is different. Irish

literature is and will be, however, the same in one thing for many a long day—in its nationality, its resolve to celebrate in verse and prose all within the four seas of Ireland. And why should it do otherwise? A man need not go further than his own hill-side or his own village to find every kind of passion and virtue. As Paracelsus wrote: 'If thou tastest a crust of bread, thou tastest of all the stars and all the heavens.'" This prophetic statement by the leader of the Irish Literary Revival certainly suggests for us, now, Joyce's method as poet—as maker, that is, not only of verses but of huge symbolic edifices which move from the crusts of personal experience toward the stars and all the heavens.

Even in the two little poems we have been investigating here, we have seen Joyce reaching out toward the Western heritage of pagan and Christian literature for the archetypes and images which will make the bridge from the personal and the Irish to the universal. In all his works, from these minor poems to the most ambitious flights of *Finnegans Wake,* the bridge is there. It is not always easy to cross, but it is worth crossing. Boccaccio observed long ago (*Genealogia,* XVI, vii) that "this fervor of poesy is sublime in its effects: it impels the soul to a longing for utterance; it brings forth strange and unheard-of creatures of the mind; it arranges these meditations in a fixed order, adorns the whole composition with unusual interweaving of words and thoughts; and thus it veils truth in a fair and fitting garment of fiction." Between the crust of bread and all the heavens lies the veil of poesy. If we do not wish to be left with the crust alone, we must seek to penetrate the veil. We must read, we must persevere, we must sit up nights, we must inquire and exert the utmost powers of our minds; so that works of poetic genius are not to us as pearls cast before swine. If we approach Joyce's works as Boccaccio insisted we must approach the works of a poet, we shall find him to be what he always meant to be—an Irish poet, and one of the greatest.

Herbert Howarth (essay date 1966)

SOURCE: "*Chamber Music* and its Place in the Joyce Canon," in *James Joyce Today: Essays on the Major Works,* edited by Thomas F. Staley, Indiana University Press, 1966, pp. 11-27.

[*In the following essay, Howarth traces the development of Joyce's lyricism, concluding that the imagery, form, and themes of the poems in* Chamber Music *foreshadow those of Joyce's later work.*]

The place of **Chamber Music** in the Joyce canon is at once first, last, and nowhere. Chronologically it is first. It is last for most critics. It is nowhere for most readers, who ignore it or read it too rapidly to gather what it can give. Joyce's own view, even at the moment when he had his worst doubts and almost withheld the volume from publication, was that the poems had "grace"; and perhaps he would also have called them "dainty," the word he uses in *A Portrait of the Artist* to describe the Elizabethan song which he sang at the piano. For the historian the book is certainly and organically what Joyce allowed it to become when he quelled his doubts and let the printer proceed: Opus I; the first stage in the evolution of the complete opera.

"It is not a book of love verses at all, I perceive," Joyce wrote to his brother. They are not love verses because they do not really attempt to reach a woman, to speak to her, to persuade her, nor do they really attempt to reflect their writer's experience of love or even of the fantasy of love. They are essays in style. This in two senses. They are essays in a style of life. Although they are not purely "Shakespearean" or "Jonsonian" or "lutanist" (since other influences from Horace to the Victorian drawing room ballads, from the Irish come-all-yous to Verlaine, converge in them), yet their singer takes shape, if a blurred shape, as a grave-mannered gentleman of a pre-industrial world, a courtier. Something must be said about him later. They are also essays in style in the more familiar literary meaning of the term: essays in the arrangement of words to please the ear. *Pulchra sunt quae audita placent.*

Read as an exhibition of the verbal skill, the more satisfying for the carefully-spun simplicity of the context, *Chamber Music* will seem a remarkable collection. It bears the sign which characterizes the poetic stylist in all languages, the deliberate invention of technical obligations and their fulfillment. In each stanza of Poem "VIII," Joyce obliges himself to renew and amplify the first line in the third line. He loves to take a word from one stanza and employ it in the next in a different position. In Poem "X" he agreeably converts two rhyming nouns of the first stanza, *streamers* and *dreamers,* into two rhyming participles in the corresponding lines of the second stanza. The craft of the disposition and redisposition of words in a short lyric might be learned from *Chamber Music.* So might the art of the reduction of large-scale effects to lyric proportions. We know how Joyce was gratified by the rhetoric with which Seymour Bushe spoke of Michelangelo's Moses, the frozen music, "which, if anything that the hand of man has wrought of noble and inspiring and beautiful deserves to live deserves to live." That immediate closure of a whole period by the iteration of a verb that has just closed a subordinate clause, Joyce uses and extends in *Ulysses,* and uses but appropriately curbs in *Chamber Music*—when he tells his sweetheart or his soul to repudiate the slanderers:

> They are sadder than all tears;
>   Their lives ascend as a continual sigh.
> Proudly answer to their tears:
>   As they deny, deny.

His literary architecture, metropolitan in *Ulysses* and *Finnegans Wake,* Joyce practices in miniature in *Chamber Music.* Parallel parentheses, parallel questions, hold stanza supported against stanza. Songs curve in elegant quasi-palindrome to end as they began.

There is a spice of absurdity in proving the talents of

rhetoric in a writer who through the course of a lifetime was to demonstrate a master's power over the styles of his precursors and contemporaries: who was to resume the prose of all the eras of English literature in the "Deshil Holles Eamus" chapter of *Ulysses;* who parodied *The Waste Land;* who dexterously plied a birthday lyric into five languages, each version authentic in tone and tune. The reminder of the obvious is to clarify the intention of Opus I. The persistent stylistic care has one predominant purpose, implicit in the title of the volume. The aim is "music."

It is legitimate to call Joyce neoclassical and to see him in the neoclassical procession of our century. Yet the term is too narrow and too broad. Joyce was a Romantic poet as well as an Archaic. And of the classical centuries he totally ignored the eighteenth, for some observers the supremely classical. He was not of the Age of Reason. He valued the lyric above all other poetry, and understood its birth and its beauty as beyond the reach of reason or observation. That is clear from his love of Mangan, from his appeal to the standard of "Es war ein König in Thule," from his rejection of Meredith's poetry for its lack of the lyrical impulse. In both *A Portrait* and *Ulysses* he describes Stephen writing a lyric, and shows with scrupulosity of introspection that it is a brimming of unconscious powers and knowledge: that it is indeed a "spontaneous overflow of powerful feeling." It overflows as music. "A song by Shakespeare or Verlaine, which seems so free and living and as remote from any conscious purpose as rain that falls in a garden or the lights of evening, is discovered to be the rhythmic speech of an emotion otherwise incommunicable, at least so fitly."

The Age of Reason judged that one of the problems of the poet was to make his sound seem an echo of the sense. Joyce worked from the opposite point. His effort was to find sense capable of carrying the sound that he heard when the inner life brimmed over. The sense must be the medium of the sound. He was a musician in search of a system of notation. When Joyce perceived that the poems of *Chamber Music* were not love poems, this was what he perceived: that he had been looking for words to register the music of the emotions of a young man of twenty-two.

The purpose was music. And the success? A partial success: the music is there for the seeking but does not invade the reader unless it is patiently sought. If we give the songs of *Chamber Music* several readings, they begin to take hold; and afterwards, when we are about other occupations, the music will stir in the memory, possibly without the accompaniment of the words; the melody will rise, fall, recur, prolong itself, offer its atmosphere and world picture.

But we do not give them so much reading, unless for [an essay] of this kind. And a writer is at least partly to blame if we read him no more than perfunctorily. He has not put in enough to detain the eye. What Joyce has not given to *Chamber Music* is enough sense to carry the music. For us on this North American continent at this period when some density is expected of literature, density and a scatter of potent symbols which we may construe and connect ad lib., the verses want substance. Together with his view of its music, Joyce seems to have had a conception of the lyric which deterred him from that necessary accumulation of sense. He seems to have thought that the lyric required frailty: a flower quality: it must be as fresh, standing, and defined as a flower, and as frail. For the taste of our time, consequently, he could never solve, in a poem, the problem of scoring his music with sense rich enough to carry it. But in prose he could. It was a pertinent comment when he said that one leaf of "A Little Cloud" was worth more than *Chamber Music.* He devoted nearly all his energy to prose because there he judged it right to impress a robust substance and score it densely, satisfyingly to the modern ear. Nevertheless, the music of the poems is worth seeking: a communication, however faint, of the voice of the world.

The better to see that the chamber *music* is what counts, I turn to a different aspect of the volume. Was it original? Joyce liked to appear before his city, his people, and his rivals as original: to upstage them with a display of easy intercourse with men of whom they had never heard but who were apparently Masters. But though the surprise performances of his youth came off, and though in his ultimate achievement he was so immensely original, he was not original at every moment of his progress. When, for example, he transposed Verlaine into Poem **"XXXV"** of *Chamber Music* he chose precisely the piece that most quickly made an appeal to the common English reader; Arthur Symons' translation of the same piece was to find its way into a popular anthology of world literature. In what might at this distance of sixty years seem to be the novelty of Joyce's affection for the lutesong, he was not novel. He was part of an English movement which has continued for another two generations, giving rise in literature to the sestinas and villanelles of the thirties, and in music to the revival of the sixteenth and seventeenth century composers and their forms and temper, and especially to the work of Benjamin Britten. He was not at the root of the movement. He was an offshoot from the main stem. The movement was a generation old when he published *Chamber Music.*

An essay by Francis Hueffer (father of Ford Madox Hueffer) is a useful signpost to the enquirer. In *Macmillan's Magazine,* November, 1880, Hueffer wrote on "Troubadours, Ancient and Modern." His modern troubadours were younger poets of the epoch, engaged in writing "rondeaux and roundels, villanelles and triolets." He named Arthur O'Shaughnessy, John Payne, E. W. Gosse, T. Marzials, Andrew Lang, Austin Dobson, and Mary Robinson, and quoted a triolet by Robert Bridges. During the two decades following his article, these troubadours were joined by others, including the Irishman whom Joyce regarded with some passion, Oscar Wilde.

So when Stephen, awaking towards dawn in a suffusion of music, experiences the word made flesh in the rhythmic recapitulations of the villanelle, he is not the first rediscoverer of the delight of this antique form. It is a glowing villanelle that he composes, shot with a romantic

ardour. He fills the form with his own melody and movement. But in his choice of the form the innovator-to-be is not yet an innovator.

How another Irishman, who was as dexterous and virtuous with poetry as Joyce was to be with prose, could draw on the troubadour fashion and innovate with it, can be seen by a glance at three poems written by Yeats in three well-separated and markedly contrasting periods of his career. Among the perfect poems of *The Wind among the Reeds* is "He wishes for the Cloths of Heaven." There Yeats borrows from the modern troubadours by hinting, scarcely hinting, at their recurring phrases, and assimilates their method to his twilight style. Twenty years later he writes lines in which "I would be ignorant as the dawn" recurs as if in a rondeau, but grows to the surprise of "Ignorant and wanton as the dawn" (the rondeau is transformed by the Yeatsian dynamic). Twenty years later still, he writes the Crazy Jane sequence and the cognate ballads that depend on a refrain—thus assimilating the troubadour convention to the interclashing violence and tenderness of his final art. Feigning in his early days, when the troubadours were most the mode, to stand apart and to leave their exercises to his less profound friends among the rhymers, Yeats in fact stole their recapitulations and refrains, and stole with genius to add to his technical resources.

My impression of the relationship between Yeats and Joyce, while close to that proposed by W. Y. Tindall in his preface and notes to the Columbia University Press edition of *Chamber Music,* differs a little from his, and particularly on a point of rhyme. The note to Poem **"XXVIII"** urges that Yeats inaugurated the technical experiments of his middle life, especially his experiments in distant and as I would say felicitous rhyme, or as Prof. Tindall says, "bad" rhyme, under the stimulus of *Chamber Music.* The argument is persuasively put, yet I am not quite persuaded. It is true that the rhymes of *Chamber Music* ring now and then like those of the later Yeats. In particular Joyce is successful, like Yeats, in rhyming monosyllable and plurisyllable. But there were already such rhymes in "To Ireland in the Coming Times." As for distant rhymes, the poet who had written "The Song of Wandering Aengus," in which an exquisite series of consonantal rhymes, "wood," "wand," "wing," threads the familiar vowel rhymes, did not need to learn the skill from Joyce. What he had to learn and did supremely learn from Joyce in due season was to face the real world: to face those "things uncomely and broken," by which he had been shocked in the nineties when they "wronged" his image of ideal beauty. But he could not learn that from *Chamber Music,* whose troubadour, another idealizer as troubadours are, had still to teach himself the lesson.

For the technique of lyric, Joyce was entirely willing to go to school with Yeats. He marvellously renders homage to Yeats the technician in the passage of *A Portrait* which recalls the playing of *The Countess Cathleen* in Dublin, the jeering incomprehension of Stephen's fellow students, and Stephen's enchantment. "A soft liquid joy flowed through the words where the soft long vowels hurtled noiselessly and fell away, lapping and flowing back and ever shaking the white bells of their waves in mute chime and mute peal and soft low swooning cry":— that is his experience of Yeats' dramatic verse. The metrical modulations of *Chamber Music* must at least have been encouraged by the iamb-qualifying metrics of *The Wind among the Reeds* and Aleel's songs in *The Countess Cathleen*. What is striking, perhaps, is that Joyce could incorporate the metrical lessons of Yeats without any of the more obvious signs of imitation. He liked to dissemble his debts to his immediate elders, at least if they shared the same language. Although the lyrics of *Chamber Music* are modern troubadour songs, they avoid a too evident association with the movement: there is not a roundel or villanelle among them; yet to the eye of the historian certain usages (the prohibition "O bend no more," and the exploitation of the adaptable noun "ways") clearly connect them with the villanelle of *A Portrait*. Joyce prefers the Shakespearean or Jonsonian song to differentiate himself from the Dobsons; and to imply, perhaps, that refrains are obstacles for schoolboys, relatively easy for a poet to leap, and that he will do the harder thing, meet the demands of an archaic form "free and living." By the same step he differentiates himself from Yeats. When Yeats heard some of the early Joyce poems in the autumn of 1902 he was amazed at their technique: ". . . much better than the technique of any young Dublin man I have met during my time. It might have been the work of a young man who had lived in an Oxford literary set." That last sentence is not ironic. It means that he saw the poems as an exacting development of the modern troubadouring of England. It also means that the form had beguiled him into overlooking his own influence, which he would have recognized in Irish forms or themes or in the smoke of theosophical imagery.

If we give the songs of *Chamber Music* several readings, they begin to take hold; and afterwards, when we are about other occupations, the music will stir in the memory, possibly without the accompaniment of the words; the melody will rise, fall, recur, prolong itself, offer its atmosphere and world picture.

—*Herbert Howarth*

But of course the form was not chosen for the sake of concealment. That was an incidental benefit. It was chosen because it belonged to a Weltanschauung, a stance, a "style" of life. In plotting the relative unoriginality of the "modern troubadour" form, I have no intention of depreciating its value or the function or the value of the Joycean stance. The archaic lyricist was an essential part of Joyce and his work.

An essential half. There were two Joyces: the lyrical and the satirical; the singer and the clown. At the beginning of his writing life they were well-split halves: he was the

complete schizophrene. The personality ascendant in *Chamber Music* was the courtier, the punctualist, the grave and dainty singer. The other personality was the obscenist, the ribald rapscallion, the brayer. In Joyce's outward daily behaviour at twenty-two the latter seems to have been better-known to the Dubliners (though Stanislaus tells of his craving for good manners even then). As he grew older the courtier became the conductor of his living; he would let no one outvie him in etiquette. The movement in his works was towards the ascendancy of the rollicker. But not, I hasten to add, to the exclusion of the lyricist. That is the subject of my story.

Thanks to Richard Ellmann's scholarship, we have a document which tells us a great deal about both personalities and their goings-on and gettings-together. It is the *Giacomo Joyce* notebook of the last prewar period in Trieste. At once lachrymose and animated, it helps to explain the lifelong survival of the Courtier in Joyce, and accordingly his role in *Chamber Music.*

We may sometimes ask ourselves why so stern a literary critic as Joyce permitted himself his luteplaying, and the idealizing daintiness to which Ellmann, nearly as stern, has attached the damning label "prettified." *Giacomo Joyce* shows that the literary critic knew the limitations of the style but also discerned a value at its core:

> Jan Pieters Sweelink. The quaint name of the old Dutch musician makes all beauty seem quaint and far. I hear his variations for the clavichord on an old air: *Youth has an end.* In the vague mist of old sounds a faint point of light appears: the speech of the soul is about to be heard.

The limitations are the distance and faintness of the revelation. The justification is, that the revelation comes: "the speech of the soul."

Written some ten years after the *Chamber Music* songs, *Giacomo Joyce* makes use more explicitly than they of an old-world setting and old-world locutions. Joyce transposes Amalia Popper's home across five centuries: "Wintry air in the castle, gibbeted coats of mail . . ." A servant interrupts the lesson with the announcement of a visitor: "There is one below would speak with your ladyship." On a later occasion Joyce seeks (but in the safe realm of interior dialogue) a rapport with Amalia, and when she apparently trembles before his adult approach he reassures her in a lutanist's phrase: "Nay, be not afraid." Later still he fancies that he has possessed her in a wordless, touchless interpenetration of looks, and accepts that as the most consummate of all possible conquests and resigns the physical Amalia to any lucky later-comer: "Take her now who will!" Listen to these phrases with not a troubadour's but a theatre-goer's sensibility, and you may contend that they are lifted from the dialogue of Victorian melodrama. There was certainly the oddest communication in the Joycean memory-chambers between the refined-and-archaic and the Victorian-and-plush. But it is evident from his castle scenery that he himself dated his language and stance as antique. That "elegant and antique phrase," which he had made as if to abjure in Poem **"XXVII"** of *Chamber Music,* alleging that he knew that the reality of love was different from the troubadour's ideal, he still uttered. It was irrepressible and indispensable.

However, the lyric gentleman who was the soliloquist of *Chamber Music* no longer has matters all to himself in 1913. The Other Joyce interrupts, halloos, heckles, and more and more asserts his counterstrain. Lyric twists into comedy. "Love me, love my umbrella." The two personae compete for the stage. If the graver affects to be alone, the Other cavorts around him and pokes him with bum and truncheon. This is a decisive development. The notebook drives a road towards *Ulysses.*

In *Ulysses* Joyce makes a masterpiece out of the cooperation of his two selves. As the current lore of our mid-twentieth-century tells, the schizophrene who elevates his conflict into art does it not by slaying either of the partners but by bringing them into a relationship where both live and fulfill themselves in a totality that is greater than their sum. The multifarious power of *Ulysses* arises from the integration of the Two Joyces, the coordination of what they both know and their different ways of saying it. The ribald comedian gets his heroic fling, and the lyricist still discourses in a flow of music. The vision opens, clearer, nearer. Tributes have been paid, as they must be, to the comedian as the vision-bidder. Our concern here is with Orpheus and his lute as visionary and instrument of the vision. Of course, the music of the epic is often rich beyond the dainty range of *Chamber Music*: "Yes, bronze from anear, by gold from afar, heard steel from anear, hoofs ring from afar . . ." But when Joyce wishes most precisely to elicit "the speech of the soul," he still uses the simplest lyrical phrase. So as he approaches the culmination of Molly's monologue: "he said I was a flower of the mountain." If we turn to that and look at it in a ruthless mood, we may feel not unfamiliar qualms about the suspension of Joyce's literary censorship. Has he relaxed the control when he should have exerted it sternly? He does not think so. He is working at full stretch here, and if he employs the lyrical method it is because he believes in it. He expects us not to turn and look at the phrase, but to come to it on the tide of continuous reading: to understand the style by going all the way with him through the vicissitudes in which it inheres; and thus to feel it and hear it as he does.

An event in the history of *Chamber Music* connects alike with the occurrence of that lyric phrase at the climax of *Ulysses* and with the whole problem of Joyce's valuation of his lyrical self. During the crisis of 1909 when Joyce fell victim to Cosgrave's slander of Nora and wrote to her in agonized abuse, then feared that he had destroyed his contact with her and that he would never repossess the pleasure and nourishment of her tenderness unless he could undo his outburst, one of his gestures of propitiation was to quote *Chamber Music* to her. And she, astonishingly, took up the volume and read it. He did not pretend that he had written the poems for her. On the contrary he admitted that they were conceived for an imaginary ceremonious lady of a tower: "a girl fashioned into a curious grave beauty by the culture of generations before her." By contrast Nora was, as we can see at this distance, Reality, earthy and sound, a physical wife, a healing force. Yet the poems *were* for Nora, he went on to say, because there was "something in you higher than anything I had put into them." Joyce was sure, and remained sure long after his love had "waxed all too wise," that in Real Woman there springs the point of light or the point of life or a flower, and that Real Woman longs for its recognition and for a man's worship of it. Molly, after she has had her romp with the large Blazes Boylan, still cares for Bloom because he feels for her and for all women with this lyric intuition:

> . . . yes so we are flowers all a womans body yes that was one true thing he said in his life and the sun shines for you today yes that was why I liked him because I saw he understood or felt what a woman is . . .

In 1909 it helped Joyce to expunge his mistake and win Nora back when the poems of *Chamber Music* reminded his wife that he "understood or felt what a woman is." They reminded her not by saying it, but singing it.

The episode may have confirmed to Joyce that the *Chamber Music* poems secrete the light of reality at the core of their idealism, and that song is the most compelling testimony of life, that the lyrical method must never be dropped. It might be enriched, but not dropped.

Wherever Joyce strove, and he strove persistently, to broach the light of reality, he relied on music. We can never go towards that point of light. It will recede if we press forward. It can only grow towards us, and will only come if beckoned, conjured—and can best be conjured by music. Joyce had been impressed, say Mason and Ellmann in their notes to *The Critical Writings,* by the last line in Verlaine's "Art Poétique": *"Et tout le reste est littérature."* It may be so; but he was more impressed by the first line: *"De la musique avant toute chose."* It was his own innate conviction, his own innate practice. We are always impressed to find that we are right to do what we do.

"The speech of the soul" formed in the vague mist of antique music, but the flower of *Ulysses* was Molly's body, not her soul. As the singer and the obscenist coalesced and Joyce's art strengthened, the speech of the soul became the song of the earth. In the last opus, *Finnegans Wake,* the world speaks: its rivers, its thunder. Since the effects of a major book spread in ripples through the ensuing decades, it has naturally followed that the better entertainment of our present time listens for the music of the world. An instance is the scene in Fellini's *La Dolce Vita* in which the tape-recorder, in the elegant room in Rome, plays back the menacing eddies of the cosmic winds.

To revisit *Chamber Music* with that outcome of the opera in mind is to seek the first tape of the speech of the soul which is also the first tape of the world-voice. Joyce recorded it in Poem **"XXXIV."** As he told Geoffrey Molyneux Palmer, the composer who set the song, Poem **"XXXIV"** is dramatically the last of the sequence (**"XXXV"** and **"XXXVI"** are tailpieces). Two forces are registered: the winter that menaces outside the door and forbids rest; the breathing of the sleep of a heart soothed by a poet's gentleness. The melancholy of the cosmic winter drifts through the music, but there is a lulling countermotion, a berceuse, the warmth, the protection of the pleasure of art; and the music involves, however faintly felt, faintly heard, an equilibrium of the two forces, the two rhythms. There are four vocative "O"s in this short poem. They are unnecessary to the meaning, almost unnecessary to the metre, for the poem would be metrically sufficient without them; but they are right for the music. A composer, and a singer, would make something of them. When the music comes to life in us in the days after the reading, they play their part.

The music of Poem **"XXXIV,"** faint but haunting, grows into the winter rhapsody of the last paragraph of "The Dead," with which Joyce begins to realize his orchestral powers. Then the maturation of a quarter of a century goes forward. In **Chamber Music** the paucity of the success, it has been suggested, lies in the paucity of the sense. In the subsequent books the sense gains in body. It engages the intellect in its own right in *Dubliners* and *A Portrait,* perhaps occasionally over-engages it to the neglect of the musical flow. In *Ulysses* there is the most satisfying interplay of sense and sound. But in certain sections of *Ulysses,* and in the whole of *Finnegans Wake* to which they look forward, a curious thing happens. "The sense must be the medium of the sound"; but Joyce plaits layer on layer of sense; and that almost defeats his purpose; not perhaps by his fault, but by our habits, which, however, he might have forseen. We are readers of literature, not listeners to music. We are much, much worse than our ancestors, of whom Ben Jonson bitterly complained that they were beginning to use their eyes and stop their ears. We are eye-folk on the verge of deafness. The glaucomatic Joyce was not. With Shakespeare, Jonson, and Milton he was all inclining ear. We go to work with our eyes on *Finnegans Wake,* as the spelling tempts us to, laboring to analyze the layers of sense into their components. It is salutary to turn repeatedly to the letter in which Joyce tells Miss Weaver that he is "considerably wound up" after proofreading *Anna Livia Plurabelle,* that the "sing-song" fills his addled head, and that till it fades he cannot deal with the news of the day. To be filled with the singsong must be the hope of every devotee of *Finnegans Wake.* We are brought to the right condition whenever we listen to an Irishman reading the work, or anyone reading it with the resources of the tenor voice. These aids failing, we must read it aloud ourselves. Even if we are non-Celts and even if we are crows, the sound will be better than anything the eye alone can afford. Yet though I say this as essential doctrine, I must not make it exclusive doctrine. Since Joyce took the risk of plying his sense closely, he obviously wanted the crisscross to play a part in the total effect; and it is doubtful whether the ear can pick up half the ambiguities that are within the comprehension of the eye. It may be that Joyce

overtaxed the capacity of every reader with so intricate a polyphony of sense and sound. I leave that topic to my wiser colleagues. Assuming *ad interim* what we like to assume of a master, that he is always right, let us justify him by saying that in *Finnegans Wake* the musical love of God and the intellectual love of God and the bodily love of God meet and merge.

One last consideration. Joyce presented himself in **Chamber Music** as a neoclassicist and as a perfectionist who shaped faultless lyrics and assembled them in an impeccable book. Yet the last lyric is ill-chosen if a book of perfect proportions is the objective, and ill-chosen if the objective of the book is consonance. Poem **"XXXVI"** has been praised to the neglect of the preceding thirty-five. It *is* a good poem. But it is not archaic, and it is not chamber music. It works in a style with which Yeats had experimented in "Do you not hear me calling" and "I hear the white horses," a style far from softness or daintiness, a style that bids for the furious energy of the horses of passion, a style that, regardless of all daedalian animadversions on the Celtic Revival, draws on the imagery of the Red Branch and the battlecars. How are we to account for its presence after Poem **"XXXIV"** and that perfect winter ending? We may contrive this reason: that Poems **"XXXV"** and **"XXXVI"** go on to register sharply the hostility of the winter, of the outer elements, within which Joyce had quietened his love to her long sleep. More, it registers the terror within the beauty, that violence in the cosmos, which lady and poet who lean their ear for the lovely sounds of the world will catch in the undersong— catch and lose and never cease to lean for till they have caught it again and noted what the sea murmurs and the thunder says. By this argument we may claim that the final poems issue organically from the volume, though as a disproportionate and fearsome cauda or coda. But we must add another reason. Joyce and his brother, who helped him to arrange the volume, subordinated their sense of perfection to a romantic passion from which neither they nor some of their foremost neoclassical coevals, including T. S. Eliot, were free: the love of the grand curtain. George Moore was, for better or worse, more genuinely neoclassical: he deliberately cultivated the "minor" ending, the dying fall. In this matter Joyce was romantic and Wagnerian. *Dubliners* culminates in "The Dead," extensive beyond any of the preceding stories, resonant beyond any of them, its own end soaring away from Dublin. *A Portrait* is *formally* neoclassical, touched with the sense of the downbeat ending as the narrative cracks into fragments of diary, utterly right to convey approaching departure and the disconnecting of the son, tissue by tissue, from the boyd of home; but *emotionally* it is romantic, fervidly charged with the ritual of self-dedication and intimations of immortality. *Ulysses* is the most famous example in literature of the concentration of every power in the final chapter and the unremitting amplification of the power through the last page and the last word. The final page of *Finnegans Wake* is correspondingly intense, cosmic, Wagnerian. But here, for his last bow, Joyce pulls one new trick from his reserves and exhilaratingly synthesizes his romantic and neoclassical modes: the purple curtain, seeming to descend on a *Liebestod,* suddenly furls back again, and by a dream-transformation everything is where it was at the start, and death is birth and there is no end but resumption. The final page of *Finnegans Wake* does on the largest scale what the lyrics of **Chamber Music** do in miniature, loops back to the first line. A nice example of the consistency and unity of Joyce's art.

Myra Russel (essay date 1981)

SOURCE: "The Elizabethan Connection: The Missing Score of James Joyce's *Chamber Music*," in *James Joyce Quarterly,* Vol. 18, No. 2, Winter, 1981, pp. 133-45.

[*In the following essay which was originally presented at the Seventh International James Joyce Symposium, Russel analyzes the rhythm and structure of* Chamber Music, *and notes its similarity to Elizabethan poetry.*]

James Joyce knew exactly what he was doing in the small volume of poems called **Chamber Music.** He might have called them Elizabethan Songs or simply Lyrics or Airs; he might even have called them A Short or Selected History of English Poetry, or Exercises in Metre or Verse. But then Joyce, even as a young man, was hardly one to provide explanations. So he accepted his brother's choice as the title, which actually does rather well in conveying the overall spirit. The range is not cosmic nor even symphonic. A small concert hall can accommodate singer, instrumentalist, and audience. Do not expect to be guided, hindsight, by *Finnegans Wake* or *Ulysses.* Here is no wild innovation, no journey through detailed particularity to the universal, none of the wordplay or archaeological delights of layered meaning for scholars to dig in. (About the only hint of that later Joyce comes in the portmanteau words: ringaround, lookingglass, poisondart, songconfessed.) Here is a recital—with one performer, a tenor voice, singing his various songs. The tempo is *andante,* the directive *cantabile,* the key a clear and bright G major. It is not enough to read the poems, or even to read them aloud; we must make an effort to hear the missing music.

The most obvious connection comes from the many direct references to music within the poems. Mood and tone are established at once in Poem **"I"**:

> Strings in the earth and air
>   Make music sweet;
> Strings by the river where
>   The willows meet.
>
> There's music along the river
>   For Love wanders there,
> Pale flowers on his mantle,
>   Dark leaves on his hair.
>
> All softly playing,
>   With head to music bent,
> And fingers straying
>   Upon an instrument.

While Pan plays sweet melodies on his pipes, an Elizabethan singer is fingering his lute. We know from his letters that Joyce played with the idea of having a lute made for him so he could "coast the South of England from Falmouth to Margate, singing old English songs" (*Letters I*). The London instrument-maker (who had once made a psaltery for Yeats) wrote back that lutes were difficult to make, difficult to play, and were very expensive. He suggested a harpsichord. Actually, a picture of a harpsichord did appear on the title page of **Chamber Music** when it was published in 1908, so perhaps it is not too fanciful to see this book of songs as a substitute for that tour.

Instruments in the poems include strings, winds, an old piano playing "an air / Sedate and slow and gay," sweet invisible harps, and the bugles of cherubim which herald surrender to Love. The lover's voice is "softer than the dew," he hears the girl "singing a merry air," and "wise choirs of faery / Begin (innumerous!) to be heard." Nature too is alive with music: thrushes call, the wind "is whistling merrily," and the "flowery bells of morn are stirred." Even at autumn when love is ended, the winds weave a "music of sights." Truly "strings in the earth and air" are everywhere.

But the significance of music to Joyce's poems goes beyond references to singers or instruments; it is intrinsic to the poetry itself. In ancient Greece the poem and the music were indivisible. Lyric poetry was not only a union of both, but the identity of the lyricist was so intermingled with the music that by comparison, says Nietzsche, ". . . our modern lyric poetry appears like the statue of a god without a head." To the German philosophers, music was feeling in quintessence, highest and most universal of the arts, dealing with a sphere beyond all phenomena.

The English Renaissance had its own theories, derived from the Greeks, about music and the rhythmic conception of the universe, and about the analogy between celestial order and human affairs. Music to the Elizabethans (and I use that term broadly to cover Tudor and Jacobean), while not always cosmic, had many aspects—all of them beneficial. Musical understanding, taste, and appreciation were expected of the Renaissance gentleman; so was the ability to sight-read and sing. Music contributed to what Sir Thomas Elyot called knowledge of "publicke weal," which in turn contained its own harmony. Music, it was believed, helped to establish harmony in personal character by ordering its contradictory parts into a harmonious relationship. Thus might music stimulate virtuous action and serene contemplation.

The English court set a high value on music. Henry VI composed songs, as did Henry VIII, who also played the lute well, sang at sight, and saw to it that his daughters were taught music at an early age. Queen Elizabeth had a regular establishment of from sixty to seventy wind and string players. Lutanists held the highest rank since they composed their own songs, sang as well as played, and arranged music for consort. The nobility emulated the court and kept a regular staff of instrumentalists and singers to perform and teach members of the family. Many composers earned their living this way, among them Joyce's favorite, John Dowland, whose airs he used to seek out and copy from the Elizabethan songbooks in the National Library in Dublin. (Did Joyce know that Dowland came from Irish stock, his father having come from County Dublin, or that his *First Book of Airs* was published while he was in residence at Trinity College in Dublin, or that he dedicated one of his later songs to "my loving Country-man Mr. John Forster the Younger, Merchant of Dublin in Ireland"?)

Music also affected middle class life: a vast store of airs and folk songs were sung or whistled at various levels of taste and education. Children learned vocal and instrumental music along with reading and writing, and it was believed that playing an instrument increased the skills of the small joints.

Given the importance of music in Elizabethan life and the value attached to it, it is hardly surprising that standards of musical taste were so high. The quality of the music is extraordinary. Anyone who has ever played or listened to the songs of Byrd, Campion, Dowland, or Morley—and the piano cannot approximate the rich quality of the lute—cannot but be struck by the purity and unearthly beauty of that combination of words and music. Poems they are, but not poems simply *set* to music. So commingled are both in their form, their rhythm, their sound and mood that one can only call them pure art.

Both poetry and music placed limitations on each other, and perhaps an understanding of those will help to explain what so many readers have seen in Joyce's lyrics as shortcomings. The conventions of Elizabethan poetry kept the content restricted and unpretentious, which is not to say unsophisticated. Emotions tend to be simple and impersonal; imagery and diction are likely to be obvious and familiar, and not necessarily original. The same is true of most of the poems in **Chamber Music,** and Joyce's brother tells us [in *My Brother's Keeper,* 1958] that one of the reasons for that title was that it "seemed suitable to the passionless love themes and studious grace of the songs." Elizabethan love lyrics, bound by strict conventions, were not exactly passionate either; lovers were ardent or shrinking, yielding or unkind, faithful or not. Also, because songs were meant to be sung, i.e., performed for others, emotions had to be diffused and generalized, made suitable for a public hearing. Treatment of love songs might be grave, light, or mock-serious, all of which are compatible with music. Another popular convention, *carpe diem,* with its sense of urgency, "Stay time awhile thy flying" or love me *now,* also lent itself to musical treatment. Occasionally the theme of a song might be quasi-philosophical, such as "Down down proud mind" or Campion's "What if a day or a month or a year." John Donne, who could and did write in the traditional lyric pattern, broke away to find a more personalized voice for his unusual conceits and his treatment of love as individual. It was he, according to one historian, who

initiated the divergence of music and poetry which widened as the seventeenth century advanced. Involved conceits and a subtle play of wit could not be reproduced musically, and the poets understood this.

Of course music imposed certain restrictions on the poet. Practical considerations, such as the divided attention of the listener, the fact that the words were harder to hear, a phrase and its significance might easily be missed, and there was little time to ponder an idea without missing the next one, had to be remembered. Some poets worked from the music, setting rhythm and line to the musical phrase. Some wrote with the music in mind; knowing the rules, they could compose *for* the music. James I pointed out that the poet must avoid breaking a word when the music requires a pause, and must be sure that the end of a phrase fall on a syllable long enough to bear a cadence. Another way in which music imposed its form involved repetition. Music requires and can absorb more repetition than poetry, so the melody was repeated in stanza form. This required that the poet keep the meter and general word pattern of subsequent stanzas parallel to the first verse, since the music would be the same. Thus a caesura or an enjambement, with its corresponding musical phrase, is usually repeated in all stanzas. Joyce follows the spirit, if not the letter of this rule. In Poem "VII" the many enjambed lines add to the light and musical quality of the poem, and the pattern is consistent in all three verses. But the middle-of-the-line pauses do not occur in the first stanza, but only in the second and third, which might have created a problem for an Elizabethan musician.

> My love is in a light attire
>   Among the appletrees
> Where the gay winds do most desire
>   To run in companies.
>
> There, where the gay winds stay to woo
>   The young leaves as they pass,
> My love goes slowly, bending to
>   Her shadow on the grass;
>
> And where the sky's a pale blue cup
>   Over the laughing land,
> My love goes lightly, holding up
>   Her dress with dainty hand.

Poem "XXVIII" is similar in its irregular rhythm:

> Gentle lady, do not sing
>   Sad songs about the end of love;
> Lay aside sadness and sing
>   How love that passes is enough.
>
> Sing about the long deep sleep
>   Of lovers that are dead and how
> In the grave all love shall sleep:
>   Love is aweary now.

Note that the last poem has four stresses to each line (except the last, which is irregular), while the first poem had an alternating 4/3 pattern. These are the most frequent rhythms in Elizabethan lyrics. The basic structure for a stanza was four measured lines with four phrases of music; usually each note had a syllable set to it. Shakespeare's songs had an extra dimension, set as they were amid the unrhymed iambic pentameters of the comedies. Airs such as "It was a lover and his lass" (*As You Like It* V iii), or "When that I was and a little tiny Boy" (*Twelfth Night* V i), or

> Sigh no more Ladies, sigh no more,
> Men were deceivers ever,
> One foote in Sea, and one on shore,
> To one thing constant never
> (*Much Ado about Nothing* II iii),

are among the most perfectly constructed, the most musical, and the most exquisitely beautiful of all the lyrics of the period.

Of the thirty-six poems in **Chamber Music,** thirteen are in the four-stress pattern. Five have an alternating 4/3 meter. Several others employ the four-stress with a variation: the last line of each stanza or of the poem or the finishing couplet has three stresses, or sometimes only two. But this too is standard practice; the short last line was favored by one of the earliest Renaissance poets, Thomas Wyatt.

The similarity between the **Chamber Music** poems and the short lyrics of the Elizabethans is most apparent in the rhyme schemes. One of the most widely used—*ababcc / dedeff*—Joyce follows in nine of his poems. Whereas Wyatt often varies his (in "Blame not my lute," for example) by using the *b* rhyme again in the second stanza, and Campion sometimes keeps the same *c* rhyme in every stanza, Joyce adheres strictly to the pattern. Another traditional rhyme scheme—*abab / cdcd*—occurs in ten of Joyce's poems. Rhyme in the second and fourth line—*abcb / defe*—is another common form and we find this in nine poems. Here it is Joyce who uses variations; an *a, b,* or *c* rhyme may turn up in the third or fourth stanza. This occurs most frequently with the sound *air* which quite fittingly runs as a motif through the first twenty-five poems, appearing twenty-four times as an end rhyme. There is *air* which surrounds the earth, the *air* in "Winds of May," and "with many a pretty *air,*" meaning demeanor—all in a book of *airs.*

Whether Joyce was testing his own talents and saw the Elizabethans as a challenge, or whether he chose to compose airs because music and poetry were a vital part of his own life—it hardly matters. The Elizabethans intrigued him.

—Myra Russel

Rhyme, of course, strikes the ear and is another of the obviously musical aspects of poetry. Most Elizabethan songs are in rhyme, although there were critics who deplored it. All regarded with horror the kind of obtrusive alliteration or rhyme which concealed an unbalanced or unrhythmical structure. Thomas Campion, who was both poet and musician, argues in his *Observations in the Art of English Poesie* that rhyme is often superfluous to lines which "close of themselves . . . perfectly" or else it covers up poor workmanship. He has this to say about Quatorzens, the French sonnet form:

> . . . the poet handles his subject as tyrannically as Procrustes the thiefe his prisoners, whom, when he had taken, he used to cast upon a bed, which if they were too short to fill, he would stretch them longer, if too long, he would cut them shorter.

Poetry to Campion was essentially audible, and the ear was both a "rational sence and a chiefe judge of proportion." His attack on rhyme notwithstanding, many of his finest poems are in rhyme; the workmanship, as well as the balance between music and poetry, is faultless.

So far the rhyme scheme has been accounted for in only twenty-eight of Joyce's poems. In the remaining ones, some have only minor irregularities. Poem I, for example, differs in its alternating rhyme only in the second verse where Joyce repeats his *a* rhyme—air—unexpectedly in the second and fourth lines as "there" and "hair," leaving the other two lines unrhymed with "river" and "mantle." Poems **"III"** and **"X"** both have clear patterns: the first having three stanzas of five lines with an *abbab* rhyme, and the other with two stanzas of eight lines with *abbc / addc*—although there seems to be no counterpart among the Elizabethans. The five-line alternating rhyme of Poem **"VI"** is uncommon, though there is one in Dowland's *2nd Book of Airs.* Poem **"IX"** becomes regular if we count "Welladay! Welladay! / For the winds of May" as one line, thus giving the stanza eight lines with every two rhyming. That has counterparts in Campion and Robert Jones. "Lightly come or lightly go," Poem **"XXV,"** is a little unusual because once again Joyce repeats his *a* rhyme (not "air" this time) in the second stanza.

The poem which has the strangest rhyme scheme, with no parallel, is **"XIV,"** the lovely one with echoes from the *Song of Solomon:*

> My dove, my beautiful one,
> Arise, arise!
> The nightdew lies
> Upon my lips and eyes.

In his letter to Palmer, the Irish musician who was setting some of the lyrics to music, Joyce wrote that this poem *was central,* and after it, all movement was downward (*Letters I*). The rhyme scheme here is *abbb,* an unusual beginning. The second stanza starts off with a new rhyme, *c,* but then goes back to *bba.*

The odorous winds are weaving
  A music of sighs:
   Arise, arise.
My dove, my beautiful one!

Next comes *deef,* and after that, the totally irregular *bfeb*:

I wait by the cedar tree,
  My sister, my love.
   White breast of the dove,
My breast shall be your bed.

The pale dew lies
  Like a veil on my head.
   My fair one, my fair dove,
Arise, arise!

The last verse jumbles any possibility of a pattern into *Chamber Music*'s only hint of chaos. However, from a musical standpoint none of this matters because the predominance of that *b* rhyme—arise, lies, eyes, sighs—gives the song its theme and continuity. Perhaps there is a connection, nevertheless, between centrality and disparity; perhaps this is a reminder that Joyce is twentieth-century and not, at the core, at one with his idealized neo-Elizabethan world. On the other hand, perhaps nowhere is Joyce more Elizabethan than in his irregularities.

If you add to the twenty-eight poems with a regular rhyme scheme another seven which are irregular, the total is not thirty-six. That is because there is no way to fit the last poem, **"XXXVI,"** into a structure even remotely like the Elizabethan. With an alternating meter of five and six stresses to a line, the rhythm is irregular and difficult. The long lines and the wild, despairing mood lessen the importance of the rhyme. No lute could provide music for this, only the rising excitement of percussion instruments, with perhaps a lone oboe. Many critics who dismissed most of the poems in *Chamber Music* as too light or too simple or too derivative have pronounced **"XXXVI,"** which creates a world of nightmare and desolation, one of the few worthy of being called Joycean. Of course Joyce himself said that the true end was "Sleep now," **"XXXIV,"** and that the last two poems were "tailpieces." Herbert Howarth, in his excellent and balanced essay "*Chamber Music* and Its Place in the Joyce Canon," says that while the last two can be seen as an organic outgrowth of winter and the end of love, as a "disproportionate and fearsome . . . coda," they might also be explained by Joyce's love of the final purple curtain (shared by his brother who helped to arrange the order of poems). Very few composers have set "I hear an army" to music. That is not to say that it is unmusical, but it is most certainly out of tune with the other poems in this volume.

If, as Pater has said, "All art constantly aspires towards the condition of music," then more must be accounted for than just rhythm, meter, and rhyme. Even if we add repetition and variation, which are common to both music and poetry, we have not reached the essence of what makes poetry musical. Both areas have their respective form and structure, rules, conventions and devices—yet something elusive at the core resists analysis. Since the time of the Elizabethans, very few poets or musicians or literary critics have attempted to unravel the perplexities. Northrop Frye is one of the few who has confronted the issue, particularly in his introduction to a collection of essays called *Sound and Poetry.*

> By "musical" I mean a quality in literature denoting a substantial analogy to, and in many cases an actual influence from, the art of music. . . . this is not what the word ordinarily means to the literary critic. To him it means "sounding nice.". . . The term musical as ordinarily used is a value term meaning that the poet has produced a pleasant variety of vowel sounds and has managed to avoid the more unpronounceable clusters of consonants that abound in modern English.

Such phrases as "smooth musical flow" or "harsh unmusical diction" indicate, according to Frye, a sentimental use of the word musical. "Harmony in its non-musical sense means a stable and permanent relationship," and of course in that sense music only achieves harmony at the very end, with the resolution into the final tonic chord. Music then is actually a series of discords, and a musical discord is defined by Frye as, "not an unpleasant sound; it is a sound which throws the ear forward to the next beat; it is a sign of musical energy, not of musical incompetence."

"A dreamy sensuous flow of sound" and "a careful balancing of vowels and consonants," according to this theory, would indicate an unmusical poet. "Sharp accents, crabbed and obscure language, and long, lumbering polysyllables" are more likely to have an affinity with the tension and driving impetus of music.

Does this help to determine what is musical in poetry? If these standards are applied to Joyce's lyrics, only Poem **"XXXVI"** would emerge as musical.

I hear an army charging upon the land,
  And the thunder of horses plunging, foam about
   their knees:
Arrogant, in black armor, behind them stand,
  Disdaining the reins, with fluttering whips, the
   charioteers.

The phrases drive on beyond their lines, throwing the ear forward with the restless energy of discord. The dominating *l*'s of the second stanza—battle-name, whirling laughter, cleave the gloom, blinding flame, clanging, clanging upon the heart as an anvil—certainly create tension.

But then how shall we listen to **"XXXV"** with its rush of run-ons and its long sad rhymes: moan, alone, monotone? This too is music, according to some closer to Verlaine. However, it is certainly not alien to the Elizabethans either. Here is an excerpt from "Love those beams" in Dowland's *Book of Airs*:

I'll go to the woods
  And alone
    Make my moan,
     O cruel!
For I am deceived
  And bereaved
    Of my life,
     My jewel.

Frye's theory may illuminate aspects of modern poetry or "I hear an army," but it cannot explain the musical richness of the Elizabethans or the thirty-five poems of *Chamber Music.*

Listen to the triplets in Poem **"XXXIV"**:

Sleep now, O sleep now,
  O you unquiet heart!
A voice crying 'Sleep now'
  Is heard in my heart.

The voice of the winter
  Is heard at the door.
O sleep for the winter
  Is crying 'Sleep no more.'

My kiss will give peace now
  And quiet to your heart—
Sleep on in peace now,
  O you unquiet heart!

The enjambed lines create a rhythmic flow; the words, even the consonants, slide easily and gracefully over the tongue and ear. The motifs of the first stanza are repeated in subsequent ones. *Sleep* is heard three times in the first, twice in the second, once in the last. The repetition is doubly effective because of the lulling quality of the word itself. "A voice crying 'Sleep now' / Is heard in my heart" becomes "The voice of the winter / Is heard at the door." Between the first and the last "O you unquiet heart" comes "My kiss will give peace now / And quiet to your heart." Even the fact that all the rhymes except one are identical contributes to the musical effect.

Or take the frequently set to music Poem **"V"**:

Lean out of the window,
  Goldenhair,
I heard you singing
  A merry air.

My book is closed,
  I read no more,
Watching the fire dance
  On the floor.

I have left my book,
  I have left my room,
For I heard you singing
  Through the gloom.

Singing and singing

A merry air,
Lean out of the window,
  Goldenhair.

Music would have to reflect the simplicity of the theme: a young man attracted away from his books to the brightness and lilt of a young woman's song. It would have to capture the lightness of "Goldenhair" and "A merry air." Fortunately the rhythm is not so simple or the poem could become doggerel, the dangers of which both Joyce and the Elizabethans were well aware. Remove the "dance" or "have" from stanzas two or three and the result is singsong. But it is the opening line which provides the essential rhythmic irregularity in each stanza. The falling meter of the last verse, "Singing and singing," is straight-forward. The rising meters of "My book is closed" and "I have left my book" with one up-beat and then two, are variations which create no problems. But how are we to scan the all-important line which opens the poem? Is it "*Lean* out of the *win*dow, Goldenhair" or "Lean *out* of the *win*dow, Goldenhair," which, with its triplets, is more regular and more in harmony (using the literary meaning) with the rest of the poem. Musically, the first is preferable. *Lean,* like the verb *bend* which Joyce was also fond of, has strong and active possibilities; its sound is rich and lingers over the rest of the line like an overtone. But it does throw the rhythm off, leaving three unaccented syllables before the next stress, somewhat in the manner of Hopkins' sprung rhythm. The ambiguities of that first line could inspire interesting music. Otherwise this is one of the lesser poems in the collection, although hardly what Anthony Burgess called [in his *ReJoyce,* 1965] "one of the most atrocious lyrics ever penned by a great writer." It is graceful and unpretentious.

Joyce's letters make it clear that he not only wanted the poems set to music, but meant them to be. He wrote to Palmer, who had already set eight of them:

> I hope you may set all of *Chamber Music* in time. This was indeed partly my idea in writing it. The book is in fact a suite of songs and if I were a musician I suppose I should have set them to music myself.

The Joyce also had his own ideas about what the music should be like is suggested by his remark to the composer that while the music was "very elegant," still "The second three songs please me better than the first five." Surprisingly enough, the three poems which were Joyce's own favorites, **"Donneycarney," "At that hour,"** and **"Gentle Lady" ("XXXI," "III," "XXVIII")**, have received very little musical treatment since Palmer. Poem **"III,"** which has some challenging rhythms and phrases, seems only to have been set to music by one composer, Hugo Kauder. The most popular choices have been **"I," "V,"** and **"XXXIV,"** with **"X"** and **"XVI"** close behind. Ten poems have not been set to music at all.

Most critics acknowledge that *Chamber Music* is both musical and Elizabethan. Once that is said they often go on to indicate disappointment: however delicate or lyric, the poems are "slight," or as Morton Zabel put it in 1930 in *Poetry*: ". . . his lyrics are the marginal fragments of his art, minor in theme and too often, for all their precise and orderly felicities, undecided." The major intent of this paper is to open up new ways of looking and judging. To be musical and Elizabethan is a very remarkable achievement. And if some of the poems fall short, it is hardly surprising when we consider how high the standards were.

[In *The Dying Gladiators,* 1961] Horace Gregory once said that when they came to Joyce's lyrics, his critics were tone-deaf. They belonged to a generation who "accepted the flaws of Pound, Eliot, and Auden as standards of excellence in writing verse and grew to admire flat lines and tone-deaf phrasing. Joyce's gift was nine-tenths auditory. . . ." It is not enough to say that Joyce's poems are indeed musical and do contain echoes of Elizabethan airs—and then dismiss them. We have only heard what Nietzsche called "the statue of a god without a head." How can we hear that exquisite blending, that felicitous balance, that unique and marvelous coherence which Campion called "Words and Music Lovingly Coupled" when we are attuned instead to the divergence and complete separation of the two arts, a divergence which began in the very century when the lyric was at its peak of perfection.

I started out by saying that Joyce knew precisely what he was doing in *Chamber Music.* Whether he was testing his own talents and saw the Elizabethans as a challenge, or whether he chose to compose airs because music and poetry were a vital part of his own life—it hardly matters. The Elizabethans intrigued and enticed him. He liked their poems; he loved their songs. It was, after all, the Golden Age, the Renaissance of English music and poetry. The strong connecting links suggest that these are the lyrics with which Joyce's poems should be compared, not those of his own day. And of course ultimately it is the music which must establish the clear and luminous connection. Until then, *Chamber Music,* like the statue, is missing a vital element.

Robert Boyle, S. J. (essay date 1982)

SOURCE: "The Woman Hidden in James Joyce's *Chamber Music,*" in *Women in Joyce,* edited by Suzette Henke and Elaine Unkeless, University of Illinois Press, pp. 3-30.

[*In the following essay, Boyle discusses the feminine imagery in* Chamber Music.]

Joyce developed his suite of songs in an effort to create in words, like Stephen Dedalus forming his Mercedes, the "unsubstantial image which his soul so constantly beheld." The youthful Joyce's interest, like that of young Stephen, focused primarily on his own soul, and only secondarily on that fragile and fragmented image which that not-so-constant soul sought to bring into unity. Thus

the woman who emerges from Joyce's arrangement of his songs reveals in many ways her varied sources and the adolescent narcissism, insecurity, and ineptitude of her creator. Yet it is the young writer's artistic power that reveals this evanescent but constantly intriguing woman who, like a rainbow on the mist, shimmers with a mysterious radiance and power.

As with Stephen's "green rose," Joyce's ideal woman had not yet found her embodiment outside his imagination. This ideal would be fulfilled only in Nora Barnacle, to whom Joyce wrote in August, 1909: "You were not in a sense the girl for whom I had dreamed and written the verses you find now so enchanting. She was perhaps (as I saw her in my imagination) a girl fashioned into a curious grave beauty by the culture of generations before her . . ." Joyce, in the smithy of his soul, "fashioned" this woman in delicate Elizabethan songs, and over some years evolved an arrangement of those songs in a two-part sequence building to and falling from the consummation of an ideal first love. Essential for retrieving the woman of *Chamber Music* is to establish Joyce's ordering of the songs—a difficult task, for when *Chamber Music* was published in 1907, the sequence which Joyce finally adopted (not without reservation) was arranged not by Joyce but by his brother Stanislaus.

In February, 1903, Joyce wrote to his brother about *Chamber Music*: "Dear Stannie, I send you two poems. The first one is for the second part . . .". The poems were **"I hear an army"** (**"XXXVI"**) and **"When the shy star"** (**"IV"**). [In *Selected Letters of James Joyce,* editor Richard] Ellmann notes: ". . . Joyce planned to divide his poems into two parts, the first being relatively simple and innocent, the second more complicated and experienced. The second group would commemorate his departure from Dublin . . .". Ellmann's adjectives may hint at some echo of Blake's songs of innocence and of experience, and perhaps at a foreshadowing of the early simplicity and later complications of a love affair, as in Elizabethan sonnet sequences like Sidney's and Shakespeare's. Ellmann's suggestion that the second "group" would, like the ending of *Portrait,* commemorate Joyce's departure from Dublin does seem to accord with an aspect of "I hear an army"; however, as a description of Joyce's plan for his sequence, the suggestion appears to be too restrictively autobiographical. As I see Joyce's own arrangement of his poems (different from the arrangement Stanislaus constructed for the long-delayed publication), it aims at building on Joyce's own experience a universal expression of youthful human love in all times and places. I suspect that from the beginning of his planning Joyce worked for a motion upward to the poem of consummation, **"My dove, my beautiful one"** (**"XIV"**), and downward gradually through the subsidence of passion, external difficulties, ultimate disillusion, and finally, as in the two poems he calls "tailpieces" in the published version, an Arnoldian listening to the noise of embattled waters.

The earliest manuscript of the suite, now owned by James Gilvarry, was sold by Sylvia Beach in 1935. Twenty-seven of the thirty-three poems are, like those Gogarty saw in Joyce's hand in 1903, beautifully written in the center of large sheets, and Litz describes the arrangement: "In the Gilvarry sequence, **"I"** and **"III"** are the opening poems, **"XXXIV"** is the close, and **"XIV"** stands squarely in the middle, flanked by thirteen poems on either side. This perfect symmetry of musical and emotional effects was spoiled slightly as Joyce added later poems, until finally in the rearrangement for the 1907 edition it was almost entirely obscured."

Of the ordering of the poems in the 1905 Yale MS, "*Chamber Music* (a suite of thirty-four songs for lovers) by James Joyce, Via S. Nicolo, Trieste, 1905," Litz says, "This obviously represents a careful and long-considered plan." The climactic Poem **"XIV"** still stands as squarely as it can in the middle, No. 17 of the thirty-four poems. And this is Joyce's final sequence before Stanislaus rearranged the poems for publication.

From the beginning Joyce took his ordering seriously. In 1902, he had shown the poems to Lady Gregory, and his concern for the form of the whole suite appears in her comment: "I think, from what you said, that you would not like to publish those poems till the sequence is complete . . .". She was less frank than Yeats was a month or so later, when he commented on a poem Joyce had sent him. It was surely Joyce's original arrangement of his poems that Yeats had seen and that he found helpful to interpret the poem "in its place with the others": "Perhaps I will make you angry when I say that it is the poetry of a young man, of a young man who is practicing his instrument, taking pleasure in the mere handling of the stops. It went very nicely in its place with the others, getting a certain richness from the general impression of all taken together and from your own beautiful reading." It is an interesting possibility that Yeats here by his pointed repetition laid in Joyce's imagination a foundation for the shift from *Stephen Hero* as a title to the final title of *A Portrait of the Artist as a Young Man.* Evidence that Joyce was impressed by Yeats's words seems to me apparent in a letter to Stanislaus written more than four years after he had read Yeats's judgment: "By the same post I received from Elkin Mathews the proofs of *Chamber Music.* It is a slim book and on the frontispiece is an open pianner! Shall I send you the proofs to correct. I don't know whether the order is correct. I don't like the book but wish it were published and be damned to it. However, it is a young man's book. I felt like that. It is not a book of love-verses at all, I perceive." But the version that had gone to Mathews was not the arrangement Joyce had submitted to so many publishers for those exhausting years. On October 9, 1906, Joyce wrote to Stanislaus about Arthur Symons's advice to submit his poems to Mathews, and for some reason—I suspect a complex of reasons—agreed to change his own arrangement for one proposed by Stanislaus. Joyce sounds tired and discouraged—"Tell me what arrangement you propose for the verses. I will follow it perfunctorily as I take very little interest in the publication of the verses"—and perhaps felt that a change in his text might bring luck. If one could probe Joyce's psychological depths, one might perceive some perverse revenge on his often-rejected

poems, some resentment at Yeats's patronizing but solidly based counsel, or some strange search for a co-author to share responsibility, like Joyce's later weird effort to recruit James Stephens to finish *Finnegans Wake.* There is no way to discover with rational certainty what motivations operated in Joyce's subconscious. He did accept Stanislaus's arrangement, in any case, and although that arrangement damages the "story line" of Joyce's own sequence, it offers decided advantages. In grouping the songs according to the music of the verse, and thus the mood, Stanislaus stressed the element Joyce valued most. And if a singer were to present the songs in an evening's entertainment, the arrangement by mood would be practical and effective.

But Joyce was certainly not comfortable with the book. If Stanislaus's recollection of Joyce's wanting to cancel the publication is accurate (Stanislaus had an Irish imagination), it would be added evidence that Joyce much disliked something about the book he had so vigorously sought to publish for four years. Since Joyce often showed great affection for individual poems, since he read them to friends and critics with full confidence, and since he spoke in *Finnegans Wake* with apparent satisfaction of "all this chambermade music," I suspect that the repulsive feature may have been the arrangement that he had "perfunctorily" agreed to.

Some evidence for my suspicion seems to emerge from Joyce's description of his sequence in a letter to G. Molyneux Palmer on July 19, 1909: "The book is in fact a suite of songs and if I were a musician I suppose I should have set them to music myself. The central song is **"XIV"** after which the movement is all downwards until **"XXXIV"** which is vitally the end of the book. **"XXXV"** and **"XXXVI"** are tailpieces just as **"I"** and **"III"** are preludes." Joyce still conceives of the movement rising to **"XIV"** and being "all downwards" to **"XXXIV,"** where he sees the end of something vital—I take it the end of the love affair. That description fits Joyce's arrangement to perfection, but it does not fit the published arrangement. For example, between **"XI"** (Joyce's 16), which bids adieu to virginity, and **"XIV"** (Joyce's 17), where virginity gives place to consummation, Stanislaus places **"XII"** (Joyce's 26), which weeps for the loss of girlhood. The formal tone of **"XII"** does fit well with the other poems with which it is grouped, but its motion is distinctly downward, as the poet rejects the counsel of remorse which the Capuchin moon gives to the poet's repenting lover. Again, Stanislaus's arrangement inserts, between two poems of parting (**"XXX"** and **"XXXII,"** 32 and 31 in Joyce's arrangement), a poem celebrating a uniting kiss (**"XXXI,"** 23 in Joyce's arrangement), a rude dislocation of the downward motion.

"XVII," which speaks of the loss of a male friend because of the lady, was number 10 in Joyce's arrangement and thus appeared before the poem Joyce called "central" (his 17, **"XIV"**). In Stanislaus's rearrangement, however, **"XVII"** is placed after the original central song. Ellmann opines that Joyce retained this poem to help the "changed mood" of the later poems; but Joyce placed it among the early poems in his series, and in any case it seems to me that the poem was important to Joyce because it carries a faint echo of Shakespeare's alienation from his male friend (*Finnegans Wake* certainly stresses in Wildean tonality the shadowy presence of Mr. W H). If my opinion is correct, then such reference to the desertion of the male friend should belong to the upward movement, where Joyce originally put it, before the poet and his lady achieve consummation and a temporary exclusive union. The poem which follows in both arrangements ("**XVIII**" and 11) depicts the lady comforting the poet sorrowing over the loss of his friend.

But there is no certitude to be had here. Joyce did accept and publish Stanislaus's arrangement, and in effect repudiated his own previous arrangement, never published. Why not then let the matter rest there? Because, as I have experienced it, a close look at Joyce's arrangement reveals new things about the poems, and furnishes them with the kind of universal human context that Joyce found important in his works, as in his arrangement of *Dubliners* according to the development of human experience through childhood, adolescence, and maturity.

In Joyce's original conception, as I now see it, the relationship of the lovers (which begins with the appearance of the girl in 4 ["**II**"]) gradually develops from the first hesitant approach up to the act of consummation (celebrated with religious tone in 17 ["**XIV**"]) and declines (with a growing intellectualizing about the nature of love and a diminishing of passion) to the death of love in 34 ["**XXXIV**"]. In an effort to reconstruct Joyce's conception, I offer the following outline of the original structure, with my own notion of each poem's theme. I will attempt to justify questionable points in my fuller discussion of the individual poems:

Ascent of the Suite

Preludes—the poet speaking to himself.

1 [XXI]—The lonely poet defies the world.

2 [I]—The poet makes music by himself, sweet but funereal.

3 [III]—The lonely poet hears a prelude to human love.

Suite Proper—The lovers' relationship begins.

4 [II]—The lonely girl plays the piano at evening.

5 [IV]—In the evening the poet comes to her gate, singing.

6 [V]—His song: I leave my books, my loneliness, to see and hear you.

7 [VIII]—She brings light and love to the richly appareled spring wood.

8 [VII]—"My love" is now fully objectified in the light, graceful girl.

9 [IX]—He longs for the girl.

10 [XVII]—He has deserted his friend, and suffers.

11 [XVIII]—He seeks his comfort in her.

12 [VI]—Like the Bridegroom in the "Song of Solomon," he longs for peace in her arms, in her love.

13 [X]—Now a new lover's song, livelier than 6 [V].

14 [XX]—He longs for them to lie together in the woods (and in a grave).

15 [XIII]—He sends the wind as herald to the physical consummation of their marriage of souls.

16 [XI]—He urges the virgin to loosen her hair.

Zenith of the Suite (the noon, the summer)

17 [XIV]—His Song of Songs!

Decline of the Suite

18 [XIX]—He consoles the sad girl, shamed by unnatural dogmas.

19 [XV]—He himself hears nature's sighs and the wisdom of accepting mortality.

20 [XXIII]—He expresses his happiness, like the unweeping birds (but, like Shelley with his skylark, he is, unfortunately, *more* wise than they).

21 [XXIV]—Her negligence begins to justify his wisdom.

22 [XVI]—The lover wants to seek Love in a cool valley, where those wise choirs of birds sing (and Love may visit, as he did in the past).

23 [XXXI]—She kisses him (but overhead a bat flies).

24 [XXII]—He is allured to prison, to sleep (to death).

25 [XXVI]—She experiences the fear that only a poet can express.

26 [XII]—She has been hoodwinked into accepting the false doctrine of everlasting love, and he counsels her to be satisfied with the passing but truthful living light in her eyes.

27 [XXVII]—In his "wisdom," he suggests the true source of her fear, her own animal nature (maybe also some mysterious malice).

28 [XXVIII]—He counsels acceptance of human reality.

29 [XXV]—He more desperately calls for laughter and song.

30 [XXIX]—He complains that she is ruining their garden.

31 [XXXII]—As they prepare to part, he mounts his wise pulpit once more.

32 [XXX]—He recalls the whole course of their love.

33 [XXXIII]—Another lover's song (maybe to himself, as in the preludes): winter ends us.

34 [XXXIV]—Final lover's song: accept the sleep (which may be the "Out, out brief candle" of Macbeth).

([XXXV] and [XXXVI]—Never in Joyce's arrangement of poems, he called these "tailpieces," and they are not part of the "upward-downward" movement of the other verses.)

Joyce's plot is simple enough, but the complexities within it offer many insights into his youthful notions of love, of art, and of woman. A glance at some of the points of interest in each poem might clarify Joyce's conceptions.

In the three preludial poems, the lonely poet addresses himself. In 1 ["XXI"], the problem, like the one which emerges occasionally in Shakespeare's sonnets, is to determine whether "his love" is subjective or objective. I incline to suppose that if the speaker really is unconsortable, then the only one he can possibly consort with is himself. In that case, "his love" is the love inside him. It is possible, no doubt, to find here what Joyce does suggest elsewhere, that he and his love become "one flesh," and then are in a position to face enemies as one being. But I find that difficult to merge with the lonely stag image which I see here, so I prefer to see this speaker "companioned" (that is, literally, "breaking bread," like a lonely Christ) with himself.

On Curran's autograph copy of the poem, given to him some months after Joyce had met Nora, the dedication "To Nora" is written, with the date September 30, 1904. But while the poem found a completion in Nora, more probably, according to the evidence I can now find, the song started out like the others, expressing the lonely "desire of my youth." (Joyce's reference to "my verses" seems to be inclusive of all). With this supposition, there is no difficulty in understanding the speaker's having found no soul to fellow his, and the inclusive nature of the stag image, so stressed in "The Holy Office," remains intact. Further, with this reading, the poem starts off the suite admirably, since the poet's desperate need for true companionship prepares the way for what follows.

Poem 2 ["I"] brings in "sweet" and "soft" music (the adjectives will be repeated *ad nauseam*), and the artist's exilic tendencies appear in the bent Narcissistic head. In 3 ["III"] that head assumes a more outgoing angle, look-

ing up, longing for light and the dying fall of more "soft sweet music." The religious wind, apparently, is antiphonally causing those invisible harps to sigh for Love. The need for a soft, sweet girl is established.

Poem 4 ["II"] brings in the girl. The body of the suite gets under way with the girl playing an actual piano, not the fancied harp (or real penis, if Tindall's view has force) that the anemic love of 2 ["I"] is fingering. In a dim but lovely natural setting, she too bends her head, shyly thinking (surely of the lover she longs for) as her hands wander willfully over the keys. The trees of the avenue, lining the "way" which leads to the girl, are lighted by lamps similar to those ("like illumined pearls") which set the scene for "Two Gallants"—a grim undertone. The twilight, starting out amethyst, has at the end moved down to darker blue, approaching that violet which gives a bottom limit to the rainbow and merges with night (and which, in my imagination at least, will have a share in "violer d'amores" on the first page of *Finnegans Wake*). The girl is the central light in all this gathering dusk ("gathering" is the climactic word in 33 ["XXXIII"]).

The shy girl melts into the shy star of 5 ["IV"], which draws and guides the poet to the girl's garden. [John Henry Cardinal] Newman's ". . . but like the morning star, which is thy emblem, bright and musical" is twice quoted in *Portrait*, the image haunting Stephen's imagination. Mary as the morning star and as closely related to the Star of Bethlehem was even more familiar to Catholic imaginations (used to dwelling daily from earliest childhood, as Stephen demonstrates, upon the titles in her litany) than were the blessings of Guinness. To this young poet, who had probably, like Stephen, vowed not too long before he wrote this poem to be a knightly votary of his Lady Mary, the maidenly shy evening star in Song 5 ["IV"], like Mercedes, the lady of mercy, would surround his beloved too with the rhetorical aura reflected from Newman's undulating prose.

This modest star of ***Chamber Music*** receives expansion through *Dubliners* into *Finnegans Wake*. Its potentialities as a Star of Bethlehem, drawing the Magi to that manger which had become the center of creation (as Gabriel in "The Dead" is drawn westward, and as the Evangelists with their Ass gather, in the Watches of Shaun, at the marital bed where Holy Shaun gleams forth), can be more readily perceived in this suite of poems when one reaches the climactic biblical force of 17 ["XIV"]. Its epiphanic role stems from the kind of emotion Joyce expressed after his visit to Nora's former room in Finn's Hotel. This was in the Advent season of 1909, leading to the season of Epiphany celebrated in "The Dead," and Joyce's feeling and words to Nora foreshadow those of Gabriel in the more elegant hotel where he and Gretta spent the night:

> Yes, I too have felt at moments the burning in my soul of that pure and sacred fire which burns for ever on the altar of my love's heart. I could have knelt by that little bed and abandoned myself to a flood of tears. The tears were besieging my eyes as I stood looking at it. I could

have knelt and prayed there as the three kings from the East knelt and prayed before the manger in which Jesus lay. They had travelled over deserts and seas and brought their gifts and wisdom and royal trains to kneel before a little newborn child and I had brought my errors and follies and sins and wondering and longing to lay them at the little bed in which a young girl had dreamed of me. . . . I leave for Cork tomorrow morning but I would prefer to be going westward. . . .

A similar sacred bed in the Watches of Shaun is the focus of "blue-blacksliding constellations" and the scene of "How culious an epiphany!"

The solitary, young wise man of this poem (his references to his "wisdom" weigh down the second, declining half of this suite of songs), sings as a visitant drawn from afar. And she, bent in revery like the Madonna who pondered marvelous things in her heart, would surely now look up as at the visit of a seraph.

His song follows in 6 ["V"]. "I have left . . . I have left" probably echoes the leaving of father and mother to cleave to a wife. He leaves the book and the possibly Rosicrucean and alchemical fire to plunge into the gloom which is then pierced by her song. The merry air, a contrast to his lonely, sad studies, brings him, longing for a sight of her, to her window.

In 7 ["VIII"] he revels in the sight of her in the green wood. Her light and love make the whole woodland gleam with a fire, soft and golden, far superior to the fire he left behind. She is light also in her movements, graceful, virginal, calling forth all that is beautiful and good in nature, which puts on its richest apparel and its sweetest sunlight to adorn and worship her. (This springtide, alas, will have been destroyed in the final song of the suite, and this brave attire all shed and ruined in 30 ["XXIX"] and 31 ["XXXII"]).

The girl in 8 ["VII"] becomes one with his love, the lonely love of 1 ["XXI"] now objectified fully in her. They join together, in the poet's mind, as the gay winds do, joining in companies. And as the winds woo the leaves, his desires woo the graceful girl.

But there is something odd about the girl's attitude. Like the Bride of the Song of Songs (also known as the Song of Solomon and the Canticle of Canticles), she is among the apple-trees, but she seems interested in her own shadow rather than in the Bridegroom. And she goes slowly and lightly. [In *Chamber Music*, the editor William York] Tindall scents creative urine, sees the sky as cup as helpful to the thematic chamber tinkling, and finds the holding up of her dress "no less prudent than relevant."

It is surely true that "goes" for Joyce operated well in a context of wine and porter and urine and copulation. In a letter to Stanislaus on August 31, 1906, speaking about George Moore, he wrote: "Italy . . . where they drink nice wine and not that horrid black porter (O poor Lady Ardilaun over whose lily-like hand he lingered some years

back): and then she goes (in all senses of the word) with a literary man named Ellis . . .". Lady Ardilaun was one of the Guinesses, and her lily-like hand may connect with a conditioned response in young Joyce's imagination, linking cups and chamber-pots with beef-tea and sacramental white wine and porter and urine. Then indeed the dainty hand of this song gains complexity and interest.

Joyce's woman . . . emerges for me a clear Irish figure—lovely, graceful, shy, talented, passionate, affectionate, selfish, sensitive, possessive, intuitive, guilt-ridden, resentful, cold, determined—a woman of infinite variety.

—Robert Boyle, S. J.

But more immediately applicable to this poem is Joyce's Epiphany 26, in which the girl "dances with them in the round—a white dress lightly lifted as she dances, a white spray in her hair; eyes a little averted, a faint glow on her cheek. Her hand is in mine for a moment, softest of merchandise." This suggests that in the song the girl's attention to her shadow may be shyness or calculation, or a combination of both, and thus might stem from a consciousness of and a reaction to her would-be lover.

In 9 ["IX"], the poet longs for the girl and speaks to the May winds, also light dancers. He asks them, with Verlainian delicacy, to find his true love and to make the divided loves of the last line truly one love.

In the midst of this longing, separated from the girl, he adverts in 10 ["XVII"] to his separation from his friend (like Stephen's from Cranly) because of her. This touch of the Mr. W H element of Shakespeare's sonnets suggests an alliance with Elizabethan sequences, and introduces the pain and betrayal motif of such interest to Joyce, enamored of romantic suffering. The soft "merchandise" of her hand, bought now with his betrayal of his friend, is again in his (the "again" suggests a more definitive grasp, I suspect, after some significant encounter with the friend). With his hand occupied, he cannot make any sign of amendment to his friend, nor, as she sings, speak a word. Her singing voice and willful hand have effectively destroyed his friendship with a man who was once at his side.

He seeks comfort for the pain, in 11 ["XVIII"], in her soft wooing. An immature, non-ancient mariner, he yet preaches a universal tale and knows that words are worthless. The union of bodies can express love as words cannot, and, like the Bridegroom, he can find in her breast comfort for the gnawing sorrow.

He sings, in 12 ["VI"], the Bridegroom's song, longing for peace in her arms, in her love. The "that" in the first line is, as Tindall beautifully develops, a distancing word, and indicates that the poet feels himself definitely outside that sweet bosom now, with rude winds threatening to visit him. The fourfold repetition of "that," Tindall further perceives, carries a suggestion that the poet, like Stephen in the villanelle, is reluctant to go along with the powerful impulse to plunge into the "lure." Thus an ironic undertone, quite alien to the Song of Song's surface, gives a faint ominous overtone to the soft knock in line 7, which seems to echo the Bridegroom's knocking (in Catholic liturgy applied to Christ knocking at the heart):

> I slept, but my heart was awake.
> Hark! my beloved is knocking.
> "Open to me, my sister, my love, my dove,
>   my perfect one;
> for my head is wet with dew. . . .
>   *Song of Solomon,* V, 2

A rogue will knock loudly in 33 ["XXXIII"], with murder in the background. Here the stress is on peace. Austerities (those rude south winds) might creep in, but in that sweet softness, or soft sweetness, they would be made gentle.

He proves this, in 13 ["X"], by the new lover's song, livelier than the "softer than the dew" song of 5 ["IV"]. This song is full of motion, of gaiety, of contempt for musing dreamers who do not *act*. The lover of 1 ["XXI"] and 2 ["I"] was such a dreamer, sinking into the past, into himself. This lover, as honied as the fragrant Bridegroom, moves fast and sings boldly, with wild bees drawn to his sweet odors. But we surely note (as Bloom discovered, "Still gardens have their drawbacks"), that productive and hummingly musical as they are, bees may sting.

In March, 1902, Joyce gave a Byronic—Little Chandlerish verse to John Byrne. It mourns the death of a gentle lover with (naturally) a "soft white bosom" and "no mood of guile or fear" (both moods strong characteristics in the woman of **Chamber Music**). Its last stanza foreshadows the remarkably more mature 14 ["XX"]. The earlier verse reads

> I would I lay with her I love—
> And who is there to say me no?

(No one says "nay" because a rhyme with "below" is called for.) In the poem in **CM,** the dark pine-wood is primarily the lovely trysting park near Dublin (quieter than the Hill of Howth with its flamboyant rhododendrons), but it doubles well as a coffin. Part of the wisdom of this young poet, clinging like Buck Mulligan to an adolescent rationalism, is that human love is intimately involved with the constantly changing human organism, which will inevitably deteriorate (". . . *whose mother is beastly dead"*). But like Byron, and in a far more subtle way like Jonson, this poet enshrines even mundane lips and hair in an inflated religious tonality:

> Where the great pine-forest
>   Enaisled is!

Interestingly, as Tindall points out, the shallowness of the religious coating trickles through the uncertain rhyming of "kiss" and "is."

The ennui after the "I come" of the previous poem (13 ["X"]) prepares for the post-coital letdown following their actual consummation in 17 ["XIV"]. In 14 ["XX"], the long vowels delay and dwell on the rhythm, and the imagined kiss in stanza 3 descends like water as her hair, in Rossetti-like disorder, sweetly and softly endews the Bridegroom's head.

This small baptism takes place at noon. At that hour, the speaker (or dreamer) of chapter 7 of *Finnegans Wake* figures we might, through "inversions of all this chambermade music," get a glimpse . . . of Shem the elusive artist, "the whirling dervish, Tumult, son of Thunder . . .". If we do link "tumult" in this poem to that liturgical (the dervish) and Evangelical (St. John) context, then this flowing hair can suggest baptismal water (so feared by Stephen), as do the letters just before the full statement of the villanelle (". . . the liquid letters of speech, symbols of the element of mystery, flowed forth over his brain" [*Portrait*]); and if we compare this seemingly simple girl in the pine-forest with the luring and destructive witch of the villanelle; and if we recall the apparition of Stephen's mother in "Circe" (". . . *her face worn and noseless, green with grave mould. Her hair is scant and lank. She fixes her blue-circled hollow eyesockets on Stephen and opens her toothless mouth uttering a silent word"* [*Ulysses*]), then we can see why Shem is like St. John, the true Son of Thunder (". . . whom we surnamed Boanerges, that is, sons of thunder . . ." [Mark, 3:17]), celebrator of the infinite and ineffable Logos. Shem too wants to find and utter the word and needs a divining woman to that end, somewhat as St. John needed the Blessed Virgin to see and hear the true Word. Thus Stephen begged his mother, who, like Hamlet's father, had come back from the dead, for the word known to all men; thus Joyce sought a woman for his *clou* to immortality. The fear that this woman of **Chamber Music** will feel in 25 ["XXVI"], rising from the mystery of her own being, is the same fear that inspires that artist to express the mystery of his own being (and thus of every human being) in imperishable ink. This noon poem, for all its prettiness, contains something of the threat of death and the dark and maybe even hell, the noonday devil's horrors. (Joyce is thinking of Psalm 91:6, the destruction in wait for those who rebel against God, ". . . nor the destruction that wastes at noonday.") Shem is ". . . noondayterrorised to skin and bone by an ineluctable phantom . . .". Some such torrent of contexts brings into my mind, as I skim over the sugared surface of this sweet noontide song, the feeling of threatening possibilities swirling deep below.

Approaching the climactic moment of their courtship, the "courtly" poet, more of a Jonson than a Spenser, in 15 ["XIII"] sends a courteous wind as herald of his coming as the Bridegroom. The wind of spices from the Song of Songs announces his coming, and it finds out her little garden and her window. Noon here is the climax of their love, the completion of the perfection of day. And the Greek "epithalamium" mingles the ancient sexual traditions of the Greeks with the greatest of Jewish love songs in preparation for the climactic song of this suite.

Now the voice of the lover himself, in 16 ["XI"], supplants that of the herald, and the lingering adieu to virginity comes from his seraphic lips. His address to the shy girl and his instruction to prepare for the loss of her maidenhood (and maidenhead) is translouted into turfish in *Finnegans Wake*:

> —Can you ajew ajew fro' Sheidam?
> He finges to be cutting up with a pair of sissers and to be buytings of their maidens and spitting their heads into their facepails.

As in *Portrait*, the lover has come as a seraph to the virgin's chamber, and as he dreamed of her wooing in 11 ["XVIII"], he now woos her. The name on the bugles of the cherubim may be just "Seraph," but more likely, considering Joyce's eucharistic treatment of the artist as Christ, it is "Logos," the Word. As the Word, this artist can be imagined as overshadowing the virgin to effect through her his own conception in transaccidentated ink (thus Joyce will deal with the Artist-Being-Made-Word, climaxing that image on *FW*). I am not suggesting that the youthful Joyce here foresees the sophisticated and faintly blasphemous meanings which he later developed for Stephen and Shem, but I do perceive that in suggesting the divine aspect of the poet (somewhat in contrast to his "disregard of the divine" in 26 ["XII"]), he opens the way for that development. The girl's veiled hair, enclosed as under the veil of a nun or in the formal cap of Hester Prynne, must come pouring down in what the poet sees as a sign of her surrender to him. That the surrender is a calculated one, like Molly Tweedy's among the Howth rhododendrons or like Hester Prynne's among the shadowy trees where she again lured the manipulated Dimmesdale, does not appear here—but the way is open for that too.

And now, in 17 ["XIV"], the climax, the celebration of Hymen! The Song of Songs provides all the material for this ecstatic expression of full, loving union, and the dew on the lover's lips and eyes foreshadows Stephen's soul "all dewy wet" as he pictures the seraph coming to the virgin's chamber.

Epiphany 24, having listed a dozen elements from the Song of Songs, focuses on "that response whereto the perfect tenderness of the body and the soul with all its mystery have gone: *Inter ubera mea commorabitur.*" The mystery involved in human love (as in human poetry) is the focus of this lovely song too.

This poem corresponds to Stephen's vision of the girl in the water, a female seraph who called him to his true vocation, "to recreate life out of life!" As a result of that call, he would dare, as in drunken bravery in "Oxen of the Sun," to challenge even God, and to call his post-creation

better than the creation of God, which Stephen judges to be mere material for the artist's sublime literary Eucharist. The girl in the water shares much imagery and language with the dove of this song—e.g., "soft white down," "dovetailed," "bosom was as a bird's soft and slight, slight and soft as the breast of some darkplumaged dove."

I wonder, though, if in the pale veil which lies on the poet's head (though the snood has fallen from hers), there is not some faint shadow of the demonie, some echo of the "ajew, ajew fro' Sheidam" cast backward here (*Sheidim* is Hebrew for demons), bouncing perhaps off the villanelle? There the demon-woman, the Shee, lurks in the liturgical smoke, the source of weariness for the uneasy lover. Weariness will come soon enough, in 28 ["XXVIII"], for this now ecstatic lover. Maybe this veil, in the fearful insecurity of the poet, is not altogether desirable.

But it would be hard to forecast, from the "beautiful one" of this song, the temptress of the villanelle, and, far more, the luscious but diseased (if that is the implication of the "injection mark" of *Ulysses* 512) Zoe of "Circe" and her enchanted days:

> (. . . *A fountain murmurs among damask roses. Mammoth roses murmur of scarlet winegrapes. A wine of shame, lust, blood exudes, strangely murmuring.*)
>
> Zoe
>
> (*Murmuring singsong with the music, her odalisk lips lusciously smeared with salve of swinefat and rosewater.*)
>
> *Schorach ani wenowach, benoith Hierushaloim*

Zoe's Hebrew, I would guess, more likely emerges from Bloom's imagination recalling his father's chanting than from the actual Zoe (where would she have learned it?), but in any case it means, "I am black but comely, O ye daughters of Jerusalem" (*Song of Songs,* 1:5). It will be a long journey from this Irish girl of **Chamber Music** to the battered, depraved Zoe, but within this perfect wreath of songs ("The *Vita Nuova* of Dante suggested to him that he should make his scattered love-verses into a perfect wreath . . ."), the poems which decline from the central poem point toward the lower circles where Bella and her women wait.

Sadness has come over the deflowered girl in 18 ["XIX"]—not, according to Tindall, because of the deflowering (as in the "curious rite" of *Ulysses* 392), but because of what people are saying about her. Tindall refers to Yeats's "Aedh Thinks of Those Who Have Spoken Evil of His Beloved." If one judges that "all men" are actually talking about the Sweetheart of this poem, of course the text does become as puzzling as Tindall finds it. But I believe that the "lying clamour" is that which the Capuchin will whisper in her ear in 26 ["XII"], or a corollary to that—namely, the religious stance of Irish Catholicism (as young Joyce read it) that sexual activity is evil unless blessed by Church and State.

If that is true, then in the first stanza the poet is saying to the girl, "All men condemn you, like the woman taken in adultery, preferring the religious lie to the natural truth. But you must realize that their belief that you are a woman without honour does not make it so." "Before you" could also carry the implication, especially in light of what follows, that "they preferred that clamour before you did," thus touching the source of her sadness in herself. He appeals to her natural pride to condemn the false and wasted tears of the men, their calls to repentance, and as they deny their natures, she should, like the defiant poet of 1 ["XXI"], hold "to ancient nobleness" and deny their false doctrine.

In 19 ["XV"], the poet demonstrates his own acceptance of nature's sighs (here signs not of sorrow but, presumably, of satisfaction and fulfillment) and the wise admonitions of leaves and flowers to arise, like the Bride and Bridegroom, to a day of love. Something of the tonality of Titania and Oberon in *A Midsummer Night's Dream* accompanies those veils of gossamer and those wise choirs of faery, votaries of the natural.

"Admonisheth," with its Elizabethan formality, probably means first of all an extension of the poet's counsel to his soul to arise from sleep and death (sleep as symbol of death will be stressed in 34 ["XXXIV"], as it is in Shakespeare's Sonnet 73). Joyce probably composed this song originally as an address to his own soul, like Stephen's "dewy wet" soul waking from ecstatic dreams or rising "from the grave of boyhood, spurning her graveclothes. Yes! Yes! Yes!" But as the poem fits into the suite, following 17 ["XIV"], "my soul" more naturally comes to mean the beloved lady lying at his side, who has just been sighing and, no doubt, trembling in sleep. The slumber-death of love at this point still seems to be only their former loneliness, now past. And the few faeries (or at least few choirs) who faintly celebrate their present union can be heard only by attentive and wakeful ears.

"Admonisheth," however, can also carry a warning, and maybe those sighs are not totally pleasant ones after all. Maybe the faeries are "innumerous" and faint because the wisdom they sing is to some degree specious. It may even be that among the veils threatened by the rising sun is that happy veil of dew on the Bridegroom's head in 17 ["XIV"]. The noonday devil may be preparing his attack. These "wise" choirs may be foreshadowing the later wisdom of the lover. Nature's sighs and gentle stirrings may signal not only the dawn's epithalamium but the evening's thanatopsis.

And sure enough, the wise birds of 20 ["XXIII"], who do not live very long, suggest an apothegm to the yet wiser lover. Like these prudent wrens, who store treasures in their nests, he has "laid" (another word of many helpful meanings) his own treasures also in "some mossy nest." The heart of his beloved "flutters" in the first line, preparing for the propriety of picturing her as a bird. His hope and riches and happiness, which he had lost when religion and other inimical chains had taught him, like Blake, to weep, he has regained and stored in her. Thus

they are—or are they?—as wise as the prudent birds. But into this wisdom of the poet creeps a question, and the possibility that evening will bring the death of love.

His beloved begins to justify that questioning in 21 ["XXIV"]. She had let down her hair for him in 16 ["XI"], and now she combs it endlessly for herself and her mirror-image. That glorious sun, which in 7 ["VIII"] she had made more beautiful in the woods, she now uses only as a means to admire herself more. She prefers her mirror to her lover, to natural sunlit life. Like the temptress of the villanelle, she is a witch and a lure to the lover, who "prays" her to leave her selfishness, to stop being "enchanted" by herself beneath the luring "pretty air." The charming negligence of her gestures embodies her negligence of her lover, about which he will complain more bitterly in 30 ["XXIX"]. Her love is declining, and she foreshadows the pretty airs of the piping poets to come (in 27 ["XXVII"]), airs which hide the selfish and destructive witchery beneath their enchanting praises of perfect, lasting love.

The lover in 22 ["XVI"], proposing to return to the valley where they once found love, reveals his uncertainty in that wavering "sometime." Now the musical and productive birds are the wise choir, calling them both away from that mirror. Almost abruptly, in proffering his pastoral invitation, he somewhat flatly asserts, "When we get there, we'll stay there." Since the lovers are not birds, who are better designed to be at home in the valley, the hesitant rhythm of the final line finds realistic justification.

She kisses him in 23 ["XXXI"], and sweetness and softness encompass him. But "murmuring" can be suspicious, as the idiot murmuring in Bloom's gazelle garden demonstrates. Especially is this true when the murmuring educes a phrase like "O, happily!" and all the time there is a bat flying overhead. Tindall lists Joyce's numerous treatments of women as bats and of bats associated with love and sex, and the vampire bat fits fairly well with the poisondart looming up in 27 ["XXVII"].

The witch "allures" him into the prison of her arms in 24 ["XXII"]. The witch of the villanelle lures seraphs from heaven, and here the "dearest" woos the lover with her soft arms, seeking to overcome the reluctance, like Stephen's, "to relent," and seeking to hold him fast, "to detain." There may have been a wooing word too, like that Joyce once heard from Nora: "I remember the first night in Pola when in the tumult of our embraces you used a certain word. It was a word of provocation, of invitation and I can see your face over me (you were *over* me that night) as you murmured it. There was madness in *your* eyes too and as for me if hell had been waiting for me the moment after I could not have held back from you." Hell does wait for fallen seraphs, in Catholic as in Miltonic imaginations, and I suspect that the "lure" of the villanelle and of **Chamber Music** finds some roots in the "swallowed bait" of Shakespeare's Sonnet 129, which also lands the prey in hell.

The demonic rivulets gyrate considerably below the surface of this saccharine song, starting with "sweet" and "soft" and ending with "sleep to . . . sleep . . . soul with soul." That last coupling seems to me allied to Newman's device as cardinal, *"Cor ad cor loquitur,"* heart speaks to heart. Some of the drooling prose of Stephen's dealing with Emma, under the aegis of the Blessed Virgin, seems allied to that same device:

> She placed their hands together, hand in hand, and said, speaking to their hearts:
>
> —Take hands, Stephen and Emma. It is a beautiful evening now in heaven. You have erred but you are always my children. It is one heart that loves another heart. Take hands together, my dear children, and you will be happy together and your hearts will love each other.

[John Henry Cardinal] Newman's "The Glories of Mary for the Sake of her Son" is quoted in *Portrait* just before that passage and in length at the end of the section. And that passage, in Newman's sermon, is preceded by a quotation from the Little Office of the Blessed Virgin: ". . . and in the glorious company of the saints was I *detained*" (Newman's italics). As Atherton points out [in the introduction to *Portrait of the Artist as a Young Man*] in his note to Stephen's discussion of "detained" with the Dean of Studies, "Newman is translating very literally *et in plenitudine sanctorum detentio mea* (*Ecclesiasticus*, 24:16): 'My abode is in the full assembly of the saints. . . .'" In this song in **Chamber Music** (24 ["XXII"]), the word is used as Newman uses it, and it draws in the whole complex of Newman's praise of Mary's glories, among which her virginity and her heroic determination to preserve it shine brilliantly. Now we can fully evaluate the "lying clamour" of those who, as in 18 ["XIX"], assert that the loss of virginity is a shameful loss (". . . those unspeakable sins by which degraded man outrages and defiles the temple of the Holy Ghost, defiles and pollutes himself). These "arms / By love made tremulous" resemble Stephen's reaction in his supposed freedom from alarms after his "penitence": "His hands were trembling, and his soul trembled . . . ." But Stephen's trembling stemmed from a lie, and so (we perceive as things develop) does this **Chamber Music** love. A clue lies in the ambivalence of "could" in "Ah, could they ever hold me there . . .": "I wish they could" balances with "they can't."

The basis for "I wish they could" from the artist is, I take it, his need to tap her "divining ear," to find there a *clou* to immortality. She listens, in 25 ["XXVI"], not to a choir of birds, but to the soft choiring of her own blood. And she hears there a sound which causes fear. The divining of this sorceress has tapped some mystery beyond her rational grasp. She may be fearing torrents of water rushing forth from grey deserts. It is her heart that fears, and north of the heart is that grey matter that, according to Molly, Bloom considered to be the actual phenomenon which some called "soul" ("he says your soul you have no soul inside only grey matter"). The poet may be asking his beloved if she fears not only the vague de-

structive evil but also the sterile, rationalistic floods from the brain which threaten to sweep away her divination of human delight welling from the loving soul and to drown out the dulcimers of the Pleasure Dome.

That it is a mystery she conjures forth, a source of fear and pain, is suggested by Joyce's cry to Nora in December, 1909: "O the sweet pain you brought into my heart! O the mystery your voice speaks to me of!" It is the lady's *ear* that hears the mystery from that full choir where, like the Virgin, she is "detained." Her sacred river of blood brings "a mad tale," or the basis for one, into her consciousness, like that of the Ancient Mariner, frightening and ghostly. The flow may lead, when the ghosts can be conjured up, to the Sacred River to which Purchas led Coleridge, or to the oceans of blood to which Holinshed led Shakespeare. The poet, through careful scanning of her mood, hopes likewise to be led to a mad tale, maybe as mad as *Finnegans Wake.*

But his "human only" wisdom first moves him to warn her about religious sentimentality. In one of the most complex and interesting poems of the suite, 26 ["XII"], Joyce, among many other things, reveals most obviously his debt to Ben Jonson. [In his *Dublin's Joyce*] Hugh Kenner, having expressed some brilliant insights on what Joyce learned from Verlaine, goes on, under the heading "Ironic Elegance and Ben Jonson," to see this poem as illustrating, in its "double-writing," the aim Joyce assigned to Stephen Hero:

> But in his expressions of love he found himself compelled to use what he called the feudal terminology and as he could not use it with the same faith and purpose as animated the feudal poets themselves he was compelled to express his love a little ironically. This suggestion of relativity, he said, mingling itself with so immune a passion is a modern note: we cannot swear or expect eternal fealty because we recognise too accurately the limits of every human energy. It is not possible for the modern lover to think the universe an assistant at his love-affair and modern love, losing somewhat of its fierceness, gains also somewhat in amiableness.

The artist as a *young* man recognized those limits more accurately than did the far more mature author of *Finnegans Wake,* who adverted to the multitude of pesky "unfacts": "Thus the unfacts, did we possess them, are too imprecisely few to warrant our certitude . . . ." Youthful faith in rational science and the certitude which results still impress this young artist. With these he attempts to insert an ironic modern undertone beneath the elegant Elizabethan surface of this song, and succeeds in echoing a truly ironic Elizabethan, the witty and acerbic Ben Jonson.

The song's echo of Jonson I find quite explicitly in "plenilune." That word enjoys the fullness of its tenuous existence in English, insofar as I can determine the matter, in Jonson's *The Fountaine of Selfe-Love or Cynthias Revels* (as the title appears in the 1601 Quarto):

> . . . . Arete, behold

Another Cynthia, and another Queene
Whose glorie (like a lasting *plenilune*)
Seems ignorant of what it is to wane!

(Act V, Scene 8)

That is precisely the doctrine of Joyce's "hooded moon," itself in its waned state contradicting its dogma, namely, that the full moon demonstrates that beauty and love and glory can last forever. Jonson's "lasting" on the surface implies that Queen Elizabeth, symbolized as usual in Cynthia the moon goddess, has been and will be plenilune forever. But she was, of course, ancient when Jonson wrote his lines, so Joyce's adjective also brings out an ironic undertone of Jonson's elegant surface. Joyce refers primarily to the old Elizabethan times, when "plenilunes" were fresh and at least verbally young. Now, he implies, the times and the word are both ancient and moribund, as Elizabeth was then and as the love this suite celebrates is now. All this speculation is contingent, I am aware, on Joyce's having actually derived the word from the author he was to read exhaustively in Paris, but my guess is that he did.

The waning and waxing of the moon in Joyce's song, the narcissism of this lady, the apocalyptic glory under her feet (not "tread out," as Tindall supposes, but rather supporting and setting off her glory), and her conviction, learned from the idealistic Capuchin, that there is a love that endures even to the edge of doom—these elements and others suggest Jonson's powerful influence. Further, Jonson himself, recently converted to Catholicism when he wrote those lines, would serve in excellent ways (with considerable irony also) as "the comedian Capuchin." The "elegant and antique phrase" of the following poem (27 ["**XXVII**"]) links with the antiquity of "ancient plenilune" to stress the courtly irony of old Ben, and to find deep roots feeding the "wisdom" of this young Dublin poet. In making his Capuchin a Jonsonian comedian, the *wise* young Joyce, who is reputed to have patronized Yeats, possibly echoes the attitude of Gabriel Harvey, set down about 1600: ". . . the younger sort takes much delight in Shakespeares *Venus & Adonis*: but his *Lucrece*, & his tragedie of *Hamlet, Prince of Denmarke*, have it in them, to please the wiser sort."

The glory, at any rate, passes from the unreal dogma of stanza 1 into the real sparkle in living eyes in stanza 2, which, while trembling in its ephemeral "moving and changing every part of the time," can be doubly possessed—but not for long, as the chime of "Mine, O Mine" links inevitably with "No more."

The poet's own doctrine, product of his "human only" wisdom—Shem's life transaccidentates into ink expressing a literary "chaos, perilous, potent, common to all-flesh, human only, mortal"—is clearly set forth in 27 ["**XXVII**"]. In November, 1906, when he was twenty-four years old, Joyce revealed to his brother his theories on the love he had known: "Perhaps my view of life is too cynical but it seems to me that a lot of this talk about love is nonsense. A woman's love is always maternal and egoistic. A man, on the contrary, side by side with his extraordinary cerebral sexualism and bodily fervour (from which women are normally free) possesses a fund of genuine affection for the 'beloved' or 'once beloved' object." This is the wisdom that falls from these "all too wise" lips, assigning categories for love according to sex, and distinguishing in the man "genuine" affection, which leaves for the egoistic though maternally tender woman a mixed, or perhaps hypocritical, or maybe more exactly, devious affection. At any rate, we see in 27 ["**XXVII**"] the rapturous satisfaction of her maternal heart operating simultaneously with the poison of her malice. The malignant and even murderous elements that may be operating in some complex and basically incomprehensible women—like Cleopatra and Hester Prynne and Molly Bloom—have in this suite developed from the lady's indifference in 21 ["**XXIV**"] to this Housmanian statement. The bat image helped to suggest it, and in his notes for "Penelope," Joyce noted "(female spider devours male after)." The malice in her tenderness stems, Joyce suggests, from her own animal desires and needs, particularly the need to be inseminated and to protect and foster her offspring. This is expressed with more than Jonsonian tenderness, but with full Jonsonian irony. "I but render," I presume, echoes Shakespeare's Sonnet 125, where the rendering is mutual:

No, let me be obsequious in thy heart,
And take thou by oblation, poor but free,
Which is not mixed with seconds, knows no art,
But mutual render, only me for thee.

This *Chamber Music* poet seems to be stressing, in his rendering, that the total giving of self is all on his side, and the significant item in his confession of his complete love is the supposition that mixed in with her tender love for him is malice.

The lying Capuchin of the previous poem, with his doctrine of perfect love, has waned, but these wise lips are waxing to bring in the modern truth. His own experience brings science to the religious and false "solemnizing" of love with pastoral and lyric pipes. Some touch of the poison dart he has found in all love (love in women, that is), and so he once more warns his beloved to believe him and to face the realities of human intercourse. But the warning seems to be spoken mostly for himself, and to be sugar-coated for her sentimental and less perceptive mind. Or perhaps he is striving to spare her feelings, while at the same time expressing the Darwinian undertones of animal courtship and fulfillment. The song does not really have the definite limits I am suggesting, but, while it suggests those, leaves matters open to some unexpressed larger context. It does not finally exclude mystery, try as it will.

The poet in 28 ["**XXVIII**"] sings this same wisdom briefly, and, in more direct fashion, counsels accepting the passing nature of human love. He points to mortality and implies that death, as this wise young man tends to judge, ends all love. Mae West in her youth taught a similar doctrine when she replied to a suitor's pledge of eternal love, "Yeah, but how about your health?" Echoes in this poem of Marvell's broodings on the sleep of love in the grave prepare for the final poems of the suite. The weariness of declining love foreshadows the disillusioned "Are you not weary" of *Portrait*'s villanelle.

More desperately, the poet in 29 ["**XXV**"] calls for laughter and song. The girl's divining heart, he knows, fears the inevitability of Time's (and Death's) victory—remotely like Margaret in Hopkins's "Spring and Fall," whose heart presaged mortality. But laugh anyway, he urges—as Joyce himself fills the cosmos with laughter in *Finnegans Wake*. Do not grieve over wasted suns like that of 21 ["**XXIV**"], but run while these winds (more familiar with the lover than they were with the virgin) loosen the tumult of your hair once more. Keep it light in all senses; the clouds that will bring darkness at evening yet attend (in the sense of await) the passing of the sun and of your love. Confess, not with stern self-revelation and acceptance of defeat, but with laughing and loving song assert a human defiance to darkness and the void.

Poem 30 ["**XXIX**"] is certainly written by ". . . a certain gay young nobleman whimpering to the name Low Swine . . . ." He whimpers out accusations of her destruction of the "rich apparel" of 7 ["**VIII**"], of her Titania-like despoiling of summer, of her having brought to the enclosed garden the desolate winds of autumn, soon to bring the wild winds of winter. Love is dissolving, and it's all her fault. He had loved her, too dear, not wisely but too well, as another self-satisfied hero once whimpered. But she, whose clear eyes remain unperturbed, justifies his wise insight of 27 ["**XXVII**"]. She is selfish. And so, in this song, he falls upon the thorns of life and bleeds.

But in 31 ["**XXXII**"], before the lovers finally part, he once more, as a determined preacher, mounts his wise soapbox. Rain indicates nature's empathy with their tears—his anyway, since the lady may have perceived she will do better without him—and the wet leaves, once so loving and joyful, cover their memories (which he will uncover in the following song). "Way" here is a singular, I suppose, because they have not yet parted; they will need separate ways in the next poem. They stay for a moment, to contemplate the path this whole suite has taken, before they look at the memories and part. In this moment of pause, the wise counselor returns once again to his "heart speaks to heart" pose.

In 32 ["**XXX**"], he recalls the whole course of their love. The main memory is the opening action of the suite in 4 ["**IV**"], where she shyly played the piano and he fearfully stood near—like Bloom, less shy, turning the pages for young Molly. "Grave" has something of the atmosphere of "The Dead" about it, as do all these dripping trees and soggy leaves. The sweetness is gone, and the anapest "at the last" suggests the almost stumbling speed of the painful yet welcome parting. The plodding hesitancy of the final line, similar to the movement in the final line of *Paradise Lost*—"Through Eden took their solitary way"—suggests the return of loneliness.

Two lover's songs end the suite. The poet may be singing just to comfort himself, as he did in the opening poems. At any rate, he takes the advice which he gave to her in 29 ["**XXV**"], to laugh and sing though heavyhearted—or at least he tries. Having expressed his resentment and hurt in 30 ["**XXIX**"], and his sorrow and resignation and determination in 31 ["**XXXII**"], he now sings, and his music contrasts with the "sweet" music of Love at the beginning. Love now (in 33 ["**XXXIII**"]) is neither the lonely harpist nor the happy lover nor the possibly divine figure softly knocking at the heart in 12 ["**VI**"], but is a "fool in motley" like the one Jaques met in the forest (like Buck Mulligan in motley), now loudly knocking perseveringly at the tree—no doubt the garden's apple tree. Loneliness has returned to them, now loveless, but nature, not really malignant but only indifferent, carries on in its merry determination to have propagation by fair means or foul. *Macbeth,* indeed, is somehow involved in that knocking, as the next and last poem makes explicit. The fall, which takes the ungrieving leaves, goes into the gathering of winter, as night seals their sad parting. But the repetition of "year" in the final line may go with the ambivalence of gathering, which means both a collection of force for a deadly attack and a preparation for new things to come. It may more specifically imply, too, at the close of the suite, a harvest of the good things in their love. He urges her, or at least (if she has already gone) his memory of her, to imitate the leaves and go the way nature calls her. The ending has some faint hint of the immensely powerful tonality of the ending of "The Dead."

But all hopeful possibilities disappear or are at least muffled in the final song, almost a lullaby. It is more likely that the poet is alone here, as in the opening poems, speaking once again to himself. The unquiet of the girl in 25 ["**XXVI**"] now settles in him (if she herself, as I imagine to be the case, is not actually present), and the voice which urged her to sleep in union with him in 24 ["**XXII**"] now sounds only in his own unquiet heart. "The voice of the winter" has replaced the lovely voice of the turtle once heard in the land ("voax of the turfur is hurled on our lande"), and it is likely the wintry voice emerges from that rogue (Jack Frost?) knocking in the previous poem. Here the sinister voice echoes the cry which Macbeth heard, and it sounds in the heart which has murdered love—"Glamours hath moidered's lieb . . ."

In the final stanza, we run into what Tindall calls "pronominal confusion." "My kiss" operating on "your heart" would argue that the lady is still there. I settle it by supposing that she is there in his imagination, and that his unquiet heart can be viewed by him as his or hers or both. Shem (as Mercius) does something like this in regard to himself and Justius (and their mother) at the end of chapter 7 in *Finnegans Wake,* mixing pronouns as he and his brother mingle in his mind and merge into the fluid mother. But in any case, the suite ends in some confusion, in frustration, incomplete and uneasy, with a wish for peace stymied by that fateful knocking.

Joyce, having just received the proofs of ***Chamber Music,*** told his brother, about March 1, 1907, that he might finally determine to become a writer: "Yet I have certain ideas I would like to give form to: not as a doctrine but as the continuation of the expression of myself which I now see I began in *Chamber Music.*" With this Wildean attitude in his mind, he goes on to say, "It is not a book of love verse at all, I perceive." Stanislaus's arrangement had treated the poems as just scattered love-verses. Joyce, as I understand him, perceived his poems, with his own suite in mind, as an attempt at a portrait of himself as artist, as a projection of the woman he desired to meet in the world outside himself (something like Stephen's "green rose"), and as a large philosophy dealing with human love.

Joyce's portrait of himself looms largest, of course, but if one listens to and stares long enough at the poems in Joyce's own imaginative scheme, not Stanislaus's, then behind that rather precious, self-centered, verbal musician emerges the outline of a woman, like the lovely Eve peering curiously out from under God's other arm in Michelangelo's "Creation of Adam." Joyce shows the woman of *Chamber Music* fulfilling Shakespeare's prophecy about his love:

'Gainst death and all oblivious enmity
Shall you pace forth . . .

(Sonnet 35)

Joyce's woman, as I attempt to unify these fragmentary glimpses, emerges for me a clear Irish figure—lovely, graceful, shy, talented, passionate, affectionate, selfish, sensitive, possessive, intuitive, guilt-ridden, resentful, cold, determined—a woman of infinite variety. She has the Jewish beauty and passion of the Bride in the *Song of Songs,* of the Queen of Sheba, of Anastashie. She has the glory of Mary, the source of the human Word; the happy purity of Beatrice; the shy virginity of Stephen's Mercedes, Lady of Mercy. She has the sensual taint of Zoe (Jewish at least in Bloom's imagination), sterile source of life, like the Dead Sea. She has the witchery of the villanelle's Temptress, of the Shee, of Circe, of Titania. She has the malice of the Vampire, seeking the poet's mouth like the Pale Vampire of *Ulysses,* the complete inversion of the *Song of Songs'* opening line: "Let him kiss me with the kisses of his mouth. . . ." She is contradictory and tantalizing and mysterious, but full of life and energy. She deserves to be restored to the ordered if fragmentary world in which Joyce placed her. Then, in spite of the flaws with which adolescent certitudes and artistic uncertainties left her, she will still do all that a girl composed of ink can do to make defect perfection.

FURTHER READING

Bibliography

Rice, Thomas Jackson. *James Joyce: A Guide to Research.* New York: Garland Publishing, 1982, 389 p.
    Annotated secondary bibliography.

Criticism

A. C. H. "Chamber Music—Old and New." *Poetry: A Magazine of Verse* XIV, No. 2 (May 1919): 98-103.
    Offers a negative assessment of *Chamber Music.*

Bowen, Zach. "Goldenhair: Joyce's Archetypal Female." *Literature and Psychology* 17, No. 4 (1967): 219-28.
    Discusses the feminine prototypes found in *Chamber Music.*

Dixon, John. "Ecce Puer, Ecce Pater: A Son's Recollections of an Unremembered Father." *James Joyce Quarterly* 29, No. 3 (Spring 1992): 485-509.
    Explores autobiographical aspects of Joyce's poem "Ecce Puer."

Gysling, Fritz. "Doctor's Look at a Neglected Poem." *James Joyce Quarterly* 7, No. 3 (Spring 1970): 251-52.
    Provides a clinical interpretation of "Bahnhofstrasse."

Jackson, Selwyn. *The Poems of James Joyce and the Use of Poems in His Novels.* Frankfurt: Peter Lang, 1978, 187 p.
    Full-length critical study on Joyce's poetry.

Kerrigan, Anthony. "News of Molly Bloom." *Poetry* LXXXV, No. 2 (November 1954): 109-12.
    Discusses the theme of love in *Chamber Music.*

M. A. "The Lyrics of James Joyce." *The New Republic* 18 (March 1919): 191.
    Offers a mixed review of *Chamber Music.*

Phul, Ruth von. "*Chamber Music* at the Wake." *James Joyce Quarterly* 11, No. 4 (Summer 1974): 355-67.
    Provides a psychoanalytical analysis of poem "VI" in *Chamber Music.*

Spoo, Robert. "Rival Confessors in *Chamber Music:* Meaning and Narrative in Joyce's Lyric Mode." *James Joyce Quarterly* 26, No. 4 (Summer 1989): 483-98.
    Notes thematic links between poems "XII" and "XXVI" of *Chamber Music,* as well as with *Stephen Hero* and *A Portrait of the Artist as a Young Man.*

Additional coverage of Joyce's life and career is contained in the following sources published by Gale Research: *Concise Dictionary of British Literary Biography: 1914-1945; Contemporary Authors,* **Vols. 104, 126;** *Dictionary of Literary Biography,* **Vols. 10, 19, 36, 162;** *DISCovering Authors; DISCovering Authors: British; DISCovering Authors: Canadian; DISCovering Authors: Most-Studied Authors Module; DISCovering Authors: Novelists Module; DISCovering Authors: Poet's Module; Major 20th-Century Writers; Short Story Criticism,* **Vols. 3, 26;** *Twentieth-Century Literary Criticism,* **Vols. 3, 8, 16, 35, 52;** **and** *World Literature Criticism.*

Kālidāsa
fl. c. 400

Indian poet and dramatist.

INTRODUCTION

Acclaimed as the greatest of Sanskrit poets, Kalidasa is renowned for the descriptive beauty of his work. His sensitivity and eloquence in treating the themes of love and the sanctity of nature are best expressed in his lengthy lyric poem *Meghaduta* (*The Cloud-Messenger*) and in his drama *Sakuntala.* The latter work, considered the finest of the seven compositions attributed to him, was one of the first Sanskrit writings to be translated into modern European languages. The play was lauded as a masterpiece by the German poet Johann Wolfgang von Goethe and prompted William Jones's estimation of Kalidasa as "the Shakespeare of India." *The Cloud-Messenger,* especially well received by Kalidasa's contemporaries, garnered similar laurels upon its translation into Western European languages and remains Kalidasa's most popular poetic work.

Biographical Information

Virtually nothing is known of Kalidasa's personal life. Various legend-based biographies of the poet exist, the most popular of these identifying him as one of the "nine gems," a group of first-century B.C. scientists and artists who resided at the court of King Vikramaditya of Ujjain, a legendary patron of the arts who may himself have been a mythical personage. More specifically, Kalidasa's play *Malavikagnimitra* (*Malivika and Agnimitra*), whose hero Agnimitra was the second king of the Sunga dynasty, indicates with certainty that the author lived sometime after about 150 B.C., the approximate date of Agnimitra's reign. The date of the Aihole inscription (634 A.D.), which contains a laudatory reference to the poet, has also been used as a chronological marker in placing Kalidasa. Furthermore, Kalidasa's works, according to K. Krishnamoorthy, indicate that he "lived in times of peace, when the leisured class would pursue the fine arts, free from threats of invasion from without or from conflicts within." Many scholars, including Krishnamoorthy, identify this golden age in which Kalidasa lived as the reign of Chandragupta II (c. 380-415), who ruled during the height of the Gupta dynasty, a period known for its achievements in art and literature. Various references in Kalidasa's works, distinctive of fourth-and fifth-century thought and practices, substantiate this conclusion, which has become the critical consensus.

Major Works

Kalidasa is the earliest Sanskrit poet whose works have been preserved. In addition to *The Cloud-Messenger,*

Sakuntala, and *Malavika and Agnimitra,* the compositions most widely attributed to him include a second lyric poem, *Rtusamhara* (*The Pageant of the Seasons*); a third drama, *Vikramorvasiya* (*Urvasi Won by Valor*); and two epic poems, *Kumarasambhava* (*The Birth of the War-God*) and *Raghuvamsa* (*The Dynasty of Raghu*). Numerous reactions of these texts are extant, but scholars generally consider the Devanagari the purest version. The texts of Kalidasa's poetry have been especially well preserved; they have traditionally played an important part in the Indic school curriculum and have attracted much scholarly discussion since the poet's day. *The Cloud-Messenger,* for example, inspired forty-five commentaries from Kalidasa's contemporaries—more than any other Sanskrit composition. While the author's works went through numerous editions in India, they were not introduced to Western European audiences until William Jones translated *Sakuntala* in 1789. Subsequent translations, most notably those of H. H. Wilson (*The Cloud-Messenger,* 1813), R. T. H. Griffith (*The Birth of the War-God,* 1853), and Arthur W. Ryder (*Shakuntala and Other Works,* 1912), have fostered the growth of worldwide interest in Kalidasa's works.

175

The Pageant of the Seasons, a lyric poem of 140 stanzas, is generally considered Kalidasa's earliest work. Less polished in content and diction than the poet's later compositions, *The Seasons* has prompted a continuing critical debate regarding its authenticity. Most commentators concur, however, that the poem is simply a less mature expression of Kalidasa's characteristic thought and artistry. *The Seasons* examines in succession the six seasons of the Indian year—Summer, Rains, Autumn, Early Winter, Winter, and Spring—describing their effects on nature and on human emotions. Kalidasa's other lyric poem, *The Cloud-Messenger,* has been universally praised as one of the finest in its genre. The poem relates in two parts the story of an exiled demigod, or *yaksa,* who asks a thundercloud to convey a message of comfort to his sorrowing wife. The first part of *The Cloud-Messenger* features the *yaksa's* brilliant description, in word-pictures, of the route his messenger should follow; the poem concludes with an imaginative depiction of the beauties of the god Kubera's divine city (the *Yaksa's* Himalayan home) and a moving account of the lonely wife's melancholy and despair.

The Birth of the War-God and *The Dynasty of Raghu* are epic poems presumably written by Kalidasa sometime after he completed *The Cloud-Messenger. The Birth of the War-God,* considered the earlier of the two, is comprised of seventeen cantos; the last nine of these, however, are generally regarded as spurious. The poem describes a threat posed by the powerful demon Taraka, who according to prophecy can be defeated only by a son born to a union of the great god Siva with his late wife, who has been reincarnated as Parvati, daughter of Mount Himalaya. Kama, the god of love, accompanies Parvati to Siva's Himalayan hermitage, where the celibate god is engaged in religious meditation. Kama's attempts to inflict Siva with an arrow of infatuation—while Parvati, as a handmaiden, attends to her former husband—are foiled by fire from Siva's third eye, and Kama is destroyed. Siva is impressed, however, with Parvati's subsequent religious austerities, and the final two cantos of the authentic portion of the epic describe the wedding and love-making of the divine couple. *The Dynasty of Raghu* treats similar themes of passion and the virtue of self-control. Essentially the story of the ancient Indian monarch Rama, eponymous hero of the epic *Ramayana,* the poem is framed by an account of the lives of Rama's progeny and forebears. The degenerate King Agnivarna, a distant descendant of Rama and the last of a host of monarchs sketched by Kalidasa in this work, graphically illustrates the author's concern for the dangers of moral decay in his own day. Neglecting public duty while indulging in the pleasures of his harem, Agnivarna dies of consumption, and the dynasty of Raghu comes to an end.

Critical Reception

Kalidasa's style has been the subject of many twentieth-century critical studies. Scholars point out that Kalidasa, who wrote essentially for an aristocratic audience, sought to convey positive and noble aspects of Indic culture, limiting himself to lofty themes and subjects. T. G. Main-kar has described the author's style as a form of "aristocratic romanticism," adding: "Images, events, persons, expression—all these are in [Kalidasa's] eyes subordinate to artistic considerations." Commentators have noted that Kalidasa also advocates an ideal to be pursued in his portrayal of the god Siva in *The Cloud-Messenger.* Siva embodies a perfect blend of *dharma* (righteousness), *moksa* (enlightenment), and *santa* (tranquillity), as well as a perfect balancing of passion and restraint; each of these virtues were championed in Kalidasa's day by the Gupta regime, whose cultural values and enthusiasm for life found their best expression in the poet's works.

Some critics have asserted that Kalidasa's achievement was limited by the narrow focus of his works. A. Berriedale Keith, for example, contends that, unlike Shakespeare, with whom Kalidasa is often compared, the poet was by philosophy and temperament "incapable of viewing the world as a tragic scene, of feeling any sympathy for the hard lot of the majority of men, or appreciating the reign of injustice in the world." Most critics, however, cite the many moving accounts of mourning and despair in Kalidasa's works as evidence that he recognized suffering as the lot of humanity. They further contend that Kalidasa's religio-philosophical understanding of suffering as expiation of past wrongs led to his essentially deterministic view of spiritual emancipation through trial and hardship. Because he intended his heroes and heroines to serve as inspirational models of morality as well as perseverance, Kalidasa selected characters who were legendary or divine personages.

Although critics continue to debate the breadth and universality of Kalidasa's philosophy, they are virtually unanimous in their praise of his artistry. Many have commented favorably on the delicacy of the poet's descriptions—the suggestive manner in which he "indicates by a touch," as Keith explains, what others express at length. Scholars further commend the accuracy of Kalidasa's literary allusions and his adept use of metaphor, noting that the author thus demonstrates his erudition in a wide variety of disciplines. Summarizing Kalidasa's achievement, Arthur W. Ryder wrote: "Poetical fluency is not rare; intellectual grasp is not very uncommon: but the combination has not been found perhaps more than a dozen times since the world began. Because he possessed this harmonious combination, Kalidasa ranks not with Anacreon and Horace and Shelley, but with Sophocles, Vergil, Milton."

PRINCIPAL ENGLISH TRANSLATIONS

Sakuntala (translated by William Jones) 1789
The Méghadúta; or, Cloud Messenger (translated by H. H. Wilson) 1813
Kumarasambhava; or, The Birth of the War-God (translated by R. T. H. Griffith) 1853
Sakoontala; or, The Lost Ring (translated by Monier Monier-Williams) 1856
The Raghuvamsa of Kalidasa (translated by Gopal Ra-

ghunath Nandargikar) 1897

Ritusamhara (translated by C. S. Sitaram Ayyar) 1897

Malavikagnimitra (translated by C. H. Tawney) 1898

Raghuvamsa; or, The Story of Raghu's Line (translated by Johnstone P. De Lacy) 1902

Vikramorvasie; or, The Hero and the Nymph (translated by Sri Aurobindo Pathamandir) 1911

Kalidasa: Translations of Shakuntala and Other Works (translated by Arthur W. Ryder) 1912

Meghaduta; or, The Cloud-Messenger (translated by Charles King) 1930

Rtusamhara; or, The Pageant of the Seasons (translated by R. S. Pandit) 1947

The Cloud Messenger (translated by Franklin and Eleanor Edgerton) 1964

Rtusamhara; or, The Cycle of the Seasons (translated by S. M. Punekar) 1966

Works of Kalidasa (edited and translated by C. R. Devadhar) 1966

Kumarasambhava; or, The Origin of the Young God (translated by Hank Heifetz) 1985

Kalidasa, The Loom of Time: A Selection of His Plays and Poems (translated by Chandra Rajan) 1991

CRITICISM

A. Berriedale Keith (essay date 1928)

SOURCE: "Kalidasa and the Guptas," in *A History of Sanskrit Literature,* The Clarendon Press, 1928, pp. 79-108.

[*In the following excerpt, Keith summarizes and discusses each of Kalidasa's poetical works.*]

The opinion of India which makes the **Rtusamhara,** cycle of the seasons, a youthful work of Kalidasa, has recently been assailed on many grounds. Thus it has been complained that the poem lacks Kalidasa's ethical quality, that it is too simple and uniform, too easy to understand. The obvious reply is that there is all the difference between the youth and the maturity of a poet, that there is as much discrepancy between the youthful work of Virgil, Ovid, Tennyson, or Goethe, and the poems of their manhood as between Kalidasa's primitiae and the rest of his work. Nor is it the slightest use to argue that Sanskrit poets differed from other poets since they were essentially learned and artificial; the poets mentioned are precisely of the analogous type, men who worked steadily at their art until at their prime they could create structures which make their youthful attempts seem childish folly. In point of fact the **Rtusamhara** is far from unworthy of Kalidasa, and, if the poem were denied him, his reputation would suffer real loss. The contention that Mallinatha commented on the other three of his poems but not on this is met effectively by the consideration that its simplicity rendered it poor game for the very learned commentator to deal with. The fact that the writers on poetics do not cite from the poem has an obvious explanation in the same fact; these authors never exhibit the slightest trace of liking what is

simple, and they could find in the later poems abundant material to use as illustration. More deplorable still are some of the æsthetical arguments adduced; complaint is made that the poet begins with the summer, whereas the spring was the usual beginning of the year, forgetting that Kalidasa was not composing an almanac or writing a *Shepheard's Calendar,* Again, heat or its derivatives *(tap)* is found seven times in Canto i, as if this did not accord with summer, as does eagerness *(samutsukatva)* with the rains and longing *(utkanth)* with autumn. The poet is censured for asserting that the swans excel maidens in beauty of gait and the branches rob their arms of loveliness; later, he was not guilty of such discourtesy. He mixes a metaphor in speaking of clouds as having the lightning as creeper; as we have seen, Vatsabhatti borrows the phrase, and exploits two other verses of the poem, proving its antiquity and rendering most probable its authorship. It is objected that he uses here only the construction *amalatah,* in lieu of the ablative, though equally once only in the *Kumarasambhava* he has *amekhalam;* the freshness and liveliness of the seven verbal forms (ii. 19) is unparalleled and, therefore, not by Kalidasa. Even the lack of developed use of figures of speech is adduced against him, and the use of *samhara* in the title has been questioned as unique. Poets happily do not feel themselves bound to be parrots.

The poem is far from a mere description of the seasons in their outward aspect, though Kalidasa exhibits delicate observation and that loving sympathy with nature which seems innate in Indian poets. Throughout he insists on the relation of the diverse moods of the year to the loves of man and maiden or husband and wife. Though the days of summer are a burden, the nights are the more delightful, when the moon is bright and coolness refreshes the earth; at midnight the young delight in song and dance and wine; the moon in jealousy of youthful love retires in sorrow. The rainy season comes in kingly guise, the clouds the elephants which bear him, the lightning his standard, the thunder his drum. The emotion of love is awakened by the sight of the clouds which bend down to kiss the peaks of the mountains. Autumn comes like a young bride, clad in a garment of sugar cane, girdled with ripening rice, and with face of lotus blooms. Winter's cold makes all the more welcome, all the more close and tender, the embraces of lovers. In the cool season the nights are cold, the moon shines chill, the lovers close the window of their chamber, wrap themselves warmly in their garments, and enjoy every moment of the still feeble rays of the sun, or rest beside the fire. But spring brings to them and to all nature new life and joy; we see now why the poet begins with summer; it enables him to end with the season in which young love, in harmony with the birth of a new year, is made perfect. The poem in every line reveals youth; the lack of the ethic touch is in perfect accord with the outlook of the young, and though Kalidasa was to write much finer poetry, he was also to lose that perfect lucidity which is one of the charms of the poem to modern taste, even if it did not appeal to writers on poetics. . . .

In distinction to the **Rtusamhara** the **Meghaduta** is unquestionably a work of Kalidasa's maturity; the mere fact that he adopts for it and maintains throughout with only occasional harshness a metre so elaborate as the Mandakranta is conclusive proof that he was no novice, though we may admit the possibility that he desired by this metrical *tour de force* to establish his capacity once and for all, and to exhibit himself as a great poet. Suggestions for the subject-matter may have been taken from the *Ramayana,* where Rama's deep longing for his lost Sita offers an obvious prototype for the Yaksa's sorrow for the wife from whom he is severed, and the description of the rainy season in iv. 28 has some points of similarity. But the idea is carried out with marked originality and beauty. A Yaksa banished for a year by Çiva his master, because of failure of duty, is reminded by the approach of the rainy season of his wife, lamenting him in their abode at Alaka, and begs a passing cloud to bear to his beloved the news of his welfare and the assurance of his devotion. From Ramagiri, his place of exile, the cloud is bidden go, in the company of the cranes and the royal swans *en route* for Lake Manasa, to the region of Mala and to mount Amrakuta. Thereafter it is to seek the Daçarna country with its city of Vidiça, and then must drink the waters of the Vetravat before proceeding to visit Ujjayin, after crossing the Nirvindhy and the Sindhu. The shrine of Mahakala must be visited, the Carmanvati crossed, and the holy Brahmavarta after passing Daçapura; there the cloud will visit the field of Kuruksetra, the scene of Arjuna's great deeds, and drink the water of the Sarasvati, for which Balarama, who fought not for love of his kin, abandoned his beloved wine. Thence it must go to where the Ganges descends from the Himalaya near mount Kanakhala, and then to Kailasa, passing through the gap of mount Kraunca which Paraçurama made as a path to the south. Then the water of lake Manasa will refresh the cloud, and on the top of the mountain is Alaka where the beloved of the Yaksa dwells. The delights of the divine city are fully depicted, and the poet then describes to the cloud the home he is to seek out; it can be seen from afar off through its archway; in the garden is a coral tree, its mistress's pet, and a flight of emerald steps leads to a well in which golden lotuses grow, and the swans, delighted, think no more even of their beloved Manasa. There is the beloved, sorrowful, and blighted by separation, emaciated, seeking by many a device to while away the long days until her husband's return. Gently she is to be wakened from her slumber by the cloud, which is to give her a message of tender love from her husband, and an assurance of his faith and certainty of reunion.

At first sight the effect of the poem seems to be marred by an element of unreality in the longing of the Yaksa, whose separation is but temporary and who as an attendant of Çiva cannot in truth fear either death or even injury for his beloved from his absence. The message would have read very differently had it been sent, as in Schiller's *Maria Stuart,* by a helpless captive awaiting in resignation or despair an ineluctable doom. But to understand the poem aright we must remember that the poet doubtless felt that it was, as later writers expressly allege, the duty of the poet to suggest rather than to say outright; the loves of the two immortals is a symbol of human love; perhaps Kalidasa had some experience of his own

which the poem indicates, for the vivid colours in which he describes the Yaksa's abode seem to be drawn from real life. Certainty is wholly unattainable, but in any event it is difficult to praise too highly either the brilliance of the description of the cloud's progress or the pathos of the picture of the wife sorrowful and alone. Indian criticism has ranked it highest among Kalidasa's poems for brevity of expression, richness of content, and power to elicit sentiment, and the praise is not undeserved.

Popularity has had the penalty of many interpolations of the text. There is a remarkable mass of evidence available; in the eighth century Jinasena, applying the art of Samasyapurana, worked the whole of the text of 120 verses as he knew it into an account of the life of the Jaina saint Parçvanatha, it exists in a Tibetan version in the Tanjur, and in a Sinhalese rendering; many stanzas are quoted in works on poetics; it was repeatedly imitated from the *Pavanaduta* of Dhoi in the twelfth century onwards; we have from that century and later many commentaries, including that of Vallabhadeva, who gives 111 verses, of Daksinavartanatha (*c.* 1200), who has 110, and of Mallinatha, who has 118.

Inevitably many other lyric poems were ascribed to Kalidasa, including two of some merit, the *Ghatakarpara* and the *Çrngaratilaka,* but there is no real probability of proving them his.

High as Indian opinion ranks the **Meghaduta,** which won also the commendation of Goethe, to modern taste the **Kumarasambhava** appeals more deeply by reason of its richer variety, the brilliance of its fancy, and the greater warmth of its feeling. The **Meghaduta** has, with reason, been ascribed the merit of approaching more closely than any other Indian poem to the rank of an elegy; the **Kumarasambhava** varies from the loveliness of the spring and the delights of married love to the utter desolation induced by the death of the beloved. The subject is unquestionably a daring one, the events which bring about the marriage of the highest god Çiva to Uma and the birth of Skanda, the war god, and Anandavardhana tells us that there were critics who deemed it wrong to depict the amour of two deities. Still less permissible does the subject naturally appear to modern taste, unless we realize that as in the **Meghaduta** we must see the poet's power of suggestion; the wedlock of Çiva and Uma is no mere sport, no episode of light love such as that of Zeus with Danae or many another. From this union springs a power destined to perform the slaying of the demon Taraka, who menaces the world with destruction; moreover, their nuptials and their love serve as the prototype for human marriage and human love, and sanctify with divine precedent the forces which make the home and carry on the race of men.

The poem begins with a brilliant piece of description of the Himalaya, the abode of Çiva. Kalidasa, unlike many a classical and even modern poet, had no hatred of mountains; his fancy makes them the dwelling of merry sprites who play in their caves, round which eddy the clouds, affording welcome screens for the maidens when they undress; the wind, wet with the drops of the streams of the Ganges as it descends from heaven, beats on the trunks of the deodars, and bends the peacock feathers, the scanty dress of the gnomes who chase the antelope. In marked contrast to this innocent frolic sits Çiva, sunk in deepest meditation, and on him with other maidens waits Uma, born of the mountain god himself, plucking flowers to offer to him, and fetching water and grass for his service. Canto ii shows us the gods in deep distress, for a demon Taraka has arisen to menace them, and Brahman himself can afford no aid, for he has accorded him his protection, and even a poison tree cannot be cut down, if one has reared it oneself. Only Çiva can aid, Çiva who surpasses Brahman and Visnu in glory, and, if Uma can win him, from them will spring a deliverer. Indra then seeks the aid of Kama, god of love, to win Çiva's heart for Uma. The next Canto shows Kama ready and willing to effect the end desired if Spring will be his comrade as well as his dear wife Rati. There follows a brilliant picture of the new life and love awakened in nature by the advent of Spring with Kama, but the sight of Çiva seated still as a flame when no wind blows, a cloud without rain, daunts even Kama's heart and he quails. But Uma with her friends appears, and Çiva is begged to hearken to their devotions; he feels himself strangely moved, and glancing sees Kama on the point of discharging at him his deadly arrow. One fiery glance from the god's eye reduces him to ashes. Then follows (iv) a brilliant and touchingly pathetic picture of the lament of Rati for her dead husband; she will not accept the consolation urged on her by Spring; instead she bids him heap the pyre so that she may follow him in death. But her fatal purpose is stayed by a voice from on high, which assures her of reunion with her beloved when Çiva shall have relented and taken Uma to spouse. In sorrowful hope Rati continues her life.

The first throw has failed and Uma is bitterly disappointed, bitterly ashamed. She determines, despite all protests, to perform asceticism until she wins her desire; in summer she exposes herself to the appalling heat and smoke of four fires, in winter lies in icy water, in the rains sleeps on the naked rock. As she is engaged in these acts a hermit appears before her and questions her; from her sighs he learns that she loves, and from her maids who that lover is. He proceeds to depict in appalling colours the god of her desire, but she fiercely and bitterly rebukes his attacks; delighted he reveals himself as Çiva incarnate (v). All now is ripe for the wedding, but Kalidasa detains us with a gay picture of the solemn scenes which lead up to it. The Seven Seers themselves with Arundhati come as wooers from Çiva to seek the maiden's hand; she stands, eyes downcast, counting the leaves on the lotus in her hand, at her father's side, while his eyes wander to the face of his consort, for in matters affecting their daughters householders are wont to obey their wives' desires (vi). The wedding follows, described, doubtless from the model of imperial ceremonies, with rich abundance of detail; the mother, in her excitement between joy and sorrow, cannot see to place correctly the painted mark on her daughter's forehead, and misplaces the woollen marriage thread which the nurse, more calm and practical, sets aright.

With this ends the poem in many manuscripts; others add ten cantos. Of these Canto viii describes, according to the principles of the Kamaçastra, the joys of the wedded pair; doubtless such frankness is abhorrent to western taste, but the doubts of its genuineness which have been expressed are clearly groundless; it seems certainly to have been known to Bharavi, to Kumaradasa, and to Magha, and quotations from it occur in the writers on poetics. Nor in poetic skill is it in the least inferior to Kalidasa's work. The case is other with the following cantos. They tell of Agni's approach, first in dove shape, then in his proper person, to Çiva as he prolongs for centuries the joys of dalliance, begging his aid. From the seed of Çiva, cast in the Ganges and shared by the six Krttikas, Pleiades, Kumara is miraculously born, and grows up delighting his parents by his childish play. But the gods are in terror, the city of the gods is dismayed through Taraka; Indra comes to demand help; Çiva grants his prayer and assigns Kumara to the task. The great host of Taraka is described in Canto xiv, then the portents which warn him not to war (xv). Blinded by pride he refuses, bids his young opponent go back to his father and mother rather than fight, assails him with his whirlwinds and magic fire, until pierced to the heart he falls dead. The poem thus goes far beyond the birth of Kumara as its title promises, and the inferiority of the new cantos is obvious on every ground. The metre is carelessly handled; in five cases caesura is neglected at the end of the first and third verses of the Çloka, a negligence quite foreign to Kalidasa; the same carelessness is seen six times in Upajati stanzas, where too weak caesuras—at the end of a compound, not of a word—are used far more often than by Kalidasa. In order to manage his metres the poet has to resort to versefillers, abhorred of really good writers; *su* is repeatedly thus used, as well as *sadyah* and *alam;* the constant use of periphrasis is doubtless due to the same cause: the writer expends much ingenuity in coining new designations for his characters, and is so fond of the superfluous *anta* at the end of compounds—which we have seen in Vatsabhatti—that Jacobi has conjectured that he was a Maratha, in view of the Marathi locative *amt.* In the later manner is the free use of prepositional compounds and the impersonal passive with subject in the instrumental; the former use just appears in Kalidasa, the latter is common from Bharavi onwards. Moreover, save occasionally, as in the battle scene, the poetical value of the cantos is small, and in confirmation of the internal evidence it may be added that neither commentators nor writers on poetics cite them nor are imitations found in later poets.

Of Kalidasa's model for his poem we know nothing, but we can trace in it the influence of Valmiki. In the *Ramayana* we have a brilliant picture of the contrast of the beauty of spring in the Kiskindha forest as contrasted with the ceaseless sorrow of Rama, bereft of Sita, nor can we doubt that this has influenced Kalidasa to draw the wonderful picture of Spring's advent and the revival of the youth and life of the world. There is a parallel too for Rati's despair; when Valin falls Tara addresses him with words not less sincere because they bear the stamp of the classic style: 'Why dost thus speak no more to thy beloved? Arise and share this fair couch with me; the best of men lie not, as thou, on the ground. Too dear dost thou hold, o lord, the earth even in death, since me thou dost leave alone and her hast clasped in thine embrace. Ended our days of joy together in the fair forest; sunken am I in a deep sea of sorrow, without joy, without sustenance, since thus hast departed. Hard my heart that it can see thee stretched on the ground and yet not break from sorrow.' Hints too for the demon Taraka are clearly taken from the description of Ravana in the *Ramayana*. There are doubtless reminders here and there of Açvaghosa, as in the description of the actions of the women of the city on the advent of Çiva and Parvati, which has a prototype in the description in the *Buddhacarita* of the entrance of the prince, and which is taken up again in the description in the *Raghuvança* of the entry of Aja and Indumati.

The problem why the poem was never finished by its author remains insoluble. The loss of the last pages of a solitary manuscript may be the explanation, but it is far more likely that the poet, deterred either by contemporary criticism of his treatment of the divine pair, or by the feeling that the legend of the birth with its strangeness and miracles was not a true theme for poetry, abandoned the purpose and left his work unfinished. It can hardly be claimed that death intervened, for there can be no doubt that the *Raghuvança* is a later work. This shows itself both in the graver tone, in the references to the Yoga philosophy and the less personal conception of the universe as compared with the magnification of Çiva in the *Kumarasambhava,* and in the growing pedantry seen in the use of similes derived from grammar, of which we have only modest suggestions in the *Kumarasambhava.* Thus Rama's army follows him to serve his purpose as the prefix *adhi* is followed by the root *i* to make the word *adhyayana;* Sugriva is put in Valin's place as king as a substitute replaces the root, and husband and wife are theme and suffix. Moreover, in the constant parallels between the two poems, as in the description of the marriage rites, the priority seems to belong to the *Kumarasambhava*; it is curious that Kalidasa shows a distinct love of using the same metre for the same theme; thus in both we have the Çloka used in prayers, death is described in the Viyogini, a ruined state in the Upajati.

Though inferior in some slight degree to the *Kumarasambhava,* the *Raghuvança* may rightly be ranked as the finest Indian specimen of the Mahakavya as defined by writers on poetics. Dandin lays down that the subject should be taken from old narratives or traditions, not therefore invented; the hero should be noble and clever; there should be descriptions of towns, oceans, mountains, seasons, the rising and setting of the sun and the moon, sport in parks or the sea, drinking, love-feasts, separations, marriages, the production of a son, meeting of councils, embassies, campaigns, battles, and the triumph of the hero, though his rival's merits may be exalted. It should not be too compressed, and it should be replete with sentiments (*rasa*) and the emotions which underlie them (*bhava*). It should have effective transitions (*sandhi*), an allusion to the five stages of action recognized by the writers on drama, by which from its opening the movement advances after a halt to the central moment, pauses, and

reaches the *dénouement.* The metres must be charming, and each Canto, which should not be too long, should end with a change of metre. The poem should begin with a prayer, paying homage or in addition invoking a blessing, or an indication of the subject-matter. It should promote the ends of Dharma, conduct, Artha, worldly success, Moksa, final release, and Kama, love.

The *Raghuvança* is true to the type, for the central figure is Rama, though in accord with the title the poem first sketches the history of the dynasty of the sun-born kings, descendants of the Iksvaku whose name occurs in the *Rgveda,* and whose family is renowned in the epic and the Puranas. This wide theme gives the poet full space to exercise his power of description; war and the coronation of a king, the choosing of her mate by a young princess at a Svayamvara, the marriage rite, the loss of a darling life and the grief of the bereaved husband, town and country, the seasons, the incidents of a great Digvijaya, the triumphal progress of a king who seeks to conquer the earth, all form occasions for the poet's skill. The poem carries us at once into an atmosphere strange to us; Dilipa is king but childless; he learns that by chance when returning from a visit to Indra he has failed to show reverence to his sacred cow, who has cursed him; to make amends he determines to follow in worship the movements of her daughter, Nandini, on earth; dutifully he carries out his vow, saves her from a lion by offering his own body in exchange, and Nandini accords him the wish of his heart. Soon the father gazes, with eyes as still as lotus blossoms shielded from the wind, on the lovely face of his son, his heart overflows as the sea at the sight of the moon. The young Raghu waxes fast, is given the rank of Crown Prince and bidden guard the horse that must wander for a year before his father can perform the sacred horse sacrifice; the steed disappears, but with Nandini's aid Raghu's eyes are opened until he can see where in the east Indra has taken the horse. Vainly he strives against the god, but pleased by his valour he accords him every wish save the return of the horse, and the gallant youth demands that his father shall have the full fruit of the sacrifice. The offering performed, Dilipa gives to his son the white parasol, emblem of sovereignty, and, true to his family's rule, retires to the life of an ascetic in the forest (i-iii). Canto iv recounts the knightly adventures of Raghu as conqueror of India; he advances against the Suhmas, defeats the princes of Bengal, and erects pillars of victory on the islands of the Ganges; neither the elephants nor the arrow hail of Kalinga stay his course, Mahendra yields, the Kaveri is crossed, the south invaded, the Pandyas pay tribute of pearls. Thence the hero bends his path north, through the Malaya and Dardura hills, the sea of his host covers the long slopes of the Sahya mountain, the dust of the army clings to the hair of the ladies of Kerala, the Murala river, the Trikuta hill witness his fame. Thence by land, as a pious king, not by the polluting sea, he advances against the Persians and the Yavanas, Greeks; the dust of the conflict hides the warring hosts whose presence is revealed by the twang of their bows alone, the bearded foemen cover thick the ground, those who escape death cast off their helms in token of submission; the victors wearied slake their thirst with wine. Next Raghu bids his steeds roll in the Indus—a variant has Oxus—sands, overthrows Hunas and Kambojas; the winds of the Himalaya set the reeds hymning his victories. The mountain folk feel his power, fire flashes from the mountain-sides beneath the rain of spears and arrows, and the folk of the Utsavas lose for ever their joy in festivals (*utsava*). The Lauhitya is crossed, Pragjyotisa subdued, and Kamarupa yields tribute of wild elephants.

In this spirited and martial narrative we may justly see the reflex in the poet's mind of Samudragupta's great conquests, and with customary skill the subject changes in Canto v to a very different theme. Raghu's generosity impoverishes him; when a Brahmin Kautsa begs him to aid him to meet the vast demands of his teacher, he resolves to storm the treasure-house of Kubera, god of wealth, but a rain of gold saves him from impiety. The Brahmin's gratitude secures him a son, Aja, who soon equals his father. Bidden to take part in the Svayamvara, at which the sister of a kingly neighbour will choose her mate, he sets forth; on the way he boldly attacks a monstrous wild elephant, which under his stroke changes to a Gandharva, condemned by a curse to wear this shape until released by the blow of an Iksvakuid's arrow, who gives him in reward a magic weapon. Canto vi presents us with a brilliant picture of the Svayamvara; the princess, with her companion Sunanda beside her, passes by prince after prince as they stand eager before her; none please her, one is a dicer, therefore bad as a man; in vain Sunanda presses on her Anga's lord; he has all merits, but tastes vary. In revenge she bids Indumati pass on, when she notes that her heart is won by Aja, but the maiden lays shame aside, and accords to him the coronal which marks him as her spouse. The marriage ceremony is performed, the young pair set out home, but the shamed princes have planned revenge, and resolved to take away by force the princess. Aja wages fierce battle with them, in the end the Gandharva's gift prevails, and he takes from his foes their honour, though he spares their lives (vii). His reign is fortunate; while Raghu as a hermit tames the senses, Aja destroys the foes of his realm, and, when Raghu dies, he pays him all the honours of a Yogin's funeral. But a fatal misfortune awaits him; a garland from the sky blown by the wind falls on Indumati's breast and slays her, though in truth for her death means release from her mortal bondage imposed on her, in reality an Apsaras, through a curse. No consolation is this thought to Aja; in vain is he reminded of the folly of mourning for the dead who are burnt by the tears of the living; in vain every consolation regarding the shortness of life and the duty of kings is urged on him; brokenhearted, he dies and Dilipa reigns in his place. Of him Canto ix has no concrete facts to tell us, until after a brilliant description of spring we are told of the fatal hunt, when, after displaying equal prowess and pity, Dilipa in pursuit of an elephant mortally wounds a Brahmin boy; he bears the dying youth to his aged parents, and hears the curse of a like doom. In Canto x we leave the realities of life to learn of the magic incarnation of Visnu in the sons born to Dilipa; in xi Rama's youth, his visit to Viçvamitra's hermitage where he slays the demon Tadaka, his journey to Janaka's court, where he wins at the Svayamvara the hand of Sita, and his overthrow of Paraçurama, who rec-

ognizes in him the godhead, are rapidly recounted. The banishment of Rama by Kaikeyi's device, the life of Rama and Sita in the forest, her capture by Ravana, the search for Lanka, the crossing of the ocean with the monkey horde, and the great battle between Rama and Ravana, described in vivid colours, bring us to Canto xii in which Kalidasa's descriptive powers find congenial subject-matter in describing the sights of India as seen from the aerial car on which Rama and Sita return to Ayodhya.

Then follows a series of brilliant sketches; Rama and Sita visit the widows of the king, who scarce can see them for their tears, which speedily change to joy. Sita alone weeps for the trouble her beauty has brought her husband, a foreboding of woe. For the moment all is brightness; the glorious ceremonial of the royal consecration follows. But disaster is at hand; malicious voices reproach the king whose one wife has stayed so long in Ravana's home. Rama places duty above love; he bids Laksmana take Sita —now pregnant—to Valmiki's hermitage, and there break to her the truth of her fate; overwhelmed, she deplores her lot but utters no reproach. Rama rules in solitude, her sculptured form his companion in his sacrifices (xiv). From his sorrow he is awakened to overthrow demon foes on the Yamuna banks, while in the hermitage Sita bears two boys who, taught by Valmiki the tale of their father's deed, console her sorrowing heart by reciting it. The day comes when Rama determines to perform the horse sacrifice; he rests in a hut beside the golden statue of his wife; he hears from the boys the song of his deeds; the people, Rama himself recognize them for his own, Valmiki begs reinstatement for the queen. Rama asks only that her stainless purity be made clear; she comes before him, swears to her truth as she drinks the holy water; the earth goddess appears and takes her in her bosom to bear her to the realm below. Rama transfers to his sons the burdens of the state, saddened by the restoration of Siti only to be lost forthwith; in due course, followed by all the people, he goes forth from the town and is caught up in a heavenly chariot.

The effective and pathetic picture of Siti's end and the return to heaven of Rama might well have closed the poem, but Canto xvi is not without merit. Kuça, Rama's son, reigns at Kuçavati; in a dream Ayodhya appears to him in the guise of a woman whose husband is afar, reproaches him with her fallen condition, and bids him return. Kuça obeys, Ayodhya once more is glorious, and a description of the delights of summer rivals, but fails to equal, that of spring in Canto ix. For the rest the poem sinks in interest, as Kalidasa has nothing to tell us but names of worthless kings whose harems supplied their sole interest in life. We cannot deny his authorship of Cantos xviii and xix; no ancient authority questions them, and they are cited, if rarely, by writers on poetics. But their brevity and the utter abruptness of the end, when the widow of Agnivarman, a worthless debauchee, is awaiting the birth of her child, suggest that we have no more than a rough draft. Yet we would gladly assign to a poetaster meaningless puns on names of kings, as when Pariyatra is merely said to have exceeded in height the Pariyatra mountains, or the incredible tastelessness of the action of a king who hangs his foot out of the window for the people to kiss.

Valmiki, of course, is the chief creditor of Kalidasa in this poem. Here and there one certainly surpasses the other; though normally the advantage lies with the younger poet, yet there are exceptions. Fine as is Kalidasa's picture of Rama's meeting with the sons who know him not, it yet is still more affecting in the leisurely march of the epic, and Kalidasa has failed to improve on the scene of Siti's vindication. But his merit shines out in such cases as his description of the return to Ayodhya; future poets were to imitate it, but not one to equal it.

No other epic of Kalidasa has come down to us, and the relation in time of his epics to his dramas is insoluble. The suggestion that he is responsible for the *Setubandha,* which relates the tale of Rama from the advance against Ravana and the building of the bridge to Lanka down to Ravana's death, is excluded by the style, with its innumerable plays on words, alliterations, recondite similes, exaggeration, and its enormous compounds. Its date is uncertain, as of Pravarasena of Kashmir its author or patron we know nothing definite. Still more ludicrous is the suggestion that the *Nalodaya* is his; that rimed poem of intolerable affectation is perhaps not the production of Ravideva, author of the *Raksaskavya,* of equal demerit, before the seventeenth century, but the work of Vasudeva, Protégé of Kulaçekhara and Rama.

As Sophokles seems to have found his perfect *milieu* in the Athens of Perikles' happy days, so Kalidasa appears to us as the embodiment in his poems, as in his dramas, of the Brahmanical ideal of the age of the Guptas, when order had been restored to a troubled earth, foreigners assimilated or reduced, and prosperity broadcast. Ingenuity has traced in the history of the first five of the rulers in the *Raghuvança* an exemplar of the exploits of the first five of the Gupta kings; granted that Kalidasa may have known and profited by the literary activity of Harisena, which doubtless extended far beyond the one inscription which has come down to us, still we may safely doubt any such parallelism. But Kalidasa does represent, if we may judge from his poetry, the complete carrying out of the rule of life laid down for a Brahmin or a warrior or clansman. Youth, in this view, is the time for study under a teacher, then follows the period of manhood with its happy wedlock, then in stages that of the hermit whose mind is set on things eternal. The scheme is in many ways perfectly adapted to Indian life; it starves no side of man's life; four aims of existence are recognized by Kalidasa himself, who finds them embodied in the sons of Dilipa, themselves reflexes of Visnu himself. They are duty, governing man's whole life; the pursuit of wealth and of love, the occupations of his manhood; and release, the fruit of his meditations in old age. We may not share the affection of Indian and even of a section of modern taste for the erotic scenes of the last cantos of the *Raghuvança,* but we must not regard them as the outpourings of a sensual mind. The sages of the Upanisads themselves deemed marriage obligatory and the *Brhadaranyaka* gives the spell to obtain a male son; the saintly Çvetaketu is deemed an authority on the *Kamasutra,* and Kalidasa expressly claims the divine precedent of Çiva and Uma as sanction for the most passionate married love. Statecraft

again is essentially part of the material ends of life, and not only does he paint in Rama an ideal ruler, but throughout the *Raghuvança* we are reminded of the duties of kings to the subjects. Let us grant that his vision was Brahmanical; he deliberately repeats the condemnation of the *Ramayana* on the Çudra who threatens the security of established order by venturing to expose himself, head downwards, hanging from a tree to fire, in order by penance to acquire merit. This reminds us of Fa-hien's emphatic testimony of the degradation of the Candalas in the Gupta realm.

Youth and manhood are no time for deep philosophic views, and the Kalidasa of the *Rtusamhara, Meghaduta,* and *Kumarasambhava* remains within narrower limits. We feel, however, a growing sense of the greatness and glory of Çiva; the remote figure of the *Meghaduta* is definitely brought nearer to us in the *Kumarasambhava.* Even Brahman and Visnu are less than he, and the term Lord, Içvara, is his *par excellence;* moreover, despite his all-embracing majesty, he is intensely personal. Yet neither Brahman nor Visnu is forgotten; to Brahman in the *Kumarasambhava* itself, to Visnu in the *Raghuvança* two noble prayers are addressed in which in the true spirit of kathenotheism either appears as the greatest of gods, as more than the world, as beyond all comprehension. The inconsistency, however, is rather apparent than real; it is possible to ascertain with fair certainty the view Kalidasa took of the universe, and this affords a reconciliation of his diverse views.

Both epics, but especially the *Raghuvança,* show that Kalidasa accepted Samkhya and Yoga views of the nature of the universe. The three constituents of nature, goodness, passion, and dullness, in their ethical aspect afford themes for simile; the Brahman sea as the source of the Sarayu is like the unmanifested (*avyakta*) whence springs intelligence. Yoga practices are recognized; the aged king practises concentration (*dharana*) as he sits on Kuça grass; the difficult posture known as Virasana of ascetics is compared to trees standing motionless; Sita by asceticism seeks to secure reunion in her next life with her spouse; the power to pass through closed doors may be won, and the Yogin needs not cremation, but like Raghu is buried in mother earth. But we cannot hold that the godhead envisaged by Kalidasa is the pale Içvara of the Yoga; in Brahman we are told are united both matter and spirit as they are known in the Samkhya, and this we may fairly take as indicating that to Kalidasa, as to the author of the *Katha Upanisad,* over the spirits and matter stood the absolute, who to Kalidasa takes specially the form of Çiva but who is also Brahman and Visnu, the spirit that perishes not beyond the darkness. With this absolute man is merged on death if he has attained enlightenment, for this is the sense of *brahmabhuyamagatim ajagama* in the *Raghuvança.* If enlightenment is not his but good deeds, he has heaven for his share, for knowledge alone burns up man's deeds which else force him to life after life. We need have the less hesitation to accept this view in that it is essentially the standpoint of popular Vedantism and that it afforded to a man of thought and good sense an effective means of reconciling belief in the three great gods. What is clear is that in his advancing years Kalidasa's mind turned more and more to the conception of the all-embracing character of the godhead and of the efficacy of Yoga practices to attain union with him.

From such a philosophy it would be idle to seek any solution for essential conflicts in the heart of man, or to demand any independent criticism of man's aims and fate. India knew atheists enough, but their works have all but perished, and we must rather be grateful that we have preserved in such perfection the poetic reflex of the Brahmanical ideal both in its strength and in its weakness. Nor, let us remember, does such an ideal shut out deep human feeling such as we may suspect in the longing of the *Meghaduta,* the lament of Aja over the dead Indumat , of Rati for Kama slain. But it does demand resignation, and if in perfection of form Kalidasa's poems proclaim him the Virgil of India, we may admit that he was incapable of the vision and imagery of the sixth book of the *Aeneid. . . .*

In Kalidasa we have unquestionably the finest master of Indian poetic style superior to Açvaghosa by the perfection and polish of his work, and all but completely free from the extravagances which disfigure the later great writers of Kavya. Dandin ascribes to his favourite style, the Vaidarbha, qualities which we may fairly sum up as firmness and evenness of sound, avoiding harsh transitions and preferring gentle harmonies; the use of words in their ordinary sense and clearness of meaning; the power to convey sentiment; beauty, elevation, and the employment of metaphorical expressions. He assures longevity to a poem which, in addition to conforming to the rules for a Mahakavya, is rich in ornaments (*alamkara*), and Kalidasa is not sparing in his use of these means of adding grace to his work. But he has the fundamental merit that he prefers suggestion to elaboration; his successors too often thought that they could only prove their capacity by showing all of what it was capable; he was content to produce a definite effect, and to leave well alone; his was the golden mean of Virgil between rustic simplicity and clumsiness and that over-refinement which is specially fatal. Thus it results that his miniature-painting in its polished elegance often attains relative perfection.

The truth of his delineation is seen in the picture of the sorrowing bride in the *Meghaduta:*

> utsange va malinavasane saumya niksipya vinam
>   madgotrankam viracitapadam geyam udgatukamam
> tantrim ardram nayanasalilaih sarayitva kathamcit
>   bhuyo bhuyah svayam api krtam murcchanam
>   vismaranti.

'Or perhaps, placing her lute on her lap, whose dark garment proclaims her grief, she will seek to sing a song wherein she has worked my name, but, scarce able to move the string which her tears have bedewed, she will forget the air which she herself hath made.' Or, again:

tvam alikhya pranayakupitam dhaturagaih çilayam
  atmanam te caranapatitam yavad icchami kartum
asrais tavan muhur upacitair drstir alupyate me
  kruras tasminn api na sahate samgamam nau krtantah.

'When I have portrayed thee in love's anger on the rock with my colours and seek to add myself lying at thy feet, my tears well up and ever blot out my sight; cruel the fate which even thus will not permit our union.' There is a brilliant picture of Uma's confusion and of her joy when Çiva reveals himself:

> adya prabhrty avanatangi tavasmi desah
>   kritas tapobhir iti vadini candramaulau
> ahnaya sa niyamajam klamam utsasarja
>   kleçah phalena hi punar navatam vidhatte.

'"From this moment, o drooping maiden, I am thy slave, bought by thy penance," so spake he whose crest is the moon, and straightway all the fatigue of her self-torment vanished, so true is it that fruitful toil is as if it had never been.' There is perfect simplicity of passionate longing in Rati's address to the dead Kama:

> krtavan asi vipriyam na me: pratikulam na ca te
>   maya krtam
> kim akaranam eva darçanam: vilapantyai rataye na
>   diyate?

'Thou hast never displeased me; thee I never have wronged; why then, without cause, dost thou hide thyself from thy weeping Rati?' The timid shyness of the new-made bride and her lover's ruses are delicately drawn:

> vyahrt prativaco na samdadhe: gantum aicchad
>   avalambitançuka
> sevate sma çayanam paranmukhi: sa tathapi rataye
>   pinakinah.

'Addressed she could not answer; when he touched her gown she sought to leave him; with head averted she clung to her couch; yet none the less did she delight the lord of the trident.'

> atmanam alokya ca çobhamanam: adarçabimbe
>   stimitayataksi
> Haropayane tvarita babhuva: strinam priya
>   lokaphalo hi veçah.

'When with her long eyes fixed on her mirror she saw the reflection of her radiant loveliness, swift she hastened to seek Çiva, for the fruit of woman's raiment is the light in the lover's eyes.' Equally complete in its own effectiveness is the description of the tragic shock received by Rati:

> tivra bhisangaprabhavena vrttim: mohena
>   samstambhayatendriyanam

ajnatabhartrvyasaua muhurtam: krtopaka reva Ratir babhuva.

'The bitterness of the blow cast Rati into a faint which dulled her senses and for the moment with true kindness robbed her of memory of her husband's ruin.'

Aja's tears have their excuse in nature itself:

vilalapa sabaspagadgadam: sahajam apy apahaya dhiratam

abhitaptam ayo'pi m rdavam: bhajate kaiva kath çar risu?

'He wailed aloud, his voice broken by sobs, forgetting the high courage that was his; iron in the fire yieldeth its strength; how much more feeble mortals?' He feels that his wife has doubted his love:

dhruvam asmi çathah çucismite: viditah kaitavavatsalas tava

paralokam asamnivrttaye: yadanaprcchya gatasi mam itah.

'Surely, sweet smiling one, thou hast judged me traitor whose love was feigned that thou hast gone from me to the world whence there is no return and hast not bidden me even a word of farewell.' No woman could desire a more perfect eulogy:

grhini sacivah sakhi mithah: priyaçisya lalite kalavidhau

karunavimukhena mrtyuna: harata tvam vada kim na me hrtam?

'Wife, counsellor, companion, dearest disciple in every loving art; in taking thee tell me what of me hath not pitiless Death taken.' The fatal blow is depicted:

ksanamatrasakhim sujatayoh: stanayos tam avalokya vihvala

nimimila narottamapriya: hrtacandra tamaseva kaumudi.

'For a moment she gazed on the garland as it lay on her rounded breasts, then closed her eyes in unconsciousness, like the moonlight when the darkness obscures the moon.' There is humour, on the contrary, in Indumati's rejection of the Anga prince:

athangarajad avatarya caksur: yahiti janyam avadat kumari

nasau na kamyo na ca veda samyag: drastum na sa bhinnarucir hi lokah.

'But the princess turned away from Anga's lord her gaze, and bade her maiden proceed; it was not that he had not beauty nor that she could not see it, but folk have different tastes.' This has the same graceful ease as often in the **Rtusamhara**:

vivasvata tiksnatarançumalina: sapankatoyat saraso 'bhitapitah

utplutya bhekas trsitasya bhoginah: phanatapatrasya tale nisidati.

'As the sun's garland of rays grows ever hotter, the frog sore tormented leaps up from the muddy water of the lake only to fall into the mouth of the thirsty snake, who spreads his hood to shade him from the glare.' There is a pretty picture of girlish haste:

alokamargam sahasa vrajantya: kayacid udvestanavantamalyah

baddhum na sambhavita eva tavat: karena ruddho 'pi ca keçapaçah.

'As she rushed to the window, her garlands fell from their place, and she did not even trouble to knot the abundant hair which she caught together in her hand.'

The structure of each of these cameos is simple; throughout it is normal to have each verse complete in itself, a single verb serving to support a number of adjectives and appositions, though relative clauses with verb expressed or implied are not rare. The compounds are normally restricted in length, but this is less closely observed in the Mandakranta metre, though even then clearness is aimed at and normally achieved. The order of words is very free, partly no doubt by reason of metrical necessity. Of the figures those of sound are employed not rarely but usually with skill. Beside the ordinary forms of alliteration as in *nirmame nirmamo 'rthesu*, we find the more important Yamaka, in which the same syllables are repeated, in the same or inverted order, but with different sense. There is a certain liberality in the process; thus Kalidasa is able to match *bhujalatam* with *jadatam*, for *l* and *d*, like *r* and *l*, *b* and *v*, are admitted as similar, and the same principle is clearly to be seen in

cakara sa mattacakoranetra: lajjavati lajavisargam agnau.

'She with the eyes of the intoxicated Cakora, in modesty (*lajj*) made offering of fried rice (*laja*) in the fire.' In Canto ix of the *Raghuvança* Kalidasa deliberately shows his skill in Yamakas; there is no doubt that this offends the sound rule of Anandavardhana that to seek deliberately such a result destroys the function of poetry which is to suggest—or express—not merely to exhibit form, and we can only conjecture that in this canto, which also is marked out by the amazing number of metres employed, Kalidasa was seeking to prove that he could vie with any rival in these niceties. In Canto xviii also, Yamakas are superabundant. Throughout, however, we feel Kalidasa seeking for the matching of sound and sense, to which the Indian ear was clearly more susceptible than our own.

Of figures of sense Kalidasa excels in Indian opinion in the simile, and the praise is just. The Indian love of simile appears freely in the *Rgvcda*, and is attested by the elaborate subdivisions of Indian poetics. The width of Kalidasa's knowledge and the depth of his observation of nature and life are here shown to the highest advantage.

But his world is not ours, and doubtless at times his figures seem grotesque to our taste, as when the king comes from his bath and plays with his harem like an elephant on whose shoulder still clings a shoot of the lotus sporting with the females of his herd. But often there can be only admiration; the chariot of the prince is so covered by the arrows of his foes that only by the point of its standard can it be discerned, as the morning wrapped in mist by the feeble rays of the sun; the wound torn by the arrow is the door of death; with joyful eyes the women of the city follow the prince as the nights with the clear stars of autumn the polar star. Characteristic is the love of elaboration of a comparison; the reader is not to be contented with a mere hint, the comparison must be drawn out in full. The Pandya king is peer of the lord of mountains, for the necklaces which hang over his shoulders are its foaming cascades, and the sandal that reddens his limbs the young sun which colours its peaks. Or again, the princes who hide their jealousy under the semblance of joy are compared to the pool in whose calm depths lurk deadly crocodiles. Or again, the ruined city, with towers broken, terraces laid down and houses destroyed, is like the evening when the sun sets behind the mountains and a mighty wind scatters the clouds.

To us, no doubt, both similes and metaphors sometimes seem far-fetched; those from grammar leave us cold, but there is wit in the assertion that the wearing by Rama of the royal dress when the ascetic's garb revealed already his fairness is equivalent to the vice of repetition (*punarukta*). The bowmen whose arrows strike one another are like disputants whose words conflict. The king seeks to subdue the Persians as an ascetic his senses through the knowledge of truth. Kalidasa is rich also in plays of fancy which present a vivid picture (*utpreksa*); it is natural to him to think vividly, to attribute to the mountains, the winds, the streams the cares, sorrows, joys, and thoughts of men. He loves also the figure corroboration (*arthantaranyasa*); indeed, its careless use reveals the hand of the forger of the last cantos of the *Kumarasambhava*. But the *double entendre* is rare indeed; the instances of it are very few, and they lend no credit whatever to the suggestion that v. 14 of the *Meghaduta* is an attempt obliquely to praise Nicula and damn Dignaga. Of the former we know nothing, and it was doubtless the later love for Çlesas which bade men find them in Kalidasa, where not one elaborate case even can be proved to exist.

Kalidasa's metrical skill is undoubted. In the *Rtusamhara* he used normally the Indravajra and Vançastha types, with Vasantatilaka and Malini; one stanza only in Çardulavikridita occurs. The *Meghaduta* shows the more elaborate Mandakranta used without variation; a few slight roughnesses as regards caesura may be adduced as proof of the relatively early date of the poem, but the evidence is too slight to weigh seriously in itself. In the *Kumarasambhava* we find the normal rule that the canto is written in a single metre with change, as the writers on poetics require, at the close. Thus i, iii, and vii are written in the Indravajra; ii and vi in the Çloka, iv in the Vaitaliya, and v in the Vançastha, while viii is in the Rathoddhata. The closing changes are furnished by Puspitagra, Malini, and Vasan-

tatilaka. The *Raghuvança* follows on the whole this principle, but exhibits greater variety, suggesting later date. The Indravajra type serves for ii, v-vii, xiii, xvi, xvi, and xviii; the Çloka for i, iv, x, xii, xv, and xvii; the Vaitaliya for viii, and the Rathoddhat for xi and xix. Canto ix is orthodox up to v. 54, being in Drutavilambita, then it deliberately displays the poet's skill in new metres, each with a verse or so, Aupacchandasika, Puspitagra, Praharsini, Manjubhasini, Mattamayura, Vasantatilaka, which is also used for II verses in v, Vaitaliya, Çalini, and Svagata. There occur also odd verses in Totaka, Mandakranta, Mahamalik , and iii is written in Vançastha, with a concluding verse in Harini. There are thus nineteen metres in all to eight in the earlier epic. Detailed efforts to find some sign of development in any of the metres in respect of caesuras &c. have failed to yield any results worthy of credence.

In the Çloka the rules had already been established by epic practice, and Kalidasa observes them carefully. Of the four Vipula forms he uses the last once only; the figures for the other three out of 1410 half-stanzas in the epics are 46, 27, and 41, or 8·15 per cent., showing that the third Vipula was Kalidasa's favourite. It is interesting to note that in the form of the syllables preceding the first Vipula Kalidasa shows special care to select that form . . . which is not allowed in the second Vipula as against that . . . which is permitted in both. The *Kumarasambhava* has II cases of the first to 3 of the second form, the *Raghuvança* 31 to 1; this doubtless indicates increasing care to secure elegance, and it accords with this that in the *Kumarasambhava* alone is the fourth Vipula found.

Daniel H. H. Ingalls (essay date 1976)

SOURCE: "Kalidasa and the Attitudes of the Golden Age," in *Journal of the American Oriental Society,* Vol. 96, No. 1, January-March, 1976, pp. 15-26.

[Ingalls is an American educator and critic specializing in the study of Sanskrit literature. In the following essay, he examines Kalidasa's milieu, noting the manner in which the spirit of the author's age is reflected in his thought and artistry.]

Within a few years of A.D. 320 there arose in northeast India a dynasty of rulers which was to produce what some scholars have called the Indian Golden Age. Whether the Gupta Empire deserves that title is a matter of aesthetic and moral judgment. I shall not hide my own judgment in the matter, but I shall concern myself chiefly with the facts on which a judgment must be based.

Within the first seventy years of their accession the Guptas succeeded in subjecting nearly the whole of northern India to their sway. They then moved their capital from the east to the west, from Pataliputra on the Ganges to Ujjain in Malwa. For the next eighty years they enjoyed a wide and prosperous reign and it was within this period, between A.D. 390 and 470, that the poet Kalidasa lived. The invasion of the Ephthalite Huns then destroyed the prosperity of the Guptas and ultimately robbed them of their western possessions. The Guptas moved again from the west back to the east and for a century or so continued, in steadily decreasing glory, to use the royal title. Thus the Gupta Empire counted 150 years of power and a century or so of decay. The record has been equalled by many other Indian dynasties and exceeded by several.

What first distinguishes the Guptas from other dynasties of India is that they brought about a revival of native Indian power after a long period of foreign dominance. For five hundred years prior to A.D. 320 the greater part of northwestern and western India had been ruled by foreigners: by Greco-Bactrians, Persians, Scythians, Kushans. Local rule had begun to reassert itself in the third century, but with the advent of the Guptas there appeared for the first time in half a millenium a native Indian government in the north that was also a united and a strong government.

The gaining of this empire was the work of two men, Samudragupta and Candragupta II, the second and third emperors respectively of the dynasty. We are given a list of Samudragupta's conquests in the Allahabad Pillar Inscription, composed in elegant Sanskrit by one of his generals, a man named Harisena. The beginning of the inscription is fragmentary due to the peeling of the surface of the sandstone and in what remains we are not told of the chronological order of the conquests, simply the names of the kings and sometimes of the kingdoms which the emperor conquered. But if we pinpoint the identifiable names on the map, we get very nearly a complete circle of the Indian subcontinent. Only the west coast, with the possible exception of the extreme southwest, remains without certain identification points. So it is not too fanciful to speak of Samudragupta as a *cakravartin* as the term had been understood from time immemorial. The *cakravartin,* or wheel-turner, shall make a circuit of conquest like the sun's, turning always to the right until he has sanctified the earth by his circumambulation of it. The ideal goes back to Indo-European antiquity. The high kings of pagan Ireland were expected to perform the same feat. Of course it is easier to get around Ireland than around India.

Certainly what else we know of Samudragupta points to a conscious effort to revive the customs of the Hindu and the Vedic past. One particular set of titles came to be associated with his name and is repeated as a formula in inscriptions of later emperors wherever Samudragupta's name appears in the list of their ancestors.

> Samudragupta, the conqueror of all kings, unopposed upon earth, whose fame has extended to the four oceans, equal to the gods Kubera, Varuna, Indra, and Yama, the axe of death, giver of millions in cattle and gold that he had rightfully acquired, reviver of the horse sacrifice that had long been in abeyance . . .

By way of explanation: the four gods here mentioned are the world protectors, the traditional guardians of the four compass points. Cattle and gold are the traditional gifts to brahmins. It is an important claim that the wealth so used

was acquired rightfully, that is, not by oppression of his own people. The horse sacrifice was the most prestigious of the Vedic rites and served the political purpose of confirming the performer in the high kingship. The last previous performance of which we have record was by Pravarasena I, perhaps thirty years or so before. But that was in the Deccan. It may have been centuries since a horse sacrifice had been performed in the north. Finally, one should emphasize that these titles, as indeed all Gupta inscriptions, are given in the sacred language, Sanskrit. Previously, royal inscriptions had usually used one or another of the spoken tongues.

With this evidence before us, we should expect the Gupta emperors to have been conservative to the core. Certainly that was their attitude. On the other hand, their performance was far from it. The Gupta age was remarkable for its innovations.

Samudragupta had not annexed all the lands through which he had marched. A *cakravartin* is not supposed to rule the outer regions of the earth directly. Harisena's inscription mentions twelve specific kings who were captured and then liberated. Kalidasa, whose description of the conquests of the legendary Raghu parallels in many instances that of the actual Gupta emperor, says that Raghu treated the Bengalis like rice plants: one pulls up young rice only to transplant it. One takes the glory and treasury from distant kings but leaves them their land. Only in the case of his close neighbors had Samudragupta acted otherwise. "He uprooted Acyuta and Nagasena"; and there is no word in the inscription of his replacing them. At his death, the lands directly held by the Guptas were limited to a strip along the Ganges and Jumna rivers.

The acquisition of the west was the work of his son, Candragupta II (A.D. 375-415). The work seems to have been done by politics rather than by war. I shall omit the melodrama contained in the recently recovered fragments of the *Devicandragupta,* as I doubt its truth. From the inscriptions one can see that the Guptas allied themselves with the Vakatakas, who were masters of the Vindhya hills. Candragupta II married his daughter Prabhavati Gupta to a Vakataka prince. With Vakataka's aid, it would seem, Candragupta drove the Scythian satraps out of Malwa. After doing so, he moved his capital from the east to Ujjain. Meanwhile Prabhavati's prince became king and then after five years of rule died. For the next twenty years, during the minority first of one son and then of the next, Prabhavati Gupta ruled as queen regent over a large portion of central India. To the northwest her father and later her brother put down roots in Malwa. The royal family had been and continued to be Vaisnava in religion. On the other hand, Ujjain, their new capital, was a center of Saiva worship. Candragupta solved the conflict of religion by compromise. His reign is remarkable for compromise in other respects as well.

Candragupta's government was a compromise between the bureaucracy of ministerial control which had been exercised by the western foreigners and the old ideal of personal rule through members of the royal family. The new provinces in the west, which are called *desas* in the inscriptions, were ruled by ministers. The old homeland in the east was divided into *bhuktis* governed directly by royal princes. In the choice of his ministers we are struck by his remarkable religious tolerance. The emperor himself, like his father, his son, and his grandson, is styled *parama-bhagavata,* a worshipper of Visnu especially in the incarnation of Krishna. But his minister Sikharasvamin and his hereditary Minister of Peace and War Saba-Virasena were Saivas, and we have a donative inscription in which Amrakardava, a military officer "in the employ of the emperor Candragupta," donates a village and 25 dinars for the perpetual upkeep of ten Buddhist monks and two lamps in the monastery of Sanchi.

If we look beyond the inscriptions we see a wealth of new ideas germinating in north India in the Gupta period. I shall mention only two sorts. Greek astronomy had been introduced to west India in the second century. The source of the *Yavana Jataka* was an Alexandrian manuscript which was first translated into Sanskrit prose in A.D. 149/150, then reworked into Sanskrit verse by Sphujudhvaja in A.D. 269/270. The astronomers of the Gupta period developed what the foreign rulers had imported. By the end of the period longitudes had been rereckoned from Ujjain in place of Alexandria in Egypt. More important, the mathematicians began to work seriously with astronomical problems. Aryabhata, writing at the end of the Gupta period in A.D. 499, calculated the past and future conjunctions of planets from the distance between them. He furnishes a table of sine differences from the first sine. He is the first author in the world to deal effectively with square and cube root and with arithmetical progressions. He is also the first author to furnish a general solution of indeterminate equations of the first degree.

It was also in this period that Indian logic had its beginnings. The earlier texts such as the *Nyayasutras* and Nagarjuna show no real comprehension of logic. What they furnish are patterns of debate. The analysis of inference into major and minor terms, the doctrine of the syllogism and of the faults of the syllogism appear first in Dinnaga and Prasastapada in the Gupta period.

The period of Gupta glory continued for two reigns after Chandragupta II. There was the long reign of Kumaragupta (A.D. 415-455), ineptly named, for Kumara is the epithet of the Hindu war god and Kumaragupta seems to have been singularly inactive as a military leader, and the brief reign of Skandagupta (455-467), probably his younger son and probably a usurper to the throne. Skandagupta made a valliant attempt to repel the Ephthalite Huns who were invading from the north. He defeated them in a battle recorded in the Bhitari inscription. After that, as often happens after a war, the coinage was devalued. The coins were made heavier, but the gold content was reduced. In later battles the Guptas were less successful.

What I have spoken of: politics, astronomy, logic, gold coinage, are matters somewhat removed from common life. Neither the inscriptions nor Sanskrit literature have much to say of common folk. Kalidasa in his *Sakuntala* gives us

one vulgar scene, in which an honest fisherman and three venal policemen take part. But policemen in Sanskrit plays are invariably dishonest, just as they always speak in a barbarous dialect. In these traits there is nothing peculiar to the Gupta Empire. Better evidence for the actual state of affairs under the Guptas comes from a foreign traveler.

The late Sylvain Lévi dug out a Chinese reference to a diplomatic correspondence between Magadha and Ceylon just before the advent of the Guptas. The king of Ceylon wanted to make some provision for maintenance of his subjects who might want to go on pilgrimage to the Bodhi Tree. "Wang-hsuan says that the first two monks reported, 'There is no place in the whole of India where one may live in peace'." Against this one may put the remarks of Fa Hsien, the first man to leave a record of walking from China to India. He arrived in India in A.D. 404 under the reign of Chandragupta II and he speaks of the "Middle Kingdom," that is, the homeland of the Guptas, in part as follows [The quotations are from H. A. Giles, *The Travels of Fa-hsien,* 1923]:

> To the south of this [viz., of Muttra] is the Middle Kingdom. The people are prosperous and happy, without registration or official restrictions. Only those who till the king's land have to pay so much on the profit they make. Those who want to go away, may go; those who want to stop, may stop.

> [Fa Hsien was writing with a view to his fellow Buddhists in China. Under the Wei Dynasty official regulations were burdensome, especially to Buddhists.] The king in his administration uses no corporal punishments; criminals are merely fined according to the gravity of their offenses. Even for a second attempt at rebellion the punishment is only the loss of the right hand. The men of the king's body-guard all have fixed salaries.

> [I might point out that this has been the touchstone of good government in India. When soldiers were paid directly by the king, they fought only against foreigners. When treasuries went bankrupt, soldiers were left to live off the land and consequently fought against their own people.]

> Rooms, with beds and mattresses, food and clothes, are provided for resident and travelling monks without fail; and this is the same in all places . . . When travelling priests arrive, the old resident priests go out to welcome them and carry for them their clothes and alms-bowls, giving them water for washing and oil for annointing their feet, as well as the liquid food allowed out of hours.

The general picture we get from Kalidasa is also of a happy land. But one might suspect the impressions of a court poet and a brahmin, so I have quoted the often-quoted traveler as a control. In intellectual development and poetry the Gupta age was certainly golden. From the small evidence at our disposal it seems, in the days of its prosperity, to have been a kindly environment for common men too.

The most famous author of the Gupta age is Kalidasa. He owes his fame to a number of factors. He is the oldest of the classical poets preserved in the school tradition of Sanskrit. I am here distinguishing Classical Sanskrit, the language purified by the grammarians, from the older literature of the epics and the Veda. For centuries it has been with Kalidasa's **Dynasty of Raghu,** or his **Birth of the Prince,** or his **Cloud Messenger** that Indian children have begun the study of Sanskrit poetry. The **Dynasty of Raghu** relates the legends of the solar kings of Ayodhyya: of pious Dilipa, warlike Raghu, of King Aja and the tragic death of his queen, of Rama into whose body God entered in order to destroy the demon Ravana. The **Birth of the Prince** is a poem in which one would expect to be told—of the birth of the prince. The prince, Kumara, is the Indian war god. But the poem, at least the genuine part of it, ends before the prince is born. What we are told of are the love, the marriage, and the honeymoon of the Father-god and Mother-goddess who are the prince's parents. In the **Cloud Messenger** a noble of Kubera's court, banished to South India, sends a message by means of a cloud to his wife in the Himalayas. The poem describes the various rivers and mountains and cities across which the cloud will pass.

These poems were taught by school teachers verse by verse, explaining the formation of each word, furnishing the appropriate rule for each construction, and defining each figure of speech. We have in manuscript form the lectures of some fifty of these schoolmasters from the tenth century down to the present. That Kalidasa's poetry could survive such treatment is evidence of the author's invulnerable genius. For these children grew up to love what they had memorized and to imitate Kalidasa when they came to write poetry of their own.

Again, Kalidasa is the only author of the classical tradition who wrote plays as well as poems. Other classical authors specialized in one or the other. The plays, until recently, did not form part of the school tradition; no ancient commentaries on them are preserved. They were works that were read for pleasure or which you might see performed at court or in a temple. Their text is less well preserved than that of the poems, having been added to or altered to suit successive companies of actors. We have three plays of Kalidasa, which for 1,500 years have furnished Indians with models for the aesthetic enjoyment of laughter, love, and compassion.

Finally, there is the inherent merit of Kalidasa's work. It is not that he casts all other Indian authors into the shade. Sanskrit is too traditional and anti-individualistic a medium to have produced a concentration of all its genius in a single man, as English did in Shakespeare. Kalidasa's merit is rather a merit of balance: he combines convention and originality, reason and emotion, worldly values and mystical values, with invariable taste. One can find each of these elements separately in other Sanskrit authors; and in works that pursue one of these elements single-mindedly one may find it expressed perhaps more brilliantly than in Kalidasa. But no other Sanskrit author keeps the various strands of literature, the various goals of human life, in

such perfect harmony. It has seemed to me that this balance, this harmony, of Kalidasa, may be illuminated by a comparison with the attitudes of the age in which he lived, that is, of the early fifth century, the period of Candragupta II and Kumaragupta.

I have spoken of the professed conservatism of the Guptas. One may quote Kalidasa in full support. In the **Dynasty of Raghu** the pattern is set by the first of the legendary kings that Kalidasa describes.

> Under Dilipa's guidance
> the people, like the tire of his chariot wheel,
> swerved not a hair's breadth
> from the track of the first king, Manu.
>
> > (**Ragh.** I, 17)

The next of the legendary kings is the handsome conqueror Raghu. Kalidasa speaks of the beauty of Raghu's eyes, and then adds,

> But his real eyesight
> consisted in his seeing the answer to problems
> by the light of the sacred books.
>
> > (**Ragh.** IV, 13)

The veneration of scripture, of the *sastras,* appears in Kalidasa's innumerable descriptions of ceremonies: consecrations of kings, weddings, birth ceremonies. He tells us of the haircutting and *godana* ceremonies of Raghu. Ritual had a physical effect on Kalidasa. In speaking of the smell of smoke from a sacrificial fire, he says that it cleans and lightens the soul (**Ragh.** XIII, 37). But more than this, ritual was associated in Kalidasa's mind with beauty. As the old chamberlain in the *Vikramorvasiya* views the palace where he has performed his duty for so many years, he says,

> How beautiful the king's palace in the evening!
> The peacocks, as motionless as statues,
> are sleeping on their perches.
> The smoke of incense, rising from the windows,
> settles like grey doves along the eaves.
> The older ladies of the household, purified for
> their ritual,
> set out the lamps of evening worship on the altars,
> bright lamps among the offerings of flowers.
>
> > (**Vikr.** III,2)

In the **Birth of the Prince** there occurs a wonderful chain of similes. The Mother-goddess grew up in the Himalaya, which she purified and beautified by her presence. "As the altar lamp by means of its flame, as the night sky by means of the Ganges that flows through it as the Milky Way, as speech by means of the Sanskrit language, so was the mountain purified by the goddess and thereby rendered beautiful." (**Kum. S.** I, 18) This association of ritual, cleanliness, purity, beauty, is founded on brahmin tradition and is passionately conservative.

There is no doubt where Kalidasa's heart lay. But his eyes and mind took in a broader world than the world of sacred books. To begin with geography, we might expect him to describe the city of Ujjain, for he was probably born near Ujjain and was certainly a votary of Siva to whom its chief temple was dedicated. He describes the city in the **Cloud Messenger** as a sight that the cloud should not miss.

> When you come to Avanti
>   where the villagers know the stories of Udayana,
> you must pay a visit
>   to the broad and royal city of Ujjain.
> Those who built it
>   must have come from heaven where, as their merit
>   lessened,
> they garnered what was left,
>   and left the sky to build this heaven on earth.
>
> Here the breeze at dawn,
>   rising from the Sipra with its opening lotuses,
> carries over the city
>   the sharp and liquid calling of the paddy birds;
> touching the body softly,
>   soothing the weariness of ladies from their night of love,
> it whispers
>   like a skilful lover who would ask for more.
>
> The townsfolk tell relatives
>   who have come from far to see city's sights,
> "Here is the spot
>   where King Udayana carried off Pradyota's daughter.
> This very place
>   is where his golden palm grove used to be.
> And here the elephant,
>   Nalagiri, tore up his post and broke away."
>
> In the market
>   you will see precious necklaces set out,
> the great central gems
>   and little pearls by millions;
> emeralds as dark as grass
>   with rays of light shooting from each stone,
> mother-of-pearl and coral:
>   everything the ocean holds except its water.

The **Cloud Messenger** contains similar descriptions of Vidisa, the old capital a hundred miles to the east, famous to modern archeologists for the ruined Buddhist stupa of Sanchi, famous to Kalidasa for the nearby rock chambers where the prostitutes of the town plied their trade; and of Dasapura, the modern Mandasor, some eighty miles to the north, where he describes the great temple of Kumara but fails to mention the Sun Temple although we happen to have an inscription from that temple of A.D. 473.

But Kalidasa's geographical descriptions extend far beyond his own province. They occur in several places in his works: in the **Cloud Messenger,** in the account of Raghu's conquests, in Rama's air journey from Ceylon back to Ayodhya. All of these passages furnish small details so accurate that one is led to suppose that Kali-

dasa had traveled widely, for accuracy is a virtue seldom found in Sanskrit geography. He tells us of the toddy palms that grew on the coast of Bengal (**Ragh.** IV, 34), the coconuts and betyl trees of Orissa (**Ragh.** IV, 42). He mentions the doves that fluttered in the pepper trees of Malabar and the cardamom that grew and still grows in the same area (**Ragh.** IV, 46-47). He knew that the best pearls came from the sea just off the Tamraparni River (**Ragh.** IV, 50). He might have learned that from jewelers. But his information from the northwest can scarcely have come otherwise than by personal observation. The Persians he notes wear beards and indicate submission by taking off their helmets (*Ragh.* IV, 63-64). He places the Huns on the Oxus River and notes that when Hun chieftains had fallen in battle, their wives gouged open their cheeks as a sign of mourning. I believe this fact is noted by no other Indian author although it is recorded in Chinese and Latin sources and is pictured in the art of the Huns themselves. And he had been to sea. Kalidasa is the first Sanskrit author to report on the spouting of whales. Rama sights them from his flying palace, and though we may doubt the reality of that lovely airship from which Sita had only to stretch her hand to have it braceleted with lightning, there is no doubt of the reality of what he saw. I quote literally from *Ragh.* XIII, 10:

> Yonder whales, closing their open mouths, take in the water that issues from the rivers together with the fish that are therein; then through the holes of their heads they pump jets of water upward.

And in one of his plays Kalidasa notes incidentally that property of the ocean known to all who have lived close to it, but rarely expressed in landlocked literatures, that the ocean at every moment appears something new to one's eyes (*Mal.* I, 11).

Kalidasa is equally at home at court and in the retreats of brahmins. It is in his works that we first meet with the full luxury and sensuousness of Indian palace life. Doubtless there was a tradition of describing such scenes. But the contrast between the vague descriptions of golden halls and sky-towering palaces that we find in the epic and Kalidasa's specific detail is marked. Even Asvaghosa's palace scenes, composed two centuries before, are pale in comparison. One finds the décor in the *Malavikagnimitra* and in the last canto of the **Dynasty of Raghu**: separate villas within the palace compound for each queen, hedged gardens with summerhouses and artificial hills; a painting gallery, a theater with its dancing masters and ballet. There are underground rooms cooled by water where the king may relax. Agnivarna has such a chamber in the middle of a lake, where he gives drinking parties, drinking the chilled wine from the lips of his latest favorite.

Within this courtly setting conversations attain a polite elegance that is hard to render in modern English. Indeed, this politeness runs through all Kalidasa's plays, even when the simple friends of Sakuntala are speaking. A young lady to a stranger: "I am put at ease, sir, by your kind words; and so I would ask to what royal and saintly family you belong. What land has been made homesick by your absence?" (*Sak.* II, 20 + 22) When a girl is late in arriving, she apologizes, to which the gentleman answers, "But no. The pleasure that ensues on pain has a greater relish." (*Vikr.* III, 21)

In the *Malavikagnimitra* a king is thwarted in his pursuit of a new love affair by his two wives. If you are ever placed in that difficult position, there is much you might learn from the play. The king, out of courtesy, restrains himself until the machinations of his Vidusaka have brought the elder queen to relent. By her relenting of course she wins a permanent advantage over the younger queen. But the reconciliation represents courtly politeness at its best. Queen Dharina invites the king to an offering at an *asoka* tree in her garden that has been brought to bloom only by the beauty of his new inamorata, whom she now presents to the king. The king in a verse of double meaning refers to his own restraint in terms of the *asoka* tree and implicitly subjects the tree and himself to her kindly rule.

> Your Majesty is not mistaken
> in doing honor to this *asoka* tree
> that scorned the dictates of the lovely spring
> and let its blossoms only waken respectfully
> beneath your care.
>
> (*Mal.* V, 8)

Triangles and quadrangles occur in modern literature also. But so far as my reading goes, their solutions are messier.

There is a danger in this courtly fluency. It makes it too easy to lie. Kalidasa is among the very few court poets of Sanskrit to resist the temptation. Sometimes his resistence takes the form of ridicule, as when the clown ridicules the general's praise of hunting in the **Sakuntala**. In dealing with the scriptures where ridicule would be out of place, Kalidasa uses other means. He tells the cruel story of Rama's renunciation of Sita after she had been rescued. The people refused to credit Sita's purity and Rama bowed to the will of the people. Kalidasa is forced to tell the story because it was part of the Uttarakanda of the *Ramayana*. But where the *Ramayana* criticizes Rama only once, through his brother Laksmana as Laksmana leaves the pregnant Sita in the forest, Kalidasa criticizes him three times: through his brothers, through Mother Earth, and through the sage Valmiki. These are very brief criticisms, which a reader might easily overlook, though I see that Walter Ruben has caught them. [in his *Kalidasa, die menschliche Bedeutung seiner Werke,* 1956]. What is decisive is not a criticism but an omission. At the first meeting of Rama and Sita, at their marriage, even when she is abducted by Ravana, there is not a word in Kalidasa of Rama's love of Sita. All we are given are a few conventional verses on the memory of sadness in separation, not when the sadness might have occurred, but on the return journey to Ayodhya. This reticence is extraordinary in the light of other *Kavyas* written on the Rama story. The answer, I think, is that Kalidasa could not believe in Rama's love. Rather than write hypocritically, he refrained.

Ridicule and restraint are methods of dealing with the antipathetic and uncongenial. But there are problems in life that cannot be ridiculed or silenced. There remains with Kalidasa, as with all idealists who take part in the world, the very real problem of how one can face the rough world of action, which is often cruel and usually cynical and at the same time preserve a vision of a permanent goodness and beauty.

In the optimum life the world of action and the world of goodness should not diverge. Dilipa punished the wicked for the good of others and married in order to have children. Thus his *artha* and *kama,* his pursuit of power and sex, were in accord with *dharma,* with morality (**Ragh.** I, 25). So with Atithi, whom Kalidasa describes as the perfect embodiment of political wisdom: he never injured morality for the sake of wealth and pleasure, nor them for it. He had no need to lessen his power to gratify his senses, or to lessen his pleasure to increase his power. He was in equipoise in respect to the three aims (**Ragh.** XVII, 57). This equipoise is the sign of a born hero. Dusyanta is so sure of his inner equipoise that when he sees a maiden who rouses his desire, he immediately knows that she must be of suitable caste and marriageable. Otherwise his heart would not have responded (*Sak.* I, 19).

Unfortunately we are not all of us born heroes. For those who suffer from the divergeance of human aims, Kalidasa offers two solutions, one of which I would call conservative and one innovative. The conservative solution is not to harmonize two basic ways of life but to put them side by side. This had been done by earlier authors. The *Mahabharata* had already furnished the names by which these two life styles are known throughout Sanskrit literature: the *pravrttilaksano dharma;* the active way of life, and the *nivrtti-laksano dharma,* the introverted or contemplative.

When the world becomes burdensome, or false, or cruel, one may look forward to retiring to the contemplative life, or more specifically, to life in ana*sarama*. The *asrama* is Kalidasa's antidote to the court. One wonders just what Kalidasa's pictures of *asrama* life were built on. Traditionally of course the *asrama* was the abode of an ascetic in the forest. The epics are full of references to these druid-like sanctuaries. But such forests as existed near Ujjain in Kalidasa's time seem to have been inhabited by singularly bloodthirsty mountaineers. The easy answer, of course, is to say that Kalidasa simply made use of a literary tradition. Both easy and, I think, wrong. Because the *asramas* of Kalidasa are very different from those of the literary tradition. In Kalidasa such a community is headed by a brahmin who practises the Vedic rites. He may or may not be celibate, but in no case is he an anchorite. He has pupils and attendants. The community contains men and women, boys and girls. It differs from other communities not socially but ritually and economically. The members dwell in thatched huts. They engage in no agriculture, but they have cattle and orchards and they gather wild rice. I would equate Kalidasa's *asramas* with those land grants of the Gupta Empire where a private donor buys the unplowed land on the outskirts of a village and donates it to a brahmin family; or with the land grants of the Vakatakas where the royal family assigns the revenue of a village to a brahmin teacher. Not only did brahmins, and possibly brahmin poets, grow up in such communities; they served also as occasional retreats for royalty. We know that Queen Prabhavati Gupta visited the saint Rámagirisvamin on several occasions. In fact she made her last official grant in the saint's presence. True, it is part of the literary tradition to place the *asrama* in a forest. The epic tale of *Sakuntala* is laid in a forest. But how little Kalidasa was thinking of a real forest is obvious from the first act of the play. I know something of deer hunting in the forests of Virginia; and I am quite certain that one cannot hunt deer in a forest from a galloping chariot.

It is in the *asrama* life, which I suppose to be conservative brahmin life on the outskirts of a village, that Kalidasa achieves his most wonderful harmonies of man and nature. Everyone who knows anything of his poetry will remember Kanva's *asrama* where akuntal was brought up, learning her sidelong glances from the deer, marrying the *nomalia* creeper to the mango, feeding with her hand her pet fawn. Life is ordered by the seasons and by the calender of religious ritual. But as the children grow up there is room for love. Human love in Kanva's retreat is expressed entirely in animal and vegetable images. The sudden appearance of Dusyanta is heralded by the stinging bee. Sakuntala is parched by the fever of love as the *madhavi* vine by the wind of summer. The king arrives as the cooling rain. When the lovers are in danger of being surprised, Sakuntala's friends call out to her that it is time for the shelldrakes to part. As opposed to the court, there is no luxury in the *asrama,* no polygamy, no jealousy.

Sakuntala was brought up in an *asrama.* Dilipa and Rama visited such communities in the prime of life. All who have lived in this closeness to nature and to the Vedic past have a yearning to return. It is an almost invariable rule of the kings of Raghu's dynasty that in old age they appoint their sons yuvaraj and retire, either to a garden in the suburb or to an *asrama.*

In Kalidasa's treatment of nature there is an emotional suggestiveness that was new to Sanskrit and that George Hart in a recent thesis has argued owes much to the poetic sensibilities of Dravidian India. But I have called this yearning for the *asrama* a conservative response to the problems of life because the life of forest sages had been idealized by earlier authors even if they had been speaking of a different institution and even if they had lacked Kalidasa's sensibility. More than this: the prospect of the life of contemplation is essentially uncreative. It offers solace rather than a cure.

Kalidasa had another solution, more original and much grander, for it is his personal religious vision. I find no comparable expression of it in earlier Sanskrit, though it was to be imitated many times in the centuries that followed.

Kalidasa's religion can easily be misunderstood, for he was as tolerant of religious differences as were his Gupta masters. The ninth canto of the Raghu contains a hymn to Visnu, the second book of the Prince a hymn to the

upanishadic Brahma. In no way can one establish a superiority of the one over the other. The two gods differ only by their traditional attributes. Visnu has one head and Brahma has four. But both are authors of the creation, preservation, and destruction of the world. Both are essentially without qualities but become qualified in the phenomenal world. In fact both hymns would serve almost as well as hymns to Siva except that they lack the emotional commitment that Kalidasa brings to Siva. One might say that to Kalidasa Visnu and Brahma are simply the way other people look at Siva. And Kalidasa is tolerant of other people's views. Even for Buddhism, which he has little occasion to refer to, as his poems deal with the eras of legend and myth before the birth of Buddhism, he still shows sympathy. In the *Malavikagnimitra* a Buddhist nun tells how her brother had been killed and how she had been left destitute. "After burning my brother's body," she says, "I assumed the yellow robes." To which the king replies, "You did right. That is the path of the virtuous." (*Mal.* 5.11 + 11)

But just as the Gupta emperors had their own religion as opposed to their policy of official tolerance, so also did Kalidasa have his personal religion of Saivism. It is in the figure of Siva that he found that reconciliation of good and evil, of beauty and ugliness, of life and death, that made the anticipation of retirement unnecessary, for the vision solved all problems and could transmute a man's present suffering into joy.

The first fullscale description of Siva that we are given in the **Birth of the Prince** pictures him in the trance of yoga. The description is remarkable for its suggestions of power. The god has withdrawn his senses within himself not in an act of nihilism but in an exercise of preparation. One is not sure whether the action for which he is preparing will be his dance of creation or his burning of the universe.

The god of love had accompanied the mountain princess to Siva's retreat on a plateau of the Himalayas. There he

> saw at the foot of a tall pine tree
> sitting on a seat covered with tiger skin
> in perfect self-control the three-eyed god,
>
> who sat cross-legged, motionless,
> tall torso straight, shoulders relaxed,
> hands joined palm upward in his lap
> as if he held an opening lotus.
>
> A serpent bound high his heavy locks,
> the sacred cord twisted about his ear,
> the mark of poison on his throat
> intensified the blackness of his knotted buckskin.
>
> With rigid pupils he was staring downward,
> the rays of sight emitting a faint light
> through lashes that never stirred beneath brows
> completely motionless.
> Like an unraining cloud,
> like an ocean without waves:

as he held his breath in yoga, he seemed to be
a lamp unwavering without a breath of wind.

Escaping from the opeing of his forehead eye
there rose above his head a few tendrils of fire,
thinner than the root filiments of a water lily,
brighter than the crescent of a day-old moon.

(*Kum, S.* III. 44-49)

It is from this volcanic stillness that Siva wakes to take
part in the world. In the poem, following the passage I
have quoted, he awakes to destroy the god of love. But
elsewhere he is as likely to recreate him. Siva dances the
dance of creation as well as the dance of death. The dance
of creation has been given dramatic representation, as in
the temple of Chidambaram, down to the present day. And
it is the creative, erotic, nature of Siva that is suggested
by the dancers described in the **Cloud Messenger.** The
message-sender addresses the cloud:

Being black as Siva's throat
  you will be welcomed with all honor by the
  servants
at Mahakala,
  the temple of Candisvara, master of the universe.
Its garden is perfumed
  by breezes sweet with lotus pollen
and pungent sandalwood
  used by the temple girls who bathe in the
  Gandhavati.

Though you come, O cloud,
  at any other time to Mahakala Temple,
wait at least
  until the sun descends from sight
that you may play the drum
  to the Trident-bearer's evening dance
and thereby win
  reward forever for your low-pitched thunder.

The temple girls,
  their girdles jingling at each footstep of the dance,
their arms weary
  from graceful waving of the yaktails with their
  jeweled handles,
will welcome you
  with sidelong glances as long as swarms of bees
for your drops of rain
  soothing to the lovers' nail wounds on their
  bodies.

The dance of the temple girls would have represented
Siva's *pravrtti,* his engagement in creation, sex, and
love. The opposite side of Siva's character would doubtless have been portrayed in such rituals as we read of
in Kaundinya's *Pasupatasutra-bhasya* I, 8, which the
yogi is directed to enact at temples of Mahakala the
terrifying laughter and the dance of Siva's destruction.
For in Saiva temples the worlds of *pravrtti* and *nivrtti*

confronted one another. The temple was both a palace
and a practice ground for yogis. There was no attempt
to minimize the contrast, for Siva was the god of contrasts.

How Kalidssa conceived of this paradox he tells us in
the words of the mother-goddess Parvati. She had failed
to win Siva by her beauty, even with the help of the god
of lust. So she practised yoga under the sun and between four fires while the seasons came and went, pu-
rifying herself for the sacred marriage. Finally Siva came
to her in the disguise of a young brahmin, apparently to
dissuade her from her infatuation, actually to test her
love. Siva in disguise spoke all the ill that man can speak
of God. God is a figure of terror, for he includes *all* the
world, its ugliness and its cruelty as well as its beauty
and kindness. Siva wears a garland of serpents. He
rides on a bull like a poor peasant, or wanders naked
through the graveyard with a skull for begging bowl.
And Parvati answered each of his reproaches.

I shall let Kalidasa speak for himself from the **Birth of the
Prince** V, 65-82.

The ascetic spoke: "I know God well
and here I see you striving for him once again.
As I think of his delight in ugly things,
I must say that I condemn your course.

You who persist in wanting a wrong object,
how will this wrist of yours, bound with the
  marriage thread,
endure the first touch of Siva's hand
embraceleted by serpents?

Take counsel for a moment with yourself
whether these two were ever fit to meet:
the silken bridal gown with its border of wild geese
and the flayed elephant hide dripping drops of
  blood.

Would even an enemy be pleased to see
your feet, which with their lacquered steps
have painted flowers on palace courtyards, now
leave their print on graveyards strewn with bones?

Or what could be less suitable than this:
that Siva's breast should be your place of rest;
that on your bosom, in its golden sandal paste,
should lie the mark of ashes from the grave?

On the first day will the farce begin, when you,
who should be mounted high on Indra's elephant,
shall ride the ancient bull, the beggar's only mount.
How all the crowd will laugh!

Yes, we shall have two objects now for pity,
two who have sought for union with the Bowman:

the lovely crescent of the immortal moon
and you, the moonlight of all mortal eyes.

His body is deformed of eye; no one knows his
    birth;
his poverty is shown by his nakedness.
Of what one looks for in a bridegroom, O gazelle-
    eyed bride,
the three-eyed god lacks every single grace.

Turn back your heart from what you have wrongly
    seen!
How far apart is Sambhu from one so blessed as
    you!
What man would offer on the spit of execution
the Vedic rites that sanctify the sacred pole?"

From the brahmin speaking thus against her wish
she cast her eyes askance,
curving her eyebrows in a frown
over lips whose trembling showed her anger.

She spoke to him: "You cannot know the Lord
if thus you speak of him.
The stupid hate the actions of the great,
who act from motives that common men cannot
    conceive.

It is they who fight misery, they who yearn for
    wealth,
only they, who look for lucky things.
What use are those things that chain the soul
to him who lacks desire, to the Refuge of the
    World?

He owns nothing, who is yet the source of wealth;
lord of the universe, he wanders in the graveyard.
His form is fearful, but they call him the Benign.
No one knows what Siva truly is.

He blazes in jewelry, or twines himself in snakes;
he wears the flayed hide, or wears the silken robe.
He bears a skull for begging cup, or wears the
    lunar orb within his headdress.
His form is unlimited who informs all things.

Those ashes from the graveyard, from contact with
    his limbs
are able to effect the cure of chaos,
for as he flings them off in the dance of his
    creation
the gods of heaven humbly place them in their
    crowns.

And when he rides, the poor man on his bull,
great Indra from his mighty elephant
descends to bow before his feet, which his chaplets
    turn to gold
with pollen from the trees of paradise.

In your cursed telling of Siva's faults
you spoke one word of truth:
of him who gave birth to Brahma the unborn
how would the place of birth be manifest?

But enough of argument. Let him even be
in every way just as you say he is.
My heart is set upon him; my heart flows with
    love of him.
One who is in love can see no faults."

Here in Saiva mythology and at the summit of Kalidasa's
poetry one finds a vision of the harmony of life and death.
Within that immense circle the eye of love can see the
lesser orbits of man and nature, male and female, action
and contemplation to be harmoniously interwoven. This
vision also is not unconnected with the vision of other
men of Kalidasa's time. It is the vision that justified the
building of Mahakala and of the other palace-temples of
the classical period. Hindu temples were very simple affairs before the Gupta period. Larger structures were built
by the Buddhists: stupas to house their relics and monasteries to house their monks. But the palace-temple or
city-temple of the Hindus can scarcely antedate Kalidasa's
time by as much as a century. Kalidasa's most innovative
response to the needs of religion seems to me to bear an
elective affinity with what we know of the ritual and architecture of these new temples.

In conclusion I should point out that comparisons of this
sort, between an artist and the spirit of the age in which
he lived, are at best enlightening, not explanatory. They
throw light on the artist's choice of subject and on his
scale of values. They do not explain his art, which in the
case of one like Kalidasa is his most precious gift. So I
would apologize for my essay by using the words of the
oldest commentator on Kalidasa whose work has survived.
Vallabhadeva in the tenth century in Kashmir wrote a
Panjika, or Notebook, on Kalidasa's **Birth of the Prince.**
To his notebook he prefaced the following verse:

What are the works of Kalidasa
and what is a commentator such as I?
I have entered a dragon's cavern
with only a weak lamp to show its beauty.
And yet, I have written this Notebook
on the **Birth of the Prince.**
for I was eager to let shine upon myself
the great light of that noble mind.

Steven F. Walker (essay date 1977)

SOURCE: "Pastoral and Kalidasa's 'Cloud Messenger':
An East-West Generic Comparison," in *Literature East &
West,* Vol. XXI, Nos. 1-4, January-December, 1977, pp.
112-120.

[*In the following essay, Walker compares Kalidasa's* Cloud-
Messenger *to the Western notion of pastoral poetry.*]

The ***Cloud Messenger*** (***Meghaduta***), perhaps the master-piece of Kalidasa, the greatest of the classical Sanskrit poets, has long been familiar to Western readers through numerous translations. Goethe sent a copy of Wilson's to a friend in 1817, and alluded to the gift in the following verses [quoted in Walter Ruben, *Kalidasa,* 1956]:

Und Meghaduta, den Wolkengesandten,
Wer schickt ihn nicht gerne zu Seelenverwandten!

Yet it has always proved a difficult work to classify generically. An American Indologist concluded recently that the ***Cloud Messenger*** "to all intents and purposes stands alone . . . It is such a chef d'oeuvre that it must be considered a genre by itself" [Edwin Gerow, "The Sanskrit lyric: a genre analysis," *The Literatures of India,* ed. Edward C. Dimock, 1974]. Of the traditional terms employed by Indian estheticians, *mahakavya* or heroic poem with numerous lyric descriptions and digressions, is too general; and *saindesha-kavya* ("messenger poem") constitutes a generic tautology, since the ***Meghaduta*** is the only note-worthy example of such a poem. The American Sanskritist Arthur Ryder wrote that "it is fair enough to call it an elegiac poem, though a precisian might object to the term" [*Shakuntala and Other Writings,* 1954]. It is true that the end of the poem, where the protagonist imagines that, through the intermediary of the cloud, he is speaking words of consolation to his lonely wife (stanzas 97-108), is at first rather "elegiac." But the term does no justice to the effect on the reader of the sunny and often humorous descriptions of nature and idyllic erotic scenes which make up the bulk of the poem.

In fact, the ***Cloud Messenger*** is an impersonalized, idealized and slightly dramatized treatment of certain topics relating to love, poetry and nature which in the West we have come to associate with the pastoral tradition. The humble *protagonist* is an unhappy lover (a husband in exile), and a creature of great poetic ability. The *theme* of the poem is his transcendence of the pain of erotic isolation through a heightened sense of the powers of his poetic imagination to transform Nature into Art. In the long sequence of descriptions of idyllic images and scenes are to be found many of the *motifs* associated with Western pastoral poetry. In short, wherever the themes of love, poetry and nature are treated from a generally idyllic perspective, we are in Arcadia, East or West.

The first critic to associate Kalidasa's ***Meghaduta*** with the Western pastoral tradition was André Lefèvre, who, in the book *Virgile et Kalidasa* (Paris, 1866) gave a text and facing translation of Virgil's *Eclogues,* and followed it with a verse translation of "le Nuage Messager," which he qualifies as an "idylle lyrique." But the reason for this critical choice remains a secret; his not very intelligent accompanying essay merely exalts the artistic genius of Virgil over that of Kalidasa, whose floridity was apparently the mark of an inferior civilization! No doubt, there is a certain similarity in form between the ***Meghaduta*** and the pastoral monologue as illustrated by Virgil's *Second Eclogue.* There is a brief introductory section which iden-tifies the speaker and his situation (stanzas 1-5), while the rest of the work consists of the words of the lone protagonist (6-110), and takes the form of a song or flight of the poetic imagination. The length and the variety of topics of ***The Cloud Messenger*** are greater than those of a Western pastoral monologue, but a similarly idyllic imagination is at work throughout.

The first stanza of the ***Meghaduta*** casts the protagonist of the poem into what, from the standpoint of the Western tradition, would be called a pastoral role. First of all, he is an unhappy lover, punished by exile from his beloved. He has also lost the social position he once enjoyed, and is thus a brother in exile to those Renaissance lovers living in humble status in the countryside. His present home is a *locus amoenus* of shady trees and flowing streams which was once the scene of Rama and Sita's pastoral exile in the forest. As is frequent in Pastoral, he has no strong individuality beyond these traits. The now humbled lover in exile is simply called "kascit" (first word of stanza one), "yaksah", i.e. "a certain . . . yaksha". Yakshas were demi-gods on the order of Greek fauns, nymphs and satyrs; generally harmless to human beings; originally perhaps tree-spirits, but in Kalidasa's time given the function of serving the god of Wealth Kubera. The fact that he had been a careless servant of Kubera explains his present plight. In appearance, yakshas were grotesque (like the Cyclopes, fauns and satyrs), but Kalidasa does not take any notice of this particular iconographical trait in the poem.

At the opening of the poem he is wasting away with grief, and his golden bracelet slips down his thin and wasted arm. But he is not to remain thus "sick from love" (5d "kamarta") for long; a new playful and erotic note is contributed to this sorrowful scene by the arrival of a storm cloud, the first sign of the rainy season (the season for leisurely love-making) which will be an especially poignant period for the lover to live through, separated as he is from his beloved. But the cloud itself is a happy sight, embracing the mountaintop lovingly, and playfully suggesting an elephant sporting with its tusks against an embankment (2cd). This ironic contrast between the cloud's playful appearance and its poignant reminder of more long lonely months to come is enough to bring out the poet in the yaksha.

At this point Kalidasa introduces that crucial structural element which will make the poem what it is: the yaksha frames a message. At the origin of Western Pastoral, Theocritus' genius hit on the idea of transforming the traditional characters of the urban mime into rural herdsmen, and then of presenting them in their natural role as rustic singers. The "device" which Kalidasa invented was of equal importance, since it allowed the birth in India of another version of pastoral: the yaksha suddenly perceives the cloud as a potential messenger whose northward progress towards the Himalayas could bring it near the lonely wife who is waiting for her husband in a little cottage in the divine city of Alaka. His intuition is the primary intuition of pastoral poetry, that of a world of nature which responds *sympathetically* to the unhappy lover:

"Those who are sick with love naturally endow with feeling sentient and insentient beings alike"

This intuition also calls forth from him the creative and active response of song. Thus his plight is not irremediable, for in the plot which Kalidasa has devised, the cloud will bear a message of consolation to the yaksha's lonely wife, and the very framing of that message will cure the yaksha's mind of its sorrow.

The yaksha, at first isolated in his grief, now that help seems to be at hand, suddenly becomes aware of a whole world of sympathetic nature and pastoral society, with simple people everywhere enjoying the pleasures of love in charming country or garden landscapes. His imagination delays the framing of the message as he visualizes in the mind's eye what this journey to the North will be like for the cloud as it moves slowly onward (9 "mandam-mandam" "slowly, slowly"); and he evokes this progress in the "slowly progressing" *mandakranta* meter, thus making a possible allusion to the symbolic identification of the cloud with the poem itself, of which the cloud is the vehicle in a very special way. Stanza by stanza, various scenes will be described, corresponding to the brief stops which the cloud could make on its journey to Alaka, scenes which the cloud's own refreshing beauty, playful thunder, etc. will play no small role in creating.

Although the yaksha purports to describe more or less everything that will be passed over by the cloud on its northward journey, including the great cities, it is clear that only the more pastoral aspects of the landscape attract his attention for long. If the city Vidisha is mentioned, (24), it is for the beauty of the river Vetravati, here compared to a loving woman—a frequent conceit with Kalidasa. Several stanzas (30-8) in praise of the city of Ujjayini (probably the home of Kalidasa) interrupt the journey, and include an elaborate evocation of the evening ceremonies at the great temple of Shiva there. But the city is seen primarily as the home of langorous ladies and their assiduous lovers, a paradise of idyllic eroticism. And the cloud's participation in the rites of Shiva is singularly fanciful and humorous: first its rumbling thunder is to take the place of the temple drum (34); and then, bathed in the reddish colors of sunset, it is to be emblematic of the bloody elephant skin which Shiva holds over his head in his dance. Even the description of the final goal of the cloud's pilgrimage, the divine city of Alaka in the Himalayas, gives way quickly to an evocation of that elegant *locus amoenus* which is the suburban retreat of the yaksha and his wife. Thus, potentially nonpastoral elements of description are subordinate to the pastoral theme of the poem.

Other descriptive passages are unequivocally pastoral, concerned as they are with all the more pleasing aspects of country life and with the specific beauty of flowers, streams, animals, birds, cool breezes, forests and mountains. All of these give delight to the lovesick mind of the yaksha, and these delights are no less therapeutic for being enjoyed *through the imagination alone.* For the yaksha, of course, has not stirred an inch from his spot on Rama's Mountain—nor has the cloud, for that matter. In the yaksha's imagination, the cloud will not merely be the spectator of idyllic scenes (this would have been interesting enough already), but by its very presence will help to create them. The interaction of the cloud and the landscape is a way of infusing Nature with the pastoral ideal of harmony, humor and sympathy; in the end, this same sense of harmony is made to reign in the mind of the poet who "humors" his ill-spirits as he enlivens his poetic visions of the pastoral world. It is as if a complete circuit of idyllic feeling were set flowing, the ultimate effect of which is the stimulation of good spirits and of poetic and imaginative vigor—both of which the yaksha sorely lacked at the opening of the *Meghaduta.* Thus, the arousal of the faculty of poetic vision is the crucial element of drama which lies behind the more lyric descriptive passages.

Kalidasa's presentation of this *long sequence* of idyllic images and scenes (a characteristically pastoral device, here given epic amplification) is worthy of special attention. In the yaksha's imagination, the true locus of this idyllic scenery, the cloud is co-partner with the landscape in the production of charming vignettes of country and idyllic life. The unhappy yaksha imagines, for example, how the cloud's shade will bring smiles to the faces of sweating flower-pickers (26); how the cloud will awaken the beauty of trees and flowers with its brief showers; and how the sight of it will make peacocks cry out with joy at their approaching mating season (32). This active embellishing of Nature is part of the cloud's natural role, and reminds the Western reader of many similar passages in Shelley's poem "The Cloud." For Shelley and Kalidasa alike, the cloud is a genius of eternal transformation and poetic activity. In the *Meghaduta,* such activities run parallel with the active effort which the imagination of the yaksha makes to transcend his unhappy state: the power to imagine delightful images takes the sting out of his suffering.

The last part of the poem is an evocation of the home and of the lonely wife of the exiled yaksha. Just as the cloud brought consolation to the yaksha's own heart, so it will console the longing of the wife through the message given by its rumbling thunder. Stanza 96 makes explicit the tie-in with the epic theme of the *Ramayana* first alluded to in stanza 1. Here, the wife looking up at the cloud who is delivering its message from the window, is compared to Sita raising her eyes respectfully to Hanuman. The cloud's first words introduce it as the one who "with deep yet gentle sound speed(s) on the way the throngs / of weary wanderers who yearn" to be home with their wives at last (95). The cloud is the bearer of a message which, for the lovesick yaksha and his wife, is the best thing next to actual reunion:

"Tidings brought by a friend from her true love are but little less than reunion."

As at the beginning of the poem, the identification of the cloud with the actual material (verbal) body of the poem itself lies close to the surface, along with the theme of poetry as the cure for the lovelorn state of mind.

The framing of the message itself causes at first a reopening of the old wounds of frustration and loneliness for the yaksha. As he imagines the arrival of the cloud, and the loveliness and sorrow of his lonely wife, a momentary disgust with art and with vain imaginings breaks through—thus his evocation and subsequent dismissal of the charms of pastoral Nature compared with those of his beloved:

> In the shyama vine I see thy body; in the eye of
> the startled doe, thy glance;
>
> In the moon, the sheen of thy cheek; in the
> peacock's massive plumes, thy hair;
>
> In the delicate river-ripples I descry the play of
> thine eyebrows;
>
> Nowhere, alas, O gentle one, is thy likeness found
> in a single place.

For a while, the unreality of these fancies is not proof against the reality of his suffering and longing; but he soon regains a certain serenity, and, in a playful parody of the mystical injunctions of the Bhagavad Gita, justifies his recourse to imagination and the therapeutic effects of it in his case:

> See, do I not bear myself up by my self alone,
> musing
> on many thoughts?

The yaksha reminds his wife that his exile will end in four months, and that what they now can only imagine, will soon become reality:

> Afterwards in nights of full autumn moonlight, we
> twain shall enjoy
>
> Divers heart's desires, imagined while we were parted.

The poem ends on this happy note; the yaksha is sure to enjoy reunion with his wife, and he has framed a message—and a poem—that has bridged the gulf of loneliness that first lay before him. In the meantime, he has also found a friend and consoler in the cloud who, from the standpoint of pastoral thematics, is both the listening companion and the pastoral poem itself, the airy breath of poetic utterance directed here and there by an idyllic imagination.

Gary A. Tubb (essay date 1984)

SOURCE: "Heroine as Hero: Parvati in the *Kumarasambhava* and the *Parvatiparinaya*," in *Journal of the American Oriental Society,* Vol. 104, No. 2, April-June, 1984, pp. 219-36.

[*In the following essay, Tubb examines problematic alterations made to the plot of the Sanskrit play* Parvatiparinaya *and the poem upon which it is based,* The Birth of the War-God.]

The late sanskrit play *Parvatiparinaya* ("The Wedding of Parvati") has the same subject as that of Kalidasa's famous poem, the ***Kumarasambhava*** (***Birth of the Prince***): both works tell the story of the goddess Parvati's marriage to Siva and of the events leading up to that marriage. The play is so closely modeled on the poem, not only in the sequence of events it depicts but even in much of its actual wording, that the *Parvatiparinaya* may be regarded as the result of an attempt to transfer an epic poem into the form of a play. Yet the play does alter some of the characteristics of Kalidasa's plot, and in doing so it often introduces touches that are reminiscent of several well-known Sanskrit plays. Analyses of the *Parvatiparinaya* have traced the details of the play's dependence on Kalidsa's poem and have identified the minor influences of plays dealing with other subjects, but they have done little to explain the reasons for making changes in the plot.

Many small changes are clearly due to the basic practical requirements of the dramatic genre, and in particular to the necessity of finding ways to present events that could not be acted out on the stage. The author of the play had to introduce additional characters and do some minor reshuffling in order to provide for the verbal reporting of actions whose direct presentation on the stage is difficult or prohibited: the violent death of Kama, the dressing of Parvati in preparation for the wedding, the effects of Springtime's unexpected arrival in the forest, and so on. The author of the play was attentive to these obligations in his own clumsy way, even though the high point of the entire *Parvatiparinaya,* the acting out of the marriage ceremony to which the title of the play refers, is itself prohibited by many authorities.

Such obvious requirements explain several of the more trivial alterations and additions, but they leave some important features of the play unaccounted for. What makes these unexplained alterations significant is that most of them are involved in a basic change in emphasis: they fall into a general pattern of minimizing the importance of Parvati's own actions in bringing about the marriage, and shift the focus of narration in such a way as to give much greater prominence to the role of the gods.

Why was this shift made? In other respects the author of the play stays as close as possible to Kalidasa's plot, even when it proves quite awkward to do so, and he shows himself so devoid of imagination that to suspect him of developing on his own accord an independent conception of the overall plot would be too optimistic. Furthermore, most readers of the play would agree that if his intention was to enhance the interest of his work, the result was a dismal failure. The most logical explanation is that this shift, like the other changes, was one of necessity. The change in emphasis can in fact be connected with the requirements of the dramatic genre: the prominence given to the activity of Parvati in the ***Kumarasambhava*** is difficult to reconcile with the statements in the theoretical treatises concerning the role of female characters in Sanskrit plays. This same problem helps to explain the use by the author of the *Parvatiparinaya* of touches drawn from the treatment of heroines in famous plays, for he seems to have been trying to adjust the character of Parvati in the direction of that of a more conventional heroine.

These conflicts between Sanskrit dramatic theory and the role of Parvati in the **Kumarasambhava** are worth examining, not so much for the help they give in explaining the treatment of the plot in the *Parvatiparinaya*—a very minor work in itself—but rather for what they can tell us about the construction of the **Kumarasambhava** and about the theories of criticism that were available to those within the Sanskrit tradition who attempted to analyze the plot of Kalidasa's poem. Many of the changes in plot in the play point to theoretical problems in the poem that were noticed by Sanskrit critics long before the *Parvatiparinaya* was composed. The difficulties that these critics felt in dealing with the plot of the **Kumarasambhava** in terms of theory specifically addressed to that poem's own genre, the reasons why they considered doctrines of dramatic theory relevant to the analysis of a non-dramatic poem, and the further difficulties that arose in their attempts to apply dramatic theory to the poem all serve to illumine important aspects of the innovative place of Kalidasa's poem in the history of Sanskrit literature. In what follows I propose to examine the problems that the role of Parvati in the **Kumarasambhava** has raised for critics of the poem within the Sanskrit tradition, before returning briefly to an explanation of how the author of the *Parvatiparinaya* attempted to deal with these problems.

The most direct discussions of the theoretical problems connected with the plot of the **Kumarasambhava** are to be found in the remarks that the authors of running commentaries on the poem have made while attempting to analyze its plot. That these commentators freely use the canons of dramatic criticism in discussing the plot of the **Kumarasambhava,** which belongs rather to the genre of the *mahakavya,* or artificial epic poem, is an indication of the peculiar nature of the poem within its genre. Discussions of this genre in the works on poetics, while they usually include long lists of traditional subjects of description to be taken up in the poem, have very little to say about the construction of the plot, for the simple reason that most *mahakavyas* have only a very rudimentary plot. Typically a poem of this genre merely uses the skeleton of a well-known story as a framework for long series of descriptions. The **Kumarasambhava** is certainly not deficient in description, and yet, despite its being unusually short for a *mahakavya,* it also presents a story so rich in dramatic action that its plot both supports and requires the fuller apparatus of plot-analysis that is available only in the works on dramatic criticism.

The basic outline of this plot, and its focus on events in the life of Parvati, can be summarized through a brief look at the titles of the **Kumarasambhava**'s eight cantos as they are given in many editions of Mallinatha's commentary on the poem:

1. Parvati's Birth

2. The Audience with Brahm

3. The Burning of Kama

4. The Lament of Kama's Wife

5. The Success of Parvati's Austerities

6. Parvati's Betrothal

7. Parvati's Wedding

8. Parvati's Honeymoon

In the first canto Siva's divine wife Sati abandons her body and is reborn as Parvati, the daughter of Himalaya. The divine sage Narada predicts that Parvati will become Siva's wife, but Himalaya, who resolves to accept no other suitor for her, will not presume to bring the matter up with Siva. Instead he simply waits until Parvati has reached adolescence, and then places her in the service of Siva, who is engaged in deep meditation at a remote spot in the mountains. At this point begins a subplot to which the next three cantos are devoted. In Canto 2, the gods, oppressed by the demon Taraka, seek advice from the creator-god Brahma, who tells them that only a son of Siva's can defeat the demon, and that they must therefore try to induce Siva to produce a son by drawing his mind from meditation with the charms of Parvati. In Canto 3, Indra, the king of the gods, sends an expedition against Siva, led by the love-god Kama, who is to shoot Siva with his enamoring arrow. Although Siva has shown signs of wavering in the presence of Parvati, this attack provokes him to destroy Kama with the fire from his third eye. The resulting lament of Kama's wife fills Canto 4. After this disaster Parvati decides that the only way to win Siva is to undertake rigorous yogic austerities, and Canto 5 narrates her performance of these austerities, her angry defence of Siva against the criticisms of a mysterious visitor, the visitor's revelation of his true identity as Siva, and Siva's declaration that Parvati has won him with her austerities. The titles of the remaining cantos are self-explanatory.

When viewed in terms of the doctrines of Sanskrit literary theory, the overwhelming emphasis on the life of Parvati that appears clearly in this version of the titles of the poem's cantos is anomalous, whether one consults the treatises dealing specifically with the *mahakavya* or attempts, as some commentators do, to apply the canons of dramatic criticism as well.

To begin with the theories on the *mahakavya:* none of the definitions or theoretical discussions of the genre has anything to say about a heroine. Women appear in the definitions only as recommended objects of description and as accessories in the sensual enjoyments included in the standard lists of topoi. This omission is in accord with the early history of the genre, for it is clear that the *mahakavya* was traditionally a poem on political and military subjects rather than a love poem, and with minor exceptions the role of women as propounded in Sanskrit literary theory is confined to matters of love. The great *mahakavyas* regularly contain cantos describing wine-drinking, love-making, playing in the water, picking flowers, and so forth, and women are essential in such descriptions, but these women are anonymous and are only incidentally connected with the hero's actions in pursuit of his major goal. The prominence of an individual woman would require an underlying emphasis on a relationship of love with the hero, and although Kalidasa himself employed such emphasis in a couple of the stories that are strung together in his other *mahakavya,* the **Raghuvamsa,** aside from the **Kumarasambhava** the earliest major *mahakavya* that is devoted as a whole to love rather than to war is the twelfth-century *Naisadhacarita* of Sriharsa, based on the old story of Nala and Damayanti. Changes in Sanskrit literary theory came even more slowly: it was not until the fourteenth century, some nine hundred years after Kalidasa, that the theory on *mahakavyas* began to contemplate the possibility of the genre's including a real love poem, in which a heroine could play an important part.

With this belated acknowledgement of the possibility of an emphasis on love in a *mahakavya,* theoretical discussion of the *mahakavya* as a separate genre came to an end. Throughout the entire previous history of Sanskrit literary theory, however, the essentially martial nature of the *mahakavya* was unobscured, and many of the peculiarities of the plot developed by Kalidasa in the **Kumarasambhava** seemed to reflect a conscious toying with the traditional requirements of the genre. The only characters mentioned in the definitions of the *mahakavya* as necessary elements of the plot are the hero (*nayaka*) and his opponent (*pratinayaka*), with the story narrated in the poem to consist of a conflict between the two in which the hero is ultimately victorious. In the treatises that give further details, even where the definitions are embellished with long lists of optional descriptions the basic stages in the plot are purely military: a council of war, the sending of spies to reconnoiter, a march against the enemy's forces, the arranging of battle lines, and finally the major conflict, in which the hero proves victorious, and in which the death of the opponents may optionally be described. In the **Kumarasambhava** this military theme obviously does not fit the story of the poem as a whole, but the traditional formula does appear within a portion of the poem, curiously worked out stage by stage in the episode of Kama's expedition that is told in the third canto, with Siva as the opponent. In effect this episode is a parody of the traditional *mahakavya*-plot, since all the necessary martial elements appear only in the form of counterparts drawn from the world of love. Of the major stages outlined above, the council of war occurs in the discussion between Indra and Kama, in the course of which Indra reveals the reports of his spies, the beautiful nymphs of heaven. Kama then marches forth with his friend Springtime as lieutenant and his wife Passion as aide, and their progress through the forest arouses sentiments of love on all sides. When the lines of battle are formed at Siva's camp, Kama is encouraged by the presence of the charms of Parvati to aid his cause, and he draws his bow of flowers. Then the entire lovely campaign is suddenly destroyed in the fire of Siva's violent anger.

While Kama may have functioned as a sort of *nayaka* or hero within the episode of his quaint expedition, his disastrous defeat makes it clear that in the larger context of the poem his role is quite different. The commentators who discuss the character of Indra and of his henchman Kama explicitly connect them with the theoretical descriptions of the *pratinayaka* or antagonist, and the hero whom they oppose is obviously Siva. Siva is automatically taken to be the *nayaka* in the poem by every Sanskrit writer who comments on the matter, and within the tradition the **Kumarasambhava** is repeatedly described as an account of the deeds of Siva. But in examining these deeds as they are actually presented in the poem, two serious difficulties arise. The first is that even after the failure of the efforts of the gods Siva continues to be presented not as an active agent in pursuit of the goal of the plot, but rather as the stubbornly resisting object in the attempts to achieve that goal, for like the gods Parvati strives to win over Siva, and the attracting of Siva's mind has been identified by at least one Sanskrit critic as the general goal (*karya*) of the entire plot. The second problem is that even if Siva's contribution is ultimately more active than it may at first appear to be, the precise nature of his role is kept very much in the background of the narration until the end of the poem. He is not even the direct subject of most of the narration in the poem, because Kalidasa deliberately conceals a great part of the motives and even the actions of Siva. At times Kalidasa refuses to explain the purpose of the hero's acts, as when he says that Siva was practising austerities "with a certain desire" (*kenapi kamena,* 1.57). At other times we must infer from what little the poet says that Siva was involved in an incident not described, as when Siva says in verse 6.29 that the gods have asked him to produce a son, from which statement we must suppose, as the commentator Arunagirinatha points out, that Siva was visited by the gods sometime between his destruction of Kama and his appearance before Parvati.

Both these problems are ultimately reflections of Kalidasa's personal religious conception of Siva. I shall discuss below the connection between Siva's divine nature and his role as object, rather than agent, in the pursuit of the goal of the poem; the policy of keeping Siva in the background of the narration can be further explained by assuming the Kalidasa would not presume to attempt an analysis of the unfathomable ways of his God, the ineffability of whose nature is eloquently expounded by Parvati in the fifth canto. The practical consequence of Kalidasa's treatment of Siva is the placing of the burden of the action in the primary plot on Parvati. It is significant that, with the sole exception of Siva's conversation with the Seven Sages (a conversation brought about by Parvati's request for action on the part of Siva), each time that Siva is seen in the poem Parvati is either present or on the verge of appearing. In effect, we see Siva largely through the eyes of Parvati. Parvati herself, in contrast, appears alone throughout the greater part of the crucial fifth canto, and she is the subject of extended treatment by the poet long before Siva is introduced in the poem. The whole narrative focus in the poem is on the events of her life.

It is this focus on the life of the heroine that the theory on *mahakavya,* with its omission of any discussion of a heroine, is unable to elucidate. The commentators on the **Kumarasambhava** are therefore forced to turn to the treatises on the dramatic genre, which have a great deal to say about the types of heroines and the ways in which they should be presented. Even in these texts, however, the prevailing confinement of the literary role of female characters to matters of love is clear; the categories offered for the analysis of heroines pertain, for the most part, to those characteristics of women that are relevant in their relationships with men, rather than to more general characteristics such as are employed in the classifications applied to male characters. Thus heroines are categorized according to which man they belong to, or the extent of their sexual experience, or the various ways in which they are attractive to men; and finer levels of classification depend upon the particular responses of the heroine to the romantic endeavors of the man with whom she is involved.

This theoretical emphasis on the connections between the heroine and the mood of love (*srngara-rasa*) is useful, as far as it goes, in analyzing the descriptions of Parvati in the **Kumarasambhava,** for the theme of her physical charms is constantly present, beginning with the elaborate blazon that depicts her in the bloom of her youth; and even before her first appearance in the poem this general mood is already being set by the many overtones of *srngara* scattered through the description of the setting of her birth that opens the poem. In fact this is what we should expect in a work in which the mood of love is clearly predominant. Even in dealing with Parvati's most heroic actions, Kalidasa never loses sight of this theme of physical attractiveness: the descriptions of her austerities routinely include some mention of her beauty and inherent tenderness, either by pointing out the contrast with her former life of luxury or by remarking that even under such difficult circumstances she seems to have become even more beautiful.

Yet these remarks do not involve a recognition of the contrast between the usual activities of beautiful and the ascetic practices that Parvati has undertaken, and it is in dealing with the austerities performed by Parvati that the inadequacies of the dramatic theory begin to appear. At the same time, it is important to observe that this asceticism is not in itself considered inconsistent with the traditional character of a heroine. Parvati's right to undertake this course of action is supported by the remarks both of the other characters in the poem and of the Sanskrit commentators who have discussed the matter. Significantly, however, in all these justifications of Parvati's activity the approval of the performance of austerities by a woman retains the emphasis on the woman's relationship with a man (and, specifically, on her obtaining a good husband).

Within the poem the clearest statement of a woman's right to undertake austerities is made by Siva himself when he visits Parvati in disguise. After offering a string of opening compliments in which he simultaneously praises her physical beauty and ascetic accomplishments, he explicitly discusses the circumstances under which "such a course of action might be possible for ladies," finally deciding that Parvati must be trying to win a husband. The same motive is cited in the explicit approval of Parvati's actions by the women in her home town who, when they see the bridegroom Siva arriving in the procession for the wedding, declare:

It was right for Parvati, tender though she is, to perform austerities to win him. A woman would be fulfilled even by becoming his slave—not to speak of gaining repose in his lap.

Kalidasa touches on the same subject in his remarks on Arundhati, who is the wife of the sage Vasistha and the model of the woman who combines yogic austerities with wifely duty. In describing the appearance of Arundhati and the Seven Sages before Siva, Kalidasa follows praise of their austerities with a flat assertion of equality:

The Lord (Siva) looked on both her and the sages with no difference in respect. There should be no concern for whether one is a man or a woman, for it is the conduct of the good that is honored.

But the setting of this statement is instructive. The verse that precedes this one depicts Arundhati, "like the embodiment of the success of austerities," standing with her eyes directed toward her husband's feet, and the verse that follows places her excellence in the usual perspective:

At the sight of her, Siva's desire to have a wife became greater. As is well known, a good wife is the prime cause of righteous actions.

So once again a woman's asceticism is praised chiefly in its effect on her relationship with her husband.

Nevertheless, the characters in the poem assume that Parvati will do what is necessary to win Siva, and they acknowledge that asceticism is a valid means by which to attain this goal. For them the only question is whether or not Parvati is undertaking something too difficult for her tender body. Throughout the description of her austerities constant reference is made to the contrast between her innate physical delicacy and the rigors of her asceticism, and it on these grounds that her mother tries at first to turn her toward the simpler domestic religion more commonly resorted to by women:

Our tutelary deities are in the temples. How great is the difference between austerities and this body of yours! A delicate *sirisa*-blossom could bear the foot of a bee, but not the foot of a bird.

But her mother's reluctance is overruled by the consent of her father, who is "pleased with her suitable perseverance," and who also seems relieved to have Parvati take matters into her own hands. When Parvati goes off to the forest and begins her ascetic endeavors, the descriptions of her are replete with references to the contrasts between the austerity of her new mode of life and the great delicacy of her former circumstances. Siva's first words when he arrives in disguise express the hope that Parvati is not engaged in something too difficult for her (5.33), and, after several remarks contrasting Parvati's present condition with the life of ornaments and luxury she formerly enjoyed, he offers to give her half the accumulated power of his own austerities so that she can end her asceticism (5.50). In reply Parvati's friends explain why she has "made her body into the instrument of austerities, as if making a lotus into a sunshield." And, as we have seen, the women of her home town refer to Parvati's tenderness in proclaiming that her decision to undertake austerities was nonetheless proper. For all these characters within the poem, the propriety of the heroine's undertaking is acknowledged; it is only the obvious difficulty of that activity in contrast with the apparently delicate body of Parvati that alarms them.

The commentators on the poem approach the matter somewhat differently. For them the contrast between the rigors of the heroine's austerities and the tenderness of her body is viewed as a foundation of charming poetic ornaments, and they seem to assume tacitly that asceticism is as good an instrument as any for a woman bent on winning a husband. The question that bothers the commentators is whether a woman is ever justified to begin with in interfering so actively in the process of finding a husband. That this question was taken seriously by the commentators who deal with the matter is shown by the great pains they take to explain how Parvati's active pursuit can be permissable; they justify it morally and legally by quoting high authorities. A long section is taken from the *Kamasutra* to show that a girl who has lived by the rules of her family and caste but has nevertheless not been asked for by a suitable man should try to obtain a marriage through her own efforts (in this case, they explain, the only suitable husband is Siva, whose motives for not seeking her hand are entirely inscrutable, since his nature is "quite unlike that of ordinary people"). And from the *dharmasastra* is cited the statement that a girl who has reached puberty should wait three years to see what happens, but may then seek a husband (and it is puberty, the commentator Arunagirinatha reminds us, that has awakened in Parvati her inborn love for Siva).

Thus for the commentators as well, although their uneasiness when confronted with Parvatis austerities has a focus somewhat different from that of the reservations expressed within the poem, those austerities are justifiable. From the point of view of dramatic criticism, the real problem lies not in Parvati's ascetic activity in itself, but rather in the prominence that this activity is given as the primary cause of progress toward the goal in the poem; and beyond this particular activity the real problem with the descriptions of Parvati throughout the poem lies not in any failure to conform to the traditional interest in the qualities of the heroine that are relevant to the mood of love, but rather in the prominence given to the events of Parvati's life as the framework on which the entire poem is constructed.

These problems may be made clearer by comparing Kalidasa's treatment of Parvati in the **Kumarasambhava** with his treatment elsewhere of two other heroines, Sakuntala in his play *Abhijnanasakuntala* and Sita in the portion of his *Raghuvamsa* that deals with the story of Rama. The common theme in the lives of these three heroines has often been pointed out: each is rejected by her husband (in Parvati's case, her former and future husband, and in a sense her eternal husband), each then enters a life of asceticism in the resulting separation from him, and each

is later reunited with the husband. Despite these similarities, Parvati's role as presented by Kalidasa differs from that of the two other heroines in the two important ways I have just mentioned as problems.

First, the activity of Parvati differs from that of the other heroines in the emphasis placed upon it as an unassisted endeavor undertaken deliberately for the purpose of effecting the reunion and serving as the fundamental moving force in the progress toward that reunion. When rejected by their husbands, both Sakuntala and Sita are received into the protection of wise elders in holy surroundings, where, as pregnant wives without their husbands, they stay, give birth to sons, and fall more or less inevitably into lives of ascetic simplicity, with no real expectation of ever seeing their husbands again in their lifetime (although Sita does initially express the hope that her asceticism will lead to reunion with Rama in a future life). And when the reunion finally does occur, the conduct of the heroines is only one part of a whole complex of contributing factors, including the intervention of the protecting elders (the gods for Sakuntala, Valmiki for Sita), the important role of the sons (through whom contact with the husbands is first reestablished), and the differing roles of the husbands themselves and their own progress through suffering—in the case of Sakuntala, the development of Dusyanta is at least as important as her own, and he is eager to take her back even before he learns of what has happened to her, and in the case of Sita, there is no real development in Rama, with the result that Sita promptly disappears again. Parvati, in contrast, leaves behind the protection of her parents and strikes out on her own despite her mother's advice, resolving to practise austerities until Siva accepts her. She then proceeds to accomplish singlehanded what even the gods had failed to bring about, as Siva himself declares unequivocally when he reveals his true identity: "From this day forth," he tells her, "I am your servant, bought by your austerities."

Second, the actions of Parvati differ from those of the other heroines in serving as the framework upon which the story is told. In this respect Parvati corresponds not to Sakuntala and Sita, but rather to their husbands Dusyanta and Rama. When the stories begin in the *Abhijnanaskuntala* and in the Rama-portion of the *Raghuvamsa,* it is Dusyanta and Rama we are first told about, just as the **Kumarasambhava** begins with a description of Parvati and her family. When the hero and heroine in each work meet for the first time, it is Dusyanta and Rama who go to Sakuntala and Sita, just as it is Parvati who comes to Siva. After the separations, it is Sakuntala and Sita who disappear, and Dusyanta and Rama who suffer without knowing what is happening to their wives, while their own actions are reported to Sakuntala and Sita, just as it is Siva who disappears, and Parvati who undergoes her suffering without knowing where Siva is, while Siva is aware of her project of austerities. Finally, the overall narrative focus is on the lives of Dusyanta, Rama, and Parvati, rather than on those of their spouses: in the *Abhijnanasakuntala,* Dusyanta appears nine times when Sakuntala is not present, and beyond this he watches her four times from hiding places, while Sakuntala appears only once when

Dusyanta is not present (although it is true that this is a long appearance, and that in another scene a friend of Sakuntala's watches Dusyanta); in the *Raghuvamsa,* although we do see Sita briefly after the separation, we see much more of Rama, and his story in the poem had been in progress well before Sita entered his life and continues after she is gone; in the *Kumarasambhava,* the story focuses on the events in the life of Parvati in ways that I have already mentioned.

It follows from all of this that in the plot presented by Kalidasa in the *Kumarasambhava* Parvati is the principal protagonist. And when the prominence of Parvati is viewed in terms of Sanskrit literary theory—particularly when one observes that the opening descriptions in the poem, traditionally devoted to the hero, are of Parvati and her parents, and that the five stages (*avasthas*) in the action, theoretically to be found in the deeds of the hero, are most straightforwardly connected with the activity of Parvati—it also follows that Parvati must be granted a role that the treatises do not contemplate for a female character: she acts as the de facto hero in the poem. The commentators on the *Kumarasambhava* come close to recognizing this status of Parvati's when they connect the description of her austerities with the heroic mood (*vira-rasa*) while associating Siva's own austerities with the mood of peace (*santa-rasa*). And in describing the character of Parvati as depicted in the poem they are forced to take the unusual step of applying to her the definitions of categories prescribed in theory not for the heroine, but for the hero. When, for example, they reach the point in the poem at which Parvati first undertakes her austerities and her hero-like activity thus begins to be especially conspicuous, they apply to her the definition of the "exalted" type of hero, for "the definition of an exalted hero—'A self-controlled and exalted hero is one who is steadfast and whose egotism lies deeply hidden'—is to be applied to an exalted heroine as well," even though the basis in theory for this extrapolation is difficult to find.

Judging from further remarks made by the commentators, some analysts attempted to downplay the heroism of Parvati by resorting to the same procedure that, as we shall see, underlies the alterations in plot in the *Parvati-parinaya*—emphasizing the role of the gods in bringing about the union of Siva and Parvati. It appears to be the gods who make the first overt effort to accomplish this union, and the commentators mention the view that the gods' attempt constitutes the first of the major stages in the progress toward the goal as outlined in dramatic theory, the stage of the initial undertaking (*arambhav-astha*). This view is presented as an objection to the construction of the plot in the *Kumarasambhava,* since the five stages laid down in the treatises on dramatic theory are supposed to be stages in the action of the hero. But the commentators reject the idea that the gods are the ones who perform the real undertaking, explaining that our heroine had intended to bring about her marriage to Siva even before her birth as Parvati, and that the endeavors of the gods constitute merely a subordinate plot that serves to further the main plot.

The role of the gods, however, persists even beyond the failure of their overt attempt and the success of Parvati's austerities, for even though it was the asceticism of Parvati that won over Siva to her, as he himself declared, his reasons for assenting to the actual marriage—at least in the version he gave his fellow ascetics, the Seven Sages—were the result of further intervention by the gods:

> I have been begged for a son by the gods, who are afflicted by their enemy, as a cloud is begged for rain by *cataka*-birds who are tormented by thirst.

> Hence I wish to marry Parvati for the purpose of begetting offspring, as a sacrificer desires a piece of wood for the production of fire.

This declaration raises an obvious question: if the gods could induce Siva to marry Parvati simply by asking him to produce a son, why did they take the trouble of sending out the disastrous expedition of Kama? It would appear that the actions of Parvati were in fact a necessary prerequisite, and the rest is explained by the commentator Arunagirinatha in his remarks on the verses just quoted:

> But if Siva was inclined toward marriage because of the request of the gods, then why did the poet set down the episode of Kama? (Because) it was useful as the foundation for Parvati's performance of austerities. And this is demonstrated at the beginning of the fifth canto.

The passage referred to by Arunagirinatha at the end of this remark declares that Parvati's decision to perform austerities was a reaction to the defeat of Kama:

> After her hopes had thus been shattered by Siva when he burned the love-god before her eyes, Parvati inwardly condemned her beauty, for loveliness has the affection of a lover as its goal.

> She wished to make blameless beauty for herself, practising concentration with austerities. How else could she attain that pair—such a love and such a husband?

In fact the episode of Kama is a foundation for Parvati's actions in a much more important way than simply by serving as an impetus, for the whole second half of the poem, beginning with these verses at the start of the fifth canto, constitutes a step-by-step retracing of the events in the first half of the poem. The single most striking feature in the composition of the *Kumarasambhava*'s plot is the arrangement of the poem in these two corresponding halves—two groups of four cantos each, presenting in parallel fashion two different attempts to bring about the union of Siva and Parvati. The recognition of this arrangement is crucial for an understanding of the true role of the gods in the poem.

I have already outlined the events in the first half of the poem, which describes the growth of Parvati to physical maturity and the attempt of the gods to bring about her union with Siva through external force by sending Kama to shoot him with his enamoring arrow in her presence. With the fifth canto begins the second half of the poem, in which the attempt that is described relies on internal forces—internal in the sense that the attempt depends upon a process of spiritual maturing brought about within Parvati through her own efforts. The essence of this process, as Kalidasa suggests in many beautiful ways, is the gradual growth of Parvati into the perfection of her status as a living counterpart of the earth. This role of Parvati as the "goddess of earth and fertility," and the manner in which Kalidasa suggests the perfection of this role at the end of Parvati's austerities, have been nicely explained by Daniel H. H. Ingalls [in *Sanskrit Court Poetry*], and overtones of this theme are present in the earlier part of the poem as well.

The plot of the **Kumarasambhava** consists, in its larger aspects, of this process of internal transformation in Parvati—in essence, the perfection of her incarnation as the immanent Goddess—and the reunion of Parvati with Siva—the transcendent God—that results from its success, as set against the earlier process of purely external development combined with the employment of external force, and the rejection of Parvati by Siva that results from its inadequacy. The smaller "events" organized by this plot consist partly of situations conveyed through descriptions, and partly of incidents of action conveyed through narration. In Kalidasa's design of the overall plot, the internal growth and consequent reunion in the second half of the poem are successful counterparts of the external growth and subsequent rejection in the first half, and what I should like to emphasize here is the impressively thoroughgoing way in which the poet has made this general parallelism apparent even in his treatment of the smaller aspects of the plot: the presentation of most of the events in the second half of the poem proceeds in a sequence that corresponds even in fairly small detail to the sequence of events in the first half.

In accordance with the contrast between the failure of the attempt to unite Siva and Parvati in the first half of the poem and the success of that made in the second, most of these correspondences between events involve some sort of reversal, based either on the contrast between negative responses to such events and positive responses. Thus when the action begins early in the first canto, we are told that our heroine abandoned her body through yoga out of contempt for her father; early in the corresponding canto, with the express consent of her father—a more auspicious beginning—she gives her body over to yogic austerities and initiates this process of spiritual growth, the depiction of which parallels the description of her physical growth in the first canto.

In the interests of space I can mention here only the most obvious of the pairs of corresponding events that follow these parallel beginnings at the start of each half of the poem. In most of these pairs this same sort of reversal of the earlier event is clear. For example, the mention in the first canto of Siva's avoidance of all contact with women finds its reverse in the fifth canto when Siva voluntarily comes to visit Parvati; and while the first canto ends with the placement of Parvati in the services of Siva, who is

engaged in yogic austerities, the fifth canto ends with Siva's declaration that he has become the servant of Parvati, won by her own austerities. Among the subsequent events in each half, compare the visit of the gods to the grandfather Brahma, and his advice that they should try to unite Siva and Parvati, with the visit of the sages to Parvati's father, and his permission for the marriage to take place; compare the decoration of the earth by the arrival of Springtime with the decoration of the Earth-goddess Parvati in preparation for the wedding; compare the depiction of Siva's terrible yogic withdrawal from the world with the description of his showing himself benignly in public procession; compare his resistance to the effects of Parvati's presence with his later response to the touch of her hand at the wedding, and, finally, compare the submission of the love-god's widow to the full realization of the loss of her husband with the submission of Parvati to the full realization of the gaining of hers.

Most of these parallels are fairly obvious once the general pattern of matching sequences has been discerned; what I have tried to bring out here is simply the fact of their pervasive occurence in the poem. This pattern of consistent parallel development has several important consequences—not the least of which, incidentally, is the clear implication that Kalidasa designed his poem to be complete in the eight cantos that we have, for this point has often been disputed. For our present purposes, however, the significance of these parallels is to make it even clearer that the actions of the gods are not the beginning of a process that is eventually brought to a successful end with the help of Parvati, but rather a model of utter failure through incorrect means, necessitating a completely fresh start by Parvati and the reversal of the mistakes made by the gods.

Ultimately the only real obstacle within the poem to the view that the role of the gods is entirely subordinate is Siva's statement to the Seven Sages that he wishes to marry Parvati because the gods have asked him to produce a son (verses 6.27-28). On this statement the commentator Arunagirinatha remarks as follows:

> Here it is only the request of the gods that is presented as the reason for his desire for marriage, and not the austerities of Parvati, because these sages know the behavior of Siva and Parvati as it really is. For those two are (in reality) never separated from each other at any time. And therefore the austerities of Parvati were not really performed for the purpose of union with Siva, but rather for the purpose of giving instruction in the proper conduct of women in the world, by demonstrating that a woman born in a good family should strive with all her power to obtain a husband suitable for her. Just as all the actions of Siva are done for the benefit of others, so also are those of his *Sakti* (i.e., his active power, in the person of his consort).

While many readers must feel the presence of a deeper motive than the straightforward didacticism offered in this pious explanation. Arunagirinatha is surely correct in his emphasis on the special identities of the hero and heroine in the **Kumarasambhava** as the underlying reasons for the unorthodox focus of the plot. To begin with, the transcendence of Siva that goes hand in hand with the status of Parvati as his *sakti* helps to explain the keeping of Siva in the background of the action, together with the emphasis on the active role of Parvati; the distinction I have mentioned between the heroic mood of Parvati's austerities and the peaceful mood of Siva's meditation fits well with this conception of Siva and Parvati as Absolute Consciousness and Dynamic Power respectively. The deeper theme that I have tried to identify in my remarks on the growth of Parvati into a counterpart of the earth may also be connected with a further aspect of the divine nature of these two—namely, the interpretation of them as Purusa and Prakrti, an interpretation that was sensitively explored by Sri Aurobindo [in *Kalidasa,* 1929]. Rabindranath Tagore analyzed the role of Parvati along similar lines ["The Religion of the Forest," in *Creative Unity,* 1922], and Kalidasa's treatment of Parvati provides rich material for further theological and philosophical explanations as well.

Whichever interpretation we choose to emphasize, it is clear that the special nature of the divine relationship between Siva and Parvati is central in the working of the plot, and that it necessitates both the subordinate status of the endeavors of the gods and the focus on the activity of Parvati. The implications of the special nature and eternal existence of this relationship for the way in which the marriage had to be brought about are handled very beautifully by Kalidasa within his description of the wedding itself, and the importance of this same relationship can be traced throughout the poem with little difficulty.

Once the status of Parvata as the *sakti* of Siva is clearly understood, it becomes apparent that she and Siva together, as two aspects of the same godhead, serve jointly as the protagonist in the poem, with the degree of activity exhibited by one or the other at any point in the plot dependent upon the progress of Parvati's development in her earthly form. Until Parvati has perfected her incarnate form through austerities so as to make possible a full relationship with Siva, the story can only be told from the point of view of Parvati, since Siva himself cannot yet be actively involved. But once that process of self-perfection is complete, Parvati's experience of Siva is elevated to the level at which the presence of the transcendent God can be experienced in its full power, and at this point the role of Siva changes dramatically. From the latter part of the fifth canto onward he becomes gradually more active, and in the eighth canto, describing the honeymoon, he is clearly the more active partner. Parvati becomes the recipient of his outpouring of bliss and knowledge, culminating in the description, at the end of this final canto, of the complete remerging of the divine couple into each other.

The more advanced stages of this assumption by Siva of a more active role once the necessary conditions had been met could not be incorporated into the play based on Kalidasa's poem, because the explicit scenes of lovemaking through which the activity of Siva is most strikingly expressed in the eighth canto of the **Kumarasambhava** obviously could not be presented on stage, and even their

inclusion in the original poem has been a source of considerable scandal. The *Parvatiparinaya* therefore makes use of only the first seven cantos of the poem, ending with the completion of the wedding ceremony, and thus must face the problem of the emphasis on Parvati's activity in an even stronger form than that present in the poem itself.

The objections to the supposed impropriety of depicting the lovemaking of Siva and Parvati in the poem are met by Arunagirin tha, in his remarks at the beginning of the eighth canto in the **Kumarasambhava,** with condemnation of the folly of those who declared themselves reluctant to comment on that canto:

> The fault here belongs purely to him who thinks that these activities are real, when in fact they are merely the playing of these two Great Actors, acting out the actions of famous ordinary heroes and heroines of the exalted type.

Of course the lovemaking even of mortals cannot be acted out explicitly on an Indian stage, and the author of the *Parvatiparinaya* had no choice in omitting Kalidasa's depiction of the honeymoon. But something akin to what Arunagirinatha has in mind—that the account of the actions of Siva and Parvati is intended not as a literal recitation of actual events, but rather as a representation, in terms understandable to humans, of inexpressible divine realities—operates throughout the earlier portions of the poem as well, and we have seen how the focus of the plot in the **Kumarasambhava** can be understood only in the light of Kalidasa's religious view of Siva and Parvati.

The author of the *Parvatiparinaya* seems unaware of the implications of such a view, central as it is to Kalidasa's conception of the plot, and he doggedly attempts to circumvent the theoretical problems that arise when the roles of Siva and Parvati prior to the honeymoon are subjected to analysis in terms of the rules applicable to ordinary heroes and heroines. This attempt, as I have said, is carried out chiefly by emphasizing the role of the gods and downplaying that of Parvati at every step. The result is such an unhappy one that to trace the process in full detail would be depressing, but a brief outline of the changes made in the plot will be enough to make the nature of these alterations clear.

At the beginning of the play the divine sage Narada appears, and in a lengthy monologue he flatly declares that he is setting out to accomplish the task of the gods by seeking to unite Siva and Parvati; in the **Kumarasambhava** Narada merely makes a casual prediction, with no apparent motive in doing so, and this occurs long before the necessity of uniting the two has been revealed to the gods by Brahma. While in the poem this prediction is the only appearance of Narada, in the play his part is completely rewritten to give him the active role of a scheming brahmin minister like that of Yaugandharayana in the plays dealing with the story of King Udayana; in discussions of these plays in well-known treatises on dramatic criticism, the deeds of Yaugandharayana who is thought of as an agent of the king, are construed as preserving the predominance of the king's role despite the prominent activity of Vasavadatta and other women in the plays. In the *Parvatiparinaya* the role of the other gods is also made more extensive and positive: among their activities presented explicitly in the play, they follow events on earth with great interest even after the defeat of Kama, and carry on negotiations with Siva. Siva himself participates in further heavenly activity by sending out spies of his own to check up on Parvati.

The activity of Parvati is correspondingly pushed into the background. Her austerities, which are so firmly a part of the traditional story that they could not be ignored, are merely described in a few verses, and her heroic defense of Siva against the accusations of the mysterious visitor are reduced to one brief outburst; she speaks only three times in the entire play. By expanding the role of her friends along the lines of the friends of Sankuntala in the *Abhijnanasakuntala,* Parvati is assimilated as far as possible to the character of that heroine she appears in the earliest part of the play, so that Parvati's confrontation with the disguised Siva, presented so boldly in the *Kumarasambhava,* becomes awkwardly coy in the *Parvatiparinaya.*

Other alterations in the plot, together with the introduction of several new characters whose activity takes place within the world of the gods, shift the focus away from the heroine. Many of the developments in the play are not incompatible with the facts of the story told by Kalidasa, but the selection and relative prominence of these events involves a substantial change in priorities. Yet the heroic actions of Parvati, however briefly they are described or referred to, inescapably remain the real driving force in bringing about her union with Siva, so that all the attempts by the author of the *Parvatiparinaya* to shift the focus result in a play that is grotesquely uneven and ineffective.

In the course of making his changes in emphasis, the author of the *Parvatiparinaya* also inevitably abandons the impressive structural achievements of the *Kumarasambhava.* It might have been possible to preserve the pattern of parallel halves even in the play; Kalidasa himself, for example, had used a similar though less thoroughgoing technique in his play *Abhijnanasakuntala.* But in the *Kumarasambhava* this pattern operates primarily through the strong emphasis placed on the activities of Parvati in the second half of the work, and in the *Parvatiparinaya* it is precisely this emphasis that is avoided, with the result that the fundamental conception underlying the details of construction in the original poem is torn away.

Despite their unhappy results, the alterations in plot made by the author of the *Parvatiparinaya* have been useful in highlighting two significant, and certainly more successful, features of the *Kumarasambhava*: the focus on the inner development of Parvati as a dramatically effective way of reshaping a traditional story in the light of personal religious insight, and the related technique of presenting that story in a tightly and symmetrically structured poem.

The difficulties faced by the commentators on the *Kumarasambhava* who attempted to analyze these same fea-

tures in terms of traditional Sanskrit literary theory are also useful, as an indication of the degree to which Kalidasa's achievements in the poem are innovations going beyond the usual characteristics of Sanskrit *mahakavyas.* In fact the structure of each of Kalidasa's non-dramatic poems involves some innovation that the tradition of poetics, with its conservative repetition of the old definitions of genres, was slow to recognize. In his *Meghaduta* he created a new genre, that of the *dutakavya,* which has never found a clear place in the traditional discussions of the types of poetry, despite the scores of poems composed in imitation of it. And in the *Raghuvamsa* Kalidasa experimented with a polycentric *mahakavya* describing a series of different heroes—a structure that has scarcely been mentioned in traditional accounts of the *mahakavya* genre. The inner development and balance that inform the plot of the *Kumarasambhava* are among the most fortunate of these structural innovations. The system of literary theory that fails to recognize many of these features abounds in painstaking descriptions of the characteristics of the more typical works within the tradition; that they ignore the innovations in the *Kumarasambhava* is perhaps an indication not of their inadequacy in dealing with a genre, but rather of the inventive genius of an individual poet.

D. K. Gupta (essay date 1985)

SOURCE: "Kuntaka's Critique of Kalidasa as a Master of Sukumara Style," in *Vishveshvaranand Indological Journal,* Vol. XXIII, June-December, 1985, pp. 267-79.

[*In the excerpt below, Gupta places Kalidasa's work in the* sukumara *or "delicate" style, which is characterized as being free from affectation and growing organically out of the poet's imagination.*]

Although Sanskrit poetics is characterised by a rare richness of poetical theories or doctrines of literary criticism, yet at the same time it is, unfortunately enough, very poor in representing, in a real sense, the practical aspect of literary criticism which is hardly traceable, in a noble form, in the long range of works on poetical theory excepting in the *Dhvanyaloka* of Anandavardhana (*c.* A.D. 875) and the *Vakroktijivita* of Kuntaka (*c.* A.D. 950). Of these two works also, the *Vakroktijivita* represents this aspect of literary criticism in a more comprehensive form and with greater critical insight than the other work. Kuntaka, in his treatise, attempts, in his own characteristic way, a critical appreciation of a good number of classical writtings with reference to the poetic elements propounded by him and makes a critical assessment of them in perspective.

Of the classical writers of note, Kalidasa (*c.* A.D. 400) enamours Kuntaka the most and naturally draws, therefore, his foremost attention. He is represented in his treatise as the master *par excellence* of the *sukumara* style, one of the three styles critically elaborated by him in the first chapter of his work. The *sukumara* or the delicate style, according to him, reveals itself in the work of a poet with a soft and gentle temperament endowed with a rich gift of poetic imagination (*pratibha*) which finds its full expression in his poetry. A work composed in this style, free from affectation, reminds one, as Kuntaka observes, of the supreme artistic creation of the universe by the Creator. Whatever artistic turn (*valcitrya* or *vakrokti*) is there in the work written in this style, it is the result of the poet's creative imagination alone. Even the slightest amount of figurative beauty in it is entirely due to the poet's creative power; it is never externally imposed or laboriously created. It thus positively conveys flashes of delicacy or gentle grace (*saukumarya*) which, in this context, is the same as *abhijatya* or nobility that creates beauty of deep aesthetic appeal through its animated touch. Kuntaka illustrates his point by quoting the following verse from Kalidasa's **Raghuvamsa,** which depicts the summer season at Ayodhya that provides a befitting setting for Kusa's water-sport in the Sarayu river: . . .

> The day (during this season) became exceedingly hot and the night turned extremely slim (i.e. of smaller duration). The two, separated from each other through their conflicting actions, appeared like husband and wife filled with jealous anger.

As Kuntaka comments, the ornamental beauty here, having a tinge of paronomasia, which is brought about by the poet's creative imagination alone and is not externally or artificially imposed, contributes to unique aesthetic charm. The words, *prayrddha-tapah,* in masculine gender, for the day and *tanvi,* in feminine gender, for the night, have been so used here as to bring out essentially the charming nature of the two. Though they do not directly signify any other shade of meaning, yet the poet's artistic skill has made them suggest the other meaning also, which, being quite in tune with the original meaning, delights the aesthetic mind. The other meaning is suggested by the artistic use of the words, *virodha-kriya* and *vibhinna,* in the verse. With reference to the objects described, that is, day and night, their *virodha-kriya* signifies absence of co-existance and their being *vibhinna* or separated from each other rests on their difference in nature. With reference to the standard of comparison or *upamana,* that is, husband and wife, *virodha-kriya* signifies their jealous quarrel and their being *vibhinna* or staying away from each other is occassioned by their feeling of anger. The two adverbs, *atimatram* and *atyartham,* signify a high degree of the state of things in both the cases, and as such strike us as extremely charming. The charm of paronomasia which is generally secured with great effort has been brought about here without an effort, and hence deeply appeals our aesthetic sense.

Some of the other special features characterising this *marga* have also been illustrated in Kuntaka's work by the verses from Kalidasa's writings. One of such features of this *marga* is the sprouting forth of fresh words and meanings by virtue of the poet's creative imagination capable of fresh invention. The "word" in the context of poetry, as explained by Kuntaka elsewhere, signifies that unique expression which alone can fully convey the poet's intended meaning out of a hundred alternatives before him, and the

"meaning" is that alone which delights the aesthetic mind by its own refreshing natural beauty and adds force to the sentiment intended to be developed. Kalidasa excels others in the cultivation of such words and meanings. He commands the gift of unique expression, and as one of the instances of this gift in him Kuntaka cites the following verse from the **Kumarasambhava**: . . .

> By your craze for union with Siva who puts on a string of skulls round his neck, now two have become the object of pity, namely, the shining digit of the moon and you—the shining moonlight for the eyes of the entire world.

Commenting on the words used in the verse, the critic in Kuntaka observes, that though a number of other synonyms were possible to refer to the lord Siva, the poet has chosen here the word *kapalin,* which signifies "one wearing skulls round his neck". This word, suggesting disgust appropriate to the context, endows the verse with artistic beauty of expression. Again, the words, *samprati* and *dvayam,* are extremely charming, since they implicitly convey a sense of ridicule that "while heretofore there was only one to be pitied for this indecent craving, *now* with your joining him *two* have become the object of pity for such craze." The word *prarthana* has also been happily used; if it were a mere coincidence there would be no point in censuring the union, but "the asking" for it certainly invites public censure. The conjunctive particle *ca* used twice to requate the moon's digit to Parvati is very effective, suggesting as it does the excessive charm of both The poet's preference for words *kalavatah* and *kantimati* with possessive suffixes in respect of both is also a means of excellence. None of the above senses, thus, could be conveyed by replacing the words used by their synonyms.

As an example of aesthetically delightful meaning in Kalidasa's poetry, Kuntaka cites the following verses from the **Meghaduta**: . . .

> Know me, O fortunate lady, to be a bosom friend of your husband. I am a cloud, come to you with his message treasured up in my heart—a cloud that urges, by his deep and pleasant rumblings, the wearied travellers on the road, eager to loosen the braids of their pining beloveds, to hurry back home.

Commenting on the aesthetic charm in the meaning of the verse, Kuntaka observes that it has, in the first place, a very significant vocative, *avidhave,* which infuses confidence in the mind of the Yaksa's love The qualifying word, *mitram,* points to the cloud-messenger's respectability and the epithet, *priyam,* indicates the intimacy of his friendship and inspires her confidence so that she may entrust him with a message in reply. Having thus put her at ease, the messenger comes to the main subject of the message for her. The epithet, *hrdayanihita,* for the message reveals his great care in preserving it. One might ask why some other person endowed with keen senses and talents was not entrusted with the task. The messenger, therefore, adds that he alone possesses special qualifications in this regard. He is a "carrier" of water by nature, and carrying something is his speciality. He hastens the hosts of travellers sinking with fatigue on the road by his rumbling sounds to reach their beloveds. The plural throughout (in *prosita* and *vrnda*) brings out his repeated act of helping others His "deep and pleasant" rumblings point to the pleasing words of the ideal messenger. The word *pathi* (on the road) shows how help is rendered by him even to those not related to him; thus it is implied that much more would be his sense of urgency with regard to a message entrusted to him by his bosom friend The word *abala* for the women emphasises how they are feeling dispirited owing to separation from their lovers, and the epithet, *abalavenimoksotsuka,* for the latter display their deep attachment to their beloveds. To sum up, the messenger means to emphasise that it is a self-chosen solemn mission with him to effect the joyous union of lovers that might have been torn apart by fate in spite of their deep love for each other. The beauty of thought created here by the poet constitutes the very essence of his poem named "Cloud-messenger", and is supremely delightful to the aesthetic mind.

Another special feature of the *sukumara* style is the sparse and effortless and, consequentially, charming use of poetic figures. The verse chosen to illustrate this feature is from Kalidasa's ***Kumarasambhava,*** which describes the advent of the vernal season providing an effective excitant for Siva's love for Parvati: . . .

> The Palasa flowers, not fully opened and hence curved like the crescent moon and exceedingly red, looked like the fresh nail-imprints of the Spring (*Vasanta,* in masculine gender) as it were on the limbs of the Sylvan Lands (*Vanasthali,* in feminine gender) during their first intimate union.

As Kuntaka elaborates, the expressions, *balendu-vakra-ni, atilohitani* and *sad yo vasantena samagatani,* have, in a delicate manner, been used just to present a simple description of natural state of things; still the delightful figure of speech (i.e. simile) involved in the words, *nakhaksataniva,* gets naturally related to them without the slightest strain on the reader's mind, and creates genuine aesthetic delight.

Again, the *sukumara marga* consists in giving prominence to the intrinsic or natural form of an object in preference to the external and artificial touch given to it by learning or technical skill (*vyutpatti*). This feature has been illustrated by Kuntaka by the description of Dasaratha's hunting excursion in the vernal season to introduce the episode of the death of the ascetic boy, Sravana, at his hands, contained in the ***Raghuvamsa,*** IX. 55-71. The following verse, cited in particular by him in this context, captures a side-glimpse of the hunting scene: . . .

> Before him (Dasaratha) appeared a herd of dear with *kusa* grass in their mouths, led by a proudly strutting spotted antelope. The female deer, in the herd, were frequently obstructed in their movement

by their younglings who fondly clung to their udder for milk.

Kuntaka illustrates this particular feature also by the depiction, in the ***Kumarasambhava,*** of amorous actions of animal creatures, stimulated by the onset of the spring season in the grove where Siva was practising austerities. He quotes, in particular, the following half-verse: . . .

> The spotted antelope started gently tickling the doe with his horn, thus making her close her eyes in ecstasy at its pleasing touch.

An important feature of the *sukumara* style is its capacity to create mental empathy in men of taste, expert in enjoying the essence of sentiments (*rasas*), to make them imaginatively experience the poet's experiences and identify these with their own. Kuntaka illustrates this feature by the ***Raghuvamsa*** verses (XIII. 2-63) reproducing words of Rama to Sita on his way back to Ayodhya in the aerial car after regaining her. These verses, depicting the extreme agony once felt by Rama during his separation from Sita in place after place coming now to view again, are eminently capable of creating mental empathy in the rearders of taste. One of these verses cited by Kuntaka is as follows: . . .

> At night I would remember, O Sita, your past embrace accompanied by tremors of fear (caused by the sudden thunder of clouds resounding in the caves), and with a great difficulty could I endure the rumblings of clouds as they resounded long in the caves.

Again, this style is very pleasing by a kind of beauty which is ineffable and eludes the critic's power of analysis. Though Kuntaka has not illustrated his point by citing an instance, he appears to be referring here to the poetic beauty which would defy a clear-cut assessment in terms of sentiments, poetic figures etc., the known elements of poetic charm. We may have a number of such verses of Kalidasa's composition cited in Kuntaka's work as would aptly illustrate this kind of poetic beauty. We may quote here the following verse from the *Abhijnanasakuntala,* which represents Dusyanta as so totally lost in his love's thought that he takes her painted figure to be the real Sakuntala and addresses the bee portrayed near her face thus: . . .

> O bee, if you dare to touch my darling's lip, as red as the *bimba* fruit and as charming as the fresh sprouts of soft plants, which I kissed but gently even in my festive amours, I shall put you into the prison of a lotus-bud.

Dusyanta's words here, as Kuntaka observes, betray his sweet recollection with the deep impress of his darling and have a direct appeal to our aesthetic sensibility, though the verse in question may not be said to display any tangible figurative beauty.

The four *gunas* or poetic excellences which, in their slightly varying form, constitute distinctive features of the three styles, are *madhurya* (sweetness), *prasada* (perspicuity), *lavanya* (grace) and *abhijatya* (nobility). Of these, *madhurya,* as conceived with reference to *sukumara marga,* consists in the beauty both of word and meaning, artistic arrangement of vocables and avoidance of a profusion of compounds. Curiously enough, Kuntaka has not illustrated this *guna* by a verse from Kalidasa, while he has invariably cited from the great poet in explaining the nature of the other three *gunas* with reference to the *sukumara* style. May be, the verse of an unknown source cited by Kuntaka to illustrate his *guna* belonged to Kalidasa and occurred in some lost work of his. In fact, Kalidasa's poetry is distinctly characterised by *madhurya* of the highest order, and any verse from his works may well be cited as an instance of this excellence. We give below a verse from the *Kumarasambhava,* quoted by Kuntaka in some other context, to illustrate this *guna* with reference to the delicate style: . . .

> The moon, with his fingers in the form of rays, holds fast the dark braided hair of the Night and kisses her face as it were, making her close her lotus-like eyes in ecstasy.

The second excellence, *prasada,* in this style, signifies perspicuity which brings out the poet's intent without any effort on the part of the reader. It conveys the meaning in an instant as it were, and addresses itself to *rasas,* sentiments, and *vakrokti,* an expression with artistic turn, i. e. a figurative expression. The factors which bring about perspicuity in an expression are (i) absence of long, and not easily intelligible compounds, (ii) direct meanings, and (iii) uninvolved constructions. Kuntaka cites the following verses from Kalidasa to illustrate this excellence: . . .

(1) . . .

> As the snowy winter came to a close, the lips of the Kimpurusa damsels began to shine bright, the complexion of their faces started glittering yellowish white, and drops of perspiration made their first appearance on the painted designs on their faces.

Commenting on the figurative charm which this verse commands, the critic in Kuntaka observes that the beauty of the face primarily caused by the various painted designs is further embellished as it were by the appearance of the pearl-like drops of perspiration.

(2) . . .

> Indumati, you may please agree to marry this king (of Kalinga) and sport in his company on the shores of the ocean rustling with groves of palmyra trees. May the winds, wafting the scent of cloves from remote islands, wipe away the drops of perspiration from your body (tired in amorous sport).

(3) . . .

(Already cited and explained above).

The third *guna, lavanya,* in this style, consists in the charm of syntax (*bandha-saundarya*) resulting from even a little beauty in respect of alliterative syllables and in the choice of diction. It is, in effect, a graceful ease and tenderness in words and meanings. This excellence has been illustrated by Kuntaka by the following verses from the ***Raghuvamsa***:

(1) . . .

> Cupid, whose spirit diminished at the close of the spring season, found a new source of strength in the tresses of damsels, wet and let loose after their bath, richly scented by fumigation and decked with jasmine flowers fresh in the evening.

As Kuntaka observes, the strikingness of beauty in construction here cannot be explained in words and may just be felt by men of taste.

(2) . . .

> [Introducing Aja to Indumati, Sunanda says: "Here is the king Aja who, having climbed on the mountain Mahendra as if on a great bull and hence commanding the lustrous appearance of iva,] deprived for ever the cheeks of the Asura queens of their ornamental paintings through the showers of his arrows [in the battle].

Here too, as Kuntaka observes, the beauty in the case of syllables and in the choice of diction, which is responsible for the exquisite charm in syntax, is strikingly manifest.

The fourth excellence, *abhijatya,* is the quality of being smooth on the ear and capable as it were of intimate embrace by thought and commanding the effect of spontaneous sparkle in poetry. This excellence has been illustrated by Kuntaka by the following half-verse from the ***Meghaduta***: . . .

> [Thereafter, O Cloud, with your thunderings prolonged by their being echoed by the mountain-caves, you may make Skanda's that peacock dance, the outer corners of whose eyes are brightened by the lustre of Siva's moon], and whose moulted feather, bearing circles of streaks of starlight, Parvati puts on her ear, usually the seat of a blue lotus-petal, out of affection for her son.

As Kuntaka observes, the half-verse commands the spontaneous sparkle owing to a smooth sensation on the ear, which may well be appreciated by men of taste.

The above examination of Kuntaka's treatment of the *sukumara marga,* with its characteristic features and excellences almost exclusively illustrated by the verses from Kalidasa's works, makes it abundantly clear that Kuntaka viewed Kalidasa as a poet with soft and gentle temperament and gifted with a delicate creative power, which, aided by an equipment in tune with it, directed the course of his poetic endeavours along the *sukumara* or delicated path, aptly likened by him to the grove of full-blown flowers and gave birth to the rich crop of his poetry of soft and tender appeal. Kalidasa's poetry, according to him, is eminently characterised by all the features and excellences which form ingredients of the *sukumara* style. Even though Kuntaka does not subscribe, in theory, to the idea of gradational assessment or categorisation of the three styles, his predilection, in practice, for the *sukumara marga,* where *pratibha* or the creative power of the poet reigns supreme with *vyut patti* or learning and technical skill subordinating and attuning itself to the former, is more than evident. This is in perfect consonance with his genuine preponderance for Kalidasa's poetry, typically exemplifying the *sukumara* style, which, significantly enough, gets the largest representation in the wide range of the illustrative material embodied in his treatise. Again, it may not be less significant to note that it is in Kuntaka's work, in the whole range of works on Sanskrit poetics, that Kalidasa has been cited the most and in the maximum quantum and has received the greatest applause for his poetry of supreme aesthetic appeal. In fact, in Kuntaka's view, Kalidasa's poetry is enshrined in a diction which is singularly adorned by *vakrokti* or artistic turn of speech and is happily fashioned in the *sukumara* style, which has a general resemblance to the Vaidarbha-*marga* or Vaidarbhi-*riti,* long associated, in literary tradition, with his name.

Martha Ann Seeby (essay date 1994)

SOURCE: A review of *The Seasons: Kalidasa's Rtusamhara,* in *The Journal of Asian Studies,* Vol. 53, No. 2, May, 1994, pp. 610-11.

[*In the following review, Seeby criticizes the translator of* A Round of Seasons *for his over-reliance on prosody.*]

The *Rtusamhara, A Round of Seasons,* is a fairly early, if not the earliest, example of Sanskrit *laghukavya* composed on the popular theme of *sadrtuvarnana,* "description of the six seasons." According to inscriptional evidence, this poem was most likely composed at some point prior to the mid-fifth century C.E. There is no doubt that it is an erotic poem. It is verbal seduction, Sanskrit style, spoken by a man to his beloved, and its very movement through the year is designed to titillate. The poem begins in the heat of summer. The speaker asks his love to wait: because of the oppressive heat of the season, it is too hot for lovemaking, and he proceeds to describe all six seasons of the year for her, ending in the bursting fertility of spring.

The *Rtusamhara* is popularly ascribed to Kalidasa. One of the commentators on the text, Manirama, describes the poem as only "Kalidasa-ish," and he is probably right: it has its charms, to be sure, but it is an extremely immature work. Much of it is labored and repetitive, and it was not at all valued by the later Sanskrit critics, who unanimously chose to ignore it. If the poem does belong to Kalidasa, it could only be characterized as a very early "sketchbook" of this great master and standard-setter of classical Sanskrit lyric.

Doubts of these sorts—my own and those of the classical rhetoricians—lead me to ask John Roberts why he chose to do a full translation of this work. If the choice is made to accept the poem as an early piece by Kalidasa, this text takes on a certain literary-historical significance if one wishes to engage in a historical study of Kalidasa's "style." But, unfortunately, the text itself is of very little poetic value.

I greatly admire Roberts's effort—and downright courage—in producing this translation which amounts to a verse-rendering in English that precisely reflects Sanskrit prosodical patterns of rhyme and meter. It is a labor of love, certainly, and an idea that most Sanskritists who specialize in *kavya* toy with, and then abandon, during the translation process. But it seems that poetry, to Roberts, is all prosody and rhyme, and it is for this reason that I cannot admire the result.

Because of the nearly obsessive emphasis that Roberts has placed on prosody, he has sacrificed sense for the sake of meter in too many instances to mention, resulting in a translation that is as utterly baroque as the "richly gilded poetic frames" in which the translator describes these verses as having been set, and, due to the nature of the original work itself, Roberts has not gilded a lily but rather a dandelion. This is not a poet's translation, but one produced by a poetaster. The hallmark of a truly excellent sonnet is that the reader is not aware that a poem is a sonnet at all until secondary readings and analyses. Prosody is the heartbeat of any language, Sanskrit or English, and when English is forced into the rather elaborate and beautifully algebraic meters of classical Sanskrit, the result is not subtle, quiet heartbeat but hiccoughs. In the second *uddyota* of his *Dhvanyaloka,* ninth-century critic Anandavardhana wisely cautions against the use of sequential alliteration (*anuprasa*) or paranomastic alliteration (*yamaka*), devising an uncluttered aesthetic for love poetry in general. This prescription is one that has stood the test of time, and is something that I see just as applicable to classical Sanskrit verse as to late twentieth-century translations.

The only readable translation of the *Rtusamhara* is Emile Senart's, published in 1938 by the Societé d'Édition "Les Belles Lettres" in Paris as an appendix to Senart's translation of the *Meghaduta.* I would direct readers to that particular edition if they are interested in an accurate translation of the *Rtusamhara* that reads smoothly and well.

Rather than producing a translation of this work, Roberts would have better written a scholarly book on Sanskrit prosody, a task he is well equipped to undertake, using the *Rtusamhara* as a source from which to draw examples. The book as it stands would serve well as a "workbook" for students who are beginning to read Sanskrit *kavya.* As well, one could memorize verses from Roberts's translation as mnemonic devices for remembering Sanskrit metrical schemes, but one could just as well memorize a Sanskrit verse or two. It would certainly be more edifying.

FURTHER READING

Bibliography

Mandal, Paresh Chandra. *Kalidasa as a Dramatist: A Study*. Dhaka, Bangladesh: University of Dhaka, 1986.
> In addition to a section on Kalidasa's dramas, provides a list of critical editions and works touching on broader issues.

Criticism

Bandyopadhyay, Pratap. "Did Kalidasa Complete the *Kumarasambhava?*" *Journal of the American Oriental Society* 106, No. 3 (July-September 1986): 559-64.
> Asserts that some of Cantos VIII to XVII, although inferior to the earlier cantos, were written by Kalidasa, then lost, and rewritten by a second hand.

Dwivedi, R.C. "Asvaghosa and Kalidasa—Point and Counter-Point of Moksa and Dharma in Poetic Tradition of India." *Annals of the Bhandarkar Oriental Research Institute* LXVII, Nos. 1-4 (1986): 259-63.
> A comparison of the two poets' ideals, pointing out the value of the latter's asceticism.

Robinson, Richard. "Humanism Versus Asceticism in Asvaghosa and Kalidasa," in *Journal of South Asian Literature* XII, Nos. 3 & 4 (Spring-Summer 1977): 1-10.
> Traces two varying states of mind in *The Birth of the War-God* and Asvaghosa's *Career of the Buddha: raga* (sensual desire) and *tyaga* (detachment).

Sarma, Dimbeswar. *An Interpretive Study of Kalidasa*. Calcutta: Chowkhamba Sanskrit Series Office, 1968, 383p.
> A dissertation outlining and describing the poet's philosophies, ethics, and religious beliefs.

Sinharay, Haridas. "An Aesthetic Evaluation of the Rhetorical Devices in Kalidasa." *Indian Studies: Past and Present* IX, No. 2 (1968): 133-6.
> Explores rhetorical devices in *Meghaduta* and *Raghuvamsu*.

Additional coverage of Kalidasa's life and career is contained in the following source published by Gale Research: ***Classical and*** *Medieval Literature Criticism, Vol. 9.*

Philip Levine
1928-

American poet and autobiographer.

INTRODUCTION

Best known for his poetry celebrating the working class, Levine's verse extolls the virtues of blue-collar factory workers and gives voice to the inequities suffered on the lines. Levine's background—born and raised in Detroit—mirrored those people he wrote about. For a time, Levine himself worked on an assembly line in the automobile factories of his hometown. Over the years, Levine's subject matter and poetic form have changed little, resulting in mixed critical reviews.

Biographical Information

Levine was born in Detroit, Michigan, on January 10, 1928 to immigrant parents of Russian-Jewish ancestry. His youth and early adulthood typified the experiences of most lower and middle income people in Detroit, taking their place within the great industrial machine that drove the American economy: the automobile assembly plants at the height of the industry's power. Working in assembly plants, experiencing first-hand the long work days and poor conditions, inspired Levine to vow to use poetry to give a voice to the voiceless. He attended Wayne University (to later become Wayne State University) in Detroit where he received both his B.A. in 1950 and his M.A. in 1955. While attending Wayne, Levine became intrigued with the Spanish poet Federico Garcia Lorca. He later recalled the experience: "I stood in the stacks of Wayne State University Library with my hands trembling and read my life in his words."

After leaving Wayne State, Levine went on to receive an M.F.A. from the University of Iowa in 1957, where he studied with Robert Lowell and John Berryman. Later that same year he was awarded the Stanford University Fellowship in Poetry and moved to California. The following year, Levine joined the faculty of Fresno State College, where his students included the poets Luis Omar Salinas, Sherley Anne Williams, and Gary Soto (whose work is often considered similar to Levine's).

In 1961, Levine published his first volume of poetry, *On the Edge*. During the 1960s, Levine's fascination with Spanish literature and culture caused him to move to Spain with his family for two separate periods. The time spent in Spain profoundly influenced his poetry, the history and politics of the region becoming subjects for his work. For example, *The Names of the Lost*, dedicated to Buenaventura Durruti, a leader of the anarchist move-

ment during the Spanish Civil War, contains the elegy "For the Fallen," written in Durruti's honor.

1979 was a banner year for Levine, as he received both the American Book Award and the National Book Critics Circle Prize for *Ashes* (1979). He met with similar success in 1991 when *What Work Is* earned both the Los Angeles Times Book Prize and the National Book Award for Poetry. Levine won the Pulitzer Prize in Poetry for *The Simple Truth* in 1994.

Major Works

Since his first collection, *On the Edge*, Levine has remained faithful to his vow to tell the stories of "the problematic, the painful, the disorderly, [and] the ugly" with little deviation from that theme. Critics have noted an intensity of purpose in Levine's poetry from the 1960s and '70s, spanning the volumes *On the Edge* through *They Feed They Lion* (1972). During this time, his narrow focus on the bleak life of the laborer earned his poetry the reputation of being drab and somewhat jaded. Beginning with *1933* (1979), however, Levine professes to have undergone a change of style and subject matter, describing his poetry as "less aggressive." Increasingly sentimental and nostalgic, he turns his attention towards relatives, friends, and notable figures of the Spanish Civil War. Such poems as "1933," "On the Murder of Lieutenant Jose Del Castillo," "For the Fallen," "Montjuich," and "Francisco, I'll Bring You Red Carnations," are examples of this trend. Beginning with *Ashes* (1979), Levine's style shifts again as he moves from an examination of the "sad realities of a hostile world" to an acceptance of the natural world. It is in these later volumes that Levine is at his most inventive.

Critical Reception

Levine's work has received mixed reviews since the appearance of *On the Edge*, although the overall critical response has been more positive than negative. Levine's commitment to bring to light the travails of the working class and the downtrodden poor, however, along with his abandonment of conventional metrical forms and rhyme scheme, has created a critical divide over the interpretation and quality of his work. On one side, such well-known critics as Herbert Leibowitz and Helen Vendler downplay his poetic ability and contend that his style is more like prose than poetry, and drab prose at that. Harold Bloom leads the opposing viewpoint, admiring Levine's ability to control the pathos in his verse and subject matter, apparently not put off by the bleak and gritty picture of the working-class world. Other critics support Bloom, considering Levine's poetry as characteristic of the world in these modern times, describing the dreary circumstances of everyday life and creating a forum where the voices of the (traditionally) voiceless can be heard. In the end, what is irrefutable is that Levine's distinct poetic voice speaks volumes for a segment of society unaccustomed to being championed in popular literature, and for that he will be remembered, despite critics' less than enthusiastic opinion of his meter and form.

PRINCIPAL WORKS

Poetry

On the Edge   1961
Silent in America: Vivas for Those Who Failed   1965
Not This Pig   1968
5 Detroits   1970
Thistles: A Poem Sequence   1970
Pili's Wall   1971; revised edition,   1980
Red Dust [illustrated by Marcia Mann]   1971
They Feed They Lion   1972
1933   1974
New Season   1975

On the Edge and Over: Poems Old, Lost, and New   1976
The Names of the Lost   1976
7 Years from Somewhere   1979
Ashes: Poems New and Old   1979
One for the Rose   1981
Selected Poems   1984
Sweet Will   1985
A Walk with Tom Jefferson   1988
New Selected Poems   1991
What Work Is   1991
The Simple Truth   1994

Other Major Work

The Bread of Time: Toward an Autobiography   1994

CRITICISM

Ralph J. Mills, Jr.   (essay date 1975)

SOURCE: "'The True and Earthy Prayer': Philip Levine's Poetry," in *Cry of the Human: Essays on Contemporary American Poetry*, University of Illinois Press, 1975, pp. 251-65.

[*In the following essay, Mills traces the development of Levine's themes from* On the Edge *to* Red Dust *and* They Feed They Lion.]

> We live
> the way we are
>   —P.L., **"The Sadness of Lemons"**

The poetry of Philip Levine, from *On the Edge* (1963) to his two latest collections, *Red Dust* (1971) and *They Feed They Lion* (1972), has always displayed technical skill, a dexterous handling of both formal and, more recently, informal modes, and a command of the resources of diction and rhythm. Yet these aspects of technique seem in a way secondary, absorbed as they are by a central, driving intensity peculiar to this poet's approach. Such intensity leads him to a relentless searching through the events of his life and the lives of others, through the particulars of nature as these signify something about the processes of living, the states of existence, in order to arrive not at Eliot's transcendence, Roethke's "condition of joy," or Whitman's ideal of progress and brotherhood (though the sharing of suffering and the common ties of humanity are basic to Levine's attitude) but to the sort of awareness suggested by Yeats's phrase, "the desolation of reality": an unflinching acquaintance with the harsh facts of most men's situation which still confirms rather than denies its validity. If this is a difficult prospect, we must acknowledge how familiar it has become of late through the poems of Robert Lowell, David Ignatow, James Wright, Allen Ginsberg, and Galway Kinnell, to mention a few obvious names. In the writing of these poets, as in Levine's, the range of human sympathies, the frankness, perseverance, and sensitivity create of themselves an affirmative, life-sustaining balance to the bleak recognition of religious deprivation, war, social injustice, moral and spiritual confusion.

Levine's early poetry is taut, sharp, formal but gradually alters to accommodate his desire for greater freedom in line length and overall construction. A prominent theme of his first book is the reversal or defeat of expectations. Put another way, it motivates a struggle on the poet's part to view life stripped of the vestiges of illusory hope or promise, a type of hard spiritual conditioning which helps to engender his fundamental responsiveness to the dilemmas of the poor, embittered, failed lives of the "submerged population" (the late Frank O'Connor's term) in modern society, a responsiveness that accounts for much of both the energy and the deep humaneness of all his work. A firm grip on existence itself takes priority for Levine from the start, though with it necessarily comes an acceptance of pain and the admission that failure, defeat, and imperfection—but not surrender!—are unavoidable in men's affairs. The penetrating look he gives himself in **"The Turning"** from *On the Edge* points the direction he follows to maturity, which depends on the realization of flaws as well as the capacity to exist, to continue, made sturdier by this self-knowledge:

> . . . . no more a child,
> Only a man,—one who has
> Looked upon his own nakedness
> Without shame, and in defeat
> Has seen nothing to bless.
> Touched once, like a plum, I turned
> Rotten in the meat, or like
> The plum blossom I never
> Saw, hard at the edges, burned
> At the first entrance of life,
> And so endured, unreckoned,
> Untaken, with nothing to give.
> The first Jew was God; the second
> Denied him; I am alive.

Committed to a fallen, unredeemable world, finding no metaphysical consolations, Levine embraces it with an ardor, anguish, and fury that are themselves religious emotions. In a brief comment on his work contributed to *Contemporary Poets of the English Language* (1970) he lists among his "obsessions" "Detroit" (where he was born, did factory labor, and studied), "the dying of America" (a recurrent theme in various guises), and "communion with others," which incorporates its predecessors as well as specifying what is for him a primary poetic impulse. Writing frequently of persons whose lives are distinct yet touch his own, he increases his consciousness and imaginative powers, and a chord of compassion and understanding reverberates within and beyond the boundaries of his poems. This is not to say that Levine puts himself out of the picture or chooses a mask of impersonality, but that his presence in a poem, whether overt or concealed, constitutes an enlargement of personality, a stepping out of the ego-bound "I" into the surrounding life. Paradoxically, he reaches inward, far into the re-

cesses of the psyche, at the same time he reaches outward, thus fulfilling a pattern of movement Robert Bly has long advocated as essential to a modern poetry rich in imaginative potentialities.

Among the poems of Levine's initial volume, this self-extension appears most complete when he adopts the voices of different persons—the Sierra Kid, four French Army deserters in North Africa, the unnamed officer of **"The Distant Winter"**—to replace his own. Another sort of identification, of a crucial kind for the line of development his work pursues, occurs in the title poem **"On the Edge,"** and also in **"My Poets"** and **"Gangrene."** In these instances he does not assume the role of another speaker but takes up the question of a poetic vocation and the destiny of poets in society today. In one shape or another, each of these poems really considers the problem of speechlessness, the lacerating irony of the mute poet imprisoned by circumstances which thwart or oppose his art, making its practice unlikely or impossible. So Levine sorts through the probabilities of his own future. The poet/speaker of **"On the Edge"** describes himself as the insane, alcoholic Poe of the twentieth century, born, as Levine was, "in 1928 in Michigan." This latter-day Poe plays the part of an observer who doesn't write, only watches the actions and prevarications of nameless people. In the last stanza he repeats a refusal of his art, though we are provided in its statement of alienation, perceptiveness, and silence with a poetry of angry eloquence:

> I did not write, for I am Edgar Poe,
> Edgar the mad one, silly, drunk, unwise,
> But Edgar waiting on the edge of laughter,
> And there is nothing that he does not know
> Whose page is blanker than the raining skies.

This abstention from writing, or persecution for telling the truth by means of it, occupies the other poems mentioned. Levine's effort here is to indicate the need for honest speech, the conditions which militate against it, and the frustrating atmosphere of separateness the poet faces. Thematically, the poem **"Silent in America"** from *Not This Pig* (1968), Levine's second collection, brings such matters to a critical climax and to a moment of transformation and decision. Though it is not the first poem in the book, dramatically speaking it should be thought of as a pivotal piece, for its procedure and resolution make possible what Levine is doing elsewhere in the same volume: breaking down those barriers which prevent him from entering areas of otherwise lost or unapprehended experience requisite to the poetry he wants to write. At the outset the poet announces his silence, which fashions for him a state of remoteness and solitude that border on anonymity. Watching ordinary things— a sprinkler wetting a lawn—stirs him toward utterance, but he stays quiet. A doctor's examination uncovers no defect. Details of nature engage him with the elusive tracery of their being; still, the animate *something* he notices in trees, water, and flowers defies his wish to name it, and thus his muteness persists. Locked in isolation, Levine now falls victim to inner torments, to his "squat demon, / my little Bobby," a splintered apparition of the self who plagues him with insatiable sexual demands. The poem develops rapidly toward hysteria and derangement until the poet bursts out with a negative cry of resistance. A section ensues in which he articulates the aims of his writing—to give voice to the varied experience of lost, unknown, or forgotten individuals he has met, speaking with and for them—but he is likewise forced to assent to the fact that each person remains finally impervious to total comprehension and communion. The following passage handsomely summarizes Levine's intentions and concerns:

> For a black man whose
> name I have forgotten who danced
>   all night at Chevy
>   Gear & Axle,
>   for that great stunned Pole
> who laughed when he called me Jew
>   Boy, for the ugly
>   who had no chance,
>
>   the beautiful in
> body, the used and the unused,
>   those who had courage
>   and those who quit—
>   Rousek and Ficklin
> numbed by their own self-praise
>   who ate their own shit
>   in their own rage;
>
>   for these and myself
> whom I had loved and hated, I
>   had presumed to speak
>   in measure.
>   The great night is half
> over, and the stage is dark;
>   all my energy,
>   all my care for
>
>   those I cannot touch
> runs on my breath like a sigh;
>   surely I have failed.
>   My own wife
>   and my children reach
> in their sleep for some sure sign,
>   but each has his life
>   private and sealed.

Levine's anxiety arises from the profoundly felt impulse to put his language, as poetry, in the service of others' lives, in addition to his own. The walls of privacy and individuality he cannot traverse cause him regret and a feeling of loss. Yet, just as surely, he *does* speak for others to the very limit of his abilities, not only here but also in the rest of this book, as well as in his subsequent poetry. If he is unable to appropriate the entirety of another life, like a second skin, it is still possible for him to go with others, moving to the rhythms of their existence and assimilating the details which his imagination requires. This kind of correspondence and kinship receives treatment in the closing section of the poem, where

Levine meets a friend, H., in a Los Angeles bar and talks with him. H. is perhaps a writer too; in any event, he is described as doing essentially what an artist does: he creates a world composed of half-real, observed figures and half-fictitious ones who fit in with their actual counterparts, and he lives with them in imagination and sympathy. In the tavern Levine senses the presence of a person of fabulous name, apparently a wholly fictive man, conjured by his mind, who imposes himself no less strongly on the poet's awareness and emotions because of that:

> Archimbault is here—
> I do not have to be drunk
>   to feel him come near,
>
> and he touches me with his
>   life, and I could cry,
> though I don't know who he is
>   or why I should care
> about the mad ones, imagined
>   and real, H. places
> in his cherished underground,
>   their wounded faces
>
> glowing in the half-light of
>   their last days alive,
> as his glows here.

Whatever his self-questioning, Levine clearly cares, and his expressed wish in the next lines merges his own existence with that of such persons as fill the bar, until all seems to become part of poetry itself: "Let me have / the courage to live / as fictions live, proud, careless, / unwilling to die." So he would have his life speak itself as poems do, tenacious of their being. At the conclusion Levine and H. leave the bar and "enter the city." The poet urges his readers to join him, to blend into the mass of humanity thronging the streets in their restlessness, at last to go "beyond the false lights / of Pasadena / where the living are silent / in America." This invitation is as much a definition of his own poetic pursuits as it is a gesture by which the poet makes his reader a partner to what he sees. Levine will invade those areas of the unspoken life and lend them words.

Rich and complex though they usually are, the poems of Levine's first two collections are relatively direct, proceeding by certain logical, sequential, narrative, or other means which provide the reader with support and guidance. Levine never altogether abandons poems of this sort, but even in *Not This Pig* he begins to widen his fields of exploration to include experiences which manifest themselves in irrational, dreamlike, fantastic, or visionary forms, doing so variously in such poems as **"The Rats," "The Business Man of Alicante," "The Cartridges," "The One-Eyed King," "Animals Are Passing from Our Lives," "Baby Villon," "Waking an Angel," "The Second Angel,"** and **"The Lost Angel."** These pieces prepare the way for the surrealist atmosphere of *Red Dust,* the elliptical, disjunctive composition evident there, and further visible in portions of *They Feed They Lion.* Levine has cited the Spanish and

Latin American poets Hernandez, Alberti, Neruda, and Vallejo, in addition to postwar Polish poetry, as having presented new possibilities available to him. The freedom, vigorousness, metaphorical and imagistic daring of these poets plainly has had a tonic effect on Levine's more recent writing, releasing him to new boldness and strength.

So, by any but a narrow or restrictive view, Levine's latest books must be judged extraordinarily successful, exhibiting an access of inventiveness and vision. In **Red Dust** the elements of experience move into different focus; they are less "distanced," talked about, or pointed to than rendered dramatically as the very substance of language and image in the poems. The general character of these poems is also freer, more intuitive, and thus occasionally more difficult, unyielding to logical analysis. From the beginning we find an openness in the structure of poems, in the sense that they are not brought to a tidy conclusion but often end in a startling, seemingly irrational—yet, on consideration, perfectly apt—statement. Here is the final section of **"Clouds,"** a poem which gathers considerable momentum by associative leaping among apparently random details whose disconnectedness actually pulls together a grim portrait of the contemporary world. Over the shifting scenes and figures the aloof clouds travel, absorb, and spill out their rain, giving the poem coherence while at the same time implying a universal indifference to which the poet responds with vehemence in the striking lines at the close:

> You cut an apple in two pieces
> and ate them both. In the rain
> the door knocked and you dreamed it.
> On bad roads the poor walked under cardboard
>   boxes.
>
> The houses are angry because they're watched.
> A soldier wants to talk with God
> but his mouth fills with lost tags.
>
> The clouds have seen it all, in the dark
> they pass over the graves of the forgotten
> and they don't cry or whisper.
> They should be punished every morning,
> they should be bitten and boiled like spoons.

In poems of this sort the components are set down in combinations which resist or contradict ordinary rational expectations for them. The reader, thus perceptually thrown off balance, has the option either to give up or give in, and so to see and feel the particulars of experience fused in vivid, evocative ways. Gradually, the shifting shapes, the elisions and abrupt juxtapositions will disclose their significance, if the reader will only accept them on their own terms. As indicated previously, Levine's social and moral preoccupations retain their urgency, but, as in the work of the Spanish-speaking poets he admires, such interests tend at times to be integral with the immediate, elliptical, or surreal orderings of imagery and statement. Frequently now, the poems seek out specific details of landscape, cityscape, even veg-

etation and animal life, though these directly or obliquely correspond with aspects of human existence. Sensitivity to place—whether Detroit, California, or Spain (where Levine lived for two years recently)—the imagination exercised on what is perceived there, leads readily into poems of large expressive force. The figures inhabiting these pieces may be quite separate and distinct, with Levine himself only a transparent or invisible speaker (though, of course, an indirect commentator, sometimes a savage one), as in **"The End of Your Life"** or **"Where We Live Now";** or they may involve the poet openly, as he tries to define himself and his life, or when he captures a moment's affective resonance, a mood charged with implications, of the kind we observe in **"A Sleepless Night," "Told," "Holding On,"** and **"First."** In **"Noon"** he draws self and others together beautifully within the frame of a landscape:

> I bend to the ground
> to catch
> something whispered,
> urgent, drifting
> across the ditches.
> The heaviness of
> flies stuttering
> in orbit, dirt
> ripening, the sweat
> of eggs.
>
>   There are
> small streams
> the width of a thumb
> running in the villages
> of sheaves, whole
> eras of grain
> wakening on
> the stalks, a roof
> that breathes over
> my head.
>
>   Behind me
> the tracks creaking
> like a harness,
> an abandoned bicycle
> that cries and cries,
> a bottle of common
> wine that won't
> pour.
> At such times
> I expect the earth
> to pronounce. I say,
> "I have been waiting
> so long."
>
>   Up ahead
> a stand of eucalyptus
> guards the river,
> the river moving
> east, the heavy light
> sifts down driving
> the sparrows for
> cover, and the women

bow as they slap
the life out
of sheets and pants
and worn hands.

In this poem, as in many of Levine's newest, man's common attachments with earth, his relationship with objects, the hard, painful climate in which most lives are lived, are evoked through a skilled interweaving of images, the particulars of the world suddenly caught up to view, suffused with the "reek of the human," to borrow a phrase from Donald Davie. "How much earth is a man," Levine asks in another poem; his answer indicates an indissoluble, fateful bond: "a hand is planted / and the grave blooms upward / in sunlight and walks the roads." In the three angel poems from *Not This Pig,* which create a little sequence among themselves, the realm of transcendence, of the spiritual ideal, dissolves or collapses before the spectacle of flawed earthly reality. What aspects of the spiritual can become evident belong not to a hidden or remote sphere but radiate, if possible, from the ingredients of day-to-day mundane affairs. So, in Levine's work, life is circumscribed by the finality of death, but this inevitability is countenanced with toughness, stoicism, staying power. As he says of his fist in the final stanza of the poem bearing that title:

It opens and is no longer.
Bud of anger, kinked
tendril of my life, here
in the forged morning
fill with anything—water,
light, blood—but fill.

Between the poems of *Red Dust* and those of *They Feed They Lion* no alterations occur in Levine's attitude toward such matters; two poems, **"The Space We Live"** and **"How Much Can It Hurt?"**, are even reprinted from the earlier book. In general, however, Levine employs less of the dense irrational or associative manner so prominent in *Red Dust,* though with no loss of concentrated force. The opening poems, **"Renaming the Kings"** and **"The Cutting Edge,"** for instance, dramatize personal incidents in a direct, sequential way quite appropriate to the experiences. These pieces, along with several others, examine the poet's encounters in the midst of natural settings, with each occasion revealing some facet of a relation between the things of earth and a man—a relation sometimes assuring and harmonious, sometimes disturbing or painful. In **"The Cutting Edge"** a stone under water gashes the poet's foot; he casts it out of the stream and hobbles away. Later he returns, discovers it, and pauses to wonder before deciding what to do with it:

I could take it home
and plant it in a box;
I could talk about
what it did to me
and what I did to it,
or how in its element
it lives like you or me.
But it stops me, here

on my open hand,
by being a stone, and I send
it flying over the heads
of the fishing children,
arching alone above
the dialogue of reeds,
falling and falling toward water,
somewhere in water to strike
a conversation of stone.

A very different type of "conversation" takes place in **"To a Fish Head Found on the Beach Near Málaga,"** where Levine, walking alone, comes upon the ravaged body and head, hanging by its shred of bone, then confides his "loneliness," "fears," and torments to it. The result of his strange speech makes him sense the contours and characteristics of his own face and head, and, at last, "throw the fish head to the sea. / Let it be fish once more." The poem's concluding lines assert the speaker's comprehension of the unalterable cyclicism of existence, the ironic necessity of destruction for renewal:

I sniff my fingers
and catch the burned essential oil
seeping out of death. Out of the beginning,
I hear, under the sea roar, the bone words
of teeth tearing earth and sea,
anointing the tongues with stone and sand,
water eating fish, fish water,
head eating head to let us be.

This volume also includes sequences of varying length, as well as groups of obviously connected poems. **"Thistles,"** the longest of them, dedicated to the poet George Oppen, is composed of discrete pieces each of which focuses on a singular occasion, perception, or ambiance of feeling. The same may be said for the shorter sequence, "Dark Rings." These poems are not bound tightly together, though the thistle appears in the first and last pieces of that sequence, and the "dark rings" refer not only to a specific detail in one poem but also to images in most and the mood of all of them. Yet their swift, free, occasionally abbreviated notation and arrangement give an impression of accuracy, deftness, and assurance in the handling of experience. The poems are full of nuances and overtones which linger on. One must place with these sequences most of the poems in the book's second section, dealing with Levine's Detroit life among the automotive workers and the abandoned, hopeless, silent figures we have seen him desirous to know and to speak for. The angels return in this section in shifting but always earthly forms, evanescent protective spirits hovering about the poet, presences in his closet, or incarnate in someone of his acquaintance, as in the fourth poem of "The Angels of Detroit" group. Here "the angel Bernard," trapped and frustrated by the massive industrial system for which he labors and cannot escape, writing poems no one will read, aching for love, release, even death, awakens as always to find himself surrounded by the debris of manufacture, our values and lives rupturing from the shapes of steel and rubber in which we have conceived them:

At the end of the mud road
in the false dawn of the slag heap
the hut of the angel Bernard.
His brothers are factories and
bowling teams, his mother is the
power to blight, his father
moves in all men like a threat,
a closing of hands, an unkept
promise to return.
                              We talk
for years; everything we
say comes to nothing. We drink
bad beer and never lie. From
his bed he pulls fists
of poems and scatters them
like snow. "Children are guilty,"
he whispers, and the soft mouth
puffs like a wound.

He wants it all tonight.
The long hard arms of a black woman,
he wants tenderness, he wants
the power to die in the
chalice of God's tears.

True dawn through the soaped window.
The plastic storm-wrap swallows wind.
'37 Chevie hoodless, black burst
lung of inner tube, pot metal
trees buckling under sheets.
He cries to sleep.

Such a poem gives notice of the incredible strength, the economy and muscle with which Levine endows the majority of his poems. Two of the most amazing and powerful pieces, **"Angel Butcher"** and **"They Feed They Lion,"** bring the book's second section to a climactic level of prophetic vision; the latter poem is dazzling in its syntactic, linguistic, and dramatic invention, its use of idiomatic effect. But both poems need to be read in their entirety and are too long for quotation here. It remains now simply to say for the purposes of this brief commentary that Levine's poetry, praiseworthy at the start, has developed by momentous strides in the past decade. His new poems make it impossible for him to be ignored or put aside. He stands out as one of the most solid and independent poets of his generation—one of the best poets, I think, anywhere at work in the language. It is time to begin listening.

Can you hear me?
the air says. I hold
my breath and listen
and a finger of dirt thaws,
a river drains
from a snow drop
and rages down
my cheeks, our father
the wind hums
a prayer through my mouth
and answers in the oat,
and now the tight rows of seed

bow to the earth
and hold on and hold on.

> **Hayden Carruth reviews Levine's *Not This Pig*:**
>
> To distinguish exactly the quality of Philip Levine's poems is not easy. He falls outside our categories. In some respects his horror poems, reciting the barbarities of our time, seem old-fashioned, reverberations from the days of early Jarrell and Shapiro, twenty-five years ago when we were all so intent upon, for example, the painting of Hieronymus Bosch. Levine gives us that inspired loathing, that humane coldbloodedness. But his contempt is even fiercer than his forebears', I should say, and he writes without their neo-metaphysical ornamentation. Face to face with the bomb, what is the use of wit? Levine's first book, which appeared four years ago, was remarkable for its individuality, its poems in a classical acerbic voice, including a long poem, **"The Distant Winter,"** which is one of the most hard-boiled anti-war poems I have read. Now in his new book, ***Not This Pig,*** Levine writes with an easier, freer, more fluent and versatile command. His scene is California, the cities in whose corroded streets angels are flaying one another with bicycle chains. Over them the air thickens with the ultimate explosion to come. Why in these twenty years have we had so few poems about the extinction we all never cease to expect? No doubt there are many reasons; but one is that the event itself, so overwhelmingly dreadful, is too *simple* for our poetry; when we stick it in a poem the result looks silly and embarrassing. We have all tried to overcome this, to give total meaninglessness some meaning, even the meaning of not having a meaning; but how hard it is.
>
> *Hayden Carruth, "Making It New," in* The Hudson Review, *Vol. XXI, No. 2, Summer, 1968.*

Calvin Bedient (review date 1976)

SOURCE: "Four American Poets," in *The Sewanee Review,* Vol. LXXXIV, No. 2, Spring, 1976, pp. 355-59.

[*In the following excerpt, Bedient asserts that Levine's poetry has shifted from "bereft and skeptical" towards romanticism.*]

The drama of Levine's career lies in his movement away from his origins—industrial and Jewish immigrant, bereft and skeptical—toward American romanticism, that faith of the senses in an intimate bigness beyond even the bigness of the land. From Detroit, a "city pouring fire," to "the one stove of earth"—such has been his progress.

"The first Jew was God," he wrote at the outset, in ***On the Edge*** (1964); "the second / Denied him; I am alive." History had left him nothing, so it seemed, except a legacy of horror, such as the horse that survived Hiroshima "without skin, naked, hairless, without eyes and ears, searching for the stableboy's caress." Like the classic American he was beginning anew, but not trustingly. Quite the contrary: "And I say 'balls,' / the time will never come," says one of the tough burned poems of *Not This Pig* (1968), "nor ripeness be all." Would he turn to bite the boy who led him to market? "No. Not this pig."

Yet by the third volume, *Red Dust* (1971), he was saying, "A man has every place to lay his head." In this poem and that, one could see forming the vast innocence, the sensuously crucified mysticism, of the romantic. The more Levine came to know of time and death the more he loved and was warmed by the "one stove"—and the more he needed to save things from its consumption. In words from his next volume, *They Feed They Lion* (1972), he developed the "ferocity of pig driven to holiness." He fed he lioned. His subject, when he could get past his finite griefs, was "the one poem born / of the eternal and always going back."

In *1933* the "one poem" consists, in part, of the natural world, its usual American form. The triumphant instance is **"Once in May"**; then "the earth seemed / all there was, all there had to be," and the poet stood with water in his pockets, salt in his socks, "naming / the grains of the sea."

> The moon rose slowly
> showing its broken face,
> the ring of stars climbed
> to the tips of my fingers,
> one bright planet crowned my hair
> and hummed until dawn.
> The sea gray and sliding,
> small boats coming in,
> the men tired, gray, unloading
> hake, merluza, squid in handfuls,
> sea bass, prawns, sword fish,
> great finned flat fillets,
> the cold meats of the deep.

The murderous variety of the many, the irrefragable One—both press their reality upon him. His poem simply bears it, stretched between pain and ecstasy.

But for Levine (and here he is exceptional as a romantic) the "one poem" is also human beings, above all his family. He is with Whitman and James Agee, his spiritual distinction an immense tenderness for those who have come near him. The romanticism of *1933* lies in part in remembered love—in love that time has transmuted into ecstasy. So it is, for instance, in the final poem, **"Hold Me"**:

> In May, like this May, long ago
> my tiny Russian Grandpa—the bottle king—
> cupped a stained hand under my chin
> and ran his comb through my golden hair
>
> Sweat, black shag, horse turds on the wind,
> the last wooden cart rattling down
> the alleys, the clop of his great gray mare,
> green glass flashing in December sun. . . .

And then, suddenly, space calls together the above and below and time closes back on itself, on a child defying mortality, separation, loss:

> I am the eye filled with salt,
> his child climbing the rain, we are
> all the moon, the one planet, the hand
> of five stars flung on the night river.

So in parts of *1933* Levine turns back to his childhood as to the gate to sempiternity. Back to 1933, when his father died, and back to the subtly doomed subsequent years. And indeed he finds he is "always a boy swimming up / through the odors of beer and dreams / to hear my name shivering / on the window. Beside me mother / curls on her side. . . ."

Then, again, he is not that boy, any more than he can really climb the rain: "The table is cleared of my place / and cannot remember." He enters a bedroom and his father, it may be, looks up but sees nothing. "Was I dust that I should fall?"

Once he was diffuse enough to confuse himself with others and now, in making this family album, he is the many in search of the one he may have been, the one in search of the many he was. And if finally, in the closing lines, he succeeds in being borne up by the past, it is only by having first been weighed down by it, painfully, throughout the book. Memory, *1933* shows us, is the least if the last of romantic kingdoms, because the ally as well as the adversary of separation and death.

Levine's manner has altered with his matter—indeed has at last become part of it. At first, rather than merging with, rather than transforming its subjects, it presented them. If poetic enough by conventional standards, his voice had a clothes-hanger stiffness, the intentionality of a diagram: "I have not found peace / but I have found I am where / I am by / being only there / by standing in the clouded presence of the things I observe."

Gradually Levine learned to entice the reader into his words, so as to dream them. And finally he could write a line as bafflingly simple and right, as inexhaustible, as "his child climbing the rain." How grasp such a line except with a thrill of the emotional imagination?

Levine developed a unique manner of plain emotional language and braced rhythms. He was spare with adjectives, so that old romantic properties—dawn, moon, stars, roots, stones, sun, ocean, trees, darkness, burning, angels, snow, rain, eyes—emerged with a contemporary astringency. The thrifty procedure gave an effect of precision. Once perfected in *They Feed They Lion,* the result was both chaste and lyrical. And as in these lines on his father it could turn the ordinary into miracle:

> Dusk is a burning
> of the sun.
> West of Chowchilla
> The Lost Continent of Butterflies
> streams across the freeway.

Radiators crusted,
windshields smeared with gold
and you come on
rising into the moons
of headlights.

In *1933,* with its hazards of nostalgia, the style occasionally lapses, it is true, into the infantile, the fey—as in "Why do the hills cry?" and "After the water bled / the toad grew a shell" and "the stars are burned eyes that see." The mode pretends the wonder that is elsewhere painstakingly earned. Yet for the most part the style is unusually pure, with a mature taste behind it, the pathetic element subtly risked and judged. "And a breeze woke / from the breathing river"—such is its typical tenor, reticently oracular.

Levine's words now join those before them as if this were the sweetest pleasure, with a pull and affinity and satisfaction of contact like magnetism. The poet's ear for sequence has become impeccable. A few simple words, a little alliteration or assonance, some clearly delineated rhythms—somehow from these humble ingredients again and again a consummate irresistible order is formed.

No one has managed short lines better or broken them with a surer hand. Here is a passage on fishing boats from **"One by One"**:

> All afternoon
> they steamed on the sand
> and the fishermen dozed
> in the buzzing shade and woke
> blinking in the first
> chill winds. Now
> in the deepening rose
> of day's end, they slide
> into the breakers and bob out
> to meet the moon.

Almost every line-break justly emphasizes the local meaning. Typically the sinuous syntactical forms play the short lines for a raised yet restrained lyricism. And the pauses yield a suspense that is like the awaiting of a revelation.

The chief limitation of the manner is its undying poignancy. Telling us over and over how all life excites and hurts in the same way since it is all caught up in the same coming and going, it makes the volume virtually "one poem" but by proving much of a sameness. The poems, too, are cut alike. They linger among memories and close either in imitation of death or, conversely, with an absolving embrace of all that has been, is now, or will be. Monotony is avoided only by frequent changes of scene and cast and by the continual creative pilgrimage of the language.

On the other hand the holding power of Levine's taut manner is so great that he can risk the "flung" structures which his love of the "one poem" incites. His poems reflect the indetermination of memory. They feel their

way. A few—"I've Been Asleep," "Harvest," "One by One"—juxtapose adventure and death, pleasure and pain, uncompromisingly, in separate sections. The procedure is interestingly bold but not quite satisfying: we cannot make the ends meet; the parts remain fractional. The more traditional structure of **"Once in May"** merges contraries without annihilating them, and here we feel the striking iron of vision.

I wish that Levine would cease starting poems over near the end, as in **"Bad Penny"** (which yet ends wonderfully) and **"War"** (which ends in an apocalyptic bash). The practice seems to elbow aside what has already been composed. For the rest, even his most innovative structures pay their way, uncertain as their necessity, their triumphs, may be. In all *1933* is at once daring and exquisite: an extraordinary volume.

Peter Stitt   (review date 1980)

SOURCE: "The Sincere, the Mythic, the Playful: Forms of Voice in Current Poetry," in *The Georgia Review,* Vol. 34, No. 1, Spring, 1980, pp. 202-04.

[*In the following review, Stitt compares* 7 Years from Somewhere *with* Ashes, *contending* Ashes *is a more powerful and imaginative work.*]

Because lyric poetry is spoken in a direct and seemingly intimate voice, it is by its very nature a personal form of utterance. Such recent movements as confessionalism have sometimes led us to believe that lyric poetry, being personal, is also inherently sincere. In the sense that the poet means what he or she says, of course, poetry (except for the ostensibly ironic) is generally sincere. But in the sense that the poet is writing about his or her *own* life, feelings, and thoughts, poetry is never necessarily sincere. In one way or another—whether it appears only in the form or also in the content—artifice must be a component of the poem, and artifice is inevitably a dilutant of absolute sincerity. Without art there would be no poem; artificiality forms the musculature of poetic structure, and when a writer cuts too close to the white bone of unadulterated truth, it is the fiber of art which is damaged. A literal poem, one which shows no figurations, neither comparisons nor transformations, no renderings of fact into metaphor, is a poem in which the artistry is dead.

In terms of content, Philip Levine has always written a poetry that is generally both personal and sincere, a poetry based on the facts, feelings, and experiences of his own life. On one day last year, Levine published two books which, between them, illustrate both directions that this kind of verse can take. The poems in *Ashes* (many of which first appeared in Levine's 1971 volume, *Red Dust*) show everywhere signs of the transforming power of the artistic imagination; the raw materials of experience and emotion have been converted, through metaphor, through music, into poetry. In *7 Years from Somewhere,* on the other hand, the writing is generally flat, the poems literal. At his best, Levine has always been a rhetorician, ever willing to set the devices of poetry working for him; it is a disappointment to find these elements so lacking in his most recent poems. One's sense of disappointment is all the more acute given Levine's obviously strong sense of commitment to his material. The poems are all, in one way or another, elegies—some lament the passage of time, the coming of age; some lament the deaths of friends, heroes; some lament the progressive passing of the poet himself, the loss of his childhood and youth. These are affective subjects, possessed of considerable power in and of themselves. It is understandable that Levine often relies on this inherent strength to carry his poems, but the results here are not compelling. **"Words,"** for example, tells how time takes its toll on a family; the speaker seems to be trying, but failing, to extricate himself from a sense of depression. The poem ends: "My wife will say nothing / of the helplessness / she feels seeing her / men rocking on / their separate seas. / We are three people / bowing our heads to / all she has given us, / to bread and wine and meat. / The windows have gone / dark, but the room is / quiet in yellow light. / Nothing needs to be said." The form of this poem is, in a curious way, appropriate to the subject; both reveal an endemic emptiness.

Elsewhere there is an altogether direct and artless expression of excess emotion, artistically unjustified, as in these lines: "I did cry. I put my hands between / my legs, alone, in the room I came / to love because it was all the room / I had, and pitched forward and cried / without hope or relief, for myself. . . ." The poems in this book are generally narrative in form and often epiphanic in structure; in poem after poem, the speaker tells of incidents in his life which led to one revelation or another. Many are good poems too—like **"Peace," "Let Me Begin Again," "You Can Have It,"** and the title poem **"7 Years from Somewhere"**—but none is as good as even the average poem in *Ashes*. There is a progression evident in Levine's work from the lush rhetorical intensity of his earlier poems to the relatively plain style of these later volumes. But Levine's natural voice is not well suited to the plain style, and that is why there is so much flatness in *7 Years from Somewhere.*

Ashes embodies a stylistic compromise. The pounding rhythms and insistent repetitions of the early work are largely absent here, with the formal emphasis being placed upon Levine's figurative imagination. The ability to double, to see one thing within another, to spot the latent form lurking in the block of stone—always notable in his work—is the chief feature of *Ashes*. As many critics have demonstrated, metaphor is a complicated and elusive literary device, virtually impossible to pin down and describe in all its many forms; but it is the essence of poetry, an essence of life. One kind of metaphor, sometimes called surrealism, involves ascribing to an object characteristics which in nature that object could not possess. Metaphorically, we might call this a kind of synesthesia, which itself allows a stimulation to be registered by the wrong sense, as hearing the scent of a rose or

tasting the color blue. Levine's poem **"Noon"** is built of such metaphors; we read of "The heaviness of / flies stuttering / in orbit, dirt / ripening, the sweat / of eggs"; "the villages / of sheaves, whole / eras of grain / . . . a roof / that breathes." Each of these figures is an expression of the oppressiveness of a hot noontime; "At such times," says Levine later, "I expect the earth / to pronounce"—as indeed it has. The poem ends on a similar transference of function: "the women / bow as they slap / the life out / of sheets and pants / and worn hands." This sort of thing can easily become too clever, but here the purpose is admirably served.

Elsewhere Levine's images can be close to the purely descriptive, the literal, but still work brilliantly because of their profusion; for example, this stanza from **"Clouds"**: "Morning is exhaustion, tranquilizers, gasoline / the screaming of frozen bearings, / the failures of will, the TV talking to itself." The relative literality of these lines prepares us well to appreciate the metaphorical power of this later depiction of the clouds: "In their great silent pockets / they carry off all our dead." In his best poems, Levine reinforces his images with, and places them within, an insistent rhetorical flow. **"How Much Earth"** attempts to show man's inherent mortality through a metaphorical description of the progress of his life; it is an example of Levine at his recent best:

> Torn into light, you woke wriggling
> on a woman's palm. Halved, quartered,
> shredded to the wind, you were the life
> that thrilled along the underbelly
> of a stone. Stilled in the frozen pond
> you rinsed heaven with a sigh.
>
> How much earth is a man.
> A wall lies down and roses
> rush from its teeth; in the fists
> of the hungry, cucumbers sleep
> their lives away, under your nails
> the ocean moans in its bed.
>
> How much earth.
> The great ice fields slip
> and the broken veins of an eye
> startle under light, a hand is planted
> and the grave blooms upward
> in sunlight and walks the roads.

The texture of Levine's poetry has ever been emotional, revealing a strong commitment both to his subjects and his art. The feeling in this poem verges continually on the edge of an extreme, as is shown in certain crucial words ("torn," "shredded," "thrilled," "stilled," "rush," "fists," "startle") and in many phrases. This kind of verbal, imagistic intensity is central to Levine's art, and the retreat from it (and from metaphor) in *7 Years from Somewhere* is unfortunate. Happily, *Ashes* shows him easily in command of his full powers; it is a stunning book from one of our most powerful and masterful poets.

Robert Hosmer   (review date 1992)

SOURCE: "What We See and Feel and Are," in *The Southern Review,* Vol. 28, No. 2, Spring, 1992, pp. 433-36.

[*In the following excerpt, Hosmer counters criticism that espouses the view that Levine is not a poet but "simply a memoir writer in prose."*]

Ever since the publication of his first major book, *Not This Pig* (1968), Philip Levine has acquired ardent champions and severe critics. The latter often single out his limited range of subject matter and style, some going so far as to say that what he writes isn't poetry at all ("simply a memoir writer in prose," said Helen Vendler, who asked of *One for the Rose* [1981], "Is there any compelling reason why it should be called poetry?"). Well, yes there is, if you're willing to be flexible in developing an enlarged, somewhat nontraditional and nonmusical understanding of what poetry can be. Though he once wrote a poem "after Keats" (**"Having Been Asked 'What Is A Man?' I Answer"**), Levine inscribes no Grecian urns, tunes no unearthly music in his verse. Rather, something like Ashbery's poem "What Is Poetry" springs to mind, with its vigorous dismissal of academic ideas of "poetry" and its emphasis on an exploration of what is thought, felt, known at a particular moment.

Levine writes in free and blank verse, displaying, typically, in this latest collection, *What Work Is,* a fondness for shorter poems of approximately forty to seventy lines. Evidently traditional forms are no longer valid for Levine: unlike Ashbery, with his delight in virtuoso feats like single, even double, sestinas, Levine offers no pyrotechnical displays: he manifests no interest in the music of what happens: the natural rhythms of human speech, often captured in a three- or four-beat line, dominate here. What matters to him is simplicity—simplicity of rhythm, of speech, of sentiment. The product of working-class Detroit during the Depression, himself the veteran of factory work, Levine determined early on that he would "write poetry for people for whom there is no poetry . . . [those who] lived and worked beside me," and the are of his career, now spanning twelve major volumes, testifies to his fidelity to that vow. He has never rejected what he has been or who he was: this is what has been called "blue-collar poetry," not only because of its largely working-class subject matter, but also because it can be read and understood without elaborate preparation, without cumbersome textual apparatus, without scholarly "explanation."

The recently published *New Selected Poems* and *What Work Is* demonstrate to a degree beyond convincing that Philip Levine is a deeply introspective, very much American poet drawn to elemental materials—ashes, snow, earth, salt pigs, dogs, smoke—and to everyday working-class lives of drudgery, boredom, sweat, and beer. His is an extraordinarily meditative presence who continues to be concerned with those who have no voice, the working-class men and women, the lost children, and the forgotten aged.

The titles of two poems in *What Work Is* describe the essential activities of Levine's poetry: **"Coming Close,"** in which he takes us to a woman at a polishing wheel in a factory; and **"Scouting,"** in which "getting the feel of the land," charting the physical and psychic landscape, assumes major significance. One point of decided appeal and excellence lies in those poems which create a resonance with the world of adolescent male experience. Levine is particularly skilled at crafting a "coming-of-age poem" and here he does it a number of times with effect: in **"Growth,"** the poignant tale of a fourteen-year-old boy working in a soap factory oven; in **"Gin"** ("The first time I drank gin I thought it must be hair tonic"); in **"Coming of Age in Michigan"**; and in **"The Seventh Summer,"** which tells of a seven-year-old Jewish boy's perception of his essential difference from three Christian companions.

While *What Work Is* is a different Levine collection, it is not a departure in formal or technical terms, though the eighteen-page sequence **"Burned"** is among the longest poems Levine has written. Like [John Ashbery's] *Flow Chart, What Work Is* is an autumnal work, the labor of a poet now past sixty years old. Here may be a greater concern with the lives of aged parents, yet nothing to equal the clear-eyed force of the title poem from *1933* ("My father entered the kingdom of roots / his head still as a stone") or of **"Letters for the Dead,"** also from *1933.* Both are included in an extraordinarily judicious, representative, and echoing gathering of 111 poems in *New Selected Poems,* meant to supersede *Selected Poems* (1984).

What is most striking about *What Work Is,* is the long poem **"Burned"** set at the opening of the second half of the collection and comprising all of Section III. **"Burned"** belies the received notion that Levine's is an accessible poetry. It is a series of memory panels with the poet-narrator demonstrating a clearly felt and explicitly stated imperative: "I have . . . to hold it all in my eyes." In another poem, **"Scouting,"** the narrator engages in the essential activity of the title, "getting the feel of the land" of memory and experience, attempting to make a meaningful whole of past and future, but satisfied that, "in the dark you can love this place." Evidently what he has to hold is nearly everything, for here we have a poet of later middle age ("my hand . . . burning now to autumnal rust") tracing streams of memory to his Detroit childhood, his married life, his move to the West Coast. The poet pokes among ruins, rooting among shards of memory and experience, to find a garden. The central metaphor of burning applies not just to structures that have been incinerated, not just to people burned, but to the burning within the poet to construct a structure of self that will, against the ravages of reality, endure. This poet is haunted by the central problem of identity: "When this passes, how will I know I was and I was alive?"

A problematic "you" haunts the sequence as well. Is it addressed to anyone in particular? At times it would appear to be a particular individual—say the poet-narrator's wife; at other times, its identity blurs as the poet tries to invest it with self-significance, as when he declares, "If I called you `my soul,' you'd laugh in my face." Yet this is nearer the center of activity than anything else: in *What Work Is,* Levine engages in a search for the very soul of individuals. The quest that leads him to come close to others also brings him close to himself; the search for the defining, essential dignity of others embraces the poet himself. Surrounded by other poems which render the lives of others with stark dignity and chaste feeling, **"Burned"** is a self-portrait of the artist himself; it offers a series of snapshots of the poet doing his own work. As Levine noted in **"Facts,"** "I am an enormous man given to long bouts of silence as I brood on facts." The poem's lack of effective closure, the very absence of a satisfactory solution, reminiscent of **"A Poem With No Ending"** from *Sweet Will* (1985), the failure to find home and to delineate a sharply focused self, seem emblematic of Levine's sense of the human condition. Like Ashbery, he echoes Amy Clampitt's understanding that "Nothing stays put. The world is a wheel. All that we know, that we're made of, is motion."

In **"Scouting,"** the narrator extrapolates from experience, coming to a conclusion of sorts: "What is it like to come to, nowhere, in darkness, not knowing who you are, not caring if the wind calms, the stars stall in their sudden orbits, the cities below go on without you, screaming and singing? I don't have the answer." In **"Every Blessed Day,"** the poet says of an anonymous worker, "Where he's going or who he is he doesn't ask himself, he doesn't know and doesn't know it matters." In *What Work Is,* Philip Levine has asked these questions about others and about himself; though he may not know the answers with the certainty and clarity he—and we—would all like, he does know how very much it matters. At his best, and he often is at his best in *What Work Is,* Philip Levine writes what he has striven to write: "a powerful, authentic, politically relevant poetry" that rarely fails to catch at the heart and mind. Whether or not that poetry is, as he hopes, potent enough to change lives, remains to be seen.

Carol Frost   (review date 1992)

SOURCE: "Philip Levine at Work," in *New England Review,* Vol. 14, No. 4, Fall, 1992, pp. 291-305.

[*In the following review, Frost discusses Levine's poetic influences and favorably reviews* New Selected Poems *and* What Work Is.]

I

Exceptional poets come in two kinds: those whose territory is small (the neighborhood or garden, privately walled, perhaps) and those who speak for a wider locale. Both—like mapmakers, blues singers, and revolutionaries—are remarkable in their reinventions of common ground. It comes down to an act of mind, the imagination's ability to inhabit a place and time so deeply that the names for it are transformed. Philip Levine is a poet of wide territory, primarily interested in portraying the lives of ordinary working class people in America, shore to shore (Detroit, Gary, Pasadena, New York City, Dubuque, Akron, Baltimore, Wheeling, L.A.), in Spain (Barcelona, Malaga, Valladolid), and, with more passing reference, in Italy, Thailand, France, Hungary, Poland, Russia, Mexico, Canada, and Germany.

The Midwest exerts the strongest pull on his imagination, with its auto industry and its foundries, fertile ground for his treatment of the American work ethic, human will, and fatedness. Such places as Detroit and Belle Isle take on a nearly mythic glow, lit by the iron-colored fires of the transmission and chemical factories. "We burn the city every day," he says in **"Coming Home,"** and references to fire and iron appear again and again throughout the 292 pages of his *New Selected Poems* and in *What Work Is.* Levine's poetry forges, out of a wide and common geography, terms for a new understanding of late-twentieth-century experience, rooted in the lives of second- and third-generation immigrants who continue their manual labors for a living and for their sense of dignity. But for all of that interest in the lives of others, Levine's poems are strongly personal; he so thoroughly empathizes with his characters, remembered and invented, that their experience becomes his own, and ours.

Levine's ideal is similar to Whitman's, who talks about his preference for the common over the heroic in notes for a lecture under the heading *Beauty:*

> [N]ot the beautiful girl or the elegant lady . . . but the mechanic's wife at work . . . not the scenery of the tourist, picturesque, but the plain landscape, the bleak sea shore, or the barren plain, with the common sky and sun.

Everywhere in Levine's new collections are touches of a nearly journalistic plainness. Other features of Levine's work underscore his affinities with Whitman: colloquial speech, oratorical devices (in such poems as **"They Feed They Lion"**), parallel sentence structure, enumeration, very direct presentation of human experience, and the exclusion of conventional literary subjects. Levine has stated that Garcia Lorca's poetry offered him a model for "all the eloquence and fury a poet could master" ("The Poet in New York in Detroit," *NER* Fall 1991), and that Keats's poetry and theory, "being in uncertainties," added to his evolving sense of how to write a poetry no one else could write. The influences, one comes to understand as one reads through all the poems in the *New Selected Poems,* are numerous. Levine's mature line, for instance, is most closely related to the free verse of William Carlos Williams—a much less oceanic phrasing and a thinner profile on the page than Whitman or Lorca, less sensual than Keats. Furthermore, his imagery, rather than being exclusively realistic, is sometimes highly surreal, particularly in the poems selected from his earlier books, where the pressure of statement and emotion cause a more extravagant crafting of the poem, as in some of Dickinson and in Stephen Crane, and certainly in Lorca.

To mention Whitman, Emily Dickinson, and Stephen Crane in this context is to open up for myself one chapter in literary history out of which Levine's work seems surely to come, and which, therefore, helps to explain the thematic development in these chronologically arranged selections of poems, as well as Levine's methods. His belonging to the continuum of realism-to-naturalism and his affinities with late-nineteenth-century poetry hardly make his work seem old-fashioned, narrowly American, or derivative. Levine's poetry is most notable for its freshness and originality. A freshness so apparent misdirects you, and you take the poems for granted as individual specimens of formally heightened emotion at its best; but then as the weight of your interest in the poems increases and you want to know what makes them tick and where they come from, common sense points to earlier poets, both like and unlike the one you are reading now, for new ways into the work. Levine writes what he writes not only because of his experiences in the "real world," but also because he has read what he has read and because of his accord in temperament, method, and theme with some of those poets. Fully invented as they are, the poems were not written in a literary vacuum.

II

The literary territory that Levine stakes out for himself is largely realistic, both in method and attitude. Verisimilitude is one of his virtues, and many of his poems present journalistic detailing: dates, place names and addresses, the exact time ("he woke at 3," "40 miles from Malaga," "Detroit, 1951, Friday night," and, in speaking of Barcelona, "Here / is the Plaza of San Jaime, here the Rambla / of San Pedro"). Even his most fantastic poems are faithful to realistic detail, as in a poem like **"Angel Butcher,"** where the angel hoses out the abattoir prior to receiving Christophe, who asks the angel for "all the names of / all the tools and all / their functions," then "lifts / and weighs and / balances, and runs a long / forefinger down the tongue / of each blade" prior to his being stunned for slaughter. The surreal scene is made to appear tangibly true—as if in heaven such a place exists. Perhaps the clearest statement of Levine's method is made in **"Silent in America,"** a poem which depicts the speaker's feelings of inadequacy ("Fresno's / dumb bard, America's last / hope") to speak for the downtrodden and the beautiful: Jews, Poles, the fated, and "those who had courage"—a full range of Americans. "Surely I have failed," he says. In section five, the speaker explains that what he surely knows about the world comes from a close scrutiny of physical details:

> I tell time
> by the sunlight's position
>   on the bedroom wall:
> it's 5:30, middle June.
>   I rise, dress,
>   Assume my name
>
>   and feel my
> face against a hard towel.
>   My mind is empty;
> I see all that's here to see:
>   the garden
>   and the hard sky;

> the great space
> between the two has a weight,
>   a reality
> which I find no burden,
>   and the height
>   of the cot tree
>
>   is only
> what it has come to deserve.
>   I have not found peace,
> but I have found I am where
>   I am by
>   being only there,
>
>   by standing
> in the clouded presence of
>   the things I observe.

This section of the poem goes on to take note of the fact that there is an unobservable force in the air which "moves / when it is still" and "speaks / of being alive." It is in part in response to the unknowable, the answers to questions—why, for instance, there is little "to choose / but failure" (**"Lights I have seen Before"**) for the ordinary people who populate the cities and neighborhoods of the America Levine talks about, why "half / the men in this town / are crying in the snow," why fathers die young ("the mouth asking everybody and nobody / *Why Why*" in **"Letters for the Dead"**), why people want earth to be heaven and for there to be a heaven, and why "the earth / would let the same children die day / after day, let the same women curse / their precious hours, the same men bow / to earn our scraps" (**"Ashes"**)—that Levine's realism shades into naturalism.

The details of the lives that Levine depicts, particularly in the selections of poems from his first eight books, are grim, and the speaker's tone frequently angry. As with Emily Dickinson, Levine's close observation of natural detail results in poems which sound naturalistic. It seems not to be his intention (or hers) to follow the tenets of the naturalists as much as it is the objective outcome of such close scrutiny of the physical world which makes him doubt human ability to overcome the difficulty ordinary living provides.

The seeds of Levine's naturalistic view appear early in his work in his references to fate, the incontrovertible nature of death, and the "failures of will" he finds all around him. He also early expresses anger toward what he perceives as an indifferent universe. In one early poem, **"Noon"** (*Red Dust*), in a landscape of abandoned bicycles, "ripening dirt," and washerwomen slapping the life out of laundry with worn hands, the speaker says, "At such times / I expect the earth / to pronounce." He seems to expect some benevolent word from the natural world, and gets none. In **"Clouds,"** another early poem, Levine expresses his anger at a similar silence, this time from the clouds. Below them the wreckage of civilized living— abandoned cars, "the TV talking to itself," pollution, war, and death—is met by silence from the clouds who "have seen it all." In a characteristic statement which carries with it the presumption of nature's power and the notion that nature ought to be benevolent, the speaker says that the clouds

> . . . should be punished every morning,
> they should be bitten and boiled like spoons.

This bitterness is reminiscent less of Dickinson than of Stephen Crane, although many of Dickinson's ironies concerning the absence of an intervening God or universe when one faces death (in fact, nature's complicity suggested in such lines as "The blonde Assassin passes on—/ That Sun proceeds unmoved / To measure off an Approving God" and "When Winds take Forests in their Paws—/ The Universe—is still") seem to mock the conventions of nature and God. In Crane, however, particularly in **"The Open Boat,"** a reader finds a rationale for a bitterness toward nature, a bitterness that matches Levine's. Crane writes, "When it occurs to a man that nature does not regard him as important, and that she feels she would not maim the universe by disposing of him, he at first wishes to throw bricks at the temple, and he hates deeply the fact that there are no bricks and no temples."

There are expressions of anger toward nature's indifference throughout the first half of the *New Selected Poems,* but the greatest concentration of this attitude occurs in the selections from *The Names of the Lost.* Speaking to his dead uncle in **"No one remembers,"** the speaker says, "The earth is asleep, Joe, it's rock, steel, ice, / the earth doesn't care / or forgive." In **"Gift for a Believer,"** speaking to a patriot who still believes in a dream of goodness, in politics righting political and social wrongs, despite historical evidence to the contrary, the speaker tells how the wind and the snow obliterate "your childhood / and all the promises." Then, near the end of the poem, the speaker describes the earth as cold and says "on cold stones, the great Pacific / that blesses no one breaks / into water." In *Ashes* there are several other such references to a cruelly indifferent world. In **"On a Drawing by Flavio,"** though the Jews have been incinerated in Auschwitz, the sun seems to say, "Do as you please," and the implication is that it ought somehow to have put a stop to the killing. In **"Ashes,"** the speaker wonders why the earth allows children to hunger and men to sacrifice their dignity for the little that they can earn and provide.

Levine also expresses anger at a god and a heaven which, if they existed, ought to provide solace and answers. God, it seems, does not care and probably doesn't exist, which is why in **"Fist"** (*Red Dust*) a fist is described as "a flower / that hates God," why in **"Blasting from Heaven"** (*Not This Pig*) the sounds issuing from heaven in response to the sad lives of a little family are the 8 o'clock whistle, and why in **"Angel Butcher"** (*They Feed They Lion*) at least one of the seraphim is responsible for the slaughter of the good and innocent who "come up the long climb." In a later poem, **"Uncle"** (*1933*), Levine mocks religious faith when he has the speaker remember that his uncle "taught / the toilet the eternal." There seems to be nothing substantial to be found in the pursuit of

religious faith, for, as Levine tells us, "heaven was nowhere" (**"On the Murder of Lieutenant Jose del Castillo by the Falangist Bravo Martinez, July 12, 1936"**). If God has given people anything, it is each other and it is the corporeal.

And while realism turns Levine to a scrutiny of the common particulars of our experience, it also turns him to certain unhappy truths. The conflict that is presented through the first half of the *New Selected Poems* is between the ideals of human will, aspiration, and hard work on the one hand—all that represents promise—and reality on the other. Levine is angry about broken promise, about the discrepancy between the wish "for a new world and a new home" (**"A New Day"**) and people's willingness to work for it, "putting their lives / into steel" (**"The Helmet"**), working until they are often too tired to stand up; and he is angry about the reality of poverty, the essential uselessness of work.

In **"Hear Me,"** Levine says that the notion that work presents "salvation" is laughable. Men work hard, and get nowhere; children seem to follow in their fathers' footsteps. The poems in *1933* are poems about the real or imagined lives of parents and other relatives whose lives are repeated in the lives of their children. "The lie is retold in the heart," the speaker says in **"Letters from the Dead,"** a poem which tells the story of a young man's remembrances of his family, the father a drunk who dies young, the mother vain and disappointed. The events of the father's life are reflected in the son's. He too leaves home, traveling on a hot bus to "the dawn of a new world," which provides nothing. As the speaker remembers this journey and then his father's death by suicide, he feels the air that "crackles with their angers," and later recalls his violence toward his "strange tall son." Disappointments seem generational, if not hereditary; in the unpromising environment depicted in these poems, children are caught up in a fate they do not quite understand. More particularly, the premature death of the father, "himself a child," ensures his son's loneliness. How can the future be anything more than the "scar" the grown child with his own nearly grown son calls it in **"New Season"**? Violence leads naturally and generationally to violence. A working class father spawns a working class son, and neither seems able to control his environment; neither seems fully to understand what forces are at work to prevent the promise of something wonderful.

In **"No One Remembers,"** the speaker, addressing his uncle, indicts him for his violence toward his own wife— "She'll cry like always / when you raise your voice / or your fist." The speaker says it is his hand, not the uncle's, that the woman will take and will "feel / slowly finger by finger / like so many threads back / to where the blood dies / and our lives met / and went wrong, back / to all she said she'd be, / woman, promise." The identification with the uncle by the speaker shows the essential relationship of the generations to the conflict I mentioned earlier between promise and doomed hopes. In these poems the family is not presented without fondness: a grandfather in **"Zaydee"**—small and vulgar, a dandy, card

cheat, cigar smoker, thief, excon, sensualist—is presented as wise and loving, for instance. A war veteran and a
woman, who in the context of the other poems seem to
be the speaker's relatives, fall in love at a dance in **"At
the Fillmore,"** and their illusions, "the promises again,"
are presented with a sweet regard. But the poems clearly
set out the notion that the past traps the future.

It is only after his first eight books that Levine comes to
an understanding which allows him, if not to love the
experiences of living, at least to accept what can't be
altered. The pivotal poem in *New Selected Poems* is **"Lost
and Found"** (*Ashes*). Levine's quarrel with the world is
partly resolved in this poem, which has the speaker take
responsibility for his boyhood and the familial past, so
that "father and child / hand in hand, the living and / the
dead, are entering the world." What has allowed the speaker to reach this point of maturity is stated in the beginning of the poem:

> How long it takes to believe
> the simplest facts of lives—
> that certain losses are final,
> death is one, childhood another.

As a consequence of his acceptance of the unalterable
nature of the starkest realities, Levine's speaker is able
to escape the angers and victimizations of experience.
He has "come home from being lost, / home to a name
I could accept, / a face that saw all I saw / and broke in
a dark room against / a wall that heard all my secrets /
and gave back nothing." That becoming aware of the limitations of life is an act of adulthood is echoed in **"Salts
and Oils"**; the speaker says that his fully digesting the
"filth and glory / of the palatable world" happens "because I have to grow up."

In both these poems the moment of mature understanding
occurs in the morning—"one quiet morning" in **"Salts
and Oils,"** and at the end of "the night which seemed so
final" in **"Lost and Found."** There are seventy references to dawn or a new day in the 292 pages of *New Selected
Poems,* as well as a few references to a new world or
season as part of the same thematic indication. In the
poems before **"Lost and Found,"** dawn is most often
symbolic of nature's cheat. The expectations for nature's
benevolence are shown as illusory in such lines as "A
gray light coming on at dawn, / no fresh start and no bird
song" (**"A New Day"**) and "has anyone fallen on his knees
/ and begged the dawn to reconsider" (**"Ask the Roses"**).
However, starting with **"Lost and Found,"** dawn's symbolic value changes. Nature is no longer seen as cruelly
indifferent or even malignant, and the new light of day
more often shines on a world worth calling home. For
instance, in **"Rain Downriver,"** the speaker says, "the
earth gives each of us / a new morning," and in the end
he is able to declare that "the world is mine." This is a
reversal of the earlier sentiment, as expressed in **"Told,"**
where the speaker says that the world "was not home."
When Levine comes to accept that the experience of living is a mixture of good and bad news, the new sun, the
new day, the new light, and the new season are much less

often treated ironically. Overall, the positive and negative references to dawn are about equal, thirty-six to
thirty-four—but it is most interesting to note that in the
one hundred sixty-nine pages before **"Lost and Found,"**
the ratio of positive to negative is 1:3, and with that poem
the ratio reverses itself.

A similar shift occurs in Levine's numerous references
to tears. That the world gives people ample reason to cry
is made clear by the variety of those who weep (grown
men, children, mothers, wives, fathers, lost souls, an angel,
laborers), and the inanimate objects that also do (the hills,
the sea, the radio). These are tears of despair for the
most part, the sadness relating to Levine's sense of injustice and hopelessness, and there is no shame in them.
Still, when Levine's change of heart occurs in **"Lost and
Found,"** the expressions of sadness diminish considerably, even if the reasons for tears don't entirely alter.
There are fifty-five early references to tears and only
eighteen after *Names of the Lost*. The nature of tears
changes slightly, with four of the later references suggesting stoicism: "He didn't like to cry" (**"Nitrate"**),
"cry without a sound" (**"A Poem with No Ending"**),
"the tears held back so long" (**"28"**), "She's not going to
cry about it" (**"These Streets"**).

The thematic shift in Levine's work from a strong emphasis on the sad realities of a hostile world, wherein
humanity is fated to failure through no fault of its own,
to an acceptance of the natural world (a shift not accompanied by any shift in his method of closely observing
and recording the physical world) is consistent with a
major strain of the American literary tradition. Where
for a romantic the ideal dominates—nature and God are
benevolent and an individual can affect his or her fate—
for the naturalist physical reality dominates. Many naturalists eventually look for consolation. For Dickinson,
the same forces that beheaded flowers bring the consolations of summer and autumn ("Summer makes her light
escape / Into the Beautiful") and for Hemingway the
consolation is how human beings perform in the face of
danger and death; the conditions of his world are
naturalistic, but his characters face them, so they seem
idealized, even in failure. For Levine, the conditions of
the world are bleaker than for either of the two writers
mentioned, so it might be argued that his need for consolation is even greater. He introduces several: nature,
courage in the face of impossible odds, love—"each other" (**"Sources"**)—and, as in Whitman and Stephen Crane,
camaraderie. The fellowship between the shipmates in
Crane's "The Open Boat" is similar to the camaraderie
that factory workers and other laborers share in **"And
the Trains Go On," "Sweet Will,"** and **"An Ordinary
Morning."**

In Levine's later poems, a kind of comfort comes through
realizing that nature's indifference, which once seemed
cruel, is benign, even when its natural processes result in
death. The speaker in **"The Face,"** for instance, notes
that the streets of the "battered" Spanish city are "filled
with dirty children," but still listens for the "one word"
from his dead father, who he imagines tells him "of why

the earth takes / back all she gives." Knowing that earth does this, and having imagined his father's voice, "even that," he says, "comes to be enough." Imagining himself as dead in **"Let Me Begin Again,"** the speaker says, "Let / me come back to land after a lifetime / of going nowhere." He wants to begin again in the world he knows is nothing more than "salt water and dark clouds" because, despite the "black wastes," his life is like no other. In **"Snow,"** the "foolishness of the world" and "the filthy waters of their river" are givens, but what is left over from those who have died, their tears (snow), "given their choice chose then / to return to earth." Earth, the speaker in **"Voice"** says, "is my one home, as it always was," echoing the last lines in **"Rain Downriver":** "The fall of evening / glistens around my shoulders that / also glisten, and the world is mine." Once death is seen as a part of living, a reality that is painful ("No one believes that to die is beautiful"), an understanding and even a little joy are possible: "Do you hear the wind / rising all around you? That comes / only after this certain joy."

Perhaps the most complete statement of this new attitude occurs in **"The Poem of Flight,"** spoken by the Wright brother who was the first to fly. Concerning his flight, he has this to say:

> . . . the time has come to say something
> to a world that largely crawls, forwards
> or backwards, begging for some crust
> of bread or earth, enough for a bad life
> or a good death. I've returned because
> thin as I am there came a moment
> when not to seemed foolish and difficult
> and because I've not yet tired
> of the warm velvet dusks of this country
> of firs and mountain oak. And because
> high above the valleys and streams
> of my land I saw so little of what is here,
> only the barest whiff of all I eat each day.
> I suppose I must square my shoulders,
> lean back, and say something else,
> something false, something that even I
> won't understand about why some of us
> must soar or how we've advanced beyond
> the birds or that not having wings
> is an illusion that a man with my money
> refuses to see. It is hard to face
> the truth, this truth or any other,
> that climbing exhausts me, and the more
> I climb, the higher I get, the less I
> want to go on, and the noise is terrible,
> I thought the thing would come apart,
> and finally there is nothing there.

As this poem makes clear, the truth for Levine is that earth—with the fouled lakes, broken bottles, and shoddy trees, wrong turns, sulking gray factories, mentally deranged and violent people we continue to be reminded of—is what we've got, and as his own acceptance grows, he begins to be able to treat the notion of perfecting the world with some humor, as in **"The Suit."** As his zoot suit tatters from over-wearing and abuse, so do the speak-

er's "other hopes for a singular life in a rich / world of a certain design: / just, proportioned, equal and different / for each of us and satisfying like that flush / of warmth that came with knowing / no one could be more ridiculous."

Levine is less and less apt to be furious, or to demand change, in the face of the bad he continues to see in American experience; the good he now allows. The earth is "amazing," according to the poor black man Tom Jefferson in **"A Walk with Tom Jefferson,"** despite racism, plunder, and his neighborhood—the "dumping ground" for "mangled chifforobes" and "ice boxes / yawning at the sky." Tom Jefferson is "six feet of man, unbowed." There are other heroes in Levine's universe, stoics most of them—old boxers, uncomplaining peasants, and especially political idealists from the same war Hemingway idealized in *For Whom the Bell Tolls*. In **"Francisco, I'll Bring you Carnations,"** the conditions of the working people for whom the leftists fought during the Spanish Civil War have not, the speaker says, improved. The Barcelona which Francisco knew is gone, "swallowed / in industrial filth"; the "smiling masters" and the police remain, but despite the slums and Francisco's early death (half his life before that spent in prison), "that dream / goes on," the dream "where every man / and every woman gives / and receives the gifts of work / and care." Those who manage to believe in a better future despite evidence to the contrary, who keep on with the belief even in quiet ways, are worthy of our admiration, Levine tells us in **"To Cipriano, in the Wind,"** where the speaker praises a simple man's dignity. Cipriano, who presses pants, believes that "Some day the world / is ours," just as he believes spring follows the icy winter. Addressing Cipriano at the end of the poem, the speaker asks him to "enter my dreams / or my life" because he also would like to believe that "this / world will be ours." And he would like to live with dignity. Just as Hemingway's essentially nihilistic vision is repeatedly modified by his assertion of the possibility of living with courage, so in this poem is Levine's; but it isn't until after working through the journalistically recorded grimness of working class life and a period of youthful anger and wishful thinking—the position that the universe needs to be amended and God or nature was to blame for the lack of change, Crane's position—that Levine comes fully to appreciate the idea of grace under pressure, a faithfulness to the ordeal of living and dying. Two earlier poems featuring political heroes, **"Gift for a Believer"** and **"On the Murder of Lieutenant Jose del Castillo by the Falangist Bravo Martinez, July 12, 1936,"** early as they are in Levine's thematic evolution, are basically negative; the characters' ideals turn into gray mist and smoke when they die, reality defeating promise.

During the twenty-five years it took for the books from *On the Edge* to *A Walk with Tom Jefferson* to be published, Levine's themes evolved in ways similar to the evolution of realism through seventy-five years. Faithfully recording the physical, social, and psychological facts of the American working class, Levine moves from a youthful anger at the way things are, at the machine of the natural universe which seems to grind up essentially innocent people, toward an acceptance of palpable reality, inimical nature, including the certainty of death he earlier railed against. In the last poems his attitude seems to be that human beings can persevere in the face of such realities, and that they have a responsibility toward the "amazing" planet that is home (**"A Walk with Tom Jefferson"**).

This development is hardly casual; it is a growing process, a maturing of vision, and it is large. It is as if more than seventy-five years of American literary history have been telescoped into Levine's twenty-five years of writing and publishing poems, twenty-five years of living and seeing blended into what he has read and what he creates out of it—poems impressionistic, paradoxical, often ironic, and highly original.

III

The Levine line to which his readers have become accustomed is an orthodox free verse line, broken syntactically. He has a knack for rising action and for succinct detail, and can quickly establish the tone of narration, as in **"Sweet Will,"** the title poem of a book published in 1985:

> The man who stood beside me
> 34 years ago this night fell
> on to the concrete, oily floor
> of Detroit Transmission, and we
> carefully stepped over him until
> he wakened and went back to his press.
> It was Friday night, and the others . . .

Most of Levine's mature poems are informed by a similar strong narrative impulse, and it would seem that he is remembering events from his personal past, so that the story of his life is made to stand for the story of many. There are, however, so many exceptions to this that it would be a mistake to label Levine's *oeuvre* as narrowly autobiographical. An early example of a Levine poem which sounds like a personal narrative is **"The Midget"** (*Not This Pig,* 1968). In a quickly unfolding drama in a bar "lined with factory workers" who are drinking alone and heavily, Levine describes a midget with a potbelly and a cummerbund who singles out the speaker, asking him to verify his manhood by feeling part of his anatomy. The poem is so carefully detailed that it is reasonable for a reader to think that Levine has depicted an event from his own life, and that the *I* is Levine himself. The question might simply be where the real event stopped and the poet's imagination took over, perhaps at the point where the midget climbs into the speaker's lap, or when the speaker begins to sing a lullaby to him, "this late-born freak / of the old world swelling in my lap." It's a surprising poem, and when I mentioned it to Levine this fall, he told me there wasn't a midget, that he hadn't existed. What matters, of course, is the semblance of existence, *artistic* reality. One of Levine's particular strengths as a writer is his ability to imagine and empathize with invented characters to the point that readers assume they are acquaintances or relatives.

"On my Own," a poem from his tenth book *One for the Rose* (1981), further illustrates Levine's empathic powers.

The piece also has intertextual significance, inasmuch as it serves to amplify and lend clarity to those of the older poems which owe a debt to the surreal. In **"On my Own,"** a supernatural being describes his entry into the ordinary stream of life on earth as a seven-year-old. Having chosen the house of an old woman who "opened her door expecting milk" and instead got the youngster with plastered-down hair and a suitcase filled with earthly paraphernalia (children's books, clothing, a stuffed toy), he must choose a name and go off to school for the first time, as if he's just moved into the neighborhood:

> I chose Abraham Plain
> and went off to school wearing a cap
> that said "Ford" in the right script.

The boy slowly gets used to the simple pleasures of earth, "the beauty of sleep" and being able to dream of "seascapes / at the other end of the world," and it is in the guise of this fictive character that Levine reveals his belief in the "infinite" powers of the imagination to enliven reality. The boy addresses the reader as if he had been present as a crossing guard:

> Sure, now you
> know, its obvious, what with the light
> of the Lord streaming through the nine
> windows of my soul and the music of rain
> following in my wake and the ordinary air
> of fire every blessed day I waken with the world.

Though it has been argued that Levine's poetry is more concerned with his personal life than with the life of the imagination, the two together seem equally to inform his poems. Indeed, Levine claims imaginary, idealized truths as his prerogative in **"I was born in Lucerne"** (*One for the Rose*): to have had a beautiful young woman as his mother, "A woman of independence and courage / who sang the peasant songs of her region," who turned the past of his father and other male relatives into myth, and helped protect the speaker from the facts about poverty and war. Balanced against the grayer truths "in the fields or in the factories" is Levine's sun-touched and, strangely, more defiant idea of reality:

> Look in my eyes!
> They have stared into the burning eyes of theearth,
> molten metals, the first sun, a woman's face,
> they have seen the snow covering all
> and a new day breaking over the mother sea.
> I breathed the truth, I was born in Lucerne.

The act of articulation resides in imagining the scene as vividly as memory, in careful reformulations of the way things are or seem to be. Levine's many references in the *New Selected Poems* to silence are accompanied by his personae's expressions of fear that he, and others, and reality itself, might lie. His strategy for telling the truth involves stepping bodily into the lives of all sorts of people—boxers, rabbis, stonecutters, young girls (*Pili's Wall*), fathers, sons, wives—who experience the weight of disappointment and death, as well as joy. In the best of his poems, the stories of their lives unfold swiftly through a series of precise images which delineate mood and tone and psychological motivation. In some of the weaker poems—under the influence of the style of the time, perhaps—the images are more vivid and easily associated with a feeling or attitude but the reason for the feeling exists off the page. A few of the poems in *Red Dust* (1971) contain exotic images of anger. The mood poem **"Fist,"** for instance, suffers from a lack of context. A reader knows the terrible power of the speaker's anger in similes for his clenched hand, "a flower / that hates God, the child / tearing at itself," but would have to try to guess at the motivation for the anger unless he or she had read more of Levine's work.

If in a few poems Levine creates riddles while talking of real things, making impossible combinations of them, normally he ascribes to the ideals of style articulated in Aristotle's *Poetics*. His narratives and lyrics use the "regular words for things," but his language also varies from the "common element," largely in his use of metaphor, though also by changing the traditional value of a word by altering the syntax of his sentences, as in **"They Feed They Lion."** Anaphoric, syntactically parallel and at the same time syntactically wrenched, the poem makes use of high and low speech and a mixture of ordinary and extreme metaphors. Here are the first lines:

> Out of burlap sacks, out of bearing butter,
> Out of black bean and wet slate bread,
> Out of acids of rage, the candor of tar,
> Out of creosote, gasoline, drive shafts, wooden
>   dollies,
> They lion grow.
>   Out of gray hills
> Out of industrial barns, out of rain, out of bus ride,
> West Virginia to Kiss My Ass, out of buried aunties,
> Mothers hardening like pounded stumps, out of
>   stumps,
> Out of the bones' needs to sharpen and the
>   muscles' to stretch,
> They lion grow.

In **"A Theory of Prosody"** (*A Walk with Tom Jefferson*), Levine refuses to reveal his poetic intentions as they relate to the line, and the poem establishes, humorously (the tone that he employs with greater and greater frequency in his later poems), that chance is at least as operative in his decisions about line breaks as theory. Of the cat Nellie, the speaker says

> She would sit behind me
> as I wrote, and when the line
> got too long she'd reach
> one sudden black foreleg down
> and paw at the moving hand, the offensive one. The
>   first
> time she drew blood I learned
> it was poetic to end
> a line anywhere to keep her
> quiet.

Though she is described as "alert," the speaker says it is the artist's pretense to say that nothing is left to chance. The poem's charm is a mixture of hyperbole and modesty. In lines which communicate Levine's refusal to acknowledge the skill that attends an intuitive sense of how a line should sound, the poem illustrates the simple authority of a well-schooled writer of free verse in the tradition of Williams. None of the lines in this particular poem are by themselves memorable, but overall they get the job done, with an occasional modest gesture in the direction of form repeating content. In a poem that is about accidental line breaks, Levine writes such a line as "quiet. After all, many morn-," yet he seems to be ribbing the theorist who would expect such a break. The authority of his lines often appears to derive solely from establishing a length and staying with it. Their integrity is related to narrative image; the poem unfolds, the details of the story are interesting, and the line carries those details with no visible show of artistic adornment. The rhythms of language and life grow out of one another. Despite Levine's rigorous schooling in the tradition (as a student he wrote sonnets for John Berryman), and despite evidence throughout the anthology of syllable- and accent-counting, it might be as simple as that.

IV

What Work Is (1991) is a continuation of Levine's dual attempt to give voice to the complicated lives of men and women and to make that voice something closer to simple song than ordinary speech. The reasons for song are not the usual—happy, happy love or the beauties of nature—although Beauty does matter in the world Levine creates, and love is redemptive. Whistling in the dark is, perhaps, a better description of the kind of song sung by the people of whom Levine tells us. Life, he says, is not easy, not even for children, who in **"Among Children"** are asleep "so as to be ready for what is ahead, / the monumental boredom of junior high / and the rush forward tearing their wings / loose and turning their eyes forever inward." Their fathers "work at the spark plug factory or truck / bottled water"; the children's backs already "have thickened," and their hands are "soiled by pig iron." The speaker would like to

> sit down among them and read slowly
> from the Book of Job until the windows
> pale and the teacher rises out of a milky sea
> of industrial scum, her gowns streaming
> with light, her foolish words transformed
> into song, I would like to arm each one
> with a quiver of arrows so that they might
> rush like a wind there where no battle rages
> shooting among the trumpets, Ha! Ha!

What this poem contends is that the teacher's lessons on history, math, and civics will be of less importance to the children of Flint, Michigan, than laughter and song in the face of the stupefying boredom and difficulties of working people. The songs are the songs of grandfathers who sing themselves to sleep (**"Burned"**), of jazzmen like John Coletrane "playing his music with such joy / and contained energy and rage" that a woman twice his age, who has heard the solo in a dream, recognizes it as a gift that she passes along to her son, of hymns sung by women on a bus returning from church (**"Coming Home from the Post Office"**); of a boy at his first job at the soap factory, "singing / my new life of working and earning" (**"Growth"**); and of the blue morning glories along a fence whose existence is described as both music and laughter. "They blared all day," Levine tells us, "though no one could score their sense or harmony / before they faded in the wind and sun."

There are harmonies in these people's confrontations with reality—the daily labors of the workplace, where who you are and "what it takes to be known among women and men" (**"Fear and Fame"**) is revealed by the normal effort expended at work, the dirt and grime associated with work, the hunger for a better position, the meals prepared and eaten, the rise and fall of day and season and man and woman, familial ties and personal histories out of which the rational and irrational hopes for the future come. It is work to find these harmonies, Levine tells us, work to "enter the fires of your own making, naked / day after day, until the burning becomes / a sweetness" (**"Burned"**). To transform a life, and life itself, into more than its angry and sad bits of experience, into "the final truth" of the same poem, one must enter the fires of the past, "stare into fire," and risk burning:

> I have to climb
> the slag hills again, but this time not
> as a child, and look out over the river of iron,
> and hold it all in my eyes,
> the river, the iron mountains, the factories
> where our brothers burned. I have to repeat
> the prayer that we will all go back
> to earth one day soon to become earth,
> that our tears will run to the sea
> a last time and open it, and our fires
> light the way back home for someone.

This is the work of living, and it exists as a monumental task. It includes "the mythology of boys growing into men," "girls fighting to be people" (**"Coming of Age in Michigan"**), and the lies attending the relationships between young men and women:

> We even lied back in return, inventing squadrons
> of blondes and serious brunettes driven by love
> to wait on our doorsteps until we returned
> by bus, filthy and broken by the long days
> of breaking the earth, women with new cars
> and old needs content to take their turns.
>
> (**"Innocence"**)

"It isn't easy," the speaker says in **"On the River,"** to "get a better / look" at one's "own life" through the smoke "of our own making," and even though this smoke is really the dirty residue from factories, it also seems to be representative of all that we allow to get in our way—

fears, "false Gods" (**"Burned"**), facts, "foolish hopes" (**"My Grave**), and forgetfulness, "an old pillow of forgetting, / a way out before the world got in" (**"Perennials"**).

Levine's attempt to find out truth, to work for it and make it work for him, is accompanied by modest demurrals throughout the book. "I don't have the answer," he says in **"Scouting"** in reply to the question "What is it Like?" When in **"Snails"** the speaker is at the point of saying "something final" about the autumn beauty, he says he "kept quiet." By listening to the ticking of the leaves, and watching the shadows, letting the world "escape / to become all it's never been," Levine practices the art of the poet who has made a tangible commitment to truth; he lets the world speak for itself.

The bright, sung conversations of the earth and the earthbound are what the poems in *What Work Is* records. If these are nearly the same stories, about trying to live with dignity in a very difficult century, that he told in *New Selected Poems,* they are worth their retelling. They continue Levine's quest for ways to understand the paradoxes of isolation and community, Godlessness and spirituality, death and beauty, tears and "deep song" (Lorca's phrase) which are synonymous with the experience of living. Firemen, steelworkers, boxers, women, dead poets and other ghosts, young and old, get a say. What they have in common he simultaneously turns into myth and demythifies. How they are different he acknowledges. The territory of this poetry keeps coming back to a center—praise for the common person, an American, probably with immigrant parents, who having gotten "off the bus / at the bare junction of nothing / with nothing" (**"Scouting"**) manages to find a way home.

Joyce Carol Oates attempts to describe Levine's "unclassifiable poetry":

The poems in [*Red Dust*] that strike me as unforgettable are those that in some ultimate way do not 'make sense'— at least to me. I doubt that they make sense to Levine either. But they are near-perfect creations in which the restless, scrutinizing, analytical mind has forced some shape upon that inchoate reservoir of the Unconscious—the famous 'voix surréaliste'—and made it horribly recognizable, though never comprehensible. Purely surrealistic poetry is always disappointing, because it seems so arbitrary; Levine's unclassifiable poetry weaves violent and not-to-be-softened images in and out of a single sensibility's monologue of awe. The poems move back and forth from a mystical affirmation of the earth to a fragmented, ceaselessly questioning consciousness that excites us, sometimes against our will, with the prospect of a good fight. My first impulse is to say *He should write novels!*—but my more reasoned instinct is *He has no need to write novels.*

Joyce Carol Oates. "A Cluster of Feelings: Wakoski and Levine," in American Poetry Review. *Vol. 2, No. 3. May/June 1973.*

Philip Levine   (interview date 1995)

SOURCE: "A Conversation with Philip Levine," in *Tri-Quarterly,* Winter, 1995-96, pp. 67-82.

[In the following interview, Levine answers questions from students at Davidson College regarding his method and style of writing, the political relevance of poetry, and his most recent collection, The Simple Truth.*]*

[Chris Wyrick] *Congratulations on the big prize! [The Pulitzer Prize in Poetry for* **The Simple Truth** *(1994)]*

[Philip Levine] Well, thank you. Yes. It's been a long time coming. But, you see, patience does pay off. Actually, I think it's better to get it when you're old. Ah, I'm happy to win it.

[George Weld] *I think now especially a lot of young writers feel a tension between the feeling that they need to be activists in their work for social change and a feeling that, as Auden says, "Poetry makes nothing happen," that poetry is irrelevant or elitist, and I'm wondering whether you feel this tension yourself.*

Well, frankly, I think that Auden is wrong. Poetry *does* make things happen. And I think that if a young person is troubled by the idea that he or she is practicing an elitist art, then he ought to do something else. I mean, if you have grave doubts about being a poet because you will thereby not achieve your social ambitions, then don't write poetry. Poetry will make it without you. And the question you have to ask yourself is, "Can I make it without poetry?" And if the answer is fuzzy and hazy, do something else. The answer had better be very loud and very clear: "I *can't* make it without poetry." Because there's so much in a life of poetry that can defeat you. And the apparatus for rewarding you is so abysmal, and the rewards themselves, aside from the writing of the poems, so small, that there's no point in doing it unless you're utterly confident that that's your vocation, that's your calling. I was very lucky when I was your age. T. S. Eliot came to see me. He said, "American poetry just needs you, Phil." He took the bus. In Detroit. I was surprised to see him in a Jewish neighborhood, but there he was. I said, "You're Tom Eliot." He said, "Say Sir, son." Of course, I'm kidding. It was a long bus ride from London, from Faber and Faber.

When I was your age I had no doubt. I also had social goals, and I was naive enough at eighteen or nineteen to think that poetry or fiction could have a vast social influence because it had a vast influence on the way I felt and thought. It wasn't very long before I realized that if I wasn't being read I wasn't going to influence many people through my writing. I was aware of the fact that while I was reading poets like Eliot, Auden, Spender, Wilfred Owen, Lowell, Stevens, and Hart Crane, my neighbors weren't. They wouldn't have known who the hell I was talking about, so I didn't talk about them. I'd guess much of my family was puzzled. They must have thought, "What is this infatuation and how long will it last?" I was the

only member of my family ever to finish college. There's a Yiddish expression that translates, "For this you went to college?" That's exactly what my grandfather said to me when I graduated from college and told him I wanted to be a poet. He told me about this man who lived in his village back in Russia before he left in '04 to come to the United States. This guy was some sort of lunatic who went from house to house; people fed him and listened to his terrible poems. My grandfather said, "At least he didn't go to college. Why did you go, for this?" I tried to explain to him that I didn't go to college to become a poet, that while I was there my romance with poetry deepened. He just shrugged.

But poetry does make things happen. You know that already. It changes all of us who read it. But it will not change legislation.

[Rachel Newcomb] *I have another question that's along those same lines. In an interview in 1988 you said that perhaps American poetry had stopped believing in itself, and I was wondering if you felt that contemporary American poetry has become marginal and, if so, how can poetry attract a wider audience?*

I don't know why I said that in '88. I can't recall the occasion. Perhaps I was reading a lot of boring poetry. I talk to a lot of younger poets and most of them don't seem to feel their generation has found itself as yet. I had a conversation for publication recently with a wonderful younger poet, Kate Daniels—she must be thirty-eight or so—and she felt her generation hadn't yet found what it wanted to do, but she felt that my generation had to assert itself early because we were under the shadows of the giants. If you looked at the magazines in which I first published, you'd see I'm in there with Stevens, Marianne Moore, Williams. I wasn't awed by them. I knew how good they were, I knew they were writing far better than I, but I thought, given enough time, they will vanish from the earth in their bodily incarnations and then maybe my writing will get as good as theirs. Well, the first part did happen, and I'm still waiting for the second.

You asked about the audience for poetry in our country. I think it's the largest it's ever been. I know we're told otherwise. There's this "expert," Joseph Epstein, who published something like "Who Killed Poetry?" or something like that. Nobody killed poetry. Guys like Epstein like to hearken back to some dreamland America in which people got up in the morning and opened their windows to the birds singing and when they felt their souls elevated they recited American poetry to the waiting world. Bullshit! If you go back to the time when Stevens, Eliot, Williams were first publishing, exactly the same things were being said in the middlebrow press: "Look at this generation of turkeys. You can't understand a word they write. They're so obscure and so negative. Give us back our uplifting verse!" That was the middlebrow response to one of the great outpourings of poetry in the history of the English language, which took place early in this century. What happened in American poetry was extraordinary: Frost, Stevens, Williams, Pound, Moore, Eliot, all writing at the same time, E. A. Robinson, the whole Imagist thing. And the Epsteins of that hour were griping just as they are now. My guess is that today it still has something to do with class; they can't stand the idea of all these poets coming out of Turkey Tech and Fresno State and Puma J. C. They're from the fancy places that once owned our poetry. We had the same response from the Eastern lords when the Beats hit the press.

I think poetry now is very healthy. There is no such thing as an official style. It's open house. It doesn't matter how tall or short you are, what color you are or what sex you are or what nine sexes, you can put anything in your work.

You can write about anything. No matter how badly you write you can find somebody who'll publish you. Time will sift the good stuff from the bad. As far as readership goes it's the largest it's ever been. I know, we're told no one is reading it, but that's nonsense. Go back and discover how large, say, an edition of William Carlos Williams was in 1944. His last book, *The Wedge,* was published in fewer than 500 copies. In '54 his great book, *The Desert Music,* was published by Random House; I'd be surprised if they did more than 1,200 copies. How big was the first edition of Lowell's incredible *Lord Weary's Castle?* One thousand copies? Berryman's *The Dispossessed?* I'd bet fewer than 1,000. The first edition of my new book is 7,500. And Sharon Olds and Adrienne Rich outsell me; they must do 10,000 of theirs. My editor told me the other day that Galway Kinnell's *The Book of Nightmares* had sold 60,000 copies and is still selling. I remember a year ago reading with Galway in Portland, and afterwards they had a book-signing, and for over an hour people kept lining up with old battered copies of his books. Those books had been read, God knows by how many people. There is a huge readership. We're told otherwise by the naysayers, but it's not true.

[Patrick Malcor]: *You said that there is no specific style of poetry right now. Do you think poetry is beyond the point where it can have a movement, a certain mass style, or do you think that it needs that?*

There will always be movements. We have one right now that began in California, the Language Poets. Do you know their work? [Blank looks.] You don't, God bless you. Young poets begin movements to have something to belong to, something potentially exciting: "We're going to change American poetry!"

Ever since I began writing I've noticed that certain movements are there mainly to help people without talent write something they can pass off as poetry. If you can't tell a decent story, denounce poems that tell stories. If you can't create characters, denounce poems with people in them. If you can't create images, write boring generalities. If you have no sense of form, imitate the formlessness of the sea. If you have no ear, disparage music. If everything you write is ugly and senseless, remind your readers that the world is ugly and senseless. Bad poets are incredibly resourceful. But those are movements that are easily forgotten. About fifteen years ago we had something called the New Formalism, and it seems to have vanished already. Very curious movement, a sort of nostalgia for the poetry of the fifties and perhaps for the decade itself, and it occurred at a time when the best formal poets of the fifties—Wilbur, Merrill, Hecht, Nemerov—were still writing incredibly well. The important movements change the way we see poetry or poetry sees us.

When I was your age a poet friend of mine, Bernie Strempek, and I founded a revolutionary poetry movement. We called it The New Mysticism; that was Bernie's idea. I believe he truly believed in the majesty and burning of the invisible whereas I was about as mystical as a sofa. Clearly we didn't change anything, not even the way we saw ourselves, but for a few weeks we had great fun talking about how we were going to change the country. Both the Language poets and the New Formalists strike me as less interesting than the New Mystics, though I am hardly objective. They're such conservative movements: neither seems in the least interested in shouldering a social or spiritual or political agenda. Both are academic and largely praised by academic critics and by the poets themselves, but perhaps they will have a healthy impact on our writing. They probably find my work and the contemporary work that resembles it garbage, which is fine. What's important is there is not a single official, accepted style. Today someone entering poetry can take any number of directions and find other poets who will validate his or her work. I hate the notion that any style, mine or anyone else's, is *the* style.

We have had very important, essential movements in this century. For me the most important one was the Imagist movement, which included such poets as Williams, Pound, Ford Madox Ford, D. H. Lawrence, and profoundly changed both English and American poetry. One in England right after the end of World War II changed the entire focus of their poetry. It was labeled "The Movement" and was something of a repudiation of the high-flown rhetoric of poets like George Barker, Dylan Thomas and Henry Treece. Suddenly we got these hard-assed poems from poets like Thom Gunn and Philip Larkin. They seemed more interested in what went on in a department store than what went on after you died and went to heaven. They'd write about trying to pick up a girl or spinning out on your motorcycle or finding a pair of pants that made you look sexy. In their poems people sound like people and not holy texts. In "Church Going" Larkin writes about a man with no religious faith who goes into an empty church and wonders what the hell it's for. At one point in the poem he says "up at the holy end"; he can't think of the name for that part of the church, if he ever knew it. It's a marvelous poem about the need for religious feelings in people without religious feelings.

And then in the late fifties we had the Beat or Black Mountain thing, all the poets represented in Donald Allen's anthology *The New American Poetry.* If you can still find that book have a look at it. You'll find it contains some of the best American poets of the second half of the century: Gary Snyder, Creeley, Ginsberg, Robert

Duncan, Denise Levertov. All of us who write poetry owe those poets a great debt for ending the absolute domination of the official Eastern establishment; that was a great service. Maybe you folks would like to start a movement: the Davidson Suicide Squad or the North Carolina Stompers. It couldn't do any harm, and it might enliven things. They're a little dull right now.

[Todd Cabell]: *You mention in the first essay in your book,* **The Bread of Time,** *that anybody can become a poet, that we have democratized poetry, and then you mention creative-writing classes in colleges and high schools. I wonder, being a teacher yourself, what exactly do you view as bad in that movement?*

Nothing. I think it's a wonderful thing. When I started writing there was not the sense that everybody could become a poet. Chicano poetry did not exist, Asian-American poetry did not exist, such giants as Robert Hayden and Sterling Brown were not represented in the official anthologies. I'm having fun in that essay, and I'm also being serious because I do think there are too many writing programs and many are staffed by people who can't write themselves. I visit places where poetry writing is taught in graduate programs, and I can't believe the level of writing. Then I see the poetry the teachers write, and I know why. And you visit a class, and everything is praised: the MO seems to be, "Let's pretend all this writing is poetry." Once you create a program you require students, so you let everyone in and you keep them in by making them happy. I also visit writing programs in which real standards are operating, the students have talent and are reading and working like mad; the teachers are dedicated, demanding, fair, and they are gifted and productive poets themselves. There are two things you must have for a valuable writing program: first and most importantly, the right students. Then the teachers. You could have mediocre teachers if you had great students because the students will teach each other and inspire each other. The problem is great students rarely gravitate to mediocre teachers.

[Chris Wyrick]: *I'd like to ask a question about your method of writing. In* **What Work Is,** *in the poem* **"Scouting,"** *you say, "I'm scouting, getting the feel of the land," and in the poem* **"What Work Is,"** *"Forget you. This is about waiting, shifting from one foot to another." And I want to ask you if you could tell us more about this process of scouting that you engage in your poems.*

That's a difficult and interesting question. How do you research a poem, which is what scouting is? Or at least that's one of the things I'm scouting for in the poem, the poem itself. You know you're constantly obliged when you apply for grants or things like grants to describe the specific steps you're going to take to write the book you're asking for financial support to write, and of course you rarely know exactly what you'll have to do. If you've been doing it as long as I, you have some idea, and I'd call it a kind of scouting. It's a circling and circling, quite literally—a cityscape, a landscape, a subject, an emotion-

al obsession. I'll give you an example. I have this fascination with Spanish anarchism, so back in the seventies I went to one of the great collections of anarchist literature, The International Institute for Social Study in Amsterdam. The records of the CNT and the FAI—the National Workers Confederation and the Iberian Anarchist Federation—were stored there. Most of the stuff is in Spanish, and at the time my Spanish was good enough to read it. The people who worked in the library there were very helpful and generous; they brought me whatever I wanted to see, old newspapers, posters, memoirs, manifestoes, anything I asked for, and I sat there for hours, day after day, reading. The poetry I finally got had nothing to do with Spanish anarchism, though I have written many poems out of that obsession; this "scouting" produced poems that had to do with being in a library. They had to do with the quality of light, the sadness that invades a library late in the afternoon when you've been there all day from 9:00 in the morning until 5:30 and suddenly you realize the light has changed and the day is ending. In Amsterdam the weather can change very suddenly, and I would glance out the window and dark clouds were blowing in from the North Sea, and the day was totally different from the one I left when I entered the library. My heart was always yearning to go out in the streets and to be in Amsterdam; it's such a beautiful and lively city. I learned a hell of a lot about Spanish anarchism and I wrote about my hours in the library, the people I met there, the yearning for the city, the shocking realization of how quickly time was passing and the light going.

And **"Scouting,"** the poem itself, is about my days in North Carolina, your dear state, where I lived the summer of 1954 in a mountain town called Boone. I thought I'd made a drastic step that might mean I would never become the amazing poet I had seemed destined to become. I had just gotten married. I had fallen in love with a woman who had a young child, and so we married. I thought, "Look what a foolish thing love has driven me to do. I must now be a responsible human being. I'm only twenty-six years old and I've thrown my young life away." You know, men at twenty-six are total idiots. I would go for long walks most days. I didn't have to work, my new wife was working and supporting all of us. I was supposed to be writing poems, but my mother-in-law had come for the wedding, and no one can write with his mother-in-law in the house, even, as in my case, if she's a lovely woman. So I went on these long walks and began to discover the landscape of those mountains and the people. I'd knock on doors of these little cabins and say, "Could I have a drink of water?" And besides the water, which I always got, I'd get different responses. "Where you from, son?" "What are you doing here?" They'd hear my accent and know I was not local, these gracious country people sharing their water with me, their time; we'd have wonderful conversations. It was a kind of scouting. As I got further and further into it I realized I was carrying out research, I was researching myself as well as these people and their place. My mother-in-law left, so in the mornings I'd work for hours on poetry; I found Saintsbury's *History of English Prosody* in the local library, never had been read, pages uncut, and I poured over that. I'd been trying to write poetry for ten years, and I still didn't know how to do it and knew I didn't know. But I was getting clues and I was also learning how to research poems: you keep your eyes open, your ears open, all your senses open. The world responds to you, and you respond to the world. It goes on that way; it never ends.

Keats has a late letter to Shelley. I don't think he ever truly cared for Shelley. It might have been a class problem, Shelley coming from the rich and famous family and living his "spontaneous" life. Like Byron, Shelley wrote all the time. Keats had long bouts of silence, what we too easily call writer's block. He suggests to Shelley that his poetry might be richer if he "loaded every rift with ore," if he wrote less and did it with more intensity. He goes on to say that he has sat as long as six months without writing. I think Keats believed, as I have come to believe, that not writing is part of the process of writing. Not in the beginning—for first you have to learn what the hell it is you're doing—then you must write, as Berryman said to me, everything that occurs to you.

I've been very lucky. I've never had one of those terrible droughts. Three or four months is the longest I've ever gone without writing poetry or something I could regard as poetry. I've come to think part of the process, an essential part, is waiting, being patient, and avoiding what one might call busy work. There's the temptation to construct what you secretly know is second-rate and keep working at it because it beats not working at anything. I think you're better off not writing at all than just soothing yourself with busywork. I'm not talking about beginning writers; they have no idea where anything will go and should plow ahead with whatever comes to them. By the time you've been at it fifteen years you know when you're just imitating yourself.

"Scouting" is also about that dreadful moment here in North Carolina when I said to myself, "Philip, you have o'erstepped your usual timidity and entered upon marriage." You know I was just like any other jerk my age. No one had told me how to become a poet, and I'd figured out that if you didn't have money there were two ways to live: you can have a family or you can write poetry, but you ain't going to do both. How the hell are you going to take care of kids, help dress and feed them, get them off to school, and then write a poem? What kind of nonsense is that? I figured I should have someone coming into my study with toast and tea, I should have silence interrupted at intervals for wonderful meals. Wasn't that how Rilke lived? How many nights do you think he sat up with a sick kid? You know at one point or another in your life you have to wake up and become a person. The irony of all this is I was incredibly lucky. I was marrying a woman who had a profound regard for poetry and this kid I adopted turned out to be one of my best friends. It was probably one of the three or four intelligent decisions I've made in my whole life. Another was buying the house I work in in Fresno. Another was not going to the Korean War. I can't think of another one, but there must be a fourth.

[Mary Stephens]: *I'm interested in how memory works in the writing process because so many of your poems are retrospective. How does this process differ from poems that are observed at the moment of conception? And how important is looking back, not only on your own experiences, but on your earlier writing?*

I don't know if I can answer the second part. It seems to me that you made a distinction between writing a poem that would come out of memory and one that would come out of an experience that was before you. But you'll notice that in my poems it almost doesn't seem to matter what's before me: I go back into memory and try often to twine what I remember with what I'm observing. And I'm not sure why I do this, although it's obviously something that I do. I think that a lot of it has to do with the fact that I feel an urgency to record things because they seem so transitory. And I am now a kind of archive of people, places and things that no longer exist. I carry them around with me, and if I get them on paper I give them at least some existence. And that seems like a legitimate thing to be doing with poetry. To be granting some form of permanence—I mean, however permanent the poems are—to the things, to a way of life and the people who made up that way of life.

As far as looking back at my own writing, I try not to. I purposely don't memorize my poems. When I'm on the brink of memorizing a poem I stop using it at readings. I wait for time to erase it because I don't want to memorize it. I don't mind memorizing other people's poems, but I'm not going to sit down and write a poem that I've memorized by Hardy or Wyatt or Dylan Thomas. I'm not going to do that. Whereas a poem that's my own may haunt me if I go back to it. I don't want to go back to it. I don't want to look at it. And sometimes when I look at them I'm a little depressed by the fact that they're better than what I'm writing now. That's another thing: I believe some of the older poems have more imagination, more vitality. I know that these last two books have won all these honors, but I actually prefer some of the older books.

People ask me, for example, what's the book I'm working on now, what's it about, and when I tell them the truth they think I'm putting them on. I say, "I don't know yet. I won't know until I'm done." But that's the truth. That's happened with every book I've ever written. I didn't know what the book was about until I finished it or got close to finishing it. And then I saw, "Oh, that's what I've been obsessed with!" For example, in writing the last book, *The Simple Truth,* I saw at a certain point that there were three poems I needed. I had taken out a group of poems that either weren't good enough or didn't belong. I said to myself, "I need three poems to go right there," and in the next month I wrote them. That was very rare for me.

With the book *What Work Is,* I suddenly realized I needed a long poem at the center, so I revived a poem I'd been working on for at least a dozen years and had failed to finish, **"Burned."** I looked at what I had and knew the time had come to finish it. And I got it. I didn't get it right, but I think I got it as right as I would probably ever get it. Sitting over it another year wouldn't have made it any better, so I let it out into the world. And it was well treated. Have I answered your question?

[Geordie Schimmel]: *What if not poetry? If not the dialogue with stars and trees at thirteen, what would you have chosen?*

It would have been the dialogue at fourteen. That's what I was going to do. I don't have the least doubt about it. Before I was ten I was utterly fascinated with language, with the shape and flavor of words. And I got so much pleasure out of using language, and I used it with snap. Besides, there weren't that many other options. I couldn't have been a dancer, I'm too awkward. I can't draw so I couldn't have been a painter. Maybe an Abstract Expressionist, except my sense of color stinks. I can't carry a tune worth a damn, so although I love music it wasn't for me. I might have become a critic. No, never a *cricket,* as Mark Twain calls them. Better to be an honest huckster and sell Buicks. I might have become a novelist. When I was in college I worked as hard at fiction as I did at poetry, but back then my temperament wasn't suited for it; I hadn't yet developed the incredible patience a novelist requires.

[William Robert]: *I'd like to return to your works for a minute and ask you a question about them. Pretty consistently, from the earliest ones to the ones that just came out in* **The Simple Truth,** *you develop many philosophical threads. And one of the most fundamental seems to me to be the lack of, the impotency of, even the impossibility of, true communication between individuals. Do you see this as an ironic stance for a poet, namely one who depends on communication, to take?*

No, no, I don't. Failing to communicate is part of what we live with, part of our condition. Poetry is about as good as we can get at communicating without the aid of gestures, without the aid of our bodies. Rilke wrote somewhere that without our bodies we cannot love. Also with our bodies, with our gestures, with our facial expressions, we can communicate far more fully than with merely words on the telephone or words in a letter. Poetry is as close as we can get to complete communication with words alone. And I think it's good enough. I believe that when I'm reading Keats or Hardy—another of my favorite poets—I'm getting it, the essence of what they have to say and even more than the essence, lots of the particulars. Obviously I'm not getting it all. There's no such thing as perfect communication. Hardy's experience of the world is not mine, though our lives overlapped by some months. Keats's experience of the London of his era is not mine; their experience with the words they use is so different from mine. But the miracle of poetry is that it can cross so many of these barriers. Approximate communication seems so amazing itself when you consider how separate we are or how separate we have conceived of ourselves. I believe that we aren't nearly as separate as we think we are. If, for example, someone in this room were running a fever we would all heat up a bit, we'd feel it even though we might not know we felt it.

Our eyes tell us we're more separate than we actually are, and our conscious experience tells us, and we've conditioned ourselves to believe we're more separate. But to get back to poetry, given who we've created out of ourselves, poetry is miraculous.

But you're right: there is an obsession in much of my work with the failures of people to communicate, but those failures are usually very specific. I'm usually concerned with a few people, perhaps only two, and how they fail to communicate. A book that moved me enormously when I was young, maybe eighteen, was *Winesburg, Ohio.* I remember a story about two very lonely people, a man and a woman, who have no one to communicate with and whose experience of love is very limited. As I recall—I haven't read the story in ages—they get together and they discover they have these mutual needs and they could be dear friends. As I recall the man oversteps the bounds of this budding friendship; while the woman is trying to speak out of her joy that she has a listener he shuts her up by kissing her. There's this awful and wonderful irony that he has chosen to communicate his love or joy in the occasion this way, and she wants to communicate it another way and you can't do both at the same time. She says something like, "But, Harold, let me tell you what it was like to be six and a solitary girl," and he goes smack, smack, as if to say, "Let me show you what it's like to be twenty-seven and a man in the company of a woman." I thought Anderson had captured something amazing: How even when we fail each other the miraculous happens, they cross that great divide that separates one person from another. I believe it's possible. I believe I've done it, totally. I try to record it in my poem **"The Escape."** The communication between the speaker and the woman is total, and he becomes a creature endowed with two sexes, an angel with no wings. They don't do it merely with words, but they do it. He touches the woman and discovers he's also touching himself because they've become one being.

[Kristina Nevius]: *Through this interview you've mentioned languages. What effect have foreign languages and cultures had on your poetry?*

When I go to a foreign country where I don't speak the language I usually make no effort to learn it. I'm just "The Ugly American," as Eugene Burdick called us in his novel years ago. I enjoy the ignorance, I use it. Say I go into the Campo Fiori, the great open market in Rome. I stop and listen to two people standing in line to buy eggs. The man says to the woman, "Was there ever a more perfect shape than an egg? And the luminosity! The amazing delicacy of the color, the way it takes the hues of the air. Not only does the egg contain sustenance for us, for our bodies which feed our souls, but within each egg is the potential of a creature that can fly." Amazing, they say such rare things in such common places in Rome; Italians are angels. Of course that's not what they're saying at all. The guy has turned to his cousin Elfonzina and said, "Holy shit, the bastard raised the price again!" Because I don't speak Italian I've endowed him with poetry, and I say to myself, "How fortunate you are, Philip, to be living among such profound people when in fact they're saying the same trivial things they'd be saying in Fresno or Detroit."

One invaluable thing I learned from studying Spanish was how great our own poetry is, how many things it can do that Spanish poetry hasn't done. We appear in American poetry and we speak in our daily voices. It gave me a new regard for American poetry. Discovering the great poetry written in Spanish in this century was intoxicating. There's also much more awful poetry written in Spain than in the U.S. because anyone who goes to the university in Spain publishes a book of poetry. The dentist will hand you a beautifully printed book of poems—each dentist has one— all about the perfume of flowers, the brightness of the moon, the tenderness of kisses, the sweetness of the night air of Andalusia, the kindness of wild herbs. The poetry of love, dreams, moonlight, fantasy. Absolute garbage. It's so bad they couldn't even sing it in Nashville, and they can sing anything in Nashville. The great poetry is able to use the same vocabulary and break all the silly conventions and astonish you.

Even though I had to work like a demon on my Spanish, I got a great kick out of being able to speak it and understand it. I also found it exhausting to speak it for hours on end. One day I got so tired I went into a little park near the *futbol* stadium in Barcelona, flopped on a bench and slept for hours. Once I started dreaming in Spanish I got scared I'd lose my American English, so I would go down to the port and speak to American sailors and marines off the ships.

I think, too, it's very good to read poetry in another language to discover the immense possibilities we're not taking advantage of in our poetry. I know you can discover much of that reading translations, say of Zbigniew Herbert or Tomas Tranströmer, but I think you get an even keener sense when you read someone like García Lorca or César Vallejo in the original. And you're inspired in the same way you're inspired when you read Whitman or Dickinson or Williams. I can still struggling with the poems of Miguel Hernández in the original and those sudden glimpses of how astonishing the poetry was, how brutal and lyrical at exactly the same moment. I'd never read anything like it; it reconfirmed my belief in the power and beauty of poetry in the face of the worst life can dish out. These are poems that grew out of the most tragic circumstances. They are full of indescribable pain, which he foresees. They are very great and very difficult poems; I had to work hours, and then I would get this glimpse of their majesty. Going to Spain, living there, was a wonderful experience for me. I owe the discovery of the poetry mainly to Hardie St. Martin, the poet and translator I met in Barcelona. He was working on his great anthology, *Roots and Wings,* and generously took me into his stable of translators.

[Alex Crumbley]: *Did it take you long to become comfortable writing persona poems? And when you do, do you have trouble with people assuming you're the narrator when you're not?*

First thing, it didn't take long at all. Once I decided I wanted to do it, I just did it. I had written a lot of fiction, at least a dozen stories and large chunks of two novels, so I was used to the problem of getting into the heads of other characters and getting them to speak in my writing.

As far as people misreading, I don't much care. I remember a review I got, I think it was in the *Village Voice,* in which a woman wrote that one of my poems from *7 Years from Somewhere* was very curious. The poem, **"I Could Believe,"** is in the voice of a guy who has come back from the Spanish Civil War. This woman wrote something like, "Levine is an autobiographical poet, so it's amazing to discover that he fought in the Spanish Civil War, which ended when he was eleven." She mused over this, and then wrote, "Perhaps he's trying something different." Perhaps if I'd written in the voice of someone coming back from the American Civil War she wouldn't have missed it, but you can't be sure. If you're troubled by being misunderstood then you'd better not publish.

Even our fellow poets and friends read our poetry differently. I remember going to a class at the University of Minnesota and having a conversation with them; it was much like today. At the end someone asked if I would read one poem. I said, "Sure, let me read something I'm working on and we'll see what you think of it." I read **"Listen Carefully"** in an early draft. After I was done a young woman asked me if I would publish the poem. I said, "Yeah, if I ever get it right." "But if your sister read it, how would she feel?" I said, "I don't have a sister." She was shocked. My host, Michael Dennis Browne, an English poet who has become a fine American poet, then told an interesting story.

He said, "You know, Sharon Olds was sitting in that same chair last year, and for some reason she got on the subject of Phil's poetry. She told us how she had asked Phil where she might get `chocolate cookies in the shape of Michigan,' cookies Phil refers to in one of his poems. To Sharon's surprise Phil said he just made it up." Michael quoted her in a surprised voice, "He made it up!" as though that were unheard of. Sharon is a dear friend of mine, and my guess is she was having fun. It's very possible it's not something she would do in her own poems, but I'm sure she knows it's something I do all the time. To me it's always open house; if you want it and it doesn't exist, just make it up. This poem with the cookies in it is about an amazing kid, a kid so amazing he's not human and yet he is. He's what human beings would be if human beings were totally themselves. Now how would I know what human beings would be if they were totally themselves? I'll tell you how; I've been totally myself. I've experienced it. That's what you become when you're inspired, you become totally yourself. We pray to the muse and all the rest of that. Poets tell us, Coleridge and Keats for example, that they wrote some of their most inspired works when they were invaded by a force not their own. Maybe they're right, but I have a different notion: I don't believe there is this outside force. I believe that we are so rarely totally ourselves that when we are we don't know who we are. I think it's similar to what athletes refer to as being "in the zone."

That's what poets live for, those days when we are totally ourselves. I know when I'm there. I awaken in the morning, and I know I'm there, that today it's going to happen. I've been working toward that day for ages, and when it comes I'm in no hurry. I learned from Alberto Giacometti to take my time when *the* day comes. I think it was in 1968 I read a book called *A Giacometti Portrait,* by James Lord. One chapter describes a day on which Alberto knows he's going to do great work, he just has it, so he just goes about his day very slowly. He wants to touch and perhaps bless as much of his daily life as he possibly can, the people and the places and the things that make up his daily life. He takes a long walk, he visits his usual haunts, he talks to people, and then he gets down to work. I had no idea you could do that until I was forty or forty-one; I didn't know the poem wouldn't run away from me. When you're inspired there's no rush; it's who you've become. Take your time, move around, absorb all you can, reach out as far as possible. You're not going to lose it. It's there. It's you.

FURTHER READING

Criticism

Buckley, Christopher, ed. *On the Poetry of Philip Levine: Stranger to Nothing.* Ann Arbor: The University of Michigan Press, 1994, 359 p.

 Provides reviews, essays, and bibliography through

Levine's 1988 publication of *A Walk with Tom Jefferson.*

Disch, Thomas M. "The Occasion of the Poem." *Poetry* CLX, No. 2 (May 1992): 94-107.

 Stresses the element of grievance in Levine's poetry.

Hirsch, Edward. "The Visionary Poetics of Philip Levine and Charles Wright." In *The Columbia History of American Poetry,* pp. 777-805. New York: Columbia University Press, 1993.

 A detailed critical overview of Levine's poetry.

Murphy, Bruce. "The State of the World." *Poetry* CLXVII, No. 3 (December 1995): 156-59.

 Reviews *The Simple Truth* unfavorably with comparison to *New and Selected Poems* by Gary Soto, Levine's former student.

Vendler, Helen. "All Too Real." *The New York Review of Books* SSSVIII, No. 20 (17 December 1981): 32-6.

 Reviews *One for the Rose* stating that Levine seems to be "simply a memoir-writer in prose" and asks "is there any compelling reason why it should be called poetry?"

Yenser, Stephen. "Bringing It Home." *Parnassus: Poetry in Review* 6, No. 1 (Fall/Winter, 1977): 101-17.

 Describes Levine as a poet who is "Prospero-dominated," meaning Levine is more concerned with truth than with beauty.

Interview

Simpson, Mona. "The Art of Poetry XXXIX: Philip Levine." *The Paris Review* No. 107 (Summer 1988): 157-86.

 Levine comments on his education, influences, themes, politics, and the process of writing.

Additional coverage of Levine's life and career is contained in the following sources published by Gale Research: *Contemporary Literary Criticism,* **Vols. 2, 4, 5, 9, 14, 33;** *DISCovering Authors: Poets Module; Contemporary Authors,* **Vols. 9-12R;** *Contemporary Authors New Revision Series,* **Vols. 9, 37, 52; and** *Dictionary of Literary Biography,* **Vol. 5.**

Marie de France
Circa Twelfth Century

French poet.

INTRODUCTION

Marie de France is the earliest known female French writer and is regarded as one of the finest poets of the twelfth century. She wrote during a western European cultural renaissance marked by the expansion of urban life and the rise of a new class of intellectuals, which included women. As a member of this class, Marie was able to obtain an extensive education and pursue a writing career. Although most modern scholars attribute to Marie a collection of fables and a translation of the legend of Saint Patrick, she is best known for her *Lais,* a collection of twelve verse tales written in octosyllabic rhyming couplets. Historians speculate that Marie may have been the originator of this form, but they concede that the absence of extant Breton lays, upon which Marie claimed to have based her own *Lais,* makes it difficult to determine the extent of her originality. Whether or not Marie de France invented the genre, critics assert that her *Lais* form an important part of medieval literature.

Biographical Information

Very little is known for certain about Marie's life; therefore, much of the information cited by biographers is conjectural. In each of her three works Marie names herself as author, providing a clue to her identity and implying a concern for protecting her authorship. Biographers generally agree that Marie was born in France in the last half of the twelfth century and that she lived for many years in England. Many critics point to her vocabulary, style, and knowledge of Latin, French, and English as proof that she was an aristocrat. It is possible that she was associated with the English court, which was French-speaking at the time. Marie in fact dedicated her *Lais* to a "noble King," who, critics note, may be either the English monarch Henry II or his son Henry, known as the Young King. A commonly asserted theory of Marie's identity is that she was the illegitimate daughter of Geoffrey Plantagenet, thus the half-sister of Henry II, and that she later became the abbess of Shaftesbury. Alternatively, several critics have suggested that Marie was the daughter of Anglo-Norman nobles Galeran de Meulan and Agnes de Montfort. The name by which Marie is known today was coined by Claude Fauchet in 1581. While consulting a manuscript that included a collection of fables, Fauchet read in the epilogue, "Marie is my name and I am from France," and thereafter referred to the author as Marie de France.

Major Works

Marie's *Lais,* a collection of twelve lays or narrative songs, is thought to be her first literary work. In her prologue to the *Lais,* Marie states her intention and her source: she had heard Breton lays and decided to document them for posterity and for her own fame. Scholars believe that *Les Fables d'Ysopet,* a collection of twenty-three fables she translated from English into French, constitutes Marie's second work. The title of this work cites "Ysopet," or Aesop, as Marie's model, but in the epilogue she acknowledges Alfred the Great, whose fables have been lost, as her source. As with the *Lais,* the lack of preserved literary antecedents for the *Fables* makes it difficult to determine the level of Marie's originality. *L'Espurgatoire Saint Patriz,* which is believed to be her third and final work, is a close translation into French of Henricus Salteriensis's Latin version of the legend of St. Patrick.

In the *Lais,* Marie places her characters in a variety of circumstances covering the fundamental issue of love in human relationships. As the narrator of events, she acts as a quiet observer, relating details of clothing, speech, and courtly lifestyles, as well as facets of social behavior. Although her *Lais* has a subtly didactic tone, Marie refrains from analysis or outright judgment, presenting an assortment of conflicts with unpredictable resolutions. Many of Marie's characters live in a hostile world, trapped literally by a jealous husband or figuratively by social or familial obligations, and they seek an ideal love as a means of escape. Some critics conclude that Marie presents marital love as the ideal, while others surmise that she treats adultery as a more dangerous and, therefore, stronger expression of passion. A love that is loyal, generous, and pure results in success for the lovers, regardless of marital ties, while a love that is selfish or impure ends in tragedy or punishment. Like the *Lais,* Marie's *Fables* shows her concern for individual growth and well-being. Many of the lessons taught by these stories affirm the injunction set forth in the epilogue to the collection: "one who neglects one's own interests acts foolishly." Through the actions of characters in the fables, Marie asserts her disdain both for manipulators and those careless enough to become victims. She also warns against corrupt and villainous officials. Didactic by nature, the fables instruct readers to fight the oppression of the weak, to root out corruption and greed, and to choose a simple and free life over a luxurious but enslaved existence.

Critical Reception

The number of manuscripts of Marie's work that have survived through the centuries serves as evidence of her importance as a medieval writer. However, the bulk of

English criticism of her works did not appear until the nineteenth and twentieth centuries. Scholars note one mention of her by a contemporary, Denis Piramus, who in his work *La Vie Seint Edmund Le Rei* (1190-1200) speaks of a "lady Marie who wrote in rhyme and composed the verses of lais." Critics today describe Marie de France as a storyteller of great charm and imagination who wrote with wit, intelligence, and economy. On the other hand, what certain critics refer to as charming simplicity in Marie's writing some view as a lack of sophistication. Her character depiction, for example, has been judged by some to be two-dimensional; others, however, have asserted that Marie intentionally established fixed types so that the slightest deviation would be noticeable, thereby contributing to the definition and differentiation of her characters. Some critics cite as a weakness her tendency to create absurd situations—as in the lai "Yonec" in which a pregnant woman jumps twenty feet from the tower where she is imprisoned, lands unhurt, and journeys to find her lover. But others argue that Marie's *Lais* is purposely absurd and thereby intent on conveying both humor and irony. Finally, scholars note that Marie's narratives depict not only the style of dress and manner of speech but also the behavioral codes and societal attitudes of the late twelfth century. Her vivid portrait of life in the medieval Anglo-Norman court has attracted the attention of critics and historians throughout the centuries, but it is her insightful treatment of love and human relationships that has secured her universal appeal.

PRINCIPAL ENGLISH TRANSLATIONS

Guingamor, Lanval, Tyolet, Bisclaveret (translated by Jessie L. Weston) 1900

Marie de France: Seven of Her Lays Done into English (translated by Edith Rickert) 1901

French Mediaeval Romances from the Lays of Marie de France (translated by Eugene Mason) 1911

The Lays Gugemar, Lanval, and a Fragment of Yonec (translated by Julian Harris) 1930

Marie de France: Fables (translated by Alfred Ewert and R. C. Johnston) 1942

Marie de France: Lais (translated by Alfred Ewert) 1944

The Lais of Marie de France (translated by Robert Hanning and Joan Ferrante) 1978

The Fables of Marie de France (translated by Mary Lou Martin) 1984

The Lais of Marie de France (translated by Glyn S. Burgess and Keith Busby) 1986

Fables (translated by Harriet Spiegel) 1987

CRITICISM

William S. Woods (essay date 1970)

SOURCE: "Marie de France's 'Laüstic'," in *Romance Notes*, Vol. XII, No. 1, Autumn, 1970, pp. 203-07.

[*In the following essay, Woods examines the structure of the* lai *"Laüstic," demonstrating how Marie de France used concision, understatement, and powerful symbols to tell this brief tale effectively.*]

The present discussion of the literary skill of Marie de France is a brief analysis of some of her poetic techniques in the *lai, "Laustic"* and is a demonstration of her ability at its best. A careful and sensitive reading of this story reveals the use of aesthetic devices which we value today as much as Marie evidently did.

An examination of **"Laüstic"** discloses a build-up of dramatic tension through Marie's use of understatement, linking, symbol, irony and concision. The latter is evident in the structure of the poem and in her handling of the components. The work consists of 160 lines, of which the first six are her introduction and the last four are the conclusion. Since neither of these sections is part of the intrigue, they are being considered only incidentally here. The plot is told in 150 lines which are divided into nine parts of nearly equal length.

I. (7-22) The Exposition. There are sixteen lines which furnish the exposition of elements needed in Marie's story. They give the setting, describe the situation and present the characters. The locale is Saint-Malo where there are two knights of great worth and who are assets to the city. One has married a wise, courtly and comely wife and the other remains a bachelor. This latter, Marie's hero, is known among his peers for prowess, honor, for love of tourneys and for his generosity. The last line (22), "E bien denot ceo qu'il aveit," serves as a link with the next part and actually anticipates its first line (23).

II. (23-38) The Plot. The First Obstacle. The opening line, "La femme sun veisin ama," renders specific and dramatic in its suddenness the generosity of the knight mentioned generally in line 22. In an unexpected heightening of interest we learn of his gift to his neighbor's wife—his love. The first obstacle is revealed in the one succinct line which also gives us the classic courtly love triangle—the hero's love for a married lady. The remaining lines tell of his successful suit for her love and of their apparent acceptance of the circumstances. Marie uses 15 of the 16 lines to present a banal and pallid courtly situation. The final line provides a fresh barrier suggesting the frustration to be detailed in the following part, "Fors un haut mur de piere bise (38).

III. (39-56) Frustration. The third division is of 18 lines. For the first eight we hear of their mutual pleasure at talking and exchanging gifts. Line 46 reads "Mut esteient amdui a eise." Lines 47-48 reveal the frustration of pleasure. "Fors tant k'il ne poënt venir / Del tut ensemble a lur pleisir." So the obstacles interfere with the love and intensify the suspense. Marie uses irony in lines 53-56 in stating that no one could prevent their coming to the window and seeing each other. This stands in ironic contrast to what actually does happen in the fourth division where the husband materializes for the first time and in the fifth section where he sets about negating lines 53-56 and destroying their innocent joy.

IV. (57-58) Preparation for Conflict and Symbol. The fourth segment is of 22 lines and is the longest. Lines 57-58, "Lunguement se sunt entr'amé / Tant que ceo vient a *un* esté," bring us to a specific summer and we can assume that the drama is commencing. This is corroborated by lines 77-78, "Delit aveient al veer, / Quant plus ne poeient aver." The resignation of II and III is no longer acceptable. They *do* want more. The husband is introduced on stage in lines 70-71. The remainder of IV is a tender description of the arrival of spring, the green thickets and meadows, the flowering orchards and the singing birds which delight all lovers. This charm-drenched setting is preparatory to the presentation of the symbol—the nightingale—in V and it provides sharp contrast to the horror of the dénouement. In the fashion of true lovers our lovers derive happiness from the birds' song. One is led here to speculate as to whether or not the wife commits two faults. Does she overindulge her pleasure, or fail to observe "mesure," and does her overindulgence reveal the love to her husband? An affirmative answer is suggested by the "tant . . . tant" of the opening line (79) of V and we can conclude that the wife and her lover bring tragedy on themselves and the bird. Marie merely suggests this and we must admire her understatement again.

V. (79-94) The Threat. This division is of 16 lines telling of the reaction of the husband who, disturbed by his wife, asks why she gets up and where she goes. His question is the result of her "desmesure" and it forces her to attempt to conceal her love by using a symbol. This attempt is, of course, a failure which means that the wife has revealed her love. The obstacles to love mentioned earlier and which were passive are now personalized in the husband who begins to participate actively in the action.

This is the central of the nine sections and in it Marie introduces her love symbol—the nightingale. The bird is named for the first time in line 85 of the poem's 160 or in line 79 of the plot's 150. We thus meet this charming and poetic symbol at approximately the mid-point of the *lai*. The subterfuge of the wife infuriates the husband who decides to trap the inoffensive bird-symbol. It should be noted that from this section on to the end of the poem the author and the three protagonists speak and act within the frame-work of the symbol. Once it is introduced there is no mention of love again.

VI. (95-110) Vengeance. This part has 16 lines wherein the husband carries out his resolution against the bird with a thoroughness which, through its disproportion, vividly suggests his restrained and silent anger at his wife. He controls his rage to the point that he never reproaches

her overtly. The extent of his fury is conveyed by his actions and Marie's understatement makes that fury all the more intense. His efforts against the bird are successful and his sardonic joy reflects his bitterness at his wife. Once more Marie uses irony—bitter irony, this time—in the words of the husband to the wife as he disposes of the symbol, "J'ai le laüstic englué / Pur quei vus avez tant veillé. / Desor poëz gisir en peis: / Il ne vus esveillerat meis," It is ironic because the bird's capture is the last thing that the wife wants; ironic because it will be a long time before she can sleep in peace; ironic because she, a true lover who should love the bird, has been the cause of its capture; ironic finally because the threat to the nightingale-symbol is a veiled threat to her and the love.

VII. (111-125) The Tragic Climax. There follows a section of 15 lines where the wife makes the mistake of asking for the symbol. Had she not asked for it, the bird would probably have survived. When he learns that she values the nightingale, the husband—again acting within the frame-work of the symbol—twists its neck, kills it and throws it on his wife. It falls on her breast and bloodies her *chainse*. The location of the blood stain, "Un peu desor le piz devant," (119) is meant to symbolize her wounded and bleeding heart or is a threat to her and her love.

VIII. (126-140) Dénouement. The Wife. The following fifteen lines present the reaction of the wife to the murder. Those who captured the bird have taken from her *grant hait* and the implication of the rest of her meditation is that the death of the love-symbol will impede and possibly destroy the love. To prevent any misunderstanding by her lover she sends him the body with the story of the bird's death. Logic forces us to ask why she can never get up again at night to see her lover or why she cannot see him at the window during the day or during her husband's absence. Logic also forces us to ask if the love relationship must remain permanently frustrated by the death of the bird. The answer must lie within the symbolism that Marie attached to the nightingale. The death of the symbol must mean the end of the love for nothing in the remainder of the poem suggests that the lovers will ever see each other again.

IX. (141-156) Dénouement. The Lover. Nothing is left to interest us and Marie except the reactions of the lover. They are told in 16 lines in which he conducts himself with the grief and sensitivity befitting a courtly lover. He has the body placed in a precious *chasse* as a reliquary which he will always carry with him.

The final four lines of the poem tell us that the *lai* was composed about the event and was called **"Laüstic."** Hence the name of the poem derives from the bird and the prominence of the symbol in the title and the plot indicates its importance.

It is of interest that Marie does not quote conversation between the lovers. We are told three times that they speak together (23, 41-42, 68) but we never hear them. A similar lack of words is most effective in the scenes between the husband and wife. The former never verbalizes his anger and jealousy and his silent bitterness is translated into cruel action rendered all the more intense by his wordless frustration. Similarly, the death of the bird is accompanied by silence. Apparently Marie felt that verbal expression of emotions would slow down the actions of her drama and would dilute the intensity of the suggested reactions which are all the more powerful for being left to the imagination of the audience. The poem also ends on a silent note. No words are exchanged directly between the lovers and no promises or reassurances are expressed. The story of frustrated love ends on a note of silence and of quiet acquiescence.

Marie uses direct conversation only three times (83-90, 105-110, 126-134). The first is the wife's explanation of her sleeplessness and the explanation introduces the symbol. The second quotation is the ironic joy of the husband at his capture of the bird. The final example is the wife's monologue about the death of the nightingale and the effect on the lover. It is of interest that the bird is the subject of the only direct discourse in the poem. Marie uses conversation to dramatize and emphasize the importance of the nightingale-symbol.

This study has attempted to demonstrate Marie's poetic and dramatic devices which are as valid today as they were in her day. Her use of symmetry and understatement enhance the dramatic quality of her tale. Her use of linking lines between sections serves to make a more cohesive poem. Her irony and contrast add poignancy and drama to the story. The symbol is a most poetic and felicitous one which enlists the sympathy and concern of the audience. Its use is also a means of economy and understatement. Finally, the use of concision, understatement and symbol forces us to contribute, through our imagination, to the drama which unfolds before us all the more effectively because of our creative participation in the tragedy.

Rupert T. Pickens (essay date 1973)

SOURCE: "'Equitan': Anti-'Guigemar'," in *Romance Notes,* Vol. XV, No. 2, Winter, 1973, pp. 361-67.

[*In the following excerpt, Pickens compares "Equitan" to the* lai *"Guigemar" and defends "Equitan" against those critics who call it an inferior* lai.]

No other *lai* of Marie de France has suffered more at the hands of critics than **"Equitan"** To Hoepffner it is nothing more than "un médiocre fait-divers sans grandeur qui fournirait plutôt matière à un fabliau ou à un conte drôlatique qu'à un de ces contes sentimentaux qui sont dans la manière de notre poétesse" [Ernest Hoepffner, *Les Lais de Marie de France,* n.d.]. Without its love casuistry, according to Moshé Lazar, "'**Equitan**'" n'aurait été qu'un fabliau de peu d'intérêt." [*Amour courtois et* fin'amors *dans la littérature du XIIe siècle,* 1964]. And Jeanne Wathelet-Willem wonders if such an embarrassing work

can really be by Marie de France, though she finally concludes that, despite Hoepffner, it is an "œuvre de début. Il est lourd, maladroit, sent le procédé d'école," and only out of a sense of motherly affection "pour un mal venu parmi ses enfants" did Marie slip it in among the other poems in her collection ["Equitan dans l'œuvre de Marie de France," *Le Moyen Age,* Vol. LXIX, 1963]. What offends these critics most is the last part of the *lai* (197-305), where the lovers hatch their unbelievable plot and come themselves to a cruelly ludicrous end and where adulterous "courtly" love seems to be heavy-handedly condemned—elements which would resemble most closely a *fabliau. Quandoque bonus dormitat Homerus.*

"Equitan" may be an *œuvre de jeunesse*—or, if Hoepffner is correct, one of the last *lais,* but which happens to be textually less rich than a **"Guigemar"** or an **"Eliduc"**; but it is completely worthy of Marie's art. It is more than a fable meant to illustrate a commonplace, more than a "mere" *fabliau.* It exemplifies the psychological and narrative subtelty typical of Marie, and "faults" in the tale such as the lack of verisimilitude in the lovers' plot are not due to Marie's lack of concern for construction and should be atributed to defects in the characters themselves rather than to ineptitude on the part of the author. **"Guigemar"** far from being out of place in Marie's work, has a definite function in the collection as a whole. It serves as an "anti-'**Guigemar**'"—not as a counterbalance which condemns a form of love seemingly extolled in **"Guigemar"** but rather because it illustrates that destiny and love operating in two men of essentially similar character can relentlessly push them in opposite directions.

Critics have long recognized the differences in the characters of Guigemar and Equitan, but the similarity of the heroes, in light of which the differences become significant, have not been stressed. Both heroes have positions of political pre-eminence in their countries. Equitan is already king of the Nantais, while Guigemar stands to succeed his father as lord of Saint-Pol-de-Léon. Both are urged to take a wife, certainly in order to stabilize the government and to insure their succession; but both are unwilling to do so because of their devotion to their ladies. Thus, in both heroes love is seen to interfere, at least temporarily, with the political processes which demand orderly succession and, therefore, with the social effectiveness of each man in his country. These points of comparison are obvious. Less apparent, however, is the fact that both men are presented as being socially ineffective even as their stories begin. Guigemar's initial "problem" is reported by Marie in terms of the hero's inability to function in a courtly society. He has no interest in any kind of love and has not paid court to ladies, and it is the opinion of society that, therefore, he is "peri." When he returns to Brittany after his forced separation from his lady and refuses to marry, he is just as ineffective as before, though not now because of any lack of interest in love. Equitan, likewise, is socially and politically ineffective even before he falls in love. He is indeed "jostise e reis" of Nantes (12), but it is his seneschal who wields the real power in his kingdom: "Tute sa tere li gardout / E meinteneit e justisout" (23-24). After Equitan falls in love, it is still the seneschal who "la curt teneit, / Les plaiz e les clamurs oiet" (195b-196), and when the king refuses to marry, he turns out, like Guigemar, to be no less effective than before.

The initial reasons why the heroes do not function in society are only superficially different. Equitan yields his authority to the seneschal because "Deduit amout e druërie" (15), because he passes his time hunting, jousting, and engaging in numerous short-lived courtly relationship with women. Guigemar, on the other hand, similarly hunts and jousts, but it is disinterest in sexual matters, rather than pursuit of pleasure, which causes him to be ineffective. However, both heroes are equally unaware of the power of Amurs and are unconscious of their destiny until they are forced into a fatal permanent relationship with a lady which is signified by wounds from the arrows of Amurs. Unlike Guigemar, Equitan may be predisposed to enter into a lecherous affair, and it is clear that his initial intentions are to make just another conquest (38 ff.); but once he is struck and wounded by Amurs, his passion assumes exactly the same characteristics as that suffered by the "innocent" Guigemar.

Both heroes suffer the usual physical and psychological pains of love once wounded and fall into a state of senselessness. Marie's statement about Equitan, "Tels est la mesure d'amer / Que nuls n'i deit reisun garder" (19-20), applies equally well to Guigemar. Guigemar forgets his country completely (382), recklessly engages in an adulterous affair hidden in the very bedchamber of a married woman, and, once discovered, boldly—and foolishly—fends off armed attackers with a mere clothes pole. At least Equitan and his lady are more discreet, realistically timing their assignations to correspond with apparently normal periodic bleedings (185 ff.), although, on the whole, love's unreason affects them just as profoundly as Guigemar and his lady.

Equitan's mental confusion is illustrated in the processes by which he reaches his "cynical" conclusion about his love and his lady: "Que devendreit sa curteisie, / S'ele n'amast de druërie?" (81-82). The king's "night thoughts" are a series of non-sequiturs and betray the absence of sens and cointise (58) concomitant with the arrow-wound. Beginning with a question about destiny (65-66), he recognizes the lady as the source of his anguish (67-69) and concludes that it is inevitable that he love her (70); however, he understands that he will do badly to love her because she is the wife of his seneschal (71-72), to whom he owes mutual faith and trust (73-74). He then speculates that should the seneschal discover it (what? the inevitability of his love is all that he has established thus far, not the decision to enter into an illicit relationship), he would be grieved (75-76). Nevertheless, it is better that the seneschal should suffer than that he be crazed for love of his lady (77-78). It would be better that such a beautiful lady had not been born if she did not take a lover (79-80); any man who loved her would be improved (81-82). Even so, if the seneschal did find out about it (!), he ought not to be grieved too much (85-86); rather, he cannot keep her for himself alone, and Equitan will share

her with him (87-88). [Emanuel J.] Mickel rightly sees the passage as a development of specious reasoning; it shows the ramblings of a man out of his senses with desire. ["A Reconsideration of the Lais of Marie de France," Speculum, vol. XLVI, 1971]. Equitan's disparate thoughts, grouped in one- and three-, but principally two-line sentences, are to be contrasted with the lady's far more sober four-line progressions in 117 ff.

If, as Mickel says, the processes of love are the same in **"Equitan"** and **"Guigemar,"** is the quality of the love all that different because in the one lai love is redemptive and in the other it brings about the destruction of the adulterers? The answer must be negative, for love in **"Guigemar"** is redemptive despite the "quality" of that love. The love of Guigemar and his lady leads, as in **"Equitan,"** the hero to commit adultery and to attempt murder; it also pushes the heroine to the brink of suicide in despair (a state of mortal sin) and causes the destruction of Meriadu and his castle. It also (temporarily) diminishes the hero by causing him to fail in his social and political roles. In strict moral terms, are Guigemar and his lady, adulterers who variously contemplate murder and suicide, any more pure than Equitan and his lady, adulterers who undertake to commit premeditated murder? Even in "courtly" terms, is the one love less intense, less everlasting than the other? Not at all. What apparently distinguishes the love in one lai from the love in the other is the narrator's attitude, what she emphasizes in one situation and neglects in the other. The husband in **"Guigemar"** is an old jaloux, Guigemar is uninitiated in the pleasures of love, the lady is mistreated by her husband and by Meriadu; the husband in **"Equitan"** is an upright man, Equitan is a past master at lechery, the lady is well treated by her husband. But these extenuating circumstances do not alter the essential similarities of the two pairs of lovers and the quality of their love, once the heroes are wounded by the arrows of Amurs.

The fundamental difference in the loves is the mere fact that the one turns out to be redemptive and the other destructive. Guigemar is destined by the marvellous hind and the Power whose voice it is to be redeemed by fatal love and to return to his country with his lady as his wife, to be a whole man and effective ruler despite the crimes which the love leads him to contemplate and commit. It is the destiny of Equitan, on the other hand, to be destroyed by fatal love and to fail in his attempt to make his lady his wife and thereby become an acceptable king, to remain subservient to the conventions of courtly love, because of the crimes which the love leads him to contemplate and commit. Guigemar wins despite his senselessness; Equitan loses because of it. Guigemar is destined to be saved by the magic boat and the hand of God; positive divine intervention does not operate in the life of Equitan.

The obvious sign of the difference in the destinies of the heroes is the character of the ladies whom they are meant to love. Guigemar's destiny leads him to love a woman presented as a worthy object of his passion. Physically as attractive as Equitan's lady, she is distinguished by being totally passive. Led by her bolder servant, she hesitates to enter the magic boat, where she finds Guigemar; she awaits Guigemar's declaration of love, even though she burns with desire; she suffers imprisonment by her husband and by Meriadu. Her only active undertaking is, ironically, a passive attempt at suicide. By contrast, Equitan's lady is active, bold, self-interested. Once the hero makes his tormented declaration, she immediately assumes control by directing the casuistic debate on the equality of lovers (this appears not to be her first affair), by reacting to the news that Equitan's advisors urge him to take a wife, and, finally, by formulating the fantastically inept murder plot. (That she would devise such a scheme indicates that, even so, she is still subject to an unreason paralleling that of Equitan, who accepts the plan without question.)

By no means is it suggested that the implied worthiness of the lady has anything to do *per se* with the character of the hero, that the hero is proved unworthy because he chooses to love a lady who is imperfect. Neither Guigemar nor Equitan has, in fact, a choice in the matter. Nor, therefore, can the character of the lady have anything to do with the "good" or "bad" quality of the hero's love. At the most, the ideal perfection of the lady is an indication of the kind of destiny to which the hero is subject.

"Guigemar" and "Equitan" are "about" fatal love and the two directions which an all-consuming passion can take. In one *lai* love leads to redemption; in the other, to ignoble defeat. Love itself is an amoral force and becomes "good" or "bad" only in terms of the happy or unfortunate outcome of the hero's destiny, of which it is an instrument. Circumstances which are conditions of destiny—Guigemar's opportunity to escape the jealous old husband somehow renders his love less adulterous once he is back in Brittany, while Equitan's immorality seems clearer because the loyal seneschal is always nearby—seem to color the moral picture, as does the apparent attitude of the narrator; but ultimately the similarities in the quality of the two kinds of love are not altered. It is in the sense that destiny leads the hero to destruction that "Guigemar" is an anti-"Guigemar."

One may agree, with Mme. Wathelet-Willem, that "Equitan" is the earliest *lai,* or, with Hoepffner, that it is the last; one may agree with the opinion of Robertson and Hoepffner that, *when she wrote it,* Marie fashioned a condemnation of Provençal love and lecherous passion or with the contention of Moshé Lazar that she was affirming the conventions of courtly love [see D. W. Robertson, Jr., "Love Conventions in Marie's *Equitan," RR,* vol. XLIV, 1953]. What matters more is the function of "Equitan" in the whole collection of *lais,* where it comes into association with "Guigemar" and ten others. The evidence of the Harley manuscript and the Old Norse translation, the existence of the two prologues, and line 22 of "Guigemar" indicate that Marie chose "Guigemar" to appear first in the collection, even though it is probably not first in order of composition. Less positive statements can be made about the intended position of "Equitan," but it does follow "Guigemar" in the Harley manuscript and the Old Norse translation, and the "bridge" at the end of "Equitan" indicates that it was meant to

precede "Fresne" (rather than follow, as in B.N., nouv. acq. fr. 1104). It seems to me that there is, therefore, a strong possibility that "Guigemar" and "Equitan" together were selected to introduce the collection of *lais.* If the suggestion is acceptable, then their function for "setting the tone" of the collection by presenting contrastive destinies is clear, and more might be said about the role of destiny in the entire collection. Even if not, however, "Equitan" would still stand as an anti-"Guigemar" in a more loosely defined system of organization.

Frederick Hodgson (essay date 1974)

SOURCE: "Alienation and the Otherworld in 'Lanval,' 'Yonec,' and 'Guigemar'," in *Comitatus,* Vol. V, 1974, pp. 19-31.

[*In the following essay, Hodgson discusses Marie's use of the supernatural in her* lais *to highlight the conflict between society and love that her characters face.*]

Much of the critical attention devoted to the *lais* of Marie de France has been directed toward tracing the origin of the motifs which constitute their framework. By determining the nature of the tradition which inspired Marie, source critics have hoped to measure her originality, her role in the creation of one of the richest of medieval genres. Since the results of such historical investigation have been ambiguous, critics like Emmanuel Mickel have recently focused on a more internal examination of the *lais* in a search for their common themes. But even this intrinsic analysis, when confronted with the numerous motifs from Celtic folklore which consistently buttress the action of the *lais,* either fails to assimilate these elements or dismisses them as superfluous structural devices. Such is the conclusion of Mickel in his article "A Reconsideration of the *Lais* of Marie de France" [in *Speculum,* Vol. 42, 1967] when he writes: ". . . the Celtic folklore motifs, often connected with the magical element, have yielded little help in making an over-all interpretation. The tracing of various motifs and their elucidation in terms of Celtic lore have not provided the key, but have added only another source of difficulty for one who tries to assimilate the action of the *lais* and the motifs."

It is my purpose to demonstrate, through an internal analysis of the role of the Celtic Otherworld in the *lais* of "Lanval," "Yonec," and "Guigemar," the crucial importance of the *merveilleux celtique* in the evolution of Marie's art. Through these *lais* can be traced an evolving relationship between the social reality which initially confronts the characters and the Celtic Otherworld which offers itself as an alternative. Marie profits from the readily available Otherworld of Celtic mythology because it lends itself so well to a portrait of an alienated character who must transcend the social circumstances of his *malaise* in order to love.

Gerhart B. Ladner, in his article "*Homo viator:* Medieval Ideas on Alienation and Order," [in *Speculum,* Vol. 42,

1967] provides an excellent survey of the ideas of alienation as they evolved from medieval Christian thought. He emphasizes the importance of the period between the eleventh and the thirteenth centuries for the ascendance of a missionary *habitus* in the monastic orders and points out that this ideological shift could also be seen both in the evolution of a feudal order which was to produce the chivalric ideals of the High Middle Ages and in a literature wherein appeared the figure of the knight-errant "who must seek out the hostile forces of the world and find his own self in a ceaseless course of *avanture*." The early doctrinal alienation of the monastic orders had become, in the literature of the later Middle Ages, a search for identity and values. Examined in terms of this search, Marie's Otherworld *lais* reveal a sophisticated concept of character and the priority of theme over the content of her sources.

Tom Peete Cross, in his article "Celtic Elements in the Lays of 'Lanval' and 'Graelent,'" [in *Modern Philology*, Vol. 12, 1914-15] has demonstrated the Celtic origin of many of the motifs which Marie uses in **"Lanval."** An examination of the *lai* reveals, within this Celtic framework, a detailed portrait of alienation. Lanval, the stranger at Arthur's court, is so incessantly denied the socially recognized tributes generally afforded worthy knights that an entirely different reality will for him supplant the world of the court and become the source of the love interest of the *lai*. The first twenty lines constitute the introduction in which the undeserved alienation of Lanval from Arthur's court is reinforced by a description of royal affluence which renders more severe the injustice Lanval suffers as the king forgets to reward him for his services.

> Asez i dona riches duns
> E as cuntes e as baruns
> A ceus de la table r[o]ünde—
> N'ot tant de teus en tut le munde—
> Femmes e tere departi,
> Par tut, fors un ki l'ot servi:
> Ceo fu Lanval, ne l'en sovient. . . .

To underline Lanval's solitude, Marie has emphasized the richness of the court for ironic purposes and included women among the prizes denied Lanval, thus removing this world's love from his future. The description of Lanval which follows will reinforce the unfairness of the oversight in that he is not only noble, but far away from the comfort of familial rights. Marie adds that the unjust treatment has lasted so long that Lanval has been left destitute.

After presenting this portrait of alienation, Marie describes Lanval's departure from the court and his arrival at the meadow where the servants of the fairy mistress will come to meet him. The contrast between Lanval's state of mind when he first reaches the meadow ("Il ne veit chose ke li plaise" v. 52) and his vision of the fairy servants ("Unc n'en ot veü[es] plus beles" v. 56) foreshadows the reversal of fortune the Otherworld will bring. The Otherworld will become an alternative to the injustice of Arthur's court.

An essential part of the relevant Celtic mythology is that the fairy mistresses visit the *real* world to search for a lover they have already decided upon. The fairy's servants are definitely coming for Lanval and Lanval only.

> 'Sire Lanval, ma demeisele,
> Que tant est pruz e sage e bele,
> Ele nus enveie pur vus;
> Kar i venez ensemble od nus!
> Sauvement vus i cundurums.
> Veez, pres est li paveilluns!'
>
> (vv. 71-76)

The result of the fairy's predisposition is a sense of fatality which envelops the characters. Their respective situations are similar in that the fairy, like Lanval, is a stranger in the land.

> 'Lanval,' fet ele, 'beus amis,
> Pur vus vienc jeo fors de ma tere;
> De luinz vus sui venu[e] quere.'
>
> (vv. 110-112)

This parallel characterization will be thoroughly developed in **"Yonec"** and **"Guigemar."** In **"Lanval,"** the fairy mistress bestows upon Lanval unlimited wealth with which he shall attempt to re-establish his value at Arthur's court. Thus the Otherworld, responding immediately to the injustice of the Arthurian world, presents Lanval with an alternative reality.

> Lanval donout les riches duns,
> Lanval aquitout les prisuns,
> Lanval vesteit les jugleurs,
> Lanval feseit les granz honurs:
> N'i ot estrange ne privé
> A ki Lanval n'eüst doné.
>
> (vv. 208-214)

Lanval uses his wealth to help those whose alienated plight reflects his own. The incantation of Lanval's name underlines his newfound opportunity to establish a deserved identity and foreshadows the attention he will bring upon himself, not only that of the other knights, but also of the queen who is struck by his worthiness.

Unfortunately, Lanval's wealth creates a new obstacle. The Celtic motif of the exacted promise of confidence reflects the fact that the values of the two worlds are incompatible. Forbidden to reveal his love to the Arthurian court, he must remain different, estranged. The incompatibility of the two realities bursts forth in the episode of the queen's infatuation. Finally, love in the Arthurian court is offered to Lanval. Ironically enough, what better way might there be to escape all alienation than to become the queen's lover, and thus a surrogate king? But Lanval remains faithful to his fairy mistress, and his alienation is nowhere more evident than in the reaction of the disappointed queen who, accusing Lanval of being a misfit at the court, touches upon a thing which could cause him to betray his secret.

> 'Lanval,' fet ele, 'bien le quit,
> Vus n'amez gueres cel delit;

Asez le m'ad hum dit sovent
Que des femme n'avez talent.
Vallez avez bien afeitez,
Ensemble od eus vus deduiez.
Vileins cuarz, mauveis failliz,
Mut est mi sires maubailliz
Que pres de lui vus ad suffert . . .

(277-285)

This accusation, put in terms of a dislike for women and an unfitness for duty, reflects all the problems Lanval has had with the Arthurian court and succeeds, by the strength of its invective, in forcing Lanval to break his promise of secrecy.

The queen's jealous, unjust reaction to the revelation that he has a lover represents the apex of Lanval's estrangement from the court since he stands accused, as a criminal, of solliciting her favors. This repetition of injustice reinforces the fatality with which the story unfolds and by which the appearance of another reality seems thematically justified. Note also the presence of the parallels, which had previously been suggested only by the similarity between Lanval and the fairy mistress, between the court reality and the Otherworld; for the movement of alienation is now double. In the same moment that Lanval becomes an accused criminal in Arthur's court, he loses his fairy mistress's love by a defensively proud impulse which leads to his breaking faith. The height of this spiraling alienation is suggested by mention of suicide, solitude, and insanity.

The dénouement of **"Lanval"** involves the gradual, albeit momentary, merging of the Arthurian and fairy worlds, a merging which makes possible the dispensing of justice with which Marie always rewards her morally deserving couples. The preliminary apparition of the fairy servants prepares for the appearance of the fairy mistress whose arrival immediately establishes, on account of her unsurpassed beauty, the legitimacy of Lanval's love in the eyes of the court. His spiriting away to the only world where his deserved love can be consummated is consistent with the theme of alienation. Thus the resolution of **"Lanval"** reveals a love which transcends the single reality of the Arthurian court whose unjust, restricted nature is demonstrated by the movement of the alienated principal character. Social reality is surpassed by the evocation of a deeper, psychological one. This multivalence of reality realized by Marie through her choice and use of source material will be reproduced, with similar effects, in **"Yonec"** and **"Guigemar."**

Different critical approaches have been used to associate the *lai* of **"Yonec"** with **"Lanval."** For example, Ernest Hoepffner sees the influence of *Brut* and the *Roman de Thèbes* in **"Yonec"** and **"Lanval,"** and consequently judges this relative youth by its increasing influence. "'Yonec' se placerait donc chronologiquement dans le voisinage de 'Lanval' et l'un comme l'autre assez au début de l'activité de Marie" ["Pour la chronologie des lais de Marie de France," *Romania*, Vol. 60, 1934]. However, an important development takes place in the course of these *lais*,

a development whose foundation was carefully laid in **"Lanval."** The relationship between the Arthurian court and the fairy world in **"Lanval,"** the momentary merging of the real and the fantastic which permitted a just resolution of the plot, and the intense character portrayal made possible by this multiplicity of realities are all manifested in their general outlines and their thematic implications suggested in **"Yonec."**

The theme of the *mal mariée* which introduces us to the action of **"Yonec"** is a particularly apt point of departure for a portrayal of alienation. The psychological *distance* between the lady and her husband is illustrated both in terms of age and in the *convenience* character of the marriage which had been effected to produce heirs. The description of the lady's beauty clashes ironically with the motif of imprisonment, a motif which is enriched by the presence of the husband's old, widowed sister who is more a guard than a potentially friendly interlocutor. Marie depicts the lady's alienation by describing her personal solitude, her physical suffering, and her consequent loss of beauty. Preparing the way for the lady's soliloquy in which she curses her destiny, Marie describes the departure of both the husband and the old woman and mentions for the first time the closing of the imprisoning doors which, repeated several times in the *lai*, represents well the way in which Marie chooses peripheral detail to support larger themes. Solitude allows the lady to vent her frustrations and she does so, touching upon her birth, her fate, her isolation from God and individuals, and the emptiness of her life with this oppressive husband. In short, she covers the gamut of alienation in her despair; and in her unhappiness, begins to reject her present reality.

First she blames her relatives who are responsible for the arrangement of her marriage, then begins to dream of valiant knights in a temporal context completely removed from her present state. The immediate appearance of the falcon and its subsequent metamorphosis represents the advent of a different reality which could correspond to the lady's needs. A merging of these two realities is manifested in the *courtly* behavior of this figure from folklore and its subsequent demonstration of Christian behavior. This shape-shifting character insists that he, too, has been the victim of years of frustration while waiting for the lady's summons. Thus we see the same kind of necessity coupling these characters from ostensibly different realms that we saw in **"Lanval"** and an even stronger suggestion of the merging of realities, of their rapprochement at the stimulus of an intense love.

It is at this point that the theme of the lady's appearance becomes pivotal. We remember the consistent decline of her beauty during the period of increasing oppression in her imprisoned reality. Her new reality, however, restores her condition, just as the Otherworld had re-established Lanval's position at Arthur's court. Unfortunately she repeats Lanval's mistake, violating *mesur*, for this sudden recovery of beauty brings about the suspicions which lead to the husband's knowledge of their love. The subsequent brutal wounding of the knight in his animal form shows the incompatibility of the two realities. Here, however, Marie carries the rapprochement between the realms much further than in **"Lanval."** During the lady's adventure into the Otherworld she sees other knights seemingly available to fulfill the needs of reality-rejecting damsels. In addition, her own knight warns her that his world would be just as hostile to her as hers is to him if she were discovered there. More importantly, the folklore motif of the predicted childbirth provides a framework on which will rest the ultimate dénouement where the appearance of the knight's *this-world* tomb can only signal the fusion of the various realities which the alienation and love had originally revealed.

Besides the observations concerning the relationship between the Otherworld and the theme of alienation which our internal analysis of **"Lanval"** and **"Yonec"** has provided, a highly interesting progression between the two *lais* deserves comment, for it is relevant to an analysis of **"Guigemar."** The essential difference between the two *lais féeriques* resides in the tragic tone which pervades the dénouement of **"Yonec"** but finds no analogue in the tone of **"Lanval."** The death and vengeance which mark **"Yonec"** are totally absent from **"Lanval."** Both of the *lais* have as their point of departure two realities which allow a portrait of alienation and unfound love. And yet, the autonomy and integrity of the realities which allow Lanval to escape the oppression of the Arthurian world to *live happily ever after,* dissolve in **"Yonec"** where the similarity of the two worlds receives, as we have shown, greater emphasis. The fusion of the two realities, first indicated in the motif of a child born of one mortal and one supernatural parent, becomes complete in the dénouement where the supernatural knight from the fairy world has been transformed into a *this-world* king whose tomb provokes Yonec's revenge. The combination of the two realities, foreshadowed by the important change in the lady's appearance, results in the violence perpetrated against the fairy knight and allows the ultimate justice provided by Yonec's vengeance. In other words, Marie suppresses the Otherworld framework once it has provided for a certain psychological portrait as well as the unfolding of the destiny of similar characters. Without undermining the importance of the *cadre féerique* in the portrait of certain psychologies, the progression from **"Lanval"** to **"Yonec"** is the gradual disappearance of the Otherworld. The theme, the psychological ramifications of repressed love and its ultimate effect on reality, outweighs the motif, the Otherworld. This tendency is clearly manifest in **"Guigemar,"** where the fairy mistress disappears from the Celtic scenario, leaving a purely human setting.

Source critics have spent much time trying to establish the origins of the various motifs used in **"Yonec."** The most conclusive result of their investigations is an affirmation of the originality of at least the combination of motifs, whatever their origins. Nevertheless, the closest a source critic comes to admitting Marie's creative role is in this statement of R. N. Illingworth's: "Not only do the very obvious inconsistencies between the various parts of the *lai* suggest that this combination of originally diverse

material was made in recent versions, but the possible influence of the Tristan legend on the precise manner in which [the knight] is wounded and of the *mal mariée* tradition would both seem to indicate that the story was considerably modified by the hands of an author familiar with Old French literary traditions" ["Celtic Tradition and the Lay of *Yonec, Etudes Celtiques,* Vol. 9, 1961]. The progression between **"Lanval"** and **"Yonec"** manifest in the evolution of character and the increasing rapprochement of different realities whose function has been to describe alienated characters surely explain the logic of these motifs' juxtaposition. Marie has used the revenge story to manifest the verisimilitude of the characters' love and its capacity to justify itself through vengeance against the reality which had tried to reject it. The source controversy involved with **"Guigemar"** is remarkably similar; and the similar explanation we shall offer will hopefully emphasize the originality of the thematic design in these *lais.*

The rather bizarre structure of **"Guigemar"** has been the object of numerous critics who consistently point out the incongruities of the plot, analyzing them in terms of a somewhat awkward combination of stories of different origins. Illingworth sees in **"Guigemar"** the simple juxtaposition of two stories. "They are a story on which 'Guigemar' 11. 27-554 was based, which described how an all powerful fairy lured a chosen mortal to her fairy island, and a story on which 'Guigemar' 11. 693-882 was modelled, which told how a lady, held against her will in a castle by an amorous knight, was rescued by her lover." However, he assumes that this plot conception preceded characterization when he writes: "When these two themes were combined to form the lay as we know it, the compiler recognized the paradox which was created in the character of the lady and realized that it would have to be eradicated if the new composite story was to possess any unity. He attempted to eradicate the fault by making the supernatural elements . . . appear independent of the lady." The question of why a *compiler* would link such seemingly disparate stories together, a process involving the dismissal of a main character—the fairy mistress—half way through the plot without some previous thematic conception does not occur to Illingworth. The *éléments féeriques* offer a very suitable opportunity for the portrayal of an alienated individual who must ultimately turn away from the available reality to find the love which has been absent from it. We have already seen this thematic conception in **"Lanval"** and **"Yonec"** where the emphasis on a detailed representation of one kind of alienation or another, so carefully carried out, has not gained sufficient critical attention. In **"Guigemar"** we see a logical result of such structuring which had been increasingly accompanied by an equalizing of the realities involved which had the effect of underlining the fatality of the love. By replacing the fairy mistress with a mortal woman and retaining the fairy elements useful in a portrait of the fated love of alienated characters, Marie has maintained in her story the multiplicity of realities and simultaneously produced a purely human conflict. While **"Guigemar"** is traditionally placed at the head of the *recueil* of Marie, most critics agree that it is younger than "Lanval" and "Yonec." Hoepffner, who has already substantiated for us the temporal proximity of "Lanval" and "Yonec," writes: "'Guigemar' n'est pas le plus ancien des lais, malgré la place que Marie lui attribue en tête de son oeuvre. 'Lanval' a dû chronologiquement le devancer. . . ." We need now to examine the alienation in "Guigemar," the role of the Otherworld, and the parallel characterization permitted by the replacement of the fairy mistress by a mortal woman, a *mal mariée.*

Although Guigemar has accomplished all the exploits necessary to become a knight he is unable to love. Marie devotes twelve lines to a description of his repressed nature which denies love and has led to his being singled out by others. She highlights the regressive nature of this alienation by mentioning that Guigemar returns to his family *en la fleur de sun meillur pris (v. 69).* The family generally plays no part in knightly adventure. That his repression involves this kind of regression is surely a tribute to Marie's psychological insight, an insight which appears in the hunting scene where Guigemar comes upon a doe with stag horns and a fawn—a familial setting against which Guigemar vents aggression which cannot be explained in terms of the hunt, since the larger party has left him behind. This is another example of his regression, his separation from others, and, hence, his alienation. We see the arrow of Guigemar's aggression rebound against him, reinforcing the solitary focus of his *malaise* which is dramatized in his journey, a movement of explicit self-distancing.

> Puis est muntez, d'iluec s'en part;
> Ke esloignez seit mult li est tart:
> Ne volt ke nul des suens i vienge,
> Kil desturbast ne kil retienge.
>
> (vv. 141-144)

Marie uses a series of Celtic motifs to describe Guigemar's search for a cure. The apparent ease with which he finds the supernatural ship is a result of the suppression in the story of the fairy mistress who would be drawing Guigemar towards her—the motif of the fairy disguised as a speaking, antlered white hind being the first example, as Illingworth points out, of this undercover character used to emphasize the fatality of the events unfolding. Illingworth calls this *the Otherworld induction motif.*

The similarity between the lovers which had been suggested in "Lanval" and more extensively developed in "Yonec," is most clearly portrayed in "Guigemar." Once the fantastic voyage has been made, we focus on the character of the lady who, trapped as a *mal mariée,* reflects the loveless plight which is also Guigemar's condition. Familiar now with the subtle relationship between source and theme, we should no longer be bothered by what most critics call the *incongruities* of the composition of this *lai.* Illingworth, failing to consider the possibility of the priority of theme over source, sees the Celtic induction motif in "Guigemar" as truncated, dismissed as soon as the *compiler* realized the contradiction it seems to create in the character of the powerless lady. In actuality, Marie has used the induction motif to invoke the

realities which can serve to demonstrate the course of alienation as well as to paint a deterministic view of love's fatality. But she has simply chosen a human counterpart for Guigemar's affections.

In "Yonec," we saw Marie depict the alienation and isolation of her character using a point of departure in the *mal mariée* tradition, the woman trapped in a tower by a jealous husband. With this same starting point in the second part of "Guigemar," Marie waxes literary to underline the lady's alienation. She describes murals in the lady's chamber which depict Venus, goddess of love, in the act of burning Ovid's *Remedia amoris.* Stephen Damon sees this as a projection of the mental state of an unhappy woman wishing for love, since a jealous husband would surely not allow such suggestive art in the room of an imprisoned wife.

The construction of the *lai* represents an attempt to confront both characters, similar in their repressed love, with an alternative reality. The extensive use of allusions to Ovid's work is interesting in this respect for it provides a detailed perspective on suppressed love, the suffering which is the result of its *infection,* and the happiness which comes from its open avowal. Ovidean love is appropriate in view of the alienated, solitary psychology of both her characters for whom the expression of love must involve the conquest of a lifelong repression. Hoepffner used the growing influence of Ovid, an influence which he ascribes to Marie's familiarity with the *Enéas,* in his chronological analysis of the *lais* without noticing the strong thematic affinity this source has with previous *lais.* "Entre 'Lanval' d'un part, 'Guigemar' et 'Eliduc' de l'autre, se place donc cet événement capital [knowledge of the *Enéas*]. Elle y apprend surtout à voir et à traiter les problèmes psychologiques de l'amour. De ceux-ci il n'y a pas trace dans 'Lanval.'" Although Hoepffner underestimates the psychological portrait of Lanval, it is true that the earlier *lai* lacks the psychological profundity which characterizes the love interest in "Guigemar." Nevertheless, this new profundity seems possible precisely because of the kind of psychological foundation exemplified extensively in both "Lanval" and "Yonec." The Otherworld elements preserve the background of dual reality which Marie uses to show the transcendent value of the love and the fatality which envelops even the most alienated personalities. The Ovidean motifs carry this conception further into the psychologies of these characters who suffer in the struggle to consummate their love in the face of social obstacles.

The evolution of these Otherworld *lais* illustrates a definite progression of artistic inspiration, centering upon the relationship of different realities. In "Lanval" the distinctness of the two realms allows an almost *deus ex machina* resolution to the love of the alienated pair. In "Yonec" we see the distance between the realities fade. When they merge they provide a tragic resolution to their incompatibility. In "Guigemar" the Otherworld provides a very efficacious structure from which a purely human conflict is launched, the fairy herself being absent from the plot. In each *lai* the fairy elements underline the fatality of the love involved and serve simultaneously to portray, through their function as an alternative reality, the profound alienation of the characters. The clear progression which the manipulation of Otherworld motifs in these *lais* represents reveals an artistic interest in alienated characters which thematically unites these stories and explains what critics have called their conceptual *incongruities*. The Otherworld *lais* contain the most penetrating characterizations of Marie's *oeuvre* and are fertile ground for the demonstration of her evolving, synthesizing genius.

Emanuel J. Mickel, Jr. (essay date 1975)

SOURCE: "The Unity and Significance of Marie's 'Prologue'," in *Romania,* Vol. 96, No. 1, 1975, pp. 83-91.

[*In the following essay, Mickel offers a line-by-line analysis and reinterpretation of the difficult "Prologue" to Marie de France's* Lais.]

The importance of Marie's **"Prologue"** has been recognized by scholars since the earliest studies of the **Lais.** To early scholars, interested in the origin of the *lai* as a literary form and in establishing the sources which Marie used, the interpretation of lines 33 to 42 of the **"Prologue"** was crucial to an understanding of the literary history of the text. Because they did not relate to the problem of the origins of the genre and collection, the first 27 lines received less attention. Although lines 33 to 42 present difficulties of interpretation, the first 27 lines are more obscure from a grammatical and syntactic standpoint and have long presented a problem.

In the past thirty or forty years scholars have become increasingly aware of the sophisticated nature of mediaeval literature and the multiple levels of meaning which writers of the period consciously threaded through the fabric of their texts. Professor Spitzer's 1943 article on Marie's **"Prologue"** changed the focus of attention to the first 27 lines. He related her statement in the opening lines of the **"Prologue"** to other mediaeval poetics of the period and asserted that Marie was aware of her role as "poeta philosophus et theologus" in writing the **Lais** [Leo Spitzer, "The Prologue to the *Lais* of Marie de France and Medieval Poetics," *Modern Philology,* Vol. 41, 1943]. Continuing Professor Spitzer's argument, D. W. Robertson suggested [in "Marie de France, *Lais,* Prologue, 13-15," *Modern Language Notes,* Vol. 64, 1949] that the threefold level of meaning found in many mediaeval texts was actually indicated by Marie in lines 11 to 15:

> Pur ceus ki a venir esteient
> E ki aprendre les deveient
> K'i peüssent gloser la lettre
> E de lur sen le surplus mettre.

Professor Robertson interpreted the expression "gloser la lettre" in terms of the grammatical structure (littera), the term "sen" as the apparent meaning of the text (sensus)

and the "surplus" as the doctrinal content (sententia) which the interpreters could find in the text's meaning.

In his explanation of lines 9-22, Professor Spitzer basically followed the interpretation rendered by R. Meissner, but with significant alterations. He agreed that the implication of the passage is that future generations, wiser and more intelligent, will be able to add significantly to the understanding of the text. However, following the lead of E. R. Curtius, he extends considerably the meaning of "li philosophe":

> . . . she tells us that the ancients (probably the pagan poets) expressed themselves *obscurement . . . pur cels qui a venir esteient,* that is to say, for future interpreters or readers (not only for the *authors* to come, as Meissner would have it). Marie de France, thinking "medievally" as did the Archpriest, sees her own book as only another "text", which will be "glossed", after the model of the Old Testament commented on by Tertullian, Augustine, Jerome, etc.—after the model of Virgil and Ovid "moralized". The *lur sen (sen* = Germ. *sin, sens)* is obviously the "Christian" attitude (the *intelletto sano* of Dante) in which the interpreters consult the pagan authors—authors whose *purpose* it was . . . to veil, with the obscurity of poetic form, the eternal verities; doubtless, Marie feels constrained to excuse, in harmony with the apologists, the fictional matter of which she treats as well as the poetic form of her *lais.*

The "philosophe" of line 16 are the "poetae theologi-philosophi":

> These philosophical poets have themselves experienced the changes brought about by time: time has given the correct, the Christian, interpretation of the ancient authors. . . .

This interpretation caused Professor Spitzer to make a basic alteration in his reading of lines 20-22:

> For *cels qui a venir esteient,* the generations to come, interpreters or 'just readers', will guard against deviating, in their 'glosses', from the true contents (*ceo qu'i ert*) of the ancient works. All the instinctive orthodoxy of the Middle Ages is here in this *ceo qu'i ert;* in any poetic work there is only one doctrine, the Christian doctrine, the 'right' ("Paiens unt tort, Chrestiens unt *dreit*"). Marie knows that her poetic tales have a Christian significance and that the 'subtlety' of future commentators will be exercised to discover that immutable Christian truth. . . .

Thus the future commentators do not simply elucidate the obscurities of the text by means of their increased learning. Because of the passage of time, they are able to render the true, Christian meaning now apparent. Hence, Spitzer joins Meissner in denying a didactic meaning to lines 21 and 22. Instead, he translates these lines to mean that the future readers "will guard against deviating, in their 'glosses', from the true contents (*ceo qu'i ert*) of the ancient works".

In 1961 Professor Donovan [in "Priscian and the Obscurity of the Ancients," *Speculum,* Vol. 36, 1961] sought to clarify lines 9-16 of the **"Prologue"** where Marie makes reference to the Latin grammarian, Priscian, apparently referring to the opening line of the *Institutiones*. In essence, he objects to the notion that Priscian stated that the ancients deliberately wrote obscurely and he further attempts to demonstrate that the 12th and 13th century writers themselves did not understand Priscian in this way but rather in a progressive sense. If the ancients wrote obscurely (according to Priscian) it was not because of any intent to include multiple levels of understanding, but because of ignorance: they would not live to see the unfolding of events. If moderns could add the "surplus", it is because of their knowledge of events since the writings of the ancient texts. In proof of his interpretation, Professor Donovan attempts to prove that contemporaries of Marie did not understand Priscian's opening line as indicating deliberate obscurity. The few writers cited by Professor Donovan who actually commented on the Priscian text do indeed emphasize the enlightenment of later generations. However, each individual cited was referring directly to the line from Priscian in its context and specifically intended his comments to pertain to grammar or history. Is not Marie's reference to Priscian clearly out of context, divorced from the opening line's emphasis on grammar, and is it not rather simply a reference to Priscian's statement corroborating the fact that the ancients wrote obscurely? I believe that Marie's meaning must be interpreted in the context of the first 27 lines of her **"Prologue"** and not in terms of contemporaries commenting directly on the meaning of Priscian's opening line in the context he employs. In his interpretation Professor Donovan used the translation of the **"Prologue"** offered by Professor Ewert, a version which supports his thesis. It is my contention that this section of the **"Prologue"** has long been misinterpreted and that Professor Donovan's thesis is not consistent with the meaning of Marie's text or with the rhetorical development of the passage.

The interpretation of the first eight lines of the **"Prologue"** presents few problems:

> Ki Deus ad duné escïence
> E de parler bon' eloquence
> Ne s'en deit taisir ne celer,
> Ainz se deit volunters mustrer.
> Quant uns granz biens est mult oïz,
> Dunc a primes est il fluriz,
> E quant loëz est de plusurs,
> Dunc ad espandues ses flurs.

Marie begins with the general maxim or thesis that God-given talents should be developed. It is the obligation of the writer who has been granted both *"escience"* and *"eloquence"* to make use of his gifts. In good mediaeval style, lines four to eight develop the thesis metaphorically in using the flower imagery to illustrate the beneficent results when the *"granz biens"* is sown and allowed to flourish.

It is at this point that scholars begin to differ on the interpretation of the text. Often lines 9-16 are seen as a unit. It is my contention that they simply form the basic thesis of which lines 17-27 are the amplification or show the results. The structure restates the two-part rhetorical development of the first eight lines. Lines 9-16 represent an amplified restatement of the original thesis (lines 1-4). Just as lines 1-4 are followed by the metaphorical development in lines 4-8, so do lines 17-27 illustrate the thesis in lines 9-16:

> Custume fu as ancïens,
> Ceo tes[ti]moine Precïens,
> Es livres ke jadis feseient
> Assez oscurement diseient
> Pur ceus ki a venir esteient
> E ki aprendre les deveient,
> K'i peüssent gloser la lettre
> E de lur sen le surplus mettre.

It seems clear from the text that Marie believed that the ancients wrote obscurely for those who would study the texts at a later time and who might be able to comment on the text and to add their understanding to it. Before deciding that Marie does not mean what she says (because her sense seemingly contradicts contemporary opinion), one should see if the text is consistent with what follows. It seems to me that this is where the real misunderstanding lies. Professor Ewert's translation [Oxford, 1965] of lines 17-22 implies a sense of progress which is alien to the sense and rhetorical development of the text:

> Li philosophe le saveient
> E par eus memes entendeient,
> Cum plus trespasserunt le tens,
> Plus serreient sutil de sens
> E plus se savreient garder
> De ceo k'i ert, a trespasser.

Lines 17 and 18 are clear enough, but in line 19 the third person plural verb in the future tense, *trespasserunt,* poses a problem. It is clear that *tens* is the object of the verb and that the subject is implied in the verb ending. But does this mean, then, that the verb *trespasserunt* refers to the aging of the *philosophe*? If so, is one to believe then that man gains in intelligence and perspicacity as time goes by or with the arrival of successive generations? If this be the meaning, then where is the relationship to the preceding lines concerning the study and glossing of texts? And how does this meaning relate to lines 23-27? I believe that line 19 refers directly to the statement or thesis of lines 12-16: The philosophers knew it (understood the importance of the study and elucidation of the obscure texts) and understood among themselves that the more they (future commentators) will spend time, the more they would become subtle of mind (the more they would gain in intellectual perspicacity) and the more they would know how to keep themselves from suffering or going through that which was contained therein (i. e., that those who would study the texts would profit from its lessons and would thereby be able to avoid similar situations in their own lives). *Trespasserunt* refers not to their growing old, but to the time they spend studying the difficult texts. Grappling with these texts sharpens the mind and the lessons in the texts cause them to gain in wisdom. Their increased acumen and understanding has the practical moral consequence of equipping them to cope with life and to avoid some of life's misery.

Not only is this interpretation consistent textually, but it conforms precisely to the sense of lines 9-16. In fact, it is clearly the elaboration or result of the general statement presented in these lines. Moreover, lines 23-27 confirm the interpretation and complete the rhetorical development:

> Ki de vice se volt defendre
> Estudïer deit e entendre
> E grevos' ovre comencier:
> Par [ceo] se puet plus esloignier
> E de grant dolur delïvrer.

Line 23 relates directly to the preceding lines. It is the immediate consequence of Marie's thesis: "Whoever wishes to keep himself from vice must study and understand and begin a 'grevos ovre'. By this means one is able to remove and deliver himself from great grief".

At this point one can see how carefully Marie has joined the two prominent theses of her **"Prologue"**. It is the phrase, "grevos' ovre", which is the key. It refers both to the scholar who begins the serious study of the obscure texts, from which he gains the "granz biens", as well as to the writer whose obligation it is to use his talents by beginning such a work. This is manifest in lines 28-30 ("Pur ceo comencai a penser / De aukune bone estoire faire / E de latin en romaunz traire"), where Marie relates her own reason for undertaking this work to the preceding argument.

In the context of this **"Prologue"**, it would be amiss not to stress the beautiful integrity of the text: when God-given talents are sown, the *"granz biens"* can then flourish (l. 1-8). As an example she chooses the ancients. They wrote obscurely with the knowledge that later generations would pore over the texts (l. 9-16). These later generations reap the *"granz biens"* which was sown (l. 17-22). But it should be noted that the writer who spreads the *"granz biens"* to others receives as much as he gives (l. 23-30). It is perhaps no accident that the philosophical implications of the "Prologue" accord so harmoniously with the sentiment and basic meaning of two of Marie's most important and attractive *lais*, **"Le Fresne"** and **"Eliduc"**.

Samuel T. Cowling (essay date 1975)

SOURCE: "The Image of the Tournament in Marie de France's 'Le Chaitivel'," in *Romance Notes,* Vol. XVI, No. 3, Spring, 1975, pp. 686-91.

[*In the following essay, Cowling refutes critical opinion that the lady in the* lai *"Chaitivel" is selfish and cruel.*]

That the *lais* of Marie de France concentrate upon delicate feelings and exquisite emotions has long been recog-

nized. Years ago J. D. Bruce wrote [in *The Evolution of Arthurian Romance From the Beginnings Down to the Year 1300,* 1928] of the romantic charm and grace of the *lais,* and Gaston Paris characterized the tone of Marie's work as "tendre et mélancolique" [*La Litterature française au moyen age,* 1909]. More recently John Stevens has argued that in the *lais* Marie creates images—objects, incidents, or characters—which convey or serve as the focus for the "feeling" of the narrative ["The granz biens of Marie de France," *Patterns of Love and Courtesy,* 1966]. Thus, in **"Le Chevrefeuil"** the image of the honeysuckle twined about the wand of hazel is the imaginative focus of the story of the lovers' union, the natural, non-civilized wildness of the growth suggesting the quality of the love between Tristan and Iseult.

The one exception Stevens finds to this mode of development is **"Le Chaitivel,"** which he calls "imageless and unmemorable." It is to this exception that I propose to address myself in this essay, and what I shall argue is that this *lai,* rather than being imageless, actually grows out of an image in Stevens' own sense of the term—specifically, out of the central incident of the tournament.

After the introductory identification of the *lai,* Marie tells the story of a beautiful lady who is loved by four knights and who loves each of them in return. At a tournament the four knights, after winning much honor, are defeated. Three of them, in fact, are slain, while the fourth is maimed. In the final scene of the narrative, the characteristic discussion of the title is presented dramatically in the dialogue between the lady and her one remaining knight. The lady intends to compose a *lai* telling the story of her loss and she will call it *"Quatre Dols."* The knight, however, objects:

> Mes jo, ki sui eschapé vif,
> Tut esgaré e tut cheitif
> Ceo qu'al siecle puis plus amer
> Vei sovent venir e aler,
> Parler od mei, matin e seir,
> Si n'en puis nulle joie aveir,
> Ne de baisier, ne d'acoler,
> Ne d'autre bien, fors de parler,
> Teus cent maus me fetes suffrir:
> Meus me vaudreit la mort tenir.
> Pur ceo ert li lais de mei numez:
> *Le Chaitivel* iert apelez.
>
> (ll. 215-226)

The lady graciously agrees with the knight's argument, but Marie closes the poem with her own judgment:

> Chescun des nuns bien i afiert,
> Kar la matire le requert.
>
> (ll. 235-236)

As Stevens notes, the close of the *lai* thus presents a tension between two ways of viewing the narrative action. Indeed, the narrator's commentary upon the naming of this *lai* explicitly restores in an unresolvable equilibrium the impulses that have been operating throughout: the comprehensive mastery of the lady who is the focus and the justification for the lovers' actions; and the personal desire of the lovers subordinated to civilizing conventions.

Both impulses are particularly evident in the tournament, which comprises the central narrative incident in the *lai*. Although the tournament in the twelfth century was a relatively informal affair in comparison with the highly stylized tournaments of succeeding centuries, it nevertheless represented a more ennobled and ideal form of chivalric action than the everyday military life outside the tournament. Marie carefully brings out the formality and nobility of the action in her initial description of the participants:

> Tant qu'aprés une Paske vient
> Que devant Nantes la cité
> Ot un turneiement crié.
> Pur acointer les quatre druz,
> I sunt d'autre païs venuz
> E li Franceis e li Norman
> E li Flement e li Breban;
> Li Buluineis, li Angevin
> E cil ki pres furent veisin;
> Tuz i sunt volenters alé,
> Lunc tens aveient surjurné.
> Al vespres del turneiement
> S'entreferirent durement.
> Li quatre dru furent armé
> E eisserent de la cité.
> Lur chevaliers viendrent aprés,
> Mes sur eus quatre fu le fez.
>
> （ll. 72-88).

In addition, Marie gives special attention to the lady, who watches the tournament from a tower and who carefully marks the activities of her four champions:

> La dame fu sur une tur,
> Bien choisi les suens e les lur.
> Ses druz i vit mut bien aidier,
> Ne seit lequeil deit plus prisier.
>
> （ll. 107-110)

The climactic point in the incident comes after the downfall of the knights. Their bodies are placed on their shields and borne back to their mistress, who pays tribute to them and defines the achievement to which each of them has contributed:

> Lasse, fet ele, quei ferai?
> Ja mes haitie ne serai.
> Ces quatre chevaliers amoue
> E chescun par sei cunveitoue.
> Mut par aveit en eus granz biens,
> Il m'amoent sur tute riens.
> Pur lur beauté, pur lur pruesce,
> Pur lur valur, pur lur largesce,
> Les fis d'amer a mei entendre:
> Nes voil tuz perdre pur l'un prendre.
> Ne sai lequeil jeo dei plus pleindre,
> Mes ne puis m'en covrir ne feindre:

> L'un vei nafré, li treiz sunt mort;
> N'ai rien el mund ki me comfort.
>
> （ll. 147-160)

In this speech we can recognize the expression of an ideal code which has been realized in the actions of the lady and her knights. All the splendor of this code, however, has been maintained, as we further recognize, at the expense of the personal sufferings of those who have submitted to it.

A similar paradox appears in the closing dialogue between the lady and her knight, when the image of elegant love represented by the memory of the lady and her four faithful knights is paid for by the personal sorrow of *"le chaitivel."* Marie, as Stevens points out, does not resolve the tension between the lady's ideal loss and the knight's personal anguish, but it does not seem quite fair to say, as he does, that she leaves the matter with a toss of the head. Quite properly, Marie recognizes the validity of both names proposed for the *lai,* for the values portrayed in the poem are both abstract or ideal—*"quatre dols"*—and personal—*"le chaitivel."*

The reading offered here for this *lai,* though in disagreement with some of Stevens' particular comments, does support his general theme concerning Marie's work, which is that she relies on images to convey feeling. In **"Le Chaitivel"** the image of the tournament, which is made up of the triptych of the lady standing on the tower, the knights riding out together in their blazoned coats and shields, and finally the lady lamenting over the bodies of the four knights, serves as the focus for the feeling of accomplishment and loss, of the attainment of the ideal and of human limitation.

Besides lending support to Stevens' general argument, the preceding analysis is also consistent with his implicit view of the lady herself as an essentially sympathetic figure. This view has recently been opposed by Emanuel J. Mickel, Jr., who judges the lady as grossly selfish and insists accordingly that the delineation of her throughout the *lai* is ironic ["A Reconsideration of the Lais of Marie de France," *Speculum,* Vol. XLVI, 1971]. Mickel's interpretation, however, is largely based on extra-literary considerations—in particular, on a synthetic theory of medieval love psychology according to which "there is only one love worthy of the name and . . . this love transcends suffering, in that its happiness resides not in the self but in the happiness of another." Yet nothing within **"Le Chaitivel"** suggests that the lady's character should be judged in relation to such a standard. Undoubtedly, one can judge her in this way and there may even have been moralists among Marie's audience who did so, but the judgment does not account in any precise way for the narrative development in the *lai* and provides a distorted reflection of the image at the center, which we have just examined.

The lady is no more grossly selfish than the knights are grossly over-confident. She does, obviously, look beyond the bounds of practical, conventional behavior in evaluating the courtly love relationship of which she is the focal point, just as the four knights are guilty of foolhardiness in the tournament, when they fail to take into consideration the realities of normal human competitiveness in their pursuit of glory:

> Li reng crurent, mut espessa.
> Devant la porte meinte feiz
> Fu le jur mellé le turneiz.
> Si quatre dru bien le feseient,
> Si ke de tuz le pris aveient.
> Tant ke ceo vient a l'avesprer
> Que il deveient deseuver,
> Trop folement s'abaundonnerent
> Luinz de lur gent, sil cumpererent,
> Kar li treiz i furent ocis,
> E li quart nafrez e malmis
> Par mi la quisse e enz el cors,
> Si que la lance parut fors.

(ll. 112-124)

None of the characters, however, is gross. Rather, all are basically admirable, though their achievement is necessarily tentative, it being after all a human achievement.

The setting of the closing scene is important to the final mood of the poem. The lady and her one remaining knight are together. Implicit in her words to him as well as in his condition is the fact that she has lost any possibility for happiness. The lady will not take some new lover. Indeed, romance for her is over just as irrevocably as it is for the maimed knight. It is too great an injustice, I think, to accuse the lady of selfishness. She has nothing left to be selfish about.

Patrick John Ireland (essay date 1977)

SOURCE: "The Narrative Unity of the 'Lanval' of Marie de France," in *Studies in Philology,* Vol. LXXIV, No. 2, April, 1977, pp. 130-45.

[*In the following essay, Ireland divides the story line of "Lanval" into four "stages" while demonstrating the* lai's *connections with later Arthurian romances.*]

In perhaps the best book to date on Marie de France, Emanuel Mickel, Jr. has done much to clarify for the more peripheral reader the complex issues surrounding the medieval *lai* [*Marie de France,* 1974]. According to Professor Mickel's résumé of the scholarship, not only does the relationship between Marie's narrative *lais* and earlier Breton sources remain critically enigmatic, but also there continues to be widespread disagreement whether in fact Marie called her own works *lais.* Moreover, generic definitions of the *lais* based on content somehow miss the mark in describing the breadth of her narrative poems, and those based on external features blur still further the already vague distinctions between *conte, aventure, roman, fabliau,* and *lai.* What Professor Mickel does seem to establish quite clearly is that Marie consciously created highly original, imaginative, and diverse narrative poems from folk material, probably without an accurate understanding of the nature of that original material, and that her poems have a sophisticated internal unity, the central focus of which is the nature of human, not courtly, love.

The chief appeal of Mickel's human love theme is that it affords us a plausible contributing factor to the subsequent supersession of the *lai,* as a genre, by the more didactic *fabliau.* Given a sophisticated audience, such a drift toward a more didactic expression seems not only natural but also inevitable. The narrative unity of Marie's "Lanval," the subject of this study, is a case in point. Though the well-known parallel refinement of Arthurian material from folk legend to complicated theological treatments in Grail romances stems from Chrétien [de Troyes] rather than from Marie, the elements of human love and compassion in "Lanval" have, nonetheless, a certain kinship with the profound religious expression in Von Eschenbach's *Parzival* more than a hundred years later, a kinship best understood by an examination of the "Lanval's" narrative unity.

Structurally, the "Lanval" shares with several of its analogues a common story pattern. Some years ago G. V. Smithers defined three types of story patterns characteristic of the Breton *lais* and their derivatives ["Story-Patterns in Some Breton Lays," *Medium Aevum,* Vol. XXII, 1953]. Type I, which he called the Lanval plot, embraces, in varying degrees, "Lanval," *Graelent, Sir Landevall,* and *Sir Lambewell.* The "Lanval"'s variances from the Type I pattern are readily apparent. But most evident are the four main stages which its plot has in common with the other *lais:* the obstructive circumstance; the amorous liaison with a fairy; the breach of the taboo; and the resolution of the crisis.

On examination, these stages take on a singular quality in the "Lanval" in that they follow rather neatly defined time sequences: lines 1-38, the obstructive circumstance, in which Lanval finds himself bereft of King Arthur's largesse, takes place on the feast of Pentecost; lines 39-218 reveal how one day Lanval goes off in search of diversion from his sorrows, establishes a liaison with a fairy, whereby he accepts the imposition of a taboo, and how on his return late that same evening, he discovers himself the continuous recipient of the fairy's largesse, thus enabling him to exercise the same; lines 219-414 recount how "meïsmes l'an, / Aprés las feste seinte Johan" (ll. 219-20) Lanval is forced to break the taboo in order to defend his chivalric honor against the queen who seeks to seduce him, and how his boastful insult to the queen necessitates his trial as a felon; lines 415-644 narrate the circumstances of Lanval's trial—"Al jur que cil orent numé" (415)—and his subsequent acquittal with the arrival of the fairy mistress. Of themselves the time sequences seem to be of little or no symbolic import. Feast day notations are conventional and legion in medieval narratives, and when of some consequence, the meaning is usually clear and large. However, the neat plot junctures betray the essential unity of the *lai* divisions, and the relationship these divisions bear to each other is a subject worthy of further consideration.

STAGE I—THE OBSTRUCTIVE CIRCUMSTANCE—LINES 1-38

King Arthur is holding summer court at Carlisle, in Logres, because he is at war with the Picts and Scots. At Pentecost he exercises great largesse to all save one:

> Asez i duna riches duns
> E as cuntes e as baruns.
>
> . . . . .
>
> N'ot tant de tels en tut le munde—
>
> . . . . .
>
> Fors a un sul ki l'ot servi:
> Ceo fu Lanval; ne l'en sovint
> Ne nuls des soens bien ne le tint.
>
> (13-20)

Lanval was born to wealth and nobility, but his home is far away, his money all spent, and "Kar li reis rien ne li dona / Ne Lanval ne li demanda" (31-2). Lanval is, to say the least, "mult entrepris, / Mult est dolenz, mult est pensis!" (33-4).

Such is his obstructive circumstance. It is a peculiar situation in that as a "foreigner" he has no lands, no English means, except the largesse of the lord King Arthur in whose feudal service he functions as a vassal. Such sins of omission on the part of royalty are not uncommon in medieval literature, even where, as in the **"Lanval,"** the king is "li pruz e li curteis" (6). Lanval's valor looms rather large at the court and whatever a modern logician might think of the king's motives, they are understandable and calculated: in time of war, why provide one's most heroic knight with great rewards, the means by which he might leave one's service? The point is that by his pecuniary omission Arthur slights the chivalric code in failing as a lord to do justice to his vassal. His calculation is his error. Stage I thus opens the way for Stage II, in which Lanval the mortal forges a new comitatus with the fairy queen at her Court of Love.

In using the phrase "Court of Love" here, I do not mean to suggest a clear-cut identification with the strict conventions of courtly love. Marie de France has at best only a peripheral interest in the courtly love tradition. Certainly, the tradition is not fully expressed in her work, and after a fashion she seems even to find fault with it. For Marie, love is a human force controlled by man with great difficulty; it is a spontaneous, natural, and all-consuming power, the experience of which leads to an almost blind passion at times. In that emotional respect her *lais* appear courtly; but Marie generally avoids the familiar courtly conventions, such as adultery. Given that distinction, the two worlds of **"Lanval"** used as structural elements are not, properly speaking, the faerie and the courtly, but rather the chivalric (that is, the civil comitatus realistically expressed in the imperfect mortal world) and the faerie (that is, the comitatus of human love marvelously expressed in the perfect faerie world). In that sense at least, the "Court of Love," as used here, is not specifically a "courtly" term.

STAGE II—THE AMOROUS LIAISON—LINES 39-218

The second part of **"Lanval"** opens with the hero, "Ki tant aveit le rei servi" (40), mounting his horse one day and leaving the city and court behind him. In search of divertissement he rides into a meadow through which runs a stream. But upon approaching the stream, "sis chevals tremble forment" (46). The horse is aware of a preternatural presence. Lanval dismounts, rests beside the stream, and contemplates his "mesaise" (51). But as Marie tells us, "Il ne veit chose ki li plaise" (52). Two beautiful maidens dressed in regal purple suddenly appear; they come to fetch Lanval for their mistress, who is encamped in a royal pavilion nearby. The lavish description of the fairy queen's entourage suggests a wealth beyond the mortal; and her beauty cannot be excelled. The feé, seated on a rich couch in dishabille, salutes Lanval as "pruz e curteis" (113) and promises him joy (and presumably her love) as no "Emperere ne quens ne reis" (114) has ever known. Certainly, the fairy is no miserly Arthur. Clearly, Lanval is at the Court of Love, for "Amurs le puint de l'estencele, / Ki sun quer alume e esprent" (118-19). And it is not without significance that Lanval's immediate response, which is a pledge of undying love, closely parallels a vassal's plight of servitude to his lord:

> "Bele . . . se vus plaiseit
> E cele joie m'aveneit
> Que vus me volsissiez amer,
> Ne savriez rien comander
> Que jeo ne face a mun poeir,
> Turt a folie u a saveir.
> Jeo ferai voz comandemenz,
> Pur vus guerpirai tutes genz.
> Ja mes ne quier de vus partir:
> Ceo est la riens que plus desir!"
>
> (121-30)

What Lanval does not realize is that in renouncing "tutes genz" he effectively renounces the mortal world and mortal allegiances. It is this renunciation that provides the basis of his conflict of allegiances in Stage III. In pledging himself to the Court of Love, he unknowingly surrenders his chivalric allegiance to King Arthur.

The fairy's response to Lanval's pledge of service is the highest boon possible—"S'amur e sun cors li otreie" (133). Unlike Arthur's court, where loyalty goes unrepaid, the Court of Love repays the loyal with largesse: "Ore est Lanval en dreite veie!" (134). The gifts bestowed upon Lanval are beyond anything dreamed at the Round Table. However, a taboo is imposed that Lanval never mention his mistress to another mortal, the penalty for the violation of which being an eternal loss:

> "A tuz jurs m'avriez perdue,
> Se ceste amur esteit seüe;

Ja mes ne me porrez veeir
Ne de mun cors seisine aveir."

(147-50)

One should not underestimate the significance of the penalty, even though the fairy herself confounds it by her appearance at the trial in Stage IV. The removal of the penalty is the basis of the justice ethic at work in the narrative by which, later, we recognize Lanval's absolute allegiance to the chivalric ideal of the other worldly Court of Love; his very loyalty affords the feé a rationale in forgiving him his breach of the taboo.

Their love is apparently consummated as a final submission to the fairy court, wherein at last, in a scene reminiscent of a knight's dubbing on bended knee, the fairy commands her vassal to arise and depart (159-61). On his return to Carlisle, Lanval receives full benefit of the feé's largesse and by the very act of wishing has her at his side day and night, unseen by other mortals. The obstructive circumstance of Stage I is thus removed. Lanval's wealth is in direct contrast to his initial poverty; and his own concomitant largesse, so dramatically described at the end of Stage II, is a refutation of Arthur's earlier skirting of his chivalric duties:

Lanval donout les riches duns,
Lanval aquitout les prisuns,
Lanval vesteit les jugleürs,
Lanval faiseit les granz honurs!
N'i ot estrange ne privé
A qui Lanval n'eüst doné.

(209-14)

Our knight's experience seems to him unreal. Even as he departed from the fairy pavilion, his rumination suggests he is unaware of all he has undertaken and, if you will, foreshadows the conflict of loyalties that is to follow:

Suvent reguarde ariere sei:
Mult est Lanval en grant esfrei!
De s'aventure vait pensant
E en sun curage dotant:
Esbaïz est, ne set que creire,
Il ne la quide mie a veire.

(195-200)

The transition between the hero's discovery of his poverty and consequent despair in Stage I and his meeting with the fairy and consequent joy in Stage II is not as abrupt as it first patently seems. We forget that in the feé we are dealing with a miracle-worker. Even Lanval wonders at the change, but it should be remembered that the hero's fate is in the hands of an other-worldly force.

STAGE III—THE BREACH OF THE TABOO—LINES 219-414

In Stage III the breach of the taboo comes swiftly, "meïsmes l'an / Aprés la feste seinte Johan" (219-20). That it occurs but two months after Lanval's pledge is in no way inartistic; in fact, the point of the taboo in the conflict of loyalties is such that the swiftness of its breach contributes to its artistry.

Thirty knights and Lanval retire to a meadow beside the queen's tower to disport themselves; the hero abandons his hostel (and presumably his fairy mistress) only because entreated to do so. The queen and thirty of her most beautiful maidens join them. A pairing off suggests itself. Lanval, however, separates himself from the others:

. . . mult li est tart
Que s'amie puisse tenir,
Baisier, acoler e sentir;
L'altrui joie prise petit,
Se il nen a le suen delit.

(254-8)

It is clear Lanval has not forgotten his pledge; he is in the meadow by request and with great reluctance. There is even the suggestion he has not, these past two months, been much in the world. Nonetheless, the libidinous queen's profession of love is swift, as was the fairy's, and Lanval's rejection of her is equally abrupt, as was his acceptance of the feé's love:

"Dame . . . laissiez m'ester:
Jeo n'ai cure de vus amer!
Lungement ai servi le rei:
Ne li vueil pas mentir ma fei;
Ja pur vus ne pur vostre amur
Ne mesferai a mun seignur."

(269-74)

The paradox is that he regards the queen's proffer as duplicitous—he cannot serve Arthur and the queen, too, whereas he does not regard his service to the fairy sovereign as a conflict with his obligations to Arthur. The queen's unseemly promise of favors requires a violation of both the mortal chivalric code and the strictures of the Court of Love. Lanval's subsequent attempt to be loyal to both Arthur and the fairy queen demonstrates his desire to persevere in two allegiances; the queen's request, on the other hand, is treasonous in two worlds. What Lanval does not yet know, however, is that he cannot serve God and Mammon too.

Arthur's queen then shifts in her strategy, seeking to humble Lanval into submission. Her accusation of the standard "secret vice" is not only uncourtly but also in vivid contrast to the idealistic stance taken earlier by the feé. The crude accusation challenges his manhood, his very ability to serve the Court of Love, but primarily it is an affront to the dignity of the feé herself. The consequent anger of Lanval's boast—his regret is immediate because the boast violates the taboo—derives not from personal humiliation, nor from pride, but from a desire to defend the fairy mistress:

"Dame . . . de cel mestier
Ne me sai jeo nïent aidier.
Me jo aim, e si sui amis,
Cele ki deit aveir le pris
Sur tutes celes que jeo sai.
E une chose vus dirai,
Bien le saciez a descovert:

Une de celes ki la sert,
Tute la plus povre meschine,
Valt mielz de vus, dame reïne,
De cors, de vis e de bealté
D'enseignement e de bunté!"

(291-302)

The implicit contrast therein between the feé and the queen demonstrates the ironically culpable selflessness of his *vantance*. For that reason and because of his subsequent loyalty and nobility, the feé is able to exonerate him by an exercise of largesse.

The scene is both psychologically sophisticated and artistically apt. Lanval's breach of the taboo so soon after its imposition indicates neither weakness of character nor poor plotting. The force of Lanval's love has carried him beyond the realm of all that is rationally politic. The crisis, in effect, poses a question of choice for Lanval: to defend the feé's honor or to reveal her existence. To do the one is to violate the other. For him the choice is unconscious and immediate. He must defend her honor without personal regard for the penalties of the taboo. It is a question of higher obligations. Thus Lanval "fails," if that is the word, as he inevitably must, the first moment the taboo is put to the test. Moreover, in both Stage II and Stage III the presence of the queen's highest handmaidens is a beautiful antithesis to Lanval's comparison of her to the lowest of the feé's servants, and the scene itself, the meadow, is an appropriate parallel to the meadow in Stage II. The climaxes of the two stages are also parallel in that in Stage II Lanval returns to the city from the forest after a search for diversion from sorrow, and in Stage III it is Arthur who returns from a literal "hunt." The response of each on his return, however, is quite different: Lanval's is one of joy; Arthur's, one of anger.

After their confrontation, the queen distorts the facts and Lanval finds himself accused not only of a felony (insulting the queen) but also of treason (her slander is that he attempted to seduce her). The latter charge is, of course, dropped by the Duke of Cornwall because Lanval is a "foreigner" in the service of the king, and hence not subject to the law, and because there are not the two required witnesses. The other charge stands, however, inasmuch as Lanval admits the *vantance* and asserts the truth of it. Because he is an alien, Lanval's admission is itself legally inconsequential: the only penalty is dismissal from Arthur's service. Extraordinary penalties are possible only if the felonious boast, once admitted, is also invalid, which possibility provides the mainstay of suspense in Stage IV inasmuch as Lanval lacks the necessary proof of the fairy's beauty. The situation is interesting in that the felony was committed as an act of honor (love's) in defense of one court and the consequent penalty (dismissal from Arthur's service) is a question of honor (chivalric) in the other court. And thus a day for judgment is fixed, at which time the fairy must be produced.

The ending of Stage III is both ironic and paradoxical: ironic, because in defense of a double allegiance Lanval becomes an outcast in two worlds; and doubly paradox-

ical, because first, he breaks the taboo in defense of the fairy-mistress, and secondly, it is out of love for the feé that he apparently loses her love.

What is most apparent in Stage III, however, is Lanval's transformation. It would be patently absurd, of course, to regard him as having, in the modern sense of the term, a divided self. But after violating the taboo, he does reach a kind of extra-mortal awareness that his life and love lie in the other world: his mortality hangs heavily on him; and he knows that his first allegiance should have been to the Court of Love and its rule of silence. His sense of grief and loss is thus boundless: variously, he is seen as near the point of madness; he wishes to be slain or else, we are told, it is a wonder he does not slay himself. Equally depressing is the fact that the sureties required of Gawain and others of Lanval's friends before the trial emphasize the hero's ironic return to the poverty of his original predicament in Stage I. Once again he is out of favor with the king; once again Arthur does him an injustice. The dramatic difference, however, is Lanval's knowledge—in accordance with the taboo—that his loss of faerie is eternal and with it lost also is any hope of acquittal in Arthur's court. Thus, the knight's open admission of the boast and of the truth of it, and his willingness to make amends as the court sees fit, is testament to his ideal loyalty to both mortal king and fairy queen. On that basis the feé will pardon him in Stage IV, rendering to him once again that justice which is his due and in which Arthur is lacking.

STAGE IV—THE RESOLUTION OF THE CRISIS—LINES 415-644

The trial motif that dominates Stage IV—"Al jur que cil orent numé" (415)—effects the resolution of Lanval's conflict of allegiances. The legalistic rendering of the motif goes beyond Marie's topical interest in law. Its purpose is two-fold, and the reader does not escape the feeling that two trials, in effect, are being conducted. First, the much-ado about Lanval's foreign birth and possible exemption from Arthur's jurisdiction merely heightens the reader's awareness that the bonds of love extend far beyond those of law or reason. The trial is extra-legal for reasons beyond questions of nationality: as a mortal trial it is illicit because Lanval is a vassal in the service of the Court of Love and no longer subject to the laws of Arthur or of any other mortal court. And secondly, Lanval's subsequent acquittal in the court of Arthur functions as an echo or kaleidoscope for his acquittal in the higher Court of Love.

The dramatic rendering of such a conclusion is effected by a series of parallels and contrasts. As to the truth of Lanval's *vantance*, the barons' adopted policy of judgment is one of "seeing is believing." Lanval's admitted inability to produce the fairy provides the suspense, and his assertion of the truth of the *vantance* allows the fairy queen to exercise a *deus ex machina*. Arthur and the fairy are in contrast to each other as the plaintiffs; both are offended sovereigns. Whereas Arthur and his queen continually press for a judgment of guilt, the actual judgment of innocence is gradual, delayed as it is by the arrival of the fairy. Hers is the higher law, and the trial progresses by her ordination, by the control of extra-mortal forces, as it were. Throughout, the actions of the feé and her handmaidens are ever decisive and deliberate. All the mortals are torn by indecision or by a conflict between desire and fate: the king and queen seek angrily for a judgment that eludes them; the barons, who are split between those who favor Lanval and those who favor the king, are unable to come to an accord; the comrades of the hero hope that each succeeding maiden entering the city is the fairy and each time Lanval's answer is a negation; and Lanval himself repeatedly is offered hope by his friends' alarms and each time is disillusioned by his own witness.

Thus the double procession of the fairy's handmaidens heightens the suspense and counterbalances what might otherwise have been an abruptly inartistic final judgment. The onlookers of the city, the court, the judging barons—all gradually see the truth of Lanval's *vantance:* they see and believe.

The glorious appearance of the fairy in the city is a striking contrast to the world of Arthur and his queen:

> En tut le siecle n'ot plus bele!
>
> . . . . .
>
> Riche atur ot el palefrei:
> Suz ciel nen a cunte ne rei
> Ki tut le peüst eslegier
> Senz terre vendre u enguagier.
>
> (550-8)

Whereas Lanval had lost his ability to see her, now all the world is allowed that vision. Lanval's shout is triumphant:

> "Par fei . . . ceo est m'amie!
> Or ne m'est guaires ki m'ocie,
> Se ele n'a merci de mei,
> Kar guariz sui quant jeo la vei!"
>
> (597-600)

All who gaze at her conclude, "De sa bealté n'est mie gas" (579), and the knights declare, "Ceo est la plus bele de mund, / De tutes celes ki i sunt!" (591-2). The judgment of the court is "Que Lanval a tut desraisnié: / Delivrez est par lur esguart" (628-9). Lanval's acquittal in the court of mortals is complete. His extirpation from mortal difficulty simultaneously exonerates him in the fairy's eyes. His breach of the taboo while a vassal in her service was in defense of her beauty, which all now adjudge true. Had Lanval been convicted of a lie, his would have been an enforced exile (458-60). The irony of his acquittal, therefore, is his self-chosen exile in the service of the *feé.*

What is actually being adjudicated is his love for the fairy mistress. It is as constant as has been Lanval's service to her, the broken taboo notwithstanding. It is perhaps a fitting climax that as the fairy mistress exists past a crowd of onlookers, we are told, "Asez ot gent a li servir" (632).

Thus the lay comes full circle with the couple's departure from the city. As the fairy rides forth, Lanval takes his place upon "Un grant perrun de marbre bis" (634)—from whence, no doubt, he mounted his horse on leaving the city in Stage II—and leaps upon the palfrey behind her. In Stage IV, however, his departure is final: his journey is to Avalon in service of the Court of Love. As the late Professor Hoepffner has so eloquently observed [in *Les Lais de Marie de France,* 1935], ". . . en effet, la brusque décision de Lanval est la preve qu'elle attendait. Elle l'emmène sans mot dire, et dans ce geste, plus éloquent que des paroles, comme si souvent chez Marie, elle lui accorde le pardon définitif . . . Le 'happy end' n'est donc pas une concession factice que l'auteur fait aux âmes sensible de ses lecteurs et de lectrices; il émane du sens profond qu'elle a de la justice et de l'équite."

What we have then in the **"Lanval"** is a highly unified structure having several distinguishable features. First, the time sequence of this marvelous *lai* is realistically probable. The wondrous events of Stage II and Stage IV do not render the human qualities of Lanval artificial but rather, given the brief interlude between the stages of the plot, add to the likelihood of his consequent actions.

Secondly, the divisions reveal a sophisticated integration of material. Stage I dramatizes a feudal relationship between king and knight that is inequitable. The new allegiance in Stage II, between knight and fairy, is effected in part by the unhappy circumstances of the original allegiance, and the benefits of such a relationship are in direct contrast to that situation depicted in Stage I. Stage III represents the conflict that arises between the twin loyalties the first time their obligations run counter to each other, with the result that the hero's noble defense effects a breach in both relationships. And Stage IV dramatizes the hero's perseverance by justifying his actions in Stage III.

Thirdly, there is a highly complex interplay between the two ideals of love and chivalry. A great many parallels and contrasts are drawn between the characters, scenes, and situations of the plot. Arthur and the fairy are played off against each other as sovereigns, Arthur and Lanval as adherents to the chivalric code, the queen and the fairy as regal beauties, Lanval against himself in two allegiances, and so on. The excesses and imperfections of Arthur and his court are not themselves so condemnable, nor are they of central interest. Rather, they act as a human backdrop against which the ideals of love and honor are configured in the person of our hero, Lanval.

Thus in the **"Lanval"** our hero stands fixed between the finite world of Arthur and the more perfect world of faerie, with all its promises of reward. As Dr. Mickel has, I think, clearly explained the central issue of the *Lais,* it "is not 'courtly love,' not the development of the psychology of characters, but the nature of love itself, the love so often personified in medieval literature, so often treated as a natural force, formidable and powerful precisely because it does subvert the reason and cause man to react in a way that ultimately brings him suffering and grief."

This is not to suggest that in so secular a piece of literature Lanval's agonizing struggle on the road to perfect servitude allegorically represents the struggle of mankind in some religious sense. Lanval is not Dante, nor is he a Parzival in quest of the Holy Grail. At the time of Marie's writing, the Arthurian tradition was still in its embryonic stage; the *lais* were yet to succumb to the more didactic *fabliaux;* and still further off are the Arthurian romances of the human soul. But for those of us who see in the hero's selfless admission of error something beautiful and exquisite, it is enough to relish the **"Lanval"**'s position within the tradition as the promise of grander things to come. Similar to the error of Von Eschenbach's later hero, Lanval's mistake renders Marie's fairy Munsalvesche inaccessible, a lost and invisible Eden. Both heroes, too, are driven to a fine madness as they stand twixt two worlds. And it is love which brings both men to a knowledge of a higher world and a very human love, unfailing but faulty, which deprives them of it. Though Lanval pronounces no formulaic "Oeheim, waz wirret dir" to amend a lack of compassion for some fisher-king, his selfless acquiescence to the judgment of the court and to the rightness of his loss of the fairy is witness to the profound depth of his love. As a human being, Lanval may lack rational control; but as a man of nobility possessing boundless love, he is deserving of Avalon.

Brewster E. Fitz　(essay date 1979)

SOURCE: "Desire and Interpretation: Marie de France's 'Chievrefoil'," in *Yale French Studies,* No. 58, 1979, pp. 182-89.

[*In the following essay, Fitz uses deconstructionist theory to reveal the "truth" in the* lai *"Chievrefoil."*]

The *Lais* of Marie de France are rimed narratives that tell how, why, where and by whom apparently obscure lyric poems, also called *lais,* were composed. In these narratives the personages themselves tell, sometimes write, read and in two instances (**"Chaitivel"** and **"Chievrefoil"**) make lays of their own adventures. (In the ten other texts these lays are said to have been made by anonymous, ancient Bretons.) In other words, these narratives show personages whose actions are protoliterary in that they constitute the object of the exegetical activity Marie performs.

Marie's intention is to tell the truth of these lays, as declared for example in the initial verses of **"Chievrefoil"**:

> Asez me plest e bien le voil,
> Del lai qu'hum nume Chievrefoil,
> Que la verité vus en cunt
> Pur quei fu fez, coment e dunt.

> [It pleases me and gladly I want to tell you the truth of the lay called Chievrefoil, why it was made, how and where.]

In the initial and final verses of each of the eleven other texts attributed to her, similar passages disarm and disori-

ent the modern interpreter who sets out to integrate them into a coherent reading of the text. How can one accept as truth the story of Tristan's making the *Lai du Chievrefoil*? It seems that one must either assume that these passages are commonplaces used by Marie (and by many other medieval writers as well) in order to lend verisimilitude to fictitious narratives, and as such are detachable from the text, of little or no interest to the interpreter; or one must assume that Marie really believed that Tristan composed the lay, thereby relegating the truth of her text to a corpus of pre-scientific errors. Yet this *either/or* of common sense judgment is not necessarily binding in a reading of Marie's text. In this paper an attempt is made to show that Marie's integral text is a truth-producing system in which the conceptual oppositions taken for granted by the modern reader, viz., story/history, poet/critic, fiction/criticism, and, of course, either/or, are suspended. In such a text the truth is telling the story itself, or in other words, Marie's text is exegetico-literary, or in the parlance of one contemporary tendency in narrative analysis, Marie's text intends its own intertextuality.

The initial verses of **"Chievrefoil"** have been quoted above. In the following summary the passages that critics have found problematic (verses 53-78; 107-113) are quoted in full in the original:

> Marie declares that she has heard from many persons (and found in writing) the story of Tristan and the queen, of the love from which they suffered greatly and died in one day.

> Tristan has been sent to South Wales, owing to his love for the queen. After a year in exile he returns to Cornwall, where he hides in the forest. From peasants he learns that King Mark has called for the Court to assemble at Tintagel during Pentecost. On the day that the royal cortège is due to leave for Tintagel, Tristan goes into the forest, through which the queen must pass, cuts down a hazel tree and squares a rod.

> Quant il ad paré le bastun,
> De sun cutel escrit sun nun.
> Se la reïne s'aparceit,
> Ki mut grant garde s'en perneit—
> Autre feiz li fu avenu
> Que si l'aveit aparceü—
> De sun ami bien conustra
> Le bastun, quant el le verra.
> Ceo fu la summe de l'escrit
> Qu'il li aveit mandé e dit
> Que lunges ot ilec esté
> E atendu e surjurné
> Pur espïer e pur saveir
> Coment il la peüst veeir,
> Kar ne poeit vivre sanz li.
> D'euls deus fu il tut autresi
> Cume del chievrefoil esteit
> Ki a la codre se perneit:
> Quant il s'i est laciez e pris
> E tut entur le fust s'est mis,
> Ensemble poënt bien durer,

Mes ki puis les voelt desevrer,
Li codres muert hastivement
E li chievrefoilz ensement.
"Bele amie, si est de nus:
Ne vus sanz mei, ne jeo sanz vus."

[When he has pared the rod, he wrote his name
[message?] with his knife. If the queen, who took great
care, perceives—Another time it had befallen her that
she had thus perceived it—she will know her friend's
rod when she sees it. This was the sum of the writing
that he had sent and said to her, that he had been
there, and waited and stayed for a long time, in order
to espy and to know how he might see her, for he
could not live without her. The two of them were like
the honeysuckle that was attached to the hazel: When
it had enlaced itself and taken hold there, and put
itself around the trunk, together both could survive;
but let someone separate them; the hazel would die
rapidly and likewise the honeysuckle. "Beautiful friend,
thus it is between us, neither you without me, nor I
without you."]

The queen approaches on horseback, sees the rod,
recognizes the letters on it, and stops her escorts in
order to go into the forest, where she talks with Tristan.
Before parting she promises him a reconciliation with
Mark. Tristan returns to Wales, where he remains until
his uncle calls him.

Pur la joie qu'il ot eüe
De s'amie qu'il ot veüe
E pur ceo k'il aveit escrit
Si cum la reïne l'ot dit,
Pur les paroles remembrer,
Tristram, ki bien saveit harper,
En aveit fet un nuvel lai.

[Because of the joy that he had had from his friend
whom he had seen and because of that which he had
written, as the queen had said it, in order to remember
the words, Tristan, who knew how to harp well, made
of them a new lai.]

Critics have been unable to agree on where Marie meant
the *summe de l'escrit* to have been written. Some believe
these words were meant to have been contained in a letter
Tristan sent to the queen prior to the meeting in the forest. Others believe Marie meant that Tristan carved these
words (in ogam letters) on the rod. Still others believe
that the words are the full meaning of Tristan's name
engraved on the rod as they were understood and spoken
by the queen. Whatever Marie may have "meant," the
comparison of the hazel-honeysuckle symbiosis to the two
lovers is given as Tristan's message and as the truth of
the lay. Even if Marie's narrative unequivocally specified
the location of these written words, this symbiosis, by
virtue of its being what Richard Klein has called metaphor of metaphor [in "Straight lines and arabesques:
metaphors of metaphor," *Yale French Studies,* Vol. 45,
1970], would make a literal interpretation difficult, if not
impossible, for as the truth of the lay, this self-reflexive
metaphor effects an incessant reversal of signifieds and

signifiers, of literal and figurative meanings, designating
semiotic reversability, metaphoricity itself as its truth.

This truth, according to Marie's text, is already written in
a space that E. R. Curtius called the Book of Nature [in
European Literature and the Latin Middle Ages, trans. W.
R. Trask, 1973]. Tristan's activity is a reading and a
writing of the hazel-honeysuckle symbiosis within this
topos. Whether he "literally" carved these words on the
rod, wrote them in a letter, or had them clearly (or even
obscurely) in mind when writing his name on the rod, is
irrelevant to the truth of the lay, for each of these acts
relates the lovers to the symbiosis in a paradigm of a
secondary language (that of narrative), and thereby orig-
inates the exegetico-poetic act that Marie's text repeats
and glosses. The writing Marie was concerned with—the
signified of her text—is the symbiosis, the "natural" script
and likewise the signifier of the encounter in the woods,
and the model of the entire story of Tristan and the queen.
This script makes the repetition possible; it subtends both
Tristan's message, Marie's narrative, and the multiple
readings of subsequent critics.

The comparison of Tristan to the hazel and the queen to
the honeysuckle establishes a parallel not only between
persons and plants, but also—and of greater importance
for reading the text—between *that which* relates the hazel
and honeysuckle and *that which* relates the lovers. The
term that describes the relation of the latter two is obviously a part of everyone's vocabulary: love, or desire;
whereas the term that describes the relation of the sym-
bionts does not immediately come to mind. Whatever term
one may ultimately choose for this relation (e.g. Divine
Will, natural law, or tautologically, symbiosis itself), the
status of the relation is linguistic, not empirical. In other
words, the hazel and honeysuckle are related by interpretation. (Today one would say they are related by misinterpretation, that is, the symbiosis is relegated to a corpus
of inaccurate, pre-scientific lore.)

In Marie's text, Tristan and the queen, like all literary
personages, have a purely linguistic existence. Their life,
death and desire are the message they themselves are said
to send and receive. Given the linguistic status of their
existence and the exegetico-literary intention of the narrative, one can say that the truth of Marie's text is that
desire is like interpretation, and for literary personages,
desire is interpretation; in terms of literal and figurative
meanings, one can say that Tristan is to the queen what
the letter is to the voice: the lasting, dead letter (Tristan-
hazel) and the perishable, live voice (queen-honey-suckle)
are linked by the desire of interpretation and separated by
the interpretation of desire. The drama of Tristan and the
queen is an instance of what Richard Klein calls the "drama of the metaphor . . . its spiraling movement to rejoin
itself, to signify its signifying, and thereby to halt the
movement, to silence the text that it has become—or,
rather, that it has always been."

Tristan and the queen are caught in a similar self-defeat-
ing spiral. Their desire binds them, giving them life, a
living-together (symbiosis), but also their desire results in

their separation, bringing death, and thus it is a dying-together, as the end of the Tristan story shows. Their attempts to silence the stories of their adultery (to silence the text) in order to live in harmony with Mark, or their definitive separation, would amount to a literary, textual suicide. Thus owing to the comparison of desire to the symbiosis and to interpretation, Tristan and the queen are destined to die of desire and interpretation, at the hands of either the mimetic or the structural reader.

Critics, with the exception of the couple, Spitzer-Hatcher, have failed to recognize the double comparison [See Leo Spitzer, "La 'Lettre sur la baguette de coudrier' dans le Lai du Chievrefueil," *Romania* 69, 1946; and Anna Granville Hatcher, "Lai du Chievrefueil," *Romania* 71, 1950]. The *Débat du Chievrefoil* is a discourse-producing parody of literary criticism and of Tristan's and the queen's drama. The proliferation of hypothetical readings explaining when and where the words of the *summe de l'escrit* were written simply repeats the medieval proliferation of episodes in which Mark never really finds a decisive proof of the queen's and Tristan's adultery. The missing letter, which some critics contend to have found, would be a plausible proof. Spitzer and Hatcher, instead of looking for a specific letter, turn instead to that which relates the letter and the voice, glimpsing, as it were, for a moment through a glass *clearly* into that textual space (the *topos* of the Book of Nature) where letter/voice, poet/critic, story/history, fiction/criticism are conceptual symbioses in the matrix of Biblical and secular poetics and exegesis. According to their reading, love enables the queen, who saw only the letters of Tristan's name engraved on the rod, to interpret this inscription, producing the *summe,* just as the Holy Spirit allegedly enables the Biblical exegete to arrive at the profound truth of obscure passages of Scripture. The terms of the conceptual systems of Latin, religious and Old French, secular lyric, as Pierre Guiraud has elaborated them [in "Les structures étymologiques du 'Trobar'," *Poétique*, 8, 1971], can be used to describe this exegetico-poetico-erotic reading of the **"Chievrefoil"**: the queen, owing to love (*amur-amor*), reads the letters Tristan, owing also to love, has written on the rod. The former finds (*trouver-tropare*) in the Book of Nature what the latter composes (*trouver-tropare*), owing to joy (*joie-gaudium*) in the forest. This is exactly what the second problematic passage states (see verses 107-113 above): Because of the joy that he had had from his friend whom he had seen and because of that which he had written, as the queen had said it, in order to remember the words, Tristan, who knew how to harp well, made of them a new lay.

Critics have asked: "What words?" In so doing they start on a search for the missing voice. In Marie's **"Chievrefoil"** the elusiveness of letter and voice is prescribed not only in the truth of her text, the metaphor of metaphor, but also in the double reversal of a schema that seems to belong to occidental prejudices about writing and speaking: letter as reminder/live voice as memory. Marie's exegetico-literary activity makes this double reversal manifest: Tristan's lay, a vocal and musical production, is made in order to remember the written and spoken words.

It is thus the vocal reminder of written reminder and vocal memory. When Marie tells the truth of how the lay was made, she re-reverses the schema, treating the vocal production, the lay, as the exegete treats the silent letter.

In such a system, the conflicts among personages become original *re*-petitions—the paradoxical prefix is the equivalent of verses 57-58 where the *other time* opens an infinite regress of episodes and interpretations into the text—of the exegetical conflict between the live, but perishable voice and the dead, but lasting letter. The conflicts are repetitions because there is always a previous script, the Book of Nature, of which and out of which the personages' adventures are readings. This script is the perfect conflation of the perishable voice and the lasting letter; it is the Word as Creation.

The reader sympathetic with the criticism usually leveled against those who use Biblical poetics and exegesis as a model for reading secular texts will probably point out that this paper treats Marie's text as if it were Scripture, thereby secularizing the commonplace of Biblical exegesis: *in divino eloquio non verba, sed etiam res significare habent* (in Divine Speech not only words, but also things have to signify). A closer reading absolves this writer of such a charge. It is the couple, Tristan and the queen, who want to make the *res* signify in their speech. In so doing they treat Tristan's rod in a way that recalls the speaking tree-Cross (also found alongside a path) in the *Dream of the Rood.* This speaking Cross (which links the desert, the exile of this world to Paradise, fallen man to the Father etc.) is to Divine Love as Tristan's "silent" rod (which links his exile to the joyous reunion in the forest and which, at least according to the queen's promise in verses 97-101, seems to be a step towards reconciling the exiled nephew with the avuncular stepfather) is to adulterous love. Linguistically, both Cross and rod relate "this-worldly" primary languages (Latin, Anglo-Saxon, Old French) to "otherworldly" secondary languages (that of exegesis, that of narrative analysis).

Marie, of course, does not explicitly judge the two lovers; this she leaves to sterner writer-readers, such as Dante (see *Inferno*, V, where Francesca mentions that Tristan is among the swarm of damned lovers). She does, however, explicitly say that the two died of their love, thereby peremptorily defending herself against charges of glorifying desire. As is fitting in a text where truth is metaphoricity, where desire is interpretation, Marie suspends her judgment, leaving the two textual lovers in a *neither/nor* (rather than in an *either/or*) world—purgatory rather than hell—where they wait the verdict of reader-writers.

Ann Tukey Harrison (essay date 1980)

SOURCE: "Marie de France As Naturalist," in *Romance Notes*, Vol. XXI, No. 2, Winter, 1980, pp. 248-53.

[*In the following essay, Harrison suggests that in her* lais *and fables, Marie is not interested in plant and animal lore except insofar as it can be used to symbolize or reflect upon human behavior.*]

Although Marie de France is certainly the author of courtly works infused with great sensitivity and perception about the human psyche, she frequently resorts to flora and fauna of diverse form and type to advance the intrigue, to instruct a character or the reader, to serve as symbol, and to amuse or ornament. Even the most casual reader must note that the *Ysopet* is, first of all, a collection in which 85% of the stories are animal centered, while five of the twelve *lais* are named either for a plant (honeysuckle), for a bird (nightingale), or for a character related to a plant (ash tree) or to animals (werewolf, Yonec son of a hawk-knight). How serious a naturalist is Marie de France?

Four of the *lais* are without animal or plant life ("**Chaitivel**," "**Les Deus Amanz**," "**Equitan**," and "**Lanval**") although mention is made of hunting in "**Equitan**" and Lanval does once lie in the meadow grass, hands behind his head, of a fine summer's day. "**Le Fresne**" provides an example of an undeveloped reference, a plant form chosen for its own sake or at random. This is no Druid tree cult wherein ash is purposefully preferred to oak, nor is there developed Christian symbolism, and other story tellers recounting this same *lai* do not always name the heroine Ash Tree, an indication that the name itself is not significant. If there is an underlying meaning, Marie neither develops nor transmits it.

What of the tree itself? In four lines Marie describes it:

> Un freisne vit le e branchu
> E mut espes e bien ramu;
> En quatre fors esteit quarre;
> Pur umbre fere i fu plante.

The impression given is a general one; the tree is thick, healthy, unnaturally balanced, an example of cultivated nature, subdued in the service of man who deliberately planted it for his pleasure. The tree is second to the person.

In "**Chevrefoil**" natural elements fulfill messenger or sign-bearing functions. The plant receives its meaning from the person, who literally carved it. It is fair to call the Goteleaf plant secondary and subservient to the characters of the story. So it is in three other *lais* as well, "**Guigemar**," "**Eliduc**," "**Milun**," where a white hind, two weasels, and a swan are the bearers of messages for those humans who send and receive them. Although, as Ewert notes with reference to "**Milun**," "there is no parallel in medieval literature for the use of a swan as a messenger," we can recognize an analogue to Ash Tree—nature subdued or trained for the benefit or use of man, in this case, to accomplish the lengthy correspondence between the separated lovers [Marie de France, *Lais,* ed. Alfred Ewert, 1947]. At its appearance, the swan is obviously a pet, introduced by the phrase "k'il mut ama," but one could wonder whether it is black or white and whether its life span is typical or magical.

The white hind and the weasels are messengers of a different order because they do not merely convey, they enlighten or instruct. The hind speaks, the weasels merely behave, but in both stories the animals advance plot by informing a major character. The animal's arrival on the scene is initially animal-like: the white hind and fawn startled, immobile in the forest, easy targets for the crashing hunter, the weasel scampering across the chapel floor, skittering frantically away from the sexton's broom. In both cases also man is on the attack, the animal is the victim, and eventually the man's teacher. But the initial natural image is less important than the message or lesson which the animal teaches.

How does this compare with the nightingale of "**Laüstic**"? Although the nightingale could be termed a message-bearer in this *lai,* it is also much more. First, the bird neither states (like the hind), nor carries imprinted (like the honeysuckle), nor acts out (like the weasels) the message: the nightingale is the message incarnate. Second, the bird brings to the *lai* a traditional lore or symbolic value of its own; any nightingale's song represents love and the nocturnal tryst or longing. Every use of the *laüstic* is laden with double meaning: the first song echoing the lovers' murmuring, the explanation by the wife of what she feels by the window expressed in terms of the nightingale, the husband's vow to trap the bird, its violent death literally thrown in the face of the wife, and the quasi-eternal reliquary where the love symbol will be ever remembered by the once happy lover. This is the culmination of a natural element used as sign, symbol, or message-bearer. The nightingale comes closest to escaping a secondary role, nay some might say it does escape, but I think it is still nature in the service of man. Again, Marie does not describe the bird, its natural habitat, or its behavior.

Two *lais* present a peculiar phenomenon for our consideration: "**Yonec**" and "**Bisclavret**" are about man-animal creatures who transform from one state to the other. Although we might call these supernatural, there is every indication that many medieval people found them credible denizens of nature. Yet, the image we receive of them is only the most vague and impressionistic. Yonec's hawk-father first arrives as the shadow of a great bird in the window, something that seemed to be a hawk, five or six moltings in age. No plumage color, no wing span, no eye type, no beak, no size except the word "grant." And the werewolf is, above all, frightening, not specifically furry, not depicted with teeth, no wolf-like body, no tail. The werewolf is never in motion except when he miraculously eludes the hounds and keepers to kiss the legs and feet of the king. Where do the hawk and wolf eat? Where do they live? How do they look in their forest habitat? Do they even inhabit the forest?

Certainly the reader could expect some comment about the transformation itself, but alas, nothing. Like Yonec's mother, one watches:

> E ele l'ot bien esgarde,
> Chevaler bel e gent devint.

Nothing else is shown, there are no stages. The were-wolf even speaks of his wolf state as "naked" since wolves wear no clothing. The change from man to wolf is a form of enslavement, and the reverse a liberation from confinement.

In the *lais,* animals are not interesting for their own sakes, they are not described from observation, at best they are messengers for man, and animal life, though instructive in certain restricted circumstances is inferior.

The *Ysopet* contrast with the *lais* in many ways; Marie here is not the creator, selecting animal or plant life to suit her aesthetic purposes, but she acts instead as transmitter and translator. A second even more obvious difference from the *lais* is that the overwhelming majority of the fables are animal centered. [Emanuel J.] Mickel classifies them into three groups: those where there are only animals (60), only people (18), and a mixture (nearly 20) [*Marie de France,* 1974]. In spite of this apparent wealth of animal lore, for every accurate account of a recognizable plant or animal, there are two fantastic though amusing fictions, and a careful reading of all 102 fables is most convincing as to the author-translator's interest, which is primarily human behavior. The true naturalist's mood of patient, affectionate data-gathering is wholly absent, and Mickel correctly notes that the *Ysopet* "is clearly not the personal observation of the author from a rustic scene."

Marie in the *lais* describes sparsely but accurately. Medievally acceptable supernatural behavior aside (the talking hind, the hawk-knight, the werewolf), she normally presents mimetic (the weasels, the nightingale) or at least plausible behavior (a swan that flies). Marie as translator neither corrects nor augments the view of nature she receives from the Latin model; that model leads her not only along conventionally inaccurate paths of the genre (*i.e.,* animals talking, imitating human behavior), but often it involves deliberate contradiction or distortion of reality as we and they know it, without the slightest discomfort to us or them. The reader here enters the realm of whimsy or fantasy, and he must be a willing accomplice (not a critical learner) to help it succeed. As Mickel states, referring to the *Ysopet*: "There is little evidence to indicate that the author carefully chose the actions based on their mimetic or symbolic appropriateness to the actors. Rather, the actions of personified inanimate objects, animals, and people are all appropriate to the situation and general truth which they serve to illustrate."

Mickel mentions in passing yet another aspect of this work: "In the fables where only animals are involved one finds the animals acting according to their natures and endowed with rational characteristics suitable to the roles they play within the animal hierarchy." "According to their nature"—the phrase is Marie's before it is Mickel's and for both of them, it is a convenient working hypothesis as well as a pseudo-naturalistic attitude. Marie clearly believes that it is an important phrase, for she places it in both the first and last fables. In Fable I, the hen "sulunc nature purchaçot sa viande" while in Fable CII the hen actually

speaks the phrase herself to insist upon her own identity which she refuses to violate: "sulunc ma nature e mun us."

Only one other fable (LXXIX) directly iterates the same principle. Hawk and owl share a nest, also sharing the responsibilities for raising the young. In spite of this, young hawks grow up to behave like hawks and owlets take after the owl. As one of the older birds says ruefully:

> Legiere chose est a saveir;
> de l'œf les poi jeu bien geter
> e par chalur e par cover,
> mais nient fors de lur nature.

Eight lines later, the moral concludes:

> Sa nature puet hum guenchir,
> mes nuls n'en puet del tut eissir.

The nature of the beast is changeless, no matter what his aspirations.

What is the source of information about the specific nature of the animals under consideration, since Marie is not an observer? There is no source. The phrase itself signals authority, similar to the many topic references to the ancients or the great songs and romances of the past. The reader nods his head, in complicity, and the phrase stills his curiosity before it even had a chance to be piqued.

In the *lais,* man is consistently superior to animals, though he may occasionally be instructed by them. In the fables, because so many animals imitate men in speech and action, the boundary between man and animal is less distinct. No animal bests a man except the serpent (Fable LXX), a watch-dog (Fable XLIII) and perhaps a beetle (Fable LXIII), but the people tricked are peasants and a thief. For the most part, animals and humans do not interrelate, they co-exist, and man is the superior creature, emulated by animals with mixed success since their animal nature limits potential at every turn. In genre the *Ysopet* is closest to the *Bestiaire d'amour,* a sub-type of bestiary; as the latter is a treatise about love, not animals, the former is a study of human behavior, not natural science.

Marie de France is a representative 12th-century courtly author, and the prevalence of plant and animal life in her writings affords the medievalist an opportunity to document attitudes toward the natural world which may be considered typical of Marie's era and its many courtly writers. Marie does not write from direct observation. She transmits the lore of others with no apparent concern for truth or accuracy. When animals or plants do appear, they are not well described, and they do not interest the author. Animals are used most often as messengers or illustrations, in the service or for the edification of man, who is the author's major concern. She is, at most, a pseudo-naturalist, to whom flora and fauna are useful, attractive, beloved, whimsical and fantastic in turn, but never *sui generis* commanding of her undivided attention.

Robert Sturges (essay date 1980)

SOURCE: "Text and Readers in Marie de France's *Lais*," in *Romanic Review,* Vol. LXXI, No. 3, May, 1980, pp. 244-64.

[*In the following essay, Sturges contends that readers of Marie's* Lais *are obliged by the structure of the* Lais *themselves to interpret the words and to become immersed in the stories as attempts at meaning, not as depictions of reality.*]

Although criticism in recent years of the **Lais** of Marie de France has done much to enhance the understanding of each of her individual tales, little attention has been devoted to the common themes and structures which unite them. Judith Rice Rothschild in her study *Narrative Technique in the Lais of Marie de France* [1974] has pointed out a number of themes reappearing in several tales; she believes that these common themes point toward an "artistic unity for the ensemble." To Rothschild's list of themes I would like to add the theme of interpretation. Many of the *lais* present figures who act as readers or interpreters analogous to the reader of the **Lais** themselves. Since the interpreting figures within the *lais* are invariably lovers, a further analogy, between the activities of love and of reading, is also suggested. Some of the *lais* pose problems raised by these analogies, while others suggest solutions.

Marie's book, considered as a whole, presents the reader with a variety of fictional worlds, some of which seem faithfully mimetic (the world of **"Laüstic,"** for example, or of **"Chaitivel"**) while others are more overtly fabulous (such as **"Bisclavret,"** whose hero is a werewolf, or **"Lanval,"** with its population of fairies). The mimetic worlds seldom come into contact with the fabulous worlds, and therefore neither of these two basic types calls the other's reality into question. There is, however, an ever-present tension between the apparent reality of whatever kind of world is being presented, and the self-conscious textuality of the *lai* itself. Each *lai* continually acknowledges, even emphasizes, the fact that it is a verbal, fictional creation, a text; self-reflexive details subvert any impression the reader may have gained of a reality other than the purely textual one, the reality that words alone, and not a world, are present in the work.

Perhaps the clearest example of the **Lais'** self-reflexiveness is to be found in the *lai* of **"Yonec."** The unnamed heroine, locked in a tower by her jealous husband, wishes that she might gain her freedom by becoming what the author and the reader know her to be: the heroine of a *lai*. At the end of her first speech, she expresses her desire for liberation in terms strongly reminiscent of those in which Marie de France herself, speaking in her own authorial voice in the **"Prologue"** to her book, describes how she came to write it. The heroine says:

> Mut ai sovent oï cunter
> Que l'em suleit jadis trover
> Aventures en cest païs

Ki rehaitouent les pensis.
Chevalier trovoent puceles
A lur talent, gentes e beles,
E dames truvoent amanz
Beaus e curteis, pruz e vaillanz,
Si que blasmees n'en esteient
Ne nul fors eles nes veeient.
Si ceo peot estrë e ceo fu,
Si unc a nul est avenu,
Deus, ki de tut ad poësté,
Il en face ma volente!

(ll. 91-104)

She wishes, in other words, for her life to become like one of the stories she has heard. Her words, especially the first four lines of the quotation above, inevitably recall what Marie has to say about similar stories:

> Des lais pensai, k'oïz aveie.
> Ne dutai pas, bien le saveie,
> Ke pur remambrance les firent
> Des aventures k'il oïrent
> Cil ki primes les comencierent
> E ki avant les enveierent.
> Plusurs en ai oï conter,
> Nes voil laissier ne oblier.

(**"Prologue,"** ll. 33-40)

This heroine, then, does not simply desire sexual freedom and adventure; her speech makes it clear to the reader that, whether she realizes it or not, the attainment of what she desires involves entering a story, or becoming like a text. She wants to be like a fictional character, and the fictions she wants to emulate correspond closely to this very collection of *lais*. When in the following lines her wish is granted in a particularly extravagant manner (a bird flies in through her window and magically becomes just such a lover as she had dreamed of), the reader is made aware that the tale he is reading is, indeed, exactly parallel to the tales the heroine has heard; it does not present him with any genuine reality, but simply with a fictional text conscious that it is like other fictional texts. Whatever suspension of disbelief the reader may have experienced is here subverted, not by the tale's fantastic elements, but by its textuality. The lady's passage from a presumed reality into fictionality can only emphasize the *lai*'s self-consciousness as a text.

The heroine's situation at this point is, in one way, similar to the reader's. She is an audience to ancient tales of love and adventure, just as the reader is an audience to Marie de France's similar tales; Marie from time to time (ironically or paradoxically, considering her simultaneous emphasis on the work's fictionality) even tells her readers that her *lais* are historically true, as the heroine of **"Yonec"** believes the tales she has heard to be true (in Marie's straight-faced conclusion to **"Bisclavret,"** for instance, she assures us that this tale of a werewolf "veraie fu," l. 316). The lady, however, is a far more naive reader than Marie's **Lais** allow their readers to be; the heroine wishes only for the reality recounted in those tales to become her own reality. She believes them to be faithful representations of what life could be like (as, within the tale, they are). This justifiable naiveté on her part makes it impossible for **"Yonec"**'s reader to be similarly naive: her desire to be like a character in a tale emphasizes the fact that she is indeed only a character in a tale, a verbal creation and not a possible model for the reader to emulate as this character emulates fictional heroines. The reader, unlike this lady, remains highly conscious of the tension between the *lai*'s representational and purely textual aspects.

If the reader becomes aware of the lady's textuality because of the resemblance between the tales she wishes to imitate and the text he is reading, the *lai*'s resemblance to a somewhat different kind of text-within-the-text makes it clear that her lover, Muldumarec, also contributes to the tale's self-consciousness. Fatally wounded by the suspicious husband, Muldumarec prophesizes that his son Yonec will avenge him when the boy learns his father's story:

> Par une tumbe k'il verrunt
> Orrunt renoveler sa mort
> E cum il fu ocis a tort.
> Ileoc li baillerat s'espeie.
> L'aventure li seit cuntee
> Cum il fu nez, ki l'engendra:
> Asez verrunt k'il en fera.
>
> (ll. 430-6)

The "aventure" whose narration will be prompted by the sight of Muldumarec's tomb is, of course, the plot of this very *lai* of **"Yonec."** When Yonec, along with his mother and her husband, finally does see his father's tomb, the story we have just read is gradually pieced together for him by the tomb's guardians and by the heroine, who also reveals its relevance to her son:

> Cil comencierent a plurer
> E en plurant a recunter
> Que c'iert li mieudre chevaliers
> E li plus forz e li plus fiers,
> Li plus beaus e li plus amez
> Ki jamés seit el siecle nez.
> De ceste tere ot este reis,
> Unques ne fu nuls si curteis.
> A Carwent fu entrepris,
> Pur l'amur d'une dame ocis.
> "Unques puis n'eümes seignur,
> Ainz avum atendu meint jur
> Un fiz qu'en la dame engendra,
> Si cum il dist e cumanda."
> Quant la dame oï la novele,
> A haute voiz sun fiz apele:
> "Beaus fiz, fet ele, avez oï
> Cum Deus nus ad menez ici?
> C'est vostre pere ki ci gist,
> Que cist villarz a tort ocist.
> Or vus comant e rent s'espee,
> Jeo l'ai asez lung tens gardee."
> Oiant tuz li ad coneü
> Qu'il l'engendrat e sis fiz fu;

> Cum il suleit venir a li
> E cum sis sires le trahi,
> La verité li ad cuntee.
>
> (ll. 513-39)

The heroine wished to be like a character in a story; Muldumarec ends as the main character in this story told to his son. She projected herself into a tale of the past by means of her memory, while he projects himself into a future tale by means of his prophecy. Both of these texts, remembered tale and predicted narration, are reflections in miniature of the *lai* of **"Yonec"** itself: the heroine's ideal stories are very much like this *lai,* and Muldumarec's projected narrative turns out to be an exact recapitulation of it. In this way, both of the tale's main characters demonstrate their own textuality: by projecting themselves into texts which are reflections of the *lai* itself, they insure the reader's consciousness of the tale as text.

Self-consciousness is not, however, an end in itself for Marie's *Lais*. These tales do not point out their own fictionality simply in order to demonstrate the lack of genuine human contact between tale and reader that such self-reflexiveness might imply. The *Lais'* emphasis on their own textuality is only the first step toward engaging the reader's awareness of, and responses to, a thematic concern central to all of them: the problem of interpretation, which is first approached by Marie herself in her "Prologue":

> Custume fu as anciens,
> Ceo testimoine Precïens,
> Es livres ke jadis feseient,
> Assez oscurement diseient
> Pur ceus ki a venir esteient
> E ki aprendre les deveient,
> K'i peüssent gloser la lettre
> E de lur sen le surplus mettre.
>
> (ll. 9-16)

These lines have sparked an ongoing critical debate. Leo Spitzer and D. W. Robertson, Jr., have argued that the *sen* or *surplus* to be added by the reader "is obviously the 'Christian' attitude" or *sententia* [Spitzer, "The Prologue to the *Lais* of Marie de France and Medieval Poetics," *Modern Philology,* Vol. 41, 1943-44; Robertson, "Marie de France, *Lais,* Prologue, 13-16," *Modern Language Notes,* Vol. 64, 1949]. This is not what Marie's words (*lur* sen) say, however; and, as a more recent critic has said of the problem of glossing in a somewhat different context,

> The question has been needlessly obscured by the fact that some modern critics have sought to justify their claims by appealing to one or more theoretical discussions of the problem in medieval philosophy instead of seeing how the poets treat glossing in their poems
>
> [Mary Carruthers, "Letter and Gloss in the Friar's and Summoner's Tales," *Journal of Narrative Technique,* Vol. 2, 1972].

Tony Hunt has provided a much more convincing reading of these lines with greater fidelity both to the text as it stands and to certain theories of interpretation current in Marie's period ["Glossing Marie de France," *Romanische Forschungen,* Vol. 86, 1974]. He paraphrases the lines in question (ll. 15-16) thus: "'they might construe their writing and through their wits add the rest (that was necessary to complete elucidation).'" The *sen* to be added, then, is not a predetermined Christian doctrine, but something the reader brings to the text himself. This point is necessary to an understanding of the theme of interpretation in the *lais.* Marie sees herself as an emulator of the ancient writers, that is, as one who writes obscurely so that later readers might gloss her text and add (as Marie added to the *aventures* she remembered hearing) their own interpretations to the work. The "grevose ovre" referred to in l.25 is presumably the work the reader is now beginning, the *Lais* themselves; Marie has provided her readers with an especially difficult text so that they, too, might fully experience the joys of interpretation. Since she made it clear in the earlier lines that the addition of the reader's own *sen* or meaning to the work is an important aspect of the interpretive act, Marie de France seems to invite the reader's interpretation as a valid expansion of her work. What she desires is not simply that he understand the story, if by "understanding" is meant only an acceptance of her own point of view toward it; equally necessary is the reader's very act of engagement with the text, the process itself of interpretation.

The heroine of **"Yonec"** is not the only figure of the reader, naive or otherwise, to be found in the *Lais.* The plot of each of the *lais* depends at one point or another upon the interpretation by one character of a sign of some kind made by another character. These signs range from complex verbal narratives and expressions of emotion to simple love-tokens, but all are made specifically to be interpreted. Characters in these tales spend an inordinate amount of time "reading" each other by means of these texts and tokens, and if the making of signs self-consciously reflects the making of the *lais* themselves, the reading of them necessarily projects a far more active role for the reader than the simple contemplation of a self-reflexive work having no relevance to his own reality. The reader's awareness that the text is a text is only the preparation for a more important realization: that the text, even the self-conscious text, is interpretable, that it requires his participation if meaning is to emerge from it. By signaling their own status as texts, the *Lais* are able to move beyond that mere, static textuality into a kind of dialogue with the reader.

In **"Chievrefoil,"** the shortest and perhaps best-known of Marie de France's *Lais,* most of the action is concerned with the making of a text by one character, Tristan, for the benefit of another, Iseut. This *lai* makes no secret of the fact that it is about the making of a *lai,* that it records the history of its own composition; its four-line prologue and twelve-line conclusion tell the reader directly that such is its subject-matter:

> Asez me plest e bien le voil,
> Del lai qu'hum nume *Chievrefoil,*

> Que la verité vus en cunt
> Pur quei fu fez, coment e dunt

(ll. 1-4)

> Pur la joie qu'il ot eüe
> De s'amie qu'il ot veüe
> E pur ceo k'il aveit escrit
> Si cum la reïne l'ot dit,
> Pur les paroles remembrer,
> Tristram, ki bien saveit harper,
> En aveit fet un nuvel lai.

(ll. 107-13)

Between its beginning and its ending, however, **"Chievrefoil"** presents a more subtle consideration of the creation and interpretation of symbols, of the relationship between a writer of words and an interpreter of writing. The plot of this tale is simple: Tristan, exiled from King Mark's court, learns that Iseut is about to undertake a journey. He hides in a wood through which she must pass, and leaves a message of some kind written on a piece of wood by the road for her to see. When Iseut sees and understands the message, she joins Tristan in the woods for a brief encounter before continuing on her way. Tristan composes a *lai* on the subject of the message and their meeting; Marie de France herself composes a *lai* on the subject of the composition of Tristan's *lai.*

The brevity of this *lai* causes Marie to be somewhat elliptical; the longest continuing debate among scholars writing on Marie's work concerns the exact nature of Tristan's message in **"Chievrefoil."** It is interesting to note that, although none of them mention the problem specifically, all of these critics are mainly concerned with just how much interpreting Iseut has to do. Their own interpretations are many: did Tristan write only his name on the famous piece of wood, leaving Iseut to supply the interpretation which occupies lines 63-78? Did he write out the entire message himself? Was the piece of wood an ogam, and was Iseut versed in the interpretation of ogamic characters? Had he written her a letter beforehand containing the interpretation? There is no way of knowing what Marie intended; line 53 states that Tristan carved his name, while lines 61-62, referring to the long interpretation that follows, say:

> Ceo fu la summe de l'escrit
> Qu'il li aveit mandé e dit.

"umme" is defined by Greimas as either "résumé" or "l'essentiel," and whether this gist or meaning was written out or meant to be divined by Iseut from the sight of Tristan's name alone is impossible to determine.

What is certain is Tristan's intention, for he, like Marie, is an artist, as the *lai*'s conclusion, on his abilities as a harpist and composer of *lais,* informs us. Whether or not he writes in ogamic characters, he is, as an artist, well-versed in the creation of other kinds of symbols, and what he intends is for Iseut, his reader, to interpret his symbols correctly. Whether lines 63-78 represent what Tristan actually wrote or what was to be divined by Iseut, at the heart of this message lies a sign created by Tristan to be read by Iseut:

> D'euls deus fu il tut autresi
> Cume del chievrefoil esteit
> Ki a la codre se perneit:
> Quant il s'i est laciez e pris
> E tut entur le fust s'est mis,
> Ensemble poënt bien durer,
> Mes ki puis les voelt desevrer,
> Li codres muert hastivement
> E li chievrefoilz ensemble.
> "Bele amie, si est de nus:
> Ne vus sanz mei, ne jeo sanz vus."
>
> (ll. 68-78)

The medium here is clearly the message: the branch on which the message is carved is of "codre" (l. 51), probably hazel, and presumably the "codre" entwined with honeysuckle ("chievrefoil") mentioned in line 70. Tristan has combined a written text with a physical object of symbolic value demanding and encouraging interpretation from the audience for whom it is intended. He winds up composing a *lai* about that very process (l. 109), and Marie herself ends the tale with the information that she, an audience to his composition, has created a similar composition about Tristan's *lai:*

> Dit vus en ai la verité
> Del lai que j'ai ici cunté.
>
> (ll. 117-8)

"Chievrefoil," then, is a poem about the creation of a *lai* about the creation of a poetic, or at least verbal and interpretable, symbol. It seems likely, therefore, that these three creations are to be seen as parallels, and at the basis of all three there lies the demand for a reading, for interpretation. Just as Iseut's reading of Tristan's wooden sign prompts the composition of his *lai* (whose subject is, in part, her response to the original sign), so Marie's "reading" of that *lai* prompts her own composition aimed, in turn, at readers, who will necessarily occupy a position similar to Iseut's and Marie's: that of responsive audience to an artistic performance. **"Chievrefoil"** presents a chain of compositions and their audiences leading to itself and its own audience; implicit is the likelihood that the active reader, seeing himself reflected in the images of previous readers in the chain, Iseut and Marie, might emulate their responses and, by means of his own interpretive reading, also join in this creative process. By providing characters who perform functions corresponding to the reader's, Marie draws her own readers into an active involvement with her creation.

Marie de France also demonstrates an interest in entirely non-verbal signs whose need to be interpreted by an engaged reader is emphasized. She provides a number of examples; the best are to be found in her collection's first *lai,* **"Guigemar."** This tale's self-conscious textuality is demonstrated, at certain points, in the same way **"Yonec"**'s is: the lovers recapitulate to each other the story of their lives that the reader already knows, much as Yonec's mother recapitulates Muldumarec's story; each of the

lovers thus makes the other a reader and himself or herself a narrative to be read (as in lines 311-358, for example). The necessity for interpretation, however, is given greater emphasis in the episode of their exchange of love-tokens. Fearing that they might be separated (as they soon will be), each devises an ingenious method of assuring himself or herself of the other's fidelity:

> —Amis, de ceo m'aseürez!
> Vostre chemise me livrez;
> El pan desuz ferai un plait:
> Cungié vus doins, u ke ceo seit,
> D'amer cele kil defferat
> E ki despleier le savrat.
> Il li baile, si l'aseüre.
> Le plet i fet en teu mesure,
> Nule femme nel deffereit,
> Si force u cutel n'i meteit.
> La chemise li dune e rent.
> Il la receit par tel covent
> Qu'el le face seür de li;
> Par une ceinture autresi,
> Dunt a sa char nue la ceint,
> Par mi le flanc aukes l'estreint:
> Ki la bucle purrat ovrir
> Sanz depescier e sanz partir,
> Il li prie que celui aint.
>
> (ll. 557-75)

Untying the knot and unbuckling the belt are forceful images of the interpretive process; it is an essential feature of these devices that they are not simply a means of preserving the beloved for the lover, but are also a means by which the beloved can identify the lover, that is, a way of recognizing or of reading the other's identity. The correct interpretation of these signs would lead to the recognition of the lover. It seems, in fact, curiously enough, that it is only through these signs that the other can be recognized, that without them, the lovers would not know each other: when they meet again after having been separated, the sight of his beloved is not apparently enough to convince Guigemar of her identity:

> "Est ceo, fet il, ma duce amie,
> M'esperaunce, mun quor, ma vie,
> Ma bele dame ki m'ama?
> Dunt vient ele? Ki l'amena?
> Ore ai pensé mut grant folie;
> Bien sai que ceo n'est ele mie:
> Femmes se resemblent asez,
> Pur nient change mis pensez.
>
> (ll. 773-80)

Even verbal communication is not enough proof; only when they have formally solved the puzzles posed by the knot and the buckle does recognition take place:

> Quant ele ot le comandement,
> Le pan de la chemise prent,
> Legierement le despleiat.
> Li chevaliers s'esmerveillat;
> Bien la conut, mes nequedent

Nel poeit creire fermement.
A li parlat en teu mesure:
"Amie, duce creature,
Estes vus ceo? Dites mei veir!
Lessiez mai vostre cors veeir,
La ceinture dunt jeo vus ceins."

(ll. 809-19)

Direct apprehension of each other cannot exist between
these lovers; they require the assistance of interpretable
signs, both the puzzle-devices themselves and the process
of solving or undoing them serving as signs whose correct reading will lead to union with the other.

The making of signs and texts that require a reader's interpretation serves a double purpose in each of these *lais.*
It serves to reveal the lovers to each other, and to conceal
their relationship from the world at large. This point is
made most specifically in **"Yonec"**; Muldumarec's dying
gifts to his mistress are a magic ring, whose magical properties cause the jealous husband to forget what he knows
of the lady's infidelity, and a sword, which is to serve as
a reminder of their love, a sign to be used when revealing
the truth to their son, Yonec:

Un anelet li ad baillé,
Si li ad dit e enseigné,
Ja tant cum el le gardera,
A sun seignur n'en membera
De nule rien ki fete seit,
Ne ne l'en tendrat en destreit.
S'espee li cumande e rent,
Puis la conjurë e defent
Que ja nuls hum n'en seit saisiz.
Mes bien la gart a oés sun fiz.

(ll. 415-24)

These interpretable signs are meant to be interpreted only
by those characters actually involved in the love-relationship, Muldumarec, his mistress, and their child; in the
relationship between that group and the rest of the world,
the signs serve precisely the opposite function: they actually prevent interpretation, concealing, by their very existence, their true meaning, and preventing any reading on the
part of others. The same functions are served by Tristan's
text in **"Chievrefoil"**; although Iseut interprets it correctly—

Le bastun vit, bien l'aparceut,
Tutes les lettres i conut.—

(ll. 81-2)

its meaning and even, apparently, the very fact that it is
a sign demanding that someone read it, is lost on her
companions:

Les chevaliers ki la menoent
E ki ensemble od li erroent
Cumanda tuz a arester:
Descendre voet e reposer.
Cil unt fait sun commandement.
Ele s'en vet luinz de sa gent.

(ll. 83-8)

Again, in **"Guigemar,"** the love-tokens both identify the
members of the love-relationship and prevent others from
joining in that relationship:

Le plet i fet en teu mesure,
Nule femme nel deffereit,
Si force u cutel n'i meteit.

(ll. 564-6)

Numerous other examples of the sign or text interpretable
by the lover but preventing interpretation by the world
outside the relationship might be cited from Marie's *Lais;*
the swan-messenger in **"Milun"** comes to mind, or the
nightingale in **"Laüstic."**

The point here is that in any love-relationship presented
in the *Lais,* the lover is always an interpreter, and that
interpretation, or at least correct interpretation, is a function only of the lover. To love, for Marie, is to interpret
the signs and texts which identify the beloved, and to
interpret those signs and texts correctly is to achieve the
union or reunion of lovers. In a sense, then, the active
participation in the creative process allowed the reader by
Marie's *Lais* might be perceived as an activity parallel to
that which unites the lovers within the tales: to read or
interpret the text correctly is to enter into an erotic relationship with it. Love and interpretation are metaphors
for each other.

Marie suggests this relationship subtly, but more directly
than might at first be imagined, in the interplay between
a passage in her **"Prologue"** to the whole book of *Lais*
and several suggestive passages in the individual *lais* themselves. Near the end of the **"Prologue"** Marie, speaking
as the author of her book directly to her readers, describes
her method of composition:

Rimé en ai e fait ditié,
Soventes fiez en ai veillié!

(ll. 41-2)

The problem of composition, that is, of interpreting her
predecessors and of creating a work obscure enough to
allow interpretation by her readers (as discussed above),
often kept Marie awake at night. This issue of someone's
inability to sleep at night because he or she is beset by
problems of interpretation is one that comes up often
throughout the *Lais,* but only here in the **"Prologue"** is
it applied to an author's attempt at literary creation. Every time this problem is raised in the *lais* themselves, the
victim of sleeplessness is not a reader/author figure like
the **"Prologue"**'s authorial voice, but a lover trying to
interpret the behavior of his or her beloved.

Several examples can be cited from the various tales. In
"Guigemar," the man and the woman each pass a sleepless night wondering how the other feels. Of Guigemar
himself the author says:

Tute la nuit ad si veillé
E suspiré e travaillé,

(ll. 411-12)

and his work consists of attempts to determine whether or not the lady will prove "orgoilluse e fiere" (1. 404) and refuse him. The lady, meanwhile, experiences the same difficulty:

> Veillé aveit, de ceo se pleint;
> Ceo fet Amur, ki la destreint,
>
> (ll. 429-30)

the problem being her lack of knowledge of Guigemar's feelings, *"s'il l'eime u nun"* (1. 436). In a similar fashion, the king in **"Equitan"** *"veilla tant que jur fu"* (1. 101) because, as he says,

> Uncor ne sai ne n'ai seü
> S'ele fereit de mei sun dru.
>
> (ll. 93-4)

Again, the young lady in **"Eliduc"**

> Tute la nuit veillat issi,
> Ne resposa ne ne dormi.
>
> (ll. 331-2)

and for the same reason.

Finally, and most strikingly, the entire plot of **"Laüstic"** revolves around the problem of being kept awake by love. The lovers in this tale, already aware that their feelings are reciprocated, stay awake because only at night are they sure of the privacy necessary for their secret communication. The lady's excuse to her husband for staying awake, that she is listening to the nightingale's song, thus becomes a doubly meaningful symbol like the ring in **"Yonec"**: to the lovers it is a sign of their love, while it conceals that love from the rest of the world. Ultimately, when the jealous husband kills the nightingale to remove the lady's excuse for staying awake, the symbol of a living bird becomes an ornate but lifeless text substituted for the lovers' oral communication:

> "Lasse, fet ele, mal m'estait!
> Ne purrai mes la nuit lever
> N'aler a la fenestre ester . . . ."
>
> (ll. 126-28)

> En une piece de samit
> A or brusdé e tut escrit
> Ad l'oiselet envolupé;
> Un suen vaslet ad apelé,
> Sun message li ad chargié,
> A sun ami l'ad enveié.
>
> (ll. 135-40)

Their relationship destroyed by the destruction of its symbol, all that remains is this text created by the lady for her lover.

In her **"Prologue,"** then, Marie de France chooses to speak of the activity of literary interpretation in terms otherwise reserved for her characters' interpretations of their lovers' emotions. That these activities might be regarded as parallels is suggested by the similarity of the situations in which the literary interpreter of the **"Prologue"** and the lovers in **"Guigemar,"** **"Equitan,"** and **"Eliduc"** find themselves, kept awake by problems of interpretation. The parallel can only be strengthened by reference to **"Laüstic,"** whose heroine substitutes the creation of a text for the love which had kept her awake. All these tales suggest that love is related metaphorically to literary creation and interpretation; in **"Laüstic,"** the reader of the lady's text is her former lover, who responds to her message by creating his own work of art as a commemoration of their love:

> Quant tut li ad dit e mustré
> E il l'avait bien escuté,
> De l'aventure esteit dolenz;
> Mes ne fu pas vileins ne lenz.
> Un vaisselet ad fet forgier;
> Unques n'i ot fer ne acier,
> Tuz fu d'or fin od bones pieres,
> Mut precïuses e mut chieres;
> Covercle i ot tres bien asis.
> Le laustic ad dedenz mis.
>
> (ll. 145-54)

To love is to interpret, that is, to read the beloved's text and react to it; thus the reader of Marie's *Lais* is to the text as a lover within the text is to his beloved. Text and reader form an erotic alliance.

The text reveals itself gradually to the reader, as characters in the tales slowly reveal themselves to each other. In **"Eliduc,"** for example, the reader gleans as little information from observing the hero as the heroine does, even though he has heard two fairly complex theories of interpretation from the lady and from her chamberlain. Before hearing them, the reader has been made aware that Eliduc, though still faithful to his wife, Guildeluëc, also feels a strong attachment to a second lady, Guilliadun; suspense as to whether or not he will, in fact, love Guilliadun is maintained as the poet documents Eliduc's vacillations:

> Tuz est murnes e trespensez,
> Pur la belë est en effrei,
> La fille sun seignur le rei,
> Ki tant ducement l'apela
> E de ceo k'ele suspira.
>
> (ll. 314-18)

> De sa femme li remembra
> E cum il li asseüra
> Que bone fei li portereit
> E leaument se cuntendreit.
>
> (ll. 323-6)

At this point the narrative leaves Eliduc in a state of indecision, and turns to Guilliadun, who has already fallen in love with him, and to her chamberlain; these two share the reader's suspense about Eliduc's feelings toward the lady, and discuss the possibility of arriving at a correct interpretation of them:

"Dame, fet il, quant vus l'amez,
Enveiez i, si li mandez;
Ceinturë u laz u anel
Enveiez li, si li ert bel.
Si il le receit bonement
E joius seit del mandement,
Seüre seiez de s'amur . . . ."

(ll. 355-61)

La dameisele respundi,
Quant le cunseil de lui oï:
"Coment savrai par mun present
S'il ad de mei amer talent?
Jeo ne vi unques chevalier
Ki se feist de ceo preier,
Si il amast u il haïst,
Que volentiers ne retenist
Cel present k'hum li enveast.

(ll. 365-73)

The chamberlain believes that Eliduc's reaction to a token sent by Guilliadun will serve as an interpretable sign
of whether or not he loves her, while Guilliadun herself
maintains that appearances might be deceiving, without
proposing any more effective plan. These attempts to read
Eliduc's emotions can only emphasize the closeness of
the parallel between the reader's situation with regard to
the text, and the lover's, Guilliadun's, situation with regard to the beloved, Eliduc: each is in suspense about the
outcome of events, looking forward to a sign (whether
from the author or from the beloved) which will allow a
correct interpretation of the mystery.

Guilliadun at last consents to the chamberlain's plan; the
reader then witnesses a scene which, according to the
theory of interpretation proposed by the chamberlain,
should provide such an interpretable sign, a clue to Eliduc's feelings:

Li chamberlencs mut se hasta.
A Eliduc esteit venuz.
A cunseil li ad dit saluz
Que la pucele li mandot,
E l'anelet li presentot;
La ceinture li ad donee.
Li chevaliers l'ad mercïee,
L'anelet d'or mist en sun dei,
La ceinture ceinst entur sei;
Ne li vadlez plus ne li dist
Ne il nïent ne li requist
Fors tant que del suen li offri.
Cil n'en prist rien, si est parti.

(ll. 402-14)

The surprise, of course, is that we learn nothing from this
anxiously awaited interview; Guilliadun's suspicions that
appearances might be deceiving prove disappointingly
accurate. Eliduc remains opaque even to the watchfulness
of the chamberlain, and of the reader as well, who learns
that Eliduc is willing to give his love to Guilliadun only
when she herself learns it. In this way the text teases the
reader into involvement, giving him in Guilliadun a representative within the tale who demonstrates the process
of interpretation and who eventually allows the reader to
become a party to the lovers' secret. If the purpose of
signs and texts is to reveal lovers to one another while
concealing their relationship from the rest of the world,
then the reader interpreting the text becomes a member of
that relationship, as it is revealed to him.

The very nature of literature, however, and especially the
nature of these *lais,* as Marie seems to conceive of them,
complicates this seemingly private, erotic encounter between reader and text. Marie continually emphasizes, in
the brief prologues and epilogues to her various tales, the
public nature of literature, the fact that she is giving the
secret away by writing about it. **"Laüstic,"** for example,
whose plot's major concern is with the attempt to conceal
a love-affair from the outside world, ends with an admission that the attempt failed precisely because it was turned
into a *lai:*

Cele aventure fu cuntee,
Ne pot estre lunges celee.
Un lai en firent li Bretun:
Le Laüstic l'apelë hum.

(ll. 157-60)

Marie is clearly contributing to this public knowledge of
the lovers' relationship by writing her own version of the
lai; if the individual reader can be seen as a participant in
the private encounter of lovers, it is also true that he can
be seen as a member of the public to whom that relationship is revealed, against the lovers' will Publicity, we
learn over and over again in the tales themselves, can
destroy the love-relationship; this is the reason for using
symbols interpretable only by the lovers themselves in
"Guigemar," "Yonec," "Milun," "Chievrefoil," and
others. This is as true of the reader-text relationship as of
the lovers' relationship within the text. If the reader becomes engaged in the text through the private interpretation of signs, the public revelation of those signs must
vitiate his engagement, making him a member of the
outside world rather than the love-relationship. And yet
publicity is the very reason for making a *lai,* the point
being to bring a private story to the attention of others
"pur remembrance," as Marie says in her **"Prologue"** (1.
35). The encounter between reader and text cannot be
hidden from the rest of the world, because the reader is
a part of that world.

Several of Marie's *lais* seem to propose solutions to this
paradox of the reader's position as a member both of a
private love-relationship and of the public whose knowledge destroys love. What is needed are texts that allow
the reader to enter into the erotic, interpreting relationship with them without wholly exposing their secrets to
the public knowledge, texts that engage each reader as an
individual without imposing any single solution to their
mysteries upon him. Marie's description in the **"Prologue"**
of how a reader should approach a text—"de lur sen le
surplus mettre" (1. 16)—can, then, be seen as an invitation to personal interpretation, to the private solution of
problems or mysteries the text itself refuses to solve.

One such text which invites the reader's active interpretation is the well-known *lai* of **"Lanval."** The major emphasis of this tale's plot is entirely upon the maintenance of secrecy, specifically Lanval's maintenance of the secret of his fairy-mistress's identity. The danger of publicity to the love-relationship is spelled out even more specifically than usual in this *lai;* the lady, speaking with the authority of the supernatural, tells Lanval:

> ". . . Ne vus descovrez a nul humme!
> De ceo vus dirai ja la summe:
> A tuz jurs m'avrïez perdue.
> Si ceste amur esteit seüe;
> Jamés nem purrïez veeir
> Ne de mun cors seiseisine aveir."
>
> (ll. 145-50)

Love here clearly depends upon mystery; and the lady is as mysterious to the reader as she is to Lanval and, later, to the members of King Arthur's court. Emphasis is placed on the enigmatic nature of this lady from the first moment she appears; her handmaidens carry ritual objects whose significance is never explained, and she herself explains her presence without ever mentioning her origins or identity:

> "Lanval, fet ele, beus amis,
> Pur vus vinc jeo fors de ma tere:
> De luinz vus sui venue quere! . . . .
>
> (ll. 110-12)

Her parting words to Lanval remind him that she must remain a mystery to all:

> ". . . Nul hum fors vus ne me verra
> Ne ma parole nen orra."
>
> (ll. 169-70)

The question of who this lady is remains unanswered in the text, even though Lanval disobeys her command and reveals the existence of their relationship to the queen when she mocks him for refusing her love. Indeed, the point is made more forcefully here than in any other *lai* that the lady's existence is revealed, as is her beauty, directly to a public gathering of people outside the relationship. Lanval having been condemned because of his boast that his lady's beauty exceeds the queen's, she refuses at first to appear and thus justify him, because he has broken her rule of secrecy. She finally relents in order to save him by proving that his boast was the truth:

> Devant le rei est descendue,
> Si que de tuz iert bien veüe.
> Sun mantel ad laissié cheeir,
> Que mieuz la peüssent veeir.
>
> (ll. 603-6)

But in spite of such publicity, this lady remains a tantalizing enigma; although often called the "fairy-mistress" by critics, nowhere is the reader given direct information on her nature. In fact, when her hand-maidens appear to announce her arrival. even Lanval must admit that

> . . . ne seit ki sunt
> Ne dunt vienent n'u eles vunt.
>
> (ll. 483-4)

Although we learn that she takes Lanval away to Avalon, we also learn that that information comes second-hand ("Ceo nus recuntent li Bretun," l. 642); Marie in this line joins the puzzled audience as one who knows only what she has heard, but cannot tell if it is the true story. She prefers to end on a note of mystery:

> Nuls hum n'en oï plus parler
> Ne jeo n'en sai avant cunter.
>
> (ll. 645-6)

Although Lanval may have violated the lady's secrecy, then, the text refuses to do so. It presents the reader with an enigmatic character and refuses to explain her. It does, however, try to tempt the reader into explaining her himself; clues like the unexplained ritual objects and the second-hand Breton speculation about the isle of Avalon tease the reader to provide an interpretation. Lanval's ignorance about her identity points out to the reader that he is in the presence of a mystery waiting to be solved. The reader must interpret without the author's assurance that his reading will be correct; he must be willing to find a *sen* on his own. In this way he engages himself in the text without violating it; his reading remains a private, erotic encounter rather than a public one with meaning imposed by the author. The act of interpretation will not be vitiated by public explanation in this tale, because no explanation is forthcoming. The reader thus remains a full participant in the tale to the end.

The love-relationship, as well as the relationship between reader and text, is presented more poignantly in the *lai* of **"Chaitivel."** This tale's consciousness of its own textuality is as pronounced as that of **"Chievrefoil"**: almost one-fifth of the entire *lai* concerns the manner in which the heroine made her experiences into a *lai,* and the problem of choosing a correct title for it. Four knights love the same lady, who is unable to choose among them; all fight in a tournament to prove their worth, and three are killed while the fourth is badly wounded. The lady is unable to love the survivor because of her memories of the others; she decides to compose a *lai* about them to be called *Quatre Dols* ("Four Sorrows"). The surviving knight protests that *Chaitivel* ("Wretched One") is a better title. Marie ends by saying that either title would do.

The problem confronted in the final sections of this *lai* is the difficulty of reconciling two different perceptions of an event, of bringing two points of view into harmony. The lady's preferred title, "Quatre Dols," refers to her own perspective on the events just recounted: she alone experiences them as four separate sorrows, one for each dead or wounded suitor. Her reasons for preferring that title take the form of an explanation of her own state of mind:

> ". . . Pur ceo que tant vus ai amez,
> Voil que mis doels seit remembrez;

De vus quatre ferai un lai
E *Quatre Dols* le numerai."

(ll. 201-4)

The surviving knight, on the other hand, does not seem to recognize her point of view at all; his explanation of his own title takes into account the sufferings of the other knights, which ended in their deaths, but not the lady's sorrow. His sorrow alone, he implies, is worthy of mention in the *lai*'s title:

". . . Mes jo, ki sui eschapez vifs,
Tuz esgarez e tuz cheitifs,
Ceo qu'el siecle puis plus amer
Vei sovent venir e aler,
Parler od mei matin e seir,
Si n'en puis nule joie aveir
Ne de baisier ne d'acoler
Ne d'autre bien fors de parler.
Teus cent maus me fetes suffrir!
Mieuz me vaudreit la mort tenir!
Pu c'ert li lais de meiz nomez:
Le Chaitivel iert apelez . . . .

(ll. 215-26)

The lady finally agrees to use his title, but it is clear that he has not understood her point of view at all, perhaps believing that "Quatre Dols" refers not to her own sorrows, but to those of the dead knights and himself. Marie's brief epilogue to the tale proper emphasizes, not the fact that her own version bears the title **"Chaitivel,"** but the unresolved tension that remains between the two points of view as represented by the two titles, the difficulty or even impossibility of choosing one as more appropriate than the other:

Issi fu li lais comenciez
E puis parfaiz e anunciez.
Icil kil porterent avant,
Quatre Dols l'apelent alquant;
Chescuns des nuns bien i afiert,
Kar la matire le requiert;
Le Chaitivel ad nun en us.

(ll. 231-7)

In the final lines, in fact, the narrator specifically says that no more satisfactory conclusion could be reached:

Ici finist, nen i ad plus,
Plus n'en oï ne plus n'en sai
Ne plus ne vus en cunterai.

(ll. 238-40)

This disclaimer, the narrator's inability to give any more information or provide a solution, is reminiscent of the smilar conclusion to **"Lanval."** In each case, the narrator leaves the reader with a problem or mystery requiring resolution, refusing to speculate any further or even to provide more information. Although **"Chaitivel"**'s problem is more concrete and presents a more limited number of possible solutions than the mystery of the lady's identity in **"Lanval,"** the two tales do have in common the

narrator's final withdrawal into silence. Both present the reader with a situation requiring interpretation, and with clues or possible points of view that tempt him to try and provide that interpretation himself; neither imposes an authoritative reading upon him. They allow the engaged reader to supply the tale's meaning.

The reader is free, at the end of **"Chaitivel,"** to find its meaning not in either the lady's point of view or the knight's, but in the remaining tension between the two, in the knowledge that one consciousness is inevitably isolated from another, that direct apprehension by one mind of another is impossible. An easy union of perceptions cannot be accomplished; what can be accomplished, however, is mutual contact through interpretation. This concept can ultimately be applied to all of Marie's other *lais,* which can thus be seen, in part, as a reaction to a basic fact of human existence. The reason for placing interpretable signs and texts as mediators—both barriers and bridges—between lovers is the same as the reason for creating interpretable texts to stand between an author and a reader: people cannot apprehend one another directly, cannot read one another's minds, but need, on the one hand, rings or belts as in **"Eliduc"** or **"Guigemar,"** swans as in **"Milun,"** human manners as in **"Bisclavret,"** and all the other interpretable signs discussed above; and, on the other hand, stories. Lovers can read each other's signs even when, as in **"Guigemar,"** they cannot recognize each other; and readers can participate in the chain of creation and interpretation best when meaning is not imposed upon them, because Marie's texts allow it. When, as in **"Milun,"** whose characters communicate secretly for years without coming together, love is exclusively a matter of signs and texts that substitute for contact, it becomes clear just how closely the two activities are linked. For Marie, both love and literature involve a frustrated desire for contact, and both try to deal with frustration through symbol-making and interpretation; if her lovers are like readers and her readers are like lovers, it is because these functions are analogous means of engaging another by inviting his participation in the creation of meaning through interpretation. The **Lais** both represent for their characters and present to their readers a condition of life: the independent consciousness confronting all that is not itself, and trying to make sense of it.

Glyn Burgess (essay date 1983)

SOURCE: "Chivalry and Prowess in the *Lais* of Marie de France," in *French Studies,* Vol. XXXVII, No. 2, April, 1983, pp. 129-42.

[*In the following essay, Burgess observes that most of the characters in Marie's* Lais *belong to the upper classes, and thus issues of loyalty, service, and expertise in battle and hunting predominate.*]

The world of Marie de France's **Lais** is fundamentally one of *chevaliers* and their ladies. There are 126 examples of the term *cheval(i)er* in the twelve poems and only seven of *vassal,* five of which occur in **"Lanval."** Almost all the male characters whose attitudes and activities Marie clearly supports are described as *chevaliers:* Guigemar and his father, the seneschal in **"Equitan,"** Gurun in **"Le Fresne,"** Bisclavret, Lanval, Muldumarec and his son Yonec, the lover in **"Laüstic,"** Milun and his son, the four lovers in **"Chaitivel,"** and Eliduc. A notable exception is the lover in the **"Deus Amanz,"** who is called an *enfant* (3, 241), a *damisel* (49, 143, 168, 188), a *danzel* (73, 126), and a *vallet* (68, 117, 159). Although the son of a count (50) and manifestly capable of exceptional physical effort, he does not live long enough to be knighted. In **"Chevrefoil"** Tristram is not referred to specifically as a knight, but Marie here is relying on a well-known story for the framework of her tale. The conflict between Tristram's role as knight and as lover is at the core of the legend; 'Oublïé ai chevalerie, / A seure cort et baronie', mourns Béroul's hero, when the effect of the potion wanes (2165-66); 'Ge sui essillié du païs, / Tot m'est falli et vair et gris, / Ne sui a cort a chevaliers' (2167-69).

Of the other important male characters in the *Lais* several are kings: Arthur, Mark, Bisclavret's protector, the girl's father in the **"Deus Amanz,"** Eliduc's first lord and also his second wife's father. None of these is called a *chevalier,* but they are referred to, as one would expect, as *sire/seignur:*

> Une cité fist faire uns reis
> Que esteit sire de Pistreis.
>
> **("Deus Amanz,"** 13-14)

> Elidus aveit un seignur,
> Reis de Brutaine la meinur.
>
> **("Eliduc,"** 29-30)

Meriaduc in **"Guigemar"** is described once as a *chevaler* (832) and also as *li sire* (691), the term used for the lady's husband, lord of the *antive cité* (209, 229, etc.). Equitan, 'sire de Nauns, jostis' e reis' (12), is never explicitly called a *chevalier,* but we are told that his love of pleasure led him to uphold the principles of chivalry:

> Deduit amout e drüerie:
> Pur ceo maintint chevalerie.
>
> (15-16)

Le Fresne's father is a wealthy knight, as is his neighbour:

> En Bretaine jadis maneient
> Dui chevaler, veisin esteient;
> Riche humme furent e manant
> E chevalers pruz e vaillant.
>
> (3-6)

When Bisclavret's wife learns that he is a part-time wolf, she turns to a former admirer, 'un chevaler de la cuntree' (103). In **"Laüstic"** the lady's husband is a *chevaler* (9), possessed of a substantial house and able by his *bunté* to contribute towards the good reputation of the town. The lover is said to be a *bacheler* (17) and a *chevaler* (9), so

the one attribution clearly does not exclude the other. A *bacheler* can evidently be a man of means and status. Like his neighbour he possesses a *fort maisun* (10), a *domus fortis,* doubtless of the type regularly constructed by the *milites* by way of imitation of the seignorial castles. Both houses have a *sale* and a *dungun* (36); the husband's house at least has an extensive *vergier* (97). The father of Milun's beloved is described as a *barun* (21). She has her own *barun,* 'husband', a 'mut riche humme del païs, / Mut esforcible e de grant pris' (127-28), to whom she is given by her father (126).

So Marie offers us in the *Lais* a discussion of the behaviour and problems of the later twelfth-century knight set against a background of his superiors in rank and power, who have the capacity to protect or destroy him. On the positive side one thinks notably of Eliduc's reception by Guilliadun's father in England and of Bisclavret's rescue by the king from his life as a savage beast. Less happy cases are unfortunately more numerous. Lanval and Tristram are badly treated in Marie's view by Arthur and Mark, who has caused Tristram also to live the life of a wild beast, spending his days hiding in the forest. Eliduc is banished by the King of Brittany without just cause and Muldumarec's death is caused by the man who is *avouez* of Caerwent ('the acknowledged holder of the fief,' Ewert) and 'del païs sire' (**"Yonec,"** 13-14). The seneschal in **"Equitan,"** a 'bon chevaler, pruz e leal' (22), is treated outrageously by King Equitan, who makes him do his work for him, commits adultery with his wife (seducing her in the seneschal's own castle and kindly suggesting that he should not mind if he found out) and then attempts to murder him. The characters Marie favours all possess, of course, exceptional personal characteristics and are involved in an interesting *aventure,* but it is clear that socially they are fairly well placed. Guigemar is the son and heir of a *barun,* who was 'sire de Lïun' and a 'chivalier pruz e vaillanz', intimate (*privez*) with his lord, King Hoilas (27-33). Gurun is described as a 'bon seignur' (243), with his own *chastel,* serving-men and vassals (309), one of whom is the archbishop of Dol, who officiates at his wedding (361-62). Bisclavret is 'un ber', well liked, an intimate of his lord, like Guigemar's father (15-20), with his own *meisun* (30) and *tere,* which is restored to him by the king (309). Lanval is one of the select band of knights belonging to Arthur's *meisnee* (29). Son of a *riche rei* (232) he is 'de haut parage' (27), a foreigner ('Mes luin ert de sun heritage', 28), with long service to Arthur, desperately in need of material reward as his *aveir* has been exhausted. He has his own *ostel* and *hummes* (201-02). Muldumarec is king over the territory reached by his lady through a *hoge* set in the hillside near her home in Caerwent (346-47, 355, 450). His kingdom turns out to be the area around Caerleon (517). We have seen that the lover in **"Laüstic"** is a man of substance with his own property. The lovers in **"Chaitivel"** are 'gentiz hummes del païs' (40), and Tristram is the king's nephew and heir. Eliduc has his own *ostel* (953) and *tere* (1125, 1156) and possesses the necessary means to found an *abeïe* and an *eglise* (1155). To the latter he gives 'tut son or e sun argent' (1157, see also 1151).

The conflicts which occur in the **Lais** between male protagonists are thus normally between a respectable and highly respected member of the community and a man or men of equal or higher social status. Each of the lovers in **"Chaitivel"** is engaged in a potentially dangerous amatory rivalry with three other knights. The lover in **"Laüstic"** is thwarted by another *chevalier,* but one who may have the edge in prestige. He is certainly surrounded by an army of servants who trap the nightingale. When the bird is caught Marie refers to him as a *seigneur:* 'Al seignur fu rendu tut vis' (102). He may be a little or even substantially older than his neighbour and is clearly not sexually attractive to his wife. It would appear that Marie has a tendency to use for those male personages she does not like the appellation *li sires.* She does this for the husbands in **"Laüstic"** (91), in **"Guigemar"** (209, 229, 585), and in **"Yonec"** (41, 53, 58, 242, 258, 279, 298, 470, 494). It is thus possible for her to play on the ambiguity of the term *sire/seignur,* 'lord, husband'. If *li sires* is 'the lord', *mis/sis sires* is 'my/her husband' (**"Guigemar,"** 339, 352, 580; **"Yonec,"** 178, 221, 228, 536; **"Laüstic,"** 70, 80, 113; **"Milun,"** 152, 501, 518). Ladies evidently wish to *aveir seignur* (**"Milun,"** 136), but not one imposed upon them. Thus Guilliadun wants Eliduc and no one else:

> Ele l'amat de tel amur,
> De lui volt faire sun seignur.
> E s'ele ne peot lui aveir [. . .]
> Jamés n'avra humme vivant.
>
> ("**Eliduc,**" 513-15, 517)

Meriaduc in **"Guigemar"** is also described as *li sires* (691) and this *lai* offers in fact an exploration of the concept of *seigneurie,* with two 'good' lords, Guigemar's father and Meriaduc's adversary (693, 863-68), and two 'bad' ones, the lord of the *antive cité* and Meriaduc. The husband denies freedom to the lady who is destined to cure Guigemar's wound and enable him to fulfil his social responsibilities. Meriaduc too wishes to impose his will brutally on the lady and on his neighbour.

The *chevaliers* whose fortunes Marie relates to us are lords, potential lords or intimates of lords. Her concern is manifestly to create for them, where possible, a successful marriage as a basis for harmony in personal and social relationships. She is certainly suspicious and critical of a good number of the members of the feudal establishment who ride roughshod over others' rights and inclinations. Those who do down the favoured *chevalier* are often subject to vengeance. Guigemar kills Meriaduc, Equitan is scalded to death, Bisclavret's rival is forced into exile, and Yonec decapitates his father's murderer. The case of Milun is interesting. Although possessed of all the chivalric and courtly virtues, he seems not to be regarded as a fitting match for the girl he loves and whom he has made pregnant. As Edgard Sienaert has recently pointed out [in *Les Lais de Marie de France,* 1978], by suggesting that chivalric achievements, although not allied to social position, make an individual a worthy partner for a girl of distinguished birth, Marie is making a bold statement of principle. She presents us here with one of the crucial and most delicate issues of twelfth-century society, the degree of integration of the *milites* into the *nobilitas.* As T. Hunt writes [in "The Emergence of the Knight in France and England 1000-1200," *Forum for Modern Language Studies,* Vol. 17, 1981]: 'The constant genealogical interests of the aristocracy were promoted through patronage and neither training in the skills of warfare nor the quality of being *dives et potens* was sufficient to confer *nobilitas.'* In **"Milun"** Marie is enhancing the chivalric ideal at the expense of the old order. Having been given by her father to a *barun,* the lady is given to Milun by her son, at the end of the story:

> E cum sis peres la duna
> A un barun de sa cuntre[e].
>
> (492-93)

> Lur fiz amdeus les assembla,
> La mere a sun pere dona.
>
> (529-30)

Brought together by the fruit of their love relationship, the couple live happily ever after.

In her description of Milun, Marie stresses his outstanding personal and military virtues:

> Mut par esteit bons chevaliers
> Frances [e] hardiz, curteis e fiers.
>
> (13-14)

He has an international reputation and his prowess is a cause of envy (15-18). It is also a source of love and honour:

> Pur sa prüesce iert mut amez
> E de muz princes honurez.
>
> (19-20)

> Ele ot oï Milun nomer;
> Mut le cumençat a amer.
>
> (25-26)

Through the agency of his beloved's sister, Milun's fine qualities are communicated to his son:

> Puis li ad dit ki est sa mere
> E l'aventure de sun pere,
> E cum il est bon chevaliers,
> Tant pruz, si hardi et si fiers,
> N'ot en la tere nul meillur
> De sun pris ne de sa valur.
>
> (297-302)

Milun and his son are united by their desire and capacity to be a *bon chevaler:*

> Milun i est alé primers,
> Que mut esteit bons chevalers.
> Le bon chevaler demanda.
>
> (391-93)

As we have seen, **"Milun"** is described by Marie as *franc, hardi, curteis, fier* and *proz*. He thus is possessed of the military prerequisites of courage (*proz*) and martial skills and training (*hardi*). Apart from *bon,* used nine times, *pruz* with eight examples is the adjective most frequently found qualifying *chevalier* directly (**"Guigemar,"** 33; **"Equitan,"** 22; **"Le Fresne,"** 6; **"Yonec,"** 426; **"Milun,"** 300; **"Chaitivel,"** 37; **"Eliduc,"** 6, 272). In all Marie employs the adjective *proz* 27 times in the *Lais.* It refers to Guigemar's father (33), Guigemar as a young man (43), Arthur, Gauvain and Lanval (6, 113, 227, 516), the lover in the **"Deus Amanz"** (59, 74), Yonec (328, 426, 461), Milun and his son (300, 526), the four lovers in **"Chaitivel"** (37), Eliduc (6, 272) and the *nobles reis* to whom the *Lais* are dedicated (44), presumably Henry II. With the exception of Arthur, Marie clearly calls *proz* only the favoured male protagonists of her stories. As applied to Arthur and Henry *pruz* and *curteis* probably represent courtesy epithets. But it is not only male characters who merit the use of the adjective *proz.* Le Fresne (482), the girl in the **"Deus Amanz"** (228), the fairy mistress in **"Lanval"** (72), Eliduc's wife (710), and a hypothetical perfect woman in **"Chaitivel"** (196), are all described as *pruz, sage* and *bele.* The sister of Milun's beloved is called 'pruz e senee' (70). A study of the substantive *pruesce* confirms that prowess is one of the qualities of which Marie approves in a man and a woman. *Pruesce* is used eight times, with reference to the Bretons in **"Equitan"** (3), Lanval (22), the *bacheler* in **"Laüstic"** (19), Milun and his son (19, 339), the lovers in **"Chaitivel"** (153) and Eliduc (35, 547). In the case of the *bacheler* in **"Laüstic,"** who is 'coneu de prüesce' (18-19), it helps him to gain a good reputation in the community and acts as one of the factors in his success as a lover. Eliduc is retained by the King of Brittany by virtue of his *pruesce* ('Pur sa prüesce le retint', 35). Prowess is a means of serving one's lord (32-34). Eliduc enjoys similar success with Guilliadun's father and his followers: 'Mut fu preisez par sa prüesce' (547). For Eliduc, Milun and the four lovers in **"Chaitivel,"** *pruesce* is a major component in the love they inspire in a woman. In the case of Milun's son it gives rise not only to his reputation but to his name itself: 'Puis ad tant fet par sa prüesce, / [. . .] / L'apel[ou]ent par tut Sanz Per' (339, 342). If Marie has any reservations about *pruesce,* they are that it can lead to envy and to alienation from the community (**"Lanval,"** 22-23, **"Milun,"** 345-46, **"Eliduc,"** 41). *Pruesce,* as we have seen, is not a male prerogative and it is not restricted to achievement on the battlefield. The Bretons, who have been thoughtful enough to preserve interesting *aventures* for posterity by composing *lais,* are praised for their *prüesce* (**"Equitan,"** 3). *Pruesce* is evidently the ability to adapt skill and power to a particular need. For the *chevalier* the need is principally military.

Marie uses three other military adjectives in direct association with the term *chevalier: hardi* (**"Milun,"** 14, 300; **"Eliduc,"** 6), *fier* (**"Milun,"** 14, 300; **"Yonec,"** 514; **"Eliduc,"** 6) and *vaillant* (**"Guigemar,"** 33; **"Le Fresne,"** 6; **"Yonec,"** 426; **"Chaitivel,"** 37). The adjective *hardi* is used to describe Lanval (516), Milun (14, 300) and Eliduc (6), but always accompanied by *proz* or *fier* (there is

an additional example of *hardiz e fiers* applied to Milun, v. 392, in MS S, a reading incorporated by Rychner but not by Ewert). This may suggest that Marie regards *hardement* not as a permanent characteristic or attitude of mind but as a supporting virtue. It is the dimension of boldness added to an individual's other qualities and can be inspired or tempered by circumstances. Guigemar is stimulated by love to the point of confessing his feelings to his lady:

> Amur li dune hardement:
> Il li descovre sun talent.
>
> (499-500)

If *pruesce* is the opposite of cowardice, *hardement* is the opposite of fear. When Guigemar's boat is seen arriving the lady begins to flee. Her companion is bolder:

> La dame volt turner en fuie:
> Si ele ad poür n'est merveille;
> Tute en fu sa face vermeille.
> Mes la meschine, que fu sage
> E plus hardie de curage,
> La recunforte e aseüre.
>
> (270-75)

The meaning 'bold' is appropriate for the last two occurrences, in which the syntax is *si hardi* + relative caluse. No forester would be bold enough to challenge Eliduc, so favoured was he by the king (37-40). On his arrival in England Eliduc demands that none of his men should be bold enough to accept gifts or money during the first forty days (141-44). *Hardement* must be kept in check, otherwise it leads to acts which we could call foolhardy. One can be too *hardi,* but not too *proz.*

Marie calls *vaillant* Guigemar's father (33), Le Fresne's father and his neighbour (6), Yonec (38, 426, 461) and the hypothetical lover so ardently desired by the lady in this text (98), the *prudume* who attempt to carry the girl up the mountain in the **"Deus Amanz"** (152), the lovers in **"Chaitivel"** (37), Eliduc (8), Lanval's lady (370) and Bisclavret's wife (21). When used to describe a male character *vaillant* is, like *hardi,* a supporting epithet employed principally in the formula *pruz e vaillanz* in the second hemistich, e.g., 'Chivaliers ert pruz e vaillanz' (**"Guigemar,"** 33); 'E chevalers pruz e vaillant' (**"Le Fresne,"** 6). The precise meaning of *vaillant* is not easy to determine from the contexts in which Marie uses it. It is clearly employed as a means of indicating approval of the individual in question. Its use in association with *proz* and in other texts suggests strongly that military skills are implied. The original Latin senses of the verb *valere*—having strength, effectiveness, influence or worth—combine to produce a concept of *valur* seen as particularly successful on the field of battle: 'Bien coneü entre ses pers / De prüesce, de grant valur' (the lover in **"Laüstic,"** 18-19). Lanval (21), Milun (302), and the lovers in **"Chaitivel"** (53, 154) are also said to possess *valur.* As a general social quality *valur* is especially prized when in association with *sen(s):* 'Ki en sei eit valur ne sens' (**"Guigemar,"** 520); 'Si en sei ad sen e valur' (**"Equitan,"** 139). It is as highly valued in women as in men (520, **"Chaitivel,"** 31).

Another positive virtue attributed by Marie to knights she favours (Muldumarec, Milun and Eliduc) is *fierté*. No explanation is required or offered. It is eminently clear from all Old French texts dealing with warfare that *fierté* is an essential part of the warrior's make-up, representing an attitude of mind, a dynamic view of battle, fierceness and confidence. In the *Lais* the adjective *fier* (Marie does not use the substantive) when designating male characters is always associated with other military qualities, *hardi* ("Milun," 14, 300, 392 in MS S; "Eliduc," 6), *proz* ("Milun," 14, 300; "Eliduc," 6) and *fort* ("Yonec," 514).

The *Lais* present three categories of *chevaliers*. There are those who receive passing mention as such, but whose behaviour is abhorrent to Marie: Meriaduc, Equitan, the lover in "Bisclavret," the husband in "Laüstic." These individuals are not given the benefit of positive military or social epithets, but they are powerful men who create difficulties for the favoured *chevaliers*. The latter are all lovers or sons of lovers. But in as far as they are wealthy or the sons of the wealthy both these categories of *chevaliers* have as their retainers other knights ('Chevalers manda e retient,' "Guigemar," 747; 'Plusurs bons chevalers retient,' "Milun," 383). These knights can be summoned, given instructions, used as companions ("Guigemar," 77, 741, 754; "Lanval," 478, 496; "Eliduc," 79, 284), etc. They perform whatever function is necessary, acting as escort to the queen in "Chevrefoil" (83), as reinforcements at a tournament ("Chativel," 104), as soldiers in "Eliduc" (155, 219, 232). Several references make it clear that *chevaliers* were a common sight in Marie's society:

Alez i est mut richement,
Chevalers meine plus de cent.

("Guigemar," 753-54)

Asez eurent joie e deduit,
De chevalers eurent plenté.

("Milun," 488-89)

A vus revendrai volenters
Od grant esforz de chevalers.

("Eliduc," 639-40)

Living in towns ("Guigemar," 857, "Lanval," 205) or courts, doubtless sometimes in cramped conditions, many of these knights will have been poor:

Les povres chevalers amot:
Ceo que des riches gaainot
Lur donout e sis reteneit.

("Milun," 327-29)

A sun manger feseit venir
Les chevalers mesaeisez
Quë al burc erent herbergez.

("Eliduc," 138-40)

Others had their own fiefs. The 'chevaler fiufé' put pressure on Gurun to marry, threaten disaffection if he refuses ("Le Fresne," 325-27), and are powerful enough to make him risk his personal happiness in order to satisfy their demands for a legitimate heir. Gurun is in fact the only *chevalier* whose conflict is with his social inferiors. Their behaviour gives us a glimpse of the latent power of the small-time landed knight.

The knights who with their ladies occupy the centre of the stage in Marie's stories are *proz, hardi, fier, vaillant* and *fort*. They are sound all-round warriors. But they also possess social and physical qualities. They are *franc, curteis, bel* and *gent*. They look the part of the lover, do and say the right thing at court. Marie's knights are brave and handsome young men, well equipped to be a success on the battlefield, in the banqueting hall and in the bed-chamber. In many cases their military qualities have to be taken on trust. The seneschal in Equitan, Gurun, Bisclavret, Lanval, the lover in "Laüstic," the lovers in "Chaitivel," and Tristram are not called upon in the context of their *aventures* to perform deeds of bravery on the field of battle. There are of course three main areas of activity for an active knight in the twelfth century—war, tournaments and hunting—the two latter acting as a source of pleasure and as keep-fit classes for the former. Jean Larmat has recently pointed to the connection between hunting and war: 'La chasse et la guerre sont parentes, surtout dans la société féodale' ["La Chasse dans les *Lais* de Marie de France," *La Chasse au Moyen Age,* 1981]. The motif of hunting appears in nine of the *Lais,* the exceptions being "Le Fresne," the "Deus Amanz" and "Chaitivel." In "Guigemar" the action is initiated by a hunt and brought to a conclusion by a tournament and a war. In "Eliduc" it is a war which brings Eliduc Guilliadun's love and a hunt which produces the *dénouement*: '*Dans* "Eliduc," Guilliadun, l'amie du héros, est ressuscitée grâce à une double chasse à la belette'. Marie clearly expects her young heroes to attend tournaments and one has the impression that she takes an interest in them. They are also useful for her plots. Gurun attended a tournament as an excuse for returning via the abbey where Le Fresne lived (247-49). The *bacheler* in "Laustic" was a frequent and generous visitor to tournaments: 'Mut turnëot e despendeit / E bien donot ceo qu'il aveit' (21-22). Tournaments were a way of building and maintaining a reputation and displaying virtues such as generosity (cf. "Milun," v. 323, 'La despendi e turneia'). They are also places where knights can enjoy the admiring glances of the ladies:

La dame fu sur une tur,
Bien choisi les suens e les lur;
Ses druz i vit mut bien aidier:
Ne seit [le] queil deit plus preisier.

("Chaitivel," 107-10)

In "Chaitivel" the tournament is at the very heart of the matter, and is described with careful attention to detail. In "Guigemar" it leads to the *dénouement*. Meriaduc uses the tournament as a device to attract Guigemar to his castle (744).

The jousting field offers an opportunity for financial gain, from the horses and armour taken from the vanquished ("Milun," 328, 402) and for damaging an opponent both physically and mentally:

Kar li treis [i] furent ocis
E li quart nafrez e malmis
Par mi la quisse e einz al cors
Si que la lance parut fors.

("Chaitivel," 121-24)

Si justera al chevalier
Pur lui leidier e empeirer;
Par ire se vodra cumbatre,
S'il le pout del cheval abatre:
Dunc serat il en fin honiz.

("Milun," 353-57)

Milun is reunited with his son on the occasion of a tournament. Ironically, having created for himself the reputation of a man who has never been unhorsed (11-12), he is brought down by his own son (420-21), for whom the tournament is merely another in a sequence in which he had manifested stunning prowess:

De tutes les teres de la
Porta le pris e la valur.

(332-33)

The quest for *pris* is the hallmark of the perfect knight in the **Lais**. As Milun's son knows, it can be found in tournaments (see also **"Chaitivel,"** v. 116). Milun leaves his own land to acquire *pris* by means of paid military service:

Milun eissi fors de sa tere
En sude[e]s pur sun pris quere.

(123-24)

His son, 'ki passa mer pur [sun] pris quere' (338), followed in his footsteps, and was even keen to gain greater *pris* than his father (311-12), whose *pris* and *valur* were second to none in his land (301-02).

Marie evidently likes this form of ambition in a young man. The *damisel* in the **"Deus Amanz"** has his eye on success:

De bien faire pur aveir pris
Sur tuz autres s'est entremis.

(51-52)

The young Guigemar knows that his *pris* will be enhanced by foreign service:

En Flandres vait pur sun pris quere:
La out tuz jurz estrif e guerre.

(51-52)

Tournaments are obviously closely linked to wars. Like the cricket season, they both begin just after Easter:

Tant que aprés une paske vient,
Que devant Nantes la cité
Ot un turneiement crïé.

("Chaitivel," 72-74)

De s[i] que pres la paske vient,
K'il recumencent les turneiz

E les gueres e les dereiz.

("Milun," 384-86)

Milun tells his son what an active life he has led:

Mut ai cerchiees autres teres.
Par turneiemenz e par gueres.

(441-42)

The act of jousting can apply both to tournaments (**"Milun,"** 353, 416) and to an engagement in war: ' *"Poet cel estre, nus justerums"* ' (**"Eliduc,"** 170). Similarly we encounter a *grant medlee* in **"Chaitivel"** (105), as the lovers' opponents rescue their companions, and in **"Eliduc"** Guilliadun's father has no one in his castle bold enough to 'estur ne mellee tenir' with his enemy (102). Meriaduc proclaims a tournament against his enemy:

De ci que a un turneiement,
Que Meriadus afia
Cuntre celui que il guerreia.

("Guigemar," 744-46)

Meriaduc maintains that he is not sufficiently afflicted by any war to be forced to surrender Guigemar's lady to him (848-50). Guigemar challenges him (*defier*, 855), retreats to the castle of Meriaduc's opponent in war, and uses the participants in the tournament as a fighting force (857-68). He liberates his lady and puts an end to the *guere* (868). One assumes that Guigemar will inherit his father's land and aid his own lord, Hoilas, whose land is 'sovent en peis, sovent en guere' (28).

Not all Marie's heroes are so effective in battle. But another notable exception is Eliduc who, having impressed one lord by his prowess, arrives in war-torn England: 'Plusurs reis [i] ot en la tere, / Entre eus eurent estrif e guere' (89-90). He is delighted that he has 'found' a war, as he now has a chance to offer *auxilium* and act as a mercenary:

Quant iloc ad guere trovee;
Remaner volt en la cuntree [. . .]
Vodrat aider a sun poeir
E en soudees remaneir.

(105-06, 109-10)

The search for *soudees* is Eliduc's principal motivating force: 'Mes puis avient par une guere / Quë il alat soudees quere' (13-14); 'E s'il nel voleit retenir, /[. . .]/ Avant ireit soudees quere' (116, 118). As in the case of Milun the display of prowess, wherever it is needed, is his *raison d'être*. He is defined by Marie as 'li bon chevaler' (340) and as 'le bon soudeer' (1074, see also 246, 339). Like Milun he wins through his prowess the love of a beautiful and loyal maiden of higher social status than his own. Like tournaments wars offer an opportunity for financial gain: 'Del herneis pristrent a espleit, / Merveillus gaain i unt fait' (**"Eliduc,"** 223-24). They enable the victor to inflict material damage on an opponent and at the same time to dishonour him: 'Bien tost les purreit damagier / E eus laidier e empeirier' (**"Eliduc,"** 183-84).

The acts of *gaainier* and of *damagier* are also a source of *pris*:

> 'Si nus poüm rien gaainier,
> Ceo nus iert turné a grant pris
> De damagier noz enemis.'
>
> ("Eliduc," 198-200)

P. Le Gentil argues that Marie was insufficiently interested in prowess and that Chrétien was better able to satisfy public demand in this area [*La Littérature française du moyen âge,* 1972]. Be that as it may, my impression is that Marie became more committed to action and chivalric pursuits as time passed by. In what I think were her later *lais*—"**Milun,**" "**Guigemar**" and "**Eliduc**"—more space is allotted to the hero's development in military matters and all the occurrences of the terms *guere* and *estur* are found in these *lais*. These three *lais* are also dominated by the theme of loyalty, particularly the loyalty of the man to the woman ("**Chevrefoil,**" probably another of the later *lais,* belongs to this category). These are the *lais* of real commitment by the knight, to a lady and to the service of others. Service and action are rather more specifically directed in Marie than in Chrétien, to a community rather than to an individual. But the chivalric ideal is certainly there and "**Guigemar**" at least, and "**Yonec**" in its own way, provide examples of the rescue of a damsel in distress. Larmat may be right that Marie does not like hunting and that she sees man, with his variety of weapons, as possessing an artificial superiority over the tracked animal, whose blood can leave a trail of anguish, as in the case of the nightingale in "**Laüstic,**" the hawk in "**Yonec**" and the wounded hind in "**Guigemar.**" She seems to have contempt for Equitan who will only sacrifice the pleasure of the hunt in times of war (25-28). But if it is true that hunting represents for Marie 'la métonymie des rapports entre les hommes' and an 'image de la vie humaine,' this could be seen as constituting the pessimistic strain which undoubtedly forms part of her vision of the world, especially in the earlier stage of her career. But I do not find in the *Lais* as a whole the 'pessimisme assez radical' of which J.-C. Payen has spoken. [*Le Lai narratif,* 1975]. Milun, Guigemar and Eliduc are alive and happy at the close of their *aventures* and they have the girl of their choice as marriage partner. Eliduc enjoys the luxury of being able to choose to go beyond a happy marriage to embrace the service of God. In "**Guigemar,**" "**Milun**" and "**Eliduc**" prowess and love come together to form an effective partnership to the benefit of both self and society.

Joan Brumlik (essay date 1988)

SOURCE: "Thematic Irony in Marie France's 'Guigemar'," in *French Forum,* Vol. 13, No. 1, January, 1988, pp. 5-16.

[*In the following essay, Brumlik shows how "Guigemar" is different from conventional love* lais.]

The opening lines of Marie's "**Guigemar**" expand upon the hero's place in a serious "this-worldly" world of feudal and family solidarity and dependence (27-56). The links in the chain of dependence begin at the top with King Hoilas and move down, first to Oridial, a good and trusted knight and lord of Liun, and then to his wife and children, a son and a daughter, Guigemar and Noguent.

In a period intermittently troubled by wars in Brittany, Guigemar is cherished at home until he leaves to serve his king and be dubbed by him. Then he leaves the court to establish a reputation for himself in Flanders, where, Marie tells us, there is always a war going on (52). In a romance type of tale such as this appears to be, one might expect Guigemar to find both adventure and love upon leaving home, returning to his family and *seigneur* only to marry. However, our expectations are not realized. Guigemar surprises us, not by his refusal to love (57-68), which merely announces to the reader that this situation will be reversed, but by coming home, once his reputation as a soldier is made, to see his family and his *seigneur* (69-75). These 30-odd lines of introduction do not exist simply to tell us that Guigemar is of good family, "bel" (38), "sages e pruz" (43), and a peerless knight (55-56), although that is all we need to know in order to begin a love story. Marie is incorporating into an otherwise unexceptional introduction of a hero-lover a description of an ordered society, a bulwark against potential destruction by war, in order to imply the need for heirs in this illustrious and important family.

The only son of a noble family has an obligation at some point in his life to take a wife and produce heirs. When this is implied in the introduction to a love story, the reader is encouraged to expect the tale to end in a marriage, preferably in a family or a court setting, with much rejoicing on all sides. It is the fundamental thematic irony of this *lai* that the ending takes place in a realistic landscape of total destruction:

> Guigemar ad la vile assise,
> N'en turnerat si serat prise.
> Tant li crurent ami e genz
> Que tuz les affamat dedanz.
> Le chastel ad destruit e pris
> E le seignur dedenz ocis.
> A grant joie s'amie en meine:
> Ore ad trespassee sa peine!
>
> (875-82)

If Guigemar and his lady are accompanied in their departure, we are told nothing of it. If there is a marriage to be arranged, it is not mentioned. There is, however, finality. We know that all of Guigemar's troubles are over and that he is happy. We know nothing at all of the feelings of the lady.

The ending thus fails to convey any idea of communal joy or of a reintegration into the society so clearly drawn at the outset. Even more curious, the conclusion, like the introduction, does not address the dynastic concerns which become explicit when Guigemar is able to reject all those who try in vain to untie the knot made in his shirt by his lady. In consideration of this omission let us recall the fact that Guigemar's lady is, so far as we know, still a married woman, and suggest that Marie has been playing thematic games with us from the very beginning.

Only five of Marie's *Lais* end in a reunion of the lovers. **"Eliduc"** has an edifying ending: the married lovers follow the example of the former wife, devoting their remaining years to the worship of God. **"Milun"** and **"Fresne"** alone end in marriage. In **"Fresne"** reintegration into the family is stressed. In **"Milun"** the lovers' happiness accompanies the reuniting of the family. There remains **"Lanval,"** in which the hero follows his beloved fairy mistress to Avalon:

> La fu raviz li dameiseaus!
> Nuls hum n'en oï plus parler
> Ne jeo n'en sai avant cunter.
>
> (644-46)

Since Lanval did what he wanted to do, one must suppose that the ending is happy, although Marie appears to regret not having any more definite news to pass on to us. **"Guigemar"** is closer in its conclusion to **"Lanval"** than to those *lais* which end in marriage as an affirmation of a character's reintegration into his social group. It is therefore pertinent to recall that Lanval permanently opts out of a society which rejects him. Since in **"Guigemar"** the lady is still married at the end of the *lai,* one may propose that Guigemar does the same.

Dynastic concerns are present in most of Marie's *lais.* In the **"Deus Amanz"** the king, who does not listen to his people's desire to see his only daughter married, ends by destroying the girl and her young lover. Equitan, another king, ignores the growing discontent of his people with his failure to take a wife. Indeed, Equitan so neglects all his royal obligations that it is with some satisfaction that Marie sees him destroyed in an exemplary fashion: "Ki bien vodreit reisun entendre, / Ici purreit ensample prendre" (307-08). In the *lai* **"Eliduc"** the hero's loss of feudal stability is rapidly followed by political and marital disloyalty, which brings him to the brink of disaster. There is an implied relationship in these *lais* between feudal and marital responsibility. It is perhaps significant that Lanval's problems are like those of Eliduc in that they stem from an ill-defined falling from favor:

> Femmes e teres departi,
> Fors a un sul ki l'ot servi:
> Ceo fu Lanval: ne l'en sovint
> Ne nuls des soens bien ne li tint.
>
> (17-20)

Here marriage itself depends upon acceptance by the political hierarchy.

There is, however, a notable exception to these observations, in **"Le Fresne."** This *lai* presents us with a very unusual disregard for the relationship between dynastic concerns and marriage. The girl is barren. Gurun, her lover, is urged to put her aside and marry a woman by whom he may have children. He submits, very matter-of-factly, when his vassals threaten to renounce their loyalty to him if he does not comply with their demands. Marie has unsentimentally described a medieval problem complete with its legal remedy. One is, however, puzzled that following the dramatic and realistic portrayal of a twelfth-century feudal crisis, the vassals' ultimatum has been completely forgotten when the lovers marry. Since there is no need to incorporate into a story of this kind the rather unseemly question of whether the heroine can bear children or not, the "fairy-tale" ending must be seen as provocatively overriding feudal necessity in order to satisfy the mother's need to return her long-lost daughter to the family. In other words, in this *lai,* which contains no *merveilleux,* the ending itself is supernatural, or at least usurps the function of the supernatural.

It is recognized that in Marie's *Lais* the *merveilleux* frequently offers what a given character needs or wants, something otherwise unobtainable. A fairy mistress comes to Lanval when all others forsake him. He becomes rich and loved. A fairy lover comes to the unhappy wife in **"Yonec"** in an incident which clearly demonstrates what Dafydd Evans calls "the compensatory function of the supernatural" ["Marie de France, Chrétien de Troyes, and the *malmariée, Chretien de Troyes and the Troubadors,* 1984]. In this context it should be noted that the supernatural may protect an individual from his social context without regard for conventional morality. In **"Eliduc"** the wife's discovery of a magic herb which saves the life of Eliduc's beloved provides the only means of resolving Eliduc's problems, not the least of which is the fact that he would have been responsible for the lady's death, had she not recovered, and his role in the death of an innocent sailor might have been brought to light.

When Marie introduces the *merveilleux* or the supernatural, she allows it to merge with the real world to which it is so frequently an antidote. The dramatic quality of the *merveilleux* makes it obvious to the reader that it supplies something which the real world cannot offer. Less dramatically, in **"Fresne"** the happy ending is similarly at odds with its feudal context. The same is true in **"Milun,"** although to an even lesser extent, when the husband dies the minute he is obviously *de trop.* This fortunate occurrence saves us the shock of his being put to death by Milun's well-meaning but overenthusiastic son. Eliduc's first wife takes the veil so that her husband can remarry. The second marriage in **"Eliduc"** resembles the second marriage in **"Fresne"** in that both ignore the Church's position in the latter half of the twelfth century regarding divorce and remarriage. These are fairy-tale elements designed to accommodate the characters. They belong to the *jadis,* the once-upon-a-time, and, although they may merge with the twelfth-century world evoked by Marie, for example through the participation of the Archbishop of Dol in the weddings in **"Fresne,"** they do not belong to it. While it might be tempting to assume that the twelfth century exists simply as a background for Marie's tales, one cannot help but notice the needless confrontation between fiction and reality brought about by Marie's merging of the two. Hanning remarks of the magic boat in **"Guigemar"** that it "functions as an emblem of the new romance fiction of Marie's age. Such fiction requires from its audience a commitment of faith in the artist, unlike the epic, 'historical' narratives of feudal Europe which retell . . . stories from a shared past, stories that control storyteller and audience alike" [R. W. Hanning, "Courtly Contexts for Urban *Cultus:* Responses to Ovid in Chrétien's *Cligés* and Marie's *Guigemar*," *Symposium,* Vol. 35, 1981-82]. I would go further than Hanning by proposing that, rather like Chrétien de Troyes, Marie is aware, and wishes her audience to be aware, that fiction is itself a form of *merveilleux,* creating worlds which are both appealing and, ultimately, false. Neither the *merveilleux* nor fiction can offer a permanent refuge from reality.

Let us look then at the implications of this for **"Guigemar"** by establishing at the outset the hero's rather negative attitude towards women and marriage. We are told at the beginning that Guigemar has no apparent interest in love, that he will neither seek the love of those who idolize him nor accept the advances women make to him (57-68). When he is judged "peri" (67), this is a social judgment upon a man who does not care for the type of love offered to him. It is significant that he does not turn to the women he knows when he must cure his hunting wound:

> Il set assez e bien le dit
> K'unke femme nule ne vit
> A ki il aturnast s'amur
> Ne kil guaresist de dolur.
>
> (129-32)

The doe had prophesied that he would die unless cured by a woman whose love and suffering for him and his for her would be a marvel to all (106-22). He rejects the women he knows because he does not love them and they, in his view, do not really love him enough to cure him. It would seem, then, that Guigemar is not disinclined to love, but does not wish to involve himself in loveless courtly games. Our suspicion that Guigemar is uncourtly, or in Hanning's terms not *cultus,* is confirmed by his blunt request for his lady's love, to cure a wound which is purely metaphorical:

> "Dame, fet il, jeo meorc pur vus!
> Mis quors en est mut anguissus;
> Si vus ne me volez guarir,
> Dunc m'estuet il en fin murir.
> Jo vus requeor de druërie:
> Bele, ne m'escundites mie!"
>
> (501-06)

This is unusually terse and unembellished. When the lady, not unreasonably, suggests that she would like time to consider his request, he as much as accuses her of either hypocrisy or deceit, by saying that only women accustomed to affairs do not accept such offers immediately. We can see in this speech his judgment of all the women he has hitherto encountered:

> —"Dame, fet il, pur Deu merci!
> Ne vus ennoit si jol vus di:
> Femme jolive de mestier
> Se deit lunc tens faire preier
> Pur sei cherir, que cil ne quit
> Que ele eit usé cel deduit;
> Mes la dame de bon purpens,
> Ki en sei eit valur ne sens,
> S'ele treve hume a sa maniere,
> Ne se ferat vers lui trop fiere,
> Ainz l'amerat, s'en avrat joie.
> Ainz que nuls le sachet ne l'oie
> Avrunt il mut de lur pru fait.
> Bele dame, finum cest plait!"
>
> (513-26)

Guigemar clearly has no patience with love-games. It is also pertinent that he considers his situation ideal for a love from which they may both profit before being found out. He obviously does not see the affair as a long-term commitment or as leading to one. Moreover, he anticipates that their being found out will end the affair forever.

We have a further glimpse of his view of women when the two meet again after their separation. More than two years have passed, but the lady is still beautiful (704). Guigemar has serious doubts that the lady before him is his *mal mariée:* "Bien sai que ceo n'est ele mie: / Femmes se resemblent asez" (779-80). His response supports the presumption that he did not expect to see her again and had put her out of his mind. It also suggests that his great suffering, which the doe had prophesied, was limited to the short time it took for the ship to return him home (621-31). Although he is subsequently "maz e pensis" (644), he is rather like Aucassin, content to mourn, but disinclined to attempt to be reunited with his love. Indeed, were Guigemar to find her, the tokens would make of her a lady he was destined to marry, whereas he knows that his liaison with a married woman cannot lead to marriage. His adventure has succeeded in protecting him against marriage, and that is no doubt exactly what he wanted.

On the assumption that the *merveilleux* or supernatural in Marie usually answers the needs of one of the characters, one can see the logic of a *merveilleux* which provides Guigemar with a lady who is married and remains married for the duration of the *lai.*

Marie, tongue in cheek, has been playing thematic games with us throughout **"Guigemar."** In general terms, her procedure is to introduce a motif or a theme for which the audience has fairly precise expectations. Before these expectations are realized, she shifts to another motif or theme, for which the audience has quite different expectations. Each theme has the potential of culminating in marriage, a closure for which we have been prepared by the family-oriented opening lines of the *lai,* but which never materializes.

Let us consider Guigemar's departure from home via the magic ship, as a result of a hunt and an encounter with a white doe. Our expectations are that he will be led to fairy mistress who has convoked him and who might, if the contemporary *Partonopeu de Blois* is our guide, even marry him. However, in place of the fairy mistress figure, Marie gives us a *mal mariée.* This is the first and most surprising reversal of convention that the audience experiences. It is sufficiently startling to alert us to other such reversals which will have the effect of precluding marriage. Following the example in Marie's own **"Milun"** or in Chrétien's *Cligés,* we might expect the married woman's husband to die, but he does not. He sends Guigemar home on the magic ship which had brought him, and shuts his wife in a tower. The love tokens which the lovers had exchanged in anticipation of their separation lead us to assume that they will meet again when the husband is no longer an obstacle, so that the lady can untie the knot in Guigemar's shirt and Guigemar can undo the belt fastened around his lady's waist. We expect that as soon as all the ladies of the country have tried in vain to undo the shirt, and all the knights of the country have attempted to undo the belt, the two lovers will be brought together. With the public undoing of the respective garments, we expect a public recognition that the couple belong to each other and may marry.

From the very beginning of the last episode, the tokens do not function as they should. Guigemar must be summoned to his friend Meriaduc's castle on the occasion of a tournament with a neighboring enemy. Meriaduc knows he will come, not only as "ami e cumpaniun" (750), but because Guigemar owes Meriaduc a service, "par gueredun" (749). Meriaduc, who loves the lady, wants a confrontation with Guigemar, certain that his friend with the knotted shirt is his unknown rival.

When Guigemar arrives, he is altogether unaware of his lady's existence at Meriaduc's castle, notwithstanding all the knights who have tried in vain to undo the belt. When he sees her, his behavior is equally singular. He steps back a pace. He recalls his lady with great affection, considers the possibility that it might be she, but ultimately rejects it:

> "Est ceo, fet il, ma duce amie,
> M'esperaunce, mun quor, ma vie,
> Ma bele dame ki m'ama?
> Dunt vient ele? Ki l'amena?
> Or ai pensé mut grant folie;
> Bien sai que ceo n'est ele mie:
> Femmes se resemblent asez,
> Pur nïent change mis pensez."
>
> (773-80)

However, because she resembles the lady he loved, he then advances, kisses her, and seats her beside him. He does not speak to her except to ask her to sit down (786-87). It is Meriaduc who takes the initiative, commanding the lady to attempt the knot. The shirt has to be fetched. Guigemar has it carried around by his chamberlain so that prospective wives may try the knot and fail. He has thus distanced himself from the symbol of his fidelity, as if aware from the outset that as a married woman his lady

can never come to take her place beside him. Even when she unties the knot effortlessly, Guigemar is still unwilling to believe that it is she (812-14). He asks her to show him the belt, saying:

> "Amie, duce creature,
> Estes vus ceo? Dites mei veir!
> Lessiez mei vostre cors veeir,
> La ceinture dunt jeo vus ceins."
>
> (816-19)

He then places his hands around her waist to feel the belt under her clothes, but does not undo it. At his request, she joyfully tells her story and appeals to him to take her away with him.

The belt and the knot are not supposed to be used for recognition purposes as are the ring and the cloth in **"Fresne,"** yet for Guigemar they are necessary in that function. The lady recognizes him when she hears of a knight living in the same country who has a knot in his shirt no lady can undo (727-36), she recognizes his name (765-68), and she recognizes the knot (801). But for Guigemar the belt must function as a token of recognition of this nameless *dame,* a title which distinguishes her from Meriaduc's unmarried sister, who is referred to as a *pucele.*

The placing together of a *dame* and a *pucele* in this new environment reminds us that we have been informed of no change in the marital status of the *dame* in question. We now understand Guigemar's hesitation to recognize his lady and his refusal to undo the belt. He cannot marry this woman.

The tokens are essentially tokens of love and fidelity or, as [Philippe] Ménard puts it [in *Les Lais de Marie de France,* 1979], of the impossibility of infidelity. Guigemar's love and fidelity may not have waned, but he has voided the function of the knotted shirt by using it as a protection against marriage while falsely implying a willingness to marry. The lady, on the other hand, publicly demonstrates the constancy she has always shown by untying the knot in Guigemar's shirt. That Guigemar fails to reciprocate the gesture cannot be attributed to a sense of propriety. It was he who placed the belt around her naked waist, thereby condemning her to repeated attacks on her modesty while allowing him to avoid a public demonstration in the manner appropriate to such love tokens.

Guigemar further voids the tokens of their publicly integrating function by asking Meriaduc's permission to leave with the lady, thus drawing attention to the fact that the lady is again not his and that there has been no public recognition of their belonging to one another. With Meriaduc's declaration that he will fight to keep the lady, a conventional romance might conclude with a single combat for her possession. Such a combat would have played an integrating role supportive of the tokens' function. Instead, Guigemar leaves his lady in the castle to which he intends to lay siege. He enlists men previously loyal to Meriaduc and those of his enemy. He then starves out the inhabitants of the town, destroys the castle and kills Meriaduc. This excessive display of violence towards not only Meriaduc, but also many innocent people, puts Guigemar beyond the pale of social integration. We see him as a soldier in a context of broken loyalties, a ravaged community abandoned to the enemy, and death. Guigemar has not won a bride according to any of the criteria offered in Marie's *Lais* or in conventional romance. Everything leads to the conclusion that he has abducted a woman he loves and who has faithfully loved him, but that they will not marry.

Marie has used a personalized form of the *merveilleux* in her customary way, to answer the hero's desire for a love which involves no commitment to marriage. Her idiosyncratic use of themes and motifs, and the startling juxtapositions of fairy-tale material with twelfth-century life, consistently evoke and frustrate our expectations for a final, socially integrating marriage.

Sharon Coolidge (essay date 1992)

SOURCE: "'Eliduc' and the Iconography of Love," in *Mediaeval Studies*, Vol. 54, 1992, pp. 274-85.

[*In the following essay, Coolidge argues that through its use of such symbols as a weasel and a bed before an altar, "Eliduc" becomes Marie de France's ultimate assessment of sexual and charitable love.*]

Although many early critics of Marie de France's *Lais* focused attention on her sources, her identity, and her handling of "courtly love," more recent critics have recognized the *Lais'* artistic integrity, narrative structure, and subtle handling of love. In two studies on the *Lais,* Emanuel Mickel argues persuasively that the progression of the first three lais—**"Guigemar," "Equitan,"** and **"Le Fresne"**—introduce the three types of love seen throughout the collection: love begun in passion and ennobled through fidelity, love flawed by selfish desires and lack of restraint, and selfless love which is able to transcend the suffering that obstructs its fulfillment. ["A Reconsideration of the Lais of Marie de France," *Speculum,* Vol. 46, 1971; *Marie de France,* 1974]. After introducing these types of love. Marie continues in the rest of the collection to anatomize love on many levels: love between lovers, between parent and child, between neighbors and fellow men, love of self and personal esteem, and finally love for God. Because it concludes the collection and synthesizes types, themes, and situations of love presented earlier, **"Eliduc"** provides Marie's culminating statement on the theme of love.

To present these views on love, Marie uses deliberate ambiguity, seemingly irreconcilable conflict, conscious dilemma, and symbolic resolution as she shapes Eliduc's character. As she has done with other characters in earlier lais, Marie depicts Eliduc as neither unambiguously right nor wrong, but rather poised precariously on the narrow moral fence between a right love, which leads ultimately to charity, and a wrong love, which lacks "measure" and sinks to base passion. She further complicates his position by creating a conflict between his duty to wife and king on the one hand and his love for the princess on the other. Marie adds one last complication by placing Eliduc's dilemma within the context of God's unflinching law, which forces him to make a choice. By allowing the ambiguity to build throughout the lai, Marie focuses the conflict in the storm episode and in the scene with the weasels. There Eliduc finds his choices mirrored in the worlds of nature and religion, judged by their standards, and symbolically corrected by the weasels and the regenerative love they exemplify.

Even from the beginning of the lai, Marie carefully shades Eliduc's worthiness with ambiguity. She begins by establishing his loyalty to his king, describing him as brave, courtly, bold, and proud. In fact, the king cherishes his judgment so highly that he leaves Eliduc in charge whenever he has to travel (31-35). Consequently, the reader is surprised when Eliduc is maliciously slandered and banished from court. Marie continues to show him in a good light as he sets his affairs in order and leaves. Similarly, when he arrives in the court near Exeter, Marie initially portrays him as a loyal knight who carefully weighs right and wrong. His valiant deeds in that country later qualify him to be appointed protector of the land. Even this early in the lai, however, Marie raises questions in the reader's mind concerning Eliduc's character by having him fight his battle in Exeter not directly but through an ambush, and by having him mistaken as a traitor by the king who had sent him out. Only after the mistake is cleared up does he welcome Eliduc as a hero. Although Eliduc's victory is clear-cut, his character is not. These details, although minor, begin to temper Marie's earlier depiction of him as wholly worthy.

Marie introduces ambiguity even more directly into his character as a lover. In the short prologue to the lai. Marie tells us that he and his noble wife loved each other loyally (12). When he is forced to leave home, he vows that he will be faithful to her (84). In the other court, however, Marie emphasizes his courtly qualities (271, 291) and physical attractiveness so that we are not surprised when Guilliadun falls immediately in love with him. As his love for her begins to emerge, Eliduc becomes confused in his loyalties. Like Tristan who found himself loving one Isolde and marrying another, Eliduc finds himself torn between two women. There is the princess for whom he feels a genuine love, but he knows that consummating his love will force him to break his oath of honor to his wife. There is also his wife, who at first appears to be the obstacle to his love. It is the wife, however, guided by her Christian charity and the example of the weasel, who ultimately provides the possibility for redemption and regeneration. The love *for* one woman creates the dilemma; the love *expressed by* the other woman provides the solution.

Doubling not only performs this artistic and thematic function but also precipitates Eliduc's seemingly insurmountable dilemma between duty and love. Eliduc owes his loyalty and service to the first king, but he has also pledged himself as a mercenary to the second king and served him as protector of the land. In addition, not only has he vowed faithfulness to his wife, but he embroils himself in further complications when he pledges his love to the princess.

Having thus established the conflicts thematically and structurally, Marie focuses on the dilemma which rages within the sensitivities of Eliduc: between his passionate love on the one hand and his acute conscience on the other. Although Mickel argues [in "A Reconsideration"] that Eliduc's reason prevails over his passionate desires, keeping him from any dishonorable action that would violate his oath to his wife, Eliduc's responses and those of Guilliadun are not quite so clear-cut as Mickel would seem to imply. Instead, they are deliberately ambiguous. When Eliduc becomes aware of his love for the maiden, he savors each moment he spends with her, exulting in the relationship she offers. But he also thinks of his wife as he recalls his oath of faithfulness to her:

> He had no joy or pleasure
> except when he thought of her.
> But he considered himself unfortunate
> because, before he left his own country,
> he had promised his wife
> that he'd love no one but her.
>
> (460-65)

In his heart he wants to be true, but his flesh is weak.

And yet he does not indulge his flesh. Marie emphasizes the restraint in the relationship:

> But there was no folly between them,
> no frivolity, no shame:
> When they were together,
> their lovemaking consisted
> of courting and speaking
> and giving fine gifts.
>
> (575-80)

And just a few lines later Eliduc voices his own conscience and that of the church:

> If I were to marry my love,
> Christianity would not allow it.
> This is bad in every way.
> God, how hard it is to part.
> But whoever may blame me for it.
> I shall always do right by her.
>
> (601-6)

It would seem that Eliduc is clearly tempted but that he restrains himself at the crucial moment "because of the faith he [o]wed his wife / and because he served the king" (475-76).

Such statements would seem to support Mickel's position that reason overcomes passion at the crucial moment, but it is not so simple. Marie carefully undercuts such appar-

ent nobility with two considerations. First, Eliduc fails to tell Guilliadun that he is already married—and he feels guilty about his failure:

> she thought to have him completely
> and to hold him, if she could;
> she didn't know he had a wife.
> "Alas," he said. "I have acted very badly. . . . "
>
> (582-85)

Earlier in the *lai* when the messenger delivers Guilliadun's love tokens, Eliduc's marked silence prompts the messenger to observe,

> I find him courtly and wise,
> one who knows how to hide his feelings.
>
> (423-24)

Hiding the true reason why he cannot marry her, he cunningly evades her questions just as he later equivocates when his wife inquires about his sorrow. Here he fails a second time when he gives only a partial answer, claiming that his unfulfilled obligations to the king abroad are the cause of his grief. While he may not have sinned through commission, he is surely guilty of omission.

By carefully shaping each detail toward the climactic scene of the weasels in the chapel, Marie has highlighted his dilemma as a knight and as a lover. Then she dramatically heightens the dilemma by placing Eliduc back in his original situation—back with his own king and his own wife. What before had been an intellectual question, isolated as he was from his wife and his king, now becomes an active tempest of mind and soul, pushing Eliduc to a choice, an action, and an eventual repentence. The precarious ethical balance which Marie has taken such great pains to establish is now tipped in one direction because of the overpowering love Eliduc has for Guilliadun. Technically honest and pure, the love between them may be ethically neutral, but the means by which it is furthered not only counters human prescriptive law but offends the uncompromising dictates of God and nature.

That Eliduc strictly fulfills his oath to his wife and king cannot be contested. But his attempts to restrain his passion are successful only in terms of the letter of the law. The coldness he shows toward his wife upon his return home must be seen as reprehensible when viewed in the context of Eliduc's own banishment. Just as he had pleaded to understand the king's disfavor earlier, so Guildeluec begs earnestly to know how she has offended. Eliduc's evasive response to her must fall under the same censure as his deceitful answers to Guilliadun's proposals. Marie tells us in fact that at this point he behaved "furtively" (717). He manipulates the feud he has been called home to settle so that he can return to his love on the appointed day, chooses trusted servants, and makes them pledge to keep everything hidden.

From this point until the supposed death of Guilliadun, Eliduc's action can only be seen as deceptive. Not only has he sworn his men to secrecy, but he returns to the land that had befriended him when he had been banished and cleverly takes lodgings far from the harbor to remain unknown: "he didn't want to be seen, or found or recognized" (765-66). Eliduc sends for Guilliadun to come under the cover of night, and they meet in an enclosed wood. The deceit, stealth, and cunning that earlier characterized the negative side of Eliduc's love now becomes actualized as he carries off the maiden in the darkness, an action which he had earlier rejected because it would force him to betray his faith to her father (687-88).

Until this point in the narrative, the struggles have been primarily internal. But when his ambiguity turns into overtly wrong action, the figurative internal tempest becomes external and explicit, mirrored symbolically in the tempest at sea. Arising suddenly just when they are near his original home, the storm tests Eliduc's character when the threat of destruction prompts a crew member to reveal the hidden truth of his marriage. Like its scriptural analogue in Jonah, the sudden tempest in nature can be seen to judge Eliduc's deceit even as it pushes him to act.

By deliberately and ironically juxtaposing Eliduc's guilty action with the sailors' invocation of the saints and the Virgin, Marie foreshadows important themes she will later develop in the chapel scene: concerns of death and life, of sin and redemption, of earthly hate and heavenly love. Each of the saints invoked by name—St. Nicholas and St. Clement—has in the legends associated with him a story of a miracle at sea, either a stilling of the waves, a personal triumph of his life over the sea, or a reclaiming of a life snatched by the water. Such miracles of the sea emphasize the control of nature by Divine Providence, the restoration of life through the intercessory prayer of the saints, and selfless compassion. Thus, when Marie juxtaposes Eliduc's action at sea with the invocation of these saints, along with that of the Virgin and her Son, who stilled the waters and restored the dead to life, the irony becomes explicit. Unlike Jonah, who recognized his wrong and was willing to accept the penalty, and unlike Nicholas and Clement, who were so in touch with the Creator of the world that they could calm nature and restore life, Eliduc responds in rage to the accusation that he was attempting to marry Guilliadun "in defiance of God and the law / of right and of faith" (837-38). Failing to acknowledge the truth he had hidden so long and failing to accept human responsibility, he reacts with passion, killing the truthful squire and pushing his body into the sea.

There is a potential danger in love, a danger that becomes actualized when passions rule and when cunning and deceit usurp the place of truth and honesty. By allowing the passions of a guilty conscience to rule his actions, rather than the reasoned judgment which had characterized him earlier, Eliduc has literally killed a man and has figuratively killed any future his love might have had. This series of unambiguously wrong actions—carrying off Guilliadun by stealth, denying the truth, and slaying its spokesman—now leads to death: physical death, emotional unresponsiveness, and spiritual sterility.

At this point, Marie introduces a rich complex of symbols and implications by using the setting of the chapel, the role of the holy hermit, and the central place of the altar. It is surely significant that when Eliduc arrives at the hermit's chapel with the supposedly dead Guilliadun, the doors are locked tight against him. Because of his uncontrolled rage and murderous action, as well as his earlier deception, the chapel and the faith it represents are closed to him; the hermit, with whom he had spoken many times before, had died only eight days earlier. At this point both religion and love are apparently dead to Eliduc, and as he brings the unconscious maiden to the deserted chapel and makes a bed for her in front of the altar, various themes running throughout the lai now come together.

It is surely not without significance that Eliduc creates a bed for Guilliadun in front of the altar, since both the bed and the altar have rich associations that again underscore the ambiguity seen in the lai. On the one hand, the bed prepared for Guilliadun represents death or eternal sleep, a common meaning for a bed in the Middle Ages, and one appropriate here since Eliduc fully believes that she is dead. The bed, however, can also signify passion and physical consummation, as it does in many medieval romances. In this context, Eliduc's deceits and actions have effectively killed any hopes for consummation. Furthermore, the bed can also have very positive connotations in suggesting the marriage sacrament and the creation of life. So within itself, the bed can be both positive and negative, suggesting both death and life. But the location of this bed is also significant: it is made before the altar (929). Calling up the idea of the Eucharist as the remembrance of Christ's death, the altar seems an appropriate place for a bier or a tomb. But it paradoxically also suggests Christ's victory over death and the possibility of eternal life springing from mortal death; through the altar, death in life can miraculously become life in death. The composite image of tomb, altar, and bed, taken as a whole, implies a fusion in a heavenly, eternal love for God. Purely human love, celebrated in earthly beds of passion, ceases at death, but heavenly love, a true charity, pushes beyond the boundaries of this life to everlasting life.

In this religiously significant setting, Marie creates a scene in which the ambiguities, conflicts, and dilemmas presented earlier in the lai are resolved through the miracle of love, here presented in natural, supernatural, and human terms. Just as the tempest symbolically mirrored the inner state of Eliduc's mind, this scene at the end of the lai also unfolds through symbolic, natural doubling. After sending a servant to follow Eliduc to learn his secret sorrow, Eliduc's wife discovers the young maiden lying before the altar. As she watches, a weasel runs across the body and is struck down by the servant. A second weasel, discovering its stricken mate, runs outside to get a red flower, places it in the dead weasel's mouth, and miraculously the weasel comes back to life. Certainly the weasels and their actions mirror situations in the world of mankind, as many critics have observed. Beyond that, however, the rich meanings associated with the weasel reveal it to be the central iconographical image of the lai: the ambiguity in the symbolism of the weasel parallels the evolution of love seen in the lai, from the pure, earth-bound, and frustrated love first exhibited by Eliduc and Guilliadun to the enduring, transcending charity expressed by Guildeluec.

Even from early times, the legendary associations of the weasel are paradoxical. The weasel can be seen as either a good omen or a bad omen, feared for its demonic nature, or sought after as a guardian of treasure. In common and proverbial associations, the weasel is cited as cunning, clever, and tricky, and it is also depicted as a blood-thirsty predator. In these qualities, Eliduc is like the weasel. Although Marie presents Eliduc as a noble and worthy knight, she undercuts some of that nobility by showing his craftiness in battle, his deceitfulness with both women, and the bloodguilt which he must now bear for killing the sailor. The ambiguity is further heightened by the association of the weasel with lust. Although pure in many ways, the love Eliduc is pursuing has the potential of becoming base—especially when one considers the actions his passions have prompted. His duplicity and craftiness have one other connection to the weasel; the weasel, according to early tradition, was a shape changer. There can be no doubt that Eliduc has played many roles, appearing as one person to his wife and king and representing himself in another way to Guilliadun.

Surely these common proverbial associations of the weasel spring most readily to mind, and these negative qualities find ready analogues in the lai. But the weasel also has more positive associations, which here serve not only to judge but also to provide a corrective to his misdirected actions. The weasel has long been believed to signify judgment and to be capable of averting or turning aside evil. Furthermore, the weasel has been seen as prophetic and as an avenger of oaths. In these associations, the presence of the weasel performs a function similar to that of the storm at sea: judging the rightness or wrongness of an action and recalling the oaths Eliduc made to his wife, which, though kept to the letter, were unfulfilled in spirit. In a positive sense, these associations suggest a prodding in the right direction.

Like the marriage bed, the weasel also has a connection to birth and fertility. Long associated with the weasel is the belief that it conceives through the ear and gives birth through the mouth, a belief related to the classical story of Galanthis. At the birth of Hercules, Lucina, sent by Juno, was sitting by the altar, her arms and legs crossed in an attempt to keep the mother from giving birth. A servant of the mother, Galanthis, noticed this strange circumstance and, realizing Juno's intended mischief, spoke to Lucina as if the child had just been born. The startled goddess of birth leaped to her feet, uncrossing her arms, and thus allowed the natural passage of the child. Learning of Galanthis's deception, the goddess turned her into a weasel, condemning her to give birth through the mouth because of the falsehoods which had issued from her lips.

Not only is the weasel thus associated with childbirth and fertility, but this story of Galanthis has special relation to "Eliduc" because of the number of falsehoods Eliduc tells.

Worshipped by many as the symbol of speech, the weasel also signified in Christian terms one who willingly receives the seed of divine word, but who hides what he has heard. Marie herself, in the **"Prologue"** to the *Lais,* has used a similar truth:

> Whoever has received knowledge
> and eloquence in speech from God
> should not be silent or secretive
> but demonstrate it willingly.

Fused together in the symbol of the weasel, these concepts of falsehood, truth, and fruitfulness take on added meaning in the context of **"Eliduc."** Eliduc has known the truth of his dilemma but has kept it hidden through deceit and evasive answers. When he makes the falsehood overt by carrying off Guilliadun, it leads only to unconsciousness and death of the body (the sailor), love (Guilliadun), and spirit (the deserted chapel and hermit). To possess truth without honesty is fruitless.

Although the natural and supernatural join to censure Eliduc for this wrong on his part, they also provide the corrective through the example of the weasel and its regenerating love. Long associated with the weasel is the legend that the weasel knows the herb of life and uses it to heal the sick among its young, as well as to restore life to the dead. In **"Eliduc"** this miracle of regeneration is staged in the setting of the deserted chapel where the seemingly dead maiden lies stretched out before the altar. When the servant strikes the weasel with a stick after it runs across the girl's body, he is in many ways like Eliduc himself. He, too, is associated with cunning since he is the one who followed Eliduc to discover his secret, and he has taken life, just as Eliduc did with the sailor. When the weasel's companion discovers the lifeless corpse, it runs to the wood and returns, bearing the herb of life in its mouth. Transferring this red flower to the mouth of its mate, it restores life.

By including this story of the weasels, Marie provides a new context for falsehood and its ability to kill love. If both weasels are female, as [S. Foster] Damon suggests [in "Marie de France: Psychologist of Courtly Love," *PMLA,* Vol. 44, 1929] (and as the ambiguities of the Old French would allow), there is a clear prefiguring of the relationship between the two women. One has been figuratively slain by the deceit of Eliduc. The other, possessing true charity, miraculously restores the love between Guilliadun and Eliduc. If, on the other hand, the first weasel is male, his death parallels the sterility that Eliduc feels; only the vermeil flower of Guilliadun's love made possible by his wife's sacrifice is able to restore vitality. Regardless of the sex of the first weasel, however, the inclusion of the weasels forces us to transcend the natural to understand something of supernatural love.

That Marie has changed the color of the flower from the traditional yellow flower of the legend is also significant. Although the color red can have connotations of fire, anger, and something demonic, the meanings here seem more positive. According to Christian liturgy, red is the color of Pentecost, the coming of the Holy Spirit, and as such is associated with purification. It is also a color of martyrdom and specifically the color of Christ's passion. In a broader sense, red is the color of love and passion, of power and youth, and is associated with charity and the Virgin Mary. In these connections the color red is a far more appropriate color than yellow for the regenerating love of Guildeluec and the weasel.

Paradoxically, as the wife acts in accord with the natural life force of rebirth and fertility, she denies her own sexuality. Her action of placing the red flower in the mouth of the maiden literally restores the young girl's life and symbolically restores and purifies the love between Eliduc and Guilliadun. The wife acts out the ideal of charity: giving without thought of recompense, and in that sense, she is like a martyr who gives even though her own loss may be great. In contrast, the potentially selfish love we have seen in Eliduc nurtured by deceit, dishonesty, and an upset of natural and divine order leads only to death and sterility. It results in disorder, confusion, frustration, sorrow and grievous disunity. But true charity, which results in selfless action, yields symbolic fruit: honesty, genuine love, and a unity which draws men and women together in the hope of salvation and eternal life.

With themes and artistry such as Marie has demonstrated in this lai, **"Eliduc"** is surely a fitting conclusion to a collection of stories which focus on the nature of love and on various obstructions to true love. While other lais highlight social pressures that keep lovers apart, selfish passions that distort love, and the seeming need to keep love hidden because of these obstructions, **"Eliduc"** integrates these issues in the larger context of devotion to God. Some of the other lais do in fact depict genuine love but either focus on the reconciling power of love within the social realm alone, as in **"Le Fresne,"** or suggest that true love is possible only outside this world, as in **"Lanval."** In **"Eliduc,"** Marie demonstrates for the first time an ideal love which unites the natural and the supernatural as it overcomes the obstacles to love and reforms society. While such a love may not be a practical pattern for everyone, Marie presents it rather as a goal capable of drawing all who embrace it away from selfish indulgence and into a new level of love and life.

SunHee Kim Gertz   (essay date 1992)

SOURCE: "Transferral, Transformation, and the Act of Reading in Marie de France's 'Bisclavret'," in *Romance Quarterly,* Vol. 39, No. 4, November, 1992, pp. 399-410.

[*In the following essay, Gertz uses reader response theory to explain the changes in our reactions that occur as we read "Bisclavret."*]

Marie de France's twelfth-century *lai* **"Bisclavret"** invites its audiences to become immersed in its world, as Marie's disarmingly simple narrative style conveys com-

plex, fantastic matter. Her framing of supernatural material in the standard plot of the betrayed husband creates a sense of encountering the familiar long before reaching the conclusion, partly because so little of the marvelous occupies the narrative presentation (as opposed to the material) of this *merveille*. Rather than heightening the strangeness or even the horror so obviously a potential focus of a werewolf story, Marie ironically insists on creating a very normal, human beast.

Eliciting standard expectations from this *merveille* about a Knight doomed to a werewolf existence at the hands of his Lady creates a strange need for balance. Critical responses to the *lai,* for example, often focus on the supernatural, rehearsing the sources that inform the greater context of lycanthropy in order to extrapolate significance in Marie's use of the supernatural Bisclavret. This tendency toward imbalance is instructive, since, as examined here, Marie depicts the act of reading as a balancing, a bridge between characters as well as between the supernatural and the "real" worlds of the *lai.*

Importantly, characters and worlds become linked in **"Bisclavret"** itself only when the *lai*'s personae for readers interpret rigorously; reading well is a demanding activity. For one, Marie suggests, reading intently means understanding what lies below the literal surface, as clearly indicated by the Bisclavret's own werewolf exterior which belies his courtly self. Moreover, reading effectively also means looking beyond each narrative element or link to what precedes and follows, as the advisor's linking of common motifs to reveal the hidden story at the end of the *lai* confirms.

My premises regarding this metaliterary aspect of the *lai* rest upon assumptions examined at greater length by Michelle Freeman and Edith Joyce Benkow, who both conclude that the Lady functions as a persona for the poet [Freeman, "Dual Natures and Subverted Glosses: Marie de France's 'Bisclavret'," *Romance Notes,* Vol. 25, 1985; Benkow, "The Naked Beast: Clothing and Humanity in *Bisclavret,*" *Chimères,* Vol. 19, 1988]. It is indeed compelling to read the *lai* as one concerned with the art of storytelling, a reading supported not only by its characters and narrative movement, but also by details like the *lai*'s frequent use of terms for storytelling such as "cunter," "aventure," and "merveille." But, although the *lai* may give the impression that once the nut is cracked, it is an easily comprehended tale (the Lady is evil, the Knight is virtuous, the *lai* is self-reflexively informed), things are not what they seem, on both narrative and metaliterary levels. Even the underlying, metaliterary level becomes complex and ambiguous—rather than offering itself as a simple kernel whose husk has been hulled—mainly because Marie makes her major persona for the poet also reflect the role of the reader. Distinctions between readers and tellers become blurred in the *lai,* as each of the major characters illustrates how important it is for the good poet to be an effective reader.

How Marie expresses these underlying messages also plays into her depiction of reading as a bridge. Most notably, and ironically, she makes the act of suppression (which attempts to marginalize) prominent. Also ironic, suppression in this *lai* (which silences) nevertheless elicits active and intent reading, as it places the responsibility for deciphering messages on its readers. Marie can achieve this effect because suppression in her hands is not simply absence, as the Lady hopes it will become, an absence that would convey empty silence. On the contrary, suppression here suggests an informed silence, one that holds a message if readers only had the patience and talent to look, as Freeman argues, a message made most obvious in the hunting scene. There, the silence accompanying the Bisclavret's courtly gesture of obedience induces the King to pause and attempt an interpretation as a reader, rather than to act as a hunter ordinarily would.

Curiously, these traits marking the intent reader are reminiscent of the opening lines to the **"General Prologue"** to the *Lais,* which, however, convey an idealized portrait of the poet:

> Ki Deus ad duné escïence
> E de parler bone eloquence
> Ne s'en deit taisir ne celer,
> Ainz se deit voluntiers mustrer.
>
> (ll. 1-4)

Perhaps as early as the **"General Prologue,"** Marie gives prominence to the theme of reading well and deeply in order to create effectively by also connecting it there to silence; surely, much of the **"General Prologue"** portrays her as reading Priscian and other Latin writers.

In pursuing this theme, it will become apparent that Marie treats the metaliterary subject of reading below the surface by embedding that very message below the surface: structure mirrors content. How structure and content interact is, to complicate matters, also the very basis of the *lai,* creating, for example, the multiple ironies in the Bisclavret's life. By making the Bisclavret's immediate readers respond strongly to him, Marie further draws attention to how readers respond to ambiguity. The interplay of structure and content as well as of readerly responses to that interplay are focused in the *lai* through Marie's use of the principles of *translatio,* the principles of transferral and transformation.

In a sense, one of the most remarkable aspects of **"Bisclavret"** is its presentation. Since the *lai* evokes the mundane world of the court in spite of its subject matter, its presentation has the effect of inducing confidence in its comprehensibility. Nevertheless, the *lai* is by no means straightforward. For one, the allegorical lack of concrete detail—even to the exclusion of any names for the characters—unsettles, partly because this inability to name, to identify, operates in contrast to its framework, which constantly affirms the world of the knowable, the typical relations of men and women. Content jars with structure. Similarly provocative is how Marie ends her tale of the beast-husband and his unfaithful wife with a pun carried to its genealogical conclusion in generations of noseless daughters:

> Enfanz en ad asez eü;
> Puis unt esté bien cuneü
> E del semblant e del visage:
> Plusurs des femmes del lignage,
> C'est veritez, *senz nes sunt neies*
> *Esovent ierent esnasees.*
>
> (ll. 309-14, my italics)

Here again, the framework evokes the familiar in its structure—the Lady, like Eve, is punished for her sins in a way that redounds upon her daughters—but that known structure supports material, noseless daughters, which surprises.

It seems reasonable to assume that the provokingly normal approach to fantastic material intends to convey, metaphorically, the message that the beast, the nonrational, in every human must be tamed. Metaphors, after all, are created when some usual material is put in an unusual frame; a rose in a book on gardening is a flower, while it is something altogether different, transformed, in *Le Roman de la Rose.* Once having ascertained the obvious message of the *lai* concerning the irrational in every human, readers could easily move on: the *lai* couples a genteel beast with a beastly Lady to enhance its metaphorically transmitted message. In fact, as many critics demonstrate, that reading is almost dangled before our very eyes; it entices. More crucial here, however, is that the reading of one spouse into the other suggests a strategy that subverts the relation of framework and material, and in the process, highlights the role of *translatio.*

On the metaliterary level, **"Bisclavret"** is very much about *translatio.* The most obvious "fact" of the *lai* is the Knight's transformation into a werewolf, a transformation whose very aspect of change is enhanced by other figurative details, such as his metamorphoses being dependent upon changes in clothing. The term *translatio* itself has an array of meanings important to the Middle Ages. For one, it refers to what is understood today by the term "translation," an activity presented as necessary to the writer in the **"General Prologue"** to the *Lais,* where the narrator surveys what material she might translate from the Latin, only to decide to convey folk tales to the court. *Translatio studii et imperii,* on the other hand, refers to the transferral of power and culture from one empire to the next. In **"Bisclavret,"** this particular *translatio* pattern, which links empire to lineage, is palely refracted in the genealogical pun. Moreover, *translatio* is commonly used in the Middle Ages to refer to the transferral of a saint's remains. The literary version of the saintly *translatio* is, essentially, a *vita,* in which the life of a saint is equated with the narrative being told as well as with an actual "story" in the great Book of God's universe. As a final example, *translatio* is also the technical term for "metaphor," a figure of speech which *transfers* qualities as it *transforms* language.

The common denominator in all these uses of the term *translatio* is that the movement of transferral causes transformation. Both transferral and transformation are evident in the Bisclavret himself, for example, who transfers his beastly activities to the woods, transformed in shape. But they are also present in the Lady, who transforms from a doting wife to a disfigured type of Eve, exiled from court. As can be surmised, in **"Bisclavret,"** *translatio* occurs on a variety of levels. In this essay, I will use only the last two identified above, since with that pairing, Marie underscores the subverted relations between structure and content in the *lai*.

Most obviously, **"Bisclavret"** is a "biography," a *vita.* In the *lai*, the Bisclavret's life is told by its three major inventors: the Knight, the Lady, and the advisor. I call them "inventors" because it is how they structure what they select, or find (*invenire*), from the same material accessible to all three that creates different tales. When faced with complex material and ambiguities, each opts for a different kind of tale.

As material to be shaped into different tales, the Bisclavret's life becomes multilevelled because there is discrepancy between the surface and what underlies it—the Bisclavret himself functions as a metaphor. To begin, a *vita* to mortal readers is, macroscopically, a word, a sign, a metaphor in God's Book as well as in the author's creation. Depending on who is reading the *vita,* the vehicle and tenor of this metaphor (to name its simplest defining traits) have compelling effects. The Lady, for example, is horrified by the vehicle, while the King is moved by its tenor. It is the advisor, however, who points to the property of the metaphor identified in the Middle Ages as crucial, that of transferral. By watching the Bisclavret in different contexts, the advisor can link and transfer activity which will allow the metaphor to be decoded (by its author, the Lady).

When readers encounter some puzzle, like a three-day-a-week absence or a shaggy appearance, the silence accompanying the puzzle elicits attention from readers. In the *lai,* these readers are the King and the Lady, whose interpretations of the metaphor subsequently suppress one or the other of its parts.

At the moment of their encounter in the woods, the King and his retinue (and perhaps also Marie's readers) are, at once, surprised and encouraged to look beyond the surface to uncover deeper significance.

> "Seignurs, fet il, avent venez!
> Ceste *merveille* esgardez,
> Cum ceste beste s'humile!
> *Ele ad sen a hume,* mercie crie.
> Chaciez mei tuz ces chiens ariere,
> Si gardez que hum ne la fiere!
> *Ceste beste ad entente e sen . . ."*

> (ll. 151-57, my italics)

By discovering some meaning, many readers like the King as well as the Lady, are content to settle for that kernel of understanding. Complacency, however, cannot be accepted. *Translatio* requires movement and linkage in the deeper levels of a narrative as well as along its surface. Appropriately, this hunting episode cannot help but recall the

"General Prologue" to the entire collection of the *Lais,* which also suggests the movement of *translatio:*

> Li philosophe le saveient,
> Par eus meïsmes *entendeient,*
> Cum plus *trespassereit li tens*
> Plus serreient *sutil de sens*
> E plus se savreient garder
> De ceo k'i ert a trespasser.

> (ll. 17-22, my italics)

Through *translatio,* Marie provides a strategy that subverts the relation of framework and material. Not before too long, the King's startling revelation upon comprehending the nonverbal sign of obedience is numbed into normalcy by its familiar and repetitive patterns once the Bisclavret is at court. Indeed, he and his nobles become so singularly attached to the beast that they cannot see the motif the advisor clearly sees: the Bisclavret has only attacked the Lady and her new husband. But the comfort of familiar patterns also informs the aggressive actions of the Lady, a very different reader from the King. Conventional marital bliss becomes so necessary to her well-being that when what was previously suppressed comes to light, the Lady can only see all as changed and, as a result, turns to criminal activity in order to re-establish that marital pattern, although with new content. In other words, for the King, the tenor becomes the vehicle—the beast *is* courtly—while for the Lady, the vehicle becomes the tenor—the Knight *is* a beast. What structures the material in each case is the reader's vision.

Similarly, a framework of marital treachery can lull Marie's readers into accepting the fantastic as a merely decorative or even figurative part of that structure. As a result, readers may ignore the links that make the Bisclavret a strange metaphor and that also make the tale have its own puzzles, as articulated in the following, suppressed, literal-level dilemmas: who would want to live with a werewolf anyway?; why is the lady, not the second husband, tortured?; and finally, will the Knight transform into the Bisclavret once again, even if on a part-time basis, upon his recovery? For the King, as well as for Marie's readers, the strangeness of the Bisclavret, once shocking, nevertheless dissipates.

This is also the case with the Lady, although at first it does not appear to be so, since she is mesmerized by the vehicle. Marie portrays the transforming effect of a tale on readers through the Lady early in the *lai.* Swiftly passing over the couple's married bliss in the opening lines (21-23), the narrator portrays in quite some detail how the Lady extracts the werewolf story from her husband. She then closely observes the wife's reaction to the tale of transformation, emphasizing her fear while using the terminology of storytelling:

> La dame oï cele *merveille,*
> De poür fu tute vermeille.
> De *l'avanture* s'esfrea.

> (ll. 97-99, my italics)

It is clear that the Lady here functions as a reader, emphasized through the intensity of her readerly reactions. But here, where the Lady seems most like a reader, she is also "transformed" by fear, and in her transformation further associated with the act of creation.

In persuading her husband to tell his story, the Lady, like Eve, risks her paradise (and hence foreshadows the ending of the tale) by alternately demanding and cajoling her husband, in Delilah-like fashion, to tell her everything about his weekly three-day absences:

> Suventefeiz li demanda,
> Tant le blandi e losenga,
> Ques' *aventure li cunta;*
> Nule chose ne li cela.
>
> (ll. 59-62, my italics)

Associated with the types of Eve and Delilah, the Lady's ability at the arts of persuasion are linked with the ability to create, or more precisely, with the ability to destroy, to create negatively. Although by eliciting his story, she actively pursues the role of reader, at the same time she intends to act, to use that story for another creation, a destruction of an old world for a new one—an action also associated with both Eve and Delilah.

After the Lady assimilates all her husband has told her, not only is her love transformed into distaste, she also decides to transform his tale in some way. She hopes to marginalize the *merveille* that caused her to tremble, to transform the horrific three-day a week event into a detail. Marie gives no hint of how the Lady will extricate herself from the situation, as she is caught in the tension between readerly vision and poetic creativity. Then, very abruptly, the narrator reports that the Lady has a lover who conveniently fits into her new structure, her new perceptual framework and through whom her husband's *"vita"* becomes the conventional hurdle courtly lovers must overcome to experience their love. And Marie connects the Lady's sudden find to the metaliterary theme by emphasizing the telling of her husband's story, "Puis li *cunta* cumfaitement / Ses sire ala e k'il devint" (ll. 120-21, my italics). Marie furthermore underscores the change in structure by re-introducing the Lady as a conventional beloved (compare with her first introduction, ll. 21-22) and using the language of courtly love to do so:

> Un chevalier de la cuntree,
> Ki lungement l'aveit amee
> *E mut preiee e mut requise*
> *E mut duré en sun servise,*
> Ele ne l'aveit unc amé
> Ne de s'amur aseüre.
>
> (ll. 103-08, my italics)

Reader and creator almost at the very same moment, the Lady's choice of new *aventure* also reflects what kind of reader she is. She makes swift and clever use of the conventions of courtly love to effect this exchange. Although her remarkable productivity thus suggests familiarity with the conventions of the genre, Marie also indicates that she ignores their deeper meaning. The Lady assures her lover, for example, that he will have her love as well as her body in a manner that is straightforward and literal (ll. 110-16), and in a rather crassly manipulative manner that is contrary to at least the tone of courtly lyrics. Then she convinces her beloved to rid them of her husband, again acting contrary to conventions of courtly love, which also claim that love ennobles a lover.

At the point where the Lady has married her lover and done away with her husband (at least temporarily), readers might expect, since Marie has focused so much on the Lady's ability to transform material and to create new narrative scenarios, that she will follow the Lady in her new tale. Ironically, however, Marie marginalizes the Lady's marginalization by following the Bisclavret from the King's perspective. Indeed, the dynamics of suppression now become very prominent, as we follow a silent character, a transformed metaphor. But this very prominence reverberates back into the *lai*'s beginning, where the Knight was almost an equally ill-fitting metaphor, surrounded by silence at least three days a week. In seeming contradiction to the **"General Prologue"**'s opening lines, once the Knight speaks, he is condemned to a life of silence.

From the beginning, moreover, the Bisclavret is associated with language. In the beginning, for example, he is described as being a recipient of praise, of good words:

> En Bretaine maneit uns ber;
> *Merveille l'ai oï loër:*
> Beaus chevaliers e bons esteit
> *E noblement se cunteneit.*
>
> (ll. 15-18, my italics)

He then becomes the first teller of this *merveille* in the opening scene, a *merveille* which narrates his own life:

> "Dame, jeo devienc bisclavret.
> En cele grant forest me met,
> Al plus espés de la gaudine,
> S'i vif de preie e de ravine."
> Quant il li aveit *tut cunté. . .*
>
> (ll. 63-67, my italics)

His narration, furthermore, echoes the just preceding introductory lines voiced by the narrator, not only in its content, but also in its structure. That is, the passages both list the damages done by the werewolf before referring to the act of narration.

> Hume plusur garval devindrent
> E es boscages meisun tindrent.
> Garvalf, ceo est beste salvage;
> Tant cum il est en cele rage,
> Hummes devure, grant mal fait,
> Es granz forez converse e vait.
> Cest afere les ore ester:
> Del Bisclavret vus voil cunter.
>
> (ll. 7-14)

Most jarringly, both of these emphasized passages contradict how the *lai* presents the beast; Marie focuses on his civility rather than on his blood-thirsty rampages. And her presentation is not just a matter of selective narration. It is clear from the court's surprise at his attacks on the Lady and her second husband that he has become milder. In effect outlawed from the court by his wife, the Bisclavret suppresses that very behavior for which he was marginalized.

By referring to the viciousness of werewolves in these two passages, both the narrator and the Knight conjure up well-known knowledge, the conventional, what every reader might know. But when Marie subsequently marginalizes this knowledge, it causes dissonance. In a marginalized existence, wherein defining traits (viciousness and rapine lust) are marginalized, the traditional hallmark for civilization—courtly speech—is also suppressed, expressed only in nonverbal signs. Locked in informed silence, the Bisclavret is able to speak through his actions—content is subverted by structure—and he tries to make his message plain, just as the advisor would have the Lady speak plainly ("dire") at the end of the *lai.*

The closing movement of the *lai,* then, is movement away from principles of *translatio* as exercised so far. The inversion of structure and content, the forced movement of a metaphor from one context to another, these movements produce silent metaphors that do not keep readers intent once they have attracted attention. Indeed, it is the new violent language of the Bisclavret that ironically causes the entire court to become active interpreters, thereby revealing the dynamics of effective *translatio.* As Douglas Kelly writes: "*Translatio* is itself a lingering over old matter. But it is also an expansion of vision and knowledge about that matter. The inquiry and *studium* that *translatio* supposes show that new truths may be uncovered in what the ancients left obscure" ["*Translatio studii:* Translation, Adaptation, and Allegory in Medieval French Literature," *Philological Quarterly,* Vol. 57, 1978].

What was previously marginalized to the court and to Marie's readers is the werewolf's violence. It comes forward at this time and startles all, a response to which Marie draws attention not only through the advisor, but also through the faculty of memory, or rather, its absence. That is, on the narrative level, the advisor can link the Bisclavret's attack to the Lady and her second husband because of his active memory. On the metaliterary level, Marie provides contrasting, but also suppressed links—linking the Knight's disappearance, the court's assimilation of the werewolf, and the new couple's visit to the courts is the absence of memory. Thus, after just a year (l. 135), the Knight's disappearance is lost to memory so that nobody can link it with his Lady's new marriage; the court similarly forgets the werewolf's fearful appearance; and most provocatively, the second husband followed by the Lady, one right after the other, each of the two forgets that the werewolf is an active participant in the courtly life of the King and goes to the court without a fear in the world.

When memory is so obviously lacking, then disparate parts cannot be connected with one another to create a series of new links, one that renders a different tale or a solution to a puzzle. The Knight's tale engendered the Lady's tale as well as the King's tale of his newly found pet. Similarly, the Lady's retelling engendered her courtly romance. But unlike the later *translationes* linking instances of the Bisclavret's violent language and those linking instances of amnesia, these earlier *translationes* lack memory and diachronic significance. And as Kurt Ringger argues [in *Die Lais,* 1973], "Dichten heisst für Marie Erinnern" ["For Marie, to create poetry means to remember"].

The advisor gels references to storytelling and other metaliterary elements. He completes both tales—the werewolf's *merveille* and the Lady's courtly romance—in one movement, linking them, and further giving them the same moral message. Pointing to the *sens,* the deeper meaning lying beneath the werewolf's courtesy, the advisor demonstrates how to read perceptively, to uncover hidden meanings. He marginalizes neither a crucial structural element or the vehicle (the Bisclavret), the underlying tenor (the werewolf's civility), nor even the conventional sign system (language) but, ironically, he marginalizes "fiction" itself. He sees the pieces, but he doesn't collect them; he has the Lady put them together.

The advisor's knowledge and advice allows the Bisclavret to assume his former appearance (elegant surface) and reveals the underlying origins of the Lady's courtly tale. But at the same time as the material is rewritten to end the werewolf's tale with the *merveille* of the werewolf's transformation, when it seems as if the advisor has ended the fiction, the courtly narrative developed by the Lady is also finished with the *merveille* of the noseless daughters, a *translatio* with diachronic significance. Marie thus moves from the "non-fiction" as extracted by the advisor to the narrator's own figurative brand of sprightly, startling, and enticing truth.

With this doubled ending, balanced between the advisor's memory and the narrator's figurative play, Marie rewrites the tale yet again, implying its continual transferral and transformation, as indeed at the very same time, she transfers and transforms its essence for her own readers. In a sense, the actual *merveille* of **"Bisclavret"** is that literature can constantly transform.

Bonnie H. Leonard (essay date 1993)

SOURCE: "The Inscription of a New Audience: Marie de France's *Espurgatoire Saint Patriz,*" in *Romance Languages Annual,* Vol. V, 1993, pp. 57-62.

[*In the following essay, Leonard argues that through her* Espurgatoire Saint Patriz, *Marie offered up the story of Saint Patrick to a wider audience, translating it as she did into French from Latin and embellishing upon the story to make it accessible to people living and working outside of monasteries.*]

In her least-studied work, the ***Espurgatoire Saint Patriz,*** Marie de France is involved in the translation of one form of language into another. In the ***Lais,*** the poet transformed the orally transmitted Celtic lay into written French verse. In the ***Fables,*** Marie claims to have translated King Alfred's Aesopic fables from English into Romance. The ***Espurgatoire*** undergoes similar treatment as the ***Lais*** and ***Fables*** in that it is transformed through translation by Marie. The literary circumstances surrounding the production of the ***Espurgatoire,*** however, stand in contrast to those of the ***Lais*** and the ***Fables.*** First, the Latin text of the *Tractatus de Purgatorio Sancti Patricii,* written by an English Cistercian monk known as Henry of Saltrey, survives in many manuscripts, testifying to the various stages of its development, and therefore can be compared closely with Marie's translation of it. In contrast to the abundance of *Tractatus* source texts which exist, of Marie's 102 fables only 40 are traceable to written (Latin) sources, and the collection is supposedly the French translation of the still-elusive English fable book of King Alfred. Similarly, there is no written trace of the ***Lais*** prior to Marie's recording of them. Second, the emphasis of the narrative in the ***Espurgatoire*** has shifted from this world to the next. The ***Fables,*** which by means of their epimythia teach social morality and responsibility, do not grapple with the workings of human salvation as does the ***Espurgatoire.*** The focus of the ***Lais,*** less didactic yet than the ***Fables,*** is also obviously elsewhere. The sacred subject matter of the ***Espurgatoire,*** then, sets this text apart from the ***Lais*** and the ***Fables*** on the one hand, but its status as translation into French suggests a cohesiveness of purpose on Marie's part in the three texts. Marie's ***Espurgatoire*** is not a simple translation (as if any translation is a "simple" one), but a recontextualization of Henry of Saltrey's *Tractatus.* At the most basic level, Henry's Latin prose is transformed by Marie into French octosyllables. This in itself constitutes innovation. More importantly, Marie integrates the text's new vernacular audience into the Purgatory legend not only by means of translation, but also by her inscription of this audience into the narrative itself. The focus of this study will be on how Marie simultaneously creates and speaks to a new, larger public in her ***Espurgatoire.***

The ***Espurgatoire*** is 2,302 lines long, constituting a text more extensive than any of Marie's individual fables or lays. Of these 2,302 lines 22 are, as [Thomas Atkinson] Jenkins states in his edition of Marie's text, "entirely original matter," and have no analogue in the Latin manuscripts of the text. To the body of the *Tractatus,* Marie has added a Prologue (lines 1-8), an Epilogue (lines 2297-2302), and four couplets (lines 1019-20; 1053-54; 1119-20; 1667-68). Jenkins refers to these four couplets as "interjections (which) bear the imprint of sincerity, and afford us a glimpse into the mind of the author." Others have ignored or dismissed them as inconsequential. Without questioning the sincerity of Marie's new verses, I would nonetheless suggest that they are not mere interjections, but rather the working out in narrative form of Marie's stated purpose in her Prologue; that is, to offer a new audience the possibility of salvation through the inclusion of that audience in her text.

What Marie herself added to the evolved text of H's *Tractatus* now warrants discussion, for it is in her own reworking of the Latin text that a new public for the work was created. Before passing on to Marie's aforementioned "original" material (the Prologue, Epilogue, and four couplets), several other aspects of the poet's text that I would also call "original" merit attention.

First, there are several passages in which Henry of Saltrey and Marie de France's authorial voices become confusingly mixed. The first example of this phenomenon occurs immediately after Marie's Prologue, in what is recognized as Henry's Prologue in the Latin text, but which might appear in Marie's text to concern her own work. The text found in the BN manuscript reads as follows:

> Uns Prudom m'ad piéça requise
> Pur ço m'en sui ore entremise,
> De mettre mei en cel labur,
> Pur révérence, è pur s'onur
>
> (lines 9-12)

Henry's own Prologue speaks directly to its commissioner:

> Jussisti[s], pater venerande, ut scriptum vobis mitterem, quod de Purgatorio in vestra me retuli audisse presentia. Quod quidem eo libentius aggredior, quod ad id explendum paternitatis vestre jussione instantius compellor. (9)

Marie has already changed Henry's text in first referring to Henry's *pater venerande* in the third person (*Uns prudom*). She then addresses him in the second person (*Beau piere*). Marie seems at this point to have collapsed the levels of distinction between her own work and that of Henry, explaining that *Uns Prudom* commissioned the present work. That it is Marie's voice speaking is suggested by the manuscript's own feminine past participles in lines 9-10 (*requise/entremise*). In several published editions of Marie's text, however, the feminine endings are "corrected" to the masculine. In his edition, which retains the manuscript's feminine endings, [B. de] Roquefort explains that Marie was referring to her own patron by *Uns Prudom.* Because BN fr. 25407 is the sole manuscript containing the ***Espurgatoire***'s text, comparison with other manuscripts is impossible. If the endings were indeed altered as Jenkins suggests by a later copyist, and are not of Marie's authorship, this would simply demonstrate the difficulty on the scribe's part (as well as ours) in determining where Marie's "je" ends and where Henry's begins.

This phenomenon becomes more pronounced when read against other passages in the French translation, where Marie makes a clear distinction between herself as translator and Henry as *autor.* The following is Henry's Epilogue:

> Haec, pater venerande, predictus Gilbertus et mihi et aliis pro edificacione narravit, sic ipse ab ipso milite sepe audivit. Ego vero, sequens sensum verborum et narracionis ejus, prout intelligere potui, dixi vobis. Si quis autem me reprehendere voluerit, sciat me quod vestra hoc scribere jussio coegit. Valete. (64-65)

Marie renders the passage thus:

> Gileberz cunta icel fait
> A l'autor quil nus a retrait,
> Si cum Oweins li out cunté,
> E li moignes dunt ai parlé:
> Ço que jo vus ai ici dit
> E tut mustré par mun escrit.
>
> (lines 2057-62)

Here, the levels of transmission are more clearly discernable. Owein told his story to Gilbert, who in turn told it to the *autor* or Henry, who here is spoken of in the third person by Marie's *je,* which frames the entire process in as what she refers to as *mun escrit.*

In the passage immediately following, however, the melding together of Marie and Henry's *je* seems to reoccur:

> E puis parlai a dous abbez:
> D'Irlande erent bons ordenez.
> Si lur demandai de cel estre,
> Si ço poeit veritez estre.
>
> (lines 2063-66)

Who is speaking here? If the *je* is the same as that in the verses immediately preceding ("Ço que jo vus ai ici dit / E tut mustré par mun escrit" [lines 2061-62]), it would appear that Marie herself spoke to the two Irish abbots. But the Latin text already has an *ego* who questioned them:

> Ego autem, post quam hec omnia audieram, dous de Hibernia abbates, ut adhuc cercior fierem, super his conveni. (65)

Is this *ego* Henry? It seems unlikely, given that Henry just finished his Epilogue. Is it the voice of an interpolator, who wishes to add his "two cents' worth" to Henry's account? In any case, Marie's own level of narration has receded into and become one with that of the Latin *ego* after appearing as distinct from Henry's in the preceding passage.

A final remark about Marie's treatment of the *Tractatus* involves her audience. As we have seen, the *Tractatus*'s inscribed audience is the Abott of Sartis, whom Henry of Saltrey calls *pater venerande* and at whose request the account was recorded in writing. Marie, too, speaks to a *Beau piere* (who might or might not be this abbot), but in addition expands her textual audience to the *Seignurs* whom she directly addresses in line 49 (Seignurs, a l'eissue del cors), line 189 (Seignurs, entendez la raisun), and line 421 (Seignurs, si cum dit li escriz). These courtly gentlemen are nowhere to be found in the Latin text, and their introduction into the text by Marie reflects the general trend in the *Espurgatoire* toward greater inclusion in a salvithic literary legacy of those to whom the text had been inaccessible.

With this idea of audience expansion in mind, we arrive at Marie's "original" material, which both announces and enacts the inclusion of a new, larger public in the legend of Saint Patrick's Purgatory. In the Prologue, Marie declares her intention to render into Romance the Purgatory tale:

> Al nun de Deu, qui od nus seit,
> E qui sa grace nus enveit,
> Voeil en romanz mettre en escrit,
> Si cum li livre le nus dit,
> En remembrance e en memoire,
> Les peines de l'espurgatoire;
> Qu'a Seint Patriz volt Deus mustrer
> Le liu u l'um i deit entrer.
>
> (lines 1-8)

The poet appropriates divine authority for her text in the assertion that her work is done in the name of God. This stands in contrast to the construction of authority in the **Lais,** where Marie only indirectly justifies her undertaking with a reference to the Parable of the Talents (Matthew 25:14-30), but equally with one to Classical Antiquity's *anc ens.* In the Prologue to her **Fables,** Marie likens her translation to those of Aesop and King Alfred, but nowhere does she claim God directly as her textual authority as she does in the **Espurgatoire.** The **Espurgatoire**'s universal immediacy is apparent in Marie's prayer to God: "qui od *nus* seit / E qui sa grace *nus* enveit" (lines 1-2; my emphasis). Prefaced by this all-inclusive *nus,* what follows relates directly to each individual's relationship with God. In addition, the Purgatory which God revealed to Saint Patrick is portrayed, in both the *Tractatus* and **Espurgatoire** texts, as a geographical place to which pilgrimages, like Owein's, were possible.

Such pilgrimages to Station Island on Lough Derg (Red Lake) in County Donegal, Ireland, were becoming increasingly popular at the end of the twelfth century, and visiting Saint Patrick's Purgatory was therefore a real possibility for Marie's audience. That Purgatory was an actual place on earth to be entered is reflected in Marie's qualification of it: "Qu'a Seint Patriz volt Deus mustrer / *Le liu* u l'um i deit entrer (lines 7-8; my emphasis). In addition, *l'um* is no generalized abstraction; it is rather a reference to real individuals who could literally visit Patrick's Purgatory and be purged of their sins. While the *Lais* told fanciful tales of love set in the distant past, and the **Fables** taught social correctness in a more contemporary setting, neither work could be viewed as instrumental or necessary to its public's salvation. In contrast, the **Espurgatoire** offered a "mapping out" of the next world to speakers of French. The **Espurgatoire,** unlike Dante's later *Divina Commedia,* does not explain what sins are purged in each of the regions of Purgatory, but the basic workings of the place are made clear by the archbishops in the Terrestrial Paradise. They explain that the sinners Owein witnessed in Purgatory would eventually be purged of their sins and arrive at the Terrestrial Paradise, just as those in the Terrestrial Paradise would pass on to the Celestial Paradise. Each soul's journey after death and its ease of ascent to Paradise depended directly upon the individual's life on earth, as well as the prayers and masses offered on the departed's behalf by the living. Only the souls condemned eternally to Hell, which Owein never sees, are unable to move up the heavenly scale to eternal bliss. The *Espurgatoire* was thus of direct importance to all believers, for now speakers of Romance as well as speakers of Latin were confronted with the consequences of their earthly behavior, and apprised of what they could do to be in better standing for when the Last Judgement occurred.

The *Tractatus* not only became more accessible to the layperson through Marie's translation of it, but the story's protagonist undergoes a certain rewriting as well. In the *Tractatus,* Owein remains a knight instead of entering a religious order after his journey into the next world. In the *Espurgatoire,* however, Owein's decision to forego monastic life is amplified. The following passage is the *Tractatus*'s version of Owein's seeking advice from his lord as to whether he should enter religious orders:

> Sicque, cruce in humero accepta, Jerosolimam perrexit, et, inde rediens, regem dominum suum consulturus adiit, ut ejus concilio secundum illum religionis ordinem viveret, quem rex ipse laudaret. (61)

Marie's translation develops and expands the king's response to Owein's inquiry:

> En Jerusalem en ala
> E ariere [s'en] repaira;
> A sun seignur le rei revint
> E il volentiers le retint.
> Tut en ordre li a cunté
> De sa vie la verité:
> Cunseil li quist e demanda
> De sa vie qu'il [l']en loa:
> S'il deüst moigne devenir
> U quel religiun tenir.
> E li reis li a respundu
> Chevaliers seit, si cum il fu;
> Ço li loa il a tenir,
> En ço poeit Deu bien servir.
> Si fist il bien tute sa vie:
> Pur altre ne chanja il mie.
>
>   (lines 1917-32)

During the remainder of his life, we learn that Owein serves God faithfully as a layperson as the amplification of Owein's decision to remain part of the secular world continues. When Gilbert arrives in Ireland to found an abbey on Owein's King's land, the Latin text states that Owein, who helped Gilbert, remained a knight:

> Sique miles cum ipso Gilberto mansit, sed nec monachus nec conversus esse voluit; quin potius se servum domui reddidit. (62)

But Marie places greater emphasis upon this decision than does her Latin source:

> Issi remest od Gilebert
> Li chevaliers e bien le sert;
> Mais ne voleit changier sun estre:

> En nun de chevalier morra,
> Ja altre abit nen recevra.
>
>   (lines 1972-76)

Although the *Espurgatoire* is not a saint's life *per se,* it shares some important characteristics with the hagiographic tradition. First, important events in the life of Saint Patrick himself are depicted in the *Espurgatoire*: Patrick preaches the Gospel to the unbelieving Irish (lines 189-264), he receives the Lord's Staff and Books of the Gospel from Jesus Christ (lines 265-300), and has revealed to him the entrance to Purgatory by God himself (lines 301-50). Second, the *Espurgatoire* involved its public in an immediate and personal way. Like Owein, a secular knight who had sinned against God and had been purged of his sins by his otherworldly journey, readers or hearers of Marie's text could themselves undertake this same pilgrimage to Lough Derg in northwestern Ireland and become reconciled with their Lord. The *Espurgatoire,* like the saint's life, linked its public to the events of its narrative by challenging that public better to serve God.

Obviously, the *Espurgatoire* goes beyond the realm of the saint's life, because the main character of the text is not a saint, but rather a knight who, benefitting from a saint's communion with God, himself remains a knight in both the Latin and French texts. Although the French text further emphasizes Owein's decision to stay a knight, it is remarkable that the *Tractatus,* written by one monk (Henry of Saltrey) for another (the Abbot of Sartis), is largely concerned with a layperson's faithful service of God.

It is fitting that the exemplary account of a *layperson's* descent into Purgatory and his salvation become the object of a translation into Romance. Typically, readers and writers of Latin worked in some capacity within the Church. That the *Tractatus*'s audience was probably a monastic one is reflected by the text's inscribed audience (the Abbot of Sartis), the Homily extolling monastic life, as well as the episodes in which the monk and the priest are sorely tried by demons. The *Tractatus*'s readers, like the Abbot of Sartis, were part of a circumscribed community defined in part by the Latin it spoke, wrote, and read. Romance, on the other hand, was the language of the layperson, to whom the Latin of the Church was often incomprehensible. The *Espurgatoire,* whose hero is a layperson, stands as a most appropriate text, then, to inspire and involve laypeople in the legacy of Saint Patrick and his Purgatory. Identifying with a knight would probably have been easier for most laypeople than identifying with a monk or a priest. The integration of the layperson into the tradition of Saint Patrick's Purgatory is embodied by Owein, a good Christian layperson in both the *Tractatus* and the *Espurgatoire,* and is further achieved by Marie's translation of the narrative into Romance.

After the Prologue, the actual incorporation of Marie's Romance-speaking public into the body of the narrative occurs for the first time in lines 1019-20. Owein has just witnessed the punishments of the second field in Purgatory, where sinners are nailed to the ground, tormented by burning dragons, snakes and toads, and beaten by demons. At this point, Marie expresses her sympathy for the sinners:

> Chaitis est cil qui en tel peine,
> Par ses pechiez, se trait e meine!
>
> (lines 1019-20)

There is no Latin equivalent to this couplet in the *Tractatus* manuscripts. In addition to showing pity for those seen by Owein, Marie's exclamation is a generalizing statement, and is addressed to her present audience as a warning. *(C)il* in line 1019 is not limited to one of the sinners in the second field; rather, it includes all persons, who, because of their sins, may one day find themselves in such a horrible plight. Because this is one of Marie's so-called "original" couplets, there can be no mistake that Marie is speaking here to her own public, not to that of Henry of Saltrey. Because Marie's translation was undertaken to make the text more accessible to speakers of Romance, these lines are directed uniquely at this new public, which becomes inscribed into the narrative at this point.

Marie's next "original" material is found in lines 1053-54. His demonic guides have just shown Owein the torments of the third field, where sinners are nailed to the ground by nails so close together that a person's finger could not fit between two nails without touching one of them. A cold wind blows over the sinners, and demons beat them without pity. The following couplet is Marie's addition:

> Allas, que nuls deit deservir
> Que tel peine deüst suffrir!
>
> (lines 1053-54)

Again, what has been dismissed as a sign of Marie's sincerity offers a revealing glimpse into the dynamics between Marie and her newly-created public. It is obvious that Marie has stepped momentarily out of the narrative mode to address her present audience with regard to the terrible suffering Owein has just witnessed. Those who are punished in the third field deserve their condition, for Purgatory is part of God's plan for human purgation and salvation. Marie's interjection therefore does not question the justification for the torture of these sinners; indeed, it does not directly concern them. Marie's words are rather directed toward those who are *not yet arrived* at this place as a warning to view the sinners of the third field as a negative exemplum. Indeed, Marie's "Allas" displays sympathy for those already suffering in Purgatory, but her concern that anyone (*nuls*) need suffer such punishment as Owein has viewed is for those souls who have not yet been assigned to this realm of suffering. Those souls whose destiny is still to be decided, and to whom Marie is offering the path to salvation, are the members of her French-speaking lay public.

As the narrative follows Owein through Purgatory, the knight witnesses new terrors in the fourth field of punishment. Here, some sinners are hung by various body parts by burning chains or on burning hooks, while others are thrown into furnaces, or roasted on spits or grills. For the first and only time in the narrative, Owein sees individuals with whom he was acquainted in life. Although it is never explained what they did during their lives to deserve these purgatorial torments, the souls' cries of pain are heart-rending. When the demons attempt to subject Owein to these same punishments, the knight cries out Jesus Christ's name, as he had been advised to do by the men in white robes when he first arrived in Purgatory. When Owein speaks Christ's name, the demons are rendered powerless, and the knight passes on unharmed. It is at this point that Marie again turns from Owein to address her present audience:

> Mult est cist nuns bons a numer,
> Par quei um se puet delivrer
>
> (lines 1119-20)

In the first two of Marie's couplets discussed (lines 1019-20; 1053-54), the poet presents the punishments of the second and third fields with sympathy for the sinners, but more importantly as negative exempla to be avoided by the living. In contrast, Marie here offers Owein's speaking the name of Christ to save himself from danger as a positive exemplum. That the couplet is in the present tense reinforces its applicability to Marie's audience. Marie's couplets are not to be read in the past tense, as are some present-tense passages in medieval literature. Rather, they signal a fundamental, albeit brief, shift in time from the past to the present. What happened to Owein in the past (during the reign of King Stephen), as well as what was revealed to Saint Patrick in the more distant past, is pertinent to the hearers and readers of Marie's translation. Just as Owein counted on Jesus to protect him from the demons of Purgatory, so can the Christian believer count on Christ to keep him safe from what may befall him in life's walk, and to save him from the punishments which Owein and Marie's audience have witnessed.

The next and final couplet in Marie's text which has no apparent Latin equivalent occurs in the description of the Terrestrial Paradise, which Owein enters through a beautiful door in a high wall. Bright light floods the whole realm. Fruit and flowers grow in a pleasant meadow, a wonderful aroma and lovely melodies fill the air, and the temperature is neither too hot or too cold. Owein finds himself in a state of incredible peace. The following is Marie's exclamation in response to what the knight has seen, smelled, heard, and felt in his visit to the Terrestrial Paradise:

> Or nus doint Deus ço deservir
> Qu'a cez joies puissuns venir!
>
> (lines 1667-68)

The poet has again turned from her narrative to speak to her public. Marie hopes that we, like Owein, may one day experience the ineffable joy of the blessed in the Terrestrial Paradise, for it is obvious that the poet and her public constitute the *nus* in line 1667. The occurrence of this last and the other three audience-centered couplets in Marie's text reflects Owein's progress, both spatial and spiritual, through Purgatory. In her first two couplets (following the description of the second and third fields of punishment) Marie warns us of what we should *not* do, lest we be punished as are those suffering in Purgatory. In her third couplet (which follows the description of the fourth field) Marie informs us of what we *should* do; that is, to call on Christ to keep us from sinning. In that third couplet, Marie shifts from the negative aspect of sin to the positive side of avoiding it. Finally, in these verses which follow the description of the Terrestrial Paradise, the possibility of attaining salvation is held out to us. Like Owein, who makes his way physically through Purgatory from suffering and darkness toward beatitude and light, Marie's own audience appears in these same places textually, experiences Owein's journey linguistically, and becomes woven into the fabric of the narrative. By translating the *Tractatus* into French, Marie offers nonspeakers of Latin a textual vision of salvation through Owein's adventure that they may one day experience extratextually themselves.

Marie's brief Epilogue reiterates that she has translated the *Tractatus* into Romance:

> Jo, Marie, ai mis en memoire
> Le livre de l'Espurgatoire:
> En Romanz qu'il seit entendables
> A laie gent e cuvenables.
> Or preium Deu que par sa grace
> De noz pechiez mundes nus face.

> (lines 2297-302)

Marie has transformed the narrative in order to make it accessible to those who did not speak Latin. As we have seen. Marie's rendering of the tale into French literally *creates* a new audience by its inscription into her text. Marie's **Espurgatoire** continues the tradition of audience expansion, which was initiated by God's revelation of the Purgatorial pit to Saint Patrick, an initial audience to God's plans. Marie's text enables her audience to "see" God's plans for them, too, through letters familiar to them.

John M. Bowers (essay date 1994)

SOURCE: "Ordeals, Privacy, and the *Lais* of Marie de France," in *The Journal of Medieval and Renaissance Studies,* Vol. 24, No. 1, Winter, 1994, pp. 1-31.

[*In the following essay, Bowers defines the medieval method of judgment by ordeal and asserts that Marie's* Lais *critiques the era's shift from trial by ordeal to "more efficient" ways of violating people's privacy and personal freedom.*]

Marie de France wrote during the period c. 1170-90 when England was in transition from a feudal society toward a state-nation under Henry II. It was an era when the Church was also redefining its regulatory power over the laity under a series of strong popes culminating with Innocent III. Dealing exclusively with the secret relations between men and women—typically a clandestine love affair in some secluded place—Marie's *lais* brought into sharp definition one of the human values most at stake in these pervasive restructurings of society: personal privacy. Christianity had flourished in the enclosures of monasteries and episcopal courts, and feudalism encouraged a privatization of social life in the lord's *familia* as the core political unit. Yet privacy in the modern sense was a true anomaly in these intimate, granular communities except in the sense of "collective privacy" sustained by all members of an extended household. Since any activity that a man and woman needed to keep private could be considered antisocial, suspicion naturally arose that such activities needed to be brought to light as sinful or criminal. The ordeal became one of the signal developments for uncovering secret crimes during the period 1000-1200.

The transfer of power to distant centers of administrative activity seemed to afford new opportunities for reclaiming areas of privacy in which individuals, far from these seats of disciplinary authority, could more freely cultivate their own moral, intellectual, and spiritual lives. This did not happen. My reading of Marie's *lais* centers this issue—the individual's unsuccessful bid for freedom from social discipline—by examining the transition from the ordeal as a means for revealing publicly the contents of one's secret conduct toward new, more efficient methods for violating the privacy of people's lives: jury inquest, judicial confession coerced under threat of torture, and religious confession elicited under threat of eternal damnation. If, as Michel Foucault has argued [in *Discipline and Punish,* 1977], some great cultural divide falls between medieval spectacle, in which the many watch the few, and modern surveillance, in which the few monitor the many, the passing of the ordeal as a judicial spectacle marked an important transition for early modern England, a transition to which Marie's *lais* contribute a critique of past practices as well as intimations of future developments.

In the last of the twelve *lais* collected in the British Library manuscript Harley 978, Eliduc returned home so moody over a secret love affair that his wife Guildelüec interpreted his behavior as a sign he suspected her of concealing some sexual infidelity, so she offered to prove her innocence:

> A sei meïsmes se pleigneit.
> Ele lui demandot suvent
> S'il ot oï de nule gent
> Que ele eüst mesfet u mespris,
> Tant cum il fu hors del païs;
> Volenters s'en esdrescera
> Devant sa gent, quant li plarra.

> (She lamented to herself and often asked him whether someone had told him that she had misbehaved or done wrong while he had been out of the country, for she would willingly defend herself in front of the people, if he wished.)

The public defense to which she referred was the *judicium Dei* or ordeal. In the early twelfth century, French aristocrats almost automatically took suspicions of their wives to this proof. Based on prehistoric customs among some of the Germanic tribes, these judicial tests—bilateral ordeals by combat, and unilateral ordeals by hot water, cold water, hot iron, setting adrift at sea, and so on—were promulgated by Christian kings and granted official status by the Church through priestly participation. Ecclesiastical sanction probably began as a gesture of cultural accommodation, but later, during the Carolingian period, it developed into a more self-conscious program for extending authority and strengthening the political influence of the clergy. Sometimes defended by biblical texts such as 1 Corinthians 4:5 ("the Lord comes who both will bring to light the hidden things of darkness and will make manifest the counsels of the hearts"), these judicial rituals were conducted by churchmen with varying degrees of confidence that God's justice was immanent throughout creation, expressing itself in water, earth, fire, bread, and iron. Always the last resort, not the first, the ordeal lent itself especially to cases where reliable witnesses and solid evidence were lacking for bringing to light some secret guilt, cases typically involving theft, murder, heresy, or some sexual transgression such as adultery. (The English ordeal was rarely used to resolve civil disputes involving property.) The body of the accused afforded a kind of documentation synthesizing the past deed with the present trial to render a visible text of justification. The flesh itself became the litmus paper upon which the acid of guilt might be made legible.

As a graphic instance of the sort of ordeal invoked by Guildelüec, the Winchester Annals offered a particularly famous account dated for the year 1043 but almost certainly fictionalized at the end of the twelfth century. Queen Emma, mother of Edward the Confessor, was accused by the Norman archbishop of Canterbury of committing adultery:

> The queen was brought at the king's command from Whewell to Winchester and throughout all the night preceding her trial she kept her vigil at the shrine of St. Swithin. . . . On the appointed day the clergy and the people came to the church and the king himself sat on the tribunal. The queen was brought before her son and questioned whether she was willing to go through with what she had undertaken. . . . Nine glowing ploughshares were placed on the carefully swept pavement of the church. After these had been consecrated by a short ceremony the queen's shoes and stockings were taken off; then her robe was removed and her cloak thrown aside, and, supported by two bishops, one on either side, she was led to the torture. . . . Uncontrollable weeping broke out all over the church and all voices were united in the cry "St. Swithin, O St. Swithin, help her!". . . In a low voice the queen offered this prayer as she undertook the ordeal: "O God, who didst free Susanna from the wicked elders and the three youths from the fiery furnace, from the fire prepared for me deign to preserve me through the merits of St. Swithin."

Behold a miracle! With the bishops directing her feet, in nine steps she walked upon the nine ploughshares, pressing each one of them with the full weight of her whole body; and though she thus passed over them

all, she neither saw the iron nor felt the heat. . . . She gazed and her eyes were opened; then for the first time she looked about and understood the miracle. "Lead me," she said, "to my son, that he may see my feet and know that I have suffered no ill."

The emotion-charged description includes most of the essential features: the presiding princely authority, the administering ecclesiastical figures, the immediate involvement of a viewing public, and the helplessness of the accused to do anything other than accept the ordeal for proving her innocence. The scenario is so ideally framed that it must be understood as an archaic reconstruction, hearkening back to Anglo-Saxon times, of a judicial ritual on the eve of papal prohibition.

Though literary scholars as diverse as D. W. Robertson, Jr., and Georges Duby have drawn attention to the importance of the Fourth Lateran Council of 1215 for its decisions concerning penance and the sacraments, Pope Innocent III's convention also dealt directly with the problem of ordeals in canon 18: "Nor let anyone pronounce over the ordeal of hot or cold water or glowing iron any benediction or rite of consecration, regard being also paid to the prohibitions formerly promulgated respecting the single combat or duel." Set in the context of a general exclusion of clerics from any act that resulted in the shedding of blood, the ban on priestly involvement in ordeals came at the end of a decades-long campaign by French and Italian canonists to undermine confidence in this judicial procedure. John Baldwin's study of these intellectual preparations focuses upon the work of the chief opponent, Peter the Chanter, whose career as a teacher in Paris from the 1170s to the 1190s coincides exactly with Marie de France's active presence in Angevin culture.

In addition to pressing the objection that such rituals compelled God to perform miracles against the command "Thou shalt not tempt the Lord thy God" (Deut. 6:16; Matt. 4:7), Peter the Chanter assembled anecdotal evidence in the form of stories to make the point that ordeals often failed to perform their essential function. His anecdotal archive served as memoranda of historical precedents undermining the customary status of ordeals which, as these *petites histoires* showed, sometimes yielded spectacularly wrong conclusions. He tells one story, for example, of the English pilgrim who returned home alone from Jerusalem, was accused of murdering his traveling companion, failed the test of the water ordeal, and was summarily hanged; shortly thereafter the supposedly murdered companion returned home safe and sound. Peter's strategy accords with the view of Stanley Fish that, since students of the law examine cases rather than rules, the most devastating assault upon the ordeal or any other judicial principle would be waged in the realm of the narrative [Fish, "Fish v. Fiss," *Law and Literature*, 1988].

Marie's *lais* do not pursue a steady investigation of the ordeal and are not primarily "about" the ordeal. Indeed, the dramatic potential of the ritual is degraded by being displaced from the climactic scenes it occupies in such works as *La Chanson de Roland*. In fact the ordeal as a narrative device is conspicuous by its near absence. Her collection nonetheless offers an anecdotal critique that complements Peter the Chanter's by addressing a predominantly courtly audience with its vested interest in the private exercise of power. Almost the only contemporary notice of this elusive female author comes in the prologue to *La Vie Seint Edmund le Rei* (c. 1180) by Denis Piramus, who recounts how Marie's poems were listened to over and over again by counts, barons, and knights, as well as by aristocratic ladies. Valuable as this testimony is for locating the *lais* in a courtly context, lack of evidence for placing Marie herself in a specific court severely limits the possibilities for detailing the interaction of her poetry with its social base. Although Henry II is commonly believed to be the "nobles reis" to whom Marie dedicated her *lais* (**"Prologue"** 43), even this most important connection cannot be known for sure.

If not a specific context, a general field of cultural interplay can be extrapolated from the corpus of her writings. For example, Marie is not likely to have been a woman exclusively of the court. Since she acknowledged that she could read Latin (**"Prologue"**) and based her *Espurgatoire Seint Patrice* on a Latin original, scholars who have tried to identify the historical Marie have always nominated ladies who moved between the court and the cloister, aristocratic women with secular and religious allegiances during various periods in their lives. Someone like Countess Marie of Boulogne satisfies all the presumed criteria: the daughter of King Stephen of England, she became abbess of Romsey in Hampshire, but was removed from her convent by Henry II and married off to Matthew of Flanders, returning later in life to her convent. Though the true identity of the author is likely to remain a mystery, the range of her literary interests suggests someone who moved back and forth across the boundary between distinctive social formations, cautiously negotiating the demands of the two social definitions of nun and courtly lady. In short, she was strategically situated to register a variety of clerical issues—including the debate over ordeals—and to translate, encode, and embed those contested topics along with her abiding concern for privacy in literary forms appealing to the elite of Henrician society.

R. Howard Bloch's study of the relationship between literature and the law pays steady regard to the fact that most long French narratives of the twelfth century contain some form of trial, and yet the link between the concealed truth and the outcome of the ordeal is frequently severed at some point in the ritual process: "It can be taken only as a failure of divine judgment and, hence, of the entire set of assumptions underlying immanent procedure" [*Medieval French Literature and the Law*, 1977]. Although the ordeal was supposed to have the advantage of being strictly objective because the evidence was physically visible for the entire community to read, as was the case with Queen Emma's unharmed feet, skepticism was voiced by an increasing number of scholastics who questioned the validity of such superstitious ceremonies. Like Peter the Chanter, these other twelfth-century churchmen reviewed prior historical instances, discovering that phys-

ical evidence was not always correctly interpreted and, in some cases, not even objectively perceived. Another Winchester monk, Wulfstan Cantor, dealing with another ordeal during the late Anglo-Saxon period, recounted how an unnamed slave was subjected to the ordeal of the red-hot iron and burned his hands, which were then bound according to the prescribed procedure. When the bandages were removed and his hands examined three days later, the presiding reeve and his followers were astonished to find the hands healing cleanly, proof positive that the slave was innocent. Other onlookers were even more astonished, however, because *they* perceived the pus and infection of the hands, clear signs that the man was guilty. With the potential for a wrong or dubious outcome, King Henry II had enough suspicion of the ordeal that his Assize of Clarendon in 1166 concluded that a man of bad reputation, even if he succeeded in the test, should be banished from the kingdom.

Although Bloch nowhere mentions Marie de France in this regard, her **"Guigemar"** offers the first of a series of instances in which the ritual process does in fact break down. Guigemar, brought to a foreign city by a magical ship, enjoyed a clandestine affair with the local lord's wife for a year and a half. When he was finally discovered and forced to explain his presence, the truth of his story was referred to the *judicium Dei*:

> Il li respunt que pas nel creit
> E s'issi fust cum il diseit,
> Si il peüst la neif trover,
> Il le metreit giers en la mer:
> S'il guaresist, ceo li pesast,
> E bel li fust si il neiast.
> Quant il l'ad bien aseüré,
> El hafne sunt ensemble alé;
> La barge trevent, enz l'unt mis;
> Od lui s'en vet en sun païs.
> La neif erre, pas ne demure.
> Li chevaler suspire e plure,
> La dame regretout sovent
> E pric Deu omnipotent
> Qu'il li dunast hastive mort
> E que jamés ne vienge a port,
> S'il ne repeot aver s'amie,
> K'il desirat plus que sa vie.
> Tant ad cele dolur tenue
> Que la neif est a port venue
> U ele fu primes trovee:
> Asez iert pres de sa cuntree.

(The Lord replied that he did not believe him, but that if things were as he stated and he could find the ship, he would then put him out to sea. If he survived, he would be sorry, and if he drowned, he would be delighted. When the Lord had given this assurance, they went together to the harbor, where they found the ship and put him aboard. The ship set sail, taking him back to his own country, and got under way without delay while the knight sighed and wept, lamenting the lady frequently and praying to Almighty God to let him die a quick death without even reaching land, if he could not see again his beloved whom he desired more than his life. His grief was unabated until the ship arrived in the harbor where it had first been discovered, very close to his homeland.)

Marie's narrative appropriates the ancient ordeal of setting adrift at sea, which had been a feature in Irish law combining the test with the potential for simultaneous punishment: if the proband was guilty and failed, he was drowned at sea. Sea trials of this sort were included in the hagiographic writings of other twelfth-century authors, and since the method of judgment figured in the Celtic legends of St. Patrick, it was perhaps directly available to Marie de France as author of the *Espurgatoire Seint Patrice*.

What goes wrong with this ordeal in **"Guigemar"**? First, the lord asked the wrong question. He used the sea test for affirming the truthfulness of Guigemar's story rather than determining his guilt as an adulterer. According to Robert Bartlett, the ordeal was systemically flawed because it was intended to reveal one specific fact in light of a single, precise allegation. The judicial function was further undermined by suspicion that sometimes God used the ordeal to show mercy by allowing the proband to survive unscathed. Finally, there was a persistent fear that if supernatural powers were summoned to intervene in human affairs, these powers might be magical or even demonic. The mysterious ship that conveyed Guigemar to the foreign city is so obviously related to the fairy ships like the one that carried King Arthur to the island of Avalon (the elvish domain mentioned at the end of **"Lanval,"** l. 641) that this vessel can hardly be conceived as an unambiguous instrument of God's justice.

From the lord's point of view, the ritual of setting adrift had the advantage of subjecting Guigemar to hazards that would likely guarantee his death and, in any case, would remove him from the community without any further revelations humiliating to the offended husband. Although Foucault observed that "there was something of the ordeal and something of God's judgment that was still indecipherable in the ceremony of execution," there was something of the execution readily discernible in the methods of many ordeals. They conflated judgment and punishment into a simultaneous theatrical moment in which the determination of guilt became less a matter of the *judicium Dei* strictly supervised by the priesthood and became instead an exercise of secular power, increasingly regalian power. Frederick Barbarossa, who was ahead of his time in ridiculing the ordeal's supernatural machinery, nonetheless used its threat as an instrument of blatant political manipulation. Henry II of England also invoked the ordeal when it was to his advantage, but he punished thieves, arsonists, and murderers even if they were successful at such trials, all as part of a campaign that included establishing inquests and jury proceedings to strengthen the exercise of royal authority. The Pipe Rolls for the period provide scattered evidence for the ordeal's true beneficiaries under Henry II: in several places payments are recorded for officiating priests; in one place a fine is imposed upon a man for conducting an ordeal without a presiding royal officer. These records point to the profit that traditionally accrued to clerics and, of in-creasing importance, the judicial authority claimed by the Crown.

In **"Eliduc,"** the knight was returning home with Guilliadun when a fierce storm overtook his ship just short of the harbor. When ship-wreck appeared imminent, one of the sailors shouted to him:

> "Sire, ça einz avez od vus
> Cele par ki nus perissums.
> Jamés a tere ne vendrums!
> Femme leale espuse avez
> E sur celë autre en menez
> Cuntre Deu e cuntre la lei,
> Cuntre dreiture e cuntre fei.
> Lessez la nus geter en mer,
> Si poüm sempres ariver."

> ("Lord, you have with you the woman who will cause us to perish. We shall never make land! You have a loyal wife and now with this other woman you offend God and his law, righteousness and the faith. Let us cast her into the sea and we shall soon arrive safely.")

Eliduc was so enraged that he knocked the superstitious sailor unconscious with an oar and kicked his body overboard, then took the helm himself and steered the vessel safely to harbor. The clash between the knight and the sailor represents more than a disagreement over the impropriety of an extramarital affair; it represents the confrontation between two cultural outlooks existing side by side during the late twelfth century. Speaking for the rationalists, William of Conches complained of backward-thinking men who wanted scholars such as [in *Philosophia Mundi*] himself "to believe like peasants and not to enquire into the reasons behind things." The sailor interprets the storm as a sign of divine disfavor visited upon the ship for some transgression against God's law. For him, the voyage has been spontaneously translated into an ordeal at sea like the one to which Guigemar was subjected—though he makes the fatal error of concluding that Guilliadun, who was previously innocent of the fact that Eliduc already had a wife, was the one who ought to drown to set matters right.

Eliduc's success in piloting the ship safely to harbor seemed to confirm his view that the storm was simply a natural phenomenon having little to do with God's justice. This victory reflects what many modern historians perceive to have been a significant shift in the ways many ment (not all) saw and understood the *universitas* as an expression of the homogeneity of natural phenomena responsive to sets of self-contained laws. Thus conceived, these natural forces no longer required the regular intervention of God. [In *Nature, Man, and Society*] Chenu associates this conceptual crisis with several other notable changes, including "recourse to rational proofs in courts of law instead of the mystical expedient of trials by ordeal." If the water and fire no longer responded directly to the will of God, the ordeal's outcome assumed a more ambiguous, even random character. In the case of Eliduc, truly the rain seemed to fall on the just and the unjust.

Earlier in the same *lai,* however, events did seem to be underwritten by a more coherent divine logic. After Eliduc was exiled without being given the opportunity to defend himself against various slanders, his king suffered reversals in battle. Interpreting these military misfortunes as evidence of Eliduc's innocence, the king recalled the wronged knight and banished the envious courtiers who had slandered him. This confidence in a purposeful world, where events conspired to befriend the innocent and punish the guilty, coalesced in the concept of a just God expressing his will through the unfolding of human events, as well as the elements of material creation deployed as signs. The belief that divine retribution was inscribed in human affairs had the support of various passages from scripture—"If the just man receive in the earth, how much more the wicked and the sinner" (Proverbs 11:31)—and operated as an unproblematic plot device in many earlier works such as *La Chanson de Roland,* where the duel between Thierry and Pinabel becomes a transparent contest between right and wrong, with victory going almost automatically to the warrior whose cause was just.

But events could also be viewed as contradicting the message of an ordeal, as was the case with Peter the Chanter's English pilgrim whose "victim" later turned up alive. When about 1120 the priest Dominic William of Ivois was accused of preaching heresy, he offered to clear himself by the ordeal of the Eucharist. He vindicated himself at the test, then resumed the preaching of heresy; only later was he killed when taken in adultery and, as the chronicler was relieved to report, "met a death worthy of his wickedness." But why had God allowed him to succeed at the ordeal? The historian Galbert de Bruges wrestled with a similar predicament. He recounts how Lambert of Aardenburg participated in the 1127 murder of Charles the Good, Count of Flanders, but successfully passed the test of the hot iron, only later to be killed at the siege of Ostbourg. Puzzling over this sequence of events, Galbert decided that God had spared Lambert at the time of his ordeal in the hope that the man would eventually repent, but when time passed and there was no sign of contrition, the arrogant sinner was allowed to be killed in battle. It is perhaps significant that Galbert decided that the fortunes of war were probably a more reliable index of God's judgment than the unilateral ordeal: "So it happens that while in battle the guilty one is slain, in the judgment of water or iron the guilty one, if he is penitent, does not succumb" [Galbert de Bruges, *Historie du meurire de Charles le Bon, Comte de Flandres (1127-1128), 1891*].

The most widespread form of the ordeal, the wager of battle, was the most appealing to the chivalric orders. Trial by combat had existed among the ancient Celts, it was formalized in Burgundian law by the end of the fifth century, it was preferred over the oaths of compurgators by Charlemagne, and it became a routine practice in England from the time of William the Conqueror. Probably because the Church exercised the least control over these proceedings, the popes became persistent in their efforts to eliminate tournaments and duels. Innocent II prohibited them in 1139, Eugene III in 1148, Alexander III in 1179, and Innocent III in 1215 as a part of canon

18. Some secular rulers also had their reservations. When Frederick II abolished the wager of battle in Sicily, his materialist critique raised doubts that it was even a legitimate form of ordeal; since no supernatural forces were called upon to tip the scales of justice, his *Constitutions of Melfi* (1231) decided that battle "should be termed a form of divination rather than a genuine proof." Only might made right: "For it is almost if not quite impossible for two champions to come together so equally matched that the one is not wholly superior to the other in strength or does not excel him in some other way by greater vigor and courage or at least in cleverness." Henry II used the Grand Assize of 1179 to uphold the right of a plaintiff to refuse battle by insisting upon a jury trial in a royal court, but only two years earlier th English king had presided as arbiter over conflicting claims by the kings of Castille and Navarre in which both embassies were accompanied by professional champions as well as lawyers. If such encounters did not always bear witness to God's will, they at least rendered clear-cut decisions.

Frederick II's skepticism serves as an ironic subtext to Marie de France's **"Chaitivel,"** in which the four nameless knights were so equally matched in every respect the heroine took all four of them as her lovers. A tournament was proclaimed in which the knights had occasion for proving individual valor, although the outcome was far from decisive. Three of the knights were accidentally killed by foreign opponents, while the fourth was wounded in the thigh in a manner suggesting he was emasculated. Did this mean that a divine decision had condemned all four contestants as equally unjust? Did it mean that the lady herself was being punished for leading such an irregular love life? Did it indicate divine disfavor over a judicial encounter improperly defined and conducted? The tournament had always existed in a gray area where wager of battle, military practice, and personal duel converged. Because its judicial goals in this case were not made explicit, the function of the viewing public as an "interpretive community" was eliminated, with the result that the act of interpretation itself was permanently deferred. Such a refusal of hermeneutic disclosure, as I shall later propose, was Marie's most strategic move for preserving secrecy against the ordeal.

Trial by combat was supposed to have the effect of settling disputes that might otherwise have led to lethal cycles of vendettas. Such a ritual, jointly administered by secular and ecclesiastical authorities, could displace a recursive pattern of violence with a unilinear narrative leading to a climactic conclusion. When the plot turns upon a chivalric contest in **"Milun,"** Marie exposes the dynamics of male rivalry underlying ritual combat. The power of sexual desire, projected upon the body of the woman, could lead to family quarrels, jealous rages, and deadly fights that stood as abiding threats even to the most regulated societies.

René Girard describes the sort of sexual violations that could lead to social violence [in *Violence and the Sacred,* 1977] "Even within the ritualistic framework of marriage, when all the matrimonial vows and other interdictions have been conscientiously observed, sexuality is accompanied by violence; as soon as one trespasses beyond the limits of matrimony to engage in illicit relationships—incest, adultery, and the like—the violence, and the impurity resulting from this violence, grows more potent and extreme." Since Marie's fictions persistently concern the secret trespass of established sexual boundaries (that is, the standard "courtly love" triangle), they establish their own structures for containing the violence that results from male conflict. When in **"Milun"** the Welsh knight begot a son on a local damsel, she was terrified that she would be tortured and sold into slavery if the pregnancy were discovered—another gesture of violence visited upon females who transgressed sexual bounds. Born in secret, the boy was raised by the damsel's sister in far-off Northumbria and, coming of age, set out on a quest to win public renown through tournaments and gift-giving, then to discover his father. Milun and his son recognized each other during a joust after the older knight had been unhorsed, but the victorious son acted contrary to the expectations of modern readers schooled in Freudian psychology: "In truth, father, I shall bring you and my mother together. I shall kill her husband and marry her to you." In the sense that every ordeal is an appeal for the reimposition of social order by recourse to patriarchal authority, an authority ultimately conceived as God the Father, Marie's narrative rewrites the Oedipal myth so that generational conflict is erased. The father takes dominion over the mother, and the offspring of their union freely subordinates himself as the agent of their re-union.

When the crime of adultery involved the highest earthly representative of male-defined law in the person of the king, the ordeal itself was put to the test. Such is the case in **"Equitan."** Since the conclusion of this *lai* has proven so unsatisfactory to modern readers, it is worth examining three cultural traditions that, if I am correct, converge in such a manner as to constitute a just and probable narrative ending.

Equitan, who exercised power as both justiciary and king ("Sire de Nauns, jostis' e reis" l. 12), fell in love with the wife of his loyal seneschal, the man charged with actually administering justice in the realm ("Tute sa tere li gardoit / E meinteneit e justisoit"; ll. 23-24). The adulterous lovers decided that they could fully indulge their secret affair only if they murdered the sensechal, and so the woman devised a secret plan by which she would have two bathtubs prepared for her lover and her husband in the privacy of their bedroom:

"Sun bain si chaut e si buillant,
Suz ciel n'en ad humme vivant
Ne fust escaudez e malmis,
Einz que dedenz se fust asis.
Quant mort serat e escaudez,
Vos hummes e les soens mandez;
Si lur mustrez cumfaitement
Est mort al bain sudeinement."

("The water in his bath will be so boiling hot that no mortal man could escape scalding or destruction, before

he has settled down in it. When he has been scalded to death, summon your vassals and his. Show them how he suddenly died in the bath.")

The scheme backfired when the seneschal arrived early and discovered Equitan and his wife naked in each other's arms. In an effort to conceal his shame, the disoriented king jumped feetfirst into the tub of boiling water and was scalded to death. The seneschal then seized his wife and forced her headfirst into the same bath so that the two criminal lovers died together. The punishment of the sexual outlaws surely conforms with what Huizinga described as "the violent tenor of life" in the Middle Ages, since medieval law almost universally granted a husband the right to kill his wife and her lover when caught *in flagrante*. Yet the climactic events seem politically implausible as well as socially indecorous, anticipating the fabliau with all the comical mixups of bourgeois bedroom farce.

To readjust this view, first it is necessary to establish a clearer sense of the popular "iconography" of the bathtub that figures as the improbable instrument of divine retribution. The custom of bathing was much more widespread during the medieval period than is usually imagined, and wealthy households such as the seneschal's might possess two or more portable *cuves* so that companions could wash side by side in a sociable manner, just as planned by the wife. The sensuality of bathing nonetheless had been a persistent object of suspicion throughout the Christian centuries. Constant tension existed between the notions of bathing as a form of ablution for the health of the soul and, on the other hand, of bathing as a pretext for nudity denounced as the occasion for *luxuria*. As public bathhouses grew in numbers in the new urban centers, they caused increasing concern as places where naked men and women might rendezvous for erotic intents. In fact these establishments became synonymous in many cities with houses of prostitution (the Old French *estuves* giving us the English "stews"). Henry II issued regulations stipulating that no London bathhouse permit the owner's wife to live on the premises, or admit women by themselves, or serve food or alcoholic beverages, or (to put matters bluntly) let its customers engage in sex.

Set against the popular association of baths with sexual misconduct, traditions of religious art offered the image of the boiling bath as a standard feature in the iconography of St. Cecilia. In the version fixed in the hagiographic imagination of the early Middle Ages by the *Passio S. Caeciliae,* the female saint was condemned to be boiled to death in her own cauldron bath, as the medieval audience misconceived the Roman *therma* or hypocaust of the original legend. Going beyond the Pauline pronouncement "If I should deliver my body to be burned and have not charity, it profiteth me nothing" (I Cor. 13:3), Cecilia's body was offered as visible proof of both charity *and* chastity by surviving totally unharmed in the scalding water.

This iconographic tradition showed a naked lady completely immersed in boiling water, but unscathed because she was untouched by carnal pollution. The miracle stood as powerful proof of female chastity, one that had assumed ritual identity as part of the third cultural feature invoked at the conclusion of **"Equitan"**: the ordeal of the boiling cauldron. This was the only unilateral test mentioned in the earliest Frankish records and was a part of Irish law said to have been approved by St. Patrick. Yet the details of its application were sufficiently ill defined to allow much variation in local practices, with some probands using only their hands, others their entire arms, and others—like Cecilia and Equitan—almost their entire bodies. Though wager of battle was considered chivalric and the red-hot iron was preferred for clerics, the boiling water was stigmatized from an early period as a test appropriate for peasants and slaves. Thus the déclassé character of the boiling-water judgment added to the humiliation of Equitan's death.

Marie de France effectively adapted this ordeal to a plot involving the twin crimes of adultery and conspiracy to commit murder. Equitan's status as king in no way eliminated his guilt in this double offense, but it did compromise any appeal to normal judicial processes. Marie's narrative poses the hard questions of who will judge the judges, and who will mete out justice to a king. The ordeal, which had been sanctioned for ambiguous cases even by such skeptics as Ivo of Chartres, most often had been used for politically difficult cases. The only higher authority in these cases was God, whose immanent justice in Marie's *lai* seems to underwrite the mechanics of the plot, causing Equitan to choose as his hiding place the fatal bathtub, then revealing guilt by having the king die. Because the seneschal had no role in staging the procedures, human agency did not tempt heaven in the way found objectionable to canonists such as Peter the Chanter. And because no priest was called upon to officiate, the clergy remained unstained by the deadly outcome in anticipation of canon 18 of the Fourth Lateran Council.

Once the boiling water had functioned as divine proof and punishment of the king's secret crimes, the seneschal was doubly within his rights as an official judge and offended husband to enact retaliatica against his treacherous wife. Marie had consistently emphasized his role as administrator of the king's justice: "Li seneschal la curt teneit / Les plaiz e les clamurs oieit" (ll. 195-96). Criminal justice and poetic justice combine in a resolution made morally coherent by mediation of the ordeal ritual.

The death of the seneschal's wife stands as a rare occasion in which Marie allows a woman to suffer physically as part of a judicial outcome. In Eliduc, for example, when Guildelüec proposed defending her reputation by undergoing the test, her offer was never taken up. These omissions, especially the careful avoidance of the ordeal of the hot plowshares which invariably targeted women, are noteworthy in view of the fact that history afforded an array of illustrious ladies such as Empress Richardis, wife of Charles le Gros, and St. Cunigunda, wife of Emperor Henry II—in addition to Queen Emma—who were recorded as having undergone these brutal tests. Such cases typically concerned the sexual questions of adultery and

disputed paternity (two of Marie's favorite themes), which by their very natures were least open to resolution by producing witnesses or documentary evidence. By strategic omissions, Marie's *lais* resisted the political ideology represented by the ordeals.

These rites were calculated not only to balance the scales of justice but also to dramatize the vast dissymmetry between the individual accused of violating the law and, on the other hand, the sovereign establishment reaching for greater social control. Once set in motion for public display, this awesome dissymmetry asserted itself in the unbalanced play of forces and in the potential for physical violence. Rare indeed was the case in which the proband was left miraculously unharmed; the real test involved judging how the scalded flesh was healing. The entire apparatus of asserting dominion was inscribed as a political function within a system of coercive moral legislation, by church and state, ready to be marshaled against society's marginal members such as foreigners, servants, peasants, the unorthodox, and women.

As Marie's most extended account of a judicial process, **"Lanval"** deals explicitly with the systematic victimization of a foreigner. The hero starts off at a disadvantage, apparently belonging to the class of twelfth-century lower nobility consisting mostly of younger sons, the squireen, who lacked land and were forced to seek employment abroad. The strengthening of a centralized monarch worsened the plight of such knights, increasing their dependence upon those few feudal lords who still possessed the means to rule (land, castle, private army). Forced to prove his worth in a foreign court, Lanval aroused so much envy that his achievements went unrewarded. Falsely accused by the queen of attempted rape, which would not have been an improbable expression of frustration over the fact he had been denied any legitimate marriage, Lanval was subjected to the judicial arbitration of barons willing to convict him simply because it was the king's wish. As a foreigner without the support of friends to serve as compurgators or oath-helpers—and without the automatic privilege of appealing to wager of battle or unilateral ordeal—Lanval would have been condemned if the fairy-lady had not offered herself as visual "evidence" to vindicate his boast. The legal drama represents the dark side of the jury trial under direct royal supervision. Like nearly everything else in the *lai*, the magical acquittal represents a utopian dream of wish-fulfillment utterly at odds with the harsh realities of late feudal justice.

The ordeal was available as a political device for targeting not only those suspected of criminality but also those feared for their potential to threaten the interests of the ruling elite. Like foreign knights, aristocratic women were forced to suffer physically as evidence of their submissiveness as well as their innocence. If the hierarchies of power are provisionally realigned in Marie's *lais* and the sexual transaction becomes a private negotiation detached from male-dominated institutions and ceremonies—and concealed from the masculine gaze—the entire ethics of sexuality might be redefined and the semiotics of the ordeal itself undergo translation of a radical kind. Omission, silence, and privatization become Marie's principal ploys as she renders the test and its results illegible to the larger community by depriving these rituals of their ceremonial identity: no presiding authority, no administering clergy, no viewing public. Where there are informal tests, the outcomes provide no signature to divulge a legal or moral reality, no act of publication to disclose the proband's performance for interpretation, no signs decipherable publicly to provide a reflection of private conduct. In a move parallel to the shift from oral to textual explained in Marie's **"Prologue"** (ll. 33-42) and **"Equitan"** (ll. 1-12), it is a rejection of theatricality (public interpretation) in favor of textuality (individual interpretation). The movement to private from public is also a privileging of subjective affect over social effect, grounded in Marie's accounts of secret love over and against ceremonial marriage. In this regard, study of the ordeal has much to contribute to the emerging feminist exegesis of Marie's writings.

Historically, the erosion of confidence in the ordeal was offset by increased reliance on rational arguments based on documents and witnesses. The Norman technique of inquest was perfected by canonists under the influence of Roman law's *inquisitio:* action initiated by an official, factual evidence collected, testimony taken from witnesses, and judgment issued by the investigating judge. Institutionalization of local testimony before a jury emerged as a central theme of the Henrician reforms. Maitland's famous observation that "law and literature grew up together in the court of Henry II" suggests an important similarity between the ways knowledge can be constructed through written instruments. As part of the larger transition to what Bloch has termed the "verbalization of trial," the displacement of wager of battle transformed the customary test of martial strength and bodily purity into a test of intellectual strength and linguistic skill. By positing in her *lais* the literary counterpart to an inquisitory procedure, Marie establishes what appears to be a jurist's dual authority by purporting to be a firsthand witness to performances of stories about ancient events, then producing texts that functioned as memoranda to prevent the oral record from being forgotten. A similar twofold method of factual determination was proposed by the historian Henry of Huntingdon (died c. 1155), who was careful to distinguish between evidence documented by ancient men ("quae in libris veterum legendo reperimus") and firsthand experience ("quae videndo scimus"). The abiding paradox of Marie's entire project is her insistence that such methods of exposure should take as their target essentially private experience. The **"Prologue"** urges a secular exegetics to expose the obscurities of such accounts, and her opening four lines propose that the breaking of silence becomes, for a writer like herself, not a violation of discretion but a holy virtue:

Ki Deus ad duné escïence
E de parler bon' eloquence
Ne s'en deit taisir ne celer,
Ainz se deit volunters mustrer.

(Anyone who has received from God the gift of knowledge and true eloquence has a duty not to remain silent: rather should one be happy to reveal such talents.)

She seems to violate the cardinal rule of courtly discretion: "A transmitter of transgression through transcription, she reveals secret love affairs" [Bloch].

"Bisclavret" records the historical movement away from the ordeal and toward another, more sinister method of evidential determination. The limitation of the ordeal's binary operation had been exposed in its capacity to resolve only those questions incorporated by oath into the proceedings. Because the mystery of the domesticated wolf's behavior did not afford enough information for the king to know what question to refer to the *judicium Dei,* he was advised by a counselor to resort to another mode of investigation:

"Kar metez la dame en destreit,
S'aucune chose vus direit,
Pur quei ceste beste la heit;
Fetes li dire s'el le seit!
Meinte merveille avum veü
Quë en Bretaigne est avenu."
   Li reis ad sun cunseil creü:
Le chevaler ad retenu;
De l'autre part la dame ad prise
E en mut grant destresce mise.
Tant par destresce e par poür
Tut li cunta de sun seignur.

("Question the lady to see if she will tell you why the beast hates her. Make her tell you, if she knows! We have witnessed many marvels happening in Brittany."

The king accepted his advice. Holding the knight, he took the lady away and subjected her to torture. Pain and fear combined made her reveal everything about her husband.)

Modern historians have generally recognized that the emergence of judicial torture paralleled throughout most of Europe the demise of the unilateral ordeal as a means for obtaining the confessions necessary for arriving at definitive verdicts. It was typically used upon lower-class suspects when clandestine crimes were at issue. Marie's narrative of torture had a happy ending, so to speak, since the infliction of fear upon the lady's mind and pain upon her body (not graphically described in the text, which fails even to specify the instrument of torture) resulted in extracting the truth and enabling the king to restore the woman's husband to human form. The end justified the means as a reflex of royal power; it coincided with the moment of torture described by Elaine Scarry when "objectified pain is denied as pain and read as power." [*The Body in Pain,* 1985] As an instrument of coercive force, torture became a more reliable method because the procedure was conducted in private (the dark side of Marie's own move toward privacy) and therefore was not subject to the interpretative vagaries of public spectators. It would become widely employed as what Foucault described as "a strict judicial game" with its own system of rules and adversarial relations between the judge and the accused—but not in England. The fact that torture was not promoted after the Assize of Clarendon in 1166 is another historical phenomenon certainly to be explained in terms of Henry II's reforms regarding the grand jury and the trial jury. The use of torture in **"Bisclavret"** can therefore be read as a nostalgic feature hearkening back to what was, in England anyway, an obsolescent method of investigation.

Even after jury trial was firmly established, the real prize of judicial torture—the confession—remained for jurists the *regina probationum,* the "queen of proofs," particularly in cases lacking eyewitnesses and other forms of objective evidence (exactly those cases previously referred to the ordeal). The confession brought to light the secret details that only the guilty party could know. Although Continental canonists would approve the use of torture in civil procedures by the middle of the thirteenth century, Gratian's *Decretum* from about 1140 stood as a continuing assertion that "confession is not to be extorted by the instrumentality of torture." But there were other forms of confession and other means of extortion.

There had been a longstanding tension between the ordeal and confession: the accused might publicly confess rather than face the hot iron, or he might privately confess and cleanse his soul so that the ritual would fail to detect prior criminality. It was probably no coincidence that the same Fourth Lateran Council that abolished the ordeal also made private confession annually, to one's own priest, a universal obligation for every Christian. Though this was not the first ecclesiastical act to require confession, the canon had the authority of pope and council under pain of excommunication. If the old ordeals provoked so much fear over burned flesh and scalded limbs that most candidates "chickened out" by admitting their guilt or settling out of court, these sacramental imperatives mobilized the fear of flesh burning for all eternity by threatening damnation in hell to those who did not obey. As theologians more scrupulously defined the role of the priest pronouncing absolution on the penitent, confession came increasingly to figure in a powerful network of social discipline and sacerdotal control independent of regalian authority. As Bartlett puts it [in *Trial by Fire and Water*], "One form of priestly power, the management of the ordeal, would have to be sacrificed to another form, the authority of the confessional." Integral to this evolving system of spiritual and social regulation was the sacrament of the altar, now also obligatory, which needed to be preceded by confession in order for the communicant to avoid sacrilege. As time went by, confession became essentially a form of preparation for communion.

"Yonec" tells how an unhappy wife received a lover who arrived at her window in the form of a hawk, then transformed himself into a man. At first the lady was afraid that these shape-shifting powers indicated he was not Christian, and so the knight offered to take the sacrament of Christ's body to prove he was not an evil spirit. Performing yet another metamorphosis, the mysterious knight assumed the appearance of the lady herself so that he could receive the Eucharist privately from her priest:

"Si vus de ceo ne me creez,
Vostre chapelain demandez;
Dites ke mal vus ad susprise,
Si volez aver le servise
Que Deus ad el mund establi,
Dunt li pecheür sunt gari;
La semblance de vus prendrai,
Le cors Damnedeu recevrai,
Ma creance vus dirai tute;
Ja de ceo ne seez en dute!"

          . . . . .

L'us de la chambre ad defermé,
Si ad le prestre demandé;
E cil i vint cum plus tost pot,
Corpus domini aportot.
Li chevaler l'ad receü,
Le vin del chalice beü.
Li chapeleins s'en est alez.

("If you do not believe this of me, send for your chaplain. Tell him that an illness has come upon you and that you want to hear the service that God has established in this world for the redemption of sinners. I shall assume your appearance, receive the body of Christ, and recite all my credo for you. Never doubt me on this account!" . . .

She opened the door of the chamber and sent for the priest, who came as quickly as possible, bringing the *corpus domini.* The knight received it and drank the wine from the chalice, whereupon the chaplain left.)

When nothing dreadful happened, the lady began enjoying physical intimacy with him, although later her jealous husband set a lethal trap that resulted in his death.

Here Marie is invoking a version of the Eucharist ordeal defended on the basis of Paul's words in I Corinthians 11:28-29: "But let a man prove himself, and so let him eat of that bread and drink of the chalice; For he that eateth and drinketh unworthily, eateth and drinketh judgment to himself, not discerning the body of the Lord." Though twelfth-century canonists such as Huguccio rejected ordeals that owed their existence to popular superstition, the test of the Eucharist derived special legitimacy from its sacramental status and was considered effective for revealing innocence by a number of canonists, such as the author of the Parisian *Summa: Tractaturus Magister* (c. 1175-91). Even three centuries later, this particular ordeal retained sufficient force that it was assimilated as a dramatic spectacle in the English Corpus Christi play in which the Virgin Mary proved her chastity, anachronistically, by undergoing the test of the bread and wine. In **"Yonec"** the source of the knight's magic was left unexplained, with the strong possibility that he was empowered by those supernatural forces which could falsify the outcome of an ordeal. The ordeal's limitation in responding only to a single issue is again drawn into question: the knight swore only that he believed in God, not that God gave him permission to become the lady's lover. This may have been shrewd equivocation, like the cunning oath that allowed Isolde to clear herself in the ordeal of hot iron. His subsequent death leaves open the possibility that he suffered a "delayed reaction" like the violent death that eventually overtook Lambert, according to the chronicler Galbert.

The episode also underscores Marie's concern to minimize the participation of the clergy in the ordeal ritual, as if in accord with mounting criticism from the canonists. Although custom required a priest to consecrate the elements of the ordeal, no other judicial test in her *lais* introduced a priest to officiate in the ceremony as stipulated in the *ordinales* and dramatized in accounts such as the one involving Queen Emma. The ordeal in **"Yonec"** was removed from the church, extracted from any liturgical context, and administered without the priest's knowledge that he was participating in such a test. The anonymous chaplain was summoned privately to the lady's chamber, offering the bread and wine to someone who claimed to be so ill that she was afraid of dying. The duping of the priest becomes a moment of clerical disenfranchisement that runs counter to the century's larger campaigns leading to more sacerdotal empowerment, not less, invested specifically in the priest's role of administering the sacraments.

Peter Brown is particularly clear-sighted in noting that "the same Lateran Council of 1215 that forbade clerical participation in the ordeal sanctioned the doctrine of transubstantiation" ["Society and the Supernatural: A Medieval Change," *Daedalus,* Vol. 104, 1975]. As part of an overall redefinition of the miraculous, the ordeal was suppressed as a marvel whose sources were open to suspicion and whose signs were subject to misinterpretation. On the other hand, the Eucharist was promoted as a marvel neither contingent upon local circumstances nor coerced from God for a particular occasion: it occurred every time that a priest, and only a priest, correctly performed the ritual. The source of the miraculous transformation was immune to suspicion, though the signs of the miracle remained invisible to human eyes. Theologians propounded this doctrine, and layfolk were required to do more than accept it as an article of faith: they were obliged to participate in the sacramental ritual, first confessing their sins to their parish priest, then receiving from his hands the body of Christ.

While Henry Lea's classic *Superstition and Force* viewed the ordeal as a feature of a benighted culture succeeded by a more enlightened rationality, R. I. Moore's recent *Formation of a Persecuting Society* has concluded that both the suppression of the ordeal *and* the exaltation of rationality were moves sponsored by ecclesiastical as well as secular authorities to achieve the more efficient exercise of power in their increasingly separate spheres of operation, a separation widely associated with Gregorianism. Colin Morris agrees that ordeals were simply too unpredictable for these newly self-conscious power elites: "Just as in the courts ordeals were especially the defense of the unfree, so in politics they could be used as the weapon of the innovator or the weaker party" ["*Judicium Dei:* The Social and Political Significance of the Ordeal

in the Eleventh Century," *Studies in Church History,* Vol. 12, 1975]. Henry II's efforts at restricting the nation's judicial processes to judges and grand juries, appointed by the king himself, can easily be read as a strategy designed for greater central control of the judiciary.

For his part, Innocent III in 1215 sought to redefine the grounds of sacerdotal control, first by forbidding clerical participation in ordeals which, as rituals, were too much subject to outside interference. He then redefined the priesthood's sacramental responsibilities and made mandatory the laity's obedience in confession and receiving communion, which, as rituals, were largely immune to such compromises. Besides exercising greater social control by imposing greater spiritual discipline, one on one, the priesthood also profited financially so that the clergy became a "growth sector" in the economy of the thirteenth and fourteenth centuries. When money itself became a basis for power, the ancient contest between courtly and ecclesiastical interests was joined by the bourgeois estate to translate the terms of the theological debate, which in the late fourteenth century came to focus specifically upon confession and the doctrine of transubstantiation. John Wyclif, who asserted that aural confession and annual communion were unscriptural, traced them as products of arbitrary human decrees back directly to Innocent III.

But this line of historical trajectory takes me two centuries beyond my current account. It has been the purpose of this study to situate Marie de France's *lais* as active textual presences within a twelfth-century culture undergoing a number of transitions, specifically in the realm of legal and moral accountability. To ensure that secret crimes and sins would be exposed for correction, the newly centralized authorities of state and church were quick to discard the ordeal, which had proved itself too cumbersome and too open to local manipulation, in favor of more efficient methods for stripping away the cover from secret behavior, even unspoken beliefs and hidden desires. The great casualty of this process was the privacy considered by many today as the condition necessary for personal autonomy—and treated by Marie de France as the condition essential for human intimacy.

Sharon Kinoshita (essay date 1994)

SOURCE: "Cherchez la Femme: Feminist Criticism and Marie de France's 'Lai de Lanval'," in *Romance Notes,* Vol. XXXIV, No. 3, Spring, 1994, pp. 263-73.

[*In the following essay, Kinoshita argues that in the* lai *"Lanval," the title character's ultimate rejection of chivalric society is an expression of Marie de France's feminism.*]

In any discussion of woman's voice in medieval French literature, the works of Marie de France are a natural point of departure. The putative author of a collection of fables, the hagiographic **Espurgatoire Seint Patriz** and the celebrated **Lais,** she is among the earliest attested female poets in the Romance vernacular; together with Christine de Pizan at the other end of the Middle Ages, she has been the focus of numerous feminist rereadings. But just what does it mean to speak of the "female voice" of an author who exists as little more than a name? In this paper, I will review three different critical analyses of what constitutes the "femininity" of the *Lais* of Marie de France. Then, in a brief reading of the **"Lai de Lanval,"** I will argue the importance of taking Marie's representation of medieval feudal and familial relations into account in any attempt to assess the feminist implications of her work. My critical wager is to seek the medieval "woman's voice" neither in the style of the text nor in the way in which female protagonists negotiate a path through courtly or chivalric worlds that only thinly veil the feudal and patriarchal constraints that regulated the lives of medieval women, but in the way a tale arguably lacking any "positive" female characters challenges patriarchal practices precisely by taking to its logical extreme the courtly discourse meant to mystify the project of primogeniture.

Writing in 1950, William S. Woods treats "femininity" as a totally natural and transhistorical phenomenon evident in every aspect of the text. Making no distinction between biological sex and the social construction of gender, he refers completely unselfconsciously to Marie's "endearing . . . feminine attitude and style" which, in his opinion, "add piquancy" to her poems ["Femininity in the *Lais* of Marie de France," *Studies in Philology,* Vol. 47, 1950]. Constantly at odds in Woods's article are, on the one hand, his tendency to universalize women's tastes, character, and proclivities—"Marie was very similar to women *of all times* in her use of effective and affective speech"—and, on the other, the temptation to construct a psycho-biography of the author from the details of her texts, which, in his words, *"seem to give clues as to her personality"* (emphasis added). Not surprisingly, this individualized "personality" itself turns out to be barely distinguishable from Woods's other gendered stereotypes, as where he suggests that the author was "a worldly woman . . . who had seen used, or had, herself, used beauty for material profit." For Woods, Marie quite simply writes like a woman. Her style betrays "a true womanly love for forceful and superlative adverbs and expressions" [!], emphasized by repetition, exaggeration, diminutives, and excessively detailed descriptions which, in his opinion, have "nothing to do with the story". In addition to her "womanly interest" in "cloth, clothing, furniture, architecture, adornment, and people," he cites her "love for children" and her "womanly disinterest in the details of fighting and war." Even the vengeances Marie devises for her characters (both male and female) are, in Woods's estimation, "extremely cruel and often of a feminine subtlety." In the end, he concludes that "we must content ourselves with saying that *Marie reveals herself to be a true woman* in many of the most interesting passages of the *Lais*" (emphasis added).

Needless to say, the language of literary analysis has changed considerably in the years since Woods's article, and when in the 1980s critics returned to the question of gendered readings of Marie de France, their perspectives were substantially different. Writing in the wake of Derrida and Foucault, Jean-Charles Huchet opens his article "Nom de femme et écriture féminine au moyen âge" [in *Poétique,* Vol. 48, 1981] by explicitly relinquishing all desire for the biographical: "Le nom d'auteur n'est parfois qu'une ruse de la langue ou de l'activité littéraire elle-même. Mieux encore, la reconnaissance que l'auteur n'a d'autre identité que celle construite de toutes pièces par l'œuvre." But if the "nom d'auteur" no longer entails, as for Woods, an unproblematic spectrum of essentialized traits or interests, then in what sense might the *Lais* be considered feminine/feminist? For Huchet, Marie exhibits neither the "feminist consciousness" of a Christine de Pizan, nor the linguistically—and philosophically-disruptive stylistics of *"écriture féminine."* In fact, if feminine writing is polysemous and non-linear, then Marie's work, he writes, is conspicuously masculine: on the side of the signified, of ideology, and of a surprisingly conventional clerical misogyny.

Marie's "feminism," Huchet suggests, resides instead in the narrative resolutions she brings to the sexual problematics posed by the Tristan legend, the *"texte symptôme"* through which the twelfth century interrogated "the structure of desire and of *jouissance."* In mapping the conventional courtly triangle of husband/wife/lover onto the triangle uncle/uncle's wife/nephew, he argues, *Tristan* articulates "une faille, voire une impossibilité, inscrite au cœur de la sexualité humaine," resulting in the imbalance between male lack (wounds, scars, infirmities) and female surplus or excess. Marie's feminist project consists in strategically rewriting desire and *jouissance* in ways that emphasize the erasure of sexual difference (symbolized in **"Guigemar"**'s hermaphroditic doe) and the fusion of divisions (symbolized by the symbiotic intertwining of the honeysuckle around the cleft halves of the hazel branch in **"Chevrefoil"**). According to Huchet, the most definitive resolution of sexual difference, however, is the birth of a child, which literally incarnates the successful conjunction of the sexes: "Marie s'en tient à l'enfant comme nœud parfait qui lie ensemble ses parents. Un enfant, c'est-à-dire un fil(s) noué, un noeud et un nom, le seul qui tienne." Thus the analysis that began by bracketing the biological sex of the author reads her "feminism" precisely in her narrative representation of sexual reproduction.

Like Huchet, Michelle Freeman—in her 1984 article "Marie de France's Poetics of Silence: The Implications for a Feminine *Translatio*"—defines Marie's feminism by contrasting the *Lais* to other contemporary vernacular texts, in this case the *romans d'antiquité* [*PMLA,* Vol. 99, 1984]. Unlike the male translators of the *Roman de Troie* or the *Roman de Thèbes,* Marie rejects the monumentalizing history explicit in the linked projects of *translatio studii* and *translatio imperii.* Her feminine *translatio* concentrates instead on private codes—communicated through symbolic objects like the nightingale (**"Laüstic"**) and the hazel branch (**"Chevrefoil"**)—rather than public ones, on "peculiar and unique" stories rather than grand historical narratives "in large canvaslike proportions." Principally, however, Freeman locates the feminist dimension of Marie's text in what she calls her "poetics of silence," her strategic deployment of understatement and elision. Where Huchet sees determinacy, Freeman sees willful ambiguity. Where Woods sees a love for the forceful, the superlative, the detailed, and the excess, she finds exactly the opposite: Marie "leaves out what seems essential, what generates the whole of her discourse as well as the textual lineage that engendered it, wrapping that void or mysterious, private darkness which represents a singular exchange between two lovers and two worlds in a multiplicity of layers."

Like Woods, however, Freeman oscillates between seeing Marie's "poetics of silence" as a limited individualized or personal thematics and as a distinctly feminine mode of writing. On the one hand, she states: "To be as clear as possible, *I apply this term only to Marie* and to the specific kind of relationship that pertains to her poem as it is linked to the *lai* in question, the *aventure,* and the signal. . . . I do *not* mean that each time an author is discreet . . . or each time the motif of silence appears . . . that we are dealing with the same or even closely related material" (emphasis added); on the other, she sees Marie's text as exemplary of a "clearly feminine sort of lineage, with the deliberate portrayal of a feminine conception of poetic articulation and creativity—something akin to the feminist articulations of [Heloise or the Countess of Dia] . . . a radically new form of autobiographical narrative." Finally, while avoiding the obvious essentialisms of Woods's reading, Freeman's analysis is punctuated by an odd metaphorical biologism that, like Huchet's analysis, bespeaks a profound preoccupation with the links between textual production and sexual reproduction. If Marie (in her General Prologue) describes the *Lais* as a private offering to her patron-king, she muses, "might not the gift represent a kind of sublimation of the child not borne by the woman for her lover but a sublimation that will nevertheless have its own progeny?" As for the distinctive style of the *Lais,* she writes: "[t]o apply a sexual analogy to this practice [of elision], one might indeed understand this poetics of silence as feminine, seeing it as the paradoxical absence-presence that brings forth, that gives birth to and speaks the poem before us."

Given these widely divergent assessments of the "female voice" in the work of Marie de France, I would like to turn now to **"Lanval,"** one of the twelve *lais* that has been least subject to feminist recuperations. Feminist critics of medieval literature, E. Jane Burns suggests, have responded to the question, "How much does the author's voice condition the voices of his or her fictive characters?" in two different ways: some by looking for "some telling indication of female presence in works authored by women," others by revealing "the concerted absence of female subjectivity from texts composed by men [Burns, *Bodytalk: When Women Speak in Old French Literature,* 1993]." Burns herself focusses on female characters in *male*-authored texts, hearing in their speech a "resistant doubled discourse"—the "bodytalk" deployed by figures like Iseut or Enide in order to "speak both within and against the social and rhetorical conventions used to construct them." In the remainder of this essay, I would like to make the complementary move of focussing on the *male* protagonist of a *female*-authored text, locating the "woman's voice" less at the stylistic or thematic level than

in Marie's radical challenge to the structure of feudal society through her canny manipulation of literary codes.

At first glance, the **"Lai de Lanval"** clearly functions as, in R. Howard Bloch's words, a "fantasy of utopic plenitude" exemplifying Duby's classic description of chivalric romance as the "lower nobility's quest for material support in the form of the wealthy dowager" [Bloch, *Medieval Misogyny and the Invention of Western Romantic Love,* 1991]. Though an accomplished member of King Arthur's household, the titular protagonist—a foreigner without friends or relations at court to defend his interests—is slighted by the king when it comes to the distributions of wives and lands. In the forest, however, he meets a mysterious woman of unsurpassed wealth and exceptional beauty who gives him her love and promises to supply all his material needs—as long as he tells no one of her existence. Returning to court, Lanval wins new esteem among his companions for his free-wheeling largesse while continuing to enjoy the company of his new *amie,* who comes to him secretly whenever he calls. The trouble begins, however, when Lanval becomes the object of the queen's passion. When he spurns her, she accuses him of homosexuality; he retorts that he already has a mistress—one, moreover, who far outshines her in beauty. Outraged, the queen publically charges Lanval with having made improper advances to her, and—once *she* refused *him*—insulting her by claiming to have a mistress more beautiful than she. Arthur immediately convenes his barons and puts his vassal on trial—*not,* it seems, for having made advances to the queen, but for having dared to impugn her beauty. The barons sitting in judgment of Lanval demand that he substantiate his boast by producing his lady; but of course, by revealing her existence, he has, by the terms of their agreement, already forfeited all claims to her love. Nevertheless, as he forlornly awaits the verdict, his mistress arrives, preceded by two pairs of maids, all indisputably lovelier than the queen. Enthralled by this unlooked-for beauty pageant, Arthur's barons immediately rule that Lanval has indeed spoken the truth; delighted to have been forgiven by his mistress, he rides off with her to Avalon, never to be heard from again.

As this quick summary makes clear, **"Lanval"** is, if anything, a *male* Cinderella story in which the usual gendered stereotypes are inverted. [I borrow the notion of the "male Cinderella story" from Judith Kellogg, who uses it to describe the plight of the heroine's father in Chrétien de Troyes's *Erec et Enide.*] As a loyal and worthy vassal neglected by his overlord, Lanval is, as Bloch has observed, the male counterpart of the *mal-mariée.* Throughout much of the tale, he plays the passive or subordinate role elsewhere assigned to courtly heroines. Like the mistreated wife of **"Yonec,"** he conjures his lover at will; like Enide, he is placed under an injunction to silence. Still, despite the power they wield, the women in this text remain objects of exchange grounding the homosocial feudal bond: Arthur's "mistreatment" of Lanval consists in denying him his fair share of the *"[f]emmes e teres"* (l. 17) he distributes to his other vassals. The queen is a vain and spiteful adulteress, and the enigmatic lady a construct of male fantasy: for Lanval a "rescuing female," a "dream of possession" (Bloch), and for the Arthurian knights sitting in judgment of Lanval, the beauteous object of their appreciative gaze: "Li jugeür ki la veeient / A grant merveille le teneient: / Il n'ot un sul ki l'esgardast / De dreite joie n'eschaufast!" (ll. 581-4).

The subtlety of **"Lanval"**'s rearticulation of the relationship between the feudal and the erotic, however, emerges more clearly in comparison to Marie de France's *female* Cinderella story, **"Yonec,"** the tale of a compensatory female desire that escapes the strict regulation of women's bodies in feudal society. Ostensibly, this *lai* can be read as both liberating and subversive: the unnamed heroine escapes her loveless marriage to an old *gelos* with a young and handsome lover who comes to her in the form of a great bird whenever she calls him. Though he is eventually trapped and killed, she bears his son, whom she succeeds in passing off as her husband's. Within the bounds of the tale, however, this illicit love—and resulting contamination of the husband's lineage—is recuperable. Years later, the lady reveals to her grown son his true birth, then immediately expires on her ex-lover's tomb. Without hesitation, Yonec slays his stepfather and, at the *lai*'s conclusion, is installed by his biological father's townsfolk in the lordship vacated so many years before: "Lur seignur firent d'Yönec, / Ainz que il partissent d'ilec" (ll. 553-4). In the pseudo-escapist world of the female Cinderella, even adultery is ultimately appropriated to what Roberta Krueger has called "the project of primogeniture." ["Desire, Meaning, and the Female Reader . . . ," *The Passing of Arthur,* 1988].

In **"Lanval,"** on the other hand, the theme of compensatory love is deployed to anti-feudal ends. To a greater extent than in any of the other *lais,* the plot of **"Lanval"** turns on the multiple failures of the central mechanisms of the feudal system itself. As the tale opens, the kingdom of Logres is being ravaged by Scots and Picts (ll. 7-10), yet the knights of the court are consumed by their petty jealousies while Arthur himself neglects a worthy knight impoverished by his pursuit of chivalry precisely because he is a foreigner. All sense of the courtesy and hospitality usually associated with his court has been lost. Significantly, Lanval is far from court, lying on a grassy riverbank contemplating his ill-fortune, when the beautiful lady first appears to him. (Contrast the heroine of **"Yonec,"** visited by her bird-lover in the very tower in which her jealous husband has imprisoned her.) From the beginning, she represents for Lanval the temptation to abandon the degraded feudal world of the Arthurian court. "Pur vus guerpirai tutes genz," he tells her; "Jamés ne quier de vus partir, / Ceo est la rien que plus desir!" (ll. 128-30). She is the one who vehemently insists that he return to court, promising to supply his every material need: "Amis, fet ele, levez sus! / Vus n'i poëz demurer plus: / Alez vus en! Jeo remeindrai" (ll. 159-61). Bankrolled by his new and mysterious friend, Lanval puts on a remarkable display of largesse, highlighted by the anaphoric repetition of his name: "Lanval donout les riches duns, / Lanval aquitout les prisuns, / Lanval vesteit les jugleürs, / Lanval feseit les granz honurs! / N'i ot estrange ne privé / A ki Lanval n'eüst doné" (ll. 209-14); unlike Arthur, he does not distinguish between companion and foreigner.

But just at the moment when Lanval, thanks to his lady's assistance, seems poised to outdo the king himself in magnanimity, the Arthurian court once again betrays the degree of its corruption. Where Lanval's departure had been precipitated by the undue lack of attention from the king, his return is heralded by a surfeit of unwanted attention from the queen. Lanval rejects her advances by appealing to his feudal relationship to her husband: "Lungement ai servi le rei; / Ne li voil pas mentir ma fei. / Ja pur vus ne pur vostre amur / Ne mesferai a mun seignur" (ll. 271-4). But the queen summarily dismisses his strategic deployment of feudal ethics precisely by calling his sexuality into question: "Asez le m'ad hum dit sovent / Que des femmes n'avez talent! / Vallez avez bien afeitiez, / Ensemble od eus vus deduiez" (ll. 279-82). Where Lanval treated the feudal bond linking him to his lord the king as inviolable, Arthur, as we have seen, is less scrupulous, putting his vassal on trial for his alleged insults to the queen. Lanval is saved only when his mistress, against his own expectations, suddenly arrives to testify on his behalf. Ultimately, her declaration of his innocence is less important than her appearance itself, for her unsurpassable beauty immediately vindicates his boast. Once acquitted, Lanval without hesitation mounts his lady's palfrey and rides off with her, never to be heard from again.

In the end, **"Lanval"** is striking precisely for its titular protagonist's rejection of feudal and chivalric values alike. Taking literally all the clichés of courtly discourse—honoring his lady over his lord, choosing love over reputation—he abandons Arthur's court, voluntarily choosing an oblivion that would be unthinkable both to an epic hero like Roland and a romance hero like Erec or Yvain. Ostensibly the most blandly conventional of literary heroes, Lanval—perhaps for that very reason—is able to reject the "project of primogeniture" to which all but the most rebellious of literary heroines are inevitably conscripted. It is, I suggest, in this dissent from the fundamental premises of patriarchy that the "feminism" of the *Lais* of Marie de France might ultimately reside. In **"Lanval,"** she imagines an outside to the feudal order that relegates women to the status of objects of exchange underpinning the patriarchal system. The protagonist himself is immortalized neither by his deeds nor by his progeny, but by his very disappearance. "Nuls hum," Marie concludes, "n'en oï plus parler / Ne jeo n'en sai avant cunter" (ll. 645-6).

FURTHER READING

Boland, Margaret. "Noses and Robes, Curses and Charms in Marie de France." *Tamkang Journal* 30 (January 1991): 267-76.

　　Examines the combined cultural role of folklore and organized religion in the interpretation of the *lais* of Marie de France.

Brightenback, Kristine. "Remarks on the 'Prologue' to Marie de France's Lais." *Romance Philology* XXX, No. 1 (August 1976): 168-77.

Asserts that the "Prologue" to the *Lais* provides important information concerning Marie's reliance on and adaptation of classical mythology.

Brook, Leslie C. "A Note on the Ending of 'Eliduc.'" *French Studies Bulletin* 32 (Autumn 1989): 14-16.
    Discusses the possibility that the story of the lovers in "Eliduc" "echoes" the letters written by medieval lovers Abelard and Heloise.

Bullock-Davies, Constance. "The Form of the Breton Lay." *Medium Aevum* XLII, No. 1 (1973): 18-31.
    Speculates on the style, level of difficulty, and the popularity of the Breton lay—a genre upon which Marie de France based her own *Lais*.

Burgess, Glynn S. "On the Interpretation of 'La stic,' v. 50." *French Studies Bulletin* 42 (Spring 1992): 10-12.
    Disagrees with one translator's interpretation of a line in Marie's *lai* "La stic" and thereby draws attention to the difficulty involved in translating medieval texts.

Cottrell, Robert D. "'Le Lai du La stic': From Physicality to Spirituality." *Philological Quarterly* XLVII, No. 4 (October 1968): 499-505.
    Argues that in her *lai* "La stic" Marie de France presents a "Christian-oriented world of love."

Damon, S. Foster. "Marie de France: Psychologist of Courtly Love." *PMLA* XLIV, No. 4 (December 1929): 968-96.
    Describes Marie de France as a "medieval Jane Austen" observing the effects of the rules of courtly love on the behavior of men and women.

Daugherty, Evelyn Newlyn. "The Cupid-Psyche Myth in 'Lanval,' 'Graelent,' 'Gulingamor,' and 'Bisclavret.'" *Thoth* 16, No. 2 (Spring 1976): 15-24.
    Refers to the classical myth of the god Cupid and his mortal lover Psyche to explain the structure and thematic content of two *lais* by Marie de France and two other medieval *lais*.

Ferguson, Mary H. "Folklore in the Lais of Marie de France." *Romanic Review* LVII, No. 1 (February 1966): 3-24.
    Undertakes a "systematic examination of the motifs and tale types" in Marie de France's twelve *lais*.

Fitz, Brewster E. "The Storm Episode and the Weasel Episode: Sacrificial Casuistry in Marie de France's 'Eliduc.'" *MLN* 89, No. 4 (May 1974): 542-49.
    Provides a biblical reading of two crucial moments in the *lai* "Eliduc."

Fowles, John. "A Personal Note." In his *The Ebony Tower*, pp. 117-22. Boston: Little, Brown and Co., 1974.
    Information on Marie's life, the source of her *Lais*, and the socio-historical context in which she wrote.

Freeman, Michelle A. "Marie de France's Poetics of Silence: The Implications for a Feminine Translation." *PMLA* 99, No. 5 (October 1984): 860-83.
    Discusses the feminine voice that Marie de France brings

to her retelling of the Breton *lais*, focusing on two of the *lais*—"La stic" and "Chievrefoil"—in particular.

Frey, John A. "Linguistic and Psychological Couplings in the Lays of Marie de France." *Studies in Philology* LXI, No. 1 (January 1964): 3-18.
    Examines Marie's use of "coupling," or pairs, as a literary device in her *lais*—whether it be rhyming couplets of verse, a pair of lovers, or two adversaries.

Hanning, Robert, and Ferrante, Joan. "Introduction." In *The Lais of Marie de France*, translated by Robert Hanning and Joan Ferrante, pp. 1-27. New York: E. P. Dutton, 1978.
    Overview of Marie de Frances's twelve *lais* which focuses on the prominent themes and symbols of her narratives.

Holmes, Urban T., Jr. "A Welsh Motif in Marie's 'Guigemar.'" *Studies in Philology* XXXIX (1942): 11-14.
    Suggests that there are Welsh elements in the *lai* "Guigemar," supporting Holmes's theory that Marie de France married an Englishman and lived in the Welsh border region.

Illingworth, R. N. "Celtic Tradition and the Lai of 'Yonec.'" *Etudes Celtiques* IX, No. 2 (1961): 501-20.
    Argues that plot elements and character names in Marie de France's "Yonec" provide proof that this *lai* is Celtic rather than Classical in origin.

——. "Structural Interlace in the Lai of 'Chevrefoil.'" *Medium Aevum* LIV, No. 2 (1985): 248-58.
    Looks closely at the style and structure of "Chevrefoil," arguing that it consists of an interlacing poetic form that mimics the *lai*'s honeysuckle/hazel symbolism.

Jackson, W. T. H. "The Arthuricity of Marie de France." *Romanic Review* LXX, No. 1 (January 1979): 1-18.
    Examines Marie de France's *Lais*, specifically "Lanval," to assess the extent of their similarity to Arthurian romance.

Kemp-Welch, Alice. "A Twelfth-Century Romance-Writer, Marie de France." In her *Of Six Mediaeval Women*, pp. 29-56. London: Macmillan and Co., 1913.
    Turn-of-the-century speculation on Marie de France's life and discussion of her works.

Laurie, Helen C. R. "A Note on the Composition of Marie's 'Guigemar.'" *Medium Aevum* XLIV, No. 3 (1975): 242-48.
    Suggests possible sources for the *lai* "Guigemar" and discusses Marie de France's contributions to the *lai*'s plot.

Leupin, Alexandre. "The Impossible Task of Manifesting 'Literature': On Marie de France's Obscurity." *Exemplaria* III, No. 1 (Spring 1991): 221-42.
    Interprets the *Lais* of Marie de France in light of what she says in her "Prologue" and in light of medieval Christianity.

McCulloch, Florence. "Length, Recitation, and Meaning of the Lais of Marie de France." *Kentucky Romance Quarterly* 25, No. 3 (1978): 257-68.

Argues that Marie de France deliberately arranged her twelve *lais* in a particular order.

Mickel, Emanuel J., Jr. "A Reconsideration of the Lais of Marie de France." *Speculum: A Journal of Medieval Studies* 46 (1971): 39-65.

Looks at the manner in which the theme of love is resolved in the *Lais* of Marie de France as a whole.

————. "Marie de France's Use of Irony As a Stylistic and Narrative Device." *Studies in Philology* LXXI, No. 5 (July 1974): 265-90.

Contends that Marie de France used irony in her *Lais* to emphasize humanity's selfishness in love and to show that unhappy endings can be avoided if people instead act selflessly.

————. "Guigemar's Ebony Boat." *Cultura Neolatina* XXXVII, Nos. 1-2 (1977): 9-15.

Offers an interpretation of "Guigemar" and suggests possible sources for this *lai*.

Mudrick, Marvin. "Love, Careless Love." *The Hudson Review* XXXII, No. 3 (Autumn 1979): 429-40.

Adopts a playful tone to assess Marie de France's outlook on love and lovers in her *Lais*.

Nelson, Deborah. "'Yonec': A Religious and Chivalric Fantasy." *The USF Language Quarterly* XVI, Nos. 3-4 (Spring-Summer 1978): 33-5.

Suggests that Marie's *lai* "Yonec" combines two myths: one about the search for secular love and redemption and the other about the search for religious love and redemption.

Nelson, Jan A. "Abbreviated Style and Les Lais de Marie de France." *Romance Quarterly* 39, No. 2 (May 1992): 131-43.

Argues that Marie's *Lais* follow the rhetorical models of her day advocating brevity and that her reasons for doing so appear in her "Prologue" and several of the *lais* themselves.

Pickens, Rupert T. "Thematic Structure in Marie de France's 'Guigemar.'" *Romania* (1974): 328-41.

Asserts that the *lai* "Guigemar" "demonstrates the role of love and sexuality . . . in a social microcosm and in the universal creative scheme."

Reed, Thomas L., Jr. "Glossing the Hazel: Authority, Intention, and Interpretation in Marie de France's Tristan, 'Chievrefoil.'" *Exemplaria* VII, No. 1 (Spring 1995): 99-143.

Examines Marie de France's treatment of the Tristan and Iseult legend in her *lai* "Chievrefoil," arguing that she uses the legend to make a point about the workings of communication.

Robertson, Howard S. "Love and the Other World in Marie de France's 'Eliduc.'" In *Essays in Honor of Louis Francis Solano,* edited by Raymond J. Cormier and Urban T. Holmes, pp. 167-76. Chapel Hill: The University of North Carolina Press, 1970.

Compares the theme of love and the "other world" (dream world) as it appears in most of Marie de France's *lais* with how it is treated in her *lai* "Eliduc."

Sankovitch, Tilde A. "Marie de France: The Myth of the Wild." In her *French Women Writers and the Book: Myths of Access and Desire,* pp. 15-41. New York: Syracuse University Press, 1988.

Examines Marie's works in terms of her intention "to affirm her own different poetic identity while also claiming her place in the established tradition."

Spitzer, Leo. "The Prologue to the Lais of Marie de France and Medieval Poetics." *Modern Philology* XLI, No. 2 (November 1943): 96-102.

Notes that the "Prologue" to Marie de France's *Lais* is significant in that it contains "so much of 'literary science,' of 'literary philosophy,' [and] of medieval encyclopedic lore."

Stapleton, M. L. "Venus Vituperator: Ovid, Marie de France, and Fin' Amors." *Classical and Modern Literature* 13, No. 4 (Summer 1993): 283-95.

Looks at the ways in which Marie de France uses and reinterprets the works of the Roman poet Ovid in her own *lais*.

Steinle, Eric M. "'Le Chaitivel' (Marie de France), VV. 17-28." *Romance Notes* XXXIII, No. 3 (Spring 1993): 255-63.

Offers an interpretation of some ambiguous lines in the *lai* "Le Chaitivel."

Trindade, W. Ann. "The Man with Two Wives—Marie de France and an Important Irish Analogue." *Romance Philology* XXVII, No. 4 (May 1974): 466-78.

Argues that the plots of Marie de France's *lais* "Le Fresne" and "Eliduc" were borrowed in part from an orally transmitted Celtic tale sharing similar elements.

Vitz, Evelyn Birge. "The Lais of Marie de France: 'Narrative Grammar' and the Literary Text." *Romanic Review* LXXIV, No. 4 (November 1983): 383-404.

Attempts to define "the narrative structures and the style of the twelve Lais of Marie de France."

Warren, Nancy Bradley. "Objects, Possession and Identity in the Lais of Marie de France." *Romance Languages Annual* VI (1994): 189-92.

Asserts that in her *Lais*, Marie de France identifies her characters not through detailed descriptions of their physical appearances or personalities but by what objects they own.

Additional coverage of Marie de France's life and career is contained in the following source published by Gale Research: *Classical and Medieval Literature Criticism,* **Vol. 8.**

Sharon Olds
1942-

American poet.

INTRODUCTION

Sharon Olds is known for poetry in which she uses an intensely personal voice to explore themes of domestic violence, sexuality, and family relationships. In much of her verse, she examines her roles as daughter and mother, rendering painfully ambivalent memories of her parents in unsentimental, brutally honest, and often sexually explicit language. In addition to exploring family life, Olds expresses sorrow and outrage for victims of war and political violence. Many critics have noted that her focus on both domestic and public abuse evinces the universal scope of her poetic vision.

Biographical Information

Olds was born in San Francisco, California, in 1942. She completed her undergraduate degree at Stanford University in 1964 and received a Ph.D. from Columbia University in 1972. From 1976 until 1980, Olds was a lecturer-in-residence on poetry at the Theodor Herzl Institute and has subsequently held numerous teaching and lecturing posts at various universities and writing conferences. Olds has also served as the director of the Creative Writing Program at New York University and has been involved in the administration of the NYU workshop program for the physically disabled.

Major Works

Olds's first book of poetry, *Satan Says* (1980), is divided into four sections, "Daughter," "Woman," "Mother," and "Journeys," and addresses such subjects as family relationships, domestic abuse, adolescence, sexuality, and motherhood. In the title poem, Olds juxtaposes sexually charged imagery with feelings of outrage toward her parents, particularly her abusive father. In purging herself of violent emotions, however, the narrator unexpectedly moves toward love and reconciliation. In other poems in the collection, Olds celebrates motherhood and the experience of childbirth. In "The Language of the Brag," for example, Olds writes: "Slowly alone in the centre of a circle I have / passed the new person out. . . . / I have done this thing, / I and other women this exceptional / act with the exceptional heroic body." Olds's second book, *The Dead and the Living* (1984), is divided into two sections, "Poems for the Dead" and "Poems for the Living." In the first section, Olds's concern with victims and their emotional healing is extended into the

public sphere in poems describing crimes of political persecution and social injustice. These poems center on such characters as a Chinese man about to be executed and a starving Russian girl. In "The Issue," a poem about racial tension in Rhodesia, Olds, after describing a black baby who has been bayoneted, declares: "Don't speak to me about / politics. I've got eyes, man." The second section in *The Dead and the Living* is less political. Here, Olds returns to more familiar themes, including childhood, love, marriage, and parenthood, with many of the poems addressing Olds's tempestuous relationship with her alcoholic father. The poems in *The Gold Cell* (1987) continue the family, public, and sexual narratives of Olds's earlier books. In particular, Olds emphasizes the primacy of the body. In the poem "This," for example, Olds writes: "So this is who I am, this body / white as yellowish dough brushed / with dry flour." *The Father* (1992) is a sequence of fifty-two poems in which Olds describes the slow death of her father from throat cancer. Olds expresses both her compassion for and anger toward her father, using scatological and sexually explicit language to describe the deterioration of his body, which becomes a metaphor for his dismal failings as a parent. *The Wellspring* (1996) is divided into four sections and traces Olds's life from conception to middle age. Part one focuses on childhood, part two on sexual awakenings, part three on motherhood, and part four on love and mortality.

Critical Reception

Critical reaction to Olds's works has been mixed. Although many critics suggest that Olds's predilection for sexual description and shocking subject matter is integral to the emotional catharsis of her narrators and necessary for creating empathy for both victims and their abusers, others contend that her works are self-indulgent, over-dramatic, and exhibit a morbid obsession with violence and a puerile infatuation with profanity. *Satan Says,* in particular, has been criticized for its explicit language, violent imagery, and strident tone. Critics generally agree, however, that in most of her subsequent books, Olds gained control of her emotional topics, creating a more restrained, though still disturbing, vision of humanity. Commentators have also faulted Olds for what they consider her repetitive and predictable subject matter and her underdeveloped connections between public and private cruelties. Despite these objections, Olds has been widely praised for her compelling narration, inventive use of metaphor, and scrupulous honesty in rendering extremely personal emotions and experiences.

PRINCIPAL WORKS

Poetry

Satan Says 1980
The Dead and the Living 1984
The Gold Cell 1987
The Matter of This World: New & Selected Poetry 1987
The Sign of Saturn: Poems 1980-1987 1991
The Father 1992
The Wellspring 1996

CRITICISM

G. E. Murray (review date 1981)

SOURCE: "Seven Poets," in *The Hudson Review,* Vol. XXXIV, No. 1, Spring, 1981, pp. 155-60.

[*In the following excerpt, Murray discusses Olds's passionate treatment of such subjects as pain, love, and anger in* Satan Says.]

If there were a physics of suffering, some way to graph the pain of doubt, assessing Sharon Olds's impressive debut with *Satan Says* would be an easier affair. Lacking any exact science of emotions, it should be noted that Olds's harsh and shockingly truthful poems, often wrought in a strident pitch, will attract a sizeable following. The style also may rally detractors, for to an extent Olds makes poetry as if she were lancing boils and enjoying it.

With both her masks and straight faces, Olds considers herself, variously, a temptress, carnivore, daughter, victim, mother, survivor, "a murderer / selecting a weapon." Mainly in the fashion of Sylvia Plath and Ai, which is to say passionately lyrical and driven, she confronts her terrors two-fisted, focusing—perhaps too narrowly—a raw, primal eye on life.

The failure of parents, first love, and disillusionment are perennial favorites among "poetical" topics. But on these accounts, Olds seldom falters, as she combines the serious and the absurd, anger and remorse, apathy and desire, spirit and gut-instinct. Finally, it all breaks into intense expression, most memorably in the clever and powerful **"The Indispensability of Eyes," "Station," "Indictment of Senior Officers,"** and **"Republican Living Rooms,"** each with its own biting strategies.

This is not to imply that Olds is altogether unforgiving, though the preliminary flashes of her poetry may lead casual readers to assume that shock value is the governing principle of this work. The fact is that ultimately Olds remains "faithful to central meanings" of love and shared experience, particularly as she renders them in **"Monarchs," "Primitive"** and **"The Unjustly Punished Child."** It is with this mixing of blessings—her significant verbal skills and candid emotions—that Olds will doubtlessly gain future illumination for her painful uprootings.

William Logan (review date 1983)

SOURCE: "First Books, Fellow Travelers," in *Parnassus: Poetry in Review,* Vol. 11, No. 1, Spring/Summer, 1983, pp. 211-30.

[*Logan is an American poet, critic, and educator. In the following excerpt, he argues that Olds uses violent imagery unsuccessfully in* Satan Says, *adding that the poet is capable of writing better verse.*]

Sharon Olds's poems rely on an extremity of image and a skillful manipulation of violence. At best the violence serves as a form of detection whose fastidious tone, as in **"Photographs Courtesy of the Fall River Historical Society,"** is admirably detached:

> The lady in ruched sateen is lying
> on the Turkey carpet, belly down,
> a dropped seal, a dark pool like
> oil under the face, darkness like
> hair all over the face.

Something odd—a first shudder, perhaps—has doubled the image. There is a dead gentleman in the pictures, too, whose "face has been divided into parts, a map, / and broken up like a puzzle." These are only inert images, dead ones, however, until the final stanza:

> The daughter was let off,
> but as you look at the pictures, the long
> cracks between the sections of his face,
> the back of her skull uneven as some
> internal organ, the conviction is flat.
> Only a daughter could have done that.

It is a characteristic observation by a poet who sees herself only in terms of others, only in her relations—mother, daughter, sister, lover. She would tease out a family from even the most disparate of groups, find inlaws in outlaws, fulfilling some desperate and compulsive need to relate to others only to deny them, to define herself by her rejection of the family affair. Denial and rejection are one thing, however; murder is another. Her gruesome interest in these bloody axed bodies, these Bordens, is unexplained until the final line, which seems to reveal—in the lethal harmony of that flat rhyme—something horribly private about the author.

The harmony of rhyme is rare in Olds's work. Her poems are ordered most frequently by the accretion of aggressive metaphors which upstage what they represent:

> Now the mother is the other one,
> breasts hard bags of rock salt,
> the bluish milk seeping out, her soul
> there in the small carriage, the child in her
> risen to the top, like cream,
> and skimmed off.

("**Young Mothers I**")

The mother's alienation from her body, violated by birth, ought to allow the extenuation of these images; but they exist in such scrupulous isolation from each other that the mind is newly distracted as each snaps into position, and becomes susceptible to embarrassing questions (How do the rock-salt breasts exude this blue milk? How is the baby, emerging between its mother's legs, skimmed off the top?). Commonplace sentiments cannot be rendered spectacular by the line-by-line application of image—at least they can't if one owes more to Bly than to Shakespeare.

Like any pure fiancée, Olds has passed the blood test ("mask of blood," "streaked with blood," "blood bond," "blood-spattered," "blood-red," "blood bomb," "language of blood," "blood culture," "raised on blood," "glaze of blood," "hard blood"), dreaming not of marriage but of cutlery ("knife / hanging from my hand," "she / enters the dream of murder, mutilation, her / old self bleeding in pieces on the butcher paper," "my inner sex / stabbed again and again with terrible pain like a knife," "The sky is black as charred wood, / the moon stuck in it like an axe," "sprouts struck out their knives," "that first time / he took his body like a saw to me and / cut through to my inner sex"). The knife is Olds's instrument of the sexes—castrating weapon or lethal penis. Its Freudian effect, however, does not seem entirely substantiated by any cause.

Olds becomes so lost in revery by the effect of her images, their use, that she forgets that they have their own life (or death), and must be honored:

> The year of the mask of blood, my father
> hammering on the glass door to get in
>
> was the year they found her body in the hills,
> in a shallow grave, naked, white as
> mushroom, partially decomposed,
> raped, murdered, the girl from my class.

("**That Year**")

It is a skillfully modulated beginning; but the raped and murdered classmate is afterwards abandoned, equated with the humdrum events of puberty and the separation of the poet's parents. Such abuse of the dead, the classmate a simple prop suffering rigor mortis, seems petty when Olds suddenly introduces Auschwitz into the poem:

> There was a word for us. I was: a Jew.
> It had happened to six million.
> And there was another word that was not
> for the six million, but was a word for me
> and for many others. I was:
> a survivor.

If that odd space following the first line's colon is meant to signal the poet's discretion, it is not enough. A poet who has just outraged the memory of a raped classmate ought to have more qualms about dragging onstage the six million dead of the Holocaust, only to discard them. To call herself a survivor belittles the dead girl, the slaughtered Jews. But the images have their vengeance: they discover the vapidity of Olds's assertion. The magnitude of the suffering of the raped girl and the Jews, compared with her own domestic sorrows, reveals a pathetic lack of proportion.

It should not be so, of course. The family history of despairing mother, alcoholic father, and drugged-out sister should not be subject to such diminishment. That suggests the error of Olds's strategy: the pain of others is not an appropriate reflection of her own pain, which has not been adequately established (and if established might not require these images). Such images are an evasion, and do not propitiate unpalatable facts, unpleasant memories. To refer the reader to the pain of others, like a relentless cross-index, relieves her of the need to appease her own.

Olds's poems, for the most part, proceed not out of fidelity to imagination or experience but from a calculation of dramatic extremity. She is a poet more of effect than affect. Her images are powerful—their yoking of blood and beauty is frightening—but, as in the poems of Ai or the recent work of Carolyn Forché, they establish so quickly an economy of violence, where one horrible effect can only be succeeded, or exceeded, by another, that the poems soon depend on violence for vitality. Ai, however, successfully uses blood and cruelty as personifying agents, while Forché's horrors are grounded in politics. Olds's life, the life that ought to be driven *to* violence, or from it, seems distant and abstract.

Such violence is a form of sentiment. Exaggerating and aggrandizing emotions without justifying them, it asks us to feel in excess of situation. Olds's tendency toward sentimentality is confirmed by poems for her children:

> In the dreamy silence after bath,
> hot in the milk-white towel, my son
> announces that I will not love him when I'm dead. . .
>
> . . . . .
>
> I do not tell him
> I'm damned if I won't love him after I'm
> dead, necessity after all being
> the mother of invention.
>
> **("The Mother")**

That she mistakes mawkishness for fierceness suggests why violent images so attract her—they promise (or seem to) a severe, unsentimental attitude toward life. This perceptual error lapses into absurdity when, lost in the romance of disruption, she does not consider her implications. "I lay asleep under you," she writes, "still and dark as uninhabited / countryside. . . ."

> The inhabitants of my body began to
> get up in the dark, pack, and move.
>
> All night, hordes of people
> in heavy clothes moved south in me
> carrying houses on their backs, sacks of
> seed, children by the hand, under
> a sky like smoke.
>
> **("First Night")**

From lungs to liver. From liver to pancreas. The transports of sex, the internal disruptions it occasions, deserve less ludicrous expression. Or consider, from another poem: "the blood on his penis and balls and thighs / sticky as fruit juice."

I make fun of Olds because her poems show the lineaments of better poetry. She is much too shy about using her poetic intelligence; in three or four poems (including the first quoted), the last line blossoms into something strange and unexpected:

> All afternoon, I have been watching you.
> Finally, at sunset, the oval bay
> seems to be standing up behind you,
>
> vast as a monstrous fish, its side
> rippling with light like scales, shaped
> like the waist and hips of a woman.

> I think of your
> young mother who died here,
> and recognize the quality
> of your attention to that water. I know love
> when I see its back.
>
> **("Pilgrimage")**

These moments, though small, are superior to the violences she favors. Her similes, for example, have none of Sylvia Plath's scary exactness; and the occasional successes ("the jets / float like shark along runways," "the hooks jerking / like upholstery needles through the gills") are lost in the bloodbath.

Images divorced from necessity exhaust poet and poem. The confessional poets learned a similar lesson by talking their lives to death (late Berryman, late Sexton), but perhaps it must be rediscovered by any poet of extremity. Olds's poems don't yet have the emotional presence that would torture these lines to life—indeed, her images may prevent it. By seeming sufficient, such violent scenes discourage the artistic shaping that might warrant their use—that lack makes Anne Sexton's poems inferior to Sylvia Plath's, though the pressures that drove them were equally evident, equally fierce, and equally fatal. When Olds talks of killing, she doesn't sound dangerous at all. Her work promises hard revelations, not this Hollywood ketchup. The poems are most dangerous in what they leave unsaid, as in the one that begins:

> When two plates of earth scrape along each other
> like a mother and daughter
> it is called a fault.

and ends:

> The earth cracks
> and innocent people slip gently in like swimmers.
>
> **("Quake Theory")**

When she is most quiet she most knows the horror.

Richard Tillinghast   (review date 1984)

SOURCE: "Blunt Instruments," in *The Nation,* New York, Vol. 239, No. 11, October 13, 1984, pp. 361-63.

[*Tillinghast is an American poet whose work exhibits his skill with varied poetic styles including, like Olds, confessional and political poetry. In the following excerpt in which he reviews* The Dead and the Living, *he compares Olds's poems to Sylvia Plath's and suggests that although Olds's work is flawed, its overall impact is powerful.*]

A brutalized childhood is the storm center around which the poems in Sharon Olds's second book, ***The Dead and the Living*** . . . , furiously revolve. The actors in the drama are indelibly drawn. . . .

Olds's attempts, however, to establish political analogies to private brutalization . . . are not very convincing. For one thing, Sylvia Plath did the same thing earlier, and did it better. In **"The Departure,"** Olds asks her father, "Did you weep like the Shah when you left?" And in **"The Victims,"** she writes:

> Then you were fired, and we
> grinned inside, the way people grinned
>   when
> Nixon's helicopter lifted off the South
> Lawn for the last time.

This becomes a mannerism, representing political thinking only at the most superficial level. Was Nixon ever really thought of as a father, for example, with the instinctual trust and love that implies? Were his crimes ever as intimate and damaging to any of us as child abuse would be? There is, in short, less political insight here than meets the eye.

While reading this book I found myself thinking both of Sylvia Plath and of *Wuthering Heights*. Olds has without a doubt been influenced deeply by Plath's poetry. Love and hatred of the father are major preoccupations for both writers, and both equate violence within the family with violence within the state and between nations. But there are important differences. The father in Plath is essentially a fantasy, the creation of a mind hovering on the edge of madness. Olds is, one feels certain, recording an actual story. The thrill of horror one often feels while reading Plath is produced less by some apparently real-life situation than by the workings of a brilliant mind out of control: "the autobiography of a fever," as Robert Lowell put it. But *The Dead and the Living,* like Olds's first book, *Satan Says,* has the chastening impact of a powerful documentary. It is for this reason, too, that the comparison with *Wuthering Heights* breaks down. Sadism within the family, the spectacle of the victim becoming the victimizer—those are present in both works. But because there is no romantic masochism in Olds, or—more accurately—none that has not been closely examined, her book is not a family romance but a photographic view of a family tragedy.

While her first book was impossible to ignore because of its raw power, *The Dead and the Living* is a considerable step forward. Her earlier impulse was to turn her pain and anger into myth, analogy, metaphor, as in **"Love Fossil"** from *Satan Says*—perhaps because of the difficulty of facing it head-on:

> My da on his elegant vegetarian ankles
> drank his supper. Like the other dinosaurs
> massive, meaty, made of raw steak,
> he nibbled and guzzled, his jaw dripping weeds and
>   bourbon,
> super sleazy extinct beast my heart dug for.

This grips and shocks, yet its tone of hysterical excess reflects something of the psychic damage that the speaker has sustained. In her new book the repulsion has lost none of its intensity, witness a detail such as "the black / noses of your shoes with their large pores." But the poet—and presumably also the person one glimpses fleetingly behind the work—seems more in control of the experiences that have clearly obsessed her for most of her life. In both her books, that obsessiveness is a strength and a weakness. Even in the second, many readers will feel overwhelmed by Olds's dogged insistence on reliving and rethinking her childhood traumas.

She must have sensed as much herself, because this book moves—perhaps a bit too schematically—through sections titled "The Dead," "The Living" and "The Children," from the past into the present. Olds is a keen and accurate observer of people. Still bearing the scars if not the wounds of childhood, she is not prone to sentimentality: "It's an old / story—the oldest we have on our planet— / the story of replacement," whereby as the daughter grows up, she replaces her mother. Sharon Olds is a tough, clear-eyed survivor.

Carolyne Wright (review date 1985)

SOURCE: A review of *The Dead and the Living,* in *The Iowa Review,* Vol. 15, No. 1, Winter, 1985, pp. 151-61.

[*Wright is an American poet whose work has won numerous awards. In the following review of* The Dead and the Living, *she praises Olds's use of unadorned, concrete description to evoke sympathy and love in scenes of domestic violence and trauma. Wright also lauds the universality of Olds's political poems.*]

This second book [*The Dead and the Living*] by Sharon Olds, the 1983 winner of the Lamont Award, is a powerful follow-up to *Satan Says,* fulfilling all the expectations that first book raised. Grace Paley has said in an interview that "the act of illumination is political . . . the act of bringing justice into the world a little bit": by bringing into the light lives that have been (to use Paley's words) "unseen, unknown, in darkness," Olds has both revealed and redeemed the most painful portions of her private and public lives, and celebrated that which has brought her a palpable, full-bodied joy. By confronting her own "darkness" fairly, Olds has affirmed the humanity of those who engendered that darkness, and shown herself, in these days of sensationalized telling-all for lucrative book contracts, to be a poet of affirmation. To draw a parallel with nonfiction, we could say that Olds' poetry about family is more in the spirit of Geoffrey Wolff's *The Duke of Deception* than of Christina Crawford's *Mommie Dearest.*

As is already apparent, Olds' focus in these new poems is on themes which continue to preoccupy her—familial relationships, both those in which the speaker is daughter or granddaughter, and those in which she is wife and mother. In spite of many celebratory and humorous poems (especially in the sections of the book devoted to her chosen family—her husband and children), the dominant impression of the collection's first half is somberhued, like that of a gallery of Old Master family portraits darkening with age. In what must have been poems difficult to write, Olds gives us, in passages seasoned with anger and leavened with compassion, the cruel, hard-drinking grandfather; the submissive grandmother; the elder sister who shockingly tormented her when they were children, knowing their mother "would never believe [the] story"; the brother who as an adult is still "sending his body to hell," in a protracted attempt at suicide; the mother who "took it and / took it in silence, all those years, and then / kicked [her husband] out, suddenly, and her / kids loved it"; and the father himself, especially the father, with his double bourbons and child abuse—tying his daughters to chairs, denying his son dinner, slapping the glasses off their faces. In the magnitude of what she has to forgive, and the courage, honesty, and gentleness with which she treats the details of the familial nexus, Olds brings a little more justice into the world, and also provides us with a sympathetic view of human love persisting in spite of cruelty and emotional trauma. There is much in the complexity of nuance and interrelation of characters, moreover, in these poems, that reminds us of a good collection of short fiction; as such, these poems are accessible and believable in the same way that fiction is. Olds does not stand outside or above the people in her poems; she speaks out but does not condemn; she is part of the same emotive fabric as they are, and this identification lends the work much compassion:

> Finally I just gave up and became my father,
> his greased, defeated face shining toward
> anyone I looked at, his mud-brown eyes
> in my face, glistening like wet ground that
> things you love have fallen onto
> and been lost for good. I stopped trying
> not to have his bad breath,
> his slumped posture of failure, his sad
> sex dangling on his thigh, his stomach
> swollen and empty. I gave in
> to my true self . . .
>
>   ("Fate")

The preoccupation with the father figure points to the truth of the love-hate relationship, in the nearly equal degree of energy the speaker devotes to those two emotions; and we see the peculiar way in which one transforms to the other, as the speaker gives up the attempt to be *other* than the object of fascination, and "becomes her father"—as we all are mysteriously inseparable from our earliest origins, and are most truly ourselves when we recognize and accept this truth. There are undertones of the Oedipal complex here—in the bowing to whatever is inevitable about the identity of parents and children, the nature we are perhaps fated to possess—but here the realization of such is less immediately terrifying, more immediately a source of redemption and psychic peace.

What makes these poems gripping (I read the galley proof straight through in one sitting) is not only their humanity, the recognizable and plausibly complex rendering of character and representative episode, but their language—

direct, down to earth, immersed in the essential implements and processes of daily living:

> My daughter has turned against eggs. Age six
> to nine, she cooked them herself, getting up
> at six to crack the shells, slide the
> three yolks into the bowl,
> slit them with the whisk, beat them until they
>   hissed
> and watch the pan like an incubator as they
> firmed, gold. Lately she's gone from
> three to two to one and now she
> cries she wants to quit eggs.
>
>   ("Eggs")

No inflated diction or mannerisms here, no italicized Latin or French, no learned footnotes full of elaborate historical explanations or taxonomical nomenclature, but the basics: bread, milk, blood, water, hands, hair, eyes, birth, death, love. Of sixty-two poems in the book, nine of them end with the word *life*; could it be merely accidental that six of these endings occur in the final section, the poems about Olds' two children?

Concern for the fundamentals, however, does not mean that the poems are devoid of wit, intellect, or extended figurative play:

> When I take my girl to the swimming party
> I set her down among the boys. They tower and
> bristle, she stands there smooth and sleek,
> her math scores unfolding in the air around her.
> They will strip to their suits, her body hard and
> indivisible as a prime number,
> they'll plunge in the deep end, she'll subtract
> her height from ten feet, divide it into
> hundreds of gallons of water, the numbers
> bouncing in her mind like molecules of chlorine
> in the bright blue pool.
>
>   ("The One Girl At the Boys' Party")

The controlling algebraic metaphor is appropriate to the daughter's age and primary concerns—early adolescence and its sharpened awareness of sexuality, "to the power of a thousand from her body." The writer of these poems emerges as someone who knows, from living an "ordinary" or "typical" woman's life—marriage, child-rearing, and reflection upon her own childhood family—what is really important between people. Granted, most poets write their "family" poems, but few of these relate their private mythologies in terms of national or global events, few simultaneously keep their personal lives and the larger life of human community in mind, as Olds does here in a poem to her father:

> Did you weep like the Shah when you left? Did
>   you forget
> the way you had had me tied to a chair, as
> he forgot the ones strapped to the grille
> in his name? . . . Did you forget
> the blood, blinding lights, pounding on the door,
>   as

he forgot the wire, the goad,
the stone table? did you weep as you left
as Reza Pahlevi wept when he rose
over the gold plain of Iran, did you
suddenly want to hear our voices, did you
start to rethink the darkness of our hair,
did you wonder if perhaps we had deserved to
  live,
did you love us, then?

                                        (**"The Departure"**)

The urgent interrogative tone here echoes the mental
agony embodied in the extended figure of physical torture; the daughter, distraught and still angered by her father's cruelty, presses him, even in death, to respond. We
sense that an affirmative would redeem childhood's horrors, because the father's love still matters: even in her
anger, the speaker has not entirely cut him off, entirely
refused to forgive.

Olds is not hesitant about dealing with violence or sexuality; she neither aggrandizes these concerns nor self-
consciously flaunts them. Her treatment of physical love
is direct, unembarrassed, and affectionate, as in this poem
to her husband:

A week after our child was born,
you cornered me in the spare room
and we sank down on the bed.
You kissed me and kissed me, my milk undid its
burning slip-knot through my nipples,
soaking my shirt . . . I began to throb:
my sex had been torn easily as cloth by the
crown of her head, I'd been cut with a knife and
sewn, the stitches pulling at my skin . . .
I lay in fear and blood and milk
while you kissed and kissed me, your lips hot
  and swollen
as a teen-age boy's, your sex dry and big,
all of you so tender, you hung over me . . .

                                        (**"New Mother"**)

Sensuality is heightened here by the impossibility of
consummation, the tension between the couple's passion
and present constraints; but it is the sensuality Olds affirms of happily married love. She can also be gently
humorous, especially with that most evident of male to-
tems, treating it neither with pre-Freudian awe nor post-
Freudian resentment. Her humor, rather, bespeaks familiarity that breeds appreciation:

When I was a connoisseuse of slugs
I would part the ivy leaves, and look for the
naked jelly of those gold bodies,
translucent strangers glistening along the
stones, slowly, their gelatinous bodies
at my mercy . . . the glimmering umber horns
rising like telescopes, until finally the
sensitive knobs would pop out the ends,
delicate and intimate. Years later,
when I first saw a naked man,
I gasped with pleasure to see that quiet

mystery reenacted, the slow
elegant being coming out of hiding and
gleaming in the dark air, eager and so
trusting you could weep.

                                        (**"The Connoisseuse of Slugs"**)

The pleasure and indeed, the respect accorded here by
this lengthy retroactive comparison is reminiscent of
another treatment of a delicate and often-euphemized
subject, Maxine Kumin's famous "Excrement Poem."

If I were to fault this book in any way, it would be for one
aspect of the same urge toward clarity that makes Olds'
work accessible: a tendency in places to overwrite, to
overdescribe or explain beyond what would suffice. The
language here is generally looser, more narrative than
that of *Satan Says,* and several poems could benefit from
cutting of excess adjectives and explanatory phrases:

She had taught us to take it, to hate you and take
  it
until we pricked with her for your
annihilation, Father. Now I
pass the bums in doorways, the white
slugs of their bodies gleaming through slits in
  their
suits of compressed silt, the stained
flippers of their hands, the underwater
fire of their eyes, ships gone down with the
lanterns lit, and I wonder who took it and
took it from them in silence until they had
given it all away and had nothing
left but this.

                                        (**"The Victims"**)

The awkwardness of "pricked with her for your / annihilation," the implied mixed metaphor of slugs with flippers, the belabored parallel of the ending weaken the
poem's impact, so that it does not do justice to the intensity and importance of the subject; but with some careful
cutting, such difficulties could be eliminated.

There are many poems, nonetheless, with the same ironic
tautness, the same perceptive rigor, as those in *Satan
Says.* One of my favorites is **"Rite of Passage,"** an
observation of small boys at a party already practicing
their adult masculine roles as aggressors:

As the guests arrive at my son's party
they gather in the living room—
short men, men in first grade
with smooth jaws and chins.
Hands in pockets, they stand around
jostling, jockeying for place, small fights
breaking out and calming. One says to another
How old are you? Six. I'm seven. So?
They eye each other, seeing themselves
tiny in the other's pupils. They clear their
throats a lot, a room of small bankers,
they fold their arms and frown. *I could beat you
up,* a seven says to a six,
the dark cake, round and heavy as a

turret, behind them on the table. My son . . .
   . . . speaks up as a host
for the sake of the group.
We could easily kill a two-year-old,
he says in his clear voice. The other
men agree, they clear their throats
like Generals, they relax and get down to
playing war, celebrating my son's life.

The grimmer undertones of violence and the irony of
the son's diplomatic statement are tempered here by
loving humor, and we are able to laugh with recognition of these "men in first grade" even as we shudder
at the socialization processes that demand competitiveness and bullying, and make their relaxation contingent upon "playing war."

I have been focussing so far principally upon "Poems for
the Living," the second half of the collection, in which
Olds recollects her difficult past with relative tranquility
and generosity, and celebrates her own married life and
the lives of her two children. But it is the opening, "Public" section of the book's first half, "Poems for the Dead,"
which is likely to capture critical attention above all. These
are poems based on news photographs, visual documen-
tations of the grisly effects of civil and international
conflict, and the hapless victims thereof—starving Russian and Armenian children, dead civil rights protest-
ors, Chinese and Iranian revolutionaries, and an address, in the manner of Carolyn Forché's poems to
those struggling in El Salvador, to activist poet Margaret Randall:

You are speaking of Chile,
of the woman who was arrested
with her husband and their five-year-old son.
You tell how the guards tortured the woman,
  the man, the child,
in front of each other,
"as they like to do."
Things that are worse than death.
I can see myself taking my son's ash-blond hair
  in my fingers,
tilting back his head before he knows what is
  happening,
slitting his throat, slitting my own throat
to save us that.
           ("Things That Are Worse Than Death")

Although Olds has not gone abroad to witness or participate personally in the resistance in El Salvador, Nicaragua, Chile, or elsewhere, the reality of that which is worse
than death has entered her life as fully as it has the lives
of those who have been present. She is just as engaged,
her poetic reportage is every bit as impassioned—every
line says, "I have been there, in mind and heart." She has
not merely looked at, but truly *seen* the victims in the
photographs—photos in the magazines we all flip through,
photos in the archives we all have access to—and has
responded in a way that many of us have not, although in
theory we are all capable of doing so, if Kierkegaard's
notion of actualizing potential is to be believed. Olds

knows that we do not need to join the Peace Corps, work
as overseas correspondents, or volunteer for partisan
armies abroad in order to respond as human beings to
man's own inhumanity, and to speak out and act upon
what we have seen and heard. Here is what she saw of
Rhodesia in 1978:

Just don't tell me about the issues.
I can see the pale spider-belly head of the
newborn who lies on the lawn, the web of
veins at the surface of her scalp, her skin
grey and gleaming, the clean line of the
bayonet down the center of her chest.
I see her mother's face, beaten and
beaten into the shape of a plant,
a cactus with grey spines and broad
dark maroon blooms.
I see her arm stretched out across her baby,
wrist resting, heavily, across the
tiny ribs.
        Don't speak to me about
politics. I've got eyes, man.
                ("The Issues")

Unlike those who were there and who might have been
swept up by the fever of their side of the cause, their
immediate personal stake in the struggle; or who might
have become inured to sights as horrible and as common
in the war zone as these—if only for the sake of their
own survival and sanity—as Philip Caputo has reported
of Vietnam combatants in *A Rumor of War*; Olds' perceptions have not been blunted. She has not developed a
perceptual defense mechanism against the sight of death;
this vulnerability is one advantage, as it were, of not being
physically present, of having an aesthetic, but not an
emotional distance. Therefore, she is not fooled by political bafflegab or strategic rationales—of either the Right
or the Left: her own eyes tell her all there is to know
about "the issues," if the inevitable outcome of ideological differences is the pair of mutilated bodies on the
lawn in Rhodesia. This poet is not one of those caught up
in the glamour of revolution or revolutionary causes; her
compassion for victimized humanity is pure common
sense, a mother's feeling for the deprived, the helpless,
the trapped, the children—especially the children:

The girl sits on the hard ground,
the dry pan of Russia, in the drought
of 1911, stunned,
eyes closed, mouth open,
raw hot wind blowing
sand in her face. Hunger and puberty are
taking her together. She leans on a sack,
layers of clothes fluttering in the heat,
the new radius of her arm curved.
She cannot be not beautiful, but she is
starving . . . The caption says
she is going to starve to death that winter
with millions of others. Deep in her body
the ovaries let out her first eggs,
golden as drops of grain.
            ("Photograph of the Girl")

What is signal about Olds' approach is a fidelity to detail that amounts to a modified naturalism: if she tells accurately what she sees (after selecting the most affectively pertinent details, just as the photographer has originally singled out *that* image, *that* angle and shutter speed and focal length, out of all possible subjects and treatments), the "message" implicit in the composition will stand forth on its own, as much as is possible in the inescapable contrivances of art. The speaker's stance toward her material is evident in the tone—"Just don't tell me about the issues"; "Things that are worse than death"; "I've got eyes, man";—but her attitude emerges from and is justified by the patent horror or pathos of what she shows us. Attention to detail has its ironic function as well, to point out the beauty or economy of the implements of oppression, the skill of those who devised them, as in this photo of dissidents awaiting execution in Iran:

> The first thing you notice
> is the skill
> used on the ropes, the narrow close-grained
> hemp against that black cloth
> the bodies are wrapped in. You can see the fine
> twist-lines of the twine, dark and
> elegant, the intervals exact,
> and the delicate loops securing the bagged
> bodies to the planks like cradle boards.
> The heads are uncovered, just the eyes
> bound with rag.

("Aesthetics of the Shah")

The loveliness of the composition only underscores the terror of what is soon to befall those bound in such "delicate loops."

Olds' confidence in the power of detail, and her concomitant refusal to show off verbally, to interpose a display of verbal or prosodic pyrotechnics between subject and reader, make for clarity, a style very much at the service of the subject. In her own way, Olds has heeded Stevens' aphorism in *The Necessary Angel*—poetry as an act of the mind engaged in finding "what will suffice," to do justice to what she shows us. In a sense, then, her style at its best becomes "invisible," unobtrusive except for those moments in which the desire for clarity works against itself in an excess of adjectives or descriptive phrases. But these less effective passages do not unduly distract from the power of the poems.

I am stimulated by [*The Dead and the Living*]—by its fulfillment of earlier promise, and by the potential it suggests both for Olds' own future work and for American poetry in general. Once again we have an example of our common ability to embrace the world "out there"— we need not remain, mentally or aesthetically, in our suburbs and literary ghettoes, writing only about ourselves. What we turn our attention to in our respective "private sectors" can and does have relation to the public realm, and to the lives of others. Truly "political" poetry—that which has to do with the *polis,* the community—can function as an aesthetic semi-permeable membrane, where the personal and the public inform and interfuse each other, where we private citizens can respond as individual human beings to the fate of others across socio-economic and national boundaries. Whatever the controversies raging in the journals about the possibility for and validity of political poetry, Sharon Olds has shown us that she, at least, is able both to focus on her own family and to avail herself of information accessible to all of us to enact in literature a concern for the larger family of humanity.

Diane Wakoski (review date 1987)

SOURCE: A review of *The Gold Cell,* in *The Women's Review of Books,* Vol. IV, No. 12, September, 1987, pp. 6-7.

[*Wakoski is an American poet, essayist, critic, and educator. In the following excerpt from a review of* The Gold Cell, *she remarks that Olds's poems exhibit a fascination with destruction, suffering, and sexuality.*]

Reading **The Gold Cell** gives some of the same pleasures you get in the doctor's office reading issues of *National Geographic*. It makes the news of the world interesting with its award-winning photography and glossy pages filled with articles about esoteric aspects of this earth and our daily lives. Olds' language of physical image and metaphor is never illusory (seldom allusive); it is the perfect self-contained language that the New Critics talked about. Her subject-matter is always family, though it is finally "the family of man" which is her theme.

> The boy and I face each other.
> His feet are huge, in black sneakers
> laced with white in a complex pattern like a
> set of intentional scars. We are stuck on
> opposite sides of the car, a couple of
> molecules stuck in a rod of light
> rapidly moving through darkness.

("On the Subway")

What is actually most intriguing about Sharon Olds' poetry is not her excellent grasp of how to translate the magazine and newspaper world into poetry, though that is no small skill. No, what makes me read and admire her poems is that behind the slick facade is an obsession which runs through every poem: destruction. There is not a single poem by Sharon Olds which does not intertwine destruction and creation. In fact, the poetry is often tricky and deceptive on this subject, seeming to affirm life and creation so widely. But it is really the root of death, the root of torture and pain which obsesses Olds. Her involvement with family also disguises a deeper concern: an almost nymphomaniacal obsession with sex. While she's talking about babies and children and conjugal love, she is always really relentlessly noticing the bestial.

In the most traditional sense, this is the poetry of guilt. Guilt for being white, for being alive in America, for being well-off, for being a parent, for being happily married, for being a successful poet. In the poem just quoted, she mediates on how much the young black must hate her simply because she is white and richer than he is. She automatically assumes that his blackness is a hell, and that even if he started with the same human potential as she, he couldn't win:

> And he is black
> and I am white, and without meaning or
> trying to I must profit from his darkness,
> the way he absorbs the murderous beams of
>   the
> nation's heart, as black cotton
> absorbs the heat of the sun and holds it.
>   There is
> no way to know how easy this
> white skin makes my life, this
> life he could take so easily and
> break across his knee like a stick the way his
> own back is being broken, the
> rod of his soul that at birth was dark and
> fluid and rich as the heart of a seedling
> ready to thrust up into available light.

Psychoanalytically speaking, the poems in *The Gold Cell* are poems displaying an Oedipal fascination for the handsome father, failed and drunken and behaving badly to the martyr mother, and the incredible guilt felt for loving the father so much more than the mother. The sexual energy in the life has been channeled towards creating, loving, towards wholesome sex and parental love, but underneath these poems pulses a Greek tragedy of passions, as tangled and dark as those of Medea. Watch out, readers, you may think you're just opening the pages of a nice middle-class *National Geographic* in the doctor's—no the pediatrician's—office when you crack this book, but unless you are a stupid or insensitive reader, you are in fact going to come away with infanticide, incest, matricide, rapacious desires for power.

There is a bestiality in the poems which is oddly fascinating. One of the most beautiful examples of this is **"Liddy's Orange,"** a seemingly simple poem about the rind of an orange left on the table by her daughter.

> All here speaks of ceremony,
> the sheen of acrid juice, which is all that is
> left of the flesh, the pieces lying in
> profound order like natural order,
> as if this simply happened, the way her
> life at 13 looks like something that's just
> happening, unless you see her
> standing over it, delicately clawing it open.

These poems are tormented by the guilt of Olds' animal hungers, covered over with a thick veneer of densely packed language and imagery. She represents to me, above all, the civilization we are, which has come so far and yet will probably still obliterate itself.

Linda Lancione Moyer   (essay date 1988)

SOURCE: "Witness and Transformation," in *Christianity and Crisis,* Vol. 47, No. 19, January, 1988, pp. 453-54.

[*In the following excerpt, Moyer discusses Olds's incorporation of personal pain and tragedy into her poetry.*]

"We crave getting into each other's pain," Sharon Olds said in a workshop a summer ago, and in her three books, *Satan Says, The Dead and the Living,* and *The Gold Cell,* she lays open her own. In a poem about her parents' first meeting, she exhorts them to "Do what you are going to do, and I will tell about it." She does, the alcoholism, cruelty, incest. Through all, she is the survivor, not only recording but—with the accuracy of her pictures and the clarity of her understanding—transforming.

In the long title poem of her first collection, *Satan Says,* she pictures herself as trying to write her way out of a little cedar box:

> . . . . .Satan
> comes to me in the locked box
> and says, *I'll get you out. Say*
> *My father is a shit.* I say
> my father is a shit and Satan
> laughs and says *It's opening.*
> *Say your mother is a pimp.*
> My mother is a pimp. Something
> opens and breaks when I say that.

Later, the poet hedges:

> I love them but
> I'm trying to say what happened to us
> in the lost past.

Finally she chooses to stay in the box:

> *It's your coffin now,* Satan says.
> I hardly hear; I am warming my cold
> hands at the dancer's
> ruby eye
> the fire, the suddenly discovered knowledge of love.

Her refusal to bargain with the devil, to take the easy way out, her willingness to see clearly yet stay with her ambivalence makes her work healing, though often painful to read.

Rilke, in his letter to a poet who committed suicide, wrote: "Had you once perceived how fate may pass into a verse and not come back, how, once in, it turns image and nothing but image, but an ancestor who sometimes, when you watch him in his frame seems to be like you and again not like you:—you would have persevered." So Olds has done.

The speaker in Olds' poems is not only daughter and survivor but wife and fiercely loving mother as well. She writes tightly, with clear concrete details, their impact sometimes only fully realized in the poem's last lines, as when she writes about an injury to her son's head:

> . . . the stitches black, the slit saying taken, the
> thread
>   saying given back.

Olds not only writes very personally but from deep within the body, as mother, daughter, sexual creature. In her poem called **"Prayer,"** she holds us right down on the bed with her for birth, sex, dying, then asks

>   let me not forget:
> each action, each word
> taking its beginning from these.

>   . . . . .

Olds, by speaking of untreated, taboo subjects and using strong, explicit language, exploits the ground broken by the feminist poets of the 1970s.

Terri Brown-Davidson   (essay date 1992)

SOURCE: "The Belabored Scene, The Subtlest Detail: How Craft Affects Heat in the Poetry of Sharon Olds and Sandra McPherson," in *The Hollins Critic,* Vol. XXIX, No. 1, February, 1992, pp. 1-9.

[*Brown-Davidson is an American writer and educator. In the following excerpt, she argues that the poems in* The Gold Cell *are overdramatic and self-indulgent.*]

I am a poet of excess, *Definition,* "poet of excess": writer who craves the piled-up instead of the pared-down. I recall sitting, as a child, in the darkened classroom as the projector whirred and I waited for the first dead-gray stills of Columbus and his ships to flash onto the screen. I preferred the shock-green effect of a giant floating Gumby, the whirlagig colors of the Mother Goose doll in her bonnet who would speak to us, hectically flushed, from the faded classroom screen. What can I say? As a child I wrote murder mysteries, seminal tales of beau-crazed sisters killing each other off, lurid nature tableaux. This is temperament, I decided, and certainly *must* be exploited to satisfy that storytelling urge stamped in our bones. But how much does the listener derive from unadulterated drama? I wonder about the emotional price he pays for a constant outpouring of the excessive or extraordinary. I wonder about the reader who attempts to enter a poem and finds himself repelled by its extremes in color or emotion, by its insistence on dramatizing experience in such a way that we can't locate ourselves as human beings in an overwrought text. . . .

It is a sad fact that emotion run amuck tends to alienate a reader. As if he were visiting an accident site, he is compelled to flee. He doesn't mind reading about the essential life experiences, such as death, birth, love, sex— all the Lawrentian biggies—as long as they're presented in an underplayed or controlled-enough guise to allow him to enter the situation himself, as if he were floating through a dream state as extension of his waking life. The reader is generally no pornographer. He doesn't want to see a private act made public and thus exploitive, for such sexual grandstanding can only embarrass. So, how is the poet to make love and remain safely behind closed doors? There are a number of "antiexploitive" strategies he can consider. For example, he can choose subjects which lie close to his heart and are tinged with the reality of human experience; he can strive to present such experience honestly, without "emotional embellishing"; he can ensure that his diction matches his subject and tone (i.e., no prostitutes intoning like Shakespeare); he can employ realistic, nongeneric details to "ground" his approach; he can satisfy himself that what he's written is important by undergoing the ultimate poet's honesty-gauge test: if this villanelle were written by any other poet, would I feel compelled to read it? And, most importantly, he can continue to experiment in a variety of shapes, forms, and tones to achieve his emotional effects, to try to find the one move perfectly suited to each poem and thereby ensure that he, as poet, won't degenerate into an emotionally kneejerk, formulaic writer.

As a fellow dramatist, I can easily identify with any writer who labors under the misconception that "more is more." Hence my empathy for Sharon Olds. Like Kronos devouring his children, Olds would like to gobble life whole, to swallow the entire thrust of human experience with such gusto that no dust particle escapes her attention. Certainly this is a desirable attribute in an age of bare-bone poets afraid to hang flesh on their skeletons. But Sharon Olds is also, I believe, a poet who, in her incessant hankering after the real that can be possessed in the breadth and width of her bones, has pumped up experience to such a heightened level it no longer resembles any reality a reader wants to participate in. This tendency for excess, curbed admirably in Olds' second book, ***The Dead and The Living,*** has reared up with renewed violence in her latest collection, ***The Gold Cell.*** Consider a few of the poem titles: **"Outside the Operating Room of the Sex-Change Doctor," "The Pope's Penis," "Love in Blood Time."** If these titles don't provide some inkling of the danger of imagination unchecked by—dare I write it—*taste,* a sampling of one poem from the collection, **"A Woman in Heat Wiping Herself,"** should indicate the recent direction of Olds' work:

> High in the inner regions of my body
> this gloss is spun, high up
> under the overhanging ledge where the
> light pours down on the cliff night and day.
> No workers stand around in the
> camaraderie of workers,
> no one lays the color down on the
> lip of the braid, there is only the light,
> bands and folds of light, and the clean
> sand at the edge, the working surface—there is
> no one around for miles, no one hungry,
> no one being fed. . . .

The purpose of this poem is admirable. In the Romantic tradition (though with a contemporary twist), Olds wants to celebrate the Body Electric, the mechanism of the organism, so to speak, with all the religious/spiritual overtones which adhere to such an enterprise. And she celebrates this body in language beautifully layered, like flesh upon bone. It is all wonderfully metaphorical, wonderfully elegant. But the first problem that arises is, obviously, one of literal subject. Like the modern-day besotted who like to hail the birth of a baby as "pure miracle" without noticing all the flesh-ripping and gore that such a miracle necessitates, Olds would like to celebrate the miracle of female discharge by equating it, metaphorically, with something higher than itself, in this case, a process which takes on almost metaphysical proportions. The discharge is both "light" and "sea" since the "clean sand" lies against its periphery, and it is—holy of holies—self-perpetuating process, unadulterated, since "no workers stand around in the / camaraderie of workers" but since the work is being accomplished all the same. And with what does Olds equate this process? Godhead, I think. The function of light assumes confusing spiritual ramifications, as if the discharge were at once messy inconvenience for the woman who has to don Stay-Fresh to battle it, but also a sign of spiritual favor we can't quite grasp because it boasts the same logical illogic which made us perceive, a generation back, "the Curse" as stigma. The religious connotations pile up where Olds connects the discharge to—you guessed it—lamb-as-Christ:

> Just as in the side of the
> lamb no one is tending the hole where the
> light pours out. . . .

Now, of course, the discharge has assumed not only the figurative associations of Christ and his stigmata, but the slightly scarier, more pejorative ones of vulva as "wound," of woman as "hole." Thus the tone of the poem has begun to go awry. And Olds does not redeem herself by continuing to develop the water imagery she introduced at the beginning of this poem:

> . . . . . Deep in my sex, the
> glittering threads are thrown outward and thrown
>   outward
> the way the sea lifts up the whole edge of its body,
> the rim, the slit where once or twice in a lifetime
> you can look through and see the other world—

I would say, of this passage, a nice sentiment. And I would say I admire Olds' move here in depicting the vulva as a passageway to the transcendental, for, at the end, don't we all curl into the universe in death, haven't we all emerged from the birth canal as compressed and unseeing as if we were peering through the wrong end of a telescope, waiting to see how some distant vision resolves into a clear perspective? The trouble is that Olds presses far too hard on the image. The idea of writing a poem about discharge could, if we were to enter the always dangerous realm of aesthetics, be considered sensationalistic if not downright salacious, and certainly not compelling—would one really want to write a poem about

feces? About spit? If so, what would be the aesthetic purpose here? Another problem, a concomitant problem, arises from writing such a lush, language-gorgeous poem about a bodily process. Olds is writing here the way she always writes; she has not adapted her language to her purpose, has not considered the effect, on the already somewhat repulsed reader, of saturated language when addressing a topic such as female discharge. Thus Olds' plan of attack is out of keeping with her intent, and everything potentially powerful in this poem is sacrificed to her craving for drama, even the title, which is unnecessarily sensationalistic and fights the religious ramitications—dogs go "into heat," not women, except in B movies.

In addition, Olds sabotages her intent in other ways besides coining questionable subject matter and insisting, at any cost, on the painterly language which any poet with a dramatic leaning (see **"Two Deaths,"**) must revel in. I take it for granted that Olds' intent is not just to communicate, for this is a pedestrian word, best reserved for travel articles and bills of fare, but rather to examine, to exalt, to link the reader to experience through language and shape on a page and thus wrap that reader in the sustaining warmth of meaning. Olds undercuts her purpose by not remaining conscious of it—by converting herself, in poem after poem, into some archetypal soothsayer, a sybil who spins out words without considering the implications of craft. How, you ask, might I assume this? Dare I assume it, without being a mind reader?

The fact is, Olds might convince herself that she is conscious of craft simply because she has found an amenable shape for her work (the long, straggly column) and because she can wield a phrase with the best of them. But beautiful language is not craft, particularly when it circumvents its purpose. And dramatic subject matter is nothing more than a harkening back to the lonely child in a schoolroom who squirmed in anticipation at the Mother Goose movies because they would whirl her, for one color-packed hour, out of the beige doldrums of her life.

The poet who is truly interested in achieving an emotional impact is willing to work for this effect. This means that he will employ whatever strategies he has at his command to convey a mood or idea, and, lacking these, will invent one for his purposes. The very predictability of Olds' techniques tells us that she is after, not mere emotional impact, not artistic greatness, but something else, something indefinable which, I think, revolves around the barest need for self-expression as well as the desire to extract the juice from everyday life and thus make it more "special" than it already is. If this is an ego-stroking maneuver, I don't see it at work in Olds' collections. I see, instead, a poetics which was originally exciting, if overblown, when presented in such poems as **"Love Fossil"** in *Satan Says,* when it seemed an expansion of the late Plath's work, an attempt to move back the boundaries of confessionalism and mine this school further of its most disturbing psychological opportunities. But this work lacked the craft, even then, of Plath's *Ariel,* though of course, since the presentation seemed new, the weaknesses were not readily apparent. Actually, the long, skinny column of type which is Olds' trademark had more variety then, since more poems, such as **"Late"** and **"Seventh Birthday of the First Child,"** were at least broken into stanzas.

But the shape of her poems jelled. Started to jell in ***The Dead and The Living,*** which contains, in its poems about Marilyn Monroe and political photographs, Olds' best writing because it accrues to subjects we can care about, because it hasn't yet calcified into the sensationalism which, paradoxically enough, is less stimulating than exhausting. For an example of Olds' writing at its most fossilized, consider the opening of **"I Go Back to May 1937,"** from *The Gold Cell*:

> I see them standing at the formal gates of their
>   colleges,
> I see my father strolling out
> under the ochre sandstone arch, the
> red tiles glinting like bent
> plates of blood behind his head, I
> see my mother with a few light books at her hip
> standing at the pillar made of tiny bricks with the
> wrought-iron gate still open behind her, its
> sword-tips black in the May air,
> they are about to graduate, they are about to get
>   married,
> they are kids, they are dumb, all they know is they
>   are
> innocent, they would never hurt anybody.

This passage is pure Olds formula: the skinny but irregular column, the typical enjambment between article and noun, the overwrought similes which never quite work ("red tiles glinting like bent / plates of blood behind his head"), the relentless parallelism ("they are," "they are"). There is something really disturbing about this passage—not in the way Olds intended—in how formulaic it is. In this poem, as in others in which the speaker details her father's dying, something so rigid, so set has crept into the writing that we no longer trust the speaker's voice. It's as if someone were to announce to us, "I am now going to plumb the depths of human experience," and we were then expecting that person to put on a jolly good show. In not daring to change any aspect of her craft, in declaring, in a sense, that "This is my voice, and I'm not going to change it," Olds has set herself up for failure, for the true risk-taking poet is the one who seeks answers or who solves problems through craft, who dares to push beyond the boundaries to grow and keep growing and thus asserts, "I will never be so great, so dramatic, so emotionally all-embracing that I can't find a better way to say the unsayable." In *The Gold Cell,* her third book, Olds has found her "definitive" poetic voice, her "definitive" dramatic stance, and is thus inducing her own downfall as poet. In scene after belabored scene, the browbeating which is symptomatic of the overdramatic, rather than the deeply felt word or detail, leaks through, lacquering Olds' latest poems with a thick sheen of insincerity.

Clair Wills   (review date 1993)

SOURCE: "The Body as Matter," in *The Times Literary Supplement,* No. 4711, July 16, 1993, p. 25.

[*In the following review, Wills praises Olds's unsentimental and honest depiction of emotionally laden topics and social taboos in* The Father.]

Some years ago, Sharon Olds's father died of throat cancer; this book comprises a sequence of poems charting the death of the body, and exploring the emotions and physical sensations experienced by the daughter in the face of the loss of an unloving father. With an easy lyricism, Olds recounts the gradual achievement of a kind of closeness, based not so much on mutual understanding as on an acceptance of the physical, of the body as matter. In **"The Lifting"** her father draws his nightshirt up to his neck, forcing her to look at his body when she would have turned away. The gown

> rises the way we were promised at death it would
>   rise,
> the veils would fall from our eyes, we would know
>   everything.

The reader is similarly discomfited by Olds herself—witness not only to her father's unveiling but also to her own. This intimate confessional poetry grips partly because of its honesty, and partly because of the fear of embarrassment which is a continual danger for both poet and reader, as the father's helpless body and his daughter's feelings about it are gradually laid bare. That this danger is always finally averted, and that the poetry at no point slips into sentimentality, is a tribute to the poet's control of mood and tone. Even as she relates the intimate details of the sick-room, a kind of verbal distance is maintained. Olds manages to convey both the awkwardness and fascination which arise when vulnerability and physical intimacy enter a relationship without love. The dying man is always called "my father" (never, until after death, when a new note of familiarity is released into the poetry, is he addressed as "Dad"), suggesting that what is important is his role in her life rather than any closeness or compatibility: "this long, deep, unearned desire you made when you made me".

Because of the close, almost relentless focus on the body, the poems are not elegies in any ordinary sense of the word; again and again, an elegiac tone enters the verse only to be superseded by an unaffected and humorous refusal to be fooled about god, life after death, or the meaning of the father's life; it is on corrupted matter that their relationship depends. While at times this seems a depressing admission, Olds also conveys a sense of liberation in the realization of the corporeality of the familial relation. In **"The Pulling"**, she imagines her father being drawn towards death as her children were pulled towards life through her body, "like a napkin through a ring"; in **"Last Acts"**, she is his seed:

> I want
> to be in him, as I was once inside him,

riding in his balls the day before he cast me—
he carries me easily on his long legs up the
hills of San Francisco in war-time, I am
there between his legs where I belong,
I am his flesh, he can love me without
reserve, I will be his pleasure.

In keeping with this emphasis on the "trance of matter", Olds evinces a desire to experience fully every aspect of her father's death. She feels the weight of the urn containing his ashes as "a blessing", she lies full length on his grave, or finding that kissing his gravestone is not enough she licks it ("I ate his dust, I tasted my dirt host"). This also makes for some tense moments, such as the minutes before the other relatives arrive at the funeral, which she spends working quickly at the lid of the urn until it gives, so that she can see his ashes and come face to face for the last time with "the actual matter of his being". The volume as a whole is a risky undertaking, nearly marred simply by offering us too much of the same. Yet finally it works; with lightness and candour. Olds manages to turn her subject-matter—the slow and unlovely death of a difficult man—into something touching and strangely comforting.

Brian Dillon   (essay date 1993)

SOURCE: "'Never Having Had You, I Cannot Let You Go': Sharon Olds's Poems of a Father-Daughter Relationship," in *The Literary Review*, Vol. 37, No. 1, Fall, 1993, pp. 108-18.

[*In the following essay, Dillon examines Olds's narrative about the relationship between her and her father running throughout* Satan Says, The Dead and the Living, *and* The Gold Cell.]

In her first three books of poetry—*Satan Says* (1980), *The Dead and the Living* (1984), *The Gold Cell* (1989)—as well as recently published poems not collected into book form, Sharon Olds describes a dysfunctional family misruled by a father whose abuse of power the poems' speaker responds to both as a child and an adult. Rather than one full-length *Prelude*-like account, Olds offers snapshots, literally dozens of short poems, a few which metaphorically delineate the father damaging the family structure, and others which narrate in specific detail the father's brutal presence. One anthology of literature commonly used in introductory level classes [*The Riverside Anthology of Literature,* 1991] features three poems highlighting the speaker's relationship with her father. In "**The Chute**" (included in *The Gold Cell*) the father selects a child to suspend by the ankles inside the laundry chute, threatening to drop the helpless one: "he loved to hear / passionate screaming in a narrow space." In "**The Victims**" (included in *The Dead and the Living*), an abusive father is kicked out of the house, divorced by his wife, and fired from his job. And in "**The Race**" the adult speaker narrates a wild—nearly out of breath—dash through an airport to board a plane in order to cross the

continent and arrive at her dying father's bedside. Whether deliberate or not, the anthology selection of Olds's poems allows readers to construct a plot, a linear progression from abuse to expulsion of the abuser to the apparent death of the abuser, with (perhaps) the speaker's achievement of a peace with her past in "**The Race.**" This last poem is included in *The Father,* Olds's most recent publication, and is just one of 52 poems in this book detailing the speaker's response to her father's dying and death.

To what extent, in looking at the entire Olds canon, can a plot about the father be discerned? The title poem for *Satan Says,* which opens Olds's first book, establishes a concern the poet returns to in her next two books and in poetry published since *The Gold Cell*. In circumstances more terrifying than Alice's wonderland dreamworld, the speaker is locked in "a little cedar box," apparently a small jewelry box. The voice of Satan promises her freedom if she repeats his vulgarities: "Say shit, say death, say fuck the father." The speaker complies, but her conflicted response about her parents highlights an emotion foreign to Satan: "I love them but / I'm trying to say what happened to us / in the lost past." Her expression of love prevents her escape from the cedar box. "*It's your coffin now,* Satan says." Though burdened by familial circumstances, the "pain of the locked past," the speaker's freedom lies in "trying to say what happened," as well as, the poem concludes, "the suddenly discovered knowledge of love" (*Satan Says*).

The voice of the speaker in "**Satan Says**" certainly seems to be the same voice we hear in numerous poems published over the next decade or more. In "**The Chute,**" Olds's speaker details the chilling effect her father's behavior had on her and her two siblings. For whatever odd reason, the wiring for the doorbell was located partway down the laundry chute, and one child would be chosen by the father to be dangled down it to tape two wires together. Two features stand out. Early in the poem the description of the setting is interrupted. The speaker jumps to a later time and provides the reader with a glimpse of her father that is never explained and which seems to lie outside the concerns of "**The Chute**":

> . . . And halfway
> down there was an electric fixture for the
> doorbell—that bell my father would ring and
> ring years later when he stood at the door with that
> blood on him, like a newborn's caul,
> ringing ringing to enter.
>
> (*The Gold Cell*)

Why does he have blood on him? Why is his ringing so persistent? Olds is not forthcoming with an explanation in this or other poems that appear to refer to the same incident. Consider the opening lines to "**History: 13**" (the number referring to the speaker's age at the time of the unsettling event):

> When I found my father that night, the blood
> smeared on his head and face, I did not

know who had done it. I had loved his body
whole, his head, his face, untouched,
and now he floated on the couch, his arms
up, like Mussolini hanging
upside down in the air, his head
dangling where they could reach him with boards and
   their
fingernails, those who had lived
under his tyranny.

                              (*The Gold Cell*)

As in **"The Chute,"** the speaker fails to account for her
father's bloodied appearance; instead, she focuses on her
own initially confused and finally ambivalent response to
him. She questions whether she or anyone in her family
was responsible for his disturbing presence. And though
she concludes with a label that damns the father, her
sentiment is one of empathy: ". . . I turned my back /
on happiness, at 13 I entered / a life of mourning, of mourning for the Fascist." It seems worth noting that this poem
is placed seven poems prior to **"The Chute,"** with a variety of poems about her parents viewed from both the
child's and adult's perspective in between, suggesting that
Olds refuses to make narrative continuity easy. Nine years
earlier Olds began **"That Year"** with what appears to be
the earliest reference to this minimally detailed incident.
The poem is worth reading in full to get a sense of the
genuine anguish the father caused, Olds's tendency to
place family experiences within an easily recognizable
historical context, and the speaker's attempts to assess
her past from the perspective of an adult.

The year of the mask of blood, my father
hammering on the glass door to get in

was the year they found her body in the hills,
in a shallow grave, naked, white as
mushroom, partially decomposed,
raped, murdered, the girl from my class.

That was the year my mother took us and
hid us so he could not get at us
when she told him to leave; so there were no more
tyings by the wrist to the chair,
no more denial of food
or the forcing of foods, the head held back,
down the throat at the restaurant,
the shame of vomited buttermilk
down the sweater with its shame of new breasts.

That was the year
I started to bleed,
crossing over that border in the night,
and in Social Studies, we came at last
to Auschwitz. I recognized it
like my father's face, the face of the guard
turning away—or worse yet
turning toward me.

                              (*Satan Says*)

The loathing for the man depicted as Fascist and Nazi in
these poems does not prepare the reader in search of

narrative coherence for the adult, distanced perspective on
the father the speaker offers in **"The Chute."** The reader
who hopes Olds will reproduce experience will be disappointed in the elliptical quality of many of the poems about
the father. The reader who hopes Olds will emphasize the
speaker's evaluation of her experience will be intrigued.
The child living through the experience asks, "how could
you trust him?" But the adult speaker excuses the father's
actions as she interprets the poem in the final lines.

        . . . We hung there in the dark,
    and yet, you know, he never dropped us
    or meant to, he only liked to say he would,
    so although it's a story with some cruelty in it,
    finally it's a story of love
    and release, the way the father pulls you out of
        nothing
    and stands there foolishly grinning.

                              (*The Gold Cell*)

The conclusion appears to be at cross purposes with the
rest of the poem: the dramatic tension of the preceding
narrative, the reader is informed, should not be understood as an implied criticism of the father's threatening
behavior. The child's perspective of fear gets erased with
this conclusion. The father analogously presented elsewhere as a Mussolini or a Nazi has not changed. Instead,
the speaker makes a grand effort to understand him and
to contemplate how he has penetrated the core of her
being: "if you were / his, half him, your left hand maybe
and your / left foot dipped in the gleaming / murky liquor
of his nature, how could you / trust yourself?" The tension between the speaker's response to her father as a
child and as an adult is left unresolved here (and in other
poems treating the father-daughter relationship), which
upsets efforts at reading for the plot.

The ending of **"The Chute"** admits the desire to explain,
to provide mature, distanced explanation, however unsat-
isfying this might be for the reader. As one commentator
[Christian McEwen in "Soul Substance," a review of *The
Gold Cell* in *The Nation* April 11, 1987] on Olds has
remarked, "As readers and as human beings, we may not
agree with her; we may have other, happier versions of
'love / and release.' But Olds allows no room for such
defection. The stories are hers, and they must be understood in her terms only." Yet the lines about her father
ringing the doorbell are not fleshed out, justification for
his appearance and action is left unstated, and an intratextual reading (one created by reading it in the context of
other Olds's poems) merely restates the reference to the
incident without illuminating it. Olds's 1990 poem **"The
Prepositions"** (which is not included in *The Father*) is
worth noting here: it recalls the speaker's seventh grade
assignment to memorize a list of 45 prepositions, her
school environment, and other associations prompted by
memory of this task—"fourteen, the breaking of childhood, beginning of memory." Halfway through this poem
Olds interjects the following lines:

Over, past, since, through,
    that was the year my father came home in the

middle of the night with those heavy worms of
blood on his face, trilobites of
elegant gore, cornice and crisp
waist of the extinct form. . . .

These lines can only be understood intratextually, but
even with such a reading, the father's experience and
the speaker's response to it remain ambiguous. While
the lines describing the father's appearance strain under
the weight of lexical complexity, with the odd word
"trilobites" drawing excessive attention to itself and
away from what actually occurred, how this incident
affected the speaker, and any account justifying reference to it in this poem, is unexplained. And Olds's
characteristic avoidance of enjambment with the vertical drop induced by ending lines on weak words—
the, of—forces the reader to plunge through her account of a painful experience. Again, Olds leaves the
reader with hints and indirections, with the outlines of
a plot.

Olds forces her reader to move from book to book and
occasionally from section to section within the same book
to piece together a portrait of this father. In *The Dead
and the Living,* the speaker avenges the father who delighted in intimidating his children. The pronoun "it"
carries much ambiguous weight in **"The Victims"**:
the abuse "it" suggests remains nonspecific. "When Mother divorced you, we were glad. She took it and / took it,
in silence, all those years and then / kicked you out,
suddenly, and her / kids loved it. . . . She had taught us to
take it, to hate you and take it. . . ." The father's loss of
his job follows upon the divorce; the speaker's adult
perspective, asserted in the final lengthy sentence that
begins with an overt marker of the temporal shift—"Now
I / pass the bums in the doorways . . ."—expresses no
empathy for the father, no attempt to shrug off the pains
of the past as the final lines of **"The Chute"** attempt to
do. The lack of sympathy evident in these lines, the assumption that these "bums" earned their misery, is a rare
example of Olds venting spleen but without offering any
conflicting response to suggest tension in her feelings
toward the father. The reader's empathy with the speaker
apparently is assumed. **"The Departure"** poses questions
in an accusatory tone and equates the father with the Shah
of Iran: both are guilty of engaging in impersonal acts of
brutality. "Did you forget / the way you had had me tied
to a chair, as / he forgot the ones strapped to the grille
/ in his name?" But even this poem demonstrates the
speaker's effort to penetrate an emotional depth of the
father, one that the speaker can literally identify with.
While **"The Victims"** asserts that the speaker and her
siblings "grinned inside" when the father was "kicked"
out of the house, **"The Departure"** presents the father's
leave-taking as deserving a serious rather than giddy reaction:

> . . . Did you weep as you left
> as Reza Pahlavi wept when he rose
> over the gold plain of Iran, did you
> suddenly want to hear our voices, did you
> start to rethink the darkness of our hair,

did you wonder if perhaps we had deserved to live,
did you love us, then?

> (*The Dead and the Living*)

The father has no voice in any of these poems. Yet with
"The Departure," the speaker appears to be provoking a
dialogue, and the reader is forced to imagine what the
father would say were he allowed to speak. Since the
father is a dominant presence in so many poems in Olds's
first three books and the central subject in her fourth,
why does she choose to keep him silent? To silence the
abuser, the oppressor figure grants the speaker a degree
of control as an adult-artist that she clearly lacked as a
child. But there is a significant trade-off: non-particular-
ized as the father's acts often are presented (in **"Looking at My Father"** we are told that "he's a tease, / obsessive, rigid, selfish, sentimental," generic qualities that
could be applied to many parents; *The Gold Cell*), the
poetry risks sounding less intensely private, and, consequently, risks minimizing the damage the father caused.
In *The Father,* his silences become a recurrent theme.
When in **"His Stillness"** his doctor informs him his
cancer is beyond cure, his response is "like a holy man,"
a dignified "Thank you": "I had not remembered / he had
always held still and kept silent to bear things, / the liquor a way to keep still. I had not / known him." The
speaker's hostility toward her father evident in earlier
poems is significantly toned down in this book; the emphasis here is on the absence of love and the speaker's
coming to terms with that fact. The speaker clings to
details: his striking a match and drawing on a cigar provided "his only song . . . / it was that song or none." The reader
who complains that Olds creates a space around her poems in which plot continuity is suggested but left unfulfilled, the reader who wonders whether the speaker extracts an apology from the father and if the pains of the
past are smoothed over in a final emotionally-charged
dialogue, misses the point of this book. It is precisely
the silence of the father that creates an enormous emptiness that these poems try to fill, silence that provokes
multiple conjectures as to who the father is and why his
dying and death so confound the speaker. "I had stopped
/ longing for him to address me from his heart / before
he died," Olds writes in **"The Want."** The irony of **"Last
Kiss"** is that the father's impatience with his daughter,
with her suitcases packed as she must leave him, probably for the last time, to return to her world, prompts his
exasperated "Last kiss!": "To plead that I leave / my father
asked me for a kiss! I would not / leave till he had done
so, I will not let thee go except thou beg for it." Although
echoing Jacob's demand of the angel with whom he wrestles all night, no blessing is requested by the speaker of
her father, and none is offered.

The silencing of the father, as well as the speaker's refusal to damn the father and assert that the speaker herself emerged irreparably scarred from her seemingly traumatic childhood experiences, suggests Olds's intentional
willingness to avoid the label "confessional" poet, her resistance to make poetry centered on anger and shame. The
conventional view that confessional poetry is practiced
primarily by Lowell, Plath, Sexton, and others, has been

challenged by Laurence Lerner [in "What is Confessional Poetry?" *Critical Quarterly,* Vol. 29, 1987], who argues that the term is far more amorphous than contemporary critical practice would indicate. An attempt to define the term draws attention to these concerns: "Confession is something that causes us shame . . . confessional poetry deals with experience that it is deeply painful to bring into public, not because it is disgusting, nor because it is sinful, but because it is intensely private." The conclusion to **"The Chute"** swerves away from any expression of shame at having a sadistic father. The historical analogue for understanding the father's action in **"The Departure"** allows Olds to avoid sounding "intensely private." Lerner argues that some poetry, post 1950s American especially, which gets labelled "confessional" does reveal raw experience, the psyche under intense strain, presumably the author's own and factually accurate, and demonstrates "narrative courage," yet it does not deserve the label poetry. His concluding thought seems particularly appropriate when we think of Olds's work: "lyric poetry was never wholly detachable from confession, just as, if it is to have any claim to be poetry, it can never be wholly identified with it."

Olds is careful to avoid painful revelation overwhelming her aesthetic form. Olds's speaker never asserts that her relationship with her father significantly scarred her: the thrust in her accounts of her father is that she survived and with the tool of language will describe what it feels like. In an early poem, **"Nurse Whitman,"** she equates her task as daughter / artist with that of America's greatest poet in his finest non-literary role: "You bathe the forehead, you bathe the lip, the cock, / as I touch my father, as if the language / were a form of life" (*Satan Says*). Her language not only reclaims the past but also serves a therapeutic function for the speaker. In the same book, in two other poems which feature the father when the family was still together dysfunctionally, the speaker concludes that she is a "survivor" (**"That Year"** and **"Time-Travel"** in *Satan Says*). **"Time-Travel,"** like many of Olds's poems, replaces the father's speech with his physical presence, which is lovingly described. In a dream-like episode the adult speaker re-visits a lakeside house in the summer of '55. Looking for her father, she finds him and silently observes his appearance. What follows includes the second and part of the third stanzas.

> I can possess him like this, the funnies
> rising and falling on his big stomach,
> his big solid secret body
> where he puts the bourbon.
> He belongs to me forever like this,
> the red plaid shirt, the baggy pants,
> the long perfectly turned legs,
> the soft padded hands folded across his body,
> the hair dark as a burnt match,
> the domed, round eyes closed,
> the firm mouth. Sleeping it off
> in the last summer the family was together.
> I have learned to walk
>
> so quietly into that summer
> no one knows I am there. He rests

> easy as a baby. Upstairs
> mother weeps. . . .

The prompt for the mother's weeping can be presumed only by intratextual readings, and then only indirectly. This is the outline of a frequently brutal man in repose. The speaker's desire to "possess" the father approximates the painter's desire to accurately capture her subject on canvas: for a figure so crucial in the emotional life of the speaker, the father remains mysteriously two-dimensional. What does the speaker think of the father, then (1955) and in the present time of the poem? Olds consistently leaves a gap where one expects to find personal reflection. The adult speaker, the time-traveler, locates her teenage self in this fractured family setting literally by the shoreline, isolated, confused, wary of her family: "She does not know / any of this will ever stop / She does not know she is the one / survivor" *Satan Says*. The opening line asserts that the speaker has "learned to go back" to this scene from her past; what she has learned from it remains unstated, though the ending emphasizes the speaker's distance from the brutality of the father.

The dramatic tension is minimized as the antagonist sleeps and the speaker claims a personal victory. **"Time-Travel"** opens the section titled **"Journey"** in *Satan Says*. And the journey of the speaker's efforts to describe and understand the behavior of her father and his influence on her continue throughout her work, frequently in poems that capture the physical presence of the father. **"The Ideal Father"** contrasts two versions of the past as the speaker pries apart idealization and painful memory: the hair, skin, even the penis of the idealized father are "perfect as a textbook example," yet the speaker also must remember the man who "slapped the glasses off a / small girl's face" (*The Dead and the Living*). The honesty with which the speaker avoids blurring idealization and painful memory is evident in other poems that bluntly acknowledge the speaker's inevitable burden of the father's inheritance: "Finally I just gave up and became my father / . . . I saw the whole, world shining / with the ecstasy of his grief, and I / myself, he, I, shined . . ." (**"Fate"** in *The Dead and the Living*). Again, the reader's frustrations surface as the speaker swerves from telling *what* she sees from this new perspective of merging with the father. The speaker has adopted the "likeness" of a dangerous man, and even praises her husband's willingness to trust her: "As I see you / embracing me, in the mirror, I see I am / my father as a woman, I see you bravely / embrace him, in me, putting your life in his / hands as mine" (**"Poem to My Husband from My Father's Daughter,"** *Satan Says*). The father is both dangerous and pathetic, and the speaker's strength is her ability to turn into art the pain and weirdness. She is a survivor "possessed," as the title of another poem labels this dark passion. "Never having had you, I cannot let you go . . ." (*The Dead and the Living*). And this feeling, the speaker urges us to believe, must be reciprocal, though her father might only "realize" this after his death. The speaker fantasizes that with a newly acquired afterlife voice he will account for her effect on him: "She could / speak, you see. As if my own / jaws, throat, and larynx had come / alive in her" ("**When the Dead Ask My Father about Me**"). This poem, included in *The Father,* and the final poem of this same book, "**My Father Speaks to Me from the Dead,**" demonstrate both the speaker's flagrant ego and her quest for a love that is now—and has been for many years—impossible to achieve. He speaks of her knees, curls, face, and womb. (Olds once asked, "Is there anything that shouldn't or can't be written about in a poem?" and almost in response pushes against poetic bounds here as her father asserts, "when I touched your little / anus I crossed wires with God for a moment.") Though he recalls her baby body quite well, he stops at this surface and will not be bold to imagine her emotional core: "I made you, when I say now that I love you / I mean look down at your hand, move it, / that action is matter's love, for human / love go elsewhere."

As the dying of the father is the subject of this latest work of Olds's, he escapes, quite literally, from any effort the reader imposes to plot the father-daughter relationship. The breathless speaker of "**The Race**" runs through an airport to catch a plane in order to fly to her dying father's bedside, "to touch him again in this life." The poem concludes in an open-ended manner: "I walked into his room / and watched his chest rise slowly / and sink again, all night / I watched him breathe." Perhaps her walking suggests a last minute reluctance: she is still not mentally and emotionally prepared to discuss the unresolved conflicts that "**The Victims**" and other poems indicate she feels. No attempt is made here to bring closure on the father-daughter relationship, let alone to assess its impact on the speaker. Expectations that the poet will provide narrative coherence are frustrated.

The speaker's shift from "ran" and "raced" to "walked" also suggests a reluctance to view her dying father's body, or at least a steeling of her emotions to confront the sight of her father's disease-ravaged body. In many other poems, though, the father's body, specifically the signs of its painful decay, become the poem's subject matter. His thick, heavy sputum floats in a glass on a table next to his hospital bed—"I think of it with wonder now"—and the glass acquires symbolic proportions akin to Stevens's jar in Tennessee: it would "shimmer there on the table until / the room seemed to turn around it / in an orderly way" ("**The Glass**"). What the speaker knows when she sees her father as a victim, dying of cancer, is that they are connected, not by their shared experiences, not even the ones portrayed as traumatic for the speaker in numerous poems, but connected in their bones and blood, their bodies a physical conjunction that transcend all darker memories of abuse. How the father was transformed from a handsome man courting the speaker's mother to an abusive father to a horizontal body with his life slowly excised from him is *not* the subject of Olds's poems. The poems that treat the dying and dead father minimize who the father is. Instead, his dying and death propel the speaker into the mysteries of her assumed inheritance from him. Half of the speaker's pre-embryo state she imagines as she washes the face of her dying father in "**Last Acts**":

> . . . I want
> to be in him, as I was once inside him,
> riding in his balls the day before he cast me—
> he carries me easily on his long legs up the
> hills of San Francisco in war-time, I am
> there between his legs where I belong,
> I am his flesh, he can love me without
> reserve, I will be his pleasure.

From the testicles descended, Olds derives this physiologically sound, though fantastically imagined, image.

In one of Olds's more audacious poems, "**The Swimmer,**" the speaker throws herself into the sea, emptying herself in the process of memory and emotion as she merges with the matter of her father:

> I am like those elements my father turned into,
> smoke, bone, salt. It is one of
> the only things I like to do
> anymore, get down inside the horizon
> and feel what his new life is like, how
> clean, how blank, how griefless, how without error—
> the trance of matter.
>
> ("The Swimmer")

How else, this poem seems implicitly to be asking, can the death of the other be transcended? The emotional distance the father maintained, both when the speaker was a child and as he is dying, prohibits a communion of love between father and daughter in his final days; absent the heart, the father's body still remains as an object the speaker can attend to lovingly with language. She highlights the impersonality of the mechanism of the body: the contents of his catheter bag, the "sucking snap / when his jaws draw back" ("**Death and Morality**"), his skin, eyes, and open mouth, the weight of his ashes in their urn. But she is not crudely literal. With a motif of birthing (used throughout *The Father*), the speaker internalizes his death:

> . . . my father
> moves, hour by hour, head-first,
> toward death, I sense every inch of him moving
> through me toward it, the way each child
> moved, slowly, down through my body . . .
>
> ("The Pulling")

The poems that recall the dead father do not allow the other to remain the other: the speaker absorbs the father into herself. The speaker's breast self-examination prompts recollections of the father's cancer, dying, and death. A live connection between father and daughter prevents her from shaking free of him.

> . . . when I
> lie down and get ready to die,
> prepare to find a sphere hard as a
> wizened pea-seed buried in my breast,
> I can feel myself
> slip into my father
> wholly, deep inside his flesh

as if into a death-canoe
fitted tight to the body.

("The Exam")

For the reader to demand a level of insight beyond what Olds offers here would be to expect pat generalities or religious sentiment. Religion is referred to rarely in *The Father*: in "His Terror," only a ritual act—eating the Eucharist, symbolically, the body of the divine Father—is accounted for, an act drained of spiritual significance. The poem shifts from the father's contact with his minister to the speaker's concern that a cry of pain or terror he has long stifled will break loose. Olds's efforts to plot the father-daughter relationship and the father's death-slide always skirt the safe truism. To expect a more specific account of the speaker's revelations is simply unwarranted. Instead, the poet's fearlessness must be acknowledged.

In Olds's previous works, the speaker's sympathy expands to the past, as the father's emotionally shortchanged boyhood is imagined: "When I love you now, / I like to think I am giving my love / directly to that boy in the fiery room, / as if it could reach him in time" ("**Late Poem to My Father**," *The Gold Cell*). And her awareness of her father's idiosyncrasies stretches into the future, as the speaker recognizes the passing of his traits on to her children: "Sometimes my daughter looks at me with an / amber black look, like my father / about to pass out from disgust . . ." ("**The Sign of Saturn**," *The Dead and the Living*). No reader should be tricked into believing, though, that metaphorically pushing out the father's corpse in the canoe means the speaker is released from him. The plot of this relationship might very well continue as long as Olds writes. The past cannot be neatly confronted, interpreted, and resolved. Some plots resist a tidy closure.

Calvin Bedient (review date 1993)

SOURCE: "Sentencing Eros," in *Salmagundi,* No. 97, Winter, 1993, pp. 169-81.

[*In the following excerpt, Bedient provides a stylistic and thematic analysis of* The Father, *faulting Olds's self-indulgence but praising the force of some of the poems in the volume.*]

Sharon Olds's fourth book of poems, *The Father,* is easily one of the oddest ever published—even, one of the most outrageous. Consider: a sequence of fifty-one poems on the poet's ghoulish, erotic death-watch of her father, who was hospitalized for cancer, and the grieving aftermath. His dying both steps up and makes safe (unrealizable) her lust to be him and to have him: she is Electra, a babe who will suck from his "primary tumor," a mother who will take his dead body inside her womb, a cannibal who will eat his ashes ("There are people who will swallow whole / cars, piece by piece"—"**The Urn**"). "Isn't it something," she asks after his death, "the way I can't get over you, this / long deep, unearned desire / you made when you made

me" ("**Letter to My Father from 40,000 Feet**"). The question is self-lacerating; even so, it does not escape being a boast.

In all this, the poet exhibits shame at neither her libidinal nor aesthetic self-indulgences. In the last poem, she has her dead father enumerate, at long last, what he loves about her, including "your womb, it is a heaven to me, / I lie on its soft hills and gaze up / at its rosy vault." Of course, this woman-hater would do nothing of the kind, but it is the poet's way of healing his insults—intended and accidental—to her self-esteem. The monstrous egotism of her willful disposition of the facts, her bending of the truth for vanity's and therapy's sake, also takes the form, among others, of numerous endings of forced drama and grandiosity. What a drive to omnipotence!

But this alone does not account for the astonishing peculiarity of the book. It must be taken in conjunction with two other things: first, an equally strong appetite for the ugly, the gruesome, a horror not veiled but actually played up in her eroticization of a devastating illness. Regarded only as the pioneering work of bringing death's mucus, smells, colors, spasms, into the "lovely" world of poetry, the volume is remarkable: strong stuff. This hideousness—sensational only to the degree that it is perversely eroticized—is the negative lining of the poet's omnipotent wishes. She can be equal to it; she can not only survive it but love it; no greater love has any woman, any daughter . . .

Olds's imagination, led by passion and not by judgment, trades in extremes, whether of idealization or horror. It is sublime, it would roar like a night train across the wastes of everything her life brings to light. Yes, she's powerful, she knows it, she has won literary fame for it, she banks on it, she exploits it. (In still another poem in which her dead father speaks of her, this man who was indifferent to her says he "liked her exaggerated passions," which means, I take it, that she does). But there is no justice in such an imagination; it either blasts or blesses, in each case like a God. Frequently getting things out of whack, it doesn't notice, or expects indulgence—as when Olds twists her father's protesting "*Last kiss!*" (she has been coming back again and again to give him more) into his virtual command: "I will not let thee go except thou beg for it" ("**Last Words**"). By the evidence she herself supplies, this is so wishful a misunderstanding that she must mean us to see it as pathetic. Yet it's offered not only at face value but with happy insistence and as nothing less than the poem's climax and closure. No intelligent constraint curbs the tone. This poet gives herself nothing but license.

And yet—and here lies the third strand of the book's extreme unlikeliness—the sequence ends in several poems in which this astonishingly indulgent imagination cures itself; suddenly it works through its titanic distortions and comes out in an ordinary-sized world where real justice can be done to the tortured material. After so many resistant poems? Was the poet, then, conducting her self-education in public? Presenting the reader with 85% rant and 15% wisdom, in that order? Evidently.

The underlying issue in the book, as Olds finally acknowledges, is her egregious idealization of the father she also hated and feared. In pumping him up, she made herself small. Jessica Benjamin, in *The Bonds of Love: Psychoanalysis, Feminism, and the Problem of Domination,* is incisive about the predicament: in part a girl wishes to identify with her father, she notes, in order to beat back maternal power. Olds's father's long domestic "drunken / sleep"? "A spell laid on him—by my mother!" (**"Waste Sonata"**). The father, Benjamin says, represents independence, is an example and a trellis for the child's will to individuation and sexual agency, the more so if the mother is perceived as sour on pleasure and the bodily functions, as the mother in this sequence is: the dead father says to the poet, "I never hated your shit—that was / your mother" (**"My Father Speaks to Me from the Dead"**). (No wonder Olds make her father a god of "glistening matter," reversing the usual diagnostics of patriarchy and *female* abjection; no wonder she rejoices to think of herself as once a sperm in her father's scrotum, part of *his* pleasure, or when swimming in the ocean, as the same "seed": "arms held to her sides, . . . spine whipping"— **"The Swimmer"**). Penis envy is just an aspect of this independence envy—or better to call it, in Olds's case, omnipotence-envy:

> If anyone had ever told me
> I would sit by him and he would pull up his nightie
> and I would look at him, at his naked body,
> at the thick bud of his penis in all that
> dark hâir, look at him
> in affection and uneasy wonder
> I would not have believed it. But now I can still
> see the tiny snowflakes, white and
> night-blue, on the cotton of the gown as it
> rises the way we were promised at death it would
>   rise,
> the veils would fall from our eyes, we would know
>   everything.
>
> (**"The Lifting"**)

But if, at home, the father is blotto with alcohol? All the more aloof, like a God. And if he scorns women ("the heel of his hand beating his forehead: Women are so / stupid it destroys your mind"—**"The Want"**)? All the more reason to escape his target range by becoming like or part of him, even if he has to be dead in order to seem pliable and vulnerable enough to be thus joined:

> When the hero dies, they draw away,
> as if the dead need more space—
> I was bent above my father as he curved up,
> and when he died I wanted him to rise up
> into me or me to climb down
> into his body, we were like two baskets
> ripped at the sides which could now be woven
>   together.
>
> (**"Death"**)

Or all the more reason to be possessive: "when the girl realizes she cannot *be* the father, she wants to *have* him" (Benjamin).

It is not until the forty-third poem that Olds first tests her ability to pull the exaggerated father down, and thus gain real independence; but even there she only murmurs: "I guess I am saying / I hate you, too" and ridiculously (is she trying to excuse herself by thinking like a child?) imagines throwing his look-alike (never mind that they are both passengers on a flight) "down to the ground," there to "arm-wrestle him / and win, bang his forearm on the Earth / long after he cries out" (**"Letter to My Father from 40,000 Feet"**). She's her father's daughter even in this, one tough cookie: "he respected my spunk—when they tied me in the chair, that time, / they were tying up someone he respected" (**"Beyond Harm"**).

Then, in the forty-seventh poem, **"I Wanted to be There When My Father Died,"** the first arrestingly honest piece in the book, she says, "I wanted to watch my father die / because I hated him . . . his silence had mauled me . . . I was an Eve he took and pressed back into clay." And in the forty-ninth she asks, "What have I worshipped?" But, characteristically, she cannot see him in perspective even then: he's potentially so powerful that she must waste him by peeing in a pond:

> But now I have met you, coiling bourbon
> genie of my urine, I have read the entrails
> today, I have seen your gorgeous name
> writ on water in waste, and pulled to the
> dam and dashed down over it.
>
> (**"To My Father"**)

Omnipotence still, but now chiefly hers.

It's in the next poem, **"Waste Sonata,"** that Olds finally gets it right: not wanting "To grow old and die, a child, lying to herself," she concedes that her father "was not a shit. He was a man / failing at life." But, in a self-correction that restores, in however damaged a form, the giant mould of her idealization of him, she imagines that she, her mother, sister, and, brother are the "shits that move through him . . . in that purgatory," and can only "almost" love them, and herself. The final snap of release doesn't come until the end of the next and final poem, in the very last nick of the book:

> I am matter,
> your father, I made you, when I say now that I love
>   you
> I mean look down at your hand, move it,
> that action is matter's love, for human
> love go elsewhere.

Brusque and abrupt wisdom—but, at long last, there it is.

Abruptness is Olds's poetic stock-in-trade. Its restless and exciting guise is the impression she gives of improvising at white heat, of translating impulse into narrative and image on the spot, at a ferocious clip. Flatter, more literal, than Sylvia Plath, her work is nonetheless just as excessive, just as nerve-wrackingly exigent, in its way. But unlike Plath's performances, hers depend, paradoxically, on an air almost of amateurishness—roughness and awkwardness are essential to her success. There she is, in the very thick of life, running hard just to stay in place: can she make it? More, can she pull off the poem? Olds hooks the reader by seeming to be a prose writer who has found herself on a verse treadmill that is racing out of control, one who finally pulls fearsome resources out of herself and ends with a bang.

She may throw out similes that are dull, inconsequent, or unconvincing (for example, her father passing through her as the universe passes through God "like a napkin in a ring"—**"The Pulling'**). Or she may get off track in the middle of a poem, as if unaware of where the track is, or as if being "independent" (witness **"Last Acts"** and **"The Transformed One"**). Her syntax may be sloppy at times: "Whoever has / turned away from us, or could not / look at us, just the pressure of their weight feels like a blessing." But none of this does insuperable damage, because a certain impetus is the star, a movement, a hunger that instantly slides off everything, over the quicksilver spill of a comma-splice, towards something else, something maybe better. The comma-splices keep narrative exposition from flagging, or convey hasting feeling or a literal rush (as here in the terrific poem **"The Race"**). But Olds also seems simply addicted to them; they're part of the rhythm of her drive, her nerves.

What her performed impetus cannot save are moments of imaginative forcing. Most of these are in the interest of either her father's or her own grandiosity. Recall the lines on his lifted gown as nothing less than the apocalyptic veil that will (so it's promised) fall from our eyes, so that we may know everything: an ending that is like concluding a little song the way Beethoven concludes a symphony, the religious sentiment of revelation absurdly out of proportion to the sight of a man's penis—even a father's—and the tone of sanctity the wine in a cup of self abasement.

Improvisation as exigency, ecstasy, anxiety, rage, grief—Olds turned it into triumphs again and again in *The Dead and the Living* and *The Gold Cell*, but here it groans and wobbles, its wheels wildly out of alliance. There are even a few poems of stunning badness (e.g. **"Death and Murder,"** which senselessly and sensationally compares treating an ill person to what murderers do to one, then glorifies the act of murder as "kneeling on the bank, scooping up the supple clay"—a fantasy of omnipotent creation). The risk of a sequence book is that poems will be included because they fit, or seem to, and not because they have merit. Still, there are a few pieces of no less stunning power: **"The Race," "The Feelings,"** and **"I Wanted to be There When My Father Died,"** as well as several others that seem better than jerry-built, or forced out for the sake of the sequence, among them **"The Want," "His Smell,"** and **"When the Dead Ask My Father About Me."** Most of the work, however, is neither good nor wretched; it wavers between the plausibly and the transparently self-indulgent, while communicating some, if not all, of the poet's familiar, notoriously pungent force.

Louise Glück   (essay date 1994)

SOURCE: "The Forbidden," in *Proofs and Theories: Essays on Poetry,* The Ecco Press, 1994, pp. 53-63.

[*Glück is an American poet, critic, and educator. In the following excerpt, she faults the poems in* The Father *for being repetitive.*]

Sharon Olds is a poet of considerable achievement and a wholesome distaste for that most depressing of strategies, the obligatory elevation of the quotidian via mythic analogy. Olds' technique, her fascination with the extreme physical, the unsayable reality, makes a case for her presence here, and *The Father* seems, atmospherically, to draw on or suggest taboos it doesn't actually investigate. Olds has an astonishing gift for that part of the act of writing which corresponds to the hunting/gathering phase, or, to put it another way, that part which is generative: many of the poems in *The Father* read as improvisations around a single word or cluster of words, and their resourcefulness, Olds' sustained scrutiny and fastidious notation of detail, amazes. This method, which characterizes nearly every individual poem in the collection, characterizes the book as well, as though [William Carlos] Williams' dictum regarding things had been adapted to an emotional agenda. If the book fails, as it does for me, it does so in part because the poems grow tedious: Williams' scrutiny was democratic, or perhaps, more properly, an application of the scientific method: it was a point of honor to have no bias regarding outcome. This is Williams' vitality. But Olds uses her genius for observation to make, repeatedly, the same points, to reach the same epiphanies; the energy and diversity of detail play out as stasis. The principal figures here, the speaker and her dying father, change very little; the scenes between them change very little. While we might not expect change of a dying man (his service, to the book, might be a fixity which would permit the speaker greater range in attitude and gesture as well as feeling, since response is no longer an issue), we do expect some fluidity within the speaker. What we find instead is a recalcitrant girlishness; the voice is, here, as fixed as the father, pinned to a pre-adolescent and faintly coy obsession. To some extent the drama here, father and daughter, would seem to dictate this, and the poems do recognize the problem, though their solution is not to abandon the format but to strain it: periodically, the speaker envisions the father as her child, as a fetus inside her, and so on. What the poems do not do is move either forward or backward, backward to an earlier phase of childhood, the perspectives of which might illuminate the current confrontation, or (convincingly) forward. . . .

The Father suffers from an insufficiency of will or direction; the poems are nearly all better in their parts than as wholes, as is the collection. The aimlessness of the book itself suggests the single disadvantage of Olds' impressive facility: these poems read as great talent with, at the moment, nowhere to go.

Alicia Ostriker   (essay date 1995)

SOURCE: "I Am (Not) This: Erotic Discourse in Bishop, Olds, and Stevens," in *The Wallace Stevens Journal,* Vol. 19, No. 2, Fall, 1995, pp. 234-54.

[*Ostriker is an American poet, critic, editor, and educator. In the following excerpt from a comparative essay on Olds, Elizabeth Bishop, and Wallace Stevens, she examines Olds's treatment of the theme of Eros, or erotic love. Ostriker concludes that although there are similarities between Bishop's and Olds's concepts of Eros, Bishop successfully addresses this theme and Olds does not.*]

I would like to talk about erotic discourse in poetry in its widest and most archaic sense, beginning with the proposal that what Adrienne Rich today calls "The drive / to connect[,] The dream of a common language" ("Origins and History of Consciousness") has for millennia been understood and experienced as the body and soul's desire, as simultaneously natural and divine, and as source of intense pleasure, intense pain. As in the Song of Songs: "Let him kiss me with the kisses of his mouth, for thy love is better than wine. . . . Let my beloved come into his garden and taste his pleasant fruits" (1:2; 4:16). Or Sappho: "Mother, I can't finish my weaving. You may blame Aphrodite, soft as she is, she has almost killed me with love for that boy" (frag. 135). Or Catullus, inventing introspection and passionate ambivalence in the same moment: "I hate and love. I don't know how, but I feel it, and it is excruciating" (no. 85; my translation). Or Andrew Marvell, at the close of "To His Coy Mistress": "Let us roll all our strength, and all / Our sweetness up into one ball, / And tear our pleasures with rough strife / Thorough the iron gates of life. / Thus, though we cannot make our sun / Stand still, yet we will make him run." In and from the poetry of the ages, I would stress the idea of connection, the impulse to connect, to perceive unities across the conventional boundaries of separation, as always implicitly erotic, always a form of making love.

Making love. Poetry. An odd combination, some will think. For in postmodern, media-drenched America, eros equals pornography, both for its advocates and its attackers. Pornography, or perhaps possession, a consumer product. Many poets, and almost all critics, avoid it (except in the special category of AIDS writing, where eros equals mortality). What most contemporary critics seem to want is less body and less feeling in poetry. Less sensuousness. Less desire—these topics are so sticky, so embarrassing, so impolite, so troublesome—can't we, please, have a poetry that's *clean,* with the messy and horrifying fluids and passions scrubbed off it?

Not that academic disapproval of eros is new. It is as old as the discontents of civilization and the need to subdue desire in the name of an efficient state. Freud properly observed that libido is precisely what socialization represses. Yeats rhymes entertainingly on the scandalousness of poets to pedantss: "Lord, what would they say / Did their Catullus walk that way?" ("The Scholars"). . . .

Modernist poetics, insofar as it pursues the ideal impersonality recommended by T. S. Eliot or bows to Pound's distaste for "emotional slither," constitutes perhaps an apex of anerotic sublimation—however undermined by the practice of poets such as Frost and Williams. It is surely not coincidental that of the major women modernists, the only one to be respectfully canonized was the sexually respectable Marianne Moore, while the deviantly sexual H. D., Loy, and Stein—not to mention conventionally amorous lyricists like Millay—remain outside that particular pale. His impassioned and explicit exploration of the erotic is probably one of the many causes that keep Robinson Jeffers in critical limbo, a potential embarrassment. In our own time, as women poets occupy the terrain of eros in massive numbers, uttering both heterosexual and lesbian desire and drawing radical connections between love of bodies and love as a potential principle for the body politic, it is not surprising to find a backlash of critical opinion emphatically preferring the abstract to the sensuous, the cerebral to the emotional. In part for this reason, the austere poetry of Elizabeth Bishop is universally praised, and the physically and sexually charged poetry of Sharon Olds commonly attacked. At the same time, while critical discussion of Wallace Stevens has until very recently avoided or evaded the issue of the erotic in his poetry, it is interesting to note that several recent volumes of Stevens criticism address precisely—or almost precisely—this issue.

In the following triangulated discussion of Bishop, Olds, and Stevens, I will cite at some length the critic Vernon Shetley, who concludes his chapter on Elizabeth Bishop in *After the Death of Poetry* by describing Sharon Olds as a representative mainstream poet who fails to live up to the Bishop tradition. I will argue first that Shetley's view of Bishop is skewed toward the erasure of eros in her poetry; next that his dismissal of Olds derives from a horror of eros in hers; and third, I will suggest that notwithstanding apparently polar differences between Bishop and Olds, including where they locate themselves on a continuum of erotic desire and dread, the two poets share an understanding of what eros *is*. Finally, I will propose a tentative view of erotic discourse in Stevens that would locate him elsewhere. . . .

Nobody would say Sharon Olds disguises the erotic in her poems. The erotic in her work is ubiquitous, joining bodies of flesh, generations, natural cycles of procreation and decay, human to animal, animal to vegetable, male to female, profane to sacred, life to art, sex to food to writing. The title poem of Olds's first book, *Satan Says,* announces the program of her art. Trapped inside an ornamental box she is trying to "write [her] way out of"—her childhood, her body, a sentimentalized tradition ornamented by tacky shepherds—she is tempted by Satan to escape by saying things like "fuck," "shit," and cursing her parents; she obeys, but as the lid of the box opens and she is about to exit into Satan's mouth, she remembers, "I loved / them, too," and the lid closes. The poet will remain locked in the box that is now her coffin, but she hardly cares, as freedom to articulate rebellious hate precipitates "the suddenly discovered knowledge of love."

Olds chooses to be a poet ambivalently but firmly attached to parents. Several other poems about writing in this first volume announce corollary facets of her agenda. In **"Nurse Whitman,"** Whitman's and Olds's love of men is at once compassionate and sexual, embodied and imagined, while a fusion of present and past joins a fusion of genders in an act of writing that is also an act of conception and birthing:

> We lean down, our pointed breasts
> heavy as plummets with fresh spermy milk—
> we conceive, Walt, with the men we love, thus, now,
> we bring to fruit.

In **"The Language of the Brag,"** a poem that follows several poems describing the intensely absorbed animal life of **"Young Mothers,"** Olds asserts the act of childbirth as a "heroism" equivalent to phallic power ("I have wanted excellence in the knife-throw . . . the haft slowly and heavily vibrating like the cock") and to the creation of poems. Having lain down and passed blood, feces, water, and a new person covered with "language of blood like praise all over the body" into the world,

> I have done what you wanted to do, Walt Whitman,
> Allen Ginsberg, I have done this thing,
> I and the other women this exceptional
> act with the exceptional heroic body,
> this giving birth, this glistening verb,
> and I am putting my proud American boast
> right here with the others.

That the poems are intended to be both transgressive and sacred is made clear. **"Station"** describes the poet's husband, left to mind the children while she writes, gazing at her with "the poems / heavy as poached game hanging from my hands." **"Prayer,"** the final poem in *Satan Says,* defines "the central meanings" through linked images of copulation and childbirth, closing with a Whitmanlike vow: "let me not forget: / each action, each word / taking its beginning from these."

Where Bishop writes as a voice of loneliness, fearing and desiring connection, the self in Olds is never represented in isolation but always in relation, penetrated and penetrating, glued by memory and gaze to others. She scandalously eroticizes the bodies of children and parents, genitals and all, describes the sex act with explicit attention to a variety of orifices, is obsessed with the foodlike and procreative possibilities of human bodies, loves images of animals, soil, blood and eggs, represents her sexually greedy body as a tiger's, an anteater's, that which "takes him in as anyone in summer will / open their throat to the hose held up / hot on the edge of the sandlot," and insists "I am this, *this*" (*The Gold Cell*). Cross-gendered imagery recurs through her work, as she invokes **"My Father's Breasts"** (*The Dead and the Living*) or speculates that her mother made her deliberately in the image of the powerful father: "I feel her looking down into me the way the / maker of a sword gazes at his face in the / steel of the blade" (*The Gold Cell*). Sperm is recurrently described as milk, sexual

gratification as eating and drinking, sex as power: "The center of your body / will tear open, as a woman will rip the / seam of her skirt so she can run," she tells her daughter (*The Dead and the Living*). Olds's sacralizing of the sexual and procreative body is sometimes explicit, sometimes textually hinted, as when the daughter's maturing body is described as rising bread in a way that half represents the girl as Christ (**"Bread,"** *The Dead and the Living*).

Olds's critics complain at times that she sensationalizes the dysfunction of her natal family—cold, alcoholic grandfather and father, searingly clinging anorexic mother—overlooking the complication of the daughter's insistently expressed desire for, worship of, and identification with the father's body, which persists throughout her recent volume about his dying and death. The sensuous profusion in Olds stands in stark contrast to the austerity of a writer such as Bishop. Some readers conclude that such rich surfaces cannot possibly coexist with depth. Yet there may be important unsaid, unsayable, matter in Olds just as there is in Bishop. Consider **"Sex Without Love,"** the single Olds poem Shetley discusses, which he claims uses metaphor merely ornamentally

> How do they do it, the ones who make love
> without love? Beautiful as dancers,
> gliding over each other like ice-skaters
> over the ice, fingers hooked
> inside each other's bodies, faces
> red as steak, wine, wet as the
> children at birth whose mothers are going to
> give them away. How do they come to the
> come to the come to the God come to the
> still waters, and not love
> the one who came there with them, light
> rising slowly as steam off their joined
> skin? These are the true religious,
> the purists, the pros, the ones who will not
> accept a false Messiah, love the
> priest instead of the God. They do not
> mistake the lover for their own pleasure,
> they are like great runners: they know they are alone
> with the road surface, the cold, the wind,
> the fit of their shoes, their over-all cardio-
> vascular health—just factors, like the partner
> in the bed, and not the truth, which is the
> single body alone in the universe
> against its own best time.
>
> (*The Dead and the Living*)

The poem's opening "How do they do it?" may be construed as wondering either about technique or about morality. The question lets us know that the speaker *doesn't* do it, but not whether she envies or deplores. The following swift succession of similes implies a slippage from admiration—what we might feel if our ideas of sex without love came from watching, say, James Bond movies—to something closer to horror or pain. Sex without love is attractive in the style of art or sport, athletically and socially attractive, then it is a bit like the hanging carcasses in a Francis Bacon painting, then it parallels food, then for a brief instant it shockingly resembles the most shameful abandonment of the helpless. Significantly, Olds does not dwell on this instant, although in another poem (**"The Abandoned Newborn,"**) her topic is the condition of an infant left wrapped in plastic in a dumpster. The simile nonetheless jars and reverberates, for the mother-infant image simultaneously connotes and negates the vulnerable and utterly satisfied infantile eroticism that we strive to retrieve in adult sexuality (several other Olds poems also make this connection). The linebreak reinforces the poignance of expectation dashed, the full stop signals a dead end along one line of thinking. At the edge of the image, or our consciousness of it, especially if we happen to be mothers ourselves, might be the fact that *all* mothers (including the mother of Jesus, who was Love) give their babies away, if not sooner then later. The pain of this abandonment is not accidentally but systematically a corollary of a culture in which sexual pleasure is divided from procreation, and motherhood is sentimentally honored but institutionally disempowered and without status. It is, in other words, a real *effect* of "sex without love." Shetley's comment on this simile calls it "entirely gratuitous; since babies whose mothers are going to give them away are exactly as wet, no more and no less, as babies whose mothers are going to keep them, this elaboration serves no purpose but to remind us that sex without love may lead to unwanted pregnancy, a message better suited to public service announcements than poetry." Both tone and content of a sentence like this suggest to me a reader deeply out of touch with his topic.

Shetley fails to comment on lines 8-13, in which the speaker cannot quite articulate what sex *with* love is. But this is the core of the poem. "Come to the come to the God" works doubly. It stumbles over the inexpressible and exclaims over its own inarticulateness, much as Bishop stumbles and exclaims in "One Art." It also half implies that what love "comes" to is, precisely, God. "Still waters" reinforces and deepens this implication while echoing and redeeming the wetness of sexuality and of the newborn. Each a pool from which the other drinks, we taste a shared water of life. Sex, the speaker suggests, brings us to the pastoral oasis of the Twenty-third Psalm, our animal innocence, our divine protection. It restores our souls. Loving whoever comes to such a space with us would itself be natural. Sex, birth, nature, innocence, God, and a revisionary re-reading of scripture are all involved here. The image of light rising like steam from the lovers' "joined skin" imaginatively turns the fact of perspiration into a signal of the holy. The experience lies, however, outside the poem's discourse: the poem offers a silence that the reader must fill in.

The remainder of the poem appears to repudiate or transcend the oasis experience. Loveless lovers know better, we are told: they don't make the mistake of substituting the priest (the sexual partner) for the god (the pleasure). The true religion of eros is strenuously self-absorbed; the extended final metaphor of sex as running against one's own best time (one's own best orgasm) insists on our absolute isolation.

Shetley's comment on Olds's **"Sex Without Love"** calls its metaphors "descriptive rather than cognitive." Clearly they have not made *him* think; the assumption that women who write about sex must be brainless is a very old one, which I have documented elsewhere. His commentary concludes as follows:

> But ultimately, the poem's challenge to conventional values, both sexual and poetic, is recontained through the distance and isolation in which the poem envelops these in some sense unimaginable persons. The poet professes to admire these exemplars of lucidity. . . . But ultimately, [she] consigns them to their aloneness, professing her incomprehension; she . . . prefers to remain within the emotive comfort of false beliefs. By the poem's end, its initial challenge to conventional values of emotional warmth and mutuality has been entirely defused.

This reading seems willfully incorrect in several respects as well as tautological. Olds's "in some sense unimaginable persons" certainly exist, and sometimes might be any of us; the poet initially professes incomprehension but in the end undertakes to explain them rather convincingly. More interesting is that the sharp, best-case understanding of the loveless lovers whom she continues to call "they" means the speaker simultaneously is and is not like them. It might seem that her empathy overrides and invades their loneliness, in order to understand their experience from within. Or is it rather that their perfect and superior loneliness rebukes and explodes her empathy? Two kinds of lovers, two concepts of God, two ontologies of self, constructed as "undecidable alternatives" not unlike those we admire in Bishop, govern this poem. And although it is an atypical poem for Olds because it does not use the first-person singular, it is typical in its capacity to represent sexuality as both desirable and frightening.

In the final portion of this essay I wish to ask two questions. What sort of erotic discourse do Bishop and Olds share? And can Wallace Stevens be seen as belonging to the same general discourse, or must he be otherwise located? The first question can be answered briefly on the basis of my readings. Bishop mostly evades, Olds mostly asserts erotic connection—but for both, the erotic is a power preceding and defining the self; for both, it exists at the liminal border between language and the unsayable; for both, it abuts on a realm we may call spiritual. Technically, the metaphors of both poets enact the erotic. Olds's do so, as I hope I have shown, first of all by their excess, which is mimetic of the procreativity Olds identifies with eroticism; second by requiring us constantly to register interplays of likeness and difference across categories, and in particular by repeatedly collapsing the categories of the human, the natural, the divine, and the artistic while reminding us of their conventional separation. To say "I am this," and mean the body, is in Olds to claim complete connection with the world. Bishop's metaphoric technique works differently and so subtly that one of her most characteristic and unique strategies has scarcely been noticed. From the beginning to the end of her work, Bishop has a habit of letting metaphor attribute life and motivation to the inorganic, humanity to the inhuman.

Christine Stenstrom   (review date 1996)

SOURCE: A review of *The Wellspring,* in *Library Journal,* Vol. 121, No. 1, January, 1996, p. 104.

[*In the following review, Stenstrom favorably assesses* The Wellspring.]

In this her fifth collection [***The Wellspring***], award-winning Olds surveys her life from conception to middle age with the laserlike attention to emotional and physical detail that is her hallmark. The book's first two sections focus on childhood and adolescence; the self-portrait Olds paints is of a voracious and egocentric child who thirsts for attention and is sensually attuned to all she experiences. Her recollections of her father's casual cruelties (he composed a humiliating tongue twister for his lisping daughter to recite at Sunday breakfast), though chilling, are dispassionately recounted. The second two sections are devoted to parenthood and conjugal love. Olds's poems about her children throb with love and pathos, and her paeans to an emotionally and physically satisfying marriage are among the book's most rewarding poems. In language that is taut, clear-sighted, and frank, Olds writes powerfully of life's most elemental experiences: birth, love, and death.

Laura E. Tanner   (essay date 1996)

SOURCE: "Death-Watch: Terminal Illness and the Gaze in Sharon Olds's *The Father,*" in *Mosaic,* Vol. 29, No. 1, March, 1996, pp. 103-21.

[*Tanner is the author of* Intimate Violence: Reading Rape and Torture in Twentieth-Century Fiction. *In the following essay, she applies the concept of the gaze in film and literary theory to Olds's description of her terminally ill father in* The Father.]

The publication of Laura Mulvey's "Visual Pleasure and Narrative Cinema" in 1978 [*Screen,* Vol. 16, No. 3] initiated a dialogue about the function of the "gaze" that has subsequently moved beyond the boundaries of film theory. Mulvey's discussion of scopophilic viewing in the cinema identified a voyeuristic dynamic in which the erotic identity of the viewing subject is clearly separated from the object (usually a woman) on the screen; the viewer derives pleasure from objectifying the screen persona and subjecting that persona to the power of the controlling gaze. The success of film criticism in denaturalizing the act of looking in the cinema—i.e., exposing the way in which the viewer's gaze may be constructed to enforce hidden assumptions or authorize conclusions that appear "natural"—has led in turn to the need for unveiling the way that the gaze is constructed in other forums and the need for defining the power dynamics that result from that construction.

In relying heavily upon psychoanalytic models that stress viewing as a form of visual pleasure, however, film theorists and adaptive critics following in their wake—in literary theory, gender studies and cultural studies—have paid little attention to the consequences of a gaze that is painful or uncomfortable, a gaze that moves away from a lingering focus on the seductive fetish to a flitting confrontation with disease and death. The way in which we as individuals and as a culture look at people with terminal illness raises questions about how the act of seeing can serve to naturalize assumptions about the dying body and the embodied subject framed by that body. When the object of the gaze changes from an attractive female form that the viewer objectifies or from a screen protagonist with whom the viewer identifies to the wasting body of a terminally ill patient, the structures of looking that Mulvey located within a dynamic of visual pleasure demand to be revised. The act of looking at a person with terminal illness may perpetuate the dynamics of objectification that Mulvey associated with the fetishization of women in the cinema; it may, also, however, upset the very distinction between subject and object to allow for the possibility of a gaze that dissolves the distance between the two.

This essay attempts to understand the intimacy of the gaze not as a means of negotiating sexual difference but as a way of establishing connection between a healthy subject and a person with terminal illness. The first section of the essay lays the theoretical groundwork for my investigation; using the work of theorists such as Mulvey, Foucault and Kristeva, I will explore the way that the gaze constructs the experience of dying: both for the terminally ill patient who perceives the self as an object of the gaze and for the watcher who negotiates the idea of death through the visual apprehension of a dying body. The next section of the essay expands this dialogue of critical voices through an analysis of Sharon Olds's ***The Father*** (1992), a volume of contemporary American poetry that serves to raise important theoretical questions about how the dynamics of watching are implicated in the construction of a relationship between the dying body and the embodied subject. In this volume, which focuses on the slow process of her father's death from cancer, Olds offers an unflinching exploration of what it means to turn the gaze toward the dying body. Opening with a description of watching—"I would be there all day, / watch him nap, / be there when he woke, sit with him / until the day ended" (**"The Waiting"**)—the volume continues by probing the way that looking and being looked at not only reflect but constitute identity. ***The Father,*** I will argue, offers a response to theories of the gaze that focus exclusively on eroticized and sadistic power dynamics; Olds presents not only an unflinching investigation of the gaze's dehumanizing power but a model for balancing the uneven distribution of power that marks the projection of the healthy gaze onto the diseased body.

Michael Foucault describes his study of modern medicine, *The Birth of the Clinic* (1973), as a book "about the act of seeing, the gaze." Foucault's volume begins to raise questions about how the gaze is constructed in medicine, about the forces that dictate what a doctor sees and does not see when he looks at a patient. In his exploration of these questions, Foucault defines a dichotomization of patient and disease that underlies much of modern medicine:

> Paradoxically, in relation to that which he is suffering from, the patient is only an external fact; the medical reading must take him into account only to place him in parenthesis. Of course, the doctor must know "the internal structure of our bodies"; but only in order to subtract it, and to free to the doctor's gaze "the nature and combination of symptoms, crises, and other circumstances that accompany diseases." It is not the pathological that functions, in relation to life, as a *counter-nature,* but the patient in relation to the disease itself. . . . Hence the strange character of the medical gaze. . . . It is directed upon that which is visible in the disease—but on the basis of the patient, who hides this visible element even as he shows it. . . .

In order to render disease visible, the medical gaze must factor out the person with illness; seeing the patient as an embodied subject emerges as not only inconsequential but counterproductive. In the examining room, the person with illness becomes the white space in the picture, the absence which allows the illness to be seen.

Because the medical gaze sees disease only by blocking out the human subject whose body bears the mark of illness, illness becomes increasingly visible as it becomes increasingly incontestable. The person with terminal illness may thus feel totally abandoned, for the medical gaze, as Foucault observes, sees its logical extension in the absolute obliteration of the person by the disease, in death. In "The Patient Examines the Doctor" [*Intoxicated by My Illness,* 1972], an eloquent essay describing his experience with an untreatable cancer, Anatole Broyard charts the effect of such a gaze on its object: "There is the way a doctor looks at you. One doctor I saw had a trick way of almost crossing his eyes, so he seemed to be peering warmly, humanistically, into my eyes, but he wasn't seeing me at all. He was looking without looking." Broyard's desire to be "seen" by his doctor emerges as more than a plea for "humanistic" intention or psychological affirmation; it also suggests a struggle to sustain life in the face of death. Broyard seeks a physician willing to look hard enough at him to reclaim him from the critical illness that threatens to obscure his subjective presence: "If he could gaze directly at the patient, the doctor's work would be more gratifying. Why bother with sick people, why try to save them, if they're not worth acknowledging? When a doctor refuses to acknowledge a patient, he is, in effect, abandoning him to his illness." The "direct" gaze, in this scenario, becomes a means of reversing the process of the disease, of enacting the turn through which the person overwhelms the disease within and not vice versa.

Vision always accesses the subject through the body, and the destructive dynamics of the gaze often result from a look that reduces an embodied presence to an objectified body. When a body bears the visible marks of illness—the lesions that often accompany AIDS, the uncontrollable muscle spasms of Parkinson's disease, the gaunt, hollowed face of a person dying from cancer—its function as a multiple sign system is often ignored in favor of an interpretation that renders itself as concrete vision. Because the marks of critical illness literally overwhelm the features of the person with disease, the gaze often locates the subject in a body that seems to announce its identity as the process of its own destruction. The medical gaze, then, merely extends and exaggerates a dynamics of looking that forces the person with terminal illness to see the self rendered visible only as its impending absence.

Visual confrontation with a dying body, however, also exaggerates and problematizes the dynamics of looking for the healthy viewer. The threat that such a body poses to the gaze can be framed, in Julia Kristeva's terms, as the threat of the abject, of "death infecting life." Materiality and corporeality emerge in Kristeva's work as necessary conditions of subjectivity which the subject must nonetheless disavow in order to preserve the illusion of stability, unity, wholeness. Although Kristeva defines the corpse as "the utmost of abjection" [*The Powers of Horror,* 1982], the body of the person with terminal illness may function as even more of a threat; such a person often exhibits the bodily signs of impending death while yet resisting the inanimate coldness that helps us to classify the corpse as Other.

Mainstream film, according to Mulvey, attempts to allay the fear of castration by portraying "a hermetically sealed world which unwinds magically, indifferent to the presence of the audience, producing for them a sense of separation and playing on their voyeuristic phantasy." To look at a person with terminal illness—even through the frame of literary or visual representation—often challenges such a sense of separation. The terminally ill body assaults the healthy gaze by threatening to unveil without fetishistic mediation the viewing subject's vulnerability, a vulnerability that stems from mortality itself.

The "healthy" gaze—in order to maintain "a sense of separation," in Mulvey's words, or what Sander Gilman describes as the need for distance from the ill—may attempt to move itself outside the expanding parameters of the sick body by establishing a way of viewing that destroys the link between viewer and viewed. Whereas the fear of castration can be handled by covering up the "missing parts" that suggest sexual difference, the person with terminal illness resists such easy manipulation, and indeed seems to move over his or her boundaries into the viewing subject's own. Moreover, because in this case the object of the gaze announces not only difference but sameness, the viewer's recognition of a shared mortality lends power to the very threat that the healthy gaze would dispel. Abjection, Kristeva concludes, "is above all a revolt of the person against an external menace from which one wants to keep oneself at a distance, but of which one has the impression that it is not only an external menace but that it may menace us from inside. So it is a desire for separation, for becoming autonomous . . ." [Quoted in Kelly Oliver's *Reading Kristeva,* 1993]. The diseased body frequently refuses to maintain the distance that marks separation between subjects; when the body is overwhelmed by illness, it begins to swell, ooze, sweat and bleed until it intrudes upon public space. The healthy gaze that risks intimacy with the person with disease thus sacrifices the seeming mastery of distance.

Within Kristeva's theory of the abject, erotic pleasure emerges as a symbolic response to the uncontainable threat of mortality. Defining the erotic not merely as a response to the threat of castration but as an attempt to sustain life itself in the face of death, Kristeva defines the eroticization of abjection as "an attempt at stopping the hemorrhage: a threshold before death, a halt or a respite." Kristeva's formulation of the relationship between the erotic and the abject lays the groundwork for an interrogation of the gaze that reverses the tendency in feminist film criticism to privilege the sexual aspect of looking. Although critics like Mulvey may cite the fear of castration as the source of the look, for example, they shy away from issues of mortality to focus primarily on the erotic dynamics of the gaze.

In *Over Her Dead Body: Death, Femininity and the Aesthetic,* Elisabeth Bronfren addresses the limitations of such gendered notions of castration:

> What is put under erasure by the gendered concept of castration is the other, so often non-read theme of death, forbidden maybe because far less conducive to efforts of stable self-fashioning than notions of sexual difference. To see the phallus as secondary to the scar of the navel means acknowledging that notions of domination and inferiority based on gender difference are also secondary to a more global and non-individuated disempowerment before death.

Although Bronfren's discussion of "a notion of anxiety not based on sexual difference" is not formulated in terms of the gaze, her Freudian revisions suggest new ways of thinking about the dynamics of looking at a person close to death. Thus, focusing on Olds's *The Father,* I now wish to explore the way that the erotic dynamics of the gaze are complicated by the act of looking at a person with terminal illness, and the way that such looking becomes a means of negotiating identity in the face of death. Rather than attempting to refute or replace gendered notions of the gaze based on theories of sexual difference, my argument attempts to switch the reader's frame of vision in a way that makes it possible not only to recognize the theme of death which Bronfren describes as under erasure but also to see what is at stake in the act of seeing that constitutes the death-watch.

Calvin Bedient opens his review essay of *The Father* with words that express genuine shock:

> Sharon Olds's fourth book of poems, *The Father,* is easily one of the oddest ever published—even, one of the most outrageous. Consider: a sequence of fifty-one poems on the poet's ghoulish, erotic death-watch of her father, who was hospitalized for cancer, and the grieving aftermath. His dying both steps up and makes safe

> (unrealizable) her lust to be him and to have him: she is Electra, a babe who will suck from his "primary tumor". . .

Bedient's response to what he describes as Olds's "eroticization of a devastating illness" leads him on a critical quest to "account for the astonishing peculiarity of the book." That quest is framed in psychoanalytic terms; he locates the source of the poems' "strong appetite for the ugly, the gruesome" in what he sees as the underlying issue in the collection: Olds's final acknowledgment of "her egregious idealization of the father she also hated and feared." Invoking Jessica Benjamin's *The Bonds of Love,* Bedient usefully unveils some of the complex psychological dynamics that underlie the speaker's relationship with her father in this sequence of poems. Yet in tracing the poet's "eroticization" of her father's illness back to Olds's desire for individuation and sexual agency, Bedient relegates that illness to symptom and masks its urgent presence in the poems he discusses.

The Father's revelation of the diseased and dying body— perhaps as much as any metaphorical eroticization of the relationship between father and daughter—constitutes a violation of the cultural codes through which contemporary Western civilization renders the terminally ill body visible. If one method of containing the threat of the abject is to eroticize it, Bedient's critique of Olds's poetry can be understood in just that way. Concentrating on Olds's "outrageous" eroticism, he obliterates the embodied presence of Olds's dying father and focuses instead on the symbolic function that the father serves in the daughter's construction of sexual identity. As Olds's speaker watches her father's body deteriorate from cancer and witnesses his death, the material urgency of his embodied presence erupts again and again in the text; in glossing over the volume's representation of that bodily eruption and the poet's attempt to come to terms with her own role as spectator of it, Bedient ignores the truly "outrageous" and radical aspects of Olds's poetry.

In *The Father,* erotic metaphors serve not as "a respite" from the threat of death but as acknowledgment of the intimate consequences of looking upon her father's dying. **"My Father's Eyes"** compares the exchange of looks between Olds and her father to "the sudden flash / of sex that jumps between two people." If Freud is correct in aligning sexuality with the life force and against death, this volume of poems represents Olds's attempt to use the gaze as a means of dissolving boundaries rather than maintaining distance, as a way of claiming her father's embodied presence rather than reducing him to an objectified absence. In the process of the death-watch that she both enacts and critiques in these poems, Olds finds herself pulled across the border of her father's dying body, "turning . . . around his death" (**"The Glass"**). The awkward and sometimes forced intimacy reflected in the erotic overtones of Olds's poems, then, emerges at least in part from the dynamics of a death-watch that blurs the boundaries between seer and seen, subject and object, eye and body.

In the opening poem of the collection, **"The Waiting,"** Olds immediately testifies to the objectifying power of the look. When she descends from the guest room in her father's house each morning, the speaker (whom I will take the license of referring to throughout my argument simply as "Olds") is confronted with the motionless body of her father:

> . . . . . By then, he knew he was dying,
> he seemed to approach it as a job to be done
> which he knew how to do. He got up early
> for the graveyard shift. When he heard me coming
>   down the
> hall he would not turn—he had
> a way of holding still to be looked at,
> as if a piece of sculpture could sense
> the gaze which was running over it—
> he would wait with that burnished, looked-at look
>   until
> the hem of my nightgown came into view,
> then slew his eyes up at me, without
> moving his head, and wait, the kiss
> came to him, he did not go to it.

In this rendering, Olds's father displays himself for the gaze that he is incapable of resisting; she images him as an artifact that absorbs the look but does not return it. Indeed, the "job" of dying that the father undertakes seems to involve a kind of collapse into matter, an abdication of agency that allows only the negative expression of subjectivity.

Unlike the sculpture to which he is compared, however, Olds's father can sense the gaze that runs over him, can *know* the look that renders him material. This knowledge of his own objectification emerges as one of the few signs of the father's subjective presence; the look as gaze is rewritten as the "burnished, looked-at look" not emanating from but inscribed on the father's body. Denied both the agency of the gaze and the inviolability of the object, Olds's father is caught between the definition of himself as subject and as diseased body.

Critical illness exaggerates the vexed dynamics of embodied subjectivity by placing the person with disease under the absolute tyranny of a body at the very moment when that body seems least that person's own. In *The Body in Pain* (1985), Elaine Scarry unveils the way in which extreme pain pins the suffering subject to a body that overwhelms the outer world and the inner self until that "increasingly palpable" body appears to subsume all else. When disease acts on the human body, it assaults not only organs and tissue but the subject's very notion of agency. Bound to a body that may shrink, swell, bleed and ooze but that necessarily moves toward self-destruction, the person with terminal illness may be forced to renegotiate the construction of the self in a manner that accounts both for the body's tyranny over the subject—its essential and undeniable connection to the suffering self—and for the subject's absolute alienation from a diseased body that may be as unfamiliar as the body of a stranger.

In Olds's collection, this alienation emerges in the form of the father's seeming complicity in his own objectifi-

cation. While Olds herself becomes the real subject of the poem, her father emerges only as the "something someone has made." As his daughter's look reduces him to the material status of a body that moves steadily toward death, the father's own gaze begins to collapse into the material. Rather than registering subjective presence, the father's sidelong look—when he "slew his eyes up at me, without / moving his head"—registers the dissolution of subjectivity and its replacement with a fully conscious yet objectified self.

This collapse of vision into vacant material presence denies Olds's father the power of the gaze; her look confirms—rather than resists—the process of his objectification. In beginning *The Father* with this poem, Olds not only calls attention to the significance of the gaze as a force in constructing the person with terminal illness, but also suggests the way in which her status as artist as well as observer exaggerates her role in turning subject into artifact, human into matter. In the poems that follow, Olds attempts to negotiate a way of looking at her father that is not also a perpetuation of the objectifying dynamics of the gaze.

Instead of redirecting the look away from her father's body, Olds attempts to unsettle the strict definition of subject and object within the dynamics of vision. Although Olds continues to look upon her father's dying body, in later poems of the volume her gaze comes to serve as an extension rather than a refutation of his subjective presence. As such, it begins to realize the kind of healing gaze that Broyard defines in "The Patient Examines the Doctor": "My ideal doctor would resemble Oliver Sacks. I can imagine Dr. Sacks *entering* my condition, looking around at it from inside like a kind landlord, with a tenant, trying to see how he could make the premises more livable. He would look around, holding me by the hand, and he would figure out what it feels like to be me." The healing gaze, as Broyard images it here, is a double-edged one, a look that violates the boundaries between subject and object to locate itself variously; Broyard imagines Sacks moving outside the corporeal confines of his own gaze to enter the sick body, "looking around at it from *inside*" (emphasis mine).

Broyard's metaphorical revisioning of the gaze reveals the extent to which vision remains, despite its limitations, "the core component of the epistemophilic project" [Peter Brooks, *Body Work: Objects of Desire in Modern Narrative*, 1993]. The look as a way of knowing seems to offer a grounded, almost scientific form of accessing the "truth" of a situation that, in the case of terminal illness, is defined by a fundamental confusion about the very way in which the self can be known. Although the person with terminal illness lives *in* the dying body—experiencing disease not only in its visible manifestations on the body's surface but in its invisible assault on the nerves—that person often has no clearer sense of cause and effect than the observer who looks on from without. Indeed, part of the horror of critical illness can be located in its invisibility; because the gradual weakening of arteries to the heart or the slow spread of cancer from one organ to another often occurs invisibly, the person with terminal illness may "know" the disease within the body only by constructing it in the mind. The unpredictability of illness may emerge in the subject's experience of disease as a foreign agent within the self; frequently, that agency seems more powerful and more incontestable precisely because it refuses to make itself known directly. Broyard invites his doctor "inside" his condition so that he might "figure out what it feels like to be me"; in the process of imaging the other's entrance into the body, however, Broyard lends Dr. Sacks the power of a gaze the absence of which defines his own experience of his illness.

The disjunction between these two experiences of the diseased body emerges in the imagistic fracturing of Broyard's self. Rather than portraying Sacks looking "at me" from the inside, Broyard portrays him looking "at it," something distinct from Broyard himself. Indeed, Broyard imagines himself embodied within his body, holding Sacks's hand, both of them staring wonderingly at the strange structure around them. To say that the healthy subject does not experience itself as embodied is less true than to say that the healthy subject often naturalizes a particular, familiar body as a material extension of the self. When that body is denaturalized in the course of a critical illness, its object status is exaggerated not only for others but for the embodied subject who experiences him/herself through it. Because illness fractures the symbolic unity between the self and the body, the sick person experiences the physical self as a stranger in the mirror, while the sense of the "true" embodied self remains as an ineradicable sense memory. It is this ghostly physical self of Broyard (I in my body as I know it) that holds hands with Sacks, and helps him understand the diseased body in which he lives. In figuring out "what it feels like to be me," Sacks must relate to the embodied self within yet separate from the self's body; he must understand the fragmentation of embodied identity fundamental to the experience of illness.

Because the unity or coherence of embodied identity is always to some degree illusory, the healthy subject's temporary experience of fragmentation constitutes a very real threat to its sustaining illusion of stability; the healing gaze that Broyard images unsettles subject and object oppositions in part by exposing the terminal aspect of every human life. In her discussion of the abject, Kristeva comments on the threat posed by the collapsing of boundaries between death and life, illness and health, the dying body and its apparently healthy counterpart:

> No, as in true theater, without makeup or masks, refuse and corpses *show me* what I permanently thrust aside in order to live. These body fluids, this defilement, this shit are what life withstands, hardly and with difficulty, on the part of death. There, I am at the border of my condition as a living being. My body extricates itself, as being alive, from that border. . . .

In *The Father,* it is through eroticized language that Olds charts the difficulty of first connecting with and then extricating her body from her father's, of "thrusting aside" not only the visible signs of illness but the very experience of her own mortality. The problematic construction of identity that Bedient describes is thus embodied in the dynamics of disease that bring to a crisis the poet's connection with and separation from her father. The uneven distribution of power that marks the projection of the healthy gaze onto the diseased body can be repaired only by an imaginative merging that refuses—however temporarily—the empowerment of extrication. The "eroticization of abjection" that Kristeva describes as a means of holding off the Other within the self can also, as Olds reveals, be turned to its opposite: Olds's use of a sexual vocabulary describes the intimacy of moments in which the subject not only projects the gaze onto an object but intermingles with it.

"The Lifting" traces Olds's reaction when her father attempts to direct the gaze that renders him object in **"The Waiting."** When he exposes his naked body before his daughter's eyes, he not only receives but commands her look:

> Suddenly my father lifted up his nightie, I
> turned my head away but he cried out
> *Shar!*, my nickname, so I turned and looked.
> He was sitting in the high cranked-up bed with the
> gown up, around his neck,
> to show me the weight he had lost. I looked
> where his solid ruddy stomach had been
> and I saw the skin fallen into loose
> soft hairy rippled folds
> lying in a pool of folds
> down at the base of his abdomen,
> the gaunt torso of a big man
> who will die soon.

Sitting high above his daughter on the "cranked-up bed" with his gown around his neck, Olds's father renders himself completely exposed to the look. Not only inviting but commanding his daughter's gaze, he thrusts his dying body in the line of her vision; as he does so, he upsets both the sexual dynamics of looking and the distribution of power conventionally associated with the gaze.

The healthy gaze that would distance and separate itself from the abject is here forced to focus upon the corporeal immediacy of a body revealed in all its material excess. Although Olds's desire to turn away from her father's nakedness seems to issue from a sense of sexual decorum, the marks of disease overwhelm the signs of sexuality written on her father's body. In the course of being visually drawn toward the naked body from which she would have turned away, her gaze moves first not to the penis but to the signs of disease written on her father's sagging belly. Whereas the "solid ruddy stomach" of a healthy man reflects the gaze of desire, the gathered folds of abdominal skin that confront Olds mark the visible motion of her father's body toward death. Looking at his naked body, she is confronted not with the difference of his sex but with a transforming, almost androgynous body; even as the signs of emaciation on her father's body draw Olds's eye away from the penis, the "loose / soft hairy rippled folds" of skin on her father's stomach evoke the presence of female rather than male genitalia.

Despite the way that the father's radical assertion of agency in **"The Lifting"** distinguishes his presence from his purely material manifestation in the opening poem of the volume, he continues to exist here as an object of the gaze. Offering himself up to his daughter's vision even as he commands her look, Olds's father reveals that he can no longer construct himself as subject without apprehending himself as object. His desire to look at himself and to be looked at is a mark of both the separation that he feels from his material being and his desire to know himself in that being. No longer able to present his body as a sign of his subjectivity, his health, his fitness, Olds's father loses control of both the visible surfaces that would announce his embodied presence and the interpretive system that allows others to read him through his body.

In directing his daughter's look, Olds's father appropriates her vision to reclaim his status as subject of the gaze as well as its object. Forced in **"The Waiting"** to know himself as the object of a gaze that rendered him as artifact, in **"The Lifting"** Olds's father attempts to direct and participate in the look that he cannot avoid. As he pushes his wasting torso into the line of his daughter's gaze, the father violates the conventions of decorum to implicate himself in his body; his "rueful smile" and "cast-up eyes" signify the bemused uneasiness with which he reveals the unfamiliar object that his body has become. In inviting his daughter's "interested" gaze, Olds's father asks her to share in his own fascinated and uneasy response to a body that is both his and not his; his distance from a body transformed by illness allows him, along with his daughter, to marvel at its presence even as his discomfort registers "the lifting" as an act of exposure.

In commanding his daughter's gaze, Olds's father cultivates the distance of her look as a means of negotiating the gap that he experiences between his presence as body and embodied subject. If the experience of the person with terminal illness is defined by the ever-present body, the epistemology of sight is trapped within a material dynamic that accesses subjectivity only through the visible aspects of that body. As long as the gaze sees as its object a diseased body but not the diseased person's experience of embodiment, the look only perpetuates the dislocation experienced by the person with terminal illness. In cultivating his daughter's look, Olds's father asks her not to reverse the process of the medical gaze that Foucault describes but to redefine its dynamics so that the father can be known through his body without being reduced to it. He asks her not to see him in spite of his illness—abstracting the illness out of the subject in the way that the medical gaze might abstract the patient out of the body—but rather to locate him in the unfamiliar body that literally and figuratively frames his existence.

The experience of illness denaturalizes the body that had come to signify Olds's father's identity, rendering that body unfamiliar and disconnected at the very moment that it asserts its presence as absolute. The person with terminal illness experiences the fissure that opens up between the body and the embodied subject as a gap that may blur distinctions not only between subject and body but between one subject and another, between one body and another. Entrapped within a changing body that no longer pretends to function as an essential manifestation of his subjective presence, Olds's father looks along with her at a body that both may claim but which necessarily belongs to neither. As his tumors grow larger and more visible and his body grows gaunter and more unfamiliar, Olds's father finds himself absolutely connected to a body that seems as alien to him as the body of a distant relative, an old woman, a friend.

In exposing the contingency of the subject's relationship to the body, illness also renders malleable the problematic subject/object dynamics of the gaze. Like the patient in Broyard's essay who holds the hand of his doctor as both look at the diseased body, Olds's father serves as both subject and object of his own look. In recognizing that his connection to the dying material body is inessential but absolutely determining, Olds's father gives up the claim to agency that often accompanies the assertion of subjectivity. At the same time, however, the father's admission that his body fails to speak for, signify and enact his will as subject leads to a new flexibility that also allows him to defy the status of pure object.

In **"The Lifting,"** the power dynamics of looking that depend upon the distance between subject and object begin to dissolve, along with the perceived essential connection between subjects and bodies, opening up the possibility of using the gaze as a means of forging new connections rather than asserting difference. As he draws her look onto his wasting torso, Olds's father becomes the subject of the look as well as its object; as she confronts his starkly naked form, she finds herself written there as well:

> . . . . Right away
> I saw how much his hips are like mine,
> the long, white angles, and then
> how much his pelvis is shaped like my daughter's,
> a chambered whelk-shell hollowed out,
> I saw the folds of skin like something
> poured, a thick batter, I saw
> the rueful smile, the cast-up eyes as he
> shows me his old body, he knows
> I will be interested, he knows I will find him
> appealing. If anyone had ever told me
> I would sit by him and he would pull up his nightie
> and I would look at him, at his naked body,
> at the thick bud of his penis in all that
> dark hair, look at him
> in affection and uneasy wonder
> I would not have believed it.

If the power of the viewing subject depends upon pleasure in looking and mastery over the object of the gaze, Olds finds herself disempowered; when Olds's father commands the look and directs it onto his dying body,

Olds sees her mortality rather than her desire mirrored in the object of the gaze. Caught unaware, Olds is the subject of a look that is not preformulated, distanced or empowered; in a flash of recognition, she sees her father stripped down almost to his bones and finds those bones shockingly familiar. As illness wears away at her father's flesh, what remains is not the stark sign of essential sexual difference but the long angles of hips that the speaker compares to her own and the shared curve of a pelvis "shaped like my daughter's, / a chambered whelk-shell hollowed out."

Gaylyn Studlar's *In the Realm of Pleasure* (1988), a study of the masochistic esthetic in film, explores the way that an object can function as a subject; she traces the disruption of a mastering vision to the presence of characters in film who return the look of the audience, who become subjects of the gaze themselves. In **The Father,** the subject of the gaze identifies herself with its object; as Olds recognizes the continuity between her body and her father's, her sympathetic look undermines the distance that underlies the process of objectification. In finding herself in her father's emaciated body, Olds claims that body for him; embracing his bones, she locates herself in this almost-skeleton, resignifying the materiality that threatens to erupt from within as a mark of the link between father and daughter and a sign of shared mortality. Olds's gaze probes beneath the changing surfaces of her father's body to unearth a sameness, a continuity invisible even to him; in acknowledging connection rather than maintaining separation, her form of visual essentialism locates identity in a body that seems to speak difference to the very person who experiences his world through it.

"The Lifting," then, offers a version of the look that Mary Ann Doane has defined in another context as "the female gaze." In "The Clinical Eye: Medical Discourses in the 'Woman's Film' of the 1940s" [in *The Female Body in Western Culture,* 1985], Doane describes a form of "female spectatorship" that aligns women's way of looking with an apparent excess of emotion, sentiment and empathy:

> From this perspective, the female gaze exhibits, in contrast to male distance, a proximity to the image which is the mark of over-identification and hence, of a heightened sympathy. But the concept of sympathy is a physiological one as well, of particular interest to the female subject. . . . Sympathy connotes a process of contagion within the body, or between bodies, an instantaneous communication and affinity. . . . Unable to negotiate the distance which is a prerequisite to desire and its displacements, the female spectator is always, in some sense, constituted as a hysteric.

The medical films that Doane addresses encourage the female spectator to reject a sympathetic "feminine" way of looking in favor of a "masculine" clinical gaze; the woman who fails to do so is diagnosed with "the paradigmatic female disease" of hysteria, a disease characterized, in Doane's formulation, by a body so completely in sympathy with a psyche that there is no differentiation between them.

If the medical films that Doane describes are constructed to contain the female spectator's "over-identification" and "heightened sympathy" with the object of the gaze, in **"The Lifting"** Olds expresses the radical consequences of the sympathetic look. In this poem, the "process of contagion . . . between bodies" manifests itself in the dissolution of distance between the healthy subject and her diseased counterpart, the female looker and the male object of the gaze. Because Olds's look claims a connection with her father's emaciated body, she is able to gaze with "uneasy wonder" not only at her father's naked form but "at the thick bud of his penis in all that / dark hair." Although Olds transgresses cultural norms that would prohibit a grown daughter from looking at her father's genitalia, her identification with her father's dying body emerges as a much more dangerous consequence of the act of looking than any incestuous desire. Having exposed herself to the contagion of mortality, Olds, like Doane's female spectator, finds herself moved out of a cycle of desire and displacement predicated upon the distance of the gaze. If, as Doane argues, the danger of female looking is contained in the diagnosis of hysteria, a disease in which there is no differentiation between body and psyche, then in **"The Lifting"** the radical potential of sympathetic looking is realized in a gaze that blurs the boundaries between bodies and psyches so thoroughly that the subject/object dynamics of looking are undermined. Although critics like Bedient read Olds's sympathy as a form of sexual hysteria culminating in her "ghoulish, erotic death-watch of her father," what emerges as truly radical is the motion of this poem away from the erotic power dynamics of the gaze and into a form of looking as subjective intermingling.

In **"The Last Day,"** Olds finds herself confronted once again with the sight of her father's naked, wasting body. This time, however, her father's motion toward the purely material is exaggerated by his lapse into unconsciousness. Literally unable to present or obscure himself before the look, Olds's father becomes the object not only of the medical gaze but of his daughter's penetrating stare. As Olds gazes unchecked into her father's open mouth, the reader registers with forceful immediacy the intimacy of looking:

> The daylight was shining into his mouth,
> I could see a flake, upright, a limbless
> figure, on his tongue, shudder with each
> breath. The sides of his tongue were dotted with
> ovals of mucus like discs of soft ivory,
> I sat and gazed into his mouth. . . .

Having lost all power to control or direct the look, Olds's father collapses into a body violable in its slackness. The powerful sunlight that shines into his mouth, rendering every oval of mucus and drop of spittle visible to the eye, highlights the extent to which Olds's father is unable to arrange himself before the look. The potential horror of such exposure emerges in Olds's image of the limbless figure perched upright on her father's tongue, denied any language but an inarticulate shudder.

In looking at her father, Olds carries on his wish to look at himself. She turns to the gaze in an attempt to place her father, to locate him in the unfamiliar matter of his dying body: "I sat and gazed into his mouth, I had / never understood and I did not / understand it now, the body and the spirit." Unwilling to discard the body before her as a mere shell of a spirit soon to be liberated, Olds keeps her vigil by entering into and merging with her father's body, penetrating past its surfaces into mucous and saliva. Matter issuing from the orifices of the body, in Mary Douglas's words [in *Purity and Danger,* 1969], emerges as "marginal stuff of the most obvious kind. Spittle, blood, milk, urine, faeces or tears by simply issuing forth have traversed the boundary of the body." When her father's unconscious form begins to challenge Olds's sympathetic gaze, her look forces past the boundaries of her father's body, moving closer and closer to the "physiological" concept of sympathy that Doane describes as "a process of contagion . . . between bodies." Although Olds perceives her father's body at its most abject and encroaching, she allows her gaze to be pulled in and, in Doane's terms, infected by his embodied mortality.

In the final moments of her father's dying, then, Olds's gaze emerges as increasingly embodied. Having given up the strict separation of subject and object that would allow her to declare her difference and her distance from her father's dying body—to "extricate" herself, in Kristeva's terms—Olds "stay[s] bent" before him, varying her posture and repositioning her own body to accommodate the object of her gaze. Although Olds does not inhabit the ailing body that frames her father's every breath, her identification with him emerges when the source of her gaze is unveiled; whereas in **"The Waiting"** the father "would wait with that burnished, looked-at look" for his daughter's gaze, in **"The Last Day"** it is Olds who "wait[s] and wait[s] for the next breath," her own vision trapped in the material origin of a cramped body. Having seen herself in her father's dying body, Olds sacrifices a gaze that objectifies and masters for an embodied look that is no more omniscient than she is immortal.

Olds responds to the nurse's silent announcement of her father's death by literally abolishing the distance between her body and his:

> I put my head on the bed beside him
> and breathed and he did not breathe, I breathed and
> breathed and he darkened and lay there,
> my father.

Despite her physical proximity to her father, Olds is thrust further and further away from him; the gap between her living body and his silent form expands with each of her breaths. When Olds's imaginative merging with her father collapses under the force of his silent breathlessness, Olds is thrust back into her own pulsing body; for the first time, Olds's father emerges as the object that he has figuratively threatened to become throughout the volume.

Whereas Olds's gaze contributed to her father's objectification in the opening poem of the volume, the concluding lines of the poem recounting his death show Olds turning to the gaze as a means of locating her father in the inanimate form before her. When she turns to her father's lifeless body, Olds's look is less a distanced, detached gaze than a touch, a caress:

> . . . . I laid my hand on his chest
> and I looked at him, at his eyelashes
> and the pores of his skin, cracks in his lips,
> dark rose-red inside the mouth,
> springing hair deep in his nose, I
> moved his head to set it straight on the pillow,
> it moved so easily, and his ear,
> gently crushed for the last hour,
> unfolded in the air.

In a reversal of the conventional dynamics of the gaze, Olds uses the act of looking to negotiate the distance that physical closeness has exaggerated. Vision takes on an almost physical quality as Olds's gaze fills the gaps and sutures the wounds of the body's surface.

In an earlier poem, **"Last Acts,"** Olds describes her desire to wash her father's face before he dies, to enter along with the cloth she holds the dips and valleys of his pores as a way of pushing past the boundaries between them. **"The Last Day"** recasts that act of touching into a look; in doing so, it challenges assumptions about the dynamics of looking articulated by Irigaray in her argument about the gaze: "[The gaze] sets at a distance, maintains the distance. In our culture, the predominance of the look over smell, taste, touch, hearing, has brought about an impoverishment of bodily relations" [Quoted in Robert Stam's *Subversive Pleasures,* 1989]. Olds never eschews the gaze's focus on the body's surface to find another epistemological entry into her father's being; instead, her own gaze risks the intimacy of embodiment to overcome the "impoverishment of bodily relations" that Irigaray connects with the distance of the look. As Olds's penetrating gaze enters the cracks in her father's lips and the pores of his skin, she responds to the margins of his body not as contaminating surfaces but as points of material and emotional interface. Physical proximity yields distance whereas the kind of intimacy that Olds renders elsewhere in erotic terms surfaces here in the gaze.

When Olds looks at her father's lifeless body, the manipulative dynamics of the gaze become literalized in her ability to arrange and rearrange the pliant form before her. The gaze that in **"The Waiting"** reduces the speaker's living father to an artifact of her creation, however, here accesses the father's inanimate body through the frame of his absent agency. If seeing is always a form of creating, Olds's creation in this poem garners its authority not from her desire but from her father's. His body has literally become an object that she manipulates, but she has earned the right to do so; as she moves his head to set it straight on the pillow, she images her act as restoration rather than creation: "his ear, / gently crushed for the last hour, / unfolded in the air." The body that Olds rearranges as text is one that she owns exactly because she has owned up to it, one in which she can locate her father because she has located herself in it.

In an excerpt from his journal, Anatole Broyard observes:

> What a critically ill person needs above all is to be understood. Dying is a misunderstanding you have to get straightened out before you go. And you can't be understood, your situation can't be appreciated, until your family and friends, staring at you with an embarrassed love, know—with an intimate, absolute knowledge—what your illness is like.

Broyard's formulation of the sympathetic gaze as an "embarrassed" stare reflects the way that the death-watch both invokes and unsettles the dynamics of looking. Olds's discomfort as her father thrusts his naked body before her eyes reveals the consequences of the kind of look that Broyard invites here; such viewing is experienced as intrusive rather than distancing, as disturbing rather than empowering. If the erotic gaze sometimes lends the viewing subject intimate access to the object of desire, seeing the person with terminal illness may result in a form of uncomfortable intimacy that implicates the viewer in the experience of mortality. Broyard's description of the "embarrassed" look acknowledges the inherent difficulties of such sympathetic seeing but calls for a viewer who "stares" through such embarrassment with an unflinching, directed gaze. Such an "embarrassed" stare expresses both power and powerlessness, interest and fear, discomfort and affection. Bridging the gap between the dying and the living must involve such a radical and almost contradictory unsettling of power relations; if the look is to become a means of restoring rather than disrupting connection, the viewing subject must sacrifice the distance and autonomy of the healthy gaze by refusing the empowerment of extrication. In becoming a means of locating the presence of the embodied subject in the dying body, the death-watcher dissolves the subject/object dynamics of the gaze until the healthy subject is forced to acknowledge its own mortality, and the watcher becomes the watched.

Lucy McDiarmid (review date 1996)

SOURCE: "Private Parts: Sharon Olds's Poems Don't Shy Away from Physicality," in *The New York Times Book Review,* September 15, 1996, p. 15.

[*McDiarmid is an American educator and editor. In the following review of* The Wellspring, *she discusses Olds's celebration of the body.*]

If the body electric that Whitman sang were set in one of Eavan Boland's domestic interiors, and addressed with the affectionate wisdom of Donald Hall, it might become the kind of body Sharon Olds celebrates in *The Wellspring*—sensual, familiar, beloved. These new poems, her fifth collection, describe the poet's "apprenticeship to the mortal" from her prenatal memories through adult sexuality, from **"My First Weeks"** through **"Celibacy at Twenty"** to **"True Love."**

The bodies she writes about—her mother's, father's, lovers', children's, husband's—exist with all their genetic histories and reproductive organs fully visible to the poet. To visit her mother's college is to remember a time when "Half of me / was deep in her body, dyed egg / with my name on it"; to consider the zipper of her son's outgrown jeans is to remember that he "had waited inside me so many years, his / egg in my side before I was born, / and he sprang fresh in his father that morning." In **"The Source"** Ms. Olds imagines her father's testicles ("My brothers / and sisters are there, swimming by the cinerous / millions"), as, in **"Eggs"** (from an earlier volume, *The Dead and the Living*), she had imagined her daughter's ovaries.

Perhaps it's her California background that enables Ms. Olds to write without any apparent cultural memory of Puritan taboos. The double body of her parents engaged in intercourse has long been a composite muse for her poetry. In **"My Father Speaks to Me From the Dead,"** the final poem of *The Father,* her cremated father speaks to her with a new wisdom "where I have been / I understand this life, I am matter, / your father, I made you." In **"The Wellspring"** Ms. Olds at first visualizes with disdain her mother's temperature chart, "the little x on the / rising line."

> But when a friend was pouring
>   wine
> and said that I seem to have been
>   a child who had been wanted,
> I took the wine against my lips
> as if my mouth were moving along
> that valved wall in my mother's
>   body, she was
> bearing down, and then breathing
>   from the mask, and then
> bearing down, pressing me out
>   into
> the world that was not enough for
>   her without me in it.

Because Ms. Olds cannot imagine her parents loving each other, she rewrites her conception to attribute to each parent, singly, a desire for her birth. These genetic and obstetric intimacies must stand in for the missing nuclear family.

The family invoked in the dedication of *The Wellspring* ("For our daughter and son") and in many of its poems may have made possible the poet's revisionist reading of her own childhood. The wellspring of the title is human love envisioned as a fluid source of life. Thus it is no accident that the idea of herself as a child her mother wanted occurs "when a friend was pouring wine," or that (in **"The Source"**) she thinks of herself during intercourse as "the glass of sourmash / my father lifted to his mouth." The bliss of being breast-fed meant that "every four / hours I could have the world in my mouth."

It is not easy to sustain without sentimentality a vision that could turn into a paean to family values. *The Wellspring* sustains it for many reasons, among them the chanting rhythms of the line that make each poem a miniature somatic ritual. And like Whitman, Ms. Olds sings the body in celebration of a power stronger than political oppression. To Whitman, the slave at auction was "the father of those who shall be fathers in their turns, / In him the start of populous states and rich republics." In poems from *The Dead and the Living* Ms. Olds made a lament of that trope, mourning the starving Russian girl in a 1921 photograph by imagining that "Deep in her body / the ovaries let out her first eggs," and seeing in the penis of a murdered Armenian boy "the source / of the children he would have had."

In the new poem **"May 1968,"** a revisiting of the famous student protest at Columbia, Ms. Olds's own body lying on the street becomes a site of resistance:

> The mounted police moved, near
> us,
> while we sang, and then I began to
> count,
> 12, 13, 14, 15,
> I counted again, 15, 16, one
> month since the day on that
> deserted beach,
> 17, 18, my mouth fell open,
> my hair on the street,
> if my period did not come tonight
> I was pregnant. . . .
>
> *Give me this one*
> *night,* I thought, *and I'll give this*
> *child*
> *the rest of my life* the horses'
> heads,
> this time, drooping, dipping, until
> they slept in a circle around my
> body and my daughter.

As **"May 1968"** moves from the confrontational politics of the campus to the ultrasonic vision of the protester's womb, the occasional poem turns into a lullaby. It is a sign of the complexity of Sharon Olds's vision that the pregnant body, all that domestic future of cribs and birthday parties latent within it, can still be the body militant.

Brian Sutton   (essay date 1997)

SOURCE: "Olds's 'Sex Without Love'," in *The Explicator,* Vol. 55, No. 3, Spring, 1997, pp. 177-80.

[*In the following essay, Sutton analyzes thematic and stylistic contrasts in the poem "Sex Without Love."*]

Sharon Olds's frequently anthologized poem **"Sex Without Love"** gains power through three contrasts: a contrast between surface approval and deeper criticism of "the ones who make love / without love"; a contrast between emotional coldness and physical heat; and a contrast between the poem's solemn, philosophical tone and its reliance on sexually graphic puns.

Many images within the poem appear to suggest that the speaker admires people who partake of sex without love. They are almost immediately described as being "beautiful as dancers," and later are compared with ice-skaters, "the true religious / the purists, the pros," and "great runners." All of these comparisons seem, at first glance, favorable.

Those whose sex is loveless seem to be favorably portrayed in another respect as well: They are described as purer and more profound than ordinary lovers. We are told that they are "the ones who will not / accept a false Messiah, love the / priest instead of the God." Here, ordinary lovers seem at best unenlightened, at worst heretical, while those whose sex does not involve love seem holier, more theologically insightful because their highest urges are not grounded in the physical. And after comparing the loveless sex partners to "great runners," the speaker points out that these runners do not, finally, race against other runners but against their "own best time"—an approach which seems deeper and more refined than that of the typical runner.

But when the images are examined more closely within the context of the poem, the speaker's attitude emerges as far less approving. As Richard Abcarian and Marvin Klotz point out [in their *Instructor's Manual to Accompany Literature: The Human Experience,* 1996], "while [the images] do express admiration, it is the admiration for a virtually nonhuman . . . obsession with self." There is, after all, something narcissistic in the performance of fine dancers and ice skaters; the runners, in their concern with their "own best time," ignore their fellow humans in the race; and "the ones who will not / . . . love the / priest instead of the God," their surface purity notwithstanding, choose the abstract and reject the human. Thus, Olds suggests that the loveless sexual partners lack human warmth: They are "gliding over each other like ice-skaters / over the ice," and like great runners, they are "alone / with . . . the cold."

To underscore the partners' emotional coldness, Olds contrasts it with the physical heat they generate during sex. They are described as having "faces red as / steak"—an image which emphasizes the heat of the moment and yet, paradoxically, reduces the sexual partner to the status of a piece of raw meat. Later, there is an image of "light / rising slowly as steam off their joined / skin." Yet remarkably, the sexual techniques which have created all this heat are portrayed implicitly as impersonal if not downright hostile: The partners are described as having "fingers hooked / inside each other's bodies."

Even more jarring is the image used to portray the partners' sweat in the heat of passion: They are "wet as the / children at birth whose mothers are going to / give them away." This image dramatizes the ultimate refusal to acknowledge emotional attachment as a consequence of sexual intercourse. Moreover, as Abcarian and Klotz note, since the partners are compared not to the rejecting mother but to the rejected children, they are portrayed as "people [who] have been cut off from a profound source of our humanity."

But perhaps the strongest implicit condemnation of the loveless sexual partners is expressed in lines 8 through 11:

> How do they come to the
> come to the . . . come to the God come to the
> still waters, and not love
> the one who came there with them . . . ?

The jagged, insistent rhythm of line 9, with each repetition of "come to the" set off by extra spaces, surely mimics the rhythmic thrusting and heavy breathing of the sexual partners (the heavy breathing being another link to the runners, dancers, and ice skaters). The word "God," also set off by extra spaces, is further isolated and emphasized because it breaks the rhythm of the repeated dactylic phrase "come to the" with a spondee. Thus, "God" not only is the grammatical object of "come to the," but also stands alone as the loveless sex partners' orgasmic moan. Given the imagery of these lines, and especially the fact that the partners will "not love / the one who came there with them," the statement two lines later that these partners "will not love / the priest instead of the God" seems much more negative. For just as the priest helps people to reach God, so the unloved sexual partner has helped the person who engages in sex without love to reach orgasm. Thus, implicitly, the "God" that the sexual partners love, and seek to reach, is orgasm itself.

Besides exemplifying the contrast of emotional coolness with physical heat and the contrast of surface approval with deeper condemnation, lines 8 through 11 also exemplify the third contrast: that between the poem's solemn philosophical questions and its reliance on sexual puns. In these lines, of course, the pun involves the word "come," as the speaker questions how the sex partners can come to God/orgasm and to the "still waters" (suggesting not only the Twenty-third Psalm but also the calm after the wetness leading to and climaxing in orgasm) without loving "the one who came there with them."

The poem also begins and ends with sexual puns. When the poem begins "How do they do it, the ones who make love / without love?" the question has to do not only with the separation of sexual intimacy from emotional commitment, but also with sexual methods. The poem's later description of impersonal sexual techniques tells exactly how they "do it," in both senses of those words. And in the final lines, where the loveless sex partners are compared with great runners, those runners are concerned not with other human beings but with "the fit" (of their shoes, admittedly), as well as with "the truth, which is the / single body alone in the universe / against its own best time." The final line echoes thousands of messages on bathroom walls about phone numbers to call "for a good time."

But even if the persons described in Olds's poem do call others "for a good time," emotionally they are always alone, even when engaging in sex with someone else; their partners, priestlike, may have helped them to reach their orgasmic God, but their focus is entirely on their solitary enjoyment of that God.

Harold Schweizer   (essay date 1997)

SOURCE: "The Matter and Spirit of Death," in *Suffering and the Remedy of Art,* State University of New York Press, 1997, pp. 171-84.

[*Schweizer is an educator and critic. In the following essay, he discusses the therapeutic aspects of the poems in* The Father, *concluding that the volume "is a book in search of a catharsis and clarification of fear and pity."*]

Sharon Olds' poetic sequence **The Father** records her father's death from cancer. Each breath, cough, spit of mucus, and stool is accounted for. The book is obsessed with waiting, with breathing, with bodily functions of the most intimate and ultimate kind, as if the poet wanted to wrest a secret from the slow process of dying, being present to her father's dying so as not to miss the split second when the secret might leap out of the body. The book lingers, at times with an astonishing patience and insistence, particularly over the exact moment of his death, which is the title of one poem. Olds releases her father slowly and with costly tenderness, letting go only after he has begged for it in the manner of Jacob. The book is a work in slow motion, an anticipatory and retrospective grieving, a pity and fear, all in ritual passage reminiscent of the monastic schedule, with the poems bearing such titles as **"The Waiting," "The Pulling," "The Lumens," "His Stillness," "The Want," "The Lifting,"** and so forth.

Above all, the book is about matter. Olds seems to learn with relief that that is all it is: "I have always longed to believe in what I am seeing." The father's death, where it might have most strongly called this longing into question, most strongly reconfirms it. Indeed, it seems as if the suffering and death of the father was a last occasion to prove that truth must be in the particular, in the body, not in the soul, in history, not beyond it.

> When I come to his hospital doorway in the morning
> and see, around the curtain, the motionless
> bulge of his feet, under the sheet,
> I stop breathing. I walk in,
> the starved shape of his body rises
> and falls, and I breathe again,
>   I sit and breathe with him. . . .

The line ending on "his body rises . . ." may offer a momentary illusion or allusion to the body rising from the dead, but it is the law of matter that seeks its destiny, breath not spirit, matter not metaphor. Father and daughter lie not in heaven but "somewhere on the outskirts / of the garden of Eden. . . ."

I wish I could say I saw a long
shapely leg pull free from the chrysalis, a
wet wing, a creature unfold and
fly out through the window, but he died down
into his body. . . .

The spiritual does become—perhaps necessarily if matter wants to be truth—the narrative's dialectical opponent; it has to be called forth to be called off. How else could one say that the body is enough, other than that the poet, having known her father "soulless" all her childhood, would have descended and looked for his soul if he could have been helped? But since these possibilities are denied, even salvation will be absorbed by matter. Will matter shine with its own salvation? Will salvation matter?

The book begins and ends with matter, frames its argument with matter and with all of its declensions and conjugations, as noun and verb, material and moral truth. The opening reference to Genesis where the father is "night-/ watchman of matter, sitting facing / the water—the earth without form, and void, / darkness upon the face of it, as if / waiting for his daughter"—makes a grand, perhaps intentionally too grand, announcement of a romantic creative rivalry between God and daughter, spirit and matter. The daughter is not always creator of her own world and language and, being subject to the father-God's breath, she is also subject to the father's uncreative powers: "I was an Eve / he took and pressed back into clay. . . ." That the daughter survives is only due to the stronger power of death. Death is the daughter's liberator.

In retrospect one realizes that even the very first line of the book—"No matter how early I would get up . . ." announces, allusively, the matter of this book. But while this is a book about matter its purpose is thoroughly redemptive: it is to redeem the clay into which he had pressed her. The body of her dying father is the site of redemption. The last page closes with the father's voice from the dead, "I am matter, / your father . . ." framing, thematizing this book in between whose covers there is the body of the father, still or restless, first sitting, then lying, then sinking down, in pain and in sleep, all minutely observed. There is a veritable poetics, a creative theory, in the father's relentless decline deeper into body and ash and earth and the daughter's rising, not higher, but also deeper into her conviction that soul is nothing, matter all, and yet that death can do what life undid. The bitter memories of what life undid, or what the father did, accelerate their appearance in the second part of the book. The book therefore, one senses, is a last chance of healing and helping what could never be healed or helped in life.

Each poem is a measurement of minute increments of time, of inexorable, irreparable progress, granting only the smallest reprieves and returns to previous scenes and settings. There is only one seeming remission when the father "is better, he is dying a little more slowly"; otherwise the narrative of this sequence is obedient to the strict authority of time and disease and death. Many of the poems begin by marking time, "How early . . ." "The last morning . . ." "Every hour . . ." "Now . . ." ". . . and there are three weeks left." "I waited . . . ," and so forth. In the middle of the book, the book of waiting contracts to briefer increments of time. The diary of dying which had been a living with time, becomes now a living on the verge of timelessness. The question of whether one can continue where death ends looms somewhere in that intense narrow margin of time/lessness marked by the imminence of death. Then, after ten or so pages of return and repetition of death and reflection on the moment of death itself, time expands by leaps **"Beyond Harm," "One Year"** into the future where even memory is torn down (**"The Motel"**) and the father's death not only recedes, but also rises up again in myth and dream.

The certainty of death is the book's telos from which it derives its assurance of arrival and survival as well as its style. The breath of the author is dependent first on the breath then on the death of the father, the matter of his breath and death is finally reflected by a style marked by lucid, factual clarity. Caring for the father is equally therapeutic for the daughter. Mutuality is one of the book's themes and is frequently encountered in the father's breathing, where the dauther discovers her dependency, the source of her own breathing and writing. Nor is there a question about authorship or reference or autobiography. The unproblematic analogy between life and art suggests instead that the death need not be, cannot be, transformed through art, and that art, likewise, seeks no transformative powers beyond being simply the power of witness and attendance, a *being-there* as factual as a back rub, although as much a labor of love. It is only in the latter part of the book, in what one might call the "memory-poems," where the desire for the indifference of matter leaves the remainder of an "unearned desire" and the incompletions of love.

The narrative contingency and continuance depends on seeing the father safely through to the fire, a resistance to the pull of death and a liberation from death. But eventually the achievement of the book, when the telos of the father's death has been consummated, is to continue continuance itself. The book therefore eventually asks the question: what writing can survive a death? How does one write after the most consummating narrative event? How does one write after one has written to the end? Perhaps that is why the sequence lingers at that latter point, returning to and rewriting and repeating the death until it releases the writer into freedom: "I suddenly thought, with amazement, he will always / love me now, and I laughed—he was dead, dead!"

Many of the issues I have mentioned here in summary are addressed in a poem entitled **"I Wanted to Be There When My Father Died."** The title seems more idealistic than the qualification that follows immediately: ". . . because I wanted to see him die—." Indeed, *The Father* is a book almost exclusively of seeing. "I have always longed to believe in what I was seeing." It is a curious admission since it implies other beliefs, which are, presumably, tested out at the site of the father's dying and found wanting. It is here in **"I Wanted to Be There . . ."** that we learn one of the secret motivations of the poet's presence at her father's deathbed, a motivation that explains partially the distance implied in "seeing":

> because I wanted to see him die—
> and not just to know him, down to
> the ground, the dirt of his unmaking, and not
> just to give him a last chance
> to give me something, or take his loathing
> back.

The dimensions of the daughter's relationship with the father and her childhood are present in other poems as well where we learn that if the daughter now has "nothing for him, no net, / no heaven to catch him," it is because he taught his daughter "only / the earth, night, sleep, the male / body in its beauty and fearsomeness." But besides fear she returns to him also pity. **"The Look"** gives one of the most moving examples. The last lines of the poem read:

> . . . I could touch him from deep in my heart,
> he shifted in the bed, he tilted, his eyes
> bugged out and darkened, the mucus rose,
> I held the cup to his lips and he slid out
> the mass and sat back, a flush came into
> his skin, and he lifted his head shyly but
> without reluctance and looked at me
> directly, for just a moment, with a dark
> face and dark shining confiding eyes.

In the balance of pity and fear, these remain cherished moments, encounters of which there is not much likeness, to my knowledge, in modern American poetry. **The Father** is a book in search of a catharsis and clarification of fear and pity, that they may be offered in right measure and balance. If Sharon Olds' book wants to be such an offering, the catharsis that the narrative ought to work out for its author remains one of the book's major labors, born in poem after poem, throughout the long summer of the father's dying. "All summer he had gagged, as if trying / to cough his whole esophagus out." We read on in **"I Wanted to Be There . . ."**:

> surely his pain and depression had appeased me,
> and yet I wanted to see him die
> not just to see no soul come
> free of his body, no mucal genie of
> spirit jump
> forth from his mouth,
> proving the body on earth is all we have got,
> I wanted to watch my father die
> because I hated him. Oh, I loved him,
> my hands cherished him. . . .

The Father is an articulation, a verbal extension of the "Oh," held precariously between the two forces of love and hatred, fear and pity. But eventually even the hands that cherished him will delegate their task to "other hands" into which it might be better to "commend this spirit," for not all issues between love and hatred have been, can be, resolved in poetry.

The hands that cherished him cherished the body, meaning the particular, the historical, Aristotle's "that which was." It is no body if it can be generalized, just as one cannot generalize caring, washing, nursing, helping, witnessing. Hence, the particularity of the descriptions and accounts of mucus, spit, and stool. Even the language of the poems follows the law of material truth: it avoids poeticizing this particular death, lest it might turn into Aristotle's poetic universals and thereby into a belying of individual suffering and dying. Thus, each poem, redescending into the labor of moments and situations, also refuses to let suffering, death, and caring become transformed into art.

What we admire in this volume is firstly not the art of writing but the art of nursing. What we admire must be first the exemplary moral determination and love of the daughter to nurse her father—she who "had stopped / longing for him to address [her] from his heart." Her father, we learn progressively, at times would not speak for a week, had never asked his daughter for anything, had never really looked at her, had regularly passed out on the couch in alcoholic stupor, and had only when he sickened turned to his wife and daughter. In spite of this grim record of her youth, there is not an instant of hesitation as the book begins—significantly "early"—in the daughter's moral determination. To the father she must have appeared like a Cordelia, proving in the numerous instances of closeness and intimacy a loyalty and affection rare and difficult.

> He gargled, I got the cup ready,
> I didn't vary the stroke, he spat, I
> praised him, I let the full pleasure
> of caressing my father come awake in my body,
> and then I could touch him from deep in my heart. . . .

Such attention, merging as it does pain with pleasure and matter with spirit, reconnects the world in its deepest fundamentality. Perhaps not surprisingly, it is in this poem that we find one of the epiphanies of the book, when the father momentarily responds with his "dark shining confiding eyes." If the world needs an ethical foundation, its beginnings would be in such small, intimate, and brief mergings of pleasure and pain. "This is the world where sex lives, the world / of the nerves, the world without church, / . . . outside the world of the moral" as Olds points out in **"Death and Morality."** The book is the record of the strategies of the will, of the small, small acts of attention, measured by the paced continuance of the sequence, by which this merging of pleasure and pain could be possible and consciously attended to. The originality of Olds' book is in the particularity of the death and deed, in which service she left behind, as Kierkegaard would say, both the category of ethics and of aesthetics. **The Father** tells of the incomprehensible category beyond. Olds' denial of spiritual revelation, her insistence on the body demands that the church find itself in hospitals rather than "far away, in a field," where one can hear "the distant hymns of a tent-meeting. . . ."

FURTHER READING

Beaver, Harold. "Snapshots and Artworks." *The New York Times Book Review* (March 18, 1984): 30.
>   Positive review of *The Dead and the Living* in which Beaver discusses the volume's focus on family themes.

Gilbert, Sandra M. "Family Values." *Poetry* CLXIV, No. 1 (April 1994): 39-53.
>   Examines the treatment of family relationships in Olds's *The Father* and in the poetry of Laura Riding, Grace Paley, Marge Piercy, and Carol Muske.

Gregerson, Linda. Review of *The Dead and the Living. Poetry* CXLV, No. 1 (October 1984): 36-7.
>   Mixed review of *The Dead and the Living* in which Gregerson states that Olds's political poetry is exploitive, but that the poet is "an eloquent celebrant . . . of sexual love."

Hamill, Sam. "Lyric, Miserable Lyric (Or: Whose Dog Are You?)" *The American Poetry Review* 16, No. 5 (September-October 1987): 31-5.
>   Discusses the metrical structure of *The Gold Cell.*

Harris, Peter. Review of *The Gold Cell. Virginia Quarterly Review* 64, No. 2 (Spring 1988): 262-76.
>   Finds the poems in *The Gold Cell* emotionally gripping, but questions whether the intensity of Olds's verse is merely sensationalistic.

Hudgins, Andrew. Review of *The Gold Cell. The Hudson Review* XL, No. 3 (Autumn 1987): 517-27.
>   Offers a mixed assessment of *The Gold Cell,* admiring its powerful imagery and narrative flow but faulting its haphazard structure and sensationalistic themes.

Keelan, Claudia. "That Which Is Towards." *Poetry Flash,* No. 247 (October-November 1993): 1, 4-5, 14-15.
>   Favorable review of *The Father.*

Kinzie, Mary. Review of *The Dead and the Living. The American Poetry Review* 13, No. 5 (September-October 1984): 41-3.
>   Examines Olds's use of language and metaphor in *The Dead and the Living,* comparing Olds's verse to poems by Sylvia Plath and Louise Glück.

Lesser, Rika. "Knows Father Best." *The Nation,* New York 255, No. 20 (December 14, 1992): 748-50.
>   Examines the autobiographical focus of *The Father.*

Libby, Anthnoy. "Fathers and Daughters and Mothers and Poets." *The New York Times Book Review* (March 22, 1987): 23.

Asserts that poems in *The Gold Cell* are hampered by Olds's preoccupation with morbidity, physicality, and brutality.

Matson, Suzanne. "Talking to Our Father: The Political and Mythical Appropriations of Adrienne Rich and Sharon Olds." *The American Poetry Review* 18, No. 6 (November-December 1989): 35-41.
>   Comparative review of Olds's *The Gold Cell* and Adrienne Rich's *Your Native Land, Your Life.* Matson discusses Olds's use of metaphor as a means of articulating her painful and ambivalent feelings toward her father and as a strategy for healing.

McEwen, Christian. "Soul Substance." *The Nation,* New York 224, No. 14 (April 11, 1987): 472-75.
>   Mixed review of *The Gold Cell* in which McEwan offers general praise for Olds's poetry, but questions her fascination with voyeurism and her reliance on techniques employed in her previous books.

Mueller, Lisel. Review of *Satan Says. Poetry* CXXVIII, No. 3 (June 1981): 170-74.
>   Faults Olds's metaphors in *Satan Says,* but praises the emotional intensity of the volume.

Ostriker, Alicia. "The Tune of Crisis." *Poetry* CXLIX, No. 4 (January 1987): 231-37.
>   Praises Olds's use of intimate autobiographical details and vivid imagery in *The Gold Cell.*

Peseroff, Joyce. Review of *Satan Says. The American Book Review* 4, No. 2 (January-February 1982): 21-2.
>   Heralds Olds's treatment of female relationships and use of language in *Satan Says.*

Phelan, Peggy. "Intimations of Mortality." *The Women's Review of Books* I, No. 5 (February 1984): 16-17.
>   Offers a positive assessment of *The Dead and the Living.*

Pybus, Rodney. Review of *The Matter of This World: New and Selected Poems. Stand Magazine* 30, No. 1 (Winter 1988-89): 67-75.
>   Praises Olds's focus on physicality, autobiography, and parent-child relationships in *The Matter of This World.*

Yenser, Stephen. Review of *The Gold Cell. The Yale Review* 77, No. 1 (Autumn 1987): 140-47.
>   Examines stylistic and thematic elements of *The Gold Cell,* noting that the volume exemplifies a candid narrative handling of painful subject matter.

Zeidner, Lisa. "Empty Beds, Empty Nests, Empty Cities." *The New York Times Book Review* (March 21, 1993): 14, 16.
>   Lauds the style and realism of *The Father,* but states that the work is "unusually narrow in focus."

Additional coverage of Olds's life and career is contained in the following sources published by Gale Research: *Contemporary Authors,* **Vol. 101;** *Contemporary Authors New Revision Series,* **Vols. 18, 41;** *Contemporary Literary Criticism,* **Vols. 32, 39, 85;** *Dictionary of Literary Biography,* **Vol. 120; and** *Discovering Authors: Poets Module.*

José Garcia Villa
1904-1997

Philippine poet and short story writer.

INTRODUCTION

José Garcia Villa was an award-winning poet in both the Philippines and the United States. In 1973, he became the first Philippine writer in English to be declared a National Artist, earning a lifetime pension. American awards include the Shelley Memorial Award and numerous fellowships. Villa's poems, which are marked by technical innovation and rich imagery, have been the subject of heated debates among critics who have widely different opinions regarding their artistic value. The majority agree with Dame Edith Sitwell, however, who wrote that Villa's best poems are "amongst the most beautiful written in our time."

Biographical Information

Villa was born in Manila on August 5, 1904. His father was a doctor and Army chief of staff in the Philippine revolution against Spain. Villa attended the University of the Philippines for a short time, but was suspended for writing subversive poetry. While there, he and fellow writers founded the UP Writers Club—the oldest existing literary club in the Philippines. In 1930, Villa immigrated to the United States and attended the University of New Mexico, where he earned a B.A. in 1933. He began publishing short stories during this period, earning immediate recognition; Edward J. O'Brien's *Best American Short Stories of 1932* was dedicated to Villa. Though his interests soon turned to poetry, it was 1939 before Villa completed his first collection, which was published in the Philippines. Villa attended graduate school at Columbia University before marrying Rosemarie Lamb in 1946. Highly respected in his native land, in 1968, Villa became advisor on cultural affairs to the President of the Philippines. He died on February 7, 1997, in New York City.

Major Works

Villa's first book of poetry published in the United States, *Have Come, Am Here,* won widespread critical acclaim and was in contention for the Pulitzer Prize. In this volume, he introduced a new method of rhyming, which he termed "reversed consonance." This rhyming mode requires that consonants be reversed through word choice from one line to the next, such as "said" and "days." In Villa's *Volume Two,* he included "comma poems," which make use of a symbol shaped like a comma that is attached without space to the words on either side, thus

providing a weighted pace to the moving line. Despite such innovative techniques, Villa preferred traditional stanza forms of couplets, triplets, and quatrains. The content of Villa's poetry does not provide any identifiable cultural content, but instead contains romantic and visionary images intended to be universal and to convey the sense of a liberated spirit ascending. His poems are primarily concerned with essence, or, as Villa once claimed, with "the search for the metaphysical meaning of man's life in the Universe."

Critical Reception

Critical response to Villa's poems has varied significantly over the length of his career. Early critics, such as Edith Sitwell, wrote of Villa's poetry with unassailable praise. Sitwell observed that his "poetry springs straight from the depths of the poet's being, from his blood, from his spirit, from his experience . . ." Such critics often compared Villa's poems to those of William Blake, Emily Dickinson, and e. e. cummings. Several, pointing to the religious content of Villa's works, have compared him to the Metaphysical poets. Later critics have been more scrupulous. L. M. Grow considered the majority of Villa's poems "prosy, pretentious, and contrived," adding that "Villa, like Wordsworth, would benefit from a selective fire, one which would consume a fair portion of his published work." Even so, Grow was unduly impressed by Villa's visual imagery in certain poems, especially "Clean,like,iodoform,between,the,tall," "Because,thy,smile, is,primavera," and "The,caprice,of,canteloupes,is,to,be." According to Grow, "If any poet has ever been blessed with the visual acuity, the instinct for uncluttered composition, and the historical consciousness to make the genre viable, Villa has been."

PRINCIPAL WORKS

Poetry

Many Voices 1939
Poems by Doveglion [as Doveglion] 1941
Have Come, Am Here 1942
Volume Two 1949
Selected Poems and New 1958
A Doveglion Book of Philippine Poetry [editor as Doveglion] 1962
Poems 55: The Best Poems of José Garcia Villa as Chosen by Himself 1962
Poems in Praise of Love 1962
The New Doveglion Book of Philippine Poetry [editor] 1975

Other Major Works

Philippine Short Stories [editor] 1929
Footnote to Youth (short stories) 1933
A Celebration for Edith Sitwell [editor] (essay collection) 1946
Selected Stories 1962

CRITICISM

Babette Deutsch (essay date 1942)

SOURCE: "Have Come: A Good Poet," in *The New Republic,* Vol. 107, No. 16, October 19, 1942, p. 512.

[*In the following review of* Have Come, Am Here, *Deutsch praises the collection as "a group of poems that, for all their obscurity, which is sometimes witty, sometimes profound, are luminous and vibrant with the quality of crystal."*]

The title and even more the dedication of these poems lead one to expect the unexpected. And indeed, paradox and ambiguity leap out of the pages like so many rare and strange animals. What fascinates the observer, however, is not the difficulties that these lyrics present, though they are as singular as the work of Emily Dickinson or of

Hopkins, but rather their pure intensity. There is not one, however faulty, that lacks the burning signature of the poetic imagination. José Garcia Villa belongs to the small company of religious poets who have been able to communicate their vision. He belongs to the still smaller company of those who have not needed to cry out their doubt.

Villa is concerned with ultimate things, the self and the universe.

—Babette Deutsch

This may be because his "Divine Poems" are variations on a theme of Blake's:

> Thou art a Man, God is no more,
> Thy own humanity learn to adore.

Villa goes further than Blake: he announces that God is his miracle, his work, his creation, wearing the poet's head upon His shoulders, and, therefore, perhaps capable of immortality. But, Villa insists, only when His divinity is humanized will God be perfected. Where Emily Dickinson addressed the Diety with gentle raillery as "Papa Above," and Auden respectfully apostrophizes Him as "Sir," this young poet, rejecting the authority of the awful Father and Arch-Disciplinarian, adopts toward Him the attitude of an intimate and a peer. Nowhere is this clearer than in the poem about how he wrestles with his God:

> The way my ideas think me
> Is the way I unthink God.
> As in the name of heaven I make hell
> That is the way the Lord says me.
>
> And all is adventure and danger
> And I roll Him off cliffs and mountains
> But fast as I am to push Him off
> Fast am I to reach Him below.
>
> And it may be then His turn to push me off,
> I wait breathless for that terrible second:
> And if He push me not, I turn around in anger:
> "O art thou the God I would have!"
>
> Then He pushes me and I plunge down, down!
> And when He comes to help me up
> I put my arms around Him, saying, "Brother,
> Brother." . . . This is the way we are.

The key words here are not God and heaven, but hell, adventure, danger and anger. It is significant that in another of the "Divine Poems" Villa declares:

> First, God, if you can remember
> He is not undiscriminative love.

And yet he would agree with the poet who observed that nothing was ever created by taking thought, that the creative force is not thought, but love. "Not by the mind, O Blind!" is the divine reproof to the seeker after the "temperature / Of God's calenture."

The hunger for myth is not new, but it appears to be growing acute. For that reason a poet who has an obvious kinship with the Metaphysicals and yet wears his Christian rue with so great a difference may win adventitious praise. José Villa's work, however, satisfies not merely a need of the times. It satisfies the requirements of poetry.

Villa is concerned with ultimate things, the self and the universe. He is also on visiting terms with the world. He is more interested in himself than in the universe, and he greets the world with but a decent urbanity. Yet if his range is narrow, he soars high and plunges deep. Moreover, he is an extremely conscious craftsman. In a note at the end of the book he explains his use of a new method of rhyming that he calls "reversed consonance," examples of which are "*said*" and "*days*," "*love*" and "*reveal*," "*sound*" and "*down*." This invention, however curious, is perhaps the least token of his skill. Occasionally his pleasure in technical problems betrays him, as witness the tedious alliterations of No. 126 ["**Always and always the amaranth astir**"], and other pieces where his chief interest is in auditory values. But the flaws in certain lyrics are more than compensated for by the effects achieved elsewhere. Above all, Villa shows himself a poet in his command of imagery. And this not because he takes one into an enchanted realm, where even sea gulls are musical, a realm rich with tigers and peacocks, dark with skulls and roses, bright with fire and dew, quick with the entelechies of physical love. It is not alone that the wealth of his fantasy startles and delights, but that he has the controlling, ordering imagination of the true myth-maker. And out of his abundant store he continually drops penetrating metaphors by the way. Thus he speaks of the poem that

> must be able to hide
> What it seeks, like a bride,

of the Word, "slender as an infant fawn and / Whole without death's antlers yet." He can conceive not merely "A radio made of sea-water" with "mermaids for music," but more daringly asserts that

> a radio made of light
> Will have music of Blakes:
> Who with great tigertails
> Will beat God-musicales.

When he writes, "It's a hurricane of spirit—/ That's genius!" the definition is remarkable not only for its aptness but for the authority with which it is uttered. Villa can resurrect dead words like "Christ," "Judas," "spirit," "genius," because he is himself whirled along on that giant wind.

The fact that he is a native of the Philippines who comes to the English language as a stranger may have helped him to his unusual syntax. But no accident of birth can account for his performance save the ancient "*poeta nascitur, non fit.*" Even then the adage must be qualified, for though he was undoubtedly born a poet, he has obviously and wisely labored at his art. The result is a group of poems that, for all their obscurity, which is sometimes witty, sometimes profound, are luminous and vibrant with the quality of crystal.

Edith Sitwell (essay date 1958)

SOURCE: Preface to *Selected Poems and New,* by José Garcia Villa, McDowell, Obolensky, 1958, pp. ix-xiv.

[*In the essay below, Sitwell declares: "The best of these poems are amongst the most beautiful written in our time."*]

In the late summer of 1944, I received a book of poems from America, by an author hitherto unknown to me.

I learned afterwards that the young poet in question hailed from the Philippines, and is at present living in New York. I learned, also, that this book had been acclaimed by the principal critics of America as a work of genius, and had had, in America, an enormous success. But this I did not know at the time, and even had I known it, an enormous success does not necessarily prove that an author is a great or even an estimable writer.

Opening the book, *Have Come, Am Here,* I received a shock. For my eyes fell first upon "**Number 57,**" a strange poem of an ineffable beauty, springing straight from the depths of Being. I hold that this is one of the most wonderful short poems of our time, and reading it I knew that I was seeing for the first time the work of a poet with a great, even an astonishing, and perfectly original gift.

Next, I turned to the poem beginning with the lines

> I will break God's seamless skull
> And I will break His kissless mouth,
> O I'll break out of His faultless shell
> And fall me upon Eve's gold mouth.

which is equally beautiful, equally strange, equally fiery in its entirely different way.

This poetry springs straight from the depths of the poet's being, from his blood, from his spirit, from his experience, as a fire breaks from wood, or as a flower grows from its soil.

All the poems in this book are short. But as Blake said

> The lark is a mighty angel.

and

> A little flower is the labour of ages.

These strange, passionate, and beautiful poems are equally the labour of ages, growing from all the poet's earth.

The best of these poems are amongst the most beautiful written in our time.

—Edith Sitwell

Some of the poems, both in *Have Come, Am Here* and in *Volume Two,* are born from a religious ardour and fire, some are love poems. In some of the poems of the religious kind, the soul of Man is engaged, not only in adoration, (as in **"Number 68"**) but also, at times, in a glorifying and joyous combat with his God.

His love is not for "Christ, the, Fox," whose "beauty, is, too, sly, too, meek." His love is for the Christ who is "pure, lightning," . . . "my, bright, Lion, coming, down,"—sunlike, coming down Jacob's ladder.

His is the

Theology,
Of, rose, and,
Tiger:

and he burns with their fire, with their

Vision,
Its,
Gold, and,
Its, wars.

"All absolute sensation is religious" wrote Novalis. And this absolute sensation is known by Mr. Villa. It shines and burns in his love poems, as in the poems about God. All have a strange luminosity—as if they came from the very heart of light—alternating with an equally strange darkness, and this luminosity, this darkness, bear a certain resemblance to that in the works of Blake and of Boehme.

The ecstasy in some of the religious poems is like that of certain saints,—of St. Catherine of Genoa, for instance, in her saying "If that of which my heart is feeling, one drop were to fall into hell, hell itself would become all life eternal." Or of Meister Eckhart, when he said, "One must be blind, and strip God naked of things, to see the light which shines in darkness."

There is the feeling of this light always, and of this rapture. But with it, unlike the nakedness of which Eckhart speaks, there is a profound physical beauty. And, although the actual objects, the images, are familiar to us on another scale, they come to us, always, with an amazing impact of strangeness.

Sir, there's a tower of fire in me

says the poet in one poem. And in another,

O the brightness of my dark.

These lines, with the poem which begins with the line

The distinction is in Fire and Division

seem to epitomise the spirit in the poet, which is indeed Fire, which is indeed the

Ferocious and beautiful Leopard that thrives
On the rose-imagination.

Break the heart's thicketry: leap, Leopard-mind,
Bring figuration of Fire. Great Geometer . . .

These poems grow, often, from the language, which is the matrix: as Mallarmé said, a poem is "written, not with ideas, but with words." This is now, for the most part, forgotten. Although in the earliest poetry it was held to be "magical utterance," most of the poetry written today is verbally dead.

No book of Mr. Villa's has yet been published in England, where criticism is divided into two schools—that which demands that poetry should derive from "pure intellect," and that the senses, physical beauty, should not enter it—and the school that is clamouring for "pure poetry." The former school is satisfied with any cluster of dry bones—if sufficiently contorted. The latter school, when it is provided with pure poetry, shies away from it, and howls for what Coleridge called "the metaphysical bustard, winging its slow, laborious, earth-skimming flight over dreary and level wastes."

Mr. Villa's poems are, in some cases, "pure poetry." They are compact of both imagination and fancy.

Dr. Jung, in *The Integration of the Personality,* quotes Rulard as saying (*Lexicon Alchimae,* 1611) "Imagination is the star in man, the celestial or super-celestial body." Dr. Jung adds "The peculiar expression 'astrum' is an alchemistic term that approximately means 'quintessence.' Imagination is thus a concentrated extract of the forces of life, corporeal as well as psychic."

It should be remembered that imagination is not fancy. As Goethe said "Nothing is so atrocious as fancy without taste."—Fancy is not a concentrated essence of the *forces* of life. But fancy *with* taste is as lovely as the butterflies of summer. Of what use are they? When John Ray, the great 17th century naturalist, was asked "What is the use of Butterflies?" he replied "To adorn the fields and delight the eyes of men; to brighten the countryside, serving like so many golden spangles to decorate the fields." And he added "Who can contemplate their exquisite beauty and not acknowledge and adore the traces of divine art upon them."

Mr. Villa's lighter poems spring both from imagination and from fancy.

One of Mr. Villa's latest poems is **"The Anchored Angel."** Leaving aside the great visual beauty of this, it is of much interest technically. For some reason, in this context, the two words that end the first line "golden, father," seem sinking as the sun seems to do when it sets, into the earth from which all growth arises.

"Gentle" is an assonance to "Genesis."

The lines

> Between, the, Wall, of, China, and,
>   The, tiger, tree (his, centuries, his,
>   Aerials, of, light) . . .

are as beautiful as they are strange.

A poem can be all things to all men. The poet, alone, does not make the poem—but the reader also is the maker. To this particular reader, the Wall of China is Death, seemingly dividing us from another civilisation—the civilisation of the Living, and, also, shielding us from the dangers of Life. The tiger tree is the infinite growth of the future arising from that earth, "the, father,"

> Who, made, the, flower, principle.

Throughout almost all these poems, the "principle," the archetype, the quintessence are Mr. Villa's themes.

"The Anchored Angel" sounds more than one great depth. Take, for instance, the line

> Sanskrit, of, love,

—the language as ancient as the world, and no longer fully understood—or take the phrase

> Inventor, of, great, eyes,

—Is not every poet this?

Or take the phrase "the, light's, black, branches." Is the light, perhaps, the tree, and are the shadows the branches arising from it?

The best of these poems are amongst the most beautiful written in our time.

Leonard Casper (essay date 1966)

SOURCE: "A People of Many Pasts and Complex Parts: José Garcia Villa," in *New Writings from the Philippines: A Critique and Anthology,* Syracuse University Press, 1966, pp. 103-10.

[*In this excerpt, Casper provides an introducton to Villa's stories and poems.*]

Although five of his earliest tales were reproduced in the *Selected Stories of Jose Garcia Villa* (1962), in tribute to the first prolonged revisit by the distinguished expatriate in nearly thirty years, the fiction of Villa is mainly an academic curiosity today. When Scribner's published his collection, *Footnote to Youth: Tales of the Philippines and Others,* in 1933, Villa had already committed himself to writing exclusively as a poet. Consequently, the stories are primarily of interest as commentaries on the kinds of attitudes and techniques now associated with his poetry; and, ultimately, Villa's importance to fiction is as its critic, not as its writer.

A third of the twenty-one stories in *Footnote* are semiautobiographical and as casual as diary entries. Rarely are the great plains of the commonplace interrupted; and then by minute near-mirages, apocalyptic consolations for the hermit-protagonist who has driven himself out into the wilderness. His world is so walled in that the irony of recurrence becomes a constant theme and monotonous structural device. There is a repetitive pattern of illegitimate children, unwanted or inadequately cared for; of alienation between father and grown son, between protagonist and his temporary intimates; of a love-hate identification with Rizal as father-image whose parenthood is clouded; of rejection in courtship and marriage; of renewed self-importance recovered through (usually sentimentalized) association with the suffering Christ.

In his introduction to *Footnote to Youth,* Edward O'Brien speaks of Villa's combining a "native sensuousness of perception and impression" with the traditionally Spanish "expression of passionate feeling in classical reticence of form." In actuality, Villa contrives a sort of artificial cellular geometry, within numbered paragraphs that roughly resemble stanzas isolating act from act. Routine incident, therefore, is permitted no opportunity for rescue through dramatic association. Such configurations, at best, cover the mechanical aftermath of loss, rather than—as the story line itself suggests—the gradual process of becoming totally dispossessed, and the forestalling of this process, the recovery of person through passionate intimacy with God. Vision is proclaimed, not presented as experience. The static quality of many of the stories is antinarrative.

These stories have the same frail romantic quality that was being developed in the same period by Khalil Gibran in Boston's Chinatown. However, self-consciousness too often is pushed to the brink of self-pity, and the vision of God invoked only so that His divinity can be borrowed by man, as reprieve, as proof of importance. (Eventually in Villa's poems God was reproached as man's Foe and Suppliant—a later stage in postadolescent self-definition.) The same psychology of projection and identification is evidenced by the abundance of stories concerned with "sons," "daughters," and look-alikes of Rizal; the same sentimental piety in still other stories.

The remarks of Edward O'Brien in 1933—that Villa belonged "among the half-dozen short story writers in America who count"—have to be placed in historical context. *The Best Short Stories of 1932,* which O'Brien dedicated to Villa, is a remarkably undistinguished volume more than half of whose contributing authors have remained nonentities. The modern American short story was still in its infancy. At the very moment that O'Brien was prophesying a career for Villa as a novelist, the writer was making a more accurate assessment of himself. He found his rhythmic repetitions, his sense of the cyclic, his delight in color symbol and allegory, his inability to sustain narrative momentum, his passion for the ineffable or the aphoristic, as well as the sometimes bizarre wrenching of his words, more appropriate to experiments with lyric poetry. *Footnote to Youth* has become a footnote to Villa.

As for his poetry: Villa's *Selected Poems and New* (1958) proves that he has always struck a not incongruous revolutionary pose. As an expatriate from the Philippines, he scorns in various disguises his people's most sacred images—the father; the homeland: that residue of ancestor worship visible in oppressive family circles. (An early poem, not reprinted, is titled **"Father, on His Unsonment"** and does not seem Freudian.) Paradoxically, his work is therefore representative of his abandoned countrymen's long-standing demand for self-determination, and for personal contribution to tradition. (Even the occasional strain of pompousness is reminiscent of what Rizal once asserted: in order to be accepted as equals by their Spanish masters, Filipinos had to become superior to them.) Theirs is a peculiar kind of rebelliousness neither tolerant nor liberating, but more than willing to be bound by taboos—of its own making. In spite of himself, Villa speaks for the Filipino whose requirement is that he be defined by his own history, not by any other's. His poetry's near-blasphemy, the unconvincing pretense at repentance, have some portion of their origin in the sometimes careless religious observances among Asia's only Christian people, who were left a lasting taste of distrust by Spanish religious orders that served as arms of the Colonial Office.

What is too often mistaken for mysticism in Villa—challenging "Christ Oppositor" to single combat—is surely better understood as unmeditated defiance, resolute aspiration, the refusal to be humiliated by anyone. In this passion for denial lies Villa's strength and, unwittingly, his weakness for self-imitation.

Poems of the order of **"My most. My most. O my lost!"** kindle like a condescension into heaven. Here the theme of man's daily wrestling with God for supremacy is Promethean, therefore appropriately luminous. But more typically the fire lights only itself, failing to reveal any developed sense of even that destinate "genius" so often proclaimed. The sort of criticism by word count which Richard P. Blackmur once turned against E. E. Cummings would be disastrous in Villa's case, whose rubrics also grow repetitive, rather than resonant, in a stammer of imagery. Skull rose flame eyes Christ gold tiger ruby—the romantic vocabulary is small, solipsistic. The poems therefore tend to be more cavalier than metaphysical. The theme diminishes as what at first seemed sacred or profane poems clearly become manifestations of the same self-love; and that self is never doubted, never explored,

only praised and presumed. Villa is no modern John Donne. Despite a tightness of sound pattern and stanza often as intricate as any Provençal *trobador's* bird flight variations, an essential looseness due to the loss of substance and consequence cannot be ignored.

The same reduction to absurdity, through excess, threatens the famous "comma" poems. Before Villa, E. E. Cummings liberated syllables, letters, and conventional signs for visually dramatic, often ironic rearrangement. Villa has specialized in a small reserve of words and what looks like a comma but actually provides an overriding continuity rather than, as punctuation might, separation. Where a sort of processional measure is desirable, the "comma" in fact does distribute equality of weight among words. But for other poems it is as demonstrably malfunctional as a dragging foot. Being invariable, it allows no subtleties of suspension, syncopation, etc.; being identical, visually, with actual commas, it hinders the exploitation of punctuation in general. In **"Anchored Angel,"** a recent and otherwise considerable poem, Villa still uses the "commas" with inadequate understanding and skill, although nearly ten years after his original commitment.

Nevertheless, there would seem to be more potential in such devices (if used, for example, as equivalents to musical "holds") than in what Villa calls "reversed consonance." The consonantal order of "Si*ng*" is offered as a mirror-image of that in "be*gins,*" although clearly the *sounds* have not even a reverse identity. The ear cannot, the uninstructed eye will not, note such patterns which, in the very poem offered by Villa for illustration, are dissipated by slant rhymes, multiple alliteration, and assonance. The "purpose" of reversed consonance therefore is calisthenic only, or exhibitionistic.

Such devices, however, have long been both means and ends in Villa's poetry. Can his origins as a rebel account for the fact that he has constantly relied on reversals, negatives, and reductives; definitions by rejection? To "bring the watermelons pigeons," according to one poem, "would be artistry." Another counts the permutations on pink and blue monks eating blue and pink raisins. Again: "The wind shines, / The sun blows . . ."; or "Yesterday,I,awoke,today." These are anagrams, simple exchanges no more profound than those early pseudonyms, for instance: O. Sevilla; or Doveglion (dove-eagle-lion). Occasionally, however, the results fall into meanings:

> *Myself,as,Absence,discoverer.*
> *Myself,as,Presence,searcher.*

Here, opposite ends of an experience, curved in accordance with the geometry of narcissism, converge with all the ease of a snake devouring its tail.

Throughout the *Selected Poems* it is equally natural to encounter unnumbered deprivatives. The "not-face" and "un-ears" of the younger lyrics are preparation for

> In,my,undream,of,death,
> I,unspoke,the,word.

Such conjunctions of word-unword become as elementary as those of stress-unstress; and even if, in an age of Manichaean depressives, pompousness bears a certain attraction for readers in need of reassurance, contrived complication passes for profundity only at the risk of pretentiousness. Where Villa's meanings are most immediate, as in his "Aphorisms," their triviality is undeniable.

Villa's fifth volume of poetry (the third in America) is more representative than selective, and therefore most valuable as a little archive for the historical critic. Has the rebel run out of manifestoes and will he not bring himself to trial? The essential sameness of so many of these lyrics is not lessened by the fact that they are at a loss for titles and, despite Villa's experience with short stories, have no significant narrative order. Although a number do emerge, as does **"The,bright,Centipede,"** with distinction deserving of Dame Edith Sitwell's extravagant praise, they bear no relation as climaxes or epitomes to the others with which they are indiscriminately mingled.

One would like to say that each of these others is a point of voluminous light, a graded off-color in a Seurat painting, whose figure descends from a distance; or that each represents some slight alteration in angle of view, passage of time, the revolving interplay of attitude reflected in the portrait of an object deprived, as by a Picasso, of its inflexible uniqueness. But while the human eye locks Seurat's particles into indivisible quanta, composition in Villa is too often the result of kaleidoscopic accident. And while flux is fundamental to Picasso's multiple vision, Villa's is largely predictable and therefore, in a sense, arrested, immoble, unmatured.

These are strange conclusions to have to reach about an avowed progenitor and poetic experimenter. Still, they are borne out by his latest profession of originality, his "adaptations," the editing of imaginative prose (by Rilke, Gide, *Time,* etc.) into line and stanza. There is as yet no clear indication that such minor adaptations are moving in the direction of Robert Lowell's "collaborations" which he modestly calls *Imitations* (1961), or of the translation/accommodation/mutation pattern of Ezra Pound's development. Meanwhile, these classroom mechanics do indicate Villa's skill at restyling and arranging; and perhaps, as well, betray by this aggressive borrowing unconscious acknowlment that his own poems too long have lacked specific presence and circumstantial detail.

Nevertheless, even after the worst that can be said of Villa's poetry for corrective purposes has been said, his reputation as the premier poet of the Philippines is secure. It is difficult, therefore, to understand the repressive nature of the Villa cult among the young poetasters, except as identification with the *arrivé* or as adolescent self-defense. The cultist's own insecurity, personal and professional; his own unintelligibility and self-doubts; his own linguistic inadequacies—all these he manages to protect by refusing to discuss positively the Villa text or poetic.

Villa, of course, is partly responsible for the arrogance of the cultist: his anthology, *A Doveglion Book of Philippine*

Poetry (1962), is unique not because of the unevenness of quality in his selections—every editor is guilty of some imperfection in judgment—but because of its absolute intolerance, its disdain for all other editorial judgments. Villa is discourteous; but, worse, he is uncritical—that is, as indiscriminate in his opinions as if he had stopped reading Philippine poetry the day of his expatriation. There is something equally old-fashioned about Villa's dogmatic separation of form and meaning; or of prose and poetry: "the two disciplines," he writes, "are as antipodal as night and day—in genesis, in language, craft and all." He has conveniently forgotten the history of his own artistic growth and of the manner of his recent adaptations, in order to defend what he calls Expressive Writing (romantic poetry). Villa's place in Philippine letters is secure; but his image, as it clarifies, may be modified. The arch-rebel may prove to be even more conservative than his society; and far more anachronistic.

L. M. Grow   (essay date 1987)

SOURCE: "José Garcia Villa: The Poetry of Calibration," in *World Literature Written in English,* Vol. 27, No. 2, Autumn, 1987, pp. 326-44.

[*In the following essay, Grow explores Villa's shortcomings and eccentricities as a poet, as well as his talents.*]

> Certainty and uncertainty
> Two sides of the same flame.
>
> ["**A Certain Morning Is**"]

Jose Garcia Villa is, without question, "the premier poet of the Philippines" [Leonard Casper, *New Writing from the Philippines,* 1966]. He has been praised by Filipino, American, and British critics for both short stories and poems since his mid-twenties. Teodoro Locsin, often comparing him favorably to Blake, Chatterton, Thompson, and Shelley, recommends a government sinecure for him [*Philippines Free Press,* January 18, 1947]. Amador T. Daguio's spontaneous letter to the editor, in response to Locsin's proposal, seconds Locsin's evaluation and his sinecure proposal [*Philippines Free Press,* February 22, 1947]. Locsin cites the laudatory notices of, among others, Conrad Aiken, Babette Deutsch, Marianne Moore, Mark Van Doren, Peter Munro Jack, and Edith Sitwell. Edward J. O'Brien dedicated *The Best Short Stories of 1932* to Villa and classified Villa "among the half-dozen short story writers in America who count" [Introduction to Villa's **Footnote to Youth**]. In spite of his apparently radical and innovative approaches to both poems and short stories, Villa's critical judgement has been widely respected for many years. His annual "Best Short Stories" choices were considered definitive in the Philippines in the 1920s and 1930s and his ***Doveglion Book of Philippine Poetry*** in the Peso Series in 1962 reflected the publisher's confidence in the appeal of Villa's selections would have to a wide reading public.

What makes such an impressive reputation—consistent acclaim for short stories, poetry, and critical judgement for fifty years—surprising is that it is founded on comparatively few successful works and based to a substantial degree on what are, in my judgement at least, clearly wrong-headed reasons. Villa, like Wordsworth, would benefit from a selective fire, one which would consume a fair portion of his published work. Hopefully, the fire would terminate such demonstrable failures as:

> As in a rose the true fire moves,
> As in a fire the true mind lives,
> I beheld in a rose the eyes
> That in their pure force swing
> My bells, my voice, my heart
> The spirit and the lovely thews
> The bones and the lovely skull—
> Into the eternity structural.
>
> Eternity has a structure great
> Only the rose's eyes may meet:
> The operant beams are set
> Where none but flame may live:
> A magnitude of spermal love
> In a plasm death-devout:
> Structured thus, within a rose's eye I saw
> The rigors of immortal law.
>
>   [**"As in a rose the true fire moves"**]

This is graceless and in places nonsensical (e.g., lines 3-5; what could "I beheld in a rose the eyes / That in their pure force swing / My bells . . ." possibly mean? What lines 13-14, "A magnitude of spermal love / In a plasm death-devout" might mean I think the critic is better off not to inquire). It was bad enough that Villa at a mature age (thirty-six) included this in his first volume of poems (*Have Come, Am Here*), but that sixteen years later he chose to include this among his *Selected Poems* almost defies explanation. Even more astonishing, considering that this is far from the only poem of like quality included, is that Dame Edith Sitwell could say [in her preface to Villa's *Selected Poems and New*] that "this poetry springs straight from the depths of the poet's being, from his blood, from his spirit, from his experience . . ." or that she could describe **"I was not young long; I met the soul early"** as ". . . a strange poem of an ineffable beauty, springing straight from the depths of Being. I hold that this is one of the most wonderful short poems of our time, and reading it I knew that I was seeing for the first time the work of a poet with a great, even an astonishing, and perfectly original gift." This is excessive praise for a poem which would be awkward even if it were prose:

> I was not young long: I met the soul early:
> Who took me to God at once: and, seeing
> God the Incomparable Sight, I knelt my body
>
> Humbly: whereupon God saw the star upon
> My brow: stooped to kiss it: O then the
> Blinding radiance there! explosion of all
>
> My earthness: sparks flying till I was all
> Embers: long, long did God hold me: till
> He arose and bade me to rise saying: Now

> Go back. Now go back from where you came.
> Go back: Understanding is yours now. Only
> Beware: *beware!* since you and God have lovered.

Such phrases as "I met the soul early: / *Who* took me to God at once"; "I knelt *my body*" (my emphasis; what gymnastic feat could accomplish this?); "earthness"; and "lovered" are bad prose at best.

Villa's prominence certainly is not justified by poems of the sort that we have so far examined. These, at least, do not spring "straight from the depths of Being." In fact, they fail precisely because they are prosy, pretentious, and contrived; they are artificial, not heartfelt. As we shall see later, Villa does have an extraordinary lyric gift, but it is not visible in these productions.

Besides his "lyric gift," Villa's success is often attributed to technical innovation. But technical innovation is independent of literary excellence. One need only consider Shakespeare's borrowed plots or the nearly unbroken succession of great sonneteers since Wyatt and Surrey to realize that the form matters only insofar as the artist selects a metier compatible with his gifts. Poor selection can certainly produce failure (e.g., Henry James's abortive attempt to be a playwright), but correct selection does not guarantee success. The villanelle conventions do not account for the stunning brilliance of Dylan Thomas' "Do Not Go Gentle Into That Goodnight," for instance.

But even if technical innovation did guarantee literary success, Villa does not deserve particularly high marks for his efforts. His typographical permutations are gimmicks, which a reader cannot take seriously (to be fair to Villa, one should add that he does label poems of this sort "caprices"). The **"Sonnet in Polka Dots"** consists of fourteen rows of O's; the **"Centipede Sonnet"** consists of fourteen rows of commas; **"The Emperor's New Sonnet"** consists, predictably, of a blank page. A serious artist is entitled to his lighter moments: W. H. Auden's pornographic poems and Graham Greene's "entertainments" are cases in point. But Villa's productions lack the wit of the former and the point of the latter; they are exhibitionist rather than useful, displaying the author's schoolboyish cleverness, but they are of no appreciable value to the reader. Worse, Villa does not seem to realize this; he includes **"The Emperor's New Sonnet"** in the *Selected Poems.*

The famous "comma poems" concept is not only not original with Villa (e. e. cummings originated it), but is detrimental to poetic success. Both Meredith and Casper convincingly demonstrate that the indiscriminate employment of commas interferes with normal punctuation; Meredith also notes that the commas produce fragmentation and Casper rightly observes that they preclude "subtleties of suspension, syncopation, etc." [William Meredith, "Second Verse, Same-25 the First," *Poetry*, Vol. 75, No. 5, 1950]. Finally, the metronomically regular use of the comma often results in no improvement that might offset the aforementioned disadvantages. If the commas are omitted, the poem often reads better.

Villa's "reversed consonance," which he immodestly describes as "a method which has never been used in the history of English poetry, nor in any poetry" hardly sustains this grandiose claim. It is, as Rolando Tinio concludes, "too esoteric to be effective," ["Villa's Values," in *Brown Heritage: Essays on Philippine Cultural Tradition and Literature,* ed. Antonio G. Manuud, 1967]. It is tempting to compare reversed consonance with Hopkins' sprung rhythm as an experiment worth making but yielding too little to warrant its continued use. Many of the rest of Villa's favourite techniques—"paradox, novelty of diction, and hyperbole" in particular—have only limited applications.

Villa is often credited with carrying on the metaphysical tradition but, as Casper bluntly puts it, "Villa is no modern John Donne." Casper ascribes this to Villa's narcissistic focus, his heavy reliance on reversals, negatives, and reductives, his small and solipsistic vocabulary, and his poetry's "near-blasphemy." Villa's verses also suffer from "contrived complication," sameness of many lyrics, lack of narrative order, and composition dependent on "kaleidoscopic accident." This is a formidable, even disqualifying list of flaws; how can a poet so deeply revered survive them?

The answer is, in my estimation, that they do not infect all of Villa's poetry and that, in any case, they are effects rather than causes of Villa's unsuccessful poems. Villa's major problem is that he is not equipped to be a religious poet, especially not a neo-Metaphysical. Villa's finest form is achieved in the secular lyric, more in the direction of e. e. cummings than Emily Dickinson. When he tries to write religious poetry, he becomes too self-conscious. He adopts what he apparently considers an impressive persona as his narrative voice, rather than speaking *in propria persona.* He tries to prove, rather than present, his poetic material; his poems aim at the brain, not the soul. These poems, often relying on syllogistic logic or the enthymeme, are too contrived. Villa tries to find God by calibration rather than celebration, and the result is disappointing. The principal reason for this failure is that Villa uses logic to reject logic and, by doing so, precludes sustained thematic development. This rejection is, however, unintentional. Villa thinks that deployment of paradox, negation, and reversal will enlarge the inventory of human insight and thus bring us to knowledge of God. It of course actually has the reverse effect, since negation can only function within a designated genus.

In an effort to elevate the self in order to discover God, the persona is aggrandized to almost disturbing degrees. The most extreme case:

> I will break God's seamless skull,
> And I will break His kissless mouth,
> O I'll break out of His faultless shell
> And fall me upon Eve's gold mouth.
>
> I will pound against his skull,
> I will crack it by force of love:
> I'll be a cyclone gale and spill
> Me out of His bounding groove.

I'll be upon Eve, upon Eve,
Upon Eve and her coasts of love!
I'll be upon Eve, upon Eve,

Cataract of Adamhood. There would I be
My Lord! there would I rebuild me Thee
There alone finds my Finality.
                    [**"I will break God's seamless skull"**]

The best defence of this sonnet is that it represents a schoolboyish effort to shock the reader into attention. But were the persona not fictitious we would consider calling a psychiatrist to deal with the blasphemous and barely sublimated impulses to murder, rape, and necrophilia. Yet the last stanza is astonishingly rational, and appropriately supplicatory, showing that the earlier violent utterances are mere bombast, Villa's misguided effort to be emphatic.

In many respects, Villa's direction resembles Byron's when Byron becomes the "touring tragedian":

> Always I did want more God
> Than life could yield,
> More God than God could give.
>
> I betook me to His Rood,
> Made it my chosen Field,
> That I might truly live.
>
> I bled in direst blood
> And by Him twi-distilled,
> Yet eluded He me as through a sieve.
>
> Till He loosed again His Blood,
> And over my soul it ruby-spilled,
> And wove it into mercy's Hive.
>   [**"Always I did want more God"**]

After a quite reasonable first sentence, Villa's insistent inflation of the persona turns grotesque in stanza three and bizarre in stanza four.

However, even when such an exaggerated posture is not adopted, Villa's poems often sound forced:

> First, a poem must be magical,
> Then musical as a sea-gull.
> It must be a brightness moving
> And hold secret a bird's flowering.
> It must be slender as a bell,
> And it must hold fire as well.
> It must have the wisdom of bows
> And it must kneel like a rose.
> It must be able to hear
> The luminance of dove and deer.
> It must be able to hide
> What it seeks, like a bride.
> And over all I would like to hover
> God, smiling from the poem's cover.
>   [**"First, a poem must be magical"**]

This sonnet's wording is too much dictated by preconceived content requirements. Rose, fire and light ("luminance") are three of Villa's favourite motifs, which he is determined to include, whether the poem gracefully accommodates them or not. The results included mixed metaphor (line 8) and confused synesthesia (lines 9-10).

The strain in many of Villa's poems is reflected in the elaborate rhetorical devices which he hopes will generate epiphany. He assumes that ordinary language is insufficient and so loads his poetry with such sophistications as synecdoche:

> Two,is,*two*,because—
> Mathematics,has,childhood,
> With,a,maturity,of,
> Exactitude.
>
>   ["Aphorisms, II"]

"Two,is,*two*" here represents all mathematical manipulations. Zeugma:

> The,Lord,hideth,well—
> Yet,not,to,hide.
> He,hideth,well.
>
> To,make,Hero's Lust.
> To,make,His,heroes,last.
>
>   ["Aphorisms, II"]

Here "last" means "to survive" as well as "end of the sequence," with the latter meaning reinforced by the word's position—the last of the poem's words (cf., Wordsworth's "The marble index of a mind for ever / Voyaging through strange seas of Thought / alone").

Chiasmus:

> Purely—
> In,two,ways:
> In,two,ways,
> Purely.
>
>   ["Purely"]

Often there is a great deal of verbal intricacy compressed into deceptively brief poems. For instance, the word *"In-light"* puns on both "insight" and "in light" ("enlightened"), and contains, I think, a functional allusion to Hopkins' "inscape." It represents the epiphany which Villa's poems strive to create. Likewise, *Hush!* (snow-verb)" uses onomatopoeia to relate the softness, the quietude, of a snowscape to the impact of a command. Ambiguity is also called upon:

> The,last,word,being,uttered,
> The,next,is,not.
> But,next,to,the,last,word,
>
> The,not-word,summarizing,all.
>
>   ["Aphorisms, II"]

If "not-word" is a negative ("the word which denies"), this poem is a ringing cry of *nada.* On the other hand, if "not-word" is simply "something other than a word," the poem means that the universe is more than purely verbal. Another potential ambiguity involves the poem's placement in the *Selected Poems.* It is the last selection from *Volume Two,* but a section of "New Poems and Adaptations" follows. Is this supposed to be a clue that this poem's penultimate word summarizes the overall message of the selections from *Volume Two*? Since that word is "summarizing," we get nowhere with the speculation (does this have any bearing on the possible "*nada*" interpretation of the poem?). We are presented with rings within rings—an almost Nabokovian series of mutually reflecting mirrors of meaning.

This inclination to intricacy is also visible in Villa's proclivity for very traditional stanza forms and poetic modes. Though he generally eschews regular rhyme schemes, he is fond of the sonnet and of regular stanzaic structures, often couplets, triplets and quatrains. His traditionalism is also visible in the literary influences which he has absorbed: Whitman, cummings, Blake, Dickinson, and Hopkins especially (the influence of the latter has generally gone unnoticed by critics but is well worth remark).

It cannot come as too great a surprise to find that Villa's penchant for structure and tradition carries over into his thought. His verse is redolent with logical progressions, often in the form of syllogism or enthymeme. It is this feature which has misled some critics into associating Villa with the Metaphysical poets. But conceits, one of the staples of the Metaphysical poets, are very rare in Villa, and the result is a quite un-Metaphysical abstractness about the Villa cosmos:

> The difficulty in empathizing with the Villa universe is that it is a universe completely evacuated of values which we can easily recognize as human. The landscape is completely antiseptic, like Mondrian, where, as Adaptation 202 indicates, the trees have "vanished in squares and rectangles." . . . Pure word play means that the poet has set himself off from any kind of logicality which is external to him. . . .
>
>   [Tinio, "Villa's Values"]

Tinio's emphasis properly falls on the "logicality," since Villa frequently uses syllogistic logic, here in the form of enthymeme: "The,heat,is,not,Greek—/ It,hath,no,unities" ["Aphorisms, II"]. Syllogistic logic is one manifestation of the poet's most common motif—calibration. He attempts to calculate verbal meaning so precisely that he can discover God's co-ordinates. This is why Villa's favourite motif is mathematics, especially geometry:

> Death, corollary to Life
> But only by Chronology.
> Death, the supreme Theorem—
> Life, the Corollary.
>
> Whose antecedence—
> Paradox divine—
> Mathematics Sublime
> Created in inversed line.

A progression of wine
From fruit to poem.
Grape, the Corollary,
Wine, the Theorem.

[**"Death, corollary to Life"**]

The stress which Villa puts on celebration emerges especially in

Had I not this life decreed,
With a clarity passional,
Most self to deed
With strictest diagonal,

It had not chosen love
Nor distilled it,
Nor audited proof
So oblique and exquisite.

Not merited, not heard
The birth of that Debt,
Of that syllable of The Word
Heard only in the ricochet.

[**"Had I not this life decreed"**]

Villa's persona tries to take the "strictest diagonal" (shortest distance between two points) to distill, to audit, to arrive at The Word. But standard logic and mathematics, Villa knows, do not lead to knowledge of God. The persona's course is "diagonal"; the proof is "oblique"; the "Mathematics Sublime" has been "created in inversed line." Villa tries to reverse the polarities of logic and mathematics, trying to create unlogic and unmathematics, hoping that these will reveal a sort of parallel universe containing God:

The standstillness of unthought
Into the fury of thought:
The mind, perceptor,
Becomes preceptor.

And maddens to establish boundaries
Say, This is thought
This not thought . . .

But it is Unthought all the time,
The Diamond,
Each facet of which is thought.

[**"The standstillness of unthought"**]

This replacement of thought with "unthought" rests on a perfectly clear, though transparently fallacious, premise:

Exactly what is unexact
In unexactness is exact:
Exactness unstatic,
Precision elastic.

What princelier fact
Exhibits subtler tact
Than this exactness
Of subtle unexactness?

[**"Exactly what is unexact"**]

The problem is, of course, that "unlogic" is not a mirror half of "logic," nor is "unmathematics" the obverse side of the coin "mathematics." Certainty and uncertainty are not two sides of the same flame; when Villa assumes that they are, he leaves no realm of existence for his poetry. The Cartesian reduction consumes the poem as well as the poet, which explains Villa's difficulties with sustained thematic development.

One symptom of this problem is the "Adaptations" which Villa uses to flesh out the *Selected Poems.* Unable to compose a poem, Villa claims credit for discovering one already written. Although the "found poem" has been accepted as legitimate, at least in some quarters, it is difficult not to object when a poet claims over forty pages of them. Used to this degree, the "found poem" constitutes another gimmick, rather than authentic poetic effort.

Another symptom of Villa's problems with sustained thematic development is the brevity of his poems. No poem occupies more than a few stanzas and "Aphorisms" constitute one major division (split into three sections) of the *Selected Poems.* It is interesting that very few of these poems are actually aphorisms. Most are simply short poems, ranging in size from one word to eight lines.

Even some of the already short poems need further pruning. For instance, in **"A Song for Rosemarie"** the first two stanzas are excellent, but the last two should be dropped:

Why,lamps,are,lighted,
Why,eggs,are,gold,
I,do,not,know,no,
Sweet,heavens,no.

Pale,vermouth,ultraviolet,
And,tender,lambs,astray,
But,if,these,keep,love,beautiful,
Sweet,heavens,yes.

If,they,keep,love,beautiful,
Wych-tree,wych-bird,
Any,living,whyless,do,
In,that,living,kingdom,fire.

O,in,that,living,kingdom,love,
There's,never,living,no,
All,that's,living,is,yes,
Sweet,sweet,heavens,yes.

The last two stanzas obscure what is a clear and originally-worded statement of a time honoured theme: why are things the way they are? And these last two stanzas are anti-climactic. In the same way, the current

I think, yes, a leopard in Dufy blue would
Be incomparable. Provided his eyes are green
And see death like two flowers. Myself would

Bring him me all in dazzling gold. Lie
At his feet for God's sake awaiting death. The
Blue paw will have its incomparable law. The

Green eyes incomparable words. What voice
This blue this green can muster is weight of
Immensest love. And I am love myself awaiting

This immensity. O fall quick pure feet, pure
Eyes. Fall heavy, immortal leopard. Par death
Lift me, compare me to your incomparability.
    ["I think, yes, a leopard in Duty blue would"]

would be improved if it read

    I think, yes, a leopard in Dufy blue would
    Be incomparable. Provided his eyes are green
    And see death like two flowers. Myself would
    Bring him me all in dazzling gold.
    O fall quick pure feet, pure Eyes.

The compressed version retains thematic coherence—one should allow himself to be devoured by art—without diffusion of intensity.

Often, however, Villa's poems do not have more than one or at most a few salvageable lines. After a spectacular start, such a poem dribbles off into incoherence or inconsequence because there is nowhere for it to go. Villa has unmoored himself from logic, from mathematical order—yet he is a devotee of such disciplined poetic forms as the sonnet and rhetorical modes as sophisticated as synesthesia, chiasmus, and synecdoche. The supreme irony is that Villa, the poet of reversal, negation, and, above all, paradox—has impaled himself on the irresolvable paradox—the deep and simultaneous commitment to both employment and rejection of formal structure. So we get the wonderful openings: "Bring the pigeons watermelons, Abelard"; "In Picasso you see Blue, Rose, and the Virginity of Cubes"; "her day-rose is much sweet"; "I have observed pink monks eating blue raisins"; and "To make icecream chrysantheme."

These lines are ample evidence of Villa's lyric gift. He can produce poetry that is intense, supple, original and sensuous—but he only does so when he neglects his crippling earnestness. Again paradoxically, Villa does occasionally find God—when he stops contriving to find Him:

    I,it,was,that,saw,
    God,dancing,on,phosphorescent,toes,
    Among,the,strawberries.

    It,could,have,been,moonlight,or,
    Daylight—or,no,light,at,all.
    His,feet,cast,light,on,all.

    On,phosphorescent,feet,
    On,phosphorescent,feet,He,danced,
    And,His,eyes,were,closed:

    He,made,the,strawberries,tremble!
    Yet,He,hurt,not,the,littlest,one,
    But,gave,them,ripeness,all.
    ["I,it,was,that,saw"]

The rich allusive texture here—to Wordsworth's "I Wandered Lonely as a Cloud" and to the Shakespearean "ripeness is all" ballast with literary substance a lilting, celebratory lyric.

Villa has unmoored himself from logic, from mathematical order—yet he is a devotee of such disciplined poetic forms as the sonnet and rhetorical modes as sophisticated as synesthesia, chiasmus, and synecdoche.

—L. M. Grow

But there are very few poems like this and generally those there are result from the overriding influence of either Blake or Dickinson. Blake himself might well have produced

    A,bee,flying,to,the,end,of,the,world,
    To,find,one,flower,wherein,to,lie,curled,

    Is,a,fiction,is,a,lie,
    That,will,keep,God,in,the,sky.
    ["Aphorisms, I"]

    The,biography,of,Infinity,
    Is,little,enough,
    Were,we,only,Child.
    The,muscularity,and,the,terror,
    Approach,us,only,
    On,the,hill,of,age.
    And,we,cry,"Wolf! Wolf!"
    ["Aphorisms, III"]

The deceptively simple surface of the latter poem perfectly sets the tone for the quietly disquieting last line—spoken, we realize, from the wolf's standpoint. The poem might well join the *Songs of Innocence and Experience*.

Dickinson's impact is not hard to see in

    My,Fellowship,with,God—
    My,University,Degree?
    None. His,Fellows,go,
    Unalphabeted.
    ["Aphorisms, II"]

In general, however, Villa's vocation is the secular lyric, which he can do brilliantly when he can put aside his devastatingly serious demeanour and his intellectual quest for the Divine. He has sufficient range in size and tone of poem, from the striking single line ("Abstract,as,a,Chinese,tear" [**"Aphorisms, III"**]) to more developed lyrics, quietly assured rather than strident:

My body is a bottle of white glass:
why has not somebody poured red wine into me
that I should become beautiful?

My body is a green leaf:
why have I not dried, that I should blow away
to infinity, with many winds?

[**"INVISIBLE"**]

The content of **"INVISIBLE"** is as serious as the content
of any of Villa's shrill poems. Equally serious, but again
refreshingly low key, is

Clean,like,iodoform,between,the,tall,
Letters,of,*Death*,I,see,Life. This,
To,me,is,immortal,weather,immortal,

Spelling: The,elegant,interweaver,I,
Call,Hero. Beautiful,as,a,child,eating,
Raw,carrots: whole,as,a,child's,eyes,

Gazing,at,you: Death,builds,her,heroes,
Intensely,clean,Death,builds,her,heroes,
Intensely,whole. A,man,and,Death,indeed,

That life,may,speak: a,man,and,Death,
In,league,that,Life,may,flower: clean,
Athletic,mathematic,dancer: and,present-

Tensing,all,his,future: poises,dances,
Every,everywhere,he,go: Christ,upon,a,
Ball: Saltimbange,perpetual,in beauty.

[**"Clean,like,iodoform,between,
the,tall"**]

It may be, in fact, that Villa handles the playful poetic
material even more deftly than he does material with more
significant implications:

Because,thy,smile,is,primavera,
A,nude,Botticelli: therefore,

Do,thou,smile,at,me. Because,
Thy,neck,is,proud,as,honey,

Dream,of,Modigliani: therefore,
Do,thou,come,queen,to,me.

And,because,thy,feet,are,small,
Though,I,bid,thee,run,to,me,

Do,thou,not,come,at,all,
But,let,me,run,quick,to,thee!

[**"Because,thy,smile,is,primavera"**]

The reader only familiar with Villa's overwrought efforts
at the religious lyric would never assume that the playful
can even be carried, quite successfully, to the threshold of
the precious:

The,caprice,of,canteloupes,is,to,be,
Sweet,or,not,sweet—

To,create,suspense. A,return,
To,Greek,drama.

Their,dramaturgy,is,not,in,the,sweet,
Soil,but,in,the,eye,

Of,birds,the,pure,eye,that,decides,
To,bestow,or,

To,withhold. Shall,I,be,sweet,or,
Not,sweet?—looking,

Up,at,your,face. Till,sudden:
I,will,be,sweet!

[**"The,caprice,of,canteloupes,is,to,be"**]

It is even possible for Villa to fuse the serious and the
playful tones, producing a poem of imaginative reach,
supple syntax, and consequential implication:

A radio made of seawater
Will have mermaids for music:
Who when me they will kiss
All my senses will greet.

A radio made of birds
Will have music of grapes!
Who between their ribs
Shall carry joys without peer.

But a radio made of Light
Will have music of Blakes:
Who with great tigertails
Will beat God-musicales.

[**"A radio made of seawater"**]

It is ironic and paradoxical that Villa should exalt the
music of Blake and yet construct so much of his poetic
universe with the calculating and measuring mind of Ur-
izen. Villa should, instead, have taken caution from *Lamia*
and, with Keats, drunk a toast to the confusion of mathematics.

Had he done so, Villa might have realized the full potential of his lyric gift, by perfecting the verbal still life. If
any poet has ever been blessed with the visual acuity, the
instinct for uncluttered composition, and the historical
consciousness to make the genre viable, Villa has been.
This gift goes far beyond the talent for landscape description of Cobbett, Scott, and Clare and the widely heralded
concrete object focus of Hemingway.

Villa's successful poems have the common denominator
of clear, rich imagery, not mathematical abstraction, and
their visual effectiveness is enhanced, rather than diminished, by downplaying the data of the other four senses.
"My body is a bottle of white glass:" is a case in point.
The controlling metaphor is crisply-defined and the two
stanzas of the poem are symmetrical, counterpart to the
balance required for the painter's still life. Stanza one
suggests hydrating; stanza two suggests dehydrating. Stanza one's metaphor involves a static, inanimate object;

stanza two's metaphor centres around a mutable, animate entity. Stanza one's content is finite, bounded by the dimensions of the bottle; stanza two's content is infinity. Stanza one is anticipatory, the persona awaiting the infusion of red wine (blood?) into the white glass container (the physical body?). Stanza two is superannuatory, the persona awaiting the end.

Villa's successful poems have the common denominator of clear, rich imagery, not mathematical abstraction, and their visual effectiveness is enhanced, rather than diminished, by downplaying the data of the other four senses.

—L. M. Grow

Yet, sharply parallel though these two elemental physical entities are, both because of contrast and because of comparison, the poem is not devoid of interpretational depth. The word "wind" in the last line, for instance, provokes the question of whether the winds are the vehicle of transport or the persona's companions in infinity. If the latter, the poem has posed a significant question about the essence of the persona. Are all bodily shapes merely accidents (in the philosophical sense of the term)? To what degree does transmogrification occur when appearance yields at last to reality? In short, what is real? This is an impressive accumulation of substance in a six-line poem containing only two, commonplace, abstractions ("beautiful," "infinity") and only one other word of more than two syllables. This poem is not only unpretentious; it is deceptively simple in outward appearance. It appeals to only one of the five physical senses and relies only on the rhetorical question for rhetorical depth.

"Clean,like,iodoform,between,the,tall," likewise relies exclusively on its imagery. Death is presented as a series of letters spelling out the word; immortal is equated with weather; "hero" is represented by a child eating raw carrots. Death "builds" heros, just as, presumably, an edifice is constructed from raw materials; life and death are dancers; and Christ is situated on a Ball (I surmise that "ball" here carries the obsolete meaning of "the figure of the earth").

Even the more playful poetry uses visual acuity to convey depth of emotion and/or meaning. **"The,caprice,of,canteloupes,is,to,be,"** again is strikingly like a still life, both in its subject matter and in its clarity of layout. One can envision the fruit and the birds as the subjects, actors on the stage (perhaps a garden, as "Soil" in line 6 suggests) captured in freeze frame by the painter. The diagonal balance of canteloupes in, say, the lower left corner and the birds with large liquid eyes in the upper right corner could hardly be more explicit. Explicit does not mean

shallow, however. The interesting variation on the theme of "beauty in the eye of the beholder" is, of course, the quasi-amusing reversal by which the decision about whether to be sweet or not to be sweet is made by the sightless canteloupe on the basis of the look in the bird's eye. Beauty may be in the eye of the beholder, but who is beholding whom? This question has implications for the problem of essence broached in "My body is a bottle of white glass."

Carefully tucked away beneath the glaze of commas is an ambiguous allusion to Hamlet's "to be or not to be" soliloquy. If "sweet" is construed as a term of endearment, a noun rather than an adjective, the poem reveals the canteloupe's uncertainty about whether to exist or not. Once this is recognized, the magnitude of Villa's achievement can be appreciated. In a poem featuring birds and canteloupes Villa has set out the existential dilemma: does existence precede essence?

On the most obvious level, the canteloupes are trying to decide the essence question: should we be sweet or should we not be sweet? Either way, we will remain canteloupes and our existence is not in doubt. But on the subsurface level, the poem is a dialogue (or perhaps a dramatic monologue) in which the canteloupes finally decide to exist. The cleverness here will immediately be apprehended by the philosophically-oriented reader; since the two levels of meaning are simultaneously present, the problem of precedence between essence and existence is dispensed with. But is this an answer to the existential question, or an evasion of it?

A similarly significant poem, the depth of which has generally gone unrecognized, is **"A radio made of seawater."** This is not mere fantasia; it is chillingly meaningful. What stanza one describes is the traditional fear of sailors, and stanza one describes this fear as compellingly as Eliot's "The Love Song of J. Alfred Prufrock" does at its conclusion. The mermaids' siren songs will be broadcast on the entire wavelength of the ocean. With such breadth of coverage, who can escape them? Certainly not the narrator, whose choice of "when" rather than "if" in line 3 leaves no doubt about the outcome. But what does "senses" mean? Perhaps the narrator's five physical senses, but also perhaps his wits (as in the expression "he's finally come to his senses").

Stanza two establishes the direction of the poem (from undersea in stanza one to in the air in stanza two to in heaven in stanza three). The continuity of thought is also preserved. The birds, like the mermaids, have attractive songs—the birds are the broadcasters, the grapes the music itself. This could be meant to suggest the visual similarity between quarter notes attached to the treble or bass clef and grapes hanging on a vine. If so, the common Villa practice in his best work of visual representation of abstractions is present again.

Stanza three carries the broadcast motif to the cosmic level. The stature of the music is indicated by the capital "L" on "Light" and by the word "beat" (defeat). There may be a buried allusion to the music of the spheres here and there certainly is an allusion to Blake's poem "The Tyger." Perhaps the stanza suggests that Blake's cosmogony is merely another siren song, an enticing deception. Does Blake's cosmogony have the "tiger by the tail," as the colloquialism goes, or is the opponent ("God-musicales") merely a paper tiger? "Musicales," programs of music performed at parties or other social occasions, may be meant to suggest a very casual grappling with the challenge of Blake's alternate cosmogony and thus may be meant to brush aside Blake's objection to a universe constructed by a protractor. In other words, which is the artificial—hence incorrect—picture—the traditional Christian one or Blake's?

The problem of selecting what is real from what only appears to be is, of course, compounded by such factors as the ambiguity in the word "beat" in the last line. "Beat" may mean "to defeat," "to strike," or "to accompany" (as in beating time on a drum). The verbal ambiguity is enhanced by the relatively indeterminate visual quality. It is only by synesthetic extension that we can visualize "a radio made of seawater," "a radio made of birds," or "a radio made of Light." If these images are clear at all, they are so in the same way that seeing faces etched in the clouds in the sky is clear: the reader's imagination imposes on the external object the qualities which we attribute to that object. Making any such visualization even more tenuous is the realization that Blake, himself a painter, often provides poems and works of visual art which are ironic commentaries on one another (cf. the plate accompanying "The Tyger," which depicts a playful tabby rather than a ferocious animal with "fearful symmetry").

Villa's evocative power in these verbal still lifes is enhanced by his acquaintance with the history of art, both visual and verbal. The archaic language in **"Because,thy,smile,is,primavera"** ("thy," "thou," "thee") combines with the allusions to Botticelli and Modigliani to establish the context for "nude" and, more widely, portraiture in general. This takes us beyond the still life, but still focuses on a static natural object. The last two lines are a wry reminder that the tree cannot run to the speaker, so static are the small feet (roots).

Yet the poem does not merely suggest a nineteenth-century notion that a return to nature is good ("let,me,run,quick,to,thee!"). Syntactical ambiguity permits us to read line one as a claim that the smile exists; "primavera" is a noun of direct address, rather than a predicate adjective, and "A,nude,Botticelli" is an appositive to "primavera." This reading is congruent with the personification of the next stanza ("Thy,neck,is,proud,as,honey,") which is, of course, continued on "Dream," "queen," and "feet" in the rest of the poem. The meaning is "let me

embrace (accept) you, because, though you are a natural object, you have the aesthetic quality of fine art." This interpretation finds support in stanza three, if the dream is the dream of Modigliani rather than an injunction to the primavera to dream about Modigliani. In the last line, "quick" may mean "alive" as well as "swiftly." Otherwise it is difficult to see what purpose "quick" serves, since "run" presumably identifies with the speed of the activity. Such a reading is in keeping with Villa's penchant for the "found poem." He is suggesting that nature itself produces art, and that it is the recognition of art *qua* art when we see it that represents the satisfaction of the human quest for imaginative pleasure.

In all, it is Villa's impressive success with the verbal still life which will make him live as a poet. He presents us, in these poems, stunningly realized visuals replete with meaning. He crafts both artistic exterior and philosophical interior, developing both surface and heart with equal facility.

FURTHER READING

Abad, Gemino H. "The Self as Genius and God as Peacock: A Study of 'Mysticism' in José Garcia Villa's Poetry." *University College Journal* 8 (1964): 172-85.
     Defines the purported "mysticism" evident in Villa's poetry as "a 'theology' of Self as God."

Demetillo, Ricaredo. "José Garcia Villa vs. Savador P. Lopez." In *The Authentic Voice of Poetry,* pp. 294-321. Quezon City: University of the Philippines, 1962.
     Closely analyzes Villa's poetry in a discussion of the aesthetic conflict between the poet and his harshest critic.

Moore, Marianne. "Who Seeks Shall Find." *The Nation* 155 (October 17, 1942): 394.
     Favorable review of *Have Come, Am Here,* which emphasizes Villa's poetic technique.

Solberg, S. E. "Bulosan—Theseus—Villa: A Cryptography of Coincidence." *MELUS* 15, No. 2 (Summer 1988): 3-25.
     Compares the responses to America by Villa and fellow Filipino writer Carlos Bulosan by comparing the two authors' treatment of the mythological figure of Theseus, the subject of a poem by each.

Tinio, Rolando S. "Villas' Values; Or, The Poet You Cannot Always Make Out, or Succeed in Liking Once You Are Able to." In *Brown Heritage: Essays on Philippine Cultural Tradition and Literature,* ed. Antonio G. Manuud, pp. 722-38. Quezon City: Ateneo de Manila University Press, 1967.
     Broad survey of Villa's poems and poetic technique.

Additional coverage of Villa's life and career is contained in the following sources published by Gale Research: *Contemporary Authors, Revised Edition,* **Vols. 25-28;** *Contemporary Authors New Revision Series,* **Vol. 12;** *EXPLORING Poetry.*

Poetry Criticism
INDEXES

Literary Criticism Series
Cumulative Author Index

Cumulative Nationality Index

Cumulative Title Index

How to Use This Index

The main references

Calvino, Italo
1923–1985 .... CLC 5, 8, 11, 22, 33, 39,
73; SSC 3

list all author entries in the following Gale Literary Criticism series:

BLC = *Black Literature Criticism*
CLC = *Contemporary Literary Criticism*
CLR = *Children's Literature Review*
CMLC = *Classical and Medieval Literature Criticism*
DA = *DISCovering Authors*
DAB = *DISCovering Authors: British*
DAC = *DISCovering Authors: Canadian*
DAM = *DISCovering Authors: Modules*
     DRAM: *Dramatists Module*; *MST*: *Most-Studied Authors Module*;
     MULT: *Multicultural Authors Module*; *NOV*: *Novelists Module*;
     POET: *Poets Module*; *POP*: *Popular Fiction and Genre Authors Module*
DC = *Drama Criticism*
HLC = *Hispanic Literature Criticism*
LC = *Literature Criticism from 1400 to 1800*
NCLC = *Nineteenth-Century Literature Criticism*
PC = *Poetry Criticism*
SSC = *Short Story Criticism*
TCLC = *Twentieth-Century Literary Criticism*
WLC = *World Literature Criticism, 1500 to the Present*

The cross-references

See also CANR 23; CA 85-88;
     obituary CA116

list all author entries in the following Gale biographical and literary sources:

AAYA = *Authors & Artists for Young Adults*
AITN = *Authors in the News*
BEST = *Bestsellers*
BW = *Black Writers*
CA = *Contemporary Authors*
CAAS = *Contemporary Authors Autobiography Series*
CABS = *Contemporary Authors Bibliographical Series*
CANR = *Contemporary Authors New Revision Series*
CAP = *Contemporary Authors Permanent Series*
CDALB = *Concise Dictionary of American Literary Biography*
CDBLB = *Concise Dictionary of British Literary Biography*
DLB = *Dictionary of Literary Biography*
DLBD = *Dictionary of Literary Biography Documentary Series*
DLBY = *Dictionary of Literary Biography Yearbook*
HW = *Hispanic Writers*
JRDA = *Junior DISCovering Authors*
MAICYA = *Major Authors and Illustrators for Children and Young Adults*
MTCW = *Major 20th-Century Writers*
NNAL = *Native North American Literature*
SAAS = *Something about the Author Autobiography Series*
SATA = *Something about the Author*
YABC = *Yesterday's Authors of Books for Children*

Literary Criticism Series
Cumulative Author Index

Abasiyanik, Sait Faik 1906-1954
See Sait Faik
See also CA 123

Abbey, Edward 1927-1989 .... **CLC 36, 59**
See also CA 45-48; 128; CANR 2, 41

Abbott, Lee K(ittredge) 1947- .... **CLC 48**
See also CA 124; CANR 51; DLB 130

Abe, Kobo 1924-1993 ....   **CLC 8, 22, 53, 81;**
DAM NOV
See also CA 65-68; 140; CANR 24, 60; DLB
182; MTCW

Abelard, Peter c. 1079-c. 1142 .... **CMLC 11**
See also DLB 115

Abell, Kjeld 1901-1961 .... **CLC 15**
See also CA 111

Abish, Walter 1931- .... **CLC 22**
See also CA 101; CANR 37; DLB 130

Abrahams, Peter (Henry) 1919- .... **CLC 4**
See also BW 1; CA 57-60; CANR 26; DLB 117;
MTCW

Abrams, M(eyer) H(oward) 1912- ..... **CLC 24**
See also CA 57-60; CANR 13, 33; DLB 67

Abse, Dannie 1923- ... **CLC 7, 29; DAB; DAM**
POET
See also CA 53-56; CAAS 1; CANR 4, 46; DLB 27

Achebe, (Albert) Chinua(lumogu) 1930- **CLC**
1, 3, 5, 7, 11, 26, 51, 75; BLC; DA; DAB;
DAC; DAM MST, MULT, NOV; WLC
See also AAYA 15; BW 2; CA 1-4R; CANR 6,
26, 47; CLR 20; DLB 117; MAICYA; MTCW;
SATA 40; SATA-Brief 38

Acker, Kathy 1948-1997 .... **CLC 45**
See also CA 117; 122; 162; CANR 55

Ackroyd, Peter 1949- .... **CLC 34, 52**
See also CA 123; 127; CANR 51; DLB 155; INT 127

Acorn, Milton 1923- .... **CLC 15; DAC**
See also CA 103; DLB 53; INT 103

Adamov, Arthur 1908-1970 .....   **CLC 4, 25;**
DAM DRAM
See also CA 17-18; 25-28R; CAP 2; MTCW

Adams, Alice (Boyd) 1926- **CLC 6, 13, 46; SSC 24**
See also CA 81-84; CANR 26, 53; DLBY 86;
INT CANR-26; MTCW

Adams, Andy 1859-1935 .... **TCLC 56**
See also YABC 1

Adams, Brooks 1848-1927 .... **TCLC 80**
See also CA 123; DLB 47

Adams, Douglas (Noel) 1952- .... **CLC 27, 60;**
DAM POP
See also AAYA 4; BEST 89:3; CA 106; CANR
34, 64; DLBY 83; JRDA

Adams, Francis 1862-1893 .... **NCLC 33**

Adams, Henry (Brooks) 1838-1918 . **TCLC 4,**
52; DA; DAB; DAC; DAM MST
See also CA 104; 133; DLB 12, 47, 189

Adams, Richard (George) 1920-   **CLC 4, 5, 18;**
DAM NOV
See also AAYA 16; AITN 1, 2; CA 49-52; CANR
3, 35; CLR 20; JRDA; MAICYA; MTCW;
SATA 7, 69

Adamson, Joy(-Friederike Victoria) 1910-1980
CLC 17
See also CA 69-72; 93-96; CANR 22; MTCW;
SATA 11; SATA-Obit 22

Adcock, Fleur 1934- .... **CLC 41**
See also CA 25-28R; CAAS 23; CANR 11, 34; DLB 40

Addams, Charles (Samuel) 1912-1988 **CLC 30**
See also CA 61-64; 126; CANR 12

Addams, Jane 1860-1945 .... **TCLC 76**

Addison, Joseph 1672-1719 .... **LC 18**
See also CDBLB 1660-1789; DLB 101

Adler, Alfred (F.) 1870-1937 .... **TCLC 61**
See also CA 119; 159

Adler, C(arole) S(chwerdtfeger) 1932-   **CLC 35**
See also AAYA 4; CA 89-92; CANR 19, 40;
JRDA; MAICYA; SAAS 15; SATA 26, 63

Adler, Renata 1938- .... **CLC 8, 31**
See also CA 49-52; CANR 5, 22, 52; MTCW

Ady, Endre 1877-1919 .... **TCLC 11**
See also CA 107

A.E. 1867-1935 .... **TCLC 3, 10**
See also Russell, George William

Aeschylus 525B.C.-456B.C. ... **CMLC 11; DA;**
DAB; DAC; DAM DRAM, MST; DC 8; WLCS
See also DLB 176

Aesop 620(?)B.C.-564(?)B.C. .... **CMLC 24**
See also CLR 14; MAICYA; SATA 64

Africa, Ben
See Bosman, Herman Charles

Afton, Effie
See Harper, Frances Ellen Watkins

Agapida, Fray Antonio
See Irving, Washington

Agee, James (Rufus) 1909-1955 . **TCLC 1, 19;**
DAM NOV
See also AITN 1; CA 108; 148; CDALB 1941-
1968; DLB 2, 26, 152

Aghill, Gordon
See Silverberg, Robert

Agnon, S(hmuel) Y(osef Halevi) 1888-1970
CLC 4, 8, 14; SSC 30
See also CA 17-18; 25-28R; CANR 60; CAP 2;
MTCW

Agrippa von Nettesheim, Henry Cornelius 1486-
1535 .... **LC 27**

Aherne, Owen
See Cassill, R(onald) V(erlin)

Ai 1947- .... **CLC 4, 14, 69**
See also CA 85-88; CAAS 13; DLB 120

Aickman, Robert (Fordyce) 1914-1981 **CLC 57**
See also CA 5-8R; CANR 3

Aiken, Conrad (Potter) 1889-1973   **CLC 1, 3,**
5, 10, 52; DAM NOV, POET; SSC 9
See also CA 5-8R; 45-48; CANR 4, 60; CDALB
1929-1941; DLB 9, 45, 102; MTCW; SATA
3, 30

Aiken, Joan (Delano) 1924- .... **CLC 35**
See also AAYA 1, 25; CA 9-12R; CANR 4, 23,
34, 64; CLR 1, 19; DLB 161; JRDA;
MAICYA; MTCW; SAAS 1; SATA 2, 30, 73

Ainsworth, William Harrison 1805-1882
NCLC 13
See also DLB 21; SATA 24

Aitmatov, Chingiz (Torekulovich) 1928-   **CLC**
71
See also CA 103; CANR 38; MTCW; SATA 56

Akers, Floyd
See Baum, L(yman) Frank

Altman, Robert 1925-............................ **CLC 16**
　See also CA 73-76; CANR 43

Alvarez, A(lfred) 1929- .... **CLC 5, 13**
　See also CA 1-4R; CANR 3, 33, 63; DLB 14, 40

Alvarez, Alejandro Rodriguez 1903-1965
　See Casona, Alejandro
　See also CA 131; 93-96; HW

Alvarez, Julia 1950-............................ **CLC 93**
　See also AAYA 25; CA 147

Alvaro, Corrado 1896-1956 .... **TCLC 60**
　See also CA 163

Amado, Jorge 1912- **CLC 13, 40, 106; DAM MULT, NOV; HLC**
　See also CA 77-80; CANR 35; DLB 113; MTCW

Ambler, Eric 1909- .... **CLC 4, 6, 9**
　See also CA 9-12R; CANR 7, 38; DLB 77; MTCW

Amichai, Yehuda 1924- .... **CLC 9, 22, 57**
　See also CA 85-88; CANR 46, 60; MTCW

Amichai, Yehudah
　See Amichai, Yehuda

Amiel, Henri Frederic 1821-1881 ..... **NCLC 4**

Amis, Kingsley (William) 1922-1995 **CLC 1, 2, 3, 5, 8, 13, 40, 44; DA; DAB; DAC; DAM MST, NOV**
　See also AITN 2; CA 9-12R; 150; CANR 8, 28, 54; CDBLB 1945-1960; DLB 15, 27, 100, 139; DLBY 96; INT CANR-8; MTCW

Amis, Martin (Louis) 1949- . **CLC 4, 9, 38, 62, 101**
　See also BEST 90:3; CA 65-68; CANR 8, 27, 54; DLB 14, 194; INT CANR-27

Ammons, A(rchie) R(andolph) 1926- **CLC 2, 3, 5, 8, 9, 25, 57, 108; DAM POET; PC 16**
　See also AITN 1; CA 9-12R; CANR 6, 36, 51; DLB 5, 165; MTCW

Amo, Tauraatua i
　See Adams, Henry (Brooks)

Anand, Mulk Raj 1905- .. **CLC 23, 93; DAM NOV**
　See also CA 65-68; CANR 32, 64; MTCW

Anatol
　See Schnitzler, Arthur

Anaximander c. 610B.C.-c. 546B.C. **CMLC 22**

Anaya, Rudolfo A(lfonso) 1937-...... **CLC 23; DAM MULT, NOV; HLC**
　See also AAYA 20; CA 45-48; CAAS 4; CANR 1, 32, 51; DLB 82; HW 1; MTCW

Andersen, Hans Christian 1805-1875 **NCLC 7; DA; DAB; DAC; DAM MST, POP; SSC 6; WLC**
　See also CLR 6; MAICYA; YABC 1

Anderson, C. Farley
　See Mencken, H(enry) L(ouis); Nathan, George Jean

Anderson, Jessica (Margaret) Queale 1916- **CLC 37**
　See also CA 9-12R; CANR 4, 62

Anderson, Jon (Victor) 1940- ... **CLC 9; DAM POET**
　See also CA 25-28R; CANR 20

Anderson, Lindsay (Gordon) 1923-1994 **CLC 20**
　See also CA 125; 128; 146

Anderson, Maxwell 1888-1959 ..... **TCLC 2; DAM DRAM**
　See also CA 105; 152; DLB 7

Anderson, Poul (William) 1926- .... **CLC 15**
　See also AAYA 5; CA 1-4R; CAAS 2; CANR 2, 15, 34, 64; DLB 8; INT CANR-15; MTCW; SATA 90; SATA-Brief 39

Anderson, Robert (Woodruff) 1917- **CLC 23; DAM DRAM**
　See also AITN 1; CA 21-24R; CANR 32; DLB 7

Anderson, Sherwood 1876-1941 **TCLC 1, 10, 24; DA; DAB; DAC; DAM MST, NOV; SSC 1; WLC**
　See also CA 104; 121; CANR 61; CDALB 1917-1929; DLB 4, 9, 86; DLBD 1; MTCW

Andier, Pierre
　See Desnos, Robert

Andouard
　See Giraudoux, (Hippolyte) Jean

Andrade, Carlos Drummond de .... **CLC 18**
　See also Drummond de Andrade, Carlos

Andrade, Mario de 1893-1945 .... **TCLC 43**

Andreae, Johann V(alentin) 1586-1654 **LC 32**
　See also DLB 164

Andreas-Salome, Lou 1861-1937 .... **TCLC 56**
　See also DLB 66

Andress, Lesley
　See Sanders, Lawrence

Andrewes, Lancelot 1555-1626 .... **LC 5**
　See also DLB 151, 172

Andrews, Cicily Fairfield
　See West, Rebecca

Andrews, Elton V.
　See Pohl, Frederik

Andreyev, Leonid (Nikolaevich) 1871-1919 **TCLC 3**
　See also CA 104

Andric, Ivo 1892-1975 .... **CLC 8**
　See also CA 81-84; 57-60; CANR 43, 60; DLB 147; MTCW

Androvar
　See Prado (Calvo), Pedro

Angelique, Pierre
　See Bataille, Georges

Angell, Roger 1920-............................. **CLC 26**
　See also CA 57-60; CANR 13, 44; DLB 171, 185

Angelou, Maya 1928- **CLC 12, 35, 64, 77; BLC; DA; DAB; DAC; DAM MST, MULT, POET, POP; WLCS**
　See also AAYA 7, 20; BW 2; CA 65-68; CANR 19, 42, 65; DLB 38; MTCW; SATA 49

Anna Comnena 1083-1153 .... **CMLC 25**

Annensky, Innokenty (Fyodorovich) 1856-1909 **TCLC 14**
　See also CA 110; 155

Annunzio, Gabriele d'
　See D'Annunzio, Gabriele

Anodos
　See Coleridge, Mary E(lizabeth)

Anon, Charles Robert
　See Pessoa, Fernando (Antonio Nogueira)

Anouilh, Jean (Marie Lucien Pierre) 1910-1987 **CLC 1, 3, 8, 13, 40, 50; DAM DRAM; DC 8**
　See also CA 17-20R; 123; CANR 32; MTCW

Anthony, Florence
　See Ai

Anthony, John
　See Ciardi, John (Anthony)

Anthony, Peter
　See Shaffer, Anthony (Joshua); Shaffer, Peter (Levin)

Anthony, Piers 1934- ...... **CLC 35; DAM POP**
　See also AAYA 11; CA 21-24R; CANR 28, 56; DLB 8; MTCW; SAAS 22; SATA 84

Antoine, Marc
　See Proust, (Valentin-Louis-George-Eugene-) Marcel

Antoninus, Brother
　See Everson, William (Oliver)

Antonioni, Michelangelo 1912- .... **CLC 20**
　See also CA 73-76; CANR 45

Antschel, Paul 1920-1970
　See Celan, Paul
　See also CA 85-88; CANR 33, 61; MTCW

Anwar, Chairil 1922-1949 .... **TCLC 22**
　See also CA 121

Apollinaire, Guillaume 1880-1918 **TCLC 3, 8, 51; DAM POET; PC 7**
　See also Kostrowitzki, Wilhelm Apollinaris de
　See also CA 152

Appelfeld, Aharon 1932- .... **CLC 23, 47**
See also CA 112; 133

Apple, Max (Isaac) 1941- .... **CLC 9, 33**
See also CA 81-84; CANR 19, 54; DLB 130

Appleman, Philip (Dean) 1926- .... **CLC 51**
See also CA 13-16R; CAAS 18; CANR 6, 29, 56

Appleton, Lawrence
See Lovecraft, H(oward) P(hillips)

Apteryx
See Eliot, T(homas) S(tearns)

Apuleius, (Lucius Madaurensis) 125(?)-175(?)
CMLC 1

Aquin, Hubert 1929-1977 .... **CLC 15**
See also CA 105; DLB 53

Aragon, Louis 1897-1982 ... **CLC 3, 22; DAM**
NOV, POET
See also CA 69-72; 108; CANR 28; DLB 72;
MTCW

Arany, Janos 1817-1882 .... **NCLC 34**

Arbuthnot, John 1667-1735 .... **LC 1**
See also DLB 101

Archer, Herbert Winslow
See Mencken, H(enry) L(ouis)

Archer, Jeffrey (Howard) 1940- ...... **CLC 28;**
DAM POP
See also AAYA 16; BEST 89:3; CA 77-80;
CANR 22, 52; INT CANR-22

Archer, Jules 1915- .... **CLC 12**
See also CA 9-12R; CANR 6; SAAS 5; SATA 4, 85

Archer, Lee
See Ellison, Harlan (Jay)

Arden, John 1930- .... **CLC 6, 13, 15; DAM**
DRAM
See also CA 13-16R; CAAS 4; CANR 31, 65,
67; DLB 13; MTCW

Arenas, Reinaldo 1943-1990 ... **CLC 41; DAM**
MULT; HLC
See also CA 124; 128; 133; DLB 145; HW

Arendt, Hannah 1906-1975 .... **CLC 66, 98**
See also CA 17-20R; 61-64; CANR 26, 60; MTCW

Aretino, Pietro 1492-1556 .... **LC 12**

Arghezi, Tudor .... **CLC 80**
See also Theodorescu, Ion N.

Arguedas, Jose Maria 1911-1969 **CLC 10, 18**
See also CA 89-92; DLB 113; HW

Argueta, Manlio 1936- .... **CLC 31**
See also CA 131; DLB 145; HW

Ariosto, Ludovico 1474-1533 .... **LC 6**

Aristides
See Epstein, Joseph

Aristophanes 450B.C.-385B.C.   **CMLC 4; DA;**
DAB; DAC; DAM DRAM, MST; DC 2;
WLCS
See also DLB 176

Arlt, Roberto (Godofredo Christophersen)
1900-1942 ....
TCLC 29; DAM MULT; HLC
See also CA 123; 131; CANR 67; HW

Armah, Ayi Kwei 1939- .... **CLC 5, 33; BLC;**
DAM MULT, POET
See also BW 1; CA 61-64; CANR 21, 64; DLB
117; MTCW

Armatrading, Joan 1950- .... **CLC 17**
See also CA 114

Arnette, Robert
See Silverberg, Robert

Arnim, Achim von (Ludwig Joachim von Arnim)
1781-1831 .... **NCLC 5; SSC 29**
See also DLB 90

Arnim, Bettina von 1785-1859 .... **NCLC 38**
See also DLB 90

Arnold, Matthew 1822-1888 .   **NCLC 6, 29;**
DA; DAB; DAC; DAM MST, POET; PC 5;
WLC
See also CDBLB 1832-1890; DLB 32, 57

Arnold, Thomas 1795-1842 .... **NCLC 18**
See also DLB 55

Arnow, Harriette (Louisa) Simpson 1908-1986
CLC 2, 7, 18
See also CA 9-12R; 118; CANR 14; DLB 6;
MTCW; SATA 42; SATA-Obit 47

Arp, Hans
See Arp, Jean

Arp, Jean 1887-1966 .... **CLC 5**
See also CA 81-84; 25-28R; CANR 42

Arrabal
See Arrabal, Fernando

Arrabal, Fernando 1932- ...... **CLC 2, 9, 18, 58**
See also CA 9-12R; CANR 15

Arrick, Fran .... **CLC 30**
See also Gaberman, Judie Angell

Artaud, Antonin (Marie Joseph) 1896-1948
TCLC 3, 36; DAM DRAM
See also CA 104; 149

Arthur, Ruth M(abel) 1905-1979 .... **CLC 12**
See also CA 9-12R; 85-88; CANR 4; SATA 7,
26

Artsybashev, Mikhail (Petrovich) 1878-1927
TCLC 31

Arundel, Honor (Morfydd) 1919-1973   **CLC**
17
See also CA 21-22; 41-44R; CAP 2; CLR 35;
SATA 4; SATA-Obit 24

Arzner, Dorothy 1897-1979 .... **CLC 98**

Asch, Sholem 1880-1957 .... **TCLC 3**
See also CA 105

Ash, Shalom
See Asch, Sholem

Ashbery, John (Lawrence) 1927- .... **CLC**
2, 3, 4, 6, 9, 13, 15, 25, 41, 77; DAM POET
See also CA 5-8R; CANR 9, 37, 66; DLB 5, 165;
DLBY 81; INT CANR-9; MTCW

Ashdown, Clifford
See Freeman, R(ichard) Austin

Ashe, Gordon
See Creasey, John

Ashton-Warner, Sylvia (Constance) 1908-1984
CLC 19
See also CA 69-72; 112; CANR 29; MTCW

Asimov, Isaac 1920-1992   **CLC 1, 3, 9, 19, 26,**
76, 92; DAM POP
See also AAYA 13; BEST 90:2; CA 1-4R; 137;
CANR 2, 19, 36, 60; CLR 12; DLB 8; DLBY
92; INT CANR-19; JRDA; MAICYA;
MTCW; SATA 1, 26, 74

Assis, Joaquim Maria Machado de
See Machado de Assis, Joaquim Maria

Astley, Thea (Beatrice May) 1925- .... **CLC 41**
See also CA 65-68; CANR 11, 43

Aston, James
See White, T(erence) H(anbury)

Asturias, Miguel Angel 1899-1974   **CLC 3, 8,**
13; DAM MULT, NOV; HLC
See also CA 25-28; 49-52; CANR 32; CAP 2;
DLB 113; HW; MTCW

Atares, Carlos Saura
See Saura (Atares), Carlos

Atheling, William
See Pound, Ezra (Weston Loomis)

Atheling, William, Jr.
See Blish, James (Benjamin)

Atherton, Gertrude (Franklin Horn) 1857-1948
TCLC 2
See also CA 104; 155; DLB 9, 78, 186

Atherton, Lucius
See Masters, Edgar Lee

Atkins, Jack
See Harris, Mark

Atkinson, Kate .... **CLC 99**

Attaway, William (Alexander) 1911-198 ... **CLC**
92; BLC; DAM MULT
See also BW 2; CA 143; DLB 76

Atticus
See Fleming, Ian (Lancaster)

Atwood, Margaret (Eleanor) 1939- **CLC 2, 3, 4, 8, 13, 15, 25, 44, 84; DA; DAB; DAC; DAM MST, NOV, POET; PC 8; SSC 2; WLC**
See also AAYA 12; BEST 89:2; CA 49-52; CANR 3, 24, 33, 59; DLB 53; INT CANR-24; MTCW; SATA 50

Aubigny, Pierre d'
See Mencken, H(enry) L(ouis)

Aubin, Penelope 1685-1731(?) .... **LC 9**
See also DLB 39

Auchincloss, Louis (Stanton) 1917- **CLC 4, 6, 9, 18, 45; DAM NOV; SSC 22**
See also CA 1-4R; CANR 6, 29, 55; DLB 2; DLBY 80; INT CANR-29; MTCW

Auden, W(ystan) H(ugh) 1907-1973 **CLC 1, 2, 3, 4, 6, 9, 11, 14, 43; DA; DAB; DAC; DAM DRAM, MST, POET; PC 1; WLC**
See also AAYA 18; CA 9-12R; 45-48; CANR 5, 61; CDBLB 1914-1945; DLB 10, 20; MTCW

Audiberti, Jacques 1900-1965 **CLC 38; DAM DRAM**
See also CA 25-28R

Audubon, John James 1785-1851 ... **NCLC 47**

Auel, Jean M(arie) 1936- **CLC 31, 107; DAM POP**
See also AAYA 7; BEST 90:4; CA 103; CANR 21, 64; INT CANR-21; SATA 91

Auerbach, Erich 1892-1957 .... **TCLC 43**
See also CA 118; 155

Augier, Emile 1820-1889 .... **NCLC 31**
See also DLB 192

August, John
See De Voto, Bernard (Augustine)

Augustine, St. 354-430 .... **CMLC 6; DAB**

Aurelius
See Bourne, Randolph S(illiman)

Aurobindo, Sri
See Aurobindo Ghose

Aurobindo Ghose 1872-1950 .... **TCLC 63**
See also CA 163

Austen, Jane 1775-1817 **NCLC 1, 13, 19, 33, 51; DA; DAB; DAC; DAM MST, NOV; WLC**
See also AAYA 19; CDBLB 1789-1832; DLB 116

Auster, Paul 1947- .... **CLC 47**
See also CA 69-72; CANR 23, 52

Austin, Frank
See Faust, Frederick (Schiller)

Austin, Mary (Hunter) 1868-1934 .. **TCLC 25**
See also CA 109; DLB 9, 78

Autran Dourado, Waldomiro
See Dourado, (Waldomiro Freitas) Autran

Averroes 1126-1198 .... **CMLC 7**
See also DLB 115

Avicenna 980-1037 .... **CMLC 16**
See also DLB 115

Avison, Margaret 1918- . **CLC 2, 4, 97; DAC; DAM POET**
See also CA 17-20R; DLB 53; MTCW

Axton, David
See Koontz, Dean R(ay)

Ayckbourn, Alan 1939- .... **CLC 5, 8, 18, 33, 74; DAB; DAM DRAM**
See also CA 21-24R; CANR 31, 59; DLB 13; MTCW

Aydy, Catherine
See Tennant, Emma (Christina)

Ayme, Marcel (Andre) 1902-1967 ...... **CLC 11**
See also CA 89-92; CANR 67; CLR 25; DLB 72; SATA 91

Ayrton, Michael 1921-1975 .... **CLC 7**
See also CA 5-8R; 61-64; CANR 9, 21

Azorin .... **CLC 11**
See also Martinez Ruiz, Jose

Azuela, Mariano 1873-1952 .. **TCLC 3; DAM MULT; HLC**
See also CA 104; 131; HW; MTCW

Baastad, Babbis Friis
See Friis-Baastad, Babbis Ellinor

Bab
See Gilbert, W(illiam) S(chwenck)

Babbis, Eleanor
See Friis-Baastad, Babbis Ellinor

Babel, Isaac
See Babel, Isaak (Emmanuilovich)

Babel, Isaak (Emmanuilovich) 1894-1941(?) **TCLC 2, 13; SSC 16**
See also CA 104; 155

Babits, Mihaly 1883-1941 .... **TCLC 14**
See also CA 114

Babur 1483-1530 .... **LC 18**

Bacchelli, Riccardo 1891-1985 .... **CLC 19**
See also CA 29-32R; 117

Bach, Richard (David) 1936- .. **CLC 14; DAM NOV, POP**
See also AITN 1; BEST 89:2; CA 9-12R; CANR 18; MTCW; SATA 13

Bachman, Richard
See King, Stephen (Edwin)

Bachmann, Ingeborg 1926-1973 .... **CLC 69**
See also CA 93-96; 45-48; DLB 85

Bacon, Francis 1561-1626 .... **LC 18, 32**
See also CDBLB Before 1660; DLB 151

Bacon, Roger 1214(?)-1292 .... **CMLC 14**
See also DLB 115

Bacovia, George .... **TCLC 24**
See also Vasiliu, Gheorghe

Badanes, Jerome 1937- .... **CLC 59**

Bagehot, Walter 1826-1877 .... **NCLC 10**
See also DLB 55

Bagnold, Enid 1889-1981 .... **CLC 25; DAM DRAM**
See also CA 5-8R; 103; CANR 5, 40; DLB 13, 160, 191; MAICYA; SATA 1, 25

Bagritsky, Eduard 1895-1934 .... **TCLC 60**

Bagrjana, Elisaveta
See Belcheva, Elisaveta

Bagryana, Elisaveta .... **CLC 10**
See also Belcheva, Elisaveta
See also DLB 147

Bailey, Paul 1937- .... **CLC 45**
See also CA 21-24R; CANR 16, 62; DLB 14

Baillie, Joanna 1762-1851 .... **NCLC 2**
See also DLB 93

Bainbridge, Beryl (Margaret) 1933- **CLC 4, 5, 8, 10, 14, 18, 22, 62; DAM NOV**
See also CA 21-24R; CANR 24, 55; DLB 14; MTCW

Baker, Elliott 1922- .... **CLC 8**
See also CA 45-48; CANR 2, 63

Baker, Jean H. .... **TCLC 3, 10**
See also Russell, George William

Baker, Nicholson 1957- .... **CLC 61; DAM POP**
See also CA 135; CANR 63

Baker, Ray Stannard 1870-1946 ..... **TCLC 47**
See also CA 118

Baker, Russell (Wayne) 1925- .... **CLC 31**
See also BEST 89:4; CA 57-60; CANR 11, 41, 59; MTCW

Bakhtin, M.
See Bakhtin, Mikhail Mikhailovich

Bakhtin, M. M.
See Bakhtin, Mikhail Mikhailovich

Bakhtin, Mikhail
See Bakhtin, Mikhail Mikhailovich

Bakhtin, Mikhail Mikhailovich 1895-1975 **CLC 83**
See also CA 128; 113

Bakshi, Ralph 1938(?)- .... **CLC 26**
See also CA 112; 138

Bakunin, Mikhail (Alexandrovich) 1814-1876 **NCLC 25, 58**

Bashkirtseff, Marie 1859-1884 .... NCLC 27

Basho
See Matsuo Basho

Bass, Kingsley B., Jr.
See Bullins, Ed

Bass, Rick 1958- .... CLC 79
See also CA 126; CANR 53

Bassani, Giorgio 1916- .... CLC 9
See also CA 65-68; CANR 33; DLB 128, 177; MTCW

Bastos, Augusto (Antonio) Roa
See Roa Bastos, Augusto (Antonio)

Bataille, Georges 1897-1962 .... CLC 29
See also CA 101; 89-92

Bates, H(erbert) E(rnest) 1905-1974 .. CLC 46; DAB; DAM POP; SSC 10
See also CA 93-96; 45-48; CANR 34; DLB 162, 191; MTCW

Bauchart
See Camus, Albert

Baudelaire, Charles 1821-1867   NCLC 6, 29, 55; DA; DAB; DAC; DAM MST, POET; PC 1; SSC 18; WLC

Baudrillard, Jean 1929- .... CLC 60

Baum, L(yman) Frank 1856-1919 ..... TCLC 7
See also CA 108; 133; CLR 15; DLB 22; JRDA; MAICYA; MTCW; SATA 18

Baum, Louis F.
See Baum, L(yman) Frank

Baumbach, Jonathan 1933- .... CLC 6, 23
See also CA 13-16R; CAAS 5; CANR 12, 66; DLBY 80; INT CANR-12; MTCW

Bausch, Richard (Carl) 1945- .... CLC 51
See also CA 101; CAAS 14; CANR 43, 61; DLB 130

Baxter, Charles (Morley) 1947- . CLC 45, 78; DAM POP
See also CA 57-60; CANR 40, 64; DLB 130

Baxter, George Owen
See Faust, Frederick (Schiller)

Baxter, James K(eir) 1926-1972 .... CLC 14
See also CA 77-80

Baxter, John
See Hunt, E(verette) Howard, (Jr.)

Bayer, Sylvia
See Glassco, John

Baynton, Barbara 1857-1929 .... TCLC 57

Beagle, Peter S(oyer) 1939- .... CLC 7, 104
See also CA 9-12R; CANR 4, 51; DLBY 80; INT CANR-4; SATA 60

Bean, Normal
See Burroughs, Edgar Rice

Beard, Charles A(ustin) 1874-1948 TCLC 15
See also CA 115; DLB 17; SATA 18

Beardsley, Aubrey 1872-1898 .... NCLC 6

Beattie, Ann 1947- ..   CLC 8, 13, 18, 40, 63; DAM NOV, POP; SSC 11
See also BEST 90:2; CA 81-84; CANR 53; DLBY 82; MTCW

Beattie, James 1735-1803 .... NCLC 25
See also DLB 109

Beauchamp, Kathleen Mansfield 1888-1923
See Mansfield, Katherine
See also CA 104; 134; DA; DAC; DAM MST

Beaumarchais, Pierre-Augustin Caron de 1732-1799 .... DC 4
See also DAM DRAM

Beaumont, Francis 1584(?)-1616 LC 33; DC 6
See also CDBLB Before 1660; DLB 58, 121

Beauvoir, Simone (Lucie Ernestine Marie Bertrand) de 1908-1986   CLC 1, 2, 4, 8, 14, 31, 44, 50, 71; DA; DAB; DAC; DAM MST, NOV; WLC
See also CA 9-12R; 118; CANR 28, 61; DLB 72; DLBY 86; MTCW

Becker, Carl (Lotus) 1873-1945 ...... TCLC 63
See also CA 157; DLB 17

Becker, Jurek 1937-1997 .... CLC 7, 19
See also CA 85-88; 157; CANR 60; DLB 75

Becker, Walter 1950- .... CLC 26

Beckett, Samuel (Barclay) 1906-1989   CLC 1, 2, 3, 4, 6, 9, 10, 11, 14, 18, 29, 57, 59, 83; DA; DAB; DAC; DAM DRAM, MST, NOV; SSC 16; WLC
See also CA 5-8R; 130; CANR 33, 61; CDBLB 1945-1960; DLB 13, 15; DLBY 90; MTCW

Beckford, William 1760-1844 .... NCLC 16
See also DLB 39

Beckman, Gunnel 1910- .... CLC 26
See also CA 33-36R; CANR 15; CLR 25; MAICYA; SAAS 9; SATA 6

Becque, Henri 1837-1899 .... NCLC 3
See also DLB 192

Beddoes, Thomas Lovell 1803-1849 ...... NCLC 3
See also DLB 96

Bede c. 673-735 .... CMLC 20
See also DLB 146

Bedford, Donald F.
See Fearing, Kenneth (Flexner)

Beecher, Catharine Esther 1800-1878   NCLC 30
See also DLB 1

Beecher, John 1904-1980 .... CLC 6
See also AITN 1; CA 5-8R; 105; CANR 8

Beer, Johann 1655-1700 .... LC 5
See also DLB 168

Beer, Patricia 1924- .... CLC 58
See also CA 61-64; CANR 13, 46; DLB 40

Beerbohm, Max
See Beerbohm, (Henry) Max(imilian)

Beerbohm, (Henry) Max(imilian) 1872-1956   TCLC 1, 24
See also CA 104; 154; DLB 34, 100

Beer-Hofmann, Richard 1866-1945   TCLC 60
See also CA 160; DLB 81

Begiebing, Robert J(ohn) 1946- .... CLC 70
See also CA 122; CANR 40

Behan, Brendan 1923-1964   CLC 1, 8, 11, 15, 79; DAM DRAM
See also CA 73-76; CANR 33; CDBLB 1945-1960; DLB 13; MTCW

Behn, Aphra 1640(?)-1689   LC 1, 30; DA; DAB; DAC; DAM DRAM, MST, NOV, POET; DC 4; PC 13; WLC
See also DLB 39, 80, 131

Behrman, S(amuel) N(athaniel) 1893-1973   CLC 40
See also CA 13-16; 45-48; CAP 1; DLB 7, 44

Belasco, David 1853-1931 .... TCLC 3
See also CA 104; DLB 7

Belcheva, Elisaveta 1893- .... CLC 10
See also Bagryana, Elisaveta

Beldone, Phil "Cheech"
See Ellison, Harlan (Jay)

Beleno
See Azuela, Mariano

Belinski, Vissarion Grigoryevich 1811-1848   NCLC 5

Belitt, Ben 1911- .... CLC 22
See also CA 13-16R; CAAS 4; CANR 7; DLB 5

Bell, Gertrude 1868-1926 .... TCLC 67
See also DLB 174

Bell, James Madison 1826-1902 ..... TCLC 43; BLC; DAM MULT
See also BW 1; CA 122; 124; DLB 50

Bell, Madison Smartt 1957- .... CLC 41, 102
See also CA 111; CANR 28, 54

Bell, Marvin (Hartley) 1937- CLC 8, 31; DAM POET
See also CA 21-24R; CAAS 14; CANR 59; DLB 5; MTCW

Bell, W. L. D.
See Mencken, H(enry) L(ouis)

Bernhardt, Sarah (Henriette Rosine) 1844-1923
TCLC 75
See also CA 157

Berriault, Gina 1926- ... **CLC 54, 109; SSC 30**
See also CA 116; 129; CANR 66; DLB 130

Berrigan, Daniel 1921- .... **CLC 4**
See also CA 33-36R; CAAS 1; CANR 11, 43;
DLB 5

Berrigan, Edmund Joseph Michael, Jr. 1934-
1983
See Berrigan, Ted
See also CA 61-64; 110; CANR 14

Berrigan, Ted .... **CLC 37**
See also Berrigan, Edmund Joseph Michael, Jr.
See also DLB 5, 169

Berry, Charles Edward Anderson 1931-
See Berry, Chuck
See also CA 115

Berry, Chuck .... **CLC 17**
See also Berry, Charles Edward Anderson

Berry, Jonas
See Ashbery, John (Lawrence)

Berry, Wendell (Erdman) 1934-   **CLC 4, 6, 8,
27, 46; DAM POET**
See also AITN 1; CA 73-76; CANR 50; DLB 5, 6

Berryman, John 1914-1972   **CLC 1, 2, 3, 4, 6,
8, 10, 13, 25, 62; DAM POET**
See also CA 13-16; 33-36R; CABS 2; CANR 35;
CAP 1; CDALB 1941-1968; DLB 48; MTCW

Bertolucci, Bernardo 1940- .... **CLC 16**
See also CA 106

Berton, Pierre (Francis De Marigny) 1920-
CLC 104
See also CA 1-4R; CANR 2, 56; DLB 68

Bertrand, Aloysius 1807-1841 .... **NCLC 31**

Bertran de Born c. 1140-1215 .... **CMLC 5**

Besant, Annie (Wood) 1847-1933 ...... **TCLC 9**
See also CA 105

Bessie, Alvah 1904-1985 .... **CLC 23**
See also CA 5-8R; 116; CANR 2; DLB 26

Bethlen, T. D.
See Silverberg, Robert

Beti, Mongo .... **CLC 27; BLC; DAM MULT**
See also Biyidi, Alexandre

Betjeman, John 1906-1984   **CLC 2, 6, 10,
34, 43; DAB; DAM MST, POET**
See also CA 9-12R; 112; CANR 33, 56; CDBLB
1945-1960; DLB 20; DLBY 84; MTCW

Bettelheim, Bruno 1903-1990 .... **CLC 79**
See also CA 81-84; 131; CANR 23, 61; MTCW

Betti, Ugo 1892-1953 .... **TCLC 5**
See also CA 104; 155

Betts, Doris (Waugh) 1932- .... **CLC 3, 6, 28**
See also CA 13-16R; CANR 9, 66; DLBY 82;
INT CANR-9

Bevan, Alistair
See Roberts, Keith (John Kingston)

Bialik, Chaim Nachman 1873-1934   **TCLC 25**

Bickerstaff, Isaac
See Swift, Jonathan

Bidart, Frank 1939- .... **CLC 33**
See also CA 140

Bienek, Horst 1930- .... **CLC 7, 11**
See also CA 73-76; DLB 75

Bierce, Ambrose (Gwinett) 1842-1914(?)
**TCLC 1, 7, 44; DA; DAC; DAM MST; SSC
9; WLC**
See also CA 104; 139; CDALB 1865-1917; DLB
11, 12, 23, 71, 74, 186

Biggers, Earl Derr 1884-1933 .... **TCLC 65**
See also CA 108; 153

Billings, Josh
See Shaw, Henry Wheeler

Billington, (Lady) Rachel (Mary) 1942- **CLC 43**
See also AITN 2; CA 33-36R; CANR 44

Binyon, T(imothy) J(ohn) 1936- .... **CLC 34**
See also CA 111; CANR 28

Bioy Casares, Adolfo 1914-1984   **CLC 4, 8,
13, 88; DAM MULT; HLC; SSC 17**
See also CA 29-32R; CANR 19, 43, 66; DLB
113; HW; MTCW

Bird, Cordwainer
See Ellison, Harlan (Jay)

Bird, Robert Montgomery 1806-1854 **NCLC 1**

Birney, (Alfred) Earle 1904-1995 **CLC 1, 4, 6,
11; DAC; DAM MST, POET**
See also CA 1-4R; CANR 5, 20; DLB 88; MTCW

Bishop, Elizabeth 1911-1979   **CLC 1, 4, 9, 13,
15, 32; DA; DAC; DAM MST, POET; PC 3**
See also CA 5-8R; 89-92; CABS 2; CANR 26,
61; CDALB 1968-1988; DLB 5, 169; MTCW;
SATA-Obit 24

Bishop, John 1935- .... **CLC 10**
See also CA 105

Bissett, Bill 1939- .... **CLC 18; PC 14**
See also CA 69-72; CAAS 19; CANR 15; DLB
53; MTCW

Bitov, Andrei (Georgievich) 1937- ..... **CLC 57**
See also CA 142

Biyidi, Alexandre 1932-
See Beti, Mongo
See also BW 1; CA 114; 124; MTCW

Bjarme, Brynjolf
See Ibsen, Henrik (Johan)

Bjornson, Bjornstjerne (Martinius) 1832-1910
TCLC 7, 37
See also CA 104

Black, Robert
See Holdstock, Robert P.

Blackburn, Paul 1926-1971 .... **CLC 9, 43**
See also CA 81-84; 33-36R; CANR 34; DLB 16;
DLBY 81

Black Elk 1863-1950 .... **TCLC 33; DAM
MULT**
See also CA 144; NNAL

Black Hobart
See Sanders, (James) Ed(ward)

Blacklin, Malcolm
See Chambers, Aidan

Blackmore, R(ichard) D(oddridge) 1825-1900
TCLC 27
See also CA 120; DLB 18

Blackmur, R(ichard) P(almer) 1904-1965 **CLC
2, 24**
See also CA 11-12; 25-28R; CAP 1; DLB 63

Black Tarantula
See Acker, Kathy

Blackwood, Algernon (Henry) 1869-1951
TCLC 5
See also CA 105; 150; DLB 153, 156, 178

Blackwood, Caroline 1931-1996 .   **CLC 6, 9,
100**
See also CA 85-88; 151; CANR 32, 61, 65; DLB
14; MTCW

Blade, Alexander
See Hamilton, Edmond; Silverberg, Robert

Blaga, Lucian 1895-1961 .... **CLC 75**

Blair, Eric (Arthur) 1903-1950
See Orwell, George
See also CA 104; 132; DA; DAB; DAC; DAM
MST, NOV; MTCW; SATA 29

Blais, Marie-Claire 1939- **CLC 2, 4, 6, 13, 22;
DAC; DAM MST**
See also CA 21-24R; CAAS 4; CANR 38; DLB
53; MTCW

Blaise, Clark 1940- .... **CLC 29**
See also AITN 2; CA 53-56; CAAS 3; CANR 5,
66; DLB 53

Blake, Fairley
See De Voto, Bernard (Augustine)

Blake, Nicholas
See Day Lewis, C(ecil)
See also DLB 77

Blake, William 1757-1827   **NCLC 13, 37, 57;
DA; DAB; DAC; DAM MST, POET; PC 12;
WLC**
See also CDBLB 1789-1832; DLB 93, 163;
MAICYA; SATA 30

Bova, Ben(jamin William) 1932- .... **CLC 45**
See also AAYA 16; CA 5-8R; CAAS 18; CANR 11, 56; CLR 3; DLBY 81; INT CANR-11; MAICYA; MTCW; SATA 6, 68

Bowen, Elizabeth (Dorothea Cole) 1899-1973 **CLC 1, 3, 6, 11, 15, 22; DAM NOV; SSC 3, 28**
See also CA 17-18; 41-44R; CANR 35; CAP 2; CDBLB 1945-1960; DLB 15, 162; MTCW

Bowering, George 1935- .... **CLC 15, 47**
See also CA 21-24R; CAAS 16; CANR 10; DLB 53

Bowering, Marilyn R(uthe) 1949- ...... **CLC 32**
See also CA 101; CANR 49

Bowers, Edgar 1924- .... **CLC 9**
See also CA 5-8R; CANR 24; DLB 5

Bowie, David .... **CLC 17**
See also Jones, David Robert

Bowles, Jane (Sydney) 1917-1973 .. **CLC 3, 68**
See also CA 19-20; 41-44R; CAP 2

Bowles, Paul (Frederick) 1910-1986 ....
CLC 1, 2, 19, 53; SSC 3
See also CA 1-4R; CAAS 1; CANR 1, 19, 50; DLB 5, 6; MTCW

Box, Edgar
See Vidal, Gore

Boyd, Nancy
See Millay, Edna St. Vincent

Boyd, William 1952- .... **CLC 28, 53, 70**
See also CA 114; 120; CANR 51

Boyle, Kay 1902-1992 .... **CLC 1, 5, 19, 58; SSC 5**
See also CA 13-16R; 140; CAAS 1; CANR 29, 61; DLB 4, 9, 48, 86; DLBY 93; MTCW

Boyle, Mark
See Kienzle, William X(avier)

Boyle, Patrick 1905-1982 .... **CLC 19**
See also CA 127

Boyle, T. C. 1948-
See Boyle, T(homas) Coraghessan

Boyle, T(homas) Coraghessan 1948- ....**CLC 36, 55, 90; DAM POP; SSC 16**
See also BEST 90:4; CA 120; CANR 44; DLBY 86

Boz
See Dickens, Charles (John Huffam)

Brackenridge, Hugh Henry 1748-1816 ....
NCLC 7
See also DLB 11, 37

Bradbury, Edward P.
See Moorcock, Michael (John)

Bradbury, Malcolm (Stanley) 1932- . **CLC 32, 61; DAM NOV**
See also CA 1-4R; CANR 1, 33; DLB 14; MTCW

Bradbury, Ray (Douglas) 1920- .... **CLC 1, 3, 10, 15, 42, 98; DA; DAB; DAC; DAM MST, NOV, POP; SSC 29; WLC**
See also AAYA 15; AITN 1, 2; CA 1-4R; CANR 2, 30; CDALB 1968-1988; DLB 2, 8; MTCW; SATA 11, 64

Bradford, Gamaliel 1863-1932 .... **TCLC 36**
See also CA 160; DLB 17

Bradley, David (Henry, Jr.) 1950- .... **CLC 23; BLC; DAM MULT**
See also BW 1; CA 104; CANR 26; DLB 33

Bradley, John Ed(mund, Jr.) 1958- .... **CLC 55**
See also CA 139

Bradley, Marion Zimmer 1930- ...... **CLC 30; DAM POP**
See also AAYA 9; CA 57-60; CAAS 10; CANR 7, 31, 51; DLB 8; MTCW; SATA 90

Bradstreet, Anne 1612(?)-1672 ..... . **LC 4, 30; DA; DAC; DAM MST, POET; PC 10**
See also CDALB 1640-1865; DLB 24

Brady, Joan 1939- .... **CLC 86**
See also CA 141

Bragg, Melvyn 1939- .... **CLC 10**
See also BEST 89:3; CA 57-60; CANR 10, 48; DLB 14

Braine, John (Gerard) 1922-1986 ...... **CLC 1, 3, 41**
See also CA 1-4R; 120; CANR 1, 33; CDBLB 1945-1960; DLB 15; DLBY 86; MTCW

Bramah, Ernest 1868-1942 .... **TCLC 72**
See also CA 156; DLB 70

Brammer, William 1930(?)-1978 .... **CLC 31**
See also CA 77-80

Brancati, Vitaliano 1907-1954 .... **TCLC 12**
See also CA 109

Brancato, Robin F(idler) 1936- .... **CLC 35**
See also AAYA 9; CA 69-72; CANR 11, 45; CLR 32; JRDA; SAAS 9; SATA 97

Brand, Max
See Faust, Frederick (Schiller)

Brand, Millen 1906-1980 .... **CLC 7**
See also CA 21-24R; 97-100

Branden, Barbara .... **CLC 44**
See also CA 148

Brandes, Georg (Morris Cohen) 1842-1927 **TCLC 10**
See also CA 105

Brandys, Kazimierz 1916- .... **CLC 62**

Branley, Franklyn M(ansfield) 1915- **CLC 21**
See also CA 33-36R; CANR 14, 39; CLR 13; MAICYA; SAAS 16; SATA 4, 68

Brathwaite, Edward Kamau 1930- ...**CLC 11; DAM POET**
See also BW 2; CA 25-28R; CANR 11, 26, 47; DLB 125

Brautigan, Richard (Gary) 1935-1984 .... **CLC 1, 3, 5, 9, 12, 34, 42; DAM NOV**
See also CA 53-56; 113; CANR 34; DLB 2, 5; DLBY 80, 84; MTCW; SATA 56

Brave Bird, Mary 1953-
See Crow Dog, Mary (Ellen)
See also NNAL

Braverman, Kate 1950- .... **CLC 67**
See also CA 89-92

Brecht, (Eugen) Bertolt (Friedrich) 1898-1956 **TCLC 1, 6, 13, 35; DA; DAB; DAC; DAM DRAM, MST; DC 3; WLC**
See also CA 104; 133; CANR 62; DLB 56, 124; MTCW

Brecht, Eugen Berthold Friedrich
See Brecht, (Eugen) Bertolt (Friedrich)

Bremer, Fredrika 1801-1865 .... **NCLC 11**

Brennan, Christopher John 1870-1932 ....
TCLC 17
See also CA 117

Brennan, Maeve 1917- .... **CLC 5**
See also CA 81-84

Brent, Linda
See Jacobs, Harriet

Brentano, Clemens (Maria) 1778-1842 **NCLC 1**
See also DLB 90

Brent of Bin Bin
See Franklin, (Stella Maria Sarah) Miles

Brenton, Howard 1942- .... **CLC 31**
See also CA 69-72; CANR 33, 67; DLB 13; MTCW

Breslin, James 1930-1996
See Breslin, Jimmy
See also CA 73-76; CANR 31; DAM NOV; MTCW

Breslin, Jimmy .... **CLC 4, 43**
See also Breslin, James
See also AITN 1; DLB 185

Bresson, Robert 1901- .... **CLC 16**
See also CA 110; CANR 49

Breton, Andre 1896-1966 .... **CLC 2, 9, 15, 54; PC 15**
See also CA 19-20; 25-28R; CANR 40, 60; CAP 2; DLB 65; MTCW

Breytenbach, Breyten 1939(?)- .. **CLC 23, 37; DAM POET**
See also CA 113; 129; CANR 61

Bridgers, Sue Ellen 1942- .... **CLC 26**
See also AAYA 8; CA 65-68; CANR 11, 36; CLR 18; DLB 52; JRDA; MAICYA; SAAS 1; SATA 22, 90

Bridges, Robert (Seymour) 1844-1930 **TCLC 1; DAM POET**
See also CA 104; 152; CDBLB 1890-1914; DLB 19, 98

Capra, Frank 1897-1991 .... **CLC 16**
  See also CA 61-64; 135

Caputo, Philip 1941- .... **CLC 32**
  See also CA 73-76; CANR 40

Caragiale, Ion Luca 1852-1912 .... **TCLC 76**
  See also CA 157

Card, Orson Scott 1951- .... **CLC 44, 47, 50;**
  DAM POP
  See also AAYA 11; CA 102; CANR 27, 47; INT
  CANR-27; MTCW; SATA 83

Cardenal, Ernesto 1925- .... **CLC 31; DAM**
  MULT, POET; HLC; PC 22
  See also CA 49-52; CANR 2, 32, 66; HW;
  MTCW

Cardozo, Benjamin N(athan) 1870-1938
  TCLC 65
  See also CA 117; 164

Carducci, Giosue (Alessandro Giuseppe) 1835-
  1907 ....

TCLC 32
  See also CA 163

Carew, Thomas 1595(?)-1640 .... **LC 13**
  See also DLB 126

Carey, Ernestine Gilbreth 1908- .... **CLC 17**
  See also CA 5-8R; SATA 2

Carey, Peter 1943- .... **CLC 40, 55, 96**
  See also CA 123; 127; CANR 53; INT 127;
  MTCW; SATA 94

Carleton, William 1794-1869 .... **NCLC 3**
  See also DLB 159

Carlisle, Henry (Coffin) 1926- .... **CLC 33**
  See also CA 13-16R; CANR 15

Carlsen, Chris
  See Holdstock, Robert P.

Carlson, Ron(ald F.) 1947- .... **CLC 54**
  See also CA 105; CANR 27

Carlyle, Thomas 1795-1881 ....**NCLC 22; DA;**
  DAB; DAC; DAM MST
  See also CDBLB 1789-1832; DLB 55; 144

Carman, (William) Bliss 1861-1929 **TCLC 7;**
  DAC
  See also CA 104; 152; DLB 92

Carnegie, Dale 1888-1955 .... **TCLC 53**

Carossa, Hans 1878-1956 .... **TCLC 48**
  See also DLB 66

Carpenter, Don(ald Richard) 1931-1995 **CLC**
  41
  See also CA 45-48; 149; CANR 1

Carpentier (y Valmont), Alejo 1904-1980
  CLC 8, 11, 38; DAM MULT; HLC
  See also CA 65-68; 97-100; CANR 11; DLB 113;
  HW

Carr, Caleb 1955(?)- .... **CLC 86**
  See also CA 147

Carr, Emily 1871-1945 .... **TCLC 32**
  See also CA 159; DLB 68

Carr, John Dickson 1906-1977 .... **CLC 3**
  See also Fairbairn, Roger
  See also CA 49-52; 69-72; CANR 3, 33, 60;
  MTCW

Carr, Philippa
  See Hibbert, Eleanor Alice Burford

Carr, Virginia Spencer 1929- .... **CLC 34**
  See also CA 61-64; DLB 111

Carrere, Emmanuel 1957- .... **CLC 89**

Carrier, Roch 1937- **CLC 13, 78; DAC; DAM**
  MST
  See also CA 130; CANR 61; DLB 53

Carroll, James P. 1943(?)- .... **CLC 38**
  See also CA 81-84

Carroll, Jim 1951- .... **CLC 35**
  See also AAYA 17; CA 45-48; CANR 42

Carroll, Lewis .... **NCLC 2, 53; PC 18; WLC**
  See also Dodgson, Charles Lutwidge
  See also CDBLB 1832-1890; CLR 2, 18; DLB
  18, 163, 178; JRDA

Carroll, Paul Vincent 1900-1968 .... **CLC 10**
  See also CA 9-12R; 25-28R; DLB 10

Carruth, Hayden 1921- **CLC 4, 7, 10, 18, 84;**
  PC 10
  See also CA 9-12R; CANR 4, 38, 59; DLB 5,
  165; INT CANR-4; MTCW; SATA 47

Carson, Rachel Louise 1907-1964 ... **CLC 71;**
  DAM POP
  See also CA 77-80; CANR 35; MTCW; SATA
  23

Carter, Angela (Olive) 1940-1992 **CLC 5, 41,**
  76; SSC 13
  See also CA 53-56; 136; CANR 12, 36, 61; DLB
  14; MTCW; SATA 66; SATA-Obit 70

Carter, Nick
  See Smith, Martin Cruz

Carver, Raymond 1938-1988 .... **CLC 22, 36,**
  53, 55; DAM NOV; SSC 8
  See also CA 33-36R; 126; CANR 17, 34, 61;
  DLB 130; DLBY 84, 88; MTCW

Cary, Elizabeth, Lady Falkland 1585-1639 ...**LC 30**

Cary, (Arthur) Joyce (Lunel) 1888-1957
  TCLC 1, 29
  See also CA 104; 164; CDBLB 1914-1945; DLB
  15, 100

Casanova de Seingalt, Giovanni Jacopo 1725-
  1798 .... **LC 13**

Casares, Adolfo Bioy
  See Bioy Casares, Adolfo

Casely-Hayford, J(oseph) E(phraim) 1866-1930
  TCLC 24; BLC; DAM MULT
  See also BW 2; CA 123; 152

Casey, John (Dudley) 1939- .... **CLC 59**
  See also BEST 90:2; CA 69-72; CANR 23

Casey, Michael 1947- .... **CLC 2**
  See also CA 65-68; DLB 5

Casey, Patrick
  See Thurman, Wallace (Henry)

Casey, Warren (Peter) 1935-1988 ...... **CLC 12**
  See also CA 101; 127; INT 101

Casona, Alejandro .... **CLC 49**
  See also Alvarez, Alejandro Rodriguez

Cassavetes, John 1929-1989 .... **CLC 20**
  See also CA 85-88; 127

Cassian, Nina 1924- .... **PC 17**

Cassill, R(onald) V(erlin) 1919- ..... **CLC 4, 23**
  See also CA 9-12R; CAAS 1; CANR 7, 45; DLB 6

Cassirer, Ernst 1874-1945 .... **TCLC 61**
  See also CA 157

Cassity, (Allen) Turner 1929- .... **CLC 6, 42**
  See also CA 17-20R; CAAS 8; CANR 11; DLB
  105

Castaneda, Carlos 1931(?)- .... **CLC 12**
  See also CA 25-28R; CANR 32, 66; HW; MTCW

Castedo, Elena 1937- .... **CLC 65**
  See also CA 132

Castedo-Ellerman, Elena
  See Castedo, Elena

Castellanos, Rosario 1925-1974 ...... **CLC 66;**
  DAM MULT; HLC
  See also CA 131; 53-56; CANR 58; DLB 113; HW

Castelvetro, Lodovico 1505-1571 .... **LC 12**

Castiglione, Baldassare 1478-1529 .... **LC 12**

Castle, Robert
  See Hamilton, Edmond

Castro, Guillen de 1569-1631 .... **LC 19**

Castro, Rosalia de 1837-1885 ...**NCLC 3; DAM**
  MULT

Cather, Willa
  See Cather, Willa Sibert

Cather, Willa Sibert 1873-1947 **TCLC 1, 11,**
  31; DA; DAB; DAC; DAM MST, NOV; SSC
  2; WLC
  See also AAYA 24; CA 104; 128; CDALB 1865-1917;
  DLB 9, 54, 78; DLBD 1; MTCW; SATA 30

Catherine, Saint 1347-1380 .... **CMLC 27**

Cato, Marcus Porcius 234B.C.-149B.C. **CMLC**
  21

Cheever, John 1912-1982 .... **CLC 3, 7, 8, 11, 15, 25, 64; DA; DAB; DAC; DAM MST, NOV, POP; SSC 1; WLC**
See also CA 5-8R; 106; CABS 1; CANR 5, 27; CDALB 1941-1968; DLB 2, 102; DLBY 80, 82; INT CANR-5; MTCW

Cheever, Susan 1943- .... **CLC 18, 48**
See also CA 103; CANR 27, 51; DLBY 82; INT CANR-27

Chekhonte, Antosha
See Chekhov, Anton (Pavlovich)

Chekhov, Anton (Pavlovich) 1860-1904 .... **TCLC 3, 10, 31, 55; DA; DAB; DAC; DAM DRAM, MST; SSC 2, 28; WLC**
See also CA 104; 124; SATA 90

Chernyshevsky, Nikolay Gavrilovich 1828-1889 .... **NCLC 1**

Cherry, Carolyn Janice 1942-
See Cherryh, C. J.
See also CA 65-68; CANR 10

Cherryh, C. J. .... **CLC 35**
See also Cherry, Carolyn Janice
See also AAYA 24; DLBY 80; SATA 93

Chesnutt, Charles W(addell) 1858-1932 .... **TCLC 5, 39; BLC; DAM MULT; SSC 7**
See also BW 1; CA 106; 125; DLB 12, 50, 78; MTCW

Chester, Alfred 1929(?)-1971 .... **CLC 49**
See also CA 33-36R; DLB 130

Chesterton, G(ilbert) K(eith) 1874-1936 .... **TCLC 1, 6, 64; DAM NOV, POET; SSC 1**
See also CA 104; 132; CDBLB 1914-1945; DLB 10, 19, 34, 70, 98, 149, 178; MTCW; SATA 27

Chiang Pin-chin 1904-1986
See Ding Ling
See also CA 118

Ch'ien Chung-shu 1910- .... **CLC 22**
See also CA 130; MTCW

Child, L. Maria
See Child, Lydia Maria

Child, Lydia Maria 1802-1880 .... **NCLC 6**
See also DLB 1, 74; SATA 67

Child, Mrs.
See Child, Lydia Maria

Child, Philip 1898-1978 .... **CLC 19, 68**
See also CA 13-14; CAP 1; SATA 47

Childers, (Robert) Erskine 1870-1922 .... **TCLC 65**
See also CA 113; 153; DLB 70

Childress, Alice 1920-1994 .... **CLC 12, 15, 86, 96; BLC; DAM DRAM, MULT, NOV; DC 4**
See also AAYA 8; BW 2; CA 45-48; 146; CANR 3, 27, 50; CLR 14; DLB 7, 38; JRDA; MAICYA; MTCW; SATA 7, 48, 81

Chin, Frank (Chew, Jr.) 1940- .... **DC 7**
See also CA 33-36R; DAM MULT

Chislett, (Margaret) Anne 1943- .... **CLC 34**
See also CA 151

Chitty, Thomas Willes 1926- .... **CLC 11**
See also Hinde, Thomas
See also CA 5-8R

Chivers, Thomas Holley 1809-1858 .... **NCLC 49**
See also DLB 3

Chomette, Rene Lucien 1898-1981
See Clair, Rene
See also CA 103

Chopin, Kate .... **TCLC 5, 14; DA; DAB; SSC 8; WLCS**
See also Chopin, Katherine
See also CDALB 1865-1917; DLB 12, 78

Chopin, Katherine 1851-1904
See Chopin, Kate
See also CA 104; 122; DAC; DAM MST, NOV

Chretien de Troyes c. 12th cent. ...... **CMLC 10**

Christie
See Ichikawa, Kon

Christie, Agatha (Mary Clarissa) 1890-1976 .... **CLC 1, 6, 8, 12, 39, 48; DAB; DAC; DAM NOV**
See also AAYA 9; AITN 1, 2; CA 17-20R; 61-64; CANR 10, 37; CDBLB 1914-1945; DLB 13, 77; MTCW; SATA 36

Christie, (Ann) Philippa
See Pearce, Philippa
See also CA 5-8R; CANR 4

Christine de Pizan 1365(?)-1431(?) .... **LC 9**

Chubb, Elmer
See Masters, Edgar Lee

Chulkov, Mikhail Dmitrievich 1743-1792 **LC 2**
See also DLB 150

Churchill, Caryl 1938- ...... **CLC 31, 55; DC 5**
See also CA 102; CANR 22, 46; DLB 13; MTCW

Churchill, Charles 1731-1764 .... **LC 3**
See also DLB 109

Chute, Carolyn 1947- .... **CLC 39**
See also CA 123

Ciardi, John (Anthony) 1916-1986 . **CLC 10, 40, 44; DAM POET**
See also CA 5-8R; 118; CAAS 2; CANR 5, 33; CLR 19; DLB 5; DLBY 86; INT CANR-5; MAICYA; MTCW; SAAS 26; SATA 1, 65; SATA-Obit 46

Cicero, Marcus Tullius 106B.C.-43B.C. .... **CMLC 3**

Cimino, Michael 1943- .... **CLC 16**
See also CA 105

Cioran, E(mil) M. 1911-1995 .... **CLC 64**
See also CA 25-28R; 149

Cisneros, Sandra 1954- .... **CLC 69; DAM MULT; HLC**
See also AAYA 9; CA 131; CANR 64; DLB 122, 152; HW

Cixous, Helene 1937- .... **CLC 92**
See also CA 126; CANR 55; DLB 83; MTCW

Clair, Rene .... **CLC 20**
See also Chomette, Rene Lucien

Clampitt, Amy 1920-1994 ...... **CLC 32; PC 19**
See also CA 110; 146; CANR 29; DLB 105

Clancy, Thomas L., Jr. 1947-
See Clancy, Tom
See also CA 125; 131; CANR 62; INT 131; MTCW

Clancy, Tom .... **CLC 45; DAM NOV, POP**
See also Clancy, Thomas L., Jr.
See also AAYA 9; BEST 89:1, 90:1

Clare, John 1793-1864 **NCLC 9; DAB; DAM POET**
See also DLB 55, 96

Clarin
See Alas (y Urena), Leopoldo (Enrique Garcia)

Clark, Al C.
See Goines, Donald

Clark, (Robert) Brian 1932- .... **CLC 29**
See also CA 41-44R; CANR 67

Clark, Curt
See Westlake, Donald E(dwin)

Clark, Eleanor 1913-1996 .... **CLC 5, 19**
See also CA 9-12R; 151; CANR 41; DLB 6

Clark, J. P.
See Clark, John Pepper
See also DLB 117

Clark, John Pepper 1935- ..... **CLC 38; BLC; DAM DRAM, MULT; DC 5**
See also Clark, J. P.
See also BW 1; CA 65-68; CANR 16

Clark, M. R.
See Clark, Mavis Thorpe

Clark, Mavis Thorpe 1909- .... **CLC 12**
See also CA 57-60; CANR 8, 37; CLR 30; MAICYA; SAAS 5; SATA 8, 74

Clark, Walter Van Tilburg 1909-1971 **CLC 28**
See also CA 9-12R; 33-36R; CANR 63; DLB 9; SATA 8

Clarke, Arthur C(harles) 1917- **CLC 1, 4, 13, 18, 35; DAM POP; SSC 3**
See also AAYA 4; CA 1-4R; CANR 2, 28, 55; JRDA; MAICYA; MTCW; SATA 13, 70

Clarke, Austin 1896-1974 ..... **CLC 6, 9; DAM POET**
See also CA 29-32; 49-52; CAP 2; DLB 10, 20

Colter, Cyrus 1910- .... **CLC 58**
See also BW 1; CA 65-68; CANR 10, 66; DLB 33

Colton, James
See Hansen, Joseph

Colum, Padraic 1881-1972 .... **CLC 28**
See also CA 73-76; 33-36R; CANR 35; CLR 36; MAICYA; MTCW; SATA 15

Colvin, James
See Moorcock, Michael (John)

Colwin, Laurie (E.) 1944-1992 ... **CLC 5, 13, 23, 84**
See also CA 89-92; 139; CANR 20, 46; DLBY 80; MTCW

Comfort, Alex(ander) 1920- ..... **CLC 7; DAM POP**
See also CA 1-4R; CANR 1, 45

Comfort, Montgomery
See Campbell, (John) Ramsey

Compton-Burnett, I(vy) 1884(?)-1969 **CLC 1, 3, 10, 15, 34; DAM NOV**
See also CA 1-4R; 25-28R; CANR 4; DLB 36; MTCW

Comstock, Anthony 1844-1915 .... **TCLC 13**
See also CA 110

Comte, Auguste 1798-1857 .... **NCLC 54**

Conan Doyle, Arthur
See Doyle, Arthur Conan

Conde, Maryse 1937- ..... **CLC 52, 92; DAM MULT**
See also Boucolon, Maryse
See also BW 2

Condillac, Etienne Bonnot de 1714-1780 . **LC 26**

Condon, Richard (Thomas) 1915-1996 **CLC 4, 6, 8, 10, 45, 100; DAM NOV**
See also BEST 90:3; CA 1-4R; 151; CAAS 1; CANR 2, 23; INT CANR-23; MTCW

Confucius 551B.C.-479B.C. ... **CMLC 19; DA; DAB; DAC; DAM MST; WLCS**

Congreve, William 1670-1729 . **LC 5, 21; DA; DAB; DAC; DAM DRAM, MST, POET; DC 2; WLC**
See also CDBLB 1660-1789; DLB 39, 84

Connell, Evan S(helby), Jr. 1924- **CLC 4, 6, 45; DAM NOV**
See also AAYA 7; CA 1-4R; CAAS 2; CANR 2, 39; DLB 2; DLBY 81; MTCW

Connelly, Marc(us Cook) 1890-1980 ... **CLC 7**
See also CA 85-88; 102; CANR 30; DLB 7; DLBY 80; SATA-Obit 25

Connor, Ralph .... **TCLC 31**
See also Gordon, Charles William
See also DLB 92

Conrad, Joseph 1857-1924 ...... **TCLC 1, 6, 13, 25, 43, 57; DA; DAB; DAC; DAM MST, NOV; SSC 9; WLC**
See also CA 104; 131; CANR 60; CDBLB 1890-1914; DLB 10, 34, 98, 156; MTCW; SATA 27

Conrad, Robert Arnold
See Hart, Moss

Conroy, Donald Pat(rick) 1945- . **CLC 30, 74; DAM NOV, POP**
See also AAYA 8; AITN 1; CA 85-88; CANR 24, 53; DLB 6; MTCW

Constant (de Rebecque), (Henri) Benjamin 1767-1830 .... **NCLC 6**
See also DLB 119

Conybeare, Charles Augustus
See Eliot, T(homas) S(tearns)

Cook, Michael 1933- .... **CLC 58**
See also CA 93-96; CANR 68; DLB 53

Cook, Robin 1940- .... **CLC 14; DAM POP**
See also BEST 90:2; CA 108; 111; CANR 41; INT 111

Cook, Roy
See Silverberg, Robert

Cooke, Elizabeth 1948- .... **CLC 55**
See also CA 129

Cooke, John Esten 1830-1886 .... **NCLC 5**
See also DLB 3

Cooke, John Estes
See Baum, L(yman) Frank

Cooke, M. E.
See Creasey, John

Cooke, Margaret
See Creasey, John

Cook-Lynn, Elizabeth 1930- ... **CLC 93; DAM MULT**
See also CA 133; DLB 175; NNAL

Cooney, Ray .... **CLC 62**

Cooper, Douglas 1960- .... **CLC 86**

Cooper, Henry St. John
See Creasey, John

Cooper, J(oan) California ..... **CLC 56; DAM MULT**
See also AAYA 12; BW 1; CA 125; CANR 55

Cooper, James Fenimore 1789-1851 ..... **NCLC 1, 27, 54**
See also AAYA 22; CDALB 1640-1865; DLB 3; SATA 19

Coover, Robert (Lowell) 1932- .... **CLC 3, 7, 15, 32, 46, 87; DAM NOV; SSC 15**
See also CA 45-48; CANR 3, 37, 58; DLB 2; DLBY 81; MTCW

Copeland, Stewart (Armstrong) 1952- **CLC 26**

Coppard, A(lfred) E(dgar) 1878-1957 **TCLC 5; SSC 21**
See also CA 114; DLB 162; YABC 1

Coppee, Francois 1842-1908 .... **TCLC 25**

Coppola, Francis Ford 1939- .... **CLC 16**
See also CA 77-80; CANR 40; DLB 44

Corbiere, Tristan 1845-1875 .... **NCLC 43**

Corcoran, Barbara 1911- .... **CLC 17**
See also AAYA 14; CA 21-24R; CAAS 2; CANR 11, 28, 48; DLB 52; JRDA; SAAS 20; SATA 3, 77

Cordelier, Maurice
See Giraudoux, (Hippolyte) Jean

Corelli, Marie 1855-1924 .... **TCLC 51**
See also Mackay, Mary
See also DLB 34, 156

Corman, Cid 1924- .... **CLC 9**
See also Corman, Sidney
See also CAAS 2; DLB 5, 193

Corman, Sidney 1924-
See Corman, Cid
See also CA 85-88; CANR 44; DAM POET

Cormier, Robert (Edmund) 1925- . **CLC 12, 30; DA; DAB; DAC; DAM MST, NOV**
See also AAYA 3, 19; CA 1-4R; CANR 5, 23; CDALB 1968-1988; CLR 12; DLB 52; INT CANR-23; JRDA; MAICYA; MTCW; SATA 10, 45, 83

Corn, Alfred (DeWitt III) 1943- .... **CLC 33**
See also CA 104; CAAS 25; CANR 44; DLB 120; DLBY 80

Corneille, Pierre 1606-1684 ..... **LC 28; DAB; DAM MST**

Cornwell, David (John Moore) 1931- **CLC 9, 15; DAM POP**
See also le Carre, John
See also CA 5-8R; CANR 13, 33, 59; MTCW

Corso, (Nunzio) Gregory 1930- ..... **CLC 1, 11**
See also CA 5-8R; CANR 41; DLB 5, 16; MTCW

Cortazar, Julio 1914-1984 **CLC 2, 3, 5, 10, 13, 15, 33, 34, 92; DAM MULT, NOV; HLC; SSC 7**
See also CA 21-24R; CANR 12, 32; DLB 113; HW; MTCW

CORTES, HERNAN 1484-1547 .... **LC 31**

Corwin, Cecil
See Kornbluth, C(yril) M.

Cosic, Dobrica 1921- .... **CLC 14**
See also CA 122; 138; DLB 181

Costain, Thomas B(ertram) 1885-1965 ... **CLC 30**
See also CA 5-8R; 25-28R; DLB 9

Costantini, Humberto 1924(?)-1987 .. **CLC 49**
See also CA 131; 122; HW

Crunk
See Crumb, R(obert)

Crustt
See Crumb, R(obert)

Cryer, Gretchen (Kiger) 1935- .... **CLC 21**
See also CA 114; 123

Csath, Geza 1887-1919 .... **TCLC 13**
See also CA 111

Cudlip, David 1933- .... **CLC 34**

Cullen, Countee 1903-1946**TCLC 4, 37; BLC;
DA; DAC; DAM MST, MULT, POET; PC
20; WLCS**
See also BW 1; CA 108; 124; CDALB 1917-
1929; DLB 4, 48, 51; MTCW; SATA 18

Cum, R.
See Crumb, R(obert)

Cummings, Bruce F(rederick) 1889-1919
See Barbellion, W. N. P.
See also CA 123

Cummings, E(dward) E(stlin) 1894-1962 **CLC
1, 3, 8, 12, 15, 68; DA; DAB; DAC; DAM
MST, POET; PC 5; WLC 2**
See also CA 73-76; CANR 31; CDALB 1929-
1941; DLB 4, 48; MTCW

Cunha, Euclides (Rodrigues Pimenta) da 1866-
1909 .... **TCLC 24**
See also CA 123

Cunningham, E. V.
See Fast, Howard (Melvin)

Cunningham, J(ames) V(incent) 1911-1985
CLC 3, 31
See also CA 1-4R; 115; CANR 1; DLB 5

Cunningham, Julia (Woolfolk) 1916- **CLC 12**
See also CA 9-12R; CANR 4, 19, 36; JRDA;
MAICYA; SAAS 2; SATA 1, 26

Cunningham, Michael 1952- .... **CLC 34**
See also CA 136

Cunninghame Graham, R(obert) B(ontine)
1852-1936 .... **TCLC 19**
See also Graham, R(obert) B(ontine)
Cunninghame
See also CA 119; DLB 98

Currie, Ellen 19(?)- .... **CLC 44**

Curtin, Philip
See Lowndes, Marie Adelaide (Belloc)

Curtis, Price
See Ellison, Harlan (Jay)

Cutrate, Joe
See Spiegelman, Art

Cynewulf c. 770-c. 840 .... **CMLC 23**

Czaczkes, Shmuel Yosef
See Agnon, S(hmuel) Y(osef Halevi)

Dabrowska, Maria (Szumska) 1889-1965 ... **CLC
15**
See also CA 106

Dabydeen, David 1955- .... **CLC 34**
See also BW 1; CA 125; CANR 56

Dacey, Philip 1939- .... **CLC 51**
See also CA 37-40R; CAAS 17; CANR 14, 32,
64; DLB 105

Dagerman, Stig (Halvard) 1923-1954 **TCLC 17**
See also CA 117; 155

Dahl, Roald 1916-1990 **CLC 1, 6, 18, 79; DAB;
DAC; DAM MST, NOV, POP**
See also AAYA 15; CA 1-4R; 133; CANR 6, 32,
37, 62; CLR 1, 7, 41; DLB 139; JRDA;
MAICYA; MTCW; SATA 1, 26, 73; SATA-
Obit 65

Dahlberg, Edward 1900-1977 .... **CLC 1, 7, 14**
See also CA 9-12R; 69-72; CANR 31, 62; DLB
48; MTCW

Daitch, Susan 1954- .... **CLC 103**
See also CA 161

Dale, Colin .... **TCLC 18**
See also Lawrence, T(homas) E(dward)

Dale, George E.
See Asimov, Isaac

Daly, Elizabeth 1878-1967 .... **CLC 52**
See also CA 23-24; 25-28R; CANR 60; CAP 2

Daly, Maureen 1921- .... **CLC 17**
See also AAYA 5; CANR 37; JRDA; MAICYA;
SAAS 1; SATA 2

Damas, Leon-Gontran 1912-1978 ...... **CLC 84**
See also BW 1; CA 125; 73-76

Dana, Richard Henry Sr. 1787-1879 **NCLC 53**

Daniel, Samuel 1562(?)-1619 .... **LC 24**
See also DLB 62

Daniels, Brett
See Adler, Renata

Dannay, Frederic 1905-1982 .. **CLC 11; DAM
POP**
See also Queen, Ellery
See also CA 1-4R; 107; CANR 1, 39; DLB 137;
MTCW

D'Annunzio, Gabriele 1863-1938 **TCLC 6, 40**
See also CA 104; 155

Danois, N. le
See Gourmont, Remy (-Marie-Charles) de

Dante 1265-1321 ..... **CMLC 3, 18; DA; DAB;
DAC; DAM MST, POET; PC 21; WLCS**

d'Antibes, Germain
See Simenon, Georges (Jacques Christian)

Danticat, Edwidge 1969- .... **CLC 94**
See also CA 152

Danvers, Dennis 1947- .... **CLC 70**

Danziger, Paula 1944- .... **CLC 21**
See also AAYA 4; CA 112; 115; CANR 37; CLR
20; JRDA; MAICYA; SATA 36, 63; SATA-
Brief 30

Da Ponte, Lorenzo 1749-1838 .... **NCLC 50**

Dario, Ruben 1867-1916 .... **TCLC 4; DAM
MULT; HLC; PC 15**
See also CA 131; HW; MTCW

Darley, George 1795-1846 .... **NCLC 2**
See also DLB 96

Darwin, Charles 1809-1882 .... **NCLC 57**
See also DLB 57, 166

Daryush, Elizabeth 1887-1977 .... **CLC 6, 19**
See also CA 49-52; CANR 3; DLB 20

Dashwood, Edmee Elizabeth Monica de la Pasture
1890-1943
See Delafield, E. M.
See also CA 119; 154

Daudet, (Louis Marie) Alphonse 1840-1897
NCLC 1
See also DLB 123

Daumal, Rene 1908-1944 .... **TCLC
14**
See also CA 114

Davenport, Guy (Mattison, Jr.) 1927- ... **CLC 6,
14, 38; SSC 16**
See also CA 33-36R; CANR 23; DLB 130

Davidson, Avram 1923-
See Queen, Ellery
See also CA 101; CANR 26; DLB 8

Davidson, Donald (Grady) 1893-1968 ... **CLC 2,
13, 19**
See also CA 5-8R; 25-28R; CANR 4; DLB 45

Davidson, Hugh
See Hamilton, Edmond

Davidson, John 1857-1909 .... **TCLC 24**
See also CA 118; DLB 19

Davidson, Sara 1943- .... **CLC 9**
See also CA 81-84; CANR 44, 68; DLB 185

Davie, Donald (Alfred) 1922-1995 ... **CLC 5, 8,
10, 31**
See also CA 1-4R; 149; CAAS 3; CANR 1, 44;
DLB 27; MTCW

Davies, Ray(mond Douglas) 1944- ..... **CLC 21**
See also CA 116; 146

Davies, Rhys 1901-1978 .... **CLC 23**
See also CA 9-12R; 81-84; CANR 4; DLB 139, 191

Davies, (William) Robertson 1913-1995 ... **CLC
2, 7, 13, 25, 42, 75, 91; DA; DAB; DAC;
DAM MST, NOV, POP; WLC**
See also BEST 89:2; CA 33-36R; 150; CANR
17, 42; DLB 68; INT CANR-17; MTCW

Dixon, Stephen 1936- .... **CLC 52; SSC 16**
See also CA 89-92; CANR 17, 40, 54; DLB 130

Doak, Annie
See Dillard, Annie

Dobell, Sydney Thompson 1824-1874 ... **NCLC 43**
See also DLB 32

Doblin, Alfred .... **TCLC 13**
See also Doeblin, Alfred

Dobrolyubov, Nikolai Alexandrovich 1836-1861
NCLC 5

Dobson, Austin 1840-1921 .... **TCLC 79**
See also DLB 35; 144

Dobyns, Stephen 1941- .... **CLC 37**
See also CA 45-48; CANR 2, 18

Doctorow, E(dgar) L(aurence) 1931- ... **CLC 6, 11, 15, 18, 37, 44, 65; DAM NOV, POP**
See also AAYA 22; AITN 2; BEST 89:3; CA 45-48; CANR 2, 33, 51; CDALB 1968-1988; DLB 2, 28, 173; DLBY 80; MTCW

Dodgson, Charles Lutwidge 1832-1898
See Carroll, Lewis
See also CLR 2; DA; DAB; DAC; DAM MST, NOV, POET; MAICYA; YABC 2

Dodson, Owen (Vincent) 1914-1983   **CLC 79; BLC; DAM MULT**
See also BW 1; CA 65-68; 110; CANR 24; DLB 76

Doeblin, Alfred 1878-1957 .... **TCLC 13**
See also Doblin, Alfred
See also CA 110; 141; DLB 66

Doerr, Harriet 1910- .... **CLC 34**
See also CA 117; 122; CANR 47; INT 122

Domecq, H(onorio) Bustos
See Bioy Casares, Adolfo; Borges, Jorge Luis

Domini, Rey
See Lorde, Audre (Geraldine)

Dominique
See Proust, (Valentin-Louis-George-Eugene-)
Marcel

Don, A
See Stephen, SirLeslie

Donaldson, Stephen R. 1947- . **CLC 46; DAM POP**
See also CA 89-92; CANR 13, 55; INT CANR-13

Donleavy, J(ames) P(atrick) 1926- ... **CLC 1, 4, 6, 10, 45**
See also AITN 2; CA 9-12R; CANR 24, 49, 62; DLB 6, 173; INT CANR-24; MTCW

Donne, John 1572-1631 ....   **LC 10, 24; DA; DAB; DAC; DAM MST, POET; PC 1**
See also CDBLB Before 1660; DLB 121, 151

Donnell, David 1939(?)- .... **CLC 34**

Donoghue, P. S.
See Hunt, E(verette) Howard, (Jr.)

Donoso (Yanez), Jose 1924-1996 .... **CLC 4, 8, 11, 32, 99; DAM MULT; HLC**
See also CA 81-84; 155; CANR 32; DLB 113; HW; MTCW

Donovan, John 1928-1992 .... **CLC 35**
See also AAYA 20; CA 97-100; 137; CLR 3; MAICYA; SATA 72; SATA-Brief 29

Don Roberto
See Cunninghame Graham, R(obert) B(ontine)

Doolittle, Hilda 1886-1961 ... **CLC 3, 8, 14, 31, 34, 73; DA; DAC; DAM MST, POET; PC 5; WLC**
See also H. D.
See also CA 97-100; CANR 35; DLB 4, 45; MTCW

Dorfman, Ariel 1942- .... **CLC 48, 77; DAM MULT; HLC**
See also CA 124; 130; CANR 67; HW; INT 130

Dorn, Edward (Merton) 1929- ..... **CLC 10, 18**
See also CA 93-96; CANR 42; DLB 5; INT 93-96

Dorris, Michael (Anthony) 1945-1997 ... **C L C 109; DAM MULT, NOV**
See also AAYA 20; BEST 90:1; CA 102; 157; CANR 19, 46; DLB 175; NNAL; SATA 75; SATA-Obit 94

Dorris, Michael A.
See Dorris, Michael (Anthony)

Dorsan, Luc
See Simenon, Georges (Jacques Christian)

Dorsange, Jean
See Simenon, Georges (Jacques Christian)

Dos Passos, John (Roderigo) 1896-1970 ... **CLC 1, 4, 8, 11, 15, 25, 34, 82; DA; DAB; DAC; DAM MST, NOV; WLC**
See also CA 1-4R; 29-32R; CANR 3; CDALB 1929-1941; DLB 4, 9; DLBD 1, 15; DLBY 96; MTCW

Dossage, Jean
See Simenon, Georges (Jacques Christian)

Dostoevsky, Fedor Mikhailovich 1821-1881
NCLC 2, 7, 21, 33, 43; DA; DAB; DAC; DAM MST, NOV; SSC 2; WLC

Doughty, Charles M(ontagu) 1843-1926 ... **TCLC 27**
See also CA 115; DLB 19, 57, 174

Douglas, Ellen .... **CLC 73**
See also Haxton, Josephine Ayres; Williamson, Ellen Douglas

Douglas, Gavin 1475(?)-1522 .... **LC 20**

Douglas, George
See Brown, George Douglas

Douglas, Keith (Castellain) 1920-1944 **TCLC 40**
See also CA 160; DLB 27

Douglas, Leonard
See Bradbury, Ray (Douglas)

Douglas, Michael
See Crichton, (John) Michael

Douglas, Norman 1868-1952 .... **TCLC 68**
See also DLB 195

Douglas, William
See Brown, George Douglas

Douglass, Frederick 1817(?)-1895   **NCLC 7, 55; BLC; DA; DAC; DAM MST, MULT; WLC**
See also CDALB 1640-1865; DLB 1, 43, 50, 79; SATA 29

Dourado, (Waldomiro Freitas) Autran 1926-
CLC 23, 60
See also CA 25-28R; CANR 34

Dourado, Waldomiro Autran
See Dourado, (Waldomiro Freitas) Autran

Dove, Rita (Frances) 1952-   **CLC 50, 81; DAM MULT, POET; PC 6**
See also BW 2; CA 109; CAAS 19; CANR 27, 42, 68; DLB 120

Dowell, Coleman 1925-1985 .... **CLC 60**
See also CA 25-28R; 117; CANR 10; DLB 130

Dowson, Ernest (Christopher) 1867-1900
TCLC 4
See also CA 105; 150; DLB 19, 135

Doyle, A. Conan
See Doyle, Arthur Conan

Doyle, Arthur Conan 1859-1930 .   **TCLC 7; DA; DAB; DAC; DAM MST, NOV; SSC 12; WLC**
See also AAYA 14; CA 104; 122; CDBLB 1890-1914; DLB 18, 70, 156, 178; MTCW; SATA 24

Doyle, Conan
See Doyle, Arthur Conan

Doyle, John
See Graves, Robert (von Ranke)

Doyle, Roddy 1958(?)- .... **CLC 81**
See also AAYA 14; CA 143; DLB 194

Doyle, Sir A. Conan
See Doyle, Arthur Conan

Doyle, Sir Arthur Conan
See Doyle, Arthur Conan

Dr. A
See Asimov, Isaac; Silverstein, Alvin

Drabble, Margaret 1939-   **CLC 2, 3, 5, 8, 10, 22, 53; DAB; DAC; DAM MST, NOV, POP**
See also CA 13-16R; CANR 18, 35, 63; CDBLB 1960 to Present; DLB 14, 155; MTCW; SATA 48

Drapier, M. B.
See Swift, Jonathan

Drayham, James
    See Mencken, H(enry) L(ouis)

Drayton, Michael 1563-1631 .... **LC 8**

Dreadstone, Carl
    See Campbell, (John) Ramsey

Dreiser, Theodore (Herman Albert) 1871-1945
    **TCLC 10, 18, 35; DA; DAC; DAM MST,
    NOV; SSC 30; WLC**
    See also CA 106; 132; CDALB 1865-1917; DLB
    9, 12, 102, 137; DLBD 1; MTCW

Drexler, Rosalyn 1926- .... **CLC 2, 6**
    See also CA 81-84; CANR 68

Dreyer, Carl Theodor 1889-1968 .... **CLC 16**
    See also CA 116

Drieu la Rochelle, Pierre(-Eugene) 1893-1945
    TCLC 21
    See also CA 117; DLB 72

Drinkwater, John 1882-1937 .... **TCLC 57**
    See also CA 109; 149; DLB 10, 19, 149

Drop Shot
    See Cable, George Washington

Droste-Hulshoff, Annette Freiin von 1797-1848
    NCLC 3
    See also DLB 133

Drummond, Walter
    See Silverberg, Robert

Drummond, William Henry 1854-1907...**TCLC 25**
    See also CA 160; DLB 92

Drummond de Andrade, Carlos 1902-1987
    CLC 18
    See also Andrade, Carlos Drummond de
    See also CA 132; 123

Drury, Allen (Stuart) 1918- .... **CLC 37**
    See also CA 57-60; CANR 18, 52; INT CANR-
    18

Dryden, John 1631-1700   **LC 3, 21; DA; DAB;
    DAC; DAM DRAM, MST, POET; DC 3;
    WLC**
    See also CDBLB 1660-1789; DLB 80, 101, 131

Duberman, Martin (Bauml) 1930-....... **CLC 8**
    See also CA 1-4R; CANR 2, 63

Dubie, Norman (Evans) 1945- .... **CLC 36**
    See also CA 69-72; CANR 12; DLB 120

Du Bois, W(illiam) E(dward) B(urghardt) 1868-
    1963 .... **CLC 1, 2, 13, 64, 96; BLC;
    DA; DAC; DAM MST, MULT, NOV; WLC**
    See also BW 1; CA 85-88; CANR 34; CDALB
    1865-1917; DLB 47, 50, 91; MTCW; SATA 42

Dubus, Andre 1936-   **CLC 13, 36, 97; SSC 15**
    See also CA 21-24R; CANR 17; DLB 130; INT
    CANR-17

Duca Minimo
    See D'Annunzio, Gabriele

Ducharme, Rejean 1941- .... **CLC 74**
    See also CA 165; DLB 60

Duclos, Charles Pinot 1704-1772 .... **LC 1**

Dudek, Louis 1918-........................ **CLC 11, 19**
    See also CA 45-48; CAAS 14; CANR 1; DLB 88

Duerrenmatt, Friedrich 1921-1990   **CLC 1, 4,
    8, 11, 15, 43, 102; DAM DRAM**
    See also CA 17-20R; CANR 33; DLB 69, 124;
    MTCW

Duffy, Bruce (?)- .... **CLC 50**

Duffy, Maureen 1933- .... **CLC 37**
    See also CA 25-28R; CANR 33, 68; DLB 14; MTCW

Dugan, Alan 1923- .... **CLC 2, 6**
    See also CA 81-84; DLB 5

du Gard, Roger Martin
    See Martin du Gard, Roger

Duhamel, Georges 1884-1966 .... **CLC 8**
    See also CA 81-84; 25-28R; CANR 35; DLB 65; MTCW

Dujardin, Edouard (Emile Louis) 1861-1949
    TCLC 13
    See also CA 109; DLB 123

Dulles, John Foster 1888-1959 .... **TCLC 72**
    See also CA 115; 149

Dumas, Alexandre (Davy de la Pailleterie) 1802-
    1870 .... **NCLC 11; DA; DAB; DAC;
    DAM MST, NOV; WLC**
    See also DLB 119, 192; SATA 18

Dumas, Alexandre 1824-1895   **NCLC 9; DC 1**
    See also AAYA 22; DLB 192

Dumas, Claudine
    See Malzberg, Barry N(athaniel)

Dumas, Henry L. 1934-1968 .... **CLC 6, 62**
    See also BW 1; CA 85-88; DLB 41

du Maurier, Daphne 1907-1989   **CLC 6, 11, 59;
    DAB; DAC; DAM MST, POP; SSC 18**
    See also CA 5-8R; 128; CANR 6, 55; DLB 191;
    MTCW; SATA 27; SATA-Obit 60

Dunbar, Paul Laurence 1872-1906   **TCLC 2,
    12; BLC; DA; DAC; DAM MST, MULT,
    POET; PC 5; SSC 8; WLC**
    See also BW 1; CA 104; 124; CDALB 1865-
    1917; DLB 50, 54, 78; SATA 34

Dunbar, William 1460(?)-1530(?) .... **LC 20**
    See also DLB 132, 146

Duncan, Dora Angela
    See Duncan, Isadora

Duncan, Isadora 1877(?)-1927 .... **TCLC 68**
    See also CA 118; 149

Duncan, Lois 1934- .... **CLC 26**
    See also AAYA 4; CA 1-4R; CANR 2, 23, 36;
    CLR 29; JRDA; MAICYA; SAAS 2; SATA 1,
    36, 75

Duncan, Robert (Edward) 1919-1988   **CLC 1,
    2, 4, 7, 15, 41, 55; DAM POET; PC 2**
    See also CA 9-12R; 124; CANR 28, 62; DLB 5,
    16, 193; MTCW

Duncan, Sara Jeannette 1861-1922   **TCLC 60**
    See also CA 157; DLB 92

Dunlap, William 1766-1839 .... **NCLC 2**
    See also DLB 30, 37, 59

Dunn, Douglas (Eaglesham) 1942-   **CLC 6, 40**
    See also CA 45-48; CANR 2, 33; DLB 40; MTCW

Dunn, Katherine (Karen) 1945- .... **CLC 71**
    See also CA 33-36R

Dunn, Stephen 1939- .... **CLC 36**
    See also CA 33-36R; CANR 12, 48, 53; DLB 105

Dunne, Finley Peter 1867-1936 .... **TCLC 28**
    See also CA 108; DLB 11, 23

Dunne, John Gregory 1932- .... **CLC 28**
    See also CA 25-28R; CANR 14, 50; DLBY 80

Dunsany, Edward John Moreton Drax Plunkett
    1878-1957
    See Dunsany, Lord
    See also CA 104; 148; DLB 10

Dunsany, Lord .... **TCLC 2, 59**
    See also Dunsany, Edward John Moreton Drax
    Plunkett
    See also DLB 77, 153, 156

du Perry, Jean
    See Simenon, Georges (Jacques Christian)

Durang, Christopher (Ferdinand) 1949-   **CLC
    27, 38**
    See also CA 105; CANR 50

Duras, Marguerite 1914-1996**CLC 3, 6, 11, 20,
    34, 40, 68, 100**
    See also CA 25-28R; 151; CANR 50; DLB 83;
    MTCW

Durban, (Rosa) Pam 1947- .... **CLC 39**
    See also CA 123

Durcan, Paul 1944-   **CLC 43, 70; DAM POET**
    See also CA 134

Durkheim, Emile 1858-1917 .... **TCLC 55**

Durrell, Lawrence (George) 1912-1990   **CLC
    1, 4, 6, 8, 13, 27, 41; DAM NOV**
    See also CA 9-12R; 132; CANR 40; CDBLB
    1945-1960; DLB 15, 27; DLBY 90; MTCW

Durrenmatt, Friedrich
    See Duerrenmatt, Friedrich

Dutt, Toru 1856-1877 .... **NCLC 29**

Dwight, Timothy 1752-1817 .... **NCLC 13**
    See also DLB 37

Dworkin, Andrea 1946- .... **CLC 43**
    See also CA 77-80; CAAS 21; CANR 16, 39;
    INT CANR-16; MTCW

Eliot, T(homas) S(tearns) 1888-1965 ... **CLC 1, 2, 3, 6, 9, 10, 13, 15, 24, 34, 41, 55, 57; DA; DAB; DAC; DAM DRAM, MST, POET; PC 5; WLC 2**
See also CA 5-8R; 25-28R; CANR 41; CDALB 1929-1941; DLB 7, 10, 45, 63; DLBY 88; MTCW

Elizabeth 1866-1941 .... **TCLC 41**

Elkin, Stanley L(awrence) 1930-1995 **CLC 4, 6, 9, 14, 27, 51, 91; DAM NOV, POP; SSC 12**
See also CA 9-12R; 148; CANR 8, 46; DLB 2, 28; DLBY 80; INT CANR-8; MTCW

Elledge, Scott .... **CLC 34**

Elliot, Don
See Silverberg, Robert

Elliott, Don
See Silverberg, Robert

Elliott, George P(aul) 1918-1980 .... **CLC 2**
See also CA 1-4R; 97-100; CANR 2

Elliott, Janice 1931- .... **CLC 47**
See also CA 13-16R; CANR 8, 29; DLB 14

Elliott, Sumner Locke 1917-1991 ...... **CLC 38**
See also CA 5-8R; 134; CANR 2, 21

Elliott, William
See Bradbury, Ray (Douglas)

Ellis, A. E. .... **CLC 7**

Ellis, Alice Thomas .... **CLC 40**
See also Haycraft, Anna
See also DLB 194

Ellis, Bret Easton 1964- ... **CLC 39, 71; DAM POP**
See also AAYA 2; CA 118; 123; CANR 51; INT 123

Ellis, (Henry) Havelock 1859-1939 **TCLC 14**
See also CA 109; DLB 190

Ellis, Landon
See Ellison, Harlan (Jay)

Ellis, Trey 1962- .... **CLC 55**
See also CA 146

Ellison, Harlan (Jay) 1934- .... **CLC 1, 13, 42; DAM POP; SSC 14**
See also CA 5-8R; CANR 5, 46; DLB 8; INT CANR-5; MTCW

Ellison, Ralph (Waldo) 1914-1994 .... **CLC 1, 3, 11, 54, 86; BLC; DA; DAB; DAC; DAM MST, MULT, NOV; SSC 26; WLC**
See also AAYA 19; BW 1; CA 9-12R; 145; CANR 24, 53; CDALB 1941-1968; DLB 2, 76; DLBY 94; MTCW

Ellmann, Lucy (Elizabeth) 1956- .... **CLC 61**
See also CA 128

Ellmann, Richard (David) 1918-1987 **CLC 50**
See also BEST 89:2; CA 1-4R; 122; CANR 2, 28, 61; DLB 103; DLBY 87; MTCW

Elman, Richard (Martin) 1934-1997 **CLC 19**
See also CA 17-20R; 163; CAAS 3; CANR 47

Elron
See Hubbard, L(afayette) Ron(ald)

Eluard, Paul .... **TCLC 7, 41**
See also Grindel, Eugene

Elyot, Sir Thomas 1490(?)-1546 .... **LC 11**

Elytis, Odysseus 1911-1996   **CLC 15, 49, 100; DAM POET; PC 21**
See also CA 102; 151; MTCW

Emecheta, (Florence Onye) Buchi 1944- **CLC 14, 48; BLC; DAM MULT**
See also BW 2; CA 81-84; CANR 27; DLB 117; MTCW; SATA 66

Emerson, Mary Moody 1774-1863 **NCLC 66**

Emerson, Ralph Waldo 1803-1882 **NCLC 1, 38; DA; DAB; DAC; DAM MST, POET; PC 18; WLC**
See also CDALB 1640-1865; DLB 1, 59, 73

Eminescu, Mihail 1850-1889 .... **NCLC 33**

Empson, William 1906-1984 .   **CLC 3, 8, 19, 33, 34**
See also CA 17-20R; 112; CANR 31, 61; DLB 20; MTCW

Enchi Fumiko (Ueda) 1905-1986 .... **CLC 31**
See also CA 129; 121

Ende, Michael (Andreas Helmuth) 1929-1995 **CLC 31**
See also CA 118; 124; 149; CANR 36; CLR 14; DLB 75; MAICYA; SATA 61; SATA-Brief 42; SATA-Obit 86

Endo, Shusaku 1923-1996 .   **CLC 7, 14, 19, 54, 99; DAM NOV**
See also CA 29-32R; 153; CANR 21, 54; DLB 182; MTCW

Engel, Marian 1933-1985 .... **CLC 36**
See also CA 25-28R; CANR 12; DLB 53; INT CANR-12

Engelhardt, Frederick
See Hubbard, L(afayette) Ron(ald)

Enright, D(ennis) J(oseph) 1920- **CLC 4, 8, 31**
See also CA 1-4R; CANR 1, 42; DLB 27; SATA 25

Enzensberger, Hans Magnus 1929- ... **CLC 43**
See also CA 116; 119

Ephron, Nora 1941- .... **CLC 17, 31**
See also AITN 2; CA 65-68; CANR 12, 39

Epicurus 341B.C.-270B.C. .... **CMLC 21**
See also DLB 176

Epsilon
See Betjeman, John

Epstein, Daniel Mark 1948- .... **CLC 7**
See also CA 49-52; CANR 2, 53

Epstein, Jacob 1956- .... **CLC 19**
See also CA 114

Epstein, Joseph 1937- .... **CLC 39**
See also CA 112; 119; CANR 50, 65

Epstein, Leslie 1938- .... **CLC 27**
See also CA 73-76; CAAS 12; CANR 23

Equiano, Olaudah 1745(?)-1797 ....   **LC 16; BLC; DAM MULT**
See also DLB 37, 50

ER .... **TCLC 33**
See also CA 160; DLB 85

Erasmus, Desiderius 1469(?)-1536 .... **LC 16**

Erdman, Paul E(mil) 1932- .... **CLC 25**
See also AITN 1; CA 61-64; CANR 13, 43

Erdrich, Louise 1954- .... **CLC 39, 54; DAM MULT, NOV, POP**
See also AAYA 10; BEST 89:1; CA 114; CANR 41, 62; DLB 152, 175; MTCW; NNAL; SATA 94

Erenburg, Ilya (Grigoryevich)
See Ehrenburg, Ilya (Grigoryevich)

Erickson, Stephen Michael 1950-
See Erickson, Steve
See also CA 129

Erickson, Steve 1950- .... **CLC 64**
See also Erickson, Stephen Michael
See also CANR 60, 68

Ericson, Walter
See Fast, Howard (Melvin)

Eriksson, Buntel
See Bergman, (Ernst) Ingmar

Ernaux, Annie 1940- .... **CLC 88**
See also CA 147

Eschenbach, Wolfram von
See Wolfram von Eschenbach

Eseki, Bruno
See Mphahlele, Ezekiel

Esenin, Sergei (Alexandrovich) 1895-1925 **TCLC 4**
See also CA 104

Eshleman, Clayton 1935- .... **CLC 7**
See also CA 33-36R; CAAS 6; DLB 5

Espriella, Don Manuel Alvarez
See Southey, Robert

Espriu, Salvador 1913-1985 .... **CLC 9**
See also CA 154; 115; DLB 134

Espronceda, Jose de 1808-1842 ...... **NCLC 39**

Esse, James
See Stephens, James

Esterbrook, Tom
See Hubbard, L(afayette) Ron(ald)

Feldman, Irving (Mordecai) 1928- ...... **CLC 7**
See also CA 1-4R; CANR 1; DLB 169

Felix-Tchicaya, Gerald
See Tchicaya, Gerald Felix

Fellini, Federico 1920-1993 .... **CLC 16, 85**
See also CA 65-68; 143; CANR 33

Felsen, Henry Gregor 1916- .... **CLC 17**
See also CA 1-4R; CANR 1; SAAS 2; SATA 1

Fenno, Jack
See Calisher, Hortense

Fenton, James Martin 1949- .... **CLC 32**
See also CA 102; DLB 40

Ferber, Edna 1887-1968 .... **CLC 18, 93**
See also AITN 1; CA 5-8R; 25-28R; CANR 68;
DLB 9, 28, 86; MTCW; SATA 7

Ferguson, Helen
See Kavan, Anna

Ferguson, Samuel 1810-1886 .... **NCLC 33**
See also DLB 32

Fergusson, Robert 1750-1774 .... **LC 29**
See also DLB 109

Ferling, Lawrence
See Ferlinghetti, Lawrence (Monsanto)

Ferlinghetti, Lawrence (Monsanto) 1919(?)-
CLC 2, 6, 10, 27; DAM POET; PC 1
See also CA 5-8R; CANR 3, 41; CDALB 1941-
1968; DLB 5, 16; MTCW

Fernandez, Vicente Garcia Huidobro
See Huidobro Fernandez, Vicente Garcia

Ferrer, Gabriel (Francisco Victor) Miro
See Miro (Ferrer), Gabriel (Francisco Victor)

Ferrier, Susan (Edmonstone) 1782-1854
NCLC 8
See also DLB 116

Ferrigno, Robert 1948(?)- .... **CLC 65**
See also CA 140

Ferron, Jacques 1921-1985 ..... **CLC 94; DAC**
See also CA 117; 129; DLB 60

Feuchtwanger, Lion 1884-1958 .... **TCLC 3**
See also CA 104; DLB 66

Feuillet, Octave 1821-1890 .... **NCLC 45**
See also DLB 192

Feydeau, Georges (Leon Jules Marie) 1862-1921
TCLC 22; DAM DRAM
See also CA 113; 152; DLB 192

Fichte, Johann Gottlieb 1762-1814 ....**NCLC 62**
See also DLB 90

Ficino, Marsilio 1433-1499 .... **LC 12**

Fiedeler, Hans
See Doeblin, Alfred

Fiedler, Leslie A(aron) 1917- .... **CLC 4, 13, 24**
See also CA 9-12R; CANR 7, 63; DLB 28, 67;
MTCW

Field, Andrew 1938- .... **CLC 44**
See also CA 97-100; CANR 25

Field, Eugene 1850-1895 .... **NCLC 3**
See also DLB 23, 42, 140; DLBD 13; MAICYA;
SATA 16

Field, Gans T.
See Wellman, Manly Wade

Field, Michael ....**TCLC 43**

Field, Peter
See Hobson, Laura Z(ametkin)

Fielding, Henry 1707-1754 .... **LC 1; DA;
DAB; DAC; DAM DRAM, MST, NOV;
WLC**
See also CDBLB 1660-1789; DLB 39, 84, 101

Fielding, Sarah 1710-1768 .... **LC 1**
See also DLB 39

Fields, W. C. 1880-1946 .... **TCLC 80**
See also DLB 44

Fierstein, Harvey (Forbes) 1954- ..... **CLC 33;
DAM DRAM, POP**
See also CA 123; 129

Figes, Eva 1932- .... **CLC 31**
See also CA 53-56; CANR 4, 44; DLB 14

Finch, Anne 1661-1720 .... **LC 3; PC 21**
See also DLB 95

Finch, Robert (Duer Claydon) 1900-. **CLC 18**
See also CA 57-60; CANR 9, 24, 49; DLB 88

Findley, Timothy 1930- .. **CLC 27, 102; DAC;
DAM MST**
See also CA 25-28R; CANR 12, 42; DLB 53

Fink, William
See Mencken, H(enry) L(ouis)

Firbank, Louis 1942-
See Reed, Lou
See also CA 117

Firbank, (Arthur Annesley) Ronald 1886-1926
TCLC 1
See also CA 104; DLB 36

Fisher, M(ary) F(rances) K(ennedy) 1908-1992
CLC 76, 87
See also CA 77-80; 138; CANR 44

Fisher, Roy 1930- .... **CLC 25**
See also CA 81-84; CAAS 10; CANR 16; DLB
40

Fisher, Rudolph 1897-1934 .. **TCLC 11; BLC;
DAM MULT; SSC 25**
See also BW 1; CA 107; 124; DLB 51, 102

Fisher, Vardis (Alvero) 1895-1968 .... **CLC 7**
See also CA 5-8R; 25-28R; CANR 68; DLB 9

Fiske, Tarleton
See Bloch, Robert (Albert)

Fitch, Clarke
See Sinclair, Upton (Beall)

Fitch, John IV
See Cormier, Robert (Edmund)

Fitzgerald, Captain Hugh
See Baum, L(yman) Frank

FitzGerald, Edward 1809-1883 .... **NCLC 9**
See also DLB 32

Fitzgerald, F(rancis) Scott (Key) 1896-1940
**TCLC 1, 6, 14, 28, 55; DA; DAB; DAC;
DAM MST, NOV; SSC 6; WLC**
See also AAYA 24; AITN 1; CA 110; 123;
CDALB 1917-1929; DLB 4, 9, 86; DLBD 1,
15, 16; DLBY 81, 96; MTCW

Fitzgerald, Penelope 1916- ..... **CLC 19, 51, 61**
See also CA 85-88; CAAS 10; CANR 56; DLB
14, 194

Fitzgerald, Robert (Stuart) 1910-1985 **CLC 39**
See also CA 1-4R; 114; CANR 1; DLBY 80

FitzGerald, Robert D(avid) 1902-1987 **CLC 19**
See also CA 17-20R

Fitzgerald, Zelda (Sayre) 1900-1948 **TCLC 52**
See also CA 117; 126; DLBY 84

Flanagan, Thomas (James Bonner) 1923-
CLC 25, 52
See also CA 108; CANR 55; DLBY 80; INT 108;
MTCW

Flaubert, Gustave 1821-1880   **NCLC 2, 10,
19, 62, 66; DA; DAB; DAC; DAM MST,
NOV; SSC 11; WLC**
See also DLB 119

Flecker, Herman Elroy
See Flecker, (Herman) James Elroy

Flecker, (Herman) James Elroy 1884-1915
TCLC 43
See also CA 109; 150; DLB 10, 19

Fleming, Ian (Lancaster) 1908-1964   **CLC 3,
30; DAM POP**
See also CA 5-8R; CANR 59; CDBLB 1945-
1960; DLB 87; MTCW; SATA 9

Fleming, Thomas (James) 1927- .... **CLC 37**
See also CA 5-8R; CANR 10; INT CANR-10;
SATA 8

Fletcher, John 1579-1625 ....**LC 33; DC 6**
See also CDBLB Before 1660; DLB 58

Fletcher, John Gould 1886-1950 ..... **TCLC 35**
See also CA 107; DLB 4, 45

Fleur, Paul
See Pohl, Frederik

Flooglebuckle, Al
See Spiegelman, Art

Frazier, Ian 1951- .... **CLC 46**
See also CA 130; CANR 54

Frederic, Harold 1856-1898 .... **NCLC 10**
See also DLB 12, 23; DLBD 13

Frederick, John
See Faust, Frederick (Schiller)

Frederick the Great 1712-1786 .... **LC 14**

Fredro, Aleksander 1793-1876 .... **NCLC 8**

Freeling, Nicolas 1927- .... **CLC 38**
See also CA 49-52; CAAS 12; CANR 1, 17, 50;
DLB 87

Freeman, Douglas Southall 1886-1953 ... **TCLC 11**
See also CA 109; DLB 17

Freeman, Judith 1946- .... **CLC 55**
See also CA 148

Freeman, Mary Eleanor Wilkins 1852-1930 **TCLC 9; SSC 1**
See also CA 106; DLB 12, 78

Freeman, R(ichard) Austin 1862-1943 ... **TCLC 21**
See also CA 113; DLB 70

French, Albert 1943- .... **CLC 86**

French, Marilyn 1929- **CLC 10, 18, 60; DAM DRAM, NOV, POP**
See also CA 69-72; CANR 3, 31; INT CANR-31; MTCW

French, Paul
See Asimov, Isaac

Freneau, Philip Morin 1752-1832 ..... **NCLC 1**
See also DLB 37, 43

Freud, Sigmund 1856-1939 .... **TCLC 52**
See also CA 115; 133; MTCW

Friedan, Betty (Naomi) 1921- .... **CLC 74**
See also CA 65-68; CANR 18, 45; MTCW

Friedlander, Saul 1932- .... **CLC 90**
See also CA 117; 130

Friedman, B(ernard) H(arper) 1926- .. **CLC 7**
See also CA 1-4R; CANR 3, 48

Friedman, Bruce Jay 1930- .... **CLC 3, 5, 56**
See also CA 9-12R; CANR 25, 52; DLB 2, 28;
INT CANR-25

Friel, Brian 1929- .... **CLC 5, 42, 59; DC 8**
See also CA 21-24R; CANR 33; DLB 13;
MTCW

Friis-Baastad, Babbis Ellinor 1921-1970 ... **CLC 12**
See also CA 17-20R; 134; SATA 7

Frisch, Max (Rudolf) 1911-1991 . **CLC 3, 9, 14, 18, 32, 44; DAM DRAM, NOV**
See also CA 85-88; 134; CANR 32; DLB 69,
124; MTCW

Fromentin, Eugene (Samuel Auguste) 1820-1876 **NCLC 10**
See also DLB 123

Frost, Frederick
See Faust, Frederick (Schiller)

Frost, Robert (Lee) 1874-1963 **CLC 1, 3, 4, 9, 10, 13, 15, 26, 34, 44; DA; DAB; DAC; DAM MST, POET; PC 1; WLC**
See also AAYA 21; CA 89-92; CANR 33;
CDALB 1917-1929; DLB 54; DLBD 7;
MTCW; SATA 14

Froude, James Anthony 1818-1894 **NCLC 43**
See also DLB 18, 57, 144

Froy, Herald
See Waterhouse, Keith (Spencer)

Fry, Christopher 1907- **CLC 2, 10, 14; DAM DRAM**
See also CA 17-20R; CAAS 23; CANR 9, 30;
DLB 13; MTCW; SATA 66

Frye, (Herman) Northrop 1912-1991 **CLC 24, 70**
See also CA 5-8R; 133; CANR 8, 37; DLB 67,
68; MTCW

Fuchs, Daniel 1909-1993 .... **CLC 8, 22**
See also CA 81-84; 142; CAAS 5; CANR 40;
DLB 9, 26, 28; DLBY 93

Fuchs, Daniel 1934- .... **CLC 34**
See also CA 37-40R; CANR 14, 48

Fuentes, Carlos 1928- **CLC 3, 8, 10, 13, 22, 41, 60; DA; DAB; DAC; DAM MST, MULT, NOV; HLC; SSC 24; WLC**
See also AAYA 4; AITN 2; CA 69-72; CANR
10, 32, 68; DLB 113; HW; MTCW

Fuentes, Gregorio Lopez y
See Lopez y Fuentes, Gregorio

Fugard, (Harold) Athol 1932- **CLC 5, 9, 14, 25, 40, 80; DAM DRAM; DC 3**
See also AAYA 17; CA 85-88; CANR 32, 54;
MTCW

Fugard, Sheila 1932- .... **CLC 48**
See also CA 125

Fuller, Charles (H., Jr.) 1939- **CLC 25; BLC; DAM DRAM, MULT; DC 1**
See also BW 2; CA 108; 112; DLB 38; INT 112;
MTCW

Fuller, John (Leopold) 1937- .... **CLC 62**
See also CA 21-24R; CANR 9, 44; DLB 40

Fuller, Margaret .... **NCLC 5, 50**
See also Ossoli, Sarah Margaret (Fuller marchesa
d')

Fuller, Roy (Broadbent) 1912-1991 **CLC 4, 28**
See also CA 5-8R; 135; CAAS 10; CANR 53;
DLB 15, 20; SATA 87

Fulton, Alice 1952- .... **CLC 52**
See also CA 116; CANR 57; DLB 193

Furphy, Joseph 1843-1912 .... **TCLC 25**
See also CA 163

Fussell, Paul 1924- .... **CLC 74**
See also BEST 90:1; CA 17-20R; CANR 8, 21,
35; INT CANR-21; MTCW

Futabatei, Shimei 1864-1909 .... **TCLC 44**
See also CA 162; DLB 180

Futrelle, Jacques 1875-1912 .... **TCLC 19**
See also CA 113; 155

Gaboriau, Emile 1835-1873 .... **NCLC 14**

Gadda, Carlo Emilio 1893-1973 .... **CLC 11**
See also CA 89-92; DLB 177

Gaddis, William 1922- ... **CLC 1, 3, 6, 8, 10, 19, 43, 86**
See also CA 17-20R; CANR 21, 48; DLB 2;
MTCW

Gage, Walter
See Inge, William (Motter)

Gaines, Ernest J(ames) 1933- ... **CLC 3, 11, 18, 86; BLC; DAM MULT**
See also AAYA 18; AITN 1; BW 2; CA 9-12R;
CANR 6, 24, 42; CDALB 1968-1988; DLB
2, 33, 152; DLBY 80; MTCW; SATA 86

Gaitskill, Mary 1954- .... **CLC 69**
See also CA 128; CANR 61

Galdos, Benito Perez
See Perez Galdos, Benito

Gale, Zona 1874-1938 .... **TCLC 7; DAM DRAM**
See also CA 105; 153; DLB 9, 78

Galeano, Eduardo (Hughes) 1940- .... **CLC 72**
See also CA 29-32R; CANR 13, 32; HW

Galiano, Juan Valera y Alcala
See Valera y Alcala-Galiano, Juan

Gallagher, Tess 1943- .... **CLC 18, 63; DAM POET; PC 9**
See also CA 106; DLB 120

Gallant, Mavis 1922- ... **CLC 7, 18, 38; DAC; DAM MST; SSC 5**
See also CA 69-72; CANR 29; DLB 53; MTCW

Gallant, Roy A(rthur) 1924- .... **CLC 17**
See also CA 5-8R; CANR 4, 29, 54; CLR 30;
MAICYA; SATA 4, 68

Gallico, Paul (William) 1897-1976 .... **CLC 2**
See also AITN 1; CA 5-8R; 69-72; CANR 23;
DLB 9, 171; MAICYA; SATA 13

Gallo, Max Louis 1932- .... **CLC 95**
See also CA 85-88

Gallois, Lucien
See Desnos, Robert

Gallup, Ralph
See Whitemore, Hugh (John)

Galsworthy, John 1867-1933 .. **TCLC 1, 45; DA; DAB; DAC; DAM DRAM, MST, NOV; SSC 22; WLC 2**
See also CA 104; 141; CDBLB 1890-1914; DLB 10, 34, 98, 162; DLBD 16

Galt, John 1779-1839 .... **NCLC 1**
See also DLB 99, 116, 159

Galvin, James 1951- .... **CLC 38**
See also CA 108; CANR 26

Gamboa, Federico 1864-1939 .... **TCLC 36**

Gandhi, M. K.
See Gandhi, Mohandas Karamchand

Gandhi, Mahatma
See Gandhi, Mohandas Karamchand

Gandhi, Mohandas Karamchand 1869-1948
TCLC 59; DAM MULT
See also CA 121; 132; MTCW

Gann, Ernest Kellogg 1910-1991 .... **CLC 23**
See also AITN 1; CA 1-4R; 136; CANR 1

Garcia, Cristina 1958- .... **CLC 76**
See also CA 141

Garcia Lorca, Federico 1898-1936 **TCLC 1, 7, 49; DA; DAB; DAC; DAM DRAM, MST, MULT, POET; DC 2; HLC; PC 3; WLC**
See also CA 104; 131; DLB 108; HW; MTCW

Garcia Marquez, Gabriel (Jose) 1928- **CLC 2, 3, 8, 10, 15, 27, 47, 55, 68; DA; DAB; DAC; DAM MST, MULT, NOV, POP; HLC; SSC 8; WLC**
See also AAYA 3; BEST 89:1, 90:4; CA 33-36R; CANR 10, 28, 50; DLB 113; HW; MTCW

Gard, Janice
See Latham, Jean Lee

Gard, Roger Martin du
See Martin du Gard, Roger

Gardam, Jane 1928- .... **CLC 43**
See also CA 49-52; CANR 2, 18, 33, 54; CLR 12; DLB 14, 161; MAICYA; MTCW; SAAS 9; SATA 39, 76; SATA-Brief 28

Gardner, Herb(ert) 1934- .... **CLC 44**
See also CA 149

Gardner, John (Champlin), Jr. 1933-1982
CLC 2, 3, 5, 7, 8, 10, 18, 28, 34; DAM NOV, POP; SSC 7
See also AITN 1; CA 65-68; 107; CANR 33; DLB 2; DLBY 82; MTCW; SATA 40; SATA-Obit 31

Gardner, John (Edmund) 1926- ...... **CLC 30; DAM POP**
See also CA 103; CANR 15; MTCW

Gardner, Miriam
See Bradley, Marion Zimmer

Gardner, Noel
See Kuttner, Henry

Gardons, S. S.
See Snodgrass, W(illiam) D(e Witt)

Garfield, Leon 1921-1996 .... **CLC 12**
See also AAYA 8; CA 17-20R; 152; CANR 38, 41; CLR 21; DLB 161; JRDA; MAICYA; SATA 1, 32, 76; SATA-Obit 90

Garland, (Hannibal) Hamlin 1860-1940
TCLC 3; SSC 18
See also CA 104; DLB 12, 71, 78, 186

Garneau, (Hector de) Saint-Denys 1912-1943
TCLC 13
See also CA 111; DLB 88

Garner, Alan 1934- .... **CLC 17; DAB; DAM POP**
See also AAYA 18; CA 73-76; CANR 15, 64; CLR 20; DLB 161; MAICYA; MTCW; SATA 18, 69

Garner, Hugh 1913-1979 .... **CLC 13**
See also CA 69-72; CANR 31; DLB 68

Garnett, David 1892-1981 .... **CLC 3**
See also CA 5-8R; 103; CANR 17; DLB 34

Garos, Stephanie
See Katz, Steve

Garrett, George (Palmer) 1929- ... **CLC 3, 11, 51; SSC 30**
See also CA 1-4R; CAAS 5; CANR 1, 42, 67; DLB 2, 5, 130, 152; DLBY 83

Garrick, David 1717-1779 .... **LC 15; DAM DRAM**
See also DLB 84

Garrigue, Jean 1914-1972 .... **CLC 2, 8**
See also CA 5-8R; 37-40R; CANR 20

Garrison, Frederick
See Sinclair, Upton (Beall)

Garth, Will
See Hamilton, Edmond; Kuttner, Henry

Garvey, Marcus (Moziah, Jr.) 1887-1940
TCLC 41; BLC; DAM MULT
See also BW 1; CA 120; 124

Gary, Romain .... **CLC 25**
See also Kacew, Romain
See also DLB 83

Gascar, Pierre .... **CLC 11**
See also Fournier, Pierre

Gascoyne, David (Emery) 1916- .... **CLC 45**
See also CA 65-68; CANR 10, 28, 54; DLB 20; MTCW

Gaskell, Elizabeth Cleghorn 1810-1865
NCLC 5; DAB; DAM MST; SSC 25
See also CDBLB 1832-1890; DLB 21, 144, 159

Gass, William H(oward) 1924- ... **CLC 1, 2, 8, 11, 15, 39; SSC 12**
See also CA 17-20R; CANR 30; DLB 2; MTCW

Gasset, Jose Ortega y
See Ortega y Gasset, Jose

Gates, Henry Louis, Jr. 1950- ..... **CLC 65; DAM MULT**
See also BW 2; CA 109; CANR 25, 53; DLB 67

Gautier, Theophile 1811-1872 **NCLC 1, 59; DAM POET; PC 18; SSC 20**
See also DLB 119

Gawsworth, John
See Bates, H(erbert) E(rnest)

Gay, Oliver
See Gogarty, Oliver St. John

Gaye, Marvin (Penze) 1939-1984 ...... **CLC 26**
See also CA 112

Gebler, Carlo (Ernest) 1954- .... **CLC 39**
See also CA 119; 133

Gee, Maggie (Mary) 1948- .... **CLC 57**
See also CA 130

Gee, Maurice (Gough) 1931- .... **CLC 29**
See also CA 97-100; CANR 67; SATA 46

Gelbart, Larry (Simon) 1923- ...... **CLC 21, 61**
See also CA 73-76; CANR 45

Gelber, Jack 1932- .... **CLC 1, 6, 14, 79**
See also CA 1-4R; CANR 2; DLB 7

Gellhorn, Martha (Ellis) 1908-1998 ... **CLC 14, 60**
See also CA 77-80; 164; CANR 44; DLBY 82

Genet, Jean 1910-1986 **CLC 1, 2, 5, 10, 14, 44, 46; DAM DRAM**
See also CA 13-16R; CANR 18; DLB 72; DLBY 86; MTCW

Gent, Peter 1942- .... **CLC 29**
See also AITN 1; CA 89-92; DLBY 82

Gentlewoman in New England, A
See Bradstreet, Anne

Gentlewoman in Those Parts, A
See Bradstreet, Anne

George, Jean Craighead 1919- .... **CLC 35**
See also AAYA 8; CA 5-8R; CANR 25; CLR 1; DLB 52; JRDA; MAICYA; SATA 2, 68

George, Stefan (Anton) 1868-1933 ... **TCLC 2, 14**
See also CA 104

Georges, Georges Martin
See Simenon, Georges (Jacques Christian)

Gerhardi, William Alexander
See Gerhardie, William Alexander

Gerhardie, William Alexander 1895-1977
CLC 5
See also CA 25-28R; 73-76; CANR 18; DLB 36

Gerstler, Amy 1956- .... **CLC 70**
See also CA 146

Gertler, T. .... **CLC 34**
See also CA 116; 121; INT 121

Ghalib ....**NCLC 39**
See also Ghalib, Hsadullah Khan

Ghalib, Hsadullah Khan 1797-1869
See Ghalib
See also DAM POET

Ghelderode, Michel de 1898-1962 . **CLC 6, 11; DAM DRAM**
See also CA 85-88; CANR 40

Ghiselin, Brewster 1903- .... **CLC 23**
See also CA 13-16R; CAAS 10; CANR 13

Ghose, Zulfikar 1935- .... **CLC 42**
See also CA 65-68; CANR 67

Ghosh, Amitav 1956- .... **CLC 44**
See also CA 147

Giacosa, Giuseppe 1847-1906 .... **TCLC 7**
See also CA 104

Gibb, Lee
See Waterhouse, Keith (Spencer)

Gibbon, Lewis Grassic .... **TCLC 4**
See also Mitchell, James Leslie

Gibbons, Kaye 1960-   **CLC 50, 88; DAM POP**
See also CA 151

Gibran, Kahlil 1883-1931 .. **TCLC 1, 9; DAM POET, POP; PC 9**
See also CA 104; 150

Gibran, Khalil
See Gibran, Kahlil

Gibson, William 1914- ..... **CLC 23; DA; DAB; DAC; DAM DRAM, MST**
See also CA 9-12R; CANR 9, 42; DLB 7; SATA 66

Gibson, William (Ford) 1948- .... **CLC 39, 63; DAM POP**
See also AAYA 12; CA 126; 133; CANR 52

Gide, Andre (Paul Guillaume) 1869-1951 **TCLC 5, 12, 36; DA; DAB; DAC; DAM MST, NOV; SSC 13; WLC**
See also CA 104; 124; DLB 65; MTCW

Gifford, Barry (Colby) 1946- .... **CLC 34**
See also CA 65-68; CANR 9, 30, 40

Gilbert, Frank
See De Voto, Bernard (Augustine)

Gilbert, W(illiam) S(chwenck) 1836-1911 **TCLC 3; DAM DRAM, POET**
See also CA 104; SATA 36

Gilbreth, Frank B., Jr. 1911- .... **CLC 17**
See also CA 9-12R; SATA 2

Gilchrist, Ellen 1935- ....   **CLC 34, 48; DAM POP; SSC 14**
See also CA 113; 116; CANR 41, 61; DLB 130; MTCW

Giles, Molly 1942- .... **CLC 39**
See also CA 126

Gill, Patrick
See Creasey, John

Gilliam, Terry (Vance) 1940- .... **CLC 21**
See also Monty Python
See also AAYA 19; CA 108; 113; CANR 35; INT 113

Gillian, Jerry
See Gilliam, Terry (Vance)

Gilliatt, Penelope (Ann Douglass) 1932-1993 **CLC 2, 10, 13, 53**
See also AITN 2; CA 13-16R; 141; CANR 49; DLB 14

Gilman, Charlotte (Anna) Perkins (Stetson) 1860-1935 .... **TCLC 9, 37; SSC 13**
See also CA 106; 150

Gilmour, David 1949- .... **CLC 35**
See also CA 138, 147

Gilpin, William 1724-1804 .... **NCLC 30**

Gilray, J. D.
See Mencken, H(enry) L(ouis)

Gilroy, Frank D(aniel) 1925- .... **CLC 2**
See also CA 81-84; CANR 32, 64; DLB 7

Gilstrap, John 1957(?)- .... **CLC 99**
See also CA 160

Ginsberg, Allen 1926-1997 **CLC 1, 2, 3, 4, 6, 13, 36, 69, 109; DA; DAB; DAC; DAM MST, POET; PC 4; WLC 3**
See also AITN 1; CA 1-4R; 157; CANR 2, 41, 63; CDALB 1941-1968; DLB 5, 16, 169; MTCW

Ginzburg, Natalia 1916-1991 .... **CLC 5, 11, 54, 70**
See also CA 85-88; 135; CANR 33; DLB 177; MTCW

Giono, Jean 1895-1970 .... **CLC 4, 11**
See also CA 45-48; 29-32R; CANR 2, 35; DLB 72; MTCW

Giovanni, Nikki 1943-........... **CLC 2, 4, 19, 64; BLC; DA; DAB; DAC; DAM MST, MULT, POET; PC 19; WLCS**
See also AAYA 22; AITN 1; BW 2; CA 29-32R; CAAS 6; CANR 18, 41, 60; CLR 6; DLB 5, 41; INT CANR-18; MAICYA; MTCW; SATA 24

Giovene, Andrea 1904-......................... **CLC 7**
See also CA 85-88

Gippius, Zinaida (Nikolayevna) 1869-1945
See Hippius, Zinaida
See also CA 106

Giraudoux, (Hippolyte) Jean 1882-1944 **TCLC 2, 7; DAM DRAM**
See also CA 104; DLB 65

Gironella, Jose Maria 1917- .... **CLC 11**
See also CA 101

Gissing, George (Robert) 1857-1903..... **TCLC 3, 24, 47**
See also CA 105; DLB 18, 135, 184

Giurlani, Aldo
See Palazzeschi, Aldo

Gladkov, Fyodor (Vasilyevich) 1883-1958 **TCLC 27**

Glanville, Brian (Lester) 1931- .... **CLC 6**
See also CA 5-8R; CAAS 9; CANR 3; DLB 15, 139; SATA 42

Glasgow, Ellen (Anderson Gholson) 1873-1945 **TCLC 2, 7**
See also CA 104; 164; DLB 9, 12

Glaspell, Susan 1882(?)-1948 .... **TCLC 55**
See also CA 110; 154; DLB 7, 9, 78; YABC 2

Glassco, John 1909-1981 .... **CLC 9**
See also CA 13-16R; 102; CANR 15; DLB 68

Glasscock, Amnesia
See Steinbeck, John (Ernst)

Glasser, Ronald J. 1940(?)- .... **CLC 37**

Glassman, Joyce
See Johnson, Joyce

Glendinning, Victoria 1937- .... **CLC 50**
See also CA 120; 127; CANR 59; DLB 155

Glissant, Edouard 1928- ... **CLC 10, 68; DAM MULT**
See also CA 153

Gloag, Julian 1930-............................. **CLC 40**
See also AITN 1; CA 65-68; CANR 10

Glowacki, Aleksander
See Prus, Boleslaw

Gluck, Louise (Elisabeth) 1943- .... **CLC 7, 22, 44, 81; DAM POET; PC 16**
See also CA 33-36R; CANR 40; DLB 5

Glyn, Elinor 1864-1943 .... **TCLC 72**
See also DLB 153

Gobineau, Joseph Arthur (Comte) de 1816-1882 **NCLC 17**
See also DLB 123

Godard, Jean-Luc 1930- .... **CLC 20**
See also CA 93-96

Godden, (Margaret) Rumer 1907- .... **CLC 53**
See also AAYA 6; CA 5-8R; CANR 4, 27, 36, 55; CLR 20; DLB 161; MAICYA; SAAS 12; SATA 3, 36

Godoy Alcayaga, Lucila 1889-1957
See Mistral, Gabriela
See also BW 2; CA 104; 131; DAM MULT; HW; MTCW

Godwin, Gail (Kathleen) 1937- .... **CLC 5, 8, 22, 31, 69; DAM POP**
See also CA 29-32R; CANR 15, 43; DLB 6; INT CANR-15; MTCW

Graham, Tom
See Lewis, (Harry) Sinclair

Graham, W(illiam) S(ydney) 1918-1986 ... **CLC 29**
See also CA 73-76; 118; DLB 20

Graham, Winston (Mawdsley) 1910-　**CLC 23**
See also CA 49-52; CANR 2, 22, 45, 66; DLB 77

Grahame, Kenneth 1859-1932 .... **TCLC 64; DAB**
See also CA 108; 136; CLR 5; DLB 34, 141, 178;
MAICYA; YABC 1

Grant, Skeeter
See Spiegelman, Art

Granville-Barker, Harley 1877-1946 ... **TCLC 2; DAM DRAM**
See also Barker, Harley Granville
See also CA 104

Grass, Guenter (Wilhelm) 1927- ....**CLC 1, 2, 4, 6, 11, 15, 22, 32, 49, 88; DA; DAB; DAC; DAM MST, NOV; WLC**
See also CA 13-16R; CANR 20; DLB 75, 124; MTCW

Gratton, Thomas
See Hulme, T(homas) E(rnest)

Grau, Shirley Ann 1929- .... **CLC 4, 9; SSC 15**
See also CA 89-92; CANR 22; DLB 2; INT CANR-22; MTCW

Gravel, Fern
See Hall, James Norman

Graver, Elizabeth 1964- .... **CLC 70**
See also CA 135

Graves, Richard Perceval 1945- .... **CLC 44**
See also CA 65-68; CANR 9, 26, 51

Graves, Robert (von Ranke) 1895-1985 ... **CLC 1, 2, 6, 11, 39, 44, 45; DAB; DAC; DAM MST, POET; PC 6**
See also CA 5-8R; 117; CANR 5, 36; CDBLB 1914-1945; DLB 20, 100, 191; DLBY 85; MTCW; SATA 45

Graves, Valerie
See Bradley, Marion Zimmer

Gray, Alasdair (James) 1934- .... **CLC 41**
See also CA 126; CANR 47; DLB 194; INT 126; MTCW

Gray, Amlin 1946- .... **CLC 29**
See also CA 138

Gray, Francine du Plessix 1930- .... **CLC 22; DAM NOV**
See also BEST 90:3; CA 61-64; CAAS 2; CANR 11, 33; INT CANR-11; MTCW

Gray, John (Henry) 1866-1934 .... **TCLC 19**
See also CA 119; 162

Gray, Simon (James Holliday) 1936- ... **CLC 9, 14, 36**
See also AITN 1; CA 21-24R; CAAS 3; CANR 32; DLB 13; MTCW

Gray, Spalding 1941- ... **CLC 49; DAM POP; DC 7**
See also CA 128

Gray, Thomas 1716-1771 ....　　**LC 4, 40; DA; DAB; DAC; DAM MST; PC 2; WLC**
See also CDBLB 1660-1789; DLB 109

Grayson, David
See Baker, Ray Stannard

Grayson, Richard (A.) 1951- .... **CLC 38**
See also CA 85-88; CANR 14, 31, 57

Greeley, Andrew M(oran) 1928- ....　　**CLC 28; DAM POP**
See also CA 5-8R; CAAS 7; CANR 7, 43; MTCW

Green, Anna Katharine 1846-1935　　**TCLC 63**
See also CA 112; 159

Green, Brian
See Card, Orson Scott

Green, Hannah
See Greenberg, Joanne (Goldenberg)

Green, Hannah 1927(?)-1996 .... **CLC 3**
See also CA 73-76; CANR 59

Green, Henry 1905-1973 .... **CLC 2, 13, 97**
See also Yorke, Henry Vincent
See also DLB 15

Green, Julian (Hartridge) 1900-
See Green, Julien
See also CA 21-24R; CANR 33; DLB 4, 72; MTCW

Green, Julien ....**CLC 3, 11, 77**
See also Green, Julian (Hartridge)

Green, Paul (Eliot) 1894-1981　　**CLC 25; DAM DRAM**
See also AITN 1; CA 5-8R; 103; CANR 3; DLB 7, 9; DLBY 81

Greenberg, Ivan 1908-1973
See Rahv, Philip
See also CA 85-88

Greenberg, Joanne (Goldenberg) 1932- ... **CLC 7, 30**
See also AAYA 12; CA 5-8R; CANR 14, 32; SATA 25

Greenberg, Richard 1959(?)- .... **CLC 57**
See also CA 138

Greene, Bette 1934- .... **CLC 30**
See also AAYA 7; CA 53-56; CANR 4; CLR 2; JRDA; MAICYA; SAAS 16; SATA 8

Greene, Gael ....**CLC 8**
See also CA 13-16R; CANR 10

Greene, Graham (Henry) 1904-1991 ... **CLC 1, 3, 6, 9, 14, 18, 27, 37, 70, 72; DA; DAB; DAC; DAM MST, NOV; SSC 29; WLC**
See also AITN 2; CA 13-16R; 133; CANR 35, 61; CDBLB 1945-1960; DLB 13, 15, 77, 100, 162; DLBY 91; MTCW; SATA 20

Greene, Robert 1558-1592 .... **LC 41**
See also DLB 62, 167

Greer, Richard
See Silverberg, Robert

Gregor, Arthur 1923- .... **CLC 9**
See also CA 25-28R; CAAS 10; CANR 11; SATA 36

Gregor, Lee
See Pohl, Frederik

Gregory, Isabella Augusta (Persse) 1852-1932
TCLC 1
See also CA 104; DLB 10

Gregory, J. Dennis
See Williams, John A(lfred)

Grendon, Stephen
See Derleth, August (William)

Grenville, Kate 1950- .... **CLC 61**
See also CA 118; CANR 53

Grenville, Pelham
See Wodehouse, P(elham) G(renville)

Greve, Felix Paul (Berthold Friedrich) 1879-1948
See Grove, Frederick Philip
See also CA 104; 141; DAC; DAM MST

Grey, Zane 1872-1939　　**TCLC 6; DAM POP**
See also CA 104; 132; DLB 9; MTCW

Grieg, (Johan) Nordahl (Brun) 1902-1943
TCLC 10
See also CA 107

Grieve, C(hristopher) M(urray) 1892-1978
CLC 11, 19; DAM POET
See also MacDiarmid, Hugh; Pteleon
See also CA 5-8R; 85-88; CANR 33; MTCW

Griffin, Gerald 1803-1840 .... **NCLC 7**
See also DLB 159

Griffin, John Howard 1920-1980 .... **CLC 68**
See also AITN 1; CA 1-4R; 101; CANR 2

Griffin, Peter 1942- .... **CLC 39**
See also CA 136

Griffith, D(avid Lewelyn) W(ark) 1875(?)-1948
TCLC 68
See also CA 119; 150

Griffith, Lawrence
See Griffith, D(avid Lewelyn) W(ark)

Griffiths, Trevor 1935- .... **CLC 13, 52**
See also CA 97-100; CANR 45; DLB 13

Griggs, Sutton Elbert 1872-1930(?)　**TCLC 77**
See also CA 123; DLB 50

Grigson, Geoffrey (Edward Harvey) 1905-1985
CLC 7, 39
See also CA 25-28R; 118; CANR 20, 33; DLB 27; MTCW

Hagiosy, L.
See Larbaud, Valery (Nicolas)

Hagiwara Sakutaro 1886-1942 ... **TCLC 60; PC 18**

Haig, Fenil
See Ford, Ford Madox

Haig-Brown, Roderick (Langmere) 1908-1976
CLC 21
See also CA 5-8R; 69-72; CANR 4, 38; CLR 31;
DLB 88; MAICYA; SATA 12

Hailey, Arthur 1920- **CLC 5; DAM NOV, POP**
See also AITN 2; BEST 90:3; CA 1-4R; CANR
2, 36; DLB 88; DLBY 82; MTCW

Hailey, Elizabeth Forsythe 1938- .... **CLC 40**
See also CA 93-96; CAAS 1; CANR 15, 48; INT
CANR-15

Haines, John (Meade) 1924- .... **CLC 58**
See also CA 17-20R; CANR 13, 34; DLB 5

Hakluyt, Richard 1552-1616 .... **LC 31**

Haldeman, Joe (William) 1943- .... **CLC 61**
See also CA 53-56; CAAS 25; CANR 6; DLB 8;
INT CANR-6

Haley, Alex(ander Murray Palmer) 1921-1992
**CLC 8, 12, 76; BLC; DA; DAB; DAC;
DAM MST, MULT, POP**
See also BW 2; CA 77-80; 136; CANR 61; DLB
38; MTCW

Haliburton, Thomas Chandler 1796-1865 ...**NCLC 15**
See also DLB 11, 99

Hall, Donald (Andrew, Jr.) 1928-   **CLC 1, 13,
37, 59; DAM POET**
See also CA 5-8R; CAAS 7; CANR 2, 44, 64;
DLB 5; SATA 23, 97

Hall, Frederic Sauser
See Sauser-Hall, Frederic

Hall, James
See Kuttner, Henry

Hall, James Norman 1887-1951 ...... **TCLC 23**
See also CA 123; SATA 21

Hall, (Marguerite) Radclyffe 1886-1943
TCLC 12
See also CA 110; 150

Hall, Rodney 1935- .... **CLC 51**
See also CA 109

Halleck, Fitz-Greene 1790-1867 ..... **NCLC 47**
See also DLB 3

Halliday, Michael
See Creasey, John

Halpern, Daniel 1945- .... **CLC 14**
See also CA 33-36R

Hamburger, Michael (Peter Leopold) 1924-
CLC 5, 14
See also CA 5-8R; CAAS 4; CANR 2, 47; DLB 27

Hamill, Pete 1935- .... **CLC 10**
See also CA 25-28R; CANR 18

Hamilton, Alexander 1755(?)-1804 .... **NCLC
49**
See also DLB 37

Hamilton, Clive
See Lewis, C(live) S(taples)

Hamilton, Edmond 1904-1977 .... **CLC 1**
See also CA 1-4R; CANR 3; DLB 8

Hamilton, Eugene (Jacob) Lee
See Lee-Hamilton, Eugene (Jacob)

Hamilton, Franklin
See Silverberg, Robert

Hamilton, Gail
See Corcoran, Barbara

Hamilton, Mollie
See Kaye, M(ary) M(argaret)

Hamilton, (Anthony Walter) Patrick 1904-1962
CLC 51
See also CA 113; DLB 10

Hamilton, Virginia 1936- .... **CLC 26; DAM
MULT**
See also AAYA 2, 21; BW 2; CA 25-28R; CANR
20, 37; CLR 1, 11, 40; DLB 33, 52; INT
CANR-20; JRDA; MAICYA; MTCW; SATA
4, 56, 79

Hammett, (Samuel) Dashiell 1894-1961 ... **CLC
3, 5, 10, 19, 47; SSC 17**
See also AITN 1; CA 81-84; CANR 42; CDALB
1929-1941; DLBD 6; DLBY 96; MTCW

Hammon, Jupiter 1711(?)-1800(?) ...**NCLC 5;
BLC; DAM MULT, POET; PC 16**
See also DLB 31, 50

Hammond, Keith
See Kuttner, Henry

Hamner, Earl (Henry), Jr. 1923- .... **CLC 12**
See also AITN 2; CA 73-76; DLB 6

Hampton, Christopher (James) 1946- ...... **CLC
4**
See also CA 25-28R; DLB 13; MTCW

Hamsun, Knut ....**TCLC 2, 14, 49**
See also Pedersen, Knut

Handke, Peter 1942- .... **CLC 5, 8, 10, 15, 38;
DAM DRAM, NOV**
See also CA 77-80; CANR 33; DLB 85, 124; MTCW

Hanley, James 1901-1985 .... **CLC 3, 5, 8, 13**
See also CA 73-76; 117; CANR 36; DLB 191;
MTCW

Hannah, Barry 1942-............... **CLC 23, 38, 90**
See also CA 108; 110; CANR 43, 68; DLB 6;
INT 110; MTCW

Hannon, Ezra
See Hunter, Evan

Hansberry, Lorraine (Vivian) 1930-1965
**CLC 17, 62; BLC; DA; DAB; DAC; DAM
DRAM, MST, MULT; DC 2**
See also AAYA 25; BW 1; CA 109; 25-28R;
CABS 3; CANR 58; CDALB 1941-1968;
DLB 7, 38; MTCW

Hansen, Joseph 1923-......................... **CLC 38**
See also CA 29-32R; CAAS 17; CANR 16, 44,
66; INT CANR-16

Hansen, Martin A. 1909-1955 .... **TCLC 32**

Hanson, Kenneth O(stlin) 1922- .... **CLC 13**
See also CA 53-56; CANR 7

Hardwick, Elizabeth 1916- .... **CLC 13; DAM
NOV**
See also CA 5-8R; CANR 3, 32; DLB 6; MTCW

Hardy, Thomas 1840-1928   **TCLC 4, 10,
18, 32, 48, 53, 72; DA; DAB; DAC; DAM
MST, NOV, POET; PC 8; SSC 2; WLC**
See also CA 104; 123; CDBLB 1890-1914; DLB
18, 19, 135; MTCW

Hare, David 1947- .... **CLC 29, 58**
See also CA 97-100; CANR 39; DLB 13;
MTCW

Harewood, John
See Van Druten, John (William)

Harford, Henry
See Hudson, W(illiam) H(enry)

Hargrave, Leonie
See Disch, Thomas M(ichael)

Harjo, Joy 1951- .... **CLC 83; DAM MULT**
See also CA 114; CANR 35, 67; DLB 120, 175;
NNAL

Harlan, Louis R(udolph) 1922- .... **CLC 34**
See also CA 21-24R; CANR 25, 55

Harling, Robert 1951(?)- .... **CLC 53**
See also CA 147

Harmon, William (Ruth) 1938- .... **CLC 38**
See also CA 33-36R; CANR 14, 32, 35; SATA
65

Harper, F. E. W.
See Harper, Frances Ellen Watkins

Harper, Frances E. W.
See Harper, Frances Ellen Watkins

Harper, Frances E. Watkins
See Harper, Frances Ellen Watkins

Harper, Frances Ellen
See Harper, Frances Ellen Watkins

Harper, Frances Ellen Watkins 1825-1911
**TCLC 14; BLC; DAM MULT, POET; PC
21**
See also BW 1; CA 111; 125; DLB 50

Harper, Michael S(teven) 1938- ..... **CLC 7, 22**
See also BW 1; CA 33-36R; CANR 24; DLB 41

Harper, Mrs. F. E. W.
See Harper, Frances Ellen Watkins

Harris, Christie (Lucy) Irwin 1907- .. **CLC 12**
See also CA 5-8R; CANR 6; CLR 47; DLB 88;
JRDA; MAICYA; SAAS 10; SATA 6, 74

Harris, Frank 1856-1931 .... **TCLC 24**
See also CA 109; 150; DLB 156

Harris, George Washington 1814-1869
NCLC 23
See also DLB 3, 11

Harris, Joel Chandler 1848-1908 ... **TCLC 2;
SSC 19**
See also CA 104; 137; CLR 49; DLB 11, 23, 42,
78, 91; MAICYA; YABC 1

Harris, John (Wyndham Parkes Lucas) Beynon
1903-1969
See Wyndham, John
See also CA 102; 89-92

Harris, MacDonald .... **CLC 9**
See also Heiney, Donald (William)

Harris, Mark 1922- .... **CLC 19**
See also CA 5-8R; CAAS 3; CANR 2, 55; DLB
2; DLBY 80

Harris, (Theodore) Wilson 1921- .... **CLC 25**
See also BW 2; CA 65-68; CAAS 16; CANR 11,
27; DLB 117; MTCW

Harrison, Elizabeth Cavanna 1909-
See Cavanna, Betty
See also CA 9-12R; CANR 6, 27

Harrison, Harry (Max) 1925- .... **CLC 42**
See also CA 1-4R; CANR 5, 21; DLB 8; SATA 4

Harrison, James (Thomas) 1937- ... **CLC 6, 14,
33, 66; SSC 19**
See also CA 13-16R; CANR 8, 51; DLBY 82;
INT CANR-8

Harrison, Jim
See Harrison, James (Thomas)

Harrison, Kathryn 1961- .... **CLC 70**
See also CA 144; CANR 68

Harrison, Tony 1937- .... **CLC 43**
See also CA 65-68; CANR 44; DLB 40; MTCW

Harriss, Will(ard Irvin) 1922- .... **CLC 34**
See also CA 111

Harson, Sley
See Ellison, Harlan (Jay)

Hart, Ellis
See Ellison, Harlan (Jay)

Hart, Josephine 1942(?)- .... **CLC 70; DAM
POP**
See also CA 138

Hart, Moss 1904-1961 .... **CLC 66; DAM
DRAM**
See also CA 109; 89-92; DLB 7

Harte, (Francis) Bret(t) 1836(?)-1902 ... **TCLC
1, 25; DA; DAC; DAM MST; SSC 8; WLC**
See also CA 104; 140; CDALB 1865-1917; DLB
12, 64, 74, 79, 186; SATA 26

Hartley, L(eslie) P(oles) 1895-1972 ..... **CLC 2,
22**
See also CA 45-48; 37-40R; CANR 33; DLB 15,
139; MTCW

Hartman, Geoffrey H. 1929- .... **CLC 27**
See also CA 117; 125; DLB 67

Hartmann, Sadakichi 1867-1944 ..... **TCLC 73**
See also CA 157; DLB 54

Hartmann von Aue c. 1160-c. 1205 **CMLC 15**
See also DLB 138

Hartmann von Aue 1170-1210 .... **CMLC 15**

Haruf, Kent 1943- .... **CLC 34**
See also CA 149

Harwood, Ronald 1934- .... **CLC 32; DAM
DRAM, MST**
See also CA 1-4R; CANR 4, 55; DLB 13

Hasegawa Tatsunosuke
See Futabatei, Shimei

Hasek, Jaroslav (Matej Frantisek) 1883-1923
TCLC 4
See also CA 104; 129; MTCW

Hass, Robert 1941-   **CLC 18, 39, 99; PC 16**
See also CA 111; CANR 30, 50; DLB 105; SATA 94

Hastings, Hudson
See Kuttner, Henry

Hastings, Selina .... **CLC 44**

Hathorne, John 1641-1717 .... **LC 38**

Hatteras, Amelia
See Mencken, H(enry) L(ouis)

Hatteras, Owen .... **TCLC 18**
See also Mencken, H(enry) L(ouis); Nathan,
George Jean

Hauptmann, Gerhart (Johann Robert) 1862-
1946 .... **TCLC 4; DAM DRAM**
See also CA 104; 153; DLB 66, 118

Havel, Vaclav 1936- ..... **CLC 25, 58, 65; DAM
DRAM; DC 6**
See also CA 104; CANR 36, 63; MTCW

Haviaras, Stratis .... **CLC 33**
See also Chaviaras, Strates

Hawes, Stephen 1475(?)-1523(?) .... **LC 17**

Hawkes, John (Clendennin Burne, Jr.) 1925-
CLC 1, 2, 3, 4, 7, 9, 14, 15, 27, 49
See also CA 1-4R; CANR 2, 47, 64; DLB 2, 7;
DLBY 80; MTCW

Hawking, S. W.
See Hawking, Stephen W(illiam)

Hawking, Stephen W(illiam) 1942- ... **CLC 63, 105**
See also AAYA 13; BEST 89:1; CA 126; 129;
CANR 48

Hawthorne, Julian 1846-1934 .... **TCLC 25**
See also CA 165

Hawthorne, Nathaniel 1804-1864 ... **NCLC 39; DA;
DAB; DAC; DAM MST, NOV; SSC 3, 29; WLC**
See also AAYA 18; CDALB 1640-1865; DLB 1,
74; YABC 2

Haxton, Josephine Ayres 1921-
See Douglas, Ellen
See also CA 115; CANR 41

Hayaseca y Eizaguirre, Jorge
See Echegaray (y Eizaguirre), Jose (Maria Waldo)

Hayashi Fumiko 1904-1951 .... **TCLC 27**
See also CA 161; DLB 180

Haycraft, Anna
See Ellis, Alice Thomas
See also CA 122

Hayden, Robert E(arl) 1913-1980 ... **CLC 5, 9,
14, 37; BLC; DA; DAC; DAM MST, MULT,
POET; PC 6**
See also BW 1; CA 69-72; 97-100; CABS 2;
CANR 24; CDALB 1941-1968; DLB 5, 76;
MTCW; SATA 19; SATA-Obit 26

Hayford, J(oseph) E(phraim) Casely
See Casely-Hayford, J(oseph) E(phraim)

Hayman, Ronald 1932- .... **CLC 44**
See also CA 25-28R; CANR 18, 50; DLB 155

Haywood, Eliza (Fowler) 1693(?)-1756 .. **LC 1**

Hazlitt, William 1778-1830 .... **NCLC 29**
See also DLB 110, 158

Hazzard, Shirley 1931- .... **CLC 18**
See also CA 9-12R; CANR 4; DLBY 82; MTCW

Head, Bessie 1937-1986 .... **CLC 25, 67; BLC;
DAM MULT**
See also BW 2; CA 29-32R; 119; CANR 25; DLB
117; MTCW

Headon, (Nicky) Topper 1956(?)- ...... **CLC 30**

Heaney, Seamus (Justin) 1939- ... **CLC 5, 7, 14, 25,
37, 74, 91; DAB; DAM POET; PC 18; WLCS**
See also CA 85-88; CANR 25, 48; CDBLB 1960
to Present; DLB 40; DLBY 95; MTCW

Hearn, (Patricio) Lafcadio (Tessima Carlos)
1850-1904 .... **TCLC 9**
See also CA 105; DLB 12, 78

Hearne, Vicki 1946- .... **CLC 56**
See also CA 139

Hearon, Shelby 1931- .... **CLC 63**
See also AITN 2; CA 25-28R; CANR 18, 48

Heat-Moon, William Least .... **CLC 29**
See also Trogdon, William (Lewis)
See also AAYA 9

Hebbel, Friedrich 1813-1863 .... **NCLC 43; DAM DRAM**
See also DLB 129

Hebert, Anne 1916- ... **CLC 4, 13, 29; DAC; DAM MST, POET**
See also CA 85-88; DLB 68; MTCW

Hecht, Anthony (Evan) 1923-. **CLC 8, 13, 19; DAM POET**
See also CA 9-12R; CANR 6; DLB 5, 169

Hecht, Ben 1894-1964 .... **CLC 8**
See also CA 85-88; DLB 7, 9, 25, 26 28, 86

Hedayat, Sadeq 1903-1951 .... **CLC 21**
See also CA 120

Hegel, Georg Wilhelm Friedrich 1770-1831 **NCLC 46**
See also DLB 90

Heidegger, Martin 1889-1976 .... **CLC 24**
See also CA 81-84; 65-68; CANR 34; MTCW

Heidenstam, (Carl Gustaf) Verner von 1859-1940 .... **TCLC 5**
See also CA 104

Heifner, Jack 1946-.............................. **CLC 11**
See also CA 105; CANR 47

Heijermans, Herman 1864-1924 ..... **TCLC 24**
See also CA 123

Heilbrun, Carolyn G(old) 1926- .... **CLC 25**
See also CA 45-48; CANR 1, 28, 58

Heine, Heinrich 1797-1856 .... **NCLC 4, 54**
See also DLB 90

Heinemann, Larry (Curtiss) 1944- .... **CLC 50**
See also CA 110; CAAS 21; CANR 31; DLBD 9; INT CANR-31

Heiney, Donald (William) 1921-1993
See Harris, MacDonald
See also CA 1-4R; 142; CANR 3, 58

Heinlein, Robert A(nson) 1907-1988 **CLC 1, 3, 8, 14, 26, 55; DAM POP**
See also AAYA 17; CA 1-4R; 125; CANR 1, 20, 53; DLB 8; JRDA; MAICYA; MTCW; SATA 9, 69; SATA-Obit 56

Helforth, John
See Doolittle, Hilda

Hellenhofferu, Vojtech Kapristian z
See Hasek, Jaroslav (Matej Frantisek)

Heller, Joseph 1923- **CLC 1, 3, 5, 8, 11, 36, 63; DA; DAB; DAC; DAM MST, NOV, POP; WLC**
See also AAYA 24; AITN 1; CA 5-8R; CABS 1; CANR 8, 42, 66; DLB 2, 28; DLBY 80; INT CANR-8; MTCW

Hellman, Lillian (Florence) 1906-1984 ... **CLC 2, 4, 8, 14, 18, 34, 44, 52; DAM DRAM; DC 1**
See also AITN 1, 2; CA 13-16R; 112; CANR 33; DLB 7; DLBY 84; MTCW

Helprin, Mark 1947- ... **CLC 7, 10, 22, 32; DAM NOV, POP**
See also CA 81-84; CANR 47, 64; DLBY 85; MTCW

Helvetius, Claude-Adrien 1715-1771 ... **LC 26**

Helyar, Jane Penelope Josephine 1933-
See Poole, Josephine
See also CA 21-24R; CANR 10, 26; SATA 82

Hemans, Felicia 1793-1835 .... **NCLC 29**
See also DLB 96

Hemingway, Ernest (Miller) 1899-1961

CLC 1, 3, 6, 8, 10, 13, 19, 30, 34, 39, 41, 44, 50, 61, 80; DA; DAB; DAC; DAM MST, NOV; SSC 25; WLC
See also AAYA 19; CA 77-80; CANR 34; CDALB 1917-1929; DLB 4, 9, 102; DLBD 1, 15, 16; DLBY 81, 87, 96; MTCW

Hempel, Amy 1951- .... **CLC 39**
See also CA 118; 137

Henderson, F. C.
See Mencken, H(enry) L(ouis)

Henderson, Sylvia
See Ashton-Warner, Sylvia (Constance)

Henderson, Zenna (Chlarson) 1917-1983 **SSC 29**
See also CA 1-4R; 133; CANR 1; DLB 8; SATA 5

Henley, Beth .... **CLC 23; DC 6**
See also Henley, Elizabeth Becker
See also CABS 3; DLBY 86

Henley, Elizabeth Becker 1952-
See Henley, Beth
See also CA 107; CANR 32; DAM DRAM, MST; MTCW

Henley, William Ernest 1849-1903 ... **TCLC 8**
See also CA 105; DLB 19

Hennissart, Martha
See Lathen, Emma
See also CA 85-88; CANR 64

Henry, O. .... **TCLC 1, 19; SSC 5; WLC**
See also Porter, William Sydney

Henry, Patrick 1736-1799 .... **LC 25**

Henryson, Robert 1430(?)-1506(?) .... **LC 20**
See also DLB 146

Henry VIII 1491-1547 .... **LC 10**

Henschke, Alfred
See Klabund

Hentoff, Nat(han Irving) 1925- .... **CLC 26**
See also AAYA 4; CA 1-4R; CAAS 6; CANR 5, 25; CLR 1; INT CANR-25; JRDA; MAICYA; SATA 42, 69; SATA-Brief 27

Heppenstall, (John) Rayner 1911-1981 **CLC 10**
See also CA 1-4R; 103; CANR 29

Heraclitus c. 540B.C.-c. 450B.C. .... **CMLC 22**
See also DLB 176

Herbert, Frank (Patrick) 1920-1986 **CLC 12, 23, 35, 44, 85; DAM POP**
See also AAYA 21; CA 53-56; 118; CANR 5, 43; DLB 8; INT CANR-5; MTCW; SATA 9, 37; SATA-Obit 47

Herbert, George 1593-1633 ..... **LC 24; DAB; DAM POET; PC 4**
See also CDBLB Before 1660; DLB 126

Herbert, Zbigniew 1924- .... **CLC 9, 43; DAM POET**
See also CA 89-92; CANR 36; MTCW

Herbst, Josephine (Frey) 1897-1969 .... **CLC 34**
See also CA 5-8R; 25-28R; DLB 9

Hergesheimer, Joseph 1880-1954 ... **TCLC 11**
See also CA 109; DLB 102, 9

Herlihy, James Leo 1927-1993 .... **CLC 6**
See also CA 1-4R; 143; CANR 2

Hermogenes fl. c. 175- .... **CMLC 6**

Hernandez, Jose 1834-1886............. **NCLC 17**

Herodotus c. 484B.C.-429B.C. .... **CMLC 17**
See also DLB 176

Herrick, Robert 1591-1674 .... **LC 13; DA; DAB; DAC; DAM MST, POP; PC 9**
See also DLB 126

Herring, Guilles
See Somerville, Edith

Herriot, James 1916-1995 ... **CLC 12; DAM POP**
See also Wight, James Alfred
See also AAYA 1; CA 148; CANR 40; SATA 86

Herrmann, Dorothy 1941- .... **CLC 44**
See also CA 107

Herrmann, Taffy
See Herrmann, Dorothy

Hersey, John (Richard) 1914-1993 **CLC 1, 2, 7, 9, 40, 81, 97; DAM POP**
See also CA 17-20R; 140; CANR 33; DLB 6, 185; MTCW; SATA 25; SATA-Obit 76

Herzen, Aleksandr Ivanovich 1812-1870 **NCLC 10, 61**

Herzl, Theodor 1860-1904.............. **TCLC 36**

Herzog, Werner 1942-........................ **CLC 16**
See also CA 89-92

Hesiod c. 8th cent. B.C.- .... **CMLC 5**
See also DLB 176

Hesse, Hermann 1877-1962 **CLC 1, 2, 3, 6, 11, 17, 25, 69; DA; DAB; DAC; DAM MST, NOV; SSC 9; WLC**
See also CA 17-18; CAP 2; DLB 66; MTCW; SATA 50

Hofmannsthal, Hugo von 1874-1929 .... **TCLC 11; DAM DRAM; DC 4**
See also CA 106; 153; DLB 81, 118

Hogan, Linda 1947- .... **CLC 73; DAM MULT**
See also CA 120; CANR 45; DLB 175; NNAL

Hogarth, Charles
See Creasey, John

Hogarth, Emmett
See Polonsky, Abraham (Lincoln)

Hogg, James 1770-1835 .... **NCLC 4**
See also DLB 93, 116, 159

Holbach, Paul Henri Thiry Baron 1723-1789
LC 14

Holberg, Ludvig 1684-1754 .... **LC 6**

Holden, Ursula 1921- .... **CLC 18**
See also CA 101; CAAS 8; CANR 22

Holderlin, (Johann Christian) Friedrich 1770-1843 .... **NCLC 16; PC 4**

Holdstock, Robert
See Holdstock, Robert P.

Holdstock, Robert P. 1948- .... **CLC 39**
See also CA 131

Holland, Isabelle 1920- .... **CLC 21**
See also AAYA 11; CA 21-24R; CANR 10, 25, 47; JRDA; MAICYA; SATA 8, 70

Holland, Marcus
See Caldwell, (Janet Miriam) Taylor (Holland)

Hollander, John 1929- .... **CLC 2, 5, 8, 14**
See also CA 1-4R; CANR 1, 52; DLB 5; SATA 13

Hollander, Paul
See Silverberg, Robert

Holleran, Andrew 1943(?)- .... **CLC 38**
See also CA 144

Hollinghurst, Alan 1954- .... **CLC 55, 91**
See also CA 114

Hollis, Jim
See Summers, Hollis (Spurgeon, Jr.)

Holly, Buddy 1936-1959 .... **TCLC 65**

Holmes, Gordon
See Shiel, M(atthew) P(hipps)

Holmes, John
See Souster, (Holmes) Raymond

Holmes, John Clellon 1926-1988 .... **CLC 56**
See also CA 9-12R; 125; CANR 4; DLB 16

Holmes, Oliver Wendell, Jr. 1841-1935
TCLC 77
See also CA 114

Holmes, Oliver Wendell 1809-1894 **NCLC 14**
See also CDALB 1640-1865; DLB 1, 189; SATA 34

Holmes, Raymond
See Souster, (Holmes) Raymond

Holt, Victoria
See Hibbert, Eleanor Alice Burford

Holub, Miroslav 1923- .... **CLC 4**
See also CA 21-24R; CANR 10

Homer c. 8th cent. B.C.- .... **CMLC 1, 16; DA; DAB; DAC; DAM MST, POET; WLCS**
See also DLB 176

Honig, Edwin 1919- .... **CLC 33**
See also CA 5-8R; CAAS 8; CANR 4, 45; DLB 5

Hood, Hugh (John Blagdon) 1928- ... **CLC 15, 28**
See also CA 49-52; CAAS 17; CANR 1, 33; DLB 53

Hood, Thomas 1799-1845 .... **NCLC 16**
See also DLB 96

Hooker, (Peter) Jeremy 1941- .... **CLC 43**
See also CA 77-80; CANR 22; DLB 40

hooks, bell .... **CLC 94**
See also Watkins, Gloria

Hope, A(lec) D(erwent) 1907- .... **CLC 3, 51**
See also CA 21-24R; CANR 33; MTCW

Hope, Brian
See Creasey, John

Hope, Christopher (David Tully) 1944- ... **CLC 52**
See also CA 106; CANR 47; SATA 62

Hopkins, Gerard Manley 1844-1889 ... **NCLC 17; DA; DAB; DAC; DAM MST, POET; PC 15; WLC**
See also CDBLB 1890-1914; DLB 35, 57

Hopkins, John (Richard) 1931- .... **CLC 4**
See also CA 85-88

Hopkins, Pauline Elizabeth 1859-1930
TCLC 28; BLC; DAM MULT
See also BW 2; CA 141; DLB 50

Hopkinson, Francis 1737-1791 .... **LC 25**
See also DLB 31

Hopley-Woolrich, Cornell George 1903-1968
See Woolrich, Cornell
See also CA 13-14; CANR 58; CAP 1

Horatio
See Proust, (Valentin-Louis-George-Eugene-) Marcel

Horgan, Paul (George Vincent O'Shaughnessy) 1903-1995 .... **CLC 9, 53; DAM NOV**
See also CA 13-16R; 147; CANR 9, 35; DLB 102; DLBY 85; INT CANR-9; MTCW; SATA 13; SATA-Obit 84

Horn, Peter
See Kuttner, Henry

Hornem, Horace Esq.
See Byron, George Gordon (Noel)

Horney, Karen (Clementine Theodore Danielsen) 1885-1952 .... **TCLC 71**
See also CA 114; 165

Hornung, E(rnest) W(illiam) 1866-1921
TCLC 59
See also CA 108; 160; DLB 70

Horovitz, Israel (Arthur) 1939- ... **CLC 56; DAM DRAM**
See also CA 33-36R; CANR 46, 59; DLB 7

Horvath, Odon von
See Horvath, Oedoen von
See also DLB 85, 124

Horvath, Oedoen von 1901-1938 .... **TCLC 45**
See also Horvath, Odon von
See also CA 118

Horwitz, Julius 1920-1986 .... **CLC 14**
See also CA 9-12R; 119; CANR 12

Hospital, Janette Turner 1942- .... **CLC 42**
See also CA 108; CANR 48

Hostos, E. M. de
See Hostos (y Bonilla), Eugenio Maria de

Hostos, Eugenio M. de
See Hostos (y Bonilla), Eugenio Maria de

Hostos, Eugenio Maria
See Hostos (y Bonilla), Eugenio Maria de

Hostos (y Bonilla), Eugenio Maria de 1839-1903
TCLC 24
See also CA 123; 131; HW

Houdini
See Lovecraft, H(oward) P(hillips)

Hougan, Carolyn 1943- .... **CLC 34**
See also CA 139

Household, Geoffrey (Edward West) 1900-1988
CLC 11
See also CA 77-80; 126; CANR 58; DLB 87; SATA 14; SATA-Obit 59

Housman, A(lfred) E(dward) 1859-1936
TCLC 1, 10; DA; DAB; DAC; DAM MST, POET; PC 2; WLCS
See also CA 104; 125; DLB 19; MTCW

Housman, Laurence 1865-1959 .... **TCLC 7**
See also CA 106; 155; DLB 10; SATA 25

Howard, Elizabeth Jane 1923- .... **CLC 7, 29**
See also CA 5-8R; CANR 8, 62

Howard, Maureen 1930- .... **CLC 5, 14, 46**
See also CA 53-56; CANR 31; DLBY 83; INT CANR-31; MTCW

Howard, Richard 1929- .... **CLC 7, 10, 47**
See also AITN 1; CA 85-88; CANR 25; DLB 5; INT CANR-25

Johnson, Robert 1911(?)-1938 .... **TCLC 69**

Johnson, Samuel 1709-1784 .... **LC 15; DA; DAB; DAC; DAM MST; WLC**
See also CDBLB 1660-1789; DLB 39, 95, 104, 142

Johnson, Uwe 1934-1984 .... **CLC 5, 10, 15, 40**
See also CA 1-4R; 112; CANR 1, 39; DLB 75; MTCW

Johnston, George (Benson) 1913- ...... **CLC 51**
See also CA 1-4R; CANR 5, 20; DLB 88

Johnston, Jennifer 1930- .... **CLC 7**
See also CA 85-88; DLB 14

Jolley, (Monica) Elizabeth 1923- ..... **CLC 46; SSC 19**
See also CA 127; CAAS 13; CANR 59

Jones, Arthur Llewellyn 1863-1947
See Machen, Arthur
See also CA 104

Jones, D(ouglas) G(ordon) 1929- .... **CLC 10**
See also CA 29-32R; CANR 13; DLB 53

Jones, David (Michael) 1895-1974 ..... **CLC 2, 4, 7, 13, 42**
See also CA 9-12R; 53-56; CANR 28; CDBLB 1945-1960; DLB 20, 100; MTCW

Jones, David Robert 1947-
See Bowie, David
See also CA 103

Jones, Diana Wynne 1934- .... **CLC 26**
See also AAYA 12; CA 49-52; CANR 4, 26, 56; CLR 23; DLB 161; JRDA; MAICYA; SAAS 7; SATA 9, 70

Jones, Edward P. 1950- .... **CLC 76**
See also BW 2; CA 142

Jones, Gayl 1949- ..... **CLC 6, 9; BLC; DAM MULT**
See also BW 2; CA 77-80; CANR 27, 66; DLB 33; MTCW

Jones, James 1921-1977 .... **CLC 1, 3, 10, 39**
See also AITN 1, 2; CA 1-4R; 69-72; CANR 6; DLB 2, 143; MTCW

Jones, John J.
See Lovecraft, H(oward) P(hillips)

Jones, LeRoi .... **CLC 1, 2, 3, 5, 10, 14**
See also Baraka, Amiri

Jones, Louis B. .... **CLC 65**
See also CA 141

Jones, Madison (Percy, Jr.) 1925- .... **CLC 4**
See also CA 13-16R; CAAS 11; CANR 7, 54; DLB 152

Jones, Mervyn 1922- .... **CLC 10, 52**
See also CA 45-48; CAAS 5; CANR 1; MTCW

Jones, Mick 1956(?)- .... **CLC 30**

Jones, Nettie (Pearl) 1941- .... **CLC 34**
See also BW 2; CA 137; CAAS 20

Jones, Preston 1936-1979 .... **CLC 10**
See also CA 73-76; 89-92; DLB 7

Jones, Robert F(rancis) 1934- .... **CLC 7**
See also CA 49-52; CANR 2, 61

Jones, Rod 1953- .... **CLC 50**
See also CA 128

Jones, Terence Graham Parry 1942- ... **CLC 21**
See also Jones, Terry; Monty Python
See also CA 112; 116; CANR 35; INT 116

Jones, Terry
See Jones, Terence Graham Parry
See also SATA 67; SATA-Brief 51

Jones, Thom 1945(?)- .... **CLC 81**
See also CA 157

Jong, Erica 1942-   **CLC 4, 6, 8, 18, 83; DAM NOV, POP**
See also AITN 1; BEST 90:2; CA 73-76; CANR 26, 52; DLB 2, 5, 28, 152; INT CANR-26; MTCW

Jonson, Ben(jamin) 1572(?)-1637   **LC 6, 33; DA; DAB; DAC; DAM DRAM, MST, POET; DC 4; PC 17; WLC**
See also CDBLB Before 1660; DLB 62, 121

Jordan, June 1936- ......   **CLC 5, 11, 23; DAM MULT, POET**
See also AAYA 2; BW 2; CA 33-36R; CANR 25; CLR 10; DLB 38; MAICYA; MTCW; SATA 4

Jordan, Pat(rick M.) 1941- .... **CLC 37**
See also CA 33-36R

Jorgensen, Ivar
See Ellison, Harlan (Jay)

Jorgenson, Ivar
See Silverberg, Robert

Josephus, Flavius c. 37-100 .... **CMLC 13**

Josipovici, Gabriel 1940- .... **CLC 6, 43**
See also CA 37-40R; CAAS 8; CANR 47; DLB 14

Joubert, Joseph 1754-1824 .... **NCLC 9**

Jouve, Pierre Jean 1887-1976 .... **CLC 47**
See also CA 65-68

Jovine, Francesco 1902-1950 .... **TCLC 79**

Joyce, James (Augustine Aloysius) 1882-1941   **TCLC 3, 8, 16, 35, 52; DA; DAB; DAC; DAM MST, NOV, POET; PC 22; SSC 3, 26; WLC**
See also CA 104; 126; CDBLB 1914-1945; DLB 10, 19, 36, 162; MTCW

Jozsef, Attila 1905-1937 .... **TCLC 22**
See also CA 116

Juana Ines de la Cruz 1651(?)-1695 .... **LC 5**

Judd, Cyril
See Kornbluth, C(yril) M.; Pohl, Frederik

Julian of Norwich 1342(?)-1416(?) .... **LC 6**
See also DLB 146

Junger, Sebastian 1962- .... **CLC 109**
See also CA 165

Juniper, Alex
See Hospital, Janette Turner

Junius
See Luxemburg, Rosa

Just, Ward (Swift) 1935- .... **CLC 4, 27**
See also CA 25-28R; CANR 32; INT CANR-32

Justice, Donald (Rodney) 1925- ... **CLC 6, 19, 102; DAM POET**
See also CA 5-8R; CANR 26, 54; DLBY 83; INT CANR-26

Juvenal c. 55-c. 127 .... **CMLC 8**

Juvenis
See Bourne, Randolph S(illiman)

Kacew, Romain 1914-1980
See Gary, Romain
See also CA 108; 102

Kadare, Ismail 1936- .... **CLC 52**
See also CA 161

Kadohata, Cynthia .... **CLC 59**
See also CA 140

Kafka, Franz 1883-1924 ... **TCLC 2, 6, 13, 29, 47, 53; DA; DAB; DAC; DAM MST, NOV; SSC 5, 29; WLC**
See also CA 105; 126; DLB 81; MTCW

Kahanovitsch, Pinkhes
See Der Nister

Kahn, Roger 1927- .... **CLC 30**
See also CA 25-28R; CANR 44; DLB 171; SATA 37

Kain, Saul
See Sassoon, Siegfried (Lorraine)

Kaiser, Georg 1878-1945 .... **TCLC 9**
See also CA 106; DLB 124

Kaletski, Alexander 1946- .... **CLC 39**
See also CA 118; 143

Kalidasa fl. c. 400- .... **CMLC 9; PC 22**

Kallman, Chester (Simon) 1921-1975 . **CLC 2**
See also CA 45-48; 53-56; CANR 3

Kaminsky, Melvin 1926-
See Brooks, Mel
See also CA 65-68; CANR 16

Kaminsky, Stuart M(elvin) 1934- ...... **CLC 59**
See also CA 73-76; CANR 29, 53

Kane, Francis
See Robbins, Harold

Kenyon, Robert O.
See Kuttner, Henry

Kerouac, Jack .... **CLC 1, 2, 3, 5, 14, 29, 61**
See also Kerouac, Jean-Louis Lebris de
See also AAYA 25; CDALB 1941-1968; DLB 2, 16; DLBD 3; DLBY 95

Kerouac, Jean-Louis Lebris de 1922-1969
See Kerouac, Jack
See also AITN 1; CA 5-8R; 25-28R; CANR 26, 54; DA; DAB; DAC; DAM MST, NOV, POET, POP; MTCW; WLC

Kerr, Jean 1923- .... **CLC 22**
See also CA 5-8R; CANR 7; INT CANR-7

Kerr, M. E. .... **CLC 12, 35**
See also Meaker, Marijane (Agnes)
See also AAYA 2, 23; CLR 29; SAAS 1

Kerr, Robert .... **CLC 55**

Kerrigan, (Thomas) Anthony 1918- **CLC 4, 6**
See also CA 49-52; CAAS 11; CANR 4

Kerry, Lois
See Duncan, Lois

Kesey, Ken (Elton) 1935-   **CLC 1, 3, 6, 11, 46, 64; DA; DAB; DAC; DAM MST, NOV, POP; WLC**
See also AAYA 25; CA 1-4R; CANR 22, 38, 66; CDALB 1968-1988; DLB 2, 16; MTCW; SATA 66

Kesselring, Joseph (Otto) 1902-1967 **CLC 45; DAM DRAM, MST**
See also CA 150

Kessler, Jascha (Frederick) 1929- .... **CLC 4**
See also CA 17-20R; CANR 8, 48

Kettelkamp, Larry (Dale) 1933- .... **CLC 12**
See also CA 29-32R; CANR 16; SAAS 3; SATA 2

Key, Ellen 1849-1926 .... **TCLC 65**

Keyber, Conny
See Fielding, Henry

Keyes, Daniel 1927- ..... **CLC 80; DA; DAC; DAM MST, NOV**
See also AAYA 23; CA 17-20R; CANR 10, 26, 54; SATA 37

Keynes, John Maynard 1883-1946 **TCLC 64**
See also CA 114; 162, 163; DLBD 10

Khanshendel, Chiron
See Rose, Wendy

Khayyam, Omar 1048-1131 ...... **CMLC 11; DAM POET; PC 8**

Kherdian, David 1931- .... **CLC 6, 9**
See also CA 21-24R; CAAS 2; CANR 39; CLR 24; JRDA; MAICYA; SATA 16, 74

Khlebnikov, Velimir .... **TCLC 20**
See also Khlebnikov, Viktor Vladimirovich

Khlebnikov, Viktor Vladimirovich 1885-1922
See Khlebnikov, Velimir
See also CA 117

Khodasevich, Vladislav (Felitsianovich) 1886-1939 .... **TCLC 15**
See also CA 115

Kielland, Alexander Lange 1849-1906 **TCLC 5**
See also CA 104

Kiely, Benedict 1919- .... **CLC 23, 43**
See also CA 1-4R; CANR 2; DLB 15

Kienzle, William X(avier) 1928- ..... **CLC 25; DAM POP**
See also CA 93-96; CAAS 1; CANR 9, 31, 59; INT CANR-31; MTCW

Kierkegaard, Soren 1813-1855 .... **NCLC 34**

Killens, John Oliver 1916-1987 .... **CLC 10**
See also BW 2; CA 77-80; 123; CAAS 2; CANR 26; DLB 33

Killigrew, Anne 1660-1685 .... **LC 4**
See also DLB 131

Kim
See Simenon, Georges (Jacques Christian)

Kincaid, Jamaica 1949- ..... **CLC 43, 68; BLC; DAM MULT, NOV**
See also AAYA 13; BW 2; CA 125; CANR 47, 59; DLB 157

King, Francis (Henry) 1923- .... **CLC 8, 53; DAM NOV**
See also CA 1-4R; CANR 1, 33; DLB 15, 139; MTCW

King, Kennedy
See Brown, George Douglas

King, Martin Luther, Jr. 1929-1968 **CLC 83; BLC; DA; DAB; DAC; DAM MST, MULT; WLCS**
See also BW 2; CA 25-28; CANR 27, 44; CAP 2; MTCW; SATA 14

King, Stephen (Edwin) 1947- **CLC 12, 26, 37, 61; DAM NOV, POP; SSC 17**
See also AAYA 1, 17; BEST 90:1; CA 61-64; CANR 1, 30, 52; DLB 143; DLBY 80; JRDA; MTCW; SATA 9, 55

King, Steve
See King, Stephen (Edwin)

King, Thomas 1943- ..... **CLC 89; DAC; DAM MULT**
See also CA 144; DLB 175; NNAL; SATA 96

Kingman, Lee .... **CLC 17**
See also Natti, (Mary) Lee
See also SAAS 3; SATA 1, 67

Kingsley, Charles 1819-1875 .... **NCLC 35**
See also DLB 21, 32, 163, 190; YABC 2

Kingsley, Sidney 1906-1995 .... **CLC 44**
See also CA 85-88; 147; DLB 7

Kingsolver, Barbara 1955- ....   **CLC 55, 81; DAM POP**
See also AAYA 15; CA 129; 134; CANR 60; INT 134

Kingston, Maxine (Ting Ting) Hong 1940- **CLC 12, 19, 58; DAM MULT, NOV; WLCS**
See also AAYA 8; CA 69-72; CANR 13, 38; DLB 173; DLBY 80; INT CANR-13; MTCW; SATA 53

Kinnell, Galway 1927- .. **CLC 1, 2, 3, 5, 13, 29**
See also CA 9-12R; CANR 10, 34, 66; DLB 5; DLBY 87; INT CANR-34; MTCW

Kinsella, Thomas 1928- .... **CLC 4, 19**
See also CA 17-20R; CANR 15; DLB 27; MTCW

Kinsella, W(illiam) P(atrick) 1935- ... **CLC 27, 43; DAC; DAM NOV, POP**
See also AAYA 7; CA 97-100; CAAS 7; CANR 21, 35, 66; INT CANR-21; MTCW

Kipling, (Joseph) Rudyard 1865-1936 **TCLC 8, 17; DA; DAB; DAC; DAM MST, POET; PC 3; SSC 5; WLC**
See also CA 105; 120; CANR 33; CDBLB 1890-1914; CLR 39; DLB 19, 34, 141, 156; MAICYA; MTCW; YABC 2

Kirkup, James 1918- .... **CLC 1**
See also CA 1-4R; CAAS 4; CANR 2; DLB 27; SATA 12

Kirkwood, James 1930(?)-1989 .... **CLC 9**
See also AITN 2; CA 1-4R; 128; CANR 6, 40

Kirshner, Sidney
See Kingsley, Sidney

Kis, Danilo 1935-1989 .... **CLC 57**
See also CA 109; 118; 129; CANR 61; DLB 181; MTCW

Kivi, Aleksis 1834-1872 .... **NCLC 30**

Kizer, Carolyn (Ashley) 1925- **CLC 15, 39, 80; DAM POET**
See also CA 65-68; CAAS 5; CANR 24; DLB 5, 169

Klabund 1890-1928 .... **TCLC 44**
See also CA 162; DLB 66

Klappert, Peter 1942- .... **CLC 57**
See also CA 33-36R; DLB 5

Klein, A(braham) M(oses) 1909-1972 . **CLC 19; DAB; DAC; DAM MST**
See also CA 101; 37-40R; DLB 68

Klein, Norma 1938-1989 .... **CLC 30**
See also AAYA 2; CA 41-44R; 128; CANR 15, 37; CLR 2, 19; INT CANR-15; JRDA; MAICYA; SAAS 1; SATA 7, 57

Klein, T(heodore) E(ibon) D(onald) 1947- **CLC 34**
See also CA 119; CANR 44

Kleist, Heinrich von 1777-1811 **NCLC 2, 37; DAM DRAM; SSC 22**
See also DLB 90

Klima, Ivan 1931- .... **CLC 56; DAM NOV**
See also CA 25-28R; CANR 17, 50

Klimentov, Andrei Platonovich 1899-1951
See Platonov, Andrei
See also CA 108

Klinger, Friedrich Maximilian von 1752-1831
NCLC 1
See also DLB 94

Klingsor the Magician
See Hartmann, Sadakichi

Klopstock, Friedrich Gottlieb 1724-1803
NCLC 11
See also DLB 97

Knapp, Caroline 1959- .... **CLC 99**
See also CA 154

Knebel, Fletcher 1911-1993 .... **CLC 14**
See also AITN 1; CA 1-4R; 140; CAAS 3; CANR
1, 36; SATA 36; SATA-Obit 75

Knickerbocker, Diedrich
See Irving, Washington

Knight, Etheridge 1931-1991 ......   **CLC 40;**
BLC; DAM POET; PC 14
See also BW 1; CA 21-24R; 133; CANR 23; DLB
41

Knight, Sarah Kemble 1666-1727 .... **LC 7**
See also DLB 24

Knister, Raymond 1899-1932 .... **TCLC 56**
See also DLB 68

Knowles, John 1926- ... **CLC 1, 4, 10, 26; DA;**
DAC; DAM MST, NOV
See also AAYA 10; CA 17-20R; CANR 40;
CDALB 1968-1988; DLB 6; MTCW; SATA
8, 89

Knox, Calvin M.
See Silverberg, Robert

Knox, John c. 1505-1572 .... **LC 37**
See also DLB 132

Knye, Cassandra
See Disch, Thomas M(ichael)

Koch, C(hristopher) J(ohn) 1932- ..... **CLC 42**
See also CA 127

Koch, Christopher
See Koch, C(hristopher) J(ohn)

Koch, Kenneth 1925- ..... **CLC 5, 8, 44; DAM**
POET
See also CA 1-4R; CANR 6, 36, 57; DLB 5; INT
CANR-36; SATA 65

Kochanowski, Jan 1530-1584 .... **LC 10**

Kock, Charles Paul de 1794-1871 ... **NCLC 16**

Koda Shigeyuki 1867-1947
See Rohan, Koda
See also CA 121

Koestler, Arthur 1905-1983 ... **CLC 1, 3, 6, 8, 15, 33**
See also CA 1-4R; 109; CANR 1, 33; CDBLB
1945-1960; DLBY 83; MTCW

Kogawa, Joy Nozomi 1935- .... **CLC 78; DAC;**
DAM MST, MULT
See also CA 101; CANR 19, 62

Kohout, Pavel 1928- .... **CLC 13**
See also CA 45-48; CANR 3

Koizumi, Yakumo
See Hearn, (Patricio) Lafcadio (Tessima Carlos)

Kolmar, Gertrud 1894-1943 .... **TCLC 40**

Komunyakaa, Yusef 1947- .... **CLC 86, 94**
See also CA 147; DLB 120

Konrad, George
See Konrad, Gyoergy

Konrad, Gyoergy 1933- .... **CLC 4, 10, 73**
See also CA 85-88

Konwicki, Tadeusz 1926- .... **CLC 8, 28, 54**
See also CA 101; CAAS 9; CANR 39, 59; MTCW

Koontz, Dean R(ay) 1945- ....   **CLC 78; DAM**
NOV, POP
See also AAYA 9; BEST 89:3, 90:2; CA 108;
CANR 19, 36, 52; MTCW; SATA 92

Kopit, Arthur (Lee) 1937- ....   **CLC 1, 18, 33;**
DAM DRAM
See also AITN 1; CA 81-84; CABS 3; DLB 7;
MTCW

Kops, Bernard 1926- .... **CLC 4**
See also CA 5-8R; DLB 13

Kornbluth, C(yril) M. 1923-1958 ..... **TCLC 8**
See also CA 105; 160; DLB 8

Korolenko, V. G.
See Korolenko, Vladimir Galaktionovich

Korolenko, Vladimir
See Korolenko, Vladimir Galaktionovich

Korolenko, Vladimir G.
See Korolenko, Vladimir Galaktionovich

Korolenko, Vladimir Galaktionovich 1853-1921
TCLC 22
See also CA 121

Korzybski, Alfred (Habdank Skarbek) 1879-
1950 .... **TCLC 61**
See also CA 123; 160

Kosinski, Jerzy (Nikodem) 1933-1991 ... **CLC 1,**
2, 3, 6, 10, 15, 53, 70; DAM NOV
See also CA 17-20R; 134; CANR 9, 46; DLB 2;
DLBY 82; MTCW

Kostelanetz, Richard (Cory) 1940- .... **CLC 28**
See also CA 13-16R; CAAS 8; CANR 38

Kostrowitzki, Wilhelm Apollinaris de 1880-1918
See Apollinaire, Guillaume
See also CA 104

Kotlowitz, Robert 1924- .... **CLC 4**
See also CA 33-36R; CANR 36

Kotzebue, August (Friedrich Ferdinand) von
1761-1819 .... **NCLC 25**
See also DLB 94

Kotzwinkle, William 1938- .... **CLC 5, 14, 35**
See also CA 45-48; CANR 3, 44; CLR 6; DLB
173; MAICYA; SATA 24, 70

Kowna, Stancy
See Szymborska, Wislawa

Kozol, Jonathan 1936- .... **CLC 17**
See also CA 61-64; CANR 16, 45

Kozoll, Michael 1940(?)- .... **CLC 35**

Kramer, Kathryn 19(?)- .... **CLC 34**

Kramer, Larry 1935- **CLC 42; DAM POP; DC 8**
See also CA 124; 126; CANR 60

Krasicki, Ignacy 1735-1801 .... **NCLC 8**

Krasinski, Zygmunt 1812-1859 .... **NCLC 4**

Kraus, Karl 1874-1936 .... **TCLC 5**
See also CA 104; DLB 118

Kreve (Mickevicius), Vincas 1882-1954
TCLC 27

Kristeva, Julia 1941- .... **CLC 77**
See also CA 154

Kristofferson, Kris 1936- .... **CLC 26**
See also CA 104

Krizanc, John 1956- .... **CLC 57**

Krleza, Miroslav 1893-1981 .... **CLC 8**
See also CA 97-100; 105; CANR 50; DLB 147

Kroetsch, Robert 1927- ....   **CLC 5, 23, 57;**
DAC; DAM POET
See also CA 17-20R; CANR 8, 38; DLB 53;
MTCW

Kroetz, Franz
See Kroetz, Franz Xaver

Kroetz, Franz Xaver 1946- .... **CLC 41**
See also CA 130

Kroker, Arthur (W.) 1945- .... **CLC 77**
See also CA 161

Kropotkin, Peter (Aleksieevich) 1842-1921
TCLC 36
See also CA 119

Krotkov, Yuri 1917- .... **CLC 19**
See also CA 102

Krumb
See Crumb, R(obert)

Krumgold, Joseph (Quincy) 1908-1980 ... **CLC 12**
See also CA 9-12R; 101; CANR 7; MAICYA;
SATA 1, 48; SATA-Obit 23

Krumwitz
   See Crumb, R(obert)

Krutch, Joseph Wood 1893-1970 .... **CLC 24**
   See also CA 1-4R; 25-28R; CANR 4; DLB 63

Krutzch, Gus
   See Eliot, T(homas) S(tearns)

Krylov, Ivan Andreevich 1768(?)-1844 ... **NCLC 1**
   See also DLB 150

Kubin, Alfred (Leopold Isidor) 1877-1959
   TCLC 23
   See also CA 112; 149; DLB 81

Kubrick, Stanley 1928- .... **CLC 16**
   See also CA 81-84; CANR 33; DLB 26

Kumin, Maxine (Winokur) 1925-   **CLC 5, 13, 28; DAM POET; PC 15**
   See also AITN 2; CA 1-4R; CAAS 8; CANR 1, 21; DLB 5; MTCW; SATA 12

Kundera, Milan 1929- ... **CLC 4, 9, 19, 32, 68; DAM NOV; SSC 24**
   See also AAYA 2; CA 85-88; CANR 19, 52; MTCW

Kunene, Mazisi (Raymond) 1930- ..... **CLC 85**
   See also BW 1; CA 125; DLB 117

Kunitz, Stanley (Jasspon) 1905-   **CLC 6, 11, 14; PC 19**
   See also CA 41-44R; CANR 26, 57; DLB 48; INT CANR-26; MTCW

Kunze, Reiner 1933- .... **CLC 10**
   See also CA 93-96; DLB 75

Kuprin, Aleksandr Ivanovich 1870-1938
   TCLC 5
   See also CA 104

Kureishi, Hanif 1954(?)- .... **CLC 64**
   See also CA 139; DLB 194

Kurosawa, Akira 1910- **CLC 16; DAM MULT**
   See also AAYA 11; CA 101; CANR 46

Kushner, Tony 1957(?)- ....   **CLC 81; DAM DRAM**
   See also CA 144

Kuttner, Henry 1915-1958 .... **TCLC 10**
   See also Vance, Jack
   See also CA 107; 157; DLB 8

Kuzma, Greg 1944- .... **CLC 7**
   See also CA 33-36R

Kuzmin, Mikhail 1872(?)-1936 .... **TCLC 40**

Kyd, Thomas 1558-1594 .... **LC 22; DAM DRAM; DC 3**
   See also DLB 62

Kyprianos, Iossif
   See Samarakis, Antonis

La Bruyere, Jean de 1645-1696 .... **LC 17**

Lacan, Jacques (Marie Emile) 1901-1981
   CLC 75
   See also CA 121; 104

Laclos, Pierre Ambroise Francois Choderlos de 1741-1803 .... **NCLC 4**

La Colere, Francois
   See Aragon, Louis

Lacolere, Francois
   See Aragon, Louis

La Deshabilleuse
   See Simenon, Georges (Jacques Christian)

Lady Gregory
   See Gregory, Isabella Augusta (Persse)

Lady of Quality, A
   See Bagnold, Enid

La Fayette, Marie (Madelaine Pioche de la Vergne Comtes 1634-1693 .... **LC 2**

Lafayette, Rene
   See Hubbard, L(afayette) Ron(ald)

Laforgue, Jules 1860-1887   **NCLC 5, 53; PC 14; SSC 20**

Lagerkvist, Paer (Fabian) 1891-1974   **CLC 7, 10, 13, 54; DAM DRAM, NOV**
   See also Lagerkvist, Par
   See also CA 85-88; 49-52; MTCW

Lagerkvist, Par .... **SSC 12**
   See also Lagerkvist, Paer (Fabian)

Lagerloef, Selma (Ottiliana Lovisa) 1858-1940
   TCLC 4, 36
   See also Lagerlof, Selma (Ottiliana Lovisa)
   See also CA 108; SATA 15

Lagerlof, Selma (Ottiliana Lovisa)
   See Lagerloef, Selma (Ottiliana Lovisa)
   See also CLR 7; SATA 15

La Guma, (Justin) Alex(ander) 1925-1985
   CLC 19; DAM NOV
   See also BW 1; CA 49-52; 118; CANR 25; DLB 117; MTCW

Laidlaw, A. K.
   See Grieve, C(hristopher) M(urray)

Lainez, Manuel Mujica
   See Mujica Lainez, Manuel
   See also HW

Laing, R(onald) D(avid) 1927-1989 ... **CLC 95**
   See also CA 107; 129; CANR 34; MTCW

Lamartine, Alphonse (Marie Louis Prat) de 1790-1869 ....

NCLC 11; DAM POET; PC 16

Lamb, Charles 1775-1834 **NCLC 10; DA; DAB; DAC; DAM MST; WLC**
   See also CDBLB 1789-1832; DLB 93, 107, 163; SATA 17

Lamb, Lady Caroline 1785-1828 .... **NCLC 38**
   See also DLB 116

Lamming, George (William) 1927- . **CLC 2, 4, 66; BLC; DAM MULT**
   See also BW 2; CA 85-88; CANR 26; DLB 125; MTCW

L'Amour, Louis (Dearborn) 1908-1988 . **C L C 25, 55; DAM NOV, POP**
   See also AAYA 16; AITN 2; BEST 89:2; CA 1-4R; 125; CANR 3, 25, 40; DLBY 80; MTCW

Lampedusa, Giuseppe (Tomasi) di 1896-1957
   TCLC 13
   See also Tomasi di Lampedusa, Giuseppe
   See also CA 164; DLB 177

Lampman, Archibald 1861-1899 .... **NCLC 25**
   See also DLB 92

Lancaster, Bruce 1896-1963 .... **CLC 36**
   See also CA 9-10; CAP 1; SATA 9

Lanchester, John .... **CLC 99**

Landau, Mark Alexandrovich
   See Aldanov, Mark (Alexandrovich)

Landau-Aldanov, Mark Alexandrovich
   See Aldanov, Mark (Alexandrovich)

Landis, Jerry
   See Simon, Paul (Frederick)

Landis, John 1950- .... **CLC 26**
   See also CA 112; 122

Landolfi, Tommaso 1908-1979 ..... **CLC 11, 49**
   See also CA 127; 117; DLB 177

Landon, Letitia Elizabeth 1802-1838   **NCLC 15**
   See also DLB 96

Landor, Walter Savage 1775-1864   **NCLC 14**
   See also DLB 93, 107

Landwirth, Heinz 1927-
   See Lind, Jakov
   See also CA 9-12R; CANR 7

Lane, Patrick 1939- ..... **CLC 25; DAM POET**
   See also CA 97-100; CANR 54; DLB 53; INT 97-100

Lang, Andrew 1844-1912 .... **TCLC 16**
   See also CA 114; 137; DLB 98, 141, 184; MAICYA; SATA 16

Lang, Fritz 1890-1976 .... **CLC 20, 103**
   See also CA 77-80; 69-72; CANR 30

Lange, John
   See Crichton, (John) Michael

Langer, Elinor 1939- .... **CLC 34**
   See also CA 121

Langland, William 1330(?)-1400(?)   **LC 19; DA; DAB; DAC; DAM MST, POET**
   See also DLB 146

Langstaff, Launcelot
See Irving, Washington

Lanier, Sidney 1842-1881 ...... **NCLC 6; DAM POET**
See also DLB 64; DLBD 13; MAICYA; SATA 18

Lanyer, Aemilia 1569-1645 .... **LC 10, 30**
See also DLB 121

Lao Tzu .... **CMLC 7**

Lapine, James (Elliot) 1949- .... **CLC 39**
See also CA 123; 130; CANR 54; INT 130

Larbaud, Valery (Nicolas) 1881-1957 **TCLC 9**
See also CA 106; 152

Lardner, Ring
See Lardner, Ring(gold) W(ilmer)

Lardner, Ring W., Jr.
See Lardner, Ring(gold) W(ilmer)

Lardner, Ring(gold) W(ilmer) 1885-1933 **TCLC 2, 14**
See also CA 104; 131; CDALB 1917-1929; DLB 11, 25, 86; DLBD 16; MTCW

Laredo, Betty
See Codrescu, Andrei

Larkin, Maia
See Wojciechowska, Maia (Teresa)

Larkin, Philip (Arthur) 1922-1985 ... **CLC 3, 5, 8, 9, 13, 18, 33, 39, 64; DAB; DAM MST, POET; PC 21**
See also CA 5-8R; 117; CANR 24, 62; CDBLB 1960 to Present; DLB 27; MTCW

Larra (y Sanchez de Castro), Mariano Jose de 1809-1837 .... **NCLC 17**

Larsen, Eric 1941- .... **CLC 55**
See also CA 132

Larsen, Nella 1891-1964 ... **CLC 37; BLC; DAM MULT**
See also BW 1; CA 125; DLB 51

Larson, Charles R(aymond) 1938- .... **CLC 31**
See also CA 53-56; CANR 4

Larson, Jonathan 1961-1996 .... **CLC 99**
See also CA 156

Las Casas, Bartolome de 1474-1566 ..... **LC 31**

Lasch, Christopher 1932-1994 .... **CLC 102**
See also CA 73-76; 144; CANR 25; MTCW

Lasker-Schueler, Else 1869-1945 .... **TCLC 57**
See also DLB 66, 124

Laski, Harold 1893-1950 .... **TCLC 79**

Latham, Jean Lee 1902- .... **CLC 12**
See also AITN 1; CA 5-8R; CANR 7; MAICYA; SATA 2, 68

Latham, Mavis
See Clark, Mavis Thorpe

Lathen, Emma .... **CLC 2**
See also Hennissart, Martha; Latsis, Mary J(ane)

Lathrop, Francis
See Leiber, Fritz (Reuter, Jr.)

Latsis, Mary J(ane) 1927(?)-1997
See Lathen, Emma
See also CA 85-88; 162

Lattimore, Richmond (Alexander) 1906-1984 **CLC 3**
See also CA 1-4R; 112; CANR 1

Laughlin, James 1914-1997 .... **CLC 49**
See also CA 21-24R; 162; CAAS 22; CANR 9, 47; DLB 48; DLBY 96, 97

Laurence, (Jean) Margaret (Wemyss) 1926-1987 **CLC 3, 6, 13, 50, 62; DAC; DAM MST; SSC 7**
See also CA 5-8R; 121; CANR 33; DLB 53; MTCW; SATA-Obit 50

Laurent, Antoine 1952- .... **CLC 50**

Lauscher, Hermann
See Hesse, Hermann

Lautreamont, Comte de 1846-1870   **NCLC 12; SSC 14**

Laverty, Donald
See Blish, James (Benjamin)

Lavin, Mary 1912-1996   **CLC 4, 18, 99; SSC 4**
See also CA 9-12R; 151; CANR 33; DLB 15; MTCW

Lavond, Paul Dennis
See Kornbluth, C(yril) M.; Pohl, Frederik

Lawler, Raymond Evenor 1922- .... **CLC 58**
See also CA 103

Lawrence, D(avid) H(erbert Richards) 1885-1930 ...   **TCLC 2, 9, 16, 33, 48, 61; DA; DAB; DAC; DAM MST, NOV, POET; SSC 4, 19; WLC**
See also CA 104; 121; CDBLB 1914-1945; DLB 10, 19, 36, 98, 162, 195; MTCW

Lawrence, T(homas) E(dward) 1888-1935 **TCLC 18**
See also Dale, Colin
See also CA 115; DLB 195

Lawrence of Arabia
See Lawrence, T(homas) E(dward)

Lawson, Henry (Archibald Hertzberg) 1867-1922 .... **TCLC 27; SSC 18**
See also CA 120

Lawton, Dennis
See Faust, Frederick (Schiller)

Laxness, Halldor .... **CLC 25**
See also Gudjonsson, Halldor Kiljan

Layamon fl. c. 1200- .... **CMLC 10**
See also DLB 146

Laye, Camara 1928-1980 .... **CLC 4, 38; BLC; DAM MULT**
See also BW 1; CA 85-88; 97-100; CANR 25; MTCW

Layton, Irving (Peter) 1912- ... **CLC 2, 15; DAC; DAM MST, POET**
See also CA 1-4R; CANR 2, 33, 43, 66; DLB 88; MTCW

Lazarus, Emma 1849-1887 .... **NCLC 8**

Lazarus, Felix
See Cable, George Washington

Lazarus, Henry
See Slavitt, David R(ytman)

Lea, Joan
See Neufeld, John (Arthur)

Leacock, Stephen (Butler) 1869-1944 ... **TCLC 2; DAC; DAM MST**
See also CA 104; 141; DLB 92

Lear, Edward 1812-1888 .... **NCLC 3**
See also CLR 1; DLB 32, 163, 166; MAICYA; SATA 18

Lear, Norman (Milton) 1922- .... **CLC 12**
See also CA 73-76

Leavis, F(rank) R(aymond) 1895-1978 ... **CLC 24**
See also CA 21-24R; 77-80; CANR 44; MTCW

Leavitt, David 1961- .... **CLC 34; DAM POP**
See also CA 116; 122; CANR 50, 62; DLB 130; INT 122

Leblanc, Maurice (Marie Emile) 1864-1941 **TCLC 49**
See also CA 110

Lebowitz, Fran(ces Ann) 1951(?)- ... **CLC 11, 36**
See also CA 81-84; CANR 14, 60; INT CANR-14; MTCW

Lebrecht, Peter
See Tieck, (Johann) Ludwig

le Carre, John .... **CLC 3, 5, 9, 15, 28**
See also Cornwell, David (John Moore)
See also BEST 89:4; CDBLB 1960 to Present; DLB 87

Le Clezio, J(ean) M(arie) G(ustave) 1940- **CLC 31**
See also CA 116; 128; DLB 83

Leconte de Lisle, Charles-Marie-Rene 1818-1894 .... **NCLC 29**

Le Coq, Monsieur
See Simenon, Georges (Jacques Christian)

Leduc, Violette 1907-1972 .... **CLC 22**
See also CA 13-14; 33-36R; CAP 1

Ledwidge, Francis 1887(?)-1917 ..... **TCLC 23**
See also CA 123; DLB 20

Lee, Andrea 1953- .... **CLC 36; BLC; DAM MULT**
See also BW 1; CA 125

Lee, Andrew
See Auchincloss, Louis (Stanton)

Lee, Chang-rae 1965- .... **CLC 91**
See also CA 148

Lee, Don L. .... **CLC 2**
See also Madhubuti, Haki R.

Lee, George W(ashington) 1894-1976   **CLC 52; BLC; DAM MULT**
See also BW 1; CA 125; DLB 51

Lee, (Nelle) Harper 1926- .... **CLC 12, 60; DA; DAB; DAC; DAM MST, NOV; WLC**
See also AAYA 13; CA 13-16R; CANR 51; CDALB 1941-1968; DLB 6; MTCW; SATA 11

Lee, Helen Elaine 1959(?)- .... **CLC 86**
See also CA 148

Lee, Julian
See Latham, Jean Lee

Lee, Larry
See Lee, Lawrence

Lee, Laurie 1914-1997 ..... **CLC 90; DAB; DAM POP**
See also CA 77-80; 158; CANR 33; DLB 27; MTCW

Lee, Lawrence 1941-1990 .... **CLC 34**
See also CA 131; CANR 43

Lee, Manfred B(ennington) 1905-1971 .... **CLC 11**
See also Queen, Ellery
See also CA 1-4R; 29-32R; CANR 2; DLB 137

Lee, Shelton Jackson 1957(?)- ..... **CLC 105; DAM MULT**
See also Lee, Spike
See also BW 2; CA 125; CANR 42

Lee, Spike
See Lee, Shelton Jackson
See also AAYA 4

Lee, Stan 1922- .... **CLC 17**
See also AAYA 5; CA 108; 111; INT 111

Lee, Tanith 1947- .... **CLC 46**
See also AAYA 15; CA 37-40R; CANR 53; SATA 8, 88

Lee, Vernon .... **TCLC 5**
See also Paget, Violet
See also DLB 57, 153, 156, 174, 178

Lee, William
See Burroughs, William S(eward)

Lee, Willy
See Burroughs, William S(eward)

Lee-Hamilton, Eugene (Jacob) 1845-1907 **TCLC 22**
See also CA 117

Leet, Judith 1935- .... **CLC 11**

Le Fanu, Joseph Sheridan 1814-1873 ... **NCLC 9, 58; DAM POP; SSC 14**
See also DLB 21, 70, 159, 178

Leffland, Ella 1931- .... **CLC 19**
See also CA 29-32R; CANR 35; DLBY 84; INT CANR-35; SATA 65

Leger, Alexis
See Leger, (Marie-Rene Auguste) Alexis Saint-Leger

Leger, (Marie-Rene Auguste) Alexis Saint-Leger 1887-1975 .... **CLC 11; DAM POET**
See also Perse, St.-John
See also CA 13-16R; 61-64; CANR 43; MTCW

Leger, Saintleger
See Leger, (Marie-Rene Auguste) Alexis Saint-Leger

Le Guin, Ursula K(roeber) 1929- ..... **CLC 8, 13, 22, 45, 71; DAB; DAC; DAM MST, POP; SSC 12**
See also AAYA 9; AITN 1; CA 21-24R; CANR 9, 32, 52; CDALB 1968-1988; CLR 3, 28; DLB 8, 52; INT CANR-32; JRDA; MAICYA; MTCW; SATA 4, 52

Lehmann, Rosamond (Nina) 1901-1990 ... **CLC 5**
See also CA 77-80; 131; CANR 8; DLB 15

Leiber, Fritz (Reuter, Jr.) 1910-1992 ... **CLC 25**
See also CA 45-48; 139; CANR 2, 40; DLB 8; MTCW; SATA 45; SATA-Obit 73

Leibniz, Gottfried Wilhelm von 1646-1716 **LC 35**
See also DLB 168

Leimbach, Martha 1963-
See Leimbach, Marti
See also CA 130

Leimbach, Marti .... **CLC 65**
See also Leimbach, Martha

Leino, Eino .... **TCLC 24**
See also Loennbohm, Armas Eino Leopold

Leiris, Michel (Julien) 1901-1990 ...... **CLC 61**
See also CA 119; 128; 132

Leithauser, Brad 1953- .... **CLC 27**
See also CA 107; CANR 27; DLB 120

Lelchuk, Alan 1938- .... **CLC 5**
See also CA 45-48; CAAS 20; CANR 1

Lem, Stanislaw 1921- .... **CLC 8, 15, 40**
See also CA 105; CAAS 1; CANR 32; MTCW

Lemann, Nancy 1956- .... **CLC 39**
See also CA 118; 136

Lemonnier, (Antoine Louis) Camille 1844-1913 **TCLC 22**
See also CA 121

Lenau, Nikolaus 1802-1850 .... **NCLC 16**

L'Engle, Madeleine (Camp Franklin) 1918- **CLC 12; DAM POP**
See also AAYA 1; AITN 2; CA 1-4R; CANR 3, 21, 39, 66; CLR 1, 14; DLB 52; JRDA; MAICYA; MTCW; SAAS 15; SATA 1, 27, 75

Lengyel, Jozsef 1896-1975 .... **CLC 7**
See also CA 85-88; 57-60

Lenin 1870-1924
See Lenin, V. I.
See also CA 121

Lenin, V. I. .... **TCLC 67**
See also Lenin

Lennon, John (Ono) 1940-1980 ... **CLC 12, 35**
See also CA 102

Lennox, Charlotte Ramsay 1729(?)-1804 **NCLC 23**
See also DLB 39

Lentricchia, Frank (Jr.) 1940- .... **CLC 34**
See also CA 25-28R; CANR 19

Lenz, Siegfried 1926- .... **CLC 27**
See also CA 89-92; DLB 75

Leonard, Elmore (John, Jr.) 1925-   **CLC 28, 34, 71; DAM POP**
See also AAYA 22; AITN 1; BEST 89:1, 90:4; CA 81-84; CANR 12, 28, 53; DLB 173; INT CANR-28; MTCW

Leonard, Hugh .... **CLC 19**
See also Byrne, John Keyes
See also DLB 13

Leonov, Leonid (Maximovich) 1899-1994 **CLC 92; DAM NOV**
See also CA 129; MTCW

Leopardi, (Conte) Giacomo 1798-1837 **NCLC 22**

Le Reveler
See Artaud, Antonin (Marie Joseph)

Lerman, Eleanor 1952- .... **CLC 9**
See also CA 85-88

Lerman, Rhoda 1936- .... **CLC 56**
See also CA 49-52

Lermontov, Mikhail Yuryevich 1814-1841 **NCLC 47; PC 18**

Leroux, Gaston 1868-1927 .... **TCLC 25**
See also CA 108; 136; SATA 65

Lesage, Alain-Rene 1668-1747 .... **LC 28**

Leskov, Nikolai (Semyonovich) 1831-1895 **NCLC 25**

Little, Malcolm 1925-1965
See Malcolm X
See also BW 1; CA 125; 111; DA; DAB; DAC; DAM MST, MULT; MTCW

Littlewit, Humphrey Gent.
See Lovecraft, H(oward) P(hillips)

Litwos
See Sienkiewicz, Henryk (Adam Alexander Pius)

Liu E 1857-1909 .... **TCLC 15**
See also CA 115

Lively, Penelope (Margaret) 1933- ... **CLC 32, 50; DAM NOV**
See also CA 41-44R; CANR 29, 67; CLR 7; DLB 14, 161; JRDA; MAICYA; MTCW; SATA 7, 60

Livesay, Dorothy (Kathleen) 1909- ... **CLC 4, 15, 79; DAC; DAM MST, POET**
See also AITN 2; CA 25-28R; CAAS 8; CANR 36, 67; DLB 68; MTCW

Livy c. 59B.C.-c. 17 .... **CMLC 11**

Lizardi, Jose Joaquin Fernandez de 1776-1827 **NCLC 30**

Llewellyn, Richard
See Llewellyn Lloyd, Richard Dafydd Vivian
See also DLB 15

Llewellyn Lloyd, Richard Dafydd Vivian 1906-1983 .... **CLC 7, 80**
See also Llewellyn, Richard
See also CA 53-56; 111; CANR 7; SATA 11; SATA-Obit 37

Llosa, (Jorge) Mario (Pedro) Vargas
See Vargas Llosa, (Jorge) Mario (Pedro)

Lloyd, Manda
See Mander, (Mary) Jane

Lloyd Webber, Andrew 1948-
See Webber, Andrew Lloyd
See also AAYA 1; CA 116; 149; DAM DRAM; SATA 56

Llull, Ramon c. 1235-c. 1316 .... **CMLC 12**

Locke, Alain (Le Roy) 1886-1954 ... **TCLC 43**
See also BW 1; CA 106; 124; DLB 51

Locke, John 1632-1704 .... **LC 7, 35**
See also DLB 101

Locke-Elliott, Sumner
See Elliott, Sumner Locke

Lockhart, John Gibson 1794-1854 ... **NCLC 6**
See also DLB 110, 116, 144

Lodge, David (John) 1935- .... **CLC 36; DAM POP**
See also BEST 90:1; CA 17-20R; CANR 19, 53; DLB 14, 194; INT CANR-19; MTCW

Lodge, Thomas 1558-1625 .... **LC 41**
See also DLB 172

Lodge, Thomas 1558-1625 .... **LC 41**

Loennbohm, Armas Eino Leopold 1878-1926
See Leino, Eino
See also CA 123

Loewinsohn, Ron(ald William) 1937-   **CLC 52**
See also CA 25-28R

Logan, Jake
See Smith, Martin Cruz

Logan, John (Burton) 1923-1987 .... **CLC 5**
See also CA 77-80; 124; CANR 45; DLB 5

Lo Kuan-chung 1330(?)-1400(?) .... **LC 12**

Lombard, Nap
See Johnson, Pamela Hansford

London, Jack .... **TCLC 9, 15, 39; SSC 4; WLC**
See also London, John Griffith
See also AAYA 13; AITN 2; CDALB 1865-1917; DLB 8, 12, 78; SATA 18

London, John Griffith 1876-1916
See London, Jack
See also CA 110; 119; DA; DAB; DAC; DAM MST, NOV; JRDA; MAICYA; MTCW

Long, Emmett
See Leonard, Elmore (John, Jr.)

Longbaugh, Harry
See Goldman, William (W.)

Longfellow, Henry Wadsworth 1807-1882 **NCLC 2, 45; DA; DAB; DAC; DAM MST, POET; WLCS**
See also CDALB 1640-1865; DLB 1, 59; SATA 19

Longinus c. 1st cent. - .... **CMLC 27**
See also DLB 176

Longley, Michael 1939- .... **CLC 29**
See also CA 102; DLB 40

Longus fl. c. 2nd cent. - .... **CMLC 7**

Longway, A. Hugh
See Lang, Andrew

Lonnrot, Elias 1802-1884 .... **NCLC 53**

Lopate, Phillip 1943- .... **CLC 29**
See also CA 97-100; DLBY 80; INT 97-100

Lopez Portillo (y Pacheco), Jose 1920- **CLC 46**
See also CA 129; HW

Lopez y Fuentes, Gregorio 1897(?)-1966 **CLC 32**
See also CA 131; HW

Lorca, Federico Garcia
See Garcia Lorca, Federico

Lord, Bette Bao 1938- .... **CLC 23**
See also BEST 90:3; CA 107; CANR 41; INT 107; SATA 58

Lord Auch
See Bataille, Georges

Lord Byron
See Byron, George Gordon (Noel)

Lorde, Audre (Geraldine) 1934-1992 ... **CLC 18, 71; BLC; DAM MULT, POET; PC 12**
See also BW 1; CA 25-28R; 142; CANR 16, 26, 46; DLB 41; MTCW

Lord Houghton
See Milnes, Richard Monckton

Lord Jeffrey
See Jeffrey, Francis

Lorenzini, Carlo 1826-1890
See Collodi, Carlo
See also MAICYA; SATA 29

Lorenzo, Heberto Padilla
See Padilla (Lorenzo), Heberto

Loris
See Hofmannsthal, Hugo von

Loti, Pierre .... **TCLC 11**
See also Viaud, (Louis Marie) Julien
See also DLB 123

Louie, David Wong 1954- .... **CLC 70**
See also CA 139

Louis, Father M.
See Merton, Thomas

Lovecraft, H(oward) P(hillips) 1890-1937 **TCLC 4, 22; DAM POP; SSC 3**
See also AAYA 14; CA 104; 133; MTCW

Lovelace, Earl 1935- .... **CLC 51**
See also BW 2; CA 77-80; CANR 41; DLB 125; MTCW

Lovelace, Richard 1618-1657 .... **LC 24**
See also DLB 131

Lowell, Amy 1874-1925 ...... **TCLC 1, 8; DAM POET; PC 13**
See also CA 104; 151; DLB 54, 140

Lowell, James Russell 1819-1891 ..... **NCLC 2**
See also CDALB 1640-1865; DLB 1, 11, 64, 79, 189

Lowell, Robert (Traill Spence, Jr.) 1917-1977 **CLC 1, 2, 3, 4, 5, 8, 9, 11, 15, 37; DA; DAB; DAC; DAM MST, NOV; PC 3; WLC**
See also CA 9-12R; 73-76; CABS 2; CANR 26, 60; DLB 5, 169; MTCW

Lowndes, Marie Adelaide (Belloc) 1868-1947 **TCLC 12**
See also CA 107; DLB 70

Lowry, (Clarence) Malcolm 1909-1957 **TCLC 6, 40**
See also CA 105; 131; CANR 62; CDBLB 1945-1960; DLB 15; MTCW

Lowry, Mina Gertrude 1882-1966
See Loy, Mina
See also CA 113

Loxsmith, John
See Brunner, John (Kilian Houston)

Maclean, Norman (Fitzroy) 1902-1990 ... **CLC 78; DAM POP; SSC 13**
See also CA 102; 132; CANR 49

MacLeish, Archibald 1892-1982 ... **CLC 3, 8, 14, 68; DAM POET**
See also CA 9-12R; 106; CANR 33, 63; DLB 4, 7, 45; DLBY 82; MTCW

MacLennan, (John) Hugh 1907-1990 ... **CLC 2, 14, 92; DAC; DAM MST**
See also CA 5-8R; 142; CANR 33; DLB 68; MTCW

MacLeod, Alistair 1936- ... **CLC 56; DAC; DAM MST**
See also CA 123; DLB 60

Macleod, Fiona
See Sharp, William

MacNeice, (Frederick) Louis 1907-1963 ... **CLC 1, 4, 10, 53; DAB; DAM POET**
See also CA 85-88; CANR 61; DLB 10, 20; MTCW

MacNeill, Dand
See Fraser, George MacDonald

Macpherson, James 1736-1796 .... **LC 29**
See also DLB 109

Macpherson, (Jean) Jay 1931- .... **CLC 14**
See also CA 5-8R; DLB 53

MacShane, Frank 1927- .... **CLC 39**
See also CA 9-12R; CANR 3, 33; DLB 111

Macumber, Mari
See Sandoz, Mari(e Susette)

Madach, Imre 1823-1864 .... **NCLC 19**

Madden, (Jerry) David 1933- .... **CLC 5, 15**
See also CA 1-4R; CAAS 3; CANR 4, 45; DLB 6; MTCW

Maddern, Al(an)
See Ellison, Harlan (Jay)

Madhubuti, Haki R. 1942- .... **CLC 6, 73; BLC; DAM MULT, POET; PC 5**
See also Lee, Don L.
See also BW 2; CA 73-76; CANR 24, 51; DLB 5, 41; DLBD 8

Maepenn, Hugh
See Kuttner, Henry

Maepenn, K. H.
See Kuttner, Henry

Maeterlinck, Maurice 1862-1949 .... **TCLC 3; DAM DRAM**
See also CA 104; 136; DLB 192; SATA 66

Maginn, William 1794-1842 .... **NCLC 8**
See also DLB 110, 159

Mahapatra, Jayanta 1928- ...... **CLC 33; DAM MULT**
See also CA 73-76; CAAS 9; CANR 15, 33, 66

Mahfouz, Naguib (Abdel Aziz Al-Sabilgi) 1911(?)-
See Mahfuz, Najib
See also BEST 89:2; CA 128; CANR 55; DAM NOV; MTCW

Mahfuz, Najib .... **CLC 52, 55**
See also Mahfouz, Naguib (Abdel Aziz Al-Sabilgi)
See also DLBY 88

Mahon, Derek 1941- .... **CLC 27**
See also CA 113; 128; DLB 40

Mailer, Norman 1923- ... **CLC 1, 2, 3, 4, 5, 8, 11, 14, 28, 39, 74; DA; DAB; DAC; DAM MST, NOV, POP**
See also AITN 2; CA 9-12R; CABS 1; CANR 28; CDALB 1968-1988; DLB 2, 16, 28, 185; DLBD 3; DLBY 80, 83; MTCW

Maillet, Antonine 1929- .... **CLC 54; DAC**
See also CA 115; 120; CANR 46; DLB 60; INT 120

Mais, Roger 1905-1955 .... **TCLC 8**
See also BW 1; CA 105; 124; DLB 125; MTCW

Maistre, Joseph de 1753-1821 .... **NCLC 37**

Maitland, Frederic 1850-1906 .... **TCLC 65**

Maitland, Sara (Louise) 1950- .... **CLC 49**
See also CA 69-72; CANR 13, 59

Major, Clarence 1936- ... **CLC 3, 19, 48; BLC; DAM MULT**
See also BW 2; CA 21-24R; CAAS 6; CANR 13, 25, 53; DLB 33

Major, Kevin (Gerald) 1949- ... **CLC 26; DAC**
See also AAYA 16; CA 97-100; CANR 21, 38; CLR 11; DLB 60; INT CANR-21; JRDA; MAICYA; SATA 32, 82

Maki, James
See Ozu, Yasujiro

Malabaila, Damiano
See Levi, Primo

Malamud, Bernard 1914-1986 ... **CLC 1, 2, 3, 5, 8, 9, 11, 18, 27, 44, 78, 85; DA; DAB; DAC; DAM MST, NOV, POP; SSC 15; WLC**
See also AAYA 16; CA 5-8R; 118; CABS 1; CANR 28, 62; CDALB 1941-1968; DLB 2, 28, 152; DLBY 80, 86; MTCW

Malan, Herman
See Bosman, Herman Charles; Bosman, Herman Charles

Malaparte, Curzio 1898-1957 .... **TCLC 52**

Malcolm, Dan
See Silverberg, Robert

Malcolm X .... **CLC 82; BLC; WLCS**
See also Little, Malcolm

Malherbe, Francois de 1555-1628 .... **LC 5**

Mallarme, Stephane 1842-1898 **NCLC 4, 41; DAM POET; PC 4**

Mallet-Joris, Francoise 1930- .... **CLC 11**
See also CA 65-68; CANR 17; DLB 83

Malley, Ern
See McAuley, James Phillip

Mallowan, Agatha Christie
See Christie, Agatha (Mary Clarissa)

Maloff, Saul 1922- .... **CLC 5**
See also CA 33-36R

Malone, Louis
See MacNeice, (Frederick) Louis

Malone, Michael (Christopher) 1942- .... **CLC 43**
See also CA 77-80; CANR 14, 32, 57

Malory, (Sir) Thomas 1410(?)-1471(?) ... **LC 11; DA; DAB; DAC; DAM MST; WLCS**
See also CDBLB Before 1660; DLB 146; SATA 59; SATA-Brief 33

Malouf, (George Joseph) David 1934- . **CLC 28, 86**
See also CA 124; CANR 50

Malraux, (Georges-)Andre 1901-1976 ... **CLC 1, 4, 9, 13, 15, 57; DAM NOV**
See also CA 21-22; 69-72; CANR 34, 58; CAP 2; DLB 72; MTCW

Malzberg, Barry N(athaniel) 1939- ..... **CLC 7**
See also CA 61-64; CAAS 4; CANR 16; DLB 8

Mamet, David (Alan) 1947- ... **CLC 9, 15, 34, 46, 91; DAM DRAM; DC 4**
See also AAYA 3; CA 81-84; CABS 3; CANR 15, 41, 67; DLB 7; MTCW

Mamoulian, Rouben (Zachary) 1897-1987 **CLC 16**
See also CA 25-28R; 124

Mandelstam, Osip (Emilievich) 1891(?)-1938(?) **TCLC 2, 6; PC 14**
See also CA 104; 150

Mander, (Mary) Jane 1877-1949 .... **TCLC 31**
See also CA 162

Mandeville, John fl. 1350- .... **CMLC 19**
See also DLB 146

Mandiargues, Andre Pieyre de .... **CLC 41**
See also Pieyre de Mandiargues, Andre
See also DLB 83

Mandrake, Ethel Belle
See Thurman, Wallace (Henry)

Mangan, James Clarence 1803-1849 ..... **NCLC 27**

Maniere, J.-E.
See Giraudoux, (Hippolyte) Jean

Manley, (Mary) Delariviere 1672(?)-1724 ..... **LC 1**
See also DLB 39, 80

Martinez Sierra, Maria (de la O'LeJarraga) 1874-1974 .... **TCLC 6**
See also CA 115

Martinsen, Martin
See Follett, Ken(neth Martin)

Martinson, Harry (Edmund) 1904-1978 ... **CLC 14**
See also CA 77-80; CANR 34

Marut, Ret
See Traven, B.

Marut, Robert
See Traven, B.

Marvell, Andrew 1621-1678   **LC 4; DA; DAB; DAC; DAM MST, POET; PC 10; WLC**
See also CDBLB 1660-1789; DLB 131

Marx, Karl (Heinrich) 1818-1883 .. **NCLC 17**
See also DLB 129

Masaoka Shiki .... **TCLC 18**
See also Masaoka Tsunenori

Masaoka Tsunenori 1867-1902
See Masaoka Shiki
See also CA 117

Masefield, John (Edward) 1878-1967   **CLC 11, 47; DAM POET**
See also CA 19-20; 25-28R; CANR 33; CAP 2; CDBLB 1890-1914; DLB 10, 19, 153, 160; MTCW; SATA 19

Maso, Carole 19(?)- .... **CLC 44**

Mason, Bobbie Ann 1940-   **CLC 28, 43, 82; SSC 4**
See also AAYA 5; CA 53-56; CANR 11, 31, 58; DLB 173; DLBY 87; INT CANR-31; MTCW

Mason, Ernst
See Pohl, Frederik

Mason, Lee W.
See Malzberg, Barry N(athaniel)

Mason, Nick 1945- .... **CLC 35**

Mason, Tally
See Derleth, August (William)

Mass, William
See Gibson, William

Masters, Edgar Lee 1868-1950   **TCLC 2, 25; DA; DAC; DAM MST, POET; PC 1; WLCS**
See also CA 104; 133; CDALB 1865-1917; DLB 54; MTCW

Masters, Hilary 1928- .... **CLC 48**
See also CA 25-28R; CANR 13, 47

Mastrosimone, William 19(?)- .... **CLC 36**

Mathe, Albert
See Camus, Albert

Mather, Cotton 1663-1728 .... **LC 38**
See also CDALB 1640-1865; DLB 24, 30, 140

Mather, Increase 1639-1723 .... **LC 38**
See also DLB 24

Matheson, Richard Burton 1926- ...... **CLC 37**
See also CA 97-100; DLB 8, 44; INT 97-100

Mathews, Harry 1930- .... **CLC 6, 52**
See also CA 21-24R; CAAS 6; CANR 18, 40

Mathews, John Joseph 1894-1979 ... **CLC 84; DAM MULT**
See also CA 19-20; 142; CANR 45; CAP 2; DLB 175; NNAL

Mathias, Roland (Glyn) 1915- .... **CLC 45**
See also CA 97-100; CANR 19, 41; DLB 27

Matsuo Basho 1644-1694 .... **PC 3**
See also DAM POET

Mattheson, Rodney
See Creasey, John

Matthews, Greg 1949- .... **CLC 45**
See also CA 135

Matthews, William (Procter, III) 1942-1997 **CLC 40**
See also CA 29-32R; 162; CAAS 18; CANR 12, 57; DLB 5

Matthias, John (Edward) 1941- .... **CLC 9**
See also CA 33-36R; CANR 56

Matthiessen, Peter 1927-   **CLC 5, 7, 11, 32, 64; DAM NOV**
See also AAYA 6; BEST 90:4; CA 9-12R; CANR 21, 50; DLB 6, 173; MTCW; SATA 27

Maturin, Charles Robert 1780(?)-1824   **NCLC 6**
See also DLB 178

Matute (Ausejo), Ana Maria 1925-.... **CLC 11**
See also CA 89-92; MTCW

Maugham, W. S.
See Maugham, W(illiam) Somerset

Maugham, W(illiam) Somerset 1874-1965   **CLC 1, 11, 15, 67, 93; DA; DAB; DAC; DAM DRAM, MST, NOV; SSC 8; WLC**
See also CA 5-8R; 25-28R; CANR 40; CDBLB 1914-1945; DLB 10, 36, 77, 100, 162, 195; MTCW; SATA 54

Maugham, William Somerset
See Maugham, W(illiam) Somerset

Maupassant, (Henri Rene Albert) Guy de 1850-1893 .... **NCLC 1, 42; DA; DAB; DAC; DAM MST; SSC 1; WLC**
See also DLB 123

Maupin, Armistead 1944- ... **CLC 95; DAM POP**
See also CA 125; 130; CANR 58; INT 130

Maurhut, Richard
See Traven, B.

Mauriac, Claude 1914-1996 .... **CLC 9**
See also CA 89-92; 152; DLB 83

Mauriac, Francois (Charles) 1885-1970 ... **CLC 4, 9, 56; SSC 24**
See also CA 25-28; CAP 2; DLB 65; MTCW

Mavor, Osborne Henry 1888-1951
See Bridie, James
See also CA 104

Maxwell, William (Keepers, Jr.) 1908- **CLC 19**
See also CA 93-96; CANR 54; DLBY 80; INT 93-96

May, Elaine 1932- .... **CLC 16**
See also CA 124; 142; DLB 44

Mayakovski, Vladimir (Vladimirovich) 1893-1930 .... **TCLC 4, 18**
See also CA 104; 158

Mayhew, Henry 1812-1887 .... **NCLC 31**
See also DLB 18, 55, 190

Mayle, Peter 1939(?)- .... **CLC 89**
See also CA 139; CANR 64

Maynard, Joyce 1953- .... **CLC 23**
See also CA 111; 129; CANR 64

Mayne, William (James Carter) 1928- ... **CLC 12**
See also AAYA 20; CA 9-12R; CANR 37; CLR 25; JRDA; MAICYA; SAAS 11; SATA 6, 68

Mayo, Jim
See L'Amour, Louis (Dearborn)

Maysles, Albert 1926- .... **CLC 16**
See also CA 29-32R

Maysles, David 1932- .... **CLC 16**

Mazer, Norma Fox 1931- .... **CLC 26**
See also AAYA 5; CA 69-72; CANR 12, 32, 66; CLR 23; JRDA; MAICYA; SAAS 1; SATA 24, 67

Mazzini, Guiseppe 1805-1872 .... **NCLC 34**

McAuley, James Phillip 1917-1976 .... **CLC 45**
See also CA 97-100

McBain, Ed
See Hunter, Evan

McBrien, William Augustine 1930- ... **CLC 44**
See also CA 107

McCaffrey, Anne (Inez) 1926- **CLC 17; DAM NOV, POP**
See also AAYA 6; AITN 2; BEST 89:2; CA 25-28R; CANR 15, 35, 55; CLR 49; DLB 8; JRDA; MAICYA; MTCW; SAAS 11; SATA 8, 70

McCall, Nathan 1955(?)- .... **CLC 86**
See also CA 146

McCann, Arthur
See Campbell, John W(ood, Jr.)

McCann, Edson
See Pohl, Frederik

Melmoth, Sebastian
   See Wilde, Oscar (Fingal O'Flahertie Wills)

Meltzer, Milton 1915- .... **CLC 26**
   See also AAYA 8; CA 13-16R; CANR 38; CLR
   13; DLB 61; JRDA; MAICYA; SAAS 1;
   SATA 1, 50, 80

Melville, Herman 1819-1891   **NCLC 3, 12,
   29, 45, 49; DA; DAB; DAC; DAM MST,
   NOV; SSC 1, 17; WLC**
   See also AAYA 25; CDALB 1640-1865; DLB 3,
   74; SATA 59

Menander c. 342B.C.-c. 292B.C. ..... **CMLC 9;
   DAM DRAM; DC 3**
   See also DLB 176

Mencken, H(enry) L(ouis) 1880-1956 **TCLC 13**
   See also CA 105; 125; CDALB 1917-1929; DLB
   11, 29, 63, 137; MTCW

Mendelsohn, Jane 1965(?)- .... **CLC 99**
   See also CA 154

Mercer, David 1928-1980 .... **CLC 5; DAM
   DRAM**
   See also CA 9-12R; 102; CANR 23; DLB 13;
   MTCW

Merchant, Paul
   See Ellison, Harlan (Jay)

Meredith, George 1828-1909 ... **TCLC 17, 43;
   DAM POET**
   See also CA 117; 153; CDBLB 1832-1890; DLB
   18, 35, 57, 159

Meredith, William (Morris) 1919- **CLC 4, 13,
   22, 55; DAM POET**
   See also CA 9-12R; CAAS 14; CANR 6, 40; DLB
   5

Merezhkovsky, Dmitry Sergeyevich 1865-1941
   TCLC 29

Merimee, Prosper 1803-1870 ... **NCLC 6, 65;
   SSC 7**
   See also DLB 119, 192

Merkin, Daphne 1954- .... **CLC 44**
   See also CA 123

Merlin, Arthur
   See Blish, James (Benjamin)

Merrill, James (Ingram) 1926-1995 **CLC 2, 3,
   6, 8, 13, 18, 34, 91; DAM POET**
   See also CA 13-16R; 147; CANR 10, 49, 63;
   DLB 5, 165; DLBY 85; INT CANR-10;
   MTCW

Merriman, Alex
   See Silverberg, Robert

Merritt, E. B.
   See Waddington, Miriam

Merton, Thomas 1915-1968   **CLC 1, 3, 11, 34,
   83; PC 10**
   See also CA 5-8R; 25-28R; CANR 22, 53; DLB
   48; DLBY 81; MTCW

Merwin, W(illiam) S(tanley) 1927- ... **CLC 1, 2,
   3, 5, 8, 13, 18, 45, 88; DAM POET**
   See also CA 13-16R; CANR 15, 51; DLB 5, 169;
   INT CANR-15; MTCW

Metcalf, John 1938- .... **CLC 37**
   See also CA 113; DLB 60

Metcalf, Suzanne
   See Baum, L(yman) Frank

Mew, Charlotte (Mary) 1870-1928 ... **TCLC 8**
   See also CA 105; DLB 19, 135

Mewshaw, Michael 1943- .... **CLC 9**
   See also CA 53-56; CANR 7, 47; DLBY 80

Meyer, June
   See Jordan, June

Meyer, Lynn
   See Slavitt, David R(ytman)

Meyer-Meyrink, Gustav 1868-1932
   See Meyrink, Gustav
   See also CA 117

Meyers, Jeffrey 1939- .... **CLC 39**
   See also CA 73-76; CANR 54; DLB 111

Meynell, Alice (Christina Gertrude Thompson)
   1847-1922 .... **TCLC 6**
   See also CA 104; DLB 19, 98

Meyrink, Gustav .... **TCLC 21**
   See also Meyer-Meyrink, Gustav
   See also DLB 81

Michaels, Leonard 1933- ... **CLC 6, 25; SSC 16**
   See also CA 61-64; CANR 21, 62; DLB 130; MTCW

Michaux, Henri 1899-1984 .... **CLC 8, 19**
   See also CA 85-88; 114

Micheaux, Oscar 1884-1951 .... **TCLC 76**
   See also DLB 50

Michelangelo 1475-1564 .... **LC 12**

Michelet, Jules 1798-1874 .... **NCLC 31**

Michener, James A(lbert) 1907(?)-1997 ... **CLC
   1, 5, 11, 29, 60, 109; DAM NOV, POP**
   See also AITN 1; BEST 90:1; CA 5-8R; 161;
   CANR 21, 45, 68; DLB 6; MTCW

Mickiewicz, Adam 1798-1855 .... **NCLC 3**

Middleton, Christopher 1926- .... **CLC 13**
   See also CA 13-16R; CANR 29, 54; DLB 40

Middleton, Richard (Barham) 1882-1911
   TCLC 56
   See also DLB 156

Middleton, Stanley 1919- .... **CLC 7, 38**
   See also CA 25-28R; CAAS 23; CANR 21, 46;
   DLB 14

Middleton, Thomas 1580-1627 ... **LC 33; DAM
   DRAM, MST; DC 5**
   See also DLB 58

Migueis, Jose Rodrigues 1901- .... **CLC 10**

Mikszath, Kalman 1847-1910 .... **TCLC 31**

Miles, Jack .... **CLC 100**

Miles, Josephine (Louise) 1911-1985 ... **CLC 1,
   2, 14, 34, 39; DAM POET**
   See also CA 1-4R; 116; CANR 2, 55; DLB 48

Militant
   See Sandburg, Carl (August)

Mill, John Stuart 1806-1873 .... **NCLC 11,
   58**
   See also CDBLB 1832-1890; DLB 55, 190

Millar, Kenneth 1915-1983 .... **CLC 14; DAM
   POP**
   See also Macdonald, Ross
   See also CA 9-12R; 110; CANR 16, 63; DLB 2;
   DLBD 6; DLBY 83; MTCW

Millay, E. Vincent
   See Millay, Edna St. Vincent

Millay, Edna St. Vincent 1892-1950 ... **TCLC 4,
   49; DA; DAB; DAC; DAM MST, POET; PC
   6; WLCS**
   See also CA 104; 130; CDALB 1917-1929; DLB
   45; MTCW

Miller, Arthur 1915- .... **CLC 1, 2, 6, 10, 15, 26,
   47, 78; DA; DAB; DAC; DAM DRAM,
   MST; DC 1; WLC**
   See also AAYA 15; AITN 1; CA 1-4R; CABS 3;
   CANR 2, 30, 54; CDALB 1941-1968; DLB
   7; MTCW

Miller, Henry (Valentine) 1891-1980   **CLC 1,
   2, 4, 9, 14, 43, 84; DA; DAB; DAC; DAM
   MST, NOV; WLC**
   See also CA 9-12R; 97-100; CANR 33, 64;
   CDALB 1929-1941; DLB 4, 9; DLBY 80;
   MTCW

Miller, Jason 1939(?)- .... **CLC 2**
   See also AITN 1; CA 73-76; DLB 7

Miller, Sue 1943- .... **CLC 44; DAM POP**
   See also BEST 90:3; CA 139; CANR 59; DLB
   143

Miller, Walter M(ichael, Jr.) 1923- **CLC 4, 30**
   See also CA 85-88; DLB 8

Millett, Kate 1934- .... **CLC 67**
   See also AITN 1; CA 73-76; CANR 32, 53;
   MTCW

Millhauser, Steven (Lewis) 1943- ... **CLC 21, 54,
   109**
   See also CA 110; 111; CANR 63; DLB 2; INT
   111

Millin, Sarah Gertrude 1889-1968 .... **CLC 49**
   See also CA 102; 93-96

Milne, A(lan) A(lexander) 1882-1956 ... **T C L C
   6; DAB; DAC; DAM MST**
   See also CA 104; 133; CLR 1, 26; DLB 10, 77,
   100, 160; MAICYA; MTCW; YABC 1

Moore, Edward
See Muir, Edwin

Moore, George Augustus 1852-1933 ... **TCLC 7; SSC 19**
See also CA 104; DLB 10, 18, 57, 135

Moore, Lorrie .... **CLC 39, 45, 68**
See also Moore, Marie Lorena

Moore, Marianne (Craig) 1887-1972 ... **CLC 1, 2, 4, 8, 10, 13, 19, 47; DA; DAB; DAC; DAM MST, POET; PC 4; WLCS**
See also CA 1-4R; 33-36R; CANR 3, 61; CDALB 1929-1941; DLB 45; DLBD 7; MTCW; SATA 20

Moore, Marie Lorena 1957-
See Moore, Lorrie
See also CA 116; CANR 39

Moore, Thomas 1779-1852 .... **NCLC 6**
See also DLB 96, 144

Morand, Paul 1888-1976 .... **CLC 41; SSC 22**
See also CA 69-72; DLB 65

Morante, Elsa 1918-1985 .... **CLC 8, 47**
See also CA 85-88; 117; CANR 35; DLB 177; MTCW

Moravia, Alberto 1907-1990 ... **CLC 2, 7, 11, 27, 46; SSC 26**
See also Pincherle, Alberto
See also DLB 177

More, Hannah 1745-1833 .... **NCLC 27**
See also DLB 107, 109, 116, 158

More, Henry 1614-1687 .... **LC 9**
See also DLB 126

More, Sir Thomas 1478-1535 .... **LC 10, 32**

Moreas, Jean .... **TCLC 18**
See also Papadiamantopoulos, Johannes

Morgan, Berry 1919- .... **CLC 6**
See also CA 49-52; DLB 6

Morgan, Claire
See Highsmith, (Mary) Patricia

Morgan, Edwin (George) 1920- .... **CLC 31**
See also CA 5-8R; CANR 3, 43; DLB 27

Morgan, (George) Frederick 1922- .... **CLC 23**
See also CA 17-20R; CANR 21

Morgan, Harriet
See Mencken, H(enry) L(ouis)

Morgan, Jane
See Cooper, James Fenimore

Morgan, Janet 1945- .... **CLC 39**
See also CA 65-68

Morgan, Lady 1776(?)-1859 .... **NCLC 29**
See also DLB 116, 158

Morgan, Robin (Evonne) 1941- .... **CLC 2**
See also CA 69-72; CANR 29, 68; MTCW; SATA 80

Morgan, Scott
See Kuttner, Henry

Morgan, Seth 1949(?)-1990 .... **CLC 65**
See also CA 132

Morgenstern, Christian 1871-1914 .. **TCLC 8**
See also CA 105

Morgenstern, S.
See Goldman, William (W.)

Moricz, Zsigmond 1879-1942 .... **TCLC 33**
See also CA 165

Morike, Eduard (Friedrich) 1804-1875 **NCLC 10**
See also DLB 133

Moritz, Karl Philipp 1756-1793 .... **LC 2**
See also DLB 94

Morland, Peter Henry
See Faust, Frederick (Schiller)

Morren, Theophil
See Hofmannsthal, Hugo von

Morris, Bill 1952- .... **CLC 76**

Morris, Julian
See West, Morris L(anglo)

Morris, Steveland Judkins 1950(?)-
See Wonder, Stevie
See also CA 111

Morris, William 1834-1896 .... **NCLC 4**
See also CDBLB 1832-1890; DLB 18, 35, 57, 156, 178, 184

Morris, Wright 1910- .... **CLC 1, 3, 7, 18, 37**
See also CA 9-12R; CANR 21; DLB 2; DLBY 81; MTCW

Morrison, Arthur 1863-1945 .... **TCLC 72**
See also CA 120; 157; DLB 70, 135

Morrison, Chloe Anthony Wofford
See Morrison, Toni

Morrison, James Douglas 1943-1971
See Morrison, Jim
See also CA 73-76; CANR 40

Morrison, Jim ....**CLC 17**
See also Morrison, James Douglas

Morrison, Toni 1931- .... **CLC 4, 10, 22, 55, 81, 87; BLC; DA; DAB; DAC; DAM MST, MULT, NOV, POP**
See also AAYA 1, 22; BW 2; CA 29-32R; CANR 27, 42, 67; CDALB 1968-1988; DLB 6, 33, 143; DLBY 81; MTCW; SATA 57

Morrison, Van 1945- .... **CLC 21**
See also CA 116

Morrissy, Mary 1958- .... **CLC 99**

Mortimer, John (Clifford) 1923- ... **CLC 28, 43; DAM DRAM, POP**
See also CA 13-16R; CANR 21; CDBLB 1960 to Present; DLB 13; INT CANR-21; MTCW

Mortimer, Penelope (Ruth) 1918- .... **CLC 5**
See also CA 57-60; CANR 45

Morton, Anthony
See Creasey, John

Mosca, Gaetano 1858-1941 .... **TCLC 75**

Mosher, Howard Frank 1943- .... **CLC 62**
See also CA 139; CANR 65

Mosley, Nicholas 1923- .... **CLC 43, 70**
See also CA 69-72; CANR 41, 60; DLB 14

Mosley, Walter 1952- ... **CLC 97; DAM MULT, POP**
See also AAYA 17; BW 2; CA 142; CANR 57

Moss, Howard 1922-1987 . **CLC 7, 14, 45, 50; DAM POET**
See also CA 1-4R; 123; CANR 1, 44; DLB 5

Mossgiel, Rab
See Burns, Robert

Motion, Andrew (Peter) 1952- .... **CLC 47**
See also CA 146; DLB 40

Motley, Willard (Francis) 1909-1965 **CLC 18**
See also BW 1; CA 117; 106; DLB 76, 143

Motoori, Norinaga 1730-1801 .... **NCLC 45**

Mott, Michael (Charles Alston) 1930- ... **CLC 15, 34**
See also CA 5-8R; CAAS 7; CANR 7, 29

Mountain Wolf Woman 1884-1960 .... **CLC 92**
See also CA 144; NNAL

Moure, Erin 1955- .... **CLC 88**
See also CA 113; DLB 60

Mowat, Farley (McGill) 1921- ... **CLC 26; DAC; DAM MST**
See also AAYA 1; CA 1-4R; CANR 4, 24, 42, 68; CLR 20; DLB 68; INT CANAR-24; JRDA; MAICYA; MTCW; SATA 3, 55

Moyers, Bill 1934- .... **CLC 74**
See also AITN 2; CA 61-64; CANR 31, 52

Mphahlele, Es'kia
See Mphahlele, Ezekiel
See also DLB 125

Mphahlele, Ezekiel 1919-1983 ... **CLC 25; BLC; DAM MULT**
See also Mphahlele, Es'kia
See also BW 2; CA 81-84; CANR 26

Mqhayi, S(amuel) E(dward) K(rune Loliwe) 1875-1945 .... **TCLC 25; BLC; DAM MULT**
See also CA 153

Nemerov, Howard (Stanley) 1920-1991   **CLC 2, 6, 9, 36; DAM POET**
See also CA 1-4R; 134; CABS 2; CANR 1, 27, 53; DLB 5, 6; DLBY 83; INT CANR-27; MTCW

Neruda, Pablo 1904-1973   **CLC 1, 2, 5, 7, 9, 28, 62; DA; DAB; DAC; DAM MST, MULT, POET; HLC; PC 4; WLC**
See also CA 19-20; 45-48; CAP 2; HW; MTCW

Nerval, Gerard de 1808-1855   **NCLC 1, 67; PC 13; SSC 18**

Nervo, (Jose) Amado (Ruiz de) 1870-1919   **TCLC 11**
See also CA 109; 131; HW

Nessi, Pio Baroja y
See Baroja (y Nessi), Pio

Nestroy, Johann 1801-1862 .... **NCLC 42**
See also DLB 133

Netterville, Luke
See O'Grady, Standish (James)

Neufeld, John (Arthur) 1938- .... **CLC 17**
See also AAYA 11; CA 25-28R; CANR 11, 37, 56; MAICYA; SAAS 3; SATA 6, 81

Neville, Emily Cheney 1919- .... **CLC 12**
See also CA 5-8R; CANR 3, 37; JRDA; MAICYA; SAAS 2; SATA 1

Newbound, Bernard Slade 1930-
See Slade, Bernard
See also CA 81-84; CANR 49; DAM DRAM

Newby, P(ercy) H(oward) 1918-1997 .. **CLC 2, 13; DAM NOV**
See also CA 5-8R; 161; CANR 32, 67; DLB 15; MTCW

Newlove, Donald 1928- .... **CLC 6**
See also CA 29-32R; CANR 25

Newlove, John (Herbert) 1938- .... **CLC 14**
See also CA 21-24R; CANR 9, 25

Newman, Charles 1938- .... **CLC 2, 8**
See also CA 21-24R

Newman, Edwin (Harold) 1919- .... **CLC 14**
See also AITN 1; CA 69-72; CANR 5

Newman, John Henry 1801-1890 .... **NCLC 38**
See also DLB 18, 32, 55

Newton, Suzanne 1936- .... **CLC 35**
See also CA 41-44R; CANR 14; JRDA; SATA 5, 77

Nexo, Martin Andersen 1869-1954   **TCLC 43**

Nezval, Vitezslav 1900-1958 .... **TCLC 44**
See also CA 123

Ng, Fae Myenne 1957(?)- .... **CLC 81**
See also CA 146

Ngema, Mbongeni 1955- .... **CLC 57**
See also BW 2; CA 143

Ngugi, James T(hiong'o) .... **CLC 3, 7, 13**
See also Ngugi wa Thiong'o

Ngugi wa Thiong'o 1938- ... **CLC 36; BLC; DAM MULT, NOV**
See also Ngugi, James T(hiong'o)
See also BW 2; CA 81-84; CANR 27, 58; DLB 125; MTCW

Nichol, B(arrie) P(hillip) 1944-1988 .. **CLC 18**
See also CA 53-56; DLB 53; SATA 66

Nichols, John (Treadwell) 1940- .... **CLC 38**
See also CA 9-12R; CAAS 2; CANR 6; DLBY 82

Nichols, Leigh
See Koontz, Dean R(ay)

Nichols, Peter (Richard) 1927-   **CLC 5, 36, 65**
See also CA 104; CANR 33; DLB 13; MTCW

Nicolas, F. R. E.
See Freeling, Nicolas

Niedecker, Lorine 1903-1970 .... **CLC 10, 42; DAM POET**
See also CA 25-28; CAP 2; DLB 48

Nietzsche, Friedrich (Wilhelm) 1844-1900   **TCLC 10, 18, 55**
See also CA 107; 121; DLB 129

Nievo, Ippolito 1831-1861 .... **NCLC 22**

Nightingale, Anne Redmon 1943-
See Redmon, Anne
See also CA 103

Nik. T. O.
See Annensky, Innokenty (Fyodorovich)

Nin, Anais 1903-1977 .... **CLC 1, 4, 8, 11, 14, 60; DAM NOV, POP; SSC 10**
See also AITN 2; CA 13-16R; 69-72; CANR 22, 53; DLB 2, 4, 152; MTCW

Nishiwaki, Junzaburo 1894-1982 .... **PC 15**
See also CA 107

Nissenson, Hugh 1933- .... **CLC 4, 9**
See also CA 17-20R; CANR 27; DLB 28

Niven, Larry .... **CLC 8**
See also Niven, Laurence Van Cott
See also DLB 8

Niven, Laurence Van Cott 1938-
See Niven, Larry
See also CA 21-24R; CAAS 12; CANR 14, 44, 66; DAM POP; MTCW; SATA 95

Nixon, Agnes Eckhardt 1927- .... **CLC 21**
See also CA 110

Nizan, Paul 1905-1940 .... **TCLC 40**
See also CA 161; DLB 72

Nkosi, Lewis 1936- ...... **CLC 45; BLC; DAM MULT**
See also BW 1; CA 65-68; CANR 27; DLB 157

Nodier, (Jean) Charles (Emmanuel) 1780-1844   **NCLC 19**
See also DLB 119

Noguchi, Yone 1875-1947 .... **TCLC 80**

Nolan, Christopher 1965- .... **CLC 58**
See also CA 111

Noon, Jeff 1957- .... **CLC 91**
See also CA 148

Norden, Charles
See Durrell, Lawrence (George)

Nordhoff, Charles (Bernard) 1887-1947   **TCLC 23**
See also CA 108; DLB 9; SATA 23

Norfolk, Lawrence 1963- .... **CLC 76**
See also CA 144

Norman, Marsha 1947- .... **CLC 28; DAM DRAM; DC 8**
See also CA 105; CABS 3; CANR 41; DLBY 84

Norris, Frank 1870-1902 .... **SSC 28**
See also Norris, (Benjamin) Frank(lin, Jr.)
See also CDALB 1865-1917; DLB 12, 71, 186

Norris, (Benjamin) Frank(lin, Jr.) 1870-1902   **TCLC 24**
See also Norris, Frank
See also CA 110; 160

Norris, Leslie 1921- .... **CLC 14**
See also CA 11-12; CANR 14; CAP 1; DLB 27

North, Andrew
See Norton, Andre

North, Anthony
See Koontz, Dean R(ay)

North, Captain George
See Stevenson, Robert Louis (Balfour)

North, Milou
See Erdrich, Louise

Northrup, B. A.
See Hubbard, L(afayette) Ron(ald)

North Staffs
See Hulme, T(homas) E(rnest)

Norton, Alice Mary
See Norton, Andre
See also MAICYA; SATA 1, 43

Norton, Andre 1912- .... **CLC 12**
See also Norton, Alice Mary
See also AAYA 14; CA 1-4R; CANR 68; DLB 8, 52; JRDA; MTCW; SATA 91

Norton, Caroline 1808-1877 .... **NCLC 47**
See also DLB 21, 159

Norway, Nevil Shute 1899-1960
See Shute, Nevil
See also CA 102; 93-96

Ondaatje, (Philip) Michael 1943- .... **CLC 14, 29, 51, 76; DAB; DAC; DAM MST**
See also CA 77-80; CANR 42; DLB 60

Oneal, Elizabeth 1934-
See Oneal, Zibby
See also CA 106; CANR 28; MAICYA; SATA 30, 82

Oneal, Zibby .... **CLC 30**
See also Oneal, Elizabeth
See also AAYA 5; CLR 13; JRDA

O'Neill, Eugene (Gladstone) 1888-1953 **TCLC 1, 6, 27, 49; DA; DAB; DAC; DAM DRAM, MST; WLC**
See also AITN 1; CA 110; 132; CDALB 1929-1941; DLB 7; MTCW

Onetti, Juan Carlos 1909-1994 .... **CLC 7, 10; DAM MULT, NOV; SSC 23**
See also CA 85-88; 145; CANR 32, 63; DLB 113; HW; MTCW

O Nuallain, Brian 1911-1966
See O'Brien, Flann
See also CA 21-22; 25-28R; CAP 2

Ophuls, Max 1902-1957 .... **TCLC 79**
See also CA 113

Opie, Amelia 1769-1853 .... **NCLC 65**
See also DLB 116, 159

Oppen, George 1908-1984 .... **CLC 7, 13, 34**
See also CA 13-16R; 113; CANR 8; DLB 5, 165

Oppenheim, E(dward) Phillips 1866-1946 **TCLC 45**
See also CA 111; DLB 70

Opuls, Max
See Ophuls, Max

Origen c. 185-c. 254 .... **CMLC 19**

Orlovitz, Gil 1918-1973 .... **CLC 22**
See also CA 77-80; 45-48; DLB 2, 5

Orris
See Ingelow, Jean

Ortega y Gasset, Jose 1883-1955 ..... **TCLC 9; DAM MULT; HLC**
See also CA 106; 130; HW; MTCW

Ortese, Anna Maria 1914- .... **CLC 89**
See also DLB 177

Ortiz, Simon J(oseph) 1941- ... **CLC 45; DAM MULT, POET; PC 17**
See also CA 134; DLB 120, 175; NNAL

Orton, Joe .... **CLC 4, 13, 43; DC 3**
See also Orton, John Kingsley
See also CDBLB 1960 to Present; DLB 13

Orton, John Kingsley 1933-1967
See Orton, Joe
See also CA 85-88; CANR 35, 66; DAM DRAM; MTCW

Orwell, George .... **TCLC 2, 6, 15, 31, 51; DAB; WLC**
See also Blair, Eric (Arthur)
See also CDBLB 1945-1960; DLB 15, 98, 195

Osborne, David
See Silverberg, Robert

Osborne, George
See Silverberg, Robert

Osborne, John (James) 1929-1994 **CLC 1, 2, 5, 11, 45; DA; DAB; DAC; DAM DRAM, MST; WLC**
See also CA 13-16R; 147; CANR 21, 56; CDBLB 1945-1960; DLB 13; MTCW

Osborne, Lawrence 1958- .... **CLC 50**

Oshima, Nagisa 1932- .... **CLC 20**
See also CA 116; 121

Oskison, John Milton 1874-1947 ... **TCLC 35; DAM MULT**
See also CA 144; DLB 175; NNAL

Ossoli, Sarah Margaret (Fuller marchesa d') 1810-1850
See Fuller, Margaret
See also SATA 25

Ostrovsky, Alexander 1823-1886 ... **NCLC 30, 57**

Otero, Blas de 1916-1979 .... **CLC 11**
See also CA 89-92; DLB 134

Otto, Whitney 1955- .... **CLC 70**
See also CA 140

Ouida .... **TCLC 43**
See also De La Ramee, (Marie) Louise
See also DLB 18, 156

Ousmane, Sembene 1923- .... **CLC 66; BLC**
See also BW 1; CA 117; 125; MTCW

Ovid 43B.C.-18(?) **CMLC 7; DAM POET; PC 2**

Owen, Hugh
See Faust, Frederick (Schiller)

Owen, Wilfred (Edward Salter) 1893-1918 **TCLC 5, 27; DA; DAB; DAC; DAM MST, POET; PC 19; WLC**
See also CA 104; 141; CDBLB 1914-1945; DLB 20

Owens, Rochelle 1936- .... **CLC 8**
See also CA 17-20R; CAAS 2; CANR 39

Oz, Amos 1939- ... **CLC 5, 8, 11, 27, 33, 54; DAM NOV**
See also CA 53-56; CANR 27, 47, 65; MTCW

Ozick, Cynthia 1928- **CLC 3, 7, 28, 62; DAM NOV, POP; SSC 15**
See also BEST 90:1; CA 17-20R; CANR 23, 58; DLB 28, 152; DLBY 82; INT CANR-23; MTCW

Ozu, Yasujiro 1903-1963 .... **CLC 16**
See also CA 112

Pacheco, C.
See Pessoa, Fernando (Antonio Nogueira)

Pa Chin .... **CLC 18**
See also Li Fei-kan

Pack, Robert 1929- .... **CLC 13**
See also CA 1-4R; CANR 3, 44; DLB 5

Padgett, Lewis
See Kuttner, Henry

Padilla (Lorenzo), Heberto 1932- ...... **CLC 38**
See also AITN 1; CA 123; 131; HW

Page, Jimmy 1944- .... **CLC 12**

Page, Louise 1955- .... **CLC 40**
See also CA 140

Page, P(atricia) K(athleen) 1916- ... **CLC 7, 18; DAC; DAM MST; PC 12**
See also CA 53-56; CANR 4, 22, 65; DLB 68; MTCW

Page, Thomas Nelson 1853-1922 .... **SSC 23**
See also CA 118; DLB 12, 78; DLBD 13

Pagels, Elaine Hiesey 1943- .... **CLC 104**
See also CA 45-48; CANR 2, 24, 51

Paget, Violet 1856-1935
See Lee, Vernon
See also CA 104

Paget-Lowe, Henry
See Lovecraft, H(oward) P(hillips)

Paglia, Camille (Anna) 1947- .... **CLC 68**
See also CA 140

Paige, Richard
See Koontz, Dean R(ay)

Paine, Thomas 1737-1809 .... **NCLC 62**
See also CDALB 1640-1865; DLB 31, 43, 73, 158

Pakenham, Antonia
See Fraser, (Lady) Antonia (Pakenham)

Palamas, Kostes 1859-1943 .... **TCLC 5**
See also CA 105

Palazzeschi, Aldo 1885-1974 .... **CLC 11**
See also CA 89-92; 53-56; DLB 114

Paley, Grace 1922- ... **CLC 4, 6, 37; DAM POP; SSC 8**
See also CA 25-28R; CANR 13, 46; DLB 28; INT CANR-13; MTCW

Palin, Michael (Edward) 1943- .... **CLC 21**
See also Monty Python
See also CA 107; CANR 35; SATA 67

Palliser, Charles 1947- .... **CLC 65**
See also CA 136

Palma, Ricardo 1833-1919 .... **TCLC 29**

Pancake, Breece Dexter 1952-1979
See Pancake, Breece D'J
See also CA 123; 109

Peckinpah, (David) Sam(uel) 1925-1984 ... **CLC 20**
See also CA 109; 114

Pedersen, Knut 1859-1952
See Hamsun, Knut
See also CA 104; 119; CANR 63; MTCW

Peeslake, Gaffer
See Durrell, Lawrence (George)

Peguy, Charles Pierre 1873-1914 .... **TCLC 10**
See also CA 107

Pena, Ramon del Valle y
See Valle-Inclan, Ramon (Maria) del

Pendennis, Arthur Esquir
See Thackeray, William Makepeace

Penn, William 1644-1718 .... **LC 25**
See also DLB 24

PEPECE
See Prado (Calvo), Pedro

Pepys, Samuel 1633-1703 ... **LC 11; DA; DAB;**
DAC; DAM MST; WLC
See also CDBLB 1660-1789; DLB 101

Percy, Walker 1916-1990 ... **CLC 2, 3, 6, 8, 14,**
18, 47, 65; DAM NOV, POP
See also CA 1-4R; 131; CANR 1, 23, 64; DLB
2; DLBY 80, 90; MTCW

Perec, Georges 1936-1982 .... **CLC 56**
See also CA 141; DLB 83

Pereda (y Sanchez de Porrua), Jose Maria de
1833-1906 .... **TCLC 16**
See also CA 117

Pereda y Porrua, Jose Maria de
See Pereda (y Sanchez de Porrua), Jose Maria de

Peregoy, George Weems
See Mencken, H(enry) L(ouis)

Perelman, S(idney) J(oseph) 1904-1979 ... **CLC**
3, 5, 9, 15, 23, 44, 49; DAM DRAM
See also AITN 1, 2; CA 73-76; 89-92; CANR
18; DLB 11, 44; MTCW

Peret, Benjamin 1899-1959 .... **TCLC 20**
See also CA 117

Peretz, Isaac Loeb 1851(?)-1915 ... **TCLC 16;**
SSC 26
See also CA 109

Peretz, Yitzkhok Leibush
See Peretz, Isaac Loeb

Perez Galdos, Benito 1843-1920 .... **TCLC**
27
See also CA 125; 153; HW

Perrault, Charles 1628-1703 .... **LC 2**
See also MAICYA; SATA 25

Perry, Brighton
See Sherwood, Robert E(mmet)

Perse, St.-John .... **CLC 4, 11, 46**
See also Leger, (Marie-Rene Auguste) Alexis
Saint-Leger

Perutz, Leo 1882-1957 .... **TCLC 60**
See also DLB 81

Peseenz, Tulio F.
See Lopez y Fuentes, Gregorio

Pesetsky, Bette 1932- .... **CLC 28**
See also CA 133; DLB 130

Peshkov, Alexei Maximovich 1868-1936
See Gorky, Maxim
See also CA 105; 141; DA; DAC; DAM DRAM,
MST, NOV

Pessoa, Fernando (Antonio Nogueira) 1898-1935
TCLC 27; HLC; PC 20
See also CA 125

Peterkin, Julia Mood 1880-1961 .... **CLC 31**
See also CA 102; DLB 9

Peters, Joan K(aren) 1945- .... **CLC 39**
See also CA 158

Peters, Robert L(ouis) 1924- .... **CLC 7**
See also CA 13-16R; CAAS 8; DLB 105

Petofi, Sandor 1823-1849 .... **NCLC 21**

Petrakis, Harry Mark 1923- .... **CLC 3**
See also CA 9-12R; CANR 4, 30

Petrarch 1304-1374 ... **CMLC 20; DAM POET; PC 8**

Petrov, Evgeny .... **TCLC 21**
See also Kataev, Evgeny Petrovich

Petry, Ann (Lane) 1908-1997 ..... **CLC 1, 7, 18**
See also BW 1; CA 5-8R; 157; CAAS 6; CANR
4, 46; CLR 12; DLB 76; JRDA; MAICYA;
MTCW; SATA 5; SATA-Obit 94

Petursson, Halligrimur 1614-1674 .... **LC 8**

Phaedrus 18(?)B.C.-55(?) .... **CMLC 25**

Philips, Katherine 1632-1664 .... **LC 30**
See also DLB 131

Philipson, Morris H. 1926- .... **CLC 53**
See also CA 1-4R; CANR 4

Phillips, Caryl 1958- ... **CLC 96; DAM MULT**
See also BW 2; CA 141; CANR 63; DLB 157

Phillips, David Graham 1867-1911   **TCLC 44**
See also CA 108; DLB 9, 12

Phillips, Jack
See Sandburg, Carl (August)

Phillips, Jayne Anne 1952- ..   **CLC 15, 33;**
SSC 16
See also CA 101; CANR 24, 50; DLBY 80; INT
CANR-24; MTCW

Phillips, Richard
See Dick, Philip K(indred)

Phillips, Robert (Schaeffer) 1938- ..... **CLC 28**
See also CA 17-20R; CAAS 13; CANR 8; DLB
105

Phillips, Ward
See Lovecraft, H(oward) P(hillips)

Piccolo, Lucio 1901-1969 .... **CLC 13**
See also CA 97-100; DLB 114

Pickthall, Marjorie L(owry) C(hristie) 1883-
1922 .... **TCLC 21**
See also CA 107; DLB 92

Pico della Mirandola, Giovanni 1463-1494
LC 15

Piercy, Marge 1936- .... **CLC 3, 6, 14, 18,**
27, 62
See also CA 21-24R; CAAS 1; CANR 13, 43,
66; DLB 120; MTCW

Piers, Robert
See Anthony, Piers

Pieyre de Mandiargues, Andre 1909-1991
See Mandiargues, Andre Pieyre de
See also CA 103; 136; CANR 22

Pilnyak, Boris .... **TCLC 23**
See also Vogau, Boris Andreyevich

Pincherle, Alberto 1907-1990 ..... **CLC 11, 18;**
DAM NOV
See also Moravia, Alberto
See also CA 25-28R; 132; CANR 33, 63; MTCW

Pinckney, Darryl 1953- .... **CLC 76**
See also BW 2; CA 143

Pindar 518B.C.-446B.C. ..... **CMLC 12; PC 19**
See also DLB 176

Pineda, Cecile 1942- .... **CLC 39**
See also CA 118

Pinero, Arthur Wing 1855-1934 .... **TCLC 32;**
DAM DRAM
See also CA 110; 153; DLB 10

Pinero, Miguel (Antonio Gomez) 1946-1988
CLC 4, 55
See also CA 61-64; 125; CANR 29; HW

Pinget, Robert 1919-1997 .... **CLC 7, 13, 37**
See also CA 85-88; 160; DLB 83

Pink Floyd
See Barrett, (Roger) Syd; Gilmour, David; Mason, Nick; Waters, Roger; Wright, Rick

Pinkney, Edward 1802-1828 .... **NCLC 31**

Pinkwater, Daniel Manus 1941- .... **CLC 35**
See also Pinkwater, Manus
See also AAYA 1; CA 29-32R; CANR 12, 38;
CLR 4; JRDA; MAICYA; SAAS 3; SATA 46,
76

Pinkwater, Manus
See Pinkwater, Daniel Manus
See also SATA 8

Pound, Ezra (Weston Loomis) 1885-1972
CLC 1, 2, 3, 4, 5, 7, 10, 13, 18, 34, 48, 50;
DA; DAB; DAC; DAM MST, POET; PC 4;
WLC
See also CA 5-8R; 37-40R; CANR 40; CDALB
1917-1929; DLB 4, 45, 63; DLBD 15;
MTCW

Povod, Reinaldo 1959-1994 .... **CLC 44**
See also CA 136; 146

Powell, Adam Clayton, Jr. 1908-1972 . **CLC**
89; BLC; DAM MULT
See also BW 1; CA 102; 33-36R

Powell, Anthony (Dymoke) 1905- **CLC 1, 3,**
7, 9, 10, 31
See also CA 1-4R; CANR 1, 32, 62; CDBLB
1945-1960; DLB 15; MTCW

Powell, Dawn 1897-1965 .... **CLC 66**
See also CA 5-8R; DLBY 97

Powell, Padgett 1952- .... **CLC 34**
See also CA 126; CANR 63

Power, Susan 1961- .... **CLC 91**

Powers, J(ames) F(arl) 1917- **CLC 1, 4, 8, 57;**
SSC 4
See also CA 1-4R; CANR 2, 61; DLB 130;
MTCW

Powers, John J(ames) 1945-
See Powers, John R.
See also CA 69-72

Powers, John R. .... **CLC 66**
See also Powers, John J(ames)

Powers, Richard (S.) 1957- .... **CLC 93**
See also CA 148

Pownall, David 1938- .... **CLC 10**
See also CA 89-92; CAAS 18; CANR 49; DLB 14

Powys, John Cowper 1872-1963 **CLC 7, 9, 15, 46**
See also CA 85-88; DLB 15; MTCW

Powys, T(heodore) F(rancis) 1875-1953
TCLC 9
See also CA 106; DLB 36, 162

Prado (Calvo), Pedro 1886-1952 .... **TCLC 75**
See also CA 131; HW

Prager, Emily 1952- .... **CLC 56**

Pratt, E(dwin) J(ohn) 1883(?)-1964 . **CLC 19;**
DAC; DAM POET
See also CA 141; 93-96; DLB 92

Premchand .... **TCLC 21**
See also Srivastava, Dhanpat Rai

Preussler, Otfried 1923- .... **CLC 17**
See also CA 77-80; SATA 24

Prevert, Jacques (Henri Marie) 1900-1977
CLC 15
See also CA 77-80; 69-72; CANR 29, 61;
MTCW; SATA-Obit 30

Prevost, Abbe (Antoine Francois) 1697-1763
LC 1

Price, (Edward) Reynolds 1933- **CLC 3, 6, 13,**
43, 50, 63; DAM NOV; SSC 22
See also CA 1-4R; CANR 1, 37, 57; DLB 2; INT
CANR-37

Price, Richard 1949- .... **CLC 6, 12**
See also CA 49-52; CANR 3; DLBY 81

Prichard, Katharine Susannah 1883-1969
CLC 46
See also CA 11-12; CANR 33; CAP 1; MTCW;
SATA 66

Priestley, J(ohn) B(oynton) 1894-1984 ... **CLC**
2, 5, 9, 34; DAM DRAM, NOV
See also CA 9-12R; 113; CANR 33; CDBLB 1914-
1945; DLB 10, 34, 77, 100, 139; DLBY 84;
MTCW

Prince 1958(?)- .... **CLC 35**

Prince, F(rank) T(empleton) 1912- .... **CLC 22**
See also CA 101; CANR 43; DLB 20

Prince Kropotkin
See Kropotkin, Peter (Aleksieevich)

Prior, Matthew 1664-1721 .... **LC 4**
See also DLB 95

Prishvin, Mikhail 1873-1954 .... **TCLC 75**

Pritchard, William H(arrison) 1932- ... **CLC 34**
See also CA 65-68; CANR 23; DLB 111

Pritchett, V(ictor) S(awdon) 1900-1997 ... **CLC**
5, 13, 15, 41; DAM NOV; SSC 14
See also CA 61-64; 157; CANR 31, 63; DLB 15,
139; MTCW

Private 19022
See Manning, Frederic

Probst, Mark 1925- .... **CLC 59**
See also CA 130

Prokosch, Frederic 1908-1989 .... **CLC 4, 48**
See also CA 73-76; 128; DLB 48

Prophet, The
See Dreiser, Theodore (Herman Albert)

Prose, Francine 1947- .... **CLC 45**
See also CA 109; 112; CANR 46

Proudhon
See Cunha, Euclides (Rodrigues Pimenta) da

Proulx, Annie
See Proulx, E(dna) Annie

Proulx, E(dna) Annie 1935- ... **CLC 81; DAM**
POP
See also CA 145; CANR 65

Proust, (Valentin-Louis-George-Eugene-) Marcel
1871-1922 .... **TCLC 7, 13, 33;**
DA; DAB; DAC; DAM MST, NOV; WLC
See also CA 104; 120; DLB 65; MTCW

Prowler, Harley
See Masters, Edgar Lee

Prus, Boleslaw 1845-1912 .... **TCLC**
48

Pryor, Richard (Franklin Lenox Thomas) 1940-
CLC 26
See also CA 122

Przybyszewski, Stanislaw 1868-1927 ..... **TCLC**
36
See also CA 160; DLB 66

Pteleon
See Grieve, C(hristopher) M(urray)
See also DAM POET

Puckett, Lute
See Masters, Edgar Lee

Puig, Manuel 1932-1990 .... **CLC 3, 5,**
10, 28, 65; DAM MULT; HLC
See also CA 45-48; CANR 2, 32, 63; DLB 113;
HW; MTCW

Pulitzer, Joseph 1847-1911 .... **TCLC 76**
See also CA 114; DLB 23

Purdy, Al(fred Wellington) 1918- ... **CLC 3, 6,**
14, 50; DAC; DAM MST, POET
See also CA 81-84; CAAS 17; CANR 42, 66;
DLB 88

Purdy, James (Amos) 1923- ... **CLC 2, 4, 10, 28,**
52
See also CA 33-36R; CAAS 1; CANR 19, 51;
DLB 2; INT CANR-19; MTCW

Pure, Simon
See Swinnerton, Frank Arthur

Pushkin, Alexander (Sergeyevich) 1799-1837
NCLC 3, 27; DA; DAB; DAC; DAM
DRAM, MST, POET; PC 10; SSC 27; WLC
See also SATA 61

P'u Sung-ling 1640-1715 .... **LC 3**

Putnam, Arthur Lee
See Alger, Horatio, Jr.

Puzo, Mario 1920- ... **CLC 1, 2, 6, 36, 107; DAM**
NOV, POP
See also CA 65-68; CANR 4, 42, 65; DLB 6;
MTCW

Pygge, Edward
See Barnes, Julian (Patrick)

Pyle, Ernest Taylor 1900-1945
See Pyle, Ernie
See also CA 115; 160

Pyle, Ernie 1900-1945 .... **TCLC 75**
See also Pyle, Ernest Taylor
See also DLB 29

Pym, Barbara (Mary Crampton) 1913-1980
CLC 13, 19, 37
See also CA 13-14; 97-100; CANR 13, 34; CAP
1; DLB 14; DLBY 87; MTCW

Pynchon, Thomas (Ruggles, Jr.) 1937-   **CLC 2, 3, 6, 9, 11, 18, 33, 62, 72; DA; DAB; DAC; DAM MST, NOV, POP; SSC 14; WLC**
See also BEST 90:2; CA 17-20R; CANR 22, 46; DLB 2, 173; MTCW

Pythagoras c. 570B.C.-c. 500B.C. ... **CMLC 22**
See also DLB 176

Qian Zhongshu
See Ch'ien Chung-shu

Qroll
See Dagerman, Stig (Halvard)

Quarrington, Paul (Lewis) 1953- .... **CLC 65**
See also CA 129; CANR 62

Quasimodo, Salvatore 1901-1968 ...... **CLC 10**
See also CA 13-16; 25-28R; CAP 1; DLB 114; MTCW

Quay, Stephen 1947- .... **CLC 95**

Quay, Timothy 1947- .... **CLC 95**

Queen, Ellery ....**CLC 3, 11**
See also Dannay, Frederic; Davidson, Avram; Lee, Manfred B(ennington); Marlowe, Stephen; Sturgeon, Theodore (Hamilton); Vance, John Holbrook

Queen, Ellery, Jr.
See Dannay, Frederic; Lee, Manfred B(ennington)

Queneau, Raymond 1903-1976   **CLC 2, 5, 10, 42**
See also CA 77-80; 69-72; CANR 32; DLB 72; MTCW

Quevedo, Francisco de 1580-1645 .... **LC 23**

Quiller-Couch, SirArthur Thomas 1863-1944 **TCLC 53**
See also CA 118; DLB 135, 153, 190

Quin, Ann (Marie) 1936-1973 .... **CLC 6**
See also CA 9-12R; 45-48; DLB 14

Quinn, Martin
See Smith, Martin Cruz

Quinn, Peter 1947- .... **CLC 91**

Quinn, Simon
See Smith, Martin Cruz

Quiroga, Horacio (Sylvestre) 1878-1937 **TCLC 20; DAM MULT; HLC**
See also CA 117; 131; HW; MTCW

Quoirez, Francoise 1935- .... **CLC 9**
See also Sagan, Francoise
See also CA 49-52; CANR 6, 39; MTCW

Raabe, Wilhelm 1831-1910 .... **TCLC 45**
See also DLB 129

Rabe, David (William) 1940- .... **CLC 4, 8, 33; DAM DRAM**
See also CA 85-88; CABS 3; CANR 59; DLB 7

Rabelais, Francois 1483-1553 ...   **LC 5; DA; DAB; DAC; DAM MST; WLC**

Rabinovitch, Sholem 1859-1916
See Aleichem, Sholom
See also CA 104

Rachilde 1860-1953 .... **TCLC 67**
See also DLB 123, 192

Racine, Jean 1639-1699 .. **LC 28; DAB; DAM MST**

Radcliffe, Ann (Ward) 1764-1823 **NCLC 6, 55**
See also DLB 39, 178

Radiguet, Raymond 1903-1923 .... **TCLC 29**
See also CA 162; DLB 65

Radnoti, Miklos 1909-1944 .... **TCLC 16**
See also CA 118

Rado, James 1939-............................... **CLC 17**
See also CA 105

Radvanyi, Netty 1900-1983
See Seghers, Anna
See also CA 85-88; 110

Rae, Ben
See Griffiths, Trevor

Raeburn, John (Hay) 1941- .... **CLC 34**
See also CA 57-60

Ragni, Gerome 1942-1991 .... **CLC 17**
See also CA 105; 134

Rahv, Philip 1908-1973 .... **CLC 24**
See also Greenberg, Ivan
See also DLB 137

Raimund, Ferdinand Jakob 1790-1836 **NCLC 69**
See also DLB 90

Raine, Craig 1944- .... **CLC 32, 103**
See also CA 108; CANR 29, 51; DLB 40

Raine, Kathleen (Jessie) 1908- .... **CLC 7, 45**
See also CA 85-88; CANR 46; DLB 20; MTCW

Rainis, Janis 1865-1929 .... **TCLC 29**

Rakosi, Carl 1903- .... **CLC 47**
See also Rawley, Callman
See also CAAS 5; DLB 193

Raleigh, Richard
See Lovecraft, H(oward) P(hillips)

Raleigh, Sir Walter 1554(?)-1618 ... **LC 31, 39**
See also CDBLB Before 1660; DLB 172

Rallentando, H. P.
See Sayers, Dorothy L(eigh)

Ramal, Walter
See de la Mare, Walter (John)

Ramon, Juan
See Jimenez (Mantecon), Juan Ramon

Ramos, Graciliano 1892-1953 .... **TCLC 32**

Rampersad, Arnold 1941- .... **CLC 44**
See also BW 2; CA 127; 133; DLB 111; INT 133

Rampling, Anne
See Rice, Anne

Ramsay, Allan 1684(?)-1758 .... **LC 29**
See also DLB 95

Ramuz, Charles-Ferdinand 1878-1947 ... **TCLC 33**
See also CA 165

Rand, Ayn 1905-1982 .... **CLC 3, 30, 44, 79; DA; DAC; DAM MST, NOV, POP; WLC**
See also AAYA 10; CA 13-16R; 105; CANR 27; MTCW

Randall, Dudley (Felker) 1914- ... **CLC 1; BLC; DAM MULT**
See also BW 1; CA 25-28R; CANR 23; DLB 41

Randall, Robert
See Silverberg, Robert

Ranger, Ken
See Creasey, John

Ransom, John Crowe 1888-1974 ... **CLC 2, 4, 5, 11, 24; DAM POET**
See also CA 5-8R; 49-52; CANR 6, 34; DLB 45, 63; MTCW

Rao, Raja 1909- .... **CLC 25, 56; DAM NOV**
See also CA 73-76; CANR 51; MTCW

Raphael, Frederic (Michael) 1931- ...... **CLC 2, 14**
See also CA 1-4R; CANR 1; DLB 14

Ratcliffe, James P.
See Mencken, H(enry) L(ouis)

Rathbone, Julian 1935- .... **CLC 41**
See also CA 101; CANR 34

Rattigan, Terence (Mervyn) 1911-1977 ... **CLC 7; DAM DRAM**
See also CA 85-88; 73-76; CDBLB 1945-1960; DLB 13; MTCW

Ratushinskaya, Irina 1954- .... **CLC 54**
See also CA 129; CANR 68

Raven, Simon (Arthur Noel) 1927- .... **CLC 14**
See also CA 81-84

Ravenna, Michael
See Welty, Eudora

Rawley, Callman 1903-
See Rakosi, Carl
See also CA 21-24R; CANR 12, 32

Rawlings, Marjorie Kinnan 1896-1953 ... **TCLC 4**
See also AAYA 20; CA 104; 137; DLB 9, 22, 102; JRDA; MAICYA; YABC 1

Ray, Satyajit 1921-1992 .... **CLC 16, 76; DAM MULT**
See also CA 114; 137

Read, Herbert Edward 1893-1968 .... **CLC 4**
See also CA 85-88; 25-28R; DLB 20, 149

Read, Piers Paul 1941- .... **CLC 4, 10, 25**
See also CA 21-24R; CANR 38; DLB 14; SATA 21

Reade, Charles 1814-1884 .... **NCLC 2**
See also DLB 21

Reade, Hamish
See Gray, Simon (James Holliday)

Reading, Peter 1946- .... **CLC 47**
See also CA 103; CANR 46; DLB 40

Reaney, James 1926- **CLC 13; DAC; DAM MST**
See also CA 41-44R; CAAS 15; CANR 42; DLB 68; SATA 43

Rebreanu, Liviu 1885-1944 .... **TCLC 28**
See also CA 165

Rechy, John (Francisco) 1934-   **CLC 1, 7, 14, 18, 107; DAM MULT; HLC**
See also CA 5-8R; CAAS 4; CANR 6, 32, 64; DLB 122; DLBY 82; HW; INT CANR-6

Redcam, Tom 1870-1933 .... **TCLC 25**

Reddin, Keith .... **CLC 67**

Redgrove, Peter (William) 1932- ... **CLC 6, 41**
See also CA 1-4R; CANR 3, 39; DLB 40

Redmon, Anne .... **CLC 22**
See also Nightingale, Anne Redmon
See also DLBY 86

Reed, Eliot
See Ambler, Eric

Reed, Ishmael 1938-   **CLC 2, 3, 5, 6, 13, 32, 60; BLC; DAM MULT**
See also BW 2; CA 21-24R; CANR 25, 48; DLB 2, 5, 33, 169; DLBD 8; MTCW

Reed, John (Silas) 1887-1920 .... **TCLC 9**
See also CA 106

Reed, Lou .... **CLC 21**
See also Firbank, Louis

Reeve, Clara 1729-1807 .... **NCLC 19**
See also DLB 39

Reich, Wilhelm 1897-1957 .... **TCLC 57**

Reid, Christopher (John) 1949- .... **CLC 33**
See also CA 140; DLB 40

Reid, Desmond
See Moorcock, Michael (John)

Reid Banks, Lynne 1929-
See Banks, Lynne Reid
See also CA 1-4R; CANR 6, 22, 38; CLR 24; JRDA; MAICYA; SATA 22, 75

Reilly, William K.
See Creasey, John

Reiner, Max
See Caldwell, (Janet Miriam) Taylor (Holland)

Reis, Ricardo
See Pessoa, Fernando (Antonio Nogueira)

Remarque, Erich Maria 1898-1970 . **CLC 21; DA; DAB; DAC; DAM MST, NOV**
See also CA 77-80; 29-32R; DLB 56; MTCW

Remizov, A.
See Remizov, Aleksei (Mikhailovich)

Remizov, A. M.
See Remizov, Aleksei (Mikhailovich)

Remizov, Aleksei (Mikhailovich) 1877-1957...**TCLC 27**
See also CA 125; 133

Renan, Joseph Ernest 1823-1892 .... **NCLC 26**

Renard, Jules 1864-1910 .... **TCLC 17**
See also CA 117

Renault, Mary .... **CLC 3, 11, 17**
See also Challans, Mary
See also DLBY 83

Rendell, Ruth (Barbara) 1930- .. **CLC 28, 48; DAM POP**
See also Vine, Barbara
See also CA 109; CANR 32, 52; DLB 87; INT CANR-32; MTCW

Renoir, Jean 1894-1979 .... **CLC 20**
See also CA 129; 85-88

Resnais, Alain 1922- .... **CLC 16**

Reverdy, Pierre 1889-1960 .... **CLC 53**
See also CA 97-100; 89-92

Rexroth, Kenneth 1905-1982 ... **CLC 1, 2, 6, 11, 22, 49; DAM POET; PC 20**
See also CA 5-8R; 107; CANR 14, 34, 63; CDALB 1941-1968; DLB 16, 48, 165; DLBY 82; INT CANR-14; MTCW

Reyes, Alfonso 1889-1959 .... **TCLC 33**
See also CA 131; HW

Reyes y Basoalto, Ricardo Eliecer Neftali
See Neruda, Pablo

Reymont, Wladyslaw (Stanislaw) 1868(?)-1925   **TCLC 5**
See also CA 104

Reynolds, Jonathan 1942- .... **CLC 6, 38**
See also CA 65-68; CANR 28

Reynolds, Joshua 1723-1792 .... **LC 15**
See also DLB 104

Reynolds, Michael Shane 1937- .... **CLC 44**
See also CA 65-68; CANR 9

Reznikoff, Charles 1894-1976 .... **CLC 9**
See also CA 33-36; 61-64; CAP 2; DLB 28, 45

Rezzori (d'Arezzo), Gregor von 1914- **CLC 25**
See also CA 122; 136

Rhine, Richard
See Silverstein, Alvin

Rhodes, Eugene Manlove 1869-1934 ... **TCLC 53**

R'hoone
See Balzac, Honore de

Rhys, Jean 1890(?)-1979 ... **CLC 2, 4, 6, 14, 19, 51; DAM NOV; SSC 21**
See also CA 25-28R; 85-88; CANR 35, 62; CDBLB 1945-1960; DLB 36, 117, 162; MTCW

Ribeiro, Darcy 1922-1997 .... **CLC 34**
See also CA 33-36R; 156

Ribeiro, Joao Ubaldo (Osorio Pimentel) 1941-   **CLC 10, 67**
See also CA 81-84

Ribman, Ronald (Burt) 1932- .... **CLC 7**
See also CA 21-24R; CANR 46

Ricci, Nino 1959- .... **CLC 70**
See also CA 137

Rice, Anne 1941- .... **CLC 41; DAM POP**
See also AAYA 9; BEST 89:2; CA 65-68; CANR 12, 36, 53

Rice, Elmer (Leopold) 1892-1967   **CLC 7, 49; DAM DRAM**
See also CA 21-22; 25-28R; CAP 2; DLB 4, 7; MTCW

Rice, Tim(othy Miles Bindon) 1944- . **CLC 21**
See also CA 103; CANR 46

Rich, Adrienne (Cecile) 1929-   **CLC 3, 6, 7, 11, 18, 36, 73, 76; DAM POET; PC 5**
See also CA 9-12R; CANR 20, 53; DLB 5, 67; MTCW

Rich, Barbara
See Graves, Robert (von Ranke)

Rich, Robert
See Trumbo, Dalton

Richard, Keith .... **CLC 17**
See also Richards, Keith

Richards, David Adams 1950-   **CLC 59; DAC**
See also CA 93-96; CANR 60; DLB 53

Richards, I(vor) A(rmstrong) 1893-1979   **CLC 14, 24**
See also CA 41-44R; 89-92; CANR 34; DLB 27

Richards, Keith 1943-
See Richard, Keith
See also CA 107

Richardson, Anne
See Roiphe, Anne (Richardson)

Richardson, Dorothy Miller 1873-1957   **TCLC 3**
See also CA 104; DLB 36

Richardson, Ethel Florence (Lindesay) 1870-1946
See Richardson, Henry Handel
See also CA 105

Richardson, Henry Handel .... TCLC 4
See also Richardson, Ethel Florence (Lindesay)

Richardson, John 1796-1852   NCLC 55; DAC
See also DLB 99

Richardson, Samuel 1689-1761 ..... LC 1; DA;
DAB; DAC; DAM MST, NOV; WLC
See also CDBLB 1660-1789; DLB 39

Richler, Mordecai 1931-   CLC 3, 5, 9, 13,
18, 46, 70; DAC; DAM MST, NOV
See also AITN 1; CA 65-68; CANR 31, 62; CLR
17; DLB 53; MAICYA; MTCW; SATA 44, 98;
SATA-Brief 27

Richter, Conrad (Michael) 1890-1968 CLC 30
See also AAYA 21; CA 5-8R; 25-28R; CANR
23; DLB 9; MTCW; SATA 3

Ricostranza, Tom
See Ellis, Trey

Riddell, Charlotte 1832-1906 .... TCLC 40
See also CA 165; DLB 156

Riding, Laura .... CLC 3, 7
See also Jackson, Laura (Riding)

Riefenstahl, Berta Helene Amalia 1902-
See Riefenstahl, Leni
See also CA 108

Riefenstahl, Leni .... CLC 16
See also Riefenstahl, Berta Helene Amalia

Riffe, Ernest
See Bergman, (Ernst) Ingmar

Riggs, (Rolla) Lynn 1899-1954 ...... TCLC 56;
DAM MULT
See also CA 144; DLB 175; NNAL

Riis, Jacob A(ugust) 1849-1914 ...... TCLC 80
See also CA 113; DLB 23

Riley, James Whitcomb 1849-1916   TCLC
51; DAM POET
See also CA 118; 137; MAICYA; SATA 17

Riley, Tex
See Creasey, John

Rilke, Rainer Maria 1875-1926   TCLC 1, 6,
19; DAM POET; PC 2
See also CA 104; 132; CANR 62; DLB 81;
MTCW

Rimbaud, (Jean Nicolas) Arthur 1854-1891
NCLC 4, 35; DA; DAB; DAC; DAM MST,
POET; PC 3; WLC

Rinehart, Mary Roberts 1876-1958 TCLC 52
See also CA 108

Ringmaster, The
See Mencken, H(enry) L(ouis)

Ringwood, Gwen(dolyn Margaret) Pharis 1910-
1984 .... CLC 48
See also CA 148; 112; DLB 88

Rio, Michel 19(?)- .... CLC 43

Ritsos, Giannes
See Ritsos, Yannis

Ritsos, Yannis 1909-1990 .... CLC 6, 13, 31
See also CA 77-80; 133; CANR 39, 61; MTCW

Ritter, Erika 1948(?)- .... CLC 52

Rivera, Jose Eustasio 1889-1928 .... TCLC 35
See also CA 162; HW

Rivers, Conrad Kent 1933-1968 .... CLC 1
See also BW 1; CA 85-88; DLB 41

Rivers, Elfrida
See Bradley, Marion Zimmer

Riverside, John
See Heinlein, Robert A(nson)

Rizal, Jose 1861-1896 .... NCLC 27

Roa Bastos, Augusto (Antonio) 1917- .... C L C
45; DAM MULT; HLC
See also CA 131; DLB 113; HW

Robbe-Grillet, Alain 1922- ... CLC 1, 2, 4, 6, 8,
10, 14, 43
See also CA 9-12R; CANR 33, 65; DLB 83;
MTCW

Robbins, Harold 1916-1997 ....   CLC 5; DAM
NOV
See also CA 73-76; 162; CANR 26, 54; MTCW

Robbins, Thomas Eugene 1936-
See Robbins, Tom
See also CA 81-84; CANR 29, 59; DAM NOV,
POP; MTCW

Robbins, Tom .... CLC 9, 32, 64
See also Robbins, Thomas Eugene
See also BEST 90:3; DLBY 80

Robbins, Trina 1938- .... CLC 21
See also CA 128

Roberts, Charles G(eorge) D(ouglas) 1860-1943
TCLC 8
See also CA 105; CLR 33; DLB 92; SATA 88;
SATA-Brief 29

Roberts, Elizabeth Madox 1886-1941 ... TCLC
68
See also CA 111; DLB 9, 54, 102; SATA 33;
SATA-Brief 27

Roberts, Kate 1891-1985 .... CLC 15
See also CA 107; 116

Roberts, Keith (John Kingston) 1935- ... CLC
14
See also CA 25-28R; CANR 46

Roberts, Kenneth (Lewis) 1885-1957 TCLC 23
See also CA 109; DLB 9

Roberts, Michele (B.) 1949- .... CLC 48
See also CA 115; CANR 58

Robertson, Ellis
See Ellison, Harlan (Jay); Silverberg, Robert

Robertson, Thomas William 1829-1871
NCLC 35; DAM DRAM

Robeson, Kenneth
See Dent, Lester

Robinson, Edwin Arlington 1869-1935
TCLC 5; DA; DAC; DAM MST, POET; PC
1
See also CA 104; 133; CDALB 1865-1917; DLB
54; MTCW

Robinson, Henry Crabb 1775-1867   NCLC 15
See also DLB 107

Robinson, Jill 1936- .... CLC 10
See also CA 102; INT 102

Robinson, Kim Stanley 1952- .... CLC 34
See also CA 126

Robinson, Lloyd
See Silverberg, Robert

Robinson, Marilynne 1944- .... CLC 25
See also CA 116

Robinson, Smokey .... CLC 21
See also Robinson, William, Jr.

Robinson, William, Jr. 1940-
See Robinson, Smokey
See also CA 116

Robison, Mary 1949- .... CLC 42, 98
See also CA 113; 116; DLB 130; INT 116

Rod, Edouard 1857-1910 .... TCLC 52

Roddenberry, Eugene Wesley 1921-1991
See Roddenberry, Gene
See also CA 110; 135; CANR 37; SATA 45;
SATA-Obit 69

Roddenberry, Gene .... CLC 17
See also Roddenberry, Eugene Wesley
See also AAYA 5; SATA-Obit 69

Rodgers, Mary 1931- .... CLC 12
See also CA 49-52; CANR 8, 55; CLR 20; INT
CANR-8; JRDA; MAICYA; SATA 8

Rodgers, W(illiam) R(obert) 1909-1969 ... CLC 7
See also CA 85-88; DLB 20

Rodman, Eric
See Silverberg, Robert

Rodman, Howard 1920(?)-1985 .... CLC 65
See also CA 118

Rodman, Maia
See Wojciechowska, Maia (Teresa)

Rodriguez, Claudio 1934- .... CLC 10
See also DLB 134

Roelvaag, O(le) E(dvart) 1876-1931 **TCLC 17**
See also CA 117; DLB 9

Roethke, Theodore (Huebner) 1908-1963
**CLC 1, 3, 8, 11, 19, 46, 101; DAM POET;
PC 15**
See also CA 81-84; CABS 2; CDALB 1941-
1968; DLB 5; MTCW

Rogers, Samuel 1763-1855 .... **NCLC 69**
See also DLB 93

Rogers, Thomas Hunton 1927- .... **CLC 57**
See also CA 89-92; INT 89-92

Rogers, Will(iam Penn Adair) 1879-1935
TCLC 8, 71; DAM MULT
See also CA 105; 144; DLB 11; NNAL

Rogin, Gilbert 1929- .... **CLC 18**
See also CA 65-68; CANR 15

Rohan, Koda .... **TCLC 22**
See also Koda Shigeyuki

Rohlfs, Anna Katharine Green
See Green, Anna Katharine

Rohmer, Eric .... **CLC 16**
See also Scherer, Jean-Marie Maurice

Rohmer, Sax .... **TCLC 28**
See also Ward, Arthur Henry Sarsfield
See also DLB 70

Roiphe, Anne (Richardson) 1935- ... **CLC 3, 9**
See also CA 89-92; CANR 45; DLBY 80; INT
89-92

Rojas, Fernando de 1465-1541 .... **LC 23**

**Rolfe, Frederick (William Serafino Austin Lewis
Mary)** 1860-1913 .... **TCLC 12**
See also CA 107; DLB 34, 156

Rolland, Romain 1866-1944 .... **TCLC 23**
See also CA 118; DLB 65

Rolle, Richard c. 1300-c. 1349 .... **CMLC 21**
See also DLB 146

Rolvaag, O(le) E(dvart)
See Roelvaag, O(le) E(dvart)

Romain Arnaud, Saint
See Aragon, Louis

Romains, Jules 1885-1972 .... **CLC 7**
See also CA 85-88; CANR 34; DLB 65; MTCW

Romero, Jose Ruben 1890-1952 ..... **TCLC 14**
See also CA 114; 131; HW

Ronsard, Pierre de 1524-1585 ... **LC 6; PC 11**

Rooke, Leon 1934- .... **CLC 25, 34; DAM POP**
See also CA 25-28R; CANR 23, 53

Roosevelt, Theodore 1858-1919 ...... **TCLC 69**
See also CA 115; DLB 47, 186

Roper, William 1498-1578 .... **LC 10**

Roquelaure, A. N.
See Rice, Anne

Rosa, Joao Guimaraes 1908-1967 ...... **CLC 23**
See also CA 89-92; DLB 113

Rose, Wendy 1948- ... **CLC 85; DAM MULT;
PC 13**
See also CA 53-56; CANR 5, 51; DLB 175;
NNAL; SATA 12

Rosen, R. D.
See Rosen, Richard (Dean)

Rosen, Richard (Dean) 1949- .... **CLC 39**
See also CA 77-80; CANR 62; INT CANR-30

Rosenberg, Isaac 1890-1918 .... **TCLC 12**
See also CA 107; DLB 20

Rosenblatt, Joe .... **CLC 15**
See also Rosenblatt, Joseph

Rosenblatt, Joseph 1933-
See Rosenblatt, Joe
See also CA 89-92; INT 89-92

Rosenfeld, Samuel
See Tzara, Tristan

Rosenstock, Sami
See Tzara, Tristan

Rosenstock, Samuel
See Tzara, Tristan

Rosenthal, M(acha) L(ouis) 1917-1996 .... **CLC
28**
See also CA 1-4R; 152; CAAS 6; CANR 4, 51;
DLB 5; SATA 59

Ross, Barnaby
See Dannay, Frederic

Ross, Bernard L.
See Follett, Ken(neth Martin)

Ross, J. H.
See Lawrence, T(homas) E(dward)

Ross, Martin
See Martin, Violet Florence
See also DLB 135

Ross, (James) Sinclair 1908- ..**CLC 13; DAC;
DAM MST; SSC 24**
See also CA 73-76; DLB 88

Rossetti, Christina (Georgina) 1830-1894
**NCLC 2, 50, 66; DA; DAB; DAC; DAM
MST, POET; PC 7; WLC**
See also DLB 35, 163; MAICYA; SATA 20

Rossetti, Dante Gabriel 1828-1882 .... **NCLC
4; DA; DAB; DAC; DAM MST, POET;
WLC**
See also CDBLB 1832-1890; DLB 35

Rossner, Judith (Perelman) 1935- **CLC 6, 9, 29**
See also AITN 2; BEST 90:3; CA 17-20R;
CANR 18, 51; DLB 6; INT CANR-18;
MTCW

Rostand, Edmond (Eugene Alexis) 1868-1918
**TCLC 6, 37; DA; DAB; DAC; DAM
DRAM, MST**
See also CA 104; 126; DLB 192; MTCW

Roth, Henry 1906-1995 .... **CLC 2, 6, 11, 104**
See also CA 11-12; 149; CANR 38, 63; CAP 1;
DLB 28; MTCW

Roth, Philip (Milton) 1933- ... **CLC 1, 2, 3, 4, 6,
9, 15, 22, 31, 47, 66, 86; DA; DAB; DAC;
DAM MST, NOV, POP; SSC 26; WLC**
See also BEST 90:3; CA 1-4R; CANR 1, 22, 36,
55; CDALB 1968-1988; DLB 2, 28, 173;
DLBY 82; MTCW

Rothenberg, Jerome 1931- .... **CLC 6, 57**
See also CA 45-48; CANR 1; DLB 5, 193

Roumain, Jacques (Jean Baptiste) 1907-1944
TCLC 19; BLC; DAM MULT
See also BW 1; CA 117; 125

Rourke, Constance (Mayfield) 1885-1941
TCLC 12
See also CA 107; YABC 1

Rousseau, Jean-Baptiste 1671-1741 .... **LC 9**

Rousseau, Jean-Jacques 1712-1778 .. **LC 14,
36; DA; DAB; DAC; DAM MST; WLC**

Roussel, Raymond 1877-1933 .... **TCLC 20**
See also CA 117

Rovit, Earl (Herbert) 1927- .... **CLC 7**
See also CA 5-8R; CANR 12

Rowe, Nicholas 1674-1718 .... **LC 8**
See also DLB 84

Rowley, Ames Dorrance
See Lovecraft, H(oward) P(hillips)

Rowson, Susanna Haswell 1762(?)-1824
NCLC 5, 69
See also DLB 37

Roy, Arundhati 1960(?)- .... **CLC 109**
See also CA 163; DLBY 97

Roy, Gabrielle 1909-1983 ... **CLC 10, 14; DAB;
DAC; DAM MST**
See also CA 53-56; 110; CANR 5, 61; DLB 68;
MTCW

Royko, Mike 1932-1997 .... **CLC 109**
See also CA 89-92; 157; CANR 26

Rozewicz, Tadeusz 1921- ..... **CLC 9, 23; DAM
POET**
See also CA 108; CANR 36, 66; MTCW

Ruark, Gibbons 1941- .... **CLC 3**
See also CA 33-36R; CAAS 23; CANR 14, 31,
57; DLB 120

Rubens, Bernice (Ruth) 1923- ...... **CLC 19, 31**
See also CA 25-28R; CANR 33, 65; DLB 14; MTCW

Rubin, Harold
See Robbins, Harold

Salisbury, John
    See Caute, (John) David

Salter, James 1925- .... **CLC 7, 52, 59**
    See also CA 73-76; DLB 130

Saltus, Edgar (Everton) 1855-1921 .. **TCLC 8**
    See also CA 105

Saltykov, Mikhail Evgrafovich 1826-1889
    NCLC 16

Samarakis, Antonis 1919- .... **CLC 5**
    See also CA 25-28R; CAAS 16; CANR 36

Sanchez, Florencio 1875-1910 .... **TCLC 37**
    See also CA 153; HW

Sanchez, Luis Rafael 1936- .... **CLC 23**
    See also CA 128; DLB 145; HW

Sanchez, Sonia 1934- ...... **CLC 5; BLC; DAM
    MULT; PC 9**
    See also BW 2; CA 33-36R; CANR 24, 49; CLR
    18; DLB 41; DLBD 8; MAICYA; MTCW;
    SATA 22

Sand, George 1804-1876 ...**NCLC 2, 42, 57; DA;
    DAB; DAC; DAM MST, NOV; WLC**
    See also DLB 119, 192

Sandburg, Carl (August) 1878-1967 ... **CLC 1,
    4, 10, 15, 35; DA; DAB; DAC; DAM MST,
    POET; PC 2; WLC**
    See also AAYA 24; CA 5-8R; 25-28R; CANR
    35; CDALB 1865-1917; DLB 17, 54;
    MAICYA; MTCW; SATA 8

Sandburg, Charles
    See Sandburg, Carl (August)

Sandburg, Charles A.
    See Sandburg, Carl (August)

Sanders, (James) Ed(ward) 1939- ...... **CLC 53**
    See also CA 13-16R; CAAS 21; CANR 13, 44;
    DLB 16

Sanders, Lawrence 1920-1998 ... **CLC 41; DAM
    POP**
    See also BEST 89:4; CA 81-84; 165; CANR 33,
    62; MTCW

Sanders, Noah
    See Blount, Roy (Alton), Jr.

Sanders, Winston P.
    See Anderson, Poul (William)

Sandoz, Mari(e Susette) 1896-1966 ... **CLC 28**
    See also CA 1-4R; 25-28R; CANR 17, 64; DLB
    9; MTCW; SATA 5

Saner, Reg(inald Anthony) 1931- .... **CLC 9**
    See also CA 65-68

Sannazaro, Jacopo 1456(?)-1530 .... **LC 8**

Sansom, William 1912-1976 . **CLC 2, 6; DAM
    NOV; SSC 21**
    See also CA 5-8R; 65-68; CANR 42; DLB 139;
    MTCW

Santayana, George 1863-1952 .... **TCLC 40**
    See also CA 115; DLB 54, 71; DLBD 13

Santiago, Danny .... **CLC 33**
    See also James, Daniel (Lewis)
    See also DLB 122

Santmyer, Helen Hoover 1895-1986 ... **CLC 33**
    See also CA 1-4R; 118; CANR 15, 33; DLBY
    84; MTCW

Santoka, Taneda 1882-1940 .... **TCLC 72**

Santos, Bienvenido N(uqui) 1911-1996 ... **CLC
    22; DAM MULT**
    See also CA 101; 151; CANR 19, 46

Sapper .... **TCLC 44**
    See also McNeile, Herman Cyril

Sapphire 1950- .... **CLC 99**

Sappho fl. 6th cent. B.C.- .... **CMLC 3; DAM
    POET; PC 5**
    See also DLB 176

Sarduy, Severo 1937-1993 .... **CLC 6, 97**
    See also CA 89-92; 142; CANR 58; DLB 113;
    HW

Sargeson, Frank 1903-1982 .... **CLC 31**
    See also CA 25-28R; 106; CANR 38

Sarmiento, Felix Ruben Garcia
    See Dario, Ruben

Saroyan, William 1908-1981 ... **CLC 1, 8, 10, 29,
    34, 56; DA; DAB; DAC; DAM DRAM,
    MST, NOV; SSC 21; WLC**
    See also CA 5-8R; 103; CANR 30; DLB 7, 9, 86;
    DLBY 81; MTCW; SATA 23; SATA-Obit 24

Sarraute, Nathalie 1900- ... **CLC 1, 2, 4, 8, 10,
    31, 80**
    See also CA 9-12R; CANR 23, 66; DLB 83;
    MTCW

Sarton, (Eleanor) May 1912-1995 ... **CLC 4, 14,
    49, 91; DAM POET**
    See also CA 1-4R; 149; CANR 1, 34, 55; DLB
    48; DLBY 81; INT CANR-34; MTCW; SATA
    36; SATA-Obit 86

Sartre, Jean-Paul 1905-1980 ... **CLC 1, 4, 7, 9,
    13, 18, 24, 44, 50, 52; DA; DAB; DAC; DAM
    DRAM, MST, NOV; DC 3; WLC**
    See also CA 9-12R; 97-100; CANR 21; DLB 72;
    MTCW

Sassoon, Siegfried (Lorraine) 1886-1967
    **CLC 36; DAB; DAM MST, NOV, POET;
    PC 12**
    See also CA 104; 25-28R; CANR 36; DLB 20,
    191; MTCW

Satterfield, Charles
    See Pohl, Frederik

Saul, John (W. III) 1942- ... **CLC 46; DAM NOV,
    POP**
    See also AAYA 10; BEST 90:4; CA 81-84;
    CANR 16, 40; SATA 98

Saunders, Caleb
    See Heinlein, Robert A(nson)

Saura (Atares), Carlos 1932- .... **CLC 20**
    See also CA 114; 131; HW

Sauser-Hall, Frederic 1887-1961 .... **CLC 18**
    See also Cendrars, Blaise
    See also CA 102; 93-96; CANR 36, 62;
    MTCW

Saussure, Ferdinand de 1857-1913 ... **TCLC 49**

Savage, Catharine
    See Brosman, Catharine Savage

Savage, Thomas 1915- .... **CLC 40**
    See also CA 126; 132; CAAS 15; INT 132

Savan, Glenn 19(?)- .... **CLC 50**

Sayers, Dorothy L(eigh) 1893-1957 . **TCLC 2,
    15; DAM POP**
    See also CA 104; 119; CANR 60; CDBLB 1914-
    1945; DLB 10, 36, 77, 100; MTCW

Sayers, Valerie 1952- .... **CLC 50**
    See also CA 134; CANR 61

Sayles, John (Thomas) 1950- .... **CLC 7, 10, 14**
    See also CA 57-60; CANR 41; DLB 44

Scammell, Michael 1935- .... **CLC 34**
    See also CA 156

Scannell, Vernon 1922- .... **CLC 49**
    See also CA 5-8R; CANR 8, 24, 57; DLB 27;
    SATA 59

Scarlett, Susan
    See Streatfeild, (Mary) Noel

Schaeffer, Susan Fromberg 1941- .... **CLC 6,
    11, 22**
    See also CA 49-52; CANR 18, 65; DLB 28; MTCW;
    SATA 22

Schary, Jill
    See Robinson, Jill

Schell, Jonathan 1943- .... **CLC 35**
    See also CA 73-76; CANR 12

Schelling, Friedrich Wilhelm Joseph von 1775-
    1854 ....**NCLC 30**
    See also DLB 90

Schendel, Arthur van 1874-1946 .... **TCLC 56**

Scherer, Jean-Marie Maurice 1920-
    See Rohmer, Eric
    See also CA 110

Schevill, James (Erwin) 1920- .... **CLC 7**
    See also CA 5-8R; CAAS 12

Schiller, Friedrich 1759-1805 .. **NCLC 39, 69;
    DAM DRAM**
    See also DLB 94

Schisgal, Murray (Joseph) 1926- .... **CLC 6**
    See also CA 21-24R; CANR 48

Schlee, Ann 1934- .... **CLC 35**
    See also CA 101; CANR 29; SATA 44; SATA-
    Brief 36

Schlegel, August Wilhelm von 1767-1845
    NCLC 15
    See also DLB 94

Schlegel, Friedrich 1772-1829 .... **NCLC 45**
    See also DLB 90

Schlegel, Johann Elias (von) 1719(?)-1749 ... **LC 5**

Schlesinger, Arthur M(eier), Jr. 1917- ... **CLC 84**
    See also AITN 1; CA 1-4R; CANR 1, 28, 58;
    DLB 17; INT CANR-28; MTCW; SATA 61

Schmidt, Arno (Otto) 1914-1979 .... **CLC 56**
    See also CA 128; 109; DLB 69

Schmitz, Aron Hector 1861-1928
    See Svevo, Italo
    See also CA 104; 122; MTCW

Schnackenberg, Gjertrud 1953- .... **CLC 40**
    See also CA 116; DLB 120

Schneider, Leonard Alfred 1925-1966
    See Bruce, Lenny
    See also CA 89-92

Schnitzler, Arthur 1862-1931 ... **TCLC 4; SSC 15**
    See also CA 104; DLB 81, 118

Schoenberg, Arnold 1874-1951 .... **TCLC 75**
    See also CA 109

Schonberg, Arnold
    See Schoenberg, Arnold

Schopenhauer, Arthur 1788-1860 ... **NCLC 51**
    See also DLB 90

Schor, Sandra (M.) 1932(?)-1990 .... **CLC 65**
    See also CA 132

Schorer, Mark 1908-1977 .... **CLC 9**
    See also CA 5-8R; 73-76; CANR 7; DLB 103

Schrader, Paul (Joseph) 1946- .... **CLC 26**
    See also CA 37-40R; CANR 41; DLB 44

Schreiner, Olive (Emilie Albertina) 1855-1920
    TCLC 9
    See also CA 105; 154; DLB 18, 156, 190

Schulberg, Budd (Wilson) 1914- .... **CLC 7, 48**
    See also CA 25-28R; CANR 19; DLB 6, 26, 28;
    DLBY 81

Schulz, Bruno 1892-1942 ... **TCLC 5, 51; SSC 13**
    See also CA 115; 123

Schulz, Charles M(onroe) 1922- .... **CLC 12**
    See also CA 9-12R; CANR 6; INT CANR-6;
    SATA 10

Schumacher, E(rnst) F(riedrich) 1911-1977
    CLC 80
    See also CA 81-84; 73-76; CANR 34

Schuyler, James Marcus 1923-1991 ... **CLC 5, 23; DAM POET**
    See also CA 101; 134; DLB 5, 169; INT 101

Schwartz, Delmore (David) 1913-1966 ... **CLC 2, 4, 10, 45, 87; PC 8**
    See also CA 17-18; 25-28R; CANR 35; CAP 2;
    DLB 28, 48; MTCW

Schwartz, Ernst
    See Ozu, Yasujiro

Schwartz, John Burnham 1965- .... **CLC 59**
    See also CA 132

Schwartz, Lynne Sharon 1939- .... **CLC 31**
    See also CA 103; CANR 44

Schwartz, Muriel A.
    See Eliot, T(homas) S(tearns)

Schwarz-Bart, Andre 1928- .... **CLC 2, 4**
    See also CA 89-92

Schwarz-Bart, Simone 1938- .... **CLC 7**
    See also BW 2; CA 97-100

Schwob, (Mayer Andre) Marcel 1867-1905
    TCLC 20
    See also CA 117; DLB 123

Sciascia, Leonardo 1921-1989 .... **CLC 8, 9, 41**
    See also CA 85-88; 130; CANR 35; DLB 177;
    MTCW

Scoppettone, Sandra 1936- .... **CLC 26**
    See also AAYA 11; CA 5-8R; CANR 41; SATA 9, 92

Scorsese, Martin 1942- .... **CLC 20, 89**
    See also CA 110; 114; CANR 46

Scotland, Jay
    See Jakes, John (William)

Scott, Duncan Campbell 1862-1947 ... **TCLC 6; DAC**
    See also CA 104; 153; DLB 92

Scott, Evelyn 1893-1963 .... **CLC 43**
    See also CA 104; 112; CANR 64; DLB 9, 48

Scott, F(rancis) R(eginald) 1899-1985 ... **CLC 22**
    See also CA 101; 114; DLB 88; INT 101

Scott, Frank
    See Scott, F(rancis) R(eginald)

Scott, Joanna 1960- .... **CLC 50**
    See also CA 126; CANR 53

Scott, Paul (Mark) 1920-1978 .... **CLC 9, 60**
    See also CA 81-84; 77-80; CANR 33; DLB 14;
    MTCW

Scott, Walter 1771-1832 .. **NCLC 15, 69; DA; DAB; DAC; DAM MST, NOV, POET; PC 13; WLC**
    See also AAYA 22; CDBLB 1789-1832; DLB
    93, 107, 116, 144, 159; YABC 2

Scribe, (Augustin) Eugene 1791-1861 . **N C L C 16; DAM DRAM; DC 5**
    See also DLB 192

Scrum, R.
    See Crumb, R(obert)

Scudery, Madeleine de 1607-1701 .... **LC 2**

Scum
    See Crumb, R(obert)

Scumbag, Little Bobby
    See Crumb, R(obert)

Seabrook, John
    See Hubbard, L(afayette) Ron(ald)

Sealy, I. Allan 1951- .... **CLC 55**

Search, Alexander
    See Pessoa, Fernando (Antonio Nogueira)

Sebastian, Lee
    See Silverberg, Robert

Sebastian Owl
    See Thompson, Hunter S(tockton)

Sebestyen, Ouida 1924- .... **CLC 30**
    See also AAYA 8; CA 107; CANR 40; CLR 17;
    JRDA; MAICYA; SAAS 10; SATA 39

Secundus, H. Scriblerus
    See Fielding, Henry

Sedges, John
    See Buck, Pearl S(ydenstricker)

Sedgwick, Catharine Maria 1789-1867 ... **NCLC 19**
    See also DLB 1, 74

Seelye, John 1931- .... **CLC 7**

Seferiades, Giorgos Stylianou 1900-1971
    See Seferis, George
    See also CA 5-8R; 33-36R; CANR 5, 36; MTCW

Seferis, George .... **CLC 5, 11**
    See also Seferiades, Giorgos Stylianou

Segal, Erich (Wolf) 1937- **CLC 3, 10; DAM POP**
    See also BEST 89:1; CA 25-28R; CANR 20, 36,
    65; DLBY 86; INT CANR-20; MTCW

Seger, Bob 1945- .... **CLC 35**

Seghers, Anna .... **CLC 7**
    See also Radvanyi, Netty
    See also DLB 69

Seidel, Frederick (Lewis) 1936- .... **CLC 18**
    See also CA 13-16R; CANR 8; DLBY 84

Seifert, Jaroslav 1901-1986 .... **CLC 34, 44, 93**
    See also CA 127; MTCW

Sei Shonagon c. 966-1017(?) .... **CMLC 6**

Selby, Hubert, Jr. 1928- **CLC 1, 2, 4, 8; SSC 20**
    See also CA 13-16R; CANR 33; DLB 2

Sheridan, Richard Brinsley 1751-1816 ...NCLC
5; DA; DAB; DAC; DAM DRAM, MST;
DC 1; WLC
    See also CDBLB 1660-1789; DLB 89

Sherman, Jonathan Marc .... CLC 55

Sherman, Martin 1941(?)- .... CLC 19
    See also CA 116; 123

Sherwin, Judith Johnson 1936- ...... CLC 7, 15
    See also CA 25-28R; CANR 34

Sherwood, Frances 1940- .... CLC 81
    See also CA 146

Sherwood, Robert E(mmet) 1896-1955
    TCLC 3; DAM DRAM
    See also CA 104; 153; DLB 7, 26

Shestov, Lev 1866-1938 .... TCLC 56

Shevchenko, Taras 1814-1861 .... NCLC 54

Shiel, M(atthew) P(hipps) 1865-1947 ...T C L C
8
    See also Holmes, Gordon
    See also CA 106; 160; DLB 153

Shields, Carol 1935- .... CLC 91; DAC
    See also CA 81-84; CANR 51

Shields, David 1956- .... CLC 97
    See also CA 124; CANR 48

Shiga, Naoya 1883-1971 .... CLC 33; SSC 23
    See also CA 101; 33-36R; DLB 180

Shilts, Randy 1951-1994 .... CLC 85
    See also AAYA 19; CA 115; 127; 144; CANR
    45; INT 127

Shimazaki, Haruki 1872-1943
    See Shimazaki Toson
    See also CA 105; 134

Shimazaki Toson 1872-1943 .... TCLC 5
    See also Shimazaki, Haruki
    See also DLB 180

Sholokhov, Mikhail (Aleksandrovich) 1905-1984
    CLC 7, 15
    See also CA 101; 112; MTCW; SATA-Obit 36

Shone, Patric
    See Hanley, James

Shreve, Susan Richards 1939- .... CLC 23
    See also CA 49-52; CAAS 5; CANR 5, 38;
    MAICYA; SATA 46, 95; SATA-Brief 41

Shue, Larry 1946-1985 ... . CLC 52; DAM
    DRAM
    See also CA 145; 117

Shu-Jen, Chou 1881-1936
    See Lu Hsun
    See also CA 104

Shulman, Alix Kates 1932- .... CLC 2, 10
    See also CA 29-32R; CANR 43; SATA 7

Shuster, Joe 1914- .... CLC 21

Shute, Nevil .... CLC 30
    See also Norway, Nevil Shute

Shuttle, Penelope (Diane) 1947- .... CLC 7
    See also CA 93-96; CANR 39; DLB 14, 40

Sidney, Mary 1561-1621 .... LC 19, 39

Sidney, Sir Philip 1554-1586 ... LC 19, 39; DA;
    DAB; DAC; DAM MST, POET
    See also CDBLB Before 1660; DLB 167

Siegel, Jerome 1914-1996 .... CLC 21
    See also CA 116; 151

Siegel, Jerry
    See Siegel, Jerome

Sienkiewicz, Henryk (Adam Alexander Pius)
    1846-1916 .... TCLC 3
    See also CA 104; 134

Sierra, Gregorio Martinez
    See Martinez Sierra, Gregorio

Sierra, Maria (de la O'LeJarraga) Martinez
    See Martinez Sierra, Maria (de la O'LeJarraga)

Sigal, Clancy 1926- .... CLC 7
    See also CA 1-4R

Sigourney, Lydia Howard (Huntley) 1791-1865
    NCLC 21
    See also DLB 1, 42, 73

Siguenza y Gongora, Carlos de 1645-1700
    LC 8

Sigurjonsson, Johann 1880-1919 .... TCLC 27

Sikelianos, Angelos 1884-1951 .... TCLC 39

Silkin, Jon 1930- .... CLC 2, 6, 43
    See also CA 5-8R; CAAS 5; DLB 27

Silko, Leslie (Marmon) 1948- ..... CLC 23, 74;
    DA; DAC; DAM MST, MULT, POP;
    WLCS
    See also AAYA 14; CA 115; 122; CANR 45, 65;
    DLB 143, 175; NNAL

Sillanpaa, Frans Eemil 1888-1964 ..... CLC 19
    See also CA 129; 93-96; MTCW

Sillitoe, Alan 1928- .... CLC 1, 3, 6, 10,
    19, 57
    See also AITN 1; CA 9-12R; CAAS 2; CANR 8,
    26, 55; CDBLB 1960 to Present; DLB 14, 139;
    MTCW; SATA 61

Silone, Ignazio 1900-1978 .... CLC 4
    See also CA 25-28; 81-84; CANR 34; CAP 2;
    MTCW

Silver, Joan Micklin 1935- .... CLC 20
    See also CA 114; 121; INT 121

Silver, Nicholas
    See Faust, Frederick (Schiller)

Silverberg, Robert 1935- ... CLC 7; DAM POP
    See also AAYA 24; CA 1-4R; CAAS 3; CANR 1,
    20, 36; DLB 8; INT CANR-20; MAICYA;
    MTCW; SATA 13, 91

Silverstein, Alvin 1933- .... CLC 17
    See also CA 49-52; CANR 2; CLR 25; JRDA;
    MAICYA; SATA 8, 69

Silverstein, Virginia B(arbara Opshelor) 1937-
    CLC 17
    See also CA 49-52; CANR 2; CLR 25; JRDA;
    MAICYA; SATA 8, 69

Sim, Georges
    See Simenon, Georges (Jacques Christian)

Simak, Clifford D(onald) 1904-1988 ...CLC 1, 55
    See also CA 1-4R; 125; CANR 1, 35; DLB 8;
    MTCW; SATA-Obit 56

Simenon, Georges (Jacques Christian) 1903-
    1989 ... CLC 1, 2, 3, 8, 18, 47; DAM POP
    See also CA 85-88; 129; CANR 35; DLB 72;
    DLBY 89; MTCW

Simic, Charles 1938- ..... CLC 6, 9, 22, 49, 68;
    DAM POET
    See also CA 29-32R; CAAS 4; CANR 12, 33,
    52, 61; DLB 105

Simmel, Georg 1858-1918 .... TCLC 64
    See also CA 157

Simmons, Charles (Paul) 1924- .... CLC 57
    See also CA 89-92; INT 89-92

Simmons, Dan 1948- .... CLC 44; DAM POP
    See also AAYA 16; CA 138; CANR 53

Simmons, James (Stewart Alexander) 1933-
    CLC 43
    See also CA 105; CAAS 21; DLB 40

Simms, William Gilmore 1806-1870 ... NCLC 3
    See also DLB 3, 30, 59, 73

Simon, Carly 1945- .... CLC 26
    See also CA 105

Simon, Claude 1913-1984 ... CLC 4, 9, 15, 39;
    DAM NOV
    See also CA 89-92; CANR 33; DLB 83; MTCW

Simon, (Marvin) Neil 1927- ... CLC 6, 11, 31,
    39, 70; DAM DRAM
    See also AITN 1; CA 21-24R; CANR 26, 54;
    DLB 7; MTCW

Simon, Paul (Frederick) 1941(?)- .... CLC 17
    See also CA 116; 153

Simonon, Paul 1956(?)- .... CLC 30

Simpson, Harriette
    See Arnow, Harriette (Louisa) Simpson

Simpson, Louis (Aston Marantz) 1923- ... CLC
    4, 7, 9, 32; DAM POET
    See also CA 1-4R; CAAS 4; CANR 1, 61; DLB
    5; MTCW

Simpson, Mona (Elizabeth) 1957- ...... **CLC 44**
See also CA 122; 135; CANR 68

Simpson, N(orman) F(rederick) 1919- ... **CLC 29**
See also CA 13-16R; DLB 13

Sinclair, Andrew (Annandale) 1935- ... **CLC 2, 14**
See also CA 9-12R; CAAS 5; CANR 14, 38; DLB 14; MTCW

Sinclair, Emil
See Hesse, Hermann

Sinclair, Iain 1943- .... **CLC 76**
See also CA 132

Sinclair, Iain MacGregor
See Sinclair, Iain

Sinclair, Irene
See Griffith, D(avid Lewelyn) W(ark)

Sinclair, Mary Amelia St. Clair 1865(?)-1946
See Sinclair, May
See also CA 104

Sinclair, May .... **TCLC 3, 11**
See also Sinclair, Mary Amelia St. Clair
See also DLB 36, 135

Sinclair, Roy
See Griffith, D(avid Lewelyn) W(ark)

Sinclair, Upton (Beall) 1878-1968 ... **CLC 1, 11, 15, 63; DA; DAB; DAC; DAM MST, NOV; WLC**
See also CA 5-8R; 25-28R; CANR 7; CDALB 1929-1941; DLB 9; INT CANR-7; MTCW; SATA 9

Singer, Isaac
See Singer, Isaac Bashevis

Singer, Isaac Bashevis 1904-1991 ...**CLC 1, 3, 6, 9, 11, 15, 23, 38, 69; DA; DAB; DAC; DAM MST, NOV; SSC 3; WLC**
See also AITN 1, 2; CA 1-4R; 134; CANR 1, 39; CDALB 1941-1968; CLR 1; DLB 6, 28, 52; DLBY 91; JRDA; MAICYA; MTCW; SATA 3, 27; SATA-Obit 68

Singer, Israel Joshua 1893-1944 ..... **TCLC 33**

Singh, Khushwant 1915- .... **CLC 11**
See also CA 9-12R; CAAS 9; CANR 6

Singleton, Ann
See Benedict, Ruth (Fulton)

Sinjohn, John
See Galsworthy, John

Sinyavsky, Andrei (Donatevich) 1925-1997 **CLC 8**
See also CA 85-88; 159

Sirin, V.
See Nabokov, Vladimir (Vladimirovich)

Sissman, L(ouis) E(dward) 1928-1976 ... **CLC 9, 18**
See also CA 21-24R; 65-68; CANR 13; DLB 5

Sisson, C(harles) H(ubert) 1914- .... **CLC 8**
See also CA 1-4R; CAAS 3; CANR 3, 48; DLB 27

Sitwell, Dame Edith 1887-1964 ... **CLC 2, 9, 67; DAM POET; PC 3**
See also CA 9-12R; CANR 35; CDBLB 1945-1960; DLB 20; MTCW

Siwaarmill, H. P.
See Sharp, William

Sjoewall, Maj 1935- .... **CLC 7**
See also CA 65-68

Sjowall, Maj
See Sjoewall, Maj

Skelton, Robin 1925-1997 .... **CLC 13**
See also AITN 2; CA 5-8R; 160; CAAS 5; CANR 28; DLB 27, 53

Skolimowski, Jerzy 1938- .... **CLC 20**
See also CA 128

Skram, Amalie (Bertha) 1847-1905 ... **TCLC 25**
See also CA 165

Skvorecky, Josef (Vaclav) 1924- ... **CLC 15, 39, 69; DAC; DAM NOV**
See also CA 61-64; CAAS 1; CANR 10, 34, 63; MTCW

Slade, Bernard .... **CLC 11, 46**
See also Newbound, Bernard Slade
See also CAAS 9; DLB 53

Slaughter, Carolyn 1946- .... **CLC 56**
See also CA 85-88

Slaughter, Frank G(ill) 1908- .... **CLC 29**
See also AITN 2; CA 5-8R; CANR 5; INT CANR-5

Slavitt, David R(ytman) 1935- .... **CLC 5, 14**
See also CA 21-24R; CAAS 3; CANR 41; DLB 5, 6

Slesinger, Tess 1905-1945 .... **TCLC 10**
See also CA 107; DLB 102

Slessor, Kenneth 1901-1971 .... **CLC 14**
See also CA 102; 89-92

Slowacki, Juliusz 1809-1849 .... **NCLC 15**

Smart, Christopher 1722-1771 ... **LC 3; DAM POET; PC 13**
See also DLB 109

Smart, Elizabeth 1913-1986 .... **CLC 54**
See also CA 81-84; 118; DLB 88

Smiley, Jane (Graves) 1949- .... **CLC 53, 76; DAM POP**
See also CA 104; CANR 30, 50; INT CANR-30

Smith, A(rthur) J(ames) M(arshall) 1902-1980 **CLC 15; DAC**
See also CA 1-4R; 102; CANR 4; DLB 88

Smith, Adam 1723-1790 .... **LC 36**
See also DLB 104

Smith, Alexander 1829-1867 .... **NCLC 59**
See also DLB 32, 55

Smith, Anna Deavere 1950- .... **CLC 86**
See also CA 133

Smith, Betty (Wehner) 1896-1972 ..... **CLC 19**
See also CA 5-8R; 33-36R; DLBY 82; SATA 6

Smith, Charlotte (Turner) 1749-1806 ... **NCLC 23**
See also DLB 39, 109

Smith, Clark Ashton 1893-1961 .... **CLC 43**
See also CA 143

Smith, Dave .... **CLC 22, 42**
See also Smith, David (Jeddie)
See also CAAS 7; DLB 5

Smith, David (Jeddie) 1942-
See Smith, Dave
See also CA 49-52; CANR 1, 59; DAM POET

Smith, Florence Margaret 1902-1971
See Smith, Stevie
See also CA 17-18; 29-32R; CANR 35; CAP 2; DAM POET; MTCW

Smith, Iain Crichton 1928- .... **CLC 64**
See also CA 21-24R; DLB 40, 139

Smith, John 1580(?)-1631 .... **LC 9**

Smith, Johnston
See Crane, Stephen (Townley)

Smith, Joseph, Jr. 1805-1844 .... **NCLC 53**

Smith, Lee 1944- .... **CLC 25, 73**
See also CA 114; 119; CANR 46; DLB 143; DLBY 83; INT 119

Smith, Martin
See Smith, Martin Cruz

Smith, Martin Cruz 1942- ...... **CLC 25; DAM MULT, POP**
See also BEST 89:4; CA 85-88; CANR 6, 23, 43, 65; INT CANR-23; NNAL

Smith, Mary-Ann Tirone 1944- .... **CLC 39**
See also CA 118; 136

Smith, Patti 1946- .... **CLC 12**
See also CA 93-96; CANR 63

Smith, Pauline (Urmson) 1882-1959 ... **TCLC 25**

Smith, Rosamond
See Oates, Joyce Carol

Smith, Sheila Kaye
See Kaye-Smith, Sheila

Smith, Stevie .... **CLC 3, 8, 25, 44; PC 12**
See also Smith, Florence Margaret
See also DLB 20

Smith, Wilbur (Addison) 1933- .... **CLC 33**
See also CA 13-16R; CANR 7, 46, 66; MTCW

Smith, William Jay 1918- .... **CLC 6**
See also CA 5-8R; CANR 44; DLB 5; MAICYA;
SAAS 22; SATA 2, 68

Smith, Woodrow Wilson
See Kuttner, Henry

Smolenskin, Peretz 1842-1885 .... **NCLC 30**

Smollett, Tobias (George) 1721-1771 ..... **LC 2**
See also CDBLB 1660-1789; DLB 39, 104

Snodgrass, W(illiam) D(e Witt) 1926-**CLC 2, 6,
10, 18, 68; DAM POET**
See also CA 1-4R; CANR 6, 36, 65; DLB 5;
MTCW

Snow, C(harles) P(ercy) 1905-1980 ... **CLC 1, 4,
6, 9, 13, 19; DAM NOV**
See also CA 5-8R; 101; CANR 28; CDBLB
1945-1960; DLB 15, 77; MTCW

Snow, Frances Compton
See Adams, Henry (Brooks)

Snyder, Gary (Sherman) 1930- ... **CLC 1, 2, 5, 9,
32; DAM POET; PC 21**
See also CA 17-20R; CANR 30, 60; DLB 5, 16,
165

Snyder, Zilpha Keatley 1927- .... **CLC 17**
See also AAYA 15; CA 9-12R; CANR 38; CLR
31; JRDA; MAICYA; SAAS 2; SATA 1, 28,
75

Soares, Bernardo
See Pessoa, Fernando (Antonio Nogueira)

Sobh, A.
See Shamlu, Ahmad

Sobol, Joshua .... **CLC 60**

Socrates 469B.C.-399B.C. .... **CMLC 27**

Soderberg, Hjalmar 1869-1941 ...... **TCLC 39**

Sodergran, Edith (Irene)
See Soedergran, Edith (Irene)

Soedergran, Edith (Irene) 1892-1923 ...**TCLC 31**

Softly, Edgar
See Lovecraft, H(oward) P(hillips)

Softly, Edward
See Lovecraft, H(oward) P(hillips)

Sokolov, Raymond 1941- .... **CLC 7**
See also CA 85-88

Solo, Jay
See Ellison, Harlan (Jay)

Sologub, Fyodor .... **TCLC 9**
See also Teternikov, Fyodor Kuzmich

Solomons, Ikey Esquir
See Thackeray, William Makepeace

Solomos, Dionysios 1798-1857 .... **NCLC 15**

Solwoska, Mara
See French, Marilyn

Solzhenitsyn, Aleksandr I(sayevich) 1918-
**CLC 1, 2, 4, 7, 9, 10, 18, 26, 34, 78; DA;
DAB; DAC; DAM MST, NOV; WLC**
See also AITN 1; CA 69-72; CANR 40, 65;
MTCW

Somers, Jane
See Lessing, Doris (May)

Somerville, Edith 1858-1949 .... **TCLC 51**
See also DLB 135

Somerville & Ross
See Martin, Violet Florence; Somerville, Edith

Sommer, Scott 1951- .... **CLC 25**
See also CA 106

Sondheim, Stephen (Joshua) 1930- ... **CLC 30,
39; DAM DRAM**
See also AAYA 11; CA 103; CANR 47, 68

Song, Cathy 1955-.................................... **PC 21**
See also CA 154; DLB 169

Sontag, Susan 1933- ... **CLC 1, 2, 10, 13, 31, 105;
DAM POP**
See also CA 17-20R; CANR 25, 51; DLB 2, 67;
MTCW

Sophocles 496(?)B.C.-406(?)B.C. ..... **CMLC 2;
DA; DAB; DAC; DAM DRAM, MST; DC
1; WLCS**
See also DLB 176

Sordello 1189-1269 .... **CMLC 15**

Sorel, Julia
See Drexler, Rosalyn

Sorrentino, Gilbert 1929- ... **CLC 3, 7, 14, 22, 40**
See also CA 77-80; CANR 14, 33; DLB 5, 173;
DLBY 80; INT CANR-14

Soto, Gary 1952- .. **CLC 32, 80; DAM MULT;
HLC**
See also AAYA 10; CA 119; 125; CANR 50; CLR
38; DLB 82; HW; INT 125; JRDA; SATA 80

Soupault, Philippe 1897-1990 .... **CLC 68**
See also CA 116; 147; 131

Souster, (Holmes) Raymond 1921- ... **CLC 5, 14;
DAC; DAM POET**
See also CA 13-16R; CAAS 14; CANR 13, 29,
53; DLB 88; SATA 63

Southern, Terry 1924(?)-1995 .... **CLC 7**
See also CA 1-4R; 150; CANR 1, 55; DLB 2

Southey, Robert 1774-1843 .... **NCLC 8**
See also DLB 93, 107, 142; SATA 54

Southworth, Emma Dorothy Eliza Nevitte 1819-
1899 .... **NCLC 26**

Souza, Ernest
See Scott, Evelyn

Soyinka, Wole 1934- ... **CLC 3, 5, 14, 36, 44;
BLC; DA; DAB; DAC; DAM DRAM, MST,
MULT; DC 2; WLC**
See also BW 2; CA 13-16R; CANR 27, 39; DLB
125; MTCW

Spackman, W(illiam) M(ode) 1905-1990 ... **CLC
46**
See also CA 81-84; 132

Spacks, Barry (Bernard) 1931- .... **CLC 14**
See also CA 154; CANR 33; DLB 105

Spanidou, Irini 1946-........................... **CLC 44**

Spark, Muriel (Sarah) 1918- ... **CLC 2, 3, 5, 8,
13, 18, 40, 94; DAB; DAC; DAM MST,
NOV; SSC 10**
See also CA 5-8R; CANR 12, 36; CDBLB 1945-
1960; DLB 15, 139; INT CANR-12; MTCW

Spaulding, Douglas
See Bradbury, Ray (Douglas)

Spaulding, Leonard
See Bradbury, Ray (Douglas)

Spence, J. A. D.
See Eliot, T(homas) S(tearns)

Spencer, Elizabeth 1921- .... **CLC 22**
See also CA 13-16R; CANR 32, 65; DLB 6;
MTCW; SATA 14

Spencer, Leonard G.
See Silverberg, Robert

Spencer, Scott 1945- .... **CLC 30**
See also CA 113; CANR 51; DLBY 86

Spender, Stephen (Harold) 1909-1995 ... **CLC
1, 2, 5, 10, 41, 91; DAM POET**
See also CA 9-12R; 149; CANR 31, 54; CDBLB
1945-1960; DLB 20; MTCW

Spengler, Oswald (Arnold Gottfried) 1880-1936
TCLC 25
See also CA 118

Spenser, Edmund 1552(?)-1599 ... **LC 5, 39; DA;
DAB; DAC; DAM MST, POET; PC 8; WLC**
See also CDBLB Before 1660; DLB 167

Spicer, Jack 1925-1965 .. **CLC 8, 18, 72; DAM
POET**
See also CA 85-88; DLB 5, 16, 193

Spiegelman, Art 1948- .... **CLC 76**
See also AAYA 10; CA 125; CANR 41, 55

Spielberg, Peter 1929- .... **CLC 6**
See also CA 5-8R; CANR 4, 48; DLBY 81

Spielberg, Steven 1947- .... **CLC 20**
See also AAYA 8, 24; CA 77-80; CANR 32;
SATA 32

Spillane, Frank Morrison 1918-
See Spillane, Mickey
See also CA 25-28R; CANR 28, 63; MTCW;
SATA 66

Spillane, Mickey .... **CLC 3, 13**
See also Spillane, Frank Morrison

Spinoza, Benedictus de 1632-1677 .... **LC 9**

Spinrad, Norman (Richard) 1940- ..... **CLC 46**
See also CA 37-40R; CAAS 19; CANR 20; DLB 8; INT CANR-20

Spitteler, Carl (Friedrich Georg) 1845-1924 **TCLC 12**
See also CA 109; DLB 129

Spivack, Kathleen (Romola Drucker) 1938- ... **CLC 6**
See also CA 49-52

Spoto, Donald 1941- .... **CLC 39**
See also CA 65-68; CANR 11, 57

Springsteen, Bruce (F.) 1949- .... **CLC 17**
See also CA 111

Spurling, Hilary 1940- .... **CLC 34**
See also CA 104; CANR 25, 52

Spyker, John Howland
See Elman, Richard (Martin)

Squires, (James) Radcliffe 1917-1993 ... **CLC 51**
See also CA 1-4R; 140; CANR 6, 21

Srivastava, Dhanpat Rai 1880(?)-1936
See Premchand
See also CA 118

Stacy, Donald
See Pohl, Frederik

Stael, Germaine de 1766-1817
See Stael-Holstein, Anne Louise Germaine Necker Baronn
See also DLB 119

Stael-Holstein, Anne Louise Germaine Necker Baronn 1766-1817 .... **NCLC 3**
See also Stael, Germaine de
See also DLB 192

Stafford, Jean 1915-1979 ... **CLC 4, 7, 19, 68; SSC 26**
See also CA 1-4R; 85-88; CANR 3, 65; DLB 2, 173; MTCW; SATA-Obit 22

Stafford, William (Edgar) 1914-1993 ... **CLC 4, 7, 29; DAM POET**
See also CA 5-8R; 142; CAAS 3; CANR 5, 22; DLB 5; INT CANR-22

Stagnelius, Eric Johan 1793-1823 .. **NCLC 61**

Staines, Trevor
See Brunner, John (Kilian Houston)

Stairs, Gordon
See Austin, Mary (Hunter)

Stannard, Martin 1947- .... **CLC 44**
See also CA 142; DLB 155

Stanton, Elizabeth Cady 1815-1902 ... **TCLC 73**
See also DLB 79

Stanton, Maura 1946- .... **CLC 9**
See also CA 89-92; CANR 15; DLB 120

Stanton, Schuyler
See Baum, L(yman) Frank

Stapledon, (William) Olaf 1886-1950 ... **TCLC 22**
See also CA 111; 162; DLB 15

Starbuck, George (Edwin) 1931-1996 ... **CLC 53; DAM POET**
See also CA 21-24R; 153; CANR 23

Stark, Richard
See Westlake, Donald E(dwin)

Staunton, Schuyler
See Baum, L(yman) Frank

Stead, Christina (Ellen) 1902-1983 ... **CLC 2, 5, 8, 32, 80**
See also CA 13-16R; 109; CANR 33, 40; MTCW

Stead, William Thomas 1849-1912 . **TCLC 48**

Steele, Richard 1672-1729 .... **LC 18**
See also CDBLB 1660-1789; DLB 84, 101

Steele, Timothy (Reid) 1948- .... **CLC 45**
See also CA 93-96; CANR 16, 50; DLB 120

Steffens, (Joseph) Lincoln 1866-1936 ... **TCLC 20**
See also CA 117

Stegner, Wallace (Earle) 1909-1993 ... **CLC 9, 49, 81; DAM NOV; SSC 27**
See also AITN 1; BEST 90:3; CA 1-4R; 141; CAAS 9; CANR 1, 21, 46; DLB 9; DLBY 93; MTCW

Stein, Gertrude 1874-1946 ... **TCLC 1, 6, 28, 48; DA; DAB; DAC; DAM MST, NOV, POET; PC 18; WLC**
See also CA 104; 132; CDALB 1917-1929; DLB 4, 54, 86; DLBD 15; MTCW

Steinbeck, John (Ernst) 1902-1968 ... **CLC 1, 5, 9, 13, 21, 34, 45, 75; DA; DAB; DAC; DAM DRAM, MST, NOV; SSC 11; WLC**
See also AAYA 12; CA 1-4R; 25-28R; CANR 1, 35; CDALB 1929-1941; DLB 7, 9; DLBD 2; MTCW; SATA 9

Steinem, Gloria 1934- .... **CLC 63**
See also CA 53-56; CANR 28, 51; MTCW

Steiner, George 1929- .... **CLC 24; DAM NOV**
See also CA 73-76; CANR 31, 67; DLB 67; MTCW; SATA 62

Steiner, K. Leslie
See Delany, Samuel R(ay, Jr.)

Steiner, Rudolf 1861-1925 .... **TCLC 13**
See also CA 107

Stendhal 1783-1842 ... **NCLC 23, 46; DA; DAB; DAC; DAM MST, NOV; SSC 27; WLC**
See also DLB 119

Stephen, Adeline Virginia
See Woolf, (Adeline) Virginia

Stephen, Sir Leslie 1832-1904 .... **TCLC 23**
See also CA 123; DLB 57, 144, 190

Stephen, Sir Leslie
See Stephen, Sir Leslie

Stephen, Virginia
See Woolf, (Adeline) Virginia

Stephens, James 1882(?)-1950 .... **TCLC 4**
See also CA 104; DLB 19, 153, 162

Stephens, Reed
See Donaldson, Stephen R.

Steptoe, Lydia
See Barnes, Djuna

Sterchi, Beat 1949- .... **CLC 65**

Sterling, Brett
See Bradbury, Ray (Douglas); Hamilton, Edmond

Sterling, Bruce 1954- .... **CLC 72**
See also CA 119; CANR 44

Sterling, George 1869-1926 .... **TCLC 20**
See also CA 117; 165; DLB 54

Stern, Gerald 1925- .... **CLC 40, 100**
See also CA 81-84; CANR 28; DLB 105

Stern, Richard (Gustave) 1928- ..... **CLC 4, 39**
See also CA 1-4R; CANR 1, 25, 52; DLBY 87; INT CANR-25

Sternberg, Josef von 1894-1969 .... **CLC 20**
See also CA 81-84

Sterne, Laurence 1713-1768 ... **LC 2; DA; DAB; DAC; DAM MST, NOV; WLC**
See also CDBLB 1660-1789; DLB 39

Sternheim, (William Adolf) Carl 1878-1942 **TCLC 8**
See also CA 105; DLB 56, 118

Stevens, Mark 1951- .... **CLC 34**
See also CA 122

Stevens, Wallace 1879-1955 ... **TCLC 3, 12, 45; DA; DAB; DAC; DAM MST, POET; PC 6; WLC**
See also CA 104; 124; CDALB 1929-1941; DLB 54; MTCW

Stevenson, Anne (Katharine) 1933- ... **CLC 7, 33**
See also CA 17-20R; CAAS 9; CANR 9, 33; DLB 40; MTCW

Stevenson, Robert Louis (Balfour) 1850-1894 **NCLC 5, 14, 63; DA; DAB; DAC; DAM MST, NOV; SSC 11; WLC**
See also AAYA 24; CDBLB 1890-1914; CLR 10, 11; DLB 18, 57, 141, 156, 174; DLBD 13; JRDA; MAICYA; YABC 2

Stewart, J(ohn) I(nnes) M(ackintosh) 1906-1994
    CLC 7, 14, 32
    See also CA 85-88; 147; CAAS 3; CANR 47;
    MTCW

Stewart, Mary (Florence Elinor) 1916- ... CLC
    7, 35; DAB
    See also CA 1-4R; CANR 1, 59; SATA 12

Stewart, Mary Rainbow
    See Stewart, Mary (Florence Elinor)

Stifle, June
    See Campbell, Maria

Stifter, Adalbert 1805-1868 ... NCLC 41; SSC
    28
    See also DLB 133

Still, James 1906- .... CLC 49
    See also CA 65-68; CAAS 17; CANR 10, 26;
    DLB 9; SATA 29

Sting
    See Sumner, Gordon Matthew

Stirling, Arthur
    See Sinclair, Upton (Beall)

Stitt, Milan 1941- .... CLC 29
    See also CA 69-72

Stockton, Francis Richard 1834-1902
    See Stockton, Frank R.
    See also CA 108; 137; MAICYA; SATA 44

Stockton, Frank R. .... TCLC 47
    See also Stockton, Francis Richard
    See also DLB 42, 74; DLBD 13; SATA-Brief 32

Stoddard, Charles
    See Kuttner, Henry

Stoker, Abraham 1847-1912
    See Stoker, Bram
    See also CA 105; DA; DAC; DAM MST, NOV;
    SATA 29

Stoker, Bram 1847-1912 .... TCLC 8; DAB;
    WLC
    See also Stoker, Abraham
    See also AAYA 23; CA 150; CDBLB 1890-1914;
    DLB 36, 70, 178

Stolz, Mary (Slattery) 1920- .... CLC 12
    See also AAYA 8; AITN 1; CA 5-8R; CANR 13,
    41; JRDA; MAICYA; SAAS 3; SATA 10, 71

Stone, Irving 1903-1989 ... CLC 7; DAM POP
    See also AITN 1; CA 1-4R; 129; CAAS 3; CANR
    1, 23; INT CANR-23; MTCW; SATA 3;
    SATA-Obit 64

Stone, Oliver (William) 1946- .... CLC 73
    See also AAYA 15; CA 110; CANR 55

Stone, Robert (Anthony) 1937- .... CLC 5, 23, 42
    See also CA 85-88; CANR 23, 66; DLB 152; INT
    CANR-23; MTCW

Stone, Zachary
    See Follett, Ken(neth Martin)

Stoppard, Tom 1937- .... CLC 1, 3, 4, 5, 8, 15, 29,
    34, 63, 91; DA; DAB; DAC; DAM DRAM,
    MST; DC 6; WLC
    See also CA 81-84; CANR 39, 67; CDBLB 1960
    to Present; DLB 13; DLBY 85; MTCW

Storey, David (Malcolm) 1933- ... CLC 2, 4, 5, 8;
    DAM DRAM
    See also CA 81-84; CANR 36; DLB 13, 14;
    MTCW

Storm, Hyemeyohsts 1935- .... CLC 3; DAM
    MULT
    See also CA 81-84; CANR 45; NNAL

Storm, (Hans) Theodor (Woldsen) 1817-1888
    NCLC 1; SSC 27

Storni, Alfonsina 1892-1938 .. TCLC 5; DAM
    MULT; HLC
    See also CA 104; 131; HW

Stoughton, William 1631-1701 .... LC 38
    See also DLB 24

Stout, Rex (Todhunter) 1886-1975 ...... CLC 3
    See also AITN 2; CA 61-64

Stow, (Julian) Randolph 1935- ..... CLC 23, 48
    See also CA 13-16R; CANR 33; MTCW

Stowe, Harriet (Elizabeth) Beecher 1811-1896
    NCLC 3, 50; DA; DAB; DAC; DAM MST,
    NOV; WLC
    See also CDALB 1865-1917; DLB 1, 12, 42, 74,
    189; JRDA; MAICYA; YABC 1

Strachey, (Giles) Lytton 1880-1932 ... TCLC 12
    See also CA 110; DLB 149; DLBD 10

Strand, Mark 1934- ... CLC 6, 18, 41, 71; DAM
    POET
    See also CA 21-24R; CANR 40, 65; DLB 5;
    SATA 41

Straub, Peter (Francis) 1943- ... CLC 28, 107;
    DAM POP
    See also BEST 89:1; CA 85-88; CANR 28, 65;
    DLBY 84; MTCW

Strauss, Botho 1944- .... CLC 22
    See also CA 157; DLB 124

Streatfeild, (Mary) Noel 1895(?)-1986 ... CLC
    21
    See also CA 81-84; 120; CANR 31; CLR 17;
    DLB 160; MAICYA; SATA 20; SATA-Obit 48

Stribling, T(homas) S(igismund) 1881-1965
    CLC 23
    See also CA 107; DLB 9

Strindberg, (Johan) August 1849-1912TCLC
    1, 8, 21, 47; DA; DAB; DAC; DAM DRAM,
    MST; WLC
    See also CA 104; 135

Stringer, Arthur 1874-1950 .... TCLC 37
    See also CA 161; DLB 92

Stringer, David
    See Roberts, Keith (John Kingston)

Stroheim, Erich von 1885-1957 ...... TCLC 71

Strugatskii, Arkadii (Natanovich) 1925-1991
    CLC 27
    See also CA 106; 135

Strugatskii, Boris (Natanovich) 1933- ... CLC
    27
    See also CA 106

Strummer, Joe 1953(?)- .... CLC 30

Stuart, Don A.
    See Campbell, John W(ood, Jr.)

Stuart, Ian
    See MacLean, Alistair (Stuart)

Stuart, Jesse (Hilton) 1906-1984 ... CLC 1, 8,
    11, 14, 34
    See also CA 5-8R; 112; CANR 31; DLB 9, 48,
    102; DLBY 84; SATA 2; SATA-Obit 36

Sturgeon, Theodore (Hamilton) 1918-1985
    CLC 22, 39
    See also Queen, Ellery
    See also CA 81-84; 116; CANR 32; DLB 8;
    DLBY 85; MTCW

Sturges, Preston 1898-1959 .... TCLC 48
    See also CA 114; 149; DLB 26

Styron, William 1925- ... CLC 1, 3, 5, 11, 15, 60;
    DAM NOV, POP; SSC 25
    See also BEST 90:4; CA 5-8R; CANR 6, 33;
    CDALB 1968-1988; DLB 2, 143; DLBY 80;
    INT CANR-6; MTCW

Suarez Lynch, B.
    See Bioy Casares, Adolfo; Borges, Jorge Luis

Su Chien 1884-1918
    See Su Man-shu
    See also CA 123

Suckow, Ruth 1892-1960 .... SSC 18
    See also CA 113; DLB 9, 102

Sudermann, Hermann 1857-1928 ... TCLC 15
    See also CA 107; DLB 118

Sue, Eugene 1804-1857 .... NCLC 1
    See also DLB 119

Sueskind, Patrick 1949- .... CLC 44
    See also Suskind, Patrick

Sukenick, Ronald 1932- .... CLC 3, 4, 6,
    48
    See also CA 25-28R; CAAS 8; CANR 32; DLB
    173; DLBY 81

Suknaski, Andrew 1942- .... CLC 19
    See also CA 101; DLB 53

Sullivan, Vernon
    See Vian, Boris

Sully Prudhomme 1839-1907 .... TCLC 31

Su Man-shu .... TCLC 24
    See also Su Chien

Summerforest, Ivy B.
See Kirkup, James

Summers, Andrew James 1942- .... **CLC 26**

Summers, Andy
See Summers, Andrew James

Summers, Hollis (Spurgeon, Jr.) 1916- ... **CLC 10**
See also CA 5-8R; CANR 3; DLB 6

Summers, (Alphonsus Joseph-Mary Augustus) Montague 1880-1948 .... **TCLC 16**
See also CA 118; 163

Sumner, Gordon Matthew 1951- .... **CLC 26**

Surtees, Robert Smith 1803-1864 ... **NCLC 14**
See also DLB 21

Susann, Jacqueline 1921-1974 .... **CLC 3**
See also AITN 1; CA 65-68; 53-56; MTCW

Su Shih 1036-1101 .... **CMLC 15**

Suskind, Patrick
See Sueskind, Patrick
See also CA 145

Sutcliff, Rosemary 1920-1992 ... **CLC 26; DAB; DAC; DAM MST, POP**
See also AAYA 10; CA 5-8R; 139; CANR 37; CLR 1, 37; JRDA; MAICYA; SATA 6, 44, 78; SATA-Obit 73

Sutro, Alfred 1863-1933 .... **TCLC 6**
See also CA 105; DLB 10

Sutton, Henry
See Slavitt, David R(ytman)

Svevo, Italo 1861-1928 .... **TCLC 2, 35; SSC 25**
See also Schmitz, Aron Hector

Swados, Elizabeth (A.) 1951- .... **CLC 12**
See also CA 97-100; CANR 49; INT 97-100

Swados, Harvey 1920-1972 .... **CLC 5**
See also CA 5-8R; 37-40R; CANR 6; DLB 2

Swan, Gladys 1934- .... **CLC 69**
See also CA 101; CANR 17, 39

Swarthout, Glendon (Fred) 1918-1992 ... **CLC 35**
See also CA 1-4R; 139; CANR 1, 47; SATA 26

Sweet, Sarah C.
See Jewett, (Theodora) Sarah Orne

Swenson, May 1919-1989 ... **CLC 4, 14, 61, 106; DA; DAB; DAC; DAM MST, POET; PC 14**
See also CA 5-8R; 130; CANR 36, 61; DLB 5; MTCW; SATA 15

Swift, Augustus
See Lovecraft, H(oward) P(hillips)

Swift, Graham (Colin) 1949- .... **CLC 41, 88**
See also CA 117; 122; CANR 46; DLB 194

Swift, Jonathan 1667-1745 .... **LC 1; DA; DAB; DAC; DAM MST, NOV, POET; PC 9; WLC**
See also CDBLB 1660-1789; DLB 39, 95, 101; SATA 19

Swinburne, Algernon Charles 1837-1909 **TCLC 8, 36; DA; DAB; DAC; DAM MST, POET; WLC**
See also CA 105; 140; CDBLB 1832-1890; DLB 35, 57

Swinfen, Ann .... **CLC 34**

Swinnerton, Frank Arthur 1884-1982 ... **CLC 31**
See also CA 108; DLB 34

Swithen, John
See King, Stephen (Edwin)

Sylvia
See Ashton-Warner, Sylvia (Constance)

Symmes, Robert Edward
See Duncan, Robert (Edward)

Symonds, John Addington 1840-1893 ... **NCLC 34**
See also DLB 57, 144

Symons, Arthur 1865-1945 .... **TCLC 11**
See also CA 107; DLB 19, 57, 149

Symons, Julian (Gustave) 1912-1994 ... **CLC 2, 14, 32**
See also CA 49-52; 147; CAAS 3; CANR 3, 33, 59; DLB 87, 155; DLBY 92; MTCW

Synge, (Edmund) J(ohn) M(illington) 1871-1909 **TCLC 6, 37; DAM DRAM; DC 2**
See also CA 104; 141; CDBLB 1890-1914; DLB 10, 19

Syruc, J.
See Milosz, Czeslaw

Szirtes, George 1948- .... **CLC 46**
See also CA 109; CANR 27, 61

Szymborska, Wislawa 1923- .... **CLC 99**
See also CA 154; DLBY 96

T. O., Nik
See Annensky, Innokenty (Fyodorovich)

Tabori, George 1914- .... **CLC 19**
See also CA 49-52; CANR 4

Tagore, Rabindranath 1861-1941 ... **TCLC 3, 53; DAM DRAM, POET; PC 8**
See also CA 104; 120; MTCW

Taine, Hippolyte Adolphe 1828-1893 ... **NCLC 15**

Talese, Gay 1932- .... **CLC 37**
See also AITN 1; CA 1-4R; CANR 9, 58; DLB 185; INT CANR-9; MTCW

Tallent, Elizabeth (Ann) 1954- .... **CLC 45**
See also CA 117; DLB 130

Tally, Ted 1952- .... **CLC 42**
See also CA 120; 124; INT 124

Tamayo y Baus, Manuel 1829-1898 ... **NCLC 1**

Tammsaare, A(nton) H(ansen) 1878-1940 **TCLC 27**
See also CA 164

Tam'si, Tchicaya U
See Tchicaya, Gerald Felix

Tan, Amy (Ruth) 1952- .... **CLC 59; DAM MULT, NOV, POP**
See also AAYA 9; BEST 89:3; CA 136; CANR 54; DLB 173; SATA 75

Tandem, Felix
See Spitteler, Carl (Friedrich Georg)

Tanizaki, Jun'ichiro 1886-1965 ... **CLC 8, 14, 28; SSC 21**
See also CA 93-96; 25-28R; DLB 180

Tanner, William
See Amis, Kingsley (William)

Tao Lao
See Storni, Alfonsina

Tarassoff, Lev
See Troyat, Henri

Tarbell, Ida M(inerva) 1857-1944 .. **TCLC 40**
See also CA 122; DLB 47

Tarkington, (Newton) Booth 1869-1946 **TCLC 9**
See also CA 110; 143; DLB 9, 102; SATA 17

Tarkovsky, Andrei (Arsenyevich) 1932-1986 **CLC 75**
See also CA 127

Tartt, Donna 1964(?)- .... **CLC 76**
See also CA 142

Tasso, Torquato 1544-1595 .... **LC 5**

Tate, (John Orley) Allen 1899-1979 ... **CLC 2, 4, 6, 9, 11, 14, 24**
See also CA 5-8R; 85-88; CANR 32; DLB 4, 45, 63; MTCW

Tate, Ellalice
See Hibbert, Eleanor Alice Burford

Tate, James (Vincent) 1943- .... **CLC 2, 6, 25**
See also CA 21-24R; CANR 29, 57; DLB 5, 169

Tavel, Ronald 1940- .... **CLC 6**
See also CA 21-24R; CANR 33

Taylor, C(ecil) P(hilip) 1929-1981 ...... **CLC 27**
See also CA 25-28R; 105; CANR 47

Taylor, Edward 1642(?)-1729 ... **LC 11; DA; DAB; DAC; DAM MST, POET**
See also DLB 24

Taylor, Eleanor Ross 1920- .... **CLC 5**
See also CA 81-84

Thoreau, Henry David 1817-1862 .... **NCLC 7, 21, 61; DA; DAB; DAC; DAM MST; WLC**
See also CDALB 1640-1865; DLB 1

Thornton, Hall
See Silverberg, Robert

Thucydides c. 455B.C.-399B.C. ...... **CMLC 17**
See also DLB 176

Thurber, James (Grover) 1894-1961 ... **CLC 5, 11, 25; DA; DAB; DAC; DAM DRAM, MST, NOV; SSC 1**
See also CA 73-76; CANR 17, 39; CDALB 1929-1941; DLB 4, 11, 22, 102; MAICYA; MTCW; SATA 13

Thurman, Wallace (Henry) 1902-1934 ... **TCLC 6; BLC; DAM MULT**
See also BW 1; CA 104; 124; DLB 51

Ticheburn, Cheviot
See Ainsworth, William Harrison

Tieck, (Johann) Ludwig 1773-1853 ... **NCLC 5, 46**
See also DLB 90

Tiger, Derry
See Ellison, Harlan (Jay)

Tilghman, Christopher 1948(?)- .... **CLC 65**
See also CA 159

Tillinghast, Richard (Williford) 1940- ... **CLC 29**
See also CA 29-32R; CAAS 23; CANR 26, 51

Timrod, Henry 1828-1867 .... **NCLC 25**
See also DLB 3

Tindall, Gillian (Elizabeth) 1938- .... **CLC 7**
See also CA 21-24R; CANR 11, 65

Tiptree, James, Jr. .... **CLC 48, 50**
See also Sheldon, Alice Hastings Bradley
See also DLB 8

Titmarsh, Michael Angelo
See Thackeray, William Makepeace

Tocqueville, Alexis (Charles Henri Maurice Clerel Comte) 1805-1859 .... **NCLC 7, 63**

Tolkien, J(ohn) R(onald) R(euel) 1892-1973 **CLC 1, 2, 3, 8, 12, 38; DA; DAB; DAC; DAM MST, NOV, POP; WLC**
See also AAYA 10; AITN 1; CA 17-18; 45-48; CANR 36; CAP 2; CDBLB 1914-1945; DLB 15, 160; JRDA; MAICYA; MTCW; SATA 2, 32; SATA-Obit 24

Toller, Ernst 1893-1939 .... **TCLC 10**
See also CA 107; DLB 124

Tolson, M. B.
See Tolson, Melvin B(eaunorus)

Tolson, Melvin B(eaunorus) 1898(?)-1966 ... **CLC 36, 105; BLC; DAM MULT, POET**
See also BW 1; CA 124; 89-92; DLB 48, 76

Tolstoi, Aleksei Nikolaevich
See Tolstoy, Alexey Nikolaevich

Tolstoy, Alexey Nikolaevich 1882-1945 ... **TCLC 18**
See also CA 107; 158

Tolstoy, Count Leo
See Tolstoy, Leo (Nikolaevich)

Tolstoy, Leo (Nikolaevich) 1828-1910 ... **TCLC 4, 11, 17, 28, 44, 79; DA; DAB; DAC; DAM MST, NOV; SSC 9, 30; WLC**
See also CA 104; 123; SATA 26

Tomasi di Lampedusa, Giuseppe 1896-1957
See Lampedusa, Giuseppe (Tomasi) di
See also CA 111

Tomlin, Lily .... **CLC 17**
See also Tomlin, Mary Jean

Tomlin, Mary Jean 1939(?)-
See Tomlin, Lily
See also CA 117

Tomlinson, (Alfred) Charles 1927- ... **CLC 2, 4, 6, 13, 45; DAM POET; PC 17**
See also CA 5-8R; CANR 33; DLB 40

Tomlinson, H(enry) M(ajor) 1873-1958 **TCLC 71**
See also CA 118; 161; DLB 36, 100, 195

Tonson, Jacob
See Bennett, (Enoch) Arnold

Toole, John Kennedy 1937-1969 .... **CLC 19, 64**
See also CA 104; DLBY 81

Toomer, Jean 1894-1967 ..... **CLC 1, 4, 13, 22; BLC; DAM MULT; PC 7; SSC 1; WLCS**
See also BW 1; CA 85-88; CDALB 1917-1929; DLB 45, 51; MTCW

Torley, Luke
See Blish, James (Benjamin)

Tornimparte, Alessandra
See Ginzburg, Natalia

Torre, Raoul della
See Mencken, H(enry) L(ouis)

Torrey, E(dwin) Fuller 1937- .... **CLC 34**
See also CA 119

Torsvan, Ben Traven
See Traven, B.

Torsvan, Benno Traven
See Traven, B.

Torsvan, Berick Traven
See Traven, B.

Torsvan, Berwick Traven
See Traven, B.

Torsvan, Bruno Traven
See Traven, B.

Torsvan, Traven
See Traven, B.

Tournier, Michel (Edouard) 1924- ... **CLC 6, 23, 36, 95**
See also CA 49-52; CANR 3, 36; DLB 83; MTCW; SATA 23

Tournimparte, Alessandra
See Ginzburg, Natalia

Towers, Ivar
See Kornbluth, C(yril) M.

Towne, Robert (Burton) 1936(?)- ...... **CLC 87**
See also CA 108; DLB 44

Townsend, Sue .... **CLC 61**
See also Townsend, Susan Elaine
See also SATA 55, 93; SATA-Brief 48

Townsend, Susan Elaine 1946-
See Townsend, Sue
See also CA 119; 127; CANR 65; DAB; DAC; DAM MST

Townshend, Peter (Dennis Blandford) 1945- **CLC 17, 42**
See also CA 107

Tozzi, Federigo 1883-1920 .... **TCLC 31**
See also CA 160

Traill, Catharine Parr 1802-1899 ... **NCLC 31**
See also DLB 99

Trakl, Georg 1887-1914 .... **TCLC 5; PC 20**
See also CA 104; 165

Transtroemer, Tomas (Goesta) 1931- ... **CLC 52, 65; DAM POET**
See also CA 117; 129; CAAS 17

Transtromer, Tomas Gosta
See Transtroemer, Tomas (Goesta)

Traven, B. (?)-1969 .... **CLC 8, 11**
See also CA 19-20; 25-28R; CAP 2; DLB 9, 56; MTCW

Treitel, Jonathan 1959- .... **CLC 70**

Tremain, Rose 1943- .... **CLC 42**
See also CA 97-100; CANR 44; DLB 14

Tremblay, Michel 1942- . **CLC 29, 102; DAC; DAM MST**
See also CA 116; 128; DLB 60; MTCW

Trevanian .... **CLC 29**
See also Whitaker, Rod(ney)

Trevor, Glen
See Hilton, James

Trevor, William 1928- ... **CLC 7, 9, 14, 25, 71; SSC 21**
See also Cox, William Trevor
See also DLB 14, 139

Trifonov, Yuri (Valentinovich) 1925-1981 ... **CLC 45**
See also CA 126; 103; MTCW

U Tam'si, Gerald Felix Tchicaya
See Tchicaya, Gerald Felix

U Tam'si, Tchicaya
See Tchicaya, Gerald Felix

Vachss, Andrew (Henry) 1942- .... **CLC 106**
See also CA 118; CANR 44

Vachss, Andrew H.
See Vachss, Andrew (Henry)

Vaculik, Ludvik 1926- .... **CLC 7**
See also CA 53-56

Vaihinger, Hans 1852-1933 .... **TCLC 71**
See also CA 116

Valdez, Luis (Miguel) 1940- .... **CLC 84; DAM MULT; HLC**
See also CA 101; CANR 32; DLB 122; HW

Valenzuela, Luisa 1938- ... **CLC 31, 104; DAM MULT; SSC 14**
See also CA 101; CANR 32, 65; DLB 113; HW

Valera y Alcala-Galiano, Juan 1824-1905 **TCLC 10**
See also CA 106

Valery, (Ambroise) Paul (Toussaint Jules) 1871-1945 .... **TCLC 4, 15; DAM POET; PC 9**
See also CA 104; 122; MTCW

Valle-Inclan, Ramon (Maria) del 1866-1936 **TCLC 5; DAM MULT; HLC**
See also CA 106; 153; DLB 134

Vallejo, Antonio Buero
See Buero Vallejo, Antonio

Vallejo, Cesar (Abraham) 1892-1938 ... **TCLC 3, 56; DAM MULT; HLC**
See also CA 105; 153; HW

Vallette, Marguerite Eymery
See Rachilde

Valle Y Pena, Ramon del
See Valle-Inclan, Ramon (Maria) del

Van Ash, Cay 1918-............................. **CLC 34**

Vanbrugh, Sir John 1664-1726 ... **LC 21; DAM DRAM**
See also DLB 80

Van Campen, Karl
See Campbell, John W(ood, Jr.)

Vance, Gerald
See Silverberg, Robert

Vance, Jack .... **CLC 35**
See also Kuttner, Henry; Vance, John Holbrook
See also DLB 8

Vance, John Holbrook 1916-
See Queen, Ellery; Vance, Jack
See also CA 29-32R; CANR 17, 65; MTCW

Van Den Bogarde, Derek Jules Gaspard Ulric Niven 1921-
See Bogarde, Dirk
See also CA 77-80

Vandenburgh, Jane .... **CLC 59**

Vanderhaeghe, Guy 1951- .... **CLC 41**
See also CA 113

van der Post, Laurens (Jan) 1906-1996 ...**C L C 5**
See also CA 5-8R; 155; CANR 35

van de Wetering, Janwillem 1931- ..... **CLC 47**
See also CA 49-52; CANR 4, 62

Van Dine, S. S. .... **TCLC 23**
See also Wright, Willard Huntington

Van Doren, Carl (Clinton) 1885-1950**TCLC 18**
See also CA 111

Van Doren, Mark 1894-1972 .... **CLC 6, 10**
See also CA 1-4R; 37-40R; CANR 3; DLB 45; MTCW

Van Druten, John (William) 1901-1957 ... **TCLC 2**
See also CA 104; 161; DLB 10

Van Duyn, Mona (Jane) 1921- .. **CLC 3, 7, 63; DAM POET**
See also CA 9-12R; CANR 7, 38, 60; DLB 5

Van Dyne, Edith
See Baum, L(yman) Frank

van Itallie, Jean-Claude 1936- .... **CLC 3**
See also CA 45-48; CAAS 2; CANR 1, 48; DLB 7

van Ostaijen, Paul 1896-1928 .... **TCLC 33**
See also CA 163

Van Peebles, Melvin 1932- .. **CLC 2, 20; DAM MULT**
See also BW 2; CA 85-88; CANR 27, 67

Vansittart, Peter 1920- .... **CLC 42**
See also CA 1-4R; CANR 3, 49

Van Vechten, Carl 1880-1964 .... **CLC 33**
See also CA 89-92; DLB 4, 9, 51

Van Vogt, A(lfred) E(lton) 1912- .... **CLC 1**
See also CA 21-24R; CANR 28; DLB 8; SATA 14

Varda, Agnes 1928-............................. **CLC 16**
See also CA 116; 122

Vargas Llosa, (Jorge) Mario (Pedro) 1936- **CLC 3, 6, 9, 10, 15, 31, 42, 85; DA; DAB; DAC; DAM MST, MULT, NOV; HLC**
See also CA 73-76; CANR 18, 32, 42, 67; DLB 145; HW; MTCW

Vasiliu, Gheorghe 1881-1957
See Bacovia, George
See also CA 123

Vassa, Gustavus
See Equiano, Olaudah

Vassilikos, Vassilis 1933- .... **CLC 4, 8**
See also CA 81-84

Vaughan, Henry 1621-1695 .... **LC 27**
See also DLB 131

Vaughn, Stephanie .... **CLC 62**

Vazov, Ivan (Minchov) 1850-1921 .. **TCLC 25**
See also CA 121; DLB 147

Veblen, Thorstein (Bunde) 1857-1929 ... **TCLC 31**
See also CA 115; 165

Vega, Lope de 1562-1635 .... **LC 23**

Venison, Alfred
See Pound, Ezra (Weston Loomis)

Verdi, Marie de
See Mencken, H(enry) L(ouis)

Verdu, Matilde
See Cela, Camilo Jose

Verga, Giovanni (Carmelo) 1840-1922 ...**TCLC 3; SSC 21**
See also CA 104; 123

Vergil 70B.C.-19B.C. ..... **CMLC 9; DA; DAB; DAC; DAM MST, POET; PC 12; WLCS**

Verhaeren, Emile (Adolphe Gustave) 1855-1916 **TCLC 12**
See also CA 109

Verlaine, Paul (Marie) 1844-1896 ... **NCLC 2, 51; DAM POET; PC 2**

Verne, Jules (Gabriel) 1828-1905 ... **TCLC 6, 52**
See also AAYA 16; CA 110; 131; DLB 123; JRDA; MAICYA; SATA 21

Very, Jones 1813-1880 .... **NCLC 9**
See also DLB 1

Vesaas, Tarjei 1897-1970 .... **CLC 48**
See also CA 29-32R

Vialis, Gaston
See Simenon, Georges (Jacques Christian)

Vian, Boris 1920-1959 .... **TCLC 9**
See also CA 106; 164; DLB 72

Viaud, (Louis Marie) Julien 1850-1923
See Loti, Pierre
See also CA 107

Vicar, Henry
See Felsen, Henry Gregor

Vicker, Angus
See Felsen, Henry Gregor

Vidal, Gore 1925- ... **CLC 2, 4, 6, 8, 10, 22, 33, 72; DAM NOV, POP**
See also AITN 1; BEST 90:2; CA 5-8R; CANR 13, 45, 65; DLB 6, 152; INT CANR-13; MTCW

Walker, Joseph A. 1935- ... **CLC 19; DAM DRAM, MST**
See also BW 1; CA 89-92; CANR 26; DLB 38

Walker, Margaret (Abigail) 1915-...**CLC 1, 6; BLC; DAM MULT; PC 20**
See also BW 2; CA 73-76; CANR 26, 54; DLB 76, 152; MTCW

Walker, Ted ....**CLC 13**
See also Walker, Edward Joseph
See also DLB 40

Wallace, David Foster 1962-...............**CLC 50**
See also CA 132; CANR 59

Wallace, Dexter
See Masters, Edgar Lee

Wallace, (Richard Horatio) Edgar 1875-1932 **TCLC 57**
See also CA 115; DLB 70

Wallace, Irving 1916-1990 ... **CLC 7, 13; DAM NOV, POP**
See also AITN 1; CA 1-4R; 132; CAAS 1; CANR 1, 27; INT CANR-27; MTCW

Wallant, Edward Lewis 1926-1962 ... **CLC 5, 10**
See also CA 1-4R; CANR 22; DLB 2, 28, 143; MTCW

Walley, Byron
See Card, Orson Scott

Walpole, Horace 1717-1797 ....**LC 2**
See also DLB 39, 104

Walpole, Hugh (Seymour) 1884-1941 ... **TCLC 5**
See also CA 104; 165; DLB 34

Walser, Martin 1927- ....**CLC 27**
See also CA 57-60; CANR 8, 46; DLB 75, 124

Walser, Robert 1878-1956 .... **TCLC 18; SSC 20**
See also CA 118; 165; DLB 66

Walsh, Jill Paton ....**CLC 35**
See also Paton Walsh, Gillian
See also AAYA 11; CLR 2; DLB 161; SAAS 3

Walter, Villiam Christian
See Andersen, Hans Christian

Wambaugh, Joseph (Aloysius, Jr.) 1937-...**CLC 3, 18; DAM NOV, POP**
See also AITN 1; BEST 89:3; CA 33-36R; CANR 42, 65; DLB 6; DLBY 83; MTCW

Wang Wei 699(?)-761(?) ....**PC 18**

Ward, Arthur Henry Sarsfield 1883-1959
See Rohmer, Sax
See also CA 108

Ward, Douglas Turner 1930-...............**CLC 19**
See also BW 1; CA 81-84; CANR 27; DLB 7, 38

Ward, Mary Augusta
See Ward, Mrs. Humphry

Ward, Mrs. Humphry 1851-1920 ....**TCLC 55**
See also DLB 18

Ward, Peter
See Faust, Frederick (Schiller)

Warhol, Andy 1928(?)-1987 ....**CLC 20**
See also AAYA 12; BEST 89:4; CA 89-92; 121; CANR 34

Warner, Francis (Robert le Plastrier) 1937- **CLC 14**
See also CA 53-56; CANR 11

Warner, Marina 1946-..........................**CLC 59**
See also CA 65-68; CANR 21, 55; DLB 194

Warner, Rex (Ernest) 1905-1986 ....**CLC 45**
See also CA 89-92; 119; DLB 15

Warner, Susan (Bogert) 1819-1885 ... **NCLC 31**
See also DLB 3, 42

Warner, Sylvia (Constance) Ashton
See Ashton-Warner, Sylvia (Constance)

Warner, Sylvia Townsend 1893-1978 ... **CLC 7, 19; SSC 23**
See also CA 61-64; 77-80; CANR 16, 60; DLB 34, 139; MTCW

Warren, Mercy Otis 1728-1814 ...... **NCLC 13**
See also DLB 31

Warren, Robert Penn 1905-1989 .... **CLC 1, 4, 6, 8, 10, 13, 18, 39, 53, 59; DA; DAB; DAC; DAM MST, NOV, POET; SSC 4; WLC**
See also AITN 1; CA 13-16R; 129; CANR 10, 47; CDALB 1968-1988; DLB 2, 48, 152; DLBY 80, 89; INT CANR-10; MTCW; SATA 46; SATA-Obit 63

Warshofsky, Isaac
See Singer, Isaac Bashevis

Warton, Thomas 1728-1790 ...... **LC 15; DAM POET**
See also DLB 104, 109

Waruk, Kona
See Harris, (Theodore) Wilson

Warung, Price 1855-1911 .... **TCLC 45**

Warwick, Jarvis
See Garner, Hugh

Washington, Alex
See Harris, Mark

Washington, Booker T(aliaferro) 1856-1915 **TCLC 10; BLC; DAM MULT**
See also BW 1; CA 114; 125; SATA 28

Washington, George 1732-1799 .... **LC 25**
See also DLB 31

Wassermann, (Karl) Jakob 1873-1934 ... **TCLC 6**
See also CA 104; DLB 66

Wasserstein, Wendy 1950- .... **CLC 32, 59, 90; DAM DRAM; DC 4**
See also CA 121; 129; CABS 3; CANR 53; INT 129; SATA 94

Waterhouse, Keith (Spencer) 1929-...**CLC 47**
See also CA 5-8R; CANR 38, 67; DLB 13, 15; MTCW

Waters, Frank (Joseph) 1902-1995 .... **CLC 88**
See also CA 5-8R; 149; CAAS 13; CANR 3, 18, 63; DLBY 86

Waters, Roger 1944- ....**CLC 35**

Watkins, Frances Ellen
See Harper, Frances Ellen Watkins

Watkins, Gerrold
See Malzberg, Barry N(athaniel)

Watkins, Gloria 1955(?)-
See hooks, bell
See also BW 2; CA 143

Watkins, Paul 1964- ....**CLC 55**
See also CA 132; CANR 62

Watkins, Vernon Phillips 1906-1967 ... **CLC 43**
See also CA 9-10; 25-28R; CAP 1; DLB 20

Watson, Irving S.
See Mencken, H(enry) L(ouis)

Watson, John H.
See Farmer, Philip Jose

Watson, Richard F.
See Silverberg, Robert

Waugh, Auberon (Alexander) 1939- .... **CLC 7**
See also CA 45-48; CANR 6, 22; DLB 14, 194

Waugh, Evelyn (Arthur St. John) 1903-1966 **CLC 1, 3, 8, 13, 19, 27, 44, 107; DA; DAB; DAC; DAM MST, NOV, POP; WLC**
See also CA 85-88; 25-28R; CANR 22; CDBLB 1914-1945; DLB 15, 162, 195; MTCW

Waugh, Harriet 1944- ....**CLC 6**
See also CA 85-88; CANR 22

Ways, C. R.
See Blount, Roy (Alton), Jr.

Waystaff, Simon
See Swift, Jonathan

Webb, (Martha) Beatrice (Potter) 1858-1943 **TCLC 22**
See also Potter, (Helen) Beatrix
See also CA 117

Webb, Charles (Richard) 1939- ....**CLC 7**
See also CA 25-28R

Webb, James H(enry), Jr. 1946-.........**CLC 22**
See also CA 81-84

Webb, Mary (Gladys Meredith) 1881-1927 **TCLC 24**
See also CA 123; DLB 34

Wheelock, John Hall 1886-1978 .... **CLC 14**
See also CA 13-16R; 77-80; CANR 14; DLB 45

White, E(lwyn) B(rooks) 1899-1985 ... **CLC 10,
34, 39; DAM POP**
See also AITN 2; CA 13-16R; 116; CANR 16,
37; CLR 1, 21; DLB 11, 22; MAICYA;
MTCW; SATA 2, 29; SATA-Obit 44

White, Edmund (Valentine III) 1940- .... **CLC
27; DAM POP**
See also AAYA 7; CA 45-48; CANR 3, 19, 36,
62; MTCW

White, Patrick (Victor Martindale) 1912-1990
CLC 3, 4, 5, 7, 9, 18, 65, 69
See also CA 81-84; 132; CANR 43; MTCW

White, Phyllis Dorothy James 1920-
See James, P. D.
See also CA 21-24R; CANR 17, 43, 65; DAM
POP; MTCW

White, T(erence) H(anbury) 1906-1964 ... **CLC 30**
See also AAYA 22; CA 73-76; CANR 37; DLB
160; JRDA; MAICYA; SATA 12

White, Terence de Vere 1912-1994 .... **CLC 49**
See also CA 49-52; 145; CANR 3

White, Walter F(rancis) 1893-1955 **TCLC 15**
See also White, Walter
See also BW 1; CA 115; 124; DLB 51

White, William Hale 1831-1913
See Rutherford, Mark
See also CA 121

Whitehead, E(dward) A(nthony) 1933- **CLC 5**
See also CA 65-68; CANR 58

Whitemore, Hugh (John) 1936- .... **CLC 37**
See also CA 132; INT 132

Whitman, Sarah Helen (Power) 1803-1878
NCLC 19
See also DLB 1

Whitman, Walt(er) 1819-1892 ... **NCLC 4, 31;
DA; DAB; DAC; DAM MST, POET; PC 3;
WLC**
See also CDALB 1640-1865; DLB 3, 64; SATA
20

Whitney, Phyllis A(yame) 1903- ... **CLC 42; DAM
POP**
See also AITN 2; BEST 90:3; CA 1-4R; CANR
3, 25, 38, 60; JRDA; MAICYA; SATA 1, 30

Whittemore, (Edward) Reed (Jr.) 1919- ... **CLC 4**
See also CA 9-12R; CAAS 8; CANR 4; DLB 5

Whittier, John Greenleaf 1807-1892 ... **N C L C
8, 59**
See also DLB 1

Whittlebot, Hernia
See Coward, Noel (Peirce)

Wicker, Thomas Grey 1926-
See Wicker, Tom
See also CA 65-68; CANR 21, 46

Wicker, Tom .... **CLC 7**
See also Wicker, Thomas Grey

Wideman, John Edgar 1941- ... **CLC 5, 34, 36,
67; BLC; DAM MULT**
See also BW 2; CA 85-88; CANR 14, 42, 67;
DLB 33, 143

Wiebe, Rudy (Henry) 1934- .... **CLC 6, 11, 14;
DAC; DAM MST**
See also CA 37-40R; CANR 42, 67; DLB 60

Wieland, Christoph Martin 1733-1813 ... **NCLC
17**
See also DLB 97

Wiene, Robert 1881-1938 .... **TCLC 56**

Wieners, John 1934- .... **CLC 7**
See also CA 13-16R; DLB 16

Wiesel, Elie(zer) 1928- ... **CLC 3, 5, 11, 37; DA;
DAB; DAC; DAM MST, NOV; WLCS 2**
See also AAYA 7; AITN 1; CA 5-8R; CAAS 4;
CANR 8, 40, 65; DLB 83; DLBY 87; INT
CANR-8; MTCW; SATA 56

Wiggins, Marianne 1947- .... **CLC 57**
See also BEST 89:3; CA 130; CANR 60

Wight, James Alfred 1916-
See Herriot, James
See also CA 77-80; SATA 55; SATA-Brief 44

Wilbur, Richard (Purdy) 1921- ... **CLC 3, 6, 9,
14, 53; DA; DAB; DAC; DAM MST, POET**
See also CA 1-4R; CABS 2; CANR 2, 29; DLB
5, 169; INT CANR-29; MTCW; SATA 9

Wild, Peter 1940- .... **CLC 14**
See also CA 37-40R; DLB 5

Wilde, Oscar (Fingal O'Flahertie Wills) 1854(?)-
1900 ... **TCLC 1, 8, 23, 41; DA; DAB; DAC;
DAM DRAM, MST, NOV; SSC 11; WLC**
See also CA 104; 119; CDBLB 1890-1914; DLB
10, 19, 34, 57, 141, 156, 190; SATA 24

Wilder, Billy .... **CLC 20**
See also Wilder, Samuel
See also DLB 26

Wilder, Samuel 1906-
See Wilder, Billy
See also CA 89-92

Wilder, Thornton (Niven) 1897-1975 ... **CLC 1,
5, 6, 10, 15, 35, 82; DA; DAB; DAC; DAM
DRAM, MST, NOV; DC 1; WLC**
See also AITN 2; CA 13-16R; 61-64; CANR 40;
DLB 4, 7, 9; DLBY 97; MTCW

Wilding, Michael 1942- .... **CLC 73**
See also CA 104; CANR 24, 49

Wiley, Richard 1944- .... **CLC 44**
See also CA 121; 129

Wilhelm, Kate .... **CLC 7**
See also Wilhelm, Katie Gertrude
See also AAYA 20; CAAS 5; DLB 8; INT CANR-
17

Wilhelm, Katie Gertrude 1928-
See Wilhelm, Kate
See also CA 37-40R; CANR 17, 36, 60; MTCW

Wilkins, Mary
See Freeman, Mary Eleanor Wilkins

Willard, Nancy 1936- .... **CLC 7, 37**
See also CA 89-92; CANR 10, 39, 68; CLR 5;
DLB 5, 52; MAICYA; MTCW; SATA 37, 71;
SATA-Brief 30

Williams, C(harles) K(enneth) 1936- ... **CLC 33,
56; DAM POET**
See also CA 37-40R; CAAS 26; CANR 57; DLB
5

Williams, Charles
See Collier, James L(incoln)

Williams, Charles (Walter Stansby) 1886-1945
TCLC 1, 11
See also CA 104; 163; DLB 100, 153

Williams, (George) Emlyn 1905-1987 .... **C L C
15; DAM DRAM**
See also CA 104; 123; CANR 36; DLB 10, 77;
MTCW

Williams, Hugo 1942- .... **CLC 42**
See also CA 17-20R; CANR 45; DLB 40

Williams, J. Walker
See Wodehouse, P(elham) G(renville)

Williams, John A(lfred) 1925- ... **CLC 5, 13;
BLC; DAM MULT**
See also BW 2; CA 53-56; CAAS 3; CANR 6,
26, 51; DLB 2, 33; INT CANR-6

Williams, Jonathan (Chamberlain) 1929- ... **CLC
13**
See also CA 9-12R; CAAS 12; CANR 8; DLB
5

Williams, Joy 1944- .... **CLC 31**
See also CA 41-44R; CANR 22, 48

Williams, Norman 1952- .... **CLC 39**
See also CA 118

Williams, Sherley Anne 1944- ... **CLC 89; BLC;
DAM MULT, POET**
See also BW 2; CA 73-76; CANR 25; DLB 41;
INT CANR-25; SATA 78

Williams, Shirley
See Williams, Sherley Anne

Williams, Tennessee 1911-1983 ... **CLC 1, 2, 5,
7, 8, 11, 15, 19, 30, 39, 45, 71; DA; DAB;
DAC; DAM DRAM, MST; DC 4; WLC**
See also AITN 1, 2; CA 5-8R; 108; CABS 3;
CANR 31; CDALB 1941-1968; DLB 7;
DLBD 4; DLBY 83; MTCW

Williams, Thomas (Alonzo) 1926-1990 ... **CLC
14**
See also CA 1-4R; 132; CANR 2

Williams, William C.
See Williams, William Carlos

Williams, William Carlos 1883-1963 ... **CLC 1, 2, 5, 9, 13, 22, 42, 67; DA; DAB; DAC; DAM MST, POET; PC 7**
See also CA 89-92; CANR 34; CDALB 1917-1929; DLB 4, 16, 54, 86; MTCW

Williamson, David (Keith) 1942- .... **CLC 56**
See also CA 103; CANR 41

Williamson, Ellen Douglas 1905-1984
See Douglas, Ellen
See also CA 17-20R; 114; CANR 39

Williamson, Jack .... **CLC 29**
See also Williamson, John Stewart
See also CAAS 8; DLB 8

Williamson, John Stewart 1908-
See Williamson, Jack
See also CA 17-20R; CANR 23

Willie, Frederick
See Lovecraft, H(oward) P(hillips)

Willingham, Calder (Baynard, Jr.) 1922-1995
CLC 5, 51
See also CA 5-8R; 147; CANR 3; DLB 2, 44; MTCW

Willis, Charles
See Clarke, Arthur C(harles)

Willy
See Colette, (Sidonie-Gabrielle)

Willy, Colette
See Colette, (Sidonie-Gabrielle)

Wilson, A(ndrew) N(orman) 1950- .... **CLC 33**
See also CA 112; 122; DLB 14, 155, 194

Wilson, Angus (Frank Johnstone) 1913-1991
CLC 2, 3, 5, 25, 34; SSC 21
See also CA 5-8R; 134; CANR 21; DLB 15, 139, 155; MTCW

Wilson, August 1945- .... **CLC 39, 50, 63; BLC; DA; DAB; DAC; DAM DRAM, MST, MULT; DC 2; WLCS**
See also AAYA 16; BW 2; CA 115; 122; CANR 42, 54; MTCW

Wilson, Brian 1942- .... **CLC 12**

Wilson, Colin 1931- .... **CLC 3, 14**
See also CA 1-4R; CAAS 5; CANR 1, 22, 33; DLB 14, 194; MTCW

Wilson, Dirk
See Pohl, Frederik

Wilson, Edmund 1895-1972 ...... **CLC 1, 2, 3, 8, 24**
See also CA 1-4R; 37-40R; CANR 1, 46; DLB 63; MTCW

Wilson, Ethel Davis (Bryant) 1888(?)-1980
CLC 13; DAC; DAM POET
See also CA 102; DLB 68; MTCW

Wilson, John 1785-1854 .... **NCLC 5**

Wilson, John (Anthony) Burgess 1917-1993
See Burgess, Anthony
See also CA 1-4R; 143; CANR 2, 46; DAC; DAM NOV; MTCW

Wilson, Lanford 1937- ... **CLC 7, 14, 36; DAM DRAM**
See also CA 17-20R; CABS 3; CANR 45; DLB 7

Wilson, Robert M. 1944- .... **CLC 7, 9**
See also CA 49-52; CANR 2, 41; MTCW

Wilson, Robert McLiam 1964- .... **CLC 59**
See also CA 132

Wilson, Sloan 1920- .... **CLC 32**
See also CA 1-4R; CANR 1, 44

Wilson, Snoo 1948- .... **CLC 33**
See also CA 69-72

Wilson, William S(mith) 1932- .... **CLC 49**
See also CA 81-84

Wilson, Woodrow 1856-1924 .... **TCLC 73**
See also DLB 47

Winchilsea, Anne (Kingsmill) Finch Counte 1661-1720
See Finch, Anne

Windham, Basil
See Wodehouse, P(elham) G(renville)

Wingrove, David (John) 1954- .... **CLC 68**
See also CA 133

Wintergreen, Jane
See Duncan, Sara Jeannette

Winters, Janet Lewis .... **CLC 41**
See also Lewis, Janet
See also DLBY 87

Winters, (Arthur) Yvor 1900-1968 ... **CLC 4, 8, 32**
See also CA 11-12; 25-28R; CAP 1; DLB 48; MTCW

Winterson, Jeanette 1959- ... **CLC 64; DAM POP**
See also CA 136; CANR 58

Winthrop, John 1588-1649 .... **LC 31**
See also DLB 24, 30

Wiseman, Frederick 1930- .... **CLC 20**
See also CA 159

Wister, Owen 1860-1938 .... **TCLC 21**
See also CA 108; 162; DLB 9, 78, 186; SATA 62

Witkacy
See Witkiewicz, Stanislaw Ignacy

Witkiewicz, Stanislaw Ignacy 1885-1939 ... **TCLC 8**
See also CA 105; 162

Wittgenstein, Ludwig (Josef Johann) 1889-1951
TCLC 59
See also CA 113; 164

Wittig, Monique 1935(?)- .... **CLC 22**
See also CA 116; 135; DLB 83

Wittlin, Jozef 1896-1976 .... **CLC 25**
See also CA 49-52; 65-68; CANR 3

Wodehouse, P(elham) G(renville) 1881-1975
CLC 1, 2, 5, 10, 22; DAB; DAC; DAM NOV; SSC 2
See also AITN 2; CA 45-48; 57-60; CANR 3, 33; CDBLB 1914-1945; DLB 34, 162; MTCW; SATA 22

Woiwode, L.
See Woiwode, Larry (Alfred)

Woiwode, Larry (Alfred) 1941- ...... **CLC 6, 10**
See also CA 73-76; CANR 16; DLB 6; INT CANR-16

Wojciechowska, Maia (Teresa) 1927- ... **CLC 26**
See also AAYA 8; CA 9-12R; CANR 4, 41; CLR 1; JRDA; MAICYA; SAAS 1; SATA 1, 28, 83

Wolf, Christa 1929- .... **CLC 14, 29, 58**
See also CA 85-88; CANR 45; DLB 75; MTCW

Wolfe, Gene (Rodman) 1931- .... **CLC 25; DAM POP**
See also CA 57-60; CAAS 9; CANR 6, 32, 60; DLB 8

Wolfe, George C. 1954- .... **CLC 49**
See also CA 149

Wolfe, Thomas (Clayton) 1900-1938 ... **TCLC 4, 13, 29, 61; DA; DAB; DAC; DAM MST, NOV; WLC**
See also CA 104; 132; CDALB 1929-1941; DLB 9, 102; DLBD 2, 16; DLBY 85, 97; MTCW

Wolfe, Thomas Kennerly, Jr. 1931-
See Wolfe, Tom
See also CA 13-16R; CANR 9, 33; DAM POP; DLB 185; INT CANR-9; MTCW

Wolfe, Tom .... **CLC 1, 2, 9, 15, 35, 51**
See also Wolfe, Thomas Kennerly, Jr.
See also AAYA 8; AITN 2; BEST 89:1; DLB 152

Wolff, Geoffrey (Ansell) 1937- .... **CLC 41**
See also CA 29-32R; CANR 29, 43

Wolff, Sonia
See Levitin, Sonia (Wolff)

Wolff, Tobias (Jonathan Ansell) 1945- ... **CLC 39, 64**
See also AAYA 16; BEST 90:2; CA 114; 117; CAAS 22; CANR 54; DLB 130; INT 117

Wolfram von Eschenbach c. 1170-c. 1220
CMLC 5
See also DLB 138

Wolitzer, Hilma 1930- .... **CLC 17**
See also CA 65-68; CANR 18, 40; INT CANR-18; SATA 31

Wollstonecraft, Mary 1759-1797 .... **LC 5**
See also CDBLB 1789-1832; DLB 39, 104, 158

Wonder, Stevie ....**CLC 12**
See also Morris, Steveland Judkins

Wong, Jade Snow 1922- ....**CLC 17**
See also CA 109

Woodberry, George Edward 1855-1930 ...**TCLC 73**
See also CA 165; DLB 71, 103

Woodcott, Keith
See Brunner, John (Kilian Houston)

Woodruff, Robert W.
See Mencken, H(enry) L(ouis)

Woolf, (Adeline) Virginia 1882-1941 ... **TCLC 1, 5, 20, 43, 56; DA; DAB; DAC; DAM MST, NOV; SSC 7; WLC**
See also CA 104; 130; CANR 64; CDBLB 1914-1945; DLB 36, 100, 162; DLBD 10; MTCW

Woolf, Virginia Adeline
See Woolf, (Adeline) Virginia

Woollcott, Alexander (Humphreys) 1887-1943 **TCLC 5**
See also CA 105; 161; DLB 29

Woolrich, Cornell 1903-1968 ....**CLC 77**
See also Hopley-Woolrich, Cornell George

Wordsworth, Dorothy 1771-1855 ... **NCLC 25**
See also DLB 107

Wordsworth, William 1770-1850 ... **NCLC 12, 38; DA; DAB; DAC; DAM MST, POET; PC 4; WLC**
See also CDBLB 1789-1832; DLB 93, 107

Wouk, Herman 1915- ...... **CLC 1, 9, 38; DAM NOV, POP**
See also CA 5-8R; CANR 6, 33, 67; DLBY 82; INT CANR-6; MTCW

Wright, Charles (Penzel, Jr.) 1935- ... **CLC 6, 13, 28**
See also CA 29-32R; CAAS 7; CANR 23, 36, 62; DLB 165; DLBY 82; MTCW

Wright, Charles Stevenson 1932- ... **CLC 49; BLC 3; DAM MULT, POET**
See also BW 1; CA 9-12R; CANR 26; DLB 33

Wright, Jack R.
See Harris, Mark

Wright, James (Arlington) 1927-1980 ... **CLC 3, 5, 10, 28; DAM POET**
See also AITN 2; CA 49-52; 97-100; CANR 4, 34, 64; DLB 5, 169; MTCW

Wright, Judith (Arandell) 1915- ... **CLC 11, 53; PC 14**
See also CA 13-16R; CANR 31; MTCW; SATA 14

Wright, L(aurali) R. 1939- ....**CLC 44**
See also CA 138

Wright, Richard (Nathaniel) 1908-1960 ... **CLC 1, 3, 4, 9, 14, 21, 48, 74; BLC; DA; DAB;**
DAC; DAM MST, MULT, NOV; SSC 2; WLC
See also AAYA 5; BW 1; CA 108; CANR 64; CDALB 1929-1941; DLB 76, 102; DLBD 2; MTCW

Wright, Richard B(ruce) 1937- ....**CLC 6**
See also CA 85-88; DLB 53

Wright, Rick 1945- ....**CLC 35**

Wright, Rowland
See Wells, Carolyn

Wright, Stephen 1946- ....**CLC 33**

Wright, Willard Huntington 1888-1939
See Van Dine, S. S.
See also CA 115; DLBD 16

Wright, William 1930- ....**CLC 44**
See also CA 53-56; CANR 7, 23

Wroth, LadyMary 1587-1653(?) ....**LC 30**
See also DLB 121

Wu Ch'eng-en 1500(?)-1582(?) ....**LC 7**

Wu Ching-tzu 1701-1754 ....**LC 2**

Wurlitzer, Rudolph 1938(?)- ....**CLC 2, 4, 15**
See also CA 85-88; DLB 173

Wycherley, William 1641-1715 ...**LC 8, 21; DAM DRAM**
See also CDBLB 1660-1789; DLB 80

Wylie, Elinor (Morton Hoyt) 1885-1928 ... **TCLC 8**
See also CA 105; 162; DLB 9, 45

Wylie, Philip (Gordon) 1902-1971 .....**CLC 43**
See also CA 21-22; 33-36R; CAP 2; DLB 9

Wyndham, John ....**CLC 19**
See also Harris, John (Wyndham Parkes Lucas) Beynon

Wyss, Johann David Von 1743-1818 ... **N C L C 10**
See also JRDA; MAICYA; SATA 29; SATA-Brief 27

Xenophon c. 430B.C.-c. 354B.C. .... **CMLC 17**
See also DLB 176

Yakumo Koizumi
See Hearn, (Patricio) Lafcadio (Tessima Carlos)

Yanez, Jose Donoso
See Donoso (Yanez), Jose

Yanovsky, Basile S.
See Yanovsky, V(assily) S(emenovich)

Yanovsky, V(assily) S(emenovich) 1906-1989 **CLC 2, 18**
See also CA 97-100; 129

Yates, Richard 1926-1992 ....**CLC 7, 8, 23**
See also CA 5-8R; 139; CANR 10, 43; DLB 2; DLBY 81, 92; INT CANR-10

Yeats, W. B.
See Yeats, William Butler

Yeats, William Butler 1865-1939 ... **TCLC 1, 11, 18, 31; DA; DAB; DAC; DAM DRAM, MST, POET; PC 20; WLC**
See also CA 104; 127; CANR 45; CDBLB 1890-1914; DLB 10, 19, 98, 156; MTCW

Yehoshua, A(braham) B. 1936- .... **CLC 13, 31**
See also CA 33-36R; CANR 43

Yep, Laurence Michael 1948- ....**CLC 35**
See also AAYA 5; CA 49-52; CANR 1, 46; CLR 3, 17; DLB 52; JRDA; MAICYA; SATA 7, 69

Yerby, Frank G(arvin) 1916-1991 ...**CLC 1, 7, 22; BLC; DAM MULT**
See also BW 1; CA 9-12R; 136; CANR 16, 52; DLB 76; INT CANR-16; MTCW

Yesenin, Sergei Alexandrovich
See Esenin, Sergei (Alexandrovich)

Yevtushenko, Yevgeny (Alexandrovich) 1933-
CLC 1, 3, 13, 26, 51; DAM POET
See also CA 81-84; CANR 33, 54; MTCW

Yezierska, Anzia 1885(?)-1970 ....**CLC 46**
See also CA 126; 89-92; DLB 28; MTCW

Yglesias, Helen 1915- ....**CLC 7, 22**
See also CA 37-40R; CAAS 20; CANR 15, 65; INT CANR-15; MTCW

Yokomitsu Riichi 1898-1947 ....**TCLC 47**

Yonge, Charlotte (Mary) 1823-1901 ... **TCLC 48**
See also CA 109; 163; DLB 18, 163; SATA 17

York, Jeremy
See Creasey, John

York, Simon
See Heinlein, Robert A(nson)

Yorke, Henry Vincent 1905-1974 ....**CLC 13**
See also Green, Henry
See also CA 85-88; 49-52

Yosano Akiko 1878-1942 ......**TCLC 59; PC 11**
See also CA 161

Yoshimoto, Banana ....**CLC 84**
See also Yoshimoto, Mahoko

Yoshimoto, Mahoko 1964-
See Yoshimoto, Banana
See also CA 144

Young, Al(bert James) 1939- ... **CLC 19; BLC; DAM MULT**
See also BW 2; CA 29-32R; CANR 26, 65; DLB 33

Young, Andrew (John) 1885-1971 ....**CLC 5**
See also CA 5-8R; CANR 7, 29

Young, Collier
See Bloch, Robert (Albert)

Young, Edward 1683-1765 .... **LC 3, 40**
See also DLB 95

Young, Marguerite (Vivian) 1909-1995 ... **CLC 82**
See also CA 13-16; 150; CAP 1

Young, Neil 1945- .... **CLC 17**
See also CA 110

Young Bear, Ray A. 1950- .... **CLC 94; DAM MULT**
See also CA 146; DLB 175; NNAL

Yourcenar, Marguerite 1903-1987 ... **CLC 19, 38, 50, 87; DAM NOV**
See also CA 69-72; CANR 23, 60; DLB 72; DLBY 88; MTCW

Yurick, Sol 1925- .... **CLC 6**
See also CA 13-16R; CANR 25

Zabolotskii, Nikolai Alekseevich 1903-1958 **TCLC 52**
See also CA 116; 164

Zamiatin, Yevgenii
See Zamyatin, Evgeny Ivanovich

Zamora, Bernice (B. Ortiz) 1938- .... **CLC 89; DAM MULT; HLC**
See also CA 151; DLB 82; HW

Zamyatin, Evgeny Ivanovich 1884-1937 **TCLC 8, 37**
See also CA 105

Zangwill, Israel 1864-1926 .... **TCLC 16**
See also CA 109; DLB 10, 135

Zappa, Francis Vincent, Jr. 1940-1993
See Zappa, Frank
See also CA 108; 143; CANR 57

Zappa, Frank .... **CLC 17**
See also Zappa, Francis Vincent, Jr.

Zaturenska, Marya 1902-1982 .... **CLC 6, 11**
See also CA 13-16R; 105; CANR 22

Zeami 1363-1443 .... **DC 7**

Zelazny, Roger (Joseph) 1937-1995 .... **CLC 21**
See also AAYA 7; CA 21-24R; 148; CANR 26, 60; DLB 8; MTCW; SATA 57; SATA-Brief 39

Zhdanov, Andrei A(lexandrovich) 1896-1948 **TCLC 18**
See also CA 117

Zhukovsky, Vasily 1783-1852 .... **NCLC 35**

Ziegenhagen, Eric .... **CLC 55**

Zimmer, Jill Schary
See Robinson, Jill

Zimmerman, Robert
See Dylan, Bob

Zindel, Paul 1936- .... **CLC 6, 26; DA; DAB; DAC; DAM DRAM, MST, NOV; DC 5**
See also AAYA 2; CA 73-76; CANR 31, 65; CLR 3, 45; DLB 7, 52; JRDA; MAICYA; MTCW; SATA 16, 58

Zinov'Ev, A. A.
See Zinoviev, Alexander (Aleksandrovich)

Zinoviev, Alexander (Aleksandrovich) 1922- **CLC 19**
See also CA 116; 133; CAAS 10

Zoilus
See Lovecraft, H(oward) P(hillips)

Zola, Emile (Edouard Charles Antoine) 1840-1902 ... **TCLC 1, 6, 21, 41; DA; DAB; DAC; DAM MST, NOV; WLC**
See also CA 104; 138; DLB 123

Zoline, Pamela 1941- .... **CLC 62**
See also CA 161

Zorrilla y Moral, Jose 1817-1893 ..... **NCLC 6**

Zoshchenko, Mikhail (Mikhailovich) 1895-1958 **TCLC 15; SSC 15**
See also CA 115; 160

Zuckmayer, Carl 1896-1977 .... **CLC 18**
See also CA 69-72; DLB 56, 124

Zuk, Georges
See Skelton, Robin

Zukofsky, Louis 1904-1978 ... **CLC 1, 2, 4, 7, 11, 18; DAM POET; PC 11**
See also CA 9-12R; 77-80; CANR 39; DLB 5, 165; MTCW

Zweig, Paul 1935-1984 .... **CLC 34, 42**
See also CA 85-88; 113

Zweig, Stefan 1881-1942 .... **TCLC 17**
See also CA 112; DLB 81, 118

Zwingli, Huldreich 1484-1531 .... **LC 37**
See also DLB 179

Poetry Criticism
Cumulative Nationality Index

AMERICAN

Ammons, A(rchie) R(andolph) **16**
Auden, W(ystan) H(ugh) **1**
Baraka, Amiri **4**
Bishop, Elizabeth **3**
Bogan, Louise **12**
Bradstreet, Anne **10**
Brodsky, Joseph **9**
Brooks, Gwendolyn **7**
Bryant, William Cullen **20**
Bukowski, Charles **18**
Carruth, Hayden **10**
Clampitt, Amy **19**
Clifton, (Thelma) Lucille **17**
Crane, (Harold) Hart **3**
Cullen, Countee **20**
Cummings, E(dward) E(stlin) **5**
Dickinson, Emily (Elizabeth) **1**
Doolittle, Hilda **5**
Dove, Rita (Frances) **6**
Dunbar, Paul Laurence **5**
Duncan, Robert (Edward) **2**
Eliot, T(homas) S(tearns) **5**
Emerson, Ralph Waldo **18**
Ferlinghetti, Lawrence (Monsanto) **1**
Forche, Carolyn (Louise) **10**
Frost, Robert (Lee) **1**
Gallagher, Tess **9**
Ginsberg, Allen **4**
Giovanni, Nikki **19**
Gluck, Louise (Elisabeth) **16**
Hammon, Jupiter **16**
Harper, Frances Ellen Watkins **21**
Hass, Robert **16**
Hayden, Robert E(arl) **6**
H. D. **5**
Hughes, (James) Langston **1**
Jeffers, (John) Robinson **17**
Knight, Etheridge **14**
Kumin, Maxine (Winokur) **15**
Kunitz, Stanley (Jasspon) **19**
Levertov, Denise **11**
Levine, Philip **22**
Lorde, Audre (Geraldine) **12**
Lowell, Amy **13**
Lowell, Robert (Traill Spence Jr.) **3**
Loy, Mina **16**
Madhubuti, Haki R. **5**
Masters, Edgar Lee **1**
McKay, Claude **2**
Merton, Thomas **10**
Millay, Edna St. Vincent **6**
Moore, Marianne (Craig) **4**
Nash, (Frediric) Ogden **21**
Olds, Sharon **22**
Olson, Charles (John) **19**
Ortiz, Simon J(oseph) **17**
Plath, Sylvia **1**

Poe, Edgar Allan **1**
Pound, Ezra (Weston Loomis) **4**
Rexroth, Kenneth **20**
Rich, Adrienne (Cecile) **5**
Robinson, Edwin Arlington **1**
Roethke, Theodore (Huebner) **15**
Rose, Wendy **13**
Rukeyser, Muriel **12**
Sanchez, Sonia **9**
Sandburg, Carl (August) **2**
Schwartz, Delmore (David) **8**
Sexton, Anne (Harvey) **2**
Snyder, Gary (Sherman) **21**
Song, Cathy **21**
Stein, Gertrude **18**
Stevens, Wallace **6**
Swenson, May **14**
Toomer, Jean **7**
Wakoski, Diane **15**
Walker, Margaret (Abigail) **20**
Wheatley (Peters), Phillis **3**
Whitman, Walt(er) **3**
Williams, William Carlos **7**
Zukofsky, Louis **11**

ARGENTINIAN

Borges, Jorge Luis **22**

AUSTRALIAN

Wright, Judith (Arandell) **14**

AUSTRIAN

Trakl, Georg **20**

CANADIAN

Atwood, Margaret (Eleanor) **8**
Bissett, Bill **14**
Page, P(atricia) K(athleen) **12**

CHILEAN

Neruda, Pablo **4**

CHINESE

Li Ho **13**
Tu Fu **9**
Wang Wei **18**

ENGLISH

Arnold, Matthew **5**
Auden, W(ystan) H(ugh) **1**
Behn, Aphra **13**
Blake, William **12**
Bradstreet, Anne **10**
Bronte, Emily (Jane) **8**
Browning, Elizabeth Barrett **6**
Browning, Robert **2**
Byron, George Gordon (Noel) **16**
Carroll, Lewis **18**

Chaucer, Geoffrey **19**
Coleridge, Samuel Taylor **11**
Day Lewis, C(ecil) **11**
Donne, John **1**
Eliot, George **20**
Eliot, T(homas) S(tearns) **5**
Graves, Robert (von Ranke) **6**
Gray, Thomas **2**
Hardy, Thomas **8**
Herbert, George **4**
Herrick, Robert **9**
Hopkins, Gerard Manley **15**
Housman, A(lfred) E(dward) **2**
Hughes, Ted **7**
Jonson, Ben(jamin) **17**
Keats, John **1**
Kipling, (Joseph) Rudyard **3**
Larkin, Philip (Arthur) **21**
Levertov, Denise **11**
Loy, Mina **16**
Marvell, Andrew **10**
Milton, John **19**
Montagu, Mary (Pierrepont) Wortley **16**
Owen, Wilfred (Edward Salter) **19**
Page, P(atricia) K(athleen) **12**
Rossetti, Christina (Georgina) **7**
Sassoon, Siegfried (Lorraine) **12**
Shelley, Percy Bysshe **14**
Sitwell, Dame Edith **3**
Smart, Christopher **13**
Smith, Stevie **12**
Spenser, Edmund **8**
Swift, Jonathan **9**
Tennyson, Alfred **6**
Tomlinson, (Alfred) Charles **17**
Wordsworth, William **4**

FRENCH

Apollinaire, Guillaume **7**
Baudelaire, Charles **1**
Breton, Andre **15**
Gautier, Theophile **18**
Hugo, Victor (Marie) **17**
Laforgue, Jules **14**
Lamartine, Alphonse (Marie Louis Prat) de **16**
Mallarme, Stephane **4**
Marie de France **22**
Merton, Thomas **10**
Nerval, Gerard de **13**
Rimbaud, (Jean Nicolas) Arthur **3**
Ronsard, Pierre de **11**
Valery, (Ambroise) Paul (Toussaint Jules) **9**
Verlaine, Paul (Marie) **2**
Villon, Francois **13**

GERMAN

Bukowski, Charles **18**
Goethe, Johann Wolfgang von **5**

PC Cumulative Title Index

Title Index

Title Index

Title Index

Title Index

Title Index

See "Los cisnes"
"The Swans" (Lowell) **13**:86
The Swans' Encampment (Tsvetaeva)
See *Lebediny stan*
"The Swarm" (Plath) **1**:410, 412
"Swaziland" (Giovanni) **19**:141
"Sweeney among the Nightingales" (Eliot) **5**:184
Sweeney Astray (Heaney) **18**:215-18, 235
"Sweeney Redivivus" (Heaney) **18**:215, 228, 233
"Sweet Afton" (Burns) **6**:77
"Sweet Boy, Give me Yr Ass" (Ginsberg) **4**:90
"A Sweet Flying Dream" (Ferlinghetti) **1**:183, 188
"Sweet Hopes" (Pushkin)
See "Nadezhdoi Sladostnoi"
"Sweet Michel" (Browning) **2**:30
"The Sweet Primroses" (Hardy) **8**:130
Sweet Will (Levine) **22**:221, 224, 226
"Sweetened Change" (Ammons) **16**:63
"Sweetest love, I do not goe" (Donne)
See "Song. 'Sweetest love, I do not goe'"
Swellfoot the Tyrant (Shelley) **14**:175, 202
"Swells" (Ammons) **16**:32, 63
"Swiadomość" (Milosz) **8**:209
"Swiftly walk over the western wave" (Shelley) **14**:177
"The Swimmer" (Olds) **22**:323, 325
"Swimmers" (Swenson) **14**:265, 276, 287
"Swimming Chenango Lake" (Tomlinson) **17**:316, 319, 321, 328
"Switzerland" (Arnold) **5**:12-13
Sword Blades and Poppy Seed (Lowell) **13**:69-70, 76, 93
"A Sword in a Cloud of Light" (Rexroth) **20**:190
Swords Like Lips (Aleixandre)
See *Espadas como labios*
"Sygil" (H. D.) **5**:306
"The Syllable Pain" (Celan) **10**:102
"Le sylphe" (Valery) **9**:387, 391, 393
"Sylvia's Death" (Sexton) **2**:364, 370
"Symbolism in Painting" (Yeats) **20**:299
The Symbolism of Poetry (Yeats) **20**:336
"Symmetrical Companion" (Swenson) **14**:274, 284
"Sympathetic Portrait of a Child" (Williams) **7**:349
"Sympathy" (Dunbar) **5**:134
"Symphonie en blanc majeur" (Gautier) **18**:124-27, 129-30
"Symptoms of Love" (Graves) **6**:155
"The Syrophenician Woman" (Harper) **21**:208, 215-16
Szomoru beres (Illyes) **16**:238, 247
T. V. Baby Poems (Ginsberg) **4**:47
Ta eleýa tis Oxópetras (Elytis) **21**:134-35
"Tabacaria" (Pessoa) **20**:166, 169
"Tabibito" (Nishiwaki) **15**:229
Tabibito Kaerazu (Nishiwaki) **15**:229-36
"A Table" (Stein) **18**:320-22, 324, 328, 330, 350
"Table I" (Milosz) **8**:210
"Table II" (Milosz) **8**:210
"Tableau" (Cullen) **20**:64
"Tagore's Last Poems" (Tagore)
See "Sesh lekha"
"Tahirassawichi en Washington" (Cardenal) **22**:131
"Tahirassawichi in Washington"
See "Tahirassawichi en Washington"
"Taiyo" (Nishiwaki) **15**:240-41
"Take" (Hagiwara Sakutaro) **18**:179
"Take a whole holiday in honour of this" (Day Lewis) **11**:130
"Take from My Palms" (Mandelstam) **14**:117

"Take heed of loving mee" (Donne)
See "The Prohibition"
"Taken Aback" (McKay) **2**:221
"Taking In Wash" (Dove) **6**:111
"Taking Off My Clothes" (Forche) **10**:133, 135
"Taking the Lambs to Market" (Kumin) **15**:216
"A Tale" (Bogan) **12**:85, 111, 127
"A Tale" (Coleridge) **11**:101
"A Tale" (Finch) **21**:166
"The Tale of Custard the Dragon" (Nash) **21**:265
"Tale of Melibee" (Chaucer) **19**:26, 33, 47
"A Tale of Starvation" (Lowell) **13**:60, 84
"The Tale of the Dead Princess and the Seven Heroes" (Pushkin)
See "Skazka o Mertvoy Tsarevne"
"The Tale of the Female Vagrant" (Wordsworth) **4**:373, 419
"The Tale of the Fisherman and the Fish" (Pushkin)
See "Skazka o Rybake i Rybke"
The Tale of the Golden Cockerel (Pushkin)
See "Skazka o Zolotom Petushke"
"The Tale of the Parson and His Man Balda" (Pushkin)
See "Skazka o Pope i o Rabotnike Yego Balde"
"A Tale of the Thirteenth Floor" (Nash) **21**:270-71
"The Tale of the Tsar Sultan" (Pushkin)
See "Skazka o Tsare Sultane"
"A Tale of Two Gardens" (Paz)
See "Cuento de dos jardines"
Tales (Chaucer)
See *Canterbury Tales*
Tales of Canterbury (Chaucer)
See *Canterbury Tales*
Talifer (Robinson) **1**:475, 477, 479, 483
"A Talisman" (Moore) **4**:232
"Talking in the Woods with Karl Amorelli" (Knight) **14**:43
"Talking Late with the Governor about the Budget" (Snyder) **21**:300, 326
"Talking Oak" (Tennyson) **6**:356
"Tam Glen" (Burns) **6**:59
"Tam o' Shanter" (Burns) **6**:55-8, 73-4, 76, 78, 81, 89, 96
"Tama yo shizume" (Ishikawa) **10**:213
"Tamar" (Jeffers) **17**:106-07, 111, 116, 130-32, 135, 138, 141, 146
Tamar and Other Poems (Jeffers) **17**:122, 124, 128, 135, 138, 146
"Tamara" (Lermontov) **18**:291-92, 298
"Tamarlane" (Poe) **1**:428, 436-38, 442, 444-45, 448
Tamarlane, and Other Poems, By a Bostonian (Poe) **1**:428, 432, 437, 449
The Tambov Treasurer's Wife (Lermontov) **18**:278, 282
"Tanghi-Garu Pass" (Paz) **1**:361
"Tango" (Gluck) **16**:151, 154
"Tankas" (Borges) **22**:78
"Tanto e Amara" (Olson) **19**:320
"Tanu" (Tagore) **8**:407
"Die Tänzerin (D.H.)" (Sachs) **18**:162
"Tape for the Turn of the Year" (Ammons) **16**:31
Tape for the Turn of the Year (Ammons) **16**:3-4, 6, 21-4, 28, 35, 42-3, 47-50, 59-61, 64-5
"Tapestry" (Cassian) **17**:5
"Taproot" (Forche) **10**:142
"Tarakar atmahatya" (Tagore) **8**:405
Target Study (Baraka) **4**:38
"Tarkington Thou Should'st Be Living in This Hour" (Nash) **21**:273
"th tarot match covr uv th lovrs" (Bissett) **14**:33

"Tarrant Moss" (Kipling) **3**:183
"Tartuffe's Punishment" (Rimbaud)
See "Le châtiment de Tartuff"
"tarzan collage" (Bissett) **14**:31
"A Task" (Milosz) **8**:206
The Tasking (Sassoon) **12**:271
"Tatinir katha" (Tagore) **8**:406
"The Tattooed Man" (Hayden) **6**:195
"Tavern" (Millay) **6**:205
"The Taxi" (Lowell) **13**:93
"T-Bar" (Page) **12**:177, 183, 188
"TCB" (Sanchez) **9**:225
"Tea at the Palaz of Hoon" (Stevens) **6**:304
"Teacher" (Walker) **20**:273, 286
"Teaching a Dumb Calf" (Hughes) **7**:166
"The Teamster" (Pavese) **13**:218
"The Tear" (Pushkin) **10**:407
A Tear and a Smile (Gibran)
See *Dam 'ah wabitisamah*
"Tear Gas" (Rich) **5**:393, 396
"Tears" (Sitwell) **3**:326
"Tears" (Whitman) **3**:379
"Tears and Laughter" (Gibran)
See *Dam 'ah wabitisamah*
"Tears of an Excavator" (Pasolini) **17**:258, 289
The Tears of the Blind Lions (Merton) **10**:339
"Teatro Bambino" (Lowell) **13**:94
"The Technique of Perfection" (Graves) **6**:128
"Teddy Bears" (Swenson) **14**:273
"Television Is a Baby Crawling Toward That Death Chamber" (Ginsberg) **4**:51, 76
"Television Poem" (Sanchez) **9**:210
"Tell Me" (Hughes) **1**:244
"Tell Me" (Toomer) **7**:335
Tell Me Again How the White Heron Rises and Flies Across the Nacreous River at Twilight Toward the Distant Islands (Carruth) **10**:86-7
Tell Me, Tell Me: Granite, Steel, and Other Topics (Moore) **4**:242, 259
"tell me what attackd yu" (Bissett) **14**:32
"The Temper" (Herbert) **4**:100, 118
"The Temper I" (Herbert) **4**:101, 111
The Tempers (Williams) **7**:344, 348, 367, 378, 395, 398, 405
"Tempid: Bellosguardo" (Montale) **13**:126
"The Temple" (Herrick)
See "The Fairie Temple: or, Oberons Chappell. Dedicated to Mr. John Merrifield, Counsellor at Law"
"Le temple" (Lamartine) **16**:277
The Temple: Sacred Poems and Private Ejaculations (Herbert) **4**:99-102, 106, 110, 114-18, 120-21, 123, 126, 129, 132-33
"Il tempo passa" (Pavese) **13**:209, 226
"Le Temps et les Cités" (Hugo) **17**:88
"Temptation" (Cassian) **17**:4
"The Temptation of St. Joseph" (Auden) **1**:38-39
Temy i variatsi (Pasternak) **6**:252, 255, 261, 264-65, 269, 271, 275, 277-81, 283
Temy i var'iatsii (Pasternak)
See *Temy i variatsi*
"X" (Joyce) **22**:136, 138, 145, 153, 160, 162, 168
"The Tenant" (Brodsky) **9**:2
Tender Buttons: Objects, Food, Rooms (Stein) **18**:316-34, 336, 341-42, 344, 349-54
Tender only To One (Smith) **12**:292, 326, 340, 343, 349
"Tenebrae" (Celan) **10**:101-02, 118
"Tenebrae" (Levertov) **11**:176
"Tenjo Ishi" (Hagiwara Sakutaro) **18**:178-79

Title Index